■ THE RESOURCE FOR THE INDEPENDENT TRAVELER

"The guides are aimed not only at young budget travelers but at the indepedent traveler; a sort of streetwise cookbook for traveling alone."

—The New York Times

"Unbeatable; good sight-seeing advice; up-to-date info on restaurants, hotels, and inns; a commitment to money-saving travel; and a wry style that brightens nearly every page."

—The Washington Post

"Lighthearted and sophisticated, informative and fun to read. [Let's Go] helps the novice traveler navigate like a knowledgeable old hand."

—Atlanta Journal-Constitution

"A world-wise traveling companion—always ready with friendly advice and helpful hints, all sprinkled with a bit of wit."

—The Philadelphia Inquirer

■ THE BEST TRAVEL BARGAINS IN YOUR PRICE RANGE

"All the dirt, dirt cheap."

—People

"Anything you need to know about budget traveling is detailed in this book."

—The Chicago Sun-Times

"Let's Go follows the creed that you don't have to toss your life's savings to the wind to travel—unless you want to."

—The Salt Lake Tribune

■ REAL ADVICE FOR REAL EXPERIENCES

"The writers seem to have experienced every rooster-packed bus and lunar-surfaced mattress about which they write."

—The New York Times

"A guide should tell you what to expect from a destination. Here Let's Go shines."

—The Chicago Tribune

"[Let's Go's] devoted updaters really walk the walk (and thumb the ride, and trek the trail). Learn how to fish, haggle, find work—anywhere."

—Food & Wine

LET'S GO PUBLICATIONS

TRAVEL GUIDES

Alaska 1st edition **NEW TITLE**
Australia 2004
Austria & Switzerland 2004
Brazil 1st edition **NEW TITLE**
Britain & Ireland 2004
California 2004
Central America 8th edition
Chile 1st edition
China 4th edition
Costa Rica 1st edition
Eastern Europe 2004
Egypt 2nd edition
Europe 2004
France 2004
Germany 2004
Greece 2004
Hawaii 2004
India & Nepal 8th edition
Ireland 2004
Israel 4th edition
Italy 2004
Japan 1st edition **NEW TITLE**
Mexico 20th edition
Middle East 4th edition
New Zealand 6th edition
Pacific Northwest 1st edition **NEW TITLE**
Peru, Ecuador & Bolivia 3rd edition
Puerto Rico 1st edition **NEW TITLE**
South Africa 5th edition
Southeast Asia 8th edition
Southwest USA 3rd edition
Spain & Portugal 2004
Thailand 1st edition
Turkey 5th edition
USA 2004
Western Europe 2004

CITY GUIDES

Amsterdam 3rd edition
Barcelona 3rd edition
Boston 4th edition
London 2004
New York City 2004
Paris 2004
Rome 12th edition
San Francisco 4th edition
Washington, D.C. 13th edition

MAP GUIDES

Amsterdam
Berlin
Boston
Chicago
Dublin
Florence
Hong Kong
London
Los Angeles
Madrid
New Orleans
New York City
Paris
Prague
Rome
San Francisco
Seattle
Sydney
Venice
Washington, D.C.

COMING SOON:

Road Trip USA

BRAZIL

Luis Rego Editor
Paul Berman Associate Editor
Gabrielle A. Harding Associate Editor

Researcher-Writers
Adeline Boatin
David Bright
Leila Chirayath
Rich Frank
Ankur Ghosh
Adriana Lafaille
Camilo Mejia
Reema Rajbanashi

Evan Hudson Map Editor
Megan Brumagim Managing Editor

St. Martin's Press New York

HELPING LET'S GO If you want to share your discoveries, suggestions, or corrections, please drop us a line. We read every piece of correspondence, whether a postcard, a 10-page email, or a coconut. **Address mail to:**

Let's Go: Brazil
67 Mount Auburn Street
Cambridge, MA 02138
USA

Visit Let's Go at **http://www.letsgo.com,** or send email to:

feedback@letsgo.com
Subject: "Let's Go: Brazil"

In addition to the invaluable travel advice our readers share with us, many are kind enough to offer their services as researchers or editors. Unfortunately, our charter enables us to employ only currently enrolled Harvard students.

Distributed outside the USA and Canada by Macmillan.

ISBN: 0-312-32004-3

First edition
10 9 8 7 6 5 4 3 2 1

Let's Go: Brazil is written by Let's Go Publications, 67 Mount Auburn Street, Cambridge, MA 02138, USA.

HOW TO USE THIS BOOK

ORGANIZATION. This book starts out with a crash course in everything you need to know about Brazil—from history and culture to the logistics of planning your trip. Coverage begins in Rio de Janeiro, the country's biggest tourist draw. The rest of the book is organized along the lines of Brazil's five regions: Southeast, South, Center-West, Northeast, and North. Black tabs mark each chapter.

SOLO TRAVELERS. Unless otherwise stated, the information found in this guide assumes you are traveling alone. As such, transportation, accommodations, and food listings are geared toward the options for independent travelers. This book also lists the best places to meet locals and other travelers, as well as information for those traveling in larger groups.

FEATURES & SPECIAL COVERAGE. Throughout this book, you'll find black sidebars—built-in reading material for those long lines and long trips. You can read about researchers' tales **From the Road,** get the **Local Story** from Brazilians themselves, learn what's been going on **In Recent News,** hear about the country's **Local Legends,** get to know the **Insider's City,** decipher what's **On the Menu,** pick the best way to blow your wad on **Big Splurges,** and recover it with our favorite **Hidden Deals.** Indulge in **No Work, All Play** with our in-depth coverage of **Carnaval** (p. 46). To learn about ways of giving back through volunteering and studying in Brazil, check out our detailed listings on **Alternatives to Tourism** (p. 103). Be sure to check out the brief history of Brazilian racial politics by an emerging scholar in the field (p. 45).

PRICE RANGES & RANKINGS. Our researchers rank all establishments in this guide in order of value, starting with the best; our favorite places get the *Let's Go* thumbs-up (👍). Since the best value doesn't always have the cheapest price, establishments are also caregorized by price (❶❷❸❹❺) for quick reference. **Accommodations** ranges are based on the cheapest per night rate for a solo traveler. **Food** ranges are based on the average price of a main course. See p. ix for more info.

WHEN TO USE IT

1 MONTH BEFORE. **Discover Brazil** (p. 1) contains highlights of the country, including Suggested Itineraries (p. 7) to help you plan your trip. **Essentials** (p. 62) has practical information on pre-departure planning and logistics. Take care of insurance, and write down a list of emergency numbers.

2 WEEKS BEFORE. Read through the coverage and plan the logistics of your itinerary. Leave an itinerary and a photocopy of important documents with someone at home. Take some time to familiarize yourself with Brazilian history and culture by reading through **Life & Times** (p. 11).

ON THE ROAD. The **Appendix** (p. 523) includes a guide to pronunciation, a phrasebook of Brazilian Portuguese, a menu reader, and a glossary of important vocabulary used throughout this book.

A NOTE TO OUR READERS Information for this book was gathered by *Let's Go* researchers from February through August of 2003. Each listing is based on one researcher's opinion, formed during his or her visit at a particular time. Those traveling at other times may have different experiences since prices, dates, hours, and conditions are always subject to change. You are urged to check the facts presented in this book beforehand to avoid inconvenience and surprises.

CONTENTS

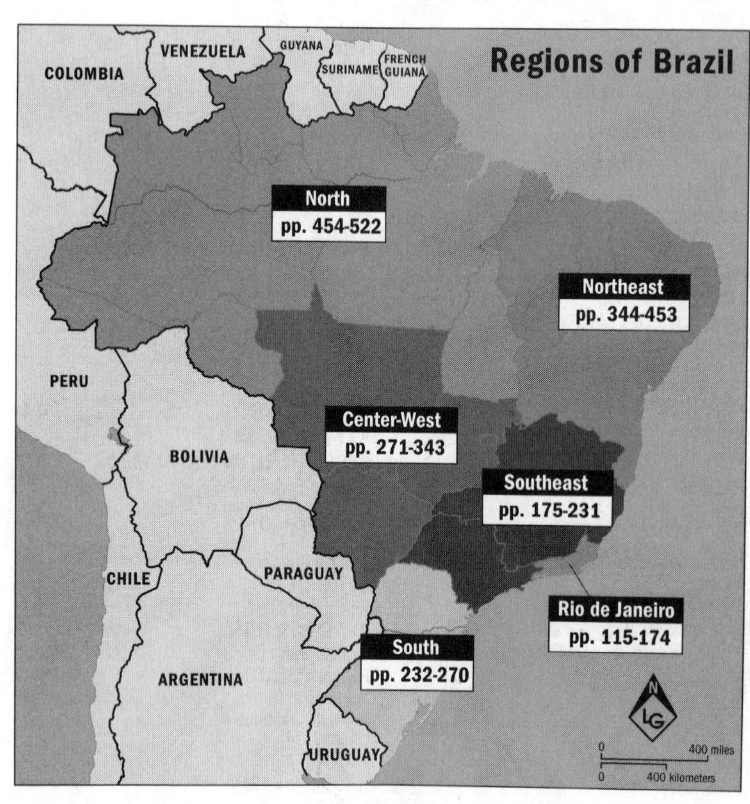
Regions of Brazil
VENEZUELA
GUYANA
SURINAME
FRENCH GUIANA
COLOMBIA
PERU
BOLIVIA
CHILE
PARAGUAY
ARGENTINA
URUGUAY
North
pp. 454-522
Northeast
pp. 344-453
Center-West
pp. 271-343
Southeast
pp. 175-231
Rio de Janeiro
pp. 115-174
South
pp. 232-270
N
LG
0
400 miles
0
400 kilometers

❶❷❸❹❺

PRICE RANGES >> BRAZIL

Our researchers rank all establishments in this guide in order of value, starting with the best value; their favorite places get the *Let's Go* thumbs-up (☒). Since the best value isn't always the cheapest price, we have a system of price ranges for quick reference. For **accommodations,** we base the range on the cheapest per night rate for a solo traveler. For **food,** we base it on the average price of a main course. Below we list what you'll *typically* find at the corresponding price range; remember, these are just guidelines.

ACCOMMODATIONS	RANGE	WHAT YOU'RE LIKELY TO FIND
❶	under R$25	Bunked hostel dorms or shared rooms in a *pousada,* with fans and a choice of common or private bath. Breakfast and hot water sometimes included, or extra.
❷	R$26-45	Hostels in big cities and most *pousadas,* all fan-cooled (A/C and hot water are usually available for a few more *reais*). Usually includes breakfast and private bath.
❸	R$46-65	Budget hotels up to and including most 3-star hotels, with A/C, private bath (hot water included), and breakfast a given. An in-room TV, phone, and *frigo-bar* may also be included.
❹	R$66-105	Similar to ❸ but with more amenities or in a more touristed area. 3-star or higher with private bath, A/C, TV, phone, *frigo-bar,* and breakfast (and maybe a pool). Sadly, price has no correlation to room size in Brazil.
❺	above R$106	A Big $plurge or luxury hotel, usually with a rating of 4 stars or more. If it's a ❺ and it doesn't have the perks you want, you've paid too much.

FOOD	RANGE	WHAT YOU'RE LIKELY TO FIND
❶	under R$7	*Lanchonetes, sucos,* and the odd fast-food joint.
❷	R$8-15	A no-frills restaurant with cheap entrees and budget-friendly *pratos feitos*. This is also the rating for all kilos (which average R$8-11 per meal; see p. 39).
❸	R$16-23	Traditional Brazilian restaurant/*botequim,* with an army of waiters and the same meat- and starch-heavy menu of pizzas, pasta, and hearty entrees (many big enough for 2). Some *churrascarias* fall into this category.
❹	R$24-31	A nicer *churrascaria* or a more upscale traditional restaurant. This includes most of the fancier ethnic and fusion eateries in the big cities.
❺	above R$32	Pricey tourist-oriented *churrascarias* or real gourmet blowouts. Eating in Brazil is cheap, so a restaurant at this price promises a lot of bang for your *real.*

RESEARCHER-WRITERS

Adeline Boatin *Santa Catarina, Rio Grande do Sul, Ceará, Piauí, Maranhão*

Having researched South Africa's coast for *Let's Go*, Adeline's love of beaches—and music, dance, and food—yielded amazing Northeast coverage. An environmental science and public policy student with a health and development focus, Adeline awed with insights into Brazil's poorest regions. Quick on her feet (even when there was nothing beneath them), she's appreciated for her hard work.

David Bright *Mato Grosso, Mato Grosso do Sul, Pantanal, Distrito Federal, Goiás, Bahia, Carnaval*

Dave's time researching *South Africa* and editing *Ireland* translated beautifully. Ever the man's man (and ladies' man), Dave did what it took to get the best coverage—donning a wet-suit to hike in the hot sun, navigating the Pantanal *sans* guide and car—while tapping the admiral and having a "dangerous amorous adventure" or two. Perfectionism paid off with flawless Pantanal coverage.

Leila Chirayath *Bahia, Tocantins, Pará, Amapá*

Last year, Leila left no stone unturned researching Mozambique and Malawi for *South Africa*. This year, she went above and beyond in her coverage of Salvador. Her expertise in African Developmental Studies and her love of dancing and diving made her the perfect choice to tackle the Afro-Brazilian capital of culture. As she spends the next year traveling around the world, she'll no doubt engage the people and places she encounters in a way very few people can.

Rich Frank *Amazonas, Pará, Roraima, Acre, Rondônia*

There's nothing Rich can't do. The knowledge he's gained as a student of the politics of international development assistance, his stamina as an aspiring triathlete, and his experience traveling from Buenos Aires to Cartagena overland along the Andes—all this and more made Rich a superstar researcher-writer. A frontiersman at heart and all-around nice guy, he's the hardest working man in the business, and consistently went the distance in the Amazon.

Ankur Ghosh *Rio de Janeiro, Carnaval*

After researching and writing the third edition of *Boston*, this former managing editor and Editor-in-Chief set his sights on Brazil. It was Ankur who laid this book's groundwork, he who wrote much of the introductory chapters, and he who will see it through final production. He combined work and play like never before, getting down and dirty in Rio, where he had skintillating adventures among the glitterati of Carnaval—with pictures to prove it. Let's Ghosh!

Adriana Lafaille *Minas Gerais, Espírito Santo, Rio de Janeiro, Bahia*

A native Brazilian, Adriana's passion for architecture and her background in Latin American studies made her the perfect match for Minas Gerais's colonial towns. Her extensive experience in the region gave her an edge covering historical background. This, coupled with a dedication to gathering all the facts, resulted in comprehensive coverage of everything from UFOs to gilded altars. Adriana is currently conducting research on urban planning in São Paulo.

Camilo Mejia *São Paulo, Paraná, Rio de Janeiro*

A student of modern Latin American history, Camilo gained first-hand experience in South America's megalopolis, São Paulo. With his experience traveling in Colombia and Peru, there was no one better to tackle sprawling Sampa. His work reflected an overwhelming dedication and enthusiasm, and he came to love São Paulo as his own. Camilo poured his heart and soles into producing incredible research, and we're sure he'll be coming back for more.

Reema Rajbanashi *Sergipe, Alagoas, Pernambuco, Paraíba, Rio Grande do Norte, Bahia*

A creative writer by trade, Reema's work was stunning. Her time on a permaculturalfarm in the *sertão* inspired her to see more of the Northeast. Reema received the Gardner Fellowship to pursue creative writing while traveling in South Asia and Southeast Asia. We hope her *Let's Go* experience will prove useful in her upcoming (and slower-paced) adventures, and wish her the best of luck.

CONTRIBUTING WRITERS

Fernando Arenas is an Associate Professor of Portuguese at the University of Minnesota. His work focuses on Brazil and Lusophone Africa.

ABOUT LET'S GO

GUIDES FOR THE INDEPENDENT TRAVELER

Budget travel is more than a vacation. At *Let's Go*, we see every trip as the chance of a lifetime. If your dream is to grab a knapsack and a machete and forge through the jungles of Brazil, we can take you there. Or, if you'd rather enjoy the Riviera sun at a beachside cafe, we'll set you a table. If you know what you're doing, you can have any experience you want—whether it's camping among lions or sampling Tuscan desserts—without maxing out your credit card. We'll show you just how far your coins can go, and prove that the greatest limitation on your adventure is not your wallet, but your imagination. That said, we understand that you may want the occasional indulgence after a week of hostels and kebab stands, so we've added "Big Splurges" to let you know which establishments are worth those extra euros, as well as price ranges to help you quickly determine whether an accommodation or restaurant will break the bank. While we may have diversified, our emphasis will always be on finding the best values for your budget, giving you all the info you need to spend six days in London or six months in Tasmania.

BEYOND THE TOURIST EXPERIENCE

We write for travelers who know there's more to a vacation than riding double-deckers with tourists. Our researchers give you the heads-up on both world-renowned and lesser-known attractions, on the best local eats and the hottest nightclub beats. In our travels, we talk to everybody; we provide a snapshot of real life in the places you visit with our sidebars on topics like regional cuisine, local festivals, and hot political issues. We've opened our pages to respected writers and scholars to show you their take on a given destination, and turned to lifelong residents to learn the little things that make their city worth calling home. And we've even given you Alternatives to Tourism—ideas for how to give back to local communities through responsible travel and volunteering.

OVER FORTY YEARS OF WISDOM

When we started, way back in 1960, Let's Go consisted of a small group of well-traveled friends who compiled their budget travel tips into a 20-page packet for students on charter flights to Europe. Since then, we've expanded to suit all kinds of travelers, now publishing guides to six continents, including our newest guides: *Let's Go: Japan* and the guide in your hands, *Let's Go: Brazil*. Our guides are still annually researched and written entirely by students on shoe-string budgets, adventurous travelers who know that train strikes, stolen luggage, food poisoning, and marriage proposals are all part of a day's work. Even as you read this, work on next year's editions is well underway. Whether you're reading one of our new titles, like *Let's Go: Puerto Rico* or *Let's Go Adventure Guide: Alaska*, or our original best-seller, *Let's Go: Europe*, you'll find the same spirit of adventure that has made *Let's Go* the guide of choice for travelers the world over since 1960.

GETTING IN TOUCH

The best discoveries are often those you make yourself; on the road, when you find something worth sharing, please drop us a line. We're Let's Go Publications, 67 Mt. Auburn St., Cambridge, MA 02138, USA (feedback@letsgo.com).

For more info, visit our website: www.letsgo.com.

ACKNOWLEDGMENTS

These books don't just put themselves together, you know. They're assembled by machines.

Team Brazil thanks: Our incredible RWs; Megan for *Cosmo Girl* and supporting us through this; Sarah, Ariel, Joanna, Emma, and Su for answering all our questions; Evan for the long hours; Nathaniel; Prod; Jesse and his army of proofers: Peter Bryce, Eric Cadin, Dan Henderson, Emi Shimokawa, Naomi Straus, Amy Young, and Allison Melia; and Ankur, for being the best sort of know-it-all.

Luis thanks: Amy and Paul for all your hard work; Nate for always being there; Lucy for telling me I should know better by now; Diane for disagreeing; Leah for fire, water, and everything in between; Aida for the prophecy of doom; Moira for that hat and that tape; Percy (no biteys on 2!); Teresa for sharing the sinking ship; Ankur for letting me baby-sit your book; Zahr for constant encouragement; and *Graceland.*

Paul thanks: Mom, Dad, Steve, Laura, Yao, Grandma and Grandpa R, and Grandma B. Also thanks to Gage, Sims, Peron, Chris and Dallas, and all the rest, plus Micah and Marissa for the apartment and Oxford St. for the furniture.

Amy thanks: Mum & Dad for being incredible parents and friends; Moira for calming me down, making me laugh, and refusing to rock the tandem; Sarah for 20 years of harebrained schemes (run, run, run, run); Leah for our world (what can I say?); Alexis for inspiration, beauty, and support; Luis for all the lists, beer(s), and pep; Ankur for all the answers; Paul B. for doing scary things like indexing; Adam for taking me on beach adventures and understanding spastic aphasia (and Earl for the chipmunk); Paul W. for tunes and evenings on the porch; David Rosenblatt for the man with a turkey head and everything after; Alex for coming home; St. Jude; all Pictou Islanders; and the guys at Toscanini's for keeping me awake.

Evan thanks: Mom, Dad, and Ryan. The Brazil book-team for patience. Megan and Nathaniel for giving me a chance.

Editor Luis Rego
Associate Editors Paul Berman, Gabrielle A. Harding
Map Editor Evan Hudson
Managing Editor Megan Brumagim
Typesetter Ankur Ghosh

Publishing Director
Julie A. Stephens
Editor-in-Chief
Jeffrey Dubner
Production Manager
Dusty Lewis
Cartography Manager
Nathaniel Brooks
Design Manager
Caleb Beyers
Editorial Managers
Lauren Bonner, Ariel Fox,
Matthew K. Hudson, Emma Nothmann,
Joanna Shawn Brigid O'Leary,
Sarah Robinson
Financial Manager
Suzanne Siu
Marketing & Publicity Managers
Megan Brumagim, Nitin Shah
Personnel Manager
Jesse Reid Andrews
Researcher Manager
Jennifer O'Brien
Web Manager
Jesse Tov
Web Content Director
Abigail Burger
Production Associates
Thomas Bechtold, Jeffrey Hoffman Yip
IT Directors
Travis Good, E. Peyton Sherwood
Financial Assistant
R. Kirkie Maswoswe
Associate Web Manager
Robert Dubbin
Office Coordinators
Abigail Burger, Angelina L. Fryer,
Liz Glynn
Director of Advertising Sales
Daniel Ramsey
Senior Advertising Associates
Sara Barnett, Daniella Boston
Advertising Artwork Editor
Julia Davidson, Sandy Liu
President
Abhishek Gupta
General Manager
Robert B. Rombauer
Assistant General Manager
Anne E. Chisholm

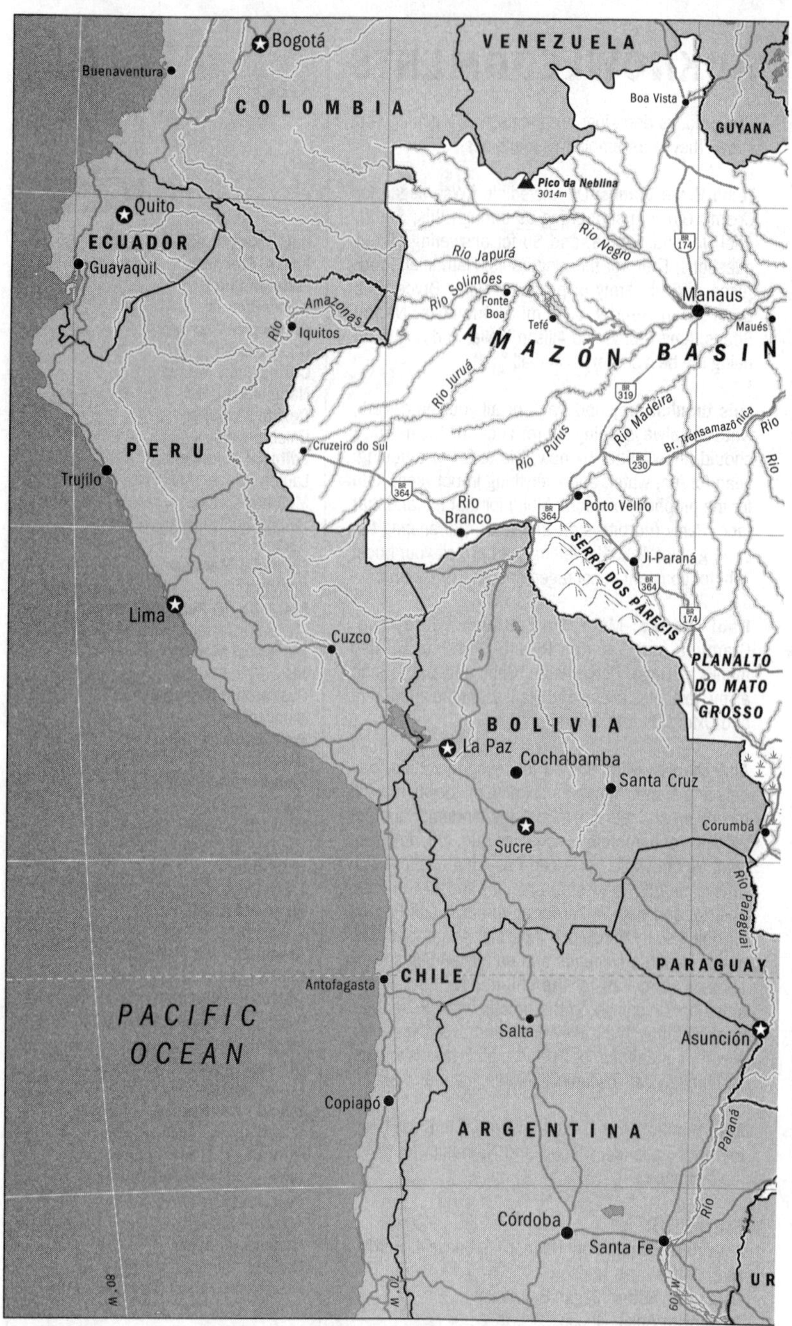

Bogotá
Buenaventura
VENEZUELA
Boa Vista
COLOMBIA
GUYANA
Pico da Neblina
3014m
Quito
ECUADOR
Guayaquil
Rio Japurá
Rio Negro
Rio Solimões
Fonte Boa
Tefé
Manaus
Maués
Rio Amazonas
Iquitos
AMAZON BASIN
Rio Juruá
Rio Purus
Rio Madeira
Br. Transamazônica
PERU
Cruzeiro do Sul
Trujilo
Rio Branco
Porto Velho
SERRA DOS PARECIS
Ji-Paraná
Lima
Cuzco
PLANALTO DO MATO GROSSO
BOLIVIA
La Paz
Cochabamba
Santa Cruz
Corumbá
Sucre
Rio Paraguai
PARAGUAY
Antofagasta
CHILE
PACIFIC OCEAN
Salta
Asunción
Copiapó
ARGENTINA
Paraná
Córdoba
Santa Fe
Rio
UR
80°W
70°W
60°W

Brazil
ATLANTIC OCEAN
BRAZIL
FRENCH GUIANA
SURINAME
Cayenne
Oiapoque
SERRA DE TUMUCUMAQUE
Macapá
Ilha de Marajó
Belém
São Luís
Parnaíba
Sobral
Fortaleza
Santarém
Rio Amazonas
Rio Tocantins
Teresina
Natal
Marabá
Imperatriz
Floriano
Juazeiro do Norte
João Pessoa
Olinda
Recife
Maceió
Juazeiro
Repressa de Sobradinho
Palmas
Alta Floresta
SERRA DO RONCADOR
SERRA GERAL DE GOIÁ
CHAPADA DIAMANTINA
Aracaju
Feira de Santana
Salvador
Valença
Ilhéus
Brasília
Cuiabá
Goiânia
Porto Seguro
Montes Claro
PANTANAL
Coxim
Uberlândia
Belo Horizonte
Campo Grande
Vitória
Juiz de Fora
Campos
Campinas
São Paulo
Rio de Janeiro
Tropic of Capricorn
Cascavel
Curitiba
Paranaguá
Joinville
Florianópolis
SERRA DO MAR
Uruguaiana
Santa Maria
Porto Alegre
Pelotas
URUGUAY

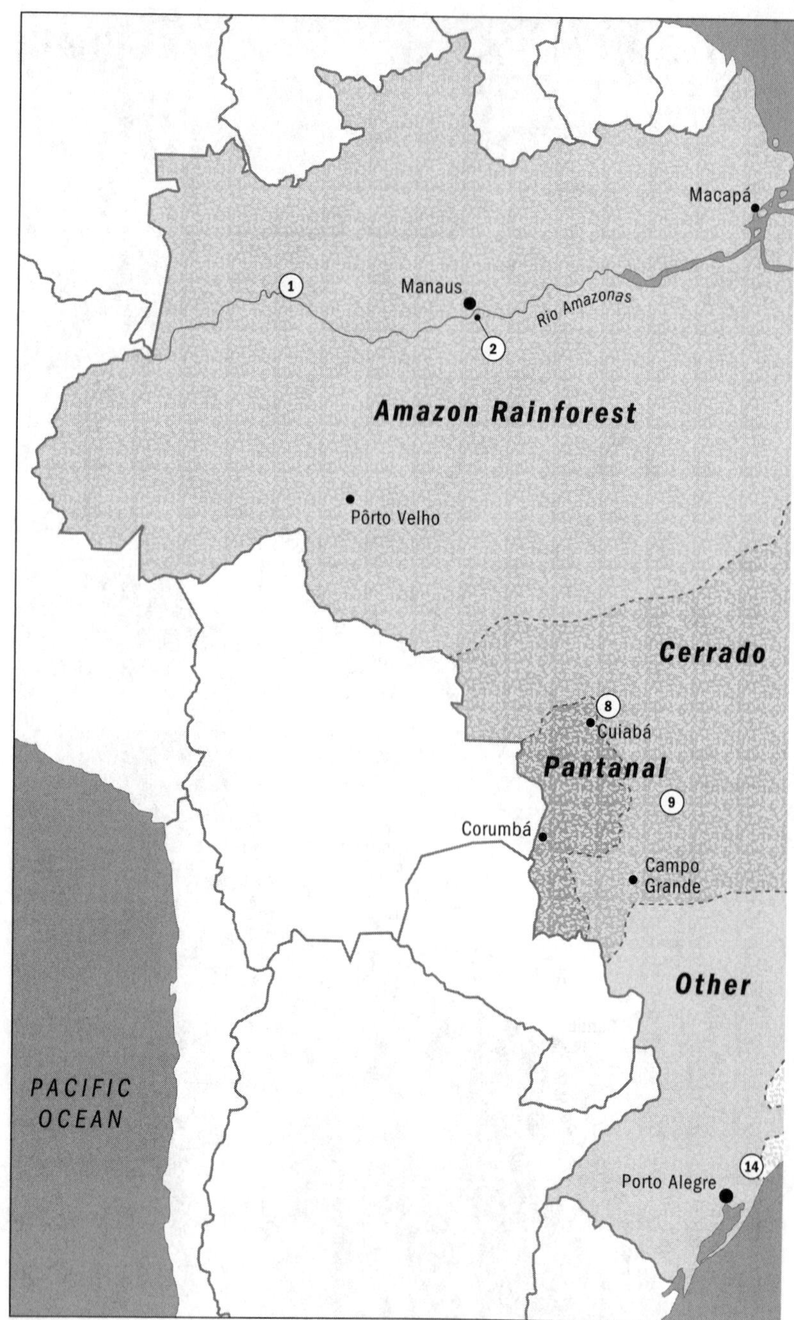
Macapá
1
Manaus
Rio Amazonas
2
Amazon Rainforest
Pôrto Velho
Cerrado
8
Cuiabá
Pantanal
9
Corumbá
Campo
Grande
Other
PACIFIC
OCEAN
14
Porto Alegre

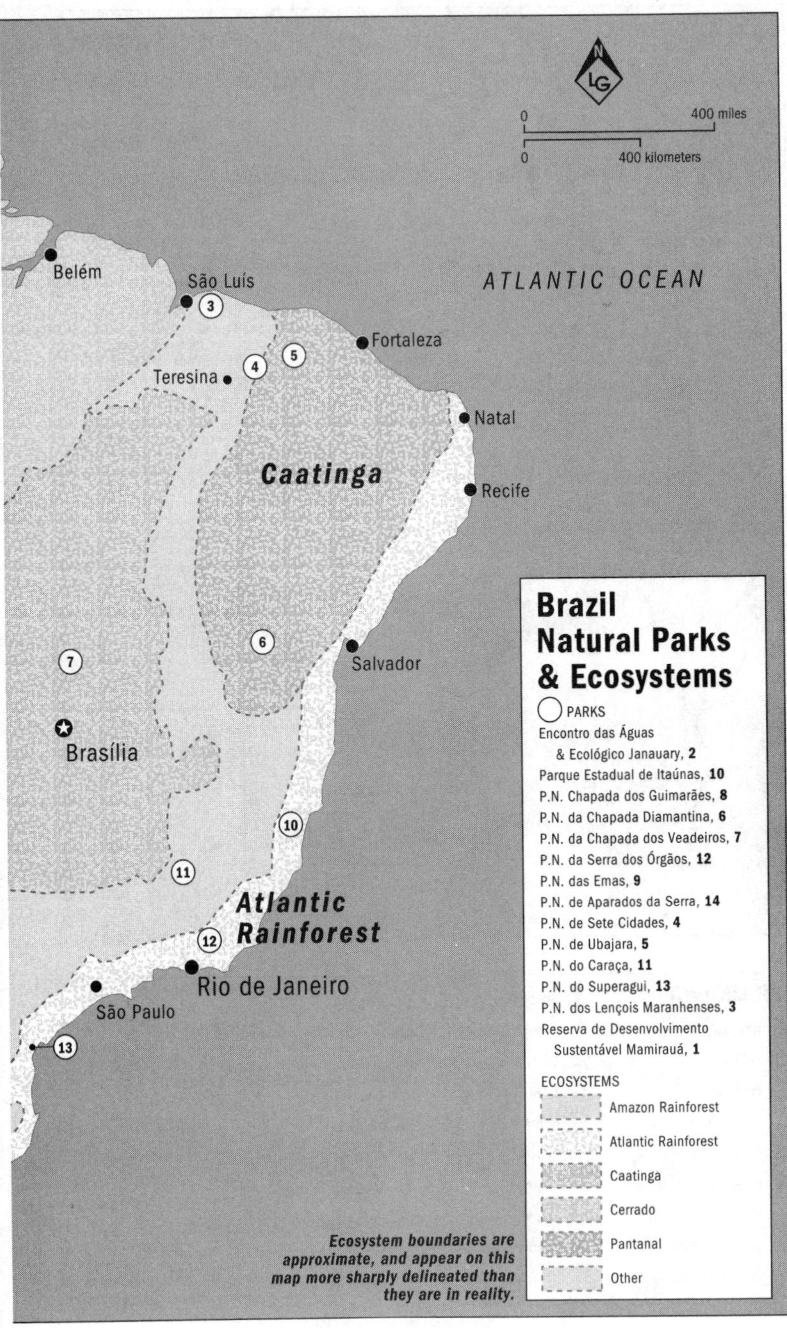

0
400 miles
0
400 kilometers
ATLANTIC OCEAN
Belém
São Luís
Fortaleza
Teresina
Natal
Caatinga
Recife
Salvador
Brasília
Atlantic
Rainforest
Rio de Janeiro
São Paulo
Brazil
Natural Parks
& Ecosystems
PARKS
Encontro das Águas
& Ecológico Janauary, 2
Parque Estadual de Itaúnas, 10
P.N. Chapada dos Guimarães, 8
P.N. da Chapada Diamantina, 6
P.N. da Chapada dos Veadeiros, 7
P.N. da Serra dos Órgãos, 12
P.N. das Emas, 9
P.N. de Aparados da Serra, 14
P.N. de Sete Cidades, 4
P.N. de Ubajara, 5
P.N. do Caraça, 11
P.N. do Superagui, 13
P.N. dos Lençois Maranhenses, 3
Reserva de Desenvolvimento
Sustentável Mamirauá, 1
ECOSYSTEMS
Amazon Rainforest
Atlantic Rainforest
Caatinga
Cerrado
Pantanal
Other
Ecosystem boundaries are approximate, and appear on this map more sharply delineated than they are in reality.

Brazil
States & Time Zones
ATLANTIC OCEAN
Equator
PACIFIC OCEAN
VENEZUELA
COLOMBIA
GUYANA
SURINAME
FRENCH GUIANA
PERU
BOLIVIA
PARAGUAY
CHILE
ARGENTINA
URUGUAY
-5 GMT
-4 GMT
-3 GMT
RORAIMA
Boa Vista
AMAPÁ
Macapá
Belém
São Luís
Fortaleza
Manaus
Rio Amazonas
AMAZONAS
PARÁ
MARANHÃO
Teresina
CEARÁ
PIAUÍ
SEE INSET MAP
ACRE
Rio Branco
Porto Velho
RONDÔNIA
Palmas
TOCANTINS
BAHIA
Salvador
MATO GROSSO
Cuiabá
GOIÁS
Brasília
DISTRITO FEDERAL
Goiânia
MINAS GERAIS
ESPÍRITO SANTO
Vitória
MATO GROSSO DO SUL
Campo Grande
SÃO PAULO
Belo Horizonte
RIO DE JANEIRO
Tropic of Capricorn
PARANÁ
Curitiba
São Paulo
Rio de Janeiro
SANTA CATARINA
Florianópolis
RIO GRANDE DO SUL
Porto Alegre
0 400 miles
0 400 kilometers
CEARÁ
RIO GRANDE DO NORTE
Natal
João Pessoa
PARAÍBA
Recife
PERNAMBUCO
Maceió
ALAGOAS
BAHIA
Aracaju
SERGIPE

MAP LEGEND
Hospital
Police
Post Office
Tourist Office
Bank or ATM
Embassy or Consulate
Sight or Point of Interest
Telephone Office
Theater or Cinema
Lighthouse
Airport
Rodoviária/Bus Station
Train Station
Internet Cafe
Beach
BR 319
Highway
Steps
Pharmacy
Church
Museum
Hotel/Hostel/Pousada
Camping
Food & Drink
Shopping
Nightlife & Entertainment
Sights/Services
Ferry Line/Stop
M
Metrô Line/Station
Trail
Pedestrian Zone
Park
Beach
Water
The Let's Go compass always points NORTH.

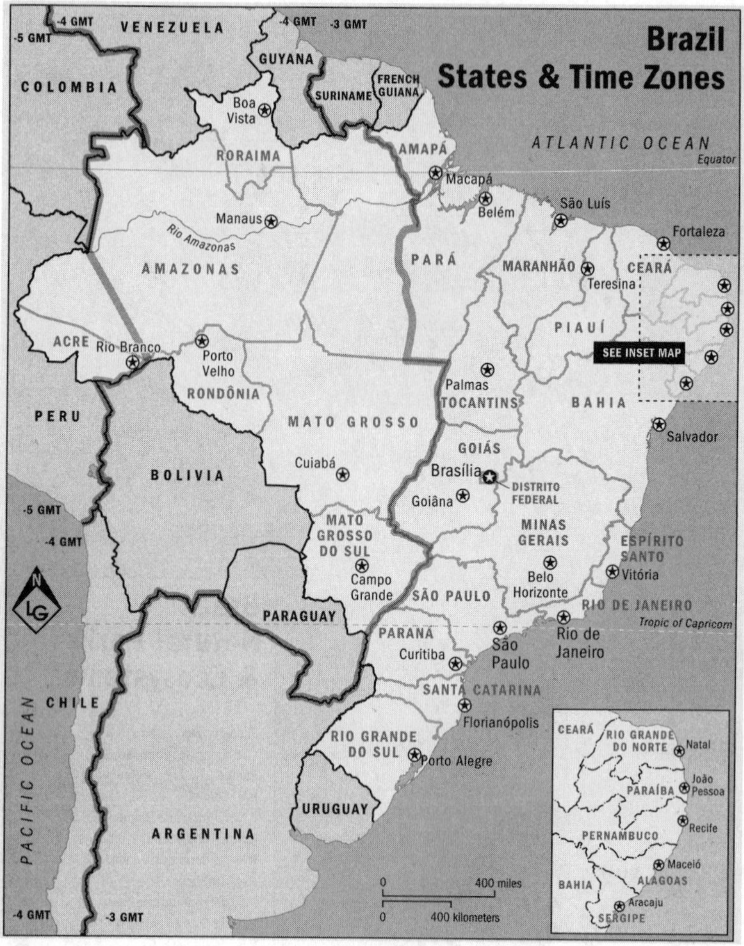

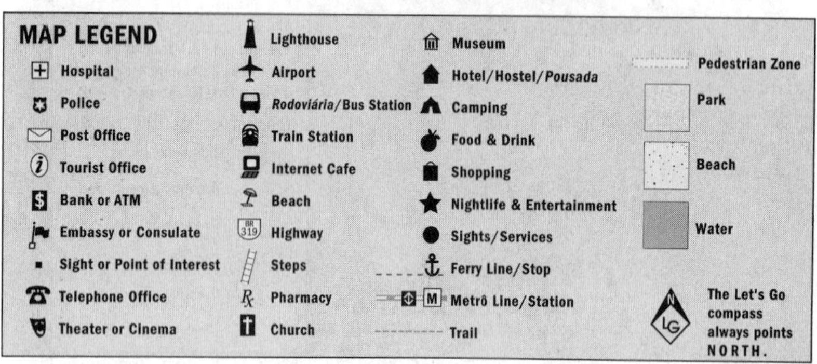

DISCOVER BRAZIL

In 1501, when Amerigo Vespucci first cruised into the Baía do Todos os Santos, the explorer encountered a seemingly deserted territory of lush palms and crystal waters. Five centuries later, the nation of Brazil is among the largest in the world, encompassing everything from unexplored equatorial rainforests to sprawling urban centers that fuel South America's economy. Bordering almost every other country on the continent, Brazil offers a vast array of attractions for travelers; from trekking in the Pantanal to learning *capoeira* from Salvador's masters to scoping the runways during São Paulo's Fashion Week. Nature lovers will find paradise in the scarcely inhabited islands and untouched stretches of the Amazon in the north, and diehard urbanites will appreciate the hustle and bustle of Brazil's major cities, set amid a unique combination of colonial and futuristic architecture. Coupled with the country's physical attractions is the incredible warmth and hospitality of the Brazilian people. Brazil's characteristic laid-back attitude is contagious, especially in the coastal towns of the Northeast, and people from all backgrounds will feel welcome here. Brazil is internationally known for its incredible beaches, raucous Carnaval, and the intoxicating sounds of *samba*, but these familiar highlights are only the beginning of what makes it such a desirable destination. Whether for a whirlwind week of partying in Rio, a month trekking through the jungle, or endless weeks of beach-hopping, Brazil must be seen to be believed.

FACTS & FIGURES

NAME: República Federativa do Brasil

GOVERNMENT: Federated republic; President Luiz Inácio Lula da Silva

CAPITAL: Brasília, Distrito Federal

LAND AREA: 8,511,965 sq. km (approx. the same size as the lower 48 US states)

BEACHES: 7491km. That's just 4cm for each person living in Brazil.

GEOGRAPHY: The world's 5th largest country, occupying over 50% of the continent. Borders every country in South America except Chile and Ecuador.

CLIMATE: Tropical; temperate in South

MAJOR CITIES: São Paulo, Rio de Janeiro, Recife, and Salvador

POPULATION: 176,030,000

INCOME PER CAPITA: US$7400

LANGUAGE: Portuguese

RELIGION: 80% Catholic, 100% *futebol!*

HIGHEST POINT: Pico da Neblina, Amazonas (3014m)

LOWEST POINT: Losing the 1998 World Cup to France

WHEN TO GO

Because of Brazil's size, there is a lot of regional variation in climate. However, 90% of the country falls within the tropical zone, so it rarely gets very cold. Because it is in the southern hemisphere, the seasons are opposite those in the northern hemisphere: summer occurs from December to March. Summer is the best time to travel to the southernmost states (Rio Grande do Sul and Santa Catarina) because parts of the region do get frost and occasional snow during the win-

TOP TEN LIST

TOP TEN BEACHES

1. Copacabana (p. 156). Brazil's most famous beach—a vibrant urban strip—is consistently ranked one of the world's best.

2. Ipanema (p. 156). Immortalized in song, Copa's slightly more relaxed neighbor is a beautiful coastline full of beautiful people.

3. Jericoacoara (p. 437). This recently "discovered" beach is great for windsurfing.

4. Ilha da Croa (p. 399). This string of beaches off Barra de Santo Antônio is near a beautiful *piscina natural* (a natural pool in the sea formed by surrounding reefs).

5. Jacumã (p. 424). This beach town near João Pessoa boasts *piscinas naturais*, colored sandbars, and mineral water springs.

6. Canoa Quebrada (p. 435). This laid-back town with huge sand dunes is a great place for weekend partying.

7. Praia do Suape (p. 412). This 24km stretch of coastline with sheltered waters is perfect for kayaking or boat trips.

8. Porto de Galinhas (p. 413). Warm, clear waters protected by a reef, plus an uncrowded shore.

9. Praia do Forte (p. 370). A popular beach with crystal waters and tropical fish, great for snorkeling, parasailing, and horseback riding.

10. Praia do Francês (p. 399). This incredible beach gets very crowded, but with good reason.

ter (June-Aug.). The coastal cities of São Paulo, Rio de Janeiro, and Salvador are consistently warm all year round, and get downright hot and humid during the summer. However, if you're looking to really let loose, Carnaval celebrations are held throughout the country in February, although prices skyrocket during this period. The Northeast has beautiful stretches of seashore; during the region's dry season (May-Nov.), the heat is tempered by constant breezes on the coast. This is also a less expensive season in which to visit; many establishments all across Brazil offer reduced rates from April to June and August to November. Travel in the Amazon is best done when much of the region floods from January to June. While this means that the humidity is higher and the rainfall more substantial, the rivers become navigable, allowing visitors to see more wildlife than during the dry season. Most travelers visit the Pantanal toward the end of its wet season in April, when the area is flooded and fauna are stranded on the remaining spots of dry land, making them easier to spot.

THINGS TO DO

HISTORY & CULTURE

HISTORY

Brazil is a young nation with a history tumultuous enough for a country three times its age. **Rio's** (p. 138) Centro was Brazil's colonial and imperial capital, with many historic buildings from and museums pertaining to that era. The city's **Museu da República** (p. 146) chronicles the beginnings of Brazil's current presidential era. **Salvador** (p. 344), Brazil's most African city, has museums dedicated to the rich historical and cultural influence of African immigrants—everything from *capoeira* to Candomblé. **Minas Gerais** (p. 203) is filled with attractions relating to the country's 18th-century mining boom.

ARCHITECTURE

Those interested in historic architecture might tire of the sight of the baroque and Rococo churches—which are literally *everywhere*—in Brazil's mining boom towns, particularly **Diamantina** (p. 223), **Goiás Velho** (p. 288), and gaudy **Ouro Preto** (p. 209). Forward-looking building buffs can head inland to **Brasília** (p. 271), Brazil's futuristic, airplane-shaped capital, littered with unconventional masterpieces by Modernist master Oscar Niemeyer (p. 24). Charming **Olinda** (p. 414) and **São Luís** (p. 445) in the Northeast of Brazil are beautifully preserved colonial-era relics. All the destinations above are designated as World Heritage Sites by UNESCO.

ARTS & CRAFTS

Art enthusiasts will enjoy the cutting-edge galleries and fine museums of **São Paulo** (p. 190), Brazil's capital of high culture. Rio's **Museu Folclórico** (p. 146) offers an excellent survey of native folk art through the years, but the best traditional works (as well as the most exciting work being done by local artists) are found in the studios *(ateliêrs)* of Salvador's **Pelourinho** (p. 358). Ceará and in particular **Fortaleza** (p. 428) are known as the center of traditional art in Brazil; the region's **lacework** is legendary, and crafts are for sale at both its **Centro Cultural Dragão** (p. 433) and the beachfront market held nightly on Praia Meireles. The North is dotted with pockets of indigenous culture, with the state of Amapá taking the national lead in pushing for conservation efforts (best exemplified in its capital, **Macapá;** p. 481). The pottery and leatherwork of the Marajó Indians, whose descendants inhabit the **Ilha do Marajó** (p. 471) near Belém, is also quite popular.

PARTY TIME

Brazilians are experts at the art of the party. The five-day debauch of Brazil's **Carnaval** (p. 46) is the world's biggest and baddest party, but there are frequent, colorful festivals all across the nation, celebrating everything from saints to seafood. There are now even Carnaval festivities outside of Carnaval season: check out the pre-season **Carnatal** (Natal; p. 425), the post-season **Fortal** (Fortaleza; p. 428), Brazil's biggest off-season celebration. The new year kicks off with a bang on Rio's Copacabana beach, site of the annual **Reveillon** (p. 42). Soon after comes **Lavagem do Bonfim** in Salvador's Pelourinho (p. 358), the world's only party for staircase-washing enthusiasts. **Semana Santa** (Holy Week) is celebrated all over the country with lavish processions and stately church services, but they're at their most awe-inspiring in historic Ouro Preto (p. 209). The truly devout can head north to Nova Jerusalém (p. 419) for the world's biggest **Passion Play.** June kicks off with the **Festas Juninas** (p. 42), a Northeastern harvest festival now celebrated throughout Brazil; Sergipe (p. 392) is our top choice for this fun-filled event. Fast on the heels of the Juninas is the hotly contested folkloric celebration of Parintins's **Boi-Bumbá** (p. 39), now one of the most popular non-Carnaval celebrations for tourists. You'll forget you're in Brazil (OK, you'll forget pretty much

TOP TEN LIST

TOP TEN FESTIVALS

1. **Carnaval** (p. 46). The world's biggest party; an obvious #1.

2. **Reveillon** (p. 115). New Year's Eve features music and fireworks across the country, with the most popular celebration in Rio.

3. **Festas Juninas** (p. 170). A nation-wide harvest festival (best in Sergipe) honoring saints, featuring bonfires and hot-air balloons.

4. **Boi-Bumbá** (p. 505). This Parintins celebration involves European and African styles of dance, music, and theater.

5. **Fortal** (p. 428). Fortaleza throws this off-season Carnaval for 4 days in July, and over 2 million people come to party in the streets.

6. **Passion Plays** (p. 419). In the 10 days before Easter, Nova Jerusalem hosts South America's largest cycle of Passion Plays.

7. **International Film Festival** (p. 196). Cinema buffs flock for films from Brazil and beyond.

8. **Celebration of Iemanjá** (p. 368). In Salvador, perfume, flowers, and jewelry are offered to the ocean for the goddess of the sea.

9. **Oktoberfest** (p. 260). Settled largely by Germans, Blumenau holds the world's 2nd largest Oktoberfest, with *bierwagons*.

10. **Lavagem do Bonfim** (p. 368). The washing of the steps of Salvador's Igreja do Bonfim is followed by prayer and late-night partying.

everything) at beer-guzzling Blumenau's **Oktoberfest** (p. 260), second in size and popularity only to Munich's. Sporting events in Brazil always call for a big celebration. Aside from giving in to the *futebol* fever that grips the country year-round, travelers flock to the **Grand Prix** held in São Paulo (p. 196) and the **Semana de Vela** (Sailing Week) in Ilhabela (p. 201). For a list of festival dates, see p. 42. Also see town **Festivals** sections for more listings.

SONG & DANCE

From the incessant drum beat of *samba* to the twangy accordion strains of *forró*, music is everywhere in Brazil, and not just during official festivities. **Samba** started in Bahia, but it is **Rio** (p. 115) that not only dedicates five days to it (during Carnaval; p. 47) but gives it its own neighborhood (Lapa; see p. 154). Rio is also the birthplace of **bossa nova,** heard in the jazz bars of Ipanema. Outside of Rio, Carnaval is synonymous with the infectious hybrid sound of **axé,** a highly danceable style heard in **Olinda** (p. 414) and from the *trios eléctricos* that drive through the streets for **Salvador's** Carnaval (p. 58). The streets of Salvador are also the best place to see *rodas* of the athletic dance/martial arts style known as **capoeira,** brought to Bahia by Angolan immigrants; the city's Pelourinho district has countless traveler-friendly *capoeira* schools to join. Pelourinho also hosts a legendary **Tuesday night music party** (p. 363) with musicians and raucous drum corps like Olodum parading through the streets until dawn. The music heard most often at local-frequented clubs is **forró** (p. 31), Brazil's own version of two-step country music; though it has yet to catch on with travelers, most still flock to the *forró* beach parties in and around **Fortaleza** (p. 428) and **Jericoacoara** (p. 437). **Reggae** (that's HEH-gee in Portuguese), though not native to Brazil, is immensely popular in this beach- and *maconha*-loving country, particularly in the laid-back state of **Maranhão** (p. 445), called the "Brazilian Jamaica."

EXOTIC EATS

In Brazil, adventurous eaters are faced with almost as many options as adventure sports enthusiasts, particularly in the North. One of the most bizarre dishes is **tacacá no tucupi** (p. 37); this manioc-based soup is eaten with a fork, served in a decorative gourd, and fwavored uthing thongue-nhumbing *jambu* weavth. The exotic fruits and berries of the nearby **Amazon** are a favorite on Brazilian menus, especially in **Manaus** (p. 490). Corner *sucos* (juice stands) all over the country sell such oddball fruits as *açaí*, *cupuaçú*, and *xoclocoatã;* **mega-bomba** versions of these juices are crammed full of everything from *guaraná* to raw eggs. The truly brave can head into the Amazon to fish for their dinner on a **piranha fishing** trip (p. 475), where they'll wade waist-deep through predator-filled waters. This activity is even more popular in the wetlands of the **Pantanal** (p. 311).

The most inventive culinary region of Brazil is **Bahia** (p. 38), where cooks use tropical and African ingredients like coconut, tongue-tingling spices, and gut-rotting palm oil *(dendê)*, plus all manner of weird creatures from the sea. The streets of **Salvador** (p. 356) are filled with stalls selling Baiano treats like *acarajé* and *tapioca;* across Bahia, restaurants brew up **moquecas,** spicy coconut stews made with everything from crab to octopus. Brazilian food is best washed down with **caipirinhas,** the national cocktail made with lime juice, ice, and **cachaça,** Brazil's gut-wrenching sugarcane rum (a.k.a. *pinga*). Connoisseurs and liver-haters head to the hills around *cachaça* capitals **Minas Gerais** (p. 203) and **Paraty** (p. 168) in search of those elusive private distilleries that ferment the best *pinga* in Brazil.

The culinarily cautious can still expand their horizons (and their waistlines) with Brazil's most famous dish, **churrascaria** (p. 39), an all-you-can-eat barbecue buffet (everything from rump roast to chicken hearts) served by waiters parading around with skewers. *Churrascarias* are all over the country, but they're best in their birthplace, among the Gaúchos of **Porto Alegre** (p. 262). Battling barbecue for the top billing is **feijoada** (p. 38), a black bean and pork tongue feast; its origins are uncertain, but few doubt the supremacy of the Saturday *feijoada* in **Rio** (p. 130).

WET & WILDLIFE

Though Brazil is probably best known for the plumed creatures of Carnaval and the tanned, bikinied wildlife of its beaches, travelers shouldn't ignore the country's spectacular array of animals. From rare rainbow-colored macaws to frisky pink dolphins, it's all here. The world's largest rainforest, the **Amazon,** blankets most of northern Brazil. Visit during the wet season (Jan.-June) and you'll canoe through treetops in search of Amazon natives like the piranha and caiman. Trips start in **Manaus** (p. 490); excellent reserves include **Ilha do Marajó** (p. 471) and **Mamirauá** (p. 507). Though the Amazon gets all the press, the **Pantanal,** sprawling wetlands in Brazil's interior, is actually the most densely packed wildlife region on the planet. On trips out of **Campo Grande** (p. 325), **Cuiabá** (p. 298), or **Bonito** (p. 338), you'll see alligators, *jabarus,* and *capybaras,* the world's largest rodent. Both regions offer wild adventures like piranha fishing and alligator wrestling.

Travelers looking for a less dangerous wildlife encounter should head to the cities along Brazil's coast, built on the remains of the vast waterfront **Mata Atlântica** (Atlantic Rainforest). The forest is home to many rare species of animals found only in the region, like the unbearably cute spider monkeys found in the streets of Rio (escaped from the **Parque Nacional da Tijuca;** p. 137). Other wildlife-friendly national parks include Rio state's **Serra dos Órgãos** (p. 164) and Paraná's **Superaguí** (p. 244). The famed waterfalls at **Foz do Iguaçu** (p. 250) are home to hundreds of cuddly, tourist-loving *coatis* as well as a rainbow array of butterfly species. Those interested in Brazil's preservation efforts should visit the **TAMAR turtle reserve** in Bahia's Praia do Forte (p. 370) or engage one of the preservation-conscious tour groups around Manaus (p. 490).

THE SPORTING LIFE

The country that gave the world Pelé, Romário, Ayrton Senna, and Guga is unsurprisingly a country of fitness and sports fanatics, especially evident in Brazil's fanatical devotion to and ability for **futebol.** Soccer fans shouldn't miss a game in Rio's **Maracanã** (p. 142), the world's largest stadium. Beach *futebol* is also popular, but it faces stiff competition from **volleyball** (Rio hosts the international championships) and other beach sports like **futevolei** (nearly impossible no-hands volleyball) and **frescobol** (beach ping-pong). A different range of aquatic sports are popular in the Northeast, including **windsurfing** in **Fortaleza** (p. 428) and **Barra de Santo Antônio** (p. 399), **snorkeling** in the *piscinas naturais* that dot the Northeast coast, and **scuba diving** on Bahia's **Morro de São Paulo** (p. 371).

Surfing is fantastic all over much of Brazil, particularly in **Saquarema** (p. 170), **Ilha do Mel** (p. 241), and expat enclave **Itacaré.** Those bored with surfing on water can try **sand surfing** down the famed dunes of **Jericoacoara** (p. 437). The sand elsewhere in Brazil is reserved for horseback riding: try it at **Praia do Forte** (p. 370) and **Natal** (p. 425), or head to the **Pantanal** (p. 311) for nighttime horseback rides. Bahia's **Lençóis** (p. 377) is known as the "Poor Man's Pantanal," and is a haven for hikers and outdoor sportsmen, particularly kayakers. Those sick of the water and the land can take to the air in a heart-stopping **hang gliding** trip either at **Arraial d'Ajuda** or in **Rio** (p. 152). The true adventure sport capital of Brazil is the Center-West's **Bonito** (p. 338), a city of kayaking, extreme hiking, rappeling, and more.

LIFE'S A BEACH

Brazil has nearly 8000km of coastline and a nearly endless string of World's Best Beach accolades. Whether you want a vibrant scene or total surf-and-sand isolation to perfect your tan, Brazil has a place for you. Rio de Janeiro's beaches (p. 150) include **Ipanema** (so sexy it spawned its own sound track; p. 30) and the world's most famous beach, **Copacabana** (p. 150). The fantastic and diverse beaches of the **Ilha da Catarina** (p. 253), near **Florianópolis,** are alone worth the trip to the oft-ignored South region. The Northeast is home to the country's highest concentration of fantastic spots. Bahia's best include hip **Porto Seguro** (p. 374) and **Arraial d'Ajuda** (p. 377) and idyllic **Praia do Forte** (p. 370). The Northeast coast is an endless string of perfection—soft sand, calm waters, and reef-ringed *piscinas naturais* (natural pools) ideal for relaxing. Rent a buggy in **Natal** (p. 425) and discover your own private piece of paradise, or head to regional highlights like **Ilha da Croa, Praia do Frances** (p. 399), **Porto de Galinhas** (p. 413), or **Jacumã** (p. 424). Excursions from **Fortaleza** (p. 428) take you to hippie-packed **Canoa Quebrada** (p. 435) or far-flung **Jericoacoara** (p. 437), once an undiscovered getaway but now one of the top backpacker destinations in the country.

LET'S GO PICKS

THE BEST OF BRAZIL

BEST TRAIN: The breathtaking ride on the **Curitiba-Paranaguá train** (p. 232).

BEST PLANE: Airplane-shaped **Brasília** (p. 271), Brazil's futuristic planned capital.

BEST AUTOMOBILE: The **dune buggies** which will take you along the beach from Fortaleza to Natal (p. 428).

BEST VARIATION ON FUTEBOL: Autoball... soccer played in cars with mansized balls (p. 41).

WETTEST WAVES: The Pororoca (p. 11), a series of Atlantic waves (up to 5m high) that sweep up the Amazon River every May between the new and full moon.

SANDIEST SURF: Boarding the **sand dunes** of Ilha de Santa Catarina (p. 253).

FRUITIEST ICON: Carmen Miranda, best memorialized in Rio's Carnaval by the **Banda da Carmen Miranda** (p. 55).

BIGGER THAN THE BEATLES: The 30m statue of **Cristo Redentor** (Christ the Redeemer) atop Corcovado in Rio (p. 137).

CHICKEN MOST FOWL: The **man-sized chickens,** carved out of palm trees, that decorate Porto do Galinhas (p. 413).

WILDEST: Carnaval (p. 46) in Rio de Janeiro, the world's biggest party.

WETTEST: Foz do Iguaçu (p. 250), the widest series of waterfalls in the world.

SAUCIEST: Tacacá no tucupi (p. 37), a mouth-numbing soup with a bite.

FLOSSIEST: The **fio dental** (string bikini, but literally "dental floss") first appeared in Rio de Janeiro.

SEEDIEST: The **Cajueiro de Pirangi,** the world's largest cashew tree (p. 425), annually produces over 60,000 cashews.

RACIEST: São Paulo's **Grand Prix** (p. 196), among the most challenging Formula 1 courses in the world.

SPACIEST: São Thomé das Letras (p. 225), Brazil's 4th highest city and home to the most reported UFO sightings in Brazil.

SUGGESTED ITINERARIES

BEST OF BRAZIL

Whether Brazil is your only port of call or just one leg of a longer South American or round-the-world trip, these suggestions will help you make the most of this vast country.

IN 2 MONTHS. Coming from Argentina's border town of Porto Iguazú, start in the South of Brazil at **Foz do Iguaçu** (p. 246, 2 days) and marvel at the world's widest waterfalls. Then it's off to **Florianópolis** (p. 253, 3 days), half of which sits on the beautiful Ilha de Santa Catarina, ringed with 42 beaches. Head north to Curitiba, where the **Curitiba-Paranaguá train** (p. 232) will take you through lush mountains and provide a spectacular view of canyons, plains, and ocean. From Paranaguá, catch a boat to **Ilha do Mel** (p. 241, 2 days), a paradise that draws surfers from all over the globe. Force yourself to leave these shores behind and head to **Brasília** (p. 271, 2 days), Brazil's futuristic capital, to scope out the fantastic architecture by Modernist master Oscar Niemeyer. In Brasília, arrange an excursion to the **Pantanal** (p. 311, 3 days), to see some of Brazil's wildlife—maybe even a *capybara*—and fish for piranha. After getting back to nature, head to urban **Rio de Janeiro** (p. 115, 7 days): learn to *samba,* watch a *futebol* game, and bake on the city's beautiful beaches. Leave the big city behind and head to the beautiful resort town of **Búzios** (p. 172, 2 days) to relax, either by snorkeling, shopping, or tanning. Next, travel inland to **Belo Horizonte** (p. 203, 2 days) to see the buildings that launched Niemeyer's career. Nearby is former gold rush town **Ouro Preto** (p. 209, 2 days), declared a UNESCO World Heritage Site; wander its lovely cobblestone streets and soak up *bandeirante* history. Then it's east to Bahia's **Porto Seguro** (p. 374, 2 days), one of the first European settlements in Brazil and the gateway to hip **Arraial d'Ajuda** (p. 377, 1 day), where you can relax with young Brazilians to the sound of reggae. Head north to beautiful **Salvador** (p. 344, 6 days), Brazil's cultural capital and the heart of its Afro-Brazilian community: stroll through pastel Pelourinho, attend a *roda da capoeira,* hear the latest fusion musical styles, sample traditional Northeastern cuisine from street vendors, and check out the infamous Tuesday night street parties. Recover with a kayak trip or scuba dive off nearby, picture-perfect **Morro de São Paulo** (p. 371, 2 days), then head back through Salvador to **Lençóis** (p. 377, 3 days) and the lush Chapada Diamantina. Surrounded by sparkling waterfalls, green mountains, and natural pools, the town is a good base for hiking in the park. After some inland adventures, it's back to **Recife** (p. 400, 1 day) and neighboring colonial wonder **Olinda** (p. 414, 2 days).

Stay on the coast while heading northward to **Natal** (p. 425); from there it's a hair-raising buggy ride past hidden beaches and dunes to **Fortaleza** (p. 428, 3 days). Learn to *forró,* visit the colossal Arts & Culture Center, enjoy incredible seafood, and then hop a bus to far-flung **Jericoacoara** (p. 437, 1 day) to windsurf or work on your tan. Head back to Fortaleza en route to Belém, where you will bid adieu to the Atlantic and sling a hammock on the deck of an **Amazonian riverboat** (p. 455, 5 days) for the breezy, enjoyable trip to the city of Manaus.

IN 1 MONTH. Fly into multicultural metropolis **São Paulo** (p. 196, 2 days), where you can check out Neoclassical

BEST OF BRAZIL: IN 1 MONTH

architecture, stroll through Parque do Ibirapuera on your way to the Museu da Arte Moderna, and spend a night barhopping in the student-filled Vila Madalena or bohemian Pinheiros. Continue your urban jaunt in **Rio de Janeiro** (p. 115, 5 days), the "Marvelous City" with its array of beaches, street *samba* parties, and the unforgettable view from Corcovado. Don't miss a *futebol* match at Maracanã, the world's biggest stadium. Take a ferry from nearby Angra dos Reis to spend a day unwinding on **Ilha Grande** (p. 166, 1 day), trekking through verdant forest to reach the island's many beautiful secluded beaches. Head back through Rio en route to historic **Ouro Preto** (p. 209, 2 days), a UNESCO World Heritage Site full of gaudy gold-leaf churches and the works of Aleijadinho, Brazil's most famous sculptor. Head east to laid-back **Arraial d'Ajuda** (p. 377, 2 days) to party nightly to reggae and *forró* before continuing north to Brazil's most culturally vibrant city, **Salvador** (p. 344, 5 days). The streets of Salvador are filled to the brim with the vibrant sights and sounds of *capoeira* and drum bands, while the air is thick with the smell of heady *dendê* oil and African-influenced cuisine. From Salvador head to **Lençóis** (p. 377, 2 days), the gateway to the waterfalls and trails of Chapada Diamantina. Then go north to cosmopolitan **Recife** (p. 400, 1 day) and neighboring relic **Olinda** (p. 414, 1 day) for beautiful beaches and rambling colonial centers. Pack light and head to Natal for a one-of-a-kind trip; the **buggy ride to Fortaleza** (p. 428, 3 days). Sample incredible seafood before making the long haul to distant **Jericoacoara** (p. 437, 2 days) for relaxing or learning to windsurf. Spend your last few days getting back to nature: either head up the coast to Belém, sling a hammock on an **Amazonian riverboat** (p. 455, 5 days) to Manaus; or, fly back to Rio or São Paulo and arrange an excursion to the **Pantanal** (p. 311, 5 days), where you'll see some of Brazil's most impressive wildlife.

STATE HIGHLIGHTS

These brief trips (10-17 days) are perfect for travelers sick of the well-trodden tourist path and eager to take more time to explore Brazil's most fascinating destinations in greater depth.

RIO DE JANEIRO STATE (17 DAYS)

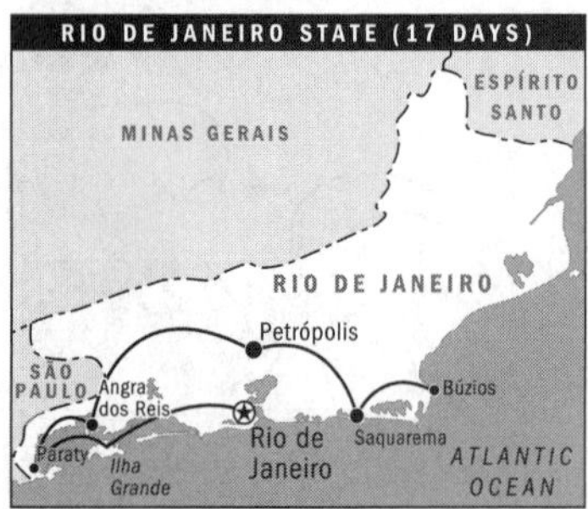

RIO DE JANEIRO STATE (17 DAYS). Start your tour in Brazil's most famous city, **Rio de Janiero** (p. 115, 5 days) and stop to watch the street performers as you explore the city's historic center and famous beaches. *Samba* on to nearby **Ilha Grande** (p. 166, 3 days) via Angra dos Reis to recover from the fast pace of Rio on seemingly endless strips of tropical sand. Hike through the Atlantic rainforest that covers much of the island, or rent a boat to find your own secluded cove. Wander through the cobblestone streets of nearby **Paraty** (p. 168, 2 days) and window shop (or splurge) at the many galleries and boutiques. From Paraty, head up the coast, passing island-hopping gateway **Angra dos Reis** (p. 165, 1 day) en route to Rio, where you can daytrip to preserved imperial getaway **Petrópolis** (p. 161, 1 day). Move on to ride the waves at **Saquarema** (p. 170, 2 days), north of Rio, or hike through the town's Ecological Reserve past cooling mineral springs and waterfalls. Wrap up your trip with downtime in **Búzios** (p. 172, 3 days), a resort town with gorgeous beaches perfect for snorkeling or sunning.

BAHIA (17 DAYS). Coming from Rio, make **Porto Seguro** (p. 374, 2 days) your first stop for its calm waters, hot sun, and pervasive *axé* and *forró* beats. Hop the ferry to laid-back **Arraial d'Ajuda** (p. 377, 2 days), then head back to the mainland and take in beautiful, bustling **Salvador** (p. 344, 5 days), Brazil's first capital and the *axé*-beating heart of the country's Afro-Brazilian culture. Immerse yourself in *rodas da capoeira,* traditional dance, museums, and spicy cuisine. Ponder colonial Brazil in historic **Cachoeira** (p. 368, 1 day): the small *centro* is packed with museums, churches, and restored buildings. Head back through Salvador and continue north to the palm-lined beaches of **Praia do Forte** (p. 370, 2 days). Take a guided trek through the *saparinga* forest to the faux-medieval castle, or stick to the coast for horseback riding and parasailing. Head back to Salvador to hop the ferry to **Morro de São Paulo** (p. 371, 2 days), Brazil's premier island paradise. Sail out to the *piscinas naturais*, rappel above the waves, or learn to scuba dive below them. After all this beach time, dry off and head west to the town of Lençóis, which is the gateway to the mountainous national park known as the **Chapada Diamantina** (p. 387, 3 days). Hike through this greenery past sparkling waterfalls or enjoy the town's charming cobblestone streets and terra-cotta roofs.

MINAS GERAIS (10 DAYS). Begin in **São João del-Rei** (p. 219, 2 days) and take in the sparkling churches of this former gold rush settlement. Scan the skies above **São Thomé das Letras** (p. 225, 2 days) for UFOs. Intergalactic getaway or not, the sunsets alone are worth the trip. Head north to **Belo Horizonte** (p. 203, 1 day) for impressive architecture and beautiful *praças* in this well-designed state capital. On the ride to **Ouro Preto** (p. 209, 3 days), prepare to be dazzled by well-preserved colonial charm. Leave the beaten track behind in **Diamantina** (p. 223, 2 days) to enjoy peace and quiet in this old mining town.

REGIONAL BESTS

Brazil's five political regions all have distinct characters, each with different cuisines, cultures, attractions, and peoples. Here's a guide to three of them:

NORTHEAST COAST (17 DAYS). This coast of Brazil is a beach-lover's dream. Coming from Salvador, stop in colorful **Recife** (p. 400, 2 days): sun on the lovely beach, explore the winding streets of the old city, and dance the night away in swinging Boa Viagem. Don't miss **Olinda** (p. 414, 3 days), Recife's charming colonial neighbor. Head to **João Pessoa** (p. 421, 2 days) to relax on the surrounding beaches. Continue north to cheerful **Natal** (p. 425, 2 days) to catch live *samba* and rent a buggy for your trip upt to **Canoa Quebrada** (p. 435, 2 days). Mingle with laid-back locals and party on weekends on the pink dunes. Push on to **Fortaleza** (p. 428, 2 day), home to a famed cultural center. Appreciate pristine **Praia da Lagoinha** (p. 436, 2 days), sample fresh seafood, then make your last stop at **Jericoacoara** (p. 437, 2 days) to take windsurfing lessons or just reflect on the *beleza natural.*

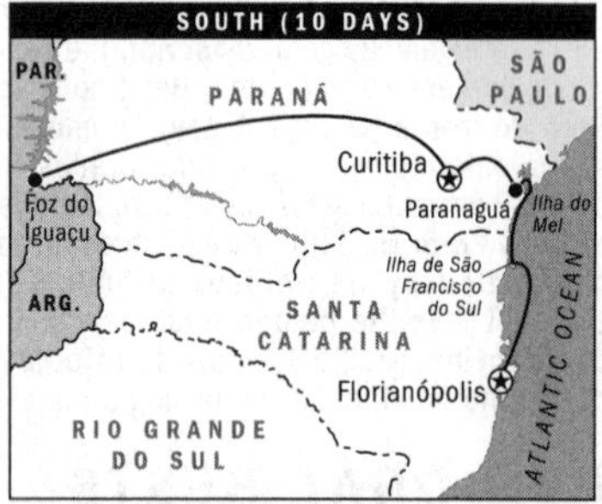

SOUTH (10 DAYS). Coming from Argentina's Porto Iguazú, begin your trip with a splash at the massive **Foz do Iguaçu** (p. 250, 2 days). Head east to **Curitiba** (p. 232, 2 days) for the neo-Gothic Catedral Basílica and the lively bar scene which leads Curitibans to call their home Brazil's "Capital Social." Hop the **Curitiba-Paranaguá train** (p. 232), which runs through lush mountains and offers views of canyons, plains, and ocean. From Paranaguá, sail to the nearby **Ilha do Mel** (p. 241, 1 day), and watch (or join) surfers on the incredible waves. Tour the bay of **São Francisco do Sul** (p. 259, 2 days), then stake out your own little patch of sand and watch the world go by. Round out your visit with **Florianópolis** (p. 253, 3 days), on the beach-filled Ilha de Santa Catarina, where you can try sandboarding on the dunes.

NORTH (17 DAYS). Cosmopolitan capital **Belém** (p. 454, 3 days) provides opportunity to experience everything from glitzy nightlife to colonial influence, at times in a strange Art Deco setting. Head north to **Macapá** (p. 481, 2 days), at the mouth of the Amazon, and learn about the region's indigenous cultures and tour the tranquil waterfront on a zippy moto-taxi. Hop a plane to Santarém to get to **Alter do Chão** (p. 480, 2 days), then relax on the white sands of the best beach in the Amazon. Once your tan is satisfactory, fly into Manaus. Discover the rainforest on one of the many **jungle trips** (p. 500, 4 days) departing from Manaus. Marvel at the lush canopy and listen to the chatter of monkeys from your canoe. Press on to **Rio Branco** (p. 512, 2 days), deep in the interior. Immerse yourself in the history of the rubber industry and the area's indigenous communities as you wander from museum to museum. Fly north to Tefé, which serves as a stepping stone to the **Mamirauá Reserve** (p. 507, 4 days). Take your camera to (legally) capture the region's amazing wildlife, as you are guided through the forest surrounding the solar-powered lodge. Relax on a starlit nighttime canoe trip, and prepare to eat or be eaten as you fish for *piranha.*

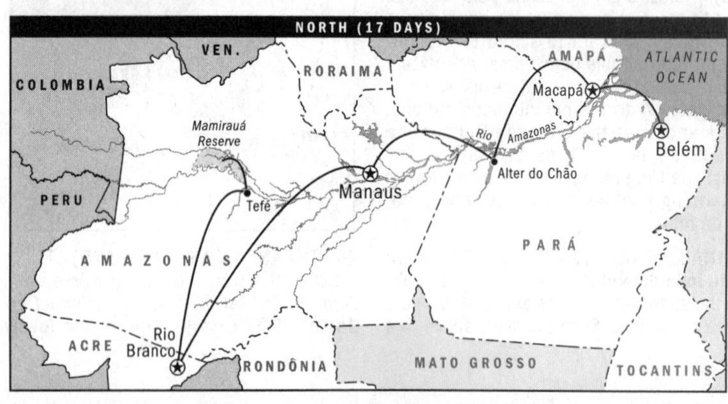

LIFE & TIMES

Brazil has an adventure for everyone, and there's much more than just soccer, *samba*, and sex. The fifth largest country in the world, the Federated Republic of Brazil is a sprawling landmass with superlative attractions to match its superior size: this is, after all, the home of the world's largest rainforest, greatest waterfall, and wildest party, to name but a few. While it's no surprise that a country of this size is not homogenous, the extent to which culture, society, geography, and climate vary within the country is astonishing. From long white beaches to ragged mountains, from lush rainforests to barren, arid plains, Brazil's spectacularly scenic panorama is almost as breathtakingly diverse as the dances, festivals, and musical styles for which the country is globally renowned. Most of Brazil's population clusters along a thin 7000km strip of Atlantic coast, which includes Carnaval capital Rio de Janeiro. However, the country's attractions are spread out over the entire nation, from the colonial architecture of Ouro Preto to the futuristic design of Brasília, from the isolated beaches of Bahia to the wilderness of the Pantanal.

LAND

With an area of over 8,500,000 square kilometers, Brazil is the world's fifth largest nation, covering about 47% of South America's continental area and sharing borders with all South American countries except Chile and Equador. Within its boundaries there are an extremely diverse collection of biomes, from dense rainforest to semiarid savanna, from mountains to rolling plains. The twenty-six states of Brazil (and the Distrito Federal, seat of the Federal government) are conventionally divided into five regions: North, Northeast, Southeast, South, and Center-West. Each of these regions contains a unique physical environment and distinct ecosystem. The two types of geographical areas which take up the majority of Brazil's landmass are the Amazon Basin (which has an area of 4,000,000 square kilometers) and the Central Highlands (a plateau south of the Amazon River, most of which consists of tablelands varying in altitude from 300 to 500m). The Southeast is the most populated region and most Brazilians live on the Atlantic coastal strip.

GEOGRAPHY

NORTH

The equatorial North is mainly comprised of the Amazon Basin and is the country's largest region, covering 45.3% of the national territory. The Basin itself contains the world's largest rainforest, which accounts for a whopping 30% of the entire world's forested areas. Moreover, this region is home to an amazing 10 of the world's 20 longest rivers (including a large section of the immense Amazon River): with so much water, it's not surprising that most transportation in this part of the nation is by water rather than by road. In addition to the rainforest, this region contains the Guiana Highlands, which are alternately forested area and rocky desert. Within these highlands is Pico da Neblina ("Mountain of the Mists"), Brazil's highest peak, which has an altitude of 3014m. The Highlands are so remote and difficult to explore that this mountain was not discovered until the early 1950s. While the North is home to the majority of Brazil's Terras Indígenas (indigenous reservations), it is nevertheless the nation's least populated region.

NORTHEAST

To the southeast of the Amazon River's mouth is the "bulge" of Brazil, the region known as the Northeast, which covers 18.3% of Brazil's total area. The Northeast consists of a narrow coastal plain (formerly the site of sugarcane plantations and still the most densely populated area in the region) and the **sertão** (semiarid interior), which is subject to recurrent droughts. Except for an isolated mountain range within the Chapada Diamantina (p. 387), the interior is on Brazil's **Great Plateau.** Those mountains cover an area of 100-150 miles (150-240km) and appear as an island of green because of their altitude, which at times reaches 5000 feet (15,000m) and allows them to collect more moisture than the surrounding *caatinga* (dry, thick thorny vegetation characteristic of the area). The states of Maranhão and Piauí are a transitional zone between this area and the North, sharing the characteristic biomes of both regions (rainforest and *sertão*). The turning point of the "bulge" is a cape known as São Roque; to the northeast lies the island of **Fernando de Noronha,** the smallest area in the world with its own time zone.

SOUTHEAST

The Southeast makes up only 10.9% of the nation's total area, but is home to 39% of Brazil's population and has many dense urban areas (including the country's two largest cities, São Paulo and Rio de Janeiro). This region was originally covered by **Mata Atlântica,** the Atlantic rainforest that has now been almost entirely destroyed but once stretched all along the Brazilian coastline up to Rio Grande do Norte (in the Northeast). More than 95% of the forest was felled for agriculture, ranching, and urban development, and farming is still prevalent. The narrow coastlines of the Southeast are bordered on the west by an escarpment, which at times extends right to the ocean in parallel steps. Each step is separated by a valley, which makes for incredible scenery. Above this escarpment is a great plateau—upon which São Paulo is located—which extends through much of the nation and finally tapers off in Rio Grande do Sul, Brazil's southernmost state.

SOUTH

Much of the characteristic geographic pattern of the South is similar to that of the Southeast: narrow, interrupted coastlines bordered on the west by an escarpment, with an inland plateau spreading westward. From the ocean, the escarpment looks like a mountain range, commonly referred to south of Rio as the **Serra do Mar** (Coastal Range). In the South, the convergence of Rio Paraná and Rio Iguaçu forms **Iguaçu Falls.** Higher than Victoria Falls and wider than Niagara Falls, the falls are formed from three sheets of water with a total width of 4.2km. In addition to the southern sea-level plains, which are covered by **pampas** (grasslands similar to those of Argentina), this region also contains pine-forested highlands and occasional patches of the original Mata Atlântica. The South is the smallest region of Brazil (accounting for only 6.8% of the nation's area), but is almost as densely settled as the Southeast, with a population even more concentrated along the coast.

CENTER-WEST

The biome for which the Center-West is best known is the **Pantanal,** an area of wetlands about the size of the US state of Florida. The second largest region in Brazil and the world's largest seasonally flooded marshes, this former inland sea is sparsely populated and submerged for most of the year. Despite the Pantanal's size, most of the Center-West (which also contains the Distrito Federal) is actually covered by the drought-resistant grasses and sparse scrub trees of the **cerrado,** which can survive the dry season most of the Center-West experiences in the middle of the year. The *cerrado* blends into tropical forest as it approaches the North.

CLIMATE

Ninety percent of Brazil's landmass falls within the tropical zone, as the country is crossed by the equator in the north and the Tropic of Capricorn in the south. However, the nation's climate is far from homogenous and ranges from equatorial to semiarid to subtropical. Because most of Brazil is in the southern hemisphere (northern Amazonas and Roriama excluded), **summer** occurs between December and March, while **winter** runs from June to August.

Near the equator, there isn't a great deal of seasonal temperature change: occasionally, during the winter months, it may be cool enough to wear a jacket. Temperatures in the Northeast's lower interior and the Pantanal can soar to 40°C during the summer, while frost is not uncommon during the winter months in the subtropical climate south of the Tropic of Capricorn. Even snow is not unheard of in the mountainous areas of Rio Grande do Sul and Santa Catarina. Precipitation, as well as temperature, can vary a great deal between regions: while the national average is about 1500mm per year, the coastal regions of Pará and western Amazonas often receive upwards of 3000mm annually. The amount of precipitation that falls in the Amazon means that areas of the rainforest *(igapos)* are flooded during the **wet season** (Jan.-June). Despite the huge amounts of precipitation the rainforest receives, much of the forest is relatively dry from May to August. However, throughout the rest of the year it is wet enough that the humidity usually remains above 97%. In stark contrast to the Amazon, the interior Northeast receives only about 500mm of rain per year and experiences severe drought in cycles of about seven years. The Northeast is not only the driest, but also the hottest part of Brazil: during the **dry season** (May-Nov.), temperatures of over 40°C have been recorded. The South and most of the Atlantic coast—as far north as Salvador—have no distinct dry season and receive an average of 1500-2000mm per year. Along the coast, Rio de Janeiro, Recife, and Salvador have warm climates (temperatures average 23-27°C), and experience constant trade winds that moderate the climate, which may explain why these areas are among the most densely populated and most frequently visited in Brazil.

FLORA & FAUNA

Within Brazil's diverse range of ecosystems are tucked away approximately one-fifth of the world's flora and fauna. South America separated from the other continents over 100 million years ago, and has been reconnected with North America for only a few million years. As a result, its animal and plant life have developed in relative isolation and Brazil itself contains hundreds of endemic species; among birds alone, there are over 200 species that do not live in the wild anywhere else in the world. The **Amazon rainforest** has been an unusually stable ecosystem, largely because the last Ice Age did not extend to this part of the globe. Very specialized evolution among indigenous plants and animals has also occurred in this region because there have been no prolonged periods of drought. It is estimated that within 2.6 square kilometers of the Amazon up to 3000 different species of plant and animal may be found. Another incredible concentration of wildlife is the **Pantanal,** the sprawling marshlands—roughly half the size of France—of the Center-West, which extends into Bolivia and Paraguay. While there are not quite as many different species of animal here as in the Amazon, the Pantanal is often better for seeing wildlife because during the rainy season (Oct.-Mar.), much of the area floods and animals shelter together on the remaining dry patches. Although the **Mata Atlântica** (Atlantic Rainforest) has—as a result of logging, clearing for agriculture, and ranching—been reduced to less than 1% of its original size, its remaining canopy forest and bamboo groves (mainly around Rio and São Paulo) are important habitats for many endangered species. Unfortunately, the Mata Atlântica is not the only forest to face destruction due to logging: the Amazon is undergoing rapid deforestation and destruction of ecosystems. Because the rainforest is so heterogeneous, the valuable trees which loggers seek to extract (like mahogany) often grow singly. In the process of cutting them down and removing them, all of the surrounding vegetation and habitat is destroyed. Another unfortunate result of this process is that the forest floor becomes littered with deadwood, which greatly increases the chance of forest fires.

PLANTS

Brazil actually gets its name from the **brazilwood tree** *(pau-brasil)*, valued by early Portuguese explorers for the brilliant red dye which could be extracted from its core. The country's biodiversity has fostered an impressive range of flora: in Bahia, studies have revealed more than 450 species of tree per square hectare. Perhaps the most commonly known is the **rubber tree,** a native of Brazil and one of early European explorers' more lucrative discoveries. A single **brazilnut tree** takes ten years to reach maturity and can produce over 450kg of nuts per year. No less impressive are Brazil's spiky-rooted palms, which have cleverly adapted to the seasonal flooding of the Amazon: the main trunk begins two or three meters above ground, supported by exposed roots which keep the trunk above floodwaters, have adapted to absorb nitrogen from the air rather than the soil, and are covered in spikes to protect themselves from whatever animals might want to gnaw on them. Within this family are the **walking palm,** which is commonly used in parquet flooring, and the **stilt palm,** which has roots that grow in a teepee-like formation and strong bark that can be taken off in a single sheet (it has long been used by indigenous peoples as flooring and wall slats). Like the animals of the Amazon rainforest, a huge number of plants actually grow in the canopy, rather than on the forest floor: such is the case with the **turtle ladder vine,** which spirals upwards to blossom in the canopy overheard and is often older than the trees around it. However, not all flowers require that you crane your neck to see them—Brazil is home to more than 200 different varieties of **orchid.** No one actually knows how many different species of plant grow in Brazil, as new ones are constantly being discovered; recently there has been a new push to uncover and catalogue new species from the Amazon in the interests of uncovering new medicinal plants. Both **Guaraná,** an energy booster, and **sacupira,** used to soothe sore throats, are indigenous to the Amazon rainforest.

ANIMALS

Brazil's wildlife is far from completely catalogued. Among those animals which have been identified are over 600 species of mammal, more than 2500 species of freshwater fish, more than 700,000 species of insect, and over 1700 species of bird (a greater variety than almost any other nation).

ENDANGERED ANIMALS. More than 160 species of animal in Brazil are considered endangered: many of them, like the tiny **golden-lion tamarin** that lives in the Mata Atlântica (Atlantic Rainforest), because of loss of habitat due to deforestation. The grassy plains of the *cerrado* have been seriously infringed upon by farming and ranching, which has depleted the population of **maned wolves** to the extent that they too are now on the endangered list. Hunting is another cause for the depletion of species like the **giant river otter** and the **giant anteater.** Poachers are a serious threat to **alligators** and some species of birds, especially **macaws.**

FISH. Of all the fish in the Amazon, the **piranha** (of which there are actually several species) is probably most widely known. However, while it is true that the piranha is an aggressive predator, it's far more likely that you will eat one of them than that they will eat you. Still, it's probably safer to keep your fingers inside the boat. Another notable fish is the **pirarucú,** which is the largest freshwater fish in the world, growing to a length of over two meters and weighing in at up to 125kg. The **tambaqui** is notable because of its eating habits—its strong jaws can crack and eat seeds and nuts from the rubber tree and *jauari* palm.

MAMMALS. Fish are not the only creatures to inhabit the waterways of the Amazon: in the black water of the Pacaya and Alfaro rivers (colored by tannins seeping into the river from decaying vegetation) you may—if you're lucky—see a **pink dolphin.** They are known as *bufeo colorado* (funny-colored), and are quite genuinely pink, owing to the blood vessels directly beneath their skin. As if this weren't cute enough, they blush even pinker when they get excited, due to increased blood flow. Another aquatic mammal in these waters is the slow-moving Amazonian **manatee.** Brazil's waterways are also home to more than 40 species of turtle, as well as five types of **alligator** and smallish crocodiles called **caimans.** On land, one of the most memorable animals is probably the **capivara,** found primarily in the Pantanal: this creature can weigh up to 66kg, making it the largest rodent in the world. The **tapir** (all four species of which are endangered) may look like a pig, but it is hooved and actually a member of the same family as the horse and rhinoceros. Among the many species of cat found in Brazil are the **puma, jaguarundi, ocelot,** and the rarely-seen **spotted jaguar,** which is the second largest feline in the world. Hidden in the canopies of the Mata Atlântica and Amazon rainforest is the distinct-smelling **tamandua tree sloth** (it uses a strong scent to mark its territory), along with many species of primate, including the **howler monkey.** This creature is far more likely to be heard than seen, although its voice is less of a howl than a roar.

INSECTS. On a slightly smaller scale, Brazil has approximately 180 species of butterfly and over 200 species of mosquito. The upside of this itchy fact is that mosquitoes serve as an important food source for Brazil's incredible population of birds. If you'll be exploring the outdoors at all, long-sleeved shirts, pants, and insect repellent are a good idea.

BIRDS. Brazil's largest bird is the flightless **rhea** (something like an ostrich), which is found in the Pantanal and *cerrado* and can grow to be one and a half meters tall. Another one of the larger birds in Brazil—and one of the most rare—is the **harpy eagle:** found primarily in the Amazon, this impressive bird of prey has a diet which includes monkeys and sloths. There are dozens of species of tiny **hummingbirds** found all over Brazil, where they are known as *beija-flor* (flower-kisser). One of Brazil's slightly less appealing birds is the **hoatzin,** which is unique enough to be the only member of the family *Opisthocomidae.* Hoatzin chicks have claws on their wings which help them clamber around before they learn to fly. This vegetarian bird also has a unique digestive system resembling that of a cow and an unpleasant smell resulting from the slow process of decay taking place inside. Brazil is also home to several species of **macaw** (most of which are endangered) and **toucan,** as well as slightly less vibrant **storks, cormorants,** and **herons.**

DANGEROUS ANIMALS. The **bicho de pé** is a parasite found near beaches and on farms in the Northeast, which burrows between ones toes and stays there until cut out. The sensible way to avoid these footworms is simply not to walk around barefoot, and to check with locals as to whether or not the beaches are safe. Another thing to keep in mind while at the beach is **sharks;** while these fish generally won't bother you without being provoked, you should still avoid swimming in non-designated areas. Certain waterways are populated by **sting-rays;** these are not aggressive fish and will only hurt you if you step on them. They can inflict a nasty wound, but the way to avoid this is to slide your feet along the river floor when walking in the water. Another reason to avoid swimming in unknown waters are the **candiru** of the Amazon. Some species of these little fish spend much of their time sucking the blood of other, bigger fish but are attracted to urine and can supposedly make their way into human urinary tracts and use their spines to lodge themselves there. There are plenty of **alligators** and **snakes** (both constrictors and poisonous varieties) in Brazil, but the same rules apply here as in other snake-heavy regions: don't wander into unknown wilderness alone, and exercise common sense.

HISTORY

INDIGENOUS COMMUNITIES (BEFORE 1500)

Human inhabitation of the North American continent can be reliably established as far back as 50,000 BC, but the figures are less certain for South America in general and the Amazonian region in particular. The established view places the first inhabitants of modern-day Brazil at approximately 10,000 BC, although there is some evidence for an earlier occupation. Brazil's indigenous population initially settled in the Amazon river basin, where they apparently stayed until climate change induced large migrations to the coasts. Those tribes that made the migration mostly adopted agricultural lifestyles and settled either in permanent villages or in semi-permanent encampments that they relocated every few years, while those who remained inland mostly retained their nomadic, hunting-and-gathering lifestyles. In both locations ample food supplies and a hospitable climate supported an estimated five million inhabitants; agriculture here was a relatively late development and never heavily employed. Brazil's two major indigenous linguistic groups divide roughly along the same lines—the Tupi-Gurani were mostly sedentary, the Tapuia mostly nomadic. However, these broad generalizations mask the heterogeneity of Brazil's indigenous cultures, as they differed nearly as much between themselves as they did with the Europeans colonists. All of them, however, remained well within the stone age, and Brazil produced no counterpart to the Mayan, Incan, or Aztec civilizations. No sprawling metropolises rose to greet Europeans in Brazil, much to the disappointment of later Portuguese adventurers.

THE PORTUGUESE (THE 1490s)

Portugal was perhaps the foremost maritime nation of Europe at the end of the 15th century; the terms of the 1494 **Treaty of Tordesillas** Portugal negotiated with Spain indicate that Portugal was at least a match for its rival Spain. The treaty granted Spain all lands discovered more than 370 leagues west of the Cape Verde archipelago, and Portugal any lands discovered east of that boundary; in effect, tiny Portugal and sprawling Spain split the globe between themselves. Historians often group Spain and Portugal together as Iberia and lump their respective New World colonies into Latin America, but this notational convenience overlooks the enormous differences in character and experience between these two nations. In the early 15th century, Spain's wealth, population, and natural resources vastly outnumbered Portugal's, and Portugal's location at the westernmost tip of the Iberian peninsula left it perpetually surrounded by the ambitious and often expansionist Spain. This constant threat lent Portugal a precarious existence, and to bolster its position Portugal poured its resources into developing overseas trade contacts and the navigational skills to reach them. In the years leading up to Spain's discovery of the New World, Portugal had already established a network of trading posts along the western coast of Africa, but an overseas route to India was the real prize that both Spain and Portugal wanted. Such a discovery would transfer the wealth and power of the Italian trading cities—who distributed to the rest of the Mediterranean goods brought from India and Asia—to the discoverer.

Columbus's claim to have reached India in 1492 had left Portugal counting its days, but it proved to be a false alarm. It became clear that whatever he had stumbled upon was neither India nor China. Meanwhile, the Portuguese court announced the successful circumnavigation of Vasco da Gama, who under their patronage had sailed westward to India. Not wasting any time, Portugal sent explorer Pedro Álvarez Cabral to retrace da Gama's route—this time, with a fleet and goods to trade in India—but strong winds blew him off course and so he inadvertently landed on what would become Brazil in April 1500. Cabral's fleet docked near present-day Porto Seguro in Bahia, in sight of Mount Pascoal. There, Cabral and crew went ashore, befriended the local population, and conducted a mass, after which Cabral divided the fleet and sailed on. One ship was sent back to Lisbon to inform the court of the discovery and arrange for a larger exploratory expedition, while the rest of Cabral's fleet went on to finish their trading expedition to India. At the time, Cabral assumed he had merely found a small island—probably no more than 20 kilometers in circumference—but he claimed it for Portugal and so began Portugal's experiences in the New World.

COLONIALISM (1500-1822)

The colonial period established the demographic structure and economic system which still exist in Brazil today. Portugal did not immediately recognize that Cabral had claimed most of a continent, but even after the extent of his discovery became apparent the territory still seemed devoid of resources. The only product of any value was the brazilwood tree—from which a red dye could be extracted and from which Brazil took its name—but even before supplies of brazilwood became depleted the trade was never very lucrative. Once Brazil's supply of brazilwood neared exhaustion the colony threatened to become economically inviable. Moreover, by 1530 the presence of French traders and colonists throughout Brazil threatened Portugal's claim, and Brazil stood in danger of falling to the French.

Portugal countered the French threat by sending Martim Alfonso de Sousa to found the colony of São Vicente, and to encourage the colony's further development divided Brazil into 12 tracts of land, which were granted to members of the Portuguese aristocracy in exchange for a promise to protect and develop the land. The only way to make such a possession profitable seemed to be the cultivation of sugarcane: the tropical climate allowed multiple harvests per season, and at the time European demand for refined sugar was increasing rapidly. Sugarcane, however, required extensive amounts of often back-breaking manual labor throughout the entire cycle of planting, growing, and harvesting; to find a workforce, the colonies turned to slavery.

Earlier, the Portuguese traders had relied on the assistance of the Tupinamba to harvest brazilwood, since the tree grew scattered all over Brazil. This arrangement suited both parties: the Portuguese found the Tupinamba efficient and inexpensive laborers, and Tupinamba culture easily accommodated this sporadic work. For sugarcane cultivation, however, it was impossible to recruit Portuguese laborers for such tedious work in an unfamiliar country, nor did the monotonous work fit into indigenous culture.

The Portuguese found the natives frustratingly inefficient laborers despite widespread attempts to make them more productive, and any remaining goodwill toward the Portuguese was quickly eradicated by the slave-hunting bands of *bandeirantes* chasing indigenous communities inland.

Plantation owners thus turned to African slaves, primarily those brought from modern-day Angola, Gambia, Guinea, and Senegal. This system had two advantages for plantation owners: the slaves had experience with agricultural labor and were less likely than indigenous laborers to rebel while separated from their clansmen and in an unfamiliar land. Nearly four million slaves arrived in Brazil in this manner, and from them descended Brazil's modern Afro-Brazilian population. During the colonial era many runaway slaves formed villages called *quilombos*, some of which, like Palmares, lasted for decades. Many *quilombos* became centers where Brazil's discontented disenfranchised communities—African, indigenous, and poor white alike—gathered and fomented rebellion. These forces aided the brief Dutch occupation of Pernambuco, as it was not uncommon for the *quilombos* to fight alongside the Dutch invaders. Had the Calvinist Dutch not alienated their Catholic conquests so rapidly, it is possible that Brazil might have become at least partially Dutch; their influence can still be seen in present-day Recife, which the Dutch held until 1654.

In 1695 a band of *bandeirantes* discovered gold in present-day Minas Gerais and sparked a gold rush, creating fervor in both Brazil and Portugal. The wealth mining created brought urban life to Brazil and the first stirrings of a movement for independence were heard in Ouro Preto, site of the failed 1789 Inconfidência Mineira. The so-called *inconfidentes* (separatists who planned to kidnap the colony's governor and battle the Portuguese) were tried and convicted of treason in Ouro Preto, but the feeling for independence was strong and the colony became a nation in 1822.

IMPERIALISM (1822-1889)

Less-expansive but longer-lived than the Spanish Empire, Portugal also had imperial ambitions and at one point had an empire stretching from South America to southern China. As the largest single component of that empire Brazil became a natural refuge for the Portuguese prince Dom João in 1807, when Napoleon's armies overran Lisbon. On his arrival João immediately undertook the modernization of Brazil: he initiated mapping and road-building efforts, lifted the ban on domestic industries, and encouraged the importation of skilled craftsmen and tradesmen from Portugal. These reforms ultimately helped pave the way to Brazilian independence.

Napoleon's defeat in 1816 gave Portugal back to the Portuguese, but João—then King João—was by then enamored of Brazil and did not return until power struggles in Portugal demanded his personal attention; he left his son Dom Pedro in charge of the colony. Jealous of Brazil's increasing wealth and power, the newly-restored Portuguese congress—against King João's wishes—passed a series of resolutions aimed at curtailing the freedoms and reforms he had implemented, but Pedro refused to obey them. As the story then goes, he grew so tired of arguing with the congress that after receiving a particularly aggravating letter while on an inland expedition near Ipiranga he declared Brazil an independent nation. With help from British negotiators Brazil quickly separated from Portugal and became an independent nation under Dom Pedro in 1822.

Dom Pedro's rule did not last long. As Emperor he had agreed to implement a system of government giving many checks on his power to congress—composed of citizens elected from Brazil's elite—but regularly ignored the congress and relied instead on imported Portuguese advisors. Mounting dissatisfaction threatened to spark a revolution, so to effectively save the Brazilian monarchy from destruction, Pedro abdicated the throne in 1831, leaving his five-year-old son Pedro II to one day take the throne.

A parliamentary coalition of Brazil's two leading political parties ruled Brazil while Pedro II grew, but the alliance grew so fractious that as soon as Pedro II reached his 14th birthday the same parliament that had forced his father to abdicate passed an act crowning the boy as Emperor of Brazil in 1840.

Pedro II became a veritable philosopher-king in the eyes of American and European observers: as a boy he had received a broad and deep education in art, literature, science, and philosophy, and was deeply sympathetic to the rationalistic currents that had coursed through European thought since the Enlightenment. Fortune favored Pedro II for a while, as coffee exports provided funding for improvements to Brazil's still-underdeveloped communication and transportation networks. Coffee cultivation—like that of sugarcane before it—required slave labor to make it economical, but Pedro II hated slavery. He was under great pressure from England and the US to emancipate Brazil's slaves, and even went so far as to free all the slaves he owned, but conditions in Brazil would have made full emancipation political suicide. Pedro II's rule was also marked by serious conflicts between church and state, but Pedro sided too often with the state to remain very popular with Brazil's conservative elite. The final blow to his rule came on May 13, 1888, when in Pedro II's absence his daughter Isabel passed the "golden law" freeing all slaves—Pedro II had always been more kind than controlling, and so had no way to defend his rule when the armed forces, backed by an elite coalition, deposed the emperor and declared Brazil a republic on November 15, 1889.

THE FIRST REPUBLIC (1889-1930)

The positivist French philosophy of Auguste Comte provided the ideological underpinnings not only for the armed forces but for most Brazilian thought at that time. Comte stressed rationality over religion, order over chaos, and scientific progress over social stasis. Brazil took its motto of *ordem e progreso* (order and progress) from Comte's writings. True to these ideals, Brazil's revolution was almost bloodless and, for a long time, was remembered as such, and those who did resist—primarily newly freed slaves loyal to their liberator—were quickly shot, buried, and forgotten. Newspapers were nonplussed by the revolution and presented it as necessary to progress, and the new republic was warmly received in the international community.

Some observers had been apprehensive about the democratic potential of a Brazilian people who would summarily dispose of a leader so dedicated to their own well-being, and their fears were not allayed by the initial difficulties establishing a republic and the army's interim rule. Brazil's first two presidents—Deodoro da Fonseca and Floriano Peixoto—were both generals, and not until 1894 under Prudente José de Morais e Barros did Brazil have a civilian leader. During this period Brazil favored order over progress: the new republic allowed most of the existing social order to remain unchanged, particularly in the rural and agricultural interior. In the cities a new middle class of scientists and engineers attained prominence and many elected officials were drawn from this class. However, power remained concentrated in the hands of the inland coffee barons, who used their economic strength to dominate national politics.

Brazilian industry came into its own after WWI. As industry enriched the middle class their growing dissatisfaction with the oligarchic coffee barons spread into the army barracks; many younger lieutenants *(tenentes)* found Brazil's agricultural back-country a premodern embarrassment and hoped to see Brazil become a modern industrial country like the US and those in Europe. The loose coalition between the middle class and the *tenentes* led to a revolutionary coup that attempted to overthrow the republic on July 5, 1922, but—after a last stand at Copacabana Fort—it was put down. However, it rose up again in 1924, far stronger than before, this time to do serious damage to the Republic's perceived legitimacy. In October 1930 the assassination of João Pessoa—the vice-presidential candidate favored by the rebels—incited an uprising that took Rio de Janeiro by November and ended the first republic.

THE VARGAS STATE (1930-1945)

The 1930 revolution brought to power Getúlio Vargas, who quickly became a near-dictator and ruled Brazil until his resignation in 1945, in the process setting Brazil's path into the 20th century. Vargas was a rancher's son who became first a lawyer and then a politician, and who thus hailed from the very backcountry elite whose political dominance had first spurred the urban middle class to revolt. Vargas saw himself as a conservative reformer making the necessary changes to Brazil's economic, political, and social structures to bring Brazil into the modern age, and these changes meant reducing the stranglehold he saw Brazil's agricultural past as having over Brazil's industrial future. Once in power Vargas curried the middle class's favor with social welfare initiatives like a minimum wage, unemployment insurance, and workplace safety regulations, but also was careful to keep the older oligarchy's approval by suppressing any dissent and maintaining order with an iron fist.

Under his watch Brazil's domestic industries flourished—at one point 90% of consumed goods were manufactured within the nation's borders—whereas before Brazil's wealth was more doled out as favors by the leadership than earned by merit. By the end of WWII Vargas agreed to resign and allow an election to choose his successor, after having sealed his own fate by sending a Brazilian regiment to fight in Italy towards the end of the war. He had done so at the request of the US in hopes that the gesture would help Brazil to claim a more prominent position in international affairs, but the populace did not fail to notice the irony of Vargas sending Brazilians abroad to defend democracy against a dictatorial onslaught.

THE FIRST DEMOCRACY (1945-1964)

The people of Brazil actually hadn't quite seen the last of Vargas: although he had alienated his original support base, he remained popular and was re-elected president in 1954, only to face charges of corruption and end his career by taking his own life. Vargas set a precedent, as two of the three succeeding presidents would fail to complete their terms.

Vargas's immediate successor, Juscelino Kubitschek, will likely always be remembered as the founder of Brasília—Brazil's current capital. This is fitting because the construction of Brasília captures Kubitschek's presidency in miniature: Brasília was elegantly designed but horribly expensive even while still on the drafting table, and during construction the project ran far over budget. Kubitschek's plans to revitalize the economy met similar fates and their failures brought the nation such high inflation that the International Monetary Fund tried to intervene. However, Kubitschek ignored their suggestions and thus doomed his successor, Jânio Quadros, to a short presidency marked mostly by ineffective attempts to bolster the currency.

Economic troubles strengthened the many leftist movements popular with Brazil's (until then largely) restive working classes, and by Quadros's election in 1961 these organizations were too powerful for the president to safely ignore. Quadros made the political mistake, however, of being too conciliatory with the groups, and even awarded revolutionary leader Che Guevara a state honor, which so terrified Brazil's military elites that Quadros resigned shortly thereafter for fear of a swift military coup.

The coup didn't materialize until 1964, during João Goulart's presidency. Goulart tried to succeed where Quadros had failed but found that Brazil's parliamentary system severely hindered his attempts to restore Brazil's economic vigor. The answer, it seemed, was to take away the congress's checks on his power, the suggestion of which alarmed Brazil's military elite far more than Quadros's pandering to the left ever had; governments worldwide began to count the days to a communist takeover. When Goulart's initiative succeeded in 1963 the military's alarm turned to panic, and it did not help matters that nearly every economic policy created by Goulart had backfired. Inflation rose, unemployment grew, subsidies shrank, and Goulart alienated nearly every sector of Brazilian society. After a series of abortive early attempts, a military coup seized power in 1964 and Brazil's democratic experiment ended.

THE MILITARY REGIME (1964-1984)

Like Brazil's earlier revolutions the 1964 military coup was short—lasting only from March 31 to April 2—and nearly bloodless. Most state governors and the economically powerful supported the insurgents, and Goulart fled to Uruguay as the insurgents passed Institutional Act #1. This suspended constitutional guarantees, gave the central government authority to ignore mandates from lower levels of government, and allowed the removal of elected officials from office. This act permitted many key political and intellectual leaders to have their rights suspended. The military regime departed sharply from Brazil's past experience. Prior political revolutions in Brazil had seen the military assist the revolution only to return power to civilian leaders once stability had been assured, but this time the military would retain authority for 20 years.

The military regime in some ways resembled the Latin American pattern of tight political control and economic austerity but, even at its worst, repression never reached the extent seen elsewhere on the continent. Brazil's military had always been the country's most democratic institution—soldiers came mostly from the lower and middle classes and from every region of Brazil—unlike the mostly elite militaries common elsewhere in South America. This kept the Brazilian military's politics moderate by comparison, but this was not enough to make the government well-liked, in particular because its first president Castello Branco chose wage freezes and foreign investment as his inflation-fighting tactics. The former aggravated Brazil's enormous income disparity and the latter ran counter to the populace's nationalistic aspirations and desire for a strong domestic economy.

Branco soon discovered how unpopular the new regime was when in 1965 he authorized direct elections for 11 governorships, only to see most of the positions fall to opposition parties; the government immediately consolidated its hold by passing Institutional Act #2, which mandated that the president and vice-president be elected indirectly, eliminated the major political parties, and gave the president authority to dissolve congress and govern as a dictator. Institutional Act #3 followed shortly thereafter and called for governors and mayors to be elected indirectly as well. An officially sanctioned opposition party, the MDB (Movimento Democrático Brasileiro; Brazilian Democratic Movement), was created to oppose the official government party, ARENA (Aliança Renovadora Nacional; National Renovation Alliance), but the MDB refused to run a candidate to oppose Artur da Costa e Silva, who took the presidency in 1967. Costa e Silva at first attempted to undo the regime's damage to Brazil's democracy, but soon internal pressure from the military led him to impose even stricter measures than his predecessor; bands of urban guerillas formed and, after some of these captured and ransomed the US ambassador, Costa e Silva was summarily removed from office and replaced with Emílio Garrastazu Médici. Like his predecessors, Médici first promised increased democracy only to retract his promise once more firmly established in office, and government repression in fact reached its peak while he ruled. Médici did succeed, however, at boosting Brazil's manufacturing base, but this success widened income disparity and he remained unpopular. Brazil's alcohol-powered vehicles also date from this era, as the global oil crisis of 1973 led Médici to attempt to wean the nation off of expensive petroleum imports.

Ernesto Geisel succeeded Médici as president and made overtures toward actual relaxation of the military regime's repression; he loosened speech restrictions, reduced the use of violence to maintain order, and where possible removed from their posts the most flagrant abusers of authority. Geisel also had the good fortune to put down a coup attempt and thus secure as successor João Baptista de Oliveria Figueiredo. Although a weak leader, Figueiredo continued Geisel's efforts at redemocratizing Brazil, which culminated in the 1984 election of Tancredo de Almeida Neves—an opposition politician—to the presidency.

RETURN TO DEMOCRACY (1984-2000)

Poor health prevented Neves from assuming office, and the presidency fell to vice-president José Sarney, who would quickly disappoint all sides. Sarney relied too heavily upon former ARENA politicos for the opposition's liking, and the economy left him by Figueiredo soon sank into crippling inflation that he was only partially able to ameliorate. Under his watch the 1986 congress began to draft a new constitution, but this strained their resources and it was not finalized and promulgated until October 1987. When the new government's first full elections were held in 1988 it became clear that the party structures had become insignificant, for no clear trend could be discerned in the composition of the nearly 50,000 officials elected that year. The presidential elections that followed were more closely contested, and most popular favorites were eliminated in the early rounds. The election came down to a contest between the former metalworker, long-time labor advocate, and political agitator Luiz Inácio Lula da Silva (known affectionately only as Lula) and the political newcomer Fernando Collor de Mello. Collor won with about 35 million votes to Lula's 31 million, and proceeded to attempt to liberalize Brazil's marketplace while implementing comparatively minor social reforms.

Collor quickly degenerated into a corrupt profiteer, embezzling billions as his reforms failed to stabilize the economy. He was impeached in 1992 and vice-president Itamar Franco took the reigns until the election of the then-minister of finance Fernando Henrique Cardoso. Cardoso stabilized the economy by introducing Brazil's current, dollar-pegged *real* and was re-elected in 1998. Both times he defeated Lula, who had emerged as Brazil's leading opposition politician, but in 2002 Lula was elected in a run-off signaling great changes for Brazil.

TODAY: AGORA É LULA

Brazil's first leftist president in over 40 years, Lula came to power on a tide of promises to cure the country's major social and economic ills—particularly Brazil's ever-growing gap between rich and poor, the widest in the world. Since the January 2003 start of his term, "the people's president" (born in the Northeast and raised in a São Paulo *favela*) has moved swiftly and often controversially to act on these promises, bringing the country's socioeconomic optimism to new highs and ushering in a new era of financial promise (evidenced in the omnipresent *Agora é*

Lula—"Now is Lula's time"—bumper stickers). Affecting everything from military spending to cinematic themes, this interest in Brazil's global powerhouse potential has colored much of Brazil's current scene, continuing on even as Lula's initial popularity has started to plummet due to beliefs that he is not doing enough. Highlights of the ongoing "Lula era" include:

FOME ZERO ("ZERO HUNGER"). One of Lula's most successful campaigns is "Zero Hunger," a wildly popular program where government funds and private business donations are used to bring food and supplies to the most economically disadvantaged communities in Brazil. Nearly two million people—most in the rural Northeast, the country's poorest region—have been helped by Fome Zero's public-meets-private program, which comes in the form of hunger "credit cards" that give them monthly *real* allotments with which to buy food. At 2003's G8 (Group of Eight) economic summit in Evian, France, Lula pushed for a proposed international version of Fome Zero, where funds from the world's economic superpowers and taxes on international arms trade would be used to assist the world's poverty- and famine-stricken nations.

WORLD SOCIAL FORUM. Lula's G8 presentation was but one example of Brazil's optimism-fueled interest in international affairs and globalization. Globalization's opponents (many of them based in Brazil) have long protested the economic hegemony of the world's superpowers, but no gathering has raised as much ire among developing nations as the World Economic Forum (WEF), an elite US$20,000-a-head annual meeting of the world's richest nations and organizations. In 1998, these WEF-opposing groups decided to formally organize, leading to the 2001 birth of the World Social Forum (Fórum Social Mundial). Held at the same time as the WEF in the Brazilian city of Porto Alegre, the event is considered the "socially conscious" version of the WEF—a similar global gathering, but this one dedicated to the needs of poorer nations and the world's social problems, rather than its economic successes. As the host of the World Social Forum and one of the developing world's major economic forces, Brazil has appropriately taken a lead in voicing the WSF's concerns on the global stage; indeed, in 2003, Lula was the first and only world leader to attend both the WSF and WEF.

TRADE AGREEMENTS. The WSF and other global watchdog groups' calls to action have met with varied success. US President George W. Bush has pushed for the **Free Trade Area of the Americas (FTAA),** which would equalize trading regulations for the 34 member nations of the Americas. Lula has stood out as one of the most vocal and prominent opposers of the FTAA (of whom there are many), making it clear that Brazil's primary interest is in **Mercosul** (a.k.a. Mercosur), a trading partnership of South American nations that he believes would benefit the continent's economy in a much more beneficial and impactive way than the FTAA.

MST (LANDLESS WORKERS' MOVEMENT). Not all of Brazil's socioeconomic mobilization has been on an international scale. Seeking—like Fome Zero—to right social wrongs and bring food to the poor, the Movimento dos Trabalhadores Rurais sem Terra (MST) began in 1985 to protest the country's land distribution laws (which the movement claims are skewed toward the wealthy). Landless farmers in search of work and food began squatting with their families on unused but arable land all over Brazil. Over 70,000 families have been provided for in this illegal manner—making it the largest social protest movement in South America—but the farmers have clashed frequently and violently with the police.

Much of the struggle died down when Lula came to power on a platform of socioeconomic cooperation across all barriers, but a recent upswing in MST-related violence has been taken by some as a symbol of Lula's imminent decline in power and effectiveness. Approval ratings for "the people's president" have dropped, with many from his own leftist party decrying Lula as growing increasingly conservative. Lula's golden image has slowly been tarnishing, and his closely watched successes in the next few months will determine whether the history books remember him as Brazil's savior or its scapegoat.

THE ARTS

Brazil's art scene has always been an amalgam of different styles and influences, all of which have contributed to its vibrant current scene. During the colonial period artists worked mostly within European schools of the day, but during the early republic the problem that would characterize much of Brazilian art arose: how to create authentically "Brazilian" art drawing on the country's indigenous, African, and European influences without exoticizing Brazil itself. The answers posed to this problem—ranging from symbolic cannibalism to a strong current of regionalism—have defined Brazilian art throughout the past century.

HISTORY

ARCHITECTURE

BAROQUE. Colonial Brazilian architecture resembles the day's style throughout South America: austere, tile-roofed buildings with whitewashed wood-and-clay walls supported by stone where available. Most early Brazilian architecture has not survived; the colonies lacked skilled labor and sturdy building materials, and most colonists were unwilling to invest in permanent settlements until mineral wealth was found. As a result, the most elaborate surviving colonial architecture can be found in Minas Gerais, particularly in Ouro Preto. This style is known as Brazilian baroque, and many examples are on UNESCO's World Heritage list.

MODERNISM. In the 20th century Brazilian architects looked to create a distinctly Brazilian architecture, motivated partly by national pride and partly by their dislike for the neoclassical architecture—often copied wholesale from European models—that dominated Brazil in the 19th century. These architects found their inspiration in the clean lines and concrete-and-glass construction techniques pioneered by the European and American modernist movements, but balked at the movement's boxy, rectangular tendencies. Brazil's so-called **free-form modernism** took modernism's materials and construction techniques and wedded them to an organic aesthetic inspired by Brazil's mountainous terrain and twisting coastlines; buildings in this style seem more drawn than built. Leading architects of this style include **Lucia Costa, Ruy Ohtake,** and, most famously, **Oscar Niemeyer.**

OSCAR NIEMEYER. Niemeyer's architecture has contributed more to the development of Brazilian free-form modernism than any other single architect in the country's history. Particular highlights of Niemeyer's extensive collection of works include Rio de Janeiro's Sambódromo (p. 47) and the Igreja São Francisco de Assis in the town of Pampulha (p. 8), as well as dozens of government and public buildings throughout the capital of Brasília (p. 280). Niemeyer and the style he pioneered brought international recognition for both Niemeyer himself and more generally for Brazilian architecture. He changed the rules of global architecture by being the first "celebrity architect"—those architects-*cum*-artists (like Frank Gehry) whose prestige garner them lucrative contracts and guarantee them near total freedom of design. Without Niemeyer, many of today's greats would have no hope of seeing their plans executed.

URBAN PLANNING. Alongside architecture, urban planning has become a major concern for Brazil. The planned capital of Brasília was laid out by Lucia Costa and houses many buildings by Niemeyer. **Curitiba** (p. 232) and **Palmas** (p. 486) were also intended as pinnacles of model urban planning. Necessity, however, drives these experiments: Brazil's urban infrastructure has struggled to adapt to the nation's rapidly expanding population, and many take as signs of its failure the growth of **favelas** (p. 30) outside Rio and other major cities.

SCULPTURE

CERAMICS. Before the arrival of the European settlers, the Cunani and Maracá cultures of modern-day Pará used clay as a medium in vases, funeral urns, and statuary. Especially in the Northeast, the ceramic tradition has been kept alive and can be seen in the work of **Servino,** who is known for working with unglazed clay, and in that of **Mestre Vitalino** (Vitalino Pereira dos Santos), who is the most famous of Brazil's "folk potters."

BAROQUE & ROCOCO. The Brazilian sculptural tradition has developed in close connection with its architecture—these two disciplines are frequently united in the churches of the nation. From the 16th century onward, Brazilians who had been trained in European styles decorated colonial churches across the nation. During the 17th and 18th centuries, baroque and rococo styles from Portugal dominated these decorations. One excellent example of this is the baroque Santuário do Bom Jesus de Matosinhos (p. 218) of Congonhas in Minas Gerais, which is surrounded by 12 statues of the Apostles and displays life-sized depictions of scenes from the life of Christ on its domed chapels. These incredible creations are the work of Brazil's most famed 18th century sculptor, Antônio Francisco Lisboa (known as **Aleijadinho,** or "the little cripple"). Alejadinho, who was the son of a Portuguese architect and an African slave, is known not only because of his self-taught skills, but also because of the fact that he suffered from an illness which so disfigured him that his assistants had to strap chisel and hammer to his deformed hands before he could begin work each day. Many of his works—including many soapstone and wood carvings—are displayed in Tiradentes and Ouro Preto: in the latter, one can visit his masterpiece, the Igreja de São Francisco de Assis (p. 215). The Matriz do NS do Pilar (p. 214), also in Ouro Preto, displays the incredible collaborative work of Aleijadinho and his friend Manuel da Costa Athayde (see **Painting,** p. 26), whose murals in this church are said to contain 748 pounds of gold dust mixed in with the paint. At Salvador's Museu da Arte da Bahia (p. 361), one can see the religious-themed works of the renowned **Manuel Inácio da Costa.**

MODERNISM. Brazilian sculpture did not end with the baroque, nor is it solely an expression of religious themes. At the beginning of the 19th century, sculptors began to move away from Christian imagery, at least through representation of famous persons. During the early 20th century, the wood carvings of **Osvaldo Goeldi** focused on the state of the lower classes, rather than commemorating the affluent. **Victor Brecheret,** in addition to being one of the greatest figurative sculptors of the 20th century, was also a major participant in the Modern Art Week of 1922. Although Brazil's Modernist movement certainly influenced much of the sculpture produced after 1922, European traditions were not wholly abandoned: the work of engraver **Marcelo Grassman** reflects the expressionistic and fantastic styles of Central Europe, in his scenes of medieval monsters, knights, and ladies. The works of **Rubem Valentim**—who took much of his inspiration from the forms and objects used in the Candomblé ceremonies of his native Bahia—again attest to the fact that there is a modern and evolving tradition of sculpture in Brazil.

PAINTING

NEOCLASSICISM. Manuel da Costa Athayde, who worked with Aleijadinho, is well known for his incredible ceilings and murals in the churches of Ouro Preto, in addition to his work as a gilder. Although **Jean-Baptiste Debret** was born in France, the influence of the neoclassical tradition established by he and his colleagues while in Brazil can be seen in the work of many Brazilian painters until well into the Republican era.

MODERN ART. Cândido Portinari is one of the first internationally renowned Brazilian painters of the modern era. His work focused on the ways of life of ordinary Brazilians, like those with whom he grew up on a small coffee plantation in São Paulo state. His experimentation with Brazilian themes involved, at one point, sending for 60 pounds of multicolored dirt from different areas of the nation and then mixing it with his paints. His international commissions included murals both at the Library of Congress in Washington, D.C. and the United Nations in New York City. The works of **Lasar Segall** are the first examples of modern art to have been exhibited (in 1913) in Brazil. **Vincente do Rego Monteiro** is known for incorporating indigenous elements from the Ilha de Marajó. The principle painters who took part in Modern Art Week were **Anita Malfatti,** whose early work shows the influence of Expressionism, **Vincente do Rêgo Monteiro, John Graz,** and **Emiliano Di Cavalcanti,** whose colorful scenes of *samba* and Carnaval have earned him a reputation as one of the most "Brazilian" painters of the era.

RECENT INNOVATIONS. In the 20th century, the work of "Nippo-Brazilian" artists (those who were born in Japan and immigrated to Brazil) like **Manabu Mabe** increased the diversity of Brazilian styles: the tradition of abstract art they developed often engaged the calligraphic lines of traditional Japanese painting. The Brazilian painters of the last few decades have often focused on political and social concerns of the people. **Siron Franco** produced a series of paintings recording the death and destruction that resulted from a leak of radioactive cesium (in 1987) in his native Goiânia. **Antônio Henrique Amaral** is best known for his series entitled *Bananas*, in which bound and tortured fruit serve as commentary upon the authoritarian regime of the 1970s.

PHOTOGRAPHY

EARLY EVENTS. The word "photography" is said to have been coined in Brazil, in the town of Campinas in São Paulo state. The French-born inventor **Hercules Florence** used this term (which means "drawing with light") to describe a process he had invented. Research done by the modern Brazilian photographer **Boris Kossoy** reveals that Florence independently discovered a photographic process in 1833, making him contemporary with photographic pioneers Niepce (1827, in France) and Talbot (1835, in England). However, his work is largely unknown and he is rarely included in the list of those considered pioneers in the development of photography as both an art form and a scientific process. According to Kossoy, Florence's experiments were inspired by the fact that some of the dyes used by indigenous peoples were light-sensitive. He quickly moved from experimenting with these dyes to photosensitive compounds of gold and silver, and eventually went on to discover that he could fix the images he produced by means of ammonia. Shortly after Florence's experimentation, in 1840, the French Abbot **Louis Compte** took the first daguerreotypes in Latin America. The young Pedro II (who would later become the Emperor of Brazil) was present at Compte's demonstration and learned how to use the process. Pedro II became an avid supporter of photography and, as Emperor, appointed the world's first royal photographers.

One of the most well-known Brazilian photographers of this early era is **Marc Ferrez,** whose attractive images of Brazilian landscapes, buildings, and people still plaster postcards all over the country.

PHOTOJOURNALISM. Brazil's role in the history of photography is not limited to the early events mentioned above, but continues into the present day: **Sebastião Salgado** has been an important player in the field of 20th century photojournalism. His pieces, which record primarily the lower classes and the struggle for better living and working conditions, have earned him several major awards. In the 1960s the prevalence of photojournalism was greatly increased by the launch of three magazines which combined political and aesthetic continent: *Realidade, Bondinho,* and the *Jornal da Tarde.* **Conrado Wessel** is known for his documentation of São Paulo as well as for establishing the first factory in Brazil for photographic paper in 1928. In 1980 **Zé de Boni** opened the **Álbum** in São Paulo, which was the first gallery in Brazil to specialize in photography. **Thomas Farkas,** who is perhaps most renowned for his images of the new capital of Brasília, is the first Brazilian photographer to have had a major museum exhibition in the country.

RECENT WORK. One of the most well-known Brazilian photographers of today is **Mário Cravo Neto,** whose work appears in museums and private collections all over the world. Although Cravo Neto stages much of his work, he is nevertheless considered to be a documenter of Afro-Brazilian culture. **Elza Lima** began working in collaboration with FUNAI in 1989, to document the lives of the indigenous tribes in the Amazon basin. **Luiz Cláudio Marigo** is one of the most widely published nature photographers in Brazil and abroad. One of **Juvenal Pereira's** major projects in the mid-1970s was to record the life and customs of Rio Grande do Sul's *gaúchos.* Pereira has also created the biennial International Photography Month.

LITERATURE

COLONIAL BEGINNINGS. The travelogue, telling of the marvels of the New World, was Brazilian literature's first prominent genre. Some literary historians trace Brazil's literature all the way back to **Pero Vaz de Caminha's** 1500 letter to Dom Manuel I, the Portuguese king, proclaiming the "discovery" of the country that would become Brazil. Others place the first work of literature considered to be "Brazilian" as **Bento Teixeira's** colonial eulogy to the captain-general of Pernambuco, *Prosopopéia* (1601). The 17th century saw a stylistic transition to baroque ornamentation, such as in **Padre Antonio Vieira's** sermons and **Gregório de Matos'** poetry, which dominated until the mid-18th century.

ARCADIANISM & INDIANISM. Arcadianism, with its idealization of the countryside and emphasis on the simple life, gained popularity in reaction to baroque decadence. Though the style was most popular in Europe, poets such as **Cláudio Manuel da Costa** and **Tomás Antônio Gonzaga** attempted to co-opt its style and themes to underscore their differences from Europeans and foster a sense of separatism. (Not surprisingly, both were involved with the failed 1789 Inconfidência Mineira (p. 17) uprising in Minas Gerais.)

Following the proclamation of independence in 1822, Romanticism was adopted in an attempt to articulate a national literature and adapted in the form of Indianism. Indianism idealizes the "noble savage," portraying indigenous characters as national heroes. **José de Alencar's** most famous Indianist novels, *Iraçéma* (trans. *Iracema the Honey-Lips*, 1865), follows the romance that develops between a colonist and an indigenous woman and concludes with the birth of their son. The novel is considered an allegory for Portuguese colonization; their son represents the recently founded Brazilian nation.

The well-regarded writer **Antônio Frederico de Castro Alves** reworked Indianism by writing about African slaves and the importance of abolition in his epic poem *O Navio Negreiro* (1868).

REALISM & REGIONALISM. As authors continued to explore Indianism, the problem emerged of how to write about local themes and use specifically Brazilian symbols without exoticizing their homeland in much the same way as the Portuguese colonists had. The move toward realism can be seen as an attempt to answer this question. **Joaquim Maria Machado de Assis** is widely regarded as one of the Brazil's greatest authors. Throughout his work, Machado de Assis chronicled Rio de Janeiro while helping introduce devices such as first-person narration, a multitude of perspectives, and self-consciousness into Brazilian literature. Among his most famous books are *Memórias Póstumas de Brás Cubas* (trans. *Posthumous Memoirs of Bras Cubas* or *Epitaph of a Small Winner*, 1881), *Quincas Borba* (trans. *Philosopher or Dog?*, 1891), and *Dom Casmurro* (trans. *Dom Casmurro*, 1899). The naturalist novel *Os Sertões* (trans. *Rebellion in the Backlands*, 1902) by **Euclides da Cunha** focused on poverty in the Northeast, while **Afonso Henriques de Lima Bareto's** *Triste Fim de Policarpo Quaresma* (trans. *The Patriot*, 1911) centered on marginalized communities in Rio.

MODERNISM & ANTHROPOPHAGY. Modernism began to take hold in the early 20th century, but its popularity is usually traced to 1922's Modern Art Week in São Paulo (p. 196), from which poets **Carlos Drummond de Andrade** and **Manuel Bandeira** emerged. **Mário de Andrade,** author of the novelistic "rhapsody" *Macunaíma, o Herói Sem Nenhum Caráter* (1928), follows the anti-hero "without character" as he leaves the rainforest for the city in order to allegorize Brazil's transition to industrialism and modernity. The same year saw the publication of **Oswald de Andrade's** *O Manifesto Antropófago*, declaring the answer to the problem of creating an authentically Brazilian literature without creating exoticism for European consumption: **cannibalism.** The manifesto demands that Brazilians instead "swallow whole" European civilization, rejecting its aspects which render Brazil exotic.

RETURN OF REGIONALISM. In the 1930s, modernist writers became interested in communicating the divergent experiences of the country's regions, particularly of the Northeast. **Graciliano Ramos's** *Vidas Secas* (trans. *Barren Lives*, 1938) is set in the Northeast interior, as is his prison memoir *Memórias do Cárece* (trans. *Memories of Prison*, 1953). **José Américo de Almeida's** *A Bagaceira* (trans. *Husk Pit*, 1937), **Raquel de Queiroz's** *O Quinze* (trans. *1915*, 1930), and **José Lins de Rego's** *Menino de Engenho* (trans. *Plantation Boy*, 1932) also chronicle the lives of various people in the Northeast.

Regionalism continued to be popular throughout the 20th century, producing sophisticated social commentaries like **João Guimarães Rosa's** masterpiece *Grande Sertão: Veredas* (trans. *The Devil to Pay in the Backlands*, 1956), **Clarice Lispector's** novel *A Hora da Estrela* (trans. *The Hour of the Star*, 1977), and poet **João Cabral de Melo Neto's** *Morte e Vida Severina* (1956). In later years, Lispector would turn to more universal themes and become one of the country's most outspoken feminists. Brazil's most popular living writer, Ilhéus-born **Jorge Amado,** is acclaimed for the quirky Baianos who populate his novels. Favorites include *Gabriela, Cravo e Canela* (trans. *Gabriela, Clove and Cinnamon*, 1958) and *Dona Flor e Seus Dois Maridos* (trans. *Dona Flor and Her Two Husbands*, 1966).

DICTATORSHIP & DEMOCRACY. The period of military rule produced a number of works confronting with the violence and political repression of the era. **Antônio Callado's** novel *Quarup* (trans. *Quarup*, 1967) focuses on religious conservatism in the Northeast. **Ignácio de Loyola Brandão's** complex *Zero, romance pré-histórico* (trans. *Zero*, 1975) is a critique of both the military government and imported consumerism. In *O Que é Isso Companheiro?* (1979), politician and former journalist **Fernando Gabeira** explores his role in the 1969 kidnapping of Charles Elbrick, the American ambassador to Brazil.

Novels during and after military rule also took as a theme life in Brazil's sprawling metropolises. **Rubem Fonseca's** *A Grande Arte* (trans. *High Art*, 1983) traces urban violence in Rio, while short-story writer **Caio Fernando Abreu's** detective novel *Onde Andará Dulce Veiga? um romance B* (trans. *Whatever Happend to Dulce Veiga? A B-Novel*, 1990?) dives into the Paulista underground.

MUSIC

Music is Brazil's most developed art form, and undoubtedly one of the country's greatest gifts to global culture. You could spend a lifetime studying the country's rich and varied tradition, spanning multiple centuries and continents. From the swagger of *samba* to the shuffling backbeats of *bossa nova* to the frenetic riffs of *forró*, music is serious business here, and it's everywhere.

ESSENTIAL BRAZILIAN MUSIC.

Elis & Tom (Tom Jobim, Elis Regina).
Getz/Gilberto (Stan Getz, Astrud & João Gilberto).
Orfeu Negro Soundtrack (Luiz Bonfá, Tom Jobim).
Tropicália (Gilberto Gil, Caetano Veloso).
Fala Mangueira! (Velha Guarda da Mangueira).
Caetano Veloso (1969, "The White Album").
A Divina Comédia (Os Mutantes).
Refazenda (Gilberto Gil).
Verde, Anil, Amarelo, Cor-de-Rosa, e Carvão (*Rose & Charcoal;* Marisa Monte).
Brazil Classics 3: Forró (comp. David Byrne).
Brazil Classics 4: The Best of Tom Zé (comp. David Byrne).
São Paulo Confessions (Suba).
Tanto Tempo (Bebel Gilberto).

SAMBA. First heard in 1917 at Rio's Carnaval, *samba* is now everywhere in Brazil, especially during Carnaval (see **Samba Schools,** p. 47), when billions of *reais* are spent in honor of this deceptively simple two-step beat. As opposed to its somewhat elite position north of the equator, in Brazil *samba* is the music of the teeming masses and the chaotic streets—as sensual, frenetically paced, and exhausting as Brazil itself.

Samba took off only after Baiano immigrants who settled in Rio at the turn of the century brought the music to the then-capital from the Northeast, where it first originated from African rhythms (like the Angolan **tam-tam**) brought to the New World by slaves. The best known style of *samba* is **samba-de-enredo** or *partido-alta*, the pounding, rhythmic samba blared by Rio *samba* schools (and their 100-strong drum corps, known as *batucadas*) during Carnaval. The 30s and 40s were considered the **Golden Age** of *samba*, with countless popular Carioca-born composers and singers gaining international acclaim. Among these were lyric guitarist/composer **Baden Powell** ("Samba da Benção") and larger-than-life **Carmen Miranda** ("Disseram que Voltei Americanizada"), a megawatt *samba* singer who made it big as a cheeky Hollywood starlet with unforgettably fruity headdresses.

The next few decades saw *samba* fall in popularity first to *bossa nova* (*samba's* brainy, laid-back cousin) and then to the "festival era" (1960-70s), when music festivals in rebellion against the military dictatorship favored loud protest styles like MPB and Tropicália. During these dormant times, *samba* went from being played by marching millions in the streets to being enjoyed in the quiet backyards of *samba* fans. Thus was the form reborn as the intimate and soft-spoken **pagode** (pa-GOH-djee), a pop-infused style that makes use of fewer percussion instruments and smaller guitars or ukuleles. The first and foremost singer of *pagode* is throaty-voiced **Beth Carvalho** ("Vou Festejar"), who also introduced Brazil to the rollicking stylings of **Zeca Pagodinho** ("Posso Até Me Apaixonar"). *Samba* has continued to evolve and adapt beyond *pagode* (though Carnaval's *sambas-de-enredo* remain popular), most notably in the rise of *axé* (p. 31), based on the fusion style of **samba-reggae.**

BOSSA NOVA (1950-60s). A sauntering, sexier version of *samba, bossa nova* is unsurprisingly the music of Rio, Brazil's capital of hedonism. In the 1950s, the beachfront bars and cafés of the newly trendy Ipanema neighborhood became *the* gathering place for intellectuals and musicians from all over the country, then in the grip of a military dictatorship. This restless creative energy burst forth in a "new style" (*bossa nova* in Portuguese) of Brazilian music: *samba* rhythms were slowed down and syncopated, harmonies were simplified, and lyrics turned to the simple pleasures. Antônio Carlos Jobim (a.k.a. **Tom Jobim**) is *bossa nova*'s most respected and prolific composer, thanks to both his swinging ode "Garota de Ipanema" (Girl from Ipanema) and the soundtrack to *Orfeu Negro (Black Orpheus)*, the film that introduced the sultry *bossa* sound to the US.

However, the true father of *bossa nova* is unquestionably Carioca composer and guitarist **João Gilberto:** his single "Chega de Saudade" launched the movement, and his crossover collaborations with international jazz greats like Charlie Parker and Stan Getz turned the world on to the movement's smooth, elevator-worthy sounds. The *Getz/Gilberto* collaboration became the best-selling jazz album of its time, and the warbling, uncredited performance on the album of João's first wife **Astrud Gilberto** ("Desafinado") helped her launch her own hit *bossa nova* career in Brazil.

TROPICÁLIA (1960-70s). *Bossa nova's* spirit may have been freewheeling, but as this studied, formal style came to dominate Brazil's musical scene, many became fed up with its strict, intellectual rules. Encouraging unbridled cross-cultural fusion and free-spirited musical synthesis, this catchy and raucously ribald musical rebellion quickly gained ground; it was christened Tropicália (Tropicalism) after a 1968 compilation considered the style's "manifesto." The movement's chief proponents were masterful singer/songwriter **Caetano Veloso** ("Alegria, Alegria"), who described Tropicália as "the opposite of *bossa nova*," and Baiano **Gilberto Gil** ("Domingo no Parque"), known for bringing African and Afro-Caribbean music to the Brazilian mainstream. Tropicalism reached its creative peak in the live *Doces Bárbaros*. This incendiary "manifesto" album starred Gil, Veloso, his sister **Maria Bethânia** ("Tempo de Guerra"), and the Tropicália era's biggest female star, fiery **Gal Costa** ("Eu Vim da Bahia"), considered by many to be the greatest Brazilian star of the 1980s.

Also popular were Rita Lee-fronted **Os Mutantes** ("Balada do Louco"), who twisted together hard-rockin' *samba*, funk, psychedelic rock, and general anarchy to much critical and popular acclaim. Controversial, surreal actor/composer/singer **Tom Zé** ("Xiquexique") was friends with fellow Baiano superstars Veloso, Gil, and Gal, but remained unknown until former Talking Head David Byrne discovered Zé's work in a used record store and re-released it under Byrne's own **Luaka Bop** label (which has done much to bring Tropicália to an international audience in the 90s). Aside from Gil's unique African influence and black pride anthems, Tropicália's biggest contribution may be the concept of the "manifesto" album, best exemplified by 2001's **Tribalistas,** a fantastic collection of neo-Tropicália tunes by MPB stars Marisa Monte, Carlinhos Brown, and Arnaldo Antunes.

MPB: MÚSICA POPULAR BRASILEIRA (1960-80s). MPB stands out as one of the hardest to classify movements in a tradition defined by eclecticism. The much-misused term specifically refers to a 1960s-80s fusion movement begun to protest the stifling military regime that then ruled Brazil, much as *bossa nova* was born from intellectual unrest resulting from that same political suppression. Like Tropicália, which often overlaps stylistically with MPB, MPB is known for its rhythmic and harmonic fusion—incorporating everything from folk to rock—and also for poetic, subversive wordplay. Many (notably Caetano Veloso) have put out MPB albums, but the genre's biggest name is poet/playwright/singer **Chico Buarque** ("Feijoada Completa"), whose catchy harmonies were often overshadowed by his overly sophisticated and (frequently censored) politicized lyrics. Perhaps the most notorious MPB star was Gaúcha spitfire **Elis Regina** ("O Bêbado é a Equilibrista"), called the Brazilian Edith Piaf for her silky singing style and over-the-top lifestyle.

Modern MPB has fallen far from the heights of Elis and Chico, so that now the term is often associated with slick, overproduced easy listening ballads. Ravishing, honey-voiced Carioca **Marisa Monte** ("Ainda Lembro")—called a "Modern-Day Elis" by many critics—has done much to bring respect back to the genre, thanks to her cutting-edge production company Phonomotor and frequent quirky collaborations (with the likes of Laurie Anderson and Phillip Glass).

OTHER STYLES. Bahia is undoubtedly Brazil's musical capital: *samba* was born here (as were superstars Gilberto Gil and Gal Costa, among others), and the region's strong African and black culture have infused countless generations of Brazilian music, including such popular **Carnaval genres** as *trio eléctrico*, *afoxé*, and *bloco afro* (see **Glossary,** p. 528). In the early 1990s, fusion-happy *bloco afro* group **Olodum** spearheaded the birth of **axé bahia** (ah-SHAY), an infectious mix of samba, funk, reggae, pop, *afoxé*, and more that is currently the most popular style of native-born music in Brazil. The most famous *axé* performers are **Daniela Mercury** ("Swing da Cor") and **Carlinhos Brown** ("Omelette Man"), who calls *axé* "music without prejudice" and is known for "funking up" the style (he took his pseudonym from funk granddaddy James Brown).

The most popular style born outside of Bahia is **forró** (foh-HOH), which is heard everywhere in Brazilian-frequented clubs and local bars. Born in the dry open plains of Brazil *sertão*, this twangy, bouncy, accordion-based music (popularized by Sertanejo singer **Luiz Gonzaga;** "Asa Branca") is often called Brazil's own "country music." Sadly, it has yet to catch on outside the country or with foreign visitors. Probably the most notorious Brazilian music "style" is **lambada,** the erotically charged thigh-to-thigh dance born in the 1970s in Belém. Infused with merengue and rhumba (unsurprising given Belém's proximity to the Caribbean), *lambada* remained fairly unknown within Brazil until it caught on in the 1990s in Europe, which in turn ignited interest in *lambada* in its home country.

DANCE

FOLK TRADITIONS & FUSION. Like many of the Brazilian arts, dance has been influenced by traditions from all over the globe (especially those of the Portuguese settlers and African slaves), and any one dance is usually a combination of several styles of different origin. The earliest fusion of styles in Brazil occurred in the 16th century, when the Jesuit missionaries used dance as a vehicle for conversion, adapting Catholic liturgy to indigenous ritual choreography.

PORTUGUESE INFLUENCES. Brazil has a long history of **folk dramas** conducted through dance, which fall roughly into four genres. These dances are Portuguese in origin but have been altered by centuries of exposure to the diverse cultures of

Brazil. *Pastoris* (shepherds) is today a secular event, but began as a performance of Christmas carols: its "characters" include the teacher, the pretty angel, the gypsy, and the North Star. *Cheganças* (arrivals) is also performed during the Christmas season, and recounts the arrival, defeat, and eventual baptism of the Moors. The *rauchos* were one of the earliest forms of Carnaval: solemn love stories acted out to a marching rhythm by dancers who competed for prizes (something like the *samba* schools of today). *Os reisados* are a cycle of 24 folk performances, the most popular of which is **Bumba-Meu-Boi,** a drama centering on the misfortunes of a prize bull.

AFRICAN INFLUENCES. Many forms of dance in Brazil's history have served functional, as well as artistic or religious ends: the **siriá** of Pará originated along the banks of the Amazon, as a sort of courtship ritual. In **maculele,** created by the African slaves of Bahia, the dancers use sticks and machetes to imitate the actions of cutting sugarcane. Today this dance is performed strictly as entertainment, but during the Paraguayan War it was actually employed in battle, much like the ritualized **capoeira** (p. 41).

The dances of the African slaves were not always well-received by the early Europeans in Brazil, for they were often perceived as erotic and inappropriate. One example of this European discomfort is illustrated by the actions of Portuguese emperor Manuel I who, while residing in Brazil during the Napoleonic Wars, went so far as to pass a law forbidding the popular **batuque** (a circle dance performed to drums and hand-clapping). Despite such censure, dances of both African and indigenous descent were not wiped out: in the 1830s, the indigenous **lundu** was combined with elements of African dance; this new hybrid form—which came to be known as **zemba queca**—rose to popularity among "high society" in Rio during the 1880s. Another variation on this popular dance was the **mesemba.** Components of the *lundu* were also fused with imported dances like the Cuban *habañera*, resulting in the **maxixe,** which became very popular in Paris at the beginning of the 20th century.

SAMBA. Undoubtedly the most well-known Brazilian dance, *samba* is thought to have originated among the Africans of Bahia. As noted above, the music and moves of *samba* are remarkably similar to the **tam-tam** of Angola. The most famous *samba* performances are those of the *samba* school parade in Rio's Carnaval, where several groups in elaborate costumes address historical themes or stories by means of dance, and are judged by a government-appointed jury (see p. 48). The ballroom *samba* was formalized in 1956 by Pierre Lavelle. Since then, various forms of *samba* have continued to evolve in conjunction with moods of modern music. Also popular at Carnaval is the **frevo,** a frenetic and acrobatic dance which originated in Pernambuco.

FILM

SILENCE & SONG. Silent film began in Brazil with **Antônio Leal's** thriller *Os Estranguladores* (*The Stranglers*, 1908) and peaked with **Mario Peixoto's** surrealist classic *Limite* (*Limit*, 1931). The 1930s marked the introduction of talkies and the *chancada* genre (slapstick musical comedies). It is here that songstress **Carmen Miranda** got her start as an actress, in films such as 1933's *A Voz do Carnaval* (*The Voice of Carnaval;* dir. Adhemar Gonzaga and Humberto Mauro). She later rose to fame as the banana-bedecked icon of Hollywood's "Good Neighbor" policy, which aimed to foster goodwill with South America during WWII (to ensure the continent's neutrality) and to allow American cinema to find new audiences to replace the lost European market.

As a result of this policy, Brazilian popular cinema became overrun with Hollywood films, including such none-too-subtle US productions like *That Night in Rio* (dir. Irving Cummings, 1941), *The Gang's All Here* (dir. Busby Berkeley, 1943), and *Copacabana* (dir. Alfred Green, 1947).

CINEMA NOVO. In 1955 director **Nelson Pereira dos Santos** set the stage for the innovative **Cinema Novo** (New Cinema) movement—which would come to dominate Brazilian cinema for the next two decades—with his *Rio 40 Grau (Rio 100 Degrees)*. The film depicts the lives of five young *favela* residents using non-professional actors (revealing the influence of Italian neorealism) to portray the life of Rio de Janeiro. Perhaps the most famous film in this style is *Orfeu Negro (Black Orpheus)*, Frenchman **Marcel Camus's** 1959 retelling of the Orpheus and Eurydice myth, set during Rio's Carnaval. Despite being French-made and -produced (though the dialog was in Portuguese), the film brought international attention to Brazilian cinema; its score, by legends Luiz Bonfá and Antônio Carlos Jobim, introduced the world to *bossa nova* (see p. 30).

Cinema Novo represented a move away from reliance on Hollywood production styles, led by intellectuals who sought to make film a more immediate experience and create a distinctly Brazilian mode of filmmaking. Cinema Novo yielded many important neorealist films, including **Anselmo Duarte's** *O Pagador de Promessas* (*The Payer of Vows*, 1962), Pereira dos Santos's *Vidas Secas* (*Barren Lives*, 1963), and **Glauber Rocha's** *Deus e Diabo na Terra do Sol* (*Black God, White Devil*, 1964). Pereira dos Santos eventually moved on to make political allegories, such as 1971's comedy about **cannibalism** *Comoe Era Gostoso O Meu Francês (How Tasty Was My Little Frenchman)*.

HORROR. The 1960s also saw the rise of a controversial horror icon, Zé do Caixão (known as Coffin Joe in English translation), the misfit mortician who wants a son. He was the star of a series of B-movies by director **José Mojica Marins.** Today the trio of films in the Coffin Joe series—namely the original, *A Meia-Noite Levarei Sua Alma* (*At Midnight I'll Take Your Soul*, 1963), its sequel *Esta Noite Encarnarei No Teu Cadaver* (*This Night I'll Possess Your Corpse*, 1966), and the self-reflective finale *O Ritual dos Sádicos* (*Awakening of the Beast*, 1969) are cult classics.

EMBRAFILME ERA. In 1969, the military regime set up the organization known as Embrafilme, a government agency charged with financing and distributing Brazilian films. It was begun in order to promote Brazilian military rule abroad, but somehow Embrafilme largely funded filmmakers opposed to the dictatorship. Embrafilme allowed Brazilian cinema to grow quite strong through its extensive funding, continuing until the agency went bankrupt and dissolved in early 1990. This so-called "Embrafilme era" resulted in films critical of the political status quo, such as **Hector Babenco's** indictment of urban poverty among children in *Pixote, A Lei do Mais Fraco* (*Pixote, Survival of the Weakest*, 1981), and **Leon Hirzman's** exploration of localized union strikes *Eles Não Usam Black-Tie* (*They Don't Wear Black-Tie*, 1981).

NINETIES. Following the end of Embrafilme, cinematic output nearly stopped altogether. Brazilian cinema has since been reinvigorated by the 1993 passing of the Audiovisual Law, which allows tax rebates for those investing in films under production. **Walter Salles, Jr.** and Daniela Thomas's *Terra Estrangeira* (*Foreign Land*, 1995) is set against the backdrop of Brazil's financial instability during Collor's administration. **Helena Sodberg's** documentary *Carmen Miranda: Bananas is My Business* (1994) found an international audience, as did Walter Salles, Jr.'s award-winning *Central do Brasil* (*Central Station*, 1998).

CURRENT SCENE

LITERATURE

The best known Brazilian writer today is novelist **Paulo Coelho,** born in 1947 in Rio's Copacabana district (where he still lives). Raised in middle-class comfort, Coelho began a long tradition of rebelliousness when he took up writing at a young age—considered such a radical act under the era's military dictatorship that his family had him repeatedly hospitalized. Incidentally, his 1998 book based on his asylum time, *Veronika Decide Morrer* (trans. *Veronica Decides to Die*), helped pass a Congressional act banning involuntary hospitalization. Coelho continued in this radical vein in the counterculture 60s and 70s, writing incendiary political tracts and subversive song lyrics. Today, Coelho is an occult figure of sorts, known as the New Age author of spiritualist, quasi-mystical novels like the symbolic best-seller **O Alquimista** (trans. *The Alchemist,* 1988). A literary "shaman" of sorts, Coelho remains a divisive figure in Brazilian letters, simultaneously dismissed as a pop phenomenon (Madonna chose *The Alchemist* as her most influential text) and worshipped the world over as the soul's premier chronicler.

Although revered in his native country as an ardent social activist, Coelho's work is actually better read outside the country's borders; the biggest literary sellers in Brazil are translated versions of works by such literary giants as John Grisham and Michael Crichton. Brazil has few, if any, other contemporary authors of note, although the country continues its tradition of turning every major novel into a blockbuster film with the 21st century flicks *Carandiru* (based on Varella's *Estação Carandiru*) and *Cidade de Deus* (from Lins's novel of the same name).

MUSIC

Many of Brazil's biggest stars are still going strong, including 2003 Oscar nominee **Caetano Veloso** and current national Minister of Culture **Gilberto Gil.** As in the rest of the world, popular music in Brazil hasn't avoided the creeping influence of pre-fab bubble-gum pop, like teeth-rottingly cheerful sibling pop stars **Sandy & Júnior** or five-girl power band **Rouge,** winners of the Brazilian *Pop Idol.* Also unfortunately popular are countless bands cut from the US-born "nü-metal" cloth—try **Charlie Brown, Jr.** or **Skank** (SKONK-ee), progenitors of "Brazilian ska." The truly cutting-edge modern music coming out of Brazil is based on techno-tweaking of traditional beats (particularly *bossa nova*), as pioneered by late Yugoslav expat **Suba.** Brazilian-born, UK-based **Amon Tobin** is a current alt-rock darling thanks to his sampled *bossa nova* and *batucada* beats. Both men helped produce 2000's sunny-smooth *Tanto Tempo*, the debut of the supposed "new voice" of *bossa nova*, **Bebel Gilberto** (daughter of João Gilberto and Miúcha and niece of Chico Buarque). The group **Bossacucanova** takes a more traditional route by mixing up *samba* and *bossa nova* standards with blipping electronic beats.

FILM

Brazilian cinema garnered international critical praise in 2002 with the ultraviolent neorealist epic *Cidade de Deus* (*City of God*, dir. **Kátia Lund** and **Fernando Meirelles**), an adaptation of Paulo Lins's novel named after the Rio *favela* around which the factually based gangster saga centers. *Cidade de Deus* has been lauded by Brazilians as making the nation confront the problems of urban poverty and drug warfare like nothing before. Also released in 2002 and based on actual events was *Ônibus 174* (*Bus 174*, dir. **José Padilha**), which follows the failed attempted robbery of a bus in Rio's Zona Sul by a young homeless man. The revival of Brazilian cinema continued in 2003 with the release of Babenco's *Carandiru*. The episodic film is loosely based on Drauzio Varella's memoir *(Estação Carandiru)* detailing his work at Carandiru, South America's largest correctional facility, in the middle of São Paulo. The novel and film culminates in the 1992 massacre of 111 unarmed prisoners by prison guards.

TELEVISION

Wondering why the streets of Brazil are deserted between 6pm and 10pm every day? It's during that time that virtually everyone in the country heads indoors to watch **novelas,** the sappy and oversexed TV soap operas that easily outrank *futebol* and *samba* as the favorite national pastime. Unlike long-running European or American soap operas, *novelas* have definite endings and tidy storyline conclusions, lasting only a few months (or as long as ratings and popularity stay high). Globo, one of the world's five biggest media conglomerates, airs the most popular *novelas* at 6, 7, and 9pm, with a break at 8pm for equally salacious news broadcasts. Each time slot is devoted to a specific *novela* type—6pm is "female empowerment;" 7pm is "bodice-ripping historical dramas;" 9pm is "minimal clothing, maximum face-sucking." Though they're overacted and hyper-dramatic, *novelas* frequently tackle topics often considered too controversial for TV, including AIDS, interracial relationships, and gay marriage. And despite their ridiculous image in foreigners' eyes, *novelas* are where the top money is in Brazil's entertainment industry, featuring the country's highest-paid actors, writers, and directors.

The rest of Brazilian TV is even trashier, consisting mostly of suggestive children's programs and groan-worthy variety shows populated by a cast of overweight hosts, brainy animal/stupid human combos, and bikini-clad go-go girls. Things get racier by the hour: the top-rated nighttime talk show is RedeTV's post-1am **Noite Afora,** a graphic sex talk show hosted on a giant fuchsia bed by former porn actress **Monique Evans** and transsexual superstar **Léo Áquilla.** Evans follows in the footsteps of **Xuxa,** a former hard-core adult film star who remade herself as an MPB singer, children's TV show host, and homemaking magazine magnate.

PEOPLE

DEMOGRAPHICS

Brazil is currently the fifth most populated nation in the world, with over 170 million inhabitants. The Southeast has historically been—and remains—the most populated area, containing just over half the nation's entire population.

It is estimated that when the first Portuguese settlers arrived in what would become Brazil in the year 1500, there were more than 1000 denominations of indigenous peoples, having a total population between two and four million. Largely due to enslavement and the spread of European diseases such as measles, this number has now dwindled to approximately 350,000 individuals, who comprise 217 discrete peoples and speak over 180 different languages. For the most part, this population is distributed among the 595 **Terras Indígenas** (indigenous reservations) spread throughout the national territory, though most are found in the Amazon Basin. As in North America, the indigenous peoples of Brazil are often referred to as "Indians," due to the first Europeans' mistaken belief that they had, upon arriving in Brazil, reached India.

While not as impressive as the diversity of the indigenous peoples, the ethnic background of the 55% of Brazilians who are of Caucasian descent is also far from homogenous. The earliest and largest group of European settlers were **Portuguese,** reflected in the fact that Portuguese is the official language. There are also many

Brazilians of Spanish, Italian, and German descent; during the 1920s, the number of Italians in São Paulo was so great that it was commonly referred to as the "City of Italians." In Santa Catarina, German roots are still celebrated in part by Blumenau's three-week-long Oktoberfest (p. 260). In addition to these larger ethnic groups, there are also Brazilians of Polish, Russian, Dutch, and Japanese ancestry. Today the Liberdade district of São Paulo is the largest community of Japanese descent outside of Japan.

Like their counterparts in North America, the European settlers of Brazil imported African slaves to work on plantations, a practice which was legally sanctioned until 1888. Largely as a result of this, an approximate 40% of Brazilians are at least partially of African descent (mostly of Yoruba and Quimbundu origin, from areas which roughly correspond to modern-day Nigeria/Benin and Angola).

In recent years, a sense of general "Brazilian" national identity has been fostered by the nation's international success in arenas such as soccer's World Cup (p. 41). However, the concept of a "racial democracy" in Brazil (p. 45) is an ideal which has not fully been reached; citizens of African and indigenous descent still face discrimination. The development of a sense of national identity—a process referred to as **brasilidade**—was first declared a national objective by President Getúlio Vargas. His decision to construct the new, centralized capital of Brasília (p. 271) was seen as an important conceptual step toward uniting the country as one nation rather than an agglomeration of large city-states. But while *brasilidade* does encourage an admirable ideal of unity, it has not at all abolished the stark economic contrasts which lie along class and racial divisions.

LANGUAGE

Portuguese—the language of the country's first European settlers—is the official language of Brazil, and is spoken by everyone. Thanks to the multicultural influences of indigenous peoples and African immigrants, among others, Brazilian Portuguese has developed its own distinct flavor: its accent, intonation, and vocabulary are quite different from those of the Portuguese spoken in Portugal (the difference is akin to that between British English and the English spoken in former British colonies like the US). Some Brazilians find continental Portuguese incomprehensible, and many joke about the "funny" way Europeans speak.

Regional accents *(sotaques)* in Brazil are very distinct. Paulistas (from São Paulo) speak at nearly inconceivable light-speed. Cariocas (residents of Rio city) speak a slightly more European Portuguese, with slurred sentences and "s" pronounced as "sh;" they also have the country's most colorful slang and local expressions. Because most *novelas* and movies are filmed in Rio, the Carioca accent and expressions are the most recognized; if you're going to learn Portuguese in Brazil, Rio is the place to do it. Southern and Central-Western Brazilians speak a more Spanish-sounding Portuguese because of their proximity to Argentina and Bolivia, respectively; Americans will also recognize a hint of a midwestern twang. Like everything else in Bahia, the Portuguese spoken by Baianos is slow, steady, and stress-free.

There are actually over 180 distinct languages spoken in Brazil, aside from Portuguese (impressive, until you consider that there were nearly four times that many before the first Europeans arrived). Virtually all these languages are indigenous tongues spoken in the Amazon, many considered endangered (spoken by fewer than 600 people) and some spoken by fewer than 200 people. Thankfully, in the past 20 years—with the help of the **Programa de Pesquisas Científicas das Línguas Indígenas Brasileiras** (Program of Scientific Research of Brazilian Indigenous Languages)—linguists have made great progress in working to document and preserve the nation's linguistic diversity.

RELIGION

Over 80% of Brazilians claim some sort of affiliation with the **Roman Catholic** church, making this nation's Catholic population the largest in the world. Despite the size of this figure, there are a vast array of faiths practiced in Brazil. When the Brazilian Constitution was ratified in 1889, the nation ceased to have an official religion (until then it had been Roman Catholic) and its citizens were guaranteed freedom of religion. Historically, this had not been the case, which resulted in the combining of Catholicism and other "forbidden" faiths. This sort of multi-faith approach to religion still exists today (although no longer because of threat of persecution), and many Brazilians choose to attend both Catholic mass and African-based ceremonies of worship.

Perhaps the best example of how religious traditions were syncretized with Roman Catholicism during slavery is **Candomblé,** one of the religions brought to Brazil by African slaves. When plantation owners forbid the practice of Candomblé rituals, its practitioners sought to preserve it by coupling their *orixás* (deities) with Catholic saints. In this way, the slaves satisfied their masters that they were worshipping the sanctioned religious figures, while still maintaining their own traditions. As such, Candomblé survived and its rituals of dance, song, and spiritual communion—led by *mães* or *pães de santo* (priestesses or priests)—are still practiced today, especially in the northeastern state of Bahia.

Another faith in which traditional Yoruba gods are still worshipped is **Umbanda,** a religion derived in part from Candomblé and exhibiting aspects of both Christian and Kardecist traditions. **Kardecism** itself is a sect of over one and a half million Brazilians who follow the doctrine of Allen Kardec, a French Spiritualist who purported beliefs in reincarnation and the idea that one could communicate with the dead. Yet another example of what anthropologists have dubbed the "hybrid religions" of Brazil is **Tambo de Mina,** practitioners of which are concentrated in Maranhão. This faith incorporates certain beliefs of the indigenous peoples of the Amazon as it preserves elements of traditions brought from Africa.

These faiths (excluding Kardecism) are only a few of the most widely-practiced African-based religions in Brazil, most of which are often incorrectly grouped together as **macumba.** While this *is* the name of one particular sect, it has come to be used as a derogatory umbrella term for all religions founded in African traditions, meant to inaccurately evoke notions of black magic and Satan-worship.

Above and beyond its diverse collection of African-based faiths, Brazil is home to a great number of Protestant religious traditions, including the Methodist, Lutheran, Baptist, Episcopal, and Pentecostal sects (the latter two having greatly increased the size of their following in the past few decades). Brazil is also home to people of Muslim, Buddhist, and Jewish faiths (Salvador is home to the first synagogue built in South America).

CULTURE

FOOD & DRINK

Brazilians have been fusing cuisines for centuries, mixing local ingredients and indigenous methods with imported African techniques and traditional Portuguese recipes. The hallmarks of Brazilian cuisine include: the liberal use of **manioc** (a.k.a. *cassava*, a stringy tuber), as both a seasoning and flour; *very* generous helpings of meat and side starches; *cozidos* (thick stews) and sauces of mixed African-European origin; and the prevalence of Brazil's many native fruits and vegetables.

The typical Brazilian restaurant menu will feature the hearty, meat-heavy traditional dishes associated with Minas Gerais *(comida mineira)*, plus European pizzas, *massas* (pastas), and salads, and the occasional Baiano specialty. *Salgados* (savory pastries) served at *lanchonetes* are common **appetizers,** as are *sopas* (soups). Entrees typically serve two but are mostly meat, so most people order side dishes *(guarnições)* of vegetables or starch. **Seafood** *(frutos do mar)* is usually only grilled *(grelhado)* or baked *(ao forno)* with potatoes. **Meats** come *simples* (grilled and ungarnished) or in the following **preparations:** *à milanesa* (fried); *à cubana* (with fried bananas and pork ends); *à francesa* (with ham, peas, and matchstick potatoes); *à grega* (with Greek rice—mixed with vegetables, raisins, and ham); *à paulista* (with sausage, fried eggs, and kale); *à piemontesa* (with cheesy rice). See p. 527 for a **Menu Reader.** Though São Paulo is considered by many the culinary capital of Latin America, outside of the major cities it's rare to find restaurants offering international cuisine. Thankfully, a country as vast and culturally diverse as Brazil has varied regional cuisines:

BY REGION

COMIDA MINEIRA (MINAS GERAIS). Miners and prospectors flooded this "heartland" of Brazil during the gold rush era, inspiring a rough-and-ready cuisine with an emphasis on easy preparations of beans, rice, and meat (especially beef and pork). Because of such humble and hearty beginnings, Minas Gerais is now considered the "motherland" of Brazilian cuisine, and anything seemingly traditional and hearty is usually classified as *comida mineira* regardless of origin; hence, *cuscuz à paulista* (a shrimp loaf from São Paulo) and the *feijoada completa* (Rio's signature Saturday stew) are both often called *mineiro* dishes. *Farofa* is the most famous *mineiro* treat, a sawdust-like bland garnish of powdered manioc baked or fried in oil.

COMIDA BAIANA (BAHIA). The African-infused cuisine of Bahia is undoubtedly the culinary highlight of Brazil. In colonial times, many African slaves were employed as plantation chefs, and added unique African touches—including Baiano basics like coconut milk, *harissa*-style spices, and *dendê* (a strong and pungent palm oil)—into heavy continental sauces and desserts. Flavorful Baiano seafood stews like *bobó*, *vatapá*, and *caruru* are now commonly found on menus all over Brazil, but no Baiano dish is as beloved as **moqueca,** a spicy stew of coconut milk, *dendê*, spices, and shrimp or fish. Also popular are **acarajé,** deep-fried brown bean fritters filled with *vatapá*, dried shrimp, and tongue-scorching chili oil. On streets and beaches all over Brazil you'll see turbaned, traditionally white-clad *baianas* selling *acarajé* and **doces** (sweets), including the sweet *crocada* (rice-and-coconut cake) and tapioca pancakes known as *biju* or *tapioquinha.*

COMIDA GAÚCHA (REGIÃO SUL). Though best known outside the country as the birthplace of supermodel Giselle Bünchen, the sprawling open plains of southern Brazil—in particular Rio Grande do Sul—are known to Brazilians as the land of the *gaúchos*, cattle-ranching cowboys famous for their meat-heavy cuisine (they recognize 37 different cuts of beef alone). The most famous *gaúcho* tradition is **churrascaria,** a giant barbecue feast served in an all-you-can-eat style called *rodízio;* it's now very popular all over the country.

COMIDA SERTANEJA (SERTÃO). The *sertão* is a region of dry grasslands in Brazil's Northeast region, with cuisine that differs markedly from the African-influenced *comida baiana* typically associated with the area. The most famous *sertanejo* dish is **carne de sol,** sun-dried beef used in both dry and rehydrated forms. As in the rest of Brazil, manioc is quite popular here, but known as *macax-*

eira. Sertaneja food is rarely served elsewhere outside the region, so the culinarily adventurous traveler who happens to be in the area would do well to take advantage of regional restaurants.

COMIDA AMAZONA (AMAZONAS). Unsurprisingly, indigenous fruits, vegetables, and freshwater fish are the centerpiece of Amazonian cuisine, with fried piranhas and catfish served up alongside exotic fruits like *cupuaçu* and *taparebá.* Local fruits—especially *guaraná* and *açaí* (see **Drinks,** below)—are quite popular all over the country, as are the many thick Indian-based stews like *tacacá.* (See p. 39 for more on fruits from the region.)

WHERE TO GET IT

Food in Brazil can be bought in both supermarkets and weekly markets called **feiras,** and is served primarily in three places: restaurants, small cafés, and street vendors. Supermarkets have more regular hours than *feiras*, but by mid-morning *feiras* have comparable prices and fresher produce, and often are the best place to buy regional products. Restaurants remain the traveler's safest and best opportunity to sample those ingredients Brazil's traditional dishes and preparations. Travelers looking for generic food items like hotdogs, hamburgers, and sandwiches will be well-served by either a **lanchonete** or a **padaria,** the former a lunch counter specializing in *salgados* (snacks) and convenience-store items, the latter resembling a mixture of a bakery and café. Some regional specialties can only be bought from street vendors. **Kilos** are bargains to watch for; here, as the name suggests, customers pay per kilogram of food.

DRINKS

Brazil's "national drink" is the potent **caipirinha,** a simple cocktail of fresh limes, sugar, and **cachaça,** a gutrot rum-style liquor. Denounced as undrinkable firewater when it was first cooked up in the 1600s, *cachaça* is still only distilled once from raw sugarcane, making it quite rough on the stomach—Pirassununga 51 is a popular brand more palatable to non-Brazilian tastes. The Fluminense city of Paraty (p. 168) and the state of Minas Gerais (p. 203) are known as the country's best producers of *cachaça;* some even go down smoothly.

The *caipirinha* may be the national drink, but it pales in popularity to the **cafezinho,** the small shots of super-strong, super-sweet coffee downed by Brazilians everywhere (they're most popular after meals and before bed, as a supposed sleep aid). *Cerveja* (beer) comes in a close second; do as Brazilians do and order a **chopp,** a small (300ml) tulip glass of the most popular local brew (usually Skol, Brahma, or Antarctica) served teeth-chatteringly cold.

Brazil's mind-boggling array of fruits and vegetables is best sampled in **sucos,** fresh-squeezed natural juices sold everywhere at juice bars (also called *sucos*) and corner *lanchonetes* (see p. 528 for a list of popular *sucos).* Brazilians take their juices very sweet, so travelers wanting things all natural should ask for *sem açúcar* (without sugar); those worried about water purity should ask for *sem gelo* (without ice). Don't miss **açaí,** a bowl of grainy purple slush made from a powdered Amazon berry of the same name (granola is often added); its purported energy- and libido-boosting qualities makes it popular with locals and travelers for post-beach refueling. **Guaraná** is an equally well-known Amazonian berry (with similar caffeine-like energy-boosting properties). It's sometimes added in powdered form to *sucos*, but is best known as a flavor of soft drink—so popular in Brazil it outsells Coca-Cola (whose own stab at *guaraná* greatness, Kuat, is reviled the country over). **Batidas** are *sucos* mixed with milk and usually *cachaça.* Note that although tap water is heavily treated in Brazil, it is recommended that travelers stick to bottled water.

CUSTOMS & ETIQUETTE

Brazilian culture is in general very informal, slow-paced, and friendly—which has its good and bad sides. Foreigners are almost always warmly welcomed (particularly in the Northeast), but many petty thieves take advantage of this, making scams abundant. Travelers will no doubt enjoy the laid-back lifestyle and Brazilian tendency to linger over *"mais um"* ("just one more drink"), but most probably won't relish the laid-back nature of most businesses and the chance to linger in interminable lines at banks, ATMs, post offices, supermarkets, and consulates.

TIME. Brazilian society places little importance on schedules, though buses do generally run on time. A half-hour late will be too early to show up for an appointment, and you should expect to wait if you show up at the agreed-upon time.

RULES. Brazilian society places less importance on abstract rules than on specific situations. For example, Brazilian drivers take traffic laws to be more suggestion than regulation, and marketplace lines are as often cut into and sidestepped as they are waited in. Visitors may be surprised by the openness with which otherwise torpid bureaucrats accept additional fees to speed their services, but should be warned that out-and-out bribery is rarer: it's far easier and less expensive to speed an aboveboard process than to create a new one.

ETHNICITY. Brazilians will often express curiosity about ethnic background, sometimes asking pointedly about race and skin color (especially of East and South Asians). In Brazil this is not considered offensive or impolite—it's small talk. Blond-haired, blue-eyed, and fair-skinned travelers may receive some extra attention, particularly in the North and Northeast regions.

SEX & SKIN. Sex is everywhere, and the heat makes minimal clothing the only way to survive. Travelers are often alternately drawn to and scandalized by how little you can get away with wearing in Rio and the surrounding areas, but should be advised that in the conservative South and the more rural areas of the Northeast, dress is generally more conservative. Business life demands suits and ties, but Brazilians dress much more casually when not at work, and very few clubs and restaurants require formal wear. Casual does not mean shabby or unfashionable, however; most Brazilians change their wardrobes as often as finances permit.

BODY LANGUAGE. Brazilian culture is very sensual, and social interactions may strike some as overly intimate. Women greet men and each other with a **kiss** on each cheek (Paulistas only kiss on one cheek); men greet other men with **handshakes.** Brazilians stand close when speaking, and often touch the forearm for emphasis. As with *Let's Go*, the **thumbs-up** is a universal symbol used constantly; it can mean OK, good job, are you sure?, where are we?, and more. The **A-OK** sign (thumb and forefinger together) is incredibly rude and should never be used.

MACHISMO. The Brazilian version of *machismo* is undoubtedly a pronounced part of the male-dominated society, but it's a watered-down, effectively harmless version compared to *machismo* elsewhere in South America. It sometimes seems like Brazilian men can't help but flirt—with everyone—but it is almost always playful and rarely dangerous. Ignoring unwanted attention is usually enough to deal with this, as flirting is an end in itself.

FAMILY. Brazilians value family life: the *parentela* (extended family) is the basic unit of Brazilian society. Children often live with parents until their late 20s, and sometimes even after marriage. Because Brazilians prefer to keep their family life private, most Brazilian social life takes place outside the home in restaurants and bars. It's rare for Brazilians to entertain visitors in their own homes.

TABLE MANNERS. Do not eat and walk: eat fast food either in the restaurant, standing still on the street, or after finding a place to eat, but not while walking to some other destination. At restaurants, the server will not stop at your table unless you signal them over, even when you are first seated. Signaling for *a conta, por favor* ("the check, please") indicates the end of the meal.

SPORTS & RECREATION

FUTEBOL

Brazil's unmatched World Cup record and its footballers' playfully improvisational style have brought Brazilian **soccer** global renown and today Brazil sends abroad more footballers than ambassadors. Brazil's vastness has stymied the development of a national league and Brazilian **futebol** remains heavily local. Brazil has the world's most football clubs per capita and this has kept fandom immediate and intense: each team usually travels with an entourage of anywhere from a few to a few hundred fans, whose presence and antics have become as much a part of the match as the game itself.

Brazil has also spawned many *futebol* variants including **futsal** (a faster, more intense soccer played on an indoor basketball court with a smaller, harder ball) and **futebol da praia** (*futebol* on the beach), both with their own leagues and championships. For a time in the 70s Brazil's elite even played **autoball,** soccer played with automobiles and a person-sized inflatable ball.

Some Brazilians complain that the sport of *futebol*—particularly at the youth level—has grown more institutional and regulated over the years, and that the increasing shortage of public space in Brazil has made informal pickup games all but impossible to arrange, but no one questions the sincerity or intensity of Brazil's love for *futebol.*

CAPOEIRA

Brazil's slave population first developed this martial art, and the domestic and international popularity of *capoeira* has surged since Brazil's government overturned its longstanding anti-*capoeira* stance in the early 1930s. *Capoeira* disguises its combat techniques as ritual dance, and correspondingly looks little like either Western boxing or wrestling or Eastern fighting styles: it almost exclusively emphasizes foot techniques and lacks blocks, and so players rely on acrobatic dodges and even-more-acrobatic counter-strikes.

Capoeiristas gather into *rodas* (circles) and provide musical accompaniment (on the *berimbau*, the single-stringed instrument associated with *capoeira*) for the two combatants in the *roda's* center. However, sparring is non-contact, competition is more friendly than fierce, and onlookers are often welcome.

BEACH SPORTS

Brazil's more than 7000km of coastline is studded with thousands of beaches fit for **surfing, windsurfing,** and the more unusual **kite surfing** and **sand surfing.** Droves of northern-hemisphere surfers descend upon them December through March, filling hotspots like Búzios, Saquarema, Angra dos Reis, and Arraial do Cabo. **Scuba diving** is also popular with locals and travelers, and most seaside destinations will have several agencies offering both expeditions and certification.

Beach volleyball is played on beaches all over the country, and increasingly common on beaches is **futevolei,** a sport similar to beach volleyball if volleyball were played entirely with the feet; despite its obvious difficulty, the sport's popularity continues to grow.

HOLIDAYS & FESTIVALS

Fun-loving Brazilians need little excuse to celebrate—this is a country known globally for its ability to throw one hell of a party. Although sweaty, sequined Carnaval is undoubtedly the most famous celebration in Brazil (if not the world), there are countless regional festivals and local parties all over the country, and all year round. Here are some of our favorites:

DATE	FESTIVAL & LOCATION	DESCRIPTION
Jan. 1	Bom Jesus dos Navegantes (Aracaju)	A procession of decorated boats; sailors who take part in this are supposedly protected from drowning.
3rd Th of Jan.	Lavagem do Bonfim (Salvador)	The washing of the steps of Bonfim Church followed by prayer and partying, with some 800,000 revelers.
Jan. 6	Three Kings Festival (Salvador)	Procession and events celebrating the magi.
Feb. 2	Celebration of Iemanjá (Salvador)	Offerings of perfume, jewelery, and flowers to Iemanjá (the goddess of the sea) are committed to the ocean.
'04: Feb. 21-24 '05: Feb. 5-8	Carnaval (most popular in Rio)	The biggest party in Brazil and possibly in the world. See p. 46 for more on Carnaval.
4th weekend in Mar.	Brazilian Grand Prix (São Paulo)	Extremely popular car racing event.
Apr.	Micareta (Feira de Santana)	Sixty-year-old local version of Carnaval, lasting 5 days.
10 days preceding Easter	Passion Pay (Nova Jerusalem)	South America's largest (and life-sized) passion play.
Apr. 21	Tiradentes (most popular in Ouro Preto)	Plays and cultural events.
May (just before Pentecost Su)	Festa do Divino (most popular in Pirenópolis)	Colorful processions with people dressed as prominent figures from Brazilian history.
June 13-14	Festas Juninas (everywhere)	Harvest festival with music, hot-air balloons, and bonfires in honor of Saints Anthony, John, and Peter.
June 22-24	Festa de São João (throughout Bahia)	Fireworks and *forró* in celebration of Saint John.
June 28-30	Boi-Bumbá (Parintins)	Dance, drums, and theater of mixed African and European origins.
Mid-June to mid-Aug.	Bumba-Meu-Boi (São Luís)	Folklore festival recreating the misadventures of a prize bull through dance and theater.
4th week of June to 1st of July	Bauernfest (Petrópolis)	Celebrates the town's German heritage.
3rd week of July	Sailing Festival (Ilhabela)	Brazil's largest sailing event.
4th week of July	Fortal (Fortaleza)	The biggest out-of-season Carnaval lasts 4 days and draws about 2 million people
F closest to Aug. 15	Festa da NS da Boa Morte (Cachoeira)	Candomblé festival organized by the Sisterhood of the Good Death, celebrating the freedom of the African slaves.
Late Sept. to early Oct.	Film Festival Rio BR (Rio)	Showcases both national and international films.
Oct.	Cocoa festival (Ilhéus)	Month-long celebration of the town's most important crop.
Oct.	Oktoberfest (Blumenau)	Second-biggest Oktoberfest in the world, testifying to the region's German influences.
2nd Su in Oct.	Círio de Nazaré (Belém)	Parade and party celebrating a statue reputed to have performed miracles in Portugal.
Mid-to-late Oct.	Jazz Festival (Rio and São Paulo)	Free 3 days showcasing Brazilian and international jazz performers.

DATE	FESTIVAL & LOCATION	DESCRIPTION
3rd and 4th weeks of Oct.	International Short Film Festival (São Paulo)	Shows films from Brazil, South America, and the world.
1st and 2nd weeks of Nov.	NS da Ajuda (Cachoeira)	Cleansing of a church followed by a street festival.
Nov. 14-21	Alejadinho Week (Ouro Preto)	Exhibits on Brazil's best-known sculptor.
Dec. 4	Santa Bárbara (Salvador)	Procession and dance celebrating Santa Bárbara and Iansã (the goddess of wind).
Dec.	Festival do Mar (Maceió)	Giant street and beach party.
1st week of Dec.	Carnatal (Natal)	Pre-season Carnaval, with lots of *forró*.
Dec. 31	Reveillon (most popular in Rio)	All-night New Year's celebration with lots of music and fireworks; Brazil's most famous party after Carnaval.

FURTHER READING & VIEWING

GENERAL HISTORY

Brazil: The Once and Future Country, by Marshall C. Eakin. A survey of major social and political issues in Brazil, as well as a brief overview of history and the arts (US$14).

The Brazilians, by Joseph A. Page. A portrait of modern-day Brazil, which looks at historic influences and events in an attempt to trace the development of Brazilian culture.

The Masters and the Slaves, by Gilberto Freyre. One of three books by the author to examine slavery on Brazil's sugar plantations.

SPORTS & RECREATION

Capoeira, a Brazilian Art Form: History, Philosophy, and Practice, by Bira Almeida. An in-depth look at the traditional ritual/dance/martial art.

Photography in Brazil, 1840-1900, by Gilberto Ferrez. The title says it all.

The Brazilian Sound: Samba, Bossa Nova and the Popular Music of Brazil, by Chris McGowan and Ricardo Pessanha. A comprehensive history of Brazilian popular music.

Brazilian Popular Music and Globalization, edited by Charles A. Perrone and Christopher Dunn. Essays tracing the movement of Brazilian pop music through the 20th century.

Futebol: The Brazilian Way, by Alex Bellos. An examination of the history, culture, and passion surrounding Brazilian soccer.

FICTION & NON-FICTION

Gabriela, Cravo e Canela (Gabriela, Clove & Cinnamon), by Jorge Amado.

Laços de Família (Family Ties), by Clarice Lispector.

Primeiros Cantos (First Verses), by Antônio Gonçalves Dias.

Macunaima, by Mario de Andrade.

Dom Casmurro, by Joaquim Maria Machado de Assis.

O Guarani (The Guaraní), by José Martiniano de Alençar.

O Alquimista (The Alchemist), by Paulo Coelho.

Global Etiquette Guide to Mexico & Latin America, by Dean Foster. See Chapter 6 (Brazil) for manners and customs of the country.

The Complete Poems, 1927-1979, by Elizabeth Bishop. Contains poems inspired by the author's time in Brazil, as well as translations of the works of Brazilian poets.

Urban Voices: Contemporary Short Stories From Brazil, edited by Cristina Ferreira-Pinto. A collection of short fiction by modern Brazilian authors.

Os Sertões (Rebellion in the Backlands), by Euclides da Cunha. A first-hand account of the 1896-97 military assaults on the interior village of Canudos.

The War at the End of the World, by Mario Vargas Llosa. A tragic novel which retells the story of the 1896 rebellion in Canudos.

Through the Brazilian Wilderness, by Theodore Roosevelt. A first-hand account of Roosevelt's 1914 voyage down the previously-uncharted River of Doubt in the Amazon.

Quarto de Despejo (Child of the Dark), by Carolina Maria de Jesus. The diary of a *favela* resident which captivated Brazilan society, becoming the best-selling book ever published in 1960s Brazil.

FILM

Copacabana (1947), dir. Alfred Green. The film whose theme song earned Rio de Janeiro the nickname *Cidade Maravilhosa* ("Marvelous City").

Orfeu Negro (Black Orpheus, 1959), dir. Marcel Camus.

A Meia-Noite Levarei Sua Alma (*At Midnight I'll Take Your Soul,* 1963); *Esta Noite Encarnarei No Teu Cadaver* (*This Night I'll Possess Your Corpse,* 1966); and *O Ritual dos Sádicos* (*Awakening of the Beast,* 1969), dir. José Mojica Marins.

Deus e Diabo na Terra do Sol (*Black God, White Devil,* 1964), dir. Glauber Rocha.

Como Era Gostoso O Meu Francês (*How Tasty Was My Little Frenchman,* 1971), dir. Nelson Pereira dos Santos.

Carmen Miranda: Bananas is My Business (1994), dir. Helena Sodberg.

Terra Estrangeira (*Foreign Land,* 1995), dir. Walter Salles Jr. and Daniela Thomas.

Cidade de Deus (*City of God,* 2002), dir. Kátia Lund and Fernando Meirelles.

Carandiru (2003), dir. Hector Babenco.

ECOTOURISM

Brazil: Amazon and Pantanal, The Ecotravellers' Wildlife Guide, by David L. Pearson and Les Beletsky. A guide for ecotravelers including information on Brazilian animals, environmental threats and conservation, parks and wildlife reserves.

Tales of a Shaman's Apprentice: An Ethnobotanist Searches for New Medicines in the Amazon Rain Forest, by Mark J. Plotkin. An account of the author's travels in the Amazon, focusing on local knowledge of plants in the rainforest.

Brazilian Pluralism

Brazil is undoubtedly one of the world's most multiracial countries, but visitors to the country generally have a different way of speaking of "race" than do the country's own citizens. In modern Brazil, "phenotypic" distinctions—skin color and facial features—have traditionally superseded "racial" distinctions like the national origins of one's ancestors. The attention paid to such physical attributes reflects a much greater focus on individuals as individuals rather than as characteristic members of stereotyped groups. Correspondingly, most Brazilians see their society as relatively tolerant and fluid with respect to racial issues. This in and of itself may lead some visitors to believe that Brazilian society compares favorably to the world's other multiracial societies, in which the historical pattern has been systematic discrimination against darker-skinned peoples; however, the truth is much more complicated than that.

Brazilians do consider their society racially harmonious, but all of the country's major socioeconomic indicators point out that the overwhelming majority of poor in Brazil are darker-skinned, and are also disproportionately of African descent. For example, the vast majority of Brazilians who live in the *favelas* (shantytowns) surrounding Rio de Janeiro are of African descent. Most Brazilians recognize that there is racism in their country but very few admit to being racist. Nazaré Soares Fonseca explored this dynamic by means of various surveys conducted in the state of Rio in 2000. These surveys found that while 93% of respondents admitted that there was racial prejudice in Brazil, 87% stated that they felt no racial prejudice, even though the same survey found that most Brazilians believe the "white race" to be more evolved than the "black race."

When trying to understand Brazilian racial politics one must contend with the prevailing myth of "racial democracy," which has been dominant throughout the twentieth century. Before that time Brazil's elite—who were largely of European descent—considered the history of Brazil to be one of "whitening" the indigenous population, both metaphorically (in terms of culture) and physically (by way of interracial marriage). This paradigm held until sociologist Gilberto Freyre revolutionized discussions on race and Brazilian national identity with his book *Casa Grande e Senzala* (trans. *The Masters and the Slaves*, 1933). Freyre's work for the first time brought attention to the importance of Afro-Brazilian cultural contributions to Brazil's formation. Freyre also argued that Portuguese colonialism was somehow more benign than Spanish colonialism, and that the Portuguese—being themselves a mixture of many peoples—showed a greater tendency toward and tolerance of racial intermixing.

In the end, the Afro-Brazilian contribution and the negative consequences of slavery were absorbed by a sociological and cultural dynamic of hybridization that resulted in a "balance between antagonisms." Herein would lie, as suggested by Freyre, the basis for the development of Brazilian nationhood and its correlative myth of "racial democracy," in which all races offer important societal contributions and all are given equal respect. Yet, as Michael Hanchard points out "phenotypic self-identification" does not make a person immune to discrimination in Brazilian society.

Fernando Arenas *is an Associate Professor of Portuguese at the University of Minnesota. His work focuses on Brazil and Lusophone Africa.*

CARNAVAL

Brazilians are always ready to party: at clubs, at bars, at the beach, at soccer games, in the street, even waiting in line, they always seem to find a way to have a good time. So just imagine what sort of party they can throw together with a few months of planning...you've probably come up with something only half as exhilarating, exhausting, and glitter-dusted as the non-stop five-day party of Carnaval.

Carnaval (a.k.a. Mardi Gras) means different things in different parts of the world—even in different parts of Brazil. Though this celebration happens all over the country, the most popular spots for travelers are Rio (p. 115) and Bahian capital Salvador (p. 344). In Rio, the holiday is synonymous with the infectious rhythms of *samba*, when a costumed menagerie of drag queens, celebrities, scantily-clad *mulatas*, and more all shake it to the pounding beat of a hundred-man drum corps during the famous Samba Parade. In Salvador, Carnaval is a raucous five-day street party throbbing to the frenetic beat of *axé* and *trios elétricos*, as people from all walks of life dance shoulder-to-shoulder every night until well past dawn.

If you're planning on being in Brazil for Carnaval, it'll help to do just that—plan. The following pages will help you maneuver once you're in Brazil, but it's best to deal with accommodations and transportation ahead of time. Hotels and hostels are booked far in advance; prices typically triple, and most places will only book for the full five-day (or seven-day) period, often requiring a deposit.

SAVE THIS DATE. The official dates for upcoming Carnaval festivities are as follows; all begin on Saturday:

Feb. 21-24, 2004
Feb. 5-8, 2005
Feb. 25-28, 2006

A BRIEF HISTORY

Carnaval supposedly has its roots in religious traditions, themselves derived from pagan celebrations. Carnaval was a five-day "last hurrah" of sinfulness and excess before the beginning of the 40-day atonement period known as Lent. The term is derived from the Latin for "farewell to meat" (*carne* "meat" + *vale* "farewell"), as Catholics are forbidden to eat red meat on Ash Wednesday. Although most Brazilians are seemingly less Catholic than their devout South American neighbors, the dates of the Carnaval holiday period (when literally everything shuts down) are still determined by the religious calendar, and it is still marked by unbridled excess and all-night partying. Carnaval begins the Saturday before Ash Wednesday (Quarta-Feira das Cinzas) and runs for five days through Fat Tuesday (Terça-Feira Gorda), celebrated elsewhere as Mardi Gras. Though the Friday before Carnaval Saturday is not an official government holiday, Friday evening is the true beginning of Carnaval, and in Salvador the holiday officially begins weeks before. In Rio, Friday before Carnaval is the day of a special ceremony (held at the City Palace, Rua São Clemente 360, Botafogo) when the mayor gives the key to the city to roly-poly *Rei Momo* (King Momo), the Ribald Regent, who "officially" rules over Rio for the five debaucherous days of Carnaval along with his sexy Queen Memo. (King and Queen are chosen in December, the requirements for the former being a good sense of humor and a minimum weight of 130kg, or about 290 lb.)

RIO DE JANEIRO

Rio's Carnaval is centered around three major activities: dancing, dancing, and more dancing. More specifically, this means dancing at the **samba parade** (p. 47), dancing at the **blocos** (street parades; p. 53), and dancing at the **bailes** (Carnaval balls; p. 56), always to *samba* and always until sunrise. The parade in particular—a ten-hour cavalcade of fantastically gaudy costumes, gigantic floats, and as much exposed, tanned flesh as possible—is known the world over, and followed minute-by-minute on TV by millions of people all over Brazil.

Officially Carnaval only lasts the five days before Ash Wednesday, but the anticipation of the holiday—particularly the main event, the lavish *escolas de samba* (*samba* schools) parade competition in Rio's purpose-built Sambódromo—means Rio is in the throes of *samba* fever long before then. The schools start preparing for next year's Carnaval parade days after this year's ends, and hold weekly open "rehearsal" parties (p. 52) as early as August—all for a brief 80min. of glory in the parade (plus a year's worth of bragging rights and unending national admiration). In the weeks before Carnaval, the streets of Rio play host to their own (more informal, but equally energetic) parade, as the itinerant *samba* bands known as *blocos* wander the streets drawing crowds of ecstatic partyers.

CARNAVAL INFO. For the most up-to-the-minute Carnaval info, try the following. The **weekend magazines** in *O Globo* and *O Jornal do Brasil* (published F; R$2) have the most comprehensive listings. The Carnaval Sa **VejaRio** insert in the news mag *Veja* (published Sa; R$5.90) has great behind-the-scenes *samba* school info. The invaluable pamphlet **Ensaio Geral** (free from Riotur) is the official word on tickets, prices, and Sambódromo safety and access. Also helpful is *samba* school governing body **LIESA's** Portuguese site (www.globo.liesa.com). When in doubt, call up Riotur's English-speaking **Âlo Rio** tourist hotline (☎2542 8080, 0800 707 1808)–Riotur is in charge of Carnaval, after all.

SAMBA PARADE

They may kiss-and-not-tell at *bailes* or march for hours with their neighborhood *bloco*, but for many Cariocas, Carnaval comes down to the *samba* parade: 80min. to display a back-breaking year's worth of hard work, blood, sweat, and sequins (not to mention glitter, feathers, fireworks, and, in 2003's parade, a levitating Moses and scuba divers doing aquarobics in giant water tanks). Some bemoan this gaudy display of seemingly pointless excess in a country where many live below poverty level—especially considering that the *samba* schools are mostly based in Rio's poorest districts, the *favelas* (shantytowns). But nothing quite expresses the scope and splendor of the Carioca lust for life like a procession of 4000+ costumed people accompanying a fleet of allegorical floats gushing glitter and shaking in rhythm to the swaying hips of topless women in elaborately adorned G-strings.

Although they're called **escolas de samba,** the *samba* "schools" are actually community groups, most named after and started in *favelas*, and staffed largely by *faveladors*. Each school chooses an annual governing theme *(enredo)*, composes a unique **samba de enredo** related to that theme, decides on floats and costumes, and begins a frenzy of sewing, building, and painting. The whole community works ridiculous hours, just for that one brief parade stint. Expectations of elaborate excess are so high now that many schools have to contract their costumes and construction out to professionals to get them done in time. Each school's *samba* gets incessant radio play (they're also compiled on a CD), and you're likely to hear a few *sambas de enredo* at street *bloco* parties.

IN RECENT NEWS

BANDAS & BANDITOS

Largely ignored for the rest of the year, Rio's *favelas* (shantytowns) are big news at Carnaval: the parades began in *favelas*, where residents sang and danced *samba* in the streets to celebrate. The resurgence of marching *bandas*—like Banda de Ipanema—recalls this tradition, as does the fact that most *samba* schools are named after the *favelas* in which they are based and in which they began.

The less festive side of the *favelas* came out in Carnaval 2003, courtesy of Fernandinho Beira-Mar, Brazil's biggest *bandito* (druglord), who was captured by US troops. Despite his arrest, Beira-Mar—named for his home *favela*—was determined to demonstrate that he was still in power. When complicated political considerations led him to be transferred to Rio's Bangú prison just a week before Carnaval, it seemed a perfect opportunity to take his message to the world. Working from his "secure" prison cell using a smuggled cell phone and coded letters, he ordered his Comando Vermelho gang to unleash a four-day wave of violence on Rio, and they proceeded to burn buses, bomb apartments, and intimidate stores into closing.

Cariocas were fearful, but not for their lives; their biggest concern was that the violence, though largely concentrated outside the city's tourist areas, would discourage travelers from seeing Rio at its

(Continued on next page)

There are countless *samba* schools in Rio, but only the top 14 (called the **Grupo Especial**) perform in the main parade, split over Carnaval Sunday and Monday (seven groups each night and into the morning). The site of the parade is the **Sambódromo,** the special parade grounds-*cum*-auditorium designed in 1984 by Oscar Niemeyer (p. 24), just west of Centro, on and around the **Avenida Marquês de Sapucaí.** The rounded "M" shape that represents Carnaval (Cariocas joke that it looks like a bikinied *derrière*) is the arch marking the end of the Sambódromo.

The schools are competing against each other in the parade, of course; the competition is hotly contested, and followed with the fanatical devotion Brazilians typically reserve for *futebol.* As they march, the schools are closely scrutinized by 40 official judges (positioned throughout the Sambódromo) on everything from costumes to theme to *bateria* (drum corps) harmony, even down to parading speed (schools must parade for at least 65min., but no more than 80min.—that's why the parade seems to be moving by so quickly).

The judges' rankings are announced on the afternoon of Ash Wednesday, at **Praça da Apoteose,** the elevated platform beneath the bikini-shaped arch. Once scores are announced, the partying continues non-stop at the *quadra* (rehearsal warehouse) of the champions—now considered bona fide national heroes—as their *samba de enredo* is played constantly on the radio. The school in last place bitterly mourns its fall from the select 14 (their spot is taken over by the winner of Saturday's smaller Grupo de Acesso parade). The following Saturday (known as **Sábado das Campeãs,** or "Champions' Saturday"), the top six schools parade again in the Sambódromo—just for show this time. A specially invited Carnevale troupe from that other major global Carnaval—Italy's—traditionally opens the show.

TICKETS

Tickets are more difficult to acquire than one would think. Riotur—which organizes Carnaval—reserves the special private booths in Sector 2 for tourists (complete with A/C, buffet, and live TV coverage), but you'll need a spare US$200+ lying around for the privilege. For more affordable tickets, get a copy of the free *Ensaio Geral* magazine from Riotur, which lists official prices *(ingressos)* and official ticket-selling agencies (usually bank branches). Unless you'll be in Rio six weeks before Carnaval and are willing to camp out overnight in front of Maracanã stadium, you're chances of getting a ticket directly from an agency and paying the price listed in *Ensaio*

Geral are non-existent. Official agencies always sell out, although there are sometimes tickets left as late as the weekend before Carnaval. The best seats are bought up instantly by tour agencies, hotels, and scalpers, to be sold for a 100%-plus profit. This means your hostel/hotel and every tour agency in Rio (including South America Experience; p. 120) will have tickets for sale. The best price you should hope for from these sources is a little more than double the price in *Ensaio Geral*, meaning about R$200-400 for the better *arquibancada* sectors (3, 4, 5, 7, 11) and around R$40-50 for the fun but far away sectors 6 and 13. Accommodations usually only have tickets for one day and one sector, while tour agencies (Riotur has suggestions on which to contact) have a much wider variety.

If you can't get tickets through the above sources—or if you want to maximize your beach time and not spend your entire holiday hunting down tickets at various travel agencies—there are plenty of scalpers around the Sambódromo and its two *metrô* stops (M: Central and M: Praça Onze); they're the people barking *"ingressos, ingressos."* Prices are obviously inflated, though not much more than at travel agencies. Scalper prices drop after more popular schools like Beija-Flor, Mangueira, and Salgueiro have paraded, and plummet sharply and quickly as the night wears on. After midnight or 1am (the parade runs non-stop until about 6am), you can easily find scalper tickets for around R$35, even for the best sections.

The racket of scalping fake or old tickets to the parade has dropped off a bit in recent years, but is still fairly rampant: inspect your ticket closely to make sure it has the right spelling, year (!), and day (different days have different colored tickets). Tickets marked *Cortesia* are a legitimate type. Tickets to all seats except those in sectors 6 and 13 have two parts: a plastic electronic ticket (resembling a credit card) and a two-piece paper ticket; you need both plastic and paper (both sheets) to get in, so don't leave a scalper without them. Sectors 6 and 13 only have plastic tickets.

If you miss the parade or can't get tickets, consider the Parade of Champions (Sábado das Campeãs) on the following Saturday, when the top six schools parade again to great applause and revelry. Although it's not quite as frenzied as the original, the Parade of Champions is just as fun and elaborate, a little bit shorter, and tickets cost about half what they do for the main parade. There are also usually always tickets left over at the official ticket agencies (check newspapers for agency info), and sometimes even at the Sambódromo ticket office.

(Continued from previous page)

best. Rio made world news on the eve of Carnaval not for toned beauties shaking their feathers but with scenes of charred buses and street violence. The violence threatened to cripple Rio's biggest event, which annually pumps US$130 million into the city; as feared, travel agencies began logging cancellations. The very concerned President Lula responded to the violence by sending in some 3000 soldiers, who stopped Beira-Mar's violence by the eve of Carnaval and moved "Freddy Seaside" (as he is known to the foreign press) to a more secure prison deep in the state of São Paulo.

Carnaval went off without any resurgence of gang violence, and if anything tourists seemed thankful for the extra police presence. In fact, perhaps the biggest surprise for most travelers is that Carnaval may well be the safest time to visit Rio. Although prices during the festival border on criminal, a classic Carioca joke says that even the thieves take a holiday for Carnaval; in any case the festival's higher prices do result in increased security. Indeed, Carnaval is Rio de Janeiro's one chance to show the world the best of the city and they pull out all the stops: so long as you keep your head about you, don't hesitate to march with a *banda* or *bloco*, or to party in the street.

SAMBÓDROMO 101. From the tiered stands of the Sambódromo, the *samba* parade seems like a teeming ocean of color, sound, and flesh rushing down Sapucaí like a tidal wave, with no possible order and only the drums to hold it all together. In reality, each school's parade *(desfile)* is tightly choreographed, with many different interlocking parts. Before the parade begins, you hear the *samba's* beating heart and soul—the drumming of the *bateria,* who march in and enter into formation between Sectors 1 and 2. They're followed by the *carro do som* (music truck) and the *puxador,* who warms up the crowd before launching into the school's official *samba.* Once the signal horn sounds, the parade begins with a burst of fireworks in the school's colors. The elegantly choreographed *comissão da frente* opens the show, followed by the breathtaking opening float and *fantasias* of the *abre alas.* Additional *alas, baianas, carros alegóricos,* and several flag-bearing *porta-bandeiras* and *mestres-sala* then follow non-stop, elaborating on the school's official theme. When it's all over, orange-suited trash collectors march in with brooms, clearing the way for the next parade. This brief glossary will help you navigate the Sambódromo:

ala: Each troupe of 100+ dancers, which collectively make up the bulk of the parade. Each *ala* has its own costume. The *abre alas* is the first, most elaborately costumed, troupe.

baianas: The *alas* of spinning older women in huge, hooped Baiano skirts, a nod to the fact that *samba* originated in the African rhythms of Bahia.

bateria: The drum corps of 100+ *batuqueiros,* fronted by the scantily clad *rainha de bateria* ("Bateria Queen"). Besides bass *(surdo)* and tenor *(atabatque)* drums, *batuqueiros* play *chucalhos* (shakers with small cymbals) and *tambourins* (rapped with 3-4 drumsticks). Also featured is the *cuica,* the drum rubbed on the inside to create *samba's* distinctive *wah-wah* sound.

carros alegóricos: The elaborate, multi-story thematic floats that gush tinsel and glitter, usually populated by *bonecos* (giant moving puppets), topless and sequin-clad *mulatas,* a few waterfalls, and the occasional celebrity.

comissão de frente: The small group of 15 or so elaborately, uniquely choreographed dancers that open the parade and introduce the school's theme.

desfile: Parade. Before the parade begins, the school gathers together in a *concentração* (in the Sambódromo, the *concentração* is in front of Sector 1).

enredo: The *samba* school's theme, echoed in its floats, costumes, and *samba de enredo,* composed specifically for Carnaval. Themes range over such diverse topics as world peace, homages to celebrities, and organ donation.

ensaio: Rehearsals, held every Sa night from mid-Aug. to Carnaval (see p. 52).

fantasia: The lavish, over-the-top costumes, which would make even Liberace blush. The most elaborate ones *(destaques)* get to ride on the floats.

passistas: The school's best *samba* dancers, who wander the parade showing off to the crowd. They typically have their own unique costume.

porta-bandeira & mestre-sala: The gaudily attired woman *(porta-bandeira)* and man *(mestre-sala)* who waltz bearing the school's official flag.

puxador: The man who sings the *samba de enredo* as he walks along with the *carro do som* (music truck), driving the parade along with the *bateria.*

samba de enredo: An original *samba,* corresponding to the school's theme *(enredo)* for the year.

velha guarda: Literally, "old guard," the *samba* school's older members who march at the end of the parade out of respect for the school's tradition.

SEATS & SECTORS

Chances are you'll be going with your hostel or hotel to the Sambódromo and won't have much of a choice where you'll be sitting. If you do have the choice of a sector, read below, and consult the map in the *Ensaio Geral*.

Aside from the pricey private booths of Sector 2, most seats in the Sambódromo are *arquibancadas*, non-numbered general bleacher seats; there are also a few *cadeiras individuais* (individual chairs set up on Sapucaí), which are comfortable, affordable, and right in the thick of the action, but at the very end of the parade route (sectors 6 and 13).

Sector 1 (Arquibancadas): Looks out on the *concentração,* so you'll see the school gear up, but won't see the parade in its full stride. Because this sector is opposite the judging booth, you'll see the dancers, marchers, and *bateria* in their finest form.

Sector 2 (Camarotes & Frisas): A/C private and semi-private booths complete with black-tie waiters, all-night buffet, TVs with live parade coverage, and so-close-you-get-tickled-by-the-feathers views. Riotur reserves these especially for top-dollar tourists (US$200+), and many luxury tours and hotels typically buy them all up.

Sectors 3, 4, 5, 7, 11 (Arquibancadas Especiais): Most budget tourists sit in these sections. Along with Sector 9, these are the best and most expensive *arquibancada* seats, giving you (and your 3000 new best friends crowded into each sector) a full view up and down the avenue. It's general admission, so arrive early to secure your spot or stay late and move closer as people leave. Sector 3 is at the official starting line, so you'll witness the amazing sight of the *bateria* arriving and entering into formation—but you'll also be forced to hear and smell the ear-splitting, smoke-spewing fireworks.

Sector 9 (Arquibancadas Turísticas): Identical to the above *arquibancadas* except that a Sector 9 ticket is for a reserved, individually numbered spot on the bleachers, and not just general admission (because tourists just *hate* to share bleacher space).

Sectors 6 & 13: These are the cheapest seats, at the very end of the parade, with the worst views of the action (they're twice as far back as any other section). To compensate, these are the most party-friendly seats, as this is where many Brazilians sit, many of them having traveled thousands of miles to be here—trust us, they came to have a good time. Many fun-loving hostels also buy seats here. Another plus: after the parade, many paraders (including celebrities) take a route out of the Sambódromo that passes by these sectors only, waving and chatting with their legions of fans.

TRANSPORTATION

Do not take the **bus** to or from the Sambódromo; it's crowded and unsafe. The **metrô** runs around the clock on Carnaval Sunday and Monday—the days of the major *samba* parade—and also on the following Saturday, for the Parade of Champions. The *metrô* is the preferred transport for paraders, who ride in their full costumes and often break out into song and dance en route to the Sambódromo. Even-numbered sectors are accessed from M: Praça Onze, while odd-numbered sections are accessed from M: Central; there are scalpers near both stops. It's a long haul from either stop to the parade grounds, and there are no signs (though there are police to point you in a general direction). Although the *metrô* is an excellent option to the Sambódromo, it is not recommended on the way back. If you leave before the parade ends, you have to walk through dark and potentially deserted areas to the station—places where Carnaval violence has taken place in the past, though there are plenty of police. If you leave at the end of the parade, the *metrô* will be packed. **Taxis** are expensive, but get you right to the Sambódromo. On the way back from the Sambódromo, taxis charge a flat, non-metered fee, and are the safest option.

THE BIG SPLURGE

DIY SAMBÓDROMO

Watching the Carnaval parade is an amazing experience, but why not march in it yourself? *Samba* schools are happy to have foreigners parade with them, as they can always use extra people and *reais*. Costumes will run R$300-500, which is much less than what Riotur charges for tickets to the tourist booths, and little more than you'll be charged by travel agencies.

To start, visit the schools' websites (p. 52) and choose your costume. Next you need to contact the school to confirm your spot, set up payment, get them your measurements, and arrange pick-up in Rio. Riotur (☎2542 8080) can help with this, and there are agencies that do all the work for you. If you'll be in Rio a few weeks before Carnaval, stop by a rehearsal (p. 52) to handle the logistics in person.

Although you'll need to arrange to march before Carnaval begins, you don't need to be in Rio any earlier than the holiday to rehearse: the *ala* (troupe) you'll be in won't have any special choreography aside from marching, twirling, and *samba*, and there will be one final rehearsal during Carnaval anyway. One caveat: there has been a recent surge of *gringos* arranging to march in the parade without ever bothering to learn the school's *samba* song or even how to *samba*. This is an insult to the school's traditions and it's hard work; don't do it.

If you take the *metrô* (either stop) to the parade, you'll get a fascinating glimpse into how the *samba* schools function, in what Riotur calls the **Samba Anteroom.** The *metrô* stations let out onto Ave. Presidente Vargas, which is also the street on which the schools line up their floats and paraders in preparation for entering the Sambódromo. This area becomes its own sort of street party, with music, dancing, food and drink vendors, and school insignia attire for sale. This is a great place to take pictures of the schools, as well as to talk to the people who help put all of this together.

REHEARSALS

Whether or not you'll be in Rio for Carnaval, you must attend one of the amazing *samba* school rehearsals *(ensaios)*. Every Saturday night from mid-August until Carnaval (beginning around 11pm or midnight), the schools hold open rehearsals where, for a small fee (R$5-20), the public is invited to join the schools in dancing and singing the school's *samba de enredo*. "Rehearsal" is a bit of a misnomer—this is more of a pre-Carnaval bash. There are bars and food stands set up, as well as a store with school insignia; there's usually an opening act as well. This might be the closest you can get to the heart-pounding, unforgettable feeling of being in the parade without actually being in it, and it's probably the loudest you'll ever hear *samba* played. Whatever you call them, these sweaty, crowded, exhausting parties are something of a miracle—how else to explain how one song, repeated over and over again, can drive a party that lasts until dawn?

Though most *samba* schools are associated with poorer neighborhoods and are in or near *favelas*, the rehearsals are quite safe, as they're held in the school's *quadra*, the secure warehouse where the school stores its floats and costumes. However, it's best to visit rehearsals in a group, and *never* to wander into the area around the *quadra*. Taxis are easy to find around the *quadras*, and are, for tourists, the only reliable means of getting to and from rehearsals.

Many hostels and hotels (and South America Experience; p. 120) organize trips to the rehearsals, including round-trip transport and admission. At R$50-55, these may cost more than a group taxi and out-of-pocket admission, but may be worth it to travelers for the guarantee of a wholly secure ride and the guidance of a local.

Always call ahead before attending a rehearsal, as schools sometimes cancel them; note that many schools now rehearse on Thursday or Friday, not Saturday. The public is welcome at any school, but tourists typically visit **Mangueira** or **Salgueiro,** the two closest to the more touristed parts of Rio (rather than in distant suburbs); both are west of Centro and no more than a R$20-25 taxi ride from Copacabana. Although both schools are in safe areas, some tours prefer Salgueiro, whose *quadra* is in a lower middle class neighborhood (whereas Mangueira's is steps from the *favela* that lends the school its name). *Ensaio Geral* has a list of school contacts and rehearsal times; below we list the 14 schools in Carnaval 2004 (all but one will parade again in 2005).

Beija-Flor, Rua Pracinha Wallace Paes Leme 1025 (☎2791 2866; www.beija-flor.com.br), in Nilópolis. After 4 straight years of 2nd placedom, Beija-Flor finally took 1st place in 2003. The one thing no one can explain: their name means hummingbird (lit. "flower-kisser"), but their school color is robins' egg blue. Rehearsals Th.

Caprichosos de Pilares, Rua Faleiros 1 (☎2592 5620; www.caprichososdepil-ares.com.br), in Pilares.

Grande Rio, Rua Almirante Barroso 5 (☎2775 8422; www.granderio.com.br), in Duque de Caxias. Rehearsals on F.

Imperatriz Leopoldinense, Rua Professor Lacê 235 (☎2270 8037; www.imperatrizle-opoldinense.com.br), in Ramos. Known for having the absolutely gaudiest and most elaborate *fantasias* (costumes) in the Sambódromo—a great choice to parade with.

Império Serrano, Ave. Ministro Edgard Romero 114 (☎3359 4944; www.imperioser-rano.art.br), in Madureira.

Mangueira, Rua Visconde de Niterói 1072 (☎3872 6786; www.mangueira.com.br), in Mangueira. The oldest school and the winner of the first competition ever held in the city, the storied *verde-e-rosa* (green and pink) is far and away Rio's most beloved and favored *samba* school.

Mocidade, Rua Coronel Tamarindo 38 (☎3332 5823; www.mocidadeindepen-dente.com.br), in Padre Miguel. Considered one of Rio's most innovative and socially conscious schools (their 2003 theme was about the joys of organ donation).

Porto da Pedra, Rua João Silva 84 (☎2605 2984; www.gresuportodapedra.com.br), in São Gonçalo. Rehearsals F.

Portela, Rua Clara Nunes 81 (☎2489 6440; www.gresportela.com), in Madureira. Rio's winningest *samba* school (21 wins since the Carnaval tradition in the Sambódromo started). MPB star Marisa Monte's school.

Salgueiro, Rua Silva Teles 104 (☎2288 3065; www.salgueiro.com.br), in Andaraí. Second only to Mangueira in popularity, the *vermelho-e-branco* (red and white) is considered by many tours and hotels to be the safest school to watch rehearse.

São Clemente, Rua São Clemente s/n (☎2580 2121; www.saoclemente.com.br), near M: Botafogo in Botafogo.

Tradição, Rua Intendente Magalhães 160 (☎3833 4611; www.grestradicao.com.br), in Campinho. Rehearsals F.

Unidos da Tijuca, Ave. Francisco Bicalho 47 (☎2516 4053; www.unidosdati-juca.com.br), in Santo Cristo.

Viradouro, Ave. do Contorno 16 (☎2628 7840; www.viradouro.com.br), in Barreto.

BLOCOS (STREET CARNAVAL)

Carnaval was born in the streets. Long before there were sexy dance parties and an over-the-top *samba* parade, Carnaval was a holiday for the people by the people, a free (and free-for-all) five-day party in the streets. Amateur *blocos* and *bandas*—itinerant marching bands of percussionists and brass players, typically residents of the *favelas*—used to wander the streets with dancing revelers in tow.

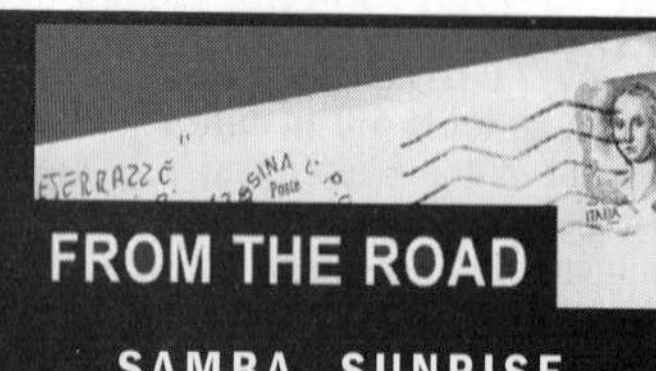

FROM THE ROAD

SAMBA, SUNRISE, SAPUCAÍ

Marquês de Sapucaí—the street on which the Sambódromo is built—is the heart of Carnaval Carioca. While the elaborate *samba* parade there is unforgettable, the old cliché holds true—getting there (and back) *is* half the fun.

The night of the parade, we decided to take the *metrô* to the Sambódromo. Our car was empty until M: Catete, where Cariocas in neon soldier/cuckoo-clock/Statue of Liberty outfits boarded. These marchers with the Portela *samba* school got the whole car singing their *samba* as they reviewed lyrics and dance steps (and saved a headdress from being crushed in the doors). Tensions rose when the popular Salgueiro's rowdy, success-drunk *bateria* (who had received rave reviews earlier in the night) boarded, but no one really gets angry during Carnaval, so things stayed calm...if the word "calm" can really be used to describe a *metrô* car full of parading neon dancers. When we finally reached the stop, we still had quite a walk to reach the parade grounds, but it was worth it; as we passed Mangueira's floats setting up, music was blasting, cameras were flashing, men in hot-pink dreidel hats chugged beer, and men fought over who got to put glitter on the oiled dancers' bodies.

The parade itself was mind-numbing sensory overload: beautiful, surreal, riotous, exhausting,

(Continued on next page)

In Salvador (from whence Rio imported its traditions), Carnaval is still a street party of itinerant *trios*, which explains why many Brazilians (and increasingly more tourists) prefer to spend Carnaval in the Bahian capital, whose street party is perceived as being closer to Carnaval's "authentic" origins.

Those in search of authenticity in fake-loving Rio, fear not: CD piracy may be so bad it was the *enredo* of a 2003 *samba* school, and silicone may be everywhere on the beach (and we don't mean in the sand), but in the past few years, the Carnaval Carioca has begun to revive the neighborhood street parade tradition, and the city's ever-increasing number of traditional *blocos* are now back with a vengeance. Many *blocos*—most with whimsical, foolish names like "What Shit is This," "Darling I'll Be Back Soon," and "Armpit of Christ"—now draw crowds upwards of 10,000. One (Monobloco) is so popular it put out its own CD (many of Bahia's favorite street Carnaval groups, like Olodum, have already cut records). Dancing, singing, and partying along in the streets with the *blocos* is one of the most exhilarating and enjoyable parts of Carnaval, and probably one of the best ways to meet Cariocas and see how the locals celebrate this increasingly touristy holiday.

I LOVE A PARADE

Most *blocos* parade several times, at least once during Carnaval (typically on the weekend or Fat Tuesday) and a few more times on the weekends preceding Carnaval. They usually have a close connection with a neighborhood, and will meet and parade (and party afterward) in that general vicinity. The bigger and more popular *blocos* parade up and down the *orlas* (beachfronts) of Copacabana and Ipanema/Leblon; you're guaranteed a good time if you head to either beach after 4pm (when most *blocos* parade) on Carnaval weekend. Like the *samba* schools, the *blocos* have a sizable *bateria* (*samba* drum corps) marching behind a *carro do som*, the truck that carries the musicians and the *puxador* (*samba* singer) and blasts music into the crowds. Unlike the schools, few *blocos* have original *sambas*, preferring to groove to the hits of Carnaval past.

Blocos gather in one area (the *concentração*), draw a crowd (and countless vendors of food, funny foam, and Carnaval masks), and lead everyone down the street in a chaotic *samba*-crazed mass, gathering people and momentum along the way. Once the *bloco* has worn itself out, the party stops moving, but continues long into the night. Anyone and everyone is welcome to join in, costumes are encouraged, and many *blocos* sell commemorative T-shirts (R$10-15).

POPULAR BLOCOS

Riotur's guide, the "VejaRio" insert, and the newspapers' weekend magazines all have full listings of *blocos* (which begin parading up to two weeks before Carnaval). The most popular *blocos* are listed below, but check the papers to confirm parade times and locations, as they often change last-minute:

Banda da Carmen Miranda. Resembling a gay pride parade—with floats and recorded music blasted into the street—this *banda* has Carnaval's most lavishly attired drag queens, many of them dressed like their namesake, sassy Carmen Miranda. *Concentração:* varies every year. Parade: Su before Carnaval.

Banda de Ipanema. Formed 40 years ago as a protest march against the country's military dictatorship (the *banda* still wears all white and sings about peace), this is now Rio's most popular and fun-loving *banda* and also the top GLS street parade, with countless drag queens and a loyal gay following. They have some 60+ *batuqueiros* (drummers) and no *carro do som,* so you'll feel that thumping *samba* beat from the top of your feathered wig down to your sequined and stilettoed feet. *Concentração:* Praça Gen. Osório, Ipanema. Parade: 2 Sa before Carnaval; Carnaval Sa and Tu.

Blocão Bicho. *Bicho* is the nickname for the popular (and yappy) *bichon frisse* dogs, and also a general term for canine companions (don't confuse this with *bicha,* a semi-derogatory term for homosexuals). This tiny *bloco* new to the Carnaval scene features a silent and silly parade of costumed, confused pets and their owners, who march at various times in Copacabana alongside other larger *blocos.*

Bloco do Bip-Bip. Formed by regulars at hole-in-the-wall bar Bip-Bip, this *bloco* traditionally opens and closes street Carnaval, parading F night at midnight (Carnaval's start) and on Fat Tuesday, after all the other major *blocos* have finished up. *Concentração:* Bar Bip-Bip, Rua Almirante Gonçalves 50, Copacabana.

Bloco das Carmelitas. Nuns + transvestites + Bohemians = Rio's most enthusiastic street party. Named for the order of Carmelite nuns whose convent tops Santa Teresa's hill, this crowded evening parade is the safest way to see the artsy neighborhood of Santa Teresa while also having a blast. *Concentração:* top of Ladeira de Santa Teresa, at Rua Dias de Barros, Santa Teresa. Parade: Carnaval F and Tu; on-site rehearsals every F before Carnaval.

Copa Bandas: While many of the truly local, intimate neighborhood *blocos* are in places unsafe for tourists, Copacabana has several local parades that let you shake your *bumbum* with hardly a *gringo* in sight. These include **Banda Sá Ferreira** and **Banda Santa**

(Continued from previous page)

and sadistically energetic. Seen from above on TV, it must have seemed a living entity of rainbow ooze: From the Sambódromo's front row, it was complete and total anarchy, as if it were the end of the world and the Four Horsemen of the Apocalypse had brought Las Vegas along for the ride. If one were trapped on American Bandstand while being dunked in a vat of glitter, it might begin to approximate the experience. Your senses are over-stimulated, and all you can think is: *keep. on. dancing.*

Carnaval is a great time to befriend Brazilians, who are known for their candor. We were all in the worst seats, but we could've been leading the *bateria* for all the fun we had. We met a group from Nilópolis, home of the Beija-Flor school, and learned moves only the *alas* learn, but I barely got to dance as one woman gossiped about each float as it passed—from who had implants to whose float had undergone a last-minute patch-up.

We left early—at least I though it was early—but by the time we made our way through the party raging on the streets outside the Sambódromo, the sun had begun to rise behind the last school's fireworks. It's too bad my eyes were too sequin-dazzled to register the gorgeous sight.

We decide to go to Arpoador, and the sunrise chased our cab through still-dark Rio. As we jumped blindly into Copacabana's dark water, the sunlight rounded the Sugarloaf. Emerging from the water, we saw the sun bathing the world's most famous beach—a perfect Carnaval capstone.

—Ankur Ghosh

Clara, found every night of Carnaval on the streets of those same names in Copacabana. If you prefer *samba* sans lyrics and sans parade, catch **Banda Bairro Peixoto** every Su before Carnaval near Posto 4 (around 4pm); they have no singer and no parade, just a powerful and quite talented *bateria*.

Cordão da Bola Preta ("Black Spot String"). This *bloco* based in Centro draws one of the biggest crowds of Carnaval (over 10,000), but it's for late partyers (or early risers) only: the *concentração* is at (!) 9am. They gather at the artsy Bola Preta *samba* club, named (like a certain Ipanema spot) after the attire of a tall and tan and young and lovely woman who once walked by the club. *Concentração:* Bola Preta, Rua 13 de Maio 13, at Rua Evaristo da Veiga, Centro (M: Cinelândia). Parade: Carnaval Sa.

Monobloco. The highlight of the Carnaval *bloco* scene is this heart-pounding powerhouse (with over 150 drummers) known for their all-original *samba recheiado* (lit. "stuffed *samba*")–*samba* infused with the Afro-Caribbean beats of funk, hip-hop, and reggae. *Concentração: orla* of Leblon, though the location varies. Parade: Su before Carnaval; unforgettable open rehearsal parties every F before Carnaval (at clubs around the city).

Simpatia é Quase Amor ("Kindness is Almost Love"). The best of both worlds: all the great things the *samba* schools have–an original *samba de enredo* and original colors, *lilás-e-amarelo* (lavender and yellow, an homage to the packaging of the anti-hangover drug Engov)–minus the schools' touristy cheese; all the unbridled, joyful energy of the local street *bloco,* without the typical *bloco* chaos and disorder. *Concentração:* Praça Gen. Osório, Ipanema. Parade: Sa before Carnaval; Carnaval Su.

BAILES (CARNAVAL BALLS)

Carnaval may have a reputation as a five-night debauch, but in reality the *samba*-related events—in the streets and the Sambódromo—are surprisingly unscandalous. (There's actually a "no full nudity" rule in the parade, although the many topless *mulatas* you'll see on Sapucaí come close—and nude women who have been body painted are permitted.) The dancing, and partying may last all night, but Carnaval revelers only truly reveal their raunchy side at Rio's infamous *bailes* (balls).

The balls were once only for aristocrats, while the poor *hoi polloi* got down and dirty in the street parades. Though people of all classes now dance with the street *blocos*, the *bailes* remain pricey and at times exclusive affairs, an option still only available to wealthier Brazilians. This doesn't detract from the excitement of the *bailes*, however, and even the higher-class *bailes* are affordable for budget travelers. Although there are several black-tie affairs, most *bailes* are just an excuse to go out drinking and dancing at the clubs wearing ridiculous outfits, partying with *gringos* and Brazilians alike in a sweaty, sexy, erotically charged atmosphere.

Crowds usually gather outside to watch the masked and scantily clad revelers arrive, parading down the red-carpet in their own X-rated version of the Sambódromo: though regular club attire is fine and most common for either sex, men sometimes choose outlandish drag or bondage attire; women have been known to slip into a sequined bikini (top optional) and flimsy wrap, baring their breasts to the camera crews vying for prime positions inside and outside the club. (The question on every TV anchor's lips is: *Quanto silicone tem?* or "How much silicone do you have?", not considered an impolite question in Brazil.)

Bailes are not for the faint of heart or those who like to keep things to themselves. The party gets going after midnight at the clubs and runs at a fever pitch all night, with non-stop kissing, grinding, and groping effectively required by anarchcic *baile* law; when it all winds down at dawn, all inhibitions have gone out the window, and anything goes.

The Riotur brochure, the "VejaRio" insert, and the newspapers' weekend magazines all have listings of the major *bailes* in the city.

BAILES AT NIGHTCLUBS

The best-known Carnaval *bailes* are at the multi-story Leblon club **Scala,** Ave. Afrânio Melo Franco 296 (☎2239 4448), which hosts a different *baile* every night of Carnaval—each more lascivious than the last. Tickets are R$70 and often sell out. For a testosterone overdose, head to Friday's sweaty **Baile do Vermelho e Preto** (Red and Black Ball), in honor of red-and-black-jerseyed Flamengo, Rio's most worshipped *futebol* team. This macho Brazilian frat party draws many more single men than women, and gets downright illegal by the end of the night.

Scala's lineup of *bailes* culminates with Fat Tuesday's legendary **Baile Scala Gay,** Brazil's GLS (gay, lesbian, and sympathizer) event of the year. Queer folk and their straight friends fly in from all over the country just to attend the ball, as much to party as to ogle the endless parade of sequined, feathered, chain-mailed, and gold-painted transvestites and transsexuals who dominate the action and bare everything (and then some) for the crowds and cameras. (Here, the most-asked question is: *É homem ou mulher? Tem virgula e é funcionado?* or "Are you a man or a woman? Do you have a penis, and does it work?") As a sort of dry run for the Scala Gay Ball, the Copacabana gay club **Le Boy** (p. 159) hosts a different themed ball every night leading up to the ball. Similarly, the Botafogo nightclub **Ballroom** (p. 158) often has a different techno- or electronica-themed *samba* dance party every night of Carnaval, with occasional guest visits from *samba* school *baterias*.

CARNAVAL

FORMAL BAILES

If you prefer actual royalty rather than drag queens, Rio has several snooty formal affairs as well. The belle of these *bailes* is held on Carnaval Saturday, when the luxurious Copacabana Palace Hotel hosts the lavishly upscale **Baile do Copa,** a tradition since a year after the luxury hotel opened in 1923. Considered *the* high society event in Rio, if not all of Brazil, this ball—which takes place in the hotel's gilded art deco ballroom, and features a live symphony orchestra—is where to go if you want to celebrate Carnaval with the incredibly rich and famous. Tickets aren't cheap (R$750-1000) and go quickly, so plan ahead, and leave some room in your pack for a Versace dress or Armani tux: this is not the place for that skimpy *fio dental*, as the Copa Palace dress code is strict black tie, designer ballgown, or *couture*-worthy costume.

OUTDOOR BAILES

During Carnaval, several outdoor areas in the city are transformed into fantastic open-air concert venues, with big concert stages and bars and food vendors—all catering to those who can't or don't want to pay the high price for tickets to the official indoor *bailes* or the *samba* parade. Consider these a cross between the open-air fun of the *blocos* and the indoor debauchery of the *bailes*.

Those who are in Rio before Carnaval will find the scene of the **Rio Folia** (Rio Follies; Carnaval Sa-Tu from 8pm) familiar. As happens every week in funky Lapa (a run-down but popular nightlife area near M: Cinelândia; see p. 154), the area at the foot of the Arcos da Lapa is transformed into a hopping outdoor bar, equipped during Carnaval with a stage that hosts live performances by cutting-edge groups playing everything from funk to *forró* to reggae. The concert is free, and you'll get a chance to hang out with Rio's young, hip, and friendly college crowd. A similar free outdoor concert area (host to better-known and *samba*-geared national acts) is just a few *bum-bum* shakes away in Pça. Floriano (at M: Cinelândia), in what is known as the **Bailes da Cinelândia** (Cinelândia Balls; Carnaval F-Tu from 8pm).

For those who want open-air revelry but don't want to be too far from the action at the Sambódromo, there's the **Terreirão do Samba,** a.k.a. **Sambaland** (Carnaval F-Tu and the following F-Sa, all night from 8pm; R$3.) Despite its name, the huge stage in this enclosed courtyard area behind Sector 1 of the Sambódromo hosts big-name national acts (like Cidade Negra) that play everything but *samba.* The courtyard is ringed by bars named after the *samba* schools parading that year. Since many Cariocas don't come to the Sambódromo for the whole parade, this is where you'll often find locals heading after the school they're rooting for has paraded. Just remember that you can't re-enter the Sambódromo once you pass out through the turnstiles (which you'll have to do to get to Sambaland.)

SALVADOR

Although the Carnaval Carioca is undoubtedly the most famous Carnaval celebration in Brazil (if not the world), other cities around the country also have fantastic and increasingly popular events scheduled for the holiday. More and more travelers are following Cariocas out of Rio during Carnaval, heading out in search of what they consider more "traditional" Carnaval festivities. **São Paulo** holds an equally gaudy and hotly contested *samba* parade at its own Sambódromo; it sees fewer tourists and corporate sponsors, yet captures much of the same frenzied joy. **Recife and Olinda** have a calmer, informal street parade and party that locals love. Beachfront beauty **Porto Alegre** features five days of fun in the sun. Rio's mid-20s college crowd typically heads north to historic **Ouro Preto** for Carnaval, partying all night with friends in the streets before crashing wherever they can.

But most travelers uninterested in Rio's "corporate" Carnaval head to **Salvador, Bahia,** considered Brazil's cultural capital and definitely one of the country's highlights. Here, the crazed street parade tradition runs strong through all five days of Carnaval. However, the newer Salvador Carnaval is gaining such popularity among travelers that it now has almost as many corporate sponsors as Rio's—but it is arguably just as much fun, if not more so. There are no spectators here or tickets to buy, just a throng of participants shaking and moving in sync, causing the city to quake to their collective beat. While Rio is a spectacle of global splendor, Salvador's Carnaval is a celebration for the masses.

CARNAVAL CAUTION. Salvador's Carnaval is one of the most exciting celebrations in the country, but it's also the most dangerous. Pickpockets are rampant throughout Brazil during Carnaval, and Salvador is particularly hard-hit. If you must carry a camera, buy a disposable. Don't get angry when you feel the first hand of a pickpocket slide down your pant leg, as it will be the first of many. The *pipoca* crowds that surround the *trios elétricos* are especially targeted (making a strong case for buying *bloco* tickets). Carry any money you bring in the bottom of your shoe or in a zipped pocket. Thieves often form a *samba* line and then rob anyone foolish enough to join on. Salvador also sees more violent crime during Carnaval than any other Brazilian city. Foreign women will be openly harassed on the streets, both verbally and physically. Gangs sometimes start fights with foreign men; once the fight has begun, the entire gang jumps in. Never travel alone–stick to small groups–and avoid confrontation at all cost.

SCHEDULE

Salvador's Carnaval is centered around two distinct events: the slow-moving but frenetic street parades of the **trios elétricos** and the small-scale street parties featuring various bands and **barracas.** Thursday marks the official beginning of Carnaval in the city, and the festivities commence when the mayor hands over the key to the city to the Rei Momo (the Carnaval king), just as in Rio.

The *trios elétricos* and *barracas* hit the streets immediately after the ceremony but things don't really heat up until Saturday, when the entire city and its three million newly acquired visitors hit the streets. Things die down slightly on Monday, and then Tuesday night is the last hurrah, the city's final salute to hedonism and debauchery. Those looking to make the most of their visit are advised to stay in the cobblestoned and historic Pelourinho area. Although it's home to most of the city's international tourists during Carnaval, it's the most central and safe location to enjoy the festivities. Tourists who opt to stay around Barra and Pça. Castro Alves where the *trios elétricos* roll by, are advised to choose lodgings away from the parade route; the party usually continues until at least 7am in the morning.

EVENTS

TRIOS ELÉTRICOS

The backbone of Salvador's Carnaval are the *trios elétricos,* huge trucks loaded with thousands of watts of sound equipment and topped with a band pounding out tunes with electric guitars. These mobile stages pump out frantic beats at deafening volume as they parade through the streets surrounded by swarms of people caught up in the festivities. They started as a joke in the 1950s, when two of the country's most famous musicians at the time, Dodó and Osmar, hopped on top of a truck and started playing electric guitars to the masses below; *trio* refers to the two musicians on top and the driver of the truck. Today you'll find close to fifty people on each truck, not including the up to 10-person band that provides the entertainment. The trucks usually travel in groups of three, and there are anywhere between 30 and 50 separate groups in each of the city's two circuits. One of the circuits can be found around **Praia do Porto da Barra;** festivities start at Av. 7 de Setembro and curve around the southern part of the beach toward Av. Pres. Vargas, where the action really gets started. The second circuit is closer to the Centro and generally begins at **Campo Grande,** running to **Praça Castro Alves.**

Gone are the days when the *trio elétrico* was a joke: today some of the best and most internationally reknowned musicians in Brazil descend on Salvador for Carnaval, so you can expect to hear quality tunes from the likes of Gilberto Gil, Carlinhos Brown, and Caetano Veloso, among others; some of the biggest stars even give special concerts on the beach during the festivities.

Whatever music may be blasting out of the trucks' speakers, you'll have to dance: the crowds surrounding the trucks are tightly packed, and there's little you can do other than dance along with them.

BARRACAS

Barracas are the small self-contained assemblies of people found throughout the city, each with their own special theme and sound systems or band. Traditionally, *barracas* are formed by local dance groups accompanied by small bands that march through the streets attracting swarms of followers, but today you'll find many groups make their own music absent of a band, dancing to the beat of their feet instead. Most of the people in the *barracas* will be festooned in elaborate costumes, while others simply have members wearing the same colored t-shirts.

To join the *barracas,* pick a group as they march by and attach yourself to the band until you spot another group wandering by that catches your interest. Among the more popular *barracas* in Salvador are the **Filhos da Gandhy** (Sons of Gandhi) and the all-female **Didá.** Though *barracas* are everywhere, the vast majority of them converge around **Pelourinho.**

TICKETS

The festivities in Salvador are free to all, but wealthy tourists still find a way to flash their cash, namely in the **camarotes** (private booths; R$100-250) that line the parade routes of the *trios elétricos*. The *trios elétricos* also sell **bloco** tickets (R$25-100) to those who want to party on top of the truck or inside the roped-off area immediately around the truck. These *bloco* tickets are actually colorful t-shirts (and sometimes shorts) that signals to the *cordão* (security officer holding the rope) that you are a member of that specific *bloco*. The *pipocas* (popcorn)—the people outside the roped-off area—usually tease those inside the ropes for spending money to be just a few feet closer to the speakers, but the additional safety these *bloco* tickets provide is well worth the money. Those who choose to brave the shoulder-to-shoulder *pipoca* crowds should expect to have their pockets and sides constantly groped over the course of the parade by eager men and/or enterprising pickpockets; keep the few *reais* you'll need inside your sock. See **Carnaval Info**, p. 47, for further safety tips. Tickets for the *blocos* and *camarotes* are available at the Bahiatursa offices in Pelourinho (p. 349), which also sells an extremely helpful guide to the Carnaval festivities for the week *(A Guide to Carnaval In Salvador)*.

ESSENTIALS

FACTS FOR THE TRAVELER

ENTRANCE REQUIREMENTS

Passport (p. 63). Required of all foreigners; must be valid for at least 6 months.
Visa (p. 63). Required for citizens of Australia, Canada, New Zealand, and the United States.
Inoculations (p. 70). Yellow fever required for some depending on country of origin; antimalarials and several other vaccinations recommended.
Work Permit (p. 105). Required for all foreigners planning to work in Brazil.
International Driving Permit (p. 96). Required for all those planning to drive.

EMBASSIES & CONSULATES

BRAZILIAN CONSULAR SERVICES ABROAD

Australia: Embassy: 19 Forster Crescent, Yarralumla, **Canberra** ACT 2600 (☎02 6273 2372, 02 6273 2373, 02 6273 2374, visa section 02 6273 4837; fax 02 6273 2375, visa fax 02 6273 4837; www.brazil.org.au). **Consulate:** Level 17, 31 Market St., **Sydney** NSW 2000 (☎02 9267 4414; fax 02 9267 4419).

Canada: Embassy: 450 Wilbrod St., **Ottawa,** ON K1N 6M8 (☎613-237-1090, 613-755-5160; fax 613-237-6144; www.brasembottawa.org). **Consulates:** Centre Manuvie, 2000 Mansfield St., Ste. 1700, **Montreal,** PQ H3A 3A5 (☎514-499-0968, 514-499-0969, 514-499-0970; fax 514-499-3963). 77 Bloor St. W, Ste. 1109, **Toronto,** ON M5S 1M2 (☎416-922-2503; fax 416-922-1832).

New Zealand: Embassy: 10 Brandon St., Level 9, P.O. Box 5432, **Wellington** (☎4 473 3516; fax 4 473 3517; www.brazil.org.nz).

South Africa: Embassy: 1267 Pretorius St., Hatfield 0083, **Pretoria** (☎12 426 9400; fax 12 426 9494; www.brazil.co.za).

United Kingdom: Embassy: 32 Green St., **London** W1K 7AT (☎020 7399 9000; fax 020 7399 9100; www.brazil.org.uk). **Consulate:** 6 St. Alban's Street, **London** SW1Y 4SQ (☎020 7930 9055; fax 020 7839 8958).

United States: Embassy: 3006 Massachusetts Ave. NW, **Washington, D.C.** 20008 (☎202-745-2837; fax 202-745-2827; www.brasilemb.org). **Consulates:** 229 Peachtree St. NE, Ste. 2306, **Atlanta,** GA 30303 (☎404-521-0061; fax 404-521-3449). The Stattler Building, 20 Park Plaza, Ste. 810, **Boston,** MA 02116 (☎617-542-4000; fax 617-542-4318). 401 N. Michigan Ave., Ste. 3050, **Chicago,** IL 60611 (☎312-464-0244; fax 312-464-0299). 1700 W. Loop S, Ste. 1450, **Houston,** TX 77027 (☎713-961-3063, 713-961-3064, 713-961-3065; fax 713-961-3070). 8484 Wilshire Blvd., Ste. 711-730, Beverly Hills, **Los Angeles,** CA 90211 (☎323-651-2664; fax 323-651-1274). 2601 S. Bayshore Dr., Ste. 800, **Miami,** FL 33133 (☎305-285-6200; fax 305-285-6229). 1185 Ave. of the Americas, 21st fl., **New York,** NY 10036 (☎917-777-7777; fax 917-827-0225). 300 Montgomery St., Ste. 900, **San Francisco,** CA 94104 (☎415-981-8170; fax 415-981-3628).

FOREIGN CONSULAR SERVICES IN BRAZIL

All foreign embassies *(embaixadas)* are in the capital, Brasília (see **Embassies,** p. 276). Rio de Janeiro, São Paulo, and several other major cities have foreign consular representation *(consulados)*, listed in the Practical Information section of those cities. In an emergency, a consulate should be able to provide legal advice, notify family members of accidents, supply a list of local lawyers and doctors, and in exceptional circumstances may be able to provide citizens with cash advances.

Australia: SHIS 09, Conj. 16 (☎248 5569, 225 2710).

Canada: SES 803, Lote 16 (☎321 2171).

Ireland: Academia de Tênis, Apt. 654, SCS, Trecho 4, Conj. 5 (☎316 6654).

South Africa: Av. das Nações, Lote 6 (☎312 9500).

UK: SES Q 801, Conj. K (☎225 2710; www.reinounido.org.br).

US: SES Q 801, Lote 3 (☎321 7272, 312 7000; www.embaixada-americana.org.br).

TOURIST OFFICES

Embratur, SCN Q2, bl. G, in Brasília, is the country's official tourist board. (☎61 429 7777; www.embratur.gov.br.) A much more helpful resource is the webpage of the Brazilian Embassy to the UK in London (www.brazil.org.uk). **Riotur,** Rua Assembléia 10, 9th fl., in Rio's Pça. XV de Novembro, is the tourist board of the continent's most visited destination, Rio de Janeiro. (☎21 2217 7575; www.rio.rj.gov.br/riotur). Riotur also runs the English-speaking **"Alô Rio"** tourist hotline (☎21 2542 8080; M-F 9am-5pm).

ESSENTIALS

DOCUMENTS & FORMALITIES

PASSPORTS

All foreign visitors to Brazil need passports (valid for at least six months) to enter the country and to re-enter their home country. Returning home with an expired passport is illegal and could result in a fine.

If your passport is lost or stolen in Brazil, immediately notify the police (☎190) and the nearest consulate of your home government (see p. 63 for a list). Any visas stamped in your passport will be lost, and must be applied for again. If you can't wait for your replacement passport request to be processed, you can ask for immediate temporary traveling papers, which allow you to re-enter your home country. Before you leave home for Brazil, photocopy your passport, visa, and any other important travel documents; carry one set of copies with you (apart from the originals), and leave another set at home.

Upon arrival in Brazil, you will receive a stamp in your passport and an **entry card** *(carteira de estrangeiros)*. Fill this card out and guard it with your life, as you will need to present it to officials to leave Brazil; the fee for lost cards is R$165.

VISAS

A visa *(visto)* is a stamp, sticker, or insert in your passport that specifies the purpose of your travel and the duration of your stay. Those who require visas for entry to Brazil must obtain them before departing for Brazil; they are available from the nearest Brazilian consular office, either in person or by post.

As of August 2003, citizens of the Republic of Ireland (and all holders of EU passports), South Africa, and the UK do not need a visa to enter Brazil as tourists. Citizens of the following countries must obtain visas (fees are in parentheses): Australia (AUS$87.50); Canada (CDN$72); New Zealand (NZ$58); the US ("free," but with a US$100 processing fee). The fees above do not include additional office or postage fees that may be levied by consulates or embassies. Beware that several visa applications (including the US) require you to have a hotel reservation or other contact in Brazil before the application can be processed. Most visas are good for five years, and valid for arrival within 90 days of issuance.

All tourists are permitted a stay of 90 days; this can be extended *(prorrogação de visto)* an additional 90 days by application to the **Polícia Federal (PF)** in major cities (**Practical Information** sections in this guide list PF offices; see www.dpf.gov.br for a full list). Those who extend their visa for 180 days and then leave Brazil are not allowed back to the country until those 180 days have passed.

Visas are required for all non-Brazilian citizens who plan to stay for more than 180 days, and for those who are planning to legally work or study in the country regardless of duration of stay. For info on work permits and student visas, see **Alternatives to Tourism** (p. 103). Note that all the info above is accurate as of August 2003; double-check with a consular office before you go, as requirements change.

IDENTIFICATION

By law you are required to carry some form of ID with you in Brazil at all times. Never carry your passport around while exploring; keep a photocopy on your person, and leave the original in a secure place. Never store all your forms of ID together, in case of theft or loss.

The **International Student Identity Card** (**ISIC;** for students) is the most widely accepted form of student ID in the world, and the only non-Brazilian student ID that will qualify you for student discounts at restaurants, accommodations, attractions, movies, and events in Brazil. ISIC membership also comes with insurance benefits (see **Travel Insurance,** p. 75) and access to a 24hr. emergency helpline (toll-free in Brazil ☎0008 145 503 844; www.isic.org). To obtain an ISIC, you must be a degree-seeking student of a secondary or post-secondary school, and must be at least 12 years old.

The **International Teacher Identity Card** (**ITIC;** for teachers), and the **International Youth Travel Card** (**IYTC;** for travelers under the age of 26 who are not students) offer the same insurance coverage and discounts as the ISIC. In most accommodations in Brazil, all three of these qualify you for HI hosteling discounts.

Each card usually costs about US$22 (cost differs from one issuer to another) and is valid for 12 months from the date of issue. Most youth-oriented travel agencies issue cards; for the location of the issuer nearest you, check www.isic.org.

CUSTOMS

Upon entering Brazil, you must declare certain items from abroad and pay a duty on the value of those articles if they exceed the allowance established by Brazilian customs. Clothes, books, toiletries, and other personal items are exempt from customs duties so long as the amount carried seems proportionate to length of stay. Moreover, travelers are allowed up to one still camera, movie camera, typewriter, computer, set of binoculars, and portable radio/audio device. Other goods intended for personal consumption are subject to duties only if their value exceeds US$500 (only US$150, however, if entering by land, lake, or river), and must be declared if their value goes over US$300. Any of the following must be declared on entry: animals, plants, seeds, foodstuffs and medications subject to health inspection, weapons and ammunition, and more than US$10,000 in cash or equivalents. Anything not duty-exempt will be taxed at 50% of its estimated value. Once in the airport, you can purchase up to US$500 in goods from **duty-free** shops. Note that duty-free merchandise is not exempt from customs duty; "duty-free" merely means that you need not pay a tax in the country of purchase. Upon returning home, you must likewise declare all articles acquired abroad and pay a duty on the value of articles in excess of your home country's allowance. In order to expedite your return, make a list of any valuables brought from home and register them with customs before traveling abroad, and be sure to keep receipts for all goods acquired abroad.

MONEY

The unit of currency in Brazil is the **real** (plural *reais*), which is divided into 100 *centavos*. Bills are color-coded and come in denominations of R$1, R$5, R$10, R$20, R$50, and R$100. (There is also a handy **waterproof plastic R$10** for taking to the beach.) Coins come in denominations of R$1 and 50, 25, 10, 5, and 1 centavos; confusingly, there are two different types of each coin.

There is a chronic lack of change and small bills *(troco)* in Brazil, especially in the Northeast, where you will often be given change in candy and sweets instead of bills. (Sometimes this supposed shortage is just laziness on the seller's part, so it can pay to be persistent.) Always ask for small bills when exchanging and get used to breaking large bills at chain restaurants, groceries, and pharmacies.

Most establishments outside the major cities are cash only, but credit cards are getting more and more common all over the country.

CURRENCY & EXCHANGE

REAL (R$)		
	AUS$1 = R$1.98	R$1 = AUS$0.50
	CDN$1 = R$2.20	R$1 = CDN$0.45
	NZ$1 = R$1.76	R$1 = NZ$0.57
	ZAR1 = R$0.37	R$1 = ZAR2.67
	US$1 = R$3.03	R$1 = US$0.33
	UK£1 = R$4.96	R$1 = UK£0.20
	EUR€1 = R$3.59	R$1 = EUR€0.28

The table above lists August 2003 exchange rates for the *real*. Daily rates are listed in newspapers and announced on the nightly news.

ATMs offer the best exchange rates, whether drawing from an international bank account or getting a cash advance on a credit card. Banks and *câmbios* (exchange houses) are the places to exchange hard currency—never convert cash on the street or with the "staff" that lurk around airports. Banks have better exchange rates than *câmbios*, but charge a high commission, especially for traveler's checks (US$20). In general, cash always gets better rates than traveler's checks. Since US$ is generally the only foreign currency accepted at exchange houses, all travelers (even those with traveler's checks) should consider carrying about US$50 for emergencies. When changing money, only go to establishments that have at most a 5% margin between their buy and sell prices. Since you lose money with every transaction, always convert large sums.

TRAVELER'S CHECKS

Because traveler's checks can be replaced or refunded if stolen or lost, they are one of the safest means of carrying money (though savvy travelers carry a combination of checks, US dollars, and credit cards). American Express and Visa are the issuers most recognized by *câmbios* and banks; AmEx is accepted at every Brazilian bank, and has offices throughout Brazil (see the **Practical Information** listings of major cities). Checks should always be purchased in US dollars.

American Express (24hr. toll-free hotline in Brazil ☎0008 145 503 382; www.aexp.com). Checks available with commission at select banks, all AmEx offices, and (for US residents only) online. Cardholders can purchase checks by phone. International AmEx service centers: In **Australia** ☎800 68 80 22; in **Canada** and **US** ☎800-221-7282; in **New Zealand** 0508 555 358; in the **UK** ☎0800 587 6023; elsewhere collect ☎+1 801 964 6665.

Visa: Checks available (generally with commission) at banks worldwide. For the location of the nearest office, call Visa's service centers: In the **US** ☎800-227-6811; in the **UK** ☎0800 51 58 84; **elsewhere** UK collect ☎+44 020 7937 8091.

Travelex/Thomas Cook: In the **US** and **Canada** call ☎800-287-7362; in the **UK** call ☎0800 62 21 01; **elsewhere** call UK collect ☎+44 173 331 8950.

CREDIT CARDS & ATM CARDS

When accepted, credit cards and ATM (debit) cards offer exchange rates that are far superior to banks and *câmbios*. ATM cards get the same exchange rate as credit cards, but often have a limit on the amount of money you can withdraw per day (around US$500). Though Brazilian ATMs don't charge foreign cards, international banks typically levy a surcharge of US$1-5 per international withdrawal.

All major credit cards are accepted in the big cities, but although credit cards are becoming more and more common, most places outside the major cities are still cash only. **Visa** is the network most widely recognized by establishments and ATMs; **Mastercard** is getting more common, while **American Express** and **Discover** remain rare. Cards are called *cartões de crédito* (singular *cartão*); do not confuse this with listings for *Credicard*, a private credit company.

ATMs are widespread in major cities, and there is usually at least one machine in even the smallest town. Unfortunately, **many ATMs in Brazil do not recognize foreign cards,** even those on the same network (Visa, Cirrus, PLUS, etc.). Get used to trying a few different machines every time you go to withdraw. **Banco do Brasil** is good for Visa, while **Bradesco** is best for Mastercard; international chain **HSBC** is one of the only banks for Cirrus. **Banco 24 Horas** (ask for *"Banco Vinte-quatro Horas"*) and **Citibank** are known for having foreign card-friendly machines.

Banks are typically open M-F 8am-4pm and Sa 8am-noon. Because most Brazilians also pay their utility bills at banks, the lines are always interminable, especially in the early morning and at lunchtime (noon-2pm).

GETTING MONEY FROM HOME

If you run out of money while traveling, the easiest and cheapest solution is to have someone make a deposit to your credit card or cash (ATM) card. Failing that, consider one of the following options.

WIRING MONEY. The only option for wiring money from your home bank to a bank in Brazil is through **Western Union** (Brazil toll-free ☎0800 785 678; www.westernunion.com), which runs its money wiring service out of **Banco do Brasil,** Brazil's national bank. Branches of the bank in major cities usually offer payout in either US dollars or in *reais* (call the number above for US currency locations), although dollars are only available to tourists, students, and holders of work visas/permits who have been in Brazil for less than one year. Those expecting a payout of more than R$4000 must inform the bank at least 48 hours in advance so the bank can have enough currency on hand. Money transfer is also available at **American Express** offices, listed in the **Practical Information** sections of major cities.

US STATE DEPARTMENT (US CITIZENS ONLY). In dire emergencies, the US State Department will forward money within hours to the nearest consulate or embassy (p. 62), which will then disburse it (according to pre-determined instructions), for a US$15 fee. For information on this service, contact the US State Department, Overseas Citizens Service (☎ +00 (21 or 23) 1-202-647-5225; after 5pm, Sundays, holidays ☎ +00 (21 or 23) 1-202-647-4000).

COSTS

Although it's among the more expensive destinations in South America, Brazil is still quite affordable and relatively inexpensive. Return/round-trip airfare will be your biggest expense, followed by accommodations (which average R$25-40 per night). Transportation is typically affordable and comfortable. Going out to eat and drink in Brazil is very cheap—almost as cheap as buying your groceries from supermarkets.

BUDGETING. A bare-bones budget for Brazil (staying in hostels or *pousadas*, eating only at cheap *lanchonetes* or supermarkets, and rarely going out at night) would cost about US$25-30 per day; a slightly more comfortable day (sleeping in nicer *pousadas* and budget hotels, eating out occasionally, and going out at night) would run about US$40. In luxury resort destinations like Rio de Janeiro, the sky's the limit, and opportunities for pampering yourself are everywhere. Don't forget to factor in emergency reserve funds (say US$200, always in US currency) when budgeting.

MONEY-SAVING TIPS. Some simpler ways to save money include searching out opportunities for free entertainment, splitting accommodations with trustworthy travelers (doubles are always cheaper per person than singles), and sharing meals (entrees at restaurants usually feed two). With that said, don't go overboard with your budget obsession. Though staying within your budget is important, don't do so at the expense of your health or a great travel experience.

TIPPING & BARGAINING

Wages are so low and unemployment so high that every spare coin or *real* note you tip is greatly appreciated. It's common to round up to the nearest *real* on **taxi** fares. Sit-down **restaurants** will automatically add 10% gratuity to your bill. In nicer hotels (three stars and higher), a tip of R$2-3 per day is the standard for porters, room service waiters, housekeepers, etc. Baggage carriers at airports are commonly given about R$1 per decent-sized bag.

Bargaining is the norm at outdoor markets and small shops. Always go into these situations with a firm idea of how much you're willing to pay, and don't be afraid to start off low. In fear of being taken for a (figurative) ride, many travelers suggest bargaining with **taxi** drivers for set fares (before getting in the taxi, of course). **Budget hotels** list their set prices at the front desk, but bargaining for a lower rate is common and always expected, especially in the low season: simply asking if there's a discount *("Tem desconto?")* or if there's a better price *("Pode fazer um melhor preço?")* will almost instantly lower the rate by up to 15%. Discounts vary depending on who you speak to and when, but they're offered for everything, including multi-day stays, cash payment, booking in advance, or just showing up.

SAFETY & SECURITY

PERSONAL SAFETY

Brazil—Rio in particular—has unfortunately earned an international reputation as a violent, unsafe destination for tourists. In reality, violent crime against travelers is very rare. The violence that makes international headlines and drives films like *Cidade de Deus* (p. 34) is almost exclusively between the police and druglords, and takes place mostly in the *favelas*, poorer suburbs, and towns where tourists

TRAVEL ADVISORIES. The following government offices provide travel information and advisories by telephone, by fax, or via the web:

Australian Department of Foreign Affairs and Trade: ☎13 0055 5135; fax-back service 02 6261 1299; www.dfat.gov.au.

Canadian Department of Foreign Affairs and International Trade (DFAIT): In Canada and the US call ☎800-267-8376, elsewhere call ☎+1 613-944-4000; www.dfait-maeci.gc.ca. Call for their free booklet, *Bon Voyage...But.*

New Zealand Ministry of Foreign Affairs: ☎4 439 8000; fax 4 434 8506; www.mft.govt.nz/travel/index.html.

United Kingdom Foreign and Commonwealth Office: ☎020 7008 0232; fax 020 7008 0155; www.fco.gov.uk.

US Department of State: ☎202-647-5225, fax-back service 202-647-3000; http://travel.state.gov. For *A Safe Trip Abroad,* call ☎202-512-1800.

ESSENTIALS

should/would never venture. This is not to say that a *gringo* (any non-Brazilian, a term not considered derogatory in Brazil) can roam risk-free through the streets. As in other major metropolitan areas throughout the world, tourists are frequently targeted in Brazil for petty theft or robbery. Although there is always a risk of these sorts of crimes, there is a spike in such activity during high tourist times, particularly during Carnaval.

PETTY THEFT & MUGGING. The best precaution against such petty theft is to not have anything worth stealing. When exploring, only carry the money you need for that trip (preferably in a belted money pouch worn underneath your clothes); stash an emergency R$20-50 away in a brassiere or sock. Don't carry any valuables—money, passports, tickets, credit cards, etc. Instead, leave them in a sealed envelope or locked bag in a safe location at your accommodations, such as a safe *(cofre)* or personal locker (secured with a lock you provide). Never wear expensive (or fake expensive-looking) jewelry or watches. Never leave your bags unattended, especially in outdoor restaurants and bars.

If you are mugged, do not attempt to fight back or negotiate. It has supposedly become common for thieves to leave victims a little cash to take the bus or a taxi, but don't count on this! Immediately report the theft to the police (☎190) and ask for a police report *(boletin de ocorrência)*; there's not much they can do, but their report is helpful for insurance claims.

EXPLORING. Avoid unwanted attention by blending in as much as possible in dress, speech, and mannerisms. Realize that regardless of clothes or carriage, fair-haired and -skinned tourists are just more likely to be singled out by locals, whether these locals have malicious intentions or not. Always familiarize yourself with your surroundings before setting out, and only consult maps and guidebooks in shops and restaurants. If you are traveling alone, be sure someone at home knows your itinerary. (See p. 98 for more tips on traveling solo around Brazil.)

At night, avoid walking alone (especially on beaches), and stick to busy, well-lit streets as much as possible. Most authorities recommend that tourists avoid riding the local bus system after 11pm; taxis are fairly inexpensive and considered by some to be more secure. Prostitution is quite prevalent in most medium-sized Brazilian cities, particularly around bus stations and near the infamous love "motels" (see **Hourly Motels,** p. 79). Red-light districts (and prostitute-frequented establishments) are sometimes high-crime areas, especially after dark. Special warnings in this guide, as well as word on the street, will clue you in to which areas of particular cities are more dangerous. If you feel uncomfortable in any situation, leave as quickly and directly as you can.

BEACHES. Tourist-frequented beaches (particularly urban beaches, like in Rio) are often targeted by petty thieves; counterintuitively, more remote beaches are actually safer. Avoid walking on beaches at night (never do it alone), though beachside *barracas* (snack stands) are fairly safe. As with exploring on land, avoid petty theft by not carrying around anything worth stealing. Do as Brazilians do and don't bring more than you need to the beach: all that's required is your (skimpy) swimsuit, sunscreen/sunglasses/sunhat, a beach towel, and a few *reais* for snacks and beer (*Let's Go* recommends the special **waterproof plastic R$10**). If you go into the water, leave belongings with a friend, a friendly local, or with the beach stands that rent umbrellas and chairs. If you want to take photos on the beach, go with a friend, take the shots, and then return the camera to your hostel.

SELF-DEFENSE. There is no sure-fire way to avoid all the threatening situations you might encounter while traveling, but a good self-defense course will give you concrete ways to react to unwanted advances. **Impact, Prepare, and Model Mugging** can refer you to local self-defense courses in the US (☎800-345-5425). Visit the website at www.impactsafety.org for a list of nearby chapters. Workshops (2-3hr.) start at US$50; full courses (20hr.) run US$350-500.

DRIVING. Cars are not recommended in Brazil, as most destinations of tourist interest are easily accessible by bus, boat, or plane. Driving is hell in the sprawling major cities where cars are the norm (Brasília and São Paulo), and carjackings are common in the latter. (This explains the Brazilian law that frees cars from having to stop at red lights after 10pm.) In cities, park your vehicle in a garage or well traveled area, and use a steering wheel-locking device. Be sure to learn local driving signals and always wear a seatbelt. Invest in an up-to-date road atlas once in Brazil, preferably one from the **Guias Quatro Rodas** line of guides (sold at every newsstand and bookstore in Brazil, and updated annually, R$29). If your car breaks down, wait for the police to assist you. For long drives in desolate areas like the South and Center-West, invest in a cellular phone and a roadside assistance program (see p. 96). **Sleeping in your car** is one of the most dangerous (and illegal) ways to get your rest. For info on the perils of **hitchhiking,** see p. 91.

FINANCIAL SECURITY

As noted above, never carry your valuables with you around town; keep them in a locked bag or sealed and signed envelope to store away in hotel or hostel safes. On any given excursion, only bring the cash you'll need for that day or that trip, preferably stashed in a discreet money belt worn underneath your clothes. Buy a few combination padlocks, to secure your luggage together and to use on hostel or bus station lockers. Keep a secondary stash of money for emergencies (about US$50) sewn into or stored in the depths of your pack, along with your traveler's check numbers and photocopies of important documents.

CON ARTISTS & PICKPOCKETS. Con artists are an unfortunately prominent aspect of large tourist-frequented cities like Rio and Salvador. Many work in groups to distract and steal, and children are among the most effective. Beware of certain classics: sob stories that require money, requests to purchases "just a few *reais*" worth of food, or sauce spilled (or saliva spit, or crotches grabbed) to distract you while they snatch your bag or your wallet. **Pickpockets** are an occasional problem on local buses and big crowds: avoid overcrowded buses at all times, and steer clear of buses after 11pm. Pickpocketing is most serious during Carnaval (especially in Salvador), when revelers crowd the streets shoulder to shoulder; fair-skinned travelers are more obvious targets than others. Money belts and zippered pockets are no use in this situation: keep your money in your socks, and turn your pockets inside-out to show that your pockets are cash-free.

ACCOMMODATIONS & TRANSPORTATION. Never leave your belongings unattended when checking in or out of hotels and hostels; crime occurs in even the safest-looking establishments. You should have no qualms about storing your valuables in safes *(cofres)* of three-star and higher hotels; for lower-end hotels, *pousadas*, and hostels, ask about safes before committing. Always store safe-bound belongings in either a signed and sealed envelope or a locked bag. Always bring along your own **locks** (both padlocks and keylocks) for use in hostel lockers.

As noted above, pickpocketing can occur on crowded local buses (though it's rare); for safety reasons, most recommend avoiding local buses after 11pm. Be careful on overnight **buses;** horror stories abound about determined thieves who wait for travelers to fall asleep. Keep your daypack where you can see it, lock your luggage to the overhead rack of the bus, and keep valuables on your person.

DRUGS & ALCOHOL

Narcotic use and possession are both illegal in Brazil, but as you can tell from the distinct smell of most beaches at sunset, most everyone in the country takes a laid-back approach to drugs—except the police. Penalties for those caught with drugs are very harsh and strictly enforced, especially with foreign travelers, who are assumed to have deep pockets. Even though marijuana *(maconha)* is used everywhere and easily obtained (especially in the major cities and hip, backpacker-friendly beach towns like Ilha Grande, Arraial d'Ajuda, Itacaré, and Jericoacoara) fines and jail time for possession and use are quite steep. Police in major cities and the aforementioned drug-friendly beach towns frequently search young people arriving on boats and buses, although they usually only inspect males in a group. A large amount of drugs is smuggled annually into Brazil from Bolivian and Paraguayan border towns, so most forms of transportation departing from Foz do Iguaçu or the Center-West region will be stopped by police, and the passengers searched. Brazil's drinking age is 18; clubs and bars rarely, if ever, ask for ID.

The Brazilian police force has a reputation for being notoriously corrupt, particularly toward foreign travelers. In reality, Brazilian police are woefully underpaid and often work additional jobs to support themselves or their families. Some travelers who have come in contact with police for infractions like drug possession or use report being offered freedom from jail time in exchange for monetary bribes.

HEALTH

Common sense is the simplest prescription for good health while you travel. The best source for travel-related health information is the **World Health Organization (WHO)** International Travel and Health Page (www.who.int/ith). Also helpful is the US **Center for Disease Control and Prevention** (☎877-394-8747; www.cdc.gov/travel).

BEFORE YOU GO

In your passport, write the names of any people you wish to be contacted in case of an emergency, and list any allergies or medical conditions. Matching foreign **prescriptions** to the Brazilian equivalent is easy as long as you have the medication's trade name and chemical name, so always carry up-to-date, legible prescriptions or a statement from your doctor stating these names as well as the manufacturer and dosage. Keep all medication with you in your carry-on luggage. For tips on packing a basic first-aid kit and other health essentials, see p. 76.

IMMUNIZATIONS & PRECAUTIONS. Travelers should meet with a health care provider at least one month before departure for Brazil to arrange vaccinations and prophylaxis (like malaria pills). A health-care provider will have up-to-date information pages on Brazil, and can tailor recommendations based on your medical history. All travelers should have the following childhood vaccines up to date: MMR (measles, mumps, and rubella); DTaP or TD (diptheria, tetanus, and pertussis); OPV (polio); HbCV (haemophilus influenza B); and HBV (hepatitis B). All visitors arriving in Brazil from areas infected with **yellow fever**—most of Sub-Saharan Africa (excluding South Africa), plus Bolivia, Colombia, Ecuador, and Peru—are required to present a yellow fever vaccination certificate. For all others, yellow fever vaccinations are recommended only if traveling outside urban areas (see **Yellow Fever,** p. 72). The yellow fever vaccine is administered weekly at free clinics in major cities in Brazil.

The other **recommended vaccines** for travel to Brazil are: hepatitis A; hepatitis B (if you'll have blood or sexual contact with the population); rabies (if you'll be visiting areas with wild animals); and typhoid. **Malaria** pills (antimalarials) are recommended for those traveling to malaria risk areas in Brazil, which are the state of Mato Grosso (the Northern Pantanal) and all states in the Região Norte (the **North** chapter of this guide). Malaria risk outside these areas is negligible or non-existent. See p. 72 for information on which antimalarials are best for you.

MEDICAL INSURANCE & SUPPORT SERVICES. Those worried about getting proper medical care in Brazil may wish to arrange special support services before they leave. The *MedPass* from **GlobalCare, Inc.** (☎800-860-1111; fax 678-341-1800; www.globalems.com), provides 24hr. international medical assistance, support, and medical evacuation resources. The **International Association for Medical Assistance to Travelers** (**IAMAT;** www.iamat.org) has free membership, lists English-speaking doctors worldwide, and offers detailed information on immunization requirements and sanitation. If your regular **insurance** policy does not cover travel abroad, you may wish to purchase additional coverage (see **Insurance,** p. 75).

Those with medical conditions may want to obtain a membership (first year US$35, annually thereafter US$20) with **Medic Alert** (☎888-633-4298; outside the US 209-668-3333; www.medicalert.org), which includes a stainless steel ID tag, among other helpful benefits.

ESSENTIALS

ONCE IN BRAZIL

GENERAL PRECAUTIONS

FOOD & DRINK. Water in urban areas is heavily treated, but not recommended for drinking; stick to sealed bottled water everywhere. Before heading out on arranged jungle trips, camping expeditions, and day-long boat tours, etc., ask about how much bottled water will be brought along or available for purchase. **Coffee** and **tea** are safe, as the water has been boiled. **Fruits** and **vegetables** bought from markets should be thoroughly washed with bottled water, and preferably peeled. Fresh fruit **juices** *(sucos)* sold at juice bars and *lanchonetes* are usually safe, though it's probably best to ask for them *sem gelo* (without ice).

MEDICAL ASSISTANCE. Medical care facilities in major cities in Brazil are usually entirely adequate for most travelers' needs, although outside the major cities quality varies greatly and is much less reliable. English-speaking doctors are less common outside tourist destinations, but there will usually be at least one English and/or Spanish speaker on staff who will be able to assist you. Free public clinics in major cities are usually sanitary and well enough equipped to deal with travelers, but private hospitals are much less of a risk. (This guide lists both public and private medical resources for major cities.) Needle reuse is less of a concern in Brazil than it once was, but those worried about it should bring spare syringes along. Whatever you do, always make sure needles are individually wrapped and opened for the first time in front of you.

In addition to selling miracle hangover cure **Engov** (a tourist favorite), all pharmacies in Brazil (known as *drogarias* or *farmácias*) sell over the counter many drugs that require prescriptions in other countries, a boon for travelers. Pharmacists will also recommend medications for certain ailments described for them, although you heed their advice at your own risk.

ENVIRONMENTAL HAZARDS

Heat exhaustion and dehydration: Heat exhaustion leads to nausea, excessive thirst, headaches, and dizziness. Avoid it by drinking plenty of fluids, eating salty foods (e.g. crackers), and abstaining from dehydrating beverages (e.g. alcohol and caffeinated beverages). Continuous heat stress can eventually lead to heatstroke, characterized by a rising temperature, severe headache, delirium, and cessation of sweating. Victims should be cooled off with wet towels and taken to a doctor. As Brazil is a tropical country most regions present some risk, but travelers should be most cautious while at the beach, attending any large festival, dancing, and when in the Southeast.

Sunburn: If you are planning on spending time near water, at high altitudes, or in the open sun, you are at risk of getting burned, even through clouds. If you get sunburned, drink more fluids than usual and apply an aloe-based lotion. Severe sunburns can lead to sun poisoning, a condition that affects the entire body, causing fever, chills, nausea, and vomiting. Sun poisoning should always be treated by a doctor.

High altitude: Allow your body a couple of days to adjust to less oxygen before exerting yourself. Note that alcohol is more potent and UV rays are stronger at high elevations.

INSECT-BORNE DISEASES

Many diseases are transmitted by insects—mainly mosquitoes, fleas, ticks, and lice. Be aware of insects in wet or forested areas, especially while hiking and camping; wear long pants and long sleeves, tuck your pants into your socks, use a mosquito net, and at night an insect net over your bed. Use insect repellents such as DEET and soak or spray your gear with permethrin (licensed in the US for use on clothing). In general, visitors to the Northeast carry the heaviest risk of infection, the Southeast carries the least risk; the North, Center-West, and South fall somewhere in between. However, conditions can vary wildly within these regions and caution is always recommended.

Malaria: Transmitted by *Anopheles* mosquitoes that bite at night. The incubation period varies from 6-8 days to as long as several months. Early symptoms include fever, chills, aches, and fatigue, followed by high fever and sweating, sometimes with vomiting and diarrhea. See a doctor for any flu-like sickness that occurs after travel in a risk area. To reduce the risk of contracting malaria, use mosquito repellent, particularly in the evenings and when visiting forested areas, and consult a doctor about taking oral prophylactics, like doxycycline. Note that mosquitoes in Brazil have developed resistance to the antimalarial mefloquine (sold under the name Lariam).

Dengue fever: An "urban viral infection" transmitted by *Aedes* mosquitoes, which bite during the day rather than at night. Early symptoms include chills, high fever, headaches, swollen lymph nodes, muscle aches, and, in some instances, a pink rash on the face. If you experience these symptoms, see a doctor, drink plenty of liquids, and take fever-reducing medication such as acetaminophen (Tylenol). *Never take aspirin to treat dengue fever.* An outbreak in Rio threatened 2002's Carnaval, and the disease remains a serious threat.

Yellow fever: A viral disease transmitted by mosquitoes; derives its name from one of its most common symptoms, the jaundice caused by liver damage. While most cases are mild, the severe ones begin with fever, headache, muscle pain, nausea, and abdominal pain before progressing to jaundice, vomiting of blood, and bloody stools. While there is no specific treatment, there is an effective vaccine that offers 10 years of protection.

The WHO recommends vaccinations for travelers to endemic areas, including rural areas in the states of Acre, Amapá, Amazonas, Goiás, Maranhão, Mato Grosso, Mato Grosso do Sul, Pará, Rondônia, Roraima, and Tocantins, as well as areas of Minas Gerais, Paraná and São Paulo.

Other insect-borne diseases: Filariasis is a roundworm infestation transmitted by mosquitoes. Infection causes enlargement of extremities and has no vaccine. The WHO has initiated an elimination program, but it considers filariasis to be endemic to Brazil. **Leischmaniasis** is a parasite transmitted by sand flies, and is also endemic to Brazil. The only initial symptom is a hard purple swelling around the fly's bite, and early signs of infection include fever, weakness, and swelling of the spleen. If left untreated, the disease can progress for years, at which point lethal heart failure is typical. There is a treatment, but no vaccine. In Brazil, **Chagas disease** (American trypanomiasis) is no longer as common as it once was, but is still a concern throughout the continent. It is transmitted by the cone nose and kissing bugs which infest mud, adobe, and thatch. Its symptoms are fever, heart disease, and later on an enlarged intestine; there is no vaccine and limited treatment.

FOOD- & WATER-BORNE DISEASES

Prevention is the best cure: be sure that your food is properly cooked and the water you drink is clean. Peel fruits and vegetables and avoid tap water (including ice cubes and anything washed in tap water, like salad; in the Amazon avoid anything cooked in river water). Watch out for food from markets or street vendors that may have been cooked in unhygienic conditions. Other culprits are raw shellfish, unpasteurized milk, and sauces containing raw eggs. Buy bottled water, or purify your own water by bringing it to a rolling boil or treating it with **iodine tablets;** note, however, that some parasites such as *giardia* have exteriors that resist iodine treatment, so boiling is more reliable. Always wash your hands before eating or bring a quick-drying purifying liquid hand cleaner.

Traveler's diarrhea: Results from drinking untreated water or eating uncooked foods. Symptoms include nausea, bloating, and urgency. Try quick-energy, non-sugary foods with protein and carbohydrates to keep your strength up. Over-the-counter anti-diarrheals (e.g. Imodium) may counteract the problems. The most dangerous side effect is dehydration; drink 8 oz. of water with ½ tsp. of sugar or honey and a pinch of salt, try uncaffeinated soft drinks, or eat salted crackers. If you develop a fever or your symptoms don't go away after 4-5 days, consult a doctor. Consult a doctor immediately for treatment of diarrhea in children.

Dysentery: Results from a serious intestinal infection caused by certain bacteria. The most common type is bacillary dysentery, also called shigellosis. Symptoms include bloody diarrhea (sometimes mixed with mucus), fever, and abdominal pain and tenderness. Bacillary dysentery generally only lasts a week, but it is highly contagious. Amoebic dysentery, which develops more slowly, is a more serious disease and may cause long-term damage if left untreated. A stool test can determine which kind you have; seek medical help immediately. Dysentery can be treated with the drugs norfloxacin or ciprofloxacin (commonly known as Cipro). If you are traveling in high-risk (especially rural) regions, consider obtaining a prescription before you leave home.

Hepatitis A: A viral infection of the liver acquired primarily through contaminated water. Symptoms include fatigue, fever, loss of appetite, nausea, dark urine, jaundice, vomiting, aches and pains, and light stools. The risk is highest in rural areas, but it is also present in urban areas. Ask your doctor about the vaccine (Havrix or Vaqta) or an injection of immune globulin (IG; formerly called gamma globulin).

Giardiasis: Giardiasis is transmitted through infectious parasites such as microbes, tapeworms, etc.; these are most commonly found in contaminated water and food, although there is a potential risk of infection by parasites if you swim in streams, lakes, or other bodies of water, or if you drink untreated water that has been taken from such sources. Symptoms of the disease include swollen glands or lymph nodes, fever, rashes or itchiness, and digestive problems.

Schistomiasis: A growing threat in Brazil, this is transmitted by parasites in freshwater streams and rivers, and is particularly common among agricultural workers and fishermen. Depending on the parasite, it may strike the intestines or urinary track, and symptoms include leg paralysis, bladder cancer, and internal scarring; no vaccine is available, but safe and effective treatments are available.

OTHER INFECTIOUS DISEASES

Rabies: Transmitted through the saliva of infected animals; fatal if untreated. By the time symptoms (thirst and muscle spasms) appear, the disease is in its terminal stage. If you are bitten, wash the wound thoroughly, seek immediate medical care, and try to have the animal located. A rabies vaccine, which consists of 3 shots given over a 21-day period, is available but is only semi-effective.

Hepatitis B: A viral infection of the liver transmitted via bodily fluids or needle-sharing. Symptoms, which may not surface until years after infection, include jaundice, loss of appetite, fever, and joint pain. A 3-shot vaccination sequence is recommended for health-care workers, sexually active travelers, and anyone planning to seek medical treatment abroad; it must begin 6 months before traveling.

Hepatitis C: Like hepatitis B, but the mode of transmission differs. IV drug users, those with occupational exposure to blood, hemodialysis patients, and recipients of blood transfusions are at the highest risk, but the disease can also be spread through sexual contact or sharing razors and toothbrushes that may have traces of blood on them.

HIV/AIDS & STDS

Brazil has the world's highest concentration of citizens infected with AIDS (Acquired Immune Deficiency Syndrome) outside of the continent of Africa. Although the spread of the disease has stabilized over the last few years within the country, much of the citizenry remains uninformed about methods of transmission of HIV, STDs, and AIDS, particularly in relation to knowledge about safe sex—so much so that the 2003 organizers of Rio de Janeiro's Carnaval made condom use the theme of the five-day holiday. Brazil does not deny entrance to those who are HIV-positive, and does not screen incoming long-term travelers and foreign workers. For more info, consult **UNAIDS,** the Joint United Nations Programme on HIV/AIDS (www.unaids.org).

Prostitution is prevalent in most Brazilian cities; for those who engage such services, the threat of **STDs** (sexually transmitted diseases) is always a concern. Hepatitis B and C can also be transmitted sexually (see p. 74). Though condoms may protect you from some STDs, oral or even tactile contact can lead to transmission. If you think you may have contracted an STD, see a doctor immediately.

WOMEN'S HEALTH

Women traveling in unsanitary conditions are vulnerable to urinary tract and bladder infections, common and very uncomfortable bacterial conditions that cause a burning sensation and painful (sometimes frequent) urination. Vaginal yeast infections flare up frequently in Brazil's hot and humid climates. Wearing loosely fitting trousers or a skirt and cotton underwear will help, as will over-the-counter remedies like Monostat or Gynelotrimin (readily available at all *drogarias* in Brazil).

Tampons, pads, and reliable contraceptives are also easy to find in most all Brazilian *drogarias* (pharmacies); travelers partial to certain brands should bring supplies with them.

INSURANCE

Travel insurance generally covers four basic areas: medical/health problems, property loss, trip cancellation/interruption, and emergency evacuation. Your regular medical insurance policy may well extend to travel-related accidents (this is true of most nationally subsidized policies and university policies, but not true of US Medicare). You might consider purchasing extra travel insurance if the cost of potential trip cancellation or emergency evacuation is greater than you can afford.

Buying travel insurance independently (apart from a larger insurance package) generally costs about $50 per week for full coverage, while trip cancellation/interruption may be purchased separately at a rate of about $5.50 per $100 of coverage. The international student and youth ID cards **ISIC, IYTC,** and **ITIC** (see **Identification,** p. 64) provide basic insurance benefits, including $100 per day of in-hospital sickness for up to 60 days, $3000 of accident-related medical reimbursement, and $25,000 for emergency medical transport. Cardholders also have access to a useful toll-free 24hr. helpline (toll-free in Brazil ☎0008 145 503 844) for medical, legal, and financial emergencies. **American Express** (US ☎800-528-4800) grants most cardholders automatic car rental insurance (collision and theft, but not liability) and ground travel accident coverage of US$100,000 on flight purchases made with the card. **Homeowners' insurance** (or your family's coverage) often covers theft during travel and loss of documents (passport, plane ticket, railpass, etc.) up to US$500.

PACKING

Pack lightly: lay out only what you absolutely need, then take half the clothes and twice the money. If you plan to do a lot of hiking, also see the section on **Camping & the Outdoors,** p. 79.

LUGGAGE. If you plan to cover most of your itinerary by foot, a sturdy **frame backpack** is unbeatable. (For the basics on buying a pack, see p. 82.) Toting a rolling **suitcase** is fine if you plan to live in one or two cities and explore from there, but not recommended for a whirlwind tour, as street conditions throughout Brazil make suitcase travel unwieldy. A **daypack** is also useful.

CLOTHING. The dress is casual and the weather is hot all over Brazil, so don't pack much clothing: a few t-shirts, a pair each of short and long pants, and one nice outfit for bars and clubs (where dress is still quite casual, and dress codes non-existent) is adequate. Many travelers buy light, weather-appropriate clothing cheaply in Brazil. *Gringos* should definitely wait to buy swimwear (*fio dentais* for women, *sungas* for men) until they're in Brazil, as tastes elsewhere are much too conservative for Brazilian beaches.

Rain gear is good for those frequent afternoon tropical showers; those heading to the South in the fall and winter (Apr.-Sept.) should also bring a sweater or warm top. Bring sturdy sandals or shoes for daytime exploring, although you may soon spend your days in the cheap but sturdy flag-emblazoned *chinelos* (flip-flops; sold everywhere) everyone wears. Hikers and outdoorsmen should check p. 81 for info on what to pack for camping.

CONVERTERS & ADAPTERS. Electrical outlets (power points) in Brazil are non-standardized, with both 110V (as in North America) and 220V (as in Europe and Australia) outlets. Most outlets have their voltage prominently displayed—ask if you are unsure. Outlets also take both round and flat pins. To deal with this, it's best to bring both an adapter (which changes the shape of the plug) and a converter (which changes the voltage); both are readily available in major cities. For more information, check out http://kropla.com/electric.htm.

TOILETRIES. Toiletries like toothbrushes, tampons, condoms, and more are readily available at *drogarias* (drugstores/chemists) in even the smallest towns in Brazil. **Contact lens** solution *(solução das lentes de contato)* is easy to find but very expensive. The same goes for **sunblock** *(proteção solar;* R$15-20): SPF 15-30 is recommended. Life-saving **bug spray** *(repelente de insetos)* is easy to find, but often only available in grocery stores.

CELLULAR PHONES. A cell phone can be a lifesaver on the road. If you own a cell phone and are traveling abroad, it most likely will not work when you arrive in Brazil. Companies like **Cellular Abroad** (www.cellularabroad.com) rent cell phones and prepaid SIM cards that work in a variety of destinations around the world, providing a more reliable option than attempting to pick up a phone in-country.

FIRST-AID KIT. Most simple medical aids can be purchased at *drogarias* (drugstores) anywhere in Brazil; however, a basic first-aid kit is absolutely required if you will be camping or in remote areas. A good kit includes: bandages, pain reliever, antibiotic cream, a thermometer, a Swiss Army knife (which can only travel in checked luggage), tweezers, moleskin, decongestant, motion-sickness remedy, diarrhea medication, antihistamine, sunscreen, insect repellent, burn ointment, and a syringe (you'll need an explanatory letter from your doctor).

FILM. Camera film is rather expensive in Brazil (about R$30-40 for a 24-exposure roll), so consider bringing along as much as you need. Disposable cameras are readily available but also expensive (R$30-40). Digital cameras and more expensive camera equipment are safe to bring with you as long as you are cautious; see p. 67 for more info on keeping your valuables safe. Always pack film in your carry-on luggage, since higher-intensity X-rays are used on checked luggage.

OTHER USEFUL ITEMS. For safety purposes, bring a **money belt** and a few **padlocks.** For quick repairs and patches of torn garments and bags, bring duct tape and a needle and thread. You can easily find detergent for hand washing your clothes. Other things you might need in Brazil (all of which can be bought there) include: an umbrella or rain gear, an alarm clock, a calculator, and a flashlight.

IMPORTANT DOCUMENTS. Don't forget your passport, traveler's checks, ATM and/or credit cards, adequate ID, and two photocopies of all of the aforementioned in case these documents are lost or stolen (see **Identification,** p. 64). Also check that you have (and have photocopied) the following, if applicable: an ISIC- and/or HI-affiliated membership card (p. 64); an International Driving Permit, if you'll be driving (p. 64); travel insurance forms; and any airpasses or onward tickets you might have bought (see **Getting Around Brazil,** p. 91).

ACCOMMODATIONS

HOSTELS

Hostels are not that common in Brazil *(pousadas* are the budget lodging of choice), but they remain the cheapest option for solo travelers and the best option for those wanting to meet fellow backpackers. Known as *albergues (da juventude)*, hostels in Brazil are all dormitory style accommodations that vary greatly in quality but little in price. (Dorm beds are rarely more than R$20-25 per night, R$35 in major cities.) Most hostels have dorm rooms (both co-ed and single-sex) with bunk beds and common hall baths, though many also offer private rooms and private bathrooms. Most have knowledgeable English-speaking staff and usually offer a variety of other services for travelers, including daily outings to local attractions, airport transfers, kitchens and/or breakfast, laundry facilities, and Internet access. Hostels will typically have either front-desk safes *(cofres)* or private lockers; bring your own locks for the latter, and use the former at your own risk. Most hostels list their room rates at the reception desk.

HOSTELLING INTERNATIONAL

Joining the youth hostel association in your home country (listed below) automatically grants you membership privileges in **Hostelling International (HI),** which offers members discounts on hostel stays at accredited hostels. (Most Brazilian HI hostels also offer the discount to ISIC and IYTC cardholders.) A new membership benefit is the Free Nites program, which earns hostelers points toward free rooms. See http://www.iyhf.org/home_gb.html for more on Hostelling International; check out www.hostelbooking.com for information about booking online.

There are about 50 HI hostels in Brazil, scattered throughout every region except the North (see the website for full listings, although this guide lists most HI hostels). These are all overseen by the **Federação Brasileira dos Albergues da Juventude (FBAJ),** headquartered at the Rio de Janeiro HI hostel (see p. 123), Rua Gen. Dionísio 63 (☎21 2286 0303; www.hostel.org.br). Though HI hostels are often more expensive than private hostels (especially if you don't have a HI card), they are almost always cleaner and more popular with international travelers. Most student travel agencies and Brazilian HI hostels sell HI cards (R$30), as do all the national organizations listed below. International hostel reservations can be made through ☎202-783-6161 in the US or online at www.hostelbooking.com. All prices listed below are valid for one-year memberships.

Australian Youth Hostels Association (AYHA), Level 3, 10 Mallett St., Camperdown NSW 2050 (☎02 9565 1699; www.yha.org.au). AUS$52, under 18 AUS$16.

Hostelling International-Canada (HI-C), 205 Catherine St. #400, Ottawa, ON K2P 1C3 (☎613-237-7884; www.hihostels.ca). CDN$35, under 18 free.

An Óige (Irish Youth Hostel Association), 61 Mountjoy St., Dublin 7 (☎01 830 4555; www.irelandyha.org). EUR€15, under 18 EUR€7.50.

Youth Hostels Association of New Zealand (YHANZ), P.O. Box 436, 193 Cashel St., 3rd fl., Union House, Christchurch (☎03 379 9970; www.yha.org.nz). NZ$40, under 18 free.

Hostels Association of South Africa, 73 St. George's House, 3rd fl., Cape Town 8001 (☎021 424 2511; fax 021 424 4119; www.hisa.org.za). ZAR70, under 18 ZAR40.

Scottish Youth Hostels Association (SYHA), 7 Glebe Crescent, Stirling FK8 2JA (☎01786 89 14 00; fax 01786 89 13 33; www.syha.org.uk). UK£6.

Youth Hostels Association (England and Wales), Trevelyan House, Dimple Rd., Matlock, Devonshire DE4 3YH, UK (☎01629 59 26 00; fax 01629 59 27 02; www.yha.org.uk). UK£13, under 18 UK£6.50.

Hostelling International Northern Ireland (HINI), 22 Donegall Rd., Belfast BT12 5JN (☎02890 31 54 35; fax 02890 43 96 99; www.hini.org.uk). UK£10, under 18 UK£6.

Hostelling International-American Youth Hostels (HI-AYH), 733 15th St. NW, #840, Washington, D.C. 20005 (☎202-783-6161; fax 202-783-6171; www.hiayh.org). US$25, under 18 free.

POUSADAS

A majority of budget travelers in Brazil stay at *pousadas,* which are often called the bed and breakfasts of Brazil. These small- or medium-sized guesthouses are run by private owners and offer fairly clean and tidy single, double, and triple rooms, most with private bathrooms and a choice of fans or A/C. (*Quartos* are rooms with communal hall bathrooms, while *apartamentos* are rooms with private bath.) Starting from as low as R$30-40 for a double, *pousadas* are quite affordable; double rooms are often cheaper per person than hostel dorm beds. Breakfast (anything from simple to sumptuous) is almost always included in the price. You should always try to negotiate for a lower room rate at *pousadas.*

HOTELS

From shabby jail cell dives with moldy mattresses to glittering Rio penthouses with private beaches, Brazil has hotels for every budget. Lower-end hotels are often indistinguishable from (or even inferior to) *pousadas,* with a choice of fairly clean single/double/etc. rooms with private bath and breakfast included in the room price. Like *pousadas,* lower-end hotels often offer a choice of rooms with *(apartamento)* or without *(quarto)* private bath. Mid- and higher-range hotels almost always include A/C, TV, phone, and *frigo-bar* (mini-fridge stocked with overpriced drinks and snacks). Higher-end hotels offer different levels of *apartamentos,* which differ greatly in price but often differ only in minor amenities like TV or view. Hotels in major cities are regulated by the local government for quality and comfort, but it's always best to check out the room before agreeing to stay. Though hotels list room rates at the reception desk, bargaining for a lower price (*Tem desconto?* "Do you have a discount?") is a given. There are discounts offered for almost anything, including multi-day stays, cash payment, booking in advance, booking online, or just showing up. At hotels with star ratings (three or higher), you should feel secure in leaving your valuables in the safe.

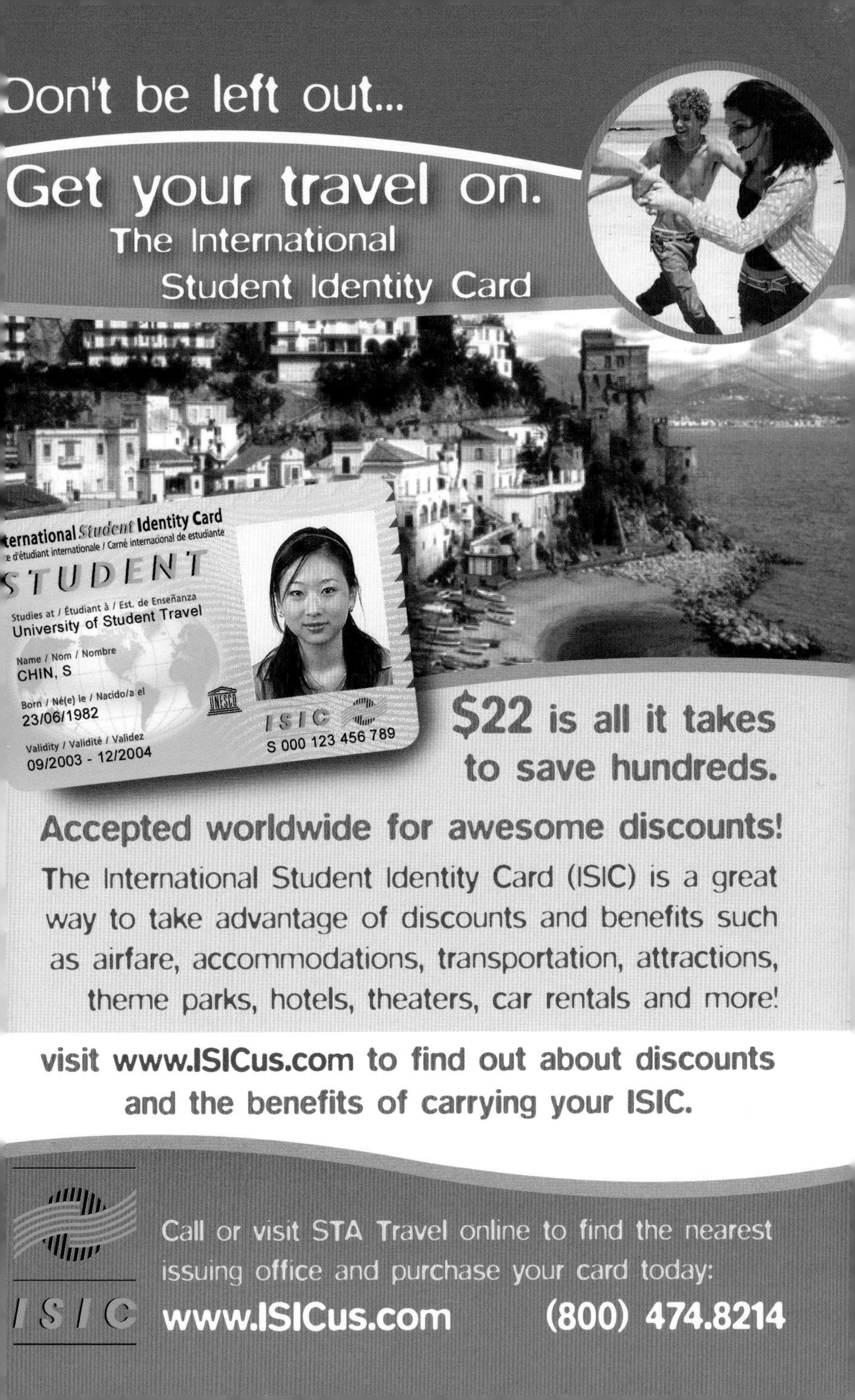
Don't be left out...
Get your travel on.
The International
Student Identity Card
ternational Student Identity Card
e d'étudiant internationale / Carné internacional de estudiante
STUDENT
Studies at / Étudiant à / Est. de Enseñanza
University of Student Travel
Name / Nom / Nombre
CHIN, S
Born / Né(e) le / Nacido/a el
23/06/1982
Validity / Validité / Validez
09/2003 - 12/2004
UNESCO
ISIC
S 000 123 456 789
$22 is all it takes
to save hundreds.
Accepted worldwide for awesome discounts!
The International Student Identity Card (ISIC) is a great way to take advantage of discounts and benefits such as airfare, accommodations, transportation, attractions, theme parks, hotels, theaters, car rentals and more!
visit www.ISICus.com to find out about discounts and the benefits of carrying your ISIC.
ISIC
Call or visit STA Travel online to find the nearest issuing office and purchase your card today:
www.ISICus.com
(800) 474.8214

HOURLY MOTELS. If you're staying in one of Rio's budget hotels, you've most likely passed by the tinted-windowed Hotel Love Time, on Rua do Catete. Despite its name, Love Time is actually a motel. Found everywhere just outside of major cities like São Paulo and Brasília, these "motels" are nothing like their North American counterparts: they're strictly for short-term stays (as in hourly) and strictly for sex. Brazil's alarmingly high urban population density–Rio's Copacabana district alone has some 5000 people crammed into every block–means privacy is at a premium in cities. Young people live with their parents until marriage, and often move in with other relatives after marriage, meaning they rarely get time alone together. Despite the illicit taste motels might leave in foreigners' mouths, motels are not considered sleazy, and are seen as perfectly acceptable by Brazilians. If you want to shell out the extra *reais* (motels are busiest and priciest on weekends), you'll find motel suites to be quite luxurious (and a little campy): these multi-floored, plush velvet pads often feature private saunas, vibrating circular beds, and room service (with pornographic movies and sex toys on the menu). For discretion, parking is always hidden from the street. The better-known motels are on the outskirts of the major cities.

CAMPING & THE OUTDOORS

Camping is a viable option in many parts of Brazil, and is usually the most inexpensive type of accommodations. Camping is permitted in many of the national parks *(parques nacionais)*, but often there are no facilities or organized sites: check with individual park information centers. *Let's Go* advises that you camp only in established sites; otherwise you may end up in trouble with local authorities or encounter unfriendly wildlife. The price per night at a campsite (which may be charged either by person or by tent, depending upon the site) is almost invariably cheaper than a hostel. In the Amazon and Pantanal, many tour operators offer organized camping excursions which are led by a guide and provide you with the necessary equipment. While these trips can be expensive, they are often the best (and sometimes only) option for these regions, where tromping off into the wilderness by yourself can be difficult or dangerous.

It is rarely necessary to make a reservation at Brazilian camping sites, but during the summer months they may be crowded, so it's always a good idea to call ahead. Be aware that campgrounds often charge higher rates during the high season. The high season is generally the summer (Dec.-Mar.), but varies somewhat by region: high season in the Pantanal occurs Apr.-May and Sept.-Oct., whereas in the Amazon it is Mar.-July.

The majority of campgrounds in Brazil are found by coastal beaches and will have basic amenities (toilets and running water); often there is also a restaurant or beach bar nearby. Many of these sites are ideal for backpackers: they tend to be accessible by public transportation, and are usually designed for tents only (rather than RVs). When camping, be particularly aware of security because there is generally no place to store your belongings. Also, keep in mind that it is always safer to camp in groups, especially for women.

The **Associação Brasileira de Pousadas e Campings (ABPC)** is Brazil's national camping association: their Portuguese-only website provides hundreds of site listings. (www.campismo.com.br. Rua dos Meninos 248, loja 2, Vila Gerti 09580-300, São Caetano do Sul, São Paulo, Brazil.) Watch for their sticker at campsites you visit—this is something like "AAA-approved accommodations" in the US—as a campground sanctioned by them has met their requirements for safety and reputability. Another useful organization for campers is the **Camping Clube do Brasil,** which has more than 40 sites all across the country. Their website provides more information about the club and its specific sites. Alternatively, you can contact their main office in Rio de Janeiro for a list of authorized campgrounds (☎21 2210 3171; www.campingclube.com.br. Rua Senador Dantas 75, 29th fl., Centro 20037, Rio de Janeiro, Brazil). A good general resource for outdoors-geared travelers is the **Great Outdoor Recreation Pages** (www.gorp.com). Although this website is not camping-specific, it does have information on adventures throughout Brazil.

USEFUL PUBLICATIONS & RESOURCES

A variety of publishing companies offer hiking guidebooks to meet the educational needs of novices or experts alike. For information about camping, hiking, and biking, download a free **South American Travel** catalogue from www.gorp.com. **Sierra Club Books,** 85 2nd St., 2nd fl., San Francisco, CA 94105, USA, publishes general resource books on hiking, camping, and women traveling in the outdoors. (☎415-977-5500; www.sierraclub.org/books.) **The Mountaineers Books,** 1001 S.W. Klickitat Way #201, Seattle, WA 98134, USA, has over 600 titles on hiking, biking, mountaineering, natural history, and conservation, including *South America's National Parks* with coverage of Brazil's park system. (☎800-553-4453; fax 800-568-7604; www.mountaineersbooks.org.)

NATIONAL PARKS

Brazil has over 40 national parks *(parques nacionais)*, only about half of which allow visitors. Of those that do, most offer tours—and some can only be visited with a guide, due to rough terrain (especially those in the Pantanal and the Amazon). In those that do not require that you hire a guide, there are often specific hiking trails, maps of which are available at the entrance to the park. It is rare that any park open to tourists does not have an information center at its entrance, but check with the local tourist office before heading out to the park. Actual transportation to parks can be complicated: in the Center-West there is usually a nearby gateway town, but there is not always public transportation into the Pantanal proper. Tour operators often run a bus to the park entrance (as do some hostels/hotels in nearby towns), and sometimes you can get there by local taxi. Make sure that you have arranged return transportation, especially from those parks where camping is not allowed. There is often an admission fee of a few *reais*, but the breathtaking scenery is generally worth it.

WILDERNESS SAFETY

THE GREAT OUTDOORS. Stay warm, stay dry, and stay hydrated. The vast majority of life-threatening wilderness situations can be avoided by following this simple advice. Prepare yourself for an emergency by always packing raingear, a first-aid kit, bugspray, a reflector, a whistle, high-energy food, and extra water for any hike. Bring a jacket, especially if you will be traveling in the Amazon or the South.

Check weather forecasts and pay attention to the skies when hiking. Since weather patterns can change suddenly, always be prepared for rain. Whenever possible, let someone (either a friend, your hostel, a park ranger, or a local hiking organization) know when and where you are going hiking. Do not attempt a hike beyond your ability—you may be endangering your life. See **Health,** p. 70, for information about outdoor ailments and basic medical concerns.

THINGS THAT WILL EAT YOU. The waters of Brazil are home to sharks, alligators, and—most famously—piranhas. The latter will probably not be able to make a meal of you, but it does have a nasty bite. Although shark and alligator attacks are rare, you should check with locals as to whether these animals inhabit the waters you might be wanting to swim in. The same general rule applies for avoiding all of these creatures: exercise common sense. Don't swim in undesignated areas, check with locals to make sure they are safe, and don't swim alone.

THINGS THAT WILL POISON YOU. Among the 230 species of snake in Brazil are several poisonous ones. Basic rules include: don't stick your hands or feet into dark holes, don't step over logs without checking to see if there's a snake on the other side, make sure to watch where you are walking (especially in tall grass or brush), and don't try to pick up snakes. It's a good idea to wear long pants and tuck them into your boots while in forests and fields. On the off-chance that you are bitten, you should seek medical attention immediately, as some snake venoms are extremely toxic.

THINGS YOU SHOULD NOT LICK. A number of the 200 species of *bufo* toad do, in fact, have parotid glands which produce bufotenine, a substance which can cause hallucinations. However, this compound is inactive if taken orally (e.g. by licking). Strangely, most *bufo* toads secrete extremely toxic poisons which *are* active if taken orally. Licking toads is a bad idea, no matter what you may have seen on TV.

THINGS THAT WILL MAKE YOU SICK. One of the less thrilling examples of Brazil's biodiversity is the over 200 species of mosquito in the country. You may want to consider taking prescription anti-malarial drugs (p. 72), especially if you are traveling in the rainforest. If you will be traveling anywhere outside of the major cities you may be required to have a yellow fever vaccination (p. 72).

THINGS THAT WILL STICK IT TO YOU. The **bicho de pé** (literally, "foot monster") is a parasite found on beaches and farms in the Northeast which will burrow into the flesh of your feet and must be cut out. The way to avoid these nasty critters is to wear shoes as much as possible, and ask locals about whether or not the beaches are footworm-free. The **candiru** also has a penchant for lodging itself in inappropriate places: this little fish, which makes its home in the Amazon, will reputedly swim into the human urinary tract, if given the opportunity. Because of its spines, it cannot be removed except by surgery. Locals do swim in waters where it is known to live and apparently avoid it by wearing tight-fitting swimwear... but it's still a good idea to ask around before you go for a dip. Another fish to watch out for is the **sting-ray,** which can inflict serious cuts with its tail. However, it is not aggressive and will only hurt you if surprised (i.e. stepped on): avoid this by dragging your feet along the river bottom or sea floor.

CAMPING & HIKING EQUIPMENT

WHAT TO BUY

Good camping equipment is both sturdy and light. If you plan to camp often, bring your equipment with you, as it is generally more expensive in Brazil.

Sleeping Bag: Most bags are rated by season ("summer" means 30-40°F or 0-4°C at night; "four-season" or "winter" often means below 0°F or -17°C). They are made either of **down** (warmer and lighter, but more expensive, and miserable when wet) or of **synthetic** material (heavier, more durable, and warmer when wet). Prices range US$70-210 for a summer synthetic to US$250-300 for a good down winter bag. **Sleeping bag pads** include foam pads (US$10-30), air mattresses (US$15-50), and Therm-A-Rest self-inflating pads (US$45-120). Bring a **stuff sack** to store your bag and keep it dry.

Tent: The best tents to buy are those that are free-standing (with their own frames and suspension systems), set up quickly, and only require staking in high winds. Low-profile dome tents are the best all-around. Good 2-person tents start at US$90, 4-person at

US$300. Remember to seal the seams of your tent with waterproofer, and make sure it has a rain fly. Other tent accessories include a **battery-operated lantern,** a **plastic groundcloth,** and a **nylon tarp.**

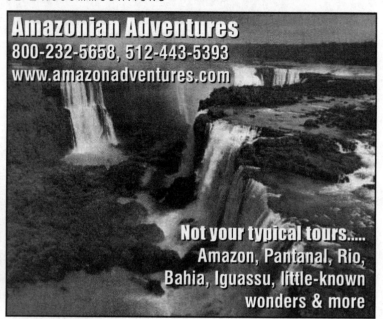

Backpack: Internal-frame packs mold better to your back, keep a lower center of gravity, and flex adequately to allow you to hike difficult trails. **External-frame packs** are more comfortable for long hikes over even terrain, as they keep weight higher and distribute it more evenly. Make sure your pack has a strong, padded hip-belt to transfer weight to your legs. Any serious backpacking requires a pack of at least 4000 in^3 (16,000cc), plus 500 in^3 for sleeping bags in internal-frame packs. Sturdy backpacks cost anywhere from US$125-420—this is one area in which it doesn't pay to economize. Fill up any pack with something heavy and walk around the store with it to get a sense of how it distributes weight before buying it. Either buy a **waterproof backpack cover,** or store all of your belongings in plastic bags inside your pack.

Boots: Be sure to wear hiking boots with good **ankle support.** They should fit snugly and comfortably over 1-2 pairs of wool socks and thin liner socks. Break in boots over several weeks before you go in order to spare yourself painful and debilitating blisters.

Other Necessities: In addition to a **rain jacket,** a broad-brimmed hat is essential to protect you from the weather: bringing **sunscreen** and sunglasses is also a good idea. **Synthetic** layers, like those made of polypropylene, and a pile jacket will keep you warm even when wet. A **"space blanket"** will help you to retain your body heat and doubles as a groundcloth (US$5-15). Plastic **water bottles** are virtually shatter- and leak-proof. Bring **water-purification tablets** for when you can't boil water. Although some campgrounds provide campfire sites, you may want to bring a small metal grate or grill of your own. For those places that forbid fires or the gathering of firewood, you'll need a camp stove (the classic Coleman starts at US$45) and a propane-filled fuel bottle to operate it. Also don't forget a **first-aid kit** (p. 76), pocketknife, lip salve, **insect repellent,** calamine lotion, and waterproof matches or a lighter.

RESPONSIBLE TOURISM. The idea behind responsible tourism is to leave no trace of human presence behind–an especially important idea in Brazil, where government-sanctioned nature preservation is still in its infancy. Some tips: a campstove is safer (and more efficient) than using vegetation to cook; if you must make a fire, use only dead branches or brush rather than cutting vegetation. Make sure your campsite is at least 150 ft. (45m) from water supplies or bodies of water. If there are no toilet facilities, bury human waste (but not paper) at least 4 in. (10cm) deep and above the high-water line, and 150 ft. or more from any water supplies and campsites. Always pack your trash in a plastic bag and carry it with you until you reach the next receptacle. See Alternatives to Tourism, p. 103, for more information. Some important organizations are:

Earthwatch, 3 Clock Tower Place #100, Box 75, Maynard, MA 01754, USA (☎800-776-0188; info@earthwatch.org; www.earthwatch.org).

International Ecotourism Society, 28 Pine St., Burlington, VT 05402, USA (☎802-651-9818; www.ecotourism.org).

National Audubon Society, Nature Odysseys, 700 Broadway, New York, NY 10003, USA (☎212-979-3000; www.audubon.org).

Tourism Concern, Stapleton House, 277-281 Holloway Rd., London N7 8HN, UK (☎020 7753 3330; www.tourismconcern.org.uk).

ESSENTIALS

WHERE TO BUY IT

The mail-order/online companies listed below offer lower prices than many retail stores, but a visit to a local camping or outdoors store will give you a good sense of the look and weight of certain items.

Campmor, 28 Parkway, P.O. Box 700, Upper Saddle River, NJ 07458, USA (☎888-226-7667; www.campmor.com).

Discount Camping, 880 Main North Rd., Pooraka, South Australia 5095, Australia (☎08 8262 3399; fax 08 8260 6240; www.discountcamping.com.au).

Eastern Mountain Sports (EMS), 1 Vose Farm Rd., Peterborough, NH 03458, USA (☎888-463-6367; www.ems.com).

L.L. Bean, Freeport, ME 04033, USA (US and Canada ☎800-441-5713; UK ☎0800 891 297; www.llbean.com).

Mountain Designs, 51 Bishop St., Kelvin Grove, Queensland 4059, Australia (☎07 3856 2344; fax 3856 0366; www.mountaindesigns.com).

Recreational Equipment, Inc. (REI), Sumner, WA 98352, USA (US and Canada ☎800-426-4840, elsewhere 253-891-2500; www.rei.com).

YHA Adventure Shop, 19 High St., Staines, Middlesex, TW18 4QY, UK (☎1784 458 625; fax 1784 464 573; www.yhaadventure.com). The main branch of one of Britain's largest outdoor equipment suppliers.

ORGANIZED ADVENTURE TRIPS

Organized adventure tours offer another way of exploring the wild, and are sometimes the only way to visit certain areas of Brazil (especially in the Center-West and the North). Activities include hiking, biking, skiing, canoeing, kayaking, rafting, climbing, diving, and fishing. These tours almost always include the necessary equipment and meals, but make sure while you are arranging your tour that the price of food is included in the overall package price. Tours arranged within Brazil are usually cheaper than those arranged from abroad, but not all operators are reputable. Check at the tourist office for a list of reliable guides and organizations in the area and *never* arrange a tour with the guides who may assail you at the bus or train station. Tourism bureaus can often suggest parks, trails, and outfitters; other good sources of information are stores and organizations that specialize in camping and outdoor equipment like REI and EMS (see above).

Specialty Travel Index, 305 San Anselmo Ave. #313, San Anselmo, CA 94960, USA (☎800-442-4922, 415-459-4900; fax 415-459-9474; www.specialtytravel.com). Offers tours worldwide, including an extensive list of tour operators in Brazil.

Brazilnuts, 1854 Trade Center Way, Ste. #101A, Naples, FL 34109 USA (☎800-553-9959; fax 239-593-0267; www.brazilnuts.com). US tour operator specializing in Brazil (especially the Amazon), including jungle lodges and riverboats.

Brazil On-Line, 1110 Brickell Ave., Ste. 502, Miami, FL 33131, USA (☎888-527-2745; fax 305 379 9397; info@brol.com; www.brol.com). Online discount booking for most tours and lodges in Brazil, as well as airlines.

KEEPING IN TOUCH

BY MAIL

SENDING MAIL FROM BRAZIL

Postal services in Brazil are quite reliable. Yellow-and-blue post offices *(correios)* are the only places that sell **stamps** *(selos)*. Speedy **airmail** is the most common way to send postcards and letters home; it takes about one week for mail sent from Brazil to arrive in North America, Europe, or Oceania. Post offices also sell **aerogramas** (R$1), printed sheets that fold into envelopes and travel via airmail; write "PAR AVION" or "POR AVIÃO" on the front. **Surface mail** is the cheapest and slowest way to send mail, taking anywhere from one to four months; it's best for shipping home stuff you won't need for a while, like souvenirs or other articles you've acquired along the way. For more information, see www.correios.com.br.

SENDING MAIL TO BRAZIL

Mark envelopes "air mail," "par avion," or "por avião;" otherwise your letter or postcard will never arrive. In addition to your country's standard postage system, **Federal Express** (www.fedex.com; Australia ☎13 26 10; US and Canada ☎800-247-4747; New Zealand ☎0800 73 33 39; UK ☎0800 12 38 00) handles express mail services from many home countries to Brazil.

RECEIVING MAIL IN BRAZIL

The most common means for travelers to receive mail is via **Poste Restante** (General Delivery in the US), which is fairly reliable in Brazil. Mail addressed as indicated below will be held at the main post office of any major city for up to 30 days. (*Let's Go* lists the main post office and postal code of every major city in the **Practical Information** section). Bring photo ID for pick-up, and check under your first and last names; there may be an unofficial "fee."

POSTE RESTANTE. Address *Poste Restante* letters like so:
Carmen MIRANDA
Poste Restante
[Post Office Address]
[City], [State]
BRASIL CEP [Postal code]

American Express travel offices throughout the world offer a free **Client Letter Service** (mail held up to 30 days and forwarded upon request) for cardholders who contact them in advance. Some offices will offer these services to non-cardholders (especially AmEx Travelers Check holders), but call ahead to make sure. *Let's Go* lists AmEx office locations for most large cities in **Practical Information** sections; for a complete, free list, call ☎800-528-4800 or check www.aexp.com.

BY TELEPHONE

PHONE CALLS

Domestic (DDD): ☎0 + carrier code + city code + number (no.)
International (DDI): ☎00 + carrier code + country code + city code + no.
International operator: ☎000 111
Directory assistance: ☎102 (Portuguese only)

CALLING ABROAD FROM BRAZIL

The most reliable way to place an international call from Brazil is from an international phone office (known as a **posto telefônico**); these are listed in the **Practical Information** section of each city in this guide. At phone offices, you place your call from a private booth and pay afterward in cash. Always ask for and settle on a minute rate for the call *before* you step in to the booth. Rates vary widely across the country, and are more expensive in more remote cities and towns. Many Internet cafés double as international phone offices.

If you plan to call abroad from Brazil using a **prepaid Brazilian calling card** *(cartão telefônico)* at a public pay phone *(orelhão)*, know that international calls cost about one unit per second, and you can't switch cards mid-call. More importantly, most *orelhões* are restricted to domestic calls (indicated on the phone as DDD, or Discagem Direta a Distância); those that allow international calls are marked **DDI (Discagem Direta Internacional).** Using an **International calling card** with a toll-free access number and PIN works fine at most DDD *orelhões.* However, you'll still need to first insert a prepaid Brazilian calling card with at least one unit on it before placing your toll-free call; no units will be used on the call, but you'll need the card to "activate" the phone.

CALLING BRAZIL FROM ABROAD. To call Brazil from abroad, dial:

1. **International dialing prefix.** Dialing out of: **Australia,** 0011; **Canada** and the **US,** 011; **Ireland, New Zealand,** and the **UK,** 00; **South Africa,** 09.
2. **Brazil's country code.** 55
3. **City/area code.** *Let's Go* lists the city codes for destinations in Brazil opposite the destination name. If the city code begins with a 0 (or 0xx), omit it.
4. **Local number.**

Let's Go has partnered with ekit.com to provide a convenient all-in-one calling card that offers a number of convenient services for travelers, including email, voice messaging, 24hr. emergency service, and an online "travel vault" for storing important documentation. The toll-free 24hr. access number in Brazil is ☎0008 145 503 844; the call must be made from a DDI phone. For more information, visit www.letsgo.ekit.com.

To place **international collect calls** *(ligações a cobrar)*, dial the English-speaking international operator at ☎000 111. Desk clerks at major hotels can also help with international phone calls (most speak English), and some hotels will even let you use their main phone line (for a fee).

If you will be in Brazil for an extended period of time, you should do like Brazilians do and spring for a mobile phone *(celular)*. Cellular phones are cheaper, more reliable, and increasingly more prevalent than land lines. For more on buying a cellular phone and SIM card that will work in Brazil before you go, see p. 76.

CALLING WITHIN BRAZIL

CARRIER CODES. Two-digit carrier codes are noted in Brazil as **xx.** Embratel **(21)** and Intelig **(23)** can call anywhere worldwide.

ESSENTIALS

Calls within Brazil (DDD) are best made from the curvaceous public phone booths known as **orelhões** ("big ears;" singular *orelhão*), named for their distinctive floppy-eared shape. Phone service within Brazil is notoriously unreliable: though finding an *orelhão* is easy (they're everywhere), finding one that works is much more difficult. *Orelhões* only accept **cartões telefônicos** (singular *cartão telefônico*), prepaid phone cards sold everywhere—at pharmacies, newsstands, and by neon-vested street vendors. Cards carry a certain number of units *(unidades)*, which the phone counts down as you make your call (all calls are timed). Cards are sold in denominations of 10 units; a good price is around R$1 per 10 units. One or two units is enough for a local call, although calls to cell phone numbers (which start with 9) eat up units much faster; a brief domestic call takes about 10-15 units. Calls to emergency personnel (police, firemen, etc.) are free.

To make a **local call,** just dial the number; dial 9090 before the number for **local collect calls** *(a cobrar)*. To place a **domestic call** to any other city in Brazil, dial ☎ **0 + carrier code (21 or 23) + city code + number** (dial all this even if the city shares a city code with the one from which you are calling); dial 9 before this in order to place a **domestic intercity collect calls.**

The **carrier code** system seems a lot more confusing than it actually is. Each state or region of Brazil has multiple private carriers (most with calling areas restricted to that region) each vying for your calls. To place any non-local call from Brazil (whether calling abroad or just the next town over), you must dial the two-digit code associated with a carrier before the city code. (The place to dial the code is indicated by **xx** in Brazilian phone numbers; hence Rio's city code is 0xx21, Manaus is 0xx92, etc.) A regional carrier code will always be plastered all over the *orelhão* you're using, but it's easiest to just remember that Embratel **(21)** and Intelig **(23)** are the two carriers that always work for anywhere in Brazil and the world.

TIME DIFFERENCES

Brazil has four time zones *(fusos horários)*. Most of the country is on Brasília time, which is three hours behind GMT/UTC. Most of the North and Center-West regions are one hour behind Brasília time (GMT-4), while the state of Acre is two hours behind (GMT-5). Fernando de Noronha, a tiny island far off the coast of Pernambuco, has the "rarest hour in the world"—the smallest full-hour time zone on the planet, one hour *ahead* of Brasília time (GMT-2). There are exceptions here and there, often within state borders; see the chart on the inside of the back cover for a state-by-state time zone breakdown.

Daylight Savings Time is observed in some states, but unfortunately observation varies widely from year to year based on annual governmental decree. This causes great confusion among travelers and locals alike—more than one traveler has missed buses, flights, or appointments from being an hour or two late. Whenever you arrive in an airport or bus station, ask what time it is.

BY EMAIL & INTERNET

Though Brazil was a little slow to jump on the Internet bandwagon, you should have no problem getting online now: even the smallest towns and most remote islands in the country have an Internet café or two, and in the big cities there are high-speed DSL places everywhere. (Where available, *Let's Go* lists Internet cafés in a city's **Practical Information** section.) Thanks to Brazil's plagued telecommunications infrastructure, rates run higher than elsewhere in South America, at around R$5-8 per hour (as high as R$15 per hour in more remote locales). Few people can afford private Internet connections, so be prepared to share your Internet experience with loud, Guaraná-guzzling adolescents playing online shoot-'em-up games or indiscreet men of all ages ogling graphic pornography.

GETTING TO BRAZIL

BY PLANE

Discounts and price wars are so common in the airline industry that students, seniors, and those under 26 should never pay full price for an airline ticket. If your plans are flexible enough to deal with the restrictions, **courier fares** are the cheapest. An unconfirmed **standby** ticket—dependent on there being an open seat on the plane—can also be a good deal, but **last-minute specials** (mostly available over the Internet) often beat these fares. Your best bets for finding a cheap fare are the budget travel agencies listed below and your own sleuthing on the Internet.

AIRFARES

The high season for travel to Brazil is the Brazilian summer (Dec.-Mar.), with airfares peaking around Carnaval (usually the end of Feb.). However, Brazil's year-round beautiful weather means you can visit in the dead of winter for half the price (and with hotels discounted) and still enjoy all the country has to offer.

ROUND-TRIP TICKETS. Midweek (M-Th morning) round-trip flights run US$40-50 cheaper than weekend flights, but they are generally more crowded and less likely to permit frequent-flier upgrades. Not fixing a return date ("open return") or arriving in and departing from different cities ("open-jaw") is pricier than booking a regular point-to-point round-trip flight.

Almost every international flight to Brazil arrives at either São Paulo's Guarulhos (GRU) or Rio de Janeiro's Galeão/Tom Jobim (GIG) international airports; most international flights to Rio stop in São Paulo en route. **Fares** for roundtrip flights to either of these cities from the US or Canada cost up to US$800, but should be closer to US$500 in the low season; high-season flights from the UK, Ireland, and most of the EU average UK£500; flights from Australia and New Zealand run up to US$1300 (AUS$2000, NZ$2000).

ROUND THE WORLD (RTW) TICKETS. For many travelers, Brazil is often just one stop on a more extensive trip, either round-the-world (RTW) or all over South America. **Round-the-world** tickets include at least five stops around the globe and are valid for a year; prices range US$1200-5000, based on either a certain number of stops or a certain allotment of miles. A popular RTW package is offered by the **Star Alliance,** a consortium of 16 airlines in 128 countries (including Brazil's Varig) that allows up to 15 stops over some 39,000 miles (US ☎ 800-241-6522; www.staralliance.com). Varig/Star Alliance also offer a regional Brazil Airpass (see p. 93).

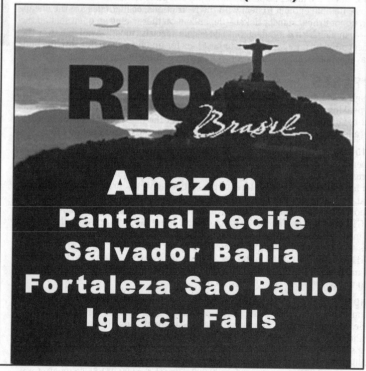

The only airpass for South America is the **Mercosur Airpass** (www.latinamerica.co.uk/mercosur.htm), which allows two or three stops each (up to nine stops total) in Argentina, Brazil, Chile, Paraguay, and Uruguay, over a maximum of 30 days. Fares are based on miles flown (from US$225 for 1200 miles up to US$870 for 4200+ miles); date and time changes can be made for a fee, but re-routes are not allowed. Tickets must be purchased before arriving in South America, and are only available to those with a round-trip ticket to a destination in the above five countries. For more info, consult a budget travel agent near you.

DISCOUNT FLIGHT OPTIONS

AIR COURIER FLIGHTS. Air couriers get deep discounts on airfare by using their checked luggage space for international cargo freight. As such, couriers must travel with carry-ons only and deal with complex flight restrictions. Most flights are round-trip only, with short fixed-length stays (usually one week) and a limit of a one ticket per issue. Couriers typically fly between major business centers, meaning flights are most common out of big cities in the US (i.e. New York, Los Angeles, San Francisco, or Miami), as well as London and Toronto; all courier flights to Brazil are to São Paulo or Rio de Janeiro. During the high season, the most popular destinations usually require an advance reservation of about two weeks (you can usually book up to two months ahead).

TICKET CONSOLIDATORS (BUCKET SHOPS). Bucket shops buy unsold tickets in bulk from commercial airlines and sell them at discounted rates; most bucket shops have tickets to Rio. The best place to look is online or in the Sunday travel section of any major newspaper, where many bucket shops place tiny ads. Call quickly, as availability is typically extremely limited. Not all bucket shops are reliable, so insist on a receipt that gives full details of restrictions, refunds, and tickets. Pay by credit card (in spite of the 2-5% fee) so you can stop payment if you never receive tickets.

The following are suggestions for bucket shops in the US and Canada; *Let's Go* does not endorse any of them: **Travel Avenue** (☎800-333-3335; www.travelavenue.com); **Rebel Tours** (☎800-227-3235 www.rebeltours.com); **Flights.com** (www.flights.com); and **TravelHUB** (www.travelhub.com).

CHARTER FLIGHTS. Charters are flights a tour operator contracts with an airline to fly extra loads of passengers during peak season. Charter flights fly less frequently than major airlines, make refunds particularly difficult, and are almost always fully booked. Schedules and itineraries may also change or be cancelled at the last moment (as late as 48 hours before the trip, but without a full refund), and check-in, boarding, and baggage claim are often much slower. **Discount clubs** and **fare brokers** offer members savings on last-minute charter and tour deals.

BUDGET & STUDENT TRAVEL AGENCIES

Below is a list of the most common budget travel-oriented travel agencies throughout the English-speaking world. Most are based primarily in one country but have branches throughout the world. In addition to selling international ID cards, all the following book airline tickets at their branch offices and through the phone numbers listed (STA also books online); some also book arranged tours and sell travel-related gear (backpacks, phone cards, etc.). Travelers holding **ISIC** or **IYTC** (see p. 64)—or those who buy them from these agencies—qualify for major discounts.

STA Travel (toll-free in the US ☎800-329-9537; www.sta-travel.com). The largest worldwide youth travel agency, with countless offices worldwide (although there are no offices in Ireland). Also books tickets online at www.sta-travel.com.

ESSENTIALS

USIT (☎01 602 1600; www.usitnow.ie). Leading Irish student/budget travel agency, with over 20 offices in the Republic of Ireland and Northern Ireland.

usit Adventures (☎086 000 0111; www.usitadventures.co.za). Runs 10 budget travel offices in South Africa.

CTS Travel (anywhere in Europe ☎020 7290 0621; www.ctstravel.co.uk). A London-based budget travel agency with branches all over Europe and 1 US office at 350 Fifth Ave. #7813, New York City, NY (toll-free US ☎877-287-6665; www.ctstravelusa.com).

Travel CUTS (toll-free in the US ☎866-246-9762; www.travelcuts.com). Canada's own budget and student travel agency, with roughly 60 agencies near college campuses throughout Canada and others throughout the world, including Brazil.

Student UNI Travel (www.sut.com.au). Australia- and New Zealand-based budget travel agency. The branch at 92 Pitt St., Level 8, Sydney (☎02 9232 8444) is the main office for the 6 Australian offices, while the branch at 7 Victoria St. E., Auckland (☎09 300 8266) heads the New Zealand offices.

BORDER CROSSINGS

Brazil shares a border with every country in South America except Chile and Ecuador. Foz do Iguaçu and Corumbá are the two busiest and most heavily patrolled border towns in the country. **Foz do Iguaçu** (p. 248) borders Puerto Iguazú, Argentina, and Ciudad del Este, Paraguay. **Corumbá** (p. 332) is near the Bolivian town of Puerto Suárez. **Cacéres** (p. 310) is near San Matías, Bolivia.

GETTING AROUND BRAZIL

BY PLANE

The vast distances between cities in Brazil mean travel by air is sometimes necessary, and much more convenient and comfortable than bus travel. Domestic flights are getting ever cheaper, and the recent growth of budget airlines like **Gol** and **Fly** means you can usually find cheap flights *(vôos)* quite easily. Most flights actually operate like bus routes, stopping for an hour or less at the major airport(s) en route (sometimes with plane changes), and often only leaving once or twice a day. Even the most infrequently used routes are run by Brazil's major international carriers, so equipment and service are very safe. As travel agencies often levy hefty fees, tickets are best purchased online or directly from airline ticket offices at the airport or within the city limits (listed online, in phone books, and in the Practical Information sections of cities throughout this guide).

NATIONAL AIRLINES

The following are Brazil's major airlines with national service. In early 2003, TAM and Varig announced plans to merge, but as of press time, this had not significantly affected travel with either of these carriers.

FLY (☎0300 313 1323; www.voefly.com.br). The cheapest airline in Brazil—too bad it only runs between Fortaleza, Natal, Rio de Janeiro, and São Paulo.

Gol (toll-free ☎0800 701 2131; www.voegol.com.br). Brazil's budget-friendliest airline, with dirt-cheap flights all over the country.

TAM (☎0300 123 1000; www.tam.com.br). Sells airpasses (US$399). Plans to merge with Varig.

Varig (☎0300 788 7000; www.varig.com). Sells airpasses (US$460; US$399 if round-trip ticket is purchased through a Star Alliance carrier; see www.staralliance.com for a list). Plans to merge with TAM. Typically the most expensive carrier in Brazil.

VASP (☎0300 789 1010; www.vasp.com.br). Flies to several cities throughout Brazil.

AIRPASSES

If you will be in Brazil for less than a month and/or hope to cover a lot of ground, an airpass is a better means of travel than buses: though it isn't cheap, flying cuts days off the time you waste in transit on buses. Airpasses can also be quite convenient for travel in more difficult or remote areas, especially the North region of the country. Passes work out to about US$100 per flight, which is about average for major destination flights (e.g, Rio-Salvador, Salvador-Fortaleza) but much cheaper than the common fare for trips between far-flung destinations (e.g., Foz do Iguaçu-Salvador, Rio-Manaus).

Valid only for foreigners and Brazilian citizens living abroad, airpasses must be purchased before arriving in Brazil, with flights booked in advance, at time of purchase. Itineraries may be changed for a US$30 fee. Holders of airpasses must also have an onward ticket out of the country. Passes (US$399) valid for 21 days and four flights, including layovers, can be bought directly from airlines or for a nominal fee from travel agencies. Additional flights (up to nine) can be added for US$100 each, but these must also be booked at time of purchase. The pass is tied to an airline (either Varig or TAM), and is good for anywhere in Brazil those airlines fly. For more info, visit www.airpasses.com or contact the airlines directly (see **National Airlines,** p. 91).

BY BUS

Long-distance buses are fairly safe and very convenient, and by far the most common and affordable means of long-distance travel within Brazil. Even overnight routes are safe and secure, although it's probably wise to keep valuables with you on the bus (in a money pouch or in your lap, rather than in the overhead storage compartments), especially if you sleep on overnight journeys.

There are three different classes of bus in Brazil; though travelers coming from luxury-coach Argentina might be disappointed, all are quite comfortable and modern. The cheapest are **convencional,** which are standard single-level buses, with only a few (if any) daily A/C routes; these are mainly for short routes, as they are not equipped for overnight travel. **Executivo** (*semi-cama* elsewhere in South America) and the more expensive **leito** are the two options for overnight trips. Both classes include very spacious double-decker buses with A/C (blasting on high—bring a sweater), bathroom, almost fully reclining seats, and a cooler of bottled water. *Leito* buses also typically show movies on board, and sometimes offer free snacks. The only major difference between the two is in price (which is nominal) and in the fact that *executivos* stop much more often than *leitos*, meaning they take at least two hours longer.

Known as **rodoviárias** (ho-doh-vee-AH-ri-ahz), bus stations can be anything from covered shacks by the side of the road to large modern complexes with showers, luggage storage, restaurants, and countless ticket booths. They're typically not in the most convenient or safest parts of a city, so it's wise to take a taxi there and back, especially if you have unwieldy luggage. In any given bus station, you'll be faced with Brazil's menagerie of bus companies *(empresas)*; often times multiple companies run on the same route, offering different schedules but identical prices. Schedules are sometimes posted at the *empresa*'s booth, but usually you have to speak with the attendant; if you don't speak Portuguese, bring along pen and paper

with your destination written clearly on it. Although Brazilians don't hold punctuality in high regard (see **Customs & Etiquette,** p. 40), buses usually leave from stations on time, so arrive a little early to buy tickets. Tickets on popular routes often sell out; it's always best to book a day or at least a few hours ahead. Tickets on all but *convencional* buses are for reserved seats *(poltronas)*, either window *(janela)* or aisle *(corredor)*. If you have a choice, book a seat in the first row of the bus, which has more leg room; avoid seats near the bathroom.

BY FERRY

Occasionally you'll have to take ferries—known in Brazil as *ferries* (FEH-hees)—to remote islands or beach destinations. Though many ferry services are legitimate and well-run, don't always expect the punctuality and reliability of Brazilian buses and airlines: ferries are often just private boats or leaky motor-equipped rowboats run unofficially by an enterprising local.

BY TAXI

Taxis are fairly common in most major cities and towns, and are relatively inexpensive. Metered taxis you flag down on the street are called **comum.** Some travelers consider the metered rate to be a rip-off and suggest negotiating with the *taxista* (driver) for a set fare before getting in the taxi. Those truly afraid of being ripped off can stick to **rádio taxis,** which have more expensive pre-set fares but are mostly scam-free. These taxis lurk outside bus stations and airports; their names typically begin with *coo-*. If you do choose to use the meter, make sure it's running when you get in and set to the right rate (1 or 2, based on the time of day and month; the higher rate 2 is for evenings and Sundays).

BY CAR

Car travel can be an adventure in Brazil: driving resembles a fast and furious free-for-all and Brazilian traffic consistently ranks with the world's worst. Many larger cities have adopted a rotation system to try to reduce congestion, but even so traffic remains thick—and often gridlocked—from early morning until late evening. Many cars in Brazil now run on *álcool*, a blend of alcohol and petroleum. Although priced less, this fuel is also less efficient; *álcool*-powered cars handle sluggishly.

RENTING

Renting an automobile in Brazil can be costly, and if you do not intend to visit many out-of-the-way places a combination of public transit and long-distance busing will be far more affordable. If you do decide to rent, you must be at least 21 years old (most companies require 25), and all agencies will require a credit card, a passport, and a valid driver's license. Also be aware that entering or exiting Brazil by car will incur stricter customs regulations (p. 64); do not rent an alcohol-powered car if you are driving to other countries, as you will be unable to refuel.

RENTAL AGENCIES. The largest national and international agencies have offices in most major airports and cities. Most metropolitan areas will have several smaller rental agencies (listed under *locadoras* in the phone book) with lower rates than the national chains. Car rental agencies with locations across Brazil include: **Localiza** (☎0800 992 000; www.localiza.com.br); **Interlocadora** (☎0800 138 000; www.interlocadora.com.br); and **Avis** (☎0800 198 456; www.avis.com).

COSTS & INSURANCE. Rental rates vary little between the national agencies and from region to region. Expect to pay at least R$100 per day (including insurance), and probably much more. Local agencies may have slightly lower rates, but may also have substandard maintenance or punitive liability clauses. Any serious driving will likely require a four-wheel-drive vehicle, which will cost several times the compact-car rate. For those planning to drive long distances, Brazil's vast expanses make paying extra for an unlimited-mileage plan likely to be less expensive, but high fuel costs make driving anywhere an expensive proposition.

Insurance is mandatory for rentals and these price estimates include it. Brazil's rough traffic and frequent auto thefts make it advisable not to skimp on insurance. Be sure to examine your rental and insurance contracts carefully, as these can leave you largely liable for any damage or theft even if you are insuranced.

ON THE ROAD. Brazil's road systems range from 12-lane expressways to unpaved back-country roads. Generally speaking, the highest-quality roads are found along the coasts and throughout the heavily industrial areas of the Southeast, but even these may have inadequate signage and confusing layouts; drive cautiously throughout the country. Driving is on the right, but drivers commonly pass on the left on Brazil's many two-lane roads. Most drivers communicate with their turn signals: they will turn on their right-turn signal if it's clear to pass on the left, and warn of oncoming traffic with the left-turn signal. Speeds over 120kmh are common on the highways, as speed limits (usually within 60-80kmh) are usually ignored, but violators pay steep fines if caught. **Petrol** (gasoline) prices vary widely between regions (as do prices for the cheaper *álcool*), but are always expensive.

DANGERS. The primary dangers presented by the roads include rough surfaces, potholes, and floods, and that most automobiles will not take kindly to the heat. Another set of dangers, however, are other drivers and automobile thieves: drive defensively to protect yourself from the former and secure your car thoroughly to hinder the latter.

DRIVING PRECAUTIONS. Remember to carry enough cash to pay for gasoline along your route, and remember to store no valuables in your car, keep your car securely locked, and park off-street whenever possible. If driving long distances, be sure to pack a map, patch kit, cell phone, tire iron, jack, extra tubes, and an extra spare tire. Avoid driving at night whenever possible: road hazards are harder to see at night, as are other cars, especially because Brazilian drivers tend not to use their headlights after dark. Check the weather: during the rainy season many roads may be impassable due to floods, particularly in the Center-West, Northeast, and North regions.

DRIVING PERMITS & CAR INSURANCE

INTERNATIONAL DRIVING PERMIT (IDP). Foreign driver's licenses are valid for 6 months, but having a **certificate of validity** from Detran (the Department of Transit) is advisable, especially for extended stays. A better option, however, is to secure an **International Driving Permit (IDP).** An IDP will greatly smooth over interactions with authorities, and is especially useful when dealing with non-English-speaking officials, as the information on the IDP is printed in 10 languages, including Spanish and Portuguese. Your IDP, valid for one year, must be issued in your own country before you depart. An application for an IDP usually includes one or two passport photos, a current local license, an additional form of identification, and a fee. To apply, contact the national or local branch of your home country's Automobile Association.

CAR INSURANCE. Car insurance is mandatory in Brazil. If you're renting a car you will purchase insurance from the rental agency; if bringing your own car, you will purchase insurance from an insurer based in your home country. Try to obtain as much coverage as possible. If you lack third-party collision coverage you may forfeit your car in an accident. Coverage for damage and theft are also recommended. Be sure to obtain an **International Insurance Certificate,** a green card certifying that you have purchased insurance valid in Brazil. These can be obtained at car rental agencies, car dealers (for those leasing cars), some travel agents, and some border crossings.

BY THUMB

Hitchhiking is not common in Brazil, thanks to the country's vast distances and fairly deserted highways. *Let's Go* strongly urges you to consider the risks if you choose to hitchhike, especially in the more remote areas; only a fool would travel by thumb in the North and Center-West.

SPECIFIC CONCERNS

WOMEN TRAVELERS

Women exploring on their own—especially in macho South America—inevitably face some additional safety concerns. *Machismo* is very much a part of male-dominated Brazilian society, but it's a watered-down, effectively harmless version compared to the catcalls and harassment women often face in other parts of the continent. Women will always get attention from Brazilian men (solo women constant attention, groups less so), but it is almost always playful and rarely dangerous. Often Brazilian men seem to have an insurmountable desire to flirt, but little concern for the actual outcome of the chase; thus, ignoring attention and walking away seem to work well. Typical solo female tactics like "wedding rings" and photos of your "husband" and "children" don't work, or prompt the popular question "How married are you?" Men rarely comment on women out loud, and violence against women is rare. If you are in a situation where you can't move away (i.e. on a bus or *metrô*), a firm, loud, and very public "Leave me alone!" (*Deixe-me em paz!* [DAY-she-may em pas]) should be enough. If harassment does not subside and others do not intervene on your behalf (which they almost always will), turn to an older local woman or seek out a police officer.

In general women attract less attention in more modest clothing, but Brazil's very liberal dress standards mean that even the skimpiest outfit won't draw too much unwarranted attention in most cities. However, in rural areas and outside the major cities and beach towns, dress codes are stricter, especially in the South; the standard bikini-and-*canga* (sarong) uniform of Carioca women is not acceptable or safe south of Rio state or in the rural areas of the North and Northeast. Other safety advice includes staying in hostels which offer single rooms that lock from the inside; sticking to safely, centrally located areas; and avoiding solitary late-night excursions. Women are usually safe traveling alone to nightlife venues, but should be ready for almost constant overtures from flirtatious men.

Always stash emergency money (for a phone call, bus, or taxi) away in a sock, shoe, or money pouch. Hitchhiking is rather uncommon in Brazil, as roads are fairly deserted, but those who do travel by thumb know that it's never safe for lone women or groups of women to hitchhike. Though nothing can prepare you for every contingency you might face in Brazil, a self-defense course should help you in case of a potential attack and raise your general level of awareness (see **Self-Defense,** p. 69). Also be aware of the health concerns that women face when traveling (see **Women's Health,** p. 74).

SOLO TRAVELERS

Brazil often seems actively set against solo traveling: restaurant portions are usually for two or more people, clubs prefer groups, single rooms are much more expensive than the per person cost of a double room, etc. Nevertheless, solo travelers are very common in Brazil, and the well-traveled backpacker trail and lively scene at most backpacker hostels make it easy for those traveling alone to find temporary traveling companions. Regardless of how many people you're traveling with—but especially if you're traveling alone—it's best to maintain regular contact with someone at home who knows your itinerary.

For detailed info on surviving solo travel, pick up *Traveling Solo* by Eleanor Berman (Globe Pequot Press; US$17) or subscribe to **Connecting: Solo Travel Network,** 689 Park Road, Unit 6, Gibsons, BC V0N 1V7, Canada (☎604-886-9099; www.cstn.org; membership US$35). **Travel Companion Exchange,** P.O. Box 833, Amityville, NY 11701, USA (☎800-392-1256, 631-454-0880; www.whytravelalone.com; US$48), will link solo travelers with companions with similar travel habits and interests. Many travelers have also met up using *Let's Go's* travel forums (www.letsgo.com).

OLDER TRAVELERS (IDOSOS)

In Brazil, senior citizens are eligible for a wide range of discounts on transportation, museums, movies, theaters, and concerts—just look or ask for discounts for the elderly *(descontos pra idosos)*. The books *No Problem! Worldwise Tips for Mature Adventurers*, by Janice Kenyon (Orca Book Publishers; US$16) and *Unbelievably Good Deals and Great Adventures That You Absolutely Can't Get Unless You're Over 50*, by Joan Rattner Heilman (NTC/Contemporary; US$13) are both excellent resources. For more information, contact one of the following organizations: **Elderhostel,** 11 Ave. de Lafayette, Boston, MA 02111, USA, organizes "educational adventures for those 55+, including a three-week package tour of Brazil. (☎877-426-8056; www.elderhostel.org.) **The Mature Traveler,** P.O. Box 15791, Sacramento, CA 95852, USA, has deals, discounts, and travel packages for the 50+ traveler. (☎800-460-6676; www.thematuretraveler.com).

GAY & LESBIAN TRAVELERS (GLS)

There is no law against homosexuality in Brazil. Flamboyant displays of queer identity—like sassy transsexual talk show host **Léo Áquilla** (p. 35) and gaudy Carnaval drag queens (see **Popular Blocos,** p. 55)—are wholeheartedly enjoyed by most all Brazilians, but their tolerance for more subtle displays varies greatly, leaning more toward intolerance thanks to the country's strong Catholic upbringing and diluted sense of South American *machismo.* Crude jokes and ridicule are common, but physical violence is thankfully getting more and more rare.

How out you can be depends on the region you're in. Homosexuality is pretty openly acknowledged in most major cities (if not totally accepted), but outside these areas it is not common and not nearly as tolerated; nowhere are same-sex public displays of affection acceptable outside of gay venues. **Rio de Janeiro** (city and state), **Salvador,** and **São Paulo** (city) are the gay-friendliest spots in the country, with substantial queer support and resources and very lively gay/mixed nightlife scenes. Rio has always been the continent's major gay travel destination, and while the Carnaval Carioca remains one of the world's biggest gay parties, São Paulo Gay Pride (mid-June) is the fifth largest pride celebration on the planet. Salvador is the top holiday choice for gay Brazilians; the city's **Grupo Gay da Bahia (GGB),** Rua Frei Vincente 24 (☎71 321 1848), is the country's oldest gay rights organization and a great resource. Queer-friendly activities are listed in papers as **GLS** *(gay, lésbica, e simpatizante;* "gays, lesbians, and supporters").

The following organizations offer materials addressing some specific concerns for gay and lesbian travelers. **PlanetOut** (www.planetout.com) has a comprehensive site addressing gay travel concerns, including special information on travel in Rio and Salvador; affiliated with it is **Out & About** (www.outandabout.com), which offers a gay travel newsletter and downloadable gay-oriented travel guides to Rio and beyond. The **Guia Gay Brasil** (www.guiagaybrasil.com.br) has comprehensive multilingual listings for queer-friendly accommodations and nightlife throughout Brazil. Gay bookstores will stock the latest editions of popular gay travel guides such as those published by **Spartacus** (www.spartacus.de) and **Damron** (www.damron.com). **Gay's the Word,** 66 Marchmont St., London WC1N 1AB, UK (☎020 7278 7654; www.gaystheword.co.uk), and **Giovanni's Room,** 1145 Pine St., Philadelphia, PA 19107, USA (☎215-923-2960; www.queerbooks.com), are mail-order bookstores. The **International Lesbian and Gay Association (ILGA),** 81 rue Marché-au-Charbon, B-1000 Brussels, Belgium, provides political information, such as homosexuality laws of individual countries. (☎+32 2 502 2471; www.ilga.org).

TRAVELERS WITH DISABILITIES

Disabled travelers will probably be able to get around the crowded major cities of Brazil with few problems (although handicapped-accessible establishments remain fairly rare). However, outside urban centers, the infrastructure is much less developed. Short- and long-distance buses are not equipped for wheelchairs. Those with disabilities must inform airlines and hotels of their disabilities when making reservations; some time may be needed to prepare special accommodations. **Guide dogs** are unheard-of in Brazil (and only the Distrito Federal has laws governing them), so visually impaired travelers with seeing-eye dogs will face a bit of a hassle getting their animal into restaurants and hotels; persistence and planning ahead should suffice.

Useful organizations with info and publications on disabled travelers include **Mobility International USA (MIUSA),** P.O. Box 10767, Eugene, OR 97440, USA (☎541-343-1284; www.miusa.org) and the **Society for Accessible Travel and Hospitality (SATH),** 347 Fifth Ave., #610, New York, NY 10016, USA (☎212-447-7284; www.sath.org). The latter is an advocacy group (membership US$45, students and seniors US$30) that also publishes free online travel information and the travel magazine *OPEN WORLD* (US$18, free for members).

MINORITY TRAVELERS

Thanks to the continuous mix of races and cultures—indigenous, African, Japanese, Portuguese, and other Europeans—Brazilians are very, very curious about ethnic background and will often inquire pointedly about race and skin color (especially of East and South Asians); this is just small talk and is not considered offensive or impolite. Those with blond hair, blue eyes, and fair skin are really the only ones who will stand out in Brazil (in case you needed more incentive to work on that tan), and should expect more attention from beggars. As far as actual discrimination, really the only skin color that garners unwanted attention is the splotchy red sunburn all too common with backpackers; i.e., a backpack and Birkenstocks will single you out more than any ethnic background ever will.

TRAVELERS WITH CHILDREN

Brazilians adore children of all ages, and they will heartily welcome young travelers to most establishments. Most accommodations, museums, and tourist attractions offer discounts for children, but few restaurants have separate menus for kids. Children will love Brazil's top two attractions—the beaches and the outdoors—but remember that children are even more susceptible to the country's blistering heat (see **Heat Exhaustion,** p. 72) than adults are. Also be sure that your child always carries ID in case of an emergency.

Children under two generally fly for 10% of the adult airfare on international flights (this does not necessarily include a seat). International fares are usually discounted 25% for children from age two to 11. The following books are also great resources: *Adventuring with Children: An Inspirational Guide to World Travel and the Outdoors*, by Nan Jeffrey (Avalon House Publishing; US$15); *Backpacking with Babies and Small Children*, by Goldie Silverman (Wilderness Press; US$10); *Gutsy Mamas: Travel Tips and Wisdom for Mothers on the Road*, by Marybeth Bond (Travelers' Tales, Inc.; US$8); *Have Kid, Will Travel: 101 Survival Strategies for Vacationing With Babies and Young Children*, by Claire and Lucille Tristram (Andrews McMeel Publishing; US$9); and *Trouble Free Travel with Children*, by Vicki Lansky (Book Peddlers; US$9).

ESSENTIALS

DIETARY CONCERNS

Brazil is not the most accommodating place for those with strict dietary restrictions. The country's many outdoor markets and groceries are chock full of fresh, cheap fruits and vegetables of every type imaginable, but on meat-heavy restaurant menus there are often only limited options (i.e., rice, potatoes, and *farofa*) for vegetarians and vegans. Even simple vegetable stews and soups (including the traditional bean feast *feijoada*, p. 38) are made with animal stocks, and many restaurants don't consider fish and chicken part of the meat family. Surprisingly, the best places for vegetarians (who can stand the sight of an endless parade of cow carcasses) are the country's many **churrascarias,** which feature huge all-you-can-eat salad bars alongside the all-you-can-eat meat. The salad bars at omnipresent kilo restaurants (p. 39) are also a good veggie option. In general, the major tourist centers tend to have more options for those with dietary restrictions.

The **Vegetarian Resource Group's** travel section (www.vrg.org/travel) has countless helpful links to travel resources and restaurant lists. For more information, visit your local bookstore or health food store, and consult *The Vegetarian Traveler: Where to Stay if You're Vegetarian, Vegan, Environmentally Sensitive*, by Jed and Susan Civic (Larson Publications; US$16).

Travelers who keep kosher should contact the synagogues in larger cities of Brazil for information. Your own synagogue or college Hillel should have access to lists of Jewish institutions across the country, but Brazil's vast number of Israeli visitors means word of mouth is often the best way to get information on kosher dining. An excellent print resource is the helpful *Jewish Travel Guide*, edited by Michael Zaidner (US$17).

ADDITIONAL RESOURCES

Let's Go tries to cover all aspects of budget travel, but we can't put *everything* in our guides. Listed below are books and websites that should prove helpful. For listings of books on history, culture, music, and more, see the **Further Reading & Viewing** section of **Life & Times** (p. 43).

TRAVEL PUBLISHERS & BOOKSTORES

Travel Bookstores: Adventurous Traveler (☎800-282-3963; www.adventuroustraveler.com), the **South American Explorers'** bookstore (☎800-274-0568; www.saexplorers.org), the **Globe Corner Bookstore** (☎800-358-6013; www.globecorner.com), and **Hunter Publishing** (☎617-269-0700; www.hunterpublishing.com) all specialize in travel books.

Books From Brazil: Both www.brazilianbooks.com and www.lusobraz.com have excellent selections of books in Portuguese imported from Brazil as well as books on Brazil in English. The author of *The Brazilian Sound* maintains a list of useful English-language works on Brazil at www.thebraziliansound.com/books.htm.

WORLD WIDE WEB

Brazil's Internet presence varies from the very good to the very perfunctory, and much of what has been placed online has not yet been translated into languages other than English. Still, much useful information on Brazil can be found online, including the following useful sites.

ESSENTIALS

GENERAL TRAVEL INFORMATION

WWW.LETSGO.COM Our website, www.letsgo.com, now includes introductory chapters from all our guides and a wealth of information on a monthly featured destination. As always, our website also has info about our books, a travel forum buzzing with stories and tips, and additional links that will help you make the most of a trip to Brazil.

Budget Travel: For tips, travelogues, and links to further information on budget travel, check out www.artoftravel.com, budgettravel.about.com, and www.travel-library.com. The **South American Explorers** (www.saexplorers.org) have information more specific to South America.

Sustainable Travel: Business Enterprises for Sustainable Travel (BEST) supports travel that helps communities to preserve natural and cultural resources and to create sustainable livelihoods. Their website (www.sustainabletravel.org) has listings of local programs, innovative travel opportunities, and internships. See **Alternatives to Tourism,** p. 103, for more helpful organizations to contact.

INFORMATION ON BRAZIL

Basics: The CIA's World Factbook entry on Brazil (at http://www.odci.gov/cia/publications/factbook/geos/br.html) is a good country profile. The Brazilian Embassy in London's website (www.brazil.org.uk) has an extensive collection of articles on Brazil.

Culture: www.gringoes.com has articles on Brazilian culture for foreigners. cinemabrasil.org.br/indexen.html has summaries and reviews of over 500 Brazilian films. www.pelourinho.com has frequently-updated listings of Brazil-themed events worldwide, and an excellent page of links. Both brazilianmusic.com and www.allbrazilianmusic.com have excellent coverage of Brazilian music.

Health: www.who.int and www.paho.org are the World Health Organization's and the Pan-American Health Organization's websites, respectively. Both have extensive information on health risks for travelers, broken down by both country and by health concern. The WHO page on Brazil (www.who.int/country/bra/en/) is a useful overview, and Portuguese-speakers may also find the Brazilian Ministry of Health's homepage (www.saude.gov.br) useful.

Language: www.linguaportuguesa.ufrn.br/english.html has a history of world Portuguese with a focus on Brazilian Portuguese, and www.sonia-portuguese.com has resources for students of Brazilian Portuguese. Also, there are online dictionaries at www.travlang-com: dictionaries.travlang.com/EnglishPortuguese/ and dictionaries.travlang.com/PortugueseEnglish/.

News: www.radiobras.gov.br/internacional/ has news in English, as do news.nabou.com/world/brazil_news.html and www.brazilnews.com. The Paulista newspaper *O Estado do São Paulo* maintains a small but useful online section in English at www.estado.estado.com.br/english/english.html. Also good is http:/www.southamericadaily.com, which as the name suggests covers all of South America. For news coverage of Brazil from all over the world, check out news.google.com.

Sports: For general *futebol* information, try www.footymundo.com; www.querobrazil.com has an excellent overview of the Brazilian national team and its history. Run by the author of the book with the same name, www.futebolthebrazilianwayoflife.com has regular articles on Brazilian *futebol.* For current *futebol* news, check out www.fifa.com/en/index.html. www.capoeira.com hosts an online magazine, discussion boards, and overview of the sport.

Other Sites: www.maria-brazil.com has extensive information on Brazilian food and etiquette. Opinion and commentary on Brazil can be found at all of the following: www.brazilianist.com, www.brazilmax.com, www.infobrazil.com, and www.brazzil.com.

ALTERNATIVES TO TOURISM

The modern world's transportation infrastructure has made travel costs dwindle even as the areas accessible to travelers have greatly expanded; places that once required long and arduous journeys to reach now have direct flights and luxury hotels. Moreover, tourism has undergone a global boom in recent years and many developing countries—particularly those lacking natural resources, substantial domestic industry, or political and economic stability—have come to see tourism as their economic salvation; over the past two decades many of these nations have developed extensive resources in hope of attracting foreign visitors and, with them, foreign currency. In so doing, however, they also have exposed formerly pristine ecosystems and formerly isolated cultures to an onrush of often-intrusive visitors, whose presence has brought with it as much environmental and cultural degradation as wealth generation. Some governments and organizations have realized this and have begun to implement programs aimed at checking tourism's impact upon local communities, but these have been slow in coming.

Perhaps the simplest and most immediate way tourists can reduce the impact of their travels is by practicing **sustainable travel,** which borrows ideas and techniques from "leave no trace" hiking. Travelers so inclined attempt to travel without being tourists, or at least the invasive, gawky, and littering type of tourists whose very presence disrupts the natural and social environments through which they pass. It has become something of a global movement: www.sustainabletravel.org provides a useful overview, and the World Tourism Organization's recently launched Sustainable Tourism Eliminating Poverty program (www.st-ep.com) has information on the history of and motivation for sustainable travel.

A much more involved approach is to **volunteer:** working directly with a community can be a richly rewarding experience, but also can present complications and concerns above and beyond those of recreational traveling. Moreover, what a particular community may find useful may not be what the volunteer would enjoy doing. Volunteer programs may require longer-than-desired stays in a particular location, and few programs in Brazil accept volunteers for fewer than two-week commitments; hordes of volunteers streaming through an area are no less disruptive than are hordes of tourists. The advantage of volunteering can be twofold: in addition to a deeper experience of their destinations, volunteers will have left their own mark on the place, and thus have made travel into more of an exchange.

Study abroad programs can be a more middle-of-the-road alternative: like volunteer programs, visitors will stay in a small region and have more direct interaction with the local community, but with less responsibility and community involvement. Studying abroad is easiest for students, and for those not enrolled at a university, studying abroad can be among the most expensive ways to travel. A further drawback comes in the way of insular study abroad programs whose students mostly interact and socialize amongst themselves, and thus limit visitors to only a very superficial exposure to the destination country and local community.

For those who seek more active involvement, Earthwatch International, Habitat for Humanity, and Operation Crossroads Africa offer volunteer opportunities all over the world. For more on volunteering, studying, and working in Brazil and beyond, consult Let's Go's alternatives to tourism website, **www.beyondtourism.com.**

A NEW PHILOSOPHY OF TRAVEL

We at *Let's Go* know that the majority of travelers mean well and are not unconcerned with the state of the communities and environments they visit, but we also know that even conscientious tourists can inadvertently damage natural wonders and rich cultures. We believe the philosophy of **sustainable travel** is among the most important travel tips we could impart to our readers: by staying aware of the needs and troubles of local communities, travelers can be a powerful force in preserving and restoring this fragile world, and can potentially counteract some of the worst trends at work in the world today.

Responsible tourism can often be more a a matter of self-awareness than self-sacrifice: spending responsibly can promote the conservation of local resources more effectively than abstaining from expenditure, and sensitive, respectful interation with local cultures can have a greater positive impact than well-intentioned, self-imposed distance between locals and visitors. Information is the responsible traveler's single most powerful tool: a little conscientious research before traveling can go a long way when combined with a healthy mix of inquisitiveness and common sense while on the road. To further the cause of responsible tourism, *Let's Go* has partnered with **BEST** (**Business Enterprises for Sustainable Travel;** see www.sustainabletravel.org), which recognizes and promotes businesses whose operational practices follow the principles of sustainable travel. The following are some suggestions for traveling responsibly.

TIPS FOR RESPONSIBLE TRAVEL: HOW TO MAKE A DIFFERENCE

Read about your destination's history, culture, and recent news before arriving. You will not only better appreciate your travels but you will also find it easier to practice responsible travel when you are informed of issues particular to your destination.

Taking classes and watching cultural performances can be excellent ways to promote the preservation of local practices and traditions, but can also promote the corruption and commercialization of ancient practices. Where possible, inquire as to the authenticity of the material presented, the intentions of the presenters, and their relationship with both the general community and other practitioners.

Use mass transportation whenever possible. Where safe and feasible, walking and bicycling can be excellent ways to see a community firsthand.

Reduce, reuse, recycle–use electronic tickets, recycle papers and bottles wherever possible, and avoid using styrofoam containers. Refillable water bottles and rechargeable batteries both efficiently conserve expendable resources.

Take care not to buy souvenirs made from non-renewable resources, like trees from old-growth or endangered forests or items made from endangered species. Where possible, purchase souveniers that help preserve local traditions, but be careful: many seeming "local handicrafts" are manufactured in far-removed locales specifically for sale to tourists, and their purchase will do little to preserve local cultures.

Buy from local enterprises, as in developing countries many people depend on the "informal economy," but try not to purchase from businesses using non-sustainable practices, even if the businesses are locally owned.

If you are inspired by the natural environment or culture of a region, donating money to a local preservation organization can help maintain the region's integrity, as can spreading the word to friends and colleagues–travelers can not only introduce friends to particular destinations but also to causes and charities that they might choose to support when they travel to those areas.

VISA INFORMATION Students and volunteers will both require appropriate visas, and both student and volunteer visas can be acquired from the Brazilian consulate in one's home country. A visa holder must enter Brazil within 90 days of the visa's issue, and once in Brazil register with the federal police (DPMAF) within 30 days. Travelers should be warned that it is illegal to study or work in Brazil on a tourist visa. Requirements differ between the two visas:

Student Visa: passport; 2 passport photos; a copy of one's criminal record (only required of those over 18); 2 completed and signed application forms; a letter from the host institution; proof of sufficient funds for the stay (working on a student visa is illegal).

Voluntary Work Visa: photocopy of the relevant pages of one's passport; 3 passport photos; 3 completed and signed application forms; a copy of one's criminal record; a letter of invitation and program description from the volunteer program (must be notarized in Brazil); a written statement from the volunteer program assuming full responsibility for the maintenance of the applicant while in Brazil and for his/her return to the country of origin; proof of health insurance valid in Brazil (must be authenticated by the Brazilian consulate); a copy of the program's constitution and registration; proof that the Brazilian institution is fully functional.

VOLUNTEERING

Brazil's motto *ordem e progreso* ("order and progress") may be emblazoned across its flag, but the country's historic struggles to fulfill those two objectives have led Brazilians to call their country "the land of the future." To many observers Brazil's vast and deep resources—both natural and human—mean that Brazil's future must one day, some day, be bright. For the time being, however, Brazil remains mired in the economic and social issues that have long hindered it, and currently faces the emerging threat of environmental devastation, a problem Brazil's age-old issues only compound in severity. Many travelers come to be seduced by Brazil's natural beauty and electrifying culture, only to find themselves developing a deep concern for Brazilian society and the nation's future; also, many of Brazil's environmental problems potentially have global impact, and thus have drawn the attention of many who have never set foot within its borders. Many of those concerned wish to help in some way, and volunteering in Brazil often seems the most direct way to do so. It certainly can be: those in the hands of the right program, in the right location, and with work tailored to their skills and interests often find their volunteer work among their most rewarding experiences, and volunteering in Brazil is no different.

On the other hand, those in poorly managed or ill-conceived projects, in uncomfortable or otherwise unsuitable conditions, or doing work either of little personal interest or requiring undeveloped or excessive skills often find their volunteer efforts a well-intentioned exercise in futility, and Brazil is no different here, either. Volunteers are responsible first and foremost for their own research, and before committing to volunteer for any program, anywhere, should do as much research as possible into the program, the nature of the work, and their own personal interest and suitability for the work. Is the program well-organized, doing work that the volunteer will find meaningful and that the local community will find useful? If possible, ask to contact prior volunteers with your questions and take their comments more into account than any glossy brochures. However, no amount of satisfied testimonials from past volunteers will guarantee that a program is right for you; do your homework before leaving home. For advice on what questions to ask regarding the program, see the box below:

Before handing your money over to any volunteer or study abroad program, make sure you know exactly what you're getting into. It's a good idea to get the names of **previous participants** and ask them about their experience; the **questions** below are a good place to start:

How many participants will there be and what will they be like? What duties will they have? In what roles will you interact with them?
What will be your living arrangements? Are room and board included? What are meals like? If you have dietary restrictions, will you be able to meet them?
What transportation is included? Is assistance for arranging transport to your destination country and to the program site available? Included?
How much free time will you have? How is the program perceived in the local community? How do volunteers spend their off hours?
What kind of safety network is set up? What medical facilities are available?

Also, be aware that in Brazil—as in most developing countries—volunteers will likely need to pay their own way. Although volunteers with special skills (such as doctors, lawyers, and engineers) may sometimes have their expenses paid by their host program, volunteers should expect to cover all their own expenses, which usually include but are not limited to transportation both to and within their destination, health and travel insurance, immunizations, passports and visas, room, board, and any ancillary expenses; host programs typically charge a flat fee that covers room and board for the program's duration, and leave the rest to you. Many volunteers choose to employ volunteering agencies that handle the logistics of finding, contacting, and arranging a volunteer opportunity with a suitable organization. This is usually simpler than finding a volunteer program on one's own, and can be safer, as such agencies usually evaluate organizations and will refuse to list deficient or derelict operations. The primary drawbacks to using such an agency are that they typically charge additional fees and can sometimes hinder direct pre-commitment contact with the program with which a volunteer is placed.

Resources for volunteers abound, though of varying quality and reliability. Good general information for potential volunteers—especially for college students—is maintained at the University of California at Irvine Center for International Education (internships: www.cie.uci.edu/iop/internsh.html; volunteering: www.cie.uci.edu/iop/voluntee.html). *How to Live Your Dream of Volunteering Overseas*, by Collins, DeZerega, and Heckscher has admirably thorough information despite the title's hyperbole (Penguin Books, US$17).

CONSERVATION

Brazil's Amazon rainforest contains some of the world's most extreme biodiversity and its most beautiful scenery. Trees more than 30m tall host thousands of species (many not yet discovered) high in their branches while freshwater streams, rivers, and lakes course between their trunks and through their often-exposed root structures; here life's teeming adaptability and endurance leave visitors in awe. The Amazon also finds itself threatened on all sides: the slash-and-burn farming tactics impoverished locals rely upon for sustenance erode its fringes, the Transamazonica Highway and related infrastructure tear through its hearts, loggers devour its regions wholesale, and the list could go on.

Conservation efforts have sprung up worldwide to fight this destruction, ranging from land purchasing plans to legislative advocacy, and from restoration efforts to research and education. In many ways these are the simplest avenues for concerned citizens to become involved in rainforest preservation. Most nations and even many communities will have local branches and organizations, and much of the work can be done from outside Brazil.

Those seeking to volunteer in or around the Amazon will have a rougher time of it, because for reasons both legal and pragmatic there are far fewer meaningful opportunities available. Volunteering in the Amazon exposes one to far more serious health hazards than most volunteer work, even by developing world standards. Moreover, due to the Amazon's unique environment, much work being done in the Amazon, whether research or restoration, requires specialized skills and specific training. Despite these impediments, however, there are some programs in the Amazon open to most volunteers, which we list below; be aware, however, that many of these are quite popular and may require reservations far in advance.

Brazil's other regions have attracted less international attention but are no less in need of conservation efforts. Interested volunteers will often have an easier time arranging an opportunity in the Pantanal or along the coast than they would trying to arrange voluntary work in the Amazon. Fortunately, the work itself will be no less engrossing and rewarding.

IN THE AMAZON

ACDI/VOCA, 50 F St. NW, Ste. 1075, Washington, D.C. 20001, USA (☎800-929-8622; fax 202-626-8726; http://acdivoca.org). Open to US residents or permanent residents who have acquired ten or more years experience in professions related to international development, such as farming, banking, conservation, and agribusiness. Programs worldwide; its current program in Brazil seeks to develop economically and environmentally sustainable agricultural cooperatives in rural communities near the Amazon basin. Qualified volunteers will have all expenses covered and logistics arranged.

Amizade, 920 William Pitt Union, University of Pittsburgh, Pittsburgh, PA 15260, USA (☎888-973-4443; fax 412-648-1492; http://amizade.org). Works to arrange opportunities for individuals and groups to volunteer with local humanitarian and conservation non-profits; its Brazilian activities center around Santarém. Programs in Brazil average 2 weeks and require a US$350 deposit with application; program costs start from US$1400 for 2 weeks and include room, board, and program fees. Volunteers are responsible for their own transportation and insurance.

Earthwatch International, 3 Clock Tower Pl., Ste. 100, Box 75, Maynard, MA 01754, USA (toll free in the US and Canada ☎1-800-776-0188, 978-461-0081; fax 978-461-2332; www.earthwatch.org). Conducts research expeditions focused on issues of biodiversity and conservation with paying volunteers. Current programs include Amazon Turtles (in Tocantins), Pantanal Conservation Research Initiative (in Mato Grosso do Sul), and Dolphins of Brazil (in Santa Catarina). Expeditions last 7-12 days (US$1760-2260). Requires US$300 deposit. Volunteers must arrange their own travel.

ELSEWHERE IN BRAZIL

i-to-i (www.i-to-i.com). National offices: 9 Blenheim Terr., Leeds, LS2 9HZ, **UK** (☎870 333 2332; fax 113 242 2171); 8 E. 1st Ave., Ste. 104, Denver, CO 80203, **USA** (☎800-985-4864, 303-765-5325; fax 303-765-5327); Exploration House, 26 Main St., Dungarvan, Co Waterford, **Ireland** (☎353 0 58 40050). Arranges volunteer opportunities worldwide; its Brazilian programs are in Olinda and Recife and range from youth development and health services to conservation and English instruction. Programs last 4-12 weeks and start at about US$2000 (including US$295 deposit) for room, board, insurance, and any necessary training; volunteers arrange their own travel.

THE LOCAL STORY

IPÊTERRAS

***Elenu Pereira Machado** talks about Ipêterras (see right), her NGO dedicated to environmentally sensitive agriculture.*

On permaculture: Permaculture is the integration of traditional [agricultural] practices with alternative ones....Alternative practices generally create situations more in equilibrium with the environment....[Conventional techniques often employ] machines that cut and ruin the soil. Alternative practices introduce plants that strengthen the soil.

On Ipêterras: Ipêterras sprang up in the agriculture school of Esagri...through the permacultural courses [taught there]. Attending these courses were a group of people who didn't want...to be satisfied with theory, [who] wanted an area to practice [in].

On the NGO's programs: Ipêterras has [several programs]. One is the farm itself, within which people develop...a natural and organic lifestyle. Another is the Projeto Flocescer, a project that works in Mocozerio, our neighbor...to provide the community with environmental education and environmental practice....Another program is with sports and music...to revitalize those traditions that existed once here....We also have diverse offices for students in the school and the community to use.

Iracambi Atlantic Rainforest Research and Conservation Center, Fazenda Iracambi, Rosário da Limeira, MG 36878-000, Brazil (☎32 3721 1436; fax 32 3722 4909; www.iracambi.com). This support center for professional researchers also has volunteer opportunities. Responsibilities range from direct conservation efforts to improving the center's infrastructure. US$500 covers room and board for up to 3 months, with additional months (to a limit of 6) US$150 each; volunteers arrange their own transportation.

Ecovolunteer, 577/579 Fishponds Rd., 1st fl., Bristol, BS16 3AF, UK (☎0117 965 8333; fax 0117 937 5681; www.ecovolunteer.org). Offers paying volunteers the opportunity to assist efforts to protect and study endangered species; each program focuses on a specific species and provides volunteers with all needed training on arrival. Programs average 2-3 weeks and US$900-1300, not including transportation.

Ipêterras, Caixa Postal 27, Irecê, BA 44900-000, Brazil (☎74 9121 0776; Ipeterras@bol.com.br). A permacultural farm in the Northeast *sertão* that runs 2 other projects—one focused on education, the other on recording and revitalizing the region's popular culture. The cost of living on the farm is approximately R$60 per week, although costs vary depending on the season and are flexible based on the needs of both the farm and the volunteer. For a more in-depth look at the program, see **The Local Story** (at left), where Elenu Pereira Machado speaks first-hand about her program.

SOCIAL WORK

A traveler to Brazil who only visited Rio de Janeiro and São Paulo states might leave convinced that Brazil stood at the threshold of joining the developed world, but outside of the industrial Southeast there are only a few isolated pockets of development. Large swathes of Brazil lack even basic health or transportation infrastructure, and the country has a staggering income disparity that leaves most Brazilians impoverished, especially those in the *favelas*; social problems remain rife throughout Brazil.

HEALTH & EDUCATION

Cross-Cultural Solutions, 47 Potter Ave., New Rochelle, NY 10801, USA (☎914-632-0022; fax 914-632-8494; www.crossculturalsolutions.org). Coordinates volunteer opportunities with local NGOs around the world; most of its Brazilian offerings are in Salvador and focus on health education and outreach. Requires an initial US$275 deposit before organizing a volunteer opportunity, and once arranged further fundraising is the volunteer's responsibility.

Volunteer Brazil, Rua Ana Bilhar 123, Apt. 401, Meireles, Fortaleza, CE 60160-110, Brazil (☎85 9121 9001; fax 85 244 2362; www.volunteerbrazil.org). Coordinates with local programs to arrange opportunities for groups of international volunteers to volunteer together in and around Paraíba, working on projects including computer training and health education and outreach. Volunteers pay a one-time transportation fee of US$150 and approximately US$90 in fees per day; these cover room, board, insurance, excursions, and local transportation. Volunteer groups must arrange their own transportation to Brazil.

Associação do Jovem Aprendiz (AJA), Caixa Postal 10570, Lago Sul, Brasília, DF 71680-920, Brazil (☎61 427 0140; fax 61 427 0139; www.aja.org.br). NGO operating out of Brasília and Praia do Rosa coordinates a large range of programs for international volunteers; currently has projects to provide free English and computer-skills instruction, promote AIDS awareness, and integrate the disabled into mainstream Brazilian society. Programs average 2-8 weeks and cost US$2300-3300, which includes lodging in an apartment, 2hr. per week of Portuguese instruction, and work-related transportation. Volunteers must arrange their own transportation and immunizations.

Amity Volunteer Teachers Abroad, Amity Institute, 3065 Rosencrans Pl., Ste. 104, San Diego, CA 92110, USA (☎619-222-7000; fax 619-222-7016; www.amity.org). Coordinates volunteer teachers with host institutions throughout the world, including Brazil. Volunteers must have prior experience living abroad and teaching, and some competency in the host country's language is preferred. Qualified volunteers will receive room, board, and a small stipend from the host institution, but will still be responsible for their own travel arrangements and immunizations, as well as a placement fee (US$500).

Amazon-Africa Aid Organization (3AO), P.O. Box 7776 Ann Arbor, MI 48107, USA (☎734-769-5778; fax 734-769-5779; www.amazonafrica.org). Arranges volunteer opportunities–mainly for doctors and dentists–through the Brazilian non-profit Fundação Esperança, which provides health care and related services to needy populations in and around Santarém. Most programs require a 1-month minimum commitment, but for qualified volunteers most expenses will be compensated if needed.

OTHER OPPORTUNITIES

AMIGOS, Amigos de las Américas, 5618 Star Ln., Houston, TX 77057, USA (☎800-231-7796; fax 713-782-9267; www.amigoslink.org). Arranges for students having completed their sophomore year of high school to volunteer in Latin America during the summer. Provides volunteers with training and assistance fund-raising. Its 7-week program in Brazil focuses on sustainable development in Rio Grande do Norte (US$3900).

World Youth International, 18 3rd St., Brompton 5007, South Australia, Australia (☎8 8340 1266; fax 8 8340 3677; http://worldyouth.com.au). Arranges volunteer opportunities around the world for Australians and New Zealanders. Their program in Brazil lasts about 10 weeks (AUS$4495) and divides its time between Campinas and Salvador, with excursions to Rio de Janeiro and the Pantanal. Volunteers receive individual projects in each location.

YMCA Go Global Program, 5 W. 63rd St., New York, NY 10023, USA (toll-free in the US and Canada ☎888-477-9622, 212-727-8800; fax 212-727-8814; www.ymcainternational.org/GOGlobal/home.htm). Runs programs in São Paulo and Belo Horizonte lasting 3 months (Feb.-Apr. or June-Aug.). Application fee US$250.

TEACHING ENGLISH

Those looking to volunteer as English teachers in Brazil have many options as most volunteer programs have some English teaching component. However, working as an English teacher in Brazil can be rough going: teaching jobs abroad

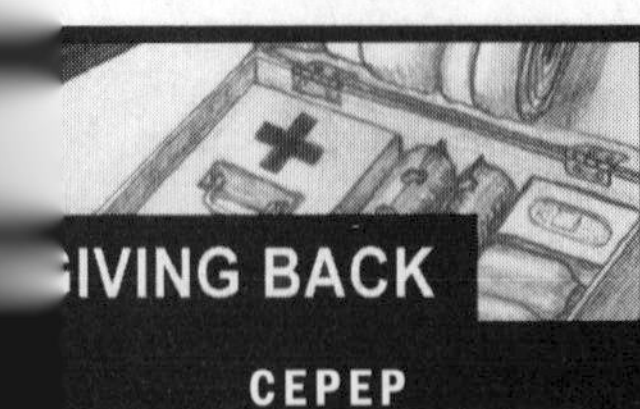

IVING BACK

CEPEP

'he shouts of happy children oreak the silence of a quiet residential neighborhood only minutes away from Belo Horizonte's argest *favelas*. This is the sound of students enjoying their stay at **CEPEP (Centro Educacional Proessor Estêvão Pinto),** the only organization in Minas Gerais to have thrice won Brazil's prestigious Prêmio Bem Eficiente, which s awarded annually to the nation's 50 most-effective NGOs.

CEPEP aims to improve the ives of local children in Belo hrough a variety of programs taiored to their changing needs as hey grow: infants and young children—and their parents—can take advantage of free day-care, while older children come to CEPEP for music instruction, outdoor activiies, art classes, and other programs. CEPEP even helps eenagers land their first jobs, and assists Brazilian youths in developing employable skills through nstructional programs. More than '00 infants, children, and adolescents currently benefit from these ree programs, and many any also eceive free medical and dental care from CEPEP.

CEPEP is currently staffed by partime volunteers, but is interested n having full-time volunteers from overseas; volunteers must speak Portuguese. For more information, vrite to cepep@metalink.com.br.

are rarely well-paid, and Brazil's educational system makes it difficult for those without some form of teaching certification to teach in any official fashion. Those seeking compensation for their labor will almost always require a bachelor's degree and specialized certification, usually the **Teaching English as a Foreign Language (TEFL)** certificate. Paid teachers will likely be expected to prepare students for one of the standardized examinations in English language proficiency, and K-12 teachers in Brazil are usually required to have an education degree.

Brazil's most widespread exam in English is the **Test of English as a Foreign Language (TOEFL),** used by US colleges and universities to evaluate foreign applicants' English language proficiency. Less typical in Brazil are the **Test of English for Foreign Communication (TOEFC), International English Language Testing System (IELTS),** and **Certificate of Proficiency in English (CPE).** The TOEFC is used by firms to evaluate applicants' English abilities and is most often taken by those seeking employment in the US. The IELTS is the United Kingdom's equivalent of the TOEFL, and the CPE is in Europe analogous to the TOEFC.

General resources for those looking to teach abroad include Dave's ESL Cafe (www.eslcafe.com) and the Teachers of English as a Second Language organization's homepage (www.tesol.org); the eclectic and astoundingly detailed English Made in Brazil webpage (www.sk.com.br) has a range of practical advice and resources for those teaching English to Portuguese speakers and an encyclopedic collection of pertinent links.

Associação Escola Graduada de São Paulo, Caixa Postal 1976, CEP 01059-970, São Paulo, SP, Brazil (☎11 3747 4800; fax 11 3742 9358; www.graded.br). One of Brazil's oldest non-missionary English language academies. Teachers here are paid salaries competitive with most offered by most US institutions, and hiring is equally competitive.

Association of American Schools in South America (AASSA), 14750 NW 77th Court, Ste. 210, Miami Lakes, FL 33016, USA (☎305-821-0345; fax 305-821-4244; www.aassa.com). Holds annual teacher recruitment conferences to help place prospective teachers in American schools throughout South America, including several schools in Brazil; website often lists positions available.

International Schools Services, 15 Roszel Rd., P.O. Box 5910, Princeton, NJ 08543, USA (☎609-452-0990; fax 609-452-2690; www.iss.edu). Consulting agency for school administrators holds annual job fairs for teachers looking to teach abroad; many private Brazilian institutions recruit primarily from these fairs.

Network Of International Christian Schools, P.O. Box 1260, Southaven, MS 38671, USA (☎800-887-6427; fax 662-796-1840; www.nics.org). A consortium of missionary schools worldwide, including Brazil. Will help find placement for those looking to teach abroad and willing to take a pledge of faith.

Search-Associates (www.search-associates.com). A consortium of agents who help find placements for experienced teachers looking to teach abroad, and help schools abroad recruit experienced teachers; used by many private institutions in Brazil.

STUDYING ABROAD

If the point of travel is to take in and come to appreciate another culture, study abroad programs may well be the ultimate form of travel. They are a chance to immerse oneself in a culture with assistance and guidance from those who have known it since birth and from experts who know best how to communicate cross-culturally. Like any other kind of travel, however, there is a great variety of study abroad programs, not all of which will be suited to a particular traveler. Although study abroad programs often aim to introduce participants to what for them is an unknown and unfamiliar culture, prospective students will benefit greatly from knowing their own objectives in studying abroad and from familiarizing themselves with their desired program's requirements. If nothing else, this will make it easier to choose from the many types of study abroad programs, which range from basic language and culture courses to college-level classes, often for credit. The usual suggestions still apply, as well: prospective students will benefit from determining a program's cost and duration, and from assessing the types of students it attracts (college students? business executives?) and the types of accommodation it arranges (homestays? apartments? hotels?).

Schools that focus exclusively or nearly exclusively on **language instruction** tend to be privately operated (i.e., not affiliated with a university) and can often be quite good and quite expensive. Typical students are executives needing crash courses in a language and college students needing intensive training; Brazil has comparatively few language schools with sizable programs for students not yet in college. The primary advantage of such schools is twofold: with language instruction as their focus, the quality of instruction is often quite high, even with a lower workload than university programs, and because they operate year-round for a diverse clientele such institutions often have very flexible schedules. Their disadvantages are that they can often be quite expensive and, for college students, often transferring any credits earned can be difficult and costly.

Many American **universities** operate study abroad programs in Brazil. These are intended primarily for undergraduate, graduate, and other degree-seeking students enrolled at accredited colleges and universities. Such programs typically run for a summer, semester, or year. Although nearly every such program offers intensive Portuguese instruction many also require past study of the language, as much of the non-language coursework will likely be related to Brazilian studies and conducted in Portuguese. For some students this can be a very affordable study abroad option, as one's regular tuition may cover most expenses involved in studying abroad. Also, transferring credits from such university-sponsored programs is usually far simpler than transferring credits earned at a language school.

There are **other options** for study abroad—many of them excellent—that are neither directly affiliated with a university nor at all resembling a language school. Another option, particularly for those already fluent in Portuguese, is to try directly contacting and enrolling at a Brazilian university; http://darkwing.uoregon.edu/~sergiok/brasil/bruniversities.html maintains an excellent list of Brazil's institutions of higher education.

LANGUAGE SCHOOLS

It goes without saying that oftentimes the most effective way to develop proficiency in a language is to study it in a country where it is spoken, particularly for languages little-spoken or little-studied elsewhere; Brazilian Portuguese is one of these. Like volunteer programs, language programs come in all costs and qualities. At the best programs beginning students will build a solid foundation in the country's language and their advanced students will leave with their skills finely polished. The worst programs often amount to little more than very expensive vacations. Language programs often can easily arrange for extended or customized instruction, although both usually cost extra. Also, language instruction programs typically have classes targeted for specific types of learners, such as programs for college students, business executives, high school students, and so forth; as with volunteer programs it will pay to research a particular program before committing.

Bridge-Linguatec International, 915 S. Colorado Blvd., Denver, CO 80246, USA (☎800-724-4210; fax 303-777-7246; www.bridgelinguatec.com). Has offerings throughout South America, including Portuguese instruction offered in Rio de Janeiro and São Paulo; instructional methods range from group classes to private immersion. Classes last 2-4 weeks (additional weeks can be arranged) and cost US$800-5000, not including transportation, insurance, and immunizations. Students mostly are housed in homestays, which provide breakfast, dinners, and weekend lunches.

Diálogo, Rua Dr. João Pondé 240, Barra, Salvador, BA 40120-411, Brazil (☎71 264 0007; fax 71 364 0053; www.dialogo-brazilstudy.com). Has a language school in Salvador offering instruction in Portuguese for individuals and groups as well as cultural enrichment programs. Various housing arrangements available. Most programs last 2-4 weeks (US$900-2000).

AFS Intercultural Programs, 198 Madison Ave., 8th fl., New York, NY 10016, **USA** (☎212-299-9000; fax 212-299-9090; www.afs.org). Travessa do Ouvidor 50, 8th fl., Centro, Rio de Janeiro, RJ 20040-040, **Brazil** (☎21 2224 4464; www.afs.org.br). Their School Year Program places high school students (ages 15-18) around the world in study abroad programs for 6-12 months, including Brazil (US$7175). Their Community Service Program arranges 5- to 6-month internships (US$4200) for volunteers (ages 19-40) with local NGOs. Program cost includes most transportation, insurance, and living expenses; participants are responsible for immunizations.

FirstStep BRAZIL, Joe Collaço 99, Corrego Grande, Florianópolis, SC 888037-010, Brazil (☎21 2267 3271; fax 21 2513 3787; www.firststepbrazil.com). Portuguese instruction in Florianópolis, which assists in acquiring university credit for coursework. Also arranges community service for a fee (US$25-100). Classes range 3-7hr. per day and last 1-4 weeks (US$345-3445). Additional weeks US$300-800.

Languages Abroad, 413 Ontario St., Toronto, ON M5A 2V9, Canada (☎800-219-9924; fax 416-925-5990; www.languagesabroad.com). Large foreign language instruction company, with programs for students, volunteers, and corporate learners. Its Brazilian options are located in Rio, Salvador, and Maceió. Classes last 2-4 weeks (can be extended on request) and cost US$800-2000, not including transportation, insurance, and immunizations. A variety of housing options are available. None of the Brazilian programs currently offer academic credit.

Council on International Educational Exchange (CIEE), 633 3rd Ave., 20th fl., New York, NY 10017, USA (☎800-407-8839; www.ciee.org/study). Sponsors work, volunteer, academic, and internship programs around the world, including São Paulo and Salvador. Programs affiliated with Pontificía Universidade Católica de São Paulo and Universidade Católica do Salvador available for a semester (US$9000-9600) or year

(US$15,250-18,500). Shorter programs affiliated with Universidade de São Paulo and Universidade Federal da Bahia lasting 5 weeks also offered (US$3000). Language programs open to students with 2 years previous instruction in Portuguese or Spanish.

Amerispan Unlimited, P.O. Box 58129, Philadelphia, PA 19102, USA (in the US and Canada ☎800-879-6640, elsewhere ☎215-751-1100; fax 215-751-1986; www.amerispan.com). Language education programs worldwide, including Brazilian Portuguese offerings in Maceió and Rio de Janeiro. For a fee, academic credits are available for coursework. Homestays can be arranged. Classes range 1-4 weeks (US$315-4340), not including transportation and immunizations. Required registration fee US$100.

UNIVERSITY PROGRAMS

All programs listed below have websites detailing their costs, offerings, and requirements; you should start your research there before applying to any institution's study abroad program. Most will also expect you to coordinate your study abroad program through the appropriate office at the school at which you are currently enrolled.

Brown in Brazil, Office of International Programs, Box 1973, Brown University, Providence, RI 02912, USA (☎401-863-3555; fax 401-863-3311; www.brown.edu/Administration/OIP/files/programs/brazil/). Students spend the fall semester (Aug.-Dec.) or a full year (July-June) studying at Pontificía Universidade Católica in Rio, with all coursework conducted in Portuguese. Program arranges homestays for students. Open to students in good academic standing having taken at least 3 semesters of college-level Portuguese and 1 course on a related topic. Tuition $14,600 for 1 semester, $29,200 for 1 year, not including living expenses and transportation.

Antioch College, Antioch Education Abroad, 795 Livermore St., Yellow Springs, OH 45387, USA (☎800-874-7986; fax 937-769-1019; www.antioch-college.edu/AEA/). Fall-term program focuses on Brazil's ecosystems and on ecological concerns specific to Brazil, dividing its time in various regions of the country. Affiliated with Universidade Federal do Paraná and Universidade Federal do Mato Grosso. Open to students in good standing having completed 2 years of college and having taken at least 1 course in ecology or environmental biology.

University of Kansas, Office of Study Abroad, Lippincott Hall, 1410 Jayhawk Blvd., Rm. 108, Lawrence, KS 66045, USA (☎785-864-3742; fax 785-864-5040; www.ku.edu/~brasilis/). June-July language and culture program in Vitória. Program fee US$2550; homestays US$430. Students must arrange transportation and immunizations.

Loyola University New Orleans School of Law, 7214 St. Charles Ave., Box 901, New Orleans, LA 70118, USA (☎504-861-5563; fax 504-861-5733; http://law.loyno.edu/fsp/brazil/). Offers a summer program on Latin American legal systems.

Temple University, International Programs, 200 Tuttleman Learning Center, Philadelphia, PA 19122, USA (☎215-204-0720; www.temple.edu/studyabroad). Summer (July-Aug.) program in Salvador features instruction in Portuguese and in Afro-Brazilian culture. Affiliated with Universidade do Estado da Bahia. Open to full-time students in good academic standing, preferably with prior coursework in or experience of topics and issues related to Latin America. Tuition US$1700-3000 plus US$100 program fee.

SUNY New Paltz, 75 South Manheim Blvd., Ste. 9, New Paltz, NY 12561, USA (☎845-257-3125, fax 845-257-3129; www.newpaltz.edu/studyabroad/prog_fasp_brazil.html). Has language and cultural programs based at Pontificía Universidade Católica in Rio; all coursework conducted in Portuguese. Open to college sophomores, juniors, and seniors in good academic standing and with 2 years of coursework in Portuguese or Spanish. Tuition US$4162.50, US$1712.50 for residents of New York state. Has semester (fall: Aug.-Dec.; spring: Mar.-July) and year (Aug.-July) programs.

OTHER STUDY ABROAD

All of the programs below are usually administered through educational institutions but are otherwise independent; this arrangement means that these programs often have the flexibility and focus of a language school and students may find it easier to transfer credits, if needed.

School for International Training, P.O. Box 676, Kipling Rd., Brattleboro, VT 05302, USA (☎888-272-7881; fax 802-258-3296; www.sit.edu). Arranges study abroad programs for credit, with curricula that focus on social and environmental issues in the host country; SIT's recent programs in Brazil have focused on Amazonian ecology and on Brazil's economic development. 1 semester averages $12,000 for room, board, and tuition. Students are responsible for transportation and immunizations.

Experiment in International Living, Kipling Rd., P.O. Box 676, Brattleboro, VT 05302, USA (toll-free in the US and Canada 800-345-2929, 802-257-7751; fax 802-258-3428; www.usexperiment.org/countries/brazil.html). Runs summer programs for high school students. Their 5-week programs in Brazil focus on community service, ecological preservation, or urban planning, and include a 2-week homestay (US$4850).

Operations Crossroads Africa, P.O. Box 5570, New York, NY 10027, USA (☎212-289-1949, fax 212-289-2526; http://oca.igc.org). Its Diaspora program spends a summer studying Afro-Brazilian culture in a *favela* outside Salvador. US$3500 covers room, board, program fees, health insurance, visas, and transportation to Salvador from New York City; applicants submit US$25 fee with application. Successful applicants are responsible for immunizations and travel to New York.

FOR FURTHER READING ON ALTERNATIVES TO TOURISM

Alternatives to the Peace Corps: A directory of third world and U.S. Volunteer Opportunities, by Joan Powell. Food First Books, 2000 (US$10).

How to Live Your Dream of Volunteering Oversees, by Collins, DeZerega, and Heckscher. Penguin Books, 2002 (US$17).

International Directory of Voluntary Work, by Whetter and Pybus. Peterson's Guides and Vacation Work, 2000 (US$16).

International Jobs, by Kocher and Segal. Perseus Books, 1999 (US$18).

Overseas Summer Jobs 2002, by Collier and Woodworth. Peterson's Guides and Vacation Work, 2002 (US$18).

Work Abroad: The Complete Guide to Finding a Job Overseas, by Hubbs, Griffith, and Nolting. Transitions Abroad Publishing, 2000 (US$16).

Work Your Way Around the World, by Susan Griffith. Worldview Publishing Services, 2001 (US$18).

RIO DE JANEIRO

Rio is less a city than a way of life. Amidst endless sunshine, endless beaches, and endless nighttime debauchery, the more than seven million residents of Rio (known as Cariocas) spend their days pursuing pleasure in all aspects of their life—be it *samba*, soccer, sand, or sex—with a determination so infectious that few visitors can resist following suit. The most famous expression of this hedonistic lifestyle is Rio's legendary **Carnaval** (see p. 47), but the city has attractions year-round to suit every taste. Crammed into a thin strip between lush mountains and ravishing beachfront—perhaps the most breathtaking setting on the planet—you'll find something that pleases, from the Floresta da Tijuca's hiking trails to Centro's historic streets, from Leblon's famous *botequins* to Lapa's sweaty dance halls—not to mention the legendary, sun-kissed sands of Copacabana and Ipanema.

While Brasília is the country's political capital, São Paulo its economic center, and Salvador its cultural highlight, Rio is unquestioningly Brazil's heart (no doubt thumping to the syncopated rhythms of a *samba* school *batucada*) and soul. South America's most visited destination and Brazil's international representative, this is the birthplace of all the country is known for: incongruously, both *feijoada* (hearty bean stew) and the *fio dental* (string bikini) first appeared here, and one ambling stroll down Ipanema's streets leaves little doubt that this is the birthplace of the smooth, sexy beats of *bossa nova.*

No paradise is without its problems, and the Cidade Maravilhosa ("Marvelous City") is no exception. Brazil's vast chasm between rich and poor is nowhere more striking (or more tense) than in Rio, where every fourth Carioca lives in the poverty of the *favelas*, literally next door to the million-dollar high-rises of the ritzy Zona Sul. In the democratic era, the former Imperial and Republican capital of Brazil has earned a reputation among travelers as one of the world's most dangerous destinations. In reality, petty crime is the main threat to travelers, but no more so than in other developed major cities. And although the gang- and drug-related violence continues, most of it occurs between police and drug lords in the *favelas* and poorer suburbs where travelers would never venture. In truth, no amount of bad press can detract from Rio's stunning attractions, both natural and naughty.

HIGHLIGHTS OF RIO DE JANEIRO

SAMBA 'TIL DAWN during Rio's ribald Carnaval (p. 46). Out-of-season revelers can get a sample of the pre-Lenten bacchanalia at a *samba* school rehearsal (p. 52).

SIP SUNSET CAIPIRINHAS atop the scenic Pão de Açúcar (p. 137) and Corcovado (p. 137) mountains. The views ain't too bad either.

GOOOOOOOL! A game at Maracanã (p. 153), where Brazil's obsession with *futebol* is at its most frenzied, is not to be missed.

FRY TO A CRISP with the tall and tan and young lovelies of Ipanema or Copacabana (p. 150).

LET LOOSE with tourists, trannies, Rastas, goths, and slumming beach bunnies at Rio's biggest baddest *samba* street party, in the shadow of the Arcos de Lapa (p. 144).

SOAR with a heart-stopping hang glide off Pedra Bonita (p. 152).

DAYTRIP Sick of Rio already? Head to tranquil island paradise Ilha Grande (p. 166) or sexy resort town Búzios (p. 172).

INTERCITY TRANSPORTATION

The *rodoviária* and both airports have luggage storage, as well as currency exchange and ATMs.

Flights: Galeão, a.k.a. Aeroporto Internacional Tom Jobim (☎3398 4106)—the only airport in the world with a *samba* written for it—is 15km north of downtown; it serves most flights. Upon arrival, ignore all rip-off offers from the gray-smocked "staff" who follow you around offering taxis, hotels, currency, etc. **Real Auto Bus** (☎2560 7041) runs a secure A/C bus route from their 1st fl. airport office all the way to Barra da Tijuca, passing the *rodoviária,* Centro's Av. Rio Branco, Aeroporto Santos Dumont, Glória/Catete, Botafogo, Copa's Av. Atlântica, and Ipanema's Av. Vieira Souto (1½hr.; every 30min. 5:30am-midnight; R$5). **Taxis:** *comum* R$30-35, *rádio* R$50 (2nd fl.). Domestic flights sometimes use Centro's **Aeroporto Santos Dumont** (☎3814 7070), accessible by Real Auto Bus, any local "Santos Dumont" bus, or taxi (R$10-25).

Buses: Rodoviária Novo Rio, Av. Bicalho 1 (☎2291 5151; www.novorio.com.br), northwest of Centro in a less than desirable area. To get there, you can take an "Integrado Ônibus" (R$2.60) from the M: Estácio stop or any local "Rodoviária" bus, but taxis (R$15-20) are considered safer. The rádio taxis outside the *rodoviária* are overpriced; there are cheaper *comum* taxis near the local bus depot just across the street. Scheduled buses include the following; call the company or check the Novo Rio website for the most updated schedules and online booking:

DESTINATION	COMPANY	DURATION	TYPE	FREQUENCY	PRICE
Angra dos Reis (RJ)	Costa Verde (☎2233 3809)	3hr.	*conv.*	18 per day 4am-10pm	R$19
Belo Horizonte (MG)	Útil (☎2518 5536)	6½hr.	*conv.* *exec.* *leito*	3 per day (time varies) 11am 11:45pm	R$40 R$52 R$67
Brasília (DF)	Itapemirim (☎2516 8284)	17hr.	*exec.* *leito*	4 per day 1:30-9pm 2:30pm	R$101 R$115-125
Búzios (RJ)	1001 (☎0300 313 1001)	3hr.	*conv.*	8 per day 7am-7pm	R$12-14
Campo Grande (MS)	Andorinha (☎2253 7289)	21-24hr.	*exec.* *leito*	4 per day 9am-9pm Su, Th 3pm	R$116 R$140
Curitiba (PR)	Itapemirim (☎2516 8284)	13hr.	*exec.* *leito*	2 per day 9:30am-8pm 2 per day 7-8pm	R$79 R$100
Florianópolis (SC)	Itapemirim (☎2516 8284)	18hr.	*conv.* *exec.* *leito*	F 3:15pm 4:30pm M, W, F 3:50pm	R$94 R$105 R$160
Foz do Iguaçu (PR)	Pluma (☎2263 9471)	20hr.	*exec.*	3 per day 8am-3pm	R$102
Mangaratiba (RJ)	Costa Verde (☎2233 3809)	2hr.	*conv.*	4 per day 5am-6pm	R$15
Ouro Preto (MG)	Útil (☎2518 5536)	7hr.	*conv.*	11:30pm	R$37
Paraty (RJ)	Costa Verde (☎2233 3809)	4hr.	*conv.*	8 per day 9am-10pm	R$21
Porto Seguro (BA)	São Geraldo (☎2263 9008)	19hr.	*exec.*	8:15pm	R$99
São Paulo (SP)	many, including Itapemirim (☎2516 8284)	5½hr.	*conv.* *exec.* *leito*	2 per day 9am-10pm 13 per day 7am-1am 3 per day 11pm-1am	R$36 R$42 R$57
Salvador (BA)	Itapemirim (☎2516 8284)	26-28hr. 24hr.	*exec.* *leito*	9:15am 2:30pm	R$145 R$170

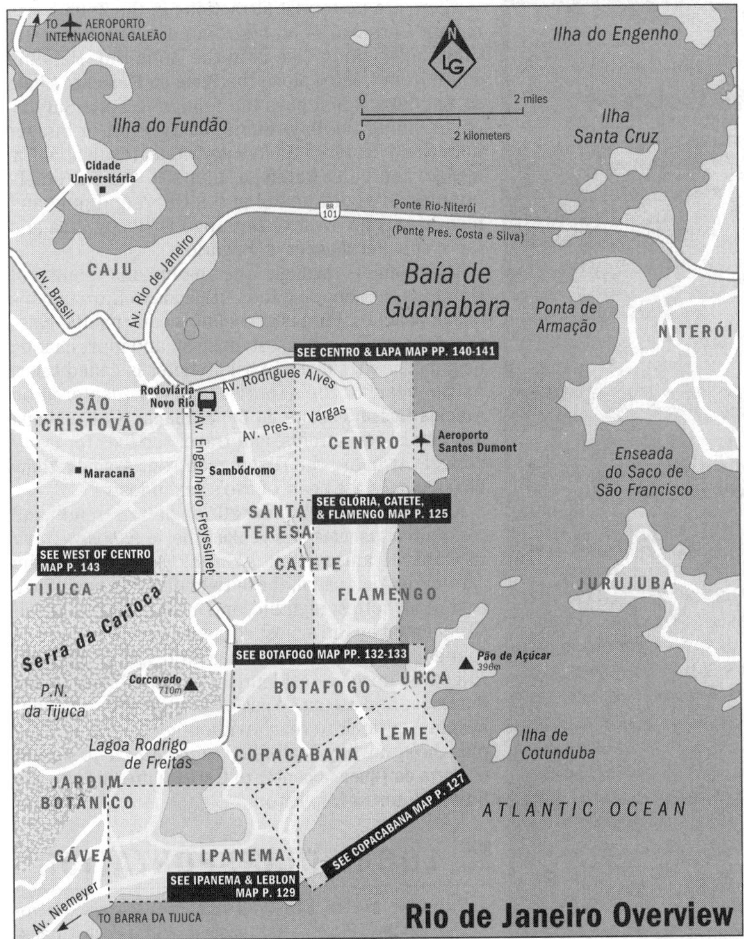

ORIENTATION

Rio de Janeiro juts out into Guanabara Bay and the Atlantic, with *bairros* (neighborhoods) hugging the coast and crammed into the thin strip of land between the mountains and the sea. The Serra da Carioca mountain range—home to **Corcovado** and the **Cristo Redentor** (Christ the Redeemer) statue—divides Rio into the industrial, lower-class **Zona Norte** (north zone) and the wealthier, beach-crazed **Zona Sul** (south zone). The two zones meet in the historic downtown business district **Centro,** centered on **Avenida Rio Branco** and **Cinelândia** (at M: Cinelândia, a.k.a. Pça. Floriano). Centro is home to most of Rio's historic sights and museums. Just southwest is the dilapidated nightlife district **Lapa** (near the Lapa Arches), and beyond that the artsy hilltop enclave **Santa Teresa.**

IN RECENT NEWS

FAVELAS

Blanketing the mountainsides on the outskirts of Rio (and many other Brazilian cities) are illegal shantytowns known as *favelas*. The gap between Rio's rich and poor has always been wide, and seems only to grow wider. Since the early 20th century, impoverished residents have squatted on government lands (mostly the mountainous parklands around the city), and these *favelas* only continue to expand. Many are located right alongside wealthy neighborhoods; Rocinha, the city's largest *favela* (which even has a designated bus line), runs right down the mountain to Gávea, the city's richest suburb. *Favelas* are unrecognized by the government, so they pay no taxes and receive nothing in return—no infrastructure, benefits, or acknowledgement on a map. *Favelas* have no paved roads, waste disposal services, or educational and health care facilities (much of the beach pollution after big rainstorms is *favela* garbage washed down the hillside). Water is scarce, electricity scarcer, and all of it is tapped unreliably and illegally from city resources. *Favelas* are also the center of Rio's illegal drug industry and its violent warring cartels, most of them run by heavily armed youths who rarely make it out of their teens.

It is estimated that one in every four Cariocas lives in a *favela;* many do cheap labor for middle-

(Continued on next page)

There are no tourist attractions in the Zona Norte except Carnaval's Sambódromo and Maracanã stadium; everything else is in the Zona Sul. Heading south from Centro along the **Praia do Flamengo/Praia do Botafogo,** you'll pass the following Zona Sul districts, lining the bay: **Glória/Catete,** full of budget hotels and centered on **Rua do Catete;** residential **Flamengo;** and quiet **Botafogo,** home to the extremely popular HI youth hostel and a thriving dining and nightlife scene. East of Botafogo is sleepy **Urca** and the scenic **Pão de Açúcar** (Sugarloaf).

The tunnel through the mountains south of Botafogo (at Shopping Rio Sul) leads to Rio's famous ocean beaches. First is glitzy but seedily middle-class **Copacabana,** Rio's densest, busiest, and most chaotic neighborhood. Copa's first kilometer is called **Leme.** As the heart of Rio's tourist industry (centered on **Avenida Nossa Senhora de Copacabana)**, Copacabana has hotels, restaurants, and travel services for every budget. At night, the ritzy beachfront **Avenida Atlântica** becomes the heart of Rio's sex industry.

Abutting Copa at a near-90° angle are trendy and residential **Ipanema** and **Leblon,** the sexy *bossa nova* to Copa's frantic urban *samba*. Separated by the Jardim de Alah canal, these twin districts have Rio's best food, hottest nightlife, and most gorgeous beach (frequented by Rio's most gorgeous people). North of Ipanema is the lagoon Lagoa Rodrigo de Freitas, ringed by upscale residential districts **Gávea, Jardim Botânico,** and **Lagoa.** West of Leblon are excellent beaches difficult to reach without a car (see p. 151), plus the sprawling, mall-filled *nouveau riche* suburb of **Barra da Tijuca,** a center of Carioca life but offering little of interest for visitors.

LOCAL TRANSPORTATION

Subway: Metrô Rio (☎3982 3600; www.metrorio.com.br). Rio's safest, easiest, and quickest transport—too bad it closes at 11pm. **Linha 1** runs between Copacabana and Centro, **linha 2** between Centro and the Zona Norte. There's no *metrô* in Ipanema, but an "Integrado Ônibus" fare (R$2.60) includes transfer between either of the Copacabana *metrô* stops and a bus to/from Ipanema's Pça. Osório. Fare R$1.88. Open M-Sa 6am-11pm.

Buses: Hold on tight! Rio's 24hr. bus system is safer during the day, but many do not recommend it for tourists after 11pm. Front windows list route number, destination, and stops en route. Flag down buses at designated stops (covered benches or posts with blue signs). Board and pay at the back and exit at the front; pull the ceiling cord to stop. Buses come with or without A/C *(ar condicionado):* the former are called *frescão* and are considered more comfortable and less unsafe. R$1.40, *frescão* R$1.60.

Vans & Kombis: These minivans darting in and out of bus queues cost R$2-4 and run directly to faraway suburbs and major destinations (you pay more for the non-stop route). They're cramped and hot, and moreover are illegal, controlled by mobsters, and unregulated by police. *Let's Go* recommends avoiding them.

Taxis: Metered **comum taxis** (yellow with a blue stripe) are cheap, omnipresent, and frighteningly fast. Drivers often take the most roundabout route (fares are by distance), and should only take 4 passengers (to ask for 5: *"Pode levar cinco?"*). Rate 1: base fare R$2.70, plus R$0.87 per km and R$0.10 per min. Rate 2 (20% higher per km rate) charged daily 9pm-5am. **Rádio taxis** have pre-arranged (pricier) fares for those wary of being overcharged. Try **Coopertramo** (☎2560 2022), **Cootr\amo** (☎2560 5442), or **Transcoopass** (☎2560 4888). Sample *comum* fares for negotiation include:

From Copacabana to: Botafogo (R$10); Centro/Lapa (R$16); Glória/Catete (R$14); Ipanema (R$7); Pão de Açúcar or Corcovado (R$12).

From Glória/Catete to: Botafogo (R$9); Centro/Lapa (R$6); Copacabana (R$14); Ipanema (R$17); Pão de Açúcar or Corcovado (R$8-10).

Car Rental: Avoid having a car in Rio—parking is scarce, roads are confusing, and drivers are crazy. International rental agencies have offices at both airports (see p. 116) and along Copacabana's Av. Princesa Isabel.

Bike Rental: Rio has 74km of *ciclóvias* (bike paths), which run around the Lagoa and along the beaches. For rentals (averaging R$2-5 per hr.), try: Copacabana's **Frente Bike Rental,** Rua Figueiredo de Magalhães 285 (☎2257 1726); Ipanema's **Special Bike,** Rua Visconde de Pirajá 135 (☎2521 2686); Leblon's **Bike Tech,** Rua Bartolomeu Mitre 455 (☎2529 3120). There are also bike rental stands along Copa Beach.

PRACTICAL INFORMATION

TOURIST & FINANCIAL SERVICES

Tourist Offices: Riotur (www.rio.rj.gov.br/riotur), the city tourist board, has the best map and the invaluable *Ensaio Geral* brochure on Carnaval (which they organize). They run **booths** at both airports, the *rodoviária,* and their Pça. XV de Novembro corporate office, Rua Assembléia 10, 9th fl. (☎2217 7575; open M-F 9am-5pm). They also run a Copacabana **tourist info center,** Av. Princesa Isabel 183 (☎2541 7522; open M-F 9am-6pm) and the English-speaking **"Alô Rio"** tourist hotline (☎2542 8080), manned M-F 9am-5pm.

(Continued from previous page)

class Brazilians, who largely ignore the existence of these shantytowns. For a long time the government's attitude toward the *favelas* was similar. Until the mid-1990s, they were systematically torn down and used for landfill or developed as pricey high-rise sites (much of the Zona Sul expanded this way). This has since given way to more constructive solutions, such as the US$350 million-plus Favela-Bairro Project, begun in 1994 with the aim of bringing basic infrastructure like electricity, sewer systems, day-care, educational centers, and transport to the *favelas*. Although the program is far from meeting its projected 2004 deadline for upgrading all *favelas* and integrating them into the city as proper *bairros* (neighborhoods), it has gone far in improving basic living conditions for many *faveladors.*

In 2002, help came in a completely different form: Fernando Meirelles' and Katia Lund's graphic film *Cidade de Deus (City of God),* which chronicles the violent, brutal life of young thugs in the eponymous *favela* outside Rio. The film was a hit in Brazil and abroad; more importantly, its critical and popular success opened the eyes of many Brazilians to the horrifying conditions of the *favelas* and helped them gain understanding of these often-ignored communities.

Under no circumstances should you walk around a *favela* on your own. Most tour agencies in Rio offer guided *favela* tours, which visit private homes and community centers to offer a glimpse into the day-to-day functioning of these communities.

PHONE CODE The phone code for the entire city of Rio de Janeiro is ☎**21.**

Tours: Grayline (☎2512 9919) has overpriced touristy trips to popular Rio sights. **Jeep Tour** (☎3890 9336; www.jeeptour.com.br) and **Just Fly** (☎9985 7540; www.just-fly.com.br) run guided open-jeep ecotours through the Parque Nacional da Tijuca. **Marcelo Armstrong** (☎3322 2727; www.favelatour.com.br) runs Rio's oldest and best-known *favela* tour. **Rio Turismo Radical** (☎2295 9947; www.rioturismoradical.com.br) specializes in outdoor adventure in the Rio area, including hiking, scuba diving, rafting, and skydiving (US$40-200). **South America Experience** has the most affordable tours and local excursions (see **Budget Travel,** p. 120).

Airlines: All airlines have airport ticket offices. The following offices are in Copacabana (unless indicated otherwise) and are open M-F 9am-5pm, Sa 9am-noon. **American** and **Continental** are both at the Copacabana Palace Hotel, Av. Atlântica 1702. **KLM,** Av. Rio Branco 311A, ste. 211 (☎2524 7744), facing Centro's Pça. Floriano. **TAM,** Pça. Floriano 19, 28th fl. (☎2524 1717), next to KLM in Centro. **Varig,** Rua Rodolfo Dantas 16A (☎2541 6343). **VASP,** Av. NS de Copacabana 262 (☎3873 4286).

Travel Agencies: Travel agencies line Copacabana's streets and Ipanema's Rua Visconde da Pirajá. Copa's helpful **Guanatur Turismo,** Rua Dias da Rocha 16A (☎2548 3275), sells bus tickets for a R$2 fee.

Budget Travel: South America Experience, Rua Raimundo Corrêa 36 (☎2548 8813; www.southamericaexperience.com), Copacabana. M: Siqueira Campos. 2-year-old South America Experience is already the top choice of savvy independent travelers. In Rio, they offer daytrips (R$85-95) to sights, hidden beaches, and hang-gliding spots, plus shorter trips (R$40-50) to soccer games and *samba* schools. They also run a fantastic hop-on/hop-off bus trip through Rio state (R$140-265) and arrange 5-7 day budget excursions to the Pantanal, Amazon, and Iguaçu Falls. The staff of fun, young, English-speaking locals is an invaluable resource on Rio (especially the city's nightlife) and on travel throughout Brazil. Affiliated with Oz and Kiwi Experience. Internet access R$0.15 per min. (1hr. free for stopping by.) Open daily 9am-7pm.

Consulates: All embassies are in Brasília (p. 276); the following countries have consular representation in Rio. **Australia,** Av. Pres. Wilson 231, 23rd fl. (☎3824 4734), Centro. Open M-F 9am-6pm. **Canada,** Av. Atlântica 1130, 5th fl. (☎2543 3004), Copacabana. Open M-F 9am-1pm. **Ireland,** Rua 24 de Maio 347 (☎2501 8455), Riachuelo. Open M-F 9am-noon. **South Africa,** Rua David Campista 50 (☎2527-1455), Botafogo. Open M-F 2-4:30pm. **UK,** Praia do Flamengo 284, 2nd fl. (☎2553 5976), Flamengo. Open M-F 8:30am-5pm; consular services M-F 9:30am-12:30pm. **US,** Av. Pres. Wilson 147 (☎2292 7117), Centro. Open M-F 8am-4:45pm; passport services M-F 1:30-3pm.

Currency exchange: At Galeão airport, only exchange money at official booths (open daily 6am-11pm); be wary of gray-smocked airport "staff" offering exchange. *Câmbios* are all over the city (most travel agencies are also *câmbios*), with most along Centro's Av. Rio Branco, Copa's Av. NS de Copacabana, and Ipanema's Rua Visconde de Pirajá.

ATMs: Galeão airport, 3rd fl. There are ATMs all over Rio, but many don't take foreign cards, even those on the same network. **Citibank** ATMs accept all cards and can be found at: Rua da Assembléia 100, **Centro;** Rua Voluntários da Pátria 450, **Botafogo;** Av. NS de Copacabana 619, **Copacabana;** Rua Visconde de Pirajá 229 and 459, **Ipanema.** All ATMs open daily 6am-10pm (some close Su).

American Express: Copacabana Palace Hotel, Av. Atlântica 1702, 1st fl. (☎3814 3312). Open M-F 9:30am-5pm.

Work & Study: Instituto Brasil-Estados Unidos (IBEU), Av. NS de Copacabana 690, 5th fl. (☎2548 8332; www.ibeu.com.br). M: Siqueira Campos. This city-wide language school often has jobs teaching English to Brazilians, and offers the city's largest choice of Portuguese language classes. **Wizard,** Av. NS de Copacabana 1199 (☎2522 0277; www.wizard.com.br), is a country-wide English language school popular with young Cariocas and travelers looking for short-term work.

LOCAL SERVICES

Luggage Storage: Available at both airports and the bus station.

English-Language Bookstores: Letras & Expressões, Rua Visconde de Pirajá 276 (☎2521 6110), Ipanema; 24hr. branch, Av. Ataulfo de Paiva 1292 (☎2511 5085), Leblon. All branches of chains **Livraria Siciliano,** Av. NS de Copacabana 755 (☎2548 2683), Copacabana, and **Livraria da Travessa,** Rua Visconde de Pirajá 462 (☎2287 5157), Ipanema, have (pricey) English-language books and travel guides.

Supermarkets: Major chains are Pão de Açúcar, Sendas, and Zona Sul. 24hr. branches are Copacabana's **Pão de Açúcar,** Av. NS de Copacabana 495, and Pça. Osório's **Zona Sul,** Rua Prudente de Morais 49. **Mundo Verde,** Rua do Catete 214A (☎2556 0983), Catete, is a major natural food chain. The Copacabana branch at Av. NS de Copacabana 630 is opposite natural food competitor **Farinha Pura,** Av. NS de Copacabana 595.

Laundromats: Chains like **Lavakilo, Laundromat,** and **Speed Queen** are everywhere, especially Catete, Copa, and Ipanema. Most charge R$4-5 per kg for *lavar e secar* (wash, dry, and fold). Hostel/hotel staff are usually willing to do washing for a few *reais.*

Public Toilets & Showers: Though most people go in the water, there are free but dingy bathrooms and showers at the numbered *postos* (lifeguard stations) that line the Zona Sul beaches. The chair/umbrella rental shacks on the beach also run showerheads (R$1). There are no public toilets in the streets, but plenty of McDonald's and Bob's.

PUBLICATIONS

The major dailies have full entertainment and film listings (in Portuguese), including Carnaval-related events; there's similar info in the *VejaRio* insert in weekly news rag *Veja* (published Sa; R$5.90). Friday weekend magazines are also great resources; *O Globo's* magazine (R$2) has the most thorough Carnaval listings. All these are available at streetside *bancas* (newsstands). International newspapers and magazines are expensive (about twice the cover price), but are readily available at most English-language bookstores and some newsstands.

EMERGENCY & COMMUNICATIONS

EMERGENCIES	The emergency numbers for all of Brazil are: **Police** ☎190. **Ambulance** ☎192. **Fire** ☎193.

Tourist Police: Rua Afrânio de Melo Franco 159 (☎3399 7170), Leblon. Open 24hr. **Polícia Federal,** Av. Venezuela 2, off Pça. Mauá in Centro, is the place for visa extensions *(prorrogação de visto).* Take any "Praça Mauá" bus. Visitors in shorts or sandals will not be allowed into the building.

24hr. Pharmacies: Drogasmil, Av. NS de Copacabana 852 (☎2572 3000), in Copacabana. **Drogaria Pacheco,** Rua do Catete 248 (☎2556 6792), in Catete, and Av. Ataulfo de Paiva 1151 (☎2472 2828), in Leblon. **CityFarma,** Rua Humaitá 95A (☎2266 6060), in Botafogo.

Hospitals: Leblon's **Hospital Miguel Couto,** Rua Bartolemeu Mitre 1108 (☎2274 6050) and Botafogo's **Hospital Rocha Maia,** Rua Gen. Severiano 91 (☎2295 2121), opposite Shopping Rio Sul, both have emergency rooms. Clinic **Galdino Campos Cárdio Copa,** Av. NS de Copacabana 492 (☎2548 9966), has English-speaking staff. Open 24hr. The **free clinic** in Copacabana's Pça. Correia gives free yellow fever inoculations every Th. **24hr. Dentist,** Av. Ataulfo de Paiva 517 (☎2274 4144), in Leblon.

Telephones: Phone offices, newsstands, and street vendors sell phone cards (most R$1 per 10 units) for use at all blue *orelhão* ("big ear") pay phones. Long-distance calls are most reliably made at the Internet cafés with phone booths (see **Internet Access,** p. 87). Portuguese-only directory assistance ☎102. International operator ☎000 111.

Internet Access: The Zona Sul is full of Internet cafés; most have English-speaking staff, international phone booths, and full tech services.

Central Fone, Rua Vinícius de Moraes 129B (☎3813 0952), in **Ipanema.** International phone booths. Internet R$2 1st 15min., R$0.14 per additional min. **Centro** branch (☎3681 7500), at entrance to M: Carioca. Both open M-F 9am-9pm, Sa 10am-4pm.

Conexão C@fe, Rua Visconde de Pirajá 3 (☎2287 4139), in **Ipanema.** Internet only. R$3.50 per 30min.; R$5 per hr. Open daily 9am-midnight.

Internet Access, Av. NS de Copacabana 374, ste. 202, in **Copacabana.** Internet only. R$2 per 20min.; R$5 per hr. Open daily 9am-10pm.

MS Depot Informática, Largo da Carioca, Shopping Av. Central, 3rd fl., in **Centro.** M: Carioca. Internet only. R$2 1st 15min., R$0.14 per additional min. Open M-Sa 9am-7pm.

South America Experience (see **Budget Travel,** p. 120) offers Internet access (R$0.15 per min.).

Telbra, Rua Hilário de Gouveia 57 (☎2236 3432), in **Copacabana.** International phone booths. Internet R$1 per 10min. Also at Av. NS de Copacabana 36. Open daily 9am-11pm.

Telenet, Rua Domingos Ferreira 59 (☎2543 0287), in **Copacabana.** International phone booths and **FedEx** shipping. Internet R$2 1st 15min., R$0.10 per additional min. Also at Av. Princesa Isabel 245. Open M-Sa 9am-11pm, Su 1-9pm.

Tudo é Fácil, Rua Barata Ribeiro 396 (☎2256 2268), in **Copacabana.** International phone booths and **cell phone rental.** Internet R$2.50 1st 15min., R$1.50 per additional 15min. Other Copa branches at Av. Prado Júnior 78 and Rua Xavier da Silveira 19. Open M-Sa 8am-midnight, Su 8am-10pm.

Post Office: *Posta restante* is held at the main post office, Rua 1 de Março 64, near Pça. XV de Novembro. M: Carioca. Galeão airport branch open 24hr. **FedEx** services available at Telenet. **Postal code:** 20000-000. Street signs list the 8-digit postal code for every block in the city.

ACCOMMODATIONS

Brazil's top tourist destination has accommodations for every budget. Copacabana has the most hotels of any neighborhood, but most of them are for top-dollar tourists; Rio's **budget hotels** (p. 124) are in Glória and Catete, near Lapa's clubs and Centro's sights but removed from the beaches and nightlife of Copacabana and Ipanema. Hotel rooms cost about double in those beach neighborhoods, where **hostels** (see below) are the preferred budget option.

Wherever you decide to stay in Rio, accommodations here will be more expensive than elsewhere in Brazil. During **New Year's** and **Carnaval,** room prices typically triple, and most accommodations only agree to book for the full holiday period (5-7 days for Carnaval), often with a deposit required. Prices below are for the high season, and (as in most of Brazil) are open to negotiation—always try to bargain down room rates.

HOSTELS

The recent flurry of *albergue* openings in Copacabana and Ipanema has left this once hostel-starved city full of many excellent options for hostelers. Hostels in Rio de Janeiro are all dormitory-style (up to six beds per dorm, with common bath), though some also offer private rooms with bath for a higher price. Most hostels (and some hotels) organize daily group outings to hiking spots, soccer games, *favelas*, *samba* rehearsals, and Rio's other attractions. For all establishments listed below, payment is in cash only unless noted otherwise.

ACCOMMODATIONS BY PRICE

UNDER R$25 (❶)

Carioca Easy Hostel (124)	Botafogo
Chave Rio–HI (124)	Botafogo
Che Lagarto Copa (123)	Copa
Hostel Mar_Rio (124)	Copa
King Albergue (124)	Catete
Rio Hostel (123)	Santa Teresa

R$26-45 (❷)

Casa 6 (123)	Ipanema
Che Lagarto Ipanema (124)	Ipanema
Copa Praia (123)	Copa
Hostel Harmonia (123)	Ipanema
Hostel Ipanema (124)	Ipanema
Hotel Caxambu (124)	Catete
Hotel Ferreira Viana (126)	Catete
Hotel Hispano Brasileiro (126)	Catete
Hotel Riazor (124)	Catete
Hotel Rio Claro (126)	Catete
Hotel Rio Lisboa (126)	Catete
Hotel Vitória (126)	Catete
Monterrey Hotel (126)	Catete

R$46-65 (❸)

Apart-Hóteis Santa Clara (126)	Copa
Hotel Angrense (128)	Copa
Hotel Leão (126)	Catete
Hotel San Marco (128)	Ipanema
Hotel Santa Clara (126)	Copa
Pousada Girassol (128)	Copa
Turístico Hotel (124)	Glória

R$66-105 (❹)

Grande Hotel Canadá (128)	Copa
Hotel Biarritz (128)	Copa
Hotel Flamengo Palace (126)	Catete
Hotel Toledo (128)	Copa
Hotel Único (126)	Catete
Imperial Hotel (126)	Catete
Martinique Hotel (128)	Copa

OVER R$106 (❺)

Acapulco Copacabana Hotel (128)	Copa
Hotel Arpoador Inn (128)	Ipanema
Hotel DeBret (128)	Copa
Hotel Ipanema Inn (128)	Ipanema
Hotel Vermont (128)	Ipanema

Rio Hostel, Rua Joaquim Martinho 361 (☎3852 0827; www.riohostel.com). Infused with the easygoing style of youthful, artsy **Santa Teresa,** this spotless, modern hostel feels like home, a welcome respite from the overdeveloped, tourist-choked Zona Sul. BBQ on-site, relax by the rooftop pool and bar, or heed helpful owner Carina's advice and explore the neighborhood to see how Cariocas really live. Even touristy things aren't touristy here: *e.g.*, the ride to Corcovado wends through rainforest and offers aerial views of Rio. Internet access. Breakfast included. Kitchen. Dorms R$35. DC/MC/V. ❷

Che Lagarto Copacabana, Rua Anita Garibaldi 87 (☎2256 2777; www.chelagarto.com), in **Copacabana.** With the most perks for the lowest price, this is one of Rio's newest and best hostels, housed in a spotless and beautifully redecorated former clinic in the Bairro Peixoto. Hopping indoor/outdoor deck and lounge with a full bar, TV/DVD, pool table, and piano. All dorms have private bath and A/C (some also have TVs). Laundry facilities. Internet access. Kitchen. Breakfast included. Dorms R$35. ❷

Copa Praia, Rua Tenente Marones de Gusmão 85 (☎2547 5422), in **Copacabana's** Bairro Peixoto. This four-story mega-hostel with a fantastic party vibe is the best place in Rio to meet fellow budget travelers. Choice of tidy, tiny dorms (with private bath) or palatial multi-person *apartamentos* (with private bath, full kitchen, and common area; some with A/C). A great long-term option. Best hostel book exchange in Brazil. Internet access. Dorms R$30. *Apartamentos* R$75-85. ❷

Hostel Harmonia, Rua Barão da Torre 175, casa 18 (☎2523 4905), in **Ipanema.** Done up like a funky international treehouse, this was Rua Barão da Torre's first hostel, and remains the top choice in Ipanema, despite crowded quarters. Friendly polyglot staff keeps things clean and lively. Internet access. Kitchen. *Quartos* R$40. ❷

Casa 6, Rua Barão da Torre 175, casa 6 (☎2247 1384), in **Ipanema.** *Casa* is right: Casa 6 feels like home, not a hostel. It has cheerful and comfortable common areas, sunny and immaculate dorms, and a gorgeous rooftop sun-deck. The cleanest of Rua Barão da Torre's hostels. Kitchen. Breakfast included. Dorms R$45. Doubles R$100. ❷

Albergue da Juventude Chave Rio (HI), Rua General Dionísio 63 (☎2286 0303), in **Botafogo.** Take Bus #172 to Rua São Clemente, then taxi (R$7). The good news: this charming townhouse keeps to its HI roots as probably the cleanest, quietest hostel in Rio.

The bad news: the inconvenient location far from beaches, buses, and *metrô* in a non-budget (but fun) area. Thankfully, the crowd here keeps things going. Breakfast included. Dorms R$30, non-members R$45. R$3 extra for A/C. ❶/❷

Hostel Ipanema, Rua Barão da Torre 175, casa 14 (☎2247 7269), in **Ipanema.** The newest and most basic of Rua Barão da Torre's hostels, though still clean and comfy with a pleasant deck. Carioca owner Paulo is a great source of Rio info and a hang gliding legend (he runs Just Fly outdoor excursions; p. 152). Laundry facilities. Internet access. Kitchen. Dorms R$40. ❷

Che Lagarto Ipanema, Rua Barão de Jaguaripe 208 (☎2247 4582), in **Ipanema.** Carrying on the Che tradition of fun-loving, party-hardy hostels, the artsy, multi-story Ipanema outpost has a rockin' in-house bar to rival the hottest Leblon nightspot, complete with a stunning view of Corcovado (to make up for the 10min. walk to the beach and the slightly beat-up baths). Internet access. Kitchen. Breakfast included. Dorms R$40, with A/C R$43, with A/C and bath R$45. Doubles R$100. ❷

Carioca Easy Hostel, Rua Marechal Cantuária 168 (☎2295 7805), in Urca, just east of **Botafogo.** Take Bus #104 to its end at Rua Marechal Cantuária. The livin' is easy at this phenomenal addition to Rio's hostel scene, though we can't decide what's best: the beach-ringed and postcard-perfect (though inconvenient) setting at the foot of the Sugarloaf, the sparkling modern baths and dorms, or the amazing rooftop pool. Breakfast included. Nov.-Mar. dorms R$40. Apr.-Oct. dorms R$35. ❷

Hostel Mar_Rio, Rua Leopoldo Miguez 10 (☎3185 6604), in **Copacabana.** Unmarked orange gate at Rua Constante Ramos. A guaranteed great time. It may not be Rio's swankiest or most private *albergue* (some dorms are divided by partitions, though all have A/C), but you'll barely notice thanks to diversions like the courtyard bar, PlayStation/DVDs, and namesake ▧ Mario himself, perhaps the friendliest and most fun-loving Carioca in Rio. Kitchen. Breakfast included. Dorms R$35. ❷

King Albergue, Rua Barão de Guaratiba 20 (☎2557 3471), in **Catete.** M: Catete. Hardly the king, this recently opened hostel *is* nevertheless a welcome addition to Catete's budget kingdom. Cleaner and cheerier than the 2 other Catete *hospedarias,* on par with (but much cheaper than) some area budget hotels. Private lockers and safe. Internet access. Breakfast included. *Quartos* R$20. ❶

HOTELS

GLÓRIA & CATETE

Most of Rio's budget hotels are in these once-aristocratic neighborhoods, where weathered colonial mansions have been converted into shabby, largely indistinguishable hotels. Though it's 20min. by bus or *metrô* from Copacabana and Ipanema's beaches and nightlife, room rates here are half what they are near the shore. The area's proximity to both Centro's sights and funky nightlife district Lapa also attracts travelers. Unless noted otherwise, the following are all in Catete (along Rua do Catete), near M: Catete. All include breakfast.

Hotel Riazor (Antiga Monte Blanco), Rua do Catete 160 (☎2225 0121). This once ornate mansion opposite the Catete Palace has seen better days, but it's still Catete's best budget bet, with low rates, friendly staff, and tidy rooms (with A/C, TV, and private bath). Easygoing hostel atmosphere. Singles R$45; doubles R$60. ❷

Hotel Caxambu, Rua Correia Dutra 22 (☎2265 9496). Very popular with budget travelers, this sunny hotel just steps from the Parque do Flamengo features modern rooms with A/C, TV, and some of Catete's cleanest bathrooms (a few with Carmen Miranda decor). Popular with Israeli backpackers. Singles R$50; doubles R$60. ❸

Turístico Hotel, Ladeira da Glória 30 (☎2557 7698), in **Glória.** M: Glória. A very clean, very quiet budget hotel with a maze-like layout and choice of private or common bath.

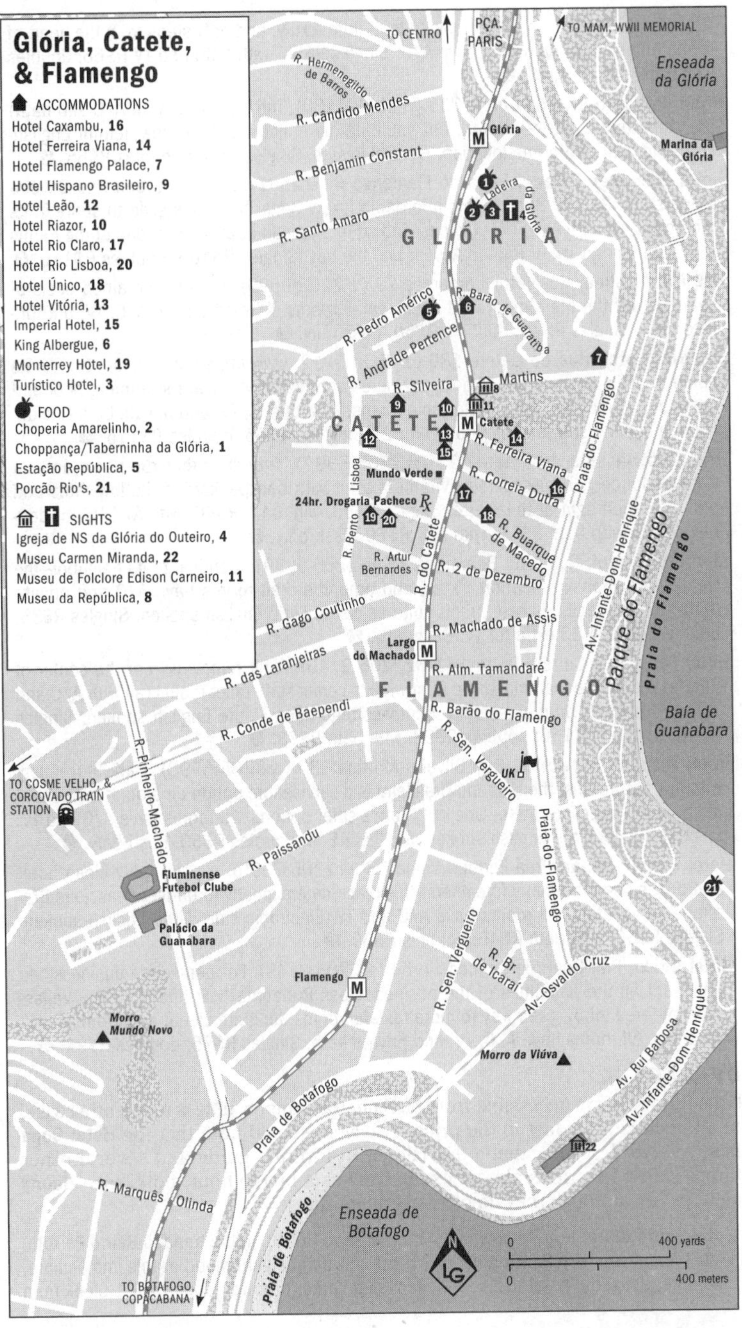
Glória, Catete, & Flamengo
ACCOMMODATIONS
Hotel Caxambu, 16
Hotel Ferreira Viana, 14
Hotel Flamengo Palace, 7
Hotel Hispano Brasileiro, 9
Hotel Leão, 12
Hotel Riazor, 10
Hotel Rio Claro, 17
Hotel Rio Lisboa, 20
Hotel Único, 18
Hotel Vitória, 13
Imperial Hotel, 15
King Albergue, 6
Monterrey Hotel, 19
Turístico Hotel, 3
FOOD
Choperia Amarelinho, 2
Choppança/Taberninha da Glória, 1
Estação República, 5
Porcão Rio's, 21
SIGHTS
Igreja de NS da Glória do Outeiro, 4
Museu Carmen Miranda, 22
Museu de Folclore Edison Carneiro, 11
Museu da República, 8
TO CENTRO
PÇA. PARIS
TO MAM, WWII MEMORIAL
Enseada da Glória
Marina da Glória
R. Hermenegildo de Barros
R. Cândido Mendes
Glória
R. Benjamin Constant
Ladeira da Glória
R. Santo Amaro
GLÓRIA
R. Pedro Américo
R. Barão de Guaratiba
R. Andrade Pertence
R. Silveira Martins
Catete
CATETE
R. Ferreira Viana
R. Correia Dutra
Praia do Flamengo
Mundo Verde
24hr. Drogaria Pacheco
R. Bento Lisboa
R. Buarque de Macedo
R. Artur Bernardes
R. 2 de Dezembro
R. do Catete
Av. Infante Dom Henrique
Parque do Flamengo
Praia do Flamengo
R. Gago Coutinho
R. Machado de Assis
Largo do Machado
R. das Laranjeiras
R. Alm. Tamandaré
FLAMENGO
R. Conde de Baependi
R. Barão do Flamengo
Baía de Guanabara
R. Sen. Vergueiro
UK
TO COSME VELHO, & CORCOVADO TRAIN STATION
R. Pinheiro Machado
R. Paissandu
Fluminense Futebol Clube
Palácio da Guanabara
R. Sen. Vergueiro
R. Br. de Icaraí
Av. Osvaldo Cruz
Flamengo
Morro Mundo Novo
Morro da Viúva
Av. Rui Barbosa
Av. Infante Dom Henrique
Praia de Botafogo
R. Marquês Olinda
Enseada de Botafogo
Praia de Botafogo
0
400 yards
0
400 meters
TO BOTAFOGO, COPACABANA

Great for budget backpackers looking for a little luxury, and only steps from the heart of Glória and Catete. All rooms have A/C. Singles R$55, with bath and TV R$66; doubles with bath and TV R$78. ❸

Hotel Rio Claro, Rua do Catete 233 (☎2558 5180). The rooms (all with A/C and bath) are small and a bit weathered, but you'll hardly notice thanks to the helpful English-speaking staff and prime location. Electronic safe. Singles R$40; doubles R$65. ❷

Hotel Flamengo Palace, Praia do Flamengo 6 (☎2557 7552), between Rua Silveira Martins and Rua do Russel. This affordable luxury 3-star hotel has style to spare in its mod pads, all with A/C, TV, *frigo-bar,* and squeaky-clean bath. Beg for one of the rooms with a stunning view of Pão de Açúcar and the bay. Singles R$105; doubles R$116. ❹

Hotel Rio Lisboa, Rua Artur Bernardes 29 (☎2265 9599). A well-maintained oasis of calm just off the main drag, with basic, small rooms. All rooms have A/C, TV, and private bath. Singles R$35; doubles R$50. Cash only. ❷

Imperial Hotel, Rua do Catete 186 (☎2556 5212; www.imperialhotel.com.br). As its name implies, you will feel like royalty here—what with the private swimming pool and many bright, modern, and comfortable rooms, all with A/C, TV, and private bath (including immaculate showers big enough for 2). Singles R$105; doubles R$115. ❹

Hotel Vitória, Rua do Catete 172 (☎2205 5397). Though rather run-down and on Catete's loudest, busiest street, Vitória is a hit with backpackers for its low rates and prime location right at the *metrô.* Singles R$35, with bath R$40, with A/C R$45; doubles R$50, with bath R$55, with A/C R$60. Cash only. ❷

Monterrey Hotel, Rua Artur Bernardes 39 (☎2265 9899). Identical to its neighbor—the Hotel Rio Lisboa—in location, rates, and amenities (all rooms have A/C and private bath), but the facilities here aren't quite as clean. Little English spoken. Singles R$35; doubles R$50. R$3 extra for TV. Cash only. ❷

Hotel Leão, Rua Correia Dutra 141 (☎2205 2146). A bit removed from the center of Catete, Leão more than makes up for it with its genial staff, quiet rooms (all with A/C and TV), and lurid red bordello-meets-country-cottage decor. Little English spoken. Singles R$46, with bath R$56; doubles R$68, with bath R$78. ❸

Hotel Hispano Brasileiro, Rua Silveira Martins 135 (☎2265 5990). Dark and musty with tiny bathrooms, the Hispano Brasileiro is a serviceable option on a quiet residential street in the heart of Catete. One of Catete's safer options. All rooms have A/C and TV. Electronic safe. Little English spoken. Singles R$45; doubles R$50. Cash only. ❸

Hotel Ferreira Viana, Rua Ferreira Viana 58 (☎2205 7396). A dark, fairly clean hotel that doesn't see too many foreigners—this place caters mostly to budget-conscious Brazilians on vacation. All rooms have A/C and TV. Electronic safe. Little English spoken. Singles R$35, with bath R$45; doubles R$60. ❷

Hotel Único, Rua Buarque de Macedo 54 (☎2205 8149). For pennywise businessmen who want all the amenities of the business-class Rondônia next door for less. Vegas-style mirrored lobby gives way to more tasteful rooms, all quite clean, comfortable, and spacious. All rooms have A/C, TV, and private bath. Singles R$75; doubles R$91. ❹

COPACABANA

All the following are accessible from M: Siqueira Campos, unless noted otherwise, and all include breakfast in the price. Travelers should note that the **Hotel Copa Linda,** Av. NS de Copacabana 956 (listed in Riotur's guide and several other sources), now functions almost exclusively as a by-the-hour motel (see **Hourly Motels,** p. 79), although they do offer overnight rates.

Hotel Santa Clara, Rua Décio Vilares 316 (☎2256 2650), in the tranquil Bairro Peixoto. You'll forget you're in South America's most crowded neighborhood at this immaculate, intimate, delightful hotel tucked in a secluded corner of rowdy Copa (just 1 block from

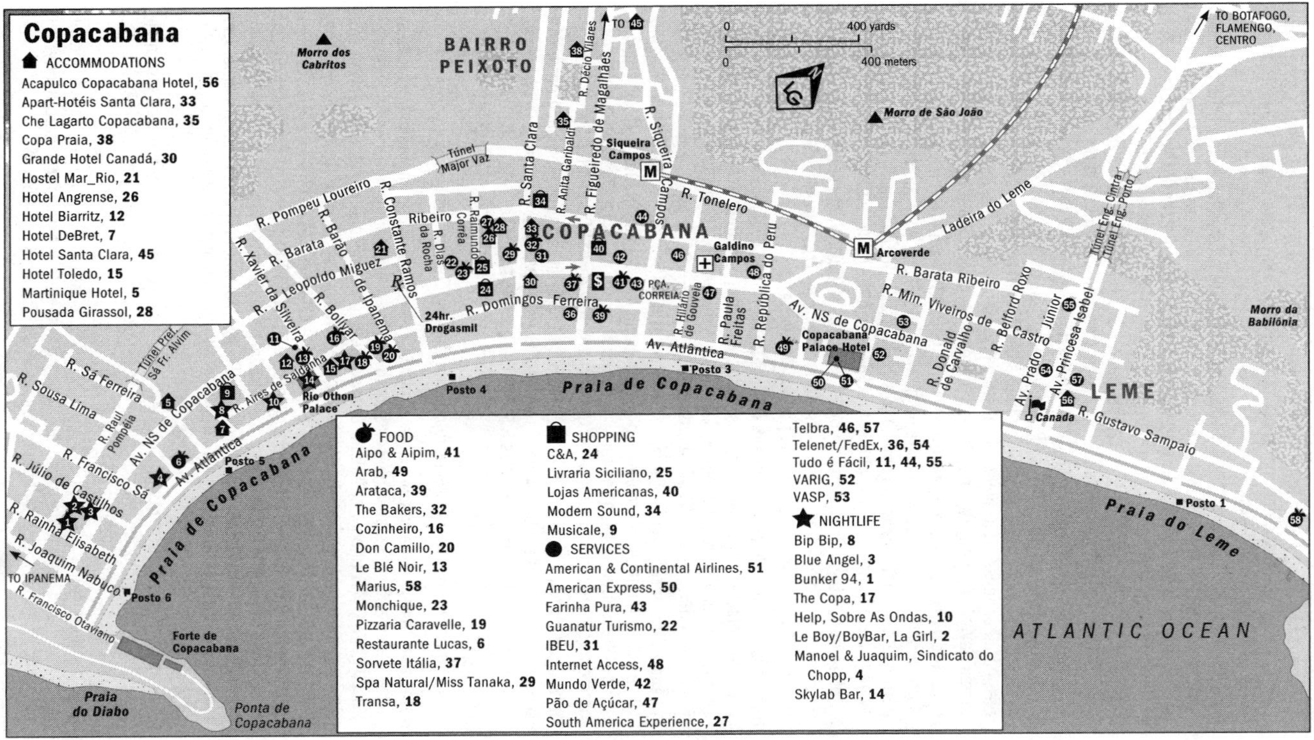

Copacabana

ACCOMMODATIONS

- Acapulco Copacabana Hotel, **56**
- Apart-Hotéis Santa Clara, **33**
- Che Lagarto Copacabana, **35**
- Copa Praia, **38**
- Grande Hotel Canadá, **30**
- Hostel Mar_Rio, **21**
- Hotel Angrense, **26**
- Hotel Biarritz, **12**
- Hotel DeBret, **7**
- Hotel Santa Clara, **45**
- Hotel Toledo, **15**
- Martinique Hotel, **5**
- Pousada Girassol, **28**

FOOD

- Aipo & Aipim, **41**
- Arab, **49**
- Arataca, **39**
- The Bakers, **32**
- Cozinheiro, **16**
- Don Camillo, **20**
- Le Blé Noir, **13**
- Marius, **58**
- Monchique, **23**
- Pizzaria Caravelle, **19**
- Restaurante Lucas, **6**
- Sorvete Itália, **37**
- Spa Natural/Miss Tanaka, **29**
- Transa, **18**

SHOPPING

- C&A, **24**
- Livraria Siciliano, **25**
- Lojas Americanas, **40**
- Modern Sound, **34**
- Musicale, **9**

SERVICES

- American & Continental Airlines, **51**
- American Express, **50**
- Farinha Pura, **43**
- Guanatur Turismo, **22**
- IBEU, **31**
- Internet Access, **48**
- Mundo Verde, **42**
- Pão de Açúcar, **47**
- South America Experience, **27**
- Telbra, **46, 57**
- Telenet/FedEx, **36, 54**
- Tudo é Fácil, **11, 44, 55**
- VARIG, **52**
- VASP, **53**

NIGHTLIFE

- Bip Bip, **8**
- Blue Angel, **3**
- Bunker 94, **1**
- The Copa, **17**
- Help, Sobre As Ondas, **10**
- Le Boy/BoyBar, La Girl, **2**
- Manoel & Juaquim, Sindicato do Chopp, **4**
- Skylab Bar, **14**

the *metrô*). With the extra-low (Catete-style) rates, breakfast in bed, and a gregarious owner, can you really complain about the 15min. walk to the beach? Singles R$95; doubles R$105. R$10 extra for balcony. ❹

Hotel DeBret, Av. Atlântica 3564 (☎2522 0132). The most affordable of the high-end beachfront hotels, DeBret offers charming (if smallish) colonial rooms, sparkling bathrooms, and the best hotel breakfast in Rio, served in their 12th fl. in-house restaurant with a wraparound view of Copacabana. Singles US$43; doubles US$63. ❺

Grande Hotel Canadá, Av. NS de Copacabana 687 (☎2257 1864). A modern, comfortable 3-star hotel on Copacabana's busiest intersection, but only 2 short blocks from the beach. All rooms have A/C and bath. Singles R$100-140; doubles R$110-156. ❹/❺

Acapulco Copacabana Hotel, Rua Gustavo Sampaio 854 (☎2275 0022). M: Arcoverde. One of Brazil's best 3-star hotels. With huge rooms, impeccable service, and pristine cleanliness, you might mistake them for their luxury neighbor, Le Meridien. All rooms have A/C, bath, TV, and phone. Singles R$125-150; doubles R$155-185. ❺

Hotel Angrense, Travessa Angrense 25 (☎2548 0509). One of the cheapest hotels in Copa. Musty but spacious rooms (all with A/C and TV) and your choice of hall or private bath (both serviceably clean) make this an average budget hotel—with a well below average price. Singles R$68, with bath R$85; doubles R$90, with bath R$110. ❹

Hotel Toledo, Rua Domingos Ferreira 71 (☎2257 1990). Very clean, very quiet, very small rooms a block from the beach. All rooms have A/C. Singles R$60, with TV and phone R$110; doubles with TV and phone R$130. ❹

Hotel Biarritz, Rua Aires de Saldanha 54 (☎2522 0542). Despite its motto ("The best place for business of pleasure"), this is not a motel (see **Hourly Motels,** p. 79) but a roomy, cool, and dead-quiet option 1 block from the beach. All rooms have A/C and TV. Electronic safe. Singles R$110; doubles R$130. ❺

Pousada Girassol, Travessa Angrense 25A (☎2256 6951), off Av. NS de Copacabana. All *girassóis* (sunflowers) and cheery yellow—complete with balconies and sunny courtyards—Girassol is pleasant enough. Too bad that sun doesn't shine on its run-down bathrooms. Large rooms all have A/C and bath. Singles R$80; doubles R$100. ❹

Martinique Hotel, Rua Sá Ferreira 30 (☎2522 1652), in sight of the beach on the far southern end of Copacabana. Rooms are modern and tidy, and all have A/C, TV, phone, and spotless private bath. Singles R$115; doubles R$145. ❺

IPANEMA

Like in Copacabana, the hotels here are not geared for budget travelers.

Hotel San Marco, Rua Visconde de Pirajá 524 (☎2540 5032). Ipanema's cheapest hotel is an excellent 3-star with a soft spot for backpackers. Rooms are cheerful and spotless, with A/C, TV, phone, and bath. Backpacker ("economico") rooms differ only in size (and not by much), and are better than Ipanema's similarly priced hostel doubles. Economico singles R$99; doubles R$110. Regular singles R$120; doubles R$140. ❸/❹

Hotel Arpoador Inn, Rua Francisco Otaviano 177 (☎2523 0060). On a quiet stretch of sand steps from both Copacabana and Ipanema's action, and in view of sunrise-friendly Arpoador Rock. This clean if antiseptic mid-range hotel with a great beach bar is also the hotel closest to the beach in all of Rio. All rooms have A/C, TV, and private bath. Singles and doubles R$130-170. ❺

Hotel Ipanema Inn, Rua Maria Quitéria 27 (☎2523 6092). A dim but pleasant mid-range hotel close to Ipanema's most coveted stretch of sand. All rooms have A/C, bath, and TV. Singles and doubles R$156-180. ❺

Hotel Vermont, Rua Visconde de Pirajá 254 (☎2522 0057). A tidy but expensive budget hotel popular with businessmen and budget travelers looking for a little luxury. All rooms have A/C, TV, and palatial private bath. Doubles R$140-150. ❺

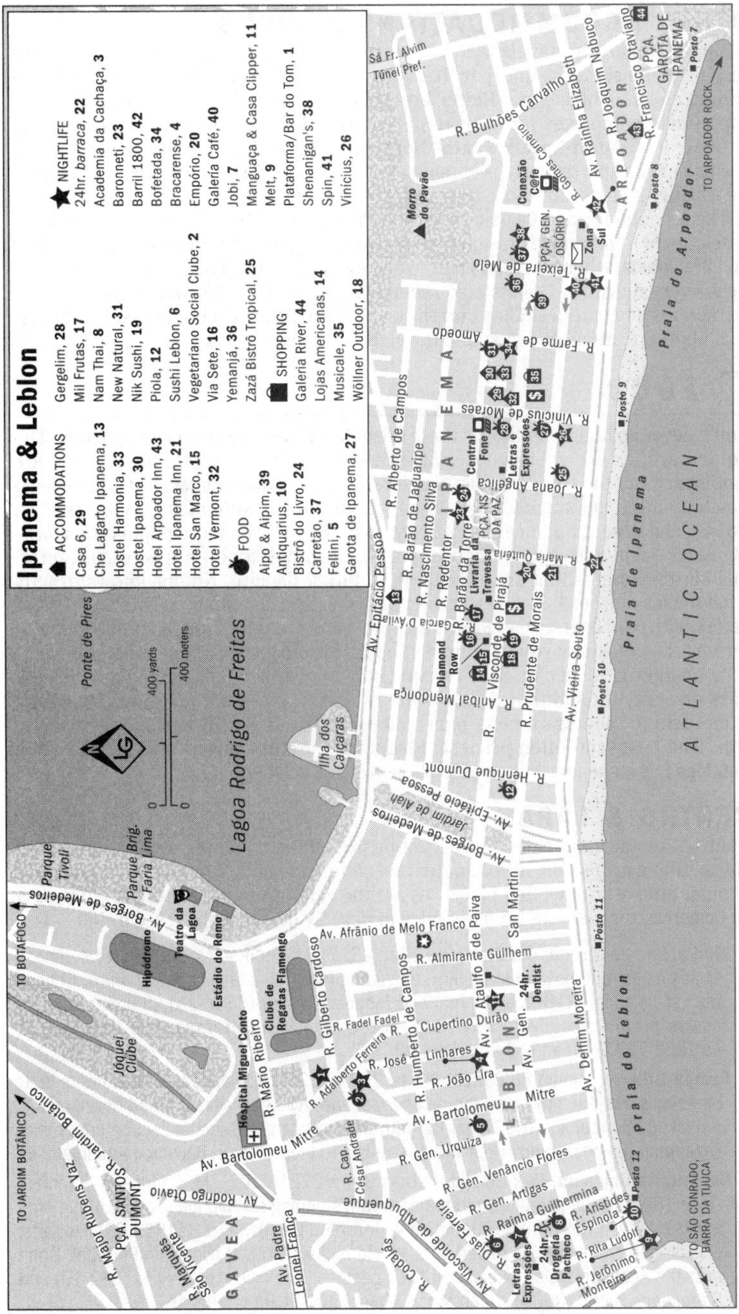

Ipanema & Leblon

ACCOMMODATIONS
- Casa 6, **29**
- Che Lagarto Ipanema, **13**
- Hostel Harmonia, **33**
- Hostel Ipanema, **30**
- Hotel Arpoador Inn, **43**
- Hotel Ipanema Inn, **21**
- Hotel San Marco, **15**
- Hotel Vermont, **32**

FOOD
- Aipo & Aipim, **39**
- Antiquarius, **10**
- Bistrô do Livro, **24**
- Carretão, **37**
- Fellini, **5**
- Garota de Ipanema, **27**
- Gergelim, **28**
- Mil Frutas, **17**
- Nam Thai, **8**
- New Natural, **31**
- Nik Sushi, **19**
- Piola, **12**
- Sushi Leblon, **6**
- Vegetariano Social Clube, **2**
- Via Sete, **16**
- Yemanjá, **36**
- Zazá Bistrô Tropical, **25**

SHOPPING
- Galeria River, **44**
- Lojas Americanas, **14**
- Musicale, **35**
- Wöllner Outdoor, **18**

NIGHTLIFE
- 24hr. *barraca*, **22**
- Academia da Cachaça, **3**
- Baronneti, **23**
- Barril 1800, **42**
- Bofetada, **34**
- Bracarense, **4**
- Empório, **20**
- Galería Café, **40**
- Jobi, **7**
- Manguaça & Casa Clipper, **11**
- Melt, **9**
- Plataforma/Bar do Tom, **1**
- Shenanigan's, **38**
- Spin, **41**
- Vinícius, **26**

OTHER ACCOMMODATIONS OPTIONS

Groups planning on staying in Rio for a week or more will often find renting a furnished **apartment** to be cheaper than staying in a hotel. The best deals are found through local contacts; the Riotur brochure also has full listings of *apart-hotéis* (apartment complexes for short-term rental) and official rental agencies. Among the latter, **Apart-Hotéis Santa Clara,** Rua Santa Clara 98 (www.rioapartments.com), is particularly recommended. Travelers fluent in Portuguese can try newspaper listings, but those are mostly for long-term rental.

The recently formed **Cama e Café,** Rua Progresso 67 (☎2221 7635; www.camaecafe.com.br), in Santa Teresa, oversees an ever-growing network of private **Bed and Breakfasts,** where travelers can live in local homes and break bread with Cariocas every morning. Guests also receive a Cama e Café discount card for local attractions and eateries. They currently only have listings in home base Santa Teresa, but there are plans to expand throughout Rio and Brazil.

FOOD

You'll never go hungry in Rio, as there are at least two eateries on every block. The golden arches are everywhere (McDonald's is the country's biggest private employer), but the true Brazilian fast food joints are **lanchonetes,** dirty, dirt-cheap lunch counters selling *choppes*, *sucos* (fruit juices), *salgados* (savory snacks; R$1-3), and decent full meals (*pratos feitos;* R$5-7). Even more popular than *lanchonetes*—and with better atmosphere and healthier food—are **botequins,** informal bar-restaurants that are a hallmark of Rio de Janeiro. No one knows exactly what makes one *botequim* better than the other, but any time you find an open-air eatery with cold beer, cheap food, late hours, and crowds of locals spilling out into the streets, you know you've stumbled upon this uniquely Carioca creation.

As an international city, Rio is second only to gourmet capital São Paulo in culinary diversity. In addition to *lanchonetes* and *botequins* you'll find everything from sushi to sauerkraut here, plus a nice cross-section of Brazilian regional cuisine. The best (and often priciest) restaurants are in **Ipanema** and **Leblon,** while **Botafogo** has a cheaper but equally globe-trotting selection.

CENTRO & LAPA

Centro's restaurants cater to hurried businessmen, meaning swift service and cheap, filling meals. The *lanchonetes* and *chopperias* off of **Avenida Rio Branco** are popular after-work meeting places, as are the eateries on the picturesque **Travessa do Comércio,** through the Arco do Teles in Pça. XV de Novembro (see p. 139).

Miako, Rua do Ouvidor 45, 2nd fl. (☎2222 2397). M: Carioca. Ascend the red staircase to this Asian food nirvana in an airy Zen setting (with table fans chanting *ohm*). Choose from so-so sushi (R$8+), a few Thai and Japanese dishes (R$14-25), or the amazing 6-course *pratos executivos* (R$13-15). Also a branch in **Botafogo,** Rua do Farini 20 (☎2552 7847). Open M-F 8am-8pm. ❸

Pampa Grill, Av. Almirante Barroso 90 (☎2524 1199). M: Carioca. 2 restaurants in 1: upstairs is a top-quality, semi-formal *churrascaria* (R$33 per person), and downstairs is a packed informal kilo (R$27 per kg) with the city's largest buffet selection and lots of vegetarian options. Happy Hour with live music Tu-F 6pm. Open daily noon-midnight. ❷

Confeitaria Colombo, Rua Gonçalves Dias 32 (☎2221 0107). M: Carioca. A landmark since 1894, this gilded old-world tearoom with stunning stained glass decor offers ordinary *salgados* (R$1-3) and extraordinary, decadent European treats (R$2.50) like tarts, eclairs, and charlottes, all based on ages-old recipes brought over from Portugal. Don't miss the April Fool's Day joke cotton-filled pastries. Fine china tea service (R$2-10) and Sa *feijoada* buffet (R$30). Open M-F 8:30am-7pm, Sa 9am-5pm. ❶

FOOD BY TYPE

BRAZILIAN	
Amarelinho (131)	Centro ❸
Bar Luiz (131)	Centro ❸
Choperia Amarelinho (132)	Catete ❸
Choppança/Taberninha (132)	Glória ❷
Garota de Ipanema (135)	Ipanema ❷
Restaurante Aurora (133)	Botafogo ❷
Restaurante Lucas (135)	Copa ❸
Transa (135)	Copa ❹
Via Sete (136)	Ipanema ❷
BRAZILIAN REGIONAL	
Arataca (Amazonas; 134)	Copa ❷
Yemanjá (Bahia; 135)	Ipanema ❺
Yorubá (Bahia; 133)	Botafogo ❺
CHURRASCARIAS	
Carretão (135)	Ipanema ❷
Marius (134)	Copa ❺
Monchique (134)	Copa ❷
Pampa Grill (130)	Centro ❷
Porcão Rio's (132)	Flamengo ❸
EUROPEAN	
Afrodite tis Milo (Greek; 133)	Botafogo ❷
Bar Luiz (German; 131)	Centro ❸
Don Camillo (Italian; 134)	Copa ❹
Le Blé Noir (French; 134)	Copa ❸
Restaurante Lucas (German; 135)	Copa ❸
HEALTH FOOD & VEGETARIAN	
Gergelim (136)	Ipanema ❸
New Natural (136)	Ipanema ❷
Spa Natural/Miss Tanaka (134)	Copa ❷
Vegetariano Social Clube (136)	Leblon ❸
ICE CREAM	
Mil Frutas (135)	Ipanema ❶
Sorvete Itália (134)	Various ❶
INTERNATIONAL	
Bistrô do Livro (135)	Ipanema ❹
Bistro do Paço (131)	Centro ❷
Botequim (133)	Botafogo ❸
Cozinheiro (134)	Copa ❸
Madam Vidal (133)	Botafogo ❹
JAPANESE	
Miako (130)	Centro ❸
Nik Sushi (136)	Ipanema ❸
Spa Natural/Miss Tanaka (134)	Copa ❷
Sushi Leblon (136)	Leblon ❹
KILO RESTAURANTS	
Aipo & Aipim (134)	Copa ❷
Estação República (132)	Catete ❷
Fellini (136)	Leblon ❸
New Natural (136)	Ipanema ❷
PASTRIES & SWEETS	
The Bakers (134)	Copa ❶
Confeitaria Colombo (130)	Centro ❶
PIZZA	
Don Camillo (134)	Copa ❹
Piola (135)	Ipanema ❸
Pizzaria Caravelle (135)	Copa ❸
Stravaganze (133)	Botafogo ❸
PORTUGUESE	
Antiquarius (136)	Leblon ❺
Confeitaria Colombo (130)	Centro ❶
Nova Capela (131)	Centro ❹
OTHER CUISINE	
Arab (Middle Eastern; 134)	Copa ❷
Nam Thai (Thai; 136)	Leblon ❹
Puebla Café (Mexican; 133)	Botafogo ❷
Zazá Bistrô (Fusion; 135)	Ipanema ❹

RIO DE JANEIRO

Bar & Restaurante Amarelinho, Pça. Floriano 55 (☎2240 8434). M: Cinelândia. Their namesake yellow tables are the best spot for Pça. Floriano people-watching. Typical Brazilian meat-and-starch menu R$15-30. *Chopp* R$1.80. Open daily 11am-midnight. ❸

Nova Capela, Av. Mem de Sá 96 (☎2252 6228), in **Lapa.** M: Cinelândia or take any "Lapa" bus. This 80-year-old traditional blue-tiled eatery (where the now-ubiquitous *frango à francesa* was invented) is a Rio legend—as famous for its hearty Portuguese and Brazilian cuisine as for its gruff waiters. Entrees for 2 R$20-30. Open daily 11am-5am. ❹

Bistro do Paço, Pça. XV de Novembro 48 (☎2533 4407). M: Carioca. Hausmannized streets and well-manicured squares aren't Centro's only Parisian influence: this café in the Paço Imperial (p. 139) offers European delights like quiche, brioche, and vegetarian options (R$6-9), plus a filling *prato feito* (R$15). Open Tu-Su noon-6:30pm. ❷

Bar Luiz, Rua da Carioca 39 (☎2262 6900). As Rio's oldest bar/restaurant, Luiz has had 12 decades to perfect the art of the *chopp* (R$2.80)—and they've succeeded. The menu hasn't changed much since they opened in 1887: still lots of German-style food like Kassler, potato salad, and bratwurst, alongside typical Brazilian fare (entrees for 2 R$15-25). Open M-Sa 11am-11:30pm. ❸

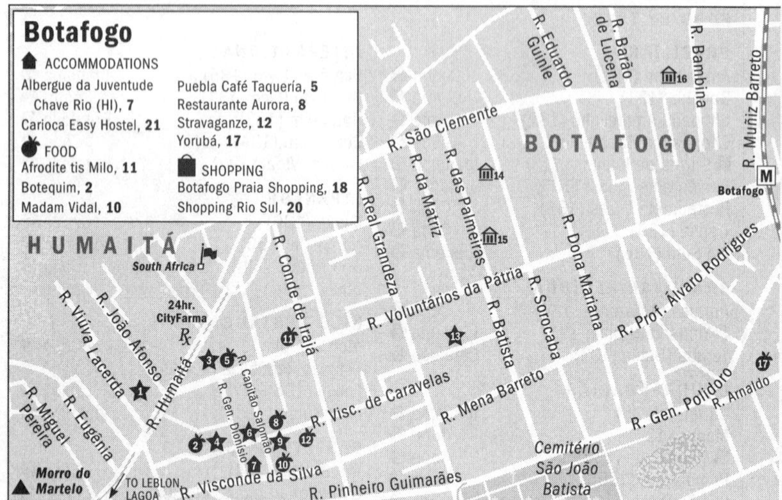

GLÓRIA & CATETE

The food in this budget hotel-filled area is nothing special, but there are plenty of cheap *lanchonetes* and kilos to satisfy hungry backpackers.

Choppança/Taberninha da Glória, Rua do Russel 32B (☎2557 7847). M: Glória. The only thing more enjoyable than Choppança's big, breezy patio is its dirt-cheap prices for typical Brazilian fare (entrees R$10-15), pizzas (R$7-15), and sandwiches (R$5-6). Excellent ice cream selection (R$5). Open daily 11am-1am. ❷

Estação República, Rua do Catete 104 (☎2225 2650). M: Catete. A popular kilo with an ample buffet and *churrascaria* (R$19 per kg). Open daily 11am-midnight. ❷

Porcão Rio's, on Av. Infante Dom Henrique (☎2554 8535), off Praia do Flamengo in **Flamengo.** Take any "Praia do Flamengo" bus; Av. Henrique (marked by Porcão's sign) is after the pyramidal Monumento do Estácio de Sá. Taxi R$12-20. *Porcão* means "big pig," and you might just start oinking after gorging at this classy *churrascaria* (R$39 per person) popular with tour groups for its top cuts and gorgeous panorama of Sugarloaf and the bay. Branches in **Copacabana,** Av. NS de Copacabana 1144 (☎2523 1497), and **Ipanema,** Rua Barão da Torre 218 (☎2522 0166). All open daily noon-1am. ❺

Choperia Amarelinho, Rua do Russel 30 (☎2558 3502). M: Catete. Branch of the famed yellow Cinelândia *botequim* (p. 131). Typical Brazilian menu (entrees for 2 R$15-30), plus a kilo (R$11.90 per kg) daily until 5pm. Open daily 11am-midnight. ❷

BOTAFOGO

Botafogo is Rio's hidden culinary treasure, with diverse, quality eateries popular with young Cariocas. Many places look upscale (the influence of Carême Bistro, one of Brazil's priciest fine dining spots), but all welcome even the most bedraggled, flip-flopped hostelers. The cheapest eats are at the **Cobal da Humaitá** (see **Bars & Live Music,** p. 155), a parking lot and produce market with a large food court and patio restaurants serving everything from *galetos* (roast chicken) to pizza to sushi. For those not staying at the hostel nearby, this culinary corner of Rio is accessible on any "Voluntários da Pátria" bus (buses just to "Botafogo" won't work).

Puebla Café Taquería, Rua Voluntários da Pátria 448, in front of the Cobal da Humaitá. A bit of Cancún in Rio, this patio hotspot offers decent Tex-Mex fare (burritos, fajitas, etc.; R$8-15) *really* far south of the border. Don't miss the rare libations (R$6-8) like fruity margaritas and jazzed-up tequila shots with wacky names (Adios Motherfucker?)–some even come to the table on fire! Open daily 9pm-2am. ❷

Yorubá, Rua Arnaldo Quintela 94 (☎2541 9387). Yorubá specializes in Baiano and African cuisine, and does both spectacularly. A Baiano *acarajé* is the perfect opener for the lengthy menu of rich African stews and curries. Entrees for 2 R$60-70. Open W-F 7pm-midnight, Sa-Su noon-8pm. ❺

Restaurante Aurora, Rua Capitão Salomão 51 (☎2539 4756). The area's cheapest sit-down restaurant, Aurora is like every other *botequim,* except for its low prices. Entrees for 2 R$15-23. *Pratos do dia* (daily special) M-Th under R$10, F-Su under R$20. Open Su-Th 8am-midnight, F-Sa 8am-2am. ❷

Botequim, Rua Visconde de Caravelas 184 (☎2537 7650). Exquisitely prepared European and Brazilian favorites (entrees for 2 R$15-23), their excellence matched by the charm of this lime-green townhouse and its romantic interior patio, ringed by rustling bamboo and flickering candles. Open Su-Th 11:30am-1am, F-Sa 11:30am-2am. ❸

Afrodite tis Milo, Rua Conde de Irajá 288 (☎2246 8430). Greek expat Adonis Nino whips up light, flavorful dishes from his homeland, including a winning *moussaka.* Often features the all-you-can-eat *banaeyeri,* a Greek food *rodízio* (R$20). Entrees R$10-20. Open Su-Th 11:30am-midnight, F-Sa 11:30am-2am. ❷

Stravaganze, Rua Visconde de Caravelas 121 (☎2535 0591). Tasty brick-oven pizzas with fresh imported toppings–light years away from the greasy cardboard you usually find in Rio (R$16-25). Wines R$5-10 per glass. Open daily 6pm-midnight. ❸

Madam Vidal, Rua Capitão Salomão (☎2246 0045). The exterior of the building may be dirty and industrial, but inside it's cozy, quiet, and candlelit–perfect for a nighttime seduction over bistro-style Mediterranean food (carpaccios, steak *au poivre,* pastas, salads, and more). Sadly, this Madam doesn't come cheap (entrees for 2 R$20-30). Open M-Th 9pm-2am, Sa-Su 9pm-3am. ❹

COPACABANA

Copacabana has some excellent restaurants, as well as Rio's highest concentration of *lanchonetes* along **Rua Barata Ribeiro.** Beachfront **Av. Atlântica** is lined with eateries, many geared toward tourists—always check your bill and change, and try to block out the incessant and annoying whistling of trinket sellers. All of these establishments are near M: Siqueira Campos.

Monchique, Av. NS de Copacabana 796A (☎2548 5140). A hit with the many hostelers in the area, this is Rio's cheapest *churrascaria,* with meat quality and buffet variety that rival classier places which charge 3-4 times more. All-you-can-eat buffet M-F R$11, Sa-Su R$14. Open daily 11am-midnight. ❷

Spa Natural/Miss Tanaka, Rua Santa Clara 95 (☎2548 5965). Veggie-friendly *lanchonete,* bakery, restaurant, and sushi bar (part of Rio's prestigious Tanaka San empire), all inside a natural food shop. Health nuts in a hurry will love the sandwiches, diet cakes, and sushi to go (all $3-5), but nothing beats the deliciously low-calorie, veggie-based *pratos feitos* (with 1 vegetarian option daily; R$9). Open daily 8am-11pm. ❷

Le Blé Noir, Rua Xavier da Silveira 15A (☎2287 1272). Charming French Provençal-style creperie that uses freshly imported ingredients in their savory (R$10-25) and sweet (R$6-9) *crepes* and *flambées.* Live French music W (cover R$6). Open Su and W-Th 7pm-1am, F-Sa 7pm-2am. ❸

Cozinheiro, Rua Bolívar 27A (☎2548 4372). A *botequim* for discerning gourmands. *Cozinheiro* (cook) Marcones de Deus definitely deserves top billing for his mouth-wateringly upscale gourmet flourishes on everyday Brazilian *botequim* fare—thankfully still at everyday prices (entrees for 2 R$15-30). Open Su-W noon-1am, Th-Sa noon-2am. ❸

Aipo & Aipim, Av. NS de Copacabana 605 (☎2549 2215). One of Rio's best, freshest kilos, with *churrascaria* (M-F R$18 per kg, Sa-Su R$20 per kg). 3 other locations on Av. NS de Copacabana (at 391, 902, and 1175) and 1 in **Ipanema,** Rua Visconde de Pirajá 145 (☎2267 8313). All open M-F 11am-11pm, Sa-Su 11am-6pm. ❷

Arataca, Rua Domingos Ferreira 41B (☎2288 6606). A tiny lunch counter inside a dingy market specializes in the authentic tastes of the Amazon, from well-known seafood stews like *vatapá* to exotic dishes like *maniçoba* (poison manioc with pork) and *galinha a gabidela* (chicken in its own blood). Entrees R$9-15. Open daily noon-midnight. ❷

Sorvete Itália, Rua Figueiredo de Magalhães 147 (☎2256 9283), with many other locations throughout the city. Rio's cheapest and largest ice cream chain is the perfect post-beach pit stop. Popsicles R$0.70. Cone R$2. Open daily 9am-9pm. ❶

The Bakers, Rua Santa Clara 86 (☎2256 7000). Bakers Allan and Dany Geller (cousins of NYC celebrity chef Monica) are the toast—and brioche, danish, and tart—of Rio thanks to this bakery and breakfast counter, serving Rio's best coffee (R$1-2), gourmet sandwiches (R$5-8), and sinfully rich Brazilian twists on European and American desserts, like the passionfruit cheesecake (R$3.50). Open M-F 9am-8pm, Sa-Su 9am-5pm. ❶

Marius, Av. Atlântica 290 (☎2543 6363), in **Leme.** Often named Rio's best all-you-can-eat *churrascaria* (R$39 per person)—hence the busloads of tourists—Marius definitely has the most variety: this spectacular parade of meats puts even the Sambódromo to shame. The attached **Marius Crustáceos** is an equally mind-boggling seafood-only *rodízio* (R$70). Open daily noon-midnight. ❺

Don Camillo, Av. Atlântica 3056 (☎2549 9958). *Al dente* meets *al fresco* at this classy, upscale Italian standout on Av. Atlântica, with prices to match. Candles, live nightly Italian music, and a hidden outdoor patio set the proper romance-and-red-sauce mood. Regionally based pastas and pizzas R$25-40. Open daily noon-2am. ❹

Arab, Av. Atlântica 1936A (☎2235 6698). Behind beachfront Arab's Alhambra-inspired facade is a sumptuous Middle Eastern feast, fit for a king but priced for a kilo (M-F R$18.60 per kg, Sa-Su R$22 per kg). After 5pm, Arab ditches the kilo and goes Franco-

Arabian a la carte, featuring a menu with everything from couscous to cassoulet (R$15-30). Open Tu-Su 11am-1am. ❷

Restaurante Lucas, Av. Atlântica 3744 (☎2521 4705). Among the best of Av. Atlântica's virtually identical Brazilian spots, this one with German specialties (pork chops, sauerkraut, and more) and Rio's best *chopp escuro* (dark-malt beer; R$2). Less of a tourist trap than others. Entrees for 2 R$16-25. Open daily 11am-2am. ❸

Transa, Av. Atlântica 3070 (☎2275 7299). A typical Atlântica patio eatery with an atypical name (don't say it in polite company), Transa softens the blow of its pricey traditional entrees (R$20-30) with excellent budget *pratos* (R$10) meant for 1 but big enough to share. Their pork offerings are the best in Rio. Open daily 11am-2am. ❹

Pizzaria Caravelle, Rua Domingos Ferreira 220B and 221A (☎2236 7151). The place that first introduced pizza to Rio still serves a decent (if greasy) pie at a great price (R$11-20). Top it off with a huge ice cream sundae (R$7.50). Open daily until midnight. ❸

IPANEMA

Along with Leblon, Ipanema has the best food in Rio and the price tag to show it. While Ipanema may not have many *lanchonetes*, its amazing array of international and fusion restaurants are sure to please.

Yemanjá, Rua Visconde de Pirajá 128 (☎2247 7004). Experience the sights, sounds, and flavors of Bahia right in Rio. Named after the Candomblé goddess of the sea, Yemanjá appropriately specializes in hearty seafood dishes, with waitresses in traditional white dresses ladling up gigantic pots of the seafood stew *moqueca* (feeds 3; R$50-90). Open Su noon-10pm, M-Th 6pm-midnight, F-Sa noon-midnight. ❺

Garota de Ipanema, Rua Vinícius de Moraes 49 (☎2523 3787). Join tourists and locals at this ordinary *botequim* with an extraordinary story: it's on this corner patio that Vinícius and Tom composed "Girl from Ipanema," inspired by a tall and tan and young and lovely girl who walked by here every day (p. 30). Thankfully, the view and the prices (entrees for 2 R$12-25) haven't changed much since then. Priceless *bossa nova* and "Garota" memorabilia (including original lyrics) on the walls. Open daily 11am-3am. ❷

Piola, Rua Paul Redfern 44 (☎2249 4881). With branches in Miami and Venice, Piola is a casually sexy pizzeria for the mod squad—thankfully not at globe-trotting prices, and *sans* any jet-set attitude. Their homemade dough is piled high with imported ingredients like Parma ham, porcinis, and provolone. Individual thin-crust pies R$11-18. Open M-F 6pm-2am, Sa-Su noon-3am. ❸

Mil Frutas, Rua Garcia D'Ávila 134 (☎2521 1384). Rio's best *sorveteria,* with exotic flavors to make any *suco* jealous (and tongue-tied): *atemoya, açaí, cupuaçu, pitanga, taperebá* with *sake...* Open M-F 10:30am-1am, Sa-Su 9:30am-1am. ❶

Zazá Bistrô Tropical, Rua Joana Angélica 40 (☎2247 9101). Mil Frutas just puts them in ice cream; Zazá has perfected the art of cooking with Rio's bounty of exotic tropical fruits—in Brazilian-Thai fusion cuisine, of course. Try the passion fruit-glazed tuna, the duck with *mangaba-taparebá* chutney (R$26-35), or let the chef surprise you (tasting menu R$115). Rio's most romantic spot, with an upstairs "harem-style" dining room. Open Su-Th 12:30pm-1am, F-Sa 12:30pm-2am. ❹

Carretão, Rua Visconde de Pirajá 112 (☎2267 3965), on Pça. Osório. A classy but informal *churrascaria* with good variety and a great price (all-you-can-eat R$16-19). No swimsuits allowed. Open daily 11am-midnight. ❷

Bistrô do Livro, Rua Barão da Torre 348 (☎2523 4842). Fantastic gourmet Euro-Brazilian fusion...in a bookstore! Browse the shelves between courses like banana-gruyère *confit, tournedos* with asparagus tempura, and mango-chantilly cheesecake. What sauce goes with Jorge Amado? (Clove and cinnamon, of course.) Entrees R$20-30. Open daily 9am-1am. ❹

New Natural, Rua Barão da Torre 167 (☎2287 0301). Looking for seitan *salgados* or an all-vegetable *feijoada?* Head to this ample, excellent vegetarian kilo (there are even a few meat options for your bloodthirsty carnivore friends). Next door to the 3 Barão da Torre hostels. M-F R$18.50 per kg, Sa-Su R$21 per kg. Open daily 7am-11pm. ❷

Nik Sushi, Rua Garcia D'Ávila 83 (☎2512 6446). A favorite local *maki*-roller with both an a la carte menu and a sprawling sushi and salad buffet, served kilo at lunch (Tu-Sa 11:30am-3:30pm, R$22.50 per kg) and all-you-can-eat at dinner (Tu-Sa 7pm-midnight, Su 7-10pm; R$30). Open Tu-Su from 11:30am. ❸

Gergelim, Rua Vinícius de Moraes 121 (☎2523 7026). A teeny slice of heaven for vegetarians and veggie sympathizers, serving low-calorie, high-flavor food like quiches and salads (R$9-10), plus more substantial carnivore fare (R$13-18), all using organic produce and healthy cuts of meat and fish. Open Tu-F noon-11pm, Sa-Su 9am-midnight. ❸

Via Sete, Rua Garcia D'Ávila 123 (☎2512 8100). Omigod, like, *picanha so* goes with a whiskey sour! *The* hangout of Rio's "expat brats," this sexy outdoor café serves potent American cocktails (cosmopolitans, apple martinis, and more; R$5-10) to wash down the mammoth burgers (R$10-17). Open Su-Tu 11am-1am, W-Sa 11am-2am. ❷

LEBLON

The food scene in Leblon is identical to that in Ipanema—unique, upscale food from around the world, in a unique, upscale setting.

Sushi Leblon, Rua Dias Ferreira 256 (☎2512 7830). Repeatedly chosen as Rio's best sushi parlor, this upscale but affordable spot has over 1hr. waits on weekends. Don't miss the exhaustive list of imported *sakes* and teas. Rolls R$7+. Open Su 1:30pm-midnight, M-Sa 7pm-1:30am. ❹

Vegetariano Social Clube, Rua Conde Bernadotte 26, loja L (☎2294 5200). A vegetarian restaurant in the land of *churrascarias?!* The shame of being Rio's *only* meatless eatery may have banished it to a hidden strip mall, but tree-huggers still flock for filling and flavorful (and animal product-free) fare like *palmito*-shiitake stroganoff. Lunch *pratos feitos* R$10. Entrees R$7-20. Open Su noon-6pm, M-Sa noon-midnight. ❸

Nam Thai, Rua Rainha Guilhermina 95B (☎2259 2962). The only Thai restaurant in Rio works tamarind-laced miracles with Rio's seafood bounty and an ever-changing menu of authentic Thai recipes, like *gruay ditov pad knee mao* (fried rice with squid, broccoli, and Thai basil). Entrees for 2 R$25-50. Open M-F from 7pm, Sa-Su from noon. ❹

Antiquarius, Rua Aristides Espinola 19 (☎2294 1049). The best Portuguese restaurant in town, though this hearty, stew-heavy taste of the motherland isn't cheap (entrees R$40-80). The specialty is traditional *bacalhau* (salt cod); order it and get a commemorative Portuguese *azulejo* (blue tile) plate. Open daily noon-2am. Discover only. ❺

Fellini, Rua Gen. Urquiza 104 (☎2511 3600). Born the year its namesake Italian *cinéaste* died, Fellini was one of Rio's first kilos, and is still one of its best (R$21.50 per kg). No *churrascaria,* but lots of gourmet options like lobster and ginger-honey duck. Open Su-Th 11:30am-midnight, F-Sa 11:30am-1am. ❷

SIGHTS

Though Rio is known more for its bikini-clad sights than any museums or buildings, the former Imperial and Republican capital of Brazil does have a few spots of historical, cultural, and artistic interest for those rainy days.

POSTCARD VIEWS (CARTAS-POSTAIS)

Rio's most recognizable (and most visited) sights are its two scenic lookouts: Pão de Açúcar (Sugarloaf) and Corcovado, the latter topped by the famous open-armed statue of Christ the Redeemer. They face each other across Botafogo.

CORCOVADO

Corcovado Train Station, Rua Cosme Velho 513, Cosme Velho, west of Flamengo. Take any "Cosme Velho" bus to the end of the line (Bus #583 from Botafogo or the beaches; Bus #180 from Centro or Glória/Catete); the station is on the left. Taxi to train station R$8-12, or you can arrange a round-trip fare (including wait) with any taxista *(around R$60). ☎2558 1329; www.corcovado.com.br. Round-trip train ticket to statue R$25. Open daily 8:30am-7pm.*

Hovering over the city with his arms outstretched, the giant statue of **Cristo Redentor** (Christ the Redeemer) atop 710m high Corcovado mountain stands as one of the most iconic and enduring images of Rio—and offers the city's most spectacular view. From the lookout points scattered at the feet of the 30m tall, 1100 ton statue (the world's largest Art Deco work), you'll see all of Rio laid out breathtakingly before you. Christ faces Botafogo and the Pão de Açúcar, in its most photographed position; his left hand stretches toward Maracanã stadium and the Zona Norte; and his right hand points to Copacabana and Ipanema, with Lagoa in the foreground and the Pedra Dois Irmãos (Two Brothers' Rock) behind. Visit at sunset and you'll cast away any lingering doubts you may have about whether Rio de Janeiro is the most beautiful place on earth. Whenever you go to Corcovado, take your time, take your camera, and always check the mountains for cloudiness and fog beforehand. For as the sign at the ticket booth says: "We are not responsible for the weather around Christ."

The trip up to the statue is on a slow-moving train that lugs you and every other tourist in Rio up the side of the jackfruit-covered mountain in about 20min. Through the right-hand window you'll catch glimpses of Ipanema, Lagoa, and the steep green mountains of Parque Nacional da Tijuca. Once the train drops you off, you used to (until 2003) have to climb 210 steep steps up to the actual statue. (When the Pope visited in 1980, he couldn't handle the uphill trek and had to be airlifted up to the chapel housed in the pedestal of the statue.) Thankfully, Brazil's Banco Real recently spearheaded a multimillion-*real* campaign to make improvements on the sight, so there is now a series of swift, sleek elevators and escalators that lead right to Christ's feet and the sweeping vistas visible from it.

A block up the street from the train station is **Museu Internacional de Art Naïf,** Rua Cosme Velho 561 (☎2205 8547), which houses the world's largest collection of *naïf* art—the strikingly vivid, at times even primitive, art of self-taught amateur artists. Brazil is one of the world's centers of *naïf* art; you'll find it for sale here and at the market held nightly on the Av. Atlântica median, near Posto 6.

PÃO DE AÇÚCAR (SUGARLOAF)

Cable Car Station, Av. Pasteur 520, Urca, east of Botafogo. Take any "Urca" bus to Pça. Gen. Tibúrcio, the end of the line (Bus #512 from the beaches; Bus #107 from Centro; Bus #571 from Botafogo or Glória/Catete); the station is in the praça's far corner. Taxi from M: Botafogo or Shopping Rio Sul R$10. ☎2546 8400; www.bondinho.com.br. Round-trip cable car ticket R$24. Open daily 8am-10pm.

Sugarloaf gets its name from its similarity to the loaf-shaped *(pão)* mountains of discarded sugarcane chaff generated by African slaves working on sugar *(açúcar)* plantations in colonial Brazil. It seems improbable that this giant ungainly rock should warrant as much attention and feelings of civic pride as the Pão de Açúcar gets—until you catch the view from the top. Though it's not as panoramic as the lookouts on Corcovado, Rio still manages to steal your breath away (rather than your wallet, camera, or watch) when seen from the famed Pão de Açúcar.

The ride to the top of Pão de Açúcar takes two trips, both on harrowingly speedy cable cars that have left more than one visitor sweaty-palmed. The first car runs up to Morro da Urca, which has lookouts facing Guanabara Bay, Niterói, and Sugarloaf itself, as well as a helipad for aerial city tours (R$200+) and a pleasant bar-restaurant that often features live music around sunset. The second car runs to the top of Pão de Açúcar, usually passing a few intrepid climbers and hikers heading to the top on foot. At the top there's a warren of balconies and lookouts facing the city, as well as a large patio bar where many stake out an early afternoon spot so they can catch the sunset with *caipirinha* in hand. Sunset is indeed the best time to visit (and everyone knows it): you'll see Centro, Copacabana, and the neighborhoods lining Guanabara Bay come twinkling to life in the dusky twilight, as the ghostly backlit statue of Christ watches over them all. It gets crowded, but you should be able to find a spot, and cloud cover is not nearly as much of a problem as it is atop foggy Corcovado.

CENTRO & LAPA

Rio's buzzing, urban downtown is also its oldest and most historic district, home to most of Rio's important (man-made) sights and cultural institutions. This is often called the most "European" part of the city, both for the old-world charm of its colonial-era buildings and for the layout of its streets: broad boulevards and beautiful *praças* inspired by Hausmann's grandiose design of Paris.

Because Centro is also Rio's major business and commercial district, it is both deserted and shut down on weekends, and should consequently be avoided then. On weekdays, however, this chaotic and lively area stays busy until that last executive finishes off his last *chopp* some time in the early evening.

CINELÂNDIA (PRAÇA FLORIANO) & ENVIRONS

The most picturesque square in a city with beauty to spare, Pça. Floriano (at M: Cinelândia, off Av. Rio Branco) is unmistakably the heart of Centro. At the end of the work day, there's no better place to down a few *choppes* than at one of the cafés or bars lining the *praça* (try Bar & Restaurante Amarelinho, p. 131).

The area is presided over by the Neoclassical facades of three of Rio's most august cultural institutions, all built just after the turn of the century: facing the *praça* across Av. Rio Branco are the **Biblioteca Nacional** (National Library) and **Museu Nacional de Belas Artes** (National Fine Arts Museum; see below); towering over it all is the gaudily lavish **Teatro Municipal,** home to Rio's ballet, opera, and symphony orchestra. In a twist only Cariocas could truly appreciate, facing these venerable grandes dames across the *praça* is the highest concentration of porn-peddling newsstands in Rio, which separate Pça. Floriano from the small park **Praça Mahatma Gandhi,** named for a statue of the freedom fighter (a gift from India) positioned at its entrance. Next to Pça. Mahatma Gandhi is Rio's oldest public park, the **Passeio Público,** where a stamp and postcard fair is held every Sunday.

MUSEU NACIONAL DE BELAS ARTES (NATIONAL FINE ARTS MUSEUM). Museu Nacional de Belas Artes has gallery after tastefully decorated gallery of largely forgettable Brazilian and European art (mostly paintings) from the 17th to 20th centuries, much of the latter brought over to Brazil by fleeing Portuguese royalty. The soothing setting—including a tiny courtyard—is the true highlight of a visit to the museum, but also worth a peek are Meireles's panoramic paintings of old Rio. Most signs and descriptions are in both Portuguese and English. *(Av. Rio Branco 199. M: Cinelândia. ☎2240 0068. Open Tu-F 10am-6pm, Sa-Su 2-6pm, tickets sold daily until 5pm. R$4, students R$1; free Su.)*

CATEDRAL METROPOLITANA. Although there are countless ornate, intimate colonial-era churches throughout Rio, the city's most important church—the home of the Archdiocese of Rio de Janeiro—is a modern concrete monstrosity built in the late 1950s. However, the cathedral's rather nondescript gray exterior belies its unique and awe-inspiring interior, which is mystically lit with shifting hues of light thanks to the design of the walls and the striking Technicolor stained-glass windows that run the height of the building. Designed by Oscar Niemeyer's colleague

Edgar de Oliveira da Fonseca in the form of a truncated cone (the cone's top has been "cut off" and placed beside it, functioning as a transparent bell tower), the church's distinct shape is meant to echo the "hunchback" shape of Rio's more famous sights, Corcovado and Pão de Açúcar. Though the floor plan is circular, the cruciform layout typical of most churches is echoed in the Greek cross-shaped skylight. The cathedral is officially dedicated to São Sebastião (St. Sebastian), who has a chapel behind the altar. Downstairs is a museum of sacred art, with colonial relics like thrones and royal baptismal fonts, taken from the archdiocese's collection. *(Av. República do Chile 245, between Centro and Lapa. M: Carioca. ☎2240 2669. Open daily 7am-5:30pm; Catholic mass M-F 11am, Su 10am. Cathedral free; museum R$4.)*

PRAÇA XV DE NOVEMBRO & ENVIRONS

Once known as the Largo do Paço (Palace Square), this large, open *praça* facing the bay just off Av. 1 de Março was the site where Portuguese fleeing Europe built their first royal palace and house of governance, the Paço Imperial. The *praça* saw important moments in Brazil's imperial era, including two coronations and the proclamation of the abolition of slavery. Once the Republic was declared, the area was renamed Pça. XV de Novembro or Pça. Quinze ("PRA-sa KEEN-zee") to commemorate the date of Brazil's independence from colonial rule, November 15. Appropriately, the *praça* is centered on an equestrian statue of Brazilian freedom fighter General Osório, who has his own square in Ipanema.

On the northern edge of the *praça* is the colonial-era **Arco do Teles** (Teles Arch), which leads to the busy Travessa do Comércio, one of the best preserved historical blocks in the city and a popular after-work hangout. In front of the Arco do Teles is the 18th-century **Chafariz da Pirâmide** (Pyramid Fountain), built by sculptor Mestre Valentim, who is also responsible for the fountain in General Osório's other square in Ipanema. Today Pça. XV de Novembro is a major city bus depot and the home of the ferry terminal for Guanabara Bay. It is also a good place to catch your breath before hoofing it to the museums south of the *praça*.

PAÇO IMPERIAL (IMPERIAL PALACE). This simple three-story "palace"—constructed in 1743—served as the seat of royal power during Brazil's colonial period. After independence, it was just a nondescript bureaucratic building, but was eventually reborn as the cultural center it is today. In addition to hosting art exhibitions, lectures, and performances, the palace has a European-style café, the Bistro do Paço; see p. 131. *(Pça. XV de Novembro 48. Open Tu-Su noon-6:30pm. Free.)*

MUSEU HISTÓRICO NACIONAL (NATIONAL HISTORY MUSEUM). Opened in 1922 to commemorate the centenary of Brazil's independence from colonial rule, this manageable, enjoyable, and informative museum (built on the site of the Fortaleza de Santiago) leads visitors on an excellent chronological walking tour through the history of Brazil, from colonial times to the present. The museum is crammed full of artifacts, clothing, paintings, and even several fully reconstructed period rooms, including a recreation of the Teixeira Novaes Pharmacy. The building is home to the world's largest collection of South American coins, as well as the world's largest collection of cannons. One of the more unusual objects on display is the unrestored portrait of Brazil's first emperor Dom Pedro I, in which his face has been scraped away by anti-imperialist Republicans. *(Pça. Marechal Âncora. From the bay side of Pça. XV de Novembro, with the bay on your left, follow the overpass–the elevated Av. Kubitschek–to Pça. Marechal Âncora. ☎2550 9224. Open Tu-F 10am-5:30pm, Sa-Su 2-6pm. R$5; free Su.)*

MUSEU DA IMAGEM E DO SOM (MUSEUM OF IMAGE & SOUND). Housed in an attractive colonial building stranded amidst cramped parking lots and dusty bus terminals, this museum has an archive of over 100,000 photos, audio tapes,

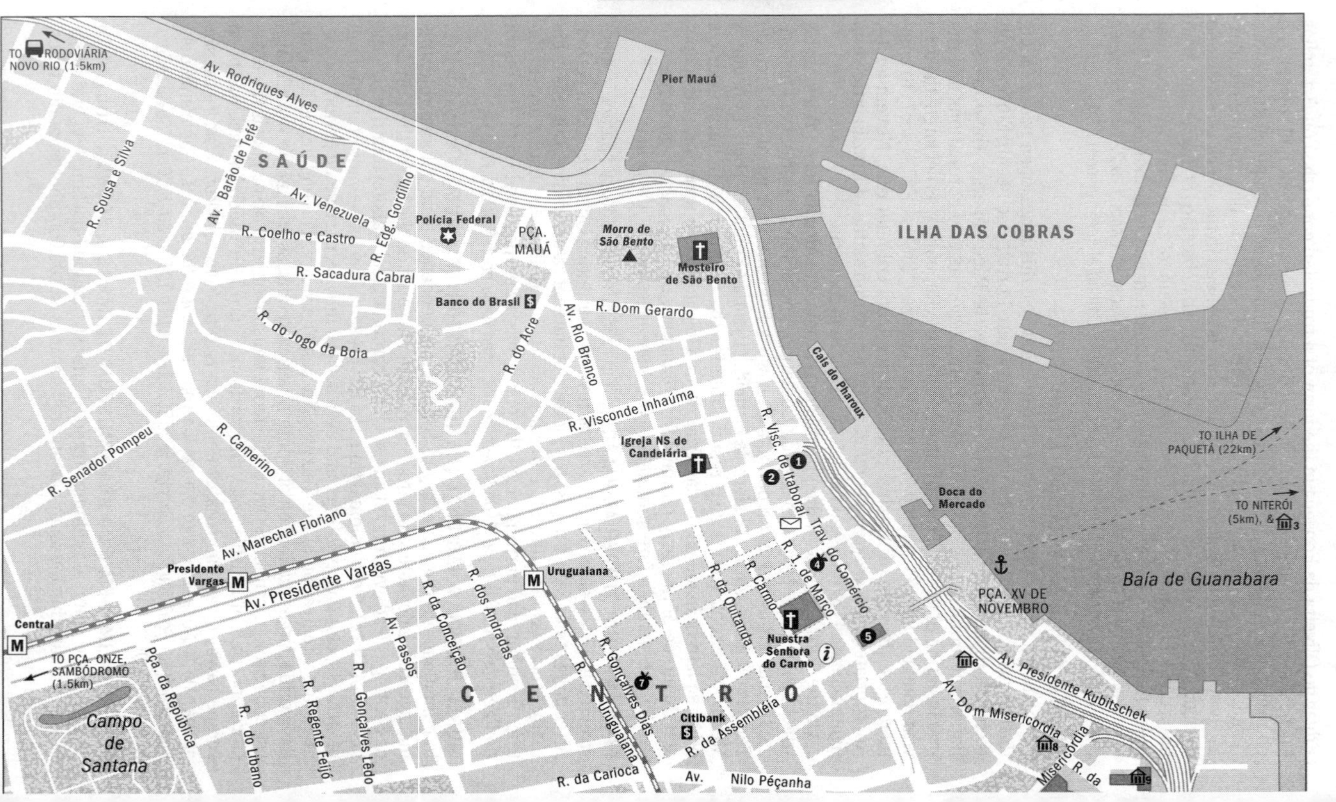

TO RODOVIÁRIA NOVO RIO (1.5km)
Av. Rodrigues Alves
Pier Mauá
ILHA DAS COBRAS
SAÚDE
R. Sousa e Silva
Av. Barão de Tefé
Av. Venezuela
R. Edg. Gordilho
R. Coelho e Castro
Polícia Federal
PÇA. MAUÁ
Morro de São Bento
Mosteiro de São Bento
R. Sacadura Cabral
Banco do Brasil
R. Dom Gerardo
R. do Jogo da Boia
R. do Acre
Av. Rio Branco
Cais do Pharoux
R. Visconde Inhaúma
R. Camerino
R. Senador Pompeu
Igreja NS de Candelária
R. Visc. de Itaboraí
TO ILHA DE PAQUETÁ (22km)
Doca do Mercado
TO NITERÓI (5km), & 3
Av. Marechal Floriano
Trav. do Comércio
R. 1. de Março
Presidente Vargas
Uruguaiana
Av. Presidente Vargas
R. Carmo
R. da Quitanda
Baía de Guanabara
PÇA. XV DE NOVEMBRO
Central
R. da Conceição
R. dos Andradas
Nuestra Senhora do Carmo
TO PÇA. ONZE, SAMBÓDROMO (1.5km)
Pça. da República
Av. Passos
R. Gonçalves Dias
Av. Presidente Kubitschek
R. Regente Feijó
R. Gonçalves Lêdo
CENTRO
Av. Dom Misericordia
Campo de Santana
R. do Libano
R. Uruguaiana
Citibank
R. da Assembléia
R. da Misericórdia
R. da Carioca
Av. Nilo Péçanha

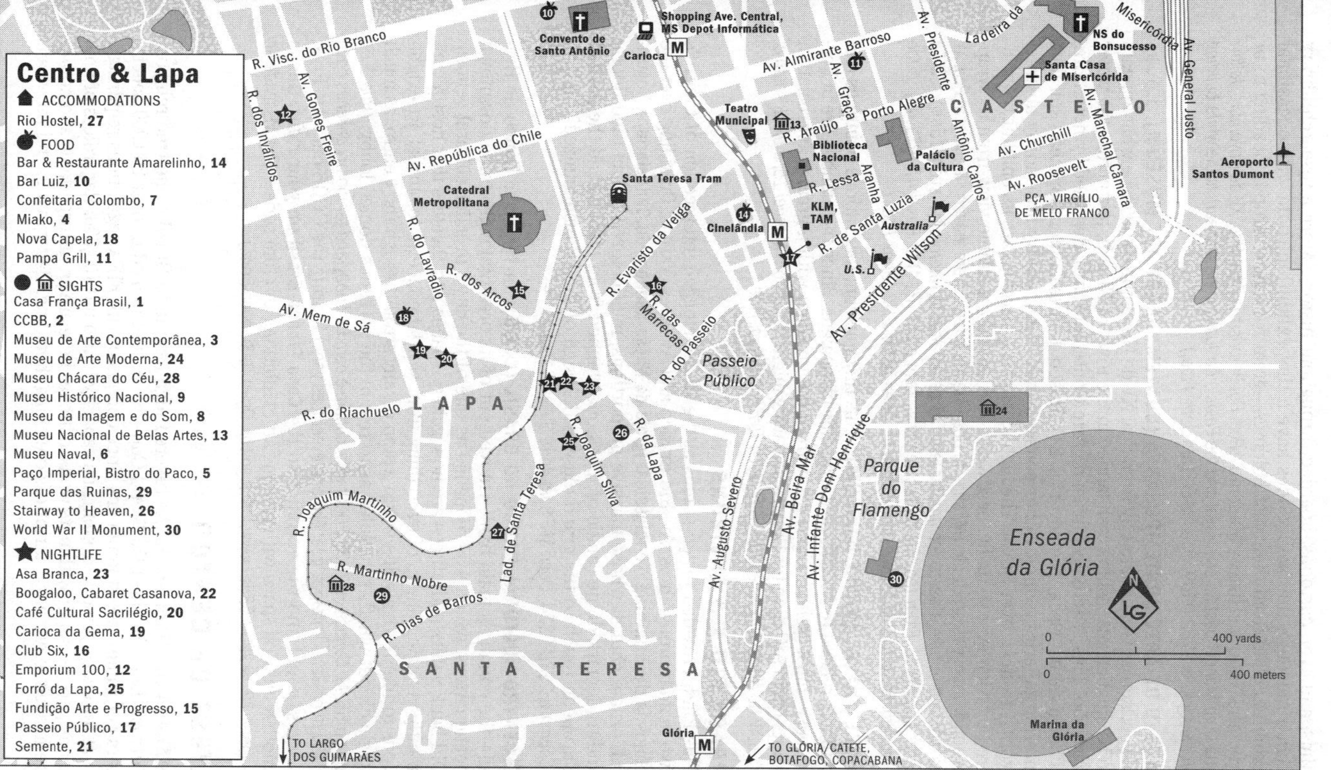
Centro & Lapa
ACCOMMODATIONS
Rio Hostel, 27
FOOD
Bar & Restaurante Amarelinho, 14
Bar Luiz, 10
Confeitaria Colombo, 7
Miako, 4
Nova Capela, 18
Pampa Grill, 11
SIGHTS
Casa França Brasil, 1
CCBB, 2
Museu de Arte Contemporânea, 3
Museu de Arte Moderna, 24
Museu Chácara do Céu, 28
Museu Histórico Nacional, 9
Museu da Imagem e do Som, 8
Museu Nacional de Belas Artes, 13
Museu Naval, 6
Paço Imperial, Bistro do Paco, 5
Parque das Ruinas, 29
Stairway to Heaven, 26
World War II Monument, 30
NIGHTLIFE
Asa Branca, 23
Boogaloo, Cabaret Casanova, 22
Café Cultural Sacrilégio, 20
Carioca da Gema, 19
Club Six, 16
Emporium 100, 12
Forró da Lapa, 25
Fundição Arte e Progresso, 15
Passeio Público, 17
Semente, 21
R. Visc. do Rio Branco
R. dos Inválidos
Av. Gomes Freire
Convento de Santo Antônio
Shopping Ave. Central, MS Depot Informática
Carioca
Av. Almirante Barroso
Av. Presidente Antônio Carlos
Ladeira da Misericórdia
NS do Bonsucesso
Santa Casa de Misericórdia
CASTELO
Av. General Justo
Aeroporto Santos Dumont
Teatro Municipal
R. Araújo
Av. Graça Aranha
Porto Alegre
Biblioteca Nacional
Palácio da Cultura
Av. Churchill
Av. Marechal Câmara
Av. Roosevelt
PÇA. VIRGÍLIO DE MELO FRANCO
Av. República do Chile
Catedral Metropolitana
Santa Teresa Tram
R. Lessa
KLM, TAM
Cinelândia
R. de Santa Luzia
Australia
U.S.
R. Evaristo da Veiga
Av. Presidente Wilson
R. do Lavradio
R. dos Arcos
R. das Marrecas
R. do Passeio
Av. Mem de Sá
Passeio Público
R. do Riachuelo
LAPA
R. Joaquim Silva
R. da Lapa
Av. Augusto Severo
Av. Beira Mar
Av. Infante Dom Henrique
Parque do Flamengo
R. Joaquim Martinho
Lad. de Santa Teresa
Enseada da Glória
R. Martinho Nobre
R. Dias de Barros
0 400 yards
0 400 meters
SANTA TERESA
Glória
Marina da Glória
TO LARGO DOS GUIMARÃES
TO GLÓRIA/CATETE, BOTAFOGO, COPACABANA

films, and even cartoons, hoarded throughout history. More a research library than a museum, the facility does have a tiny exhibition room with occasional exhibits culled from their vast holdings—great for a brief drop-in heading to or from the National History Museum. *(Pça. Rui Barbosa 1. From Pça. XV de Novembro, follow Rua Dom Manuel past Museu Naval and the Palácio da Justiça; the museum is the white building on the right. ☎2262 0309. Open M-F 11am-5pm. Free.)*

MUSEU DE ARTE CONTEMPORÂNEA (CONTEMPORARY ART MUSEUM). Looking out across Guanabara Bay from Pça. XV de Novembro, you'll see what appears to be an alien spaceship crash-landed in the town of Niterói, just across the water from Rio. This is actually Museu de Arte Contemporânea, designed by noted Brazilian architect Oscar Niemeyer (p. 24). Museu de Arte Contemporânea's spiraling interior galleries exhibit rather conservative contemporary art (mostly abstract works) from all over Brazil. The highlights of the museum are its building, considered by Niemeyer to be his best work, and the unforgettable view from its wraparound observation deck. *(Mirante da Boa Viagem, Niterói. From the ferry terminal at Pça. XV de Novembro, take a* barca *(commuter ferry) or catamaran to Niterói (M-F every 15min., Sa-Su every 1hr.; R$1). From the Niterói ferry terminal, take a taxi (R$4) or Bus #47 (R$1.40) to the museum. ☎2620 2481; www.macnit.com.br. Open Tu-Su 11am-6pm. R$5.)*

MUSEU NAVAL (NAVAL MUSEUM). This tiny museum has various paintings and artifacts related to Brazil's past maritime campaigns. Since the exhibits are in Portuguese, most visitors come away from the museum with a greater appreciation for its frigid A/C than for Brazil's seafaring might. *(Rua Dom Manuel 15, a block south of Pça. XV de Novembro. ☎2533 7626. Open Tu-F noon-4pm. Free.)*

RIO DE JANEIRO

PRAÇA PIO X & ENVIRONS

This loud, crowded *praça* stands at the traffic-clogged intersection of Centro's two main thoroughfares, Av. Rio Branco and Av. Pres. Vargas. Presiding over the chaos is the stunning Neoclassical **Igreja de Nossa Senhora da Candelária,** a beautiful, ornate church whose massive proportions, multicolored Italian tiled floors, and trademark dome (made of limestone shipped from Lisbon) add the perfect European touch to the grand old-world design of the "Hausmannized" Centro. *(Church ☎2233 2324. Open M-F 8am-4pm, Su 9am-1pm.)*

CENTRO CULTURAL BANCO DO BRASIL (CCBB). In 1989, the Banco do Brasil—the country's main bank—moved out of its breathtakingly grand downtown headquarters, which was reopened as one of the city's premier cultural venues. Old bank vaults and offices are now gallery spaces and theaters that host a constantly changing lineup of everything from *samba* concerts to surreal art exhibitions to film festivals. It's worth a stop on any stroll through the Centro, as much to check out what's scheduled as to rest in the gorgeous domed lobby. *(Rua 1 de Março 66. M: Carioca. ☎3808 2000; www.cultura-e.com.br. Lobby and temporary galleries open Tu-Su noon-8pm. Entrance free; film and event fees vary.)* Exiting the CCBB onto Av. Pres. Vargas, you'll find the entrance to the **Casa França Brasil** on your right; this is another cultural space with rotating art exhibitions and film series. *(Rua Visconde de Itaboraí 78. ☎2253 5366; www.fcfb.rj.gov.br. Open Tu-Su noon-8pm.)*

WEST OF CENTRO

MARACANÃ. Maracanã is the revered high temple to Brazil's one true religion: *futebol.* Built for the 1950 World Cup—when it crammed in over 200,000 spectators per game—the stadium has since complied with FIFA regulations requiring a seat for every person, dropping its capacity to around 100,000. Regardless of how many people can fit within its walls, matches here are an unforgettable and not-to-be-missed experience: a riot of screaming, heckling, flag-waving, and incessant

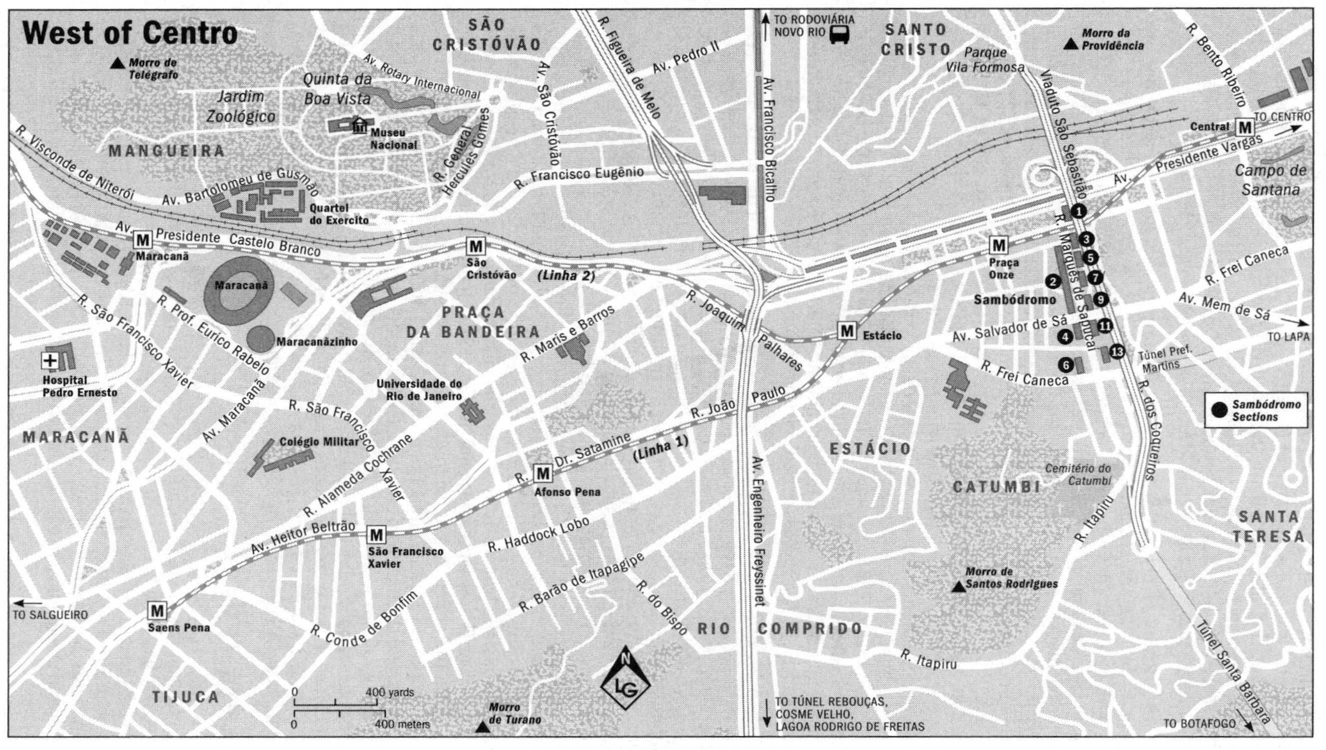

RIO DE JANEIRO

samba drumming—the perfect accompaniment to the flashy Brazilian pro-offense style of play. On non-game days, at Gate 18, you can visit the **Hall da Fama do Futebol** (Soccer Hall of Fame), featuring Brazilian *futebol* memorabilia like medals, cups, and jerseys—including the storied #10 jersey of Brazilian megastar Pelé, who scored his 1000th goal at Maracanã. *(Rua Professor Eurico Rabelo, at Av. Maracanã. M: Maracanã. ☎2568 9962. See* p. 153 *for info on seeing a game; tickets R$10+.)*

SAMBÓDROMO. During Carnaval this 600m long, 43,000+ capacity parade ground—built on and around Centro's Rua Marquês de Sapucaí—is the center of the action, where Rio's top *samba* schools strut their stuff for the five days of Carnaval. (See **Carnaval,** p. 46.) The grounds were designed in 1984 by Brasília creator Oscar Niemeyer (p. 24) specifically for the needs of Rio's *samba* parade. Before 1984, the parade took place in the streets of Centro, usually around nearby Pça. 11; to commemorate this, the Terreirão do Samba (see **Outdoor Bailes,** p. 57) is now held at Pça. 11 every year during Carnaval. At the southern end of the Sambódromo is the **Praça da Apoteose,** an elevated platform presided over by an "M"-shaped arch. It is here that the winners of the annual Carnaval parade are announced—hence the name "Apotheosis Plaza," as Carnaval champions are effectively immortalized. Outside of Carnaval, the grandstands are used as school buildings, meaning they're closed to the public. However, **Museu de Carnaval** within the Sambódromo (enter on Rua Frei Caneca) is open year-round, displaying costumes and artifacts from past Carnavals and offering an overview of *samba* and parade history. *(Rua Marquês de Sapucaí. Museum open Tu-Su 11am-5pm. Free.)*

QUINTA DA BOA VISTA. Though Brazil's royal families ruled the nation from Pça. XV de Novembro's Paço Imperial (p. 139), they made their home at the Quinta da Boa Vista, where Brazil's second emperor, Pedro II, was born. This sprawling, romantically landscaped villa west of Centro (in what is now one of Rio's most populous suburbs, São Cristóvão) has been turned into a public park popular on weekends with families from the Zona Norte. The grounds contain several lakes, waterfalls, and gardens, a small temple to Apollo, and the much-neglected (and much-graffitied) **Imperial Palace.** Like the Paço Imperial, this palace saw many important events in Brazil's history, including the declaration of independence from colonial rule, the writing and signing of Brazil's first constitution, and the royal abdication and declaration of the Republic of Brazil. The sweeping view from the upstairs balcony is what gives the villa its name (*boa vista*, "good view").

The palace is now **Museu Nacional** (National Museum), a natural history museum based on the collections of second emperor Dom Pedro II (a botanist) and his wife, Empress Teresa Cristina (an archaeologist). It has fossils, shards of pottery, minerals, and the like from around the world, plus exhibits depicting the lives and traditions of various peoples from across the nation. Behind the palace is the **Jardim Zoológico** (Zoological Garden), popular with children; admission to the zoo is included in museum admission. *(In São Cristóvão, at M: São Cristóvão (linha 2). Park ☎2503 3072, museum ☎2568 1149, zoo ☎2568 7400. Park open daily 7am-6pm; museum and zoo open Tu-Su 9am-4:30pm. Park free; museum and zoo Tu-F R$4, Sa-Su R$5.)*

SANTA TERESA

On a hill just west of Centro is Rio's own little piece of bohemia, a funky and slightly run-down neighborhood just now being discovered by tourists—even though it has been home to Rio's artists, musicians, and intellectuals for generations. Turned off by the urban chaos, skyrocketing rents, and lack of spare studio space in Rio's sea-level neighborhoods, starving artists and independent youth uninterested in living with their extended families for life have long fled to the spacious and cheap houses that line the twisting streets of this hilltop *bairro*. Though largely residential, the area does have plenty of bohemian bars, cheap restaurants, quirky craft shops, and *ateliers* (studios)—great for an afternoon of relaxed browsing. Most of the activity happens around **Largo dos Guimarães,** just beyond the first tram stop at **Largo do Curvelo.** Riding the antiquated tram (*bondinho;* see below) over cobblestoned streets, past front yard gardens and an eclectic array of architectural styles (as well as some of Rio's most imaginative street graffiti), you'll never believe this is the same city that is home to the traffic-clogged streets of Copacabana.

BONDINHO. Though it's often filled with more tourists than residents, this rickety old-time tram car (*bondinho*, or "little train") is the main form of public transportation in Santa Teresa. The tram runs from Centro over the **Arcos de Lapa** (Lapa Arches) and through the winding streets of Rio's charming bohemian enclave up to the Largo das Neves, where it loops back to Centro. You can stay on the tram for the entire round-trip loop, but on the way back to Centro many travelers get off at either Largo dos Guimarães, or the first stop, Largo do Curvelo, near the neighborhood's museums. *(Tram Station, Rua Lélio Gama, Centro, near Rua Senador Dantas, next to the Rubik's Cube-like Petrobras building. From M: Carioca, follow signs for Av. Chile/Petrobras, then cross Av. Chile to Rua Lélio Gama. Tram 15min.; every 15min. 9am-5pm; R$0.60.)*

ESCADA DO CÉU (STAIRWAY TO HEAVEN). These steps leading from Lapa's Rua Joaquim Silva to Santa Teresa's still-functional Carmelite convent (Convento de Santa Teresa) have become one of the area's most beloved landmarks. In an act complementing the artsy air surrounding this district, Chilean artist Selarón has covered the 215 steps in a mosaic of green, yellow, and blue tiles in homage to the people of Brazil. The tiles were taken from all over the world, and Selarón continues to replace tiles pieces as he finds more in his travels. Look for a blue ceramic piece broken off from one of legendary Rio eatery Antiquarius' commemorative codfish plates (p. 136), and for a yellow piece with the mark "NO8DO," a symbol of the Spanish city of Sevilla, Rio's sister city. *(Stairs branch off from Rua Joaquim Silva, just behind Lapa's Sala Cecília Meireles, Rua da Lapa 47.)*

MUSEU CHÁCARA DO CÉU. This small and enjoyable art museum is the former home of millionaire Raymundo Ottoni de Castro Maya, a prolific art collector with incredible taste in painting, sculpture, and antiques. The fully preserved rooms of his three-story late-1950s house are filled with fantastic artwork from all periods, from statues of the Buddha to Monets. The list of artists reads like a who's who of

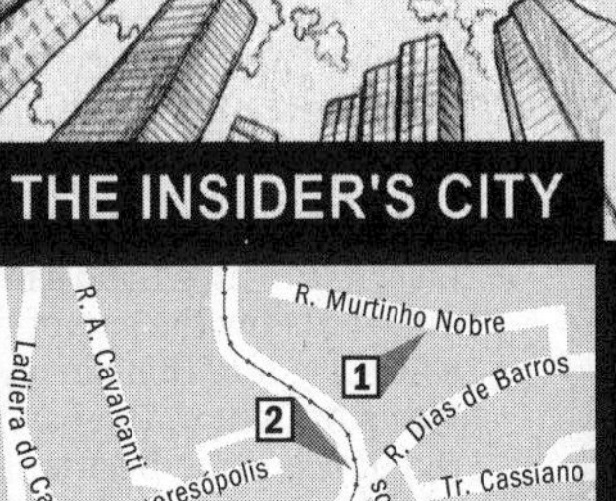

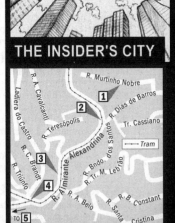

THE INSIDER'S CITY

VIVA SANTA

Santa Teresa, Rio's Bohemian hilltop enclave of arty bars and quirky shops is just now being discovered by tourists. The following spots are all along the main "Largo das Neves" bondinho *route (see left) that runs through Santa Teresa from Centro, over the Lapa Arches.*

1. The crumbling mansion inside the **Parque das Ruinas** offers a memorable view of Santa Teresa and free open-air concerts in the summer.
2. During Carnaval, catch Santa Teresa's rowdy street parade at **Curvelo Sq.,** the first tram stop.
3. Fuel up for the hike to the top of the hill at **Sobrenatural,** which serves Rio's best *bobó de camarão* (shrimp stew).
4. **Largo dos Guimarães** is the heart of Santa, with popular corner shops and bars (try Bar do Arnaudo and Bar do Mineiro).
5. Even if you don't live *la vie bohème,* dress the part with funky jewelry and clothes from the *atelier* shop/Internet cafe **Favela Hippie,** atop the hill.

the painting world's megastars—Dalí, Miró, Monet, Picasso, to name a few, as well as an impressive selection by Brazil's best-known contemporary artist, Cândido Portinari. *(Rua Martinho Nobre 93. From the tram stop at Largo do Curvelo, follow signs for the museum along Rua Dias de Barros as it curves back on itself and turns into Rua Martinho Nobre, which ends at the museum. Open W-M noon-5pm; grounds open daily 9am-5pm. R$2; free W.)*

PARQUE DAS RUINAS (RUINS PARK). The skeletal ruins of late-1930s socialite Laurinda Santos Lobo's mansion and grounds—once Rio's prime intellectual hangout—are now the site of this dusty but pleasant park. The balconies and lookouts where Isadora Duncan once danced to Heitor Villa-Lobos' music offer wraparound views of Centro, the bay neighborhoods, and the Pão de Açúcar; the top floor of the house is the best lookout. On weekends, the balcony is often the site of free outdoor concerts of *samba* and *bossa nova;* check the schedule posted at the entrance on Rua Martinho Nobre. *(Follow the walkway into the park from outside Museu Chácara do Céu, Rua Martinho Nobre 93. The exit (and alternate entrance) drops you at Rua Martinho Nobre 85, closer to the tram and Santa Teresa's main drag. Open daily 9am-5pm. Free.)*

GLÓRIA & CATETE

The historic **Parque do Catete,** at M: Catete, is home to two excellent, well-curated museums (see below) that are an enjoyable diversion on a cloudy day. Both are conveniently accessible from the area's budget hotels.

MUSEU DE FOLCLORE EDISON CARNEIRO (FOLKLORE MUSEUM). An excellent (if rather dimly lit) museum dedicated to Brazil's imaginative, colorful, and often whimsical folk art tradition, presented in five different exhibition spaces, each dedicated to one of five broad categories (technique, religion, celebration, art, life). The *festa* (celebration) section is the highlight, featuring elaborate costumes and props from Carnaval celebrations elsewhere in the country, including animal-shaped Amazonian chariots and glittering, hooped Baiano dresses; many of these even put Rio's over-the-top *samba* parade *fantasias* (costumes) to shame. The exhibits are entirely in Portuguese, but the art speaks quite eloquently for itself. *(Rua do Catete 181, next to Museu da República. M: Catete. ☎2285 0441. Open Tu-F 11am-5pm, Sa-Su 3-6pm. R$4.)*

IGREJA DE NOSSA SENHORA DA GLÓRIA DO OUTEIRO. This small, octagonal church sits on a hill peeking out at Largo da Glória. It is a baroque masterpiece, ornately decorated inside and out, but its most important feature is its location: the hill on which the church sits was the strategic point that Estácio de Sá, Rio's founder, seized from the French, allowing him to establish the first settlement in March 1565. *(Pça. NS da Glória 135. M: Glória. ☎2557 4600. Open Tu-F 9am-noon and 1-5pm, Sa-Su 9am-noon. Free.)*

MUSEU DA REPÚBLICA (MUSEUM OF THE REPUBLIC). This museum is housed in the Parque do Catete's grand **Palácio do Catete** (Catete Palace), which was the seat of the country's government during the Republican era until the new capital was built in Brasília in 1960. The exhibits on the top floor feature art and artifacts related to the Republican period and the presidents who governed in that era. A lot of space is dedicated to one of Brazil's most beloved and controversial figures, President Getúlio Vargas. Often criticized for promoting social programs and other purportedly "communist" ideas, Vargas eventually committed suicide in the palace in August of 1954; the room where he shot himself has been somberly preserved, with the fatal bullet and torn, blood-stained pajama top on display. The rooms on the second floor have been restored to their gaudy, Italianate glory, and the first floor houses temporary exhibits. *(Rua do Catete 153. M: Catete. ☎2558 6350. Open Tu and Th-F noon-5pm, W 2-5pm, Sa-Su 1-5pm. R$5, students R$2.50; free W.)*

FLAMENGO

PARQUE DO FLAMENGO (ATERRO). Hugging the bay from Botafogo to Centro is 1.2 million square meters of park officially named the Parque Brigadeiro Eduardo Gomes, usually referred to as the **Parque do Flamengo** or just the Aterro (landfill). Once entirely underwater, this area was filled in 1965 with land from the leveled hilltop *favela* Morro do São Antônio. It was landscaped as a recreational area by Roberto Burle Marx (p. 24), who is best known for the distinctive black-and-white sidewalks of Rio as well as his landscaping of Brasília. The park and adjoining Flamengo and Botafogo beaches (see p. 150) are popular with working-class Cariocas from the Zona Norte; there always seems to be a *futebol* game on at one of the park's fields. The polluted ditch that runs through the park and empties into Guanabara Bay is the remains of the Rio Carioca (Tupi for "White Man's River"), which gives the residents of Rio their name. It's better to stop in and visit the park's three museums (listed below from north to south) during the day, as the park is considered unsafe for tourists at night. *(Take any "Praia do Flamengo" or "Via Aterro" bus.)*

MUSEU DE ARTE MODERNA (MAM; MUSEUM OF MODERN ART). It may look like an airplane hangar or a futuristic fortress (and its proximity to a military school and Santos Dumont Airport doesn't help), but this giant inverted concrete pyramid on the north end of the Parque do Flamengo is in fact Rio's premier venue for cutting-edge art in all media. A 1978 fire damaged the building, closed the museum for four years, and destroyed much of the permanent collection. Thankfully, the cavernous interior has now been fully restored and hosts temporary exhibits drawn from the museum's ever-expanding collection of mostly Brazilian work. The museum's grounds were designed by the Parque do Flamengo's landscaper, Roberto Burle Marx (p. 24); his signature wavy mosaic sidewalks appear all over in red and white, including a special garden where the grass has been mowed in similar waves. *(Av. Infante Dom Henrique 85, off Praia do Flamengo. Take any "Praia do Flamengo" bus. Best approached from Centro (M: Cinelândia); at Av. Pres. Wilson, Av. Graça Aranha (which changes to Av. Calógeras) becomes a pedestrian overpass leading over the Aterro do Flamengo and the highway right to the MAM entrance. ☎ 2240 4944; www.mamrio.org.br. Open Tu-F noon-6pm. R$8, students and 66+ R$4; W everyone R$4.)*

NATIONAL MONUMENT TO THE WWII DEAD. With its surreal design, distinctive high tower, spiky sculptures, and larger-than-life roof statues, this edifice (officially known as the Monumento Nacional dos Mortos da Segunda Guerra Mundial) looks more like an escaped masterpiece from Museu de Arte Moderna next door than the somber memorial to Brazil's WWII dead that it's meant to be. The site houses a small museum with war memorabilia and uniforms, as well as the Tomb of the Unknown Soldier. *(Aterro do Flamengo, just south of Museu de Arte Moderna. Open Tu-Su 10am-4pm, but in practice opening hours vary.)*

MUSEU CARMEN MIRANDA. This small museum is unsurprisingly crammed full of memorabilia (costumes, programs, and recordings) pertaining to sassy 1940s superstar Carmen Miranda, most famous for her fruity headdresses. Born in Portugal but raised in Rio, Carmen was worshipped in her adopted homeland until she left to make it big on Broadway and in Hollywood; returning to Rio a Hollywood megastar, she was snubbed for being too American. Legend has it she was once so hurt by this frosty reception that she locked herself in a suite at the Copacabana Palace Hotel for two months. The museum has several lavish costumes worn by this gay icon, but you'll see equally impressive and florid costumes on the men in the street parades of the GLS-friendly Banda da Carmen Miranda (see **Blocos,** p. 53) during Carnaval. *(Opposite Av. Rui Barbosa 560. ☎ 2551 2597. Practically impossible to reach by bus; it's best to take a taxi (R$10-20). Open Tu-F 11am-5pm, Sa-Su 1-5pm. R$4.)*

BOTAFOGO

MUSEU DO ÍNDIO (INDIAN MUSEUM). One of the major archives of indigenous artifacts in South America, Museu do Índio is one of the only museums in Rio to utilize the concept of the interactive, multimedia exhibit—and how! The hands-on, technically innovative, at times even psychedelic exhibits (mostly in Portuguese) explore the histories, traditions, and daily lives of the various indigenous peoples of Brazil in fascinating detail. Several tribes have planted medicinal herbs and constructed traditional dwellings on the land surrounding the museum; these can be seen separately from the museum for free. *(Rua das Palmeiras 55. From M: Botafogo, walk against traffic up Rua Voluntários da Pátria and turn right onto Rua das Palmeiras. ☎2286 8899; www.museudoindio.com.br. Open Tu-F 9am-5:30pm, Sa-Su 1-5pm. R$3; tickets are only sold at the museum store, in the far left corner of the yard as you enter.)*

MUSEU CASA RUI BARBOSA. The mansion where Bahia-born politician, jurist, and diplomat Rui Barbosa spent the last 30 years of his life has been converted into a museum honoring Barbosa and his role in shaping Brazilian politics. Of little interest to anyone but the most ardent Brazilian history buff (although Barbosa's shiny late-model Mercedes-Benz may merit a peek), the real reason to stop by is for a rest and a stroll through the shady gardens surrounding the mansion—one of Botafogo's only public green spaces. *(Rua São Clemente 134. From M: Botafogo, walk against traffic up Rua Muniz Barreto and turn left onto Rua São Clemente. ☎2537 0036. Open Tu-F 9:30am-5pm, Sa-Su 2-5pm. Museum R$3; free Su. Gardens free.)*

MUSEU VILLA-LOBOS. Born and raised in the Laranjeiras suburb of Rio, classical composer Heitor Villa-Lobos is yet another major Carioca name in the world of music. Many of his works focused on Brazilian folklore and history, including the nine *Bachianas Brasileiras (1930-45)*, a series of diverse works merging the folk music traditions of Brazil and the rigid baroque style of J.S. Bach. This tiny converted house on a quiet side street has displays about Villa-Lobos's life and work, showcasing original musical scores, personal effects, and several of his instruments. *(Rua Sorocaba 200. From M: Botafogo, walk against traffic up Rua Voluntários da Pátria and turn right onto Rua Sorocaba. ☎2266 3845. Open M-F 10am-5:30pm. Free.)*

COPACABANA

Visitors to Rio are almost always taken aback by how unlike Copacabana Copacabana is. Once the most desirable address on this side of the equator—an almost fantasy destination synonymous with glamor and decadence—this now crowded, dirty, and noisy middle-class neighborhood has seen better days. Named for an extant settlement on the Bolivian shore of Lake Titicaca, this once-deserted area was cut off from the rest of Rio by the Serra da Carioca mountain range until the turn of the 20th century. When the city finally dug a tunnel through the mountains, people began trickling in, but Copa didn't become the playground of the stars until after 1923, when the luxurious white confection known as the **Copacabana Palace Hotel,** Av. Atlântica 1702, opened up on Copa's northern end.

Word of the hotel's decadence—and the city's equally hedonistic beauty—spread quickly among the world's glitterati. The Copacabana Palace Hotel single-handedly created the star-studded, upper-crust Rio myth, drawing jet-setters from around the world to this sun-dappled paradise. The 1930s and 40s were truly Rio's golden age of glamor, and indeed, it's in and around the Copacabana Palace that the era's biggest movie stars—Fred Astaire and Ginger Rogers—first danced together, in the 1933 film *Flying Down to Rio.* It remains the superstar hotel of choice, having hosted everyone from Frank Sinatra to Mick Jagger, in addition to Rio's premier high-society Carnaval event.

While the hottest bars and clubs did excellent business here for decades, by the mid-70s the "in" crowd had moved out to Ipanema and Leblon, still Rio's trendiest spots. By the late 80s Copa had fallen on really hard times, and remained quite dangerous until yet another spate of beachfront luxury hotel-building revived the area economically and physically. While hotels like the svelte **Le Meridien** (now such a vital part of the Rio landscape that it's incorporated into the logo of Riotur, the city's tourist bureau) helped revive that top-hat-and-tails image of the 1940s, the traffic-clogged modern-day Copacabana is still not the same one Fred and Ginger knew. (It's also not the Copacabana of the often-hummed Barry Manilow song "At the Copa," which refers to a Miami nightclub.) At just six kilometers long and merely four blocks wide, this is South America's densest and most crowded district, with nearly 5000 people per block.

Yet despite its shabby state, Copacabana remains Brazil's major tourist destination, thanks to the unforgettable chaos of the world's most famous beach (fronted by **Avenida Atlântica;** see p. 117), not to mention the frantic fever of the inland streets. For those who want to truly appreciate Copacabana's beauty (and we don't mean the bikini-clad kind), there's the **Forte de Copacabana,** a functional military fortress built in 1914 on the beach's southern end. There are exhibits on Brazil's army, but the main attraction here is the view. *(☎2521 1032. Open Tu-Su 10am-4pm. R$4.)*

IPANEMA

It's not surprising that the ambling, sensual beats of *bossa nova* were born in Ipanema: this is Rio's most walkable neighborhood, with a sort of sexy, sophisticated style that most travelers associate with Rio based on its early 20th-century golden age. This small (mostly residential) district of attractive, tree-lined streets and quiet squares is centered on bustling **Rua Visconde de Pirajá,** which is crowded with a diverse and enjoyable array of shopping and eating options, from cheap to chic. Though there are no real sights in Ipanema, places of interest include:

GAROTA DE IPANEMA. This corner *botequim* is where Brazilian composer Tom Jobim and poet Vinícius de Moraes wrote the song "Girl from Ipanema," based on a young woman they saw walk by this bar every day. It was this simple tune that launched a new era in Brazilian music, turning on the entire world to the slow, sexy, and brainy beat of *bossa nova* (literally, "new style"). The walls of the bar-restaurant are covered with "Garota de Ipanema" memorabilia, including original lyrics, photos, and newspaper articles. *(Rua Vinícius de Moraes 49. ☎ 2523 3787. Open daily 11am-3am. See* p. 135.*)*

DIAMOND ROW. It's time for the old marketing ploy disguised as a legitimate attraction: the museums of jewelers **Amsterdam Sauer** and **H. Stern,** on Rua Visconde de Pirajá at Rua Garcia D'Ávila. Travelers staying at five-star hotels should already have their invitations (taxi ride gratis), but any wealthy-looking tourist is encouraged to take a tour of these workshops and collections of gems and minerals, in hopes that the glittering displays will dazzle them into displaying their own credit cards. The block the museums occupy is often referred to as Diamond Row, as it is also home to similarly high-end retailers Cartier, Louis Vitton, Elle et Lui, and others, as well as the tasty but pretentious eatery **Via Sete** (p. 136).

BEYOND IPANEMA

JARDIM BOTÂNICO (BOTANICAL GARDENS). Rio's attractive botanical gardens are unfortunately not on many tourists' agendas, but those who do visit can't help but be charmed by this quiet, well-manicured park with over 5000 plant species. Built in 1808 almost immediately upon his arrival in Brazil by Portuguese prince and ardent botanist Dom João, the parklands were initially part of a gunpowder factory. Remnants of the factory still stand, including the foreman's house at the gardens' exit, Rio de Janeiro's oldest residence.

Dom João introduced imperial palms to the tropics: a descendant of the first one he planted still stands, as does the famous **Avenida Palmeira** (Grand Avenue of the Palms). Other park highlights include: the sensory garden; endangered *pau-brasil* (brazilwood) trees, the heavily harvested pigment-containing species that gave the country its name; the lake of Vitória Régia lilies, which can support up to 45kg; and several menacingly bloodthirsty carnivorous plants, kept "caged" in a greenhouse for safety. *(Rua Jardim Botânico 1008. ☎2294 9349. Take any "Jardim Botânico" or "Jóquei" bus; try Bus #571 from anywhere. Taxis R$10-20. Open daily 8am-5pm. R$4.)*

LAGOA RODRIGO DE FREITAS. Known universally as Lagoa, this large lagoon just north of Ipanema is one of the most popular recreation areas for exercise-loving Cariocas. The 8km bike and running path ringing the lake is filled with sporty types in the morning and afternoon (bike rental about R$7 per hr.), while the lake itself is filled with families tooling around in swan-shaped paddleboats (R$10 per hr.). The kiosks around the lake are also busy nightlife spots (p. 154).

BEACHES

You can easily find beaches that are more scenic than those in Rio—indeed, there are some within just a few minutes of the city. However, there's probably nowhere in the country—perhaps in the world—where the beach is as important a part of life as it is in Rio. Carioca beaches exist in a world of their own, a world with its own tribes and indigenous species, and unwritten but closely adhered to rules governing beach etiquette, attire, and attitudes. The views from atop Sugarloaf and Corcovado may be more beautiful, but nowhere in Rio is the sightseeing more interesting than from atop a beach towel. And whether you identify with Flamengo's families, Arpoador's stoner surfers, Ipanema's old hippies, Barra da Tijuca's toned beach bunnies, or none of the above, you'll find a spot for your flag-emblazoned sarong amidst the crowds of flirting, scantily clad locals. (And wherever you find yourself, the vendors will find you—selling food, drinks, hammocks, sunglasses, batteries, watches, novels, ice cream, and tattoos.)

The high tourist concentration on beaches, especially on weekends, makes them prime targets for criminals. Do as Cariocas do and bring as little as possible to the beach: leave daypacks, jewelry, and pricey equipment at your hotel or hostel, and never leave your things unattended while you go into the water (unless you don't mind losing them permanently).

FLAMENGO & BOTAFOGO. These beaches ring the Guanabara Bay, meaning the waves are calmer than at the ocean beaches but are too polluted for swimming. Popular mostly with Zona Norte Cariocas, these beaches are less crowded (but less of a scene) than elsewhere in the Zona Sul. Long, thin **Flamengo** is just steps from most of the budget hotels in Catete (p. 124), while the smaller **Botafogo** has a great view of the Sugarloaf. The cable car up the Sugarloaf departs from the small **Praia Vermelha** ("Red Beach"), so named for its distinctive dark rusty color, a result of the sand being packed much more tightly than at other beaches.

COPACABANA. Copacabana is the sole reason many travelers come to Rio, seeking that perfect combination of beautiful setting, beautiful waves, and beautiful people. While curvaceous, sun-drenched Copa doesn't disappoint on any of those fronts, it almost always surprises tourists expecting a quiet tropical paradise of waving palm trees and soothing waves. This is Rio's most inclusive beach, popular with everyone in the city, be they rich or poor, young or old, tourist or local, prostitute or john. Though not as crowded and noisy as neighboring Ipanema, things can get pretty busy here, especially on weekends. The *barraca* Rainbow and stretch of sand in front of the Copacabana Palace Hotel are popular **gay** gathering places; on weekends, look for the giant rainbow flag in the sand.

In the evening, when the beach chaos dies down, Copa's **Avenida Atlântica** comes to life. There's no better place to be at dusk than sipping ice-cold *choppes* on an Av. Atlântica patio, downing a fresh-cut *côco gelado* at a beachfront *barraca*, or strolling past the stalls on the beach-side sidewalk in search of a quick snack, handmade necklace, or more. Travelers should note that after midnight or so, Av. Atlântica becomes Rio's main prostitution strip. The beach is also deserted by then; hanging around here at night is not recommended.

ARPOADOR. This is the bend of beach between Copacabana and Ipanema, around **Arpoador Rock,** universally referred to as the *pedra* and known as the best place in Rio to catch the sunset. Most of the beach is indistinguishable from Ipanema save for the high concentration of surfers. Tucked away in a cove on the Copacabana side of the *pedra* is the small **Praia do Diabo** (Devil's Beach), popular with surfers and daring illegal nudists at sunrise.

IPANEMA & LEBLON. A continuous stretch of sand with two names, this is the best beach in Rio, sitting in the shadow of the distinctive **Pedra Dois Irmãos** (Two Brothers' Rock). The scene here is what most people imagine Rio to be like: flirty, sexy, cool, and light-hearted, like the *bossa nova* music style that was born just two blocks inland from Posto 9. Brazil's most beautiful young people flock to **Ipanema** in droves, and on any day of the week, their preferred hangout—around **Posto 9**—is filled to the brim with tall and tan and young lovelies, in a party-hardy setting even more chaotic and crowded than Copacabana. **Leblon** is noticeably quieter and more popular with families; the stretch of sand around Rua Venâncio Flores is called the **Baixo Baby** because it's popular with stroller-pushing mothers. The southern end of Leblon, known as **Alto Leblon,** is a popular surfing area.

The stretch of sand between Ruas Teixera de Melo and Rua Farme de Amoedo is a legendary **gay** hangout—the biggest and best in Rio state. On weekends, the area gets more crowded and flirty than any late-night scene, and after dark, the restaurants, bars, and clubs in this area cater to a largely gay clientele.

ELSEWHERE IN THE ZONA SUL. Beyond Leblon are some of Rio's more pristine and less crowded ocean beaches, though they're nearly impossible to reach without a car. The Surf Bus (see **Surfing,** p. 153) passes all the following beaches except Joatinga en route to Prainha, and the Real Auto Bus (see **Flights,** p. 116) runs along the beachfront avenues out to Barra. Following Av. Niemeyer out past Leblon, you'll first hit Praia São Conrado, also known as **Pepino,** a pretty and tranquil mid-sized beach best known as the landing spot for hang-gliders from Pedra Bonita (p. 152). Pepino sits in the shadow of Rocinha, Rio's largest *favela.* Separated from Pepino by the Pedra de Gávea is the long (12km, twice the length of Copacabana) stretch of **Barra da Tijuca,** the beach fronting Rio's *nouveau riche* sprawl of high-rises and malls. With the softest sand in Rio, Barra rivals Ipanema as the best Carioca beach, and is also *the* spot for tanned and toned hardbodies, particularly around the too-cool **Barraca do Pepê** (just past Barra Posto 2), named for a champion Carioca hang-glider who died in competition. A surfboard and glider monument next to the *barraca* commemorates his successes. Barra is the best spot in Rio for beach sports, from *frescobol* to parasailing. The far end of Barra is a nature reserve known as **Recreio,** which runs right into the oft-neglected beaches of **Pontal** and **Macumba.** Av. Estado da Guanabara winds through the hills past Macumba out to the awesome waves of tiny **Prainha,** considered Rio's best surfing beach.

Tucked in between Pepino and Barra is a small stretch of sand known as **Joatinga,** a isolated beach with brilliant emerald water, a beautiful view of the ocean islands, few people, and (thankfully) no vendors. To get to Joatinga by car, take the Túnel do Pepino out of São Conrado and follow the Estrada do Joá up through the mountains to the entrance. Those without wheels should check out the daytrip run by South America Experience (see **Budget Travel,** p. 120) that stops at Joatinga.

OUTDOOR ACTIVITIES & SPORTS

Rio de Janeiro's dramatic setting—crammed between forest-blanketed mountains and scalloped beach—means it's heaven for outdoor enthusiasts. The following are some options for escaping from Rio's concrete jungle; the free NOMAD guide (found at most accommodations, travel agencies, and other tourist-geared places) has lots of up-to-the-minute outdoors and sporting info.

HIKING & CLIMBING

Rio's scenic backdrop is the rolling green mountains of the largest urban forest in the world, the **Parque Nacional da Tijuca.** The section of the park with marked trails is the **Floresta da Tijuca;** the stone columns marking its entrance are in the far-flung **Alto da Boa Vista** neighborhood, most easily accessed from Jardim Botânico (which sits in the shadow of the park; p. 149). Any "Alto da Boa Vista" bus (like Bus #133 from Jardim Botânico) runs to the *floresta*'s entrance; ask for Entrada da Floresta. However, it's preferable to go by car or taxi (R$20-25) on the one-hour scenic route, which winds up through the mountains, offering lookouts all along the way. (The route begins on Rua Leão Pacheco, which is the side street off Rua Jardim Botânico that marks the northeast border of the Jardim Botânico.) A popular stop along the way is the **Vista Chinesa,** a faux-bamboo pagoda with an unforgettable view of the Atlantic and the Zona Sul—this lookout puts even Corcovado to shame. Soon after is the **Mesa do Imperador,** another (less impressive) lookout atop a Montezuma-inspired building. Entrance to the park (open daily 7am-9pm) is free; trail maps (R$1-3) are only sold at the Visitor's Center inside the park. A paved road runs from the entrance to the Visitor's Center, first passing a refreshing 35m waterfall. Those short on time can try the **Cova da Onça** trail, which begins from outside the Visitor's Center: this easy 30-minute hike cuts through the verdant forest en route to a small bridge spanning a waterfall, with a nice view of the steep mountains. Staff at the Visitor's Center offer advice on more rigorous hikes, like the all-day trek up **Pico da Tijuca** (1021m).

A highly recommended option for guided half- and full-day hikes in the park is **Rio Hiking** (☎9721 0594; www.riohiking.com.br), a certified mother-and-son team of multilingual hiking experts who lead excellent culturally- and ecologically-geared hikes all over Rio city (including hikes up the Sugarloaf and Pedra Bonita). They also lead trips in Rio state (including Paraty, Petrópolis, and the Serra dos Orgãos) as well as popular Rio nightlife excursions.

PARTICIPATORY SPORTS

HANG-GLIDING (ASA DELTA). If Rio isn't unforgettable enough on the ground, take to the air in a hang-glider—it's pretty much guaranteed that an *asa delta* trip will be one of the highlights of your time in Brazil. Sweaty-palmed tandem hang-gliding trips have long been a popular activity among thrill-seeking travelers unsatisfied by the panoramic views of Corcovado and the Sugarloaf, and the trips are totally safe. (Plus, there's only one other place in the whole country to do it—Bahia's Arraial d'Ajuda; p. 377.)

Flight preparation is easy: you and your pilot are strapped into a two-person glider, and together you take a running start off Gávea's distinctive **Pedra Bonita** into the wild blue yonder. Most travelers agree that the initial jump into thin air is the scariest part; it's all smooth sailing (or rather, floating) after that, topped off by a (sort of) soft landing on Pepino Beach. Flights average US$70 (including transportation to and from your hotel), and run—depending on your weight—from 10 to 30 minutes. The time it takes before you start breathing again varies. **South America Experience** (see **Budget Travel,** p. 120) includes a hang gliding stop in its city tour, but you can easily book directly with any licensed pilot. The best include Hostel Ipanema (p. 124) owner Paulo Celani of **Just Fly** (☎9985 7540; www.justfly.com.br) and Rui Marra of **Super Fly** (☎3322 2286; superfly@visualnet.com.br); each has over 15 years of experience.

SURFING. Rio de Janeiro state is known as one of Brazil's best surfing regions. The town of **Saquarema** (p. 170), east of Rio, is the jewel in the state's *surfista* crown, but Rio city also has great spots for those who are California Dreamin'—although most are difficult to reach without a car (see below). The huge waves at **Prainha** (p. 150), far west of Barra, make it Rio's best surfing beach. The surfing beach closest to the city is **Arpoador** (p. 150), between Copacabana and Ipanema, at Posto 7. One block inland from Arpoador closer to Ipanema you'll find **Galeria River,** Rua Francisco Otaviano 67, a surf-only shopping mall with gear and clothing shops and boards for sale or rental (around R$25 per day).

Surfistas who didn't have cars in Rio were once dead in the water, but now they have the **Surf Bus,** which runs between M: Largo do Machado and Prainha, passing all of Rio's major beaches en route. Manned by tour professionals, the bus can hold 30 surfers and 42 boards (plus a bar and entertainment center) and makes morning and afternoon trips every day; flag it down at any major hotel or along the beachfront avenues. On weekends, the last stop is at Macumba, not at Prainha. (www.oi.com.br. Departs M: Largo do Machado daily 7, 10am, 1, 4pm; departs Prainha (M-F) or Macumba (Sa-Su) 8:30, 11:30am, 2:30, 5:30pm. R$2.)

OTHER BEACH SPORTS. At dusk, crowds throng to the volleyball nets and soccer goals on the beach. Almost as popular as **beach futebol** (always played barefoot) is **beach volleyball** *(volei da praia)*, supposedly first played in Rio. Professional beach volleyball has a major following on TV, and Rio often hosts the (free) world beach volleyball championships in the summer. Combining the best of *futebol* and volleyball (not to mention gymnastics) is **futevolei,** volleyball with everything but the hands—Cariocas make it look effortless, but it's nearly impossible to master. Also popular is **frescobol,** a surf-and-sand twist on ping-pong, played with paddles and a rubber ball on the firmer shoreline sand; the game was supposedly invented between Postos 4 and 6 in the early 1950s. The Arpoador end of Copacabana is where the serious beach jocks come out to play.

SPECTATOR SPORTS: FUTEBOL

Brazil's unbridled mania for *futebol* (soccer) is undoubtedly best experienced at **Maracanã,** Rio's 100,000-person capacity soccer stadium—the largest in the world. (See p. 142 for history and info on visiting during non-game times.) The seats fill up hours before start time on game day with crazed *futebol* fanatics drinking, singing lewd songs, waving flags and firecrackers, and enjoying the incessant *samba* drums that accompany the whole game. The best and most hotly contested games are between Rio's home teams: Botafogo, Flamengo, Fluminense, and Vasco.

Tickets run R$10+ (R$20+ for championships), available at the stadium's *bilheterias* (ticket booths); they rarely sell out, so there's no need to buy from scalpers or days in advance (1-2hr. ahead of game time is a good idea). Tickets are either

RIO DE JANEIRO

for field-level *cadeiras* or bleacher *arquibancadas*. *Cadeiras* have bad views and put you far from the local fans in the stands, so stick with the bleachers. Seat sections are color-coded: the white is for foreign package tour groups and locals who couldn't get seats in the yellow or green, which is where savvy travelers and most local fans sit. The green section is meant for the more aggressive fans—as well as the drums and firecrackers—so sit here at your own risk. Despite rumors to the contrary, games rarely get violent (crowds get no wilder than at European matches), but there are armed policemen in every section. Wherever you sit, wear light clothing, as temperatures in the stadium often hit 45°C (113°F).

Let's Go recommends taking the **metrô** to the game (to M: Maracanã, linha 2) and either the *metrô* (if it's not too full) or a **taxi** (R$15-20) back to your hotel or hostel. **Buses** marked "Maracanã" run between the Zona Sul and the stadium; however, they get overcrowded and caught in bad traffic, and on the way back are not really safe for travelers (bus-riding fans have been known to smash windows and rip up seats in post-game elation or frustration). You can save yourself a lot of hassle and safety problems if you catch a game on a tour: although most hotels overcharge for trips (R$70+), **South America Experience** (see **Budget Travel,** p. 120) offers excursions for R$40 that include tickets, door-to-door round-trip transport, secure seats with locals, and the guidance of a Carioca (and ardent *futebol* fan).

NIGHTLIFE

Cariocas know how to party. Even during the 360 days a year when Carnaval isn't on, Rio keeps drinking, dancing, and celebrating every night. The popular corner *botequins* (bar-restaurants) are always busy, as are the beachfront *barracas* and sidewalk patio bars. Rio's best nightlife is in the hip bars and clubs of **Ipanema** (p. 156) and **Leblon** (p. 157) and the raucous, *samba*-paced celebration in the streets and clubs of **Lapa** (p. 154). Nothing gets going until after midnight, and it's not unusual for it to last until dawn; even Riotur recommends taking a nap to recharge between that sunset *côco gelado* and that late-night trip to a smoky dance club.

After the listings of bars and clubs below is a special section on gay and lesbian (GLS) nightlife options in Rio (p. 158).

SAMBA: LAPA

Nothing defines Rio de Janeiro like *samba:* it may have been born in Bahia, but that infectious two-step beat is very much the rhythm of Carioca life, even outside the five-day *samba* party of Carnaval. The best places to hear Carnaval's raucous *enredo*-style *samba* are the rehearsals of the 14 **escolas de samba,** held every Saturday from late August until Carnaval (see p. 52). The very best *samba* spot in Rio is **Lapa,** a run-down neighborhood just southwest of Centro. (M: Cinelândia or take any "Lapa" bus (like Bus #571); taxis (R$6-20) are safer and easier.) A dilapidated, deserted ghetto by day, Lapa transforms into the favorite nightspot for locals, a down-and-dirty street party in the shadow of the Arcos da Lapa (see p. 144). The clubs and bars all around Lapa are known as the best *samba* venues in Rio (if not the country), but at times it's wild enough just walking along the main street, **Avenida Mem de Sá,** enjoying not just *samba* but everything from funk to *forró*, plus *capoeira* and rock groups fighting for sidewalk space alongside food and beer carts. Meanwhile, nearby **Rua Joaquim Silva** becomes an outdoor bar-*cum*-hippie market, with head shops, wandering waiters, hip-hop blaring, and a distinctive sweet smell in the air. Drawn to this *alfresco* street carnival are people from all walks of life—gays, tourists, locals, trannies, ravers, surfers, goths, college kids, rastafarians, and more. Police also flock here, but it still pays to be careful: the packed crowds and dark side streets are a pickpocket's dream. Leave valuables at home (clubs rarely check ID), and take only the cash you need.

For some of the tackiest *samba* in Rio, there's Leblon's **Plataforma,** Rua A. Ferreira 32 (☎2274 4022). This dinner show embarrassment puts on a gaudy, overproduced Las Vegas-type floor show (R$40+) for package tourists who think it's "traditional" Brazilian culture. Just say no!

Carioca da Gema, Av. Mem de Sá 79 (☎2221 0043). Its name means "Carioca to the Core," and this bar adorned with works by local artists is indeed one of Rio's most authentic (and sophisticated) *samba* spots. Cover R$10; food and drink min. R$10. Live music M-Th, Sa from 8pm; F from 11pm.

Fundição Arte e Progresso, Rua dos Arcos 24 (☎2220 5070). This giant graffitied warehouse (a former foundry or *fundição*) behind the Arcos da Lapa hosts an always exciting lineup of concerts, art shows, and dance parties in an unending warren of performance halls, theaters, and dance floors. Cover R$15-20. Open daily 10pm-late.

Café Cultural Sacrilégio, Av. Mem de Sá 81 (☎3970 1461). Done up like an antique-filled haunted house renovated by music-loving bohemians, this charming, intimate bar fights with neighbor Carioca da Gema for the crowds of *samba*-loving locals. Cover Tu-Th R$8, F-Sa R$15. Open Tu-Th 7pm-1:30am, F-Sa 9pm-3:30am.

Emporium 100, Rua do Senado 53 (☎2210 0310). Rumored to be Rio's first *samba* club. It may have changed its address, but Emporium hasn't changed its reputation as Rio's hottest *samba* spot. Cover F-Sa R$8; food and drink min. W-Th R$8, F-Sa R$6. Open W-F 6pm-late, Sa 8pm-late.

Asa Branca, Av. Mem de Sá 17 (☎2224 2342). Named for Luiz Gonzaga's *forró* anthem ("White Wing," which did for *forró* what "Garota de Ipanema" did for *bossa nova*), this is Rio's most famous spot to sweat to *forró*, Brazil's twangy, immensely popular "country" music (played live Tu-Su from 10:30pm). This *gafieira* is for couples dancing, but those going alone will find partners inside. Popular *samba* and *feijoada* Sa noon-7pm. Cover R$10. Open daily 9pm-late.

Semente, Rua Joaquim Silva 138 (☎2242 5165). At night, this tiny corner eatery becomes an even tinier dance club, with live *samba* and Rio's sole mambo night. *Samba* M, Th, Sa; MPB Tu; mambo F. Cover R$10. Live music Th-Tu from 9pm.

Forró da Lapa, Rua Joaquim Silva s/n. The name says it all: a weekly lineup of infectious *forró* in a dark, dingy dance hall on Lapa's most crowded street. Cover R$2-3. Open daily 11pm-late.

BARS & LIVE MUSIC

The informal *botequins* (bar-restaurants) and *chopperias* found on every corner of Rio are great places to relax with a cold *chopp* (beer) and chat with locals. Those looking for something more formal can try one of the places below; Leblon's hot and heavy nightspots are particularly recommended.

Travelers would be wise to note that bars dubbed *boates* or "American bars" are most usually **strip clubs;** a majority of these are concentrated in Centro's Pça. Mauá and Copacabana's Av. Princesa Isabel.

BOTAFOGO

A quiet residential neighborhood with several excellent restaurants and low-key hangouts popular with Rio's under-30 crowd, Botafogo is a pleasant place to start off your evening. The food- and nightlife-heavy area is accessible by taxi (R$9-15) or any "Voluntários da Pátria" bus (*not* buses marked "Botafogo").

Cobal da Humaitá, Rua Voluntários da Patria 448. Enter through the front lot and head through the walkway. By night, the eateries ringing this parking lot put out chairs and tables that transform the whole place into one giant outdoor bar that hostelers and college-age Cariocas can't resist. Open M-Tu 9pm-1am, W-Sa 9am-4am.

O Plebeu, Rua Capitão Salomão 50 (☎2286 0699), at Rua Visconde de Caravelas. If you can't make it to Maracanã, this second-floor patio and "drive-by" sidewalk bar is the best place to join locals in cheering on local *futebol* on TV over a few beers. Brazilian fare R$15-20. Best imported liquor list in the Zona Sul (R$4-5). Open daily from noon.

Axé Santé, Rua Capitão Salomão 55 (☎2266 1065). A funky bar with fanciful bohemian decor and traditional *samba* and *choro* music nightly. Imported beer and cocktails R$5-7. Happy Hour M-F 6-9pm. Baiano cuisine buffet Su noon-8pm (R$17.90 per kg). Cover R$7. Open M-Sa noon-2am, Su noon-8pm.

Moog Bar, Rua Visconde de Caravelas 79 (☎2266 1014). Named for a synthesizer brand favored by top electronic musicians, Moog© lives up to its name with DJs spinning groove, lounge, and *bossa nova* to a hip crowd that lost its way en route to Leblon. Cover R$20-25. Open Th 7pm-2am, F-Sa 7pm-4am.

COPACABANA

Copacabana is home to all sorts of people, and **Avenida Atlântica** has watering holes for all of them, from ritzy hotel bars to informal beachside *barracas*. Though Av. Atlântica is well-policed and stays busy all night, it's best for early drinks and/or dinner: after midnight, things gets increasingly seedy as it becomes Rio's main prostitution drag (pun intended), particularly around the club **Help** (p. 158). Copacabana is also home to many of Rio's gay bars (see **Gay & Lesbian Nightlife,** p. 158).

Manoel & Juaquim, Av. Atlântica 3806B (☎2287 2398). "Manny & Jojo" (as expats call them) are the patron saints of Rio nightlife. The 12 outposts of their *botequim* empire are always voted tops for food (R$7-25), *chopp* quality (R$1.90), and infectiously friendly atmosphere. This beachfront branch is their best and busiest. Open M-Sa 5pm-2am.

Sindicato do Chopp, Av. Atlântica 3806A (☎2569 2227). Always found less than a *salgado*'s-throw away from the nearly identical Manoel & Juaquim, this city-wide *botequim* syndicate has 3 branches on Av. Atlântica alone. Open daily 5pm-2am.

Skylab Bar, Rio Othon Palace, Av. Atântica 3264 (☎2525 1500). Rivaling Corcovado for the best view of Rio, this wallet-achingly swank poolside bar atop the five-star Rio Othon is worth a visit (and an overpriced *caipirinha;* R$15) for the striking wraparound view of all the Zona Sul. Open daily until midnight.

Bip Bip, Rua Almirante Gonçalves 50 (☎2267 9696). Unmarked corner bar with copper lampposts. How did this unremarkable *botequim*—a *real* a dozen in Copacabana—gain international acclaim? Aside from having its own Carnaval *bloco,* Bip Bip's nightly live *samba* performances often draw surprise guests who happen to be Brazilian superstars, like Beth Carvalho and Zeca Pagodinho. Open daily 11am-3am.

Sobre As Ondas, Av. Atlântica 3432 (☎2522 1296), at Rua Miguel Lemos, next to Help (p. 158). Its name means "above the waves," but the choice view of Copacabana's wavy sidewalk from this second-floor bar is less alluring than the excellent live music featured here nightly—usually jazz, *bossa nova,* or *samba*. Cover R$10-20. Open daily 10pm-late.

IPANEMA

After the bars close, follow the guitar-toting young locals to Rio's only 24hr. beachfront *barraca,* on Ipanema beach (Av. Vieira Souto) at Rua Maria Quitéria (near the bar Empório).

Bofetada, Rua Farme de Amoedo 87A (☎2522 9526). Unquestionably Ipanema's most popular local hangout, this informal *botequim* gets so full at night that the crowds of Cariocas spill out onto the street. Great live Brazilian music on most weeknights from 8pm (no cover). Also a popular gay hangout. Open daily 8am-midnight.

Empório, Rua Maria Quitéria 37 (☎2767 7992). This self-proclaimed "Brazilian pub" is a backpacker favorite, a run-down old mansion that could teach the hostels a thing or two about packing in as many rowdy, rollicking locals and travelers as possible. A great place to meet young Cariocas who love swapping stories (and spit) with *mochileiros.* Open daily 9pm-late, though it doesn't get busy until well after midnight.

Barril 1800, Av. Vieira Souto 110 (☎2523 0085). For over 30 years Ipanema's prime *après-praia* spot, a classier version of the Av. Atlântica-style beachfront patio *botequim.* Great *choppes* (R$2.20) and an even greater view of the ocean. Open daily 10am-2am.

Vinícius, Rua Vinícius de Moraes 39 (☎2287 1497), opposite the similar Garota de Ipanema (p. 135), and named for the lyricist of that song. The piano bar upstairs is unsurprisingly one of Rio's best spots for live *bossa nova* and jazz. *Botequim* open daily 11am-3am (no cover). Piano bar performance days and times vary (cover R$25-30).

Shenanigan's, Rua Visconde de Pirajá 112A (☎2267 5860), upstairs from Carretão (p. 135). A raucous scene always filled beyond capacity with backpackers and expats. Because you came halfway around the world to drink at your local pub. Because you just have to have a pint of Guinness (R$19—ouch). Open Su-Th 6pm-2am, F-Sa 6pm-3am.

LEBLON

This is it, Rio's trendy nightlife nirvana. The clubs are really the places to see and be seen in Leblon, but the area's many intimate, fun-loving bars are equally popular with the flocks of attractive, affluent young locals and travelers grooving to an eclectic array of music, from breakbeats to *bossa nova.*

Academia da Cachaça, Rua Conde de Bernadotte 26A (☎2239 1542). Redefining the term "liberal arts education," this corner "academy" is *the* place to get schooled in the art of *cachaça.* Waiters help you wade through the mind-boggling list of alcohol (R$3-8; *caipirinhas* R$5-7), from smooth-as-silk Anísio to brutal Zareco. Open daily from noon.

Bracarense, Rua José Linhares 85 (☎2294 3549). Ask any Carioca to name the best *botequim* in Rio, and Bracarense inevitably comes up—little surprise given its friendly crowd, chilled *choppes* (poured through a long tube for special aeration), and a fantastic bar menu of *mineiro* treats (from Minas Gerais, the motherland of Brazilian cuisine). Open Su 9am-8pm, M-Sa 7am-midnight.

Guapo Loco, Rua Rainha Guilhermina 48 (☎2294 2915). It's just like spring break in Cancun, and young Cariocas can't get enough of this festive, slightly cheesy Mexican bar/eatery. Wash down tacos and burritos (R$15-20) with tropically tongue-in-cheek cocktails like the Tequila Mockingbird (R$8-10). Open M-F 6pm-late, Sa-Su noon-late.

Manguaça & Casa Clipper, Av. Ataulfo de Paiva 427 (☎2529 6300). Twin bar/restaurants on Leblon's busiest corner, opposite a 1st-run cinema—a great after-movie destination, with Rio's best *batatas fritas* (fries). Open Su-Th 8am-1am, F-Sa 8am-2am.

Bar do Tom, Rua Adalberto Ferreira 32 (☎2274 4022), inside Plataforma. If "Girl from Ipanema" lyricist Vinícius de Moraes gets a bar named after him (p. 157), why not composer Tom Jobim? Small wonder this is Leblon's top spot for big-name *bossa nova* acts, in an intimate setting. Cover R$20-25. Open daily 10pm-late.

Jobi, Av. Ataulfo de Paiva 1166 (☎2274 0547). A tiny and popular patio *botequim* with a scenic view of the traffic on Leblon's major thoroughfare. Open daily 9am-4am.

DANCE CLUBS

The city that shuts down for five days just to *samba* definitely takes its dance clubs seriously. While Lapa has all the *samba* clubs, the Zona Sul (especially the **Ipanema** and **Leblon**) is the place to find modern, Euro-chic discotheques spinning a dance-friendly mix of pop, rock, and house to a sweaty international crowd.

Spin, Rua Teixera de Melo 21 (☎3813 4045), in **Ipanema.** So hot it's cool. Superb DJs spin a great mix of pop, rock, and dance—everything from Björk to Beyoncé, plus occasional *bossa nova*—in a low-key setting. Choose between the sweaty upstairs dance floor or a quiet, bright-neon downstairs bar. Cover R$10-15. Open W-Sa 10pm-5am.

Melt, on Rua Rita Ludolf (☎2249 9309), in **Leblon.** The cool kids call it "Melch." This sleek, attractive 2-floor club and bar is one of Rio's sexiest nightspots, throbbing nightly with the sounds of the city's hottest electronic and live music beats. Arrive after midnight and be gorgeous if you want in. Cover R$10-15. Open M-Sa 10pm-late.

Ballroom, Rua Humaitá 110 (☎2537 7600; www.ballroom.com.br), in **Botafogo.** Spacious bar and crowded dance floor where DJs spin house and trance before and after the live, cutting-edge shows featured nightly. The best place to hear what contemporary Brazilian music is up to these days. Cover R$15+. Open daily 10pm-late.

Club Six, Rua das Marrecas 38 (☎2510 3230), in **Lapa.** One of the newest clubs in Rio, this is the best place in the city for well-spun hip-hop and rap, all in a surreal 3-floor video-game-*cum*-sex-dungeon setting. Cover R$20. Open F-Sa from 11pm.

Bombar, Av. Gen. San Martin 1011 (☎2249 2161), in **Leblon.** Yet another trendy 2-floor bar-club in Leblon, this one with DJs spinning the latest, poppiest American Top 40 dance remixes to throngs of ecstatic young Cariocas. Steep cover to keep the riffraff out: men R$40, women R$10. Open daily 10pm-late.

Passeio Público, Av. Rio Branco 277 (☎2220 1298), in **Centro** facing Passeio Público park. Steps from Lapa proper but worlds away in feel and sound, this Euro-style disco is Rio's least intimidating, most enjoyable dance club. Live *samba* and *pagode* bands share music duty with DJs spinning Brazilian and international pop and hip-hop. Cover R$15-25 (no cover Th), includes free buffet. Open M-F 5pm-late, Sa 10pm-late.

FarUP, Rua Voluntários da Pátria 448 (☎2531 1816; www.farup.com.br), in **Botafogo.** *UP* above the *Far*inha Pura grocery in the Cobal da Humaitá (p. 155) is this casual twin sister of the trendier Ballroom. Hopefully you brought your bell-bottoms and other retro togs along in your pack: on weekends, FarUP spins "flashback," the greatest hits of the 60s, 70s, and 80s. Cover R$10-30. Open daily 9pm-late.

Baronneti, Rua Barão da Torre 354 (☎2247 9100), in **Ipanema.** The unmarked white building facing Pça. NS da Paz. Oozing exclusiveness from every pore, Baronneti's sleek, sexy interior and even sleeker, sexier clientele are not for the faint of heart (or wallet). Thankfully, their winning DJs spin excellent dance and pop. Cover men R$50-60, women R$25-30. Open Tu-Su 9:30pm-late.

Bunker 94, Rua Raul Pompéia 94 (☎2521 0367; www.bunker94.com.br), in **Copacabana.** Looking for Rio's pierced, disaffected youth? They're all here, slinking along to Rio's most cutting-edge rock, trip-hop, electro-flashback, and indy pop (no grinding to indistinct techno allowed!). Three floors, game room, and naughty "Sex Box." Su gay house party "Tea Dance." Cover R$20, R$16 with website flyer. Open W-Su 11pm-late.

Casa da Matriz, Rua Henrique Novaes 107 (☎2266 1014; www.casadamatriz.com.br), in **Botafogo.** A multi-story museum, computer gaming room, bar, and dance club, with rotating exhibits and ever-changing nightly dance events (mostly electronica and dance hits). Popular with Rio's artsy crowd. Cover R$5-20. Open M, Th-Sa 10:30pm-late.

Help, Av. Atlântica 3432 (☎2522 1296), in **Copacabana.** Help! I'm a clueless horny *gringo!* Help is the place for foreign men looking to easily meet *very* friendly local women. This is Av. Atlântica's legendary prostitute hangout, so if you meet someone here, be sure you know what you're getting in to. The sidewalk outside is a frequent mugging spot. Cover R$25 (before midnight R$15). Open daily 10pm-late.

GAY & LESBIAN NIGHTLIFE (GLS)

It says a lot about South American machismo and regional attitudes toward homosexuality that Rio de Janeiro is the continent's biggest gay destination. Though there are plenty of vacationing queers in the city, Rio has only a small, largely invisible gay population, no gay neighborhoods, and little tolerance for public displays of same-sex affection.

The gay-friendly sections of Copacabana (p. 148) and Ipanema (p. 149) beaches have beachfront *barracas* that stay hopping through early evening. The two blocks of Rua Teixera de Melo and Rua Farme de Amoedo closest to Ipanema Beach is one of Rio's main gay areas, with most of the restaurants, bars, and clubs here featuring a mixed or largely gay crowd. **Lapa's** all-inclusive atmosphere makes room for everyone and anyone. **Copacabana** is home to Rio's biggest gay venue, the club **Le Boy** (see below), as well as several small gay bars and the popular Sunday gay "Tea Dance" at Bunker 94 (p. 158). All the following bars and clubs are in Copacabana unless noted otherwise.

The **Rio Gay Guide** (www.riogayguide.com) and **Guia Gay Brasil** (www.guiagaybrasil.com.br) are excellent gay nightlife resources. Both also have listings of Rio's notorious gay bathhouses and motels.

The Copa, Rua Aires Saldanha 13A (☎2255 8740). Unmarked save the mysteriously billowing red curtains opposite Cozinheiro (p. 134). Music and passion are always in fashion at The Copa, an intimate, lesser-known gay bar with kitschy 60s decor (and a lounge-lizard cocktail list to match). Rio's most beautiful waiters. Open Tu-Su 9pm-late.

Blue Angel, Rua Júlio de Castilhos 15 (☎2513 2507), 2 blocks from Le Boy. This bar-*cum*-gallery-*cum*-temple to queer icon Marlene Dietrich (vampy Lola Lola from the 30s film *The Blue Angel*) is also Rio's classiest, tiniest, and bluest gay hangout—popular with an older, sexier "in" crowd. Open W-Su 9pm-late.

Galeria Café, Rua Teixeira de Melo 31E (☎2511 3305), in **Ipanema.** Along with neighboring restaurant **Restô,** this trendy, copper-plated bar is one of Rio's main gathering places. On weekend nights, it's shoulder-to-shoulder beefcake, and quite cruisy. Called "gallery" for the local art on the walls, the finest works on display here are all in the art of the pick-up. Mixed-age crowd. Open Tu-Su 2pm-late; gallery Tu-Su 2-9pm.

Le Boy/BoyBar, Rua Raul Pompéia 102 (☎2513 4993). Homesick Frenchman Gilles Lascard's dream of a Euro-style discotheque became reality in 1992 with Le Boy, Rio's biggest gay venue. 4-story dance fl., sauna, and "dark room" packed nightly with crowds of young, flirty go-go boys sweating to gay anthems and Top 40 remixes beneath the world's largest disco ball. Strippers W, drag shows F-Sa. Raunchy balls (see **Bailes,** p. 56) Carnaval F-M. Cover R$10-15, R$5 before midnight. Open Tu-Su 11pm-late.

Boogaloo, Casa Brasil-Nigéria, Av. Mem de Sá 39, in **Lapa.** This psychedelic dance club with trippy lights and trippier music stands out from its traditional neighbors as Lapa's lone outpost of house, drum 'n' bass, and trance. Cutting-edge international DJs. Mixed gay-straight crowd. Cover R$8-10. Open Th-Sa from 10pm.

Cabaret Casanova, Av. Mem de Sá 25 (☎2221-6555), in **Lapa.** Boogaloo's dark and smoky neighbor packs in the cruisy queer Casanovas who know this is the one place in Lapa where anything goes. Cover R$5. Open Th-Sa 10pm-late.

La Girl, Rua Raul Pompéia 100 (☎2513 4993). Rio's sole lesbian bar (men are only allowed on M), brought to you by Le Boy's Gilles. Sweaty house music is kept at a dull roar for ease of flirting on the small dance floor. Cover R$5-10. Open daily 10pm-late.

ENTERTAINMENT

CINEMA

Rio's chilly cinemas (found mostly in malls like Rio Sul and Botafogo Praia Shopping; see *Veja* magazine or the newspapers for a complete list) are a popular place to beat the heat. In addition to Brazilian releases, theaters screen most foreign films a month or two after their original release, in their original language with Portuguese subtitles (dubbed films are listed as *dub.* or *cópia dublada* in the papers; subtitled films are *leg.* or *legendadas*). The major papers and the *VejaRio* insert (see **Publications,** p. 121) have daily movie listings, times, locations, and reviews. Tickets cost R$10-14 depending on day and time, with discounts for students *(estudantes)* and the elderly *(idosos)*.

LIVE MUSIC

Cariocas love music, and it's everywhere. The bars and clubs of **Lapa** (p. 154) are the best places for live *samba* and *forró*, plus great reggae. Most of **Leblon's** too-cool bars (p. 157) host cutting-edge contemporary and electronic beats; others have *bossa nova* and jazz. In summer, there are free open-air concerts on the beach. The papers' *Rio Show* sections and *VejaRio* (see **Publications,** p. 121) have full live-music listings. Rio is a frequent stop on most South American acts' tours and many international tours. During non-Carnaval season, the **Sambódromo** (see **Samba Parade,** p. 47) hosts large concerts. Rio's biggest music hall is **ATL Hall,** Av. Ayrton Senna 3000, in Barra's Shopping Via Parque. (☎2532 1919. Tickets R$25-70+.) Top Brazilian acts often perform at **Canecão,** Av. Venceslau Brás 215, in Botafogo next to Shopping Rio Sul, which you can reach by taking any "Rio Sul" bus. (☎2543 1241. Tickets R$20+.)

SHOPPING

As one of Brazil's most cosmopolitan cities, Rio has plenty of shopping. Rio's main mid-range to upscale shopping strip is **Rua Visconde de Pirajá** in Ipanema. Copacabana's **Avenida Nossa Senhora de Copacabana** is the city's most crowded shopping thoroughfare, with stores selling clothes, shoes, gifts, electronics, and more—in every price range—as well as street vendors hawking everything from bootleg DVDs to car wax.

CLOTHING

Skimpy Brazilian beachwear and snug-fitting casual wear are not only cheaper in Brazil but also a great way to blend in. Clotheshorses flock to Rio's many **malls** (imaginatively named *shoppings*), of which Rio has so many they get their own neighborhood (Barra da Tijuca). Rio's best mall is Botafogo's **Shopping Rio Sul,** Rua Lauro Müller 116, just outside the tunnel to Copacabana and accessible via any "Rio Sul" bus. (☎2545 7256. Open M-Sa 10am-10pm, Su 3-9pm.) Up the street is **Botafogo Praia Shopping,** Praia de Botafogo 400; its food court has a panoramic view of Sugarloaf, and you can reach it by taking any "Praia de Botafogo" bus. (☎2559 9559. Open M-Sa 10am-10pm, Su 3-9pm.)

The best stores for Brazilian-style swimwear are the naughtily-named **bum-bum** ("nice ass") for women and **Blue Man** for men; both have stores in Shopping Rio Sul and along Ipanema's Rua Visconde de Pirajá. Rio's cheap department stores are great options for basic clothing and travel necessities. Try Copacabana's **C&A,** Av. NS de Copacabana 749 (☎2549 8040), or **Lojas Americanas,** Av. NS de Copacabana 622 (☎2548 5327), in Copacabana, and Rua Visconde de Pirajá 526 (☎2274-0590), in Ipanema. Both are also at Shopping Rio Sul. Ipanema's **Wöllner Outdoor,** Rua Visconde de Pirajá 511 (☎2512 3867), is the city's sole outdoors outfitter and has great deals on hiking boots; there's also a branch in Shopping Rio Sul.

MUSIC

Bootleg copies of the latest national and international hits go for around R$5 from Av. NS de Copacabana street vendors, but Metallica fans and those looking for legit copies should try the following stores. **Musicale,** Rua Visconde de Pirajá 207, in Ipanema, with a branch at Av. NS de Copacabana 1103, in Copacabana, has a fantastic selection of used CDs (R$10-20) with an eclectic international and Brazilian lineup. (☎2513 0382, 2267 9607. Both open M-Sa 9am-8pm.) **Lojas Americanas** (see **Clothing,** p. 160) has the cheapest CD prices in the city, if you can bear their interminable lines. The biggest music store in Rio is **Modern Sound,** Rua Barata Ribeiro 502D, in Copacabana, which features a vast national collection (including many rare cuts) and equally large international holdings. (☎2548 5005. Open M-F 9am-9pm, Sa 9am-8pm.) **Toca de Vinícius,** Rua Vinícius de Moraes 129, in Ipanema, is a temple to *bossa nova*, with lots of classic and hard-to-find cuts, sheet music, and *bossa*-related books for sale. (☎2247 5227. Open daily 9am-6pm.)

MARKETS & FAIRS

Rio's many tourist-geared outdoor markets may not be the traditional craft fairs you'll find elsewhere in South America, but they are the best places to buy affordable souvenirs and gifts. The most popular is the **Feira Hippie** (Hippie Fair), held every Sunday (9am-6pm) in Ipanema's Pça. Osório. Also popular is the **Copacabana Night Market,** held nightly (7pm-midnight) on the median of Av. Atlântica; this is known as one of the best places in Rio to pick up *naïf* artwork (although the work in Bahia is much better). Rio's most authentic fair is the **Feira Nordestina,** an outdoor market/party featuring typical Northeastern food, music, crafts, and more, held every weekend on the Campo de São Cristóvão.

Fresh produce markets pop up everywhere in the city. A daytime farmers' market *(cobal)* is held daily at Botafogo's **Cobal da Humaitá,** Rua Voluntários da Pátria 448 (p. 155), and Leblon's **Cobal do Leblon,** Rua Gilberto Cardoso s/n, just outside Plataforma (p. 155). A convenient fruit market is also held every Wednesday outside the Copa Praia hostel (p. 123), in the Bairro Peixoto's Pça. Bitencourt.

NEAR RIO DE JANEIRO

PETRÓPOLIS ☎24

Emperor Dom Pedro I fell in love with the area where Petrópolis now is and purchased the Fazenda do Córrego Seco in 1830, and the city of Petrópolis was founded in 1843. The young city became the official summer residence of the imperial court in 1851, and a few years later a direct rail link to the capital was built; nearly 80 years later the country's first asphalt highway was built connecting Rio de Janeiro and Petrópolis. Today, the beautiful houses of Brazil's imperial court occupy tree-lined streets just next to the bustling *centro*.

TRANSPORTATION. Facil (☎2237 0101) has regular buses to Rio de Janeiro (1½hr.; every hr. 4:30am-11:15pm; R$11). **Salutaris** (☎2246 0218) has buses to São Paulo (6hr.; 11am; R$10). **Viação Teresópolis** (☎2242 2260) has buses to Teresópolis (1½hr.; M-F 7 per day 5:45am-7pm, Sa-Su 6 per day 7am-7pm; R$9).

ORIENTATION & PRACTICAL INFORMATION. The *centro's* main street is **Rua do Imperador,** which runs from the *rodoviária* to **Praça Dom Pedro II** and **Praça Expedicionários,** intersecting Rua da Imperatriz along the way. There is an obelisk at this intersection commemorating Petrópolis's 100th anniversary. **Avenida Koeler,** a block from the end of Rua da Imperatriz, has many historic mansions today used by the municipal government. **Rua Teresa,** branching from Rua Marechal Deodoro, has a seemingly endless row of clothing outlet stores. In Itaipava, **Estrada União e Industria** has many hotels, restaurants, and nightclubs.

The **tourist office,** in Pça. Expedicionários, at Rua Imperador and Rua da Imperatriz, is in the *centro.* (Open M-Sa 9am-6pm, Su 9am-5pm.) Information is also available at the *rodoviária.* (Open Su-Th 8:30am-6:30pm, F-Sa 8:30am-8pm.) There is a **tourist information line.** (☎2246 9377, toll-free 0800 241 516. Open M-Tu 9am-6:30pm, W-Sa 9am-8pm, Su 9am-4pm.) Services include: **24hr. ATM,** at the corner of Rua Marechal Deodoro and Rua General Osório; **Internet access,** Rua 16 de Março 326 (☎2231 9888; open M-F 9am-7pm, Sa 9am-6pm); **post office,** Rua do Imperador 350 (☎2242 1447; open M-F 9am-5pm). **Postal code:** 25620-000.

ACCOMMODATIONS & FOOD. Estrada União e Indústria in Itaipava has many *pousadas*, but you are better off staying in the *centro*, where there is a smattering of hotels close to the *rodoviária* and the city's sights. **Hotel Comércio ❷,** Rua Dr. Porciúncula 56, is a simple hotel in front of the *rodoviária.* (☎2242 3500. *Quarto* singles R$18; doubles R$38. *Apartamento* singles R$33; doubles R$55.) **Hotel York ❹,** Rua do Imperador 78, is a quality establishment with attractive rooms just a hop from the *rodoviária.* (☎2242 8220; www.hotelyork.com.br. Singles R$80; doubles R$100.) For Italian food, try **Massas Luigi ❹,** Rua Dr. Nelson de Sá Earp 88, in front of Pça. da Liberdade, which offers a choice of 13 types of pasta and 22 types of sauce (R$14-26). (☎2246 0279. Open Su-Th noon-midnight, F-Sa noon-1am.) **Falconi ❸,** Rua do Imperador 757, has operated for almost a century, serving *picanha gaúcha* (R$31) and *lasagna verde* (R$15); plates serve two people. (☎2242 1252. Open Su-Th 8am-midnight, F-Sa 8am-1am.) In the *centro*, **Casa d'Angelo ❷,** Rua do Imperador 700, is a classy restaurant and bar with live music Friday nights and Sundays at lunch, and a nightly buffet (R$6) of eight stews. (☎2242 0888. Open daily 5-11pm.)

SIGHTS. Once home to Brazil's royalty, Petrópolis has many elegant, richly decorated buildings. A good place to begin is **Museu Imperial,** Rua da Imperatriz 220, the summer residence of Emperor Dom Pedro II. It was used as a school after the end of the empire, until it was converted into a museum in 1943. (☎2237 8000. Open Tu-Su 11am-6pm. R$5.) **Catedral São Pedro de Alcântra,** Rua São Pedro de Alcântra 60, is an impressive Gothic church begun in 1884, with the support of Dom Pedro II and Princess Isabella. To the right is the **Capela Imperial,** which holds the royal family's remains. (☎2242 4300. Open Tu-Su 8am-noon and 2-6pm.) The **Palácio de Cristal,** Rua Alfredo Pachá s/n, was built in France in 1879 and moved to Brazil in 1884 to host events and expositions, which it does to this day. It is here that in 1888 Princess Isabela declared the abolition of slavery. (☎2247 3721. Open daily 9am-5:30pm. Free music Sa 6pm.) The museum **Casa do Barão de Mauá,** Pça. da Conflência 3, was once the summer home of one of Brazil's most important businessmen, who founded Banco do Brasil and built South America's first railway. Today it houses the Casa da Cultura, and has a tourist information table. (☎2246 9377. Open Sa 9am-6:30pm, Su and holidays 9am-5pm.) The **Palácio Rio Negro,** Av. Koeler 255, was the summer residence of Brazil's presidents throughout the 20th century; Getúlio Vargas visited it every summer of his 18 years in power. (☎2246 9380. Open M noon-5pm, W-Su 9:30am-5pm. R$2.) **Museu Casa de Santos Dumont,** Rua do Encanto 22, is commonly known as A Encantada. It was designed and built by Santos Dumont, a pioneer of Brazilian aviation. (☎2257 3158. Tu-Su 9:30am-5:30pm. R$2.) **Palácio Quitandinha,** Av. Joaquim Rolla 2, was once South America's largest casino and boasted an impressive if overdone interior; today its ceiling dome is still the world's largest. The casino was frequented by Brazil's elite until gambling was outlawed, and it now hosts events and conventions. (☎2237 1012. Open Tu-Su 9am-5pm. R$4.) The impressive **Castelo Barão de Itaipava,** Estrada União e Indústria 15243, was designed by Lúcio Costa, and built exclusively with materials from Europe. (☎2222 1088. Open Sa 10am-5pm. R$12.)

FESTIVALS. Every June, Petrópolis celebrates its colonists with **Bauemfest** (also called Festa do Colono), which features 10 days of German dances, foods, and folklore in and around the Palácio de Cristal. In April, in the Itaipava Parque Municipal, the **Exposição Agropecuária** has rodeos and livestock displays.

TERESÓPOLIS ☎21

This mountain city is named after Brazilian Empress Teresa Cristina, who often vacationed there; today it is where the national *futebol* team goes for high-altitude training. Visitors to Teresópolis can enjoy the **Parque Nacional da Serra dos Órgãos** and tour the **Circuito Turístico Tere-Fri,** a series of ranches on the road between Teresópolis and neighboring Nova Friburgo, where they can ride through the mountains on horseback. Visitors should also check out the beautiful views of the **Mirante Vista Soberba.**

ORIENTATION & PRACTICAL INFORMATION. The main avenue in Teresópolis is the so-called **Reta,** which changes names several times: in the *centro* it is **Avenida Lúcio Meira,** but it later becomes Av. Feliciano Sodré, Av. Alberto Torres, and Av. Oliveira Botelho. Av. Delfim Moreira is parallel to Av. Lúcio Meira, and on it lies **Praça Baltazar da Silveira.** The entrance to the national park and the weekend fair are in the Alto neighborhood, which also has many restaurants along Av. Oliveria Botelho. The *rodoviária* (☎2742 3352, ext. 4036) is just outside the *centro*, a block from Av. Lúcio Meira. **Viação Teresópolis** (☎2742 2676) has buses to Petrópolis (1½hr.; 6-7 per day 6am-7pm; R$8) and Rio de Janeiro (1½hr.; M-Sa 5am-10pm, Su 6am-10pm; R$13). **Salutaris** (☎2742 9818) has buses to São Paulo (7hr.; 10pm; R$41). For **taxis** call ☎2742 2656 in the *centro* and ☎2642 3390 in Alto. The **tourist office** is on Av. Lúcio Meira near Pça. Olímpica. (Open M-F 9am-6pm, Sa 9am-5pm, Su 9am-1pm.) Other services include: **currency exchange** in the Galeria, Rua Francisco Sá 179 (☎2643 1543; open M-F 10am-5pm); **supermarket,** Av. Lúcio Meira 85 (☎2742 5170; open M-Sa 8am-8pm, Su 8am-1pm); **24hr. pharmacy,** Av. Delfim Moreira 435 (☎2742 0313); **hospital,** Rua Judith Mauricio de Paula 40 (☎2642 1062); **Internet access** in Shopping Teresópolis, Rua Edmundo Bitencourt 101 (☎2742 9050; open M 1-8pm, Tu-Sa 9am-9pm, Su 1-7pm); **post office,** Av. Lúcio Meira 259 (☎2742 0252; open M-F 9am-5pm). **Postal code:** 25953-970.

ACCOMMODATIONS & FOOD. Most affordable hotels are in the *centro*. **Várzea Palace Hotel ❷,** Rua Prefeito Sebastião Teixeira 41, behind the Matriz, is a wonderfully historic hotel that retains much of its former grandeur. (☎2742 0878. *Quarto* singles R$30; doubles R$40. *Apartamento* singles R$35; doubles R$55.) **Hotel Rever ❷,** Av. Delfim Moreira 634, is a cozy house where every room is a little different. (☎2742 0176. *Quarto* doubles R$36. *Apartamento* doubles R$55.) **Hotel Comary ❶,** Av. Lúcio Meira 467, has a central location and the town's best prices. (☎2742 3463. *Quarto* singles R$15; doubles R$25. *Apartamentos* R$35.) **Hotel Teresópolis ❸,** Av. Oliveira Botelho 647, is a good option for those wanting to stay near the entrance to the park. (☎2642 5610. Singles R$45. Weekday doubles R$70. Weekend doubles R$85.)

Many restaurants offer fondue *rodízios*, appropriate in Teresópolis's chilly mountain climate. There are several nice restaurants in the Alto, and a handful of good self-service restaurants on Av. Delfim Moreira in the *centro*. **Taverna di Olicio's ❸,** Av. Oliveira Botelho 456 (☎2642 4920), is a lively restaurant offering a pizza and pasta *rodízio* (Th-Su from 7pm; R$12), as well as cheese, chocolate, and meat fondues (R$28 serves two). Between Alto and the *centro* is a good three-restaurant complex at Av. Feliciano Sodré 221; one of these is the self-service **Maria Fumaça ❷** (☎2742 3887. M-F R$9, Sa-Su R$10. Open W-M 11:30am-4pm).

P.N. DA SERRA DOS ÓRGÃOS ☎21

The Parque Nacional da Serra dos Órgãos is remarkable because of its curiously shaped peaks. The most famous of these, the Dedo de Deus ("Finger of God"), looks like a hand with extended index finger, and is something of a symbol for Teresópolis. The peaks form a stepped pattern that resembles organ pipes, and the park is known as Brazil's mountain climbing capital. Founded in 1939, the park's 11 hectares are divided between the municipalities of Teresópolis, Petrópolis, Magé, and Guapimirim. There are entrances to the park at Guapimirim and Teresópolis. The Guapimirim entrance leads to a beautiful area with several short trails to natural ponds, while the Teresópolis entrance is the starting point for several hikes to different peaks, including Pedra do Sino, the tallest peak in the range. The Teresópolis entrance is also the starting point for the Travessia, a three-day guided trek from Teresópolis to Petrópolis.

AT A GLANCE: P.N. DA SERRA DOS ÓRGÃOS

AREA: 11 hectares of mountain peaks, waterfalls, and *piscinas naturais.*

CLIMATE: The summers are warm enough to allow swimming in the *piscinas naturais*, but rainy and unpredictable weather can complicate hikes. Weather varies less during the winter, but hikers should be prepared for freezing temperatures near the peaks.

WHEN TO GO: Hiking is better attempted during winter, but swimming is only possible during the summer. The park is open Tu-Su 8am-5pm.

HIGHLIGHTS: Pedra do Sino, where sits Terra dos Gigantes, considered Brazil's hardest climb; the Dedo do Deus, Teresópolis's signature rock formation.

GATEWAY TOWNS: Teresópolis (p. 163) and Guapimirim.

FEES: Entrance R$3, additional R$9 for those seeking to climb Pedra do Sino. Motorcycles R$3, cars R$5.

CAMPING: There are three campgrounds, which cost R$6 per night, including the entrance fee.

PRACTICAL INFORMATION

Entrance fees can be paid either in Teresópolis or Guapimirim, and you can use your receipt to enter without paying again in the other. There is a Visitor's Center at each entrance (Teresópolis center open Tu-Su 9am-5pm; Guapimirim center open Th-Su 10am-5pm). Those wishing to hike Pedra do Sino or to the waterfalls must pay R$9 and sign a statement of responsibility. Mountain climbers with equipment and experience must contact Vicente at the Centro de Operações (☎2642 0659; open M-Sa 9am-5pm) for authorization to climb the park's peaks. The easiest way to get to the Teresópolis entrance is to take any "Alto" bus from the town's *centro* to the last stop and then walk along Av. Oliveira Botelho. Alternatively, buses labeled "Alto Soberbo" will leave you near the entrance, and buses to Guapimirim and Magé pass by both entrances. The park has three campgrounds, one in the Teresópolis area and two in the Guapimirim area. (R$6 per night, including R$3 entrance fee.)

OUTDOOR ACTIVITIES

In the Teresópolis leisure area near the entrance there is a waterfall and natural swimming pool, but these are often dry during winter. **Trilha Moart Catão** is an easy 30min. hike that takes you to the **Mirante Alexandre Oliveira,** from which there are beautiful views of Teresópolis. **Trilha da Primavera** is a 15min. trail through the forest. From the entrance to the park, you can walk to **Barragem** to find the **Trilha Suspensa,** a wooden walkway above the trees. The climb up to **Pedra do Sino** also begins in Barragem. The hike to the 2263m peak requires approximately fours hours, and is best done in winter, but come prepared for freezing temperatures at the top. Along the way are **Cachoeira Véu da Noiva,** a 35m waterfall that is said to have been one of Emperor Dom Pedro's favorites, and the 15m **Cachoeira das Andorinhas** is nearby. The **Travessia** trek from Teresópolis to Petrópolis begins at Bonfim and involves a hike to Pedra do Sino, a walk along the plateau to Pedra do Açu, and a descent to Petrópolis. The stretch between Pedra do Sinó and Pedra do Açu cannot be done without a guide. The three-day, 42km trip includes a night's stay at both Pedra do Sino and Pedra do Açu. **Mundo de Mato** has Travessia guides. (☎2742 0811; mundodemato@ig.com.br. R$250 for 1-2 people; R$350 for 3-5 people.) For mountain climbers, the biggest attractions are the 1692m **Dedo de Deus,** and the **Terra dos Gigantes,** considered the most difficult climb in Brazil.

RIO DE JANEIRO STATE

COSTA VERDE

ANGRA DOS REIS ☎24

Angra dos Reis is a narrow coastal town stretching across 365 islands. The best way to spend your time there is to visit a few of the bay islands, especially **Botinas, Piedade, Gipóia,** and the tiny but spectacular **Cataguases.** (5-6hr. excursions; R$25-35 per person.) Alternatively, you can charter a boat from **Associação de Barqueiros de Angra dos Reis,** Av. Júlio Maria s/n, either for the whole day or just for a drop-off on and pick-up from Cataguasas. (☎3365 3165. High season open daily 8am-late; low season daily 8am-5pm. 10-seaters R$300 per day, or R$80 drop-off/pick-up.) The city's biggest event is the **Procissão Marítima** every January 6, in which 1000 decorated boats are christened by sailing under a spray of water before setting sail from Praia das Flechas on Ilha do Gipóia to Praia do Anil on the mainland.

In the *centro*, **Avenida Júlio Maria** runs closest to the coast, while the roughly parallel **Rua do Comércio** has most of the town's shops, banks, and services. **Praia do Anil** is just north of the *centro*, and the *rodoviária* (☎3365 5138) is a little farther. **Costa Verde** (☎3365 0181) has buses to Rio de Janeiro (2½hr.; 18 per day 4am-10:45pm; R$23). **Reunícas Paulista** (☎3365 1280) runs to São Paulo (7hr.; 3-5 per day 8am-9:55pm; R$33) via Ubatuba (3½hr.; R$14). **Util** (☎3365 0565) goes to Belo Horizonte (10hr.; 8:15pm; R$44). **Colitur** (☎3365 0223) has buses to Paraty (2hr.; 28 per day 5am-10:30pm; R$5). The **tourist office,** Av. Júlio Maria 10, is in the *centro*. (☎3365 1175. Open M-Sa 8am-5:30pm, Su 8am-5pm.) In front of it there is a **24hr. ATM.** Services in town include: a **supermarket,** Av. Júlio Maria 140 (☎2365 1114; open M-Sa 8am-10pm, Su 8am-8pm); a **24hr. pharmacy,** in Angra Shopping, Av. José Elias Rabha 280 (☎3365 4893), near the *rodoviária;* **hospital** on Rua Dr. Coutinho (☎3365 0131); **Internet access,** Rua do Comércio 220 (☎3365 3721; open M-F 9am-6pm, Sa 9am-1pm); **post office,** Pça. Lopes Trovão 142 (☎3365 3020; open M-F 9am-5pm, Sa 9am-1pm). **Postal code:** 23900-970.

Hotel Jaques ❷, Rua do Comércio 144, is right in the *centro*. (☎3365 6508. *Quartos* R$15; *apartamento* doubles R$35.) **Albergue da Juventude Angra Hostel (HI) ❷,** Pça. da Matriz 152, is conveniently located. (☎3363 1234. High-season dorms R$20, non-members R$30. Low-season dorms R$15, non-members R$20; doubles R$40.)

Palace Hotel ❸, Rua Coronel Carvalho 275, has fully equipped rooms. (☎3365 0032. Singles R$40, with cable TV R$50; doubles R$60, with cable TV R$70.) **Fogão de Minas ❷,** Rua Júlio Maria 398, is the town's favorite self-service restaurant, with 45 options for only R$13 per kg. (☎3365 4877. Open daily 11am-4pm.) **Verde Mar ❶,** Pça. Lopes Trovão 35, has panoramic views of the bay, specializes in seafood, and makes a great *paella*. (☎3365 2065. Entrees R$39-49 for 2. Open daily 11am-10:30pm.) Nightlife in the *centro* is concentrated on and around Rua Coronel Carvalho, but Angrans themselves tend to spend the night farther north in **Pirata's Mall,** Estrada Municipal 91, near the city entrance, where on weekends there is always live music and dancing. There are also several bars and clubs in Parque das Palmeiras near the *rodoviária*. The open-air **Armazen,** Rua Joseá Belmiro da Paixão 320, has live MPB on Wednesday, *forró* on Thursday and Sunday, and is a dance club on Friday and Saturday. (Cover R$3 women; R$5 men. Open W 6pm-2am, Th-Sa 6pm-5am, Su 6pm-2am.)

ILHA GRANDE ☎24

Ilha Grande is a mountainous island with several small villages and beautiful, nationally renowned beaches. In colonial times Ilha Grande was a base for pirates and smugglers, but it is now a hot tourist destination. There are fewer than ten cars on Ilha Grande and visitors can still find pristine, deserted beaches. **Vila Abraão,** Ilha Grande's main village, houses most of its accommodations and restaurants. It is directly on the waterfront, with **Rua da Praia** running along the beach and **Rua Getúlio Vargas** roughly parallel to it a block away. From the dock, the main *praça* and church are to your left along Rua da Praia. **Rua da Igreja** runs next to this *praça* from Rua da Praia to Rua Getúlio Vargas. The island's inland side has many small villages and settlements, and beaches are accessible from Vila Abraão by boat. **Lagoa Azul** is popular for its calm waters, abundant fish, and view from atop the oddly shaped **Pico do Papagaio.** The seaward side has the island's most beautiful beaches, with waves ideal for surfing. The most admired beach is **Lopes Mendes,** a 30min. hike from Pouso. You can get to Pouso from Vila Abraão by boat, or by a 1½hr. trail. **Dois Rios,** between the mouths of two rivers, is the site of the **Lazareto,** a former jail, and can be reached by a 2hr. trail from Vila Abraão. From there, you can go to **Cachadaço,** a tiny beach surrounded by large rocks. Also on the seaward side is **Aventureiro,** a beautiful beach popular with surfers and accessible by boat during the high season.

Associação de Barqueiros da Ilha Grande, to the left of the dock, rents boats for up to ten people, but these small boats cannot sail to the seaward side of the island. (High season open daily 8:30am-9pm; low season daily 8:30-11am and 5-9pm. R$180-300.) **Barcas S/A** shuttles between Vila Abraão and Angra dos Reis (1½hr.; departs daily 10am; returns M-F 3:30, Sa-Su 1:30; M-F R$4.55, Sa-Su R$22.75). From Rio de Janeiro, the island is accessible via Mangaratiba (1½hr.; Sa-Th 8am, F 2 per day 8am-10pm; M-F R$4.55, Sa-Su R$22.75). The **tourist office** is right on the dock. (High season open daily 9am-1pm and 3-7pm; low season daily 9am-11am and 3pm-5:30pm.) Services include: a **pharmacy** on Rua da Praia, to your left after the bridge (☎3361 5151; open daily 8:30am-9:30pm); **health center** on Rua Getúlio Vargas just past the first bridge (☎3361 5884); **Internet access** at Ilha Grande.Com, down the first street to the left from the dock (☎3361 5985; open daily 8am-2am.).

The price of a place to stay in Ilha Grande tends to be steep, and only gets steeper in the high season. There are many small campgrounds by the beaches, and on the eastern side of the island camping is the only option. **Pousada Portal dos Borbas ❸,** Rua das Flores 4, is on the right from the second bridge on Rua Getúlio Vargas. This quaint *pousada* has sizable, fully equipped rooms. (☎3361 5085. High-season doubles R$120. Low-season singles R$50; doubles R$70.) **Pousada**

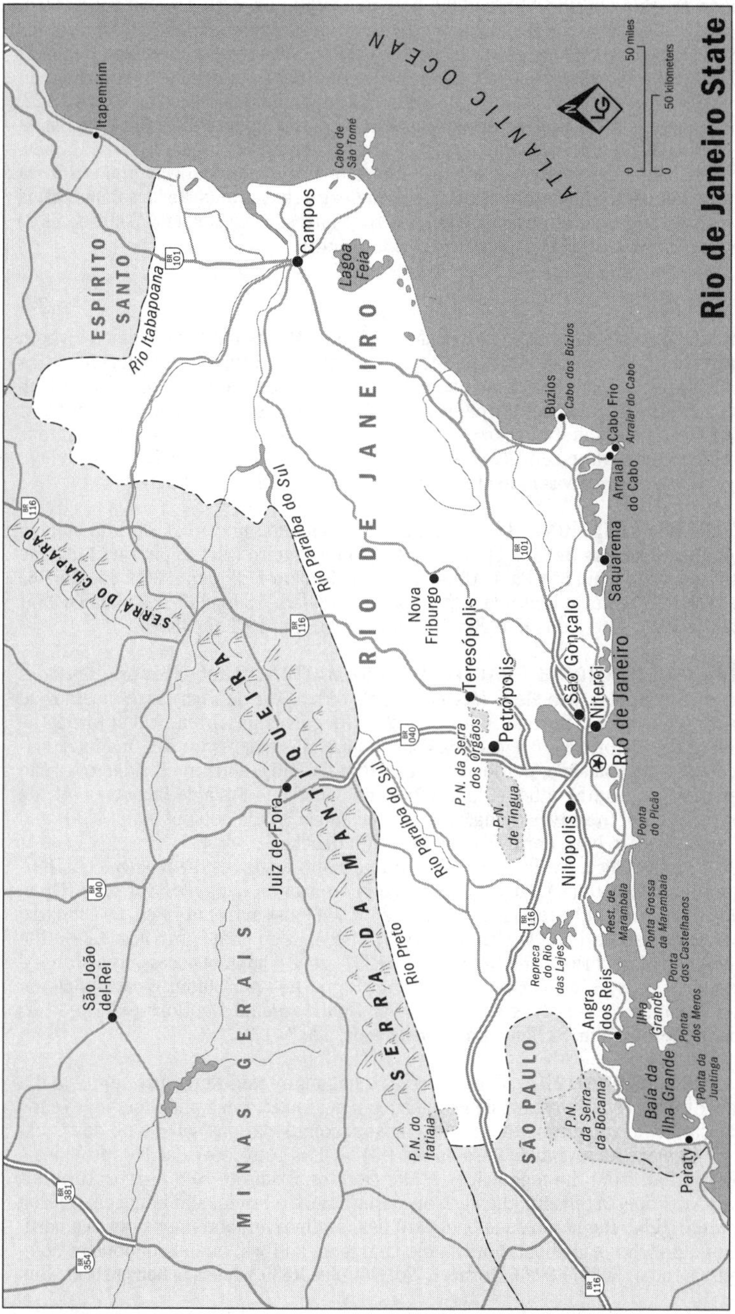
Rio de Janeiro State
ATLANTIC OCEAN
0
50 miles
0
50 kilometers
Itapemirim
Cabo de São Tomé
ESPÍRITO SANTO
Rio Itabapoana
BR 101
Campos
Lagoa Feia
RIO DE JANEIRO
Búzios
Cabo dos Búzios
Cabo Frio
Arraial do Cabo
Arraial do Cabo
Saquarema
BR 101
Nova Friburgo
Teresópolis
São Gonçalo
Petrópolis
Niterói
Rio de Janeiro
P.N. da Serra dos Órgãos
P.N. de Tinguá
Nilópolis
Ponta do Picão
Rio Paraíba do Sul
Rio Paraíba do Sul
SERRA DO CHAPARAO
BR 116
BR 116
SERRA DA MANTIQUEIRA
BR 040
Juiz de Fora
BR 040
MINAS GERAIS
São João del-Rei
Rio Preto
P.N. do Itatiaia
BR 381
BR 354
BR 116
BR 116
SÃO PAULO
Represa do Rio das Lajes
Rest. de Marambaia
Ponta Grossa da Marambaia
Ponta dos Castelhanos
Angra dos Reis
Ilha Grande
Ponta dos Meros
Baía da Ilha Grande
Ponta da Juatinga
P.N. da Serra da Bocama
Paraty

Caúca ❸, Rua Getúlio Vargas 300, has quality rooms with a beautiful garden. (☎3361 5137; www.pousadacauca.com.br. High-season singles R$105; doubles R$150. Low-season singles R$42; doubles R$60.) **Albergue da Juventude Holandês (HI) ❷**, Rua da Assembléia s/n, is on the second right after the second bridge on Rua Getúlio Vargas. (☎3361 5034. Breakfast included. High-season dorms R$22, non-members R$30. Low-season dorms R$17, non-members R$20.) **Sabor da Ilha ❷** is on the Buganville walkway past the first bridge left of the dock. (☎3361 5550. R$14 per kg. Open daily noon-9pm.) Past the Buganville walkway along Rua da Praia, there is a concentration of mid- to high-end restaurants. **Rei dos Caldos ❸**, is on the second right after the bridge, and specializes in seafood (R$28-40 serves 2) and stews. (☎3361 5511. Open Th-Tu noon-11pm.)

PARATY ☎24

Situated on a stunning stretch of coast, the city of Paraty has been blessed by both nature and history. The city began to take its present form in the 18th century, as gold mining in Minas increased its importance as a port. Paraty's *centro* was idealistically planned and uses the daily influx of high tide as a natural street cleaner. At the foot of mountains and surrounded by beautiful beaches, Paraty is also famous for its *pinga* (white rum), which is still manufactured as it was in the 19th century, when the city was home to as many as 120 *engenhos* (distilleries).

TRANSPORTATION. The **rodoviária** is just outside the *centro*, on Rua Manoel S. Pádua. **Reunídas** (☎3371 1196) runs to Rio de Janeiro (4hr.; 2 per day 11:30am-12:40am; R$31) and São Paulo (5hr.; 4 per day 9:40am-11:35pm; R$27). **São Geraldo** (☎3371 1277) runs to Ubatuba (1hr.; 3 per day 7:50am-6:30pm; R$7). **Colitur** (☎3371 1224) goes to Angra dos Reis (2hr.; 26 per day 4:50am-10:30pm; R$5).

ORIENTATION & PRACTICAL INFORMATION. Paraty's historic *centro* is closed to vehicles. **Rua Maria Jácome de Melo** (a.k.a. **Rua da Lapa**), is the main road leaving the *centro*. Beyond Rua Domingos Gonçalves de Abreu, which forms the limit of the historic *centro*, **Avenida Roberto Silveira** is where you will find most services. **Rua do Comércio,** perpendicular to Rua da Lapa, ends in a bridge over Rio Perequê-Açú. On the other side are **Praia do Pontal** and **Praia de Jabaquara.** At the southern tip of the city is **Trindade,** which became a hippie hotspot in the 1970s and is considered to have Paraty's most beautiful beaches.

The **tourist office,** Av. Roberto Silveira 1, is just outside the *centro*. (☎3371 1897. Open daily 9am-9pm.) **Currency exchange** is on Rua da Lapa. (☎3371 1295. Open daily 9am-7pm.) Other services include: **24hr. ATM** just in front of Pça. do Chafariz; **pharmacy,** also on Pça. do Chafariz (☎3371 2965; open 8am-9pm); **hospital** on the other side of the bridge and to the right (☎3371 1623); **Internet access,** Rua Marchal Deodoro 15 (☎3371 2530; open daily 9am-10pm; R$3 per 30min.); **post office,** on Rua Domingos Gonçalves de Abreu near Rua Marechal Deodoro (☎3371 1152; open M-F 9am-5pm, Sa 9am-1pm). **Postal code**: 23970-000.

ACCOMMODATIONS. Paraty's *centro* has many mid-range *pousadas* and a slew of fine restaurants, most specializing in seafood. Prices jump for New Year's and Carnaval, and during these times most accommodations sell 4- or 5-day packages. **Albergue da Juventude Casa do Rio (HI) ❷**, Rua Antônio Vidal 120, provides a slight break from the high prices in the *centro*. From the *rodoviária*, turn left onto Av. Roberto Silveira, then left onto Rua João do Prado, and left again on Rua Antônio Vidal. Its picturesque backyard lies on the river, and the owner is a certified guide who leads boat, horseback, van, jeep, and walking excursions at competitive rates. (☎3371 2223. Dorms R$20. Doubles R$35.) **Pousada Konquista ❷**, Rua

Jango Pádua 20, is a beautiful colonial-style *pousada* between the *rodoviária* and the *centro*. (☎3371 1308. High-season singles R$40; doubles R$60. Low-season singles R$30; doubles R$40. R$10 extra for A/C.) **Pousada Provence ❸,** Av. Otávio Gama s/n, is a quality riverfront *pousada* with friendly service and a cozy common area. (☎3371 1349. High-season doubles R$100. Low-season doubles R$60.) **Pousada Solar da Praia ❷,** Av. Orlando Capineli 194, has simple accommodations on lively Praia do Pontal, five minutes from the *centro* with beautiful views of the bay. (☎3371 2507. High-season singles R$20-25; doubles R$40-50.) There are two campsites by Praia do Pontal: **Beira Rio** (☎3371 1985; low-season camping R$7 per person) and **Camping Clube do Brasil** (high-season camping R$20 per person; low-season R$11 per person). **Camping Jabaquara ❶,** over the hill at Praia de Jabaquara, has large grounds. (Camping R$12 per person. Trailers R$25 per person.)

FOOD. **Sabor da Terra ❷,** Av. Roberto Silveira 180, is the town's most popular self-service restaurant. (☎3371 2384. R$13 per kg. Open daily 11:30am-5pm and 6-10pm.) **Restaurante Matriz ❹,** Pça. da Matriz 6, is a sophisticated restaurant specializing in seafood. Try their *camarão casadinho* (R$28) or *moqueca à baiana,* which comes with a banana *moqueca* on the side (R$37). Most dishes serve two. (☎3371 2820. Open Su-Th 11am-11pm, F-Sa 11am-midnight.) **Armazém do Antun ❸,** Pça. Monsenhor Hélio Pires 3, is near the river's edge, just removed from the night-time action, and serves Middle Eastern food; their *kafta michui* (R$23 for 2) is recommended. (☎3371 6266. Open Su-Th 1pm-midnight, F-Sa 1pm-2am.)

SIGHTS & OUTDOOR ACTIVITIES. The beautiful 18th-century architecture of Paraty's *centro* is the city's most impressive sight. At its edge is the **Matriz de Nossa Senhora dos Remédios,** built at the request of Maria Jácome de Melo, a Paraty native who donated part of her land so that the settlement could be moved to the city's present location. In return for her donation, the city's patron saint became Nossa Senhora dos Remédios, of whom she was a devotee. Construction of the church was begun in 1787 and lasted for 86 years. (Open Tu-Su 10am-noon and 2-5pm. R$2.) The nearby **Igreja de São Benedito** dates to 1857, and its features demonstrate the tropicalization of baroque elements; check out the pineapple wood carving containing the chandelier. (Open Su-Tu 10am-noon and 2-5pm. R$2.) **Igreja de Santa Rita** is the oldest church in the *centro,* and currently houses **Museu de Arte Sacra.** (Open W-Su 9am-noon and 1:30-5pm. R$1.)

Paraty's environs should not be missed. Horseback rides through mountain trails leading to waterfalls are the easiest way to find some beautiful spots. Paraty's 65 islands and 300 beaches should be explored. Many agencies have 5-6hr. **boat excursions** through the islands, making about five stops for beachgoing and snorkeling (trips start at R$20). Close to the *centro* are the lively **Praia do Pontal** and the beautiful **Praia de Jabaquara.** The bay view from both of these beaches is stellar, but the best beaches are farther away from the *centro.* The neighborhood of **Trindade,** 30km from the *centro,* is considered to have the city's most beautiful beaches, though some would claim that the same is also true for **Paraty-Mirim,** 27km from the *centro.* The entire northern coast is readily accessible via the bus to Angra dos Reis, and there are some accommodations near **Praia Grande** and the much-loved **Praia Prainha.** The stretch of coast between Trindade and Paraty's *centro* has many beaches with little infrastructure that are accessible only by boat or trail. The mountains around Paraty have many spectacular waterfalls, though the water is chilly year-round. **Pedra Branca** is also popular, accessible via a 1hr. trail.

NIGHTLIFE. On weekend and summer nights, there is no shortage of elegant bars spilling live music into the streets. **Café Paraty,** Rua do Comércio 253, is a spacious bar where daily live MPB, jazz, and *bossa nova* set the mood. (☎3371 1464.

Open Su-Th 9am-11pm, F-Sa 9am-late. Cover R$7 after 9pm.) Trendy **Paraty33,** Rua Maria Jácome de Melo 357, has drinks served to the tune of daily live music after 7pm. (☎3371 7311. Open Su-Th noon-midnight, F-Sa noon-4am. Cover after 7pm: Su-Th R$5; F-Sa R$5 women, R$10 men.) **Dama da Noite,** Alameda Princesa Izabel s/n, is an after-hours club just over the bridge leaving the *centro*. (☎9992 3662; www.damadanoiteparaty.com.br. Cover R$5. Open Th-Sa midnight-late.)

FESTIVALS. Paraty's five-day **Carnaval** is very popular. The most famous of its six *blocos* is the Bloco da Lama, whose participants leave from Praia de Jabaquara covered in mud. **Festa do Divino** in early June and **Festa de Nossa Senhora dos Remédios** in early September are traditional religious celebrations with ten days of processions and nighttime shows. In the third week of August, the three-day **Festival da Pinga** showcases Paraty's *pinga* (white rum).

COSTA DEL SOL (REGIÃO DOS LAGOS)

SAQUAREMA ☎21

Saquarema enjoys a relaxed lifestyle between sea, lake, and mountains. It is famous for its waves and many of its residents have practically grown up on surfboards. The town's center *(vila)* is between the Praia da Vila and the sizable Lagoa de Saquarema, just a few blocks from the coast. Close to the outlet of the lake is Pça. Oscar de Macedo Soares. On the other side of the outlet, connected by a bridge, is the neighborhood of Itaúna, which is dominated by the surfers' paradise of Praia do Itaúna. Av. Saquarema begins at the bridge and runs inland along the edge of the lake to Bacaxá, where most banks are located. Just a few blocks from the bridge on this avenue is the popular mall, Lake's Shopping.

TRANSPORTATION & PRACTICAL INFORMATION. Buses to Rio de Janeiro leave from Lake's Shopping but also stop at Pça. Oscar de Macedo Soares (1½hr.; 8 per day 5:15am-8pm; R$10.50). City buses cost R$1.30, and taxis can be called at ☎2034 7188. The **tourist office,** Rua Barão de Saquarema 253A, is just off Pça. Oscar de Macedo Soares 128. (☎2651 4112. Open M-F 9am-5pm.) There is **currency exchange** at Free Bank, Rua Segisfredo de Oliveira Bravo 139, in Bacaxá. (☎2653 3128. Open daily 8am-5:30pm.) Other services include: a **supermarket,** Av. Oceânica 169 (☎2651 2335; open M-Sa 8am-6pm, Su 8am-noon); a **pharmacy,** Rua Brão de Saquarema 231 (☎2651 3081; open M-Sa 8am-9pm, Su 8am-noon and 4-9pm); a **hospital,** Rua Adolfo Bravo s/n (☎2653 3123), in Bacaxá; **Internet access,** on Rua Dr. Luiz Januário (open daily 10am-midnight). The **post office** is in Pça. Oscar de Macedo Soares. (☎2651 2298. Open M-F 9am-5pm.) **Postal code:** 28990-000.

ACCOMMODATIONS. Itaúna is full of appealing accommodations, many of them directly on the beach, though good deals are hard to find. Prices go up during Carnaval, New Year, the International Surf Championship in late July and early August, and the Festa da Padroeira in early September. **Hotel Saquarema ❷,** Pça. Oscar de Macedo Soares 128, has simple but appealing accommodations with ceiling fan, TV, and breakfast. (☎2651 2275. Singles R$40; doubles R$50-R$60.) **Canto da Vila ❸,** Av. Salgado Filho 52, has delightful rooms right in front of Saquarema's liveliest beach, and simpler rooms in back. (☎2651 1563. High-season *quarto* singles R$40; doubles R$65, with A/C R$80; *apartamentos* R$110. Low-season *apar-*

tamentos R$90.) **Pousada Airumã ❷,** Rua das Garoupas 228, 10min. from Praia de Itaúna, is a small and cozy hotel where every detail is just right. (☎2651 6080; www.aktuell.com.br/airuma. High-season doubles R$85. Low-season singles R$45; doubles R$65.) **Pousada Solar de Itaúna ❸,** Rua das Pitangas 700, is a beautiful, fully equipped *pousada* a short walk from the beach. (☎2430 4300. High-season singles R$85; doubles R$95. Low-season singles R$65; doubles R$75.) **Itaúna Inn ❸,** Av. Oceânica 1764, is a fun beach-front *pousada.* (High-season *apartamento* singles R$55; doubles R$75. Low-season *apartamento* singles R$45; doubles R$60.)

FOOD. Should you feel strangely at home at **Algas Marinhas ❸,** Av. Oceânica 1435, it will likely be because you are, indeed, on the front porch of the couple preparing the food, which includes excellent pizzas for two (R$14-25). (☎2651 1368. High-season open daily 11am-2pm and 5-7pm.) **Marisco ❷,** Pça. Oscar de Macedo Soares 35, is a centrally located restaurant that has been around for decades. Its self-service lunch includes great seafood (R$12 per kg; *churrasco* R$14 per kg). (☎2651 1884. Open daily 11:30am-3:30pm.) **Mac Bel ❹,** Av. Saquarema 5450, is in Bacaxá and the simple restaurant is known for its excellent meat. (☎2653 3250. *Picanha* for two R$36. Open daily noon-midnight.) **Garota de Itaúna ❸,** Av. Oceânica 165, is a *barraca* serving large portions. (☎2651 2321. Entrees R$20-25. Open M-F 8am-10pm, Sa-Su 8am-2am.)

SIGHTS. Saquarema's main beach is **Praia da Vila,** near the *vila,* but it is **Praia de Itaúna** that receives the most attention. Surfers treasure its excellent waves, and it is the site of the International Surf Championship held annually in late July and early August. The best waves come in September, toward winter's end. To check the waves, go to www.saquasurf.saquarema.com.br or call the Escola de Surf. The **Escola de Surf de Saquarema,** Av. Oceânica 180, near the beginning of the beach, offers surfing lessons; an individual two-hour lesson costs R$50, but you can also join a group class, with 12 lessons over the course of a month for R$70. Board rentals are R$50 per six hours. The school also rents bicycles (R$30 per day) and serves as a de facto tourist office, helping point tourists to accommodations and other activities in the area. (☎2651 4630, 9903 6619; escoladesurfsaqua@hotmail.com.) The city of waves and lakes also has a wilderness worth exploring on foot. The **Reserva Ecológica Estadual de Jacarepiá** includes the beautiful Lagoa de Jacarepiá, a forest area in which you can find the region's characteristic wildlife, and the Praia de Massambaba. A 20min. hike cuts across the reserve. A good hike for the adventurous is **Trilha do Lago de Água Mineral,** a difficult, 8km hike leading to great views and a lake of mineral water. Continuing 3km is the **Trilha do Alto Tingüí,** which leads to further views and a waterfall. Take the bus to Sampaio Corrêa to find the trailhead. The region of Saquarema was populated in prehistoric times, and travelers can visit archaeological sites over 4000 years old. Saquarema has 18 *sambaquis,* small mounds containing the remains of ancient residents. Open for visitation is the **Sambaqui da Beirada,** where the partially unearthed remains of a 4500-year-old woman and a 4100-year-old young man, still covered in the shells with which he was ceremonially covered, are on display. Take the bus to Barra Nova or Jaconé via Coqueiral. (☎2651 9178. Open W-F 2-4pm, Sa-Su 9am-4pm.) **Igreja Matriz Nossa Senhora de Nazareth** was founded in 1630 and is the destination of hundreds of thousands of pilgrims during the annual **Festa da Padroeira,** every September 8. In back of the church is the legendary **Gruta de Nossa Senhora de Lourdes.** The images of Nossa Senhora de Lourdes and Santa Bernadete have been there since the 1940s, when a priest had them sent from France because of the stark resemblance of this cave to one where the Virgin Mary was supposedly sighted in Lourdes, France.

BÚZIOS ☎22

The picturesque, wind-swept isthmus of Armação de Búzios—home of some of Brazil's most famed beaches—has undergone tremendous development in the last few decades. Among the few reminders of its former status as a humble fishing village is a sculpture, simply titled *The Fishermen*, located on Praia Armação. Closer to the *centro* is a very different sculpture: a bronze likeness of the iconic symbol of fashion and sophistication, Brigitte Bardot, which celebrates Búzios' dramatic reincarnation as the ultimate destination for die-hard sun-worshippers. In 1965, Brigitte was photographed relaxing in remote Búzios, and according to local legend, she later asserted that her time there had been the happiest days of her life. Whether or not this is true, today Búzios attracts thousands of visitors—a majority of them from abroad—seeking to experience that same bliss. Catering to an upscale market, the area is no budget traveler's paradise, but for those willing to splurge, Búzios offers the company of beautiful people in a beautiful setting.

TRANSPORTATION. The intercity **rodoviária,** Estrada da Usina 1001 (☎2623 2050), is only two blocks from the *centro*. **Mil e Um** runs buses to Arraial do Cabo (1hr.; 6 per day 7:45am-10:45pm; R$2.10) and Rio de Janeiro (3hr.; 8 per day 7am-7pm; R$12.15-13.50). **Local buses** go to Cabo Frio (30min.; every 30min.; R$2.10). To get to some of the more remote beaches *kombis* are available, but walking or biking is usually the safest option. In the *centro*, try **Bike Tour,** Rua das Pedras 266 (☎2623 6365). The coolest way to get around town is to rent a **buggy.** Tourism agencies, many on or around Rua das Pedras, can set up affordable packages.

ORIENTATION & PRACTICAL INFORMATION. Attractions are relatively spread out, but it is easy to get from one point to another. All traffic into Búzios must pass through the **Pórtico** upon arrival. The main street, **Estrada J.B. Ribeiro Dantas,** traverses the isthmus, passing through all areas of interest. First along the road is **Manguinhos,** known for the popular **Praia Géribа,** which receives excellent surf and a young, fun-loving crowd. This is one of the most commercially developed areas. The street continues eastward to the *centro*, where the majority of services and nightlife hotspots are found. Most of the action occurs on rowdy **Rua das Pedras,** the street that never sleeps. From here, the coast curves sharply northward to hilly **Ossos,** a quiet residential area. Its tranquil beaches, particularly **Praia Azeda** and **Praia João Fernandes,** are frequented by both friendly families and hardcore sun-worshippers.

The main **tourist office** is located at the Pórtico. (☎0800 249 999. Nov.-Jan. open daily 24hr.; Feb.-Oct. daily 9am-11pm.) There is also a helpful **tourist booth,** Pça. Santos Dumont 111, in the *centro*. (☎2623 2099. Open daily 9am-9pm.) Several companies in town run **schooner tours** of the area, which leave from the pier in Praia do Canto and start at R$30; call ahead for price and schedule information. **Queen Lory** (☎2623 1179) has excursions which visit some northern beaches and Ilha Feia. **Interbúzios** (☎2623 6454) runs trips to the more untamed southern beaches and Ilha Branca, which include three snorkeling stops. **Miss Búzios Vitória** (☎2623 6454) includes stops for fishing and visits 15 of the northern beaches. There is a **24hr. ATM** at Banco do Brasil, Rua Manuel de Carvalho 70, which accepts Visa cards (☎2623 2302). For **currency exchange** in town, **Malizia,** in Shopping Praia do Centro, has good rates. (☎2623 2022. Open M-Sa 9am-5pm.) There is a **police post** in Pça. Santos Dumont (☎2623 1340), and a **first-aid post,** Estrada J.B. Ribeiro Dantas 2000 (☎2623 2447). **Internet access** is available at Internet@Búzios, Estrada J.B. Ribeiro Dantas 92. (☎2623 0956. R$4 per 30min. Open daily 11am-11pm.) The main **post office,** Rua Manoel de Carvalhos 70, loja 3, is in the *centro* (☎2623 1640. Open M-F, 9am-5pm.) **Postal code:** 28950-000.

ACCOMMODATIONS. Budget accommodations in Búzios are practically nonexistent, particularly during the busy summer season, when prices may rise by as much as R$50 per person. The majority of hotels are concentrated in the *centro*. **Albergue Praia dos Amores ❶,** Estrada J.B. Ribeiro Dantas 92, is a 20min. walk from downtown. The clean but bare rooms come with fan, private bath, and *frigo-bar* during the summer. (☎2623 2422. Dorms R$25.) **Pousada Vittoria ❸,** Rua César Augusto São Luiz 21, is only two blocks from Rua das Pedras on a surprisingly quiet street. All rooms have A/C, TV, *frigo-bar*, and private bath. It's not the best option for meeting people, but you'll be able to get your beauty sleep. (☎2623 7294. Singles R$50-60; doubles R$110-120.) **Pousadinha ❸,** Rua Manoel Turíbio de Farias 202, is a good alternative for couples. Smallish rooms have A/C, TV, and private bath. The romantic open-air courtyard makes for a wonderful breakfast spot. (☎2623 1448. Singles R$55; doubles R$70; triples R$95.)

FOOD. There's no shortage of restaurants on and around Rua das Pedras. Unfortunately, many of them can be a bit of a strain on the wallet. A good supermarket close by is **Supermercado Alves,** Av. J.B. Ribeiro Dantas 14. (☎2623 6127. Open daily 8am-9pm.) There is a branch of the popular Rio ice-cream sensation **Mil Frutas ❶,** Rua das Pedras s/n, which has a large and exotic flavor selection: try the amazing Fruta do Conde. (☎2623 6436. 1 scoop R$5; 2 scoops R$9.) The best kilo in town is **Bananaland ❷,** Rua Manoel Turibio de Farias 50. Owners Rosangela and Carlos Alberto take pride in their delectable daily buffet (R$24 per kg). Salmon, filet mignon, and a delicious *banana á milanesa* are common dishes. (☎2623 2666. Open daily 11:30am-11pm.) Pricier **Âncora ❸,** Av. J.B. Ribeiro Dantas 44 (☎9813 9859), in Praia da Armação, has wonderful sunset views, and the cool, shaded balcony is very relaxing. The international menu includes beef and chicken dishes, as well as a tasty *gnocchi* (R$15).

BEACHES. Búzios' fantastic beaches have gained international repute as some of the most beautiful in Brazil. With so many sizes and shapes to choose from, it's always possible to find your own little piece of heaven. One way to see the area is on the touristy **Búzios Trolley** (☎2623 2763), which departs from the *centro* (2hr.; 3 per day 9am-3pm; R$20 per person). Far better are the **schooner tours** that take you along the coast (tours start at R$30, and include snorkeling equipment). Generally, the beaches on the north side of the peninsula (closer to the *centro)* have calm waters and heavier boat traffic. **Praia do Canto** and **Praia da Armação** are very picturesque stretches, but due to heavy boat traffic and pollution, are not recommended for swimming. Tiny, pristine beaches on the south side—some with excellent waves—are accessible via small dirt roads and trails. **Praia da Geribá,** in Manguinhos, is one of the most popular beaches in Búzios. Adored by surfers, the waves of Geribá can reach heights of four meters. A more secluded beach is **Praia da Tartaruga,** accessible via a dirt road 1km west of the *centro*. Its calm, clear waters are perfect for a quick swim. **Praia dos Ossos,** one of the first to be "discovered" by tourists, is a yachting hotspot. Five minutes from Ossos on a narrow footpath are **Praia Azeda** and **Praia Azedinha,** arguably two of the most beautiful beaches in Búzios. The still-exotic **Praia Brava,** surrounded by rocky walls and exotic vegetation, is a mecca for surfers.

NIGHTLIFE. No matter which beach you decide to spend the day on, nighttime in Búzios belongs to the fabulous **Rua das Pedras,** where people of all ages go to show off the day's tan. During the summer, things pick up after midnight and continue past dawn. **Chez Michou,** Rua das Pedras 90, is the best spot for late-night crepes, and has a large open-air dance floor to complement the great live music. Michou also hosts a fantastic Jazz and Blues Festival in July. (☎623 2169. Open Su-Th noon-11pm, F-Sa 1pm-5am.) **Gulfstream Bar,** near the beginning of Rua das Pedras, hosts nightly pop impersonations by the highly entertaining Luís Antônio Santos. (Open daily 7pm-late.) Trendy **Fashion Café,** Rua das Pedras 151, has a balcony right over the water. Live Brazilian music, with plenty of audience participation, is a highlight. (☎2623 2617. Open daily 11pm-late.)

CABO FRIO ☎24

Roughly 23km south of Búzios is Santa Helena de Cabo Frio. Even though it was officially founded under Portuguese rule in 1615, for over 100 years before that the region was the site of violent conflict between English, French, Dutch, and Portuguese settlers, all of whom were seeking control over the *pau-brasil* (brazilwood) market. Buttressed by an economy based on salt extraction and fishing industries, Cabo Frio's population has expanded to almost 127,000 in the past few decades, and increasing numbers of tourists crowd the city's beaches. **Praia do Forte, Praia do Foguete,** and **Praia das Dunas** are particularly popular for their unique landscapes of imposing dunes and powdery sand. The more suburban **Praia do Peró, Praia das Conchas,** and **Praia Brava** (a favorite surfing spot) are a bit more difficult to reach from the *centro*. Another attraction is the 17th-century **Forte São Mateus,** at the north end of Praia do Forte. Because of its larger size and urban atmosphere, Cabo Frio is not as appealing as its glamorous northern neighbor, Búzios.

The intercity **rodoviária,** Av. Juscelino Kubitschek 38, has **buses** and **vans** departing almost all day long to Rio de Janeiro (2½-3hr.; R$15). **Taxi stands** are located across the street from the *rodoviária*. It costs R$6-10 to reach the *centro*, but it's easier to walk. **City buses** are useful to access some of the more remote beaches, such as Praia Brava and Praia das Conchas. **Morro da Guia,** a round hill with the small white chapel of **Nossa Senhora da Guia** on top, is directly to the north of the *rodoviária*. A 15min. walk toward the hill brings you to **Avenida João Pessoa** and the *centro*, where most hotels, restaurants, and services are located. The **Secretaria do Turismo,** on Av. João Pessoa, in front of Praia do Forte, has free maps. (☎2665 4145. Open M-F 9am-5pm, Sa-Su 9am-2pm). You can set up **tours** with Planeta Costa do Sol, Pça. Porto Rocha 18, loja 21 (☎2645 2023), which runs daily excursions to the dunes south of the city. **24hr. ATMs** at HSBC, Av. Assunção 793 (☎2645 1818), accept most foreign cards. Other services include: **Hospital Santa Izabel,** Rua Barão do Rio Branco 72 (☎2645 4040); **Internet access** at Cyber Café, Rua 13 de Novembro 140 (☎2647 5357); **post office,** Largo Santo Antônio 55, in the *centro* (☎2645 4466; open M-F 8am-6pm). **Postal code:** 28907-000.

Pousada Agua Marinha ❷, Rua Rui Barbosa 996, three blocks from Av. Júlia Kubitschek, is an affordable option during the low season, but prices increase as much as 50% Dec.-Mar. Whitewashed, spotless rooms have *frigo-bar*, TV, and private bath. (☎2643 8447. Singles R$35; doubles R$60. R$10 extra for A/C.) **Pousada Suzy ❸,** on Av. Júlia Kubitschek, one block from the *rodoviária*, is a convenient overnight stop, though a bit far from the beach. (☎643 1742. Singles R$50; doubles R$70.) **Branca Confeitaria ❶,** Pça. Porto Rocha 15, four blocks from the beach, is an inexpensive place for tasty food. Though they are known for their scrumptious Napoleons and ice cream sundaes (R$3.80), they also serve *salgados* (R$1) and burgers—try the Big Branca (R$4.20). (☎2643 0084.)

SOUTHEAST

Though not the largest political region in Brazil—encompassing only the small states of Espírito Santo, Minas Gerais, and Rio de Janeiro, plus the average-sized São Paulo state—the Southeast no doubt looms largest in most Brazilians' minds: every second Brazilian lives in this region, and the region is responsible for some 65% of the country's international economic output. Even excluding the Cidade Maravilhosa and its neighboring cities, a region this dense and dynamic holds countless attractions for travelers to Brazil, most of whom arrive in the country via the Southeast's unofficial capital, São Paulo. From the untamed wilds of national parks to the untamed throngs of one of the world's biggest cities, from the uninhabited beaches of Ubatuba to the intricately wrought colonial architecture of Minas Gerais, the Southeast merits a spot on any itinerary.

HIGHLIGHTS OF THE SOUTHEAST

SOAK up the sun on the beaches of **Ilhabela** (p. 201).

CONTEMPLATE *objèts d'art* in **São Paulo's** incredible Museum of Modern Art (p. 192).

SCAN the skies in **São Thomé das Letras,** Brazil's 4th highest city (p. 225).

MEANDER through the winding streets of historic **Ouro Preto** (p. 209).

RELAX in the isolated **Parque Estadual de Itaúnas** (p. 229).

SOUTHEAST

SÃO PAULO ☎11

Paulistas have a love-hate relationship with the sprawling city of São Paulo, as they attempt to shield themselves from it even while taking full advantage of the city's many cultural institutions. The world's sixth most populous city and Brazil's economic epicenter, São Paulo is responsible for 10% of Brazil's economic output and more than 70% of the country's business-related activities. The city has many names; it has been dubbed the New York of the Tropics by some and the Money-Making Machine by others, but those who know it best simply call it Sampa, echoing Caetano Veloso's famous ode to the city.

INTERCITY TRANSPORTATION

Flights: Aeroporto Internacional de Garulhos (☎6445 2945), a.k.a. **Cumbica,** is 30km from Centro. Dark, bunker-like, and full of shops, Cumbica is the busiest airport in South America. ATMs, luggage storage, and currency exchange booths can be found throughout the airport. **Comum** taxis are easy to find but hard on the wallet (R$50-70 to Centro). **Guaracoop Taxis** (☎6440 7070), with a booth in Cumbica, charges R$65 to Av. Paulista. By far the best deal is the Airport Bus Service managed by **EMTU** (☎0800 190 088, in Cumbica 6445 2505) which departs from the airport every 30min. and stops at Av. Paulista, Pça. da República, Congonhas Airport, El Dorado Shopping, and at the Tietê and Barra Funda *rodoviárias.* **Car rental** offices in the airport include: **Avis** (☎4225 8356); **Hertz** (☎0800 701 7300); **Interlocadora** (☎0800 13 8000); **Unidas** (☎0800 12 1121). **Aeroporto de Congonhas** (☎5090 9000) has more than 100 daily flights to Rio de Janeiro. Taxis (R$30 to Centro), EMTU buses, and all major rental car companies are available.

Buses: São Paulo has 3 *rodoviárias.* **Tietê,** or Terminal Rodoviário Governador Carvalho Pinto, Av. Cruzeiro do Sul 1800 (☎6221 7199), is the largest, with buses arriving from all over Brazil, as well as from Argentina, Chile, Paraguay, and Uruguay. M: Tietê is located inside the station, and provides the safest, most convenient transport. **Barra Funda,** Rua Mário de Andrade 664 (☎3612 1782), is one of the smaller *rodoviárias,* and serves destinations in Paraná, Goiás, Mato Grosso do Sul, and inland São Paulo state. It is also served by the *metrô,* and is 1 block away from the Memorial da América Latina (p. 192). **Jabaquara,** Rua dos Jequitibás (☎5012 2256), is the smallest of the 3 *rodoviárias,* serving 9 small cities in the southern region of São Paulo state.

ORIENTATION

Sprawling, massive, and constantly expanding, São Paulo might appear to the first-time visitor as one of the world's most disorienting places. Metropolitan São Paulo is a patternless crazy quilt of socioeconomic diversity: affluent residential areas are interspersed with the city's decaying slums, which are in turn indiscriminately mixed in with São Paulo's beautiful universities, famous museums, middle-class neighborhoods, and industrial zones. However, getting around is surprisingly easy, as most points of interest to the visitor are located in a relatively compact area south of **Tietê** and east of **Pinheiros.** North of Tietê spreads the **Zona Norte,** where the *metrô's* principal north-south line originates (M: Tucuvuri). Farther north is **Pico de Jaraquá,** the highest point in the São Paulo metropolitan area, which can be seen from Av. Paulista on clear days.

Directly south of the river is the **Zona Central,** the geographic and historic center of the city. Many of São Paulo's most important monuments and museums are found here. **Praça da Sé,** site of the beautifully renovated Catedral Metropolitana, is the city's geographic center and also where the *metrô's* Azul (blue) and Vermelha (red) lines meet; these are also known as lines 1 and 3, respectively. Directly to the south of this area are the city's Italian and Japanese neighborhoods, **Bixiga** and **Liberdade.**

Line 1 continues southward to the **Zona Sul,** through the neighborhoods of Vila Mariana and Saúde. To the southeast is **Ipiranga,** home of the São Paulo Zoo and Botanical Gardens. To the west is the elegant **Brooklin** and the city-within-a-city **Santo Amaro.** Farther north in the Zona Sul is **Jardins,** the most famous of the city's elite neighborhoods, full of ritzy hotels, fashionable bars and clubs, and a sizable GLS population. Along the border of Jardins runs **Avenida Paulista,** the city's financial center and popular postcard subject.

Along with the Zona Sul, the **Zona Oeste** is one of the city's most prosperous districts, encompassing the bohemian **Pinheiros** and **Vila Madalena,** as well as the **Cidade Universitária** (home of the Universidade de São Paulo, USP). Other important residential neighborhoods in the Zona Sul and Oeste are **Itaim Bibi, Higienópolis,** and **Moema,** which borders the Parque do Ibirapuera. **Zona Oeste,** known for the *favelas* on its periphery, is the area least frequented by tourists and nonresidents of the area; it is served by the *metrô* red line.

LOCAL TRANSPORTATION

Metrô: The efficient São Paulo subway (http://www.metro.sp.gov.br/ingles/index.asp) and its ultra-modern stations could be considered tourist attractions in themselves. One-way R$1.60, round-trip R$2.60; 10-trip pass R$12.50.

Kombis: These small, fast, and furious vans might cost less, but are not worth the hassle. They are illegal, and it's often difficult to know exactly where they're going or what route they will take to get there.

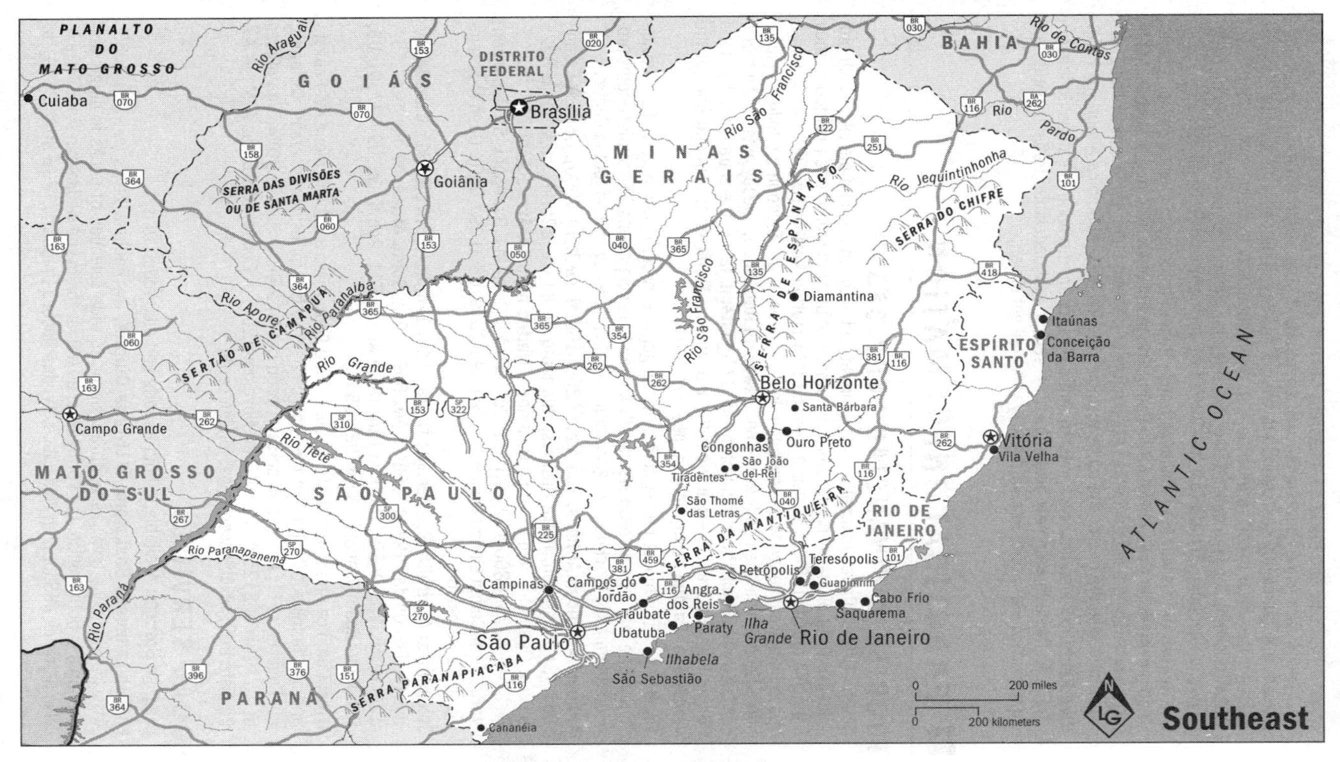
PLANALTO DO MATO GROSSO
Cuiaba
GOIÁS
DISTRITO FEDERAL
Brasília
Goiânia
SERRA DAS DIVISÕES OU DE SANTA MARTA
Rio Araguaia
BAHIA
Rio de Contas
Rio Pardo
MINAS GERAIS
Rio São Francisco
Rio Jequintinhonha
SERRA DO CHIFRE
SERRA DO ESPINHAÇO
Diamantina
Itaúnas
Conceição da Barra
ESPÍRITO SANTO
Belo Horizonte
Santa Bárbara
Ouro Preto
Congonhas
São João del-Rei
Tiradentes
São Thomé das Letras
Vitória
Vila Velha
ATLANTIC OCEAN
Rio Aporé
Rio Paranaíba
SERTÃO DE CAMAPUÃ
Rio Grande
Campo Grande
Rio Tietê
MATO GROSSO DO SUL
SÃO PAULO
SERRA DA MANTIQUEIRA
RIO DE JANEIRO
Teresópolis
Petrópolis
Guapimirim
Cabo Frio
Saquarema
Rio Paranapanema
Rio Paraná
Campinas
Campos do Jordão
Taubaté
Angra dos Reis
Paraty
Ubatuba
Ilha Grande
Rio de Janeiro
São Paulo
Ilhabela
São Sebastião
PARANÁ
SERRA PARANAPIACABA
Cananéia
0
200 miles
200 kilometers
Southeast

SOUTHEAST

Taxis: All taxis in São Paulo are metered. **Comum** taxis (☎3092 3536)—and most taxis in general—are white, and come in all shapes and sizes. Unfortunately, São Paulo's streets are sufficiently confusing that, even if you are equipped with a map, it will be easy for the driver to take a much longer, roundabout way to reach your destination. A safer, pricier option is to call a Rádio Taxi, but plan ahead: they cannot be reached from a public telephone. Try **Alô-Taxi** (☎229 7688) or **Guarucoop** (☎6440 7070).

Car Rental: Unless you are familiar with the city and its chronic, chaotic traffic, it is not recommended that you drive in São Paulo. The roads often twist and turn confusingly, and the traffic can be treacherous at all hours of day and night; avoid a pounding headache and take the *metrô*. Car rental agencies are located in Cumbica Airport (p. 175).

Bike Rental: Unless you're planning to rent a bike for an afternoon in Parque do Ibirapuera, São Paulo is extremely bike-unfriendly: vehicle and pedestrian traffic make it hard to get anywhere with a bike, and it may very well get stolen.

PRACTICAL INFORMATION

TOURIST & FINANCIAL SERVICES

Tourist Office: There are small tourist information booths throughout the city, which provide all sorts of maps, pamphlets, and other useful information, often related to their specific location. There is also a **general information hotline** (☎6224 0400) and a useful city website (www.cidadesaopaulo.com). Booths are found in the following locations, and are all open daily 9am-6pm: **Praça da República,** directly outside the *metrô* exit; **Avenida Paulista,** in front of the MASP; **Iguatemi,** facing the entrance to Iguatemi Shopping; **Luz Train Station,** near the Pinacoteca; **Tietê,** on the ground floor of the *rodoviária;* **Parque do Ibirapuera,** near gate 10.

Tours: The city's tourist bus system is no longer in service. Luxury hotels often provide tours for a fee, though these are usually limited to paying guests. The tourist booths provide informative brochures on good routes that can be covered on foot in Centro.

Airlines: American Airlines, Rua Araújo 206, 10th fl. (☎3214 4000). Open M-F 9am-5pm, Sa 9am-noon. **Delta Airlines,** Rua Marq de Itu 61, 12th fl., rm. 121 (☎3225 9120). Open M-F 9am-5pm, Sa 9am-noon. **United Airlines,** Av. Paulista 777, 10th fl. (☎3145 4225, 0800 162 323). M: Consolação. Open M-F 9am-5pm, Sa 9am-noon. **Varig,** Pça. Comdt Linneu Gomes s/n (☎5091 2009, 0800 997 000). Open M-F 9am-5pm, Sa 9am-noon.

Consulates: Australia, Rua Tenente Negrão 140, 12th fl. (☎3078 6281); **Canada,** Av. das Nacões Unidas 12901, 16th fl. (☎5509 4321); **South Africa,** Av. Paulista 1754, 12th fl. (☎3285 0433); **UK,** Rua Ferreira de Araújo 741, 2nd fl. (☎3094 2700); **US,** Rua Padre João Manuel 933 (☎3081 6511).

ATMs: Cumbica Airport has ATMs on the ground floor. ATMs are found along Av. Paulista and all throughout Centro, but they can be hard to find in residential areas. **Citibank,** Av. Paulista 1111, accepts all cards. A good bet for 24hr. access is **BBVA,** with offices at Av. Paulista 2125 and Av. 15 de Novembro 206, in Centro. **HSBC** has ATMs at Av. Paulista 949, which accept most foreign cards.

LOCAL SERVICES

Luggage Storage: Available in both airports and all 3 *rodoviárias*.

English-Language Bookstore: Livraria Cultura, Av. Paulista 2073 (☎3170 4033; www.livrariacultura.com), is worth a visit for its wide selection of books in all genres, available in both English and Portuguese, as well as for its knowledgeable staff. There is also a branch at Shopping Villa-Lobos, Av. das Nações Unidas 4777 (☎3024 3599). In

SOUTHEAST

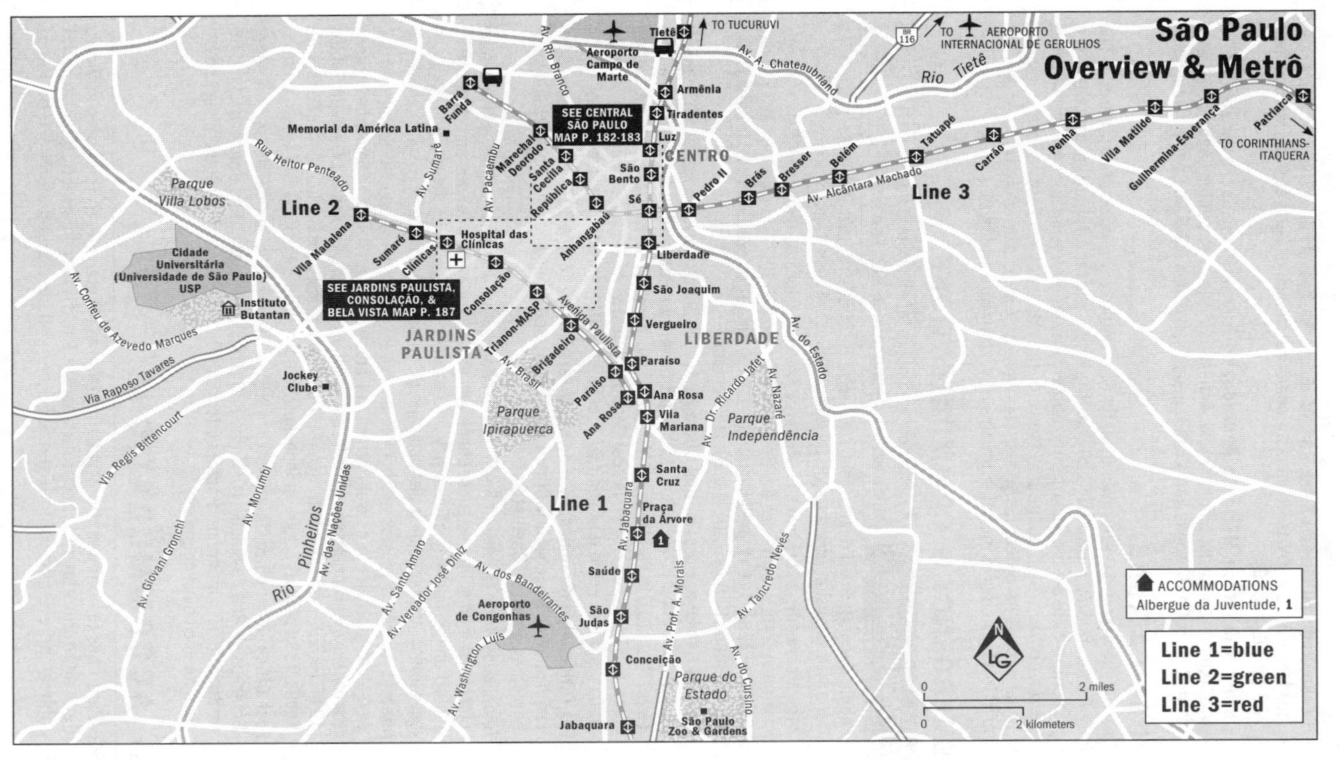
São Paulo Overview & Metrô
Line 1=blue
Line 2=green
Line 3=red
ACCOMMODATIONS
Albergue da Juventude, 1
SEE CENTRAL SÃO PAULO MAP P. 182-183
SEE JARDINS PAULISTA, CONSOLAÇÃO, & BELA VISTA MAP P. 187
TO AEROPORTO INTERNACIONAL DE GERULHOS
TO CORINTHIANS-ITAQUERA
TO TUCURUVI
BR 116
Rio Tietê
Rio Pinheiros
Line 1
Line 2
Line 3
CENTRO
LIBERDADE
JARDINS PAULISTA
Patriarca
Guilhermina-Esperança
Vila Matilde
Penha
Carrão
Tatuapé
Belém
Bresser
Brás
Pedro II
Tietê
Armênia
Tiradentes
Luz
São Bento
Sé
Liberdade
São Joaquim
Vergueiro
Paraíso
Ana Rosa
Vila Mariana
Santa Cruz
Praça da Árvore
Saúde
São Judas
Conceição
Jabaquara
Anhangabaú
República
Santa Cecília
Marechal Deodoro
Barra Funda
Brigadeiro
Trianon-MASP
Consolação
Clínicas
Sumaré
Vila Madalena
Hospital das Clínicas
Aeroporto Campo de Marte
Aeroporto de Congonhas
Memorial da América Latina
Parque Ipirapuerca
Parque Independência
Parque do Estado
São Paulo Zoo & Gardens
Jockey Clube
Instituto Butantan
Cidade Universitária (Universidade de São Paulo) USP
Parque Villa Lobos
Av. A. Chateaubriand
Av. Alcântara Machado
Av. do Estado
Av. Nazaré
Av. Dr. Ricardo Jafet
Av. Tancredo Neves
Av. do Cursino
Av. Prof. A. Morais
Av. Jabaquara
Avenida Paulista
Av. Brasil
Av. dos Bandeirantes
Av. Washington Luís
Av. Vereador José Diniz
Av. Santo Amaro
Av. das Nações Unidas
Av. Morumbi
Av. Giovani Gronchi
Via Regis Bittencourt
Via Raposo Tavares
Av. Corifeu de Azevedo Marques
Rua Heitor Penteado
Av. Sumaré
Av. Pacaembu
Av. Rio Branco
0 2 miles
0 2 kilometers

SOUTHEAST

Centro, **Red Star Livraria Sebo,** Rua São Bento 81, has an impressive selection of various LPs, CDs, and DVDs. There is an additional branch of Sebo at Rua José Bonifácio 203 (☎3024 3599).

Library: Biblioteca Mário de Andrade, on Rua da Consolação (☎256 5777; www.prodam.sp.gov.br/bib.mario). M: Anhagabaú. The largest library in the city, having more than 500,000 books and 11,000 periodicals. Open M-F 9am-9pm, Sa 9am-5pm.

PUBLICATIONS

Bancas (newsstands) are ubiquitous in São Paulo, even in residential areas. The daily *Folha de São Paulo* (R$2.20) has the city's widest circulation, and the city's most comprehensive listings of films and entertainment. Another great resource is *Guia da Folha*, which includes reviews of the city's newest restaurants, bars, and clubs as well as its oldest favorites. The weekly *Veja* is also quite popular, and its *Veja São Paulo* insert includes listings of restaurants and bars.

EMERGENCY & COMMUNICATIONS

EMERGENCIES	The emergency numbers for all of Brazil are: **Police** ☎190. **Ambulance** ☎192. **Fire** ☎193.

Polícia Federal: Rua Prestes Maia 700 (☎3225 5080). M: Luz. This is the place to go for a visa extension *(prorrogação de visita)*. Open M-F 8am-4pm.

24hr. Pharmacy: All branches of **Drogaria São Paulo,** located throughout the entire city, are open 24hr., including: Av. São Luís 34 (☎3258 8872), in Centro; Av. Paulista 2103 (☎3284 1168), in Paulista; Rua Pamplona 1130 (☎289 9494), in Jardins; Av. da Liberdade 840 (☎3207 4168), in Liberdade.

Medical Services: Hospital das Clínicas, Av. Dr. Eneãs Carvalho Aguiar 255 (☎369 6000), in Pinheiro. M: Clínicas. **Hospital de São Paulo,** Rua Borges Lagoa 783 (☎5573 2319), in Vila Mariana. M: Santa Cruz. **Hospital Santa Casa,** Rua Dr. Cesário Mota Jr. 61 (☎3224 0122), is near Centro. **Clinics,** at Av. Dr. Ab. Ribeiro 283 (☎3619 3501) and Rua Pedro de Toledo 675 (☎5571 5000), provide free vaccinations.

Fax Office: AlphaGraphics, Av. Brigadeiro Faria Lima 2941 (☎3078 4900; www.farialima.alphagraphics.com.br). Other branches located throughout the city, including several on Av. Paulista. Open M-Sa 24hr.

Telephones: As in the rest of Brazil, public phones work with phone cards, which can be purchased in most newsstands, phone offices, as well as many shops and hotels (R$2 per 10 units). Yellow Telefônico pay phones are located all over the city and are quite easy to find, thanks to their distinctive *orelhão* (big ear) markings.

Internet Access: Paulistas are hooked on *cybers,* which have popped up all over the city. Most specialize in network games, advertised as "Lan 4 Fun." Connection speeds are usually excellent. **Monkey** has locations all over the city, including: Alameda Santos 1217 (☎3253 8627), 5min. from M: Consolação, in Paulista; Rua Inácio Pereira da Rocha 988 (☎3816 5509), in Pinheiros; Rua Aracajú 66 (☎3668 5674), in Centro.

Post Office: Main office, Rua Boa Vista 88 (☎3107 7803), in Pça. da Sé, in Centro. Branches at: Rua Pamplona 1083 (☎3838 8655), in Paulista; Rua Haddock Lobo 566 (☎3083 2879), in Jardins. **Postal code:** 01000-000. Street signs list the 8-digit postal code for each block in the city.

ACCOMMODATIONS

São Paulo has accommodations ranging from the luxurious to the down-and-out. Budget accommodations are concentrated in Centro, especially in Pça. da República and eclectic Santa Ifigênia. Higher-end accommodations can be found downtown, but most are on the trendy streets of Jardins and around Av. Paulista. There are very few backpacker-friendly hostels in São Paulo, but the few that exist are clean, reliable, and cheap. By midweek traveling businessmen have filled many hotels, and consequently it is easier to secure lodging during the weekend. Budget hotels teem with visitors throughout July, Christmas break, and Carnaval, so plan accordingly. Most hotels and hostels have prices amenable to negotiation, particularly for large groups or extended stays.

CENTRO

São Paulo's Centro is the place to find many budget accommodations. The *metrô* is easily accessible from most hotels, as are many of the area's monuments and museums. Centro is currently undergoing a revival of sorts, but nevertheless locals still warn against walking around at night, particularly in Santa Ifigênia. All of the following hotels are 5-15min. from M: República. The Airport Bus Service (EMTU) also stops at Pça. da República.

Hotel Itamarati, Av. Dr. Vieira de Carvalho 150 (☎2220 4133; hotelitamarati.com.br). M: República. From the *metrô* exit, take a right and walk across Pça. República, then another right, and a left onto Av. Dr. Vieira de Carvalho. 24hr. security and easy access make this a great pick. Small balconies face the elegant old building's small inner courtyard. Breakfast included. Reservations recommended M-F. Singles R$34, with bath R$47; doubles R$48, with bath R$62; triples R$82. ❷

Hotel São Sebastião, Rua 7 de Abril 364 (☎3257 4988). M: República. From the *metrô* exit, turn left and continue straight on Rua 7 de Abril; the hotel will be on your left. A little rowdy during the day, but rooms are spotless, centrally located, and cheap. Frequented by an international crowd. Breakfast included. Check-out 10am. *Quarto* singles R$20; doubles R$35. *Apartamento* singles R$29; doubles R$42. Cash only. ❶

Las Vegas Hotel, Rua Vitória 390 (☎221 8144). M: República. From Pça. da República, head down Av. Vieira de Carvalho and take a right on Rua Vitória. Walk down about 4 blocks; the hotel is on the intersection of Av. Rio Branco and Rua Vitoria. Expect neither glitz nor glamour from this poorly-lit but otherwise well-equipped hotel. *Apartamentos* include TV, private bath, and breakfast. Singles R$35; doubles R$50; triples R$75. ❷

Hotel Rivoli, Rua Dom José de Barros 28 (☎3231 5633; www.hotelrivoli.com.br). M: República. From Pça. da República, head down Rua 7 de Abril and take your first left onto Rua Dom José dos Barros. This longtime Centro favorite may be cramped, but you'll be close to the action and only 1 block from the *metrô.* English spoken. Breakfast included. Reservations recommended M-F. Singles R$28, with bath R$33; doubles R$38, with bath R$45; triples R$58. 10% discount in June. AmEx/MC/V. ❷

Artemis Hotel, Alameda Barõ de Limeira 44 (☎221 9166; www.artemishotel.com.br). M: República. Tacky wood panels greet guests in this favorite of the business crowd. Tidy rooms all have bath. Easy *metrô* access and close to rowdy Rua Santa Ifigênia. Singles R$40; doubles R$60; triples R$76. Weekend discounts. AmEx/MC/V. ❸

São Paulo Hostel (HI), Rua Barão de Campinas 94 (☎3333 0844). M: República. Cross Pça. da República and go up Rua Vieira de Carvalho. Bear right and cross Av. São João; the hostel is on the corner of Rua Barao de Campinas and Rua Gen. Osorio. This new addition to the HI family has a hotel's body but the soul of a hostel. Unexpected luxuries include private bath, complimentary bedsheets and towels, TV, and *frigo-bar.* There is an Internet café next door, and the roomy common area has cable TV. English spoken. Dorms R$25, non-members with ISIC R$27, non-members R$35. ❶/❷

Jandaia Hotel, Av. Duque de Caixas 433 (☎3331 8322). A 10min. walk from Pça. da República, Jandaia is filled with business travelers on weekdays. All rooms are large and include sheets, towels, and private bath. Elevators offer easy access to the upper

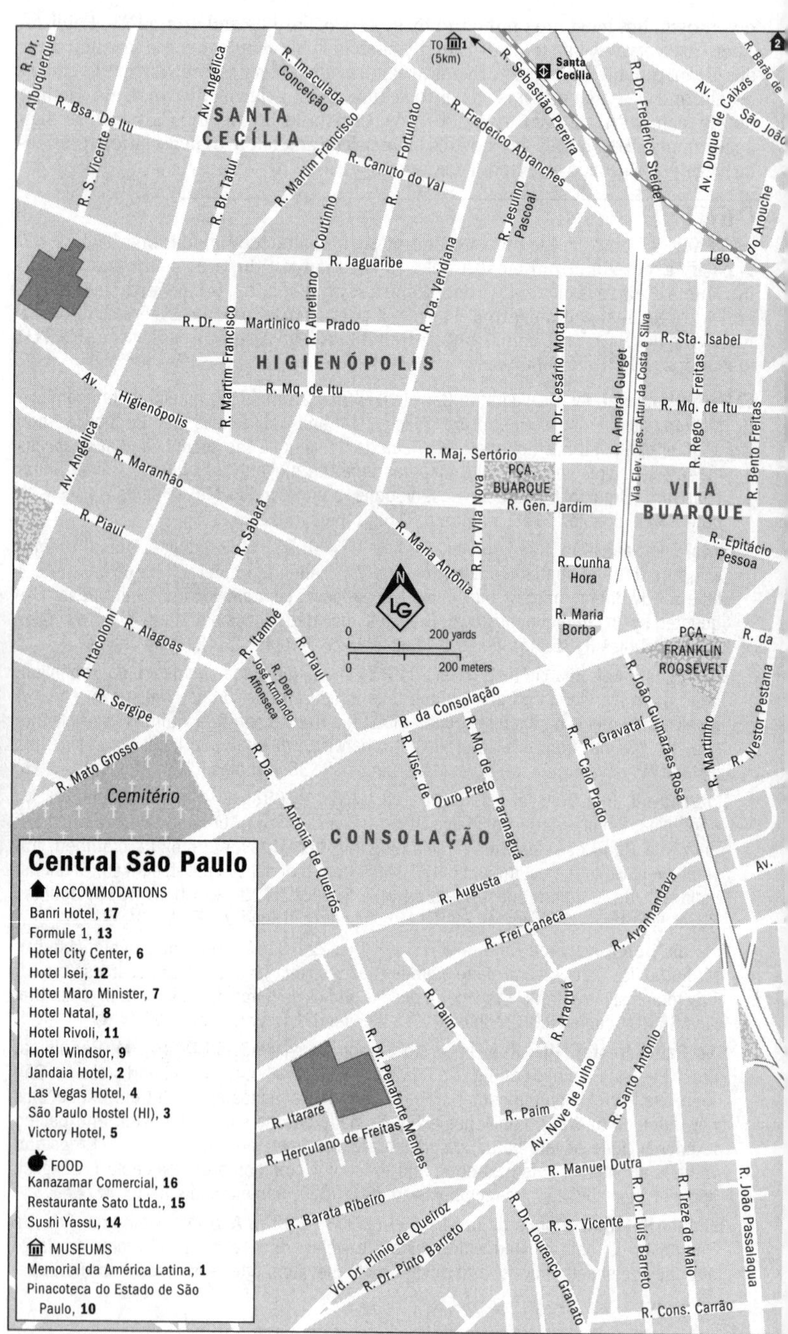
Central São Paulo
ACCOMMODATIONS
Banri Hotel, 17
Formule 1, 13
Hotel City Center, 6
Hotel Isei, 12
Hotel Maro Minister, 7
Hotel Natal, 8
Hotel Rivoli, 11
Hotel Windsor, 9
Jandaia Hotel, 2
Las Vegas Hotel, 4
São Paulo Hostel (HI), 3
Victory Hotel, 5
FOOD
Kanazamar Comercial, 16
Restaurante Sato Ltda., 15
Sushi Yassu, 14
MUSEUMS
Memorial da América Latina, 1
Pinacoteca do Estado de São Paulo, 10
TO 1 (5km)
Santa Cecília
SANTA CECÍLIA
HIGIENÓPOLIS
VILA BUARQUE
CONSOLAÇÃO
PÇA. BUARQUE
PÇA. FRANKLIN ROOSEVELT
Cemitério
Lgo.
0 200 yards
0 200 meters
R. Dr. Albuquerque
R. Bsa. De Itu
R. S. Vicente
Av. Angélica
R. Imaculada Conceição
R. Br. Tatuí
R. Martim Francisco
R. Canuto do Val
R. Fortunato
R. Frederico Abranches
R. Sebastião Pereira
R. Jesuíno Pascoal
R. Dr. Frederico Steidel
Av. Duque de Caixas
Av. São João
R. Barão de
Av. do Arouche
R. Aureliano Coutinho
R. Jaguaribe
R. Da. Veridiana
R. Dr. Martinico Prado
R. Mq. de Itu
Av. Higienópolis
R. Maranhão
R. Piauí
R. Sabará
R. Maj. Sertório
R. Gen. Jardim
R. Dr. Vila Nova
R. Dr. Cesário Mota Jr.
R. Amaral Gurget
Via Elev. Pres. Artur da Costa e Silva
R. Sta. Isabel
R. Rego Freitas
R. Bento Freitas
R. Maria Antônia
R. Cunha Hora
R. Maria Borba
R. Epitácio Pessoa
R. Itacolomi
R. Alagoas
R. Itambé
R. Dep. José Armando Affonseca
R. Sergipe
R. Mato Grosso
R. da Consolação
R. Visc. de Ouro Preto
R. Mq. de Paranaguá
R. Caio Prado
R. Gravataí
R. João Guimarães Rosa
R. Martinho
R. Nestor Pestana
R. da
R. Da. Antônia de Queirós
R. Augusta
R. Frei Caneca
R. Avanhandava
Av.
R. Paim
R. Araquá
R. Dr. Penaforte Mendes
R. Itararé
R. Herculano de Freitas
Av. Nove de Julho
R. Santo Antônio
R. Manuel Dutra
R. Barata Ribeiro
Vd. Dr. Plínio de Queiroz
R. Dr. Pinto Barreto
R. Dr. Lourenço Granato
R. S. Vicente
R. Dr. Luís Barreto
R. Treze de Maio
R. João Passalaqua
R. Cons. Carrão

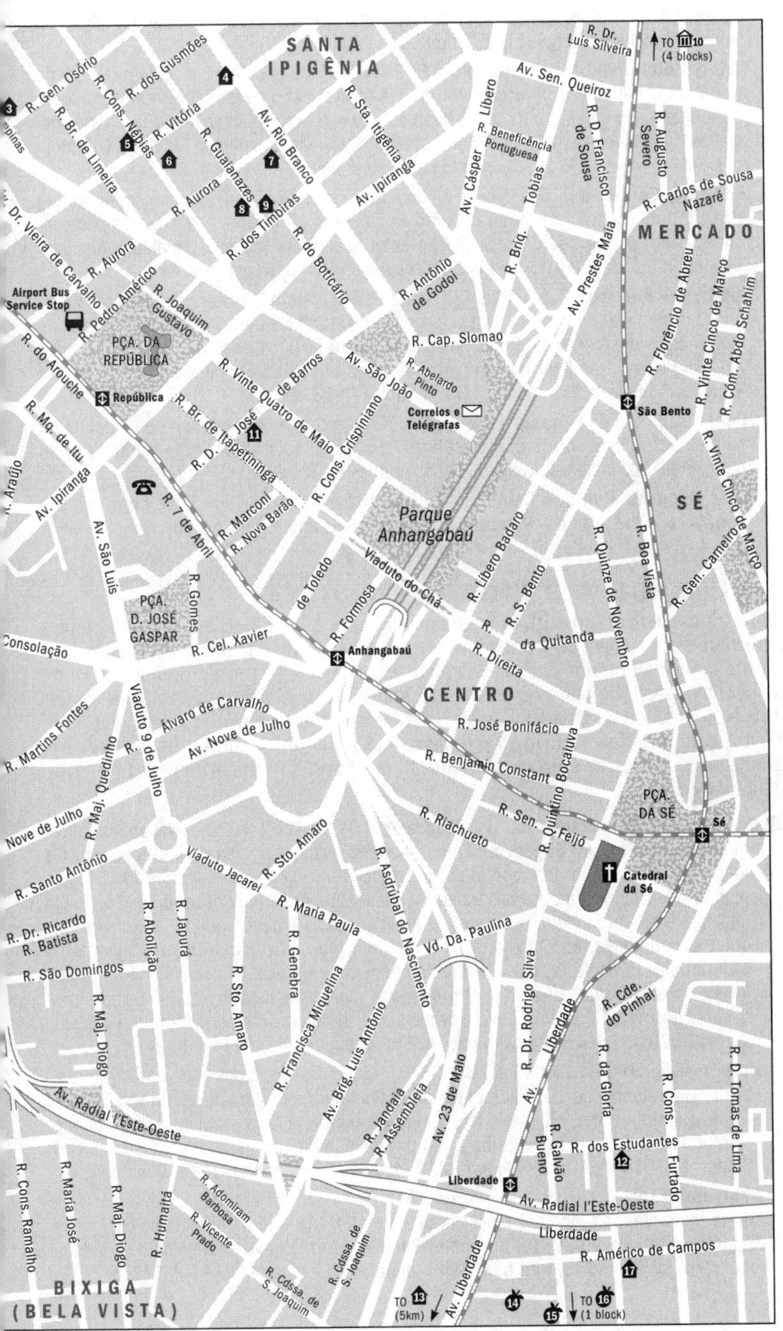
SANTA IPIGÊNIA
MERCADO
SÉ
CENTRO
BIXIGA (BELA VISTA)
TO 10 (4 blocks)
R. Dr. Luís Silveira
Av. Sen. Queiroz
R. Gen. Osório
R. Cons. Nébias
R. dos Gusmões
R. Br. de Limeira
R. Vitória
R. Guaianazes
Av. Rio Branco
R. Sta. Ifigênia
Av. Ipiranga
Av. Cásper Líbero
R. Beneficência Portuguesa
R. Tobias
R. D. Francisco de Sousa
R. Augusto Severo
R. Carlos de Sousa Nazaré
R. Aurora
R. dos Timbiras
R. do Boticário
R. Dr. Vieira de Carvalho
R. Antônio de Godoi
R. Brig.
Av. Prestes Maia
R. Florêncio de Abreu
R. Vinte Cinco de Março
R. Côm. Abdo Schahim
Airport Bus Service Stop
R. Pedro Américo
R. Joaquim Gustavo
PÇA. DA REPÚBLICA
R. Cap. Slomao
R. do Arouche
República
R. Vinte Quatro de Maio
R. de Barros
Av. São João
R. Abelardo Pinto
Correios e Telégrafas
São Bento
R. Mq. de Itu
R. Br. de Itapetininga
R. D. José
R. Cons. Crispiniano
R. Araújo
Av. Ipiranga
R. 7 de Abril
R. Marconi
R. Nova Barão
Parque Anhangabaú
R. Líbero Badaró
R. Quinze de Novembro
R. Boa Vista
R. Gen. Carneiro
Av. São Luís
R. Gomes
PÇA. D. JOSÉ GASPAR
de Toledo
Viaduto do Chá
R. S. Bento
R. Formosa
R. da Quitanda
Consolação
R. Cel. Xavier
Anhangabaú
R. Direita
R. Martins Fontes
Viaduto 9 de Julho
R. Álvaro de Carvalho
Av. Nove de Julho
R. José Bonifácio
R. Quedinho
R. Benjamin Constant
R. Quintino Bocaiuva
Nove de Julho
R. Maj. Quedinho
R. Riachueto
R. Sen. Feijó
PÇA. DA SÉ
Sé
Catedral da Sé
R. Santo Antônio
Viaduto Jacareí
R. Sto. Amaro
R. Asdrúbal do Nascimento
R. Maria Paula
R. Dr. Ricardo R. Batista
R. Abolição
R. Japurá
R. Genebra
Vd. Da. Paulina
R. São Domingos
R. Maj. Diogo
R. Sto. Amaro
R. Francisca Miquelina
Av. Brig. Luís Antônio
R. Dr. Rodrigo Silva
Av. Liberdade
R. Cde. do Pinhal
R. da Glória
R. Cons. Furtado
R. D. Tomas de Lima
Av. Radial l'Este-Oeste
R. Jandaia
R. Assembleia
Av. 23 de Maio
R. Galvão Bueno
R. dos Estudantes
Liberdade
Av. Radial l'Este-Oeste
R. Cons. Ramalho
R. Maria José
R. Maj. Diogo
R. Humaitá
R. Adomiram Barbosa
R. Vicente Prado
R. Cdssa. de S. Joaquim
R. Cdssa. de S. Joaquim
Av. Liberdade
Liberdade
R. Américo de Campos
TO 13 (5km)
TO 16 (1 block)

SOUTHEAST

floors. Ask for a room facing away from Av. Duque, which is noisy throughout the week. Breakfast included. Singles R$60; doubles R$70. ❸

Victory Hotel, Rua Conselheiro Nébias 309 (☎3361 8114). Three blocks from Pça. da República, right off Rua Vitória. Victory! A friendly and personable staff, and well-appointed, very clean rooms make Victory a great pick for backpackers. The hotel specializes in business guests, but is also amenable to long-term stays. Singles R$65; doubles R$86; triples R$118. Discounts negotiable. AmEx/MC/V. ❸

Hotel City Center, Rua Conselheiro Nébias 236 (☎3331 7234). Very accessible from Pça. República. Its dark hallways lead to similarly dark rooms, but they are clean, cheap, and, as the name suggests, the hotel is centrally located. Breakfast included. Singles R$30; doubles R$45. Discount for stays of 10 days or more. ❷

Hotel Maro Minister, Rua Aurora 427 (☎223 5611). Maro Minister compensates for its undesirable location with its own self-service restaurant, barber, manicurist, and common room with satellite TV. Spic-and-span rooms have TV, shower, and fan; deluxe have A/C. The classy 2nd floor bar is open 24hr., and often has live music. *Feijoada* served every Sat. Singles R$59; doubles R$69; triples R$93. ❸

Hotel Natal, Rua Guaianazes 41 (☎3331 6722), in Santa Ifigênia. Don't be intimidated by the narrow, long and somewhat stifling hallways: all rooms have *frigo-bar* and private bath. Breakfast included. Singles R$23; doubles R$25. ❶

Hotel Windsor, Rua dos Timbiras 444 (☎3331 5411). A 3min. walk from Pça. da República is the luxurious Windsor, with large rooms and a groovy lobby. Singles R$61, with A/C R$67; doubles R$71, with A/C R$78. ❸

SOUTHEAST

LIBERDADE & BIXIGA (BELA VISTA)

Safer than Centro and with convenient *metrô* access, Liberdade is an excellent alternative for budget accommodations. Liberdade is also within walking distance of the nightlife hotspot Bixiga, as well as Pça. da Sé's historic monuments. Don't expect to sleep late, however, as the neighborhood wakes up early and gets louder throughout the day. Bixiga, a small neighborhood in the historically Italian Bela Vista, can be quieter during weekdays, and is within walking distance of Av. Paulista. At night, the *cantinas* on Rua 13 de Maio fill to the brim with live music and lively crowds.

Pousada dos Franceses, Rua dos Franceses 100 (☎3262 4026; www.pousadadosfranceses.com.br). M: Brigadeiro. From the *metrô,* walk downhill on Av. Brigadeiro Luís Antônio 2 blocks, turn left, continue for 1 block, turn right, and continue for 1 block, then turn left onto Rua dos Franceses. The most student-friendly *pousada* in São Paulo might be a bit hard to find, but once you get there you will never want to leave: relatively quiet surroundings, and proximity to Bixiga and the *metrô* make this an unbeatable pick. Indulge in cable TV, or enjoy the company of the *pousada's* constant flow of fun-loving, mostly foreign students. Discounts available for monthly stays. Dorms have sheets, and female dorms have private bath. Breakfast included. Internet access. Dorms R$20. Singles R$25, with bath R$30; doubles R$48. Cash only. ❶

Hotel Isei, on Rua da Glória (☎3208 6677). M: Liberdade. From Pça. Liberdade, proceed downhill on Rua dos Estudantes and take your first right. The hotel will be up a flight of steps on the left. Isei's lobby might resemble a large cubicle, but its cheap, comfortable rooms with private bath will put a smile on your face. Breakfast included. Singles R$20, with TV and *frigo-bar* R$39; doubles R$60; triples R$84. Cash only. ❶

Banri Hotel, on Rua Galvão Bueno (☎3207 8877). M: Liberdade. Easily accessible down the main road, about 3 blocks from the *metrô*. Nice rooms with not-so-nice views. *Apartamentos* have A/C, TV, and bath. Simpler *quartos* have shared bath. Breakfast included. Singles R$35, with bath R$45; doubles R$72; triples R$81. MC/V. ❷

Hotel Berilo, Rua 13 de Maio 886 (☎3266 7799). M: Brigadeiro. The recently repainted Berilo could use help in other departments: its tiny rooms are bare and unimpressive. However, it's on the most happenin' street in Bela Vista, and only a 15min. walk from Av. Paulista. Try to get a room in the back, since the hotel faces a highway. Doubles with shower R$25, with private bath R$30. Cash only. ❶/❷

JARDINS PAULISTA

Five-star luxury towers dot the streets of Av. Paulista's wealthy residential neighborhood Jardins, and are concentrated in Cerqueira Cesar. There are a few affordable options in the neighborhood, all within easy access of Av. Paulista, as well as some great bars and restaurants.

Pousada Dona Ziláh (☎3062 1444; www.zilah.com). M: Consolação. From the *metrô* stop, walk 2 blocks toward the Banco do Brasil building until Rua da Consolação. Turn left and walk 4 blocks to Alameda Franca, then take a right. The *pousada* will be on your left almost at the end of the block. The *pousada* is blessed with a great location in a tranquil corner of Jardins, less than 5min. from great bars and restaurants. Owner Dona Ziláh offers an oasis of peace in the city's concrete labyrinth, with floral arrangements, and a sunny breakfast patio. Friendly staff will provide all sorts of useful information along with hours of conversation. All rooms have private bath. Breakfast included. Reservations recommended F-Su. Singles R$75; doubles R$92; triples R$115. ❹

Formule 1, Rua Vergueiro 1571 (☎5085 5699; www.accor.com.br). M: Paraíso. Walk away from Av. Paulista on Rua Vergueiro; the tall, thin building is hard to miss. Fast-paced Formule 1 is a favorite budget option for business travelers. Functional rooms all have cable TV. Public phones and vending machines are found in the hallways. All rooms can fit up to three people in a double bed and cot. Rooms R$49. ❸

Albergue da Juventude—Praça de Árvore (HI), Rua Pageú 266 (☎5071 5148; www.spalbergue.com.br). M: Pça. de Árvore. This tidy, well-equipped hostel is tucked away in a tranquil residential area south of Av. Paulista. The light traffic and relative silence are real rarities in São Paulo. Rooms are bare, and most windows face roofs or concrete walls. The common area has cable TV and is perfect for sharing stories with fellow travelers. Laundry facilities in basement. 15-night max. stay. Reception 24hr. Reservations recommended in July and Nov.-Jan. Dorms R$21, non-members with ISIC R$23, non-members R$25. Singles add R$1, doubles add R$2. ❶/❷

Hotel Pamplona, Rua Pamplona 851 (☎285 6347). M: Trianon-MASP. Downhill from Av. Paulista 1½ blocks, on the Jardins side. The whitewashed lobby corridor resembles a hospital hallway and leads to small upstairs rooms with fan, *frigo-bar,* and private bath. Rua Pamplona is one of São Paulo's major streets and is prone to heavy traffic day and night. Breakfast included. Singles R$45; doubles R$75; triples R$95. ❸

SOUTHEAST

FOOD

São Paulo is widely regarded as the culinary capital of Brazil, and the city's restaurants and cafés are packed for both lunch and dinner most nights of the week. There is no dish that would be considered specifically Paulista (even the origins of the well-known shrimp loaf *cuscuz à paulista* are debatable), but the city does have a mind-boggling selection of international cuisine, the sheer variety of which is unmatched anywhere else in the country.

Cheap, tasty snacks are readily available at the city's ubiquitous *lanchonetes.* The residential **Jardins** and trendy **Itaim Bibi** have the city's best and most expensive restaurants; wonderful and informal cafés line the appealing streets of **Vila Madalena.** Splurge on a fine meal at least once, and you will start to appreciate why so many people love Sampa.

LIBERDADE & BIXIGA (BELA VISTA)

The adjacent *bairros* of Liberdade and Bixiga have numerous culinary treasures hidden within their narrow, bustling streets. Many affluent Paulistas claim that the neighborhoods have exaggerated their immigrant roots, resulting in an inauthentic image. Even so, these lively neighborhoods are still worth a daytime stroll, complete with stops in Bixiga's small *cantinas* and Liberdade's many sushi bars.

Kanazawar Comercial, Rua Galvão Bueno 379 (☎3207 1801). M: Liberdade. About 4 blocks downhill from Pça. Liberdade, on your left. Owner Fernando Kanazawa is rightfully proud of his homemade Japanese treats, and the friendly staff will be happy to tell you their personal favorites. The *sakura niti,* with pink rice and a sweet-and-sour filling, is absolutely delicious (R$1.50). Open daily 9am-6pm. ❶

Sushi Yassu, Rua Tomas Gonzaga 110 (☎3207 8078). M: Liberdade. Facing away from the *metrô* stop, walk downhill along Rua Galvão Bueno. Turn left onto Rua Tomas Gonzaga after about 4 blocks. The restaurant will be on your left half a block uphill. Sushi Yassu has maintained its reputation as one of the city's most authentic sushi bars and is a lunchtime favorite of local businessmen. Lunch specials include the Sushi *simple* (R$31) or the *especial* (R$39; large enough for 2). Open daily noon-4:30pm and 7-10:30pm. AmEx/MC/V. ❹

Restaurante Sato Ltda., Rua Galvão Bueno 268 (☎3208 8504; reservations 3341 3072). M: Liberdade. About 2 blocks downhill from Pça. da Liberdade. Sato is an oasis of Brazilian cuisine in Japanese Liberdade, serving *feijoada* every day (R$7). Another cheap house favorite is the *frango ao molho* (R$6). Simple, white-washed and spotless interior with windows facing the busy street. Open M-Sa 10am-5pm. ❶

Mansoires, Rua 13 de Maio 210. M: Brigadeiro. Eclairs, cream-filled donuts, and other goodies. A good spot for a quick afternoon snack *para viagem* (to go). Assorted juices R$1.50. Most pastries R$1-3. ❶

JARDINS PAULISTA

Upscale, ritzy, expensive, and invariably high-quality food, the restaurants of Jardins are one of the reasons why so many tourists shell out big bucks in São Paulo. Paulistas are themselves ardent fans of eating great food in a great setting and—with its tree-lined blocks, dozens of bars, and beautiful people—Jardins is the place to do so.

Folha da Uva, Rua Bela Cintra 1435 (☎3081 0989). M: Consolação. This elegantly decorated but unassuming restaurant ranks as one of the best Middle Eastern restaurants in Jardins. The best time to go is at lunch, when the restaurant is less full and serves a buffet. The hummus appetizer (R$10) and falafel sandwich (R$11) are popular. Top it all off with some delicious baklava (R$2.50). Open daily 11am-4pm and 6-11pm. ❷

Baby-beef Rubaiyat, Alameda Santos 86 (☎289 6366). M: MASP-Trianon. Located just one block from Av. Paulista, in one of the city's poshest districts. Don't be fooled by their playful name: Baby-beef takes their meat quite seriously, and the restaurant is reputed to serve the city's best cuts. Splurge on the extraordinarily popular Saturday *feijoada* (R$49.50 per person). Open M-F 11:30am-3:30pm and 7:30pm-1:30am, Sa-Su opens at noon. ❺

Pequi, Bar and Restaurant, Rua Peixoto Gomide 988 (☎3263 0394). M: Trianon-MASP. One block from both MASP and Av. Paulista. One of the best 24hr. full-service restaurants in the city, Pequi is frequented by famous Brazilian actors, who show up late and keep the place rocking. Contemporary cuisine is the hallmark of this trendy restaurant, and ranges from simple grilled chicken to the most savory *gorgonzola risotto* you'll ever eat (R$22.50). *Caipiroskas* (*caipirinhas* with vodka; R$6) are a perfect accompaniment to pretty much anything. Open daily 24hr. ❸

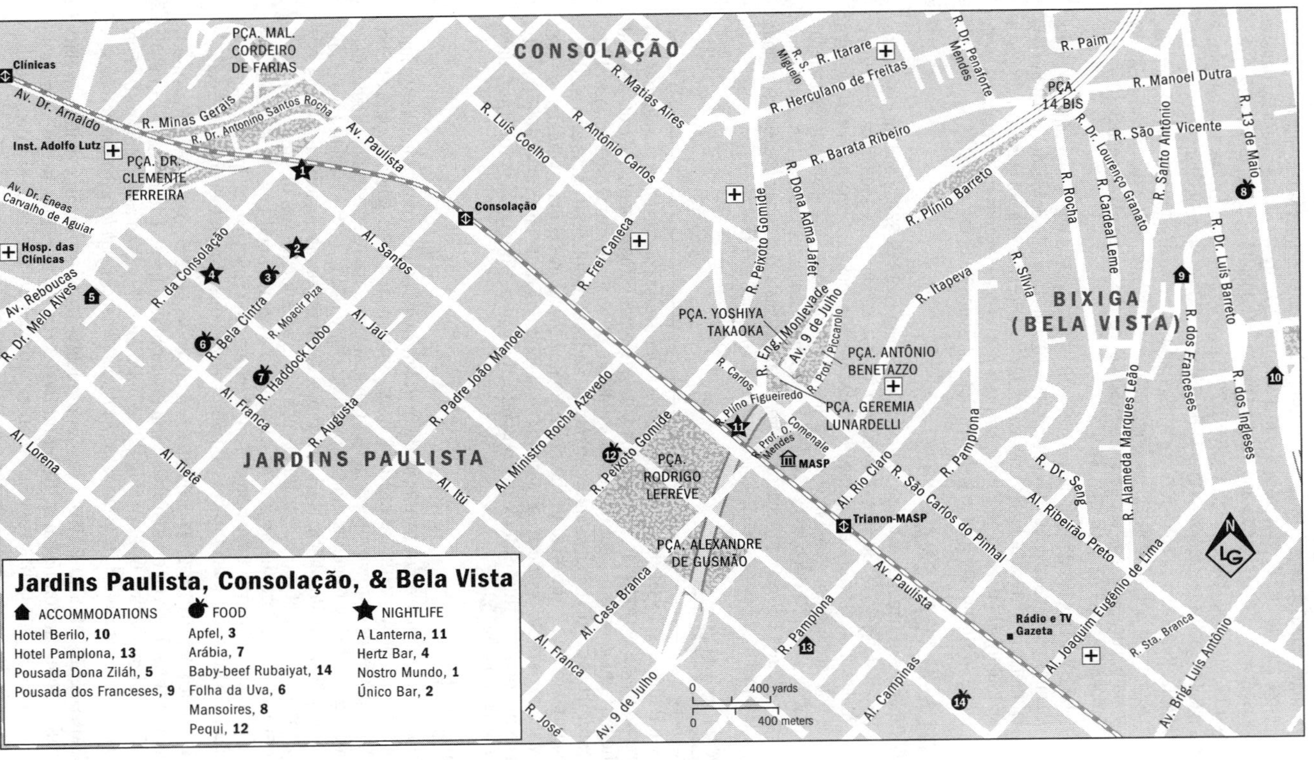
Jardins Paulista, Consolação, & Bela Vista
ACCOMMODATIONS
Hotel Berilo, 10
Hotel Pamplona, 13
Pousada Dona Ziláh, 5
Pousada dos Franceses, 9
FOOD
Apfel, 3
Arábia, 7
Baby-beef Rubaiyat, 14
Folha da Uva, 6
Mansoires, 8
Pequi, 12
NIGHTLIFE
A Lanterna, 11
Hertz Bar, 4
Nostro Mundo, 1
Único Bar, 2
CONSOLAÇÃO
BIXIGA (BELA VISTA)
JARDINS PAULISTA
Av. Paulista
Clínicas
Consolação
Trianon-MASP
MASP
PÇA. 14 BIS
PÇA. ALEXANDRE DE GUSMÃO
PÇA. RODRIGO LEFRÉVE
PÇA. MAL. CORDEIRO DE FARIAS
PÇA. DR. CLEMENTE FERREIRA
PÇA. YOSHIYA TAKAOKA
PÇA. ANTÔNIO BENETAZZO
PÇA. GEREMIA LUNARDELLI
Rádio e TV Gazeta
Inst. Adolfo Lutz
Hosp. das Clínicas
0
400 yards
400 meters

Orange, Rua Butataes 388 (☎3885 3384). This excellent vegetarian option is packed most afternoons. Food is served buffet-style (R$10); try the house specialty banana lasagna (made with ricotta and mashed bananas). Open M-F 11:30am-3pm. ❷

Apfel, Rua Bela Cintra 1343 (☎3062 3727; www. apfel.com.br). M: Consolação. A great vegetarian restaurant. Open M-F 11:30am-3:30pm, Su noon-4pm. ❷

Arábia, Rua Haddock Lobo 1397 (☎3263 0394). M: Consolação. A Middle Eastern restaurant with a limited selection. The traditional *coalhada* (R$6) is popular, as is the tomato, cucumber, and alfalfa salad (R$6). *Sucos* R$3. Open M-Th noon-3:30pm and 7pm-midnight, F-Sa noon-1am. ❶

Tiella, Rua Eugênio de Medeiros 530 (☎3812 5387). This cheap kilo with a rotating menu is guaranteed not to disappoint (R$9-10). The only real downside is that the restaurant is only open for lunch. On Wednesday the special is Mineiro cuisine, including a special *feijão tropeiro* and *costelinha* (beef ribs). Friday belongs to the *nordeste,* with plenty of shrimp and Baiano favorites. Open M-F noon-3pm. ❶

VILA MADALENA

Oficina de Pizzas, on Rua Inácio Pereira da Rocha (☎3813 8389) and Rua Purpurina (☎3816 3749). M: Sumaré. Across from the gas station at the end of Rua Luís Murat. Paulistas are discriminating when it comes to pizza, but in Oficina de Pizzas even the most selective eaters will melt with delight. The *purpurina* (with garlic and mozzarella) and *ponto chic* (with buffalo mozzarella, roast beef, and baby pickle slices) are legendary (R$28). Conveniently accessible from many of Vila's clubs and pubs, the restaurant is a perfect pre-party destination. Open daily 7pm-1:30am. ❷

SIGHTS

SOUTHEAST

São Paulo is a city of great contrast, and its sights and sounds elicit (in visitors and residents alike) extreme feelings: love, hate, disgust, amazement, frustration—but never indifference. Seemingly endless blocks of concrete sometimes conceal the natural beauty of the city's many attractive and well-manicured parks and gardens. Sights are found throughout the metropolitan area; unfortunately, many are not easily accessible by *metrô* or without a car, and bus routes in and around the city are in constant flux. Check the bus information hotline (☎158) for up-to-date routes and schedules.

CENTRO

Many Paulistas are not proud of their downtown; ignore their complaints and make your peace with the liveliest, most diverse, and most chaotic part of São Paulo. Many downtown streets have been converted into pedestrian promenades, and the best way to get around is on foot. Many of the better budget hotels are around **Praça da República,** a stone's throw from the area's historic buildings and churches. Some of the better hotels can arrange guided tours of Centro, but the best way to explore the area is to wander. The area around Pça. da República is colloquially known as **Centro Novo** (New Center), and is where Av. Ipiranga and Av. São João intersect. Caetano Veloso immortalized this area in his song "Sampa."

TEATRO MUNICIPAL. This theater is a majestic neoclassical opera house modeled after the Paris Opera. The beautiful interior has a lighted dome made from 260 individual lamps and 6000 crystals. The building still serves as a theater. *(On Rua Libero Badaró. ☎3241 3815. Open only during performances; call for schedule of events.)*

MOSTEIRO DE SÃO BENTO. This is arguably the most dazzling church in São Paulo. Construction began in 1910 and took 12 years to complete. Its interior is dominated by one of Brazil's most enormous organs, with over 6000 pipes, and the baroque wooden crucifix on the altar dates from 1777. Try to visit during the Gregorian chants. *(On Rua São Bento, just outside the* metrô *stop. M: São Bento. Chants M-F 7am, Sa 6am, Su 10am.)*

EDIFÍCIO ITÁLIA. The tallest building on Av. Ipiranga is a great vantage point from which to see Centro. Although it is not a proper tourist attraction, the panoramic restaurant on the top floor is worth a visit for the view, although it is a bit of a splurge. *(On Av. Ipiranga. M: República. Min. consumption R$25.)* The **Edifício Copan** is a strangely wave-like building: one of Oscar Niemeyer's signature works and a long-time postcard favorite. *(Next to the Edifício Itália on Av. Ipiranga. M: República.)*

EDIFÍCIO BANESPA. If São Paulo is the New York of the Tropics, this is Sampa's Empire State Building. The terrace at the top, with a 360-degree open-air view of the city, is a great place to orient yourself and is definitely worth a visit. *(On Av. São João. Open M-F 10am-5pm. Free.)*

PRAÇA DA SÉ. Praça da Sé has been the epicenter of São Paulo since the 16th century, when it served as the point of origin for all religious processions. The **Marco Zero,** the city's geographic center from which all distances are measured, runs through this *praça*. Today, Pça. da Sé is undergoing a mild resurgence due to the recently completed renovation of the **Catedral da Sé.** This grandiose neo-Gothic cathedral was first inaugurated in 1954, and is fast becoming one of São Paulo's top tourist attractions. *(On Rua 15 de Novembro. M: Sé.)*

OTHER SIGHTS. Rua Barão de Italpetininga is one of São Paulo's several pedestrian promenades. It is lined with large shops and *camelôs*, which are small street stands that buy and sell everything from trinkets to leather jackets. *(Off Av. Ipiranga.)* **Edifício Martinelli** was completed in 1929 by the self-made Italian architect Giuseppe Martinelli. This 30-floor building in the French neoclassical style was once the tallest in South America; even today Edifício Martinelli remains a prime symbol of São Paulo's Belle Epoque in the early 20th century. *(On Rua Libero Baradó, 3 blocks from the Viaduto de Cha.)*

LIBERDADE & BIXIGA (BELA VISTA)

Liberdade, home to the world's largest community of Japanese immigrants, can be easily reached by *metrô* (M: Liberdade) or by foot along Av. da Liberdade, which begins behind the Catedral da Sé. A stroll down Rua Galvão Bueno, the main street, is the best way to become familiar with the area. The only real sight—beyond the streets themselves—in Liberdade is the small **Museu da Imigração Japonesa.** *(Rua São Joaquim 381, 7th fl. M: Liberdade. ☎279 5465. Open Tu-F 1:30-5:30pm.)* Neighboring Bela Vista, the historic center of Italian immigration, is known for Bixiga, a district of large restaurants and bars along Rua 13 de Maio.

JARDINS & AVENIDA PAULISTA

One of São Paulo's most dynamic neighborhoods, affluent Jardins is home to some of the city's most exclusive addresses and luxurious hotels. The upper half of Jardins, known as **Cerqueira Cesar,** teems with bars and restaurants catering to a largely GLS clientele. The nearby residential areas are safer (if less pedestrian-friendly) than Centro. Five blocks downhill from Av. Paulista are two of the city's most exclusive shopping strips in town: **Rua Oscar Freire** and **Alameda Lorena.** Here many top international clothing and jewelry brands maintain boutiques and sell to only the ritziest Paulistas.

AVENIDA PAULISTA. This skyscraper-lined avenue is the most-photographed street in all of São Paulo. It can be hard to believe that this bustling financial hub—through which pass more than 450,000 people per day—was founded over a cen-

THE BIG SPLURGE

OUT-OF-TOWNIN'

A few days in São Paulo can leave even seasoned urbanites longing for the woods, and this desire provides the perfect opportunity to experience one of the area's most worthwhile tours. Nomad Expedições runs full-day, weekend, and weeklong expeditions intended to give travelers a taste of the Brazilian road trip, thanks to veteran travelers Luízão and Nancy and their amazing automobile. They have refurbished this former police van and added their famous *tapete voador* (flying carpet), from which guests receive an unobstructed view from the roof. They have one-day tours to the Serra da Mantiqueira, the jungles of Iperó, or the Mata Atlântica of Juréia and Tapiraí (R$130-190 per person); "mini-expeditions" of 2-3 days' length, which include overnight stays at the aforementioned spots, as well as rafting in Juquiá and a visit to the famous coffee *fazenda* of São José do Barreiro (R$305-500 per person); and very customizeable weeklong expeditions, which can range from Pantanal excursions to a journey through the *sertão*.

To arrange a tour, visit Consultoria e Planejamaneto Turismo Ltda., Rua São Paulo 125 (☎5594 3199; nomadnet@bol.com.br). All expeditions include a guide, breakfast, cold drinks, and all taxes and fees. R$130-3000 per person, depending on itinerary.

tury ago as a peaceful refuge for the city's coffee barons. Where their sprawling mansions once stood are now endless blocks of skyscrapers housing banks, corporations, and posh hotels.

OTHER SIGHTS. Conjunto Nacional and **São Carlos do Pinhal e Paulicéia** will thrill architecture fans. These two edifices are both stunning examples of Brazil's modern architecture. *(Av. Paulista 2703 and Av. Paulista 900, respectively. Closed to visitors.)* **Casa das Rosas** is a small 1935 mansion, built in the French style typical of the time, and is one of the last surviving examples of Av. Paulista's earlier days. Today it contains a small museum and occasionally hosts classical music concerts. *(Av. Paulista 3. M: Brigadeiro. ☎251 5271. Open Tu-Su 11am-8pm.)*

PARQUE DO IBIRAPUERA

Ibirapuera is an oasis of green in the concrete jungle of São Paulo. With an area of 1.6 square kilometers, the park competes with the city's *shoppings* for the title "beach of the Paulistas." On weekend and holiday afternoons, it's a favorite destination for biking, walking, and relaxing. Flora in the park includes the Australian eucalyptus trees that were imported to help tame the formerly marshy environment. Oscar Niemeyer had a hand in the park's design, contributing the **Grande Marquise,** a concrete blob that covers much of the park's center. Ugly or not, its smooth floor is perfect for in-line skating and skateboarding. The interesting **Museu da Arte Moderna** at the eastern edge of the park is a major cultural attraction (see p. 192), and there is also a tourist information booth and a bike rental station. *(The park can be reached from Av. Paulista via any "Terminal João Dias" bus. ☎5574 5177. Bike rental R$3 per hr. Open daily 6am-8pm. M-F entry through gate 10 only.)*

MUSEUMS

Art lovers have an incredible selection of museums to sample from in São Paulo. The city is the heart of Brazil's contemporary art scene; it also serves as a cultural center with over 100 art galleries, meaning the city boasts a huge array of exhibits, including everything from works by famous European masters like Bellini, Rembrandt, and Cézanne (all of whom have works in **MASP**) to works by lesser-known artists in **Museu da Imagem e do Som.** All museums below are wheelchair-accessible unless otherwise noted in listings. The Portuguese guide *Muito Prazer: São Paulo* ("Pleasure to Meet You: São Paulo") has listings and descriptions of all museums, monuments, and galleries in the city.

PINACOTECA DO ESTADO DE SÃO PAULO. Since 1905, Pinacoteca do Estado has housed an invaluable collection of Brazilian art, focusing on the great painters of the 19th and 20th centuries. Recent renovations have added a more modern interior to the building's original structure, including a clear glass ceiling that lets plenty of sunlight in throughout the day. This natural light graces the building's holdings, including sculptures by Rodin and paintings by Pedro Alexandrinho, Flávio de Carvalho, and Lasar Segall. Be sure to check out Jorge Coli's *O Violeiro*, a poignant piece which speaks volumes about life in the *sertão*. Along with these, the permanent collections on the second floor comprise an excellent survey of the past two century's most important works, as well as many portraits of important Brazilians from the same period. The first floor has temporary exhibitions, which may include photographic displays, sculpture collections, and modern art. There is also a well-stocked gift shop, which sells a general map of the building (R$1). The basement includes a 140-seat auditorium where concerts of classical music are held every Sunday at 4pm. For Portuguese speakers there are free, fascinating art lectures held every Saturday at 4pm, usually conducted by professional scholars of Brazilian art history. *(Pça. da Luz 2. M: Luz. ☎229 9844. Open Tu-Su 10am-6pm. Tours available if reserved in advance. Admission R$4, students R$2; Sa free.)*

MUSEU DE ARTE DE SÃO PAULO ASSIS CHATEAUBRIAND (MASP). The city's most important museum is in many respects a microcosm of the megalopolis. The building itself immediately elicits a response, whether admiration of its architecture or discomfort at the sight of a huge block of concrete suspended in mid-air by four immense columns. The collection was started by Brazilian communications mogul Assis Chateaubriand in 1947, and will not disappoint: Chateaubriand took advantage of the post-war depression in Europe to purchase invaluable pieces of art at very low prices. The collection was initially housed downtown, but in the mid-1960s the plot of land where the museum stands today was purchased. The former owner included a proviso that an unobstructed view of Centro must be available from the museum, and thus the building is suspended 74 meters above the ground. However, due to the construction of skyscrapers in the past few decades it is no longer possible to view the Centro from the museum's terrace. The museum is divided into four levels, two above ground and two below. The top floor houses the permanent collection, including works by the Impressionist masters Renoir, Monet, Manet, Matisse, and Toulouse-Lautrec. Other international artists represented in the collection include Picasso, Van Gogh, Eugene Delacroix, and El Greco. Brazilian art is also on display, including works by Anita Malfati and Di Cavalcanti. The first floor and top basement floor hold the temporary exhibitions, while the bottom basement floor houses a small self-service restaurant and the Escola do MASP, which offers popular (and expensive; R$300) art history classes. *(Av. Paulista 1578. M: Trianon. ☎251 0574. Open Tu-Su 11am-6pm. Tours available Tu-F 9am-5pm. R$10, students R$5, under 10 or over 60 free.)*

INSTITUTO BUTANTAN. Located close to the main entrance of the Cidade Universitária is Instituto Butantan, a global leader in the production of vaccines and serums for major diseases. Dr. Vital Brazil, the institute's founder, became famous for his extraction of curatives in 1898, when he helped end the outbreak of bubonic plague in nearby Santos. The ever-expanding institute produces roughly 79 million doses of vaccinations annually, and does extensive research.

Directly inside is **Museu da Rua,** which has a series of bilingual panels describing the institute's history. Downhill to the left is the **Historical Museum,** which includes an unimpressive collection of furniture, lab equipment, and other items used by Dr. Brazil and his colleagues. The **Biological Museum** is one of the world's finest and lies at the end of Museu da Rua. It includes over 100 different specimens of snake, lizard, iguana, and frog, and usually has groups of school children crowding the animals' cages. Uphill is the **Microbiological Museum,** the newest of the museums. Farther down the main road is the popular **Serpentário,** filled with napping snakes and rapt school children. *(Av. Vital Brasil 1500. Bus #702U, "Butantã," stops close to the institute at the entrance to the Cidade Universitária. ☎3726 7222. Open Tu-Su 9am-4pm. R$4; students R$2; W students free.)*

CASA DE ANCHIETA (PÁTEO DO COLÉGIO). On January 25, 1554, the Real Colégio de São Paulo de Piratininga was founded on the spot where Casa de Anchieta stands today. The location was originally selected for its high elevation, but is now dwarfed by mammoth towers of steel and concrete on all sides. Nothing of the original structure remains aside from a segment of wall made of *taipa de pilão*, a clay which was used in many of the buildings in the downtown area. After Brazil expelled the Jesuits in 1765, the building became a military and government headquarters and was continually altered—sometimes demolished—throughout the 19th and 20th centuries. The structure was returned to the Jesuits in the mid-1950s, and today Casa de Anchieta includes a library, a church popular for concerts, and a nearby auditorium that hosts lecture series and debates. Worth visiting is the monument *Gloria Imortal aos Fundadores de São Paulo*, built in 1925. *(Pátio do Colégio 2. ☎3105 6899. Open Tu-Su 9am-6pm. R$2, students R$1.)*

MEMORIAL DA AMÉRICA LATINA. This is one of the many buildings in São Paulo designed by Oscar Niemeyer (p. 24). The memorial was envisioned by Brazilian author Darcy Ribeiro and is meant to foster a positive relationship between Latin American countries by encouraging the dissemination of artistic material from throughout the region. The immense complex has over 84,000 square meters of exhibition space, a library, a collection of over 1500 videocassettes, and more than 2000 music samples. There is also a small museum, focused primarily on regional artifacts, clothing, and ceramics. The main auditorium hosts acts from all over Latin America. A great way to get acquainted with the museum is to visit the Portal do Memorial (www.memorial.org.br), which provides information on upcoming events and an online cultural news magazine. *(Av. Auro Soares de Moura 664. ☎3823 4600. Tours can be arranged by calling ☎3923 9686. Open Tu-Su 9am-6pm.)*

MUSEU DE ARTE MODERNA DE SÃO PAULO (MAM). São Paulo's Museum of Modern Art houses a very eclectic collection in a structure designed by Oscar Niemeyer. Its holdings include sculptures, paintings, and all sorts of interesting *objèts d'art* in four galleries. Highlights include works by Anita Malfatti, Flávio de Carvalho, and Alfredo Volpi, as well as the annual Panorama da Arte Brasileira, which showcases new work by contemporary artists. The auditorium is the site of art lectures and regular debates. Check out the sculpture garden outside. *(Parque do Ibirapuera, gate 3. ☎5549 9688. Open Tu, W, F noon-6pm; Th noon-10pm; Sa-Su 10am-6pm.)*

OUTDOOR ACTIVITIES

São Paulo's seemingly endless maze of concrete and traffic makes the great outdoors seem far away, and many Paulistas use their weekends to head for the cool breezes and open spaces of the mountains and beaches. Locals also take advantage of the city's infrastructure of sports clubs, public parks, and gyms, many of which remain open 24hr. **Parque do Ibirapuera** (p. 190) and **Parque da Aclimação,** Rua Muniz de Souza 1119 are both very popular (open daily 5am-8pm).

Younger types often head to **Playcenter,** Rua José Gomez Falcão 20, which has roller-coasters and other exciting rides. (☎3618 2700. Open Th-Su noon-8pm.) Families with children frequent the large **São Paulo Zoo,** Av. Miguel Estéfano 4241 (☎5073 0811). M: São Judas and M: Saúde. The zoo is reputed to have one of the most complete collections of animals in the entire world, featuring more than 3200 animals from 444 different species. Highlights of the zoo's collections include giant ants from the Northeastern Brazilian state of Maranhão as well as some interesting amphibians.

One of the most frequented spots for leisure activities are SESCs, huge complexes of sports facilities, tennis and squash courts, and soccer fields, as well as cultural spaces, shops, eateries, and parks. The largest is **SESC Itaquera,** Av. Fernando do Espírito Santo Alves de Mattos 1000. It contains Atlantic rainforest, a water park, and many sports facilities. (☎6523 9200. Open Th-Su 9am-5pm.)

NIGHTLIFE

Cariocas like to claim that São Paulo has no nightlife, but spend a weekend in the city and you will find that Paulistas know how to party. In fact, nightspots are a dime a dozen in sprawling São Paulo. Between Centro's historic bars and *chopperias*, trendy Vila Olímpia, student hangout Vila Madalena, bohemian Pinheiros, and GLS-friendly Jardins, it is hard to have nothing to do in Sampa. Early birds beware: many popular dance clubs and bars don't heat up until well past midnight. Moreover, Paulista bars and clubs have a high turnover rate; check the weekly *Guia da Folha* and *Veja São Paulo* for the most current information.

VILA MADALENA

Grazie a Dio!, Rua Girassol 67 (☎3031 6568; www.grazieadio.com.br). M: Sumaré. Located right off the cemetery. You'll thank God when you enter this lively, crowded venue, which has live music nightly, including Sa groove sessions and Su *sambasonics*. This is hands-down the best place for live music in Vila Madalena. Sip a *Grazie a Dio!* (R$9.40), or warm up with some *vinho quiente* (mulled wine; R$6). Casual dress. 18+. Cover R$7. Open daily 7pm-late. AmEx/MC/V.

Matrix Bar, Rua Wisard 24 (☎3241 6532). M: Sumaré. From the corner of the cemetery, head 2 blocks up Rua Girassol and turn left on Rua Wisard; the bar will be on your left. Put on your best shade of black if heading to this goth hangout. Smoky pool tables in the back. *Caipirinhas* R$8. Cover R$10. Open Tu-Sa 7pm-5am.

Quitandinha, Rua Fidalga 242 (☎3817 558). M: Sumaré. Downhill from the cemetery, turn left 1 block after the gas station, then 1 block up on your right. Smoky Quitandinha is a favorite after 1am, and great as either a warm-up to or cool-down from a night of dancing. Good *chopp* (R$3) is accompanied by a rowdy, local university crowd. Strong *caipirinhas* R$6. Open M-Sa 7pm-5am.

Brancaleone, Rua Luís Murat 298 (www.brancaleone.com.br). M: Sumaré. Directly across from Grazie a Dio!, Brancaleone is managed by the same owner as its spunkier neighbor. The spacious club serves thumping techno to the crowds on its multiple dance floors. Shell out for a *brancaleone* (vodka, Fra Angelico, milk, and pineapple; R$10), or just sit and enjoy cartoon classics on the large screen in the center of the bar. Beer R$6. 18+. Cover R$10. Open daily 7pm-5am. AmEx/MC/V.

Empanadas, Rua Wisard 489 (☎3032 2116). M: Sumaré. This place is a perfect first stop on a night out in Vila Madalena, where everyone and their mother come for the scrumptious meat and chicken *empanadas* (R$1 each), best accompanied by the unique *espanhola caipirinha* (R$4). Try the slightly sweet Xingu beer (R$2). Open M-Sa 11am-1am, Su 1pm-1am.

Astor, Rua Delfina 163 (☎3815 1364). M: Sumaré. Four blocks from the cemetery, up Rua Morato Coelho. Art Deco fans meet *mojito*-lovers in this well-decorated establishment with a funky vibe. Check out the cool lamps, and check yourself out on the mirror-lined walls. Don't leave without tasting the ultimate Cuban drink (R$7). Casual dress. Open M-F 6pm-3am, Sa noon-4am, Su noon-7pm. AmEx/MC/V.

Blen Blen Brasil, Rua Inácio Pereira da Rocha 32 (☎3815 4999). Rising acts often start in Blen Blen, which has live music nightly and one of the city's most varied musical lineups, from big bands to *forró.* Beer R$3. Open Tu-F 8pm-late, Sa-Su 9pm-late.

A Lanterna, Rua Fidalga 531 (☎3031 0483). One block past the gas station, uphill along Rua Fidalga. Things are bright and lively in this jack-of-all-trades of a club. The large, open upstairs hosts up-and-coming acts, and the downstairs has a full bar. The back has thumping dance classics and the best dancing. *Chopp,* R$3.10. Tu-W cover R$10. Min. consumption Th-Sa R$20-35. Open M-Sa 6pm-1:30am. AmEx/MC/V.

Filial, Rua Fidalga 254 (☎3813 9226), facing Quitandinha. Join the family at this effusively friendly bar smack in the heart of the Vila. The hopping yet homey Filial serves a wicked *chopp* and a mind-boggling 52 varieties of *cachaça*. Open M-Th 5pm-2:30am, F-Sa 5pm-4am, Su 5pm-1am.

Caretas Bar, Rua Aspicuelta 208 (☎3814 7581; www.caretas.com). Decorative masks stare down from the walls of this trendy bar in the heart of Vila Madalena. Its 2 floors and hopping outside deck invite patrons to imbibe and snack on the house's specialty—fried rabbit, served *en flambé* in cognac. Cool off with a bottle of Bohemia beer (R$3.70). Cover R$4. Open Tu-Sa 6pm-late. AmEx/MC/V.

PINHEIROS, JARDINS, & VILA OLÍMPIA

Bar Léo, Rua Aurora 100 (☎221 0247). M: República. In a city with so many watering holes, this bar is a favorite of beer connoisseurs. Despite its dubious location in the infamous *boca do lixo,* Léo has been pleasing its increasingly varied crowd for over 60 years. The bar serves popular *bolinhos do bacalão* (cod balls; R$6). *Chopp* R$3. Open M-F 11am-9:30pm, Sa 11am-4pm.

Teta, Rua Cardeal Arcoverde 1265 (☎3031 1641). This Pinheiro establishment serves simple meals alongside daily live jazz shows, and has a much-acclaimed piano bar. The older crowd favors whisky (R$8), but don't overlook Teta's *chopp* (R$2.50) or *gruyere* burgers (R$11). Cover R$5. Open M-Sa 6pm-5am. AmEx/MC/V.

Único bar, Rua Bela Cintra 1372 (☎3085 4310). M: Consolação. All types come to Único to enjoy MPB and *bossa nova* classics. Open M-Sa 11:30am-4am. AmEx/MC/V.

GAY & LESBIAN NIGHTLIFE (GLS)

Rio may be the continent's most popular gay destination, but São Paulo hosts the continent's biggest Gay Pride Parade (p. 98) and has its fair share of clubs catering to a mostly GLS crowd. The place to go for gay nightlife is undoubtedly the western edge of Jardim Paulista, known locally as Cerqueira César. Other notable neighborhoods include Pinheiros and Vila Madalena. The *Guia da Folha* is an invaluable resource for weekly updates. All of the following are accessible via M: Consolação, and all are located in Jardins.

Espaço Massivo, Alameda Itú 1548 (☎3083 0432). From Rua da Consolação, head downhill 2 blocks and take a right. São Paulo's best-known gay venue lures massive crowds for its varied shows, which range from hot MPB hits to trance. Flirty crowds spill into the street and continue the party until late morning. Cover R$15. Min. consumption R$15. Open Tu-Sa midnight-6am. AmEx/MC/V.

Hertz Bar, Alameda Itú 1530 (☎3064 2088). Massivo's smaller neighbor spins Madonna classics, electronica, and MPB favorites to keep the crowd grooving. *Chopp* R$2.50. Min. consumption R$8. Open Tu-Sa 6pm-3am, Su 5pm-3am. AmEx/MC/V.

Nostro Mondo, Rua da Consolação 2554 (☎3259 2945). Many years ago Nostro Mondo became São Paulo's first club to openly serve an exclusively gay clientele. Today, the club continues to please old and new patrons alike with its acclaimed drag shows. Try to come on Sa night, when it's less crowded. Cover R$10. Open F-Sa 10pm-5am, Su 6pm-midnight. AmEx/MC/V.

A Louca, Rua Frei Caneca 916 (☎3159 8889). Go crazy in this underground bar and longtime favorite of the Paulista GLS community. A mixed crowd of gay and straight twenty-somethings grind the night away to hard techno. Saturday mornings the party continues well past sunrise. *Chopp* R$3. Cover R$12-R$18. Open Th noon-6pm, F-Sa midnight-10am, Su 7pm-5am.

ENTERTAINMENT

CINEMA

There are two staples of weekend afternoons in São Paulo: shopping and movies. Many of the city's largest cinemas, like Cinemark, are inside *shoppings* (malls). Their selection tends to be a mixture of Hollywood blockbusters, popular Brazilian films, and some European releases. Smaller, artsier theaters—like the popular **Espaço Unibanco,** Rua Augusta 1475 (☎288 6780)—are also frequented by Paulistas. Full movie listings are available each week in *Guia da Folha.* Dubbed titles are listed either as *dub.* or *dublado.* Tickets average R$10-14, and student discounts are usually available. **Shopping Center Iguatemi,** Av. Brigadeiro Faria Lima 2322 (☎3812 4013), and **Shopping Ibirapuera,** Av. Ibirapuera 3103 (☎5095 2300), both have three-screen cinemas.

LIVE MUSIC

Live performances are available every day of the year in São Paulo. The city's innumerable bars and clubs keep up a fast-paced, steady beat until the wee hours of the morning, but music halls, *futebol* stadiums, and pretty much any other large open space is fair game for a great show at any time of day or night. Of particular interest are the **Memorial da America Latina** (p. 192), which is a popular spot for visiting South American musicians, and Parque do Ibirapuera, which frequently hosts free outdoor concerts. The "Shows" and "Concertos" sections of *Guia da Folha* have listings updated weekly. Contact Ticketmaster Brasil (☎6846 6000; www.ticketmaster.com.br) for up-to-date information. **Credicard Hall,** Av. das Nações Unidas 17955 (☎5643 2500), has over 7000 seats and is São Paulo's largest music venue. International stars are frequent guests, as are many of Brazil's most popular acts. **Tom Brasil,** Rua das Olimpíadas 66, smack in the middle of trendy Vila Olímpia, is known for its excellent MPB. (☎3845 2326; casatombrasil.com.br.) **Bourbon Street Music Club,** Rua dos Chanés 127, in Moema, features daily blues and jazz, played to an affluent crowd with many *reais* to spare. (☎5561 1643; www.bourbonstreet.com.br.)

THEATER

Theaters in São Paulo are organized into a few locales, the most-frequented of which is Bixiga, dubbed the "Paulistano Broadway," being home to many famous theaters. *Veijinha* and *Guia da Folha* are both great resources for finding shows. Ticket reservations can be made at Ticketmaster Brasil. (☎6846 6000; www.ticketmaster.com.br.) Two popular theaters in Bixiga are **TBC,** Rua Maj. Diogo 315 (☎3115 4622; www. novotbc.com.br), and **Oficina,** Rua Jaceguai 520 (☎3106 2818; www.teatroficina.com.br). Centro's **Teatro Itália,** Av. Ipiranga 344 (☎3257 9092; www.teatroitalia.com.br), also draws crowds.

SHOPPING

Many Paulistas take offense at the suggestion that the city's shopping malls are its beaches, but even a single Friday afternoon visit to any of São Paulo's myriad, overflowing *shoppings* will reveal that Paulistas shop until they drop. **Shopping Ibi-**

IN RECENT NEWS

THE LAW OF THE LANDLESS

Brazil's most dynamic agricultural states—including São Paulo and Paraná—have long witnessed the ongoing struggle between Brazil's impoverished rural population and affluent urbanites. In 1984, peasants in Paraná founded the **Movimento dos Trabalhadores Rurais Sem-Terra (MST),** a.k.a. the Landless Rural Workers' Movement, with a simple mission: to seize and settle upon unproductive land, then create permanent, productive collectives on that land. Predictably, the movement has encountered stiff resistance from both landowners and the government. Nevertheless, MST has expanded into São Paulo state, Santa Catarina, Rio Grande do Sul, and Mato Grosso do Sul. There are an estimated 13,000 families participating in MST, which now also includes unemployed urban laborers with only primary education.

MST's leadership considers Lula's election as a boost for the movement, for Lula was once an outspoken advocate for agricultural workers, so much so that today, many recognize him as the movement's official spokesman. The main challenge for Lula—and for Brazil as a whole—is to strike a balance between property law and the rural peasants' right to make a living. As such, this story—and the struggle of the landless—is far from over.

rapuera, Av. Ibirapuera 3130, is the biggest shopping mall in the entire country, complete with a giant food court. Other popular malls in São Paulo include: **Shopping Center Iguatemi,** Av. Brigadeiro Faria Lima 2322 (☎3812 4013); **Shopping El Dorado,** Av. Rebouças 3970 (☎3819 0688; any "Cidade Universitária" or "Butantã" bus); and **Shopping Paulista,** Rua 13 de Maio 1947 (☎3191 1100; M: Paraíso).

FESTIVALS & EVENTS

Several of this city's festivals are world-famous, and draw visitors from all over the globe. Every late June or early July, the city holds the renowned **São Paulo Fashion Week,** which showcases work by both established and up-and-coming Brazilian designers (www.uol.com.br/spfashionweek). The main events take place in Parque do Ibirapuera's Grande Marquise, and the event draws over 70,000 spectators. Slightly racier is the **Grande Prêmio Brasil.** Every April Formula 1 competitors from across the globe and hordes of racing enthusiasts descend upon São Paulo (www.gpbrazil.com). If cars aren't exactly your speed, stop by Sampa in late August to witness some of the world's best short films at the reknowned **São Paulo International Film Festival,** which is attended by some 150,000 or more film fans every year. The city's annual **Gay Pride Parade** down Av. Paulista, held every June since 1996, attracts crowds of more than 800,000 participants, and is one of the largest such celebrations in the whole world.

SÃO PAULO STATE

CAMPOS DO JORDÃO ☎12

Originally settled by German immigrants and reminiscent of a village high in the Bavarian Alps, Campos de Jordão has long been a favorite weekend destination for urbanites both Paulista and Carioca. The beautiful scenery and crisp weather draw throngs of visitors, especially during June and July, when prices skyrocket. Today, Campos's historical heritage has become more of a tourist attraction than living museum. Fortunately, the town's environs provide unfettered access to amazing opportunities for climbing, biking, and even horseback riding. To experience the area's liveliness visit during a festival: the **Festas do 20 de Janeiro** (January 20th), lasts 2 weeks and marks the town's anniversary, while on March 16, the town celebrates its political emancipation with music and dance.

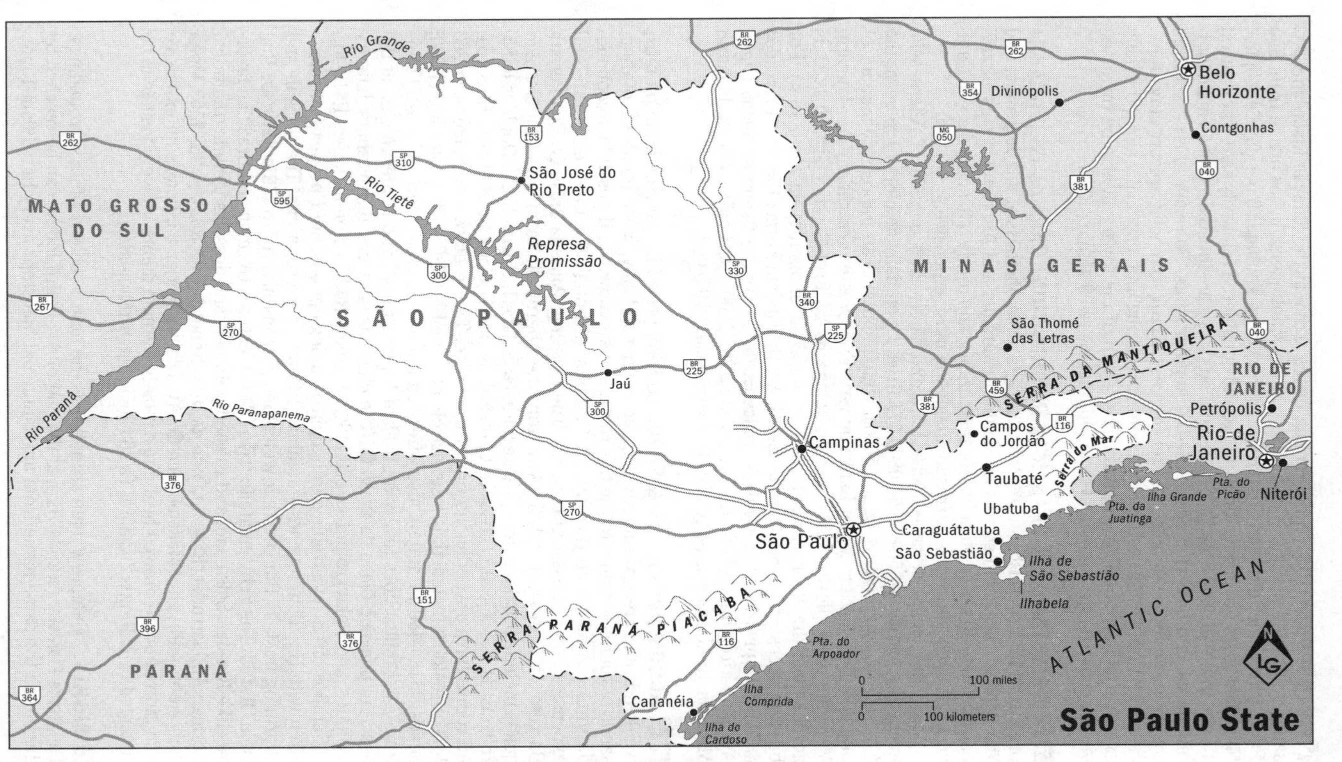
São Paulo State
Rio Grande
BR 262
BR 354
Divinópolis
Belo Horizonte
Contgonhas
BR 040
MG 050
BR 381
BR 153
SP 310
São José do Rio Preto
MATO GROSSO DO SUL
SP 595
Rio Tietê
Represa Promissão
SP 300
SP 330
BR 340
MINAS GERAIS
BR 267
SÃO PAULO
SP 270
SP 225
São Thomé das Letras
SERRA DA MANTIQUEIRA
RIO DE JANEIRO
Petrópolis
Rio-de-Janeiro
Niterói
Pta. do Picão
Ilha Grande
Pta. da Juatinga
Jaú
BR 225
BR 459
BR 381
BR 116
Rio Paraná
Rio Paranapanema
Campinas
Campos do Jordão
Serra do Mar
Taubaté
Ubatuba
Caraguátatuba
São Sebastião
Ilha de São Sebastião
Ilhabela
São Paulo
BR 376
BR 151
ATLANTIC OCEAN
SERRA PARANÁ PIACABA
BR 396
Pta. do Arpoador
PARANÁ
Ilha Comprida
Cananéia
Ilha do Cardoso
BR 364
0
100 miles
100 kilometers

SOUTHEAST

TRANSPORTATION. All incoming buses arrive at the **Estação Rodoviária,** Av. Januário Miráglia (☎262 1996), in Jaguaribe. Mantiqueira buses arrive from São Paulo (3hr.; 6 per day 6am-7pm; R$19.15) and from Taubaté (8 per day 6am-8pm). **Municipal buses** are clean, comfortable, and considered relatively safe. They run on 15min. intervals, and cost R$1; municipal bus stops are located along all main thoroughfares, and have distinctive tiled, triangular roofs. To reach Abérnessia from the *rodoviária*, cross onto Av. Frei Orestes Girardi; to reach Capivari, stay on Av. Januário Miráglia. **Taxi** stations are common throughout, especially along the main avenues and around Pça. Capivari. The length of the town can also be traversed via the **suburbio,** the municipal tram (40min.; every 30-45min.; R$1).

ORIENTATION & PRACTICAL INFORMATION. Campos do Jordão is organized into three distinct *vilas* (districts): **Vila Abernéssia, Vila Jaguaribe,** and **Vila Capivari.** The main streets Av. Januário Miráglia and Av. Frei Orestes Girardi pass through all three. Most hotels, restaurants, and tourist attractions are in Capivari, although the area is correspondingly the most expensive.

The main **tourist office** is located approximately 2km outside of Abernéssia, inside the **portal.** (☎3664 3525, 0800 771 5104. Open daily 8am-8pm.) Request the *Nosso Guia* publication (☎262 5000), which contains an impressive amount of practical information. Major banks line Av. Frei Orestes Girardi and Av. Januário Miráglia, particularly in Abernéssia. **Unibanco,** Av. Frei Orestes Girardi 1233, is across from the Abernéssia tram stop (☎262 3388; open M-Sa 11am-4pm). For Internet access, try **Cyber Café Boulevard,** Av. Dr. Djalma Forjaz 100, loja 15 (☎3663 6351) in Capivari. Other services: **police** (☎262 1155); the **Centro de Saúde** clinic, Av. Januário Miráglia 806, in Abernéssia (☎262 1600); **post office,** on Av. Januário Miráglia, in Abernéssia (☎262 6044). **Postal code:** 12460-000.

SOUTHEAST

ACCOMMODATIONS & FOOD. Lodging prices in Campos jump on most weekends and are several times higher in June and July, when hundreds of thousands of tourists cram into the tiny town. Book in advance if possible. Accommodations can be found throughout Campos, although the most elaborate and expensive hotels cluster in Capivari. The excellent **Pousada Brasil ❷,** Rua Pereira Barreto 22, is directly uphill away from the Abernéssia tram stop. Doubles and quads include breakfast and private bath. (☎262 2341. Dorms R$25. Doubles R$85-260; quads R$165-440.) Closer to Capivari's action is **Siena Hotel ❸,** Av. Brasil 64. All rooms have a wooden interior, private bath, TV, fireplace, and balcony. (☎263 1330. Breakfast included. 10% service charge. Doubles R$70-300; triples R$111-390; quads R$144-480.) Campos also offers camping: take the "Horto Florestal" bus from Av. Emilio Ribas (every hr. 6:30am-10pm; R$1.60) and request a stop at the peaceful **Camping Clube do Brasil ❶.** The club has showers, dishwashers, laundry facilities, and a playground. (☎263 1130. Members R$6-15, non-members R$18-45.)

Campos offers a veritable cornucopia of dining options, but European cuisine—often with Brazilian touches—dominates Capivari's restaurants. The sociable and charming hostess Bia Dietrich welcomes patrons nightly to **Bia Kaffe ❸,** Rua Isola Orsi 33. The Schlagplate for two (R$40) features German and Brazilian favorites like Kassler, Salsichão, and roasted potatoes, and desserts include traditional German Apfelstrudel (R$5) and *pão de mel* (honey bread; R$2). (☎263 1507. Open daily noon-midnight.) **Baden-Baden ❸,** Av. Djalma Forjaz 93, boasts an extensive selection of home-brewed beer and a mostly German menu; brewery visits can be arranged by calling ☎262 3091. (☎263 3659. Open 10am-late.)

SIGHTS. Campos's main attraction is the natural beauty of its surroundings. The **Horto Florestal** (☎263 3762), at the end of Av. Pedro Paulo, can be reached by the bus of the same name from any municipal bus stop (every hr. 6:30am-10pm;

R$1.60). Reputedly Brazil's oldest state park, it encompasses 8,341 acres of unspoiled forests and well-maintained gardens. Take the **teleférico** (cable car) from Emílio Ribas station in Capivari to the **Morro de Elefante** for pleasant views of the town. The adventurous can try climbing the **Pedra do Baú,** a peculiarly shaped rock considered one of Campos's most characteristic sights. On Av. Mario Colla Francisco, north of Abernéssia, is the **Palácio Boa Vista,** which was originally the municipal government's summer residence and today is a museum. The **train** from Campos to Santo Antônio de Pinhal is a short excursion; it begins in Capivari, provides unforgettable views of the Palácio Boa Vista and the Pedra do Baú, and includes a stop at **Alto de Lajeado** (1743m), Brazil's highest railroad point.

UBATUBA ☎12

Travelers come to Ubatuba for its more than 80 beaches—and in this easygoing coastal city your only concern may be choosing between them. Ubatuba has proclaimed itself the "Capital of Surf," and beaches here range from happening **Praia Grande** to pristine **Praia Fazenda.** North of the city, the **Parque Estadual da Serra do Mar** has many half- and full-day trails leading to *cachoeiras* hidden in thick tropical forests. To the south are extravagant resorts and apartment buildings extending along miles of shoreline. During the high season tourists (mostly Brazilian) stuff Ubatuba with ten times its normal population; those who come during the low season will have the town to themselves.

TRANSPORTATION. Ubatuba has two intercity **bus** stations and one domestic terminal. The **rodoviária** is located in the *centro* on Rua Prof. Thomaz Galhardo. (☎3832 6912. Open daily 6:30am-8pm.) **Reunidas Paulista** (☎3832 5361) runs to Paraty (3 per day 9:40am-8:40pm; R$5.50) and São Paulo (3½hr; 3 per day 8am-8:30pm; R$25.20). **São José** (☎3832 6912) goes to Taubaté (2hr.; 4 per day 6:30am-8pm; R15.05). The municipal **Rodoviária Costamar** station is located on the corner of Rua Conceição and Rua Hans Staden, facing Pça. 5 de Maio. **Costamar** runs the majority of routes to the beaches north and south of the city. (☎332 4142. Open 8am-midnight; all buses R$1.70.) Many of the stops are unlabeled so travelers should ask the driver to announce their stop. To return to Ubatuba, board any "Cidade" bus (every hr.; R$1.70). Ubatuba's *centro* is easily traversed on foot, but **taxis** to more distant destinations like beaches can be prohibitively expensive, although there are convenient **taxi stands** in Pça. 5 de Maio (☎3832 1235) and Pça. Nóbrega (☎3832 1157). Localiza has **car rental** offices outside Ubatuba Airport (☎3833 7200). There is a **bike rental** station on Rua Prof. Thomaz Galhardo; the tourist office in Pça. 5 de Maio is also helpful.

PRACTICAL INFORMATION. The **tourist office,** at the end of Rua Prof. Thomaz Galhardo near Av. Iperoig (☎3832 4255; www.ubatuba.sp.gov.br) offers the excellent **Guia Pena-Areia** (www.penaareia.com). Major **banks** are found between Rua Hans Staden and Rua Nóbrega. **Banespa,** on the corner of Rua De Maria Alves and Rua Hans Staden, exchanges traveler's checks. (☎3832 1941. Open M-Sa 9am-4pm.) **Internet access** is available at **Global LAN House,** Rua. Dr. Esteves da Silva 74. (☎3833 1603. Open daily 10am-10pm.) The **post office** is on Rua Cel. Ernesto de Oliveira (☎3832 8974). **Postal code:** 11680-000.

ACCOMMODATIONS. Ubatuba is a popular vacation spot, and its hotels and *pousadas* are often full from mid-November to Carnaval. **Barra de Farol ❶,** Rua Dr. Felix Guisard Filho, stands less than a block from the coast and is heavily frequented by beachgoers. From Pça. 5 de Maio head down Rua Conceição toward the beach, turn left onto Rua Salvador Correa, and continue along it for about five blocks; the hotel will be on your left. (☎433 3568. High season dorms R$35-40. Low season dorms R$15.) Two blocks inland—in the heart of Pça. Nóbrega—is **Hotel São Charbel ❷**, Rua Cel. Domiciano. The hotel brochure includes detailed maps of the city and major beaches. All rooms have cable TV, A/C, private bath, sheets, towels, and fully stocked *frigo-bar*. (☎3832 1090; www.saocharbel.com.br. Breakfast included. Dorms R$40-60. Doubles R$80-120; triples R$120-180. MC/V.)

FOOD. Nearly every street corner in the *centro* has a *sorveteria* or a *lanchonete*. **Supermercado Paulista,** Rua Maria Alves 218, has supplies. **Quiosques** in Praia Vermelha and Praia Grande are most popular with surfers and beach bums. The aptly named **Come-Se Bem ❹,** Rua Guarani 311, has a highly recommended *azul marino* (grilled fish with onions, spices, and rice; R$27.80)—a must for first-time visitors—as well as beef, chicken, and pasta dishes. From Praia de Cruzeiro, face the ocean, take a right, then walk toward Praia Itaguá until you see the bright sign on your left. (☎3432 2480. Open 11am-11pm.) **Bucaneros Pizza ❶/❷,** Rua Conceiçao 61, is excellent for *chopp* (R$2-3) and pizza (R$14). The inexpensive, unassuming, and filling **Sabor em Peso ❷,** Rua Dona Maria Alves 473, is a kilo with tons of *feijão* and other Brazilian favorites. Locals gather here even in low season, making it a great place to mingle. (☎3882 3751. Open daily 8am-8pm.)

BEACHES. Ubatuba's beaches spread along over 70km of coastline, and 87% of them—primarily those north of the *centro*—are in protected areas reachable only by often-unmarked trails; get a map from the tourist office. Traveling by car is the most flexible way of getting around, but the regular buses are also convenient. **Praia da Fazenda,** about 45km from the *centro*, or 50min. by bus, and the neighboring village **Picinguaba** are largely untouched and worth a visit. From Picinguaba, trails lead uphill through the **Parque Estadual da Serra do Mar** and on to **Cachoeira Promirim** and **Cachoeira Escada.** Within 5km of the *centro* are the beaches of **Praia Grande, Toninhas, Tenório,** and **Norte de Vermelha.** These beaches are also nightlife hotspots; the nearby *quiosques* and *danceterias* get crowded after midnight and continue bumping well into the morning.

SÃO SEBASTIÃO ☎12

The nearby **Parque Estadual da Serra do Mar** has the most trails in the **Litoral Paulista** and will (literally) take adventurers to new heights, but busy, buzzing São Sebastião below will not disappoint either. The town's **Maresias, Boicuçanga,** and **Barra do Una** beaches are perfect for surfing, bronzing, and even diving, and a well-developed rental infrastructure caters to extreme sports fans seeking everything from surfboards to kayaks. The neighboring island paradise **Ilhabela** (p. 201) is a playground for wave runners and beach buggies, and the unforgettable jeep tours to the far side of the island are highly recommended. To experience São Sebastião's liveliness, visit during a festival: the **Festas do 20 de Janeiro** (January 20th), lasts 2 weeks and marks the town's anniversary, while on March 16, the town celebrates its political emancipation with music and dance.

The *centro* area is easy to navigate. **Litoranea** buses arrive from Caraguátatuba (50min.; every 30min.; R$2), and from São Paulo (2½hr.; 6 per day 6am-8pm; R$25). The **Terminal Rodoviário** is on Av. São Sebastião (☎3892 1072). From there, walk toward the large gas station until you reach Av. Guarda Mor Lobo Viana, and take a right onto any of the side streets, which will lead you directly into the historic center. The *centro* consists of **Praça Major João Fernandes** and, at the coastline, **Av. Dr. Atino Arantes,** both of which offer views of the port and Ilhabela. The **balsa** (ferry) to Ilhabela departs from the end of Av. São Sebastião (every 30min. 6am-midnight). The **tourist office** Sectur, Av. Dr. Altino Arantes 174, offers trail maps that include descriptions of each trail's length and difficulty and, for the most popular trails, a listing of their unique features. Keep in mind that all trails require guides, which Sectur can arrange. **Banks** are scattered along Av. Guarda Mor Lobo Viana. **Banespa** (☎3891 3300) exchanges traveler's cheques, and **HSBC** accepts most ATM cards. Other services include: the **police** (☎452 1595) and a **post office,** Rua Antônio Candido 134. **Postal code:** 11600-000.

Pousada Ana Doce ❸/❹, Rua Expedicionário Brasileiro 196, has a homey interior that includes a lush inner courtyard, plush couches, and a second floor bungalow-style dining area overlooking the garden. (☎3892 1615; www.litoralvirtual.com.br/anadoce. Singles R$60; doubles R$80; triples R$100; quads R$120. R$25 for an extra bed. 10% discount in the low season.) Closer to the bus station, **Hotel Roma ❷/❸,** Pça. Major João Fernandes 174, offers a king's service at a pauper's price. All *apartamentos* include A/C, TV, private bath, and unstocked *frigo-bar.* Rooms can get quite hot and noisy in the summer; ask for one away from the street. (☎3892 1016. Low-season *quartos* R$25; *apartamento* singles and doubles R$40.) The freshest fish passes straight from dock to dish at **Restaurante Canoa ❷/❸,** Rua da Praia 234. This restaurant is an excellent place for people-watching, especially while eating their *calderada* (seafood and fish chowder; R$35 serves two) or steak with fries (R$20 serves two). (☎3892 1772; www.restaurantecanoa.cjb.net.) For a taste of local nightlife, São Sebastião's greatest *forró* is at **Bombordo,** Rua Dr. Altino Arantes 85, best during the annual summer migration of beautiful people to the coasts. (☎2385 3841).

ILHABELA ☎12

Even when just glimpsed from São Sebastião's ferry dock, Ilhabela's name (Beautiful Island) seems deserved, as the **Pico de São Sebastião** rises majestically from the Atlantic to a height of 1378m. Seen from offshore, Ilhabela's mountains, coast, and surrounding waters seem peaceful and quiet, but the island teems with activity both above and below the water. During the summer months (Nov.-Mar.), the island's population more than triples and everything becomes more expensive. The **Festa do Camarão** (Shrimp Feast), which takes place over the entire month of August, is both a lively and less-crowded time to visit. Ilhabela has hosted the month-long **Semana de Vela** every July for the past 30 years. Competitions and regattas make this a very fun, if crowded, time to visit. The island's most attractive sights, however, are those provided by nature, and can be enjoyed year-round. The best and most unspoiled beaches face away from the mainland. **Praia Castelhanos** lies 23km away from the town and can be reached either on foot or by off-road vehicle. **Lokal Adventures,** Av. Princesa Isabel 171, runs a daytrip that includes lunch in Castelhanos and a hike to **Cachoeira do Gato** (☎3896 5777; 3896 5770; www.lokaladventure.com.br). Scuba expeditions are available to the many wrecks along the island's southern coast—including the dive site **Príncipe de Asturias,** of the Ponta de Boi—and also to the islands of **Serraria** and **Búzios** (p. 172). Lovers of the outdoors will not be disappointed by **Praia Bonete,** which offers perhaps the island's most extraordinary opportunity to leave behind the beaten path. **Silva,** Av. Independência 840, rents bikes (R$15 per 24hr.) and offers bike tours, including a 10-hour trip inland to Cachoeira Pitu in the mountains. (Bikes, guide, and lunch, R$20 per person.)

Ilhabela is easy to navigate: it has a single major street, **Avenida Princesa Isabel,** running the full length of the island, along which are most hotels and restaurants, and off of which branch most minor roads. **Bus stops** are located along Av. Princesa Isabel; those labeled "Vila" are headed north to the main *praça,* while those going southwards are labeled either "Balsa" (ferry) or "Barra Velha." The **tourist office,** on Rua Bartolomeu de Gusnão, off Princesa in Pequeá, offers a map of the island. (☎3472 1091. Open daily 9am-6pm.) **Internet access** is available at **Cyber Café,** Rua Bandoeira 33 (☎3896 1160), in the *vila,* which also has a 24hr. convenience store on its first floor. **Emergency clinic:** ☎3895 8789.

Hotels and restaurants line the island's main avenue. At **Pousada Fita Azul ❷/❸,** Av. Força Expedicionária Brasileira 98, owner and son duo Sonia and Roberto run a tight ship: delightful, spotless rooms arranged around a brightly lit, tranquil garden in the central courtyard. (☎3896 2023. Dorms R$30-50.) Eateries are concentrated around the *vila.* **Churrascaria Badejo Piranha e Companhia ❷,** Pça. Cel. Julião 43, next to the Bradesco bank serves great *picanha* (steak). (☎3896 3025.) Top off the night at **Bartatas ❷,** Rua da Pedreira 3, where the English expat John serves roasted potatoes stuffed with nearly anything imaginable: try the Special Ilhabela stuffing (R$13.40). The highlight is the *chopp* (R$2.20-2.50), always served *estupidamente gelado* ("ridiculously cold").

CANANÉIA ☎13

Cananéia's tacky architecture and sleepy winters may fool some visitors into thinking that it is just another fishing village, but they would be mistaken: throughout summer, throngs of urbanites visit from Curitiba and São Paulo. Cananéia may be the oldest permanent settlement on the Brazilian mainland; on August 12, 1531, the Portuguese explorer Martim Afonso de Souza established a defensive post in the area that today is the *centro.* **Praça Martim Afonso de Souza** has an obelisk and two large cannons commemorating the fort, and in the same *praça* is **Igreja São João Batista,** a replica of an earlier structure from the mid-1600s.

The vast majority of visitors come to Cananéia for the natural splendor of its surroundings, particularly **Ilha Comprida** and **Parque Estadual Ilha do Cardoso.** Ilha Comprida has beaches and some minor trails, and can be reached by taking a *balsa* (ferry) from the main *praça* (pedestrians free; bikes R$2.50; cars R$5). The better sights are found in Cardoso, which can be reached by organized tours. The 11km Cachoeira do Ipanema Trail passes by many beautiful waterfalls and leads to a deserted beach, and there are several less difficult trails to the southern beaches.

Cananéia proper is best covered on foot. The main street, **Avenida Independência,** starts at the town's gate and runs directly into the historic center of town, which is relatively far from the waterfront. All buses stop at the **rodoviária,** Rua Talis Bernardis 101, on the western edge of town. (☎3851 0312. Open 6am-12:50pm and 2:50-6pm.) Buses run to São Paulo (5hr.; 2 per day 7am-4:30pm; R$35). The *rodoviária* is only a block away from Pça. Martin Afonso de Souza and the waterfront, along **Avenida Beira Mar.** One block inland from the *praça* is the **Rua do Artesão,** a pedestrian street with *quiosques* selling trinkets and fast food. One block farther is **Rua Tristão Lobo,** with bars and snack joints that range from great to gross. Tourist information is available at the **Secretaria de Esporte e Turismo,** Rua Tristão Lobo 78, in the same building as Museu Municipal. (☎6851 1753. Open M-F 9am-5:30pm.) **Escuna Lagamar,** Av. Independência 885, runs half- and full-day trips to nearby Perequê (R$15 per person) and Marujá (R$30 per person). (☎3851 3437, ask for Selma Pontes.) Other services include: **Banco Banespa,** Rua Pedro Correia 13 (open M-F 10am-3pm; ATMs open until 10pm on weekends); **Supermercado da Ilha,** in Pça. Martim Afonso de Sousa (open daily 9am-6pm); a **police station,** on Rua Francisco Chaves, down the street from the post office; **Internet access** at Kurt Kaffee, Av. Beira Mar 71 (☎6851 1262; open M-F 8am-10pm, Sa-Su 9am-1am); the **post office,** Rua Francisco Chaves 392 (open M-F 10am-3pm). **Postal code:** 11990-000.

Pousadas are expensive throughout high season (Dec.-Mar. and July), but it's possible to get some good deals during less congested times. **Hotel Recanto do Sol ❶,** Rua Pero Lobo 271, is a 10min. walk from the *rodoviária.* It has luxuries like a pool and A/C, and even its most basic rooms come with private bath, fan, TV, and

frigo-bar. (☎6851 1162. Breakfast included. Low-season *quartos* R$20.) The central **Pousada Caropa ❹**, Av. Beira Mar 13, rewards splurgers with comfy doubles with TV, bath, *frigo-bar*, breakfast, and fan. (☎6851 1601. Doubles R$90.) Food is cheap and plentiful in Cananéia's unassuming, homey restaurants. **Restaurante Caiçara ❶**, Pça. Martins Afonso 41, serves a great lunch kilo with *churrasco;* filling dinner options include *marujá* (shrimp risotto with a fish filet; R$8.50) and *milano* (breaded chicken with Greek rice and fries; R$9.90). (☎3851 0360. Open daily 9am-late.) A must for after-hours fun is **Bar da Villa,** Rua Tristão Lobo 289. Things pick up after midnight most summer nights, when live MPB blasts for the trendy crowd of young Paulistanos, who come to drink (R$4-12) or smoke (R$0.70 per cigar). (☎6851 1587. Open M-Th 11:30am-midnight, F-Sa 6pm-late.)

MINAS GERAIS

BELO HORIZONTE ☎31

In the mid-1890s, Minas Gerais conducted detailed studies to find the perfect site for a new capital, but the site it found was occupied by a small town called Belo Horizonte; the state proceeded to demolish the older Belo Horizonte and in its place build a modern capital city, which was also christened Belo Horizonte, in honor of the location's former occupant. The new capital was carefully planned for its residents' convenience and comfort, and that care still shines through today; the UN once declared Belo Horizonte's quality of life among the highest in South America. The original plan called for a central area of eight square blocks intersected by eight primary diagonals, all surrounded by the circular Av. do Contorno, with a capacity of 200,000 residents. Belo Horizonte would not reach that level of population for four decades, but when it did, then-mayor Juscelino Kubitschek planned for two additional neighborhoods: an elite settlement to the north called Pampulha, and to the west a working-class neighborhood called Cidade Industrial. Pampulha became the birthplace of Brazil's modern architecture and launched Oscar Niemeyer's career (p. 24). Although most tourists come to see Pampulha, its modern buildings are not Belo Horizonte's sole architectural attraction—its many *praças* are lined by a historical panorama of Brazilian architecture, and their beauty continues to draw travelers.

TRANSPORTATION

Flights: There are two airports in Belo Horizonte. **Aeroporto Internacional Tancredo Neves,** Confins, Estrada Velha de Confins (☎3689 2700). Unir (☎3271 1335) runs buses from the *rodoviária* to the airport (1hr.; M-F 16 per day 4:45am-10:30pm, Sa-Su 13 per day 4:45am-10pm; R$4.65). Served by American Airlines, TAM, Varig, and VASP. The second airport is **Aeroporto da Pampulha,** Pça. Bagatelle 204 (☎3490 2001). Also best reached from the *rodoviária* by Unir buses (25min.; M-F 16 per day 4:45am-10:30pm, Sa-Su 13 per day 4:45am-10pm; R$4.65). Served by Gol, TAM, and Varig. For information on carriers, see **Airlines,** p. 87.

Buses: The intercity bus station is **Estação Rodoviária,** Pça. Rio Branco s/n (☎3271 3000), and is served by several companies. **Metro Lagoinha Viação Gontijo** (☎3201 6130) has buses to: **Campo Grande** (22hr.; 2 per day 7:30-8pm; R$111); **Cuiabá** (26hr.; Tu-W 9am, Th-M 2 per day 9am-8pm; R$122); **Curitiba** (14hr.; 8pm; R$80); **Goiânia** (13hr.; 4 per day 7:45am-8pm; standard R$68, *executivo* R$85); **Salvador** (23hr.; 7pm; R$124); **São Paulo** (8hr.; 11 per day 8am-midnight; standard R$46, *leito* R$82). **Viação Penha** (☎3271 1019) goes to **Brasília** (11hr.; Su-F 4 per day 8:45-10:30pm, Sa 2 per day 9:15-10:30pm; R$82) and **Vitória** (8½hr.; 4 per day 8:45am-10:30pm; standard R$42, *semi-leito* R$55). **Viação Sandra** (☎3201 2927) runs to **Congonhas** (1½hr.; M-Th and Sa 3 per day 6:15am-2:15pm, F and Su 4 per day 6:15am-6:15pm; R$11) and **São João del-Rei** (3½hr.; M-Th 11 per day 6am-7pm, F 13 per day 6am-8pm, Sa 9 per day 6am-7pm, Su 2 per day 5-9pm; R$24). **Viação Util** (☎0800 702 0008) has buses to **Rio de Janeiro** (6hr.; 8 per day 8am-12:15am; standard R$35, *leito* R$58).

Trains: Estação Ferroviária, Pça. da Estação s/n (☎3273 5976). Open M-F 5:30am-5:30pm, Sa 5:30am-3:30pm, Su and holidays 5:30am-noon.

Public Transportation: A two-line subway system runs 5:45am-11pm.

Taxis: In the *centro* ☎3215 8081. In Mangabeiras ☎3287 0071.

ORIENTATION & PRACTICAL INFORMATION

Belo Horizonte's **historic center** consists of eight square blocks, each 120 meters long. Within this grid, streets running roughly north-south are usually named after Brazilian states or cities within Minas Gerais, while streets running roughly east-west are given indigenous names or named after national heroes. In addition, eight diagonal roads cut across this matrix, and the entire *centro* is surrounded by the circular **Avenida do Contorno.** The *rodoviária* is in the northern part of the *centro*. From the *centro* **Pampulha** is about 15 minutes north on **Avenida Antônio Carlos.**

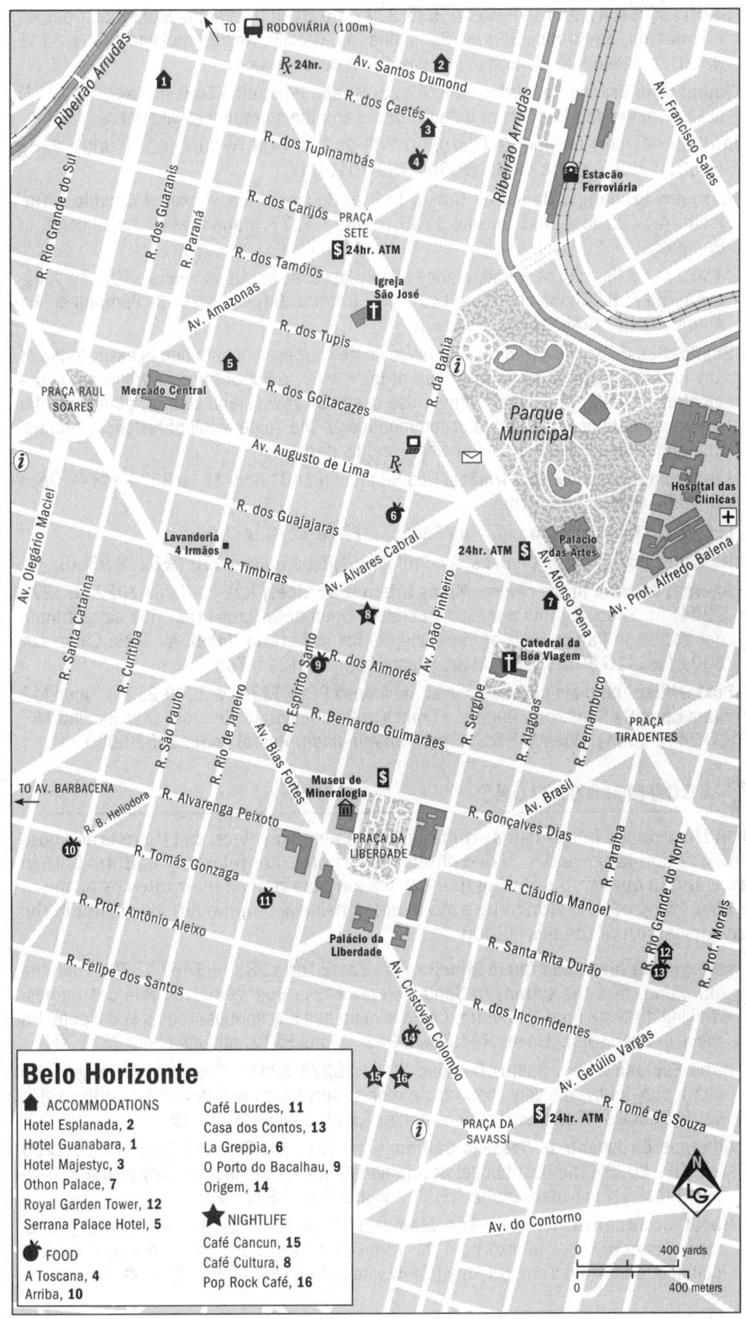
TO RODOVIÁRIA (100m)
Ribeirão Arrudas
Av. Santos Dumond
R. dos Caetés
R. dos Tupinambás
R. dos Carijós
PRAÇA SETE
24hr. ATM
R. dos Tamóios
Igreja São José
Av. Amazonas
R. dos Tupis
R. Rio Grande do Sul
R. dos Guaranis
R. Paraná
Estacão Ferroviária
Av. Francisco Sales
Parque Municipal
R. da Bahia
PRAÇA RAUL SOARES
Mercado Central
R. dos Goitacazes
Av. Augusto de Lima
Hospital das Clínicas
R. dos Guajajaras
Lavanderia 4 Irmãos
Palácio das Artes
24hr. ATM
Av. Olegário Maciel
R. Timbiras
Av. Álvares Cabral
Av. Afonso Pena
Av. Prof. Alfredo Balena
Av. João Pinheiro
Catedral da Boa Viagem
R. Santa Catarina
R. Curitiba
R. Espírito Santo
R. dos Aimorés
R. Bernardo Guimarães
R. Sergipe
R. Alagoas
R. Pernambuco
PRAÇA TIRADENTES
R. São Paulo
R. Rio de Janeiro
Av. Bias Fortes
Museu de Mineralogia
TO AV. BARBACENA
R. B. Heliodora
R. Alvarenga Peixoto
Av. Brasil
R. Gonçalves Dias
PRAÇA DA LIBERDADE
R. Tomás Gonzaga
R. Paraíba
R. Cláudio Manoel
R. Rio Grande do Norte
R. Prof. Antônio Aleixo
Palácio da Liberdade
R. Santa Rita Durão
R. Prof. Morais
R. Felipe dos Santos
Av. Cristóvão Colombo
R. dos Inconfidentes
Av. Getúlio Vargas
R. Tomé de Souza
24hr. ATM
PRAÇA DA SAVASSI
Av. do Contorno
LG
N
0
400 yards
0
400 meters
Belo Horizonte
ACCOMMODATIONS
Hotel Esplanada, 2
Hotel Guanabara, 1
Hotel Majestyc, 3
Othon Palace, 7
Royal Garden Tower, 12
Serrana Palace Hotel, 5
FOOD
A Toscana, 4
Arriba, 10
Café Lourdes, 11
Casa dos Contos, 13
La Greppia, 6
O Porto do Bacalhau, 9
Origem, 14
NIGHTLIFE
Café Cancun, 15
Café Cultura, 8
Pop Rock Café, 16

Tourist Office: Av. Afonso Pena 1055 (☎3277 7666), at the Parque Municipal. Open M-F 8am-7pm; Sa-Su 8am-3pm. In Pampulha, Av. Otácilio Negrão de Lima s/n (☎3441 9325), at Igreja São Francisco de Assis. Open daily 8am-6pm.

Tours: Ouro Branco Receptivo (☎3742 2368) and **Pampulha Turismo** (☎3372 7777) are recommended for tours of Belo Horizonte and the surrounding wilderness.

Airlines: Carriers include: **Gol** (☎0300 789 2121); **TAM** (☎0300 123 1000); **Varig** (☎0300 788 70000); **VASP** (☎0300 789 1010).

Currency Exchange: Banco do Brasil, in Pça. da Liberdade. **Portugal Câmbio e Turismo,** Av. Cel. José Dias Bicalho 1235 (☎3492 4277; viaportugal@hotmail.com), in Pampulha.

ATM: 24hr. ATMs can be found, among other places, at Av. Afonso Pena 1500; Av. Amazonas 527; R. Gonçalves Dias 1400; Av. Getúlio Vargas 1010. In Pampulha, Av. Antônio Carlos 6640 at Pça. Bagatelle.

Publications: The city's own *Guia Turístico* comes out every month and is easily found at any hotel or hostel. It includes a map of the *centro,* a list of tourist attractions, and a monthly calendar of cultural events. Also useful is www.guiabh.com.br, particularly for recommendations on food and accommodations. The guide is full of historical information about Belo Horizonte, its buildings, and its parks.

Laundromat: Lavanderia 4 Irmãos, Rua São Paulo 1401, loja 15 (☎3224 3484). Open M-F 8am-6pm, Sa 8am-1pm.

Late-Night Pharmacy: Araújo, Rua Curitiba 327 (☎3270 5000).

Hospital: Hospital das Clínicas, Av. Professor Alfredo Balena 110 (☎3248 9300).

Internet Access: In the *centro,* **Minas Internet Services,** Rua da Bahia 1022 (☎3222 2224), in Shopping Bahia is recommended. Open daily 9am-11pm. The closest Internet access to Pampulha is at Shopping del Rei in **Livraria Nobel,** Av. Pres. Carlos Luz 3001 (☎3415 8011). Open M-Sa 10am-10pm, Su 10am-7pm.

Post Office: The main post office is at Av. Afonso Pena 1270 (☎3249 2121). Open M-F 9am-6pm, Sa 9am-1pm. There is a branch in Pampulha, Av. Cel. José Dias Bicalho 187 (☎3491 1194). Open M-F 8:30-5pm, Sa 9am-noon. **Postal code:** 30530-000.

ACCOMMODATIONS

Belo Horizonte's hotels cater primarily to business travelers, and there is an abundance of mid-range and high-end hotels; these hotels are relatively uniform both in price and in quality, but during the low season may reduce their rates by as much as 60%. Many of Belo Horizonte's most inexpensive accommodations cluster in the area just south of the bus station.

Albergue da Juventude Chalé Mineiro, Rua Santa Luzia 288 (☎3467 1576). From the *rodoviária,* take the subway to Santa Tereza or take Bus #9801 on Rua dos Caetés. Walking distance from the *centro,* Chalé Mineiro has big, spotless rooms and a pool. No check-in after 10pm. Linens R$4. Towel R$1. Dorms R$12, non-members R$15. ❶

Hotel Esplanada, Av. Santos Dumond 304 (☎3273 5311). Excellent mid-range hotel with a cozy lobby and very comfortable rooms. Very near the *rodoviária. Quarto* singles R$29; doubles R$48. *Apartamento* singles R$39; doubles R$58. ❷

Albergue da Juventude Sossego da Pampulha (HI), Av. Cel. José Dias Bicalho 1258 (☎3491 8020). The best budget accommodation near Pampulha. They also rent bicycles. Breakfast included. Dorms R$22, non-members R$27. ❶

Hotel Guanabara, Av. Olegário Maciel 169 (☎3201 7387; www.hotelguanabarabh.com.br). Two blocks from the *rodoviária.* Basic but clean rooms. Breakfast included. Check-out 1pm. *Quartos* R$24, with bath R$33. AmEx/MC/V. ❶

Hotel Majestyc, Rua Espírito Santo 284 (☎3222 3390). Minimal rooms conveniently located near the *rodoviária,* but the area can sometimes be noisy. Hotel shares a building with the adjacent motel. Singles R$25; doubles with bath R$66. MC/V. ❷

Othon Palace, Av. Afonso Pena 1050 (☎0300 789 8087; central.reservas@othon.com.br). Luxury hotel famous for its spectacular views. Singles R$260; doubles R$300. ❺

Royal Garden Tower, Rua Rio Grande do Norte 1015 (☎0800 704 0022; www.royaltowers.com.br). Sleek, modern decor accents its comfortable, high-end accommodations. Singles R$130; doubles R$200. ❺

Pampulha Flat, Alameda das Latânias 1207 (☎3491 8080). Complete apartments a block from Av. Antônio Carlos and a short distance from the Lagoa da Pampulha. Singles R$73; doubles R$89. ❹

Serrana Palace Hotel, Rua Goitacazes 450 (☎3274 6020; www.hotelserrana.com.br). Centrally located, simple hotel with A/C, TV, pool, and sauna. Singles R$77; doubles R$88. AmEx/MC/V. ❹

FOOD

Belo Horizonte has Minas Gerais's broadest diversity of ethnic restaurants. Many restaurants are concentrated in the nightlife district of Savassi and also in the quieter, residential neighborhood Lourdes. A thorough list of restaurants can be found at www.guiabh.com.br, although it is not always up to date.

Casa Bonomi, Av. Afonso Pena 2600 (☎3261 3460). At the intersection of Afonso Pena and Rua Cláudio Manoel. This delightful corner bakery-turned-restaurant has everything from a quick snack to a full meal; you won't be disappointed. ❹

Casa dos Contos, Rua Rio Grande do Norte 1065 (☎3261 5853). A restaurant with a long tradition as a hangout for local intellectuals. Opens daily 11:30am. ❸

Chico do Churrasco, Rua Francisco Bicalho 2000 and 2094 (☎3454 4510 and 3413 3388). Take Bus #9403 from Av. Afonso Pena. This huge *churrascaria* became so popular that just to handle the meat-hungry crowds its owners opened another one down the street. Open Tu-F 5:30pm-1:30am, Sa-Su noon-1:30am. ❷

O Porto do Bacalhau, Rua Espírito Santo 1507 (☎3222 7300). This Portuguese restaurant's shady outdoor dining area tempts passersby to come inside and sample its variety of Portuguese favorites, including its namesake *bacalhau* (salt cod). Entrees R$25-50 for two. Open daily 11am-midnight. ❹

Sushi Naka, Rua Gonçalves Dias 92 (☎3287 2714). The city's most beloved Japanese restaurant is simple, straightforward, and always hopping. A sushi dinner will cost about R$35 a person. Open Tu-Su 11am-2pm, 6pm-midnight. AmEx/MC. ❺

Café Lourdes, Rua Tomás Gonzaga 189 (☎3291 0726). Sleek and tastefully decorated restaurant has an extensive wine list. Live jazz every W, Th, and Sa. Open M-F 6pm-late, Sa-Su noon-late. ❹

A Toscana, Rua Tupinambás 320 (☎3226 5640). A very popular kilo, with one of Belo Horizonte's largest selections of well-prepared food. Open daily 10:30am-3pm. ❷

La Greppia, Rua da Bahia 1196 (☎3273 2055). A legend in Belo Horizonte, this 24hr. restaurant features a popular dinnertime pasta *rodízio* (R$6). Be warned: while the restaurant is always open, the kitchen sometimes closes between chefs in the late afternoon and early morning. ❷

Arriba, at the corner of Rua Curitiba and Rua Tomás Gonzaga (☎3293 2262). Mexican food and international dishes in a setting which is at once sophisticated and comfortable. Open M-W 6pm-midnight, Th-Sa 6pm-1am, Su noon-11pm. ❹

ON THE MENU

FEIJOADA

Feijoada is really Brazil's national dish—a hearty, salty stew of black beans *(feijão)* simmered with pork, sausage, and other meats (whatever's left over at the end of the week—hence its popularity as a Saturday meal). Though now associated with traditional Mineiro cuisine and particularly popular in towns throughout Minas, it was first prepared in Rio (it's often called *feijoada Carioca*). It's typically eaten on Saturday as part of the *feijoada completa,* in which diverse culinary influences reflect Brazil's multicultural heritage.

The long, lingering meal begins with *caldo* (bean-based soup) and a few *caipirinhas*—or any cocktail made from *cachaça,* distilled since colonial days. *Feijoada* is served with white rice and sliced oranges, plus *farofa* (an indigenous dish of *manioc* flour baked with oil) and bitter *couve à mineira* (kale, popular with the Portuguese but typical of Mineiro cuisine). African influence is evident in both the spices used and the stew itself: in Brazil's old *fazendas* (plantations), slaves were only given kitchen scraps, and stews were the best way to make such paltry servings last.

A proper *feijoada* takes a full day to enjoy: the stock and beans must simmer for hours until they become tasty enough to eat. Thus many Brazilians head to restaurants for *feijoada,* where they can be seen happily devouring this quintessentially Brazilian feast.

Origem, Rua Tomé de Souza 1174 (☎3221 3222). Snack bar amidst Savassi's most happening clubs and restaurants. What it may lack in size it makes up for in class. Open M-F 9am-9pm, Sa 10am-2pm. ❸

SIGHTS

The **Parque Municipal** at Belo Horizonte's *centro* dates from the city's inception. Today, it houses the **Praça da Liberdade,** built in the 1890s to house the state's administrative buildings. The park is an excellent place to see a mix of architectural styles, including the late colonial **Palácio da Liberdade** and Niemeyer's modernist 1951 apartment complex. The nearby **Museu da Mineralogia,** Av. Bias Fortes 90, displays minerals from around the world. (☎3271 3415. Open Tu-Su 9am-5pm.) A few blocks away from the park is Belo Horizonte's first planned church, **Igreja São José.** Also of note is the **Catedral da Boa Viagem,** which was built over the altar of the original Belo Horizonte's Igreja Matriz de Nossa Senhora da Boa Viagem. The old Fazenda Leitão is today the **Museu Histórico Abílio Barreto,** home to colonial artworks. (Av. Prudente de Morais 202, south of the Rua Santa Caterina/Av. do Contorno intersection. ☎3277 8573. Open Tu-W and F-Su 10am-5pm; Th 10am-9pm.)

Oscar Niemeyer got his start in the **Pampulha** district, an excellent place to wander around to see the architect's early work. (Take bus #2004 from Pça. da Liberdade or Pça. Sete.) Pampulha's **Igreja São Francisco de Assis** includes Niemeyer's architecture, Burle Marx's landscaping, and a Cândido Portinari mosaic. (☎3441 9325. Open M-Sa 8am-6pm. R$1.) The curvy art gallery **Casa de Baile** (☎3277 7443; open Tu-S 9am-7pm) and casino-turned-museum **Museu de Arte da Pampulha** continue the neighborhood's artistic tradition. (Open daily 8am-5pm.)

The residents of Belo Horizonte chose as their city's symbol the **Serra do Curral.** At the mountains' feet lies the **Parque das Mangabeiras,** reached by Bus #4103 from Afonso Pena. Here you can explore any of three recreational areas. The park has excellent views of the city from the Mirante (Roteiro da Mata), beautiful natural lakes (Roteiro das Águas), and a bus that loops between all attractions (R$0.80). Outside the park is a *praça* that affords a view of which Pope John Paul II exclaimed, "What a beautiful horizon"—hence the *praça's* name, **Praça do Papa.** If you descend to the *praça's* right, you will encounter the famous **Rua do Amendoim,** which offers an interesting optical illusion for those traveling along it by car: turning your engine off at the beginning of the road and keeping the wheels straight will make your car appear to go uphill by itself.

NIGHTLIFE & ENTERTAINMENT

Belo Horizonte has more bars per capita than any other city in Brazil, and a correspondingly rich nightlife. The city is full of open-air bars, but most nightlife activity is concentrated in Savassi and Seis Pistas, which are both stocked with trendy clubs, bars, and restaurants. Fine arts events are hosted almost exclusively by **The Palácio das Artes,** Av. Afonso Pena 1537, which was designed by Niemeyer and completed in 1970. The center has three stages, three art galleries, and a movie room. More information on theater performances both at the Palácio and around the city can be found in the very helpful *PalcoBH*, published monthly.

Café Cultura, Rua da Bahia 1416 (☎3222 1347). A café and bar famous for its amazing desserts and known for a sophisticated clientele, who also come for the nightly live MPB. Open M-Th 7am-11:30pm, F-Sa 7am-3am.

Lapa Multshow, Rua Álvares Maciel 312 (☎3241 5953; www.lapamultshow.com.br). Off Av. Brasil a block before Pça. Floriano Peixoto. All live music, with *samba* every Thursday, *forró* every Sunday, and occasional rock and reggae; buy tickets in advance for better prices. Drinks R$4. Shows R$7-15. Open M-Sa 10pm late, Su 9pm-late.

Engenho de Minas, Av. Bernardo Monteiro 705 (☎3213 4666). Half a block from Hospital das Clínicas, down Av. Bernardo Monteiro, the continuation of Rua Professor Morais. You are guaranteed a good show here–most nights feature at least 3-4 bands–in either of its two showrooms or from one of its many quiet corners, which are perfect spots to sit down for dinner or drinks. Entrees R$10-50. Drinks R$4. Cover R$3-12. Open Tu-Sa 6pm-late.

Redondo: Casa de Chopp, Av. Otacílio Negrão de Lima 855 (☎3441 9604), on the Lagoa da Pampulha. This waterfront restaurant and bar is a spectacular place to watch the sunset or see the moon's reflection in the lake. Entrees R$5. Live music F-Sa 9:30pm, Su 6pm. Cover Su R$5 men. Open daily 9am-1am.

Café Cancun, Rua Sergipe 1208 (☎3287 3223), in Savassi. By day a restaurant but by night a happening club, with live pop-rock every Wednesday and on the second Tuesday of every month. 18+. Cover R$15-30.

Pop Rock Café, Rua Sergipe 1211 (☎3284 8006; www.poprockcafe.br). Belo Horizonte's hottest hot spot. Tu-Th shows R$10-25. F-Sa cover R$10-30. Open Tu-Sa 8:30pm-late.

SHOPPING

The **Mercado Central** contains over 400 stores and is an excellent place to find regional foods and crafts. The **Feira de Arte e Artesanato da Afonso Pena** (also known locally as the **Feira Hippie**) fills the broad Av. Afonso Pena. (www.feirabh.com.br. Su 8am-4pm.) A **fair** with arts, crafts, and regional food for sale is held every weekend in Pça. São Francisco de Assis. (Sa 9am-5pm.)

OURO PRETO ☎31

Ouro Preto dazzles first-time visitors with its winding cobblestone streets and extravagant churches, and was the first location in Brazil declared a UNESCO World Heritage Site. Pça. Tiradentes is the soul of this dynamic and intimate small town. Paulistano *bandeirantes* reached this mountainous region in the late 17th century. When they discovered that the area's black stones contained gold, they built a cluster of mining settlements around the base of Pico do Italocoloni. Today beautiful views of this peak can be had from nearly anywhere in the city. The discovery of gold here changed the course of Brazilian history: the colony's economic focus shifted away from sugarcane production, and the newly wealthy Southeast gave the port of Rio de Janeiro a new importance. Ouro Preto's wealth and constant activity created a new way of life in Brazil: the urban. Previous settlements had been isolated plantations, but full-fledged cities soon developed, and with them artistic and intellectual activity. Many early examples of such endeavors can be seen in Ouro Preto's numerous churches. The colony's newfound wealth dramatically altered the relationship between Brazil and Portugal, as gold led Portugal to take a more active interest in its colony. In 1719 the crown imposed a hefty tax (the *quinta*) and expelled the Jesuits—the crown's powerful rival for control in the colony—in an attempt to consolidate its hold over Brazil and its wealth.

When Ouro Preto's mines began to run dry in the 1760s, both the urban culture that had been created by Ouro Preto's mining wealth and the crown's desire for continuous mining revenue seemed well entrenched; it did not take long for these to conflict, and consequently Brazil's most important independence movement—the *inconfidência mineira*—began in Ouro Preto. Its leader was the dentist Joaquim José da Silva Xavier, known popularly as Tiradentes (literally, "tooth-puller"), but his plan to imprison the governor and fight the Portuguese was never realized: the leaders were betrayed and apprehended and the movement disbanded. Twelve of the leaders were sentenced to death, and the rest exiled to Africa; every one had their sentences commuted except for Tiradentes, who was *enforcado* (drawn and quartered) in the square that today bears his name.

TRANSPORTATION

Buses: Terminal Rodoviário 8 de Julho, Rua Padre Rolim 661 (☎3559 3252). Luggage storage R$2.50 per 24hr. Buses go to: **Belo Horizonte** (2hr.; M-Sa 16 per day 6am-8pm, Su 17 per day 7am-9:30pm; R$11); **Brasília** (11hr.; 7:30pm; R$65); **Rio de Janeiro** (7½hr.; 10pm; R$35); **Santa Bárbara** (2½hr.; M-Sa 7:30am; R$12); **São Paulo** (11hr.; 3 per day 7am-8pm; R$57); **Vitória** (11hr.; 9pm; R$36).

Public Transportation: City buses cost R$0.60 and run 6am-11pm. The Rodoviária/Padre Faria line has its westernmost stop at the *rodoviária* and easternmost stop at Capela do Padre Faria; going both ways it stops at Pça. Tiradentes.

Taxis: Taxi points are on the northwest side of Pça. Tiradentes, in front of Igreja São Francisco de Assis, and at Pça. Reinaldo Alves de Brito. Taxi numbers listed by the city government are: ☎3551 1248; 3551 2675; 3551 1977; 3551 2824; 3551 1662.

Car Rental: Localiza, Rua Amália Bernhauss 11 (☎3551 5131; 24hr. reservations at 0800 99 2000).

ORIENTATION & PRACTICAL INFORMATION

Praça Tiradentes lies in Ouro Preto's *centro*, where Antônio Dias Parish and Pilar Parish meet. From Museu da Inconfidência, Antônio Dias Parish will be on your right down **Rua Cláudio Manuel,** and Pilar Parish will be on your left down **Rua Conde do Bombadela,** which is also called **Rua Direita.** The city's monuments are evenly distributed between the two parishes, but most commerce takes place within Pilar Parish. Rua Direita and **Rua São José** are Ouro Preto's principle roads for pedestrians, and even though Ouro Preto's hilly terrain can make walking difficult Ouro Preto is a city best seen on foot.

Tourist Office: Pça. Tiradentes 41 (☎3559 3269). José de Carmo (☎9961 3355) and Alexandre (☎9961 2606) provide information in English, French, or Spanish. **Secretariat de Turismo,** Rua Cláudio Manoel 61 (☎3559 3201). Information can also be found

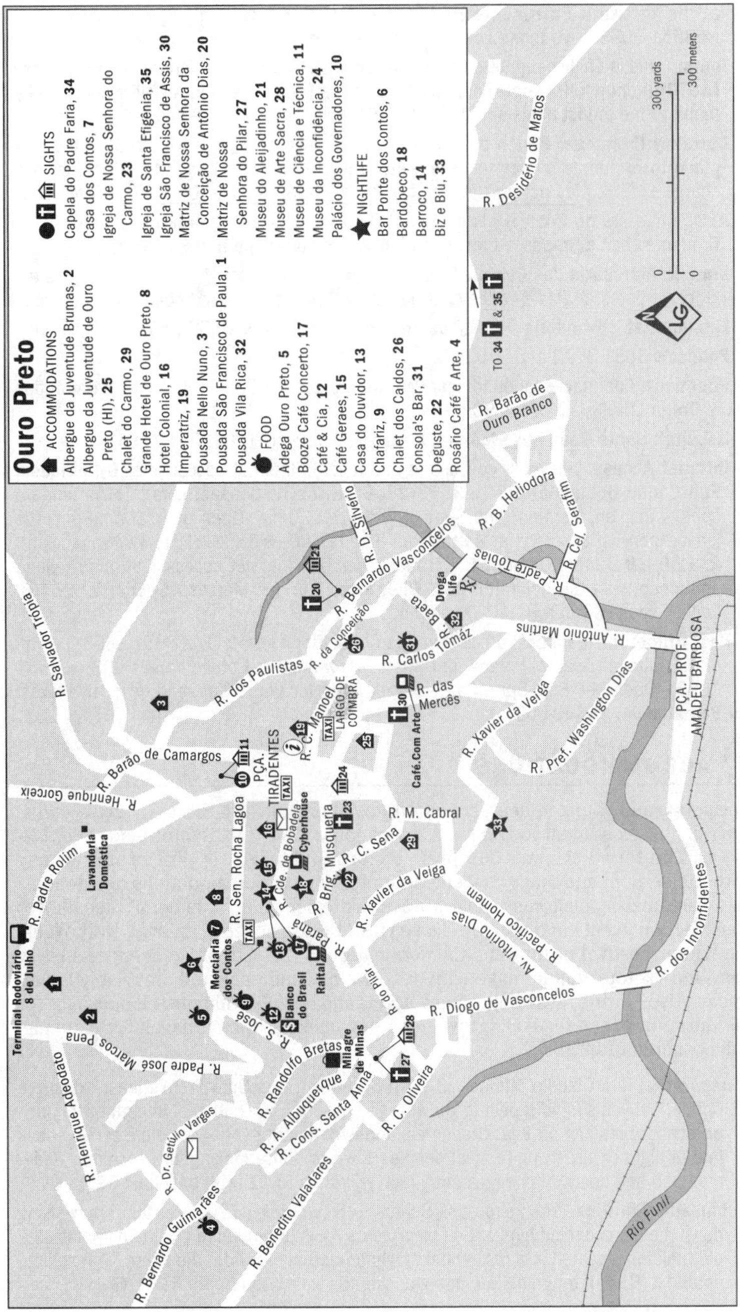

Ouro Preto

ACCOMMODATIONS
Albergue da Juventude Brumas, **2**
Albergue da Juventude de Ouro Preto (HI), **25**
Chalet do Carmo, **29**
Grande Hotel de Ouro Preto, **8**
Hotel Colonial, **16**
Imperatriz, **19**
Pousada Nello Nuno, **3**
Pousada São Francisco de Paula, **1**
Pousada Vila Rica, **32**

FOOD
Adega Ouro Preto, **5**
Booze Café Concerto, **17**
Café & Cia, **12**
Café Geraes, **15**
Casa do Ouvidor, **13**
Chafariz, **9**
Chalet dos Caldos, **26**
Consola's Bar, **31**
Deguste, **22**
Rosário Café e Arte, **4**

SIGHTS
Capela do Padre Faria, **34**
Casa dos Contos, **7**
Igreja de Nossa Senhora do Carmo, **23**
Igreja de Santa Efigênia, **35**
Igreja São Francisco de Assis, **30**
Matriz de Nossa Senhora da Conceição de Antônio Dias, **20**
Matriz de Nossa Senhora do Pilar, **27**
Museu do Aleijadinho, **21**
Museu de Arte Sacra, **28**
Museu de Ciência e Técnica, **11**
Museu da Inconfidência, **24**
Palácio dos Governadores, **10**

NIGHTLIFE
Bar Ponte dos Contos, **6**
Bardobeco, **18**
Barroco, **14**
Biz e Biu, **33**

SOUTHEAST

at the **Instituto Patrimônio Histórico e Artístico Nacional,** Pça. Tiradentes 33 (☎3551 3099; www.iphan.gov.br), which cares for national heritage sites.

Tours: Tours in English organized by the **Associação de Guias de Turismo de Ouro Preto (AGTOP)** for up to 9 people cost R$70 per 4hr. or R$110 per 8hr. AGTOP guides can be found at the tourist office and the *rodoviária.*

Currency Exchange: Banco do Brasil, Rua São José 189 (☎3551 2663) is the only place to exchange money in Ouro Preto. They will only exchange traveler's checks, charge a US$20 fee per transaction, and have a US$200 limit. Open M-F 11am-4pm.

ATM: There are no 24hr. ATMs in central Ouro Preto, but the northwest corner of Pça. Tiradentes has a Bradesco branch, and a slew of banks line Rua São José.

Market: Mercearia dos Contos, Pça. Reinaldo Alves de Brito 81 (☎3551 3266), is the grocery nearest to Pça. Tiradentes. Open M-Sa 8am-7pm, Su and holidays 8am-noon.

Laundromat: Lavanderia Doméstica, Rua Pe. Rolim 234 (☎3552 5501).

Police: ☎3551 3222 or 3551 3076.

Pharmacy: Pharmacies abound near Pça. Tiradentes, but Ouro Preto's only 24hr. option is **Droga Life,** Rua Alagoas 90 (☎3551 4723).

Hospital: Santa Casa Misericórdia, Rua José Moringa 620 (☎3551 1766).

Internet Access: The most convenient and reliable Internet access is at **Cyberhouse,** Rua Conde Bobadela 109 (☎3552 2808; www.cyberhousebr.com). The attendant speaks English, German, and Spanish. R$5 per 30min. Open daily 10am-8pm. The least-expensive access is at **Raitai,** Rua Paraná 100 (☎3551 5151; www.raitai.com). R$1.50 per 30min. Open daily 8:30am-10pm. For Internet access with more refined ambience, visit the delightful **Café.Com Arte,** Rua das Mercês 45 (☎3552 2579). English spoken. Open Tu-Su 10am-6pm.

Post Office: The main post office is at Rua Conde Bobadela 180 (☎3551 1855) just off of Rua Direita. Open M-F 9am-5pm. There is a branch at Getúlio Vargas 233 (☎3551 1020). Open M-F 8am-5pm, Sa 9am-2pm. Both locations can send or receive faxes. **Postal code:** 35400-000.

ACCOMMODATIONS

The young and young-at-heart can often stay at one of Ouro Preto's many *repúblicas* (single-sex student lodgings). A list of contact information for many *repúblicas* can be found at www.ouropreto.etc.br/republicas.htm. Prices vary widely with the season, and many low-end and mid-range accommodations decide rates on a customer-by-customer basis; always ask to see your room before deciding to stay. Certain events and holidays leave Ouro Preto packed: Carnaval, Holy Week, the Winter Festival in July, and the period around the 12th of October are all very busy and visitors should make early reservations and expected drastically higher prices. Also, during these times many hotels and hostels will only sell packages for the duration of the festival; a low-end 5-day package for Carnaval, for example, will cost about R$250.

Imperatriz, Rua Cláudio Manoel 23 (☎3551 5435). It is Ouro Preto's least expensive option, but you should expect to get what you pay for. You can't beat Imperatriz for price or location: it's just off Pça. Tiradentes, and is perfect for young travelers coming back late at night or just trying to meet people. However, those looking for peace may find it cramped and noisy. Kitchen. Laundry room. *Quartos* R$12, with breakfast R$15. ❶

Pousada Vila Rica, Rua Felipe dos Santos 145 (☎3551 4729). Get there by walking down the steps behind Igreja São Francisco de Assis. Beautiful rooms in an immaculate old building. Located in a residential neighborhood not far from the *centro,* but splurge on a taxi (R$5) if returning late at night. *Quartos* with TV and bath R$20. ❶

Camping Clube do Brasil, Rodovia dos Inconfidentes, km 92 (☎3551 1799). 1½km from the *centro.* Camping R$12.30 per person. ❶

Albergue da Juventude Brumas (HI), Rua Pe. José Marcos Pena 68 (☎3551 7809; http://brumasonline.hpg.com.br), uphill off of Rua São José. Friendly and informative staff, a lively common area, and an amazing view make Brumas a great place to stay. Breakfast included. Dorms R$18, non-members R$45. Cash only. ❶

Pousada São Francisco de Paula, Rua Padre José Marcos Pena 202 (☎3551 3456; pousadas@hotmail.com), a short walk uphill from the bus station. This picturesque *pousada* has a tidy lawn and is popular with foreign tourists. Breakfast included. 24hr. reception. Dorms R$20. Doubles with private bath R$25. Cash only. ❶

Chalet do Carmo, Rua Costa Sena 205 (☎3551 2393). Follow the path running to the left of Museu da Inconfidência until you reach this cozy hotel. Singles R$20; doubles with private bath R$50. ❶

Albergue da Juventude de Ouro Preto (HI), Rua Costa Sena 30 (☎3551 6705). The nearest HI hostel to the *centro.* Dorms R$20, non-members R$25. ❶

Pousada Nello Nuno, Rua Camilo de Brito 59 (☎3551 3375; http://br.geocities.com/pousadanellonuno/index.htm). Small, intimate, and affordable rooms with TV and private baths. Singles R$45; doubles R$60.

Hotel Colonial, Travesa Cônego Camilo Veloso 26 (☎3551 3133; www.hotelcolonial.com.br). Another excellent mid-range option located just off Rua Direita with cozy rooms. Breakfast included. Singles R$50; doubles R$80. ❸

Grande Hotel de Ouro Preto, Rua Senador Rocha Lagoa 164 (☎3551 1488; www.hoteldouropreto.com.br). Architecture by Oscar Niemeyer and sophisticated minimalist decor. Breakfast included. Singles R$79, with view R$99; doubles R$95, with view R$128. AmEx/MC/V. ❹

FOOD

Most restaurants are concentrated on Rua Direita and Rua São José. Kilos and buffets are popular with locals, and often provide the best options for vegetarians. Many restaurants are closed on Monday.

Chafariz, Rua São José 167 (☎3551 2828). Specializing in Mineiro cuisine, this lunch-only buffet is a local favorite. R$18 per person. Open daily noon-5pm. AmEx/MC/V. ❸

Casa do Ouvidor, Rua Conde de Bobadela 42 (☎3551 2141; www.casadoouvidor.com.br). Serves excellent Mineiro food with portions for two (around R$20). Open daily 11am-3pm and 7-10pm. ❷

Deguste, Rua Coronel Alves 15 (☎3551 6363; www.restaurantedeguste.com.br). Intimate and romantic place to sample the famous local cuisine, considered the traditional homestyle cooking of Brazil. Entrees R$15. Live MPB F-Sa nights. Open daily noon-4pm and 6pm-late. AmEx/MC/V. ❷

Adega Ouro Preto, on Rua Teixeira Amaral (☎3551 4171). Very popular all-you-can-eat charges R$10 for the buffet or R$14 per kg; for most appetites the kilo rate will be more economical. Open daily 11am-5pm and 7pm-late. MC/V. ❷

Café & Cia, Rua São José 187 (☎3551 6786). Popular both with locals and with international visitors. Mineiro cuisine, served in per-kilo style at lunch and with many cheeses at dinner. Open M-Th noon-4pm and 6pm-late, F-Su noon-late. ❶

Café Geraes, Rua Conde Bobadela 122 (☎3551 5097; www.cafegeraesouropreto.com; cafegeraes@bol.com.br). Welcoming establishment perfect for a light afternoon snack; try the salmon crêpe (R$8). Entrees R$15. Live jazz and MPB Sa nights. Open daily 11am-11pm. MC. ❷

Booze Café Concerto, Travessa Cônego Camilo Veloso 51 (☎3551 1482), with entrance at Rua Direita 42, below Casa do Ouvidor. An Arab restaurant turned café turned scotch bar with sweets of all sorts. Try the special *café concerto* (R$6.50). Live MPB F-Sa nights. Open daily noon-late. DC/MC/V. ❷

Rosário Café e Arte, Largo do Rosário 99 (☎3551 5097). A small café crammed with works by local artists; nothing remarkable, but everything just right. The specialty is *café rosário,* made with *jabuticaba* liquor (R$5). ❷

Consola's Bar, Rua da Conceição 18 (☎3551 4175). An excellent kilo and one of the few good dining options in Antônio Dias Parish. R$10.50 per kg. Open Th-Tu 11am-3pm and 6pm-late. ❷

Chalet dos Caldos, Rua Carlos Tomáz 33 (☎3551 3992; chaletdoscaldos@uaimail.com.br). Affordable, widely-recommended, and among the few good dining options in restaurant-starved Antônio Dias Parish; excellent *caldos* (R$3). Open Tu-Su 7-11:30pm. ❷

SIGHTS

AROUND ANTÔNIO DIAS PARISH

MATRIZ DE NOSSA SENHORA DA CONCEIÇÃO DE ANTÔNIO DIAS: 1727-1770. Antônio Dias Parish's principal church, the Matriz is a lavish example of counter-revolutionary baroque zeal. It was built where Antônio Dias (the first *bandeirante* to strike gold) had built his chapel, and like most churches of the period it has a simple exterior which hides an overpoweringly ornate interior. Aleijadinho (p. 25) frequented this church, and his gravestone has been integrated into the flooring. The Matriz also houses **Museu do Aleijadinho** (☎3551 4661). *(Open Tu-Sa 8:30-11:45am and 1:30-4:45pm, Su noon-4:45pm. R$4, which also covers admission to Igreja São Francisco de Assis.)*

CAPELA DO PADRE FARIA: 1701-1710. The oldest standing church in Ouro Preto was built as an outpost of Padre Faria, a priest and an original *bandeirante.* The Padre took the image of Nossa Senhora do Rosário (currently mounted at the church's right) when he went to perform masses in places lacking a church. There is an outdoor entrance near the side altar, and the tower separated from the primary structure reflects an older construction style. The tower bell was brought to Brasília in 1969 for the capital's inauguration, where it was rung in honor of Tiradentes. *(Take the "Padre Faria" bus from the southeast corner of Pça. Tiradentes. Open 8:30am-4:30pm. R$2, which also grants admission to Igreja de Santa Efigênia.)*

IGREJA DE SANTA EFIGÊNIA: 1733-1762. Reputedly built by the legendary Chico Rei, who is said to have been an African king sold into slavery along with the rest of his nation, and brought to work the gold mines of Ouro Preto. There he saved enough gold to buy his own freedom, bought a decaying mine and struck enough gold to purchase his nation's freedom. Igreja de Santa Efigênia was supposedly built with gold from his mine, and gold washed from the hair of slaves who had worked in the mines. Several famous artists worked on its construction, including Francisco Xavier de Brito and Manuel Francisco Lisboa. The church offers breathtaking views from the top of its very imposing staircase. *(Open 8:30am-4:30pm. R$2, which also grants admission to Capela do Padre Faria.)*

AROUND PILAR PARISH

MATRIZ DE NOSSA SENHORA DO PILAR: 1711-1733. Pilar Parish's main church is the most ornate in Minas Gerais and the second most ornate church in Brazil. Unlike most churches, it was not built on a pedestal, and its unusually complex exterior facade demonstrates later architectural influences. About 434kg of gold and 400kg of silver went into its construction, mostly in the elaborate interior. The Matriz also houses **Museu de Arte Sacra.** *(Open M-Sa 9am-10:45am and noon-4:45pm. R$4, which also grants admission to São Francisco de Paula.)*

CASA DOS CONTOS: 1787. This was the home of tax collector João Rodrigues Macedo until he fell into debt to the crown. The government then confiscated his house and used it to store gold and hold prisoners; the *inconfidente* Claudio Manuel da Costa was jailed here until he committed suicide. Today, the Casa dos Contos houses a permanent exhibition on the history of Brazilian money, a large collection of period pieces, and a sizable archive of important documents. Among these is the Livro de Ouro, a collection of signatures beginning with that of Emperor Dom Pedro II. *(Open Tu-Sa 12:30-5:30pm, Su and holidays 9am-3pm. R$1.)*

AROUND PRAÇA TIRADENTES

IGREJA SÃO FRANCISCO DE ASSIS: 1765-1810. Built by the Ordem Terceira de São Francisco, Igreja de São Francisco de Assis is among Brazil's most beautiful churches. Its curved, ornamented facade is unlike the period's typically flat facades, and the church's architecture reflects the influence of rococo on Mineiro baroque. It was built by Aleijadinho before he became crippled, and the ceilings were painted by Manuel da Costa Ataíde. *(Open daily 8:30-11:45am and 1:30-4:45pm. Mass Sa 7pm. R$4, which also grants admission to Museu do Aleijadinho.)*

IGREJA DE NOSSA SENHORA DO CARMO: 1766-1776. This church was built by the Carmelites and can be seen from anywhere in the city. Originally designed by Manuel da Costa Ataíde, this church is primarily Aleijadinho's work, who did the side altars and revised the overall plan. Its simple interior reflects the later phases of baroque. *(Open Tu-Su 1-4:45pm. R$1.)*

MUSEU DA INCONFIDÊNCIA: 1785-1855. This masterpiece of secular colonial architecture overlooking the Tiradentes monument was erected 1892-94 in the old Casa de Câmera e Cadeia. The *câmera* (assembly) was upstairs, and the *cadeia* (jail) was downstairs; in places the walls are up to 2m thick, and most doors and windows have iron bars. On the ground floor there is a mausoleum with the remains of several *inconfidentes*. *(☎3551 1121. Open Tu-Su noon-5:30pm. R$5. Free tours in Portuguese can be arranged M-F by calling ☎3351 1378.)*

PALÁCIO DOS GOVERNADORES & MUSEU DA CIÊNCIA E TÉCNICA. Governor Gomes Freiore de Andrade requested its construction and saw it inaugurated around 1750. The Palácio housed the governors of Minas Gerais until the state capital was moved to Belo Horizonte in 1897, and accordingly the building was walled off from the *praça* for the governor's protection. Today it houses **Museu de Ciência e Técnica,** which covers the history of mining and precious metals. *(Pça. Tiradentes 20. ☎3559 3118; museuct@ouropreto.feop.com.br. Open Tu-F noon-5pm, Sa-Su and holidays 9am-3pm. R$4.)*

NIGHTLIFE & ENTERTAINMENT

The student lodgings called *repúblicas* blast music day and night and are Ouro Preto's most popular places for weekend dancing and partying. The rest of Ouro Preto's nightlife is concentrated aroud Pça. Tiradentes and the uphill half of Rua Direita. At night the many people passing in and out of the bars here slow automobile traffic to a standstill, and the activity continues all the way down Rua São José. The area has options for people of all ages, but a predominantly young crowd keeps the *praça* hopping well into the night.

Those seeking schedules of classical music performances should contact Museu do Oratório and Igreja Nossa Senhora da Conceição de Antônio Dias (☎3551 4661), as both have regular concerts. The Federal University of Ouro Preto (UFOP) also has a wide variety of cultural programs, ranging from music, dance, and movies to workshops and theater. The biweekly Feira de Arte e Artesanato da Pça. da UFOP has activities for children, live music, and local arts and crafts for sale. (Sa 10am-5pm.) The Pro-Reitoria da Extensão publishes a monthly calendar of UFOP's cultural programs. (☎3559 1358; proex@ufop.br.)

Centro Acadêmico da Escola de Minas (CAEM), Pça. Tiradentes (☎3551 2452; caem@em.ufop.br). Ouro Preto's closest approximation to a traditional nightclub. The upper floor's large gymnasium-like room fills up around 2am. Th features MPB, *forró,* and other Brazilian styles. Open Th-Sa 11pm-6am. Cover R$3 women, R$5 men.

Bar Ponte dos Contos, Rua São José 56 (☎3552 6352). This bar lets its music spill into the street to attract passersby upstairs. A relaxed vibe predominates both inside and outside on the bar's vast veranda. On Fridays and Saturdays a sizable crowd gathers to listen to live MPB and drink beer, and on Sundays the bar becomes a popular *forró* club with dancing outdoors. Open Su-Th 9am-11pm, F-Sa 9am-2am. Cash only.

Bardobeco, Travessa do Arieira 15. Tucked in a quiet alley off of Rua Direita, this small bar is quiet and classy and always has the soft strum of a live guitar in the background. Bardobeco has a large selection of local *cachaças*. Open M-Th 6-11pm, F 6pm-1:30am, Sa noon-1:30am, Su noon-11pm.

Barroco, Rua Conde de Bobadela 106 (☎3551 3032). For 30 years, this bar has been the center of activity on Rua Direita. Everyone in Ouro Preto comes here, but it is particularly popular among college students. Open daily 9am-midnight.

Biz e Biu, Rua Xavier da Viega 315 (☎3551 4263). Even though it's a bit out of the way, Biz e Biu is extremely popular among local college students. Wednesdays see big crowds—they come for *videoke*—and most Fridays and Saturdays feature live music. Take a cab (R$5). Open daily 7am-2am. Full kitchen M-F after 4pm, Sa-Su after 1pm.

FESTIVALS & EVENTS

Early January brings numerous *congado* bands to Ouro Preto for the annual **Festa do Congado,** and Ouro Preto's street **Carnaval**—one of Brazil's best—and **Semana Santa** are also famous. During Semana Santa the custom of *enfeitando* (decorating) the cobblestone streets lasts throughout the night. Locally, the death of Tiradentes (April 21) is commemorated with political and popular events at Pça. Tiradentes. The locals celebrate **Dia de Santa Cruz** every May 3 by decorating all the city's crucifixes. In July the city swells with students visiting for the **Festival de Inverno,** a cultural event featuring three weeks of shows, exhibitions, and workshops. **October 12** celebrates the founding of the Federal University of Ouro Preto; alumni return for a week of wild partying.

SHOPPING

For chess sets, figurines, vases, and other souvenirs made from the rock so typical of Mineiro baroque, head to the **Largo de Coimbra Soapstone Market,** which operates in the Largo de Coimbra in front of Igreja São Francisco de Assis. (Open daily 9am-6pm.) Items range from R$2 to R$300. Also of interest are the semi-precious stones that can be found in stores throughout Ouro Preto's historic district, particularly in and around Pça. Tiradentes. Ouro Preto is also known for its *cachaça;* locals recommend **Milagre de Minas,** Rua Antônio de Albuquerque 18 (☎3551 1429).

CONGONHAS ☎31

At the highest point of the small city of Congonhas sits the **Santuário do Bom Jesus de Matosinhos**–one of South America's most impressive religious monuments—the presence of which hints at Congonhas's long and deep-seated religious traditions. The Santuário's unforgettable views of the surrounding mountains and its serenity have for two centuries drawn pilgrims from around the country; they come by the hundreds of thousands during the annual **Jublieu,** held September 7-14. Furthermore, the Santuário contains the world's largest collection of baroque statues and some of Aleijadinho's finest work.

TRANSPORTATION. **Buses** run to Belo Horizonte (1½hr.; M-Sa 16 per day 6am-8:45pm, Su 17 per day 6am-9:30pm; R$11), São João del-Rei (1½hr.; 6-7 per day 7:30am-8:20pm; R$14), São Paulo (10hr.; daily 3:18pm; R$50.25), and Rio de Janeiro (8hr.; daily 11:40pm; R$29). From the *rodoviária* a bus marked "Basílica" takes a convoluted route that eventually stops at the Santuário (25min.). For a taxi, call ☎3731 1043 or 1731 1237.

ORIENTATION & PRACTICAL INFORMATION. The main commercial street, **Avenida Júlia Kubitschek,** connects the *rodoviária* to the *centro* and **Praça Juscelino Kubitschek.** Most of the city's religious monuments lie uphill on either side of the *centro;* from the *rodoviária* the **Santuário** is at the top of the hill on the left. From the *centro*, walk up **Rua Bom Jesus,** the city's main historic street.

The **tourist office** is on Av. Júlia Kubitschek just over the bridge near the *rodoviária.* (☎3731 1300 ext. 208. Open M-F 8am-6pm, Sa-Su 9am-5pm). Several banks are near Pça. Juscelino Kubitschek, but only **Caixa Econômica Federal,** Rua Dr. Mário Rodrigues Pereira 58 (☎3731 1040), has **24hr. ATMs.** There is no currency exchange in Congonhas. A supermarket, **Supermercado Tradição,** and pharmacy, **Drogaria Congonhas do Campo,** Pça. Portugal 10 (☎3731 1486), can be found at the base of the hill that descends to the *centro* from the Santuário. The **Hospital Bom Jesus,** Rua Padre Leonardo 147 (☎3731 1820), is in the *centro* and a block from Av. Júlia Kubitschek. On the same hill as the pharmacy, there is free **Internet access** at Casa da Juventude, Rua Bom Jesus 32. Visitors must bring a photocopy of an ID in order to register, and once registered are limited to 1hr. per day. (☎3731 1490. Open M-F 7am-7pm, Sa 7am-1pm.) The **post office** is at Pça. Juscelino Kubitschek 35. (☎3731 2785.) **Postal code:** 36415-000.

ACCOMMODATIONS & FOOD. Lodging and restaurants concentrate around the Santuário and along a few blocks of Av. Júlia Kubitschek between Pça. Juscelino Kubitschek and the *rodoviária.* With a heavenly location next to the Basílica, **Hotel Colonial ❸,** Pça. da Basílica 76, offers simple but solid accommodations in a beautiful old building; its far more comfortable *apartamentos* cost little more than its ordinary rooms. (☎3731 1834. *Quartos* R$25. *Apartamentos* R$30.) The town's most inexpensive lodging is found at **Hotel Freitas ❷,** Av. Marechal Floriano Peixoto 69. From Pça. Juscelino Kubitschek, walk down the pedestrian-only street and turn right. (☎3731 1543. *Quartos* R$12, with bath R$15.) **Hotel Max Mazza ❸,** Av. Júlia Kubitschek 410, offers small but well-decorated rooms several blocks toward the *rodoviária* from Pça. Juscelino Kubitschek. (☎3731 1970. Singles R$36.) **Camping do Parque da Cachoeira ❶,** is in a well landscaped park that is itself an attraction, and draws visitors from all over the region. (☎3731 1911. Camping R$5 per person.) For fine dining near the Santuário, **Cova do Daniel ❸,** Pça. da Basílica 76, offers regional food and excellent decor underneath Hotel Colonial. Entrees for two average R$25. (☎3731 1834. Open Su-Th 9am-8pm, F-Sa 9am-10pm.) Just across the street **Casa da Ladeira ❷** specializes in regional food and pizza (R$11-15). The *centro's* most popular restaurant is **Brasa Grill ❷**, Pça. Juscelino Kubitschek 14, 2nd fl. It serves good food for R$12 per kg, and in addition has a full menu and live music most weekend nights; it is very much the center of Congonhas's nightlife. (☎3731 1799.)

SIGHTS. The story of the **Santuário do Bom Jesus de Matosinhos** begins with a Portuguese miner who believed he had been healed by Senhor Bom Jesus de Matosinhos, to whom he had pledged to build a temple in exchange for a cure. True to his word, the miner planted a cross atop the hill and began gathering donations. Construction of the Basílica began in 1757 and it still contains the miner's cross today. In front of the Basílica are six famous chapels that together contain the stations of the cross in sculptures prepared by Aleijadinho (see **Sculpture,** p. 25) and painted by Manuel da Costa Ataíde (see **Painting,** p. 26). The images were completed between 1796 and 1799, but as the chapel would not be completed for several more decades, the statues were warehoused in the interim; today two of the original statues are missing, likely stolen while in storage. The **first station** is of the Last Supper: it was also the only station completed during the period that Aleijadinho was in Congonhas. Of note are the feet missing from some statues, and also the piglet with which Aleijadinho replaced the bread, reflecting the regional traditions of Minas Gerais. In the **second station** is a statue of Peter, repositioned in a 1957 restoration, when a reexamination of the sculpture led to the conclusion that Aleijadinho had meant for Peter to be sitting rather than kneeling. After the stations were completed in 1819, a shortage of funds led work on the chapels to stop until 1964. Even then the original plan for seven chapels was revised and economized; the builders combined two of the original stations into what is now the **fourth station.** In the **fifth station** Christ's eyes are made of specially imported porcelain, but the dwarf next to Christ and the soldier in the background were only included here since the 1957 restoration; previously, they had been placed in other chapels. The **sixth station,** the crucifixion, is a good example of Aleijadinho's subtlety: the facial expressions of the two thieves crucified with Christ distinguish the good thief from the bad thief. Just in front of the Basílica are the **12 prophets** standing on pedestals placed around the stairway. (☎3731 3100. The prophets and chapels can be viewed anytime, but the Basílica is only open Tu-Su 6am-6pm. Free guided tour in Portuguese must be booked a day in advance). The nearby **Sala dos Milagres** contains an always fascinating and perpetually changing display of the pictures, notes, and art left by people thanking Senhor Bom Jesus de Matosinhos for assistance, asking for his help, or paying him homage. Just next to the Basílica is a circular building called the **Romaria.** The church funded its construction in the 1930s to house poor families on their Jubileu pilgrimages to Congonhas, but when the building changed hands in the 1960s everything but its two towers and their connecting arch was demolished. In its place was to rise a luxury hotel to house those who came to be healed by the legendary faith healer Zé Arigó, who attracted many failed by traditional medicine. Zé Arigó died, however, and with him died the plans for a luxury hotel. In 1995 the Romaria was rebuilt and it now houses the Fundação Municipal de Cultura e Turismo, as well as **Museu de Mineralogia e Arte Sacra.** (Open M-F 7am-6pm, Sa-Su and holidays 9am-5pm. Free.) Along the historic Rua Bom Jesus are **Igreja de São José** and **Museu da Memória de Congonhas.** (Open M-F 8am-6pm, Sa-Su and holidays 9am-5pm.) Continuing up the hill across the *centro* is **Igreja Matriz Nossa Senhora da Conceição,** with a frontispiece by Aleijadinho. Farther up is **Igreja do Rosário,** which is Congonhas's oldest church; it was built by slaves in the late 17th century. A trip to the well-maintained **Parque da Cachoeira,** which has ten swimming pools and a natural pool at the base of a waterfall, is also worthwhile. (☎3731 1911. Open M-F 7am-4pm R$1, Sa 7am-6pm R$2, Su and holidays 7am-6pm R$4.)

SÃO JOÃO DEL-REI ☎32

São João del-Rei has always benefited from its location as an entry point to the interior of Minas Gerais, and it has thus managed to remain prosperous long after its gold reserves ran dry. Today, thousands of tourists pass through São João's bus station while en route to Tiradentes; those who venture into the city itself find an interesting, though not always harmonious, combination of ancient and modern.

TRANSPORTATION. Intercity buses leave from the **Terminal Rodoviário Prefeito Octávio Olmeida Neves** (☎3373 4700). Buses go to Belo Horizonte (3hr.; M-F 8 per day 6am-7pm, Sa 6 per day 6am-7pm, Su 9 per day 6am-8pm; R$23.25); Brasília (15hr.; 3:15pm; R$76.50); Rio de Janeiro (5hr.; M-F 5 per day 8am-12:30am, Sa 3 per day 8am-12:30am, Su 4 per day 1pm-midnight; R$28-34); São Paulo (7hr.; 4 per day 11am-11pm; R$40); Tiradentes (M-F 10 per day 6:20am-7:30pm; Sa and holidays 9 per day 7:30am-7:30pm; Su 9 per day 8:50am-10:30pm); Três Corações (3hr.; 2 per day 9:15am-9:15pm; R$27). **City buses** run 5:30am-11pm (R$1).

ORIENTATION & PRACTICAL INFORMATION. The **Córrego do Linheiro** runs roughly east-west through São João's *centro*, and the three bridges that cross over it are important reference points. On the west is the historic **Ponte de Rosário,** which connects Igreja São Francisco de Assis to Igreja de Nossa Senhora de Rosário. A few blocks away on the river's north side there is a block-long pedestrian walkway around the base of the **Ponte da Cadeia,** another historic bridge. The third bridge is farther east, near the train station, and more modern than the other two. The city's main bus route has a stop near the *centro* on **Rua Dr. Balbino da Cunha.** The **rodoviária** is southeast of São João, and is accessed from **Rua Frei Cândido,** which runs perpendicular to **Av. Leite de Castro** and connects it to the station.

The **tourist office,** Pça. Frei Oralando 90, is located to the right of Igreja São Francisco de Assis. (☎3372 7335. Open 8am-5pm.) Coming off Ponte da Cadeia on the north side, **Drogaria Americano,** Tancredo Neves 91, is in front of the river half a block to your right. (☎3371 3699. Open daily 24hr.) The **Hospital de Nossa Senhora das Mercês,** Pça. Barom de Itambé 31, is just to the left of Igreja Nossa Senhora das Mercês, a few blocks north of Ponte da Cadeia. (☎3379 2800.) There is **Internet access** at Centercópias, Rua Ministro Gabriel Passos 314, a block and a half south from Ponte da Cadeia (☎3372 3517. Open M-F 8am-6pm, Sa 8:30am-12:30pm. R$3.50 per 30min.). The **post office,** on Av. Tiradentes, is a block south and half a block left from Ponte da Cadeia. (☎3692 6263. Open M-F 9am-5pm, Sa 9am-noon.) **Postal code:** 36307-000.

ACCOMMODATIONS. São João is an excellent alternative for those seeking to avoid the high prices and overly touristy atmosphere of Tiradentes. There are several inexpensive accommodations along the north side of the river. The **Hotel Brasil ❶,** Av. Pres. Trancredo Neves 395, is your best bet, as it still has the attractive internal spaces of its former life as a higher-end establishment. It's on the riverfront half a block east from the bridge at the train station. (☎3371 2804; hotelbrasil@ig.com.br. *Quarto* singles R$13; doubles R$26. *Apartamento* singles R$20; doubles R$40.) The nearby **Pousada São Benedito ❶,** Rua Marechal Deodoro 254, half a block from the pedestrian walkway near Ponte da Cadeia, has the *centro's* most affordable accommodations, in a large family home. (☎3371 7381. *Quartos* R$10.) **Pousada Estação do Trem ❷,** Pça. da Estação 45, offers cozy accommodations complete with breakfast, lunch, and nighttime tea, and is within a short walk of the train station. (☎3372 1985. Singles R$40; doubles R$100.) **Hotel Província de Orense ❷,** Rua Marechal Deodoro 131, also has nice, simple, and affordable rooms. (☎3371 7960. Singles R$19, with bath R$30.) **Pousada Ramon ❶,** Rua Frei Cândido

SOUTHEAST

42, is inexpensive and almost directly in front of the train station. (☎3371 5740. Dorms R$10.) **Camping del Rei ❶**, Alto da Av. 8 de Dezembro s/n, is very close to the *centro*. (☎3371 1952. Camping R$8 per person.)

FOOD. For lunch, much of São João heads to **Chafariz ❷**, Rua Quintino Bocaíuva 100, just behind the train station, and with good reason: it's an attractive kilo with plenty of good food. (☎3371 8955. Open daily 11am-3pm.) The popular **Maria Fumaça ❸**, Av. Tancredo Neves 437, has an affordable kilo buffet by day, and pricier dining with occasional live music at night. It's on the north riverfront, a block east from the bridge near the station. (☎3372 2500. Open M and W-Su 11am-1am.) **Cantina do Italo ❷**, Rua Ministro Gabriel Passos 315, is a good bet for everything from pizza and pasta to regional food. From Ponte da Cadeia, head south a block and a half; the restaurant is upstairs. (☎3371 8239. Open W-Su noon-11pm, Sa-Su noon-late.) The local favorite for meat is **Churrascaria Agostinho ❸**, Rua Eneida Sette Campos 20A. Take a bus marked "Vila Santa Cruz" or "Cidade Trevo" from the *centro* and get off in the square crossed by railroad tracks. (☎3373 2600. Live music F and Sa. Open Tu 11am-3:30pm, W-Su 11am-3:30pm and 6pm-late.)

SIGHTS. The city's oldest church, **Igreja de Nossa Senhora do Rosário,** on Largo do Rosário, stands just across from the Ponte de Rosário. Over the years it has undergone numerous modifications: its tower collapsed in 1758, as did the first replacement early in the 20th century, and its two current towers were only completed in 1936. The church contains a wooden image of Nossa Senhora do Rosário that is considered among Brazil's most beautiful wooden sculptures. (Open Tu-Su 8am-11am.) **Catedral de Nossa Senhora do Pilar,** on Rua Direita, was built in 1724 and has decorations containing the fourth-greatest amount of gold in Brazil used for such a purpose. (Open Tu-Su 6-10:30am and 1-7pm.) **Igreja de Nossa Senhora do Carmo,** in Pça. Dr. Augusto Viegas, required nearly two centuries of construction. It began in 1734 as a chapel, and underwent sporadic expansions thereafter; its sacristies and side galleries were finally completed in the early 20th century. (Open daily 8am-noon and 4:30-8pm.) Midway between the northern riverfront's two historic bridges stands **Museu Regional,** in Pça. Severiano de Resende, with well-designed exhibits of colonial furniture and sacred objects. (Open Tu-F noon-5:30pm, Sa-Su and holidays 8am-1pm. R$1.) Just to your left while crossing the Ponte do Rosário is the **Memorial Presidente Tancredo Neves,** Rua Padre Maria Xavier 7, an excellent museum commemorating the life of the first democratically elected president after Brazil's two decades of military dictatorship. Visitors must wear slippers to preserve the floor. (☎3371 7836. Open F 1-6pm, Sa-Su and holidays 9am-5pm. R$1.) **Museu Tomé Portes del-Rei,** on Rua Padre José Maria Xavier, keeps its collection of historical objects and photographs in the same house that once was home to the rebel Bárbara Heliodora and today holds the tourist office. (Open daily 8am-5pm. Free.) On the south side about halfway between the historic bridges is **Museu das Forças Armadas Brasileiras,** on Av. Hermílio Alves, which has exhibits that tell the story of a local regiment that fought in World War II. (Open daily 8am-noon and 2-4pm. R$1.) If you continue along the river toward the train station you will find **Museu da Ferrovia,** Av. Hermílio Alves 366, which contains an original train car and other relics of Brazil's railroads. (Open F-Su 1-5pm. Free.)

NIGHTLIFE. São João's small bar scene is concentrated a block south of Ponte da Cadeia. **Kalahari,** Alto da Av. 8 de Dezembro s/n, is the hottest dance spot in town, despite being all the way up the hill on Av. 8 de Dezembro. (☎3371 7593. Cover men R$12, women R$10. Open F-Sa 9pm-6am.) Those seeking live music crowd into the open-air bar **Point84,** Rua Kleber Figueiras 84. To get there take any bus marked "Vila Santa Cruz" or "Cidade Trevo" from the *centro*. (Open Th-Su

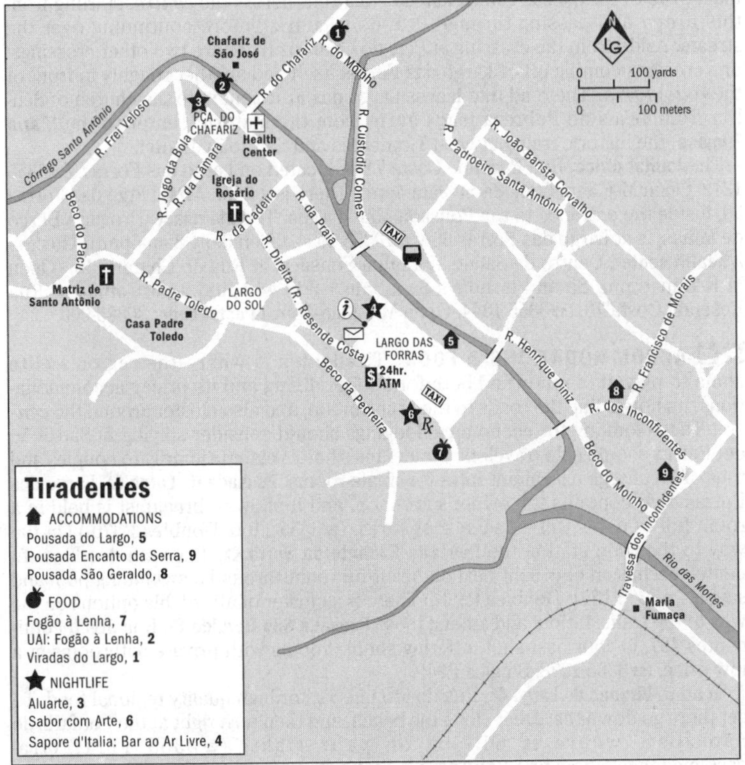

7pm-5am.) Off Av. Leite de Castro, for an otherworldly experience head to **Sarcófogo,** Rua Aureliano Pimentel 49, a rock and roll bar with decorations that will hypnotize and mesmerize; if the door is locked reach through the gate and ring the bell on the right. (☎9942 5460. Open Th-Su 9pm-4am.)

TIRADENTES ☎32

Tiradentes is probably the best-preserved colonial city in Minas Gerais. Entire neighborhoods remain unchanged from the colonial era, and the visible signs of modernization remain thankfully few; in the *centro*, the sound of a horse-drawn carriage is more likely to wake you up than is a honking automobile. Such preservation is expensive, however, and the town relies upon tourism by Brazil's wealthy elites as an economic base.

TRANSPORTATION. Access to Tiradentes is possible via a **bus** from São João del-Rei (M-F 10 per day 6:20am-7:30pm, Sa and holidays 9 per day 7:30am-7:30pm, Su 9 per day 8:50am-10:30pm).

ORIENTATION & PRACTICAL INFORMATION. Tiradentes's **centro** is built along the Ribeiro Santo Antônio, a stream running parallel to the city's historic main street **Rua Direita,** which connects the Matriz de Santo Antônio to the main *praça* of **Largo das Forras. Rua da Praia** runs across the *centro*, starting from this *praça* and passing through Pça. do Chafariz before continuing over the stream. Aside from the crossing at Pça. do Chafariz there are two other crossings: one crossing coming off of Largo das Forras itself and another roughly in front of the *rodoviária*. The road that leaves Largo das Forras next to the church of Senhor Bom Jesus de Pobreza leads away from the historic center to the **Maria Fumaça,** the historic train between Tiradentes and São João del-Rei.

The **tourist office,** Rua Resende Costa 71, is located on Largo das Forras. (☎3355 1212. Open M-F 9am-5pm, Sa-Su 9am-4pm.) There is a **24hr. ATM,** Largo das Forras 50, inside the entrance to the Pousada Mãe d'Água. The **pharmacy,** Drogaria Berço de Minas, is at Largo das Forras 66A. (☎3355 1654. Open daily 8am-6pm.). There is a **health center,** Centro de Saúde Mariquita Fonseca, at Rua do Chafariz 10. (Open M-F 7am-11pm, Sa and holidays 8am-3pm.) You will find a **post office** at Rua Resende Costa 73. (☎3355 1344. Open M-F 9am-5pm.) **Postal code:** 36325-000.

ACCOMMODATIONS & FOOD. Tiradentes is where the region's elite come to play: it is renowned both for its fine dining and its pricey accommodations. Its hotels line the roads to the train station, and also cluster around the *centro*. Those looking for economical lodgings should consider staying in São João del-Rei, as should solo travelers; Tiradentes's hotels cater primarily to couples and thus often charge exorbitant rates for single rooms. **Pousada do Largo ❹,** Largo das Forras 48A, contains the owner's art shop, and it shows—breakfast is held in a room full of delightful wooden sculptures. (☎3355 1166. Doubles R$70.) On the way to the train station the **Pousada Encanto da Serra ❹,** Travessa dos Inconfidentes 41, has an excellent deal on beautiful rooms around a swimming pool and sauna. (☎3355 1591. Doubles R$88.) There is a cluster of affordable options on the way to the train station, and among these **Pousada São Geraldo ❷,** Rua dos Inconfidentes 407, is your best shot, offering simple rooms with private bathrooms at a low price. (☎3355 1278. Singles R$40.)

SOUTHEAST

Head to **Viradas do Largo ❹,** Rua do Moinho 11, for high-quality regional food. To get there go down the street along the beach, and then turn right at the Chafariz de São José, where it will be on your right. (☎3355 1111; viradas@mgconecta.com.br.) **UAI: Fogão à Lenha ❸,** Pça. do Chafariz 73, is great for simpler, more traditional regional food very close to Mineiro cuisine's roots. (☎3355 2370. Open daily 11am-10pm.) For a break from Tiradente's high prices get a simple, solid lunch sold by the kilogram at **Fogão à Lenha ❶,** Rua dos Inconfidentes 22. It's on your right as you leave the *centro* for the train station. (☎3355 1919. Open daily 11am-4pm.)

SIGHTS & OUTDOOR ACTIVITIES. Tiradentes's main attraction is its historic *centro*, which can best be seen by walking. Those inclined can also hire horse-drawn buggies to get around town. The city's principal church is the **Matriz de Santo Antônio,** which was begun in 1710 and has a facade designed by Aleijadinho (p. 25). (Open daily 9am-5am. R$2.) The **Casa Padre Toledo** was once home to the *inconfidente* of the same name, and also hosted the first meeting of the *inconfidência* (p. 19). Today the building contains a museum of colonial art and furniture. (Open M and W-Su 9am-4pm. R$3.) Passing through the nearby alley will bring you next to **Igreja do Rosário,** a church built in the 18th century by slaves during their free hours. According to legend, all of the gold in its decorations was transported to the construction site secreted away under the slaves' fingernails, or in their hair. (Open M and W-Su noon-4pm.) Going one block left and crossing the stream will bring you to the **Chafariz de São José,** a fountain dating to 1749 and considered to be among Brazil's most beautiful colonial fountains. The historic train ride to São João del-Rei aboard the famous train **Maria Fumaça** is another of

Tiradentes's primary attractions. Emperor Dom Pedro II took part in the train's maiden voyage in 1881. (departs F-Su and holidays 1pm and 5pm; returns from São João at 10am and 3pm. R$9.)

Tiradentes's beautiful natural surroundings are great for trips on **horseback** (contact Adriano ☎9966 5864). Particularly popular hikes are the trails to **Cachoeira do Carteiro** ("Mailman's Waterfall", named after a mailman who died nearby) and to **Mangue.** The hikes require about 1½hr. and 30min., respectively, and you will find natural pools at the end of both. A less rugged outdoors experience can be had at the **Balneário de Água Santas,** a mountain resort which has waters said to have healing properties. (Open daily 7am-6pm.) Registered **guides** offer trips to the waterfalls and tours of Tiradentes's historic areas. Excursions can be arranged through the tourist office.

NIGHTLIFE. **Sapore d'Italia: Bar ao Ar Livre,** Av. Ministro Gabriel Passos 23C, is an open-air bar as the name suggests, and has some of Tiradentes's most exciting nightlife. (☎3355 1241. Open M-Th 7-11pm, F 7pm-midnight, Sa noon-4pm and 7pm-midnight, Su noon-4pm.) **Sabor com Arte,** Largo das Forras 66, a low-priced eatery during the week that becomes a popular hangout on weekends, when it usually hosts live music. (☎3355 1886. Open M and Th 11am-5pm, F-Sa 11am-2am, Su 10:30am-2am.) **Aluarte,** 1 Largo do Ò, is a very chic piano bar serving pizza to a surprisingly sophisticated crowd. (☎3355 1608. Open Th-Su 8pm-late.)

FESTIVALS. The city's main festival is its annual **Festival de Cultura e Gastronomia,** in which chefs from Brazil's most prestigious restaurants come to the city to display their latest creations every August. During the festival, special meals in the Largo das Forras and in many of the city's restaurants can cost as much as R$160. The city also hosts a 10-day **Mostra do Cinema** every January, featuring Brazilian films and short features projected onto three specially mounted screens.

DIAMANTINA ☎38

In the 1690s, when miners from Sabará came to this area looking for gold but found diamonds instead, they founded Diamantina. Today, the city's great distance from the commonly-visited regions of Minas has helped to preserve its backcountry charm, making it a rare gem among Minas's many historic mining towns.

TRANSPORTATION. The *rodoviária* is located at Largo Dom João 134, just uphill from the *centro.* **Pássaro Verde** (☎3531 1471) has buses to Belo Horizonte (5hr.; 6 per day 6am-1am; R$37). **Conjigo** (☎3531 1430) has buses to São Paulo (14hr.; 4pm; R$66). For local **taxis,** call ☎3531 1113, 3531 3795, or 3531 1413.

ORIENTATION & PRACTICAL INFORMATION. The *centro* is built in a valley. From the *rodoviária,* **Rua das Mercês** will take you to **Rua Direita,** which leads to the cathedral and the **Praça Conselheiro Mata.** Two other important *praças* connect to this *praça* in the *centro*: **Praça Juscelino Kubitschek** (a.k.a. Pça. JK), behind the church, and **Praça Barão Guaicui,** which houses the market.

Tourist information is available from the **Secretariat do Culturo e Turismo,** Pça. Antônio Eulálio 53. (☎3531 1636; sectur@citel1.com.br. Open M-F 9am-6pm, Sa 9am-5pm, Su 9am-noon.) Services in town include: **police** on the highway to Belo Horizonte, at the city entrance (☎3531 1625); **Drogaria Dom João** (☎3531 1138), on the main *praça;* **Hospital Nossa Senhora da Sáude,** Rua Macau de Baixo (☎3531 1357); **Internet access** at Rua Joaquim Feliciano 27 (open M-F 9am-6pm), or in **Livraria Espaço Café** (R$2 per 30min.; p. 224); **post office** at Pça. Dr. Prado 171, near Igreja do Rosário. **Postal code:** 39100-000.

ACCOMMODATIONS & FOOD. Diamantina's *centro* is full of pleasant accommodations. **Pousada Relíquias do Tempo ❸,** Rua Macau de Baixo 104, is by far the best, and in terms of beauty the small hotel almost outdoes the *centro* itself. (☎3531 1627; www.diamantinanet.com.br/pousadareliquiasdotempo. High-season *quartos* R$107. Low-season *quartos* R$78.) Nearby is the more affordable **Hotel Dália ❷,** Pça. JK 25, which has good accommodations right in the *centro* and peculiar antique furniture in its lobby. (☎3531 1477. High-season singles R$50; doubles R$80.) **Hotel JK ❶,** Largo Dom João 135, directly in front of the *rodoviária,* is no frills, but the price is right. (☎3531 6469. *Quartos* R$10.) **Pousada N'há Mocinha ❷,** Pça. Brasília 36, is in a flower-covered house with beautiful windows. It has a great diversity of rooms, and also occupies a second building across the street. (☎3531 1385. *Quartos* R$30.)

Restaurants are concentrated in the area between Rua Direita and Pça. Barão Guaicui. Most are self-service at lunch and a la carte for dinner. **Caipirão ❷,** Rua Campos Carvalho 15, is the local favorite for regional food. *Mineiro* standards average R$22 for two people, with *churrasco* on weekends (R$14 per kg). (☎3531 1526. Open M-Sa 8am-midnight, Su 8am-4pm.) **Apocalipse ❷,** Pça. Barão de Guaicui 78, has a great self-service lunch (R$14 per kg or R$12 all-you-can-eat) and fantastic views. (☎3531 3242. Open daily 11am-3pm.) **Cantina do Marinho ❸,** Rua Direita 113, is the place to go for meat and seafood. *Bacalhau* R$48, filet R$25; portions serve two. (Open M-Sa 10:30am-3pm and 7-11pm, Su 10:30am-3pm.) **Casa Velha ❸,** Rua Direita 106, 2nd fl., is a very attractive restaurant popular for its pizzas and regional fare. (☎3531 3538. Open Su-M 11am-2:30pm, Tu-Sa 11am-2:30pm, and 6pm-late.) **Livraria Espaço Café ❹,** Beco da Tecla 31, is a bookstore-turned-restaurant that is a quiet, charming place for coffee, wine, or a meal, often on tables covered with books. (☎3531 6005. Open M-Th 8am-midnight, F-Sa 8am-2am, Su 9am-1pm.) **Supermercado Ana e Pedro** is at Rua do Rosário 99. (Open M-Sa 7am-7pm.)

SIGHTS & OUTDOOR ACTIVITIES. While the historic center of Diamantina is a sight in and of itself, some buildings stand out. **Casa da Chica da Silva,** Pça. Lobo de Mesquita 266, is known for its unique architecture. The 1878 passageway at **Casa da Glória,** Rua da Glória 298, is one of Diamantina's characteristic images. **Casa de Juscelino Kubitschek,** Rua São Francisco 241, is the childhood home of former president Juscelino Kubitschek. (Open Tu-Th 9am-5pm, F-Sa 9am-6pm, Su 9am-2pm.) The **Mercado Velho,** built in 1835, still houses a Saturday fair featuring local crafts and agricultural products. The city's environs also have quite a few attractions. **Cachoeira da Sentinela,** 7km from town, has many small, sandy-bottomed pools. The 20m **Cachoeira dos Remédios** is 16km away, and has a sandy bottom thick with vegetation. **Cachoeira dos Cristais,** 14km away, is a favorite, with three waterfalls and a large natural pool. **Gruta do Salitre,** 7km from the city, is a quartzite cave with nine rooms. The **Caminho dos Escravos** (Slaves Road) connects Diamantina to the mining district Mendanha and passes by small waterfalls and streams. **Pico do Itambé** requires a 28km hike to reach its 2150m peak, which has great views of the entire region. The region's topography provides excellent opportunity for **climbing** and **rappeling.** The Clube do Rappel charges R$50 per person for a full day with a small group. For more information, contact Cristian at ☎9106 0231. Other recommended guides are Charles (☎3531 6527), Manoel (☎3531 8893), and André (☎8801 1802).

NIGHTLIFE. Nightlife is concentrated around the mouth of Rua da Quitanda, on the edge of the main *praça.* **A Baiúca,** Rua da Quitanda 13, has been around for decades, and is the most popular local hangout, with tables spilling into the street, and an upstairs dance club on weekends. (☎3531 3181. Open M-W 7am-2am, Th-Sa

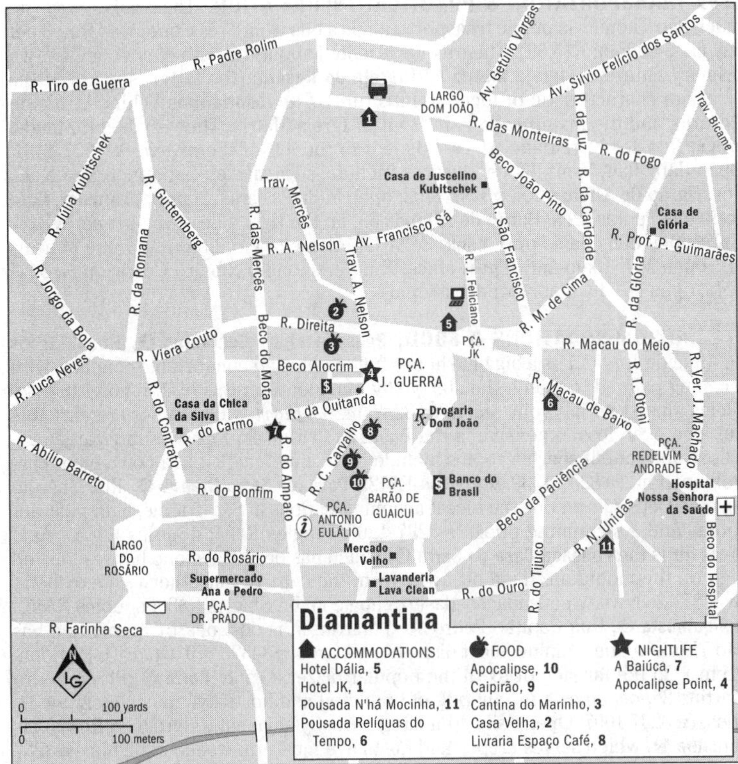

7am-5am. Th-Sa cover R$3.) Just across the street, the newer **Apocalipse Point,** Pça. Joubert Guerra 119, also spreads its tables into the street and provides a lively atmosphere. (☎3531 9296. Open Su-F 5pm-2am, Sa 10am-2am.)

SÃO THOMÉ DAS LETRAS ☎35

With far-flung São Thomé das Letras's lengthy and quite colorful history of UFO sightings, it seems that this tiny little town's popularity as a tourist destination is appreciated throughout the galaxy. The skeptical may laugh at such claims, but even skeptics must admit that São Thomé has a special relationship with the sky; it is, after all, Brazil's fourth-highest city. The amazing panoramic views are complemented by magnificent sunsets and the shooting stars which can be seen so easily in the area's thin air.

Most terrestrial (or at least temporarily earth-bound) visitors come to see the city's many nearby caves and waterfalls, each of which is so beautiful and unique that locals usually cannot decide on a favorite. The mountain underneath the city is composed mostly of a special quartzite (locally called Pedra São Thomé), and this is the predominant material in São Thomé's roads and houses; as you approach the mountaintop you will encounter many stone buildings smoothly integrated into the mountainside's exposed rock.

TRANSPORTATION & PRACTICAL INFORMATION. The only way to reach São Thomé via public transportation is a bus from Três Corações (1hr.; 3 per day 6am-4:30pm; R$5.50). The town is oriented about the path connecting its two primary churches, **Igreja Matriz** and **Igreja do Rosário** (the latter is made of the quartzite characteristic of local architecture). The **rodoviária** is behind Igreja do Rosário, and the main *praça* is in front of Igreja Matriz. The very helpful **tourist office,** Rua José Cristiano Alves 4, is just to the left of the *praça*. (☎3237 1461. Open daily 9am-5pm.) Other services include: **supermarket,** Supermercado Noel, Pça. Barão de Alfenas 39 (☎3237 1202; open M-Sa 8:30am-6:30pm); **pharmacy,** Drogaria das Pedras, Pça. Barão de Alfenas 35, on the right side of the *praça* (☎3237 1397; open daily 9am-9pm); **bank,** BEMGE, Alameda Virgílio de Andrade Martins 6B (open M-F 10am-2pm); **post office,** Rua Marcionilio Ribeiro Costa s/n (☎3237 1249; open M-F 9am-noon and 1-4:30pm).

ACCOMMODATIONS & FOOD. **Pousada Alpha Centaurus ❶,** Rua Marcos de Almeida Jorge 21, is a big blue house full of lofts and comfortable couches, with a ceiling painted to match the starry sky outside; from this hilltop hotel the sky seems almost within your reach. (☎3237 1428. *Quartos* R$15.) Less remarkable but also even less expensive is the **Pousada Central ❶,** Pça. Getúlio Vargas 23, whose adequate if spartan rooms include bath and breakfast in a convenient central location. (☎3237 1339. *Quartos* R$12.) **Pousada Serra Branca ❷,** Rua Capitão João de Deus 7, is among the nicest accommodations in São Thomé, with pleasant rooms and a swimming pool. (☎3237 1200. Singles R$35; doubles R$45.) Also pleasant is the **Pousada Casa da Serra ❷,** which has beautiful stone houses located high on the mountain. It's a bit away from the *centro*, but otherwise excellent. (☎3237 1268; www.pousadacasadaserra.hpg.com.br. Singles R$30; doubles R$45.) **O Alquimista ❷,** Rua Capitão Pedro José Martins 7, is on a nearby corner and has São Thomé's finest dining; most dishes serve two. (☎3237 1279. Open Th-Su noon-11pm.) On the far side of town the popular pizzeria **Ponto Certo ❶,** Plínio Pedro Martins 26, occupies a fascinating old building and hosts live music most weekends. (☎3237 1007. Open daily 3pm-late.) Directly adjacent to Igreja do Rosário is **Fornalha ❷,** which serves crepes and hosts live music on weekend nights. (☎3237 1373. Open F-Su 3pm-late.) An almost supernatural abundance of pool tables haunt São Thomé's nightlife establishments, but even so its nighttime activity is centered on the restaurants with live music, most of which are near the Cruzeiro on the moutainside. The groovy **Woodstock,** Rua Idorgino Alves Ferreira 1, hides behind Igreja Matriz before the slope steepens. (☎3237 1220. Open F-Su 9pm-6am.)

SOUTHEAST

SIGHTS & OUTDOOR ACTIVITIES. Mountainous São Thomé has many interesting sites within the city itself: the **Mirante** is a viewing platform, the **Cruzeiro** is a cross mounted atop a stunning rock outcropping, and the **Pirâmide** is a pyramid-shaped house; all three provide panoramas worth seeing. The caves and waterfalls outside of town are best accessed by car—bring your bathing suit and take one of the tourist office's handy maps. A relatively easy trip on foot will take you to **Cachoeira Eubiose, Cachoeira do Flávio, Cachoeira Véu de Noiva,** and **Cachoeira Paraíso.** For those traveling by car, the tourist office can arrange for accompaniment by a *guia mirin* (certified guide). For those without cars, there are many guides with jeeps who hang around the main *praça*, who charge about R$130 for a full-day excursion to your choice of waterfalls. **Cachoeira da Chuva** is exceptionally beautiful, and for those traveling by car a visit to the **Ladeira do Amendoim** will be fun—it's a hill that cars can climb even with the engine turned off. São Thomé's topography also makes it an ideal place for the adventurous to practice their rock-climbing or rappeling. A day's assistance and equipment rental will cost about R$50; call **Aventura** (☎9957 5782), or inquire at Sinhá (see food, p. 226).

PARQUE NATURAL DO SANTUÁRIO DO CARAÇA ☎31

AT A GLANCE: PARQUE NATURAL DO SANTUÁRIO DO CARAÇA	
AREA: 112.3 square kilometers.	**CAMPING:** Camping is not permitted.
CLIMATE: Average temperature 15°C.	**FEES:** Cars R$10, motorcycles R$5.
HIGHLIGHTS: Waterfalls and trails.	**WHEN TO GO:** The park is open daily, year-round, but only from 7am-9pm.
GATEWAY TOWN: Santa Bárbara.	

The sign at the park entrance proclaims that "You are arriving in paradise," and indeed you are: the church chose this area wisely for the site of a new sanctuary. Today, the sanctuary functions as a hotel for those who visit the park, its mountains, and its waterfalls.

The sanctuary and reception area are in the middle of the park. At reception, you can get a very good, color-coded map explaining all of the possible hikes. The trails—part rock, part sand, part red soil—lead to waterfalls, natural pools, and peaks, although you need a guide to reach most of the peaks. Parque Natural do Caraça is best reached from Santa Bárbara, although there are no buses from the city to the park. The 25min. taxi from Santa Bárbara costs R$38 each way (☎3832 1253). It's a good idea to schedule a return time with the taxi driver who takes you out there. The park charges a R$10 fee per car (taxis not exempt), and R$5 per moto-taxi. Moto-taxis (R$15 each way) are a cheaper option for the park, and can be found in Santa Bárbara on Rua Antônio Pereira Rocha, near the *rodoviária* (☎3832 2729). The park is only open 7am-9pm. The most popular hikes are to **Cascatona,** 6km long and easy, and **Cascatinha,** 2km long and ranked relatively difficult. **Pico do Sol** and **Pico do Inficionado** are the most popular climbs, but both peaks require guides. Recommended is João Júnior (☎3832 1889).

The only place to stay that is located within in the park is the attractive **Santuário do Caraça ❷/❸.** Visitors to the park who will not be spending the night can purchase meals (breakfast R$3.50, buffet lunch R$8, buffet dinner R$8). (☎3837 2698. All meals included. Reception Su-Th 8am-6pm, F-Sa 8am-9pm. Dec.-Jan. and July singles R$48, with bath R$82; doubles R$70, with bath R$114. Feb.-Jun. and Aug.-Nov. singles R$45, with bath R$75; doubles R$65, with bath R$105. Reserve in advance. M-F 7am-5pm.)

ESPÍRITO SANTO

VITÓRIA ☎27

Vitória sprawls across 34 islands full of fine beaches and waterfront hotels. Its main beach, **Camburi,** is an attractive 6km stretch ideal for sports and leisurely strolls. Vitória is just a short hop away from the bars and restaurants of Praia do Canto, and is the best place to sample the food of Espírito Santo. Try the local specialty, *moqueca capixaba,* which is much lighter than its Baiano counterpart.

TRANSPORTATION. National flights leave from Aeroporto de Vitória (☎3235 6300). Carriers include: **Gol** (☎3235 6420); **Varig** (☎3227 1588); **TAM** (☎0300 123 1000); **VASP** (☎3324 1499). Intercity buses leave from the **Terminal Rodoviária de Vitória** (☎3222 3366). **Águia Branca** (☎4004 1010) has **buses** to: Conceição da Barra (5hr.; 3 per day 6:40am-4pm; R$24); Porto Seguro (10hr.; 3 per day 8am-9pm; *convencional* R$43, *executivo* R$61); Rio de Janeiro (8hr.; 4 per day 11:10am-

10:50pm; *convencional* R$38, *executivo* $42, *semi-leito* R$55); Salvador (18hr.; 5pm; R$103); São Paulo (14hr.; 2-3 per day 3:35-7pm; *convencional* R$68, *semi-leito* R$99). **Itapemirim** (☎3322 0980) has buses to: Belo Horizonte (8hr.; 4 per day 8:45am-10:30pm; *convencional* R$38, *executivo* R$51); Brasília (16hr.; 11pm; R$90); Foz do Iguaçu (30hr.; Sa 6pm; R$177); Ouro Preto (7hr.; daily 9pm; R$33). Bus #111 runs the entire length of Praia do Camburi, passing by the *rodoviária* and through the *centro*. From the *rodoviária*, buses marked "Vila Velha" and "Itapuã" go to Praia da Costa and Praia de Itapuã, respectively. **Estação Ferroviária Pedro Nolasco** (☎3226 4169) has **trains** to Belo Horizonte (daily 7am; economy R$24, *executivo* R$39).

ORIENTATION & PRACTICAL INFORMATION. The *centro* is on the main island. The **Baía da Vitória** reaches inland, and **Avenida Beira Mar** runs along its edge to the *centro*. Following Av. Beira Mar toward the ocean will take you first to Shopping Vitória and then to the **Praia do Canto.** Vitória's nightlife and restaurants are concentrated in the Praia do Canto's **Triangula das Bermudas** neighborhood. A bridge connects Praia do Canto to **Praia do Camburi.** On the other side of the Baía de Vitória lies **Vila Velha,** another municipality connected to Vitória by three bridges. Two of these bridges are inland, near Vitória's *centro* and one—Terceira Ponte—is close to ocean. Vila Velha's main beach is **Praia da Costa,** which connects to happening **Praia do Itapoã.**

Tourist information is found in Shopping Vitória. (☎3382-6364. Open M-Sa 10am-10pm, Su 3-9pm.) The **Banco do Brasil,** Pça. Pio XII, is in the *centro* (☎3322 4574). Services include: **24hr. ATM** a block from Praça Pio XII on Av. Princesa Isabel; **currency exchange** at Mar Azul, in Shopping Vitória (☎3335 1187; open M-Sa 10am-10pm, Su 3pm-9pm); a **24hr. pharmacy,** Av. Princesa Isabel 261 (☎3222 6059); **Hospital São Lucas,** 1533 Rua Des. José Vicente 1533 (☎3381 3385); **Internet access** at Livraria Leitura, in Shopping Vitória (☎3335 1981; R$3 per 30min.; open M-Sa 10am-10pm, Su 3pm-9pm); a **supermarket** in Pça. Regina Frigeri Furmo (☎3227 9037; open M-Sa 8am-10pm, Su 8am-2pm); **post office,** Av. Jeônimo Monteiro 310 (☎3331 2394; open M-F 9am-5pm). **Postal code:** 29001-000.

SOUTHEAST

ACCOMMODATIONS. Vitória has a large number of very similar hotels catering to business travelers. These hotels can be great values, and their prices drop most weekends. Unusually, most of Vitória's finest luxury hotels are set aside from the beaches, so the best beachfront accommodations are often in the better rooms of mid-range hotels. Wherever you stay, be prepared to book ahead. **Pousada Itatiaia ❷**, Av. Antônio Gil Veloso 2728, is a simple hotel right in the middle of the action of Praia de Itapuã in Vila Velha. (☎3329 6513; www.pousadaitatiaia. Singles R$30; doubles R$50.) The youth hostel **Príncipe Hotel (HI) ❷,** Av. Dario L. Souza 120, is directly in front of the *rodoviária*. (☎3322 2799. *Quartos* R$20, non-members R$25. *Apartamentos* R$29.) **Ibis Vitória ❸,** Rua João da Cruz 385, tries to break out of the business-hotel mold. It has fully-equipped rooms in Praia do Canto, with the beach in walking distance and the *centro's* dining and nightlife at its doorstep. (☎3345 8600; www.accorhotels.com.br. M-F rooms R$75. Sa-Su rooms R$65.) **Hotel Cidade Alta ❶,** Rua Pedro Palácios 213, is the place for cheap beds in the historic district. (☎3223 2063. Singles R$13, with bath R$21; doubles R$19, with bath R$28.) **Hotel Camburi ❷,** Av. Dante Michelini 1007, is a relatively simple hotel on the Camburi beachfront with a swimming pool. (☎3334 0303. High-season singles R$60; doubles R$75. Low-season singles R$45; doubles R$56.)

FOOD. There are several restaurants around the Triangulo das Bermudas, in Praia do Canto. **Sarandi ❷,** Av. Marelchal Mascarenhas de Moraes 1979, has excellent meat and great service. Options include a *rodízio* (R$20) and a self-service lunch (R$13 per kg, with *churrasco* R$15), and an a la carte menu. (☎3227 6878. Open M-Sa 7am-11pm, Su 11am-4pm.) **Canto da Roça ❷**, Rua João da Cruz 280, is a popular restaurant specializing in meat and Mineiro food. They have a self-service lunch (M-F R$13 per kg, Sa-Su R$16 per kg) and an excellent *picanha na chapa* for two (R$23), as well as a daily *prato feito* (R$7-R$9) of Mineiro cuisine. (☎3227 4268. Live music Th-Sa. Open M-W 11am-3pm and 6pm-midnight, Th-Sa 11am-3pm and 6pm-2am, Su 11am-4pm.) **Shateau ❷**, Rua Comissário Octávio de Queiroz 1060, is a popular kilo close to Praia de Camburi. (☎3325 6738. Open daily 11am-3pm and 6pm-midnight.)

SIGHTS & ENTERTAINMENT. Vitória's historic *centro*, the Cidade Alta, is worth a look. **Palácio Anchieta,** upon which construction began in 1551, has housed the state government since the 18th century. Nearby is the neo-Gothic **Catedral Metropolitana.** The **Associação das Paneleiras,** Rua das Paneileiras 55, is a cooperative of women who make traditional stone pots used in cooking *capixaba*. Visitors can watch them work or purchase finished pots. (☎3327 0519. Take Bus #223 from the *centro*. Open M-Sa 7:30am-6:30pm.) Neighboring Vila Velha has several attractions worth visiting. The rare and beautiful **Convento de Nossa Senhora da Penha** is on a forested hilltop with beautiful views of Vitória and Vila Velha. The convent also holds one of Brazil's oldest oil paintings, and has a small museum. (☎3329 0420. Open M-Sa 5:30am-4:45pm, Su and holidays 4:30am-4:45pm.) Vila Velha is also famous for the **Centro de Documentação e Memória da Garoto,** the museum of the popular Brazilian chocolatier. The museum houses photographs, machines, wrappers, testimonies of workers, and more. (☎3320 1297. Open M-Th 1-5pm.) It is also possible to visit the factory itself while there. (☎3320 1709. M 2-3:15pm and 3:45-5pm, Tu-Th 8:45-10am, 10:15-11:30am, 2-3:15pm and 3:45-5pm, F 8:45-10am and 10:15-11:30am.)

Nightlife is concentrated around the Triangulo das Bermudas in Praia do Canto. **Bilac,** Rua João da Cruz 20, is a simple bar with a long history. (☎3225 0498. Open M-F 5pm-2am, Sa-Su 10am-2am.) The modern **Empório Santo Antônio,** Rua Joaquim Lírio 820, a block away, is a great place to nurse a cold *chopp*. The imposing exterior conceals a pleasant interior and lots of outdoor seating in back. (☎3345 9287. Open M-Sa 6pm-late.) **Swingers,** Av. Nossa Senhora da Penha 1297, is popular for dancing. The club plays a wide variety of music, and hosts several *forró* events. (☎3345 9404.) Beach kiosks are also lively at night. In Vitória proper, there is a lot of movement around Praia do Camburi, while an edgier crowd gathers at Curva da Jurema. In Vila Velha, the Praia do Itapuã sees the heaviest activity at night.

PARQUE ESTADUAL DE ITAÚNAS ☎27

Parque Estadual de Itaúnas is most famous for its sand dunes and breathtaking beaches, but the park also boasts a great diversity of natural environments created by the interaction of forest, river, sea, and swamp. The park can be visited year-round. If you come in late July and the summer months (Dec.-Mar.), you will find the park's main beaches at their most crowded, but this is also the best time to experience **Projeto Tamar,** an effort to save sea turtles. With patience and a bit of luck, you can see turtles hatching on the beach from January through March.

Visitors can see much of the park on their own, including the beaches, most of the swamps, and the remains of the old city of Itaúnas. The former Itaúnas was covered by sand dunes several decades ago after the trees that held the sand in place were cut down. **Praia do Riacho Doce,** on the Espírito Santo/Bahia frontier, is considered one of Brazil's most beautiful beaches. You can also visit the **Sítio do Angelim,** the home of a small community descended from nearby *quilombos*.

Casinha de Aventuras, located a short distance from the entrance to the park, rents bicycles, fishing rods, and kayaks (R$5 per hr. or R$20 per day). It also offers a variety of park excursions. (☎3762 5081; www.casinhadeaventuras.hpg.com.br.) On foot, visitors can go on a four-hour walking tours of the shoals, beaches, and ruins near the entrance of the park (R$10) or a six-hour walk along the beach to Praia da Costa Dourada, Bahia, returning by car to Itaúnas (R$13). Horseback rides go to the remarkable Praia do Riacho Doce, or the Sítio do Angelim (R$25). Bike rides through the forest include a stop at the Rio Itaúnas for a swim, or—for more experienced bikers—a climb to the Morro da Jaqueira for a panoramic view (R$15). Canoe and kayak rides along Rio Itaúnas stop at Ilha do Dominguihos or head up Rio Angelim, which empties into Rio Itaúnas (R$13). Trips by buggy are excellent for seeing dunes and the extension of beaches (R$180 for up to 4 people). Casinha da Aventura also has a rappeling class (R$20) and mountain biking excursion (R$20). The **park office** is located immediately next to the entrance to the park. (☎3762 2203; pei@simonet.com.br.)

ITAÚNAS & CONCEIÇÃO DA BARRA ☎27

Twenty kilometers from Conceição da Barra's *centro* and long past the end of the asphalt road lies Itaúnas, an isolated district of the town. This community of 1000 lives at the mouth of the **Parque Estadual de Itaúnas,** a mesmerizing area of dunes, forest, swamp, and beach. In July and the summer months (Dec.-Mar.), its population multiplies several times, and the city of sand streets takes on its role as the capital of *forró*. The **Circuito Nacional de Forró** and the **Festival Nacional de Forró,** both in the second half of July, draw the country's best *forró* bands and dancers.

Viação Mar Aberto (☎3762 2093) has buses from the *rodoviária* to Itaúnas (3-4 per day 7am-3:30pm; R$3.20). From Conceição da Barra, **Águia Branca** (☎3762 1159) has buses to Belo Horizonte (12hr.; 6:30pm; R$47) and Vitória (5hr.; 3 per day 6:20am-6pm; R$22). Itaúnas has two main streets. Av. Bento Danher ends at the entrance to Parque Estadual de Itaúnas, and Rua Demerval Leite da Silva runs parallel to it a block away. Itaúnas is reached via the *centro* of Conceição da Barra. There is a **supermarket** (☎3762 1430; open M-Sa 8am-6:30pm) and **pharmacy** (☎3762 1180; open M-F 7:30am-9pm, Sa 7:30am-5pm) in front of the *rodoviária*. The **post office** is on Av. Dr. Vellosa Silvares (☎3762 1506; open M-F 9am-4pm). **Postal code:** 29960-000.

Itaúnas is full of small, charming *pousadas*. Most offer packages for the *forró* festivals, Reveillon, and Carnaval. **Sol das Dunas Pousada Albergue ❶,** Rua Honário Pinheiro da Silva s/n, offers a good value and is run by Samuel, a local English teacher. (☎3762 5334. Doubles R$25.) **Zimbauê ❷,** Rua Theophilo Cabral da Silva s/n, is a beautiful and modern hotel. (☎3762 5023. Low-season doubles R$50.) **Pousada Carrancas ❷,** Rua Maria Ortiz Barcellos s/n, is attractive and fun, and even has a pool. (☎3762 5336; carrancas@simonet.com.br. Low-season singles R$25, with A/C R$30; doubles with A/C R$35.) **Suite da Manguete ❶,** Rua Demerval Leite da Silva s/n, has minimalist rooms but great rates. (☎3762 5030. Singles R$15; doubles R$20. During *forró* festivals doubles R$50.) **Dona Tereza ❸,** Rua Demerval Leite da Silva s/n, is a popular restaurant specializing in regional food like *moquecas* (R$20-50), fish filets (R$15), and *bobó de camarão* (R$25), with portions to feed two. (☎3762 5031. High season open daily 11am-midnight; low season daily 11am-9pm.) Itaúnas is famous for its nightlife, and throughout the summer thousands swing to some of the country's best beats. Its most famous clubs are the **Bar do Forró** and **Buraco do Tatú,** which open on alternate nights during the summer. On weekends in the off-season, you can often find *forró* at **Cachaçaria.**

You may also choose to stay in the *centro* of Conceição da Barra, particularly during Carnaval when its beach is the center of action. **Hotel Rio Mar ❷**, Av. Dr. Vellosa Silvares 11 is a centrally located, friendly, and family-run establishment. (☎3762 1223. Low-season doubles R$25. Seven-day Carnaval package for two R$600.) **Recanto Praia Hotel ❷**, Av. Carlos Castro 1, on the beach and near the *rodoviária*, has nice, simple rooms. (☎3762 1573; www.recantopraiahotel.com.br. High-season singles R$30; doubles R$54. Five-day Carnaval package for two R$700.) **Colher de Pau ❷**, Rua Barão de Tibuí 16, has a very popular self-service lunch (R$10 per kg). Its loyal customers come here for fish, chicken, *feijão tropeiro*, and many other options. (☎9931 2974. High-season open M-Sa 11am-late; low season M-Sa 11am-3pm.) **Caranguejão ❷/❸**, Av. Carlos Castro s/n, is a massive but simple beachfront restaurant popular for its *moquecas* (R$21-47), pizzas (R$13-18), and *pratos feitos* (R$8). (☎3762 1402. High season open daily 7am-3am; low season 7am-10pm.) Nightlife concentrates near the waterfront. In the high season, the beach kiosk **Kiri-Kerê** has live music. (☎3762 1945. Open Su-Th 8:30am-11pm, F-Sa 8:30am-3am.)

SOUTH

Most travelers only head to the South of Brazil (Paraná, Santa Catarina, and Rio Grande do Sul) to gasp at the epic Iguaçu Falls, which straddle the border with Argentina. Those who venture farther will find a region set apart from the rest of Brazil—and proud of it. The fiercely independent Gaúchos of the southern pampas (dry grasslands) occasionally threaten to secede, and the Old World air of the area's original non-Portuguese European immigrants still clings to the atypical architecture, culture, and language. The air here is literally different—temperate, with semi-discernible seasons (and frost!). And while the *rodízio* native to the area is the ultimate in excess, in general tastes here are more conservative in the rest of Brazil, though the coast still has its share of hedonistic beach bumming towns—this is still Brazil, after all.

HIGHLIGHTS OF THE SOUTH

MARVEL at **Foz do Iguaçu,** the world's widest series of waterfalls (p. 250).

ENJOY the panoramic views from the **Curitiba-Paranaguá train** (p. 232).

FALL under the spell of **Ilha de Santa Catarina,** a.k.a. the "island of magic" (p. 253).

LISTEN to the roar of world-famous waves on the shores of **Ilha do Mel** (p. 241).

SPOT rare wildlife in the **P.N. do Superaguí** (p. 244).

PARANÁ

CURITIBA ☎41

Visitors often underestimate the proud city of Curitiba, Paraná's state capital, treating it as little more than a stepping stone to Iguaçu. However, as the self-proclaimed "Capital Social," Curitiba has gained international recognition for its organization, cleanliness, and large public parks, which practically surround the city. Curitibans will quickly tell you how much they love it here; they show their love by keeping the streets clean, and funding an ambitious recycling program—even public trash cans sort garbage into foodstuffs and inorganic materials. Thanks to these efforts, the city boasts one of Brazil's highest quality of life indices, despite its substantial size and population. Spread out on a high plateau, Curitiba is prone to substantial seasonal variations in temperature, and frosts are common in the winter.

TRANSPORTATION

Flights: Flights leave from **Alfonso Pena International Airport,** Av. Rocha Pombo (☎381 1515). Flight carriers include **Varig** (☎282 0345), **VASP** (☎282 0345), and **TAM** (☎381 1620), all of which have offices along Rua das Flores.

Buses: National and international buses leave from the **Rodoferroviária,** Av. Pres. Afonso Camargo 330 (☎320 3000). The many destinations served include: **Florianópolis** (every 1-2 hr. 1:45-7:30pm); **Rio de Janeiro** (12hr.; 4-5 per day 7:30am-10:45pm); **São Paulo** (6hr.; 5-7 per day 7am-11:50pm; R$55).

Trains: The very popular tourist train to **Paranaguá** also leaves from the **Rodoferroviária,** Av. Pres. Afonso Camargo 330. The train is run by **Serra Verde Express** (☎323 4007). Nov.-Jan. trains depart daily at 8am, *litorina* 9am; returns from Paranaguá 3pm, *litorina*

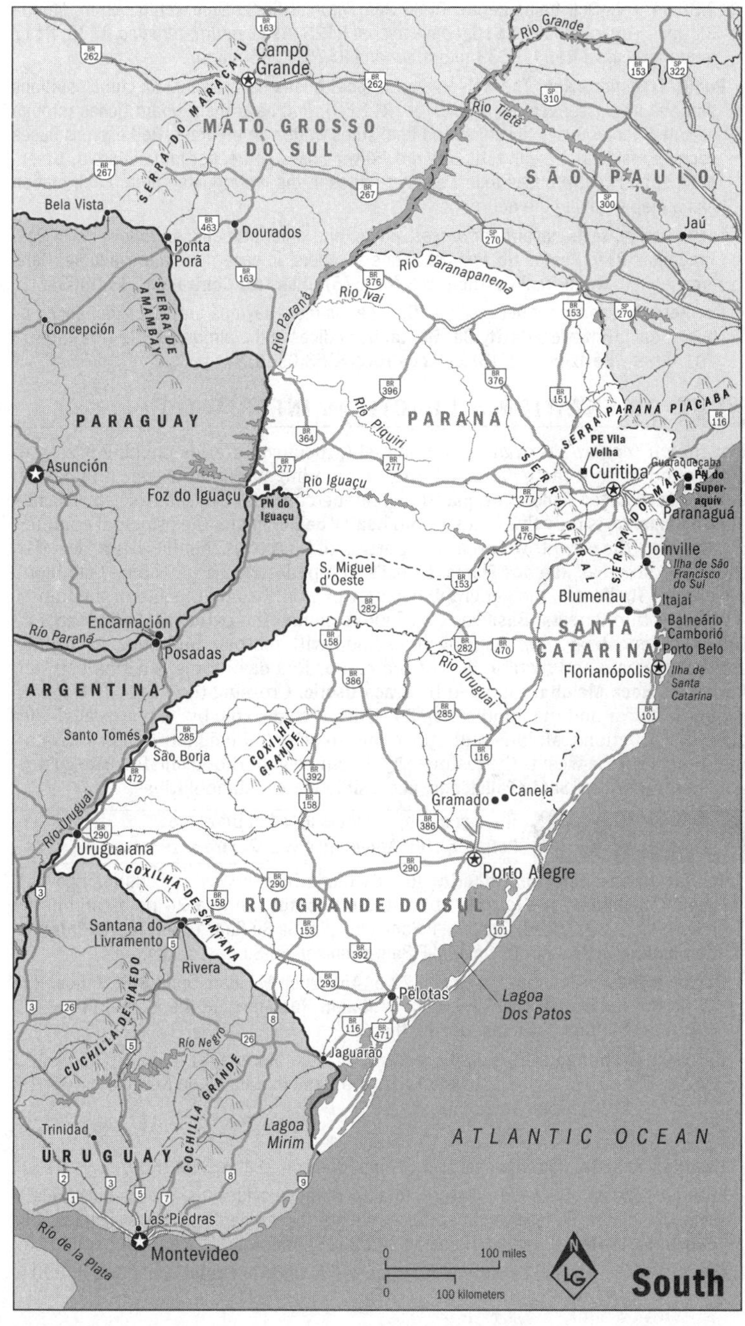
Campo Grande
MATO GROSSO DO SUL
SERRA DO MARACAIÚ
SÃO PAULO
Rio Grande
Rio Tietê
Bela Vista
Dourados
Ponta Porã
Jaú
SIERRA DE AMAMBAY
Concepción
Rio Paranapanema
Rio Ivaí
Rio Paraná
PARAGUAY
PARANÁ
Rio Piquiri
SERRA PARANÁ PIACABA
PE Vila Velha
Curitiba
SERRA GERAL
SERRA DO MAR
Guaraqueçaba
PN do Superagui
Paranaguá
Asunción
Foz do Iguaçu
PN do Iguaçu
Rio Iguaçu
Joinville
Ilha de São Francisco do Sul
S. Miguel d'Oeste
Blumenau
Itajaí
Balneário Camboriú
Porto Belo
SANTA CATARINA
Florianópolis
Ilha de Santa Catarina
Encarnación
Río Paraná
Posadas
ARGENTINA
Rio Uruguai
Santo Tomés
São Borja
COXILHA GRANDE
Gramado
Canela
Río Uruguai
Uruguaiana
Porto Alegre
COXILHA DE SANTANA
RIO GRANDE DO SUL
Santana do Livramento
Rivera
Pelotas
Lagoa Dos Patos
CUCHILLA DE HAEDO
Río Negro
Jaguarão
CUCHILLA GRANDE
Trinidad
URUGUAY
Lagoa Mirim
ATLANTIC OCEAN
Las Piedras
Montevideo
Río de la Plata
0
100 miles
100 kilometers
LG
South

SOUTH

2:30pm. Feb.-Oct. trains depart Th-Su 8am, *litorina* Sa-Su 9am; returns 3pm, *litorina* 2:30pm. *Vagão popular* R$16; *convencional* R$25, R$13 return; *turístico* R$36, R$17 return; *executivo* R$54, R$33 return; *litorina* R$75, R$35 return.

Public Transportation: The well-organized **local buses** have trademark "tube" stations that charge passengers as they enter (R$1.60), and have them board buses through elevated doors. Buses have first and final stops written on the front. **Red** express buses connect residential areas to the *centro.* **Silver** buses go deeper into suburbia. Green, orange, and yellow buses follow distinct routes in the metropolitan area. Each station has a map outlining the network.

Taxis: Orange **taxis** hover near *praças,* parks, and other attractions. *Rodoviária* to Pça. Tiradentes R$9. **Postos de taxi** list phone numbers, in case none are available. Cabs are metered. **Rádio Taxi Curitiba** (☎376 7676). **Disk Taxi Central** (☎333 0303).

Car Rental: A car is not necessary in Curitiba, as most daytrips are best experienced by bus or train. However, **Thrifty Car Rental** has offices in the airport (☎329 0099, 0800 701 0099). **Hertz** (☎381 1383). **Localiza** (☎253 0330).

ORIENTATION & PRACTICAL INFORMATION

Downtown *(centro)* is organized in straight, rectangular grids, making it easy to get around by foot there. To reach the surrounding parks, however, it is best to grab a bus. **Estação Rodoferroviária** (the combined bus and train station), on **Avenida Afonso Camargo,** is only five blocks from **Rua XV de Novembro,** the principal commercial street of the downtown area. The portion of this street that has been closed to traffic is known as **Rua das Flores,** Brazil's first pedestrian promenade. One block up is **Praça Tiradentes,** the geographic center of Curitiba and the site of the imposing neo-Gothic **Catedral Basílica.** Two blocks behind the cathedral is the **Largo da Ordem,** a pedestrian, cobblestone road lined with historic buildings, as well as some lively bars and restaurants. At the end of Rua das Flores is a small stretch known as **Boca Maldita,** followed by **Praça Osorio.** Crossing the *praça* is Rua Visconde de Nacar and the famous **Rua 24 Horas,** recognizable by its many steel-and-glass constructions. Middle- and upper-class residential neighborhoods surround the *centro.* To the west is the historically Italian neighborhood and favorite gastronomic attraction of **Santa Felicidade,** accessible via Av. Manoel Ribas.

EMERGENCIES	The emergency numbers for all of Brazil are: **Police** ☎190. **Ambulance** ☎192. **Fire** ☎193.

Tourist Offices: Tourism Authority, Rua de Glória 362 (www.viaje.curitiba.pr.gov.br). useful brochures are available at the **tourist booths,** on Rua 24 Horas and in the *rodoviária* (☎324 7036). Open M-F 8am-midnight, Sa-Su 8am-10pm. **Tourist information hotline:** ☎352 8000. Open M-F 8am-midnight, Sa-Su 8am-10pm.

Banks: HSBC, on Rua Das Flores (☎322 5445). Open M-F 8am-5pm. **BBV Banco,** Rua XV de Novembro 260 (☎232 9361). **Citibank,** Rua Marechal Deodoro 711 (☎221 6703). **HSBC,** Rua 24 Horas. Open 24hr.

Currency Exchange: AVS Cambio e Turismo, Rua Marechal Deodoro 630 (☎223 2828). Open M-Sa 9am-5pm. **Jade Turismo e Cambio,** Rua XV de Novembro 467, 1st fl. (☎322 1123). Open 9am-5pm.

Police: ☎362 2313.

Hospital: Hospital das Clínicas, Rua General Carneiro 181 (☎360 1800).

Internet Access: Digitando o Futuro, Rua 24 Horas, provides free access but space is limited and must be reserved in advance. Hotline about other free access sights ☎156. **Papelaria 24 Horas,** Rua 24 Horas (☎225 2008). R$2 per 15 min.; R$6 per hr.

Post Office: On Rua 15 de Novembro. Open M-F 8am-6pm. **Postal code:** 80200-000.

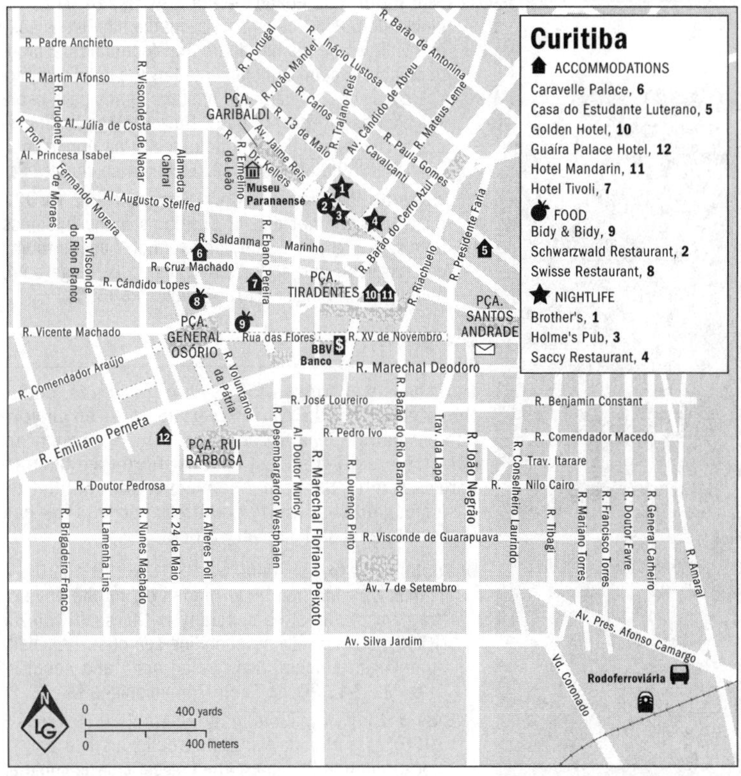

ACCOMMODATIONS

Budget hotels are clustered around the *rodoviária* and in the *centro*.

Hotel Mandarin, Travessa Tobias de Macedo 120 (☎223 8618), is conveniently near practically everything in Curitiba. It has well-lit, simple rooms with cable TV, spotless bath, and phone. The upstairs rooms also have a nice view. Breakfast included. Singles R$22; doubles R$35. Cash only. ❶

Golden Hotel, Travessa Tobias de Macedo 26 (☎324 3010), offers some of the simplest and cheapest rooms in the entire city. All rooms at Golden come equipped with private hot-water bath. Singles R$22, with cable TV and fan R$35; doubles R$40, with cable TV and fan R$55. ❶

Casa do Estudante Luterano, on Rua Carlos Cavalcanti (☎324 3313), also functions as a college dormitory. Hallways can get quite rowdy, but there is no better place to meet locals. Rooms have TV, and the shared bath has laundry facilities. Breakfast included. Dorms R$8. ❶

Guaíra Palace Hotel, Pça. Rui Barbosa 537 (☎232 9911), offers both luxury and panoramic views. All rooms are carpeted, and come with A/C, TV, and *frigo-bar.* The hotel caters primarily to a business crowd and is usually full during the week, but often offers weekend discounts. Singles R$54; doubles R$62. ❸

N THE MENU

CHURRASCARIAS

f the huge portions of meat served at most Brazilian restau- ants aren't enough for you, stop n at one of the all-you-can-eat parbecues known as *churrascar- as*, which began among the *gaúchos* (cowboys) of the South. here is usually an ample and veg- gie-friendly buffet at these estab- ishments, but the main draw is *churrasco*, giant skewers of succu- ent beef, chicken, and pork. Wait- ers roam the restaurant, foisting meat on everyone in an all-you- can-eat system known as *rodízio*. he red/green card on your table upposedly lets the staff know whether to stop or pass by your able, but the barrage of meat is pretty much constant. You'll see meats here you didn't even know existed (*gaúchos* have 53 differ- ent cuts of beef alone)—just go with it, and don't miss favorites ike chicken hearts *(corações)* or he rump roast *picanha*, Brazil's op cut. Whatever ends up on your plate, you definitely won't be hun- gry for a few days after the non- stop gorging that is *rodízio*.

Many *churrascarias* aren't cheap (costing up to R$40 per person), but they're worth it for the quality and diversity—particularly n the South region, where *churrascaria* started. And virtually anywhere in Brazil, you can always visit a sidewalk or beachfront *churrascart*, which offer skewers of lower quality) grilled meat and cheese for just R$1-2.

Tivoli Hotel, Rua Ébano Pereira 139 (☎224 0111), 2 blocks from Pça. Tiradentes. Living the high life is easy at Tivoli, where marble floors and fountains decorate the lobby, and are complemented by the hotel's impeccable service. The carpeted upstairs rooms have cable TV, phone, and private bath. However, the business-heavy clientele makes the hotel feel a bit impersonal. Singles R$59; doubles R$79. 10% service charge. ❸

Caravelle Palace, Rua Cruz Machado 282 (☎322 5757), is another one of Curitiba's many business hotels. It might feel stuffy and formal, but the rooms are excellent, and all have A/C, cable TV, large bath, and *frigo-bar*. Singles R$78; doubles R$96. ❹

FOOD

Curitiba is well known for its *churrascarias*, and is the originator of the *rodizio* serving style, an all-you-can-eat parade of different cuts of meat brought to your table until you can't eat any more (see **Churrascarias,** at left). Satisfying a sweet-tooth couldn't be easier in Curitiba, where countless *confeterias* can be found along almost every block.

Sushi Yamato, Av. Iguaçu 1730 (☎233 1730), a 10min. taxi ride from Pça. Tiradentes, on the edge of the *centro*. Yamato's specialty is the sushi *rodízio* (R$30), a seemingly never-ending sea of sushi, salad, dumplings, tempura, fish, grilled pork, and noodles. Open M-F 7-11:30pm, Sa-Su 7pm-midnight. ❹

Bidy & Bidy, Rua Comendador Araújo 170 (☎324 7966), is a cheap, filling, and delicious kilo only 1 block from Rua 24 Horas. The biggest crowds come at lunch for the savory beef stroganoff (R$12.90 per kg). Open M-F 11am-8pm, Sa 11am-5pm. ❷

Churrascaria Curitibana, Av. Iguaçu 1315 (☎233 5287), is the very best and most frequented *rodízio* in Curitiba. It makes up for a lack of ambience with succulent cuts of meat. Patrons get all the beef, pasta, and salad they can handle (M-F R$19, Sa-Su R$20); wooden hour-glass shaped markers are given to each customer to let the waiters know when to *go* get more meat (green), or *stop* the madness (red). Open M-Sa 11:30am-4pm and 7-11pm, Su 11:30am-4pm. ❸

Schwarzwald, Rua Claudio dos Santos 63 (☎223 2585), in the heart of Largo da Ordem, specializes in such German favorites as Bratwurst (R$12) and Kasseler (R$18.90 for 2). Schwarzwald's dark and somber interior makes it perfect for tranquil drinking of dark *chopp* (R$3.45). Open daily 11am-2am. ❷

Durski Restaurant, on Pça. Garibaldi (☎225 7893), specializes in Ukrainian, Polish, and Russian cuisine. The full-course banquet includes unique foods like Russian salad, grilled chicken breast in mint sauce (R$23.80), and other high-end favorites like filet mignon (R$24) and shrimp stroganoff (R$32). Open Tu-F 11:30am-2:30pm and 7-11:30pm, Sa 11:30am-4pm and 7-11:30pm, Su 11:30am-4pm. ❹

Swisse, on Rua Voluntários da Pátria (☎233 6271), is where the locals go for sweets. Caramel and chocolate *brigadeiros* are a traditional Brazilian birthday treat (R$1.60), and both the *folhados* (R$2.60) and *canoles* (R$2.60) come with all sorts of toppings and stuffings, from *doce de leite* to chocolate fudge. Open M-F 9am-8pm. ❶

SIGHTS

PARKS. Curitiba's numerous parks are spread out along the outskirts of the city. The municipal government runs the **Linha Turismo** bus, which travels to 22 points of interest, including most parks and several of the museums listed below. *(Buses depart from Pça. Tiradentes. ☎352 8000. Tu-Su every 30min. 9am-5:30pm; R$10, including 2 re-boards.)* From Tiradentes, the bus makes a brief stop at Rua das Flores, followed by **Rua 24 Horas,** a one-block strip of shops, cafés, and small bookstores that never close. The bus then heads to the delightful **Jardim Botânico,** the most recognizable landmark of the city, with meticulously groomed gardens and a unique steel-and-glass greenhouse, which is a replica of one in London's Kew Gardens. The Linha Turismo continues past the *rodoviária* to the **Passeio Público,** one of the city's most central parks. The park is nice for a weekend stroll and contains the **Memorial Árabe.** Farther north along the route is the **Bosque Alemão,** a small but densely wooded forest with a small children's library. *(On Rua Niccolo Paganini.)* Also, be sure to check out the **Torre dos Filósofos** (Philosophers' Tower), which offers panoramic views of the city and the Serra do Mar. *(In the Bosque Alemão. ☎338 6935. Open daily 6am-8pm.)* Ten minutes up the road is **Parque Tanguá,** one of the newest parks in Curitiba. From the bottom of the park it is possible to see a stunning waterfall. *(On Rua Dr. Bemben. ☎350 9163. Open M-Su 6am-8pm.)* **Parque Tingui** is smaller and less impressive, but still a favorite weekend spot for locals. *(On Av. Fredolin Wolf s/n.)*

MUSEUMS & OTHER SIGHTS. Most cultural sites are clustered close to the *centro*, and are easily accessible by foot. The grounds of the **Museu Botânico** include a dense forest, which provides opportunities to observe the unique flora and fauna of Paraná. *(On Av. Pres. Afonso Camargo, to the left of the greenhouse in the Jardim Botânico. Open M-Su 8am-6pm.)* At the top of the hill in the historic district is the newly reopened **Museu Paranaense,** which displays ancient and modern paintings and indigenous artifacts. *(Rua Kellers 289. ☎304 3300. Open Tu-F 9:30am-5:30pm, Sa-Su 11am-3pm.)* **Museu de Arte Sacra** specializes in 18th and 19th century baroque art from Paraná. *(Largo Cel. Enéas s/n, down the hill from Museu Paranaense. ☎322 1525. Open M-F 9am-6pm, Sa-Su 9am-2pm.)* **Museu Metropolitano** boasts a collection of approximately 3500 pieces from both local and international contemporary artists. *(Av. Rep. Argentina 3430. ☎322 1525. Open Tu-F 1-7pm, Sa-Su 3-7pm.)* Motorheads will enjoy **Museu do Automóvel,** in Barigui Park. *(Av. Cândido Harttmann 2300. ☎335 1440. Open M-F 9am-6pm, Sa-Su 9am-2pm.)* The **Opera de Arame (Parque das Pedreira)** is an imposing, tube-shaped opera house constructed of steel and glass that actually meshes seamlessly into the surrounding vegetation. *(Rua João Fava s/n, north of the* centro. *☎354 2662. Open Tu-Su 8am-10pm.)*

NIGHTLIFE

Curitiba's sizable university population ensures a lively nightlife scene, and there's something for everyone here. Pubs, clubs, and restaurants are particularly concentrated along the **Largo da Ordem;** most of these stay open quite late and don't even think of closing until early morning. In addition to those listed below, there are a few bars and nightclubs scattered farther to the west, along Av. Augusto Steiffeld and Rua Vicente Machado.

Holme's Pub, Largo da Ordem 159 (☎234 1254), is frequented by a college crowd, and is a good place to sing along with MPB favorites in a relaxed, informal atmosphere. On summer nights the outdoor tables are perfect for people-watching. Beer R$2. Open Tu-Th 7pm-2am, F-Sa 7pm-6am, Su 7pm-midnight.

Brother's, Rua Claudino dos Santos 44 (☎225 6712), is a narrow, crowded venue with incredible live *samba* and MPB every night. With few tables, practically everyone is on the dance floor. Beer R$2. Open M-Th 7pm-1am, F-Sa 7pm-4am, Su 7pm-3am.

Saccy, Rua São Francisco 350 (☎222 9922), is a relaxed place where you can enjoy rock and MPB. The mellow atmosphere goes well with drinks and midnight snacks like the provolone cheese plate (R$8) and grilled chicken platter (R$15). Top it off with a *caipirinha* (R$4) or a lip-smacking Guinness (R$3). Open daily 6pm-late.

The Farm, Av. Jaime Reis 40 (☎224 8654), near Pça. Garibaldi. Known for its international selection of alcohol, The Farm is unbeatable for an early evening drink; it tends to get crowded on weekends. Open M-Th 5pm-2am, F-Sa 5pm-4am, Su 10am-2am.

MORRETES ☎41

It may seem that nothing ever happens in Morretes, but that only lends its colonial *centro* a special charm. With its restaurants serving the local specialty, *barreado*, Morretes is a perfect early afternoon lunch stop overlooking the banks of the Rio Nhundiaquara. The town itself can be seen in a few hours, so it's a good idea to get off the train in Morretes, hang around town for an afternoon, and then catch one of many buses to Paranaguá or Curitiba. **Igreja Matriz** is the oldest church in town and offers a nice view of the surrounding area, including peaks in the nearby **Parque Estadual do Marumbi.**

The **rodoviária,** on Av. Odilon Negrão, is at the edge of town only three blocks from the **Centro Histórico.** On the way is the **Praça Rocha Pombo,** directly in front of the **ferroviária** (train station). Morretes's main street, **Rua XV de Novembro,** runs the length of the tiny town. During the peak season, the **train** from Curitiba continues on to Paranaguá (Th-Su 11am); schedules fluctuate in low season, so be sure to ask before departing from Curitiba. **Buses** depart for Curitiba (2½hr.; every 2hr.; R$9) and Paranaguá (1hr.; every hr.; R$2).

The **tourist office,** on Rua J. de Almeida, is housed in a fully restored colonial house, known as the Casa Rocha Bombo. The warm staff has incredibly thorough information. There is a **Banco do Brasil,** Rua XV de Novembro 198. (☎462 1204. Open M-F 6am-10pm.) The **post office** is at Rua Golmo Pereira 61 (open M-F 9am-5pm). **Postal code**: 83350-000.

The best accommodations are along the river and in Centro Historico. The **Hotel Nhundiaquara ❶,** on Rua General Carneiro, is a town landmark, but its rooms can be oppressively hot in the summer, so splurge for a fan. The hotel also has a gorgeous restaurant located directly on the riverfront, that has great *barreado* (R$9). (Singles R$13, with TV, fan, and private bath R$25; doubles R$45; triples R$75.) Owner Loizety pampers students and families alike at **Pousada Cidreira ❷,** Rua Romulo Pereira 61, where the colorful hallways give the hotel a tropical feel. Spacious rooms have satellite TV, luxurious private bath, and fan. (☎462 1604. Breakfast included. Singles R$35; doubles R$70. R$20 per additional person.)

Most restaurants are located along Morretes's busy riverfront. The much-touristed **My House ❸,** Rua das Flores s/n (☎462 1371), serves a cheap *barreado* (R$9; with seafood R$15). **Terra Nossa ❷,** Rua XV de Novembro 109 (☎462 2174), serves Italian fare (R$12-15).

PARQUE ESTADUAL MARUMBI ☎41

Officially formed in 1990, Parque Estadual Marumbi has become a favorite destination for Curitibano mountaineers. With an area of almost 24 square kilometers, Marumbi offers prime conditions for secluded camping, adventurous climbing, or just communing with nature. There are four well-marked, color-coded trails, each leading to at least one of Marumbi's summits. The park's relatively small area makes it possible to explore every trail without a guide. Camping within designated areas in the park is free year-round.

AT A GLANCE: PARQUE ESTADUAL MARUMBI	
AREA: 23.4 square kilometers. **CLIMATE:** Hiking is not recommended during rainy periods, though hikers should note that the dry winter days are also shorter, and that hiking the mountains by night can be dangerous. **WHEN TO GO:** It is possible to visit year-round, although in summer the park can be crowded.	**HIGHLIGHTS:** Hiking the 9 summits, from little Rochedinho (625m) to towering Olimpo (1539m). **GATEWAY TOWNS:** Curitiba (p. 232) and Paranaguá (p. 240), via the railway between them. **CAMPING:** There are designated campgrounds on the trails. Camping is free.

TRANSPORTATION

Serra Verde Express (☎323 4007) runs the very popular and scenic tourist train that runs to Paranaguá from the *rodoferroviária*, Av. Pres. Afonso Camargo 330, in Curitiba (Nov.-Jan. trains depart daily at 8am, *litorina* 9am; returns from Paranaguá 3pm, *litorina* 2:30pm. Feb.-Oct. trains depart Th-Su 8am, *litorina* Sa-Su 9am; returns 3pm, *litorina* 2:30pm. *Vagão popular* R$16; *convencional* R$25, R$13 return; *turístico* R$36, R$17 return; *executivo* R$54, R$33 return; *litorina* R$75, R$35 return.

ORIENTATION & PRACTICAL INFORMATION

From the Marumbi train station the mountains of the Serra de Marumbi begin a gentle climb through heavily wooded terrain. To the extreme right of the range is the summit of **Rochedinho** (625m), the most accessible peak. Unlike the tame Rochedinho, the wilder peaks of **Facãozinho** (1100m), **Abrolhos** (1200m), **Torre dos Sinos** (1280m) and **Esfinge** (1378m) are steep and dramatic, as are the higher peaks of **Boa Vista** (1491m) and **Gigante** (1487m). Reigning over all the rest is the mighty **Olimpo,** 1539m above sea level.

Emergency: COSMO, the Corpo de Socorro de Montanha (☎432 2072), is responsible for all search and rescue operations in the park. Their office is located close to the park office at the foot of the mountain. All hikers are required to fill out an identity card *(cadastro),* which allows park authorities to keep a record of all visitors, as well as to send help in case of problems.

Stations: The ranger station and first-aid office (☎432 2072) are both located close to the train stop at the beginning of the trails. The office remains open until nightfall.

Park Information: Instituto Ambiental do Paraná, Rua Engenheiro Rebouças 1375 (☎333 5044), in Curitiba.

Maps: Free maps are available in the park office. They detail the trails with average lengths and levels of difficulty.

Gear: The campground is quite basic, with a couple of showers and room for tents. Equipment can be rented or purchased in Curitiba (p. 232). Be sure to bring along all necessary toiletries, food, and water; there are no restaurants or snack bars in the park. Bringing a jacket is a good idea, especially during the rainy season.

Tours: Organized tours are not commonly available, nor are they necessary. The best way to explore the park is with a good pair of hiking boots and a couple of friends. The park staff does not recommend going it alone or bringing along very large groups.

Camping: There is one rudimentary campground approximately 1hr. along the Trilha Noroeste. The facilities include bathrooms with sinks and showers. No equipment rental is available, but camping is free year-round.

HIKING & BACKPACKING

The highlights of Marumbi are its four trails, three of which meet at the top of Olimpo. Inexperienced hikers should note that all trails except the trail known as the Trilha Rochedinho are classified as *pesadas* (difficult) and should only be attempted after consulting the park staff. Never set out without completing your identification card. The longest and most difficult trail is **Trilha Noroeste (red).** From its deceptively easy beginning the trail becomes progressively more difficult, ascending one after another the peaks of Abrolhos, Esfinge, Ponta do Tigre, Gigante, and finally the mighty Olimpo. At the top, the trail meets up with the Trilha Facãozinho and the Trilha Frontal. (18½hr. Difficulty: hard.) If you just want to climb Olimpo, the **Trilha Frontal (white)** is the most direct trail. It begins gently, passing the Cachoeira dos Marumbinistas, and then becomes increasingly steep until it ends atop Olimpo. (4hr. Difficulty: hard.) The **Trilha Facãozinho (yellow)** reaches Facãozinho, Boa Vista, and Olimpo. (11hr. Difficulty: hard.) An easier trek is the **Trilha Rochedinho (blue),** which is perfect for beginners, as it is a shorter hike. You will pass by the pleasant natural pools of the Rio Taquaral, and finish atop Rochedinho. (1½hr. Difficulty: easy.)

PARANAGUÁ ☎41

In the early 20th century Paranaguá was the point of entry for millions of European immigrants on their way to the interior of Paraná. Today, the city's modern buildings and dynamic industrial sector spread inland, and the important port exports soy. The *centro* contains about five blocks of well-preserved colonial architecture. Most hotels and restaurants are concentrated in this area. On summer weekends the **waterfront** gets lively, and the **Mercado Municipal** fills with vendors and musicians. **Rua General Carneiro** (a.k.a Rua da Praia) runs along the waterfront to the *rodoviária*. The main street, **Avenida Julia da Costa,** runs the length of the city. The *ferroviária*, three blocks from the waterfront, is on **Avenida Arthur de Abreu.** Most historic buildings, museums, and churches are in this area.

TRANSPORTATION. Buses stop at the **Terminal Municipal Rodoaviário,** Rua João Estevão, on the waterfront. (☎223 0872. Open daily 5am-10pm.) Buses go to: Curitiba (3hr.; every hr. 5am-10pm; R$11); Morretes (1hr.; every hr. 5am-10pm; R$2); Rio de Janeiro (14hr.; F 7:15pm; R$70.50); São Paulo (8hr.; Tu, Th, Su 10pm; R$53). The **Serra Express train** to Curitiba departs from the station on Av. Arthur de Abreu (3pm, *litorina* Sa-Su 2:30pm; R$35). **Ferries** depart from the dock across the street from the tourist office. During the low season (Apr.-Aug.), there are boats to Nova Brasília and Praia das Encantadas (M-F 2 per day 9:30am-3pm, Sa-Su 2 per day 9:30am-1pm). High-season schedules fluctuate depending on demand, but there are up to four boats per day to Ilha do Mel (1½hr.; R$10).

PRACTICAL INFORMATION. The **tourist office,** Rua General Carneiro 14, has some maps, but little else. (☎422 6228. Open M-Sa 8am-6pm.) **Tassi Turismo,** Rua Fria Sobrino 563, is the only place in the *centro* for currency exchange. (☎422 2166. Open M-Sa 9am-6pm.) There is an **ATM** that accepts international cards at Banco do Brasil, Largo Conselheiro Alcindino 103. (Open M-F 9am-5pm.) Other services include: **24hr. pharmacy** Drogamed, Rua Faria Sobrinho 411 (☎423 4461); **first-aid** (☎423 1422); **police** (☎422 4344). **Postal code:** 83203-000.

ACCOMMODATIONS & FOOD. Hotels are everywhere in the city; the most convenient accommodations are in the historic *centro*. Upper-end hotels are closer to the waterfront. One block from the waterfront is **Hotel Ponderosa ❷,** Rua Presciliano Corrêa 68, where spotless hallways with high ceilings lead to spacious suites with A/C, TV, and private bath. (☎423 2464. Singles R$30; doubles R$40. R$20 per additional person.) **Pousada Itiberê ❶,** Rua Heitor Ariente 142, is a clean, student-friendly joint. (☎3743 8114. Kitchen. Laundry services. High-season singles R$27; doubles R$40. Low-season singles R$17; doubles R$30.) A safe bet close to Museu de Arqueologia e Etnologia de Paranaguá is **Karibe Hotel ❶,** Rua Fernando Simas 86, where religious imagery decorates the whitewashed hallways. Some rooms have TV, A/C, and phone. (☎423 4377. Singles R$15; doubles with bath R$40; triples with bath R$66.) One block inland from the waterfront, **Dantas Executive Hotel ❹,** Rua Visconde de Nacar 740, has Paranaguá's most luxurious and old-fashioned beds; the oak-paneled lobby leads to very beige rooms. (☎421 1555. Singles R$85; doubles R$105. R$20 for an extra bed.) Fish is cheap and plentiful in the **Mercado Municipal's** many *barracas* and stands, and on weekends the market has live music. *Lanchonetes* are clustered at the far end of the waterfront area opposite the Mercado Municipal. The best and most varied kilo is **Divina Gula ❷,** Rua XV de Novembro 165, with a large Saturday *feijoada.* (☎422 2788. Su-F R$13 per kg, Sa R$14 per kg. Open M-Su 11:30am-3pm.) **Ancoradouro ❸,** Rua Benjamin Constant 706, a couple of blocks from the waterfront, serves seafood and has a full bar. (☎423 2091. Entrees R$17-20. Open M-Sa 11am-2:30pm and 6pm-midnight.)

SIGHTS. The **Museu de Arqueologia e Etnologia de Paranaguá,** Rua General Carneiro 66, is worth visiting; it's built over the Jesuit School of Paranaguá, which lasted for only five years before Jesuits were expelled in 1760. It was converted to a museum in 1962, and collections include donations from the Musée de l'Homme in Paris as well as some indigenous artifacts. (☎422 2511. Open Tu-F 9am-noon and 1-6:30pm.) Two blocks uphill is **Igreja Nossa Senhora de Rosário,** on Rua Profesor Cleto, the city's oldest church. From there it's only two blocks to **Igreja de São Benedito,** on Rua Conselheiro Sinimbu, which is a charming colonial church built in 1784. Several local boat companies run cruises through the Baía de Paranaguá, lasting 1-12hr. **Sea Blue** has regular tours around the nearby islands of Cotinga, Ilha do Mel, Ilha das Cobras, and Ilha das Peças. (☎362 7310. Departures every 1½hr. from 10am. R$20 per person. Min. 4 people.)

SOUTH

ILHA DO MEL ☎41

Ilha do Mel (the Island of Honey) consists almost entirely of luscious forests and unspoiled beaches. Arriving at the port of **Nova Brasília**—one of the island's two villages—is in itself an enthralling experience. Instead of the roar of traffic (no cars are allowed on the island), one hears the roar of crashing waves, which draw surfers from around the world. A surprisingly narrow stretch of sand divides Ilha do Mel into the **Estação Ecológica** in the north and the beaches and the settlement of **Encantadas** to the south. While visitors are common throughout the year, the vast majority of tourists invade the island during the summer (Dec.-Apr.). The island thrives on tourism, and most buildings on the island are either hotels, restaurants, or bars. Popular daytime activities include sunbathing and eating fresh seafood; at night the island has excellent live music, particularly *forró*.

TRANSPORTATION. **Ferries** from the mainland arrive daily from Paranaguá. During the low season (Apr.-Aug.), there are boats to Nova Brasília and Praia das Encantadas (M-F 2per day 9:30am-3pm, Sa-Su 2 per day 9:30am-1pm). High-season schedules fluctuate depending on demand, but there daily boats to Ilha do Mel from Paranaguá (1½hr.; 2-4 per day; R$10). Boats to Paranaguá depart from Encantadas (M-F 2 per day 8am-4:30pm) and Nova Brasília (M-Sa 2 per day 8:30am-5pm, Su 2 per day 10:30am-4:30pm). If you're stuck in Nova Brasília or Encantadas, it is possible to get transportation from one to the other by boat, though rates tend to be higher for single travelers or small groups. There is no set schedule for boats; the trip takes about ten minutes.

PRACTICAL INFORMATION. There is a **tourist information desk** directly in front of the dock in Nova Brasília. It offers a small map of the island, a list of phone numbers for most *pousadas*, and boat departure information. (☎426 8073. Open M-Su 8am-5:30pm.) There are **no banks or currency exchange** on the island. There are two **health centers** on the island: one directly inland from the port of Nova Brasília, and a second one in Encantadas, which offers 24hr. assistance. All health-related problems can be addressed by calling the **police** (☎426 8004), which faces the health center in Nova Brasília. Fast, reliable, but pricey **Internet access** is available at Praia das Conchas; follow the signs pointing to the "Blue House." (☎426 8065. Open daily 9am-9pm.) There is a small **post office** in Encantadas, in front of the pier. **Postal code:** 83521-000.

ACCOMMODATIONS & FOOD. Accommodations on the island come in all shapes and sizes—from fenced-in patches of grass to cozy cottages with ocean views—and are concentrated in Nova Brasília, Encantadas, and Praia do Farol. During high season reservations may be necessary. A quick stroll from Praia da Fortaleza in Nova Brasília is the newly renovated **Pousada Harmonia ❷**, where owner Wanderley offers clean, rustic rooms with fan. (☎426 8024. Breakfast included. Dorms R$25. Doubles R$60.) The **Praia do Farol ❶**, to the right of the docks in Nova Brasília, looks like a wooden cabin, and has two types of rooms: first-floor rooms have bath and fan, while the smaller rooms upstairs have A/C but no bath. (☎426 8014. Breakfast included. Singles R$20, with bath R$25; doubles R$40, with bath R$50.) **Camping do Arione ❶**, one of many campgrounds on the island, is a comfortable and cheap option in Nova Brasília. Rental equipment is sometimes available. Boat trips to the neighboring islands can also be arranged here. (☎9959 4603. Showers. Laundry. Grill. Camping R$10 per person.) Just to the left from the dock in Encantadas is **Pousada Tia Maria ❶**, the summer party crowd's preferred hangout. Rooms have private bath. (☎9978 3352. Singles R$20; doubles R$35.) **Pousada de Carlito ❶**, on the trail to Praia da Fora, has decent rooms for a decent price. The owner Carlito also rents a small house equipped with two bedrooms, bath, living room, and kitchen. (☎426 9012. Singles R$20; doubles R$40. House R$15 per person.) Most restaurants and *lanchonetes* along the beaches double as bars and nightclubs by night. Seafood is served everywhere, but *lanchonetes* also have lighter meals. Praia da Fora's **Praça da Alimentação** is a food court that frequently hosts live *forró* acts. **Restaurante Paraiso ❷**, on the coast of Encantadas, is adored by *forró* fanatics; try the island's strongest *caipiríssimas* (*caipirinhas* with vodka; R$5). **Toca Abutre ❷**, in Nova Brasília (☎425 8007), is a breezy restaurant facing Praia do Farol. Snack on the *camarão surf* (R$11).

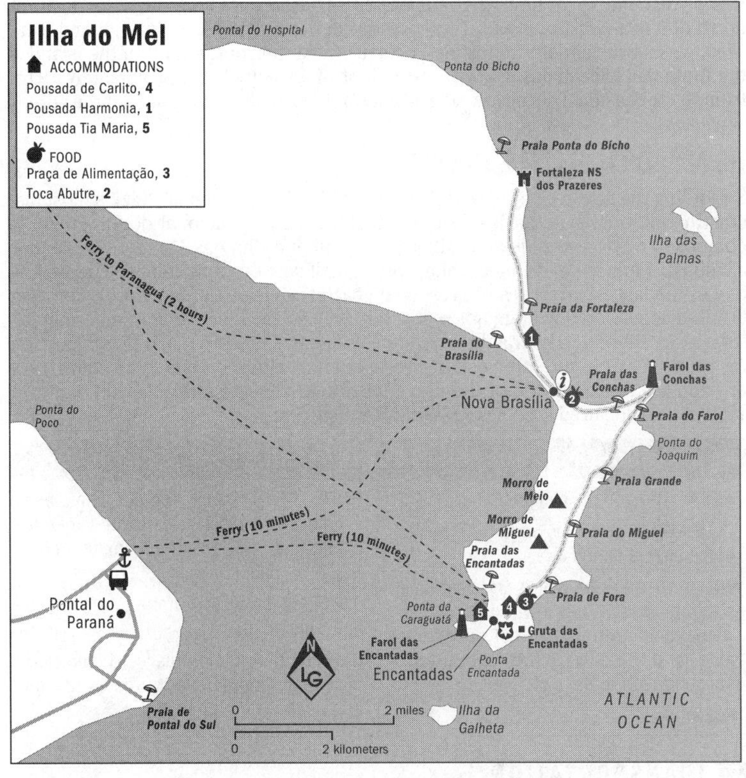

SIGHTS & OUTDOOR ACTIVITIES. The villages, beaches, and attractions of Ilha do Mel are all accessible by foot. Large maps indicating the distance, approximate time, and accessibility of various points are found throughout the island, with directions in Portuguese and English. **Green trails** (inland) are safe throughout the day, while **red trails** (running south along the beach to Encantadas and north to the fortress) can get a little tricky during high tide. **Encantadas,** on the island's southwestern tip, is about an hour from Nova Brasília. On its way south, the Nova Brasília-Encantadas trail passes through some of the most fantastic beaches on the island. Lined with a few *pousadas*, campgrounds, and bars, small **Praia do Farol** is both picturesque and convenient. A little rock-hopping through the Ponta do Joaquim brings you to **Praia Grande,** an elongated and more secluded stretch. The waves closer to the Ponta are larger and more intimidating, and even in July hardcore surfers can be spotted catching some wicked winter waves. Continuing south past **Praia do Miguel** is the **Ponta Nhá-Pinha,** a lookout spot with views of the surrounding beaches. **Praia da Fora,** one of the beaches most frequented by visitors staying in Encantadas, is very lively and has tame waves. To the north of Nova Brasília is the most family-friendly beach on the island, **Praia da Fortaleza,** which has especially calm waves. Only 15min. from Nova Brasília is the **Farol das Conchas,** built by Emperor Dom Pedro II in 1872. This still-operational lighthouse offers majestic views of the island and beyond. It is a great place to plan out which

SOUTH

beach you'd like to hit first. The **Fortaleza Nossa Senhora dos Prazeres,** about an hour north of Nova Brasília, was recently restored; the original structure, dating from 1780, was a crucial defense for the Portuguese. At the southern tip of the island is the **Gruta das Encantadas,** a gorge at the foot of a steep cliff approximately 1½hr. from Nova Brasília. During low tide, it's possible to explore the inside of the gorge.

P.N. DO SUPERAGUÍ ☎41

Straddling the northern border of Paraná and São Paulo is one of Brazil's most fascinating national sanctuaries. Formed in 1989, Parque Nacional do Superaguí is composed of two large islands (Ilha Superaguí and Ilha das Peças), the smaller islands of Pinheiro and Pinheirinho, and a small section of mainland. The park is one of the largest stretches of preserved coastal rainforest in the world. The area is still disconnected from major roads, but even so the increasing number of visitors poses a threat to its fragile ecosystem. Superaguí is still a magnificent location for spotting rare—and often endangered—wildlife, either on one of its many trails or from the decks of one of the many tour boats that pass through the park. In 1999, it was declared a UNESCO World Heritage Site.

AT A GLANCE: P.N. DO SUPERAGUÍ

AREA: 450 square kilometers.

CLIMATE: Heavy rains Sept.-Oct. The rest of the year is temperate.

WHEN TO GO: Summer is the best time, although it can be crowded. In winter, water temperatures can get uncomfortable, and it can be difficult to arrange transportation to the park.

FEES: None.

HIGHLIGHTS: Peace and quiet; rare and endangered species; vast orchards of rare plants; the Praia Deserta's uninterrupted 37km of pristine beach.

GATEWAY TOWNS: Paranaguá (p. 240) and Guaraqueçaba.

CAMPING: Extremely rustic, with no electricity and little hot water. There are over 10 *pousadas* in Superaguí.

TRANSPORTATION

Ferries to Superaguí do not operate regularly. Throughout the summer, it is easy to find boats to the park from Paranaguá (3hr.; R$200-260 for 4-6 people), though transportation will be more frequent from Guaraqueçaba (1½hr.; R$60-120 for 4-6 people). A few *pousadas* offer round-trip transportation for a fee. Pousada Superaguí charges R$220, including one night's stay in the *pousada* (☎422 2325, 9978 0821, ask for Dalton). A third option is to take a guided tour, which usually leave from Paranaguá in the morning and return the same afternoon. English-speaking Marcelo Guimarães is a reliable, knowledgeable guide. (In Curitiba ☎322 5272, in Paranaguá ☎422 1217; m.guimaraes@onda.com.br.)

SOUTH

ORIENTATION & PRACTICAL INFORMATION

The natural preserve of which Superaguí is a part encompasses more than 450 square kilometers. This area includes the town of Guaraqueçaba and its surrounding islands; these together comprise the Guaraqueçaba Environmental Research Station. The islands of Superaguí and Peças are composed of marshlands, mangrove swamps, and a few nearly impenetrable highlands. The worthwhile route from Guaraqueçaba passes through mangrove swamps and forests. **Vila Superaguí,** the most visited of the park's fishing villages, is on the southwestern tip of the island. There is only one well-marked trail to the **Praia Deserta,** which is itself one of the area's greatest attractions, and though there are some rudimentary trails in the forest, these are not recommended for visitors. Check in with the IBAMA post in Vila Superaguí (☎455 1564, ask for Irundina). The smaller Pinheiros and Pinheirinho islands to the north of the Vila are uninhabited and inaccessible.

Emergency: IBAMA, ☎322 5125.

Stations: IBAMA, the agency overseeing the park, has a small post roughly 2km from the dock in Vila Superaguí, and another station in Guaraqueçaba, Rua Paula Miranda 10 (☎482 1262). Open M-Sa 9am-5pm.

Maps: Maps are hard to get, but try the IBAMA stations or ask around in Vila Superaguí.

Gear: Outdoor equipment is not available in Vila Superaguí, although toiletries can be purchased at Mercerias do Tóninho. Bring insect repellent.

ACCOMMODATIONS & FOOD

Accommodations in Superaguí are basic, though the latest *pousadas* have TV and A/C. Campgrounds are large, with shared restrooms and showers. **Pousada Sobre as Ondas ❶**, 10min. down the beach from the main dock, is one of the few *pousadas* in Superaguí with private hot-water baths. Rooms are clean, modern, and spacious. (☎9978 4213. Singles R$20; doubles R$40.) **Pousada Crepusculo ❶**, three houses down from the main dock, has rustic rooms with fans. Guests share four clean bathrooms with hot water. (☎482 7106. Breakfast included. Dorms R$25.) Like its hotels, Superaguí's restaurants are rustic and cheap. Seafood fans will absolutely adore the selection of fish and shrimp, and lunches often come with *feijão* (beans) and *molho de camarão* (shrimp sauce). By far the best dishes are at **Restaurante dos Golfinhos ❷** (☎482 7126). Its huge meals include breaded fish, tiny fried shrimp, *feijão*, *molho de camarão*, rice, and salad (R$15).

SIGHTS & OUTDOOR ACTIVITIES

Most of Superaguí's highlights can be covered in one day. From Vila Superaguí, the easiest trip is to the **Praia Deserta,** a 37km stretch of unspoiled beach and tranquil ocean perfect for summer bathing. The migratory *maçaricos* settle along the beach throughout the summer. One of the most highly recommended boat excursions is to Ilha do Pinheiro (15min. from Vila Superaguí) to observe the *revoada dos papagaios-de-cara-roxa*. This is the period in the late afternoon, roughly 4-5:30pm, when the pink-

ON THE MENU

CHIMARRÃO

Indigenous Amazonians first drank *chimarrão* to keep warm in Brazil's harsher southern regions, but now people of every class, culture, and creed drink the bitter beverage. On almost every street corner in southern Brazil (particularly in towns close to the border), you'll see people holding a *cuia* (a distinctive wooden cup) in one hand and a thermos of hot water in the other. The drink is a tea made from the leaves of the native *erva mate* tree, and *chimarrão* drinkers continually add hot water to the leaves to brew fresh tea. *Chimarrão* is often drunk in groups, where people pass the *cuia* around. It is custom to pass and accept the *cuia* with your right hand.

To make your own *chimarrão*, fill your *cuia* three-quarters full with *erva mate*, then tilt the cup (as though you are pouring a beer) and slowly add hot water. Return the cup to an upright position; the *mate* leaves should leave a convenient place for a straw. Pour hot water in, let the tea seep, then drink and repeat.

Chimarrão is chemically similar to green tea, and like its Asian counterpart, any number of health benefits are supposedly derived from its consumption. *Chimarrão* drinkers (as well as the growers of *erva mate*) often promote the drink as a substance that increases mental alertness and improving immune system function; if nothing else, sharing a *cuia* can be a good way to make new friends.

faced parrots return to their sleeping grounds in great numbers. While it is not possible to disembark on the island, the trip offers an excellent opportunity to view these unique birds. Most *pousadas* can help arrange **boat excursions** to Ilha das Peças, Ilha do Mel, and Cachoeiras de Sibui.

FOZ DO IGUAÇU ☎45

Founded in 1914, the town of Foz do Iguaçu spent much of the past century in obscurity. Tucked in a remote corner of Paraná, this small settlement remained obscure until the 1970s when construction began on the massive Itaipu Dam. Throughout the following decades, the city experienced a boom in the hotel industry thanks to the commercial appeal of nearby Ciudad del Este in Paraguay, known for its dirt-cheap clothing and electronic goods. However, within the last decade Paraguay's economy has grown stronger, and so commercial tourism has dropped sharply. Today, Foz do Iguaçu still experiences a lot international tourism thanks to the town's namesake waterfalls (p. 249), and the area has also become an important site of ecotourism.

TRANSPORTATION

Flights: Foz de Iguaçu Airport, on Av. das Cataratas, is on the way to the park. Buses labeled "Parque Nacional" stop at the airport both on its way to the park entrance and back to the city *centro* (every 30min. 5:30am-midnight). Flights can be arranged with one of three carriers. **Varig,** Av. Juscelino Kubitschek 463 (☎523 2111). Open M-F 8am-6pm. **TAM,** Rua Rio Branco 640 (☎523 8500). **VASP,** on Av. Juscelino Kubitschek (☎529 7754).

Buses: Long-distance buses leave from the **rodoviária,** on Av. Costa e Silva, located about 6km out of town. To get to the *centro,* catch any "TTU" (Terminal de Transporte Urbano) bus from the tube-shaped bus stop outside (every 10min.; R$1.60). Buses leave for: **Asunción,** Paraguay (6hr.; 7am; R$30); **Buenos Aires,** Argentina (18hr.; 2pm; R$80); **Campo Grande** (14hr.; 4 per day 9am-6pm; R$58); **Curitiba** (5 per day 7am-9:30pm; *convencional* R$68, *leito* R$133); **Rio de Janeiro** (22hr.; 4 per day noon-8pm; R$110); **São Paulo** (15-16hr.; 7 per day; *convencional* R$81, *leito* R$155).

Public Transportation: The **Terminal de Transporte Urbano** (municipal bus station), at the corner of Av. República Argentina and Av. Juscelino Kubitschek (a.k.a. Av. JK), is in the north end of town. To get to the **P.N. do Iguaçu (Brazil),** grab any bus labeled "Parque Nacional" in the station or along Av. JK (30min.; M-Sa every 20min. 7am-6pm, Su every 35min. 7am-6pm; R$1.60). The last bus leaves the park at 7pm. To get to **P.N. de Iguazú (Argentina),** catch the "Linha Internacional (Puerto Iguazú)" bus (30min.; every 40min.; R$3) to the terminal in Puerto Iguazú, then grab the yellow "El Practico" bus labeled *Cataratas* to the park entrance (15min.; 8am-8pm every 40min.; R$3.50). Both *reais* and *pesos* are accepted once in Argentina.

PRACTICAL INFORMATION

Tourist Offices: The **main tourist office,** Pça. Getúlio Vargas s/n, is managed by the Secretaria Municipal de Turismo. The large, well-equipped office has a knowledgeable staff who can provide hotel and restaurant listings, a free map of the city, and thorough information about the parks. There are also **information booths** in the airport, the *rodoviária* (open daily 6:30am-6pm), the municipal bus station (open daily 7:30am-6pm), and on highway BR-277, on the way out of town (open daily 7:30am-6:30pm).

Tourist Hotline: ☎0800 451 516. Open daily 7am-11pm.

Currency Exchange & ATMs: Major banks are found along Av. Brasil. **Banco do Brasil,** Av. Brasil 1377, charges 10% commission on traveler's checks. It has two **ATMs** that accept most international cards. Open M-F 9am-3pm. **Safira Turismo,** Av. Brasil 567 (☎523 9966), charges 6% commission. Open M-F 8am-6pm, Sa 8am-2pm. **Caribe Turismo,** in the airport, does not charge commission.

Tourist Police: Theft should be reported to **Delegacia de Proteção Turista,** Av. Brasil 1374 (☎523 3036). Open daily 8am-5pm.

Hospital: Santa Casa Hospital, Rua Benjamin Constant 345 (☎523 1150). Open 24hr.

Internet Access: Jinius, Av. Brasil 34 (☎572 0078). R$3 per hr. Open daily 8am-11pm. **NetPub,** on Rua Rui Barbosa (☎572 5773). R$6 per hr. Open daily 9am-10:30pm.

Post Office: Pça. Getúlio Vargas 72 (☎574 2180). Open M-F 8am-4pm, Sa 8am-noon. **Postal code:** 85851-000.

ACCOMMODATIONS

As one of Brazil's major tourist magnets, Foz do Iguaçu has more than its share of hotels and *pousadas* to match every taste and budget. Bargains are plentiful, particularly in the heart of the city, so be sure to ask for a discount at the front desk, especially in some of the mid-range hotels.

BORDER CROSSING: TO ARGENTINA Be sure to carry your **original** passport when visiting the Argentine falls from Brazil; copies are not accepted, and you will be sent back. If traveling with a tourist group, you will not receive an exit stamp when leaving Brazil, but your passport will be checked. If, however, you are traveling on your own, you should receive **exit stamps** when leaving both Brazil and Argentina. Buses stop in the immigration office, where passengers disembark to have their passports checked and stamped individually. Most of the time, it is a straightforward–if time-consuming–process. If you are planning on staying at least one night in Argentina, be sure to get entry and exit stamps in both countries. For longer periods, you should verify whether Argentina requires a tourist visa for your home country. To find out, contact the **consulate** of Argentina, Travessa Eduardo Bianchi 26 (☎523 4166).

Pousada Paudimar (HI), Rodovia das Cataratas, km 12.5 (☎529 6061), on the road to the Brazilian side of the Falls. The living is easy in this relaxed hostel. Amenities include a (smallish) swimming pool, cabins, a soccer field, a game room, Internet access, and even a post office. Meet fellow backpackers in the large dining room, or set up your own tent in the clean, spacious campground. Organizes daily excursions to Iguaçu Falls (R$20). Dorms R$10, non-members with student ID R$12, non-members R$15. ❶

Hotel del Rey, Rua Tarobá 120 (☎523 2027), is a favorite with international crowds. Its spacious rooms have A/C, TV, *frigo-bar,* and private bath. Excellent tourist information office. Breakfast included. Singles R$35; doubles R$50; triples R$65; quads R$75. ❷

Lanville Palace Hotel, Av. Jorge Schimmelpfeng 827 (☎523 1511), is a surprisingly affordable option on the main nightlife strip. Luxuriously decorated rooms have A/C, TV, and private bath. The large pool with sundeck is a slice of paradise in the middle of the city. Singles R$40; doubles R$80. ❷

Pousada de Laura, Rua Naipi 671 (☎572 3374), in a quiet residential area, a 10min. walk from the municipal bus station. Rooms inside the main house have a homey feel, though there is more privacy in the second building out back. Breakfast included. Kitchen. Laundry facilities. Singles R$15; doubles R$30. ❶

Camping Internacional, Rua Manêncio Martins 21 (☎529 8183; www.campinginternational.com.br), only 1.5km from the *centro.* Offers clean, air-conditioned *apartamentos* as well as camping facilities with hot showers and restrooms. You'll never go hungry with the full-service restaurant, *lanchonete,* and barbecue spot. English spoken. *Apartamentos* R$30 per person. Camping R$10. ❶

FOOD

Large, noisy, and generally unappealing tourist-oriented restaurants are predictably plentiful in Foz do Iguaçu. Thankfully, there are also some good-quality restaurants scattered around the downtown area. Since streets are quite empty and somewhat unsafe, at night it is best to call a cab.

Restaurante Tempero da Bahia, Rua Marechal Deodoro 1228 (☎572 9187), is one of the most entertaining joints in town, as live night music complements the delicious Northeastern cuisine. Big eaters should try the *moqueca de camarão* (shrimp stew with coconut milk, spices, and *dendê* oil; R$45 serves 2). *Caipirinhas* (R$6) are the obligatory accompaniment. Open daily 6pm-late. ❷/❸

Armazém, Rua Edmundo de Barros 446 (☎572 7422), is a trendy place rumored to have the best margaritas in Foz do Iguaçu. Well-dressed locals crowd Armazém's outdoor seating, especially in the more pleasant summer months. Tasty appetizers R$5-10. Live music. Open daily 7pm-late. ❸

Bufalo Branco, Rua Rebouças 530 (☎523 9744), is the oldest *churrascaria* in town, and briskly serves delectable cuts of meat. Despite all the tourists, the food is excellent. Has a spectacular dessert buffet. R$25 per person. Open daily 11:30am-11:30pm. ❹

Pizza Park, on Av. Jorge Schimmelpfeng (☎523 3669), in front of Bar Capitão, is a top-notch post-*festa* destination. While pizza is the predictable specialty, the restaurant's claim to fame is its relaxed, lively atmosphere. Family-friendly touches include a cool playground area for the kiddies. Open daily 6pm-2am. ❷

Casa da Esfinha, Av. Juscelino Kubitschek 409 (☎523 1088), is known as a good spot for the classics: falafel, hummus, and shawerma servings are generous and very easy on the wallet, usually less that R$10 per person. Open 9am-9pm. ❶/❷

SIGHTS

Foz do Iguaçu's appeal as an internationally renowned tourist destination can be singly attributed to its most visited attraction, the majestic **Cataratas do Iguaçu** (Iguaçu Falls), which straddle the border between Brazil and Argentina. While there are certainly other things to see in and around the city proper, this massive waterfall is hands-down the most impressive sight in the area.

CATARATAS DO IGUAÇU

Catch any "Parque Nacional" bus from the Terminal de Transporte Urbano, at the corner of Av. República Argentina and Av. Juscelino Kubitschek. 30min.; M-Sa every 20min. 7am-6pm, Su every 35min. 7am-6pm; R$1.60. Park admission R$19.

It would be hard to imagine a more mesmerizing natural wonder than Iguaçu Falls. The 3300m-wide stretch of tropical waterfalls are the primary landmark of two bi-national parks: **Parque Nacional do Iguaçu** in Brazil, and **Parque Nacional Iguazú** in Argentina. Both parks can be reached from the city of Foz do Iguaçu. Virtually every hotel and hostel in town has transportation packages to both parks and tours of varying prices. While getting there on your own is certainly cheaper, packages can be more convenient. See the P.N. do Iguaçu coverage on p. 250 for extensive coverage of the Falls.

OTHER SIGHTS

ITAIPU HYDROELECTRIC POWER PLANT. This massive dam produced a record-breaking 93.4 billion kWh of energy in the year 2000, and is currently responsible for providing 91% of Paraguay's and 25% of Brazil's total energy needs. Depending on your viewpoint, the faux-Gothic concrete structure is either a high temple to modern engineering or a towering concrete monstrosity. As the boastful automated tour guide will undoubtedly let you know, Itaipu is a global leader in energy production. Its sprawling spillway, which releases excess water, can handle water-flow 40 times greater than that of the Falls. Seeing the spillway in action can be one of the most rewarding parts of any visit. The only way to see the dam is to join one of the guided tours that leave from the Visitor's Center. *(19km north of Foz do Iguaçu. Grab any "Conjunto C" bus from Av. Juscelino Kubitschek, across the street from the municipal bus stop. Tours run M-Sa 6 per day 8am-3:30pm; they last 1½hr., and information is available in English. Free.)*

ECOMUSEU. This newly renovated museum near the Itapui Dam contains a neat model of the area prior to the construction of Itaipu. There is also a large fish tank, a simulation of a working turbine from the power plant, and a room for temporary exhibitions. *(Av. Tancredo Neves 6001, 500m from the Itapui Dam. Take any "Conjuncto C" bus from Av. Juscelino Kubitschek, across the street from the municipal bus stop. ☎520 5817. Open M 2-5pm, T-Su 9-11:30am and 2-5:30pm. Free.)*

PARQUE DAS AVES. The Bird Park is easily accessible, because of its proximity to the entrance to the Brazilian side of the Falls. Over 800 birds of various species are free to fly around the five hectares of forest. The entire circuit takes about an hour to walk, and is a good way to kill time while waiting for an afternoon flight or bus. *(Rodovia das Cataratas, km11. Catch any "Parque Nacional" bus from the Terminal de Transporte Urbano, and ask to be dropped off. ☎529 8282. Open daily 8am-6pm. R$22.)*

NIGHTLIFE

Foz do Iguaçu is no mecca for night-owls, but even so the city's bars and clubs—most of which are clustered around Av. Jorge Schimmelpfeng—offer a surprisingly range of styles, genres, and crowds.

Vicius e Manias, Rua Benjamin Constant 107 (☎523 9161), has excellent live *samba* and *pagode*. An eclectic mix of wide-eyed, clumsy tourists and seasoned locals dance the night away in this well-guarded bar. Get in the mood with a few potent *caipiroskas* (R$4). Open daily 11pm-4am.

Capitão Bar, on Av. Jorge Schimmelpfeng (☎572 1512), is usually crowded with young tourists. During the high season (Nov.-Feb.), it's almost impossible to get a table unless you arrive early. The sound system blares mostly American pop. Share the *escondinho* (dip made with shredded meat, melted cheese, and *catupiry;* R$8), and wash it down with a *chopp* (R$3).

Gilles Night Bar, on the corner of Rua Benjamin Constant and Rua Belarmino de Mendonça (☎574 6833), is a popular place with high ceilings and outdoor seating for chilling on hot nights. Gay-friendly. Enter through the side door on Rua Belarmino de Mendouça. Open daily 11pm-late.

P.N. DO IGUAÇU ☎45

Parque Nacional do Iguaçu has lush and abundant tropical vegetation gracing its frontiers, which are demarcated by the mighty Rio Iguaçu and the raging waterfalls. Guided tours and expeditions can take a full day or more, and do provide access to areas otherwise inaccessible. However, most travelers just visit the impressive Iguaçu Falls (p. 252).

ORIENTATION

BRAZILIAN SIDE

The Brazilian side of the park covers an area about three times the size of the Argentine side, and contains some of the most impressive panoramic views of the falls. However, it has only one major trail that can be visited without a guide. At the entrance is the brand-new **Visitor's Center,** with ticket booths, bathrooms, a small snack bar, and a gift shop. From here, you can grab a **tour bus,** which stops at the **Macuco Safari** booth (where you can arrange guided treks) and the decaying **Hotel Tropical das Cataratas**–the only hotel inside the park—where the panoramic trail begins. Continuing roughly along the edge of this trail, the road ends at the **Espaço Porto Canoas,** another tourist magnet with cafeterias, an upscale restaurant, public phone booths, an exhibition space, a medical station, and—lest we forget—a souvenir shop. Frequent shuttle buses are available all day for the return trip.

ARGENTINE SIDE

Though smaller than its Brazilian counterpart, the portion of the falls that fall within Argentina's borders—known as the Parque Nacional Iguazú—offers a great deal more in terms of trails, and allows visitors to get closer to the falls. Sadly, the

AT A GLANCE: P.N. DO IGUAÇU	
AREA: 1852 square kilometers (Brazil); 550 square kilometers (Argentina). **CLIMATE:** Hot and muggy year-round, except for a few days in June-July, when temperatures hover around freezing. Brief but forceful summer storms are common. **HIGHLIGHTS:** Incredible waterfalls; boat rides up the Rio Iguaçu. **GATEWAYS:** Foz do Iguaçu (p. 246), Puerto Iguazú (Argentina).	**CAMPING:** Camping is not permitted, but there are plenty of accommodations near both entrances. **FEES:** Entering from the Brazilian side, R$19; entering from Argentina R$33. **WHEN TO GO:** The park is popular all year long. High season is in Nov.-Jan., when falls are more impressive due to increased rainfall. July also sees large crowds.

recent infrastructure overhaul has not left the Argentine park untouched. The **Visitor's Center** is a sprawling complex of walkways and buildings full of information booths, restaurants, phone booths, baths, a tram station, and...a large souvenir shop. There is also a path to the **Green Trail** (the old walkway to the Falls, and a great alternative to the touristy tram), and the 3km **Macuco Trail.** A 15min. tram ride leads to the **Cataratas Station,** where one can access the Falls via the Upper and Lower Circuits, well-built metallic catwalks that meander through the forest and above the Falls. The shorter **Upper Circuit** can be easily walked in about an hour. It includes balconies with amazing views of the Brazilian Falls and close encounters with the Argentine Falls (don't miss the ferocious Salto San Martín). Though longer and a bit more challenging, the **Lower Circuit** takes about 1½hr. and brings you even closer to the water. The **port** at the bottom of the circuit has free rides to and from **Isla San Martín** every 15min. The tram's final stop is **Garganta del Diablo Station,** which has bathrooms, an information booth, and a fast food joint. The newly opened catwalk leads away from the station and to the park's centerpiece, a balcony overlooking the most massive and voluminous waterfall of all, the **Cachoeira Garganta del Diablo** (Devils's Throat Waterfall). With all the tourists continually crowding around to catch a glimpse, it can be impossible to snap your own keepsake photo. But you should definitely try.

TRANSPORTATION

Virtually every accommodation in Foz do Iguaçu has tours and transport packages for both parks. Going on your own is the cheapest and probably most enjoyable way to see the parks. Guided visits start at R$30 per person, but the price depends on what the tour includes.

Buses: Buses leave for both parks from the **Terminal de Transporte Urbano** (municipal bus station), at the corner of Av. República Argentina and Av. Juscelino Kubitschek, in Foz do Iguaçu. To get to the **P.N. do Iguaçu (Brazil),** grab any "Parque Nacional" bus in the terminal, or along Av. Juscelino Kubitschek (30min.; M-Sa every 20min. 7am-6pm, Su every 35min. 7am-6pm; R$1.60). The last bus leaves the park at 7pm. To get to **P.N. Iguazú (Argentina),** catch any "Linha Internacional (Puerto Iguazú)" bus (30min.; every 40min.; R$3) to the terminal in Puerto Iguazú, then grab the yellow "El Practico" bus (labeled *Cataratas*) to the park entrance (15min.; 8am-8pm every 40min.; R$3.50). Both *reais* and *pesos* are accepted once in Argentina.

Park Transportation: On the Brazilian side, modern **double-decker buses** whisk tourists from the Visitor's Center to the Hotel Tropical das Cataras, where the main panoramic trail begins, stopping along the way at the Macuco Safari booth, which is responsible for all guided excursions through the park. From the hotel, the bus continues to Porto

Canoas, where the panoramic trail ends (every 15min.; free). In Argentina, there is a 10min. walk from the front entrance to the **electric train** station (every 20-30min.; free). The sluggish ride takes visitors to Cataratas Station, with access to the park's major panoramic trails and Isla San Martín. The train continues to Garganta del Diablo Station, with access to the footpath that leads to the gargantuan waterfall. Heavy-duty hikers can still take the old footpath all the way to the end of the tram line.

PRACTICAL INFORMATION

Stations: Brazil: Information booths are located in the Visitor's Center (at the front entrance), at the Hotel Tropical das Cataratas stop, and at the Espaço Porto Canoas. English spoken. **Argentina:** Information booths are located at the front entrance of the park, in the Visitor's Center, at Cataratas Station, and at Garganta del Diablo Station.

Fees: Brazil: R$19; under 7 R$4. **Argentina:** R$33.

Maps: The most complete and helpful map of both parks is the **Iguazú, Argentina** map, which marks trails and circuits and ranks their difficulty. It is free and can be obtained in most hotels or the park entrance in Argentina.

Gear: A **poncho** is a good idea for river trips and hiking near the falls: cheap, disposable ponchos are for sale, of course (R$3). **Insect repellent** is essential in the summer, and is available at the gift shops or any Foz de Iguaçu market or pharmacy.

Tours: Organized tours can be arranged individually with hotels. **Yaha Iguazú,** in the Hotel del Rey, has a guided daytrip to the Argentine Falls, which leaves at 9:30am and returns at 5pm. R$30 per person. Contact Luís or Rosiane (☎572 4158). **P.N. do Iguaçu (Brazil):** Macuco Safari (☎55 45 574 4244; www.macucosafari.com.br) is the only tour operator in the park, and has a monopoly on trail and boat excursions. Their office is the first stop on the bus route. **P.N. Iguazú (Argentina):** Iguazú Jungle Explorer runs all boat and certain trail excursions in the park, but on the Argentine side it is less necessary to take a tour, as more trails are accessible to the independent hiker.

HIKING & BACKPACKING

Most hikes on the Brazilian side of the Falls require a guide, except for the Catwalk, the park's most popular trail. **Macuco Safari** (☎55 45 574 4244; www.macucosafari.com.br) can arrange guided tours with English-speaking guides to other parts of the park, but you must make reservations to take part in them.

MAIN TRAIL (CATWALK). This panoramic trail is the most frequented in both parks and provides one of the most rewarding panoramic views of Iguaçu Falls. To get a general idea of the structure of the Falls, it is best to visit the Brazilian side first, then move on to the other trails in the Argentine side. With its well-marked steps and heavy traffic, it is impossible to get lost on this trail. The entire path can be walked in about an hour.

GUIDED HIKES. The **Linha Martin** hike winds through the vast ecosystem of Iguaçu National Park, and spotting wildlife along the way is possible. The tour is combined with a boat ride along the upper Rio Iguaçu. (4km, 4-5hr.) The longer **Trilha Poço Preto** can be covered either on foot or by bicycle. Emphasis is placed on the flora and fauna of the park. You have the option of kayaking and descending to Porto Canoas in a twin-engine boat, or returning via the 2km Trilha da Bananeira. (9km, 5-6hr.) For those with less time, there is a shorter excursion including the **Trilha da Bananeira,** which passes several lagoons and provides trekkers with the chance to see some of the park's wildlife. The excursion ends with a brief sail down the Rio Iguaçu. (2km, 2½hr.)

SANTA CATARINA

FLORIANÓPOLIS & ILHA DE SANTA CATARINA ☎48

Locals call it Ilha da Magia (Island of Magic), and a few days spent here will illuminate why. With 42 beaches, there's a patch of sand to suit everyone, and Ilha de Santa Catarina is a veritable island paradise. It's no wonder that many who come to Florianópolis find it hard to leave. Florianópolis is nestled between the mainland and the island: half the city sits on the continent and the other, more popular half is on Ilha de Santa Catarina. The city proper is active and bustling, while the island combines the best of urban and rural life in near-perfect harmony.

TRANSPORTATION

Flights: Aeroporto Internacional Hercílio Luz, Av. Diomício de Freitas 3393 (☎331 4000), is located on the island and services major Brazilian cities as well as some international destinations. **Gol** (☎0300 789 2121) and **TAM** (☎331 4072) have offices at the airport. Carriers with offices in the city include **Aerolineas Argentinas,** Rua Tenente Silveira 200, 8th fl., rm. 801 (☎224 7835); **Varig,** Av. Rio Branco 796 (☎224 7266); **VASP,** Av. Osmar Cunha 105, shop 1 (☎224 1122).

Buses: Intercity buses leave from **Rodoviária Rita Maria,** on Av. Paulo Fontes (☎224 2777), to: **Balneário Comboriú** (24 per day; R$12); **Blumenau** (2-3 per day 10am-6pm; R$28); **Brasília** (28hr.; 3:30am every other day; R$147); **Buenos Aires** (10:15am; R$183); **Fortaleza** (60hr.; Sa 5:45pm; R$267); **Foz do Iguaçu** (Su-M 2 per day 3-4pm; R$66); **Itajaí** (24 per day; R$14); **Joinville** (5 per day 7am-7pm; R$24); **Porto Alegre** (6hr.; 5 per day 9am-5pm; *convencional* R$34, *leito* R$46); **Porto Belo** (6pm; R$9); **Rio de Janeiro** (18hr.; M 2:15pm, Tu and Su 4pm; *convencional* R$89, *executivo* R$108, *leito* R$163); **Santiago** (W and Sa 12:35am; R$295); **São Paulo** (28hr.; 5 per day 7am-8:15pm; *covencional* R$55, *leito* R$61).

Public Transportation: There are 3 **local bus stations,** all within walking distance of each other. Getting around the island by bus costs R$0.90-2.30. Allow an hour for transportation to the beaches. There are **timetables** on the platforms, and they can also be obtained from the central office, located between the market and Terminal Urbano.

The **first station,** between Rua Francisco Tolentino, Av. Paulo Fontes, and Rua Jerônimo Coelho, has buses to the northern part of the island: Jurerê, Canasvieiras, Brava, Ingleses, and Santinho.

The **second station,** Terminal Urbano, on Av. Paulo Fontes between Rua Dos Iheus and Av. Hercílio Luz, near the public market, has buses to the eastern and southern parts of the island: Barra da Lagoa, Mole, Joaquina, Lagoa de Conceiçao, Armação, Lagoinha do Leste, and Pântano do Sul.

The **third station,** on the corner of Rua Silva Jardim and Rua Bulcãoviana, has buses running to the *continente* (mainland).

Taxi: 24hr. **Rádio Taxis** (☎240 6009).

Car Rental: The Best Rent A Car, Rua Pedro Ivo 162 (☎222 5099; fax 225 2809).

ORIENTATION & PRACTICAL INFORMATION

As a traveler you'll probably spend most of your time on the island rather than downtown. Florianopolis's *centro* is located on the western edge of the island. The main street is **Rua Felipe Schmidt,** where most shops are located. At one end of the street is Pça. XV Novembro, the public market, and the three bus stations (see **Transportation,** above). Accommodations listed for Florianópolis are all within

SOUTH

walking distance of the *centro*. Av. Jornalista Rubens de Arruda Ramos and Av. Paulo Fontes run along the coast and are popular routes for jogs or long walks. Around the island are 42 beaches; the most popular and easiest to visit are—clockwise from the *centro*—Canasvieras, Ingleses, Santinho, Moçambique, Lagoa da Conceição, Barra da Lagoa, Mole, and Joaquina.

Tourist Office, in Pça. da Alfândaega (☎224 2906), next to the public market. Open M-F 8am-7pm, Sa-Su 8am-6pm. There is a branch in the Rodoviária Rita Maria (☎2123 1080). Open daily 7am-10pm.

Tours: Passeios, Rua Felipe Schmidt 515 (☎222 0110, 224 7928). Offers various city tours, including the Centro Sul tour to historic sights in the city and the south of the island (6hr.; daily 9am and 4pm; R$30). The Floripa Total tour travels the *centro* and runs to beaches around the island (8hr.; 9am; M and W-Sa R$35, Su and Tu R$25).

Currency Exchange: Banco de Brasil, on Pça. XV de Novembro (☎221 1995). Open M-F 10am-4pm. **Câmbio e Exchange Weshelstube,** Rua Felipe Schmidt 248 (☎222 2578, 222 2293). Open M-F 11:30am-4pm. Both change cash and traveler's checks, but the Câmbio does not charge commission.

ATMs: There is an HSBC on the corner of Rua Felipe Schmidt and Rua Alvaro de Carvalho with 24hr. ATMs that accept AmEx/Cirrus/MC.

Laundromat: Lav & Lev, Rua Felipe Schmidt 706 (☎225 2629). Open M-F 7am-10pm, Sa 8am-9pm. Wash R$6.50, dry R$3.50 per 13min.

Police: Delegacia Geral da Polícia Civil (☎224 5200).

24hr. Pharmacy: On the corner of Pça. XV Novembro and Rua Conselheiro Mafra.

Hospital: The two most central public hospitals are **Hospital Celso Ramos,** Irmã Benuarda 297 (☎251 1000), and **Hospital Universitarió,** Rua Maria Flora, Pausenwang, Campus Universitarió (☎331 9000).

Internet Access: Arom@ on Rua Felipe Schmidt (☎225 4915) across from Lav & Lev. Open M-F 9am-7pm, Sa 9am-3pm. R$1 per 15min., R$3 per 1hr. Or try **Monkey,** Av. Rio Branco 797 (☎333 6883, 225 5504), which can be noisy at times as it doubles as a games center. Open 10am-6am. R$3 per hr.

Post Office, Pça. XV Novembro 242 (☎229 4336, 0800 570 0100). Open M-F 10am-4pm. **Postal code:** 88058-000.

ACCOMMODATIONS & CAMPING

During the low season (Apr.-Nov.), finding cheap, comfortable, and ideally located accommodations is relatively easy in Florianópolis. However, prices double in most hotels and *pousadas* during the summer months. Accommodations in the *centro* are the cheapest option if you are traveling alone. If you plan on staying for longer than a few days and are in a group of two or more, accommodations on the beaches become an affordable option. If you are staying for more than three days, you can rent **apartments** in Centro, Lagoa de Conceição, Praia Canasvieiras, Praia Santinhno, and Praia dos Ingleses, but you must call ahead to reserve. (☎222 4906. R$55 for a 2-person suite with bath, kitchen and, cable TV.)

FLORIANÓPOLIS

Albergue da Juventude (HI), Rua Duarte Schutell 227 (☎225 3781, 225 4515). A 15-20 min. walk from the *rodoviária*. Exit the station and turn left onto Av. Paulo Fontes, then right onto Rua Padre Roma. Turn left onto Rua Felipe Schmidt and cross over Av. Rio Branco to Rua Duarte Schutel; the hostel will be on your left. It is comfortable and the best place to stay in town, as it has a friendly atmosphere and is a good place to meet other travelers. Sheets R$4. Dorms R$20, non-members R$24. ❶

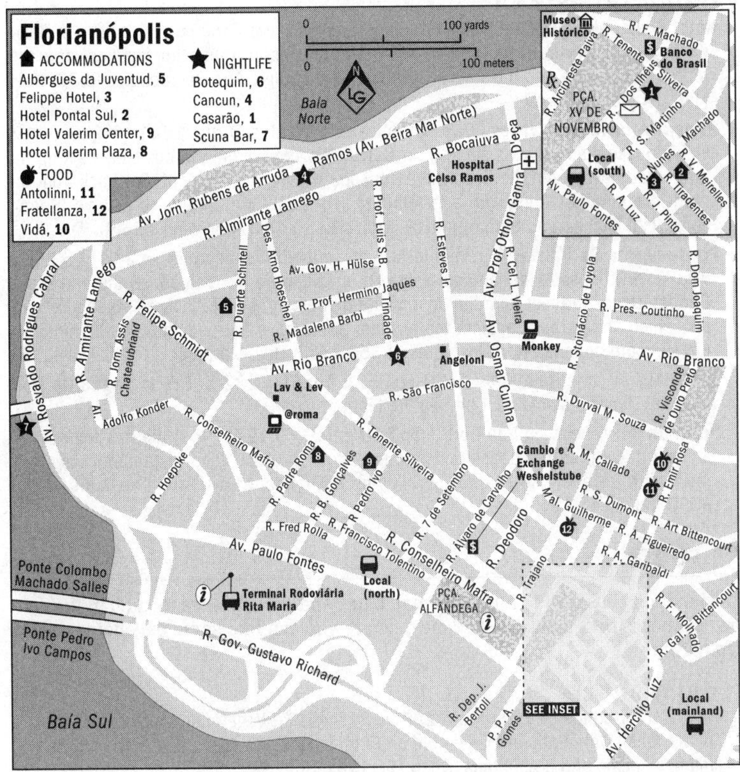

Hotel Valerim Plaza, Rua Felipe Schmidt 705 (☎225 3388). From the *rodoviária*, exit left onto Av. Paulo Fontes and take a right onto Rua Padre Roma. Follow Rua Padre Roma until you reach Rua Felipe Schmidt; the hotel is right at the intersection. More expensive than the above-listed hostel, but also more comfortable. Singles R$48; doubles R$64; triples R$79. AmEx/DC/MC/V. ❷

Hotel Valerim Center, Rua Felipe Schmidt 554 (☎225 1100). Just down the street from Hotel Valerim Plaza, on the corner of Rua Pedro Ivo. An upscale alternative in the *centro*. Singles R$48; doubles R$64; triples R$79. AmEx/DC/MC/V. ❷

Hotel Pontal Sul, Rua Tiradentes 167 (☎224 0810; fax 223 2269; www.pontalsulhotel.com.br), is about a 15min. walk from the *rodoviária*. Exit onto Av. Paula Fontes, turn right, walk until Rua dos Ihéus and turn right onto Rua Tiradentes; the hotel is on your left just after you pass Rua Nunes Machado. It has a bright and airy feel despite its location in the busy and crowded *centro*. Laundry services. Internet access. Can arrange car rentals and tours. Singles R$52; doubles R$70. ❷

Felippe Hotel, Rua João Pinto 132 (☎222 4122). Close to the Terminal Urbano. Exit the *rodoviária* on Av. Paulo Fontes, turn right and continue walking until you reach Rua dos Ihéus. Turn left onto it, and then right onto Rua João Pinto. The entrance is on the corner of the intersection. The musty rooms at Felippe are cheap, but nothing that special. Breakfast served M-Sa. Apr.-Nov. singles R$25; doubles R$50. Dec.-Mar. singles R$35; doubles R$72. ❶

AROUND THE ISLAND

Hotel Residencial Ilha Bela, Rua Altamiro Barcelos Dutra 1584 (☎232 3236), in **Barra da Lagoa.** 5min. from the beach. This hotel is a good option for families, as some rooms fit 6 people and have a small kitchen and garage. Apr.-Oct. doubles R$30. Nov.-Mar. doubles R$80. ❷

Pousada Lirio Dos Vales, Rua Altamirano Barcelos Dutra 1601 (☎232 3312; www.pousadaliriodosvales.cjb.net), in **Barra da Lagoa.** From the bus stop walk up the main road, away from the beach; the *pousada* will be on your right. Set back from the road in a small building with *apartamento*-like rooms. Call ahead to reserve. Rooms come with kitchen and bath. Apr.-Nov. rooms R$30. Dec.-Mar. rooms R$60. ❷

Pousada Ilha Da Magia, Av. Prefeito Acácio Garibaldi Santiago 23 (☎232 5468, 232 5038; www.pousadailhadamagia.com.br), in **Lagoa de Conceição,** at the end of Av. Das Rendeiras furthest from the *centro*. Rents rooms in private, colorful, triangular cabins, which are set back against the hillside. Some have front porches with hammocks. Kitchens are optional. Apr.-Nov. rooms R$50-R$89. Dec.-Mar. rooms R$90-R$160. ❷

Camping, Av. das Rendeiras 1480 (☎232 5555; fax 232 5808) in **Lagoa de Conceição.** Showers available. Camping R$15 per person. ❶

Pousada Sol & Mar, on Rua Dom João Backer (☎269 1271), in **Praia dos Ingleses.** A stone's throw from the beachfront and next door to a few good restaurants. Ask for a room with a beach view. Apr.-Nov. singles R$30; doubles R$40. Dec.-Mar. singles R$90; doubles R$110. ❷

FOOD

Florianópolis has a wide range of small cafés and *lanchonetes* located in the *centro*. Dinner is best along the beaches, where you can find some excellent seafood restaurants.

FLORIANÓPOLIS

Vidá, Rua Visconde de Ouro Preto 298 (☎223 4507). Vegetarian lunches, including a buffet lunch with elaborate vegetable and fruit salads. Also sells products such as vitamins, incense, and herbal teas. Open M-F 11am-3pm. ❶

Antolinni, Rua Visconde de Ouro Preto 248 (☎322 0707). This restaurant's homey interior and satisfying meals make it a good place to get Italian food. Buffet lunches offer a variety of pizzas and pasta dishes (R$6). Pizzas R$15-18; delivery available. Open daily 11:30am-2pm and 4pm-12:30am. ❷

Fratellanza, Rua Trajano 342 (☎222 1416), is upstairs from Rua Vidal Ramos. It doubles as a bar, with live music on Friday nights. Buffet lunch R$6. Evenings, cover R$3. Open 11am-2pm and 6pm-late. ❸

AROUND THE ISLAND

Restaurante Dois Irmãos, Rua Amaro Coelho 157 (☎232 3106), in **Barra da Lagoa,** right on the beach. Elegant, with terraced seating overlooking the bay. Entrees R$15-34. Open daily 10am-10:30pm. ❸

Restaurante Gaivota, Rua Aberlardo de Souza 163 (☎232 4114), in **Barra da Lagoa,** on the beach near Restaurante Dois Irmãos. Gaviota has good food and simple decor. Open daily 10am-6pm. ❸

Ichi-Ban, Av. das Rendeiras 200 (☎232 0039), in **Lagoa da Conceição.** A chic restaurante and sushi bar set on the lake front. Open W-M 6pm-midnight. ❸

A Casa, Rua Dom João Becker 185 (☎269 3861), in **Praia dos Ingleses.** An outdoor café, bar, and restaurant, with live music nightly. Snacks R$2-6, entrees R$22-38. Open 9am-2am. ❹

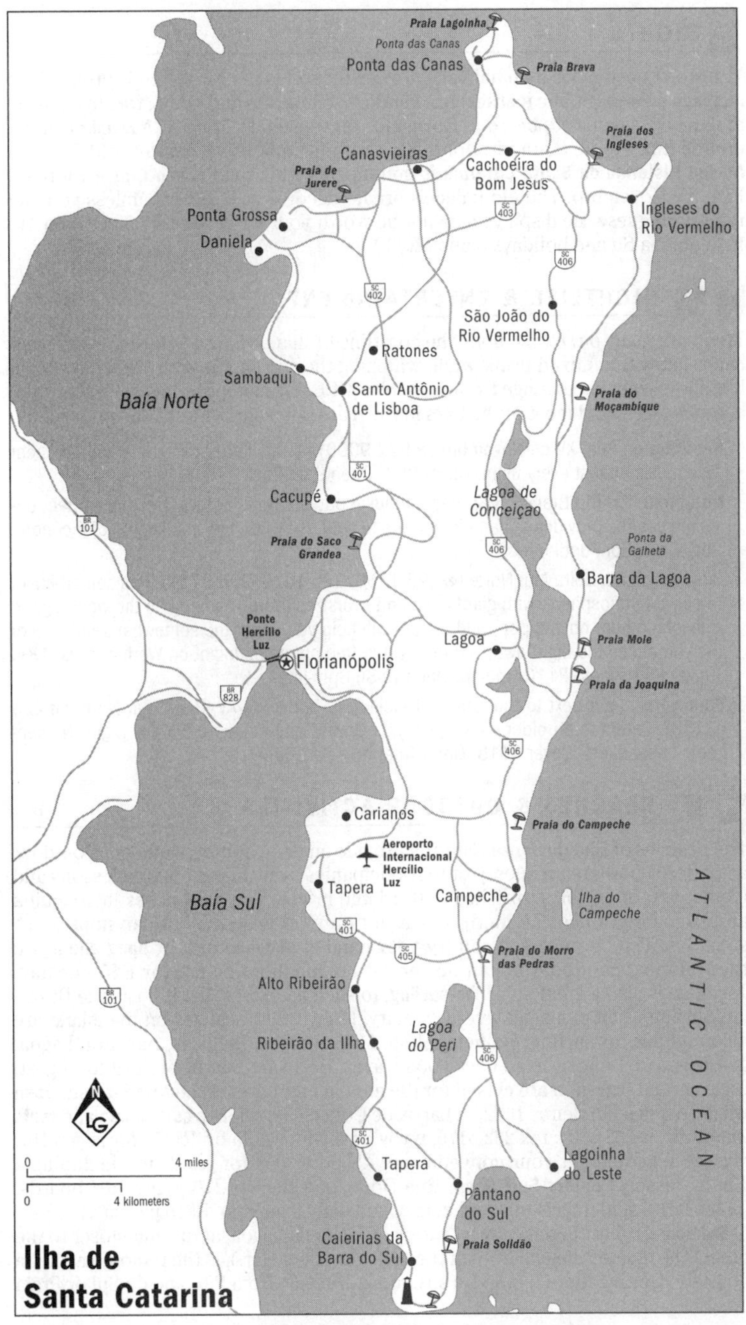
Praia Lagoinha
Ponta das Canas
Ponta das Canas
Praia Brava
Praia dos Ingleses
Canasvieiras
Cachoeira do Bom Jesus
Praia de Jurere
Ingleses do Rio Vermelho
Ponta Grossa
Daniela
SC 403
SC 406
SC 402
São João do Rio Vermelho
Ratones
Sambaqui
Santo Antônio de Lisboa
Baía Norte
Praia do Moçambique
SC 401
Cacupé
Lagoa de Conceiçao
BR 101
Praia do Saco Grandea
SC 406
Ponta da Galheta
Barra da Lagoa
Ponte Hercílio Luz
Lagoa
Praia Mole
Florianópolis
Praia da Joaquina
BR 828
SC 406
Carianos
Praia do Campeche
Aeroporto Internacional Hercílio Luz
Tapera
Campeche
Ilha do Campeche
Baía Sul
SC 401
SC 405
Praia do Morro das Pedras
ATLANTIC OCEAN
Alto Ribeirão
BR 101
Lagoa do Peri
Ribeirão da Ilha
SC 406
N
LG
SC 401
0
4 miles
Lagoinha do Leste
Tapera
0
4 kilometers
Pântano do Sul
Caieirias da Barra do Sul
Praia Solidão
Ilha de Santa Catarina

SOUTH

SIGHTS

You won't need more than half a day to see the sights in Florianópolis proper. The **mercado público** (public market) has vendors selling arts and crafts, free live music, and the occasional *capoeira* performance on weekends. **Praça XV Novembro,** at the end of Rua Felipe Schmidt, contains a rather impressive century-old fig tree. **Museu Histórico de Santa Catarina** is contained within the **Palácio Cruz e Souza** on Pça. XV Novembro. The old palace's ornate decor is striking, but unless you can read Portuguese the displays may not be worth your while. (☎221 3504. Open Tu-F 1-6pm, Sa-Su and holidays 3-6pm. R$3.)

NIGHTLIFE & ENTERTAINMENT

There are many *barracas* along the coastline of Ilha de Santa Catarina, where you can relax with a mixed drink while watching the sun sink into the sea, or catch a live show where acts range from *samba* to MPB. Florianópolis has its share of the action as well, and most of the bars in town are open almost until dawn.

Casarão, on Pça. XV de Novembro (☎222 9090). A small cozy bar where you can hear live music almost every night. Cover R$4. Open 9am-2am.

Botequim, Av. Rio Branco 632, has no music but is a popular local hangout. Open, terraced seating provides a place for crowds to chat away into the small hours of the morning. Open 6pm until late.

Cancun, on Av. Beira Mar Norte (☎225 1266, 225 1029, 225 3717). Has something of a surreal atmosphere, with giant cacti and oversized lizards hanging on the wall. A good mix of hip-hop, house, pop, and techno will help you forget the somewhat gaudy decor as you dance the night away. Women get in free before midnight on Wednesdays. 18+. Cover R$15 men, R$10 women. Open Tu-Su 8pm-late.

Scuna Bar, right next to the famous Hercilio Luz bridge on Av. Beira Mar Norte (☎225 3138). Caters to an older crowd (30+). Live MPB and *samba* on Friday night. No sandals or sneakers. Cover R$15. Open Tu and Th-Sa 10pm-late.

BEACHES & OUTDOOR ACTIVITIES

The beaches of Ilha de Santa Catarina provide an arena for any number of outdoor activities, and there are plenty of tour companies available to provide lessons and equipment, often for surprisingly affordable prices. The **sand dunes** in Joaquina and Lagoa de Conceição merit a visit not only because they are an impressive sight, but also because you can try your hand at **sandboarding** or **hang gliding** on their slopes. Sandboards can be rented on Joaquina beach for R$5 per day. Joaquina is also a great place for **surfing,** to such an extent that it hosts the Brazilian Surfing Championships every January. Many other beaches on the island are also popular for surfing: Galheta, Mole, Moçambique, Ingleses, Barra da Lagoa, and Lagoa de Conceição all have good waves. Be aware that from April to August, Ingleses and Santinho are closed for the annual migration of the *tainha* fish. **Open Winds,** Av. das Rendeiras 1672, in Lagoa de Conceição, offers a **surf course** and **rents windsurfs.** (☎232 5004; fax 232 5176; www.openwinds.com.br. R$150 for seven 1hr. classes scheduled at your convenience. R$30 per day for windsurfs including a 10min. lesson.) **Spider Surf Shop,** Rua Dom João Becker 276, rents surf boards. (☎369 0619; spidersurfshop@aol.com. Open daily 9am-9pm. R$15 per day.)

Swimming is best in the calmer waters of Barra da Lagoa, at the end closer to the point. The quietest beach, even in the summer (Dec.-Mar.), is the remote Lagoinha do Leste. Getting there requires a strenuous 1hr. **hike** from Pântano do Sul or Praia

Armação. Another quiet beach, Pinheira, is off the coast of the mainland; to get there take the bus heading to Papaguia. Inexpensive **boat tours** venture around the coast of Ilha de Santa Catarina and out to many of the smaller surrounding islands. **Scuna Sul,** with several locations on the island, arranges boat tours. (Centro ☎225 1806, 9971 1806; Canasvierias ☎266 1810, 9982 1806; Barra da Lagoa ☎232 4019, 9980 4438; www.scunasul.com.br. No children under 4. Discounts for ages 4-12. Trips from R$20-25; group rate R$15-20 per person.) Nearby is **Parque Estadual Serra do Tabuleiro,** where there are **hiking trails.** The easiest way to visit is to take a bus from the *rodoviária* south along BR-101, and ask the driver to let you off at the entrance to the park. **Trekking das Águas** offers **rafting, canoeing,** and **guided trekking** in the Parque Estadual do Serra do Tabuleiro, on the mainland. (☎245 7279, 9972 4417. Min. 3 people. Trips start at R$40.) **Ativa Rafting e Aventuras** is another company that organizes extreme sports and day trips. (☎245 7021, 9962 2420; www.ativarafting.com.br.) Companies that offer scuba diving courses and will provide equipment include: **Acquanauta Mergulho,** Rua Antenor Borges 394, in Canasvieras (☎266 1137; www.acquanauta.com.br/floripa) and **Parcel Dive Center,** Av. Luiz Boiteux Piazza 2243, Cachoeira do Bom Jesus (☎284 5564; www.parcel.com.br). **Sea Divers,** Rua Luiz Boiteux Piazza 6562, in Ponta das Canas, has similar services. (☎284 1535; www.seadivers.com.br. Open daily 7:30am-9pm.)

SÃO FRANCISCO DO SUL ☎47

The glorious white sand beaches of Ilha de São Francisco do Sul shimmer against a backdrop of rolling hills and leave visitors feeling as though they've found a little island paradise. Unlike other coastal towns in Santa Catarina, the town of São Francisco do Sul (the only town on the island of the same name) has somehow managed to develop its infrastructure while still retaining the charm of a quiet coastal community. During the high season, it may not be easy to find yourself a secluded spot on any of the island's 12 **beaches.** From December to March, droves of people—both tourists and residents of nearby Joinville—descend upon the beaches; hotels fill up, prices rise, and this quiet town becomes a lively holiday center. Of all the beaches, Praia Enseada, Praia Ubatuba, Praia Forte, and Praia do Capri are the best for **swimming,** while Praia Itaguacu, Praia Prainhan, and Praia Molhe are the hot spots for **surfing.** The most popular *praias* are Enseada, Prainha, and Grande; Enseada is the most developed. If you'd rather be on the water than in it, Ecuna Portella offers **boat tours** of the bay which leave from the port. (☎444 1579; R$15.) **Museu Nacional do Mar,** Rua Manuel Lourenço de Andrade 133, has an impressive display of maritime vessels from rowboats to submarines. (☎444 1868; www.museunacionaldomar.com.br. Open Tu-Su 9am-6pm. R$3.)

Intercity **buses** stop along the main highway, BR-280. From there, local buses run to both the *centro* and the *praias* (R$2). Buses go to Curitiba (2 per day 7am-6:30pm) and Itajaí (7:15am). For **taxi** service call ☎444 2221. The **tourist office** is on Rua Babitonga. (☎444 5257; turismo@saofranciscodosul.com.br.) There are **ATMs** at **Bradesco Bank,** Rua Babitongo 245, and **Banco do Brasil,** also on Rua Babitonga. The **post office** is at Pça. Getúlio Vargas 3. (☎444 0135. Open M-F 8am-5pm, Sa 8am-noon.) **Postal code:** 89242-000.

The best accommodations are on Praia Enseada. **Hotel Enseada ❶,** Av. Atlântica 1074, provides bright, clean, and comfortable rooms at affordable prices, and the charming and helpful host serves a great breakfast. (☎449 0122, 449 0145. Singles R$25; doubles $35, with TV and *frigo-bar* R$45.). **Hotel Turismo ❷,** Av. Atlântica 1923, is more expensive but also has terrific facilities, including an attached restaurant and Internet access (R$3 per 30min.). Rooms are comfortable and some overlook the beach. (☎449 0060; hotelturismar@ilhanet.com.br. Singles R$35; doubles R$60.) If you want to stay in the town proper, **Hotel Kontiki ❷,** Rua Babitonga

211, is right next to the port. (☎444 2232; fax 444 2024. *Quartos* R$30 per person.) Along Av. Atlântica, which runs the length of the Praia Enseada, are a number of inexpensive *choppeiras* and cafés (most of which serve only lunch). For a la carte meals, **Restaurante Panoramica ❷/❸**, is a good value and their balcony seating overlooks the beach. (Appetizers R$1.50-17. Entrees R$13-31.) The pleasant **Restaurante Portela ❷/❸**, Rua Babitonga 80, has a terrace that opens onto the bay. They serve an excellent buffet lunch as well as an a la carte dinner with a variety of options. (☎444 1579; restauranteportela@terra.com.br. Entrees R$14-25. Fish R$16-69. Pizza R$9-15. Open 9am-late. AmEx/MC/V.)

BLUMENAU ☎47

Blumenau is the home of Brazil's largest **Oktoberfest,** an 18-day street party with lots of traditional food, dancing, and *bierwagons* full of German beer. Oktoberfest is Blumenau's main attraction, and the town gets extremely crowded. The main festivities take place in the Pavilihão A da Proeb, Parque da Oktoberfest, on the corner of Rua João Pessoa and Rua Mal. Deodoro. (☎326 6798, 326 6968; fax 329 0336; www.oktoberfest.blumenau.com.br.)

ORIENTATION & PRACTICAL INFORMATION. The three main roads are the **Avenida Beira Rio, Rua XV de Novembro,** and **Rua 7 de Setembro,** which all run parallel to the Rio Itajaí Acu. The *centro* lies between the crossroads Rua Nereu Ramos and Rua João Pessoa. The **rodoviária,** Rua 7 de Setembro 1222 (☎338 1237), is on the outskirts of the town. From here, **buses** leave for: Balneário Camboriú (2 per day 12:30-7pm; R$9); Curitiba (9 per day 9:30am-11:30pm; R$19-25); Florianópolis (20 per day 6am-9pm; R$20); Foz do Iguaçu (6pm; R$56); Itajaí (14 per day 6am-11pm; R$8); Joinville (2 per day 6am-8:30pm; R$14); Penha (2 per day 6:30am-3pm; R$11); São Paulo (8pm; R$61). **Local buses** run from the *rodoviária* to the *centro* (R$1.40). To get to the *rodoviária* from town, take Bus #11 or #17 (on the Troncal-Fortaleza route) which run along Av. Beira Rio. **Taxis** between the *rodoviária* and the *centro* cost R$10; you can get one by calling Rádio Taxi (☎222 1977). The **tourist office,** Rua XV de Novembro 1050, is on the corner of Rua Nereu Ramos (☎326 6797; www.blumenau.com.br. Open M-F 8am-7pm, Sa 9am-7pm, Su and holidays 9am-3pm.) There are **ATMs** which accept AmEx/MC/V at **HSBC,** Rua XV de Novembro 534 (☎326 0133). **Casa Rowder Câmbio e Turismo Ltda.,** Rua Curt Hering 20, changes cash and traveler's checks (☎326 0287). Other services include: **24hr. pharmacy,** Drogaria Catarinese, Rua 15 Novembro 550 (☎322 1090); **Hospital Santa Isabel,** Rua Mal. Floriano Peixoto 300 (☎321 1000); and **police station,** Pça. Victor Konder 355 (☎322 9447). There is **Internet access** at Livraria Alema, Rua Dr. Amadeu da Luz 260. (Open M-Sa 9am-9pm. R$2.50 per 30min.) The **post office** is at Rua 7 de Setembro 2180. (☎326 0405. Open M-F 8am-6pm.) **Postal code:** 89010-001.

ACCOMMODATIONS & FOOD. **Hotel Hermann ❶**, Rua Mal. Floriano Peixoto 213, is the best value in town. Its architecture is reminiscent of the town's colonial history, and there is a veranda overlooking a pristine garden. (☎322 4370; fax 326 0670. *Quarto* singles R$20; doubles R$35; triples R$48. *Apartamento* singles R$30, with TV R$37; doubles R$52, with TV R$58; triples R$70, with TV R$76.) At **Blumenau Tourist Hotel ❶**, Rua Francisco Margarida 67, the rooms are somewhat musty, but it's only a minute's walk from the *rodoviária.* (☎323 4640. *Quarto* singles R$20; doubles R$36. *Apartamento* singles R$35; doubles R$60; triples R$75). **Restaurante Cantinho ❷**, Rua 7 de Setembro 2284, has a lively atmosphere and attentive staff, and is a great place to get a meal, especially the famous *feijoada* on Saturdays. (☎322 6041. Entrees R$14-23. Open M-F 7:30am-10pm, Sa 7:30am-3pm. MC/V.) If you're in the mood for something sweet, try the freshly baked pies at the

Confeitura Cafehaus Gloria ❷, Rua 7 de Setembro 954, in the Hotel Glória. They also serve a buffet lunch (R$14 per person) and a variety of light dinners. (Open M-Sa 6-10am and 11am-8pm.)

OUTDOOR ACTIVITIES. Fifteen kilometers south of town, the **Parque Ecologico Spitzkopf,** Rua Bruno Schreiber 3777, has good hiking. The more strenuous trails head toward Spitzkopf peak, which has an altitude of 960m and provides beautiful views. Less demanding trails pass by a series of natural pools. The park has campgrounds, chalets, and a *lanchonete.* You can catch a taxi from the *centro* for about R$10. The cheapest way to get there is to take a bus from the *centro* heading toward Barrio Garcia, and from there catch another bus to Barrio Progresso (R$1.40). Ask to get off at Rua Santa Maria; from there it is about a 2km walk to the park entrance. (☎336 5422; www.texart.com.br/spitzkopf.htm. Open daily 7am-7pm. R$18.)

ITAJAÍ ☎47

The indigenous Guarani named the town Itajaí, literally "the Rock's River," to describe its location at the mouth of the Rio Itajaí-Acu. Although much of the town's coastline is not good for swimming, Itajaí's scenic location is an excellent place for simply sitting back and enjoying the view. In October, Itajaí hosts the **Marejada,** Brazil's largest celebration of Portuguese seafood dishes. A huge, colorful pavilion located near the port comes alive with music, dancing, and stalls offering seafood. (☎348 1080; www.itajai.com.br.) Itajaí makes a good jumping-off point for several daytrips into the surrounding area. For a beach with excellent swimming, head to **Porto Belo,** 40km down the coast. From there you can also take a boat trip to **Ilha Porto Belo,** which has prehistoric rock carvings.

Buses from the **rodoviária,** Av. Governador Konder 1201 (☎348 6682), run to Porto Belo (every hr. until 7pm; R$6). Local buses run to the *centro* (every 15-20min.; R$1.75). There are also **taxis** available (☎348 3104, 348 1304), and **car rental** can be arranged with Localiza, Rua Lauro Muller 170. (☎348 2624.) The layout of the town can be confusing, but the *centro* lies between two parallel main roads, **Avenida Marcos Konder** and **Avenida 7 de Setembro,** and the crossroads **Avenida Joca Brandão** and **Rua Heito Liberato. Avenida Victor Konder** runs along the shoreline and past the port. Beaches are east of the *centro* and are best accessed by local buses, which display their destination clearly. One of the main stops is on Av. Marcos Konder, opposite the *praça* with the church. The **tourist office,** Av. Victor Konder 303, Pavilihão de Marejada, has a helpful staff. (☎348 1080; www.itajai.com.br. Open M-F 8am-6pm.) **ATMs** are found at **Banco Bradesco,** Rua Hecílio Luz 145 (☎348 1811) and **Banco do Brasil,** on Rua Felipe Schmidt (☎348 1211). **Exchange Tur,** Rua Hercilio Luz 53, changes cash and traveler's checks (☎348 5108). There is a **supermarket** on the corner of Av. 7 de Setembro and Rua Nereu Ramos. (Open daily 8am-9pm. AmEx/DC/MC.There are **police** at Av. Joca Brandão 112 (☎348 0123). The **post office** is on Rua Felipe Schmidt 175 (☎348 3535). **Postal code:** 88301-000.

Hotel Rota do Mar ❷, Rua Lauro Muller 97, is the best value in town, and the host speaks some English. Rooms are simple but clean. (☎348 6435, 348 4274. *Quarto* singles R$25; doubles R$45. *Semi-luxo* singles with TV and *frigo-bar* R$26, with A/C R$28; doubles with TV and *frigo-bar* R$47; with A/C R$50.) **Hotel Caicaras ❷,** Rua Pedro Ferreira 3, is more expensive but some rooms have a pleasant view of the port. It is centrally located and has a bar and an attached restaurant. (☎348 8600; www.hotelcaicaras.com.br. Restaurant open daily 11am-2pm and 6pm-1am. Singles R$40; doubles R$65.) **Yong Chin Restaurante Chinês ❷/❸,** Rua Jose Bonifacio Malburg 538, has a buffet lunch and an a la carte dinner. (☎348 4618. Open M 11:30am-2:30pm, T-Sa 11:30am-2:30pm and 7:30-10pm. DC/MC.)

SOUTH

RIO GRANDE DO SUL

PORTO ALEGRE ☎51

You'll find references to Gaúcho history at almost every turn in Porto Alegre, but the city is also home to a vibrant mix of indigenous, Azorian, African, German, and Italian traditions. Today, Porto Alegre is a flourishing and diverse urban center: grand buildings from the colonial era, the *chimarrão* drinking tradition handed down from the indigenous peoples, *churrascarias* lining the streets, and frenetic *sambas* combine in a unique cultural montage that today characterizes Porto Alegre. Appropriately, it was this city of such cultural diversity that hosted the 2003 World Social Forum. Its position as important port makes the city an active commercial and industrial hub. Nevertheless, with parks gracing the city's suburbs and protected reserves in the surrounding areas, there is enough greenery to compensate for any negative impact that industry has had here.

TRANSPORTATION. From **Salgado Filho International Airport,** Av. dos Estados s/n, there are direct flights to major Brazilian cities and some international destinations (flight information ☎343 5638, 221 1833; general information ☎3358 2000, 3358 2549). Airline offices in the city include: **Aerolineas Argentinas,** Av. Senador Salgado Filho 267 (☎/fax 3321 3300); **Air France** and **British Airways,** both at Rua dos Andrades 1234, (☎3287 8500); **American Airlines,** Av. Alberto Bins 514, loja 8, next to the Hotel Plaza São Rafael (☎3211 2088, 3211 2350; open M-F 8:30am-6pm, Sa 9am-1pm); **Lufthansa,** Pça. da Alfândega 12, 9th fl. (☎3287 3900); **Rio-Sul,** Rua 18 de Novembro 590 (☎3358 2595); **TAM,** Av. Cairú 1410 (☎3358 3000); **Varig,** Rua dos Andrades, 1107 (☎3210 3900); **VASP,** Rua dos Andrades 1320 (☎3325 6111).

The **Estação Rodoviária,** Largo Vespasiano Júlio Veppo s/n (☎3210 0101; www.rodoviaria-poa.com.br), handles both interstate and intermunicipal travel. **International buses** travel to: Asunçion (daily 7:15pm; R$103); Buenos Aires (daily 5pm; R$148); Montevideo (daily 10pm; *convencional* R$124, *leito* R$178); Santiago (36hr.; M-F 7am; R$250). **Interstate buses** leave for: Brasília (36hr.; M, W, F 9pm and Su 9am; R$182); Curitiba (3 per day 9am-10pm; *convencional* R$50, *executivo* R$75, *leito* R$99); Florianópolis (6hr.; M-F 5 per day 7:15am-midnight, Sa-Su 3 per day 7:15am-9:30pm; R$46); Fortaleza (66hr.; F 11am); Foz do Iguaçu (2 per day 6:30-7pm; R$77); Joinville (3 per day 9am-10pm; *convencional* R$46, *executivo* R$63, *leito* R$88); Santo Ângelo (6½hr.; 5 per day noon-11pm; R$43); Rio de Janeiro (24hr.; M, W, F 9am; R$151); São Paulo (18hr.; 2-3 per day 2pm-10pm; R$100). The **local bus station,** Rua Voluntários da Pátria, is next to the public market (route information ☎158; www.portoalegre.rs.gov.bris). Buses run all over the city, from the shopping areas to the suburbs (R$1.45). The **metrô** connects the *centro* to the *rodoviária* and the airport. The stop in the *centro*, Estação Mercado, is on Av. Mauá, behind the public market. Call **Rádio Taxis** (☎322 8577, 3226 1919) for cabs.

ORIENTATION & PRACTICAL INFORMATION. The city is centered on **Rua 7 de Setembro, Rua dos Andrades,** and **Avenida Alberto Bins,** which run parallel to each other. From the *centro*, Av. Borges de Medeiros, Av. Independéncia, Av. João Pessoa, and Av. Osvaldo Aranha radiate out into the surrounding suburbs where most parks, restaurants, and nightlife hotspots are located. The roads are often confusing, so it's a good idea to keep a map handy when navigating the city. Also be sure either to leave your valuables at home as you walk around, or keep them very close. The *centro* gets crowded during the day, and presents wonderful opportunity for pickpockets. At night it is not advisable to walk around the *centro*.

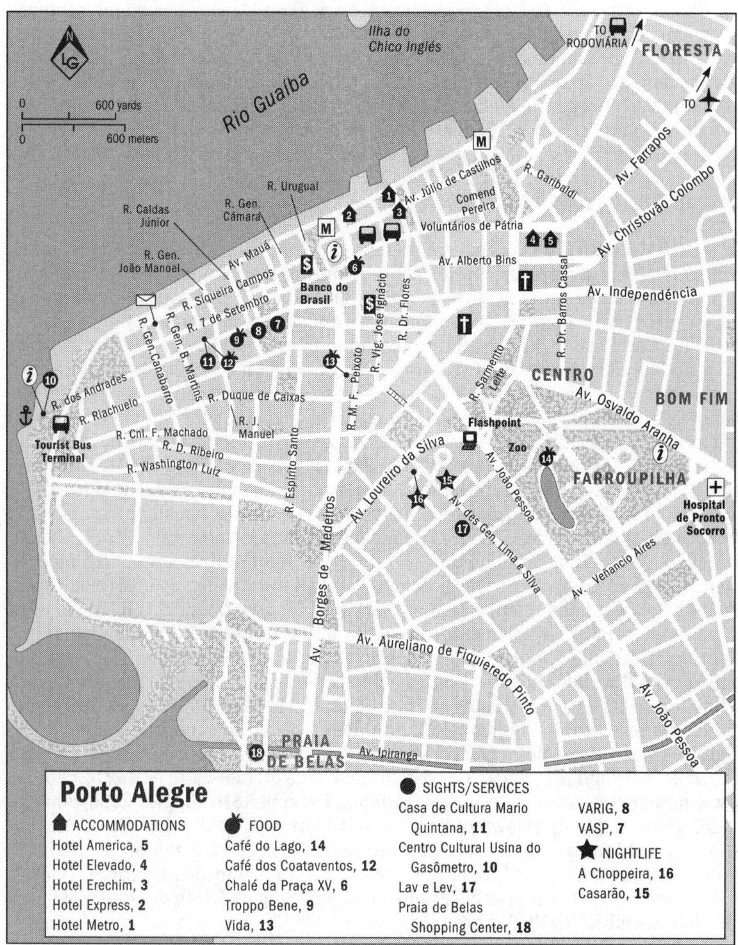

There are several **tourist offices** in the city, all with multilingual staff and information, which can be found at: the airport (☎3358 2047; open daily 7:30am-midnight); the *rodoviária* (☎225 8173; open M-F 8:30am-6pm, Sa-Su and holidays noon-6pm); Mercado do Bom Fim (☎3333 1873; open daily 9am-8pm); Mercado Público Central (open M-Sa 9am-6pm); Centro Cultural Usina do Gasômetro, Av. Pres. João Goulart 551 (open Tu-Su 10am-6pm); Praia de Belas Shopping (open M-Sa 10am-10pm). **General tourist information:** ☎0800 051 7686; www.portoalegre.rs.gov.br/turismo. **Consulates** in Porto Alegre include: **UK,** Rua Itapeva 110, ste. 505 (☎/fax 3341 0720; open M-F 9am-noon and 2:30-6pm); **South Africa,** Rua Bororó 496 (☎3249 2497; open M-F 8:30am-noon and 2-5pm); **US,** Rua Coronel Genuino 421, 9th fl. (☎226 4288, 226 4697; fax 221 2213; open M-F 2-5pm). There is **currency exchange** at **Prontut,** Av. Borges de Medeiros 445 (☎3221 6566; open M-F 9:30am-5:15pm) and **Mariotur,** Rua dos Andrades 1251 (☎3226 2102, 3226 2811; open M-F 9:30am-5:30pm). Other services include: **supermarket,** Zaffari, Av. des

Gen. Lima e Silva 606 (☎3221 6848; open M-Sa 8:30am-11pm, Su 9am-9pm); **laundry,** Lav e Lev, Av. des Gen. Lima e Silva 579 (☎3226 3755; open M-Sa 8:30am-8:30pm; wash R$6, dry R$3 per 15min.); **police,** Av. João Pessoa 2050 (☎3217 2411); **24hr. pharmacies,** Av. João Pessoa 1141 (☎228 8015), Av. Independência 1200 (☎221 9106), and Av. Borges de Medieros 628 (☎224 4407); **Hospital de Pronto Socorro,** Av. Osvaldo Aranha s/n (☎3316 9600); **Internet access,** Flashpoint, Av. des General Lima e Silva 260 (☎3227 9663; open M-Sa 9am-10pm). There is a **post office** at Rua Siqueira Campos 1100. (☎3220 8800, 3227 4871. Open M-F 9am-6pm, Sa 9am-12:30pm.) **Postal code:** 90020-000.

ACCOMMODATIONS. The quality of accommodations in Porto Alegre varies a great deal. The best places to stay are generally along Av. Júlio de Castilhos. Farther into the *centro*, the quality decreases dramatically and you will have to pay higher prices for a comfortable room. There are decent accommodations near Av. Júlio de Castilhos, within walking distance of the *metrô* stop in the *centro*, Estação Mercado. However, if you are arriving at night it is advisable to take a taxi, as the *centro* is not always safe. The cheapest accommodations are at **Hotel Elevado ❶,** Av. Farrapos 63. Rooms here are surprisingly nice for the price. The central area is bright and open with plants and cozy sofas. Rooms facing the street can be noisy; ask for a room in the back. (☎/fax 3224 5250. Parking R$5. *Quarto* singles R$16; doubles R$28; triples R$36. *Apartamento* singles R$28; doubles R$39; triples R$48.) A few minutes down the road is the almost equally pleasant **Hotel America ❶,** at Av. Farrapos 119, a 15min. walk from the *metrô* stop. From Estação Mercado, walk along Av. Júlio de Castilhos, turn right onto Rua Cel. Vicente and then left onto Av. Farrapos. This hotel has comfortable, quality rooms. (☎322 0062, 3212 4261; www.hotelamerica.com.br. Parking R$5. *Quarto* singles R$12; doubles R$25; triples R$32. *Apartamento* singles R$24; doubles R$34; triples R$48.) Another affordable option is **Hotel Erechim ❶,** Av. Júlio de Castilhos 341. From the outside you'll wonder how they managed to squeeze such comfortable rooms into what looks like a tiny place. (☎/fax 3228 7044, 3225 1090; www.hotelerechim.com.br. *Quarto* singles R$21; doubles R$35. *Apartamento* singles R$29; doubles R$42.) **Hotel Metro ❷,** Av. Júlio de Castilhos 477, has *apartamentos* with TV, *frigo-bar*, and A/C, and even basic rooms have private bath. (☎/fax 3221 5011; www.hotelmetro.com.br. Breakfast included. Parking R$10. Singles R$26; doubles R$38; triples R$50. *Apartamento* singles R$46; doubles R$68; triples R$82. AmEx/MC/V.) **Hotel Express ❷,** Av Júlio de Castilhos 342, is fancier and bigger than the Hotel Metro, with a grand foyer and spacious rooms, but higher prices. (☎3228 8080; www.hotelexpress.tur.br. English spoken. Singles R$50; doubles R$60; triples R$90. AmEx/DC/MC/V.)

FOOD. Aside from the many *churrascarias* that herald Porto Alegre's Gaúcho tradition, the city has a number of well-located cafés and restaurants with good ambience. Near the Mercado Público is **Chalé da Praça XV ❶/❷,** on Pça. XV de Novembro. If you get a good seat, you may be able to watch the street performers in the square. (☎3225 2667. Meals R$5-15. Open daily 11am-12:30am. AmEx/V.) **Café do Lago ❶,** Av. João Pessoa s/n, is situated right on the lake in Parque Farroupilha. It serves light meals and drinks, and on the weekends has live music. (☎3212 4968; www.cafedolago.com.br. Live music Sa-Su 5pm-late. Cover R$2. Open 11am-8:30pm.) Under the arches of the Casa de Cultura Mário Quintana sits **Café dos Coataventos ❷,** Rua dos Andrades 736. Elegant, refreshing, and serene, this is a great place to enjoy a meal followed by a performance in the theatre next door. (☎3226 6688. Meals R$7-21. Open M-F 11:30am-10pm, Sa-Su 2:30-10pm. MC/V.) Vegetarians can take refuge from the *churrascarias* at **Vida (Restaurante Vegetariano) ❶,** Rua Jeronimo Coelho 298, which has a wonderful buffet selection containing fruits, vegetables, pasta salads, and more for R$7 per person. (☎3212 4362. Open M-F 11am-3pm.) Another buffet-style restaurant with both meat and vegetarian dishes is **Troppo Bene ❶**, on the ground floor of Shopping Rua da Praia. This place is a healthy option amongst a sea of fast-food joints, and a great place to take a break from shopping. (☎3225 7314, 3225 4720. Open daily 11am-10:30pm.)

SIGHTS. Like many other old cities, Porto Alegre has dozens of historical buildings, monuments, churches, and museums to visit. The best way to orient yourself around these sights to is take a **city tour** offered by the tourist office **Linha Turismo.** The tour lasts about 1½hr. and has audio descriptions of the sights in Portuguese, English, and Spanish. Buses depart from the Centro Cultural Usina do Gasômetro, Av. Pres. João Goulart 551, which is at the pier end of Rua dos Andrades. (☎3333 1873. Tu-Su 5 per day 9am-4:30pm. R$5.) The tourist office also offers a **walking tour** that departs from the same place. (Tu-Su 10:30am. Free.) Take some time to look around the **Centro Cultural Usina do Gasômetro.** Originally a thermoelectric plant, it was converted into a cultural center in 1991. Surrounding somewhat ominous metal columns and open stairwells are art exhibitions, a cinema, and a theater. From the terrace there is a good view of Lagoa Guaíba. (☎3227 1383, 3212 5979. Open Tu-Su 10am-10pm.) On the way back to the *centro* is another recently renovated cultural center, **Casa de Cultura Mario Quintana,** Rua dos Andrades 736. It was constructed in the early 20th century as the Hotel Majestic, which was visited by many famous politicians and artists, including Getúlio Vargas, Vicente Celestino, Dalva de Oliveira, and the renowned Brazilian poet Mario Quintana. (☎3221 7147. Open Tu-F 9am-9pm, Sa-Su noon-9pm. Farther along Rua dos Andrades is **Praça da Alfandega,** where you'll find a mini-market with arts and crafts by local artists, and both the **Memorial de Rio Grande do Sul** and **Museu de Arte do Rio Grande do Sul.** Memorial de Rio Grande do Sul is in the old post office, and its most interesting exhibitions are those pertaining to Gaúcho history. (☎3225 8490. Open Tu-F 10am-7pm, Sa-Su noon-5pm.) The second houses famous artwork and sculptures as well as temporary exhibitions by local artists. (☎3227 2311. Open Tu-Su 10am-7pm.)

Boat tours on Lake Guaíba can be arranged with **Cisne Branco,** Av. Mauá 1050. Hour-long trips include visits to Ilha da Pintada and Ilha das Flores. (☎/fax 3224 5222. Tu-Su 4 per day 10:30am-6pm. Min. 10 people. R$10 per person.) A cheaper option is **Por do Sol V,** which offers boat tours of the same length. (☎9947 0175. Call to reserve. Min. 5 people. R$5 per person.) Both boat tours leave from behind the Usina do Gasômetro. Another way to get away from the hustle and bustle of the *centro* is to head to one of the parks in the area. The most famous is **Parque Farroupilha,** between Av. João Pessoa, Av. José Bonifácio, and Av. Osvaldo Aranha. It is also known as Redenção (Redemption), and has more than 15 acres of green, complete with its own lake, zoo, and playground. The park is nice to simply stroll or jog in, but on Sundays from 9am to 4pm the José Bonifácio end becomes a huge craft and food market with live music, *capoeira*, and street theatre. Farther removed from the city is **Parque Natural Morro do Osso,** which has been a national reserve since 1979 and encompasses an area of 114 hectares. Aside from the vibrant flora and fauna in the park, it also has an excellent view of Lake Guaíba and the surrounding area. There are various trails but hikers must be accompanied by a guide. (☎382 1518, 382 1599, 3263 3769; smam@smam.prefpoa.com.br. Open Sa-Su and holidays early-4pm.)

NIGHTLIFE & ENTERTAINMENT. There are more than 25 theatres and cultural centers in Porto Alegre, accounting for the city's dynamic arts scene. If you are in Porto Alegre for more than a couple of days and want to see a performance, you're bound to find something that suits your taste, although it will probably be in Portuguese. The best way to find out about shows is to ask at the tourist office for a free copy of *Agenda Cultural*, published monthly by the Secretaria Municipal da Cultura. Several streets in Porto Alegre are renowned for their nightlife. In Cidade Baixa, Rua Gen. Lima e Silva has bars and restaurants beckoning to passersby until the early morning. If you stop by **A Choppeira,** Rua Gen. Lima e Silva 776, you can serve yourself draft beer. (☎3221 0211. Open M-Sa 6pm-1:30am. Visa.) For live music, check out **Casarão,** Rua Sarmento Leite 892. (☎3225 7077, 3221 3330. Open Tu-F 6pm-1:30am, Sa-Su 7pm-1:30am.) Check out Rua 24 de Outubro and Rua Fernando Gomes for live jazz, blues, rock and the famous international student gathering every Tuesday night at **Bar do Goethe,** Rua 24 de Outubro 112. (☎3222 2043. Open M-F 2-10pm.)

SHOPPING. Porto Alegre's primary shopping districts are located in the *centro*. The **mercado público,** between Av. Júlio de Castiles and Rua Voluntários da Pátria, has anything and everything you have ever wanted to buy, including clothes, souvenirs, fish, fruit, and even machinery and plastics. Be wary of the numerous people shouting *"valé, valé!"*—they are selling counterfeit bus tokens, which result in being slapped with a heavy fine if you are caught using them. The market opens early in the morning and is very crowded by 11am; things get even more crowded around 4pm. It starts to wind down between 6pm and 7pm, and the area becomes unsafe at night, so it's not a good idea to wander around too late. **Rua dos Andrades** (formerly Rua da Praia) is another popular shopping district packed with shops and a pedestrian-only street. The biggest shopping malls in town are **Iguatemi,** Av. João Wallig 1800 (☎3334 4500), and **Praia de Belas,** Av. Praia de Belas 1181 (☎3231 4499; open M-Sa 10am-6pm).

GRAMADO ☎54

One hundred eighteen kilometers inland from Porto Alegre lies a mountain resort which would probably be more at home in the Alps, and chalets and chic shops make Gramado border on the slightly pretentious. Nevertheless, there is a good reason to visit: the town is known as a producer of especially delicious chocolate.

ORIENTATION & PRACTICAL INFORMATION. The main **rodoviária** (☎286 1302) is on Av. Borges de Medeiros, the major road running through the town. Walking north along Av. Borges Medeiros (toward Canela) from the *rodoviária* will get you to the *centro*, where most services and accommodations can be found. **Buses** run to Canela (every 20-30hr. 6:40am-9pm; R$1) and Porto Alegre (2hr.; 8 per day 6:15am-5:15pm; R$15). The **tourist office,** Av. Borges de Medeiros 1647, is on the same street. (☎286 1475; www.gramadosite.com.br. Open daily 9am-8pm.) There are 24hr. **ATMs** in the HSBC on Rua Garibaldi (AmEx/MC/V). **Internet access** is available at Café Cultura, Av. Borges de Medeiros 2017, near the *rodoviária* (☎286 9559. Open daily 1-11pm. R$2 per 15min.) Other services include: **supermarket** Cesa, Av. Broges de Medeiros 2497 (open daily 9am-7:30pm.); **laundromat** Lav e Lev, Rua Garibaldi 684 (☎286 3060; open M-Sa 8am-6pm; R$19.50 wash and dry; DC/MC.); **police,** Cel. João Correa, by the *rodoviária* (☎286 2222); **post office,** Rua Garibaldi 520, at Rua Augusto Zatti (☎286 2490; open M-F 9am-5pm). **Postal code:** 95670-000.

ACCOMMODATIONS & FOOD. Pricey chalet-style accommodations dominate most of Gramado, making it hard to find affordable lodging; during July, August, and December, prices go up even more. The cheapest option is the comfortable youth hostel, **Albergue Internacional de Gramado (HI) ❶,** Av. das Hortênsians 3880. To get there take the Gramado-Canela-Saiqui circular and get off in front of the Shop Saccaro and opposite Bill's Bar; the hostel is about 50m down the road. It has a kitchen, laundry room, TV room, and an exceedingly friendly English-speaking staff. (☎295 1020; www.gramado.br/albergue.htm. Laundry R$5. Dorms R$18, non-members R$22.) **Hotel Dinda ❸,** Av. Borges de Medeiros 160, is simpler than other hotels, but still rather costly. (☎286 1588; fax 286 2810. Singles R$50; 1-bed doubles R$80, 2-bed doubles R$100. R$35 for an extra bed.)

Along Av. Borges de Medeiros, you'll find lots of ritzy restaurants. **Arabian ❸,** Rua Senador Salgado Filho 190, specializes in Middle Eastern cuisine. (☎3036 0121. Platter R$10-12, for two R$15-28. Open Tu-Sa 11:30am-midnight, Su 11:30am-3pm. MC/V.) **Restaurante Kilo & Kilo ❷,** Av. das Hortênsias 1720, has a popular buffet (R$13 per person) and gets crowded in the early afternoon. (☎286 1182. Open 11:15am-3:30pm and 7-10pm.) Sample Gramado's famous chocolate at **Planalto ❶,** Rua João Carniel 689. (☎286 1701. Open daily 8am-8pm.)

SIGHTS & FESTIVALS. Gramado has a few pleasant parks. Along Av. Lago Negro, between Rua Casa da Juventude, Av. J. Renner, and Rua 25 de Julho is a small **lakeside park,** known for its beautiful *hortênsias* (hydrangeas). Gramado is also home to **Parque Knorr,** on Rua Bela Vista, off Av. das Hortênsias on the way to Canela. Parque Knorr is famous for being the home of Papai Noel (Santa Claus) but perhaps more interesting for the view it offers of the **Vale do Quilombo.** (☎286 7332. Open M-F 2-9pm, Sa-Su 10am-9pm.) Every August, Gramado and Canela jointly host a prestigious international film festival that showcases cinema from across the continent and draws movie lovers from all over the globe.

CANELA ☎54

Only six kilometers down the road from Gramado, Canela offers a very different getaway. Surrounded by six parks (see **Outdoor activities,** p. 268), the town provides opportunities for hiking, rappeling, rafting, canyoning, and horseback riding. The town itself isn't of much interest, and although each of Canela's parks are fairly small, there is enough to do that nature lovers won't get bored.

TRANSPORTATION & PRACTICAL INFORMATION. Canela is a fairly small town and most services are concentrated on the two main streets, Av. Osvaldo Aranha and Av. Júlio Castilhos. The **rodoviária** is between Ernesto Urbani and Arlindo Paso, a 2min. walk from the *centro*. **Buses** run to Porto Alegre (2hr.; 8 per day 6am-5pm; R$14.80). The **tourist office** is opposite Pça. João Correa, on Largo da Fama. (☎282 2200; www.canela.com.br; www.canelaturismo.com.br. Open daily 8am-7pm.) Nearby in the park is **Central de Aventuras** (☎282 3282) with information on the various adventure trips and the companies that run them. **Posto Telefônico,** Av. Júlio de Castilhos 319, offers **Internet access** (R$0.15 per min.), phones, and **fax** services. (☎3031 0107. Open M-F 8am-9pm, Sa 9am-8pm, Su 10am-noon and 2-6pm.) Other services include: **24hr. ATMs** that accept Visa at **Banco do Brasil,** Av. Júlio de Castilhos 465 (☎282 4100); **supermarket,** Av. Osvaldo Aranha 54 (open M-Sa 8am-7pm, Su 9am-noon); **24hr. pharmacy** Lider, Av. Júlio de Castilhos 267 (☎282 1100). **Postal code:** 95680-000.

ACCOMMODATIONS & FOOD. The cheapest place to stay in town is **Pousada do Viajante ❶,** Rua Ernesto Urban 132, right beside the *rodoviária*. The *pousada* has basic dormitories and more comfortable *apartamentos* with private bath and TV. The *pousada* also has a kitchen, and a TV room. (☎282 2017. Check-out 11am. Dorms R$15. *Apartamentos* R$30.) Farther into the town is **Hotel Turis ❶,** Av. Osvaldo Aranha 223, which has simple *quartos* and nicer *apartamentos*. (☎282 8436. *Quarto* singles R$25; doubles R$50. *Apartamento* singles R$35; doubles R$65; triples R$90.) **Pousada Veredas ❷,** Av. Júlio de Castilhos 399, has bright rooms with pine furniture, *frigo-bar*, TV, and parking. (☎278 2178; www.pousada-veredas.com.br. Singles R$40; doubles R$60.) You can pitch a tent at **Camping Clube do Brasil ❶,** RS-466, on the right just before Parque do Caracol. (☎282 4321. Camping R$4 per person.) The meat dishes at **Churrascaria Espelho Gaúcho ❷,** Rua Baden Powel 50, are sure to please. (☎282 4348. *Churrasco* R$8.90. Open 11:30am-3pm and 6-11:30pm.) For lighter meals **Café Canela ❶,** Pça. João Corrêa, is a bistro with a modern feel. (☎282 3304. Crepes R$4.40. Sandwiches R$4-8. Open daily noon-midnight.) **Boccatta ❷/❸,** Largo da Fama s/n, is a pizzeria in an old train station. From one end of the building a steam engine juts out and there is antique railway equipment inside. (☎282 7070. Pizza R$15-17. Open daily 2-11pm.)

SIGHTS & OUTDOOR ACTIVITIES. At!tude, Av. Osvaldo Aranha 391, offers a wide variety of organized half- and full-day adventure sport outings, including cycling, rafting, rappeling, canyoning, and cascading. (☎2826 3005, 3031 0345, 9982 6900; www.atitude.tur.br.) **Brilho da Serra,** Rua Melvin Jones 89, has half-day rafting trips on Rio Paranhana. (☎282 1637, 9982 4840; fax 282 4036; brilhodaserra@terra.com.br. Open M-F 8:30am-7pm, Sa 9am-4pm. Min. 6 people. R$45 per person, includes all equipment.) **JM Rafting & Expedições,** Av. Osvaldo Aranha 1038, offers an evening rafting trip on Rio Paranhana. (☎282 1255; fax 282 1542; jmrafting@jmrafting.com.br. Min. 4 people. R$50.) Horseback riding can be arranged by **Fazenda Passo Alegre.** (☎504 1800; www.passoalegre.cjb.net. Min. 2 people. 3hr. R$36; day R$75.)

Parque do Caracol, with the 131m Cascada do Caracol, is the most popular of this area's several parks. It features a number of 15-30min. trails and an observatory with impressive views of the area, as well as a restaurant, handicraft stalls, and a staircase leading to the bottom of the waterfall. The park lies 6km from the northern edge of town. (☎282 3035. Open daily 8:30am-5:30pm. R$8.) A **bus** runs to Caracol from the *rodoviária* side of Pça. João Correa, opposite the tourist office. (M-F departs 8am and noon, returns noon and 6pm; Sa departs 8am and noon, returns noon, 6, and 7:30pm; Su departs 8am and 1:30pm, returns 1:30, 6, and 7:30pm.) On the bus route to Caracol is **Parque do Pinheiro Grosso,** where there is a 700-year-old pine, standing 48m tall and 2.75m wide. (Open M-F 8:30am-5:30pm, Sa-Su 8:30am-6:30pm. R$2.) Five hundred meters past Caracol is **Floresta Encantada.** There you can hop on a cable car to witness a stunning view of the Lageana valley. There are also a number of short trails through the forests at the top of the cable ride. (☎504 1405. Open daily 9am-6:30pm. R$8.) Still farther down the road with longer trails is **Parque da Ferradura.** Trails lead to a waterfall, Cascata do Arroio Caçador, and a 420m canyon. In another part of the park, a river curves its way around a mountain peak through the Vale da Ferradura, creating the impression of an island mountain. There is no bus to the Parque da Ferradura, but you can take the bus to Caracol and hike the 7km from there. (☎282 4300. Open daily 8:30am-5:30pm. R$5.)

On the opposite end of town, 18km from Canela is **Parque da Cachoeira,** with still more opportunities for short hikes and a natural pool at the end of it to cool off. The park also has a **campsite** (R$6 per person) in case you miss your bus back. (☎504 1446, 282 2051. Open daily 8:30am-6:30pm. R$3, under 7 free.) **Buses** leave from the *rodoviária* (M, W, F departs 8:50am and 3:45pm, returns 9:10am; Sa departs 1:50pm, returns 9:10am; Su departs 7:45am, returns 7pm). Two kilometers from the southern edge of town is **Parque Sesi.** Its 17 hectares encompass ecological trails, a small waterfall, sports grounds, playgrounds, a campground, and dorm-style accommodations. (☎282 1311. Camping R$2 and R$7.) Buses leave from the *rodoviária* (departs 5 per day 7:55am-6:15pm; returns 6 per day 8:10am-6:30pm). Buses to Sesi also go to the nearby **Parque das Sequóias,** which has 90 species of conifers, some 30m high and 1.5m wide. (☎282 1373. Open daily 10am-5pm. R$2.)

P.N. DE APARADOS DA SERRA ☎54

Inland from the coast of Rio Grande do Sul lies the Serra Gaúcha mountain range, composed of magnificent peaks and spectacular cliffs with vertical drops of almost 1km. Waterfalls and rapid rivers add to the area's beauty and also give life to the great diversity of flora and fauna here. In the Parque Nacional de Aparados da Serra and its extension, the Parque Nacional da Serra Geral, Itaimbezinho and Fortaleza canyons offer the most impressive views of the Serra Gaúcha.

AT A GLANCE: P.N. DE APARADOS DA SERRA	
AREA: 102.5 square kilometers.	**HIGHLIGHTS:** Canyon Itaimbezinho; Canyon Fortaleza; Cachoeira dos Venâncios; Pedra do Segredo.
CLIMATE: Average temp of 18°C, max 32°C, min -8°C.	**GATEWAY TOWNS:** Cambará do Sul, São Francisco de Paula.
WHEN TO GO: June to August, or if you don't mind a little heat, Dec.-March. Avoid September when there is almost constant rainfall. Open W-Su 9am-5pm.	**FEES:** R$6, under 7 and over 70 free. Parking: Car R$5, Minibus R$10.
PARK INFORMATION: ☎251 1277.	**CAMPING:** Prohibited.

TRANSPORTATION

Transportation to and from the park is very infrequent: there are only two buses per day, so it's advisable to plan ahead. Buses run from Cambará do Sul's *rodoviária* to Parque Nacional de Aparados do Serra (M-Sa departs 11:45am, returns 5:30pm; R$5). Otherwise, a taxi to and from the park costs about R$65. From Cambará do Sul buses also run to São Francisco de Paula (1½hr.; 2 per day 6:30am-1:30pm), where there are connections to Canela and Porto Alegre. From São Francisco de Paula buses go to Cambará do Sul (1½hr.; 2 per day 9:45am-5pm; R$5.90) and Canela (50min.; 4 per day 7am-3:10pm; R$3.45).

ORIENTATION

As a gateway town to the park, **Cambará do Sul** is the best place to find accommodations and to stock up on any basic supplies you might need. **São Francisco de Paula,** about 1½hr. from Cambará do Sul, has banks and a post office. At Parque Nacional de Aparados do Serra there is an information station where guides (R$25) and free maps can be found. There is no similar infrastructure at Parque National da Serra Geral, where guides are more necessary and can be arranged through the tourist office in Cambará do Sul.

PRACTICAL INFORMATION

There are free **maps** available at the **tourist office** in Cambará do Sul and at the park entrance. Basic **supplies** can be bought in Cambará do Sul. **Canyon Sports** (see **Accommodations,** p. 267) sells waterproof jackets and rents sleeping pads. Otherwise, **gear** should be purchased in Canela or Porto Alegre. The best place to organize a **tour** is in Canela. **Brilho Da Serra,** Rua Melvin Jones 89, has half-day tours of Parque Nacional de Aparados da Serra. (☎282 1637; fax 282 4036; brilhodaserra@terra.com.br. Min. 6 people; R$45.) **Montes Verdes Adventure,** RS-235 521, has full-day tours of Canyon Itaimbezinho, Canyon Fortaleza, and both canyons (☎282 3282; fax 282 0568; www.montesverdesadventure.com.br. Tours 7:30am-6pm. Min. 2 people. R$125-150). **Park Information:** ☎251 1277.

ACCOMMODATIONS & FOOD

Cambará do Sul is the closest place to stay because camping in the park proper is prohibited. **Canyon Sports ❶,** Osvaldo Kroeff 54, is 5min. from the *rodoviária.* Walk left out of the station and take the first left onto Osvaldo Kroeff. Canyon is the cheapest option, providing rudimentary dorms and camping facilities with tents provided. (☎251 1700, 9999 8613. Dorms R$20. Camping R$5-7 per person.) **Pousada Itaimbeleza ❶,** Rua Dona Ursula 648, on the same road as the *rodoviária,* is an attractive cabin-like building with a warm and comfortable feel. From the *rodoviária,* turn left and walk past Osvaldo Kroeff; it's on the left just after the small rotary. (☎251 1365; www.itaimbezinnho.tur.br. *Quartos* R$25 per person. *Apartamentos* R$30 per person.) Camping is also possible at the **Fazenda Capão Alto ❶,** 15km from town; to get there you must either hike or take a taxi. From the *rodoviária,* walk left and turn left onto Osvaldo Kroeff and then right onto Av. Getúlio Vargas. Turn left after you see the restaurant Arca about 12km down the road; the campground is on the right. Facilities include showers and electricity. (☎9985 0779. Camping R$5 per person.) There are a number of *lanchonetes* with snacks and fast food in Cambará do Sul. For a more substantial meal, try **Casa-Nostra ❷,** Av. Getúlio Vargas 77, on the outskirts of Cambará do Sul as you walk toward São Francisco de Paula. Casa-Nostra is known for its *churrasco* (R$10). (☎251 1321. Open 8am-2pm and 8pm until late.) **Altos da Serva ❶,** Av. Getúlio Vargas s/n, farther into town on the main street, serves a buffet lunch (R$7) and variety of pizzas (R$14). (☎251 1395. Open M-Sa 11am-3pm and 7-10pm.)

HIKING

There are several different hikes through the park, most of which are relatively easy and short. **Trilha do Vértice** leads through the Canyon Itaimbezinho to an observation deck with views of the canyon, Cascata das Andorinhas, and Cachoeira Véu de Noiva. (1.1km, 1hr. round-trip. Difficulty: easy.) The longer **Trilha do Cota** winds through the Canyon Itaimbezinho that leads to a better view of the canyon. (6km, 2½hr. round-trip. Difficulty: easy.) The **Trilha do Pedra do Segredo** leads through the Canyon Fortaleza for a view of the monolithic rock. You'd better be quick—the rock looks like it has been ready to fall for a long time. (3km, 1½hr. round-trip. Difficulty: easy.) If you're looking for something a little more challenging, try the **Topo do Fortaleza,** a trail leading to a view of the breathtaking Canyon Fortaleza, with sharp descents of about 900m and 1172m. (2.8km, 1½hr. round-trip. Difficulty: medium to hard.)

CENTER-WEST

Including the Distrito Federal, Goiás, Mato Grosso, and Mato Grosso do Sul, the largely undeveloped Center-West region is a study in contrasts, encompassing both the meticulously planned capital district of Brasília and the untouched wilderness of the Pantanal, a vast flood plain stretching into Bolivia and Paraguay. Though the North's Amazon gets most international attention, the Pantanal's wilds (which comprise the world's largest inland wetlands) may be the best place in Brazil to see wildlife and get closer to nature. The few towns in the area have a similarly untamed flavor, with close ties to nature and a rugged frontier feel.

HIGHLIGHTS OF THE CENTER-WEST

ADMIRE the unique architecture of **Brasília,** the country's surreal capital (p. 280).

SPLASH in the waters of the **Parque Nacional Chapada dos Veadeiros** (p. 296).

TREK through the impressive **Pantanal** wetlands (p. 311).

UNWIND in the laid-back and picturesque **Pirenópolis** (p. 289).

DISTRITO FEDERAL

BRASÍLIA ☎61

Travelers often consider Brasília an unwelcome stopover on the way to or from the Pantanal. Most complain about the city's huge empty spaces and immensely wide avenues. The methodical division of city services (banks, hospitals, etc.) into separate sectors and parcelling of residential areas into small neighborhoods has also deprived the city of a heart and of a true commercial center. However, despite its functional difficulties, Brasília is still considered one of the most remarkable creations of the 20th century. With its innovative urban layout and unconventional architecture, the city presents itself like an open-air art gallery, with avenues forming the shape of a bird in flight, churches resembling pyramids and teepees, and artificial waterfalls springing from buildings. When the sun sets in the city's perpetually cloudless skies, a natural light show dances upon the skyscrapers, and the great, planned capital of Brazil is unlike any city in the world.

TRANSPORTATION

Airport: Located 12km south of the *centro* (☎365 1941). **Ônibus #102** goes directly from the airport to the *rodoviária* (25min.; every 20min. 6:40am-11pm; R$2). **Micro-Ônibus #30** travels along W3 Sul and W3 Norte (20min.; every 30min. 6am-8pm; R$2). **Taxis** to the *centro* cost R$35.

Buses: Intercity buses leave from the **Rodoferroviária** (☎363 2281) at the western tip of the Eixo Monumental. **Real Expresso** (☎361 1876) sends buses to: **Alto Paraíso** (3½hr.; 3 per day 10am-11pm; R$17); **Salvador** (18hr.; 2 per day 1-4:30pm; R$92) via **Seabre** (14hr.; R$80); **São Paulo** (12hr.; 6 per day; R$80). **Itapemirim** (☎0300 789 2020) goes to **Belo Horizonte** (15hr.; 4 per day; R$65) and **Rio de Janeiro**

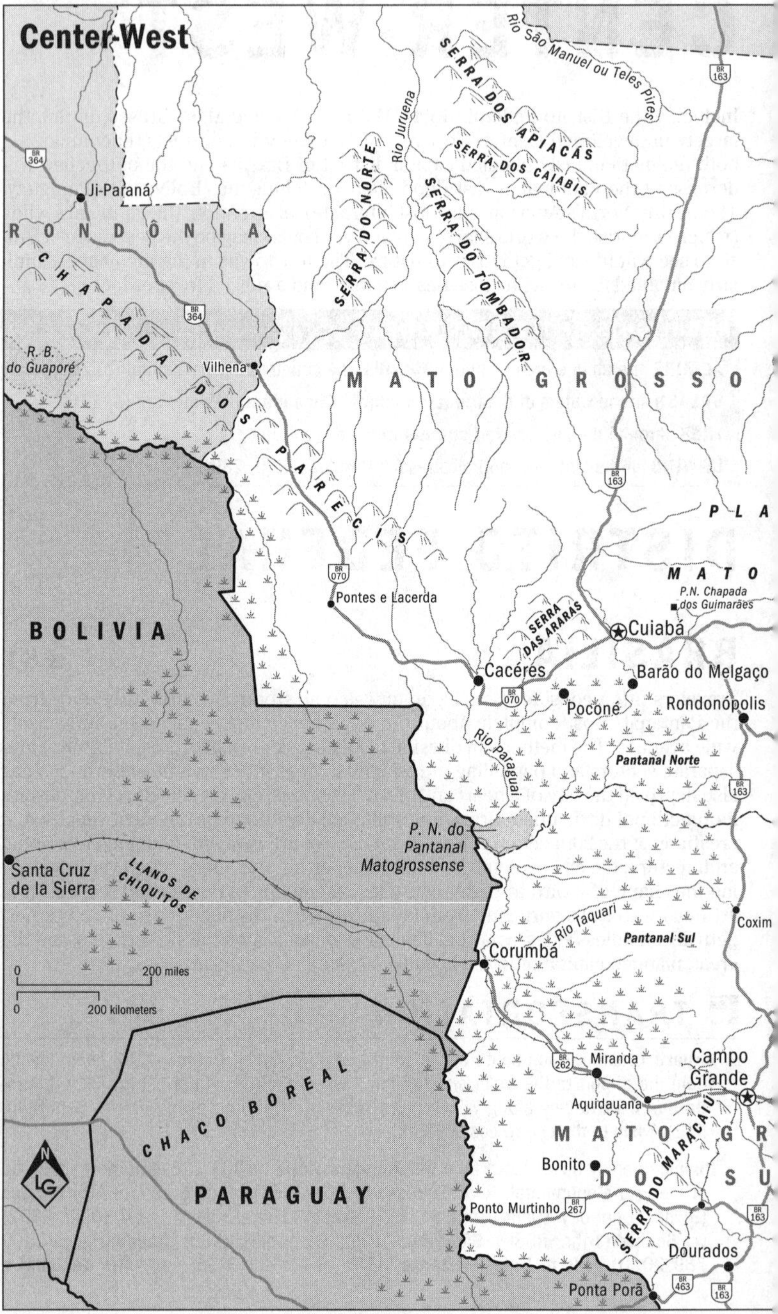

Center-West

Rio São Manuel ou Teles Pires
BR 163
SERRA DOS APIACÁS
SERRA DOS CAIABIS
Rio Juruena
SERRA DO NORTE
SERRA DO TOMBADOR
BR 364
Ji-Paraná
RONDÔNIA
CHAPADA DOS PARECIS
BR 364
R. B. do Guaporé
Vilhena
MATO GROSSO
BR 163
PLA
MATO
BR 070
Pontes e Lacerda
P.N. Chapada dos Guimarães
SERRA DAS ARARAS
Cuiabá
BOLIVIA
Cacéres
Barão do Melgaço
BR 070
Poconé
Rondonópolis
Rio Paraguai
Pantanal Norte
BR 163
P. N. do Pantanal Matogrossense
Santa Cruz de la Sierra
LLANOS DE CHIQUITOS
Coxim
Rio Taquari
Pantanal Sul
Corumbá
0 200 miles
0 200 kilometers
Campo Grande
BR 262
Miranda
Aquidauana
CHACO BOREAL
MATO GROSSO DO SUL
SERRA DO MARACAJÚ
Bonito
PARAGUAY
Ponto Murtinho
BR 267
BR 163
Dourados
BR 463
BR 163
Ponta Porã
N
LG

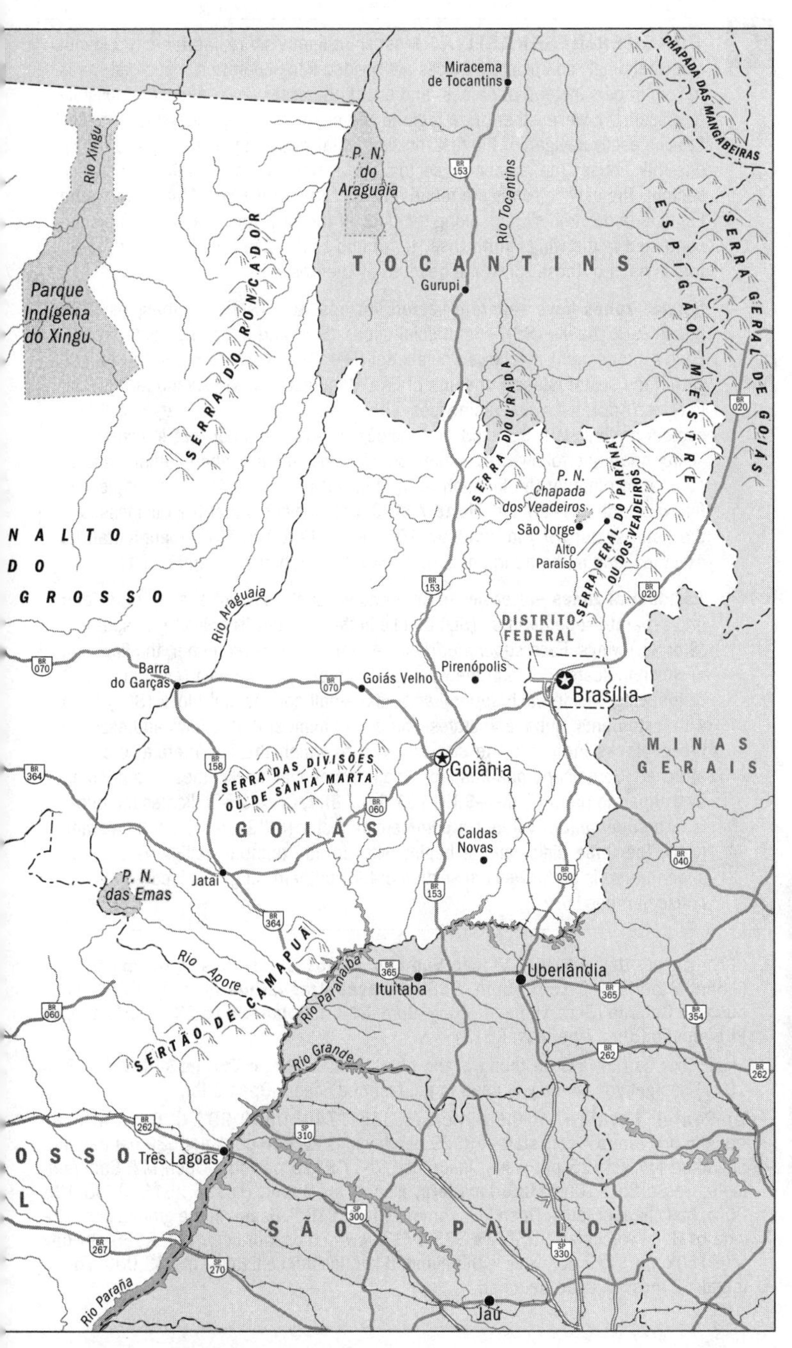
Miracema
de Tocantins
CHAPADA DAS MANGABEIRAS
P. N.
do
Araguaia
Rio Tocantins
Rio Xingu
Parque
Indígena
do Xingu
SERRA DO RONCADOR
TOCANTINS
Gurupi
ESPIGÃO MESTRE
SERRA GERAL DE GOIÁS
SERRA DOURADA
P. N.
Chapada
dos Veadeiros
São Jorge
Alto
Paraíso
SERRA GERAL DO PARANÁ OU DOS VEADEIROS
NALTO
DO
GROSSO
Rio Araguaia
DISTRITO
FEDERAL
Barra
do Garças
Goiás Velho
Pirenópolis
Brasília
MINAS
GERAIS
SERRA DAS DIVISÕES
OU DE SANTA MARTA
Goiânia
GOIÁS
Caldas
Novas
P. N.
das Emas
Jataí
SERRA DE CAMAPUÃ
Rio Apore
Rio Paranaíba
Ituitaba
Uberlândia
SERTÃO DE
Rio Grande
OSSO
Três Lagoas
L
SÃO PAULO
Rio Paraña
Jaú

CONQUERING BRASÍLIA. Most short-term visitors find the city's layout overwhelmingly confusing. Services are divided into separate city sectors, roads have numbers instead of names, and street addresses seem almost impossible to discern. However, there is a logic to the city that, once understood, makes Brasília easily navigable. The first trick is to think of the city as having two zones, one that houses the residential sectors and a second that contains the service sectors. The service zones are found on either side of the Eixo Monumental and Esplanada dos Ministérios, along the body of the bird. The residential zones are contained in the wings north (Asa Norte) and south (Asa Sul) of the body. Sectors in each of these zones are denoted by prefixes.

Service zones have separate sectors for hospitals (SMH), embassies (SE), hotels (SH), banks (SB), commercial shops (SC), and shopping centers (SD). Each sector's prefix is followed by a letter (N or S) or word (Norte or Sul) to indicate if the sector is north or south of Eixo Monumental and Esplanada dos Ministérios. Addresses for businesses within these subsections begin with the sectors prefix (SMH, SE, etc.) and include a 3-digit number that indicates the sector quadrant, followed by a more precise block number and building address number to pinpoint the location of the business (bl. H 304). For example, the following address–**SH 107 Norte / bl. C 101**–indicates that the business is in the hotel sector (SH) in quadrant 107, north (Norte) of Eixo Monumental. Its exact location in the quadrant is at block C (bl. C), building number 101.

Residential zones are easier to understand. Each residential zone is divided into separate *superquadras* (SQ) that lie in the northern (N or Norte) or southern (S or Sul) wings. Each *superquadra* has a 3-digit quadrant number, the first digit of which indicates if it is in the west (odd numbers) or the east (even numbers) of the wing. Inside each *superquadra* is a small commercial block (SCL) filled with restaurants, pubs, and stores. The 3-digit number that follows addresses in these blocks indicates the *superquadra* to which the commercial block is attached. Some *superquadras* lack small commercial blocks; these are denoted by a separate prefix (SHIG)–**SHIG 707 Sul / bl. I, Casa 15**–indicates the home is in a *superquadra* without a commercial sector (SHIG) in the southern wing (Sul). The three digit number begins with an odd number, telling us that the *superquadra* is in the western section of the southern wing. It is located at bl. I, house number 15.

(17hr.; 4 per day; R$100). **Viaçáo São Luiz** (☎361 3622) runs to **Campo Grande** (16hr.; 2 per day 5:15-6:15pm; R$86). **Viaçáo Araguarima** (☎233 7566) sends buses to **Goiânia** (3hr.; 16 per day 6am-9pm; R$22). **Goianésia** (☎233 7891) goes to **Pirenópolis** (3hr.; 7 per day; R$13).

Taxis: Taxis can always be found in the hotel sectors. **Rádio Taxi** (☎344 3060, 344 1020) can get you where you need to go, fast and cheap. Open 24hr.

Car Rental: Localiza, at the airport (☎365 1748, 0800 992 020; www.localiza.com.br). Group A cars start at R$29 per day plus R$0.46 per km; R$89 per day with unlimited km; R$525 per week. Insurance R$17-R$25 per day. Open M-F 6am-midnight, Sa-Su 8am-10pm. **Interlocadora,** also at the airport (☎365 2511, 0800 138 000), has cheaper rates. Open M-F 7am-midnight. **CTR Turismo,** in the ground floor galleria of Hotel Nacional, SHS 1 (☎323 1713; www.ctrlocadora.com.br). R$65 per day with 150km; R$420 per week with unlimited km. Insurance liability of R$2,000. For all rentals: 21+, credit card required.

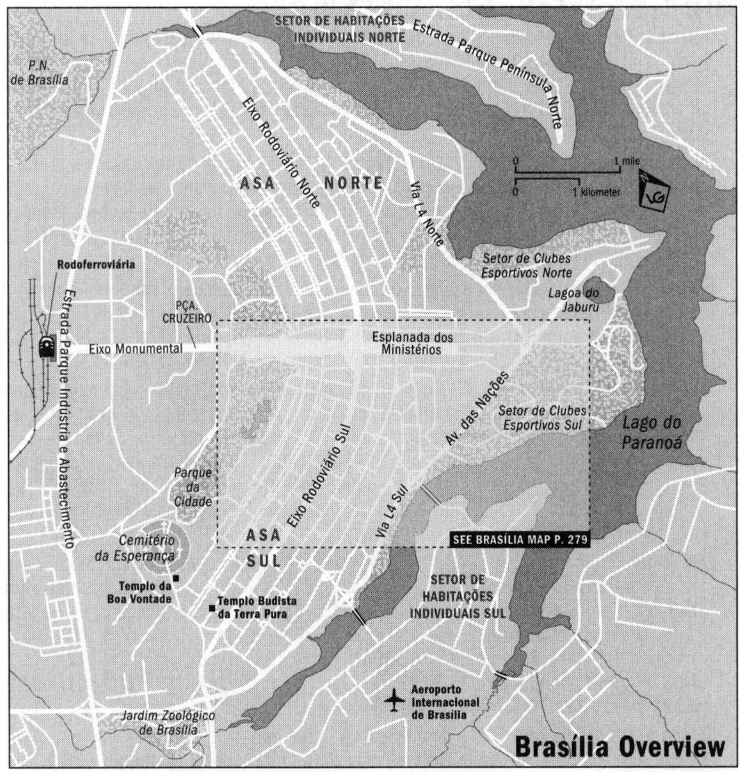

Local Transportation: To survive Brasília you must master the following public transportation routes, all of which depart from the central **rodoviária** (☎327 4631). **Bus #107** goes from the *rodoviária* to the southern residential section, traveling down W3 Sul and returning via L2 Sul. **Bus #116** covers the northern residential section, traveling up W3 Norte and returning via L2 Norte. **Buses #104** and **#108** travel between the *rodoviária* and the parliament buildings in Pça. dos Três Poderes. **Bus #131** connects the *rodoviária* and *rodoferroviária.*

PRACTICAL INFORMATION

Seen from above, the city proper resembles a bird in flight. In the "wings" are the northern and southern residential sectors. In the "tail" is **Eixo Monumental,** a broad avenue that connects the long-distance *rodoferroviária* to the *centro*. In the city's figurative "head" are the government buildings and most of Brasília's monuments of tourist interest. In the literal and figurative heart of Brasília is the *rodoviária,* surrounded by the city's commercial, hotel, and banking sectors.

The vast distances that separate most of the sectors of Brasília make public transportation essential. Although sights and services are often separated by walking distances of up to an hour, everything is within a 10min. bus ride of the central *rodoviária*. See **Conquering Brasília,** p. 274, for tips on deciphering Brasília's complicated sector and address notation system.

TOURIST & FINANCIAL SERVICES

Tourist Office: The **Airport Tourist Center** (☎365 1024) is the best resource for travel information. Their *Adetur Brasília Map,* with information about the city's sights, is extremely useful. Open 7am-8pm. Tourist information booths can also be found at the **JK Memorial** (☎225 9451), **Pça. dos Três Poderes** (☎325 6163), and **Torre de Televisão** (☎335 5735).

Budget Travel: CTR Turismo, on the ground floor galleria of Hotel Nacional, SHS 1 (☎323 1713; www.ctrlocadora.com.br). Arranges day tours, flights, and cheap car rentals. Open M-F 8am-6:30pm, Sa 9am-1pm. **Berlin Turismo,** also on the ground floor galleria of Hotel Nacional, SHS 1 (☎225 3030; berlintur@terra.com.br). Books flights and hotels. Open M-F 8:30am-6:30pm, Sa 9am-2pm.

Airlines: All airlines listed have offices on the ground floor galleria of the Hotel Nacional, SHS 1. **Air France** (☎233 4152). **British Airways** (☎226 4164). **Gol** (☎0300 789 2121; www.gol.com.br). **Lufthansa** (☎233 8202). **TAM** (☎365 1560, 0300 789 2121; www.tam.com.br). **Varig** (☎365 1550, 365 1169). **VASP** (☎321 3636).

Tours: AeroVan Turismo, SCLN 308, bl. B, rm. 208 (☎340 9251). The most reliable and longest running tour agency. For English-speaking guides call ☎911 0434 directly. Be sure to request the ever-helpful Leonardo de Campos Bezerra Costa, by far the best guide in town. Tours leave Tu-Su 9am and 2pm; night tours of the city can be arranged. 3hr. tour R$40 per person. Bookings by phone only. **Delpho's Turismo,** SCLN 104, bl. D, loja 118 (☎328 9968, 9971 8418; delphos@loreno.net), runs similar 3hr. tours, also departing Tu-Su 9am and 2pm. Bookings by phone only.

Embassies: As the capital of Brazil the city is home to all the major players, all of which are located in the Setor de Embaixadas Sul (SES), near Av. das Nações. **Australia:** SHIS 09, Conj. 16 (☎248 5569, 225 2710). **Canada:** SES 803, Lote 16 (☎321 2171). **Ireland:** Academia de Tênis, Apt. 654, SCS, Trecho 4, Conj. 5 (☎316 6654; irishembassyBrasília@eircom.net). **South Africa:** Av. das Nações, Lote 6 (☎312 9500). **UK:** SES Q 801, Conj. K (☎225 2710; www.reinounido.org.br). **US:** SES Q 801, Lote 3 (☎321 7272, 312 7000; www.embaixada-americana.org.br).

Currency Exchange and ATMs: Money can be changed at most banks, though many charge ruthless fees. Hotels sometimes offer better rates; **Hotel Nacional,** SHS 1, is a good bet. **Banco do Brasil,** SCS Q5, bl. B, loja 158 (☎321 5666). Open M-F 11am-4pm; currency exchange 11am-3pm. Branches can also be found at SCRS 508 Sul, bl. B, loja 12, and at the airport. All locations change traveler's checks (US$20) and have Visa **ATMs. Bradesco,** SCS Q2, bl. B, loja 181 (☎218 1002). Open 11am-4pm. **Citibank,** SCS Q6, bl. A, loja 208 (☎218 8000), charges mercifully low fees. Open M-F 11am-4pm; currency exchange M-F 11am-3pm.

LOCAL SERVICES

Supermarkets: Pão de Açúar, SCL 304/305 Sul, loja 128 (☎224 8835). Open M-Sa 7am-11pm, Su 7am-10pm. **Bom Motivo,** SCL 505 Sul, bl. B, loja 36 (☎242 5020). Open M-Sa 7am-11pm, Su 8am-10pm.

Public Markets: A large crafts market gathers south of the *rodoferroviária,* just off Estrada Parque Indústria, in **Ceasa.** Smaller—but more accessible—are the ad-hoc markets spread throughout **Sector Comercial Sul (SCS)** and **Sector Municipal Hospital Sul (SMHS).**

Laundromats: Most *superquadras* have a laundromat in their local commercial center (SCL or SCR). **Lavanderia Ouro Fino,** SCR 508 Sul, bl. C, loja 73 (☎242 2424). R$10 per kg with ironing. Open M-F 8am-6pm, Sa 8am-3pm. **Lavanderia Copacabana,** SCL 201 Sul, bl. A, loja 5 (☎226 9427). R$16 per kg with ironing. Open M-Sa 8am-7pm.

Public Showers: Free showers are available at the *rodoferroviária* and the Parque da Cidade, both open 24hr.

EMERGENCY & COMMUNICATIONS

EMERGENCIES	The emergency numbers for all of Brazil are: **Police** ☎190. **Ambulance** ☎192. **Fire** ☎193.

Police: The **Pelotó Turístico** (☎325 5700) are best contacted through one of the CAT Tourist Information Booths located at the city's major sights, including the JK Memorial (☎225 9451), Pça. dos Três Póderes (☎325 6163), and Torre de Televisão (☎335 5735).

Pharmacy: Drogaria Nossa Genérica, loja 16 (☎327 7281), located in the *rodoviária.* Open M-F 7am-10pm, Sa 8am-10pm. **Drogaria Família,** SCL 305 Sul, bl. B, loja 13 (☎242 1525). Open M-Sa 7am-9pm. **Drogaria Santa Mõnica,** SCL 307 Sul, bl. B, loja 11 (☎242 1147). Open 7:40am-11pm.

Hospital: General services can be found at **Da Base do Distrito Federal,** SMH 101 Sul (☎325 5050), and **Santa Lúcia,** SHL 716 Sul, bl. C (☎245 3344).

Internet Access: Lan Blaster, SCR 507 Sul, bl. B, loja 11 (☎242 8621), in the back of the *lanchonete* next to the Banco do Brasil, offers super-fast, super-cheap Internet connections. Internet R$3 per hr. Open M noon-10pm, Tu-Sa 10am-midnight, Su 2pm-10pm. **CLA** (☎322 8060), in the Patio Brasil Shopping complex. Internet R$5 per hr. Open M-Sa 10am-10pm, Su noon-10pm. **Cyberpoint,** in the Conjutu Nacional, offers 10min. free Internet access. Only 4 computers and high demand ensure long waits.

Post Office: The main **post office** (☎325 1784) is found in the hotel sector at SHS Q2, bl. B, in front of St. Paul's Hotel. Posta Restante and fax services available. Open M-F 9am-5pm. A second branch (☎244 2490) is located in the residential sector at SCR 508 Sul, bl. C, loja 1/7. Open M-F 9am-5pm, Sa 8am-noon. **Postal code:** 70312-000.

ACCOMMODATIONS

Budget accommodations in the city range from bad to worse—expect tight spaces, odd characters, and many unidentifiable smells. Most tourists avoid the hassle and opt instead to spoil themselves on the excellent deals offered by the mid- to upper-end hotels next to the *rodoviária.*

POUSADAS

There are a few *pousadas* in the northern residential wing but the majority line W3 Sul in the south. Bus #107 travels from the local *rodoviária* along W3 Sul every 10min. Most singles are makeshift cubicles that offer little privacy and gloomy lighting. All include breakfast but none accept credit cards.

Pousada Sossego, SHIG 705 Sul, bl. A, casa 43 (☎443 2609). A pleasantly refreshing change from the rest of the boys on the block. The singles are the largest around and the top-floor suites are actually inviting, with large double bed, *frigo-bar,* TV, and fan. Plush couches in the common area make for a more social atmosphere. Singles R$25. Suites R$50. ❷

Pousada dos Querubins, SHIG 703 Sul, bl. A, casa 15 (☎233 5177, 233 6686), right next door to Santuário Dom Bosco, is a great option for those who want to remain close to the *centro.* Excellent suites, clean bathrooms, comfortable beds, and humidifiers in all of the rooms. The top-floor suites are worth the extra money. Singles R$25. 1st fl. suites R$30; 2nd fl. suites R$35. ❷

Pousada Sul 705, SHIG 705 Sul, bl. M, casa 43/51 (☎244 6879, 244 6672), next to Pousada Sossego. The price of standard rooms is slightly less than average; suites are a particularly attractive option. The large common area makes for a good place to escape the small singles. Singles R$25. Suites R$40. ❷

CENTER-WEST

Cury's Solar, SHIG 707 Sul, bl. I, casa 15 (☎244 1899, 433 6252). More personable than the others in the area, it draws a more international crowd. Its location away from the main road makes for quieter nights than those in other *pousadas.* Singles R$30. ❷

Pousada Sul 707, SHIG 707 Sul, bl. A, casa 73 (☎443 3503). Splurge on the suites or save some money and settle for the surprisingly spacious dorms. Dorms R$15. Singles R$25. Suites R$30. ❷

HOTELS

Hotels are confined to the sectors north and south of the local *rodoviária.* Almost all hotels charge a 10% service charge at the end of your stay. Always request a discount at the hotels, as no one actually pays the advertised price; expect discounts of up to 40% during the off-season (Mar.-May and Aug.-Nov.) and a little more if you show up on the weekend.

Manhattan Plaza, SH Q2 Norte, bl. A (☎319 3543). A 5-star hotel with 3-star prices during the weekends and low season. *Luxo apartamentos* come with a living room, bar area, and excellent view of the government towers in the distance; standard rooms lack the view. Small roof-top pool, sauna, and excellent gym. Internet free for 15min., R$20 per hr. thereafter. All rooms sleep 1-3 people. High-season standard rooms R$250; *luxo rooms* R$270. Low-season standard rooms R$145; *luxo* rooms R$170. ❸

Bristol Hotel, SH Q4 Sul, bl. F (☎321 6162; bristol@bristolhotel.com.br). A 3-star hotel with lots of alluring amenities; ultra-comfy beds, swimming pool, and super cheap Internet (R$4 per hr.). The friendly staff arranges inexpensive tours and can provide maps for DIY tours. Well-stocked *frigo-bars* and cable TV. No service charge. High-season singles R$135; doubles R$170; triples R$195. Low-season singles R$100; doubles R$135; triples R$160. Weekend discounts. ❹

Aristus Hotel, SH Q2 Norte, bl. O (☎328 8675; www.aristushotel.com.br). The most attractive of the low-rise hotels. Basement rooms are cheaper and not much different from the rooms found on the 1st floor. All come with good lighting, modern bathrooms, and *frigo-bar.* Basement singles R$109; doubles R$134. 1st fl. singles R$121; doubles R$149. 30% off-season and weekend discount. ❹

Hotel Nacional, SH Q1 Sul, bl. A (☎321 7575; www.hotelnacional.com.br). One of Brasília's older accommodations, this 5-star hotel has all the amenities you'd expect. Huge discounts and an outside galleria home to a number of tourist and airline offices distinguish it from other higher-end places. Singles R$264; doubles R$286. *Luxo* singles R$306, doubles R$330. 70% off-season and weekend discount. ❹

CENTER-WEST

FOOD

With all the walking that travelers are forced to do in Brasília, food is often top priority. Luckily, the city is blessed with a couple of excellent places to find it. The better restaurants can be found in the southern residential section, especially at SCL 405 Sul, a.k.a. "restaurant row." Cheaper eats can be found at the *rodoviária* and near the hospital sector. Most restaurants have a 10% service charge.

Zimbrus, SCL 305 Sul, bl. D, loja 1 (☎242 0000). Home of the best sandwich and the best *sorvete* in town. Extensive dessert selection includes a score of *açaí* gelato options. The sandwiches are served fresh on soft baguettes; the Chicken Superb (with chicken, mozzarella, mushrooms, and mayonnaise) is the favorite (R$5.90). Also offers delivery, useful for those tired from exploring the city. Open daily 11am-midnight. ❶

Pizza Dom Bosco, SCL 107 Sul, bl. D, loja 20 (☎443 7579). Excellent pizza for cheap. The lack of seats and standing space necessitates on-the-run dining, but don't go too far as you'll probably want to come back for seconds. Most order the *duplo* (2 slices of pizza folded on top of each other; R$2). Slice R$1. Open daily 7am-11pm. ❶

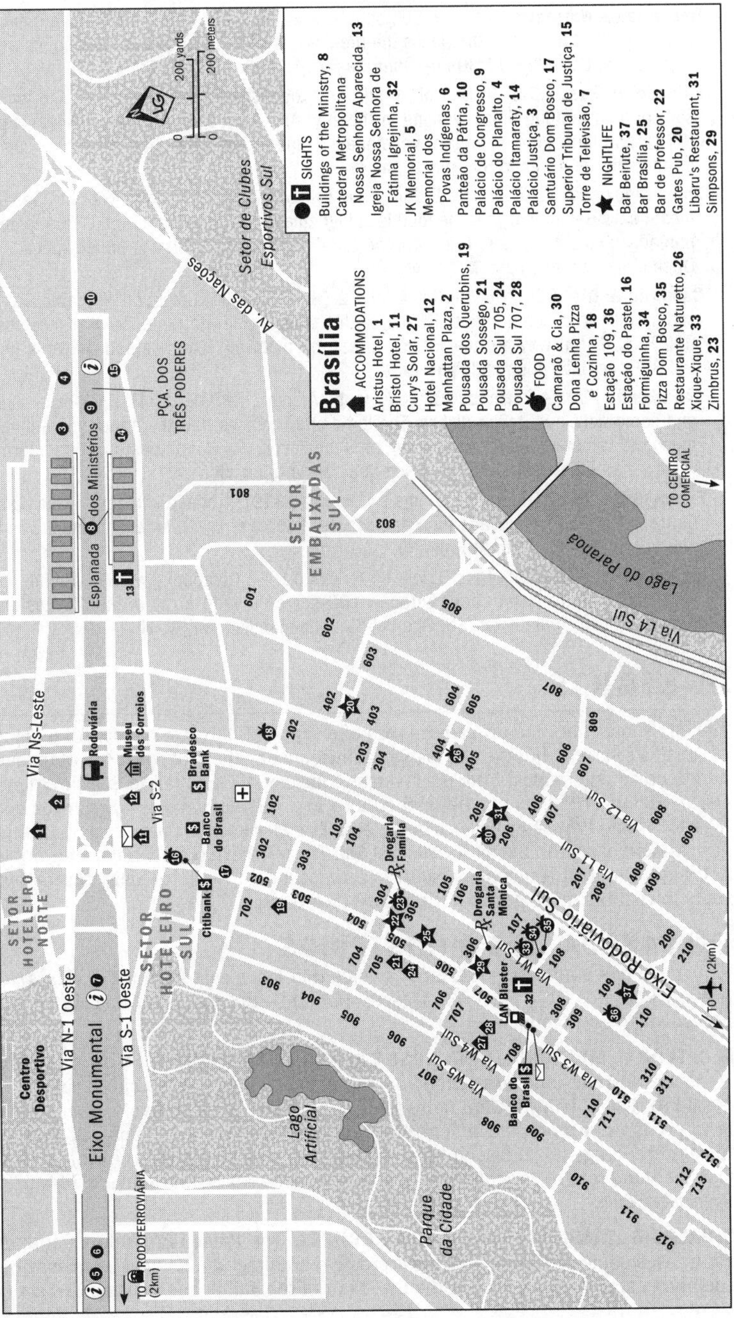

Brasília

ACCOMMODATIONS
- Aristus Hotel, **1**
- Bristol Hotel, **11**
- Cury's Solar, **27**
- Hotel Nacional, **12**
- Manhattan Plaza, **2**
- Pousada dos Querubins, **19**
- Pousada Sossego, **21**
- Pousada Sul 705, **24**
- Pousada Sul 707, **28**

FOOD
- Camaraõ & Cia, **30**
- Dona Lenha Pizza e Cozinha, **18**
- Estação 109, **36**
- Estação do Pastel, **16**
- Formiguinha, **34**
- Pizza Dom Bosco, **35**
- Restaurante Naturetto, **26**
- Xique-Xique, **33**
- Zimbrus, **23**

SIGHTS
- Buildings of the Ministry, **8**
- Catedral Metropolitana Nossa Senhora Aparecida, **13**
- Igreja Nossa Senhora de Fátima Igrejinha, **32**
- JK Memorial, **5**
- Memorial dos Povas Indígenas, **6**
- Panteão da Pátria, **10**
- Palácio de Congresso, **9**
- Palácio do Planalto, **4**
- Palácio Itamaraty, **14**
- Palácio Justiça, **3**
- Santuário Dom Bosco, **17**
- Superior Tribunal de Justiça, **15**
- Torre de Televisão, **7**

NIGHTLIFE
- Bar Beirute, **37**
- Bar Brasília, **25**
- Bar de Professor, **22**
- Gates Pub, **20**
- Libaru's Restaurant, **31**
- Simpsons, **29**

Centro Desportivo
SETOR HOTELEIRO NORTE
Via Ns-Leste
Via N-1 Oeste
Eixo Monumental
Rodoviária
Esplanada dos Ministérios
Via S-1 Oeste
TO RODOFERROVIÁRIA (2km)
SETOR HOTELEIRO SUL
Museu dos Correios
Via S-2
PÇA. DOS TRÊS PODERES
0 200 yards
0 200 meters
Citibank
Banco do Brasil
Bradesco Bank
Av. das Nações
Setor de Clubes Esportivos Sul
Lago Artificial
SETOR EMBAIXADAS SUL
Drogaria Família
Parque da Cidade
Via W5 Sul
Via W4 Sul
Drogaria Santa Mônica
LAN Blaster
Banco do Brasil
Via W1 Sul
Via W3 Sul
Eixo Rodoviário Sul
Via L1 Sul
Via L2 Sul
Via L4 Sul
Lago do Paranoá
TO CENTRO COMERCIAL
TO (2km)

Restaurante Naturetto, SCL 405 Sul, bl. A, loja 22 (☎242 3532), on "restaurant row." A superb vegetarian joint that lacks the pretensions of its neighbors. Hearty soups and tasty juices. Open M-F 11:30am-10pm, Sa-Su 11:30am-3:30pm. ❷

Estaçáo do Pastel, SC Q6 Sul, bl. A, loja 140, opposite Patio Shopping. A kilo lunch spot popular among those working in the city. Also serves sandwiches (R$4), soups (R$3), and fairly good espresso. Vegetarians come for the salad bar; carnivores come for the chicken. Open M-Sa 7am-10pm. ❷

Xique-Xique, SCL 107 Sul, bl. E, loja 2 (☎244 5797), just off noisy W1 Sul. Serves meat-heavy Baiano cuisine. The food is of high quality, and the restaurant is frequented primarily by local families. The *Carne de Sol Completa* (R$28) is the house speciality. Open daily 8am-midnight. MC/V. ❹

Camarão & Cia, SCL 206 Sul, bl. A, loja 2 (☎443 4849). The *bobó de camarão* (a shrimp dish in coconut sauce; R$20), is this place's claim to fame. Most dishes cost R$20-R$24, but why try one when you can try them all? The seafood buffet is just R$23. Open daily noon-midnight. ❸

Dona Lenha Pizza e Cozinha, SCL 201 Sul, bl. A, loja 1 (☎332 1234). Brick-oven pizza and some delicious Italian dishes. The low-arched ceilings trap the appetizing aromas much the same way as the brick oven traps the flavors. *Da Nonna* pasta (prepared with white wine and sausage; R$13). Open M-Sa 10am-8pm. ❶

Formiguinha, SCL 107 Sul, bl. D, loja 24 (☎244 1919). A cheap kilo serving the standard fare with above-average food and service. R$11 per kg. Open M-F 11am-2:30pm and 5-9pm, Sa-Su 11am-3:30pm. ❷

Estação 109, SCL 109 Sul, bl. D, loja 35 (☎244 7161). Competing with Bar Beirute for the resident Arab population, Estação 109 serves a wide array of Middle Eastern dishes. Spiced *Quibe Frilo* R$6. Open M-Sa noon-midnight. MC/V. ❷

SIGHTS

The city's museums and art galleries are of disappointingly low quality for a place of Brasília's stature, but the city is itself a museum or gallery of sorts, full of unique architecture and surreal buildings—most courtesy of Brazilian master architect Oscar Niemeyer. Sights can be divided into four distinct sectors—**Esplanada dos Ministérios** and **Praça Três Poderes** in the east, **Eixo Monumental Oeste,** and the southern residential sector, **Sector Residencial Sul.** The northern residential sector holds nothing of interest. Immense distances prompt most to join the daily three-hour tours to visit the more popular attractions (see **Tours,** p. 276).

CENTER-WEST

ESPLANADA DOS MINISTÉRIOS

Esplanada dos Ministérios is a large avenue that leads east from the *rodoviária* toward Pça. dos Três Poderes. Buses #104 and #108 travel up and down the Esplanada every 10min.

CATEDRAL METROPOLITANA NOSSA SENHORA APARECIDA. Supported by 16 concrete arches and surrounded by a large reflecting pool, Brasília's cathedral is said to resemble a wigwam more than a church. Representative of Niemeyer's most progressive work, the underground entrance is encased in fine black marble. Inside three huge angelic sculptures dangle suspended from the roof top above. Outside stand four huge sculptures of Matthew, Luke, Mark, and John. *(☎244 4073. Open daily 8-6pm.)*

PALÁCIO ITAMARATY (PALACE OF ARCHES). The Palace of Arches building showcases some of Niemeyer's most creative architecture, as well as many fine sculptures and works of art. On the first floor of the building is a suspended staircase (designed by Niemeyer, of course), which seems to defy all laws of gravity. The roof that hangs overheard is one of the largest in the world to lack pillars or support beams. From the second floor you can look down on a small Amazonian garden and see the desk upon which Princess Isabela signed the declaration that emancipated Brazil's slaves in 1888. The open-air third floor reception room holds some magnificent artworks which include a serpentine chandelier made of iron and silver, a large Persian rug, and several chairs and tables cut from the now extinct Jacacanda tree. *(☎411 6148. Open M-F 2-5pm, Sa-Su 10am-4pm.)*

BUILDINGS OF THE MINISTRY. Along Esplanada dos Ministérios on the way to Pça. dos Três Poderes, you pass by the city's 17 buildings of the ministry. There are ten buildings to the left and seven to the right; from the top of Torre de Televisão, they look like giant dominoes. Their shabby appearance is due in large part to Niemeyer's refusal to include a central cooling system in the system's design; obnoxious A/C units protrude offensively and the windows regularly crack as a result of extreme temperature changes.

PALÁCIO DA JUSTIÇA (MINISTRY OF JUSTICE). The most striking features are the six concrete funnels that extend from the front of the building. From these funnels flow artificial cascades designed to create a relaxing atmosphere. There is little of interest inside the palace, and the building can be adequately viewed as you pass by it on the bus back to the local *rodoviária*. *(Across from Palácio Itamaraty. ☎429 3401. Open M-F 10am-noon and 3-5pm.)*

PRAÇA DOS TRÊS PODERES

Pça. dos Três Poderes is located in the figurative "head" of the city. Dominating the *praça* are the twin towers of the Congresso Nacional; to either side are the Palácio do Planalto and Supremo Tribunal Federal (Supreme Court). Across the *praça*, opposite the Congresso Nacional, is the Panteão da Pátria. Buses #104 and #108 connect the *praça* to the *rodoviária*.

PRAÇA DOS TRÊS PODERES. Conceived by Lúcio Costa and designed by Oscar Niemeyer, this *praça* unites the three branches of Brazil's democratic government. The judiciary's Supremo Tribunal Federal, the executive Palácio do Planalto, and the legislative Congresso Nacional rest in the center. The spacious *praça* is adorned with several sculptures and monuments. In the northeast corner stands the famous **Os Candangos** made to honor those from the Brazilian northeast who helped with the city's construction. To the east of the *praça* stands the **Pavilhão Nacional,** a 100m flag pole flying South America's largest flag. Beneath the *praça* is the **Lúcio Costa Hall,** an underground chamber which contains a 170m model of the city. *(Lúcio Costa Hall. ☎325 6163. Open Tu-Su 9am-6pm.)*

PALÁCIO DO CONGRESSO. The 28-story twin towers of the Palácio do Congresso are one of the city's most famous symbols. In front of the two towers lie two large concrete dishes that resemble flying saucers; it is here that the legislative branches of Brazil meet. The House of Representatives meets under the upright convex dish; the Senate meets under the concave one. The Congress building was placed on this specific spot because, on April 21, the anniversary of the city's inauguration as the capital of Brazil, the sun sets directly between the two towers, making for spectacular pictures. *(Tours of the House of Representatives every 30min. M-F 9:30am-noon and 2:30-4:30pm, Sa-Su 9am-1pm. Tours of the Senate every 30min. M-F 9:30-11:30am and 2:30-4:30pm, Sa-Su 10am-2pm.)*

PALÁCIO DO PLANALTO. The Brazilian flag always flies high outside—if a green flag is raised it means the President is paying a visit. Otherwise, this building houses the administrative offices of the President and some works of art similar to those found at Palácio Itamaraty, including some modern works by Bruno Georgi. The building's sensual curves are most evident in the twisting slope that leads to the palace's main door. *(☎441 1221. Open Su 10am-4pm.)*

SUPERIOR TRIBUNAL DE JUSTIÇA. The smooth curves and winding columns of this building symbolize a departure from the rigidity of Brazil's former judicial systems. Less interesting than the other buildings in the area, it has a small library and museum. Tours of the Justice Tribunal are held only on weekends. *(Setor Adm. Fed. Sul Z 06, Lote 1. ☎217 3000. Library and museum open M-F 9am-noon, Sa-Su 9am-1pm. Justice Tribunal tours leave every 30min. Sa-Su 10am-4pm.)*

PANTEÃO DA PÁTRIA (NATIONAL PANTHEON). To the right of the Pavilhão Nacional flagpole, on the eastern side of Pça. dos Três Poderes, lies a small memorial built in the shape of a dove. The structure was built to honor the nation's fallen heroes and the eternal flame that burns outside represents their enduring spirits. Inside is a large metal book with their names inscribed on its heavy pages, as well as an extraordinary skylight mosaic created by Athos Bulcão. *(☎325 6244. Open Tu-Su 11am-5pm.)*

EIXO MONUMENTAL OESTE

Eixo Monumental Oeste runs from the local *rodoviária* in the *centro* of the city to the *rodoferroviária* five kilometers away. Bus #131 connects the two stations, stopping at all the major sights along the way.

TORRE DE TELEVISÃO (TELEVISION TOWER). One of the city's few structures not constructed by Oscar Niemeyer, this 224m high broadcasting center was instead designed by the city's urban planner, Lúcio Costa. The 75m observation deck provides a magnificent view of the city, and from the mezzanine you can visit the **Museu Nacional de Gemas. Helicopter rides** are also available near the base. On weekends the area surrounding the Torre becomes a popular market. *(☎325 5735. Open M 2-6pm, Tu-Su 9am-6pm. Museum ☎332 3227. R$3, under 12 free. Open M-F 10am-6pm, Sa-Su 8am-6pm. 10min. helicopter rides ☎323 8777. R$180. Max. 3 people. MC/V.)*

JK MEMORIAL. This memorial was constructed in 1981 to honor the man most responsible for the city's construction, Juscelino Kubitschek. The towering sculpture, visible on the bus ride between the *rodoferroviária* and the local *rodoviária*, looks rather like a giant question mark, inside of which stands a statue of JK looking down and waving to his city below. At the foot of the sculpture is a small museum that resembles a pyramid. The first floor contains JK's private library, a research room, and an exhibition of photographs pertaining to the city's construction. Upstairs in the museum lie the remains of the former president bathed in an eerie natural light filtered through a mosaic skylight above. *(☎225 9451, 226 7860; www.memorialjk.com.br. R$2; students R$1. Open Tu-Su 9am-6pm.)*

MEMORIAL DOS POVOS INDÍGENAS. This museum was constructed to pay tribute to Brazil's indigenous cultures and was designed to resemble a Yanomami hut. In addition to the many photographs of modern indigenous societies there are small collections of ceramics, woven baskets, and feathered headdresses. The museum spirals downward and eventually leads to a large *praça*. *(In front of the JK Memorial. ☎226 5206. Open Tu-F 10am-6pm, Sa-Su 11am-5pm.)*

SECTOR RESIDENCIAL SUL

A number of fascinating churches are located within the confines of the Southern Residential Sector. Santuário Dom Bosco is the only one within walking distance of the *centro*—the others lie 30min.-1hr. away. Bus #107 travels along W3 Sul and stops near each one.

SANTUÁRIO DOM BOSCO. The Santuário Dom Bosco is supported by 80 neo-Gothic columns, each 16m high, and is encased by stained-glass walls fashioned in 12 different hues of blue. Resembling the nighttime sky filled with stars, the walls bathe the entire church in a soothing natural light. The heavy doors, made from iron and bronze, are engraved with scenes from the prophetic dream of Dom Bosco (see **The Local Legend: A Link to the Past,** at right). Overhead hangs a colossal chandelier that weighs nearly 2600kg, holds 180 lightbulbs, and was constructed using 7400 pieces of delicate Venetian glass. *(W3 Sul Q702. ☎223 6542. Open daily 7am-6pm.)*

TEMPLO DA BOA VONTADE. A new-age temple for people of all faiths, this 18m pyramid holds in its center the largest crystal in all of Brazil. Upon entering the Temple da Boa Vontade (Temple of Good Will), visitors must take off their shoes and walk along a spiraling black path that moves ever inward toward the center of the complex. Negative energy is supposed to be released during this spiraling walk. Suspended from high above, the temple's giant crystal is said to transmit positive energy to believers who stand near it. After receiving the energy of the crystal, you spiral outward along an adjacent white path, as time is allowed for mediation and an embracing of positive energy.

The temple also has an **Egyptian Meditation Room** (R$2) decorated with Egyptian iconography and Greek lounge chairs, a **Hall of Nobles** with pictures of benevolent celebrities (including Helen Keller, John Lennon, and Charlie Chaplin), and a **Modern Art Gallery** definitely worth checking out. *(SGAS 915 Lote 75/76. ☎245 1070. Temple open 24hr. Egyptian Meditation Room and Modern Art Gallery open 10am-6:30pm.)*

IGREJA N.S. DE FÁTIMA IGREJINHA. This rather tiny church was the first built in Brasília. Constructed by Niemeyer in 1958, it can only hold 25-30 people at a time. The interior was decorated by Athos Bulcão and is dominated by ceramic tiles portraying peaceful doves. The incredibly original temple resembles a tent. *(EQS 307/308. ☎242 0149. Open M 9am-9pm, Tu-Sa 6am-8pm, Su 6am-9pm.)*

TEMPLO BUDISTA DA TERRA PURA. Located at the end of a large green *praça*, the Buddhist Pure Earth Templ was built in a non-Modernist style that differentiates it from all other buildings in Brasília—the temple is actually a replica of the 13th-century Eihiji Temple found in Japan's Fukui prefecture. It definitely seems out of place in its nearby surroundings. The altar is entirely gold-plated. *(EQS 315/316. ☎245 2469. Open Su 9am-11pm.)*

THE LOCAL LEGEND

A LINK TO THE PAST

Many describe Brasília—a plannec city of innovative architecture designed to look like a bird ir flight—as unlike any other in the world. However, some believe tha it may well have had not only ar equal, but an exact duplicate ir the world of the past: the Egyptiar city of **Ahketaton.** Both cities were built from scratch in a span o under four years, were located ir the center of their respective coun tries, and were designed to loo like a bird. Also, each city is (o was) their country's administrative capital and is (or was) dividec into separate residential anc administrative districts.

The marked similarities between the two cities have giver rise to nearly 1000 cults arounc Brasília that believe in an other worldly connection between the distant capitals, based upon the prophetic dream of the Italiar Dom Bosco. In 1883 he dream that a great city would resurrec itself in South America, next to a lake, between the 15th and 20th parallels. The cults believe tha Brasília, located on the 16th par allel and sitting next to an artificia lake, is that city. Reinforcing thei claims are the words of Brasília's designer, Lúcio Costa, who ofter said that the blueprint for the city was something "that I had no been looking for but that emergec already completed." Interestingly Brasília's Eixo Monumental, where Juscelino Kubitschek's remains lie, resembles an Egyptian tomb.

NIGHTLIFE

Restaurants usually pull double duty as the nighttime destinations of choice, though most lack flavor. There are good clubs sprinkled throughout the residential sectors and many in the local shopping plazas; Pier 21 has several popular clubs.

Gates Pub, SCL 403 Sul, bl. D, loja 34 (☎225 4526). This British-style tavern with an all-wooden interior is entirely different from anything else in town and a favorite among university students. Long lines advertise the pub's popularity and help identify the otherwise inconspicuous entrance. Especially busy on W nights. F rock, Sa blues, Su disco and techno. Cover R$3-15. Open daily 9am-4am.

Bar Beirute, SCL 109 Sul, bl. A, lojas 2/4 (☎244 1717). The oldest and most established of the restaurant/bar combos, Bar Beirute has been operating since 1966. Tables are crowded with glasses of beer and hummus plates and surrounded by Brasília's beautiful people. Open daily 11am-2am.

Simpsons, SCL 307 Sul, bl. D, loja 135 (☎443 4251). Another restaurant/bar a short stumble from the *pousadas* that line W3 Sul. The big-screen TV draws *futebol* fans on the weekends and during Happy Hour most of the city can be found sitting around its tables. Mostly twenty-somethings. Happy Hour 6-8pm. Open daily 7am-2am.

Libaru's Restaurant, SCL 206 Sul, bl. C, loja 36 (☎244 9795). The city's biggest, busiest, and most social restaurant/bar, offering better opportunities to meet locals than in most other bars. Attracts a hodgepodge of characters, from the up-and-coming to the down-and-out. Open daily 11:30am-2am.

Bar Brasília, SCL 506 Sul, bl. A, loja 14 (☎443 4323), next to Blockbuster Vídeo. A classy little joint serving homemade brews. No music, no TVs, no distractions, just spirited conversation, and lots of it. University intellectuals and seasoned professionals mingle the city's businessmen and politicians. Open daily 5pm-2am.

Bar de Professor, SCL 305 Sul, bl. D, loja 37 (☎9976 2808). The city's primary provider of *cachaça*. Over 100 varieties make for extensive taste-testing opportunities often followed the next morning by horrendous hangovers. Open daily 11:30am-2am.

GOIÁS

GOIÂNIA ☎62

Goiânia was the second planned city in Brazil. Founded in 1933 and designed by urban planner Armando de Godói, the city succeeds in many ways that Brasília does not. Its leafy *avenidas* provide shade from the blistering sun, and its urban parks offer pleasant weekend escapes for locals. City services are concentrated in the *centro*, and the city's circular design makes walking a better way to explore the city than car. In spite of a conspicuous lack of architectural gems, the cool climate and cheap prices make it an attractive place for travelers to break up their trip between Salvador and the Pantanal.

TRANSPORTATION

Buses: The **rodoviária** on Av. Goiás (☎224 8466), is housed in a large shopping mall with 24hr. food court, **post office** (☎229 0070), and **luggage storage** (☎9942 2392; R$2 per day). **Empressa Moreira** (☎225 1459) sends buses to **Goiás Velho** (3hr.; every hr. 6am-8pm; R$16). **Goianésia** (☎224 1552, 223 1362) goes to **Pirenópolis** (2½hr.; 5pm; R$16). **Parauna** (☎224 6063) runs to **Caldas Novas** (3hr.; 10 per day

6am-8pm; R$18). **Real Expresso** (☎225 3626) goes to **Rio de Janeiro** (20hr.; 4pm; R$127). Bus #404 runs along Av. Goiás from the *rodoviária* to the *centro*.

Taxis: Taxis between the *rodoviária* and *centro* cost R$8. **Bandeirantes Rádio Taxi** (☎210 4952) and **Rádio Taxi ABC** (☎285 1366) have cars available 24hr.

Car Rental: Localiza, Av. Anhanguera 3530 (☎261 1711). **Hertz,** Av. Caiapó 1103 (☎207 4848). 120km per day for R$75 per day. Both open M-F 8am-6pm.

Moped Rental: Motasa, Rua 90 Sul 883 (☎541 8778). Mopeds R$25 per day. Dignity-restoring VT600 Shadow motorbikes R$132. 18+. Open M-F 9am-5pm, Sa 9am-noon.

ORIENTATION & PRACTICAL INFORMATION

Government offices are centered on **Praça Cívica** in the *centro*. The residential sector is south of the *centro* and the commercial district is in the north near **Avenida Anhanguera** and **Rua 3. Avenida Araguaia** leaves from Pça. Cívica and goes all the way to Parque Mutirama, passing **Praça Antônio Lisita** on the way. To reach **Praça Tamandaré,** 20min. from the *centro*, follow Av. Anhanguera west and turn left when you reach Av. República do Libano.

Tourist Office: The state **tourist office** (☎217 1100), at the corner of Rua 4 and Rua 30, is on the 2nd fl. of the Centro de Convenções. The office is filled with brochures about the city and nearby attractions. Some English spoken. Open M-F 8am-6pm.

Budget Travel Offices: Transworld Viagens, Rua 3 516 (☎213 1310). Offers an inexpensive 10-day Pantanal trip (R$700; min. 4 people). Open M-F 8am-6pm, Sa 8am-noon. **Mundial Turismo,** Rua 2 277 (☎224 6999). Books flights and offers pricey city tours (R$250). Open M-F 8am-6pm, Sa 8am-noon. **City Tour Turisticas,** Rua 25 473 (☎225 2836) offers cheaper city tours (R$30) and are best contacted by phone.

Currency Exchange: Banco do Brasil, Av. Goiás 980 (☎216 5500). Charges 3% commission for currency exchange and US$20 fee for traveler's checks. Open M-F 10am-4pm. Another branch at Rua Anhanguera 4932. **Bradesco,** Av. Goiás 547 (☎212 3344). Open M-F 10am-4pm. Most upscale hotels have better exchange rates.

English Bookstores: Bookstores line Rua 4, especially near its intersection with Rua 9. Most have small selections of books in English. The best bet is **Feirão do Livro,** Rua 4 1077 (☎223 1040). Open M-F 8am-6pm, Sa 8am-2pm.

Laundromat: Lavanderia Araguaia, Av. Araguaia 855 (☎223 3450), 4 blocks north of Pça. Antônio Lisita. R$8 per kg. Open M-F 8am-6pm, Sa 8am-noon.

Late-Night Pharmacy: Drogaria Santa Móinica, Av. Anhanguera 3312 (☎224 1628), next to Bandeirantes Hotel. Open M-Sa 8am-8pm. Also **Drogaria Drogatti,** Rua 4 682 (☎212 6900). Open daily 7am-9pm.

Hospital: Inamps Hospital, Av. Anhanguera 4379 (☎223 5601).

Internet Access: Internet na Hora, on Rua 3 (☎213 3309), off Av. Araguaia next to Transworld Viagens. R$3 per hr. Open M-F 8am-6pm, Sa 8am-noon. **On Line Goiânia** (☎212 6205), in Banana Shopping at the intersection of Rua 3 and Rua 21. Internet R$4.50 per hr. Open M-F 9am-7pm, Sa 9am-3pm.

Post Office: The main post office is in Pça. Cívico (☎226 2110). Open M-F 9am-5pm, Sa 9am-noon. More convienently located is the branch at Rua 4 780 (☎212 1185), on the corner of Rua 8. Open M-F 9am-5:30pm. **Postal code:** 74001-000.

ACCOMMODATIONS

Goiânia's wide accommodations selection is disappointing. Most hotels are along Av. Anhanguera or Rua 4, with better hotels clustered around Pça. Antônio Lisita. Cheaper beds are near the *rodoviária* but are only suitable for short-term stays.

Goiânia Palace Hotel, Av. Anhanguera 5195 (☎224 4874). Extremely spacious rooms with lots of furniture. Suites come with separate living rooms that sometimes include a small couch or chair. Kitchen. *Quarto* singles R$16; doubles R$25; triples R$34. *Apartamento* singles with A/C R$33; doubles with A/C R$42. ❷

Hotel Araguaia, Av. Araguaia 664 (☎212 9800), in Pça. Antônio Lisita. A good location and friendly service make this an attractive choice. Also serves one of the best breakfasts in town. All rooms have *frigo-bar,* TV, phone, and much needed A/C. Free Internet available during the day. Singles R$40; doubles R$60; triples R$85. AmEx/MC/V. ❷

Hotel Karajás, Rua 3 360 (☎224 9666). The rooms are pleasant enough, though the *luxos* are worth the splurge. The hotel has a game room with table tennis and a pool table. Internet access can be found on the 6th fl. (R$10 per hr.). Singles R$20; doubles R$40. *Luxo* singles R$58; doubles R$70. ❸

Hotel Dom Bosco, Av. Araguaia 655 (☎225 3732), near Pça. Antônio Lisita. The posh lobby is misleading: expect simple but welcoming quarters. Most rooms have a sink but no bath. Singles R$25, with bath R$36; doubles R$44, with bath R$45. ❷

Vila Rica Palace Hotel, Av. Anhanguera 5308 (☎223 2733, 223 2025). A good 2-star hotel with a comfortable TV lounge. The mattresses are thicker than most and the rooms are brightly lit. Internet access R$8 per hr. Singles R$40; doubles R$65. MC/V. ❷

Plazza Inn, Rua 20 930 (☎212 8500; www.plazainn.com.br). Plazza offers plenty of ways to amuse yourself, including a roof-top pool, restaurant, and free Internet access. Doubles have a large living room and *frigo-bars.* A great option for families and couples. Singles R$89; doubles R$98. ❹

Príncipe Hotel, Av. Anhanguera 4780 (☎224 0085, 224 0962). The reception desk is on the 2nd fl. Rooms come with a hodge-podge collection of furniture and decent beds. Breakfast R$5. Singles R$27, with bath R$40; doubles R$40, with bath R$60; triples R$55, with bath R$85. ❷

FOOD

Most of the restaurants in the *centro* close relatively early, in the late evening. Late-night dining options are restricted to fast-food deliveries or long walks to Pça. Tamandaré, where the best restaurants can be found.

Argu's Executivo Restaurant, Rua 2 139 (☎224 8429). An overwhelming selection of freshly prepared dishes has inspired a loyal following that crowds the place for lunch. More expensive than other kilos, but many claim the food is worth it. A large salad spread and several plates of fruit accompany the meat and chicken dishes. R$15 per kg. Open M-F 11:30am-3pm, Sa-Su noon-3:30pm. ❷

Torre do Pizza, Rua 2 56 (☎225 4802). This popular pizza joint serves all the classics and some originals (like chocolate). Try the *California,* with olives and pepperoni. Also serves fresh fruit desserts. Pizzas R$6-11. Open M-F 7am-9:30pm, Sa 7am-6pm. ❷

China Restaurant, Rua 7 623 (☎215 1122), on Pça. Tamandaré. Your standard Chinese restaurant, serving dishes like broccoli and noodles (R$8) and tofu plates. The lunchtime buffet (M-F R$14, Sa-Su R$20) includes more meat and chicken options than elsewhere in town. Open daily 11am-2pm and 6:30-11pm. ❷

Buffalo Grill, Rua 7 780 (☎215 3935), in Pça. Tamandaré, 15min. from the *centro.* All meat dishes are freshly grilled and kept warm over a wood fire. The *frangalo* burger (two filets of chicken and slabs of bacon; R$4.30) is the most filling option. Open 24hr. ❶

Modiglianni, Rua 7 754 (☎215 4155). A pizzeria with comfortable seating and a pleasant atmosphere in Pça. Tamandaré that doubles as a popular nightspot. Huge selection of pizzas, lasagna, and spaghetti. A large Neapolitan pizza costs R$14, but the *calzone a moda* (R$10) is a better value. Open daily 6pm-midnight. ❷

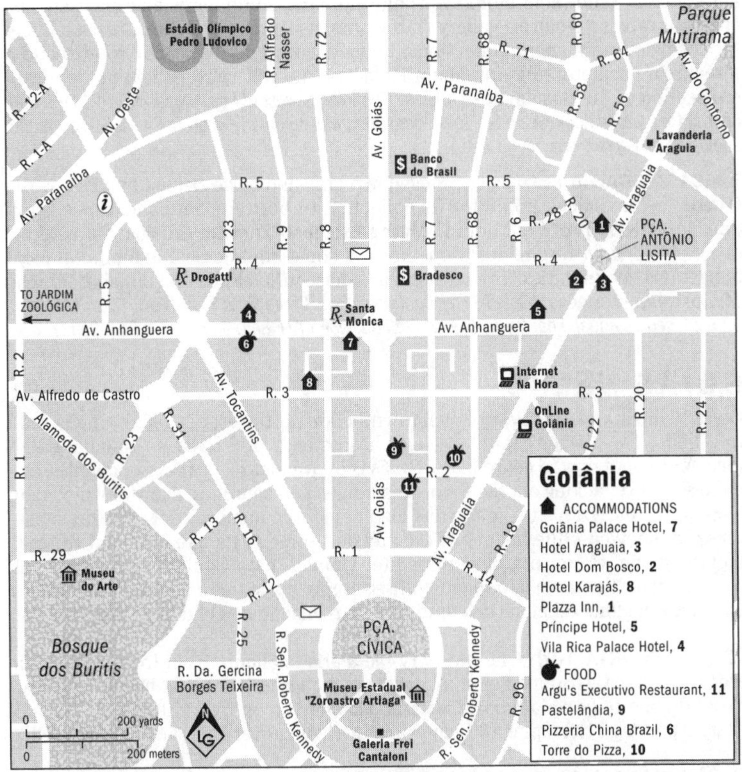

Pizzeria China Brazil, Av. Anhanguera 100 (☎224 2978). A pizzeria popular for take-away. Try the unconventional *banana pizza.* The complete lack of Asian dishes leaves you wondering about the name. Open M-F noon-8pm, Sa noon-6pm. ❷

Pastelândia, Rua Goiás 382 (☎212 5389), has 50 types of *salgados* (R$1-3) guaranteed to leave you aching for more. Heavy lunchtime traffic. Open M-Sa 9am-11pm. ❶

SIGHTS

PARQUE MUTIRAMA. This large wooded area is popular with skaters for its half-pipes and with families for its wonderful amusement park. Though seemingly small, the amusement park has a mini-rollercoaster, Ferris wheel, and bumper cars. *(Intersection of Av. Araguaia and Rua Contorno. Park open 24hr.; amusement park open M-F noon-4pm, Sa-Su 10am-6pm.)*

BOSQUE DOS BURITIS. This urban park is full of artificial waterfalls and lakes filled with giant goldfish. White herons congregate around the lakes, while the more timid birds hide in the forested areas. The park also has a large fountain and contains Museu do Arte. **Jardim Zoológica,** just off Av. Anhanguera about a kilometer west of town, is home to several lakes, sporting fields, and hikes. The park's main attraction is its fantastic zoo with over 1000 animals from nearly 200 different species. Semi-tame monkeys roam the park, as do emus and giant storks. **Museu do Arte** is a small art gallery with works by contemporary local artists. It features several permanent collections, including works by Antônio Poteiro and a three-figure sculpture by Ann Maria Pacheco. The gallery is located in the northern section of the Bosque dos Buritis. *(Two blocks west of Pça. Cívica. ☎524 1190. Park open 24hr.; Jardim Zoológica open Tu-Su 8am-5pm; Museu do Arte open Tu-Su 9am-9pm. Jardim Zoológica R$2, children under 3 free.)*

PRAÇA CÍVICA. In Pça. Cívica, housed in a gray-and-beige striped building, is the **Galeria Frei Cantaloni,** noted for its collection of portraits and landscapes. Next door to Galeria Frei Cantaloni is **Museu Estadual "Zorastro Artiaga,"** an eclectic museum filled with religious stone art and some ethnological exhibits on local indigenous communities. The museum also has stuffed birds and old photographs of Goiánian pioneers. *(Galeria Frei Cantaloni, Pça. Cívica 2. ☎212 4606. Open M-F 9am-6pm. Museu Estadual, Pça. Cívica 3. ☎223 1763. Open Tu-F 8am-6pm, Sa-Su 9am-2pm.)*

GOIÁS VELHO ☎62

Goiás Velho is an attractive colonial town 144km northwest of Goiânia on the road to Cuiabá. The former capital of Goiás has actively preserved its colonial buildings. A pleasant way to get to know Goiás is by wandering its narrow, cobblestone streets while checking out the renovated homes and churches, many of which date back to the early 1700s. The town is also home to a number of interesting museums that showcase the history of the city and some of its more famous citizens, including poet Cora Coralina and painter Goiandira do Coulo. During the week before Easter the town is flooded with visitors who come to see **Festa da Semana Santa,** a weeklong religious celebration with reenactments and huge processions.

TRANSPORTATION. The intercity **rodoviária** is 30min. from town; save your feet and ask to be dropped of at the **local bus station** (☎371 1510), beside the river. From the intercity *rodoviária* **Empressa Moreira Ltd.** (☎371 1510) goes to Aruanã (3hr.; 2 per day 11am-5pm; R$9) and Goiânia (2½hr.; every hr. 6am-7:40pm; R$15).

ORIENTATION & PRACTICAL INFORMATION. Most activity takes place around **Praça da Liberdade.** Uphill along Rua Luís do Couta is **Praça do Chafariz,** from which **Rua Moreti Foggio** leads across a small river toward **Praça do Rosário,** home to the town's most impressive church. For **guided tours** of the city and nearby trails contact **Eco Trilhas,** Rua Boa Vista 30, opposite Pousada de Ipê. (☎371 3760, 9651 2515. Guided walks R$35 per day.) **Supermercado Vila Boa,** Rua 15 de Novembro 7, opposite the city bus station, has groceries. (☎371 1605. Open M-Sa 7am-8pm.) **Bradesco,** Pça. Liberdade 6, offers **no currency exchange** and does not change traveler's checks; stock up on funds in Goiânia. (☎371 1607. Open M-F 10am-3pm.) **Farmácia Bom Jesus,** Pça. Castelo Branco 4, is well-stocked for emergencies. (☎371 1305. Open 7:30am-8pm.) **Hospital São Pedro,** on Rua do Carmois (☎371 1417, 371 1954), is the local medical facility. The **post office** is on the edge of Pça. do Chafariz. (☎371 8881. Open M-F 9am-5pm.) **Postal code:** 76600-000.

ACCOMMODATIONS & FOOD. **Pousada do Ipê ❷,** Rua do Forum 28, behind Igreja do Rosário on the other side of the river, has a shaded garden with flowering trees, a lovely pool, and hammocks along its verandas. (☎371 2065. Singles R$39, with A/C and *frigo-bar* R$49; doubles R$49, with A/C and *frigo-bar* R$57. Suites with hydromassage bath R$63-73.) **Pousada do Sol ❷,** Rua Americano do Brasil 17, two blocks from the *rodoviária,* is the best of the cheapies. The rooms are light and airy and the beds quite comfortable. (☎371 1717. Kitchen. Singles R$25; doubles R$35; triples R$45; quads R$60.) Slightly more economical lodging can be found next door at **Pousada Lua ❶**, Rua Americano do Brasil 19. The rooms are small but comfy, all with wardrobe, fan, and bath; doubles are more spacious. (☎371 1041. Rooms R$20 per person.) **Pousada Casarão ❶**, Rua Minette Foggin 8, is in the *centro* overlooking Pça. Coreto. The *pousada's* central location can sometimes make for noisy nights, but the rooms are attractive and the staff are friendly. (☎371 2874. Laundry R$1 per piece. Singles R$20; doubles R$35; triples R$55. Suite with bath R$50.)

FOOD. Pousada Casarão also runs a small restaurant, **Lanchonete Casarão ❶**, which overlooks the *praça* and serves simple but appetizing meals. (Open M-F 10am-8pm, Sa-Su 10pm-10pm.) **Beco do Sertão ❸**, Rua 13 de Maio 17, is most famous for its *peixe na telha* (sliced *pintado* fish with tomato sauce and rice served on a terra-cotta tile; R$22), but has a wide selection of dishes. (☎371 2956. Open daily 3pm-midnight.) A few doors down is the **Dalí Restaurante ❸**, Rua 13 de Maio 26, which serves everything from pizza to chicken curry. (☎372 1640. 10% service charge. Open Tu-Su 11am-11pm.)

SIGHTS. Goiandira do Coulo has been painting in Goiás for almost eighty years. She has gained international recognition for her innovative style, which involves the application of colorful sands on freshly painted oil landscapes. Her museum, **Espaça Cultural Goiandira do Caulo,** Rua Joaqin Bonafacio 19, contains paintings that date all the way back to 1926. The attraction of the museum lies in the guided tours offered by Goiandira herself. Cross the river and turn left along Rua Jardim at Igreja do Rosário. Turn right at Rua Hugo Ramos and left at Rua Joaqin Bonafacio. (☎371 1303. Open Tu-Su 9am-noon and 1-5pm. R$2.) **Casa Coralina,** Rua Dom Cândido Penso 20, pays homage to Cora Coralina, another of the city's famous citizens. Born in 1889, Cora became well known in Brazil for her enchanting poetry, though her unconventional lifestyle was a topic of much consternation. The museum houses some of her old furniture, including her writing desk. (☎371 1990. Open Tu-Su 9am-5pm.) **Museu das Bandeiras,** Pça. do Chafriz, is housed in the old city council building, the Casa de Câmara. Included in the museum's displays are some finely decorated porcelain vases, a small statue collection of plump cherubs, and artifacts from the local Marará community. On the bottom floor of the museum guests can visit one of the cells from the old city jail. (☎371 1087. Open Tu-F 9-11am and 1-5pm, Sa noon-5pm, Su 9am-1pm. R$2.) **Museu de Arte Sacra,** in Pça. Liberdade, is housed in Igreja da Boa Morte and is packed with artifacts ranging from elaborate altar chalices to vibrantly colored religious sculptures. There are also old pictures of Goiás hanging on the walls. (☎371 1207. Open Tu-F 8am-5pm, Sa 9am-5pm, Su 9am-4pm. R$2.) **Palácio Conte dos Arcos,** Pça. Dr. Tasso de Camargo s/n, has been fully restored to reflect what the building would have looked like in its glory day as the state governor's residence. Each of the palace's rooms is lavishly decorated with antique furnishing and colonial portraits. (☎371 1200. Open Tu-Sa 8am-7pm, Su 8am-noon. R$2.)

PIRENÓPOLIS ☎62

Picturesque Pirenópolis is an old mining settlement resting serenely in a green valley. Horse-drawn carts and beat-up Volkswagon Beetles pass in front of the colonial facades lining its cobblestone streets. Weekend visitors from Goiânia and Brasília often swamp Pirenópolis, but during the rest of week Pirenópolis moves at a much slower pace than the rest of Goiás. Declared a National Heritage site in 1989, the town is known for its Festa das Cavalhadas (p. 32), in which locals dress as Christian knights and reenact Charlemagne's battle against the Moors.

TRANSPORTATION

Buses: The **rodoviária** (☎331 1248), on Av. Neco Mendonça, is a few blocks from the *centro*. **Goianésia** (☎331 1080) runs to **Brasília** (3hr.; 7 per day 6am-7pm; R$13) and **Goiânia** (2½hr.; 6am; R$15).

Taxis: Taxis commonly transport visitors between the town and nearby natural attractions. Some drivers will serve as guides for a little extra. **Pirenópolis Taxis** (☎9903 3366, 9608 3805) runs 24hr. per day. Cheaper **moto-taxis** can be hired from **Moto Taxi Central** (☎331 1948).

Horse Rental: For information about renting a horse contact Mr. Aristofones (☎331 1372); he generally charges R$25 per day.

ORIENTATION & PRACTICAL INFORMATION

Avenida Neco Mendonça leads from the *rodoviária* to **Praça do Rosária Matriz,** the city's central *praça*. From this *praça*, **Rua do Rosário** leads toward the lower part of the city, where most restaurants are located. Taking a right from the *praça* will lead you to **Rua Sizenando Jayme,** where the banks and pharmacies are found.

Tourist Office: Associação do Conductores de Visitantes de Pirenópolis (☎331 2729), has lots of information about the nearby waterfalls and parks, and can provide guides for the day (R$50, not including transportation). Open 8am-6pm.

Tours: Pirenópolis Adventura, Rua Barbosa 31 (☎331 2494, 9991 1170), organizes rappeling trips (R$30 per person, min. 4 people), mountain biking, and canyon excursions. The office also sells hiking equipment. Open M-F 8am-5pm, Sa-Su 8am-noon.

Banks: Banco do Brasil, Rua Sizenendo Jayme 1 (☎331 1182). No currency exchange. Open M-F 11am-4pm. **Bradesco,** Rua Sizenendo Jayme 5 (☎331 1044), has a Visa ATM. Open M-F 11am-4pm.

Police: Delegacia de Polícia, on Pça. Bernando Sayão (☎331 1105).

Late-Night Pharmacy: Drogaria St. Antõnio, Rua Sizenendo Jayme 2 (☎331 1132), on the corner of Rua do Rosário. Open daily 7am-10pm.

Hospital: Hospital Nossa Senhora do Rosária (☎331 1897), Av. Neco Mendonça, opposite the *rodoviária*.

Public Telephones: International phone calls are best made at **Telegoiás,** Rua Sizenendo Jayme s/n (☎331 1267). Open daily 7am-10pm.

Post Office: Post office, Pça. Emmanuel Jaime Lopes s/n (☎331 1282). Open M-F 9am-5pm. **Postal code:** 72980-000.

ACCOMMODATIONS

The town is popular as a weekend getaway for those living in nearby cities, leading most hotels to increase their prices by 30-40% from Friday to Sunday.

Pousada Imperial, Rua Sizenando Jayme 21 (☎331 1382). Friendly *pousada* with good facilities and an excellent breakfast. The rooms are brightly lit and most have *frigo-bar* and A/C. They offer group discounts that make the *pousada* particularly attractive for families. Laundry R$2 per piece. Singles R$30; doubles R$50. ❷

Pousada Vivenda Verde, Rua do Rosário 14 (☎331 1468), at the bottom of the hill. Though the rooms are simple, the *pousada* compensates with a lovely pool, small game room, and a TV lounge. All rooms have fan and private bath. Laundry R$1 per piece. Singles R$15; doubles R$20. ❶

Pousada Lara, Rua Direita 11 (☎331 1294), near Pça. do Rosário. Behind the unassuming entrance is a swimming pool, sauna, and lounge area. The best rooms are found on the 2nd fl., and all have TV, fan, and *frigo-bar*. One of the smaller *pousadas* in town, so book ahead during holidays. Singles R$30; doubles R$50; triples R$75. ❷

Pousada Rancho do Ralf, Rua Benjamin Constant 17 (☎331 1162; www.pirenopolis.tur.br/ranchodoralf), near Banco do Brasil. A gold-mining themed and decorated *pousada*. Palm trees provide shade for the pool and the large garden is filled with various flowering shrubs. All suites have *frigo-bar*, A/C, and TV. Singles R$60; doubles R$95. ❸

Pousada das Cavalhadas, Pça. do Matriz 1 (☎331 1261), in front of Igreja Matriz. Provides a quite central location without the noise. The inviting couches in the lounge area provide a good place for travelers to meet, as does the cozy breakfast room. The rooms all come with comfortable beds and private bath. Doubles come with A/C, TV, and *frigo-bar*. Singles R$25; doubles R$58; triples R$75. ❷

FOOD & NIGHTLIFE

There is a large group of restaurants at the bottom of the hill on Rua do Rosário. High prices tend to mean that they are frequented only by tourists.

Restaurante dos Pireneus, Chácara Mata do Subrado, Bairro do Carmo (☎331 1345), about 15min. from the *centro* on the opposite side of the river. International cuisine and a limited selection of regional dishes served in a huge cabana overlooking the surrounding hills. It offers both a la carte and buffet options. The bottomless bowls of soup with garlic bread are delicious and feed 2-3 people; try the *creme de palmito* (R$10). Buffet R$18. 10% service charge. Open daily noon-3pm and 8-11pm. MC/V. ❷

Com Sabor e Som, Rua do Rosário 20 (☎9997 3683), on the corner of Rua do Lazer. A wide selection of dishes served in a simple outdoor area. The tasty thin crust pizza with choice of three toppings is a bit expensive (R$21), but the fish dishes, including *delícia de bacalhau* (R$23), are among the cheapest in town. Turns into a busy bar as the night goes on. Open Th-Sa 5pm-2am, Su noon-5pm. ❸

Singapura, Rua do Rosário 22 (☎331 3779). A haven for vegetarians and lovers of pan-Asian cuisine. Dishes mostly revolve around noodles and rice, but they also have large plates of sushi (R$40 serves 2). Bamboo furniture and Chinese art create a classy dining area. Open Th-Su 7pm-midnight. ❸

NO WORK, ALL PLAY

FESTA DAS CAVALHADAS

Every year, Pirenópolis plays hos to one of Brazil's most curious fes tivals, which celebrates Charle magne's expulsion of the Moor from Iberia. The festival was trans planted from Portugal in 1819 and has been celebrated eve since with a combination of moc battles, jousting competitions fireworks, and fanciful costumes Pirenópolis is decorated as European village from the Middl Ages during the festival.

On the festival's first day a kin is crowned, followed by muc singing and dancing. On the sec ond day the king watches over a elaborate battle between th Moors and Charlemagne's Chris tian forces, who win the battle an convert the vanquished Moors t Christianity amidst further singin and dancing. The third and fina day of celebration involves joust ing competitions like the Tir Cabeças (Removal of Heads) which challenges riders to spear papier-mâché head while riding a full gallop, and the infinitely mor difficult Arganlinhas, in which small metallic ring replaces th paper head. The town's popula tion swells during the festival an hotels are often booked up week in advance, so make reservations.

The Cavlhadas are held 50 day after Easter every year. Contac the tourist office (p. 290) or Mari Pereira de Pina at Museu das Cav alhadas (p. 292) for more info.

Ô Xente Vai! Restaurante, Rua do Carmo 34 (☎331 1903), across the river. Specializes in regional meat dishes and offers friendly, attentive service. The owner is especially proud of her *galinha caipira à moda Mineira* (chicken stew, served with rice and local palm vegetables; R$22 serves 2), but most come for the *carne do sol* (R$12). Often live music on weekends. Open F-Su 8-11pm. ❷

Nena Restaurante, Rua Aurora 4 (☎331 1450, 331 1470), in a small white house; enter through the front door and walk through the kitchen to reach the dining area. A modest kilo that serves surprisingly fresh food (R$10). Vegetarians will be interested in the salad spread. Weekend buffet R$11. Open Tu-Th noon-3pm, F-M noon-5pm. ❷

Crepiri, Rua do Rosário 26 (☎331 3520). A quirky café with desert crepes and some more filling dinner options. Each table comes with a set of crayons and blank paper for patrons to entertain themselves while they wait for their meal. *Sucos* R$2. Banana and chocolate crepe R$5. Savory crepes R$7-R$10. Open daily noon-10pm. ❶

SIGHTS

CHURCHES. Igreja Nossa Senhora do Rosário was built between 1727 and 1732, and was the first church in Goiás. It has long been a symbol of Goiás and the pride of the town, but a recent fire ripped through the church and destroyed everything but the imposing facade; restoration efforts are underway. From afar the church appears intact and postcard snapshots can still be taken; Pousada dos Pireneus has the best views. **Igreja Bonfim** was built shortly after Igreja Rosário and is famed for its Virgin Mary statue, brought from Portugal over 250 years ago. The statue is normally covered in a purple shroud and rests framed by two lavishly decorated shrines above the altar. *(Igreja Nossa Senhora do Rosário, Pça. do Rosário s/n. Igreja Bonfim, at the end of Rua Bonfim do Serra dos Pireneus. Open M-F 8am-5pm, Sa 9am-noon.)*

MUSEU DAS CAVALHADAS. This museum holds a wonderful and eclectic collection of costumes from the Festa das Cavalhadas. Maria Pereira de Pina runs the museum in the front two rooms of her home, which are filled with brightly colored outfits and elaborate masks used during the festival. Maria has been living in Pirenópolis for over sixty years and offers a wealth of information about the events that take place during the celebration. *(Rua Direita 39, just off Pça. do Rosário. ☎331 1166; call in advance. Open M-Sa 8am-5pm. R$2.)*

PARKS & TRAILS. The town's biggest attraction is the **Santuário Cachoeira Bonsucesso.** The park's six waterfalls are accessible via an easy 1200m trail, and although lacking in grandeur and size, some end in deep pools good for cliff-jumping and others have small beaches. Avoid going on a tour and either walk or hire a *mototaxi* to get there. **Estadual Serra dos Pireneus** was named by an excited pioneer who thought the mountain range resembled the French Pyrenees. In addition to several peaks (the highest at 1385m), the park also contains an abundance of waterfalls, including Cachoeira da Fumaça, popular as an rappeling spot for tour groups. Closer to town is **Fazenda Vagafogo,** a private wildlife sanctuary. The reserve has received visitors like Elizabeth I and Prince Philip, and is home to antelopes, armadillos, and monkeys. *(Santuário Cachoeira Bonsucesso 6km from town. ☎331 1299. Open 7am-5pm. R$5. Estadual Serra dos Pireneus 18km from town, best visited with guide. ☎331 2729. Open daily 7am-5pm. R$5. Fazenda Vagafogo 6km from town. Open 8am-5pm. R$9.)*

ALTO PARAÍSO ☎62

Alto Paraíso is a good place to stock up on supplies before continuing to the more charming São Jorge, only one kilometer from the entrance of Chapada dos Veadeiros (p. 296). Long-term stays may be attractive to flower-children, as the streets are lined with crystal healers and other mystics. There are several alternative communities on nearby farmlands that have become popular as spiritual retreats. In addition to a number of beautiful waterfalls, the area around Alto Paraíso is also home to several annual raves, including the lively **Transcendance Festival** which takes place in the second week of July.

TRANSPORTATION. The **rodoviária** (☎446 1359) is one block from the main street, Av. Ary Filho. **Real Expresso** (☎446 1861) sends buses to Brasília (3hr.; 2-3 per day; R$18). **São José** (☎446 1359) goes to Goiânia (6hr.; 10:30pm; R$33). **Santo Antônio** goes to São Jorge (45min.; 4pm; R$4). **Taxis** often meet passengers as they come off the buses.

PRACTICAL INFORMATION. **Transchapada Turismo,** in the same *praça* as the *rodoviária*, arranges guides, **bike rental** (R$5 per hr.), and **horse rental** (R$10 per hr.). They also have a "mystics tour" that visits the local temples, sanctuaries, and meditation spots. (☎446 1345. Open M-F 8am-7pm.) **Travessia Ecoturismo,** Av. Ary Filho 979, arranges popular rappeling trips (R$40-70 per person) to the nearby waterfalls. (☎446 1595. Open M-F 8am-7pm, Sa-Su 10am-2pm.) **Centro de Atendimento ao Turismo,** Av. Ary Filho, 10min. from the *rodoviária*, is well-equipped to answer questions and arrange tours. (☎446 1159. Open M-F 8am-5pm.) The only bank in town, **BEG,** Av. Ary Filho 767, has **no ATMs or currency exchange.** The **police** (☎446 1127) are on Av. João Bernardes Rabelo. There's a **pharmacy,** Medianeira, on Av. Ary Filho. (☎446 1152. Open M-F 8am-10pm.) Near the *rodoviária* along Rua São José Operário is the **Hospital Municipal de Alto Paraíso** (☎446 1103). The **post office** is on Rua das Araras, 25min. from the *rodoviária*. (☎446 1520. Open M-F 8am-4pm.) **Postal code:** 73770-000.

ACCOMMODATIONS & FOOD. **Pousada do Sol ❶,** Rua Barbosa 911, has more character and energy than other accommodations in town but is hard to find and far away; avoid the frustrating three-kilometer trek and get a taxi. Guests are encouraged to pick fruit from the avocado and *maracujá* trees or relax in the many hammocks. (☎446 1201. Dorms R$25.) **Pousada Alfa & Omega ❸,** on Rua Joaquim de Almeida, is similar to Pousada do Sol but more expensive and closer to town. From the *rodoviária* follow Av. Ary Filho for 15min. until you reach Rua Joaquim de Almeida. Turn right and it will be one block down on the corner. Its indoor swimming pool and meditation room filled with crystals and tapestries set it apart from its faraway cousin. Each private suite has a *frigo-bar* and TV; doubles come with complimentary condoms. (☎446 1225. Suites R$50 per person.) **Numes Hotel ❶,** on Av. Ary Filho, one block from the *rodoviária*, is a convenient option for those arriving late. (☎446 1170. Breakfast included. Dorms R$15.)

For regional meals, check out **Jató Saladas e Grelhados ❷,** on Rua Coleta Paulion. From the *rodoviária*, walk down Av. Ary Filho and it will be on your left. This self-service restaurant (R$11 per kg) has excellent food including plenty of vegetarian options. (☎446 2339. Open Th-M 10am-6pm.) **Pizza 2000 ❸,** Av. Ary Filho 690, is the busiest and best of the town's several pizzerias. Served with turkey, onions, and olives, *pizza paraíso* (R$18) is the local favorite. (☎446 1814. Open daily 6pm-midnight.) **Creperie Alfa e Omega ❶,** Av. Ary Filho s/n, is good for those with a sweet tooth. In addition to chicken and meat crepes the restaurant serves some very tasty desserts; the *fondu de chocolate* (R$55 serves 4) is an enticing option for hungry groups. (☎446 1163. Open daily noon-midnight.)

SIGHTS. A number of attractive waterfalls can be found on the outskirts of Alto Paraíso. **Cachoeira Água Fria** is a popular rappeling spot for local tour companies and is among the area's most visited. The 50m falls are surrounded by flower-filled fields and shimmering rocks flecked with crystals. The falls are a seven-kilometer drive from town followed by a 1.5km walk. **Cachoeira Almécegas,** a multi-tiered 45m waterfall that drops like a bride's veil into a deep canyon below, is probably the most beautiful of the falls. The falls are on the grounds of the São Bento farm 10km from town; R$3 is charged for access to the falls via a 2.5km trek. Also on the property is the **Cachoeira São Bento.** The swimming pool at its base is perfect for cliff-diving, and on the pool's left bank is a partially submerged cave. From **Crystal Streams,** a series of small waterfalls with natural pools, one can enjoy a sweeping view of the Moinho Valley. The streams are 7km from town toward Pouso Alto. Tour companies in town offer **package tours** that include visits to most of the falls (R$50-90 per person). Alternatively, you can hire a guide and bikes or horses for the day, though this option can be more expensive than tours.

NEAR ALTO PARAÍSO: SÃO JORGE ☎62

Visitors to Chapada dos Veadeiros often base themselves in the attractive little town of São Jorge. Settled in the late 1900s by miners, the town has since been overrun by environmentally conscious residents who are concerned with protecting the surrounding hills rather than exploiting them. Though the town's main attraction is the nearby national park (p. 296), the surrounding countryside boasts spectacular natural formations and hiking opportunities of its own, including the otherworldly **Vale da Lua** and tranquil **Raizama Nature Reserve** (p. 298).

São Jorge is 35km from Alto Paraíso along GO-239. **Buses** depart from the main *praça* to Alto Paraíso (45min.; 9am; R$5). **Bike rental** can be arranged through Fernando at Camping Quarto Crescent (R$15 per day). Pousada São Jorge organizes **horse rental** (R$60 per day, including guide) and also offers **Internet access** (R$30 per hr.). The **tourist office** has information on the park and local guides, and sells admission to Chapada dos Veadeiros. (☎446 1690. Open Tu-Su 8am-noon.) There is no bank in town, but some *pousadas* will exchange currency.

Pousada São Jorge ❷ is the town's most inviting place to stay. Huge king-size mattresses take up most of the bedroom's floor space but there's plenty of room to relax in the cozy TV lounge upstairs. (☎9998 5384. Laundry R$1 per piece. Singles R$25.) **Pousada Águas de Marco ❸,** has charming *quartos,* each with a double bed and windows made from green and blue bottles. The *pousada* also has a swimming pool and a small sauna. (☎347 2082. Doubles R$100.) Cheap camping can be found at **Camping Quarto Crescent ❶,** behind the tourist office. The grounds are managed by the ever-helpful Fernando, who also runs a tasty pizzeria on the premises. (☎939 9483. Pizza R$6-8. Camping R$5 per person.) **Lua de São Jorge ❷,** on the road leading out of town, serves more expensive pizzas (R$11-22) and other Italian dishes. (☎9973 3044. Open Th-Su 5pm-midnight.) Just off the main *praça,* **Papa Lua ❶** offers a lunch buffet of traditional dishes and an a la carte dinner menu of pasta and pancakes. (☎455 1085. Open F-M 3-6pm and 7-10pm.)

CALDAS NOVAS ☎64

Caldas Novas is an upscale resort town popular with Brazilian tourists for its hot springs. The springs are believed to have healing powers, and are reputed to cure everything from rheumatism to impotence. There are several water parks around the springs, and during holidays the town can be saturated with tourists. During these times it's best to make advance reservations.

TRANSPORTATION & PRACTICAL INFORMATION. The *rodoviária* is on **Rua Professor Brutas.** This street is connected by **Rua Antônio de Godov** to the main *praça,* **Praça Mestre Orlando.** Most shops and hotels are found on **Rua Capitão**

Crisostómo, one block east of Pça. Mestre Orlando. The road leading into the city from Goiânia, **Rua São Cristóvão,** is where most of the water parks are located. **Afla Luz** (☎453 1136) sends buses to Brasília (6hr.; 2 per day 7am-2pm; R$25). **Viação Paraúna** (☎453 1135) runs **buses** to Goiânia (3hr.; 10 per day 6:30am-7:30pm; R$18). The **tourist office,** in Pça. Mestre Orlando, is housed in a beige circular building. It has brochures for all the major water parks, and the staff speak English. (☎453 1868. Open M-F 8am-6pm, Sa 8am-noon.) There is **no currency exchange** in town. Other services include: **police,** at the corner of Rua Crisostómo and Alameda do Contono (☎453 1190); a **pharmacy,** Drogaria Nacional, Rua Pedro Branco de Souza 71, one block from the *rodoviária* (☎453 6250; open daily 7:30am-10pm); **Hospital Aparecida,** Rua Eça de Queiroz 13 (☎453 1290); **Internet access** at City On Line, Rua Antônio Godoy 421 (☎453 0626; R$3 per hr.; open M-F 8am-9pm, Sa 8am-3pm); and a **post office,** Rua Crisostómo 361 (☎453 1733; open M-F 9am-5pm, Sa 9am-noon). **Postal code:** 75690-000.

ACCOMMODATIONS & FOOD. The best inexpensive option is **Pousada Paulista ❶,** Rua São Cristóvão 384. The *pousada* has a welcoming lobby and large rooms with TV, *frigo-bar*, and lots of light. Some of the rooms at the front of the hotel also have small verandas. (☎453 2261. Singles R$18; doubles R$40.) **Aguas Claras ❸,** Rua São Cristóvão 1, is a chain hotel with two pools, an outdoor game room with a pool table, and a small sauna. All rooms have A/C; the *luxo* rooms also have *frigo-bar* and TV. (☎453 1738; aclaras@ih.com.br. Singles R$50; doubles R$65. *Luxo* singles R$60; doubles R$75. Low-season discounts.) A good four-star option is **Hotel Itataia ❹,** Rua Crisostómo 171. The rooms are a bit small, but most people spend their time lounging at the poolside bar. Included in room prices is an excellent lunch buffet. (☎453 1628; www.itatiaiadasthermas.com.br. Singles R$75; doubles R$80. *Luxo* singles R$85; doubles R$90.) Cheaper lodging can be found at **Pousada San Marco ❶,** Rua 18 108, on the corner of Rua São Cristóvão. The rooms are simple but comfortable, and the staff is friendly. (☎453 2234. R$20 per person.)

For an excellent breakfast, try **Casa dos Pães ❶,** two blocks west of the tourist office on Rua Antônio de Goday. In addition to espresso and cappuccino, the café also serves freshly baked pies (R$0.80-2) and French pastries. (☎453 1600. Open M-F 6am-8pm, Sa-Su 7am-noon.) The local favorite for dinner is **Nonna Mia ❷,** Av. Orcalino Santos 45, on the corner of Rua Major Nictor. The menu includes several pasta dishes (R$15) and some regional cuisine, but most tourists opt for pizza. (☎453 7030. Open daily 11:30am-3pm and 6:30-11pm. MC/V.) Vegetarians and meat-lovers alike flock to **Chão das Goianas ❷,** Av. Orcalino Santos 7140, for its huge buffet. Slabs of meat and pots of pasta are kept warm over a wood fire. (☎453 6715. R$11.90 per kg. Open daily 11am-midnight.)

SIGHTS. Tourists come to Caldas Novas to play in its water parks. Undoubtedly the most popular is **Hot Park,** 28km from the city on the road to São Paulo. It features a number of water slides, banana boats, several heated pools, and a wet-and-wild zipline. A morning bus leaves for the park at 9am and returns to the city later in the afternoon (1pm and 6pm). Transportation and packages to the park, including accommodations, can be arranged at Av. Orcalino Santos 380. (☎453 7857. Round-trip bus ticket R$3. Park open Tu-Su 9am-8pm. Park admission R$25.) Just 15min. from the *centro* is **Parque Aquatico Recreio,** Rua São Cristóvão 805, on the left as you drive towards Goiânia. This park contains artificial waterfalls, five pools, and a 360m waterslide. There is also a kiddie pool, which has lifeguards to watch over the young ones. (☎453 2191. Open Mar.-May and Sept.-Dec. W-Su 8am-7:30pm; June-Aug. and Jan.-Feb. daily 8am-7:30pm. R$20.) Slightly more modest is **Thermas di Roma,** on Rua São Cristóvão, across from Parque Aquatico Recreio. In addition to the eight pools in the recreation area there are also hot tubs with hydromassage and a poolside bar. (☎453 1718. Open daily 8am-8pm. R$20.) When visitors grow weary of the sunbathing and swimming they often escape to **Jardim Japonés,** Av. Santo Amaro 1600, a 40min. walk from town on the highway toward Goiânia. This small, beautifully sculpted garden has ponds filled with colorful fish, sprawling trees, a gazebo, and small reproductions of ancient Japanese buildings. (☎453 2930. Open daily 7am-6pm. R$1.50.)

P.N. CHAPADA DOS VEADEIROS ☎61

The sparkling streams and gushing waterfalls of Chapada dos Veadeiros dominate its strikingly beautiful terrain. The park is full of canyons, rock formations, and impressive deposits of quartz crystals that cause trails to twinkle in the sun. The scenery changes every step of the way, from views of 120m cascades to mangled trees twisting and turning in colorful, flowered meadows. The national park was established in 1961 to protect the area's rare, high-altitude *cerrado* flora, and is one of Brazil's few parks to have succeeded in its aims: the pristine countryside is almost exactly as it was 40 years ago. Among the park's many inhabitants are the spotted leopard, armadillo, macaw, parakeet, maned wolf, and ostrich.

AT A GLANCE: P.N. CHAPADA DOS VEADEIROS

AREA: 2350 square kilometers.

ALTITUDE: 1400-1640 meters.

FEATURES: Canyons, waterfalls, and natural swimming holes.

CLIMATE: The waterfalls are most spectacular during the wet season (Nov.-Mar.) though the heavy rainfall usually makes Canyon 2 inaccessible.

GATEWAY TOWNS: Alto Paraíso (p. 292) and São Jorge (p. 294).

HIGHLIGHTS: Trekking to the 120m twin waterfalls of **Salto do Rio Preto;** peering down at rushing waters as they rip through canyons below, bouncing from rock to rock at the extraordinary **Vale do Lua;** power-showering at **Cachoeira Cariocas** and **Cachoeira Garimpão.**

FEES: Entrance tickets to the park (R$3) are available at the tourist office in São Jorge. Visitors must be accompanied by an accredited guide (R$30-60 per day).

TRANSPORTATION

The official entrance to the national park is just one kilometer from São Jorge. **Santo Antônio** sends a daily bus along the 35km gravel road from Alto Paraíso to São Jorge (45min.; departs 4pm, returns 9am; R$4). This makes a two-night stay in São Jorge necessary for those who want to go on either of the park's two hikes. **Vale da Lua** and the **Raizama Nature Reserve,** both located outside the park about seven kilometers from São Jorge, are accessible by taxi, horse, bike, and some hard-to-follow trails—it's best to take a guide. Expensive package tours to these sights can also be arranged by tour companies in Alto Paraíso (p. 293).

PRACTICAL INFORMATION

The park is located three hours north of Brasília and six hours northwest of Goiânia, making it a popular weekend retreat for families seeking escape from those cities. Access to the park is greatly restricted, however, as a result of the attempts to protect the park's vegetation; only two trails are open to the public. Both of these begin at the park entrance, one kilometer from the town of São Jorge. Hikers must be accompanied by an accredited guide to enter the park; guides can be arranged at the tourist office in São Jorge (R$30 per day). The park is open Tu-Su 8am-5pm.

Park Information: There is no tourist infrastructure or park information available at the entrance to Chapada dos Veadeiros. **Tickets** to the park (R$3) must be purchased at the tourist office in São Jorge (☎508 3388). Tourist offices in both São Jorge and Alto Paraíso provide maps and guides.

Supplies: There are no camping stores in either Alto Paraíso or São Jorge, though hats, hiking boots, and small backpacks are easily found in the supermarkets. Sunscreen can be purchased at the pharmacies in Alto Paraíso or at the tourist office in São Jorge. **Travessia Ecoturismo** (☎446 1595), in Alto Paraíso, rents outdoor equipment.

Groceries: Supermercado Paineiras, Rua São José Operário 180, opposite the *rodoviária* in Alto Paraíso, is the best place to stock up on the basics. (☎445 1665. Open M-Sa 7am-7pm, Su 7am-1pm.) **Frutaria Mercearia,** Rua 12, in São Jorge around the corner from Pousada São Jorge, has the freshest fruit and bread in town. (☎9667 2401. Open daily 7am-9pm.)

Maps: Maps are difficult to find in São Jorge or Alto Paraíso. One of the more readily available is the IBAMA map available at any of the tourist offices. The *Guia da Chapada dos Veadeiros* is filled with useful information about services and restaurants in São Jorge and Alto Paraíso, but its maps are of little use.

Tours: Tour companies in Alto Paraíso offer daytrips (p. 292) to the sights just outside the national park (R$120). Hiring a guide in São Jorge and hiking to the sights is a more economical option (R$30), though most opt for a guide with a car (R$90).

Guides: The **Associaçao dos Conductores de Visitantes de Chapada dos Veadeiros (ACVCV)** has offices at the tourist centers in São Jorge and Alto Paraíso (☎646 1690). Both offices can refer you to English-speaking guides. One of the best guides in São Jorge is **Fernando** (a.k.a. Tatu), who also runs **Camping Quarto Crescent** behind the tourist office. (☎939 9483, 455 1026). Guides charge R$30 per day; with car R$90.

ACCOMMODATIONS

There are no campsites or shelters inside the park, as overnight visits are forbidden, but several farms offer excellent accommodations just outside the park. **São Bento Farm ❹,** 25km from São Jorge and 10km from Alto Paraíso along GO-239, offers more services and comfort than most. On the property are Cachoeira Almécegas and Cachoeira São Bento, connected to the main cottage by 45min. trails. Hammocks are strung up around the grounds and the large living area in the main cottage has a fireplace surrounded by cushions for chilly nights. Some of the private cottages come with four-poster beds and showers. (☎459 3000; www.pousadasaobento.com.br. Horse rental R$10 per hr. Cottages R$90 per person. Two-person luxury cottage with hydromassage bath R$250.) **Aldeia da Lua ❹,** near Vale da Lua 6km from São Jorge, attracts tourists with its large swimming pool, colorful pet parrots, and huge restaurant serving tasty buffets for lunch and dinner. Access to Vale da Lua is free for guests, as is the sauna. Each private chalet has a thatched roof and faux-marble bathroom. (☎9904 4932, 9955 6637; www.aldeiadalua.com.br. Chalets R$75. Children ages 6-14 R$35; under 6 free.)

SIGHTS & HIKING

Chapada dos Veadeiros has just two hiking trails, both of which are about 11km long. The first trail highlights the canyons and waterfalls of the park while the second takes you to the park's most photographed sight, the 120m Saltos do Rio Preto. **Hikers must be accompanied by an accredited guide.** Outside the park, near São Jorge, there are three sights that also merit a visit: Vale da Lua, the Raizama Nature Reserve, and Morando do Sol. All can be combined into a long daytrip, and though hiring a guide is not necessary it is highly recommended.

SALTOS DO RIO PRETO TRAIL. This superb trail first goes to **Saltos do Rio Preto,** the park's most impressive attraction. Here two separate waterfalls, one 80m and the other 120m high, fall side by side from atop a steep cliff and plunge into a deep pool below. Though access to the bottom of the falls is prohibited, the view from the trail is magnificent. After the five-kilometer uphill trek to the falls the trail follows an old miners' path toward **Cachoeira do Garimpão,** an 80m waterfall that spills into a huge pool almost 300m across, where you can take a much-needed dip. The trail then continues to the natural pools at **Pedreiras** and a natural stone staircase leads into the pools, where the gentle cascades give revitalizing water massages. The trail finishes with 5km of backtracking to the park entrance. *(11.5km round-trip, 3-5hr. Difficulty: medium.)*

CANYONS & WATERFALLS TRAIL. This trek is the easier of the park's two hikes, and probably the prettier. The hike leads through lush forests and meadows that show off the best of the park's diverse vegetation, and large deposits of sparkling crystals line the path. The two canyons visited along the trail—creatively named Canyon 1 and Canyon 2—are about four kilometers from the park's entrance. Curiously the first canyon reached is **Canyon 2,** a narrow gully filled with rushing rapids. At the end of the canyon the water pours out into a large pool where there are ledges suitable for cliff-jumping. The trail then leads to **Cachoeira Cariocas,** a 10m waterfall surrounded by a small white beach perfect for sunbathing. Before returning to the park's entrance the trail passes by **Canyon 1,** which boasts unique rock formations and a beautiful waterfall. *(10km round-trip, 3-5hr. Difficulty: easy.)*

VALE DA LUA, RAIZAMA NATURE RESERVE, & MORANDO DO SOL. Just outside the park, along Rio São Miguel, lies **Vale da Lua,** one of the area's most visited attractions; its smooth gray boulders and craters make for a stunning lunar landscape. The valley is nine kilometers by road from São Jorge, but is connected to the town by a pleasant five-kilometer hiking trail along the river. The trail is easily navigated, but **flash floods** can make taking a guide useful. Farther down the river, where the São Miguel meets the Raizama, is the **Raizama Nature Reserve,** a sanctuary of wildflowers, streams, and gentle waterfalls. The reserve lacks the grandeur of the park's waterfalls and mountains but has a subtle beauty that makes it an extremely relaxing place to visit. Nearby, also on Rio São Miguel, is **Moranda do Sol,** a collection of waterfalls and pools surrounded by slabs of slate similar to those found at Vale da Lua. Both Raizama and Moranda are about four kilometers west of São Jorge, connected to the town by the GO-239.

MATO GROSSO

CUIABÁ ☎65

A sign at the airport reads "Welcome to the hottest city in the world," and though this sign may exaggerate slightly, Cuiabá is still the hottest city in all of Brazil, with summer temperatures that often break 40°C. Many tourists use Mato Grosso's capital city only as a base to explore the state, spending as little time here as possible while taking advantage of its strategic position at the meeting point of three separate ecosystems. To the north of the city lie the dense jungles of the Amazon, to the east are the highlands of the *cerrado*, and to the south lie the Pantanal wetlands. Cuiabá has some wonderful museums, but most tourists come here only to sign up for a Pantanal tour (p. 316). Competition between tour operators is more civilized here than in the south; tourists who shop around are often rewarded with the best guides and tours in the entire Pantanal.

TRANSPORTATION

Airport: Aeroporto Marechal Rondon, Av. João Ponce de Arruda s/n (☎614 2511), located in the suburb of Várzea Grande, across the river about 10km from town. The airport has 24hr. **lockers** (R$2) and several car rental agencies. To get to the *centro* take any "Tuiuiú" bus to Marajuara.

Bus Station: Rodoviária de Cuiabá, Rua Jules Rimet s/n (☎621 3629, 621 2429), is 25min. from the *centro*. Turn right upon leaving the *rodoviária* and walk along Av. Marechal Deodoro for 1km; turning left when you reach Av. Getúlio Vargas will bring you to the *centro*. The *rodoviária* has showers (R$4), a 24hr. Visa **ATM,** and a post office (open M-F 9am-noon and 2-5pm). **24hr. Luggage Storage** R$3 per day. From here **Expresso São Luís** (☎621 2904) sends buses to: **Brasília** (20hr.; 5 per day 9am-7:30pm; R$83); **Cacéres** (3½hr.; 7 per day 6:30am-6pm; R$24); **Goiânia** (20hr.; 2 per day 6-7:30pm; R$69); **São Paulo** (26hr.; 7 per day 8am-11pm; R$150). **Integraçáo** goes to **Campo Grande** (10hr.; 8 per day; R$55). **Expresso Rubi** (☎621 1764) goes to **Chapada dos Guimarães** (1¼hr.; 12 per day; $4). The "Bispo" **local bus** connects the *rodoviária* to the *centro* (15min.; every 20min. 6am-midnight; R$1.50).

Car Rental: Unidas (☎682 4062), located at the airport. Class A cars with 100km R$76; with unlimited km R$91. **Localiza** (☎682 7900), located at the airport. Class A cars with unlimited km R$89. Both rental agencies require that renter be at least 21 years of age and have a credit card. Both open their offices when flights arrive.

Taxi: For cheap taxi rides call **Taxi Colorado** (☎322 1121, 9977 2127). **Moto-taxis** (☎624 7046) are a better option for those with no luggage.

ORIENTATION & PRACTICAL INFORMATION

Most tourist attractions are around **Praça Repúblico** and the nearby **Praça Alencastro,** both of which are on **Avenida Getúlio Vargas.** South of this area, between Av. Getúlio Vargas and **Av. Issac Póvoas,** the streets of Cuiabá follow a loose grid system, bound to the east by **Rua 13 de Junho** and to the west by **Rua Commandante Costa** and **Rua Barão de Melgaço.** North of these two main *praças* the serpentine streets of Cuiabá twist and turn confusingly; **Rua Pedro Celestino,** which runs north from Pça. Alencastro, cuts though the area.

TOURIST & FINANCIAL SERVICES

Tourist Office: Pça. Repúblico 131 (☎624 9060; www.sedtur.mt.gov.br), has stacks of pamphlets about the Pantanal and free Internet access. Little English spoken. Open M-F 8am-noon and 2-6pm.

Currency Exchange: Mato Câmbio, Rua Comandante Costa 465 (☎624 1667), on the corner of Rua Cándido Mariano. Excellent rates. Open M-F 8am-6pm, Sa 8am-noon. **Ousominas Câmbio,** Rua Cándido Mariano 401 (☎624 9400), on the corner of Rua Comandante Costa. Open M-F 8am-5pm, Sa 8am-noon.

Banks: Banco do Brasil, Rua Getúlio Vargas 915 (☎611 2209, 611 2121). Charges US$15 for currency exchange and US$20 for cashing traveler's checks. Open M-F 11am-4pm. **Bradesco,** Rua Barão de Melgaço 3475 (☎624 1845). Has several 24hr. **ATMs** that accept Visa cards. Open M-F 11am-4pm.

LOCAL SERVICES

Airlines: Gol (☎682 1666). **VASP** (☎682 3737). **VARIG** (☎682 3682).

Ticket Agencies: Confiança, Av. São Sebastião 2852 (☎314 2700). Books flights, bus tickets, *fazenda* stays, and everything else a tourist could need. Open M-Sa 9am-5pm. **Mundial Viagens,** Av. Issac Povoas 557, (☎623 3499; mundialtour@terra.com.br). Arranges transportation and car rental. Open M-F 8am-6pm, Sa 8am-noon.

Tour Operators: Anaconda Tours, Av. Marechal Deodoro 2142 (☎624 4142, 9981 0171), on the right as you walk toward the water. Arranges expensive tours of the city (R$81 for 2 people), Chapada dos Guimarães (R$255 for 2 days), and Aguas Quentes (R$200 for 2 people). Open M-F 9am-6pm, Sa 9am-noon. **Confiança,** Av. São Sebastião 2852 (☎314 2700; www.confiancaturismo.com.br). Also arranges tours, including adventure trips like rappeling and rafting excursions in Parque Nacional Jaciara (R$150 per day). For information about Pantanal tours, see p. 311.

Markets: Supermercado Central, Av. Marechal Deodoro 1247 (☎623 0770), next to the bakery, is the only supermarket close to the *centro.* Open M-Sa 7am-7pm.

EMERGENCY & COMMUNICATIONS

Police: Delegacia Distrital de Polícia, Rua Nova Mata Grosso s/n (☎661 2132).

Late-Night Pharmacy: Drogaria São Bento, Av. Getúlio Vargas 220, on Pça. da República across from the post office. Open M-F 7am-7pm, Sa 7am-5pm.

Hospitals: Hospital Municipal de Confresa, Rua Marcos Pereira Luz 75 (☎642 3771). Closer to the *centro* and easier to find is **Hospital Geral,** Rua 13 de Junho 2101 (☎616 7000, 624 1233).

Internet Access: NET Games, Av. Isaac Povoas 898 (☎624 0063). Offers fast, cheap Internet access. R$3 per hr. Open M-F 10am-8pm, Sa 9am-7pm. **Copy Center,** Av. Mato Grosso 415 (☎623 2554). R$4 per hr. Open M-F 8am-6pm, Sa 8am-noon.

Post Office: Pça. Repúblico 101 (☎611 1146), next to the tourist office. Open M-F 9am-5pm, Sa 9am-noon. **Postal code:** 78005-000.

ACCOMMODATIONS

Most budget hotels can be found near Pça. Ipiranga, at the intersection of Av. Issac Póvoas and Rua 13 de Junho, but you should expect only basic services. A few upscale accommodations are on Av. Issac Póvoas.

Eco-Verde Pousada, Rua Pedro Celestino 391 (☎624 1386, 9282 3201), a few blocks north of Av. Getúlio Vargas. An oasis of green in the concrete jungle, run by local Pantanal guide extraordinaire Joel Souza, who also arranges his Pantanal tours from the *pousada*. The rooms are simple and the facilities basic, but the great service has made it a favorite among international travelers. Eco-Verde also has a small library, a wealth of information about the Pantanal, and hammocks strung up in the sprawling backyard garden. Free airport pick-up. Laundry R$1 per piece. Dorms R$15. ❶

Hotel Plaza, Rua Antônio Maria 428 (☎623 2018), in a small one-story blue building on the corner of Travessa Des. Lubo. Flower paintings line the bedroom walls, funky 70s-style beds provide comfort, and the "hot" *and* "cold" taps in the shower offer more control over your bathing experience than any other hotel in the city. The hotel has just 10 *apartamentos,* all with A/C, TV, and *frigo-bar,* so call ahead. Singles R$30; doubles R$40; triples R$60; quads R$75. Visa. ❷

Real Palace Hotel, Rua 13 de Junho 102 (☎321 5375), on Pça. Ipiranga near the intersection with Av. Getúlio Vargas. Real Palace offers more bang for the buck than nearby hotels in town, with huge *apartamentos* and private baths. All rooms come with TV, phone, ample space, and dim lighting. *Luxo* rooms have A/C and *frigo-bar.* Breakfast included. Singles R$25; doubles R$35; triples R$45. *Luxo* singles R$38; doubles R$48; triples R$56. ❷

Hotel Ipanema, Rua Jules Rimet 12 (☎621 3069), in front of the *rodoviária.* A good option for those who arrive late or wish to leave early. Ipanema's rooms all have closet, TV, and clean bath. The reception area is a good place to meet other travelers passing through town. Singles R$15, with bath R$22, with A/C R$20; doubles R$24, with bath R$30, with A/C R$50. Visa. ❶

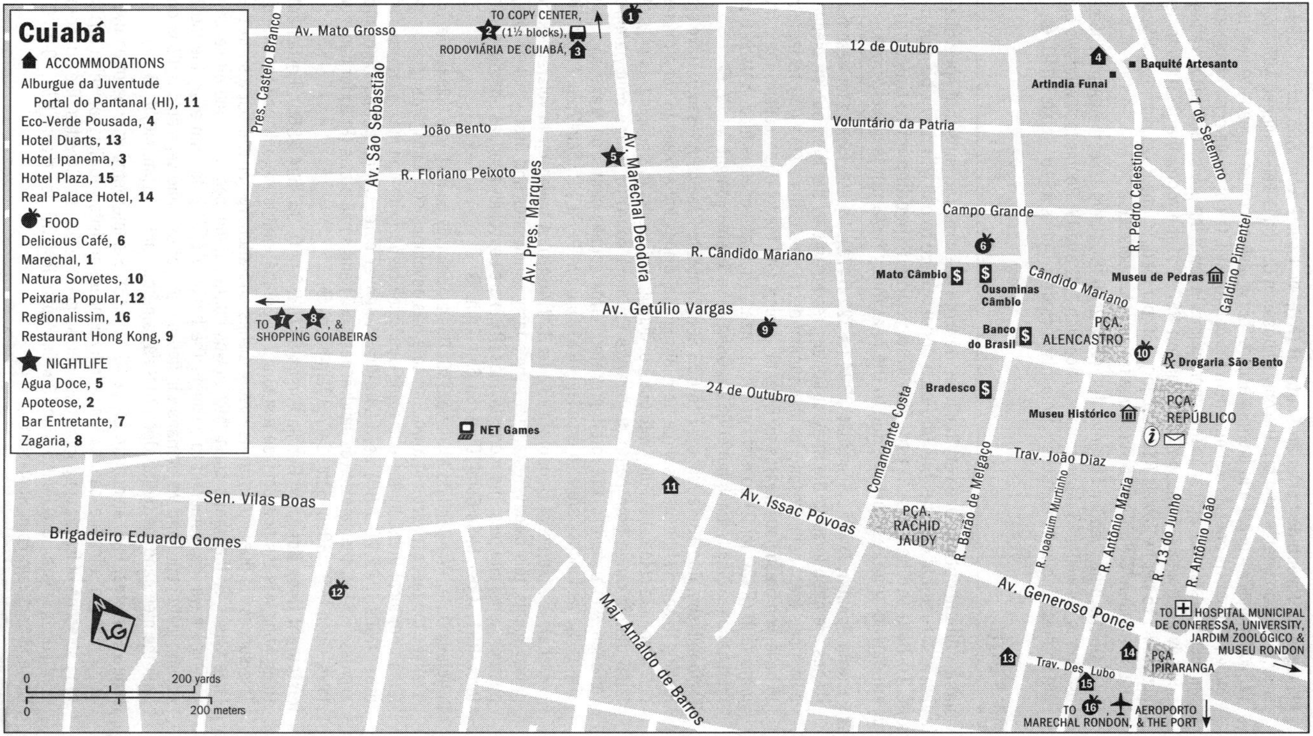

Cuiabá

ACCOMMODATIONS
Alburgue da Juventude
Portal do Pantanal (HI), **11**
Eco-Verde Pousada, **4**
Hotel Duarts, **13**
Hotel Ipanema, **3**
Hotel Plaza, **15**
Real Palace Hotel, **14**

FOOD
Delicious Café, **6**
Marechal, **1**
Natura Sorvetes, **10**
Peixaria Popular, **12**
Regionalissim, **16**
Restaurant Hong Kong, **9**

NIGHTLIFE
Agua Doce, **5**
Apoteose, **2**
Bar Entretante, **7**
Zagaria, **8**

TO COPY CENTER, 2 (1½ blocks),
RODOVIÁRIA DE CUIABÁ, 3
Av. Mato Grosso
12 de Outubro
Baquité Artesanto
Artindia Funal
7 de Setembro
Pres. Castelo Branco
Av. São Sebastião
João Bento
Voluntário da Patria
R. Floriano Peixoto
Av. Pres. Marques
Av. Marechal Deodora
Campo Grande
R. Pedro Celestino
Galdino Pimentel
R. Cândido Mariano
Cândido Mariano
Mato Câmbio
Ousominas Câmbio
Museu de Pedras
TO 7, 8, & SHOPPING GOIABEIRAS
Av. Getúlio Vargas
Banco do Brasil
PÇA. ALENCASTRO
Drogaria São Bento
24 de Outubro
Bradesco
Comandante Costa
Museu Histórico
PÇA. REPÚBLICO
NET Games
Trav. João Diaz
Sen. Vilas Boas
Av. Issac Póvoas
PÇA. RACHID JAUDY
R. Barão de Melgaço
R. Joaquim Murtinho
R. Antônio Maria
R. 13 do Junho
R. Antônio João
Brigadeiro Eduardo Gomes
Maj. Arnaldo de Barros
Av. Generoso Ponce
TO HOSPITAL MUNICIPAL DE CONFRESSA, UNIVERSITY, JARDIM ZOOLÓGICO & MUSEU RONDON
PÇA. IPIRARANGA
Trav. Des. Lubo
TO 16, AEROPORTO MARECHAL RONDON, & THE PORT
0 200 yards
0 200 meters

CENTER-WEST

Albergue da Juventude Portal do Pantanal (HI), Av. Issac Póvoas 665 (☎624 8999; www.portaldopantanal.com.br). The only HI hostel in Cuiabá is well-equipped with cable TV, communal kitchens, and Internet access, but a lack of character leads to very few foreign visitors, as does its distance from the *centro*. Still, the beds are comfortable and the facilities are cleaner than many other options in town; the private doubles are a particularly good value. Transport to the airport R$25; to the *rodoviária* R$20. Internet access R$15 per hr. Towels R$2. Laundry R$5 per load. Dorms R$21, with A/C R$26. Doubles with A/C R$50. R$5 surcharge for non-members. ❶

Hotel Duarts, Rua Joaquim Murtinho 490 (☎322 4538). Offers 16 of the town's cheapest dorms, as well as 3 decent suites, each with A/C and TV. Rooms lack windows but are spotless and well-maintained. Breakfast included. Dorms R$15. Suites R$40. ❶

FOOD

Cuiabá's dining options are very basic aside from a few restaurants that specialize in fish and regional cuisine, but finding a decent place to eat will never be a problem. To beat the heat you'll probably find yourself spending more time in ice cream parlors than restaurants; due to the heat many restaurants close 2-5pm.

Peixaria Popular, Av. São Sebastião 2324 (☎322 5471). Tourists looking for fresh fish dishes are often lured to the array of floating restaurants by the river, but knowledgeable locals feast here. Despite its unassuming decor, this is the state's only restaurant to have won prestigious awards for 5 years running, and the food is excellent. The daily *prato feito* (R$30 for 2) consists of five courses, such as boneless fried *pintado* and fried banana. Quality lunch buffet R$24. Open M-Sa 11am-midnight. MC/V. ❸

Regionalissim, Rua 13 de Junho 27 (☎623 6881), next to Casa de Artesanto. Travelers looking to sample the state's more popular regional dishes are advised to eat a dinner or 2 here. In a colonial building with outdoor dining, Regionalissim's heaping servings of local dishes range from *caldo de piranha* (piranha soup) to *frango com palmito* (chicken with *palmito*). The rotating *pratos feitos* usually center on stews and fish dishes. Buffet lunches are also excellent (R$14). Open Tu-Su 11:15am-2pm. MC/V. ❷

Marechal, Av. Marechal Deodoro 1232 (☎322 4648). A haven for travelers sick of greasy meals, this bakery/restaurant serves tasty sandwiches and freshly baked rolls, pastries, tarts, and pies. The *meringue* pies (R$2) are especially good, as are the lemon tarts (R$1). Open M-Sa 6am-10pm, Su 6am-2pm. ❶

Delicious Café, Rua Cándido Mariano 376. This ambitiously named café tells no lie, as it serves the tastiest *sucos* in town. The café has developed some invigorating concoctions from local fruits; try the energizing *açaí* juice blend (with banana, *guaraná*, and other fruits; R$2.20-2.80) as a sure-fire hangover cure. Cheap cappuccino and expresso R$1-2. The café serves sandwiches (R$2) and small pizzas (R$2) for hungrier folks. Open M-F 7:30am-6pm, Sa 7:30am-noon. ❶

Restaurant Hong Kong, Av. Getúlio Vargas 647 (☎622 0535, 624 2866). Restaurant Hong Kong was the first Chinese restaurant in Cuiabá, and is the only one to survive. This success is due in part to its savory dishes and attentive service, but also to the large screen TV that draws big nightly crowds during *futebol* season; in the off season you may have the restaurant to yourself. The buffet (R$12) is far and away the most economical option, and vegetarians will find a mass of tofu and vegetable options on both the menu and the buffet. Open Tu-Su 11am-3pm and 6-11pm. MC/V. ❷

Natura Sorvetes, Pça. Alencastro 32 (☎624 4836). Summer temperatures often over 40°C make locating the ice cream a primary concern of visitors to Cuiabá, which has a wide selection of ice cream parlors but none so great as Natura Sorvetes. The *abobora com coconut* is an excellent option. Banana splits R$6.30. Ice cream R$1.70-2.70. Open M-Sa 10am-7pm, Su 4-7pm. ❶

SIGHTS

Some sights in Cuiabá are centrally located, but most of them lie on the outskirts and require a taxi ride to be visited. Those who want to save some money can grab a bus to the university from Pça. Ipiranga (Bus #501 or #505), or catch a bus from Pça. Alencastro toward Shopping Cuiabá, which is a couple of blocks from the university campus.

AROUND THE CITY CENTER

MUSEUS HISTÓRICO, DE HISTÓRIA NATURAL, & DE ANTROPOLOGIA. Museu Histórico is housed in a yellow colonial building to the left of the cathedral. The sign on the front of the building reads "Fundação Cultural de Mato Grosso 1975" and the museum is on the second floor. Pictures of the city that date back to the late 19th century are displayed throughout the museum, local heroes are honored with small tributes, and there is a collection of furniture and silverware dating from the mid-1800s. Museu de Antropologia contains stuffed animals from the Pantanal, and Museu de História Natural has some fossils and crystals. *(Pça. República s/n. ☎321 3391. Open M-F 8am-noon and 2-5:30pm. R$1, students R$0.50.)*

MUSEU DE PEDRAS. Run by local historian Ramis Bucair, this unusual, fascinating museum displays a marvelous collection of gems and crystals, crudely stuffed animals, and a hodgepodge of miscellany, like a dried catfish tongue once used by indigenous tribes while making *guaraná*. *(Rua Galdino Pimentel 195. ☎321 9328. Open M-F 7-11am and 1-5pm. R$3.)*

ARTINDIA FUNAI. This is the best place in Cuiabá to buy indigenous crafts. The ground floor is full of standard tourist fare, but the second floor holds the items of real interest, like traditional dolls and headdresses. The store is licensed by IBAMA, and proceeds benefit local indigenous communities. *(Rua Pedro Celestino 301. ☎623 11675. Open M-F 7:30-11:30am and 1:30-5:30pm.)*

BAQUITÉ ARTESANATO. This large purple building opens to greet visitors with brightly colored carvings, elaborate necklaces, and some interesting found-art items made from toy cars, calculators, door knobs, and computer parts (R$10). The artists welcome visitors to learn a little about local crafts; those wishing to learn more should inquire about the weekly classes. *(Rua Pedro Celestino 300. ☎624 9480. Open M-F 8am-6pm, Sa 8am-3pm.)*

UNIVERSITY OF CUIABÁ CAMPUS

JARDIM ZOOLÓGICO. Divided into two separate parts, this innovative zoo provides its animal inhabitants with the utmost freedom while ensuring pleasurable viewing for its human visitors. The zoo rotates its animals between the southern area's wide-open park and the northern area's individual cages; the former keeps the animals happy and healthy, while the latter makes for convenient viewing by visitors and easier checkups by the zookeepers. The southern area has a fenced walkway from which visitors can watch tapirs, anteaters, and foxes. *(☎615 8007. Open Tu-Su 7:30-11:30am and 1:30-6pm.)*

MUSEU RONDON (MUSEU DO ÍNDIO). Run by volunteers from local indigenous communities, the museum functions primarily as an information center for people with questions about the surrounding indigenous cultures. Among the limited number of items on display are some ceramic pots and terra-cotta bowls, blowguns, spears, woven baskets, and clothing. The collections of photographs and ceremonial masks are especially interesting. *(Near the swimming pool; ask for directions. ☎615 8489. Open Tu-F 7:30-11:30am and 1:30-5:30pm, Sa 7:30-11:30am.)*

NIGHTLIFE

Nightlife venues are concentrated on Av. Lavapés, near Shopping Goiabeiras. To reach Av. Lavapés, follow Av. Vargas west toward Pça. 8 de Abril; Av. Vargas curves to the left and becomes Av. Lavapés. The *centro* tends to be quiet, though there are a few places worth exploring, especially Agua Doce.

Bar Entretante, Av. Lavapés s/n (☎624 9665), on the corner of Rua Miguel Sutil about 2 blocks from Shopping Goiabeiras. The premier local nightlife spot, attracting fashionable twenty-somethings. The outdoor seating area (with retractable roof for starry nights) is spotted with leafy palms and funky decorations. A live band plays nightly, pumping out everything from reggae to rock. Sundays draw the largest crowds. To avoid long lines show up before 11pm and dress casual-sharp. Cover R$3. Open Su and W-Sa 7pm-1am.

Zagaria, Av. Lavapés s/n (☎624 5318), at the corner of Rua Miguel Sutil. When Bar Entretante closes at 1am its patrons flood this chic *discoteca,* along with the rest of the city's glitterati. The club is split into 3 sections: the pub area entertains the 30-40s crowd, the dance floor offers room for a slightly younger crowd to shake their stuff, and the small outdoor bar gives patrons the chance to get some fresh air. Big-screen TVs beating out MTV classics, pulsating lights, and frantic trance propel the dance floor crowd. *Chopp* R$4. Mixed drinks R$15. Cover R$25. Open F-Sa 10pm-5am.

Agua Doce, Rua Marechal Deodoro s/n (☎322 8446), on the corner of Rua Floriano Peixoto. A laid-back bar in the *centro* that draws a social, less pretentious crowd. Famous for its variety of *cachaça* shots (over 180 types). Each *cachaça* is rated by its potency and taste (2-star R$1.50, 3-star R$2.50, 5-star R$5); *Let's Go* recommends nothing less than the 3-star options. Saturday night is dominated by couples in their 30s and 40s; Thursdays draw the 20-30s crowd. Happy Hour, with free snacks daily 4-8pm. Th-Sa live music. Cover R$3. Open daily 4pm-2am.

Apoteose, Av. Mato Grosso 442 (☎623 5159, 623 6220), housed in a seemingly abandoned building. Apoteose used to be the top club in town but is now a crowded mosh pit with a cheap cover and punk rock. Cover R$8. Open Th-Sa 11:30pm-5am.

P.N. CHAPADA DOS GUIMARÃES ☎65

Located on a rocky plateau 52km northeast of Cuiabá, Parque Nacional Chapada dos Guimarães is one of the most accessible parks in the Center-West. It enjoys an unusually cool climate for the area and contains some of Brazil's largest sandstone caves, but it lacks the grand peaks and dramatic waterfalls of the region's other parks. The park is often visited by those who make the journey to Mirante da Geodésica, the geographic center of South America which lies 20km to the northeast, and the nearby rock formations of Cidade da Pedra.

TRANSPORTATION

The park entrance is 52km northeast of Cuiabá and just 12km southwest of the town of Chapada dos Guimarães. **Expresso Rubi** (☎301 1280) sends buses between **Cuiabá** and **Chapada dos Guimarães;** these buses pass by the park entrance, but be sure to tell the driver to stop at the entrance, which is unmarked. (From Cuiabá: 50min.; 14 per day 5:45am-7:30pm; R$3. From Chapada dos Guimarães: 20min.; 14 per day 5:45am-7:30pm; R$1.) The park gate is 300m from the main road and the Visitor's Center is 400m farther, on the right. Taxis (☎301 1211, 9972 0773) go to Cidade da Pedra and Mirante da Geodésica.

AT A GLANCE: P.N. CHAPADA DOS GUIMARÃES

AREA: 330 square kilometers.

ALTITUDE: 600-850 meters.

FEATURES: Walking trails, waterfalls, caves, and lookout points. Nearby the park is Mirante da Geodésica, the geographical center of South America.

CLIMATE: Cooler than the rest of the state (average 24°C). Rains June-Aug.

GATEWAY TOWNS: Chapada dos Guimarães.

HIGHLIGHTS: Peering down from the top of the 86m Véu da Noiva; enjoying the spectacular sunsets from Cidade da Pedra; trekking to the Morro de São Jerônimo; tanning on the beach at the foot of Cachoeira Andorinha.

FEES: Tickets to the park (R$3) are available at the park's entrance. Guides are available for hire in the town of Chapada dos Guimarães (R$50-60 per day); there are no guides available at the park itself.

ORIENTATION & PRACTICAL INFORMATION

Two trails are open to the public, both of which begin at the Visitor's Center inside the park. The grueling 19km Caminho das Pedras leads to the park's tallest peak, while the more popular 4km Caminho das Aguas is a leisurely trek that passes by most of the park's principal waterfalls, including the 86m Cachoeira Véu da Noiva. The rock formations at Cidade da Pedra are accessible only by car, as is Mirante da Geodésica, located 8km from the town—independent travelers usually hire cabs from the town of Chapada dos Guimarães. Visitors to the park must enter between the hours of 8am-5pm, though they may stay in the park until sunset; Cidade da Pedra and Mirante da Geodésica are open 24hr.

Park Information: For information on the sights outside the park visit the **tourist office,** Rua Penn Gomes s/n (☎301 2045, 301 1690), in Chapada dos Guimarães. Open M-F 8am-6pm, Sa-Su 8:30-11:30am and 2-5pm. The **Visitor's Center** (☎301 1133, 301 2146), at the park's entrance, has a helpful model of the park and a knowledgeable staff. Park entrance: R$3; students R$1.50; over 60 free. Open Tu-Su 8am-5pm.

Bank, Hospital, Post Office: There are no services in the park, but in Chapada dos Guimarães there are **ATMs** at Bradesco, Rua Fernando Correa 808 (☎301 1205). Open M-F 10am-3pm. **Medical assistance** in town can be found at Fundação Assistencial, Rua Quinco Caldas s/n (☎301 1116). The town has a **post office,** Rua Fernando Correa 848 (☎301 1333). Open M-F 9am-5pm. **Postal code:** 78195-000.

Supplies: Supermercado Junior, on the corner of Fernando Corrêa (☎301 1350), in town opposite the *rodoviária*. The store has a limited stock of canned goods and hiking boots. Open M-Sa 7am-8pm, Su 7am-noon. **Mercado Ouro Fino,** on Pça. Dom Wunibaldo (☎301 1251), has a broad selection of food. Open M-Sa 5:30am-10pm.

Maps: Maps of the park are extremely difficult to find and aren't really necessary; your best bet will be an IBAMA map from the Cuiabá tourist office.

Tours: For adventure trips into the park contact **Atmà Turismo,** Rua Quinco Caldas 33 (☎301 3391; www.atmaturismoecologico.com.br). Rappeling trips R$100-250; rafting can be cheaper. Open M-F 9am-7pm, Sa-Su 8am-7pm. To get to Cidade da Pedra (R$60) and Mirante da Geodésica (R$40) you are best off hiring a cab (☎301 1211, 9972 0773); the driver will usually include a small tour in the price.

Guides: Guides are not required, but can be helpful on the park's winding paths. **Eco-Turismo Cultural,** Pça. Dom Wunibaldo 464 (☎301 1393, 9952 1989; www.chapadadosguimaraes.com.br), in Chapada dos Guimarães, has excellent guides for hire. R$50-60 per day. Open M-Sa 8am-noon and 1-5pm, Su 8-11:30am.

ACCOMMODATIONS

There are no accommodations in the park. Those looking to spend a few days exploring the park should stay at **Pousada Rios ❶**, Rua Tiradentes 333, on the corner of Rua Homer Mouser, about three blocks from the *rodoviária* in Chapada dos Guimarães. (☎301 1126. Singles R$20, with TV R$30; doubles R$30, with TV R$40; triples R$40, with TV R$50. Suite singles with TV, A/C, and *frigo-bar* R$40; doubles with TV, A/C, and *frigo-bar* R$60; triples with TV, A/C, and *frigo-bar* R$70. MC/V.) Brazilian tourists flood **Hotel São Benedito ❶**, Rua Tiradentes 89, which offers the cheapest digs in town. Rooms are simple, with fan, mattress, and not much else, but cheap. (☎301 1908. Dorms R$15.)

SIGHTS & HIKING

The **Caminho das Aguas** walking trail highlights the park's several waterfalls, while the **Caminho das Pedras** trek leads hardcore hikers to the park's tallest peak, Morro de São Jerõnimo. Other attractions include the 86m **Cachoeira Véu da Noiva,** the **Casa da Pedra** cave, and the **Cidade de Pedra** lookout. Near the park is **Mirante da Geodésica,** the geographic center of South America.

CAMINHO DAS AGUAS. This leisurely trail begins at the Visitor's Center and brings hikers to seven of the park's most attractive waterfalls. First on the list is **Cachoeira Véu da Noiva** (Bridal Veil Waterfall), the park's tallest and most impressive. The next waterfall visited is **Cachoeira Andorinha,** which has a small beach popular with locals at its base. The trail then passes by the top of **Cachoeira Independência.** Most guides tend to sidestep the trek to the bottom of Cachoeira Independência; make the hike and you'll be rewarded with a tranquil setting free from the tourist hordes. The remaining waterfalls boast deep pools and cool swimming areas, though some are closed off to bathers and offer only views. *(7km, 3-4hr. round-trip. Difficulty: easy.)*

CAMINHO DAS PEDRAS. This exhausting hike takes you to the park's highest mountain, **Morro de São Jerõnimo.** Though most of the trek is flat, it is also largely unshaded, which makes the hike difficult for many; be sure to bring plenty of water and protection from the sun. The unimpressive 850m peak wouldn't be worth the grueling effort if not for the peculiar rock formations it passes along the way: among the more interesting are **Jacaré de Pedra** (Alligator Rock), **Pedra Furada** (Mushroom Rock), and **Mesa de Sacrifício** (Altar Rock). The crown jewel of rock formations, however, is **Casa da Pedra,** a large cave about 6km from the Visitor's Center. The crystal-clear river that flows through this cave has molded it into the shape of a house, complete with formations that look like tables and chairs. *(19km, 7-9hr. round-trip. Difficulty: hard.)*

CIDADE DE PEDRA. The most impressive views in the park are of the granite formations known as **Cidade de Pedra** (City of Stone). The tall grass around the rocks conceal steep, 350m cliffs, so it's advisable to bring along a guide. The scenery is spectacular at sunset, which is when most people make the journey. Cidade de Pedra is located 28km from the town of Chapada dos Guimarães along the dirt road to Agua Fria. Its not advisable for tourists to drive to the area, as the main road branches in very confusing ways; most people opt for a taxi.

MIRANTE DA GEODÉSICA. For over a hundred years it was thought that the **geographical center of South America** was located on the corner of Rua Barão de Melgaço and Rua Del. Elzira in Cuiabá; a statue celebrating that fact stands there today. It wasn't until the 1990s, however, that satellite imaging was able to pinpoint the actual location, which is in the highlands to the northeast. A small marker stands 8km north of the town of Chapada dos Guimarães, indicating the exact location. Grand views of the national park and glimpses of the Cuiabá skyline are visible in the distance but most tourists are too busy snapping pictures of the marker to notice. To reach the marker follow the main road in the opposite direction of Cuiabá; the road goes off to the right and eventually turns into a dirt track. To ensure you don't pass the marker it's best to take a taxi.

BARRA DO GARÇAS ☎66

More developed than most other towns along the Rio Araguaia, Barra do Garças, with its beautiful location at the foot of two verdant hills, is a good place to break up the long bus ride between Cuiabá and Goiânia. Tourists usually spend their time fishing on the river and sunbathing on the fine stretches of sand that emerge during the dry season in June and July. On holidays it becomes a raging beach town, with most of the activity centering on Parque Salome José Rodrigues. During the rest of the year, visitors come for the nearby hot springs and waterfalls.

TRANSPORTATION. The **rodoviária** is inconveniently located five kilometers from town in the middle of the industrial sector (☎401 5361, 401 1217). From here **Barrattur** (☎401 1303) goes to Cuiabá (7hr.; 2 per day noon-11:30pm; R$43) and São Paulo (18hr.; M, W, F, and Su noon; R$73). **Viaçáo Araguarina** (☎471 1110) sends buses to Brasília (12hr.; 3pm; R$43) and Goiânia (8hr.; 6 per day 8am-11pm; R$28). A **taxi** from the *rodoviária* to the *centro* costs about R$10. For those traveling light, **moto-taxis** make the journey for R$2.50.

ORIENTATION & PRACTICAL INFORMATION. Across from the city on the opposite side of the river lies the town of Aragarças, where most beaches are located. Between the two towns is a small island with its own beach; the bridges connecting the towns cross the island. **Avenida Min. João Alberto** runs from the bridge to the *centro*, passing through the main *praça*, **Praça dos Garimpeiros.** Turning right after crossing the bridge will lead you along the waterfront down **Avenida Antônio Bilego** and eventually to **Parque Salome José Rodrigues.**

The state-run **tourist center,** Rua Mato Grosso 652, is one block from Pça. dos Garimpeiros along Rua Waldir Rabelo. Most of the staff speaks English and the office is well-stocked with brochures about the surrounding area. (☎401 1604. Open M-F 7:30am-noon and 1:30-5pm.) **Adventur Turismo,** Av. Min. João Alberto 12, organizes fishing excursions and tours to nearby hot springs and waterfalls. (☎401 1709. Open M-F 8am-6pm, Sa-Su 8am-2pm.) **Boat rental** is possible at Porto da Baé, along the waterfront beside Botos, the floating restaurant in Parque Salome José Rodrigues. Pousada Sol do Araguaia can also help arrange boat rental. Boats normally cost R$60 per day, not including gas. You can purchase **camping equipment** at Matrinchã, Av. Min. João Alberto 389. (☎401 3192. Open M-F 7:30am-5pm, Sa 7:30am-1:30pm.) The biggest **supermarket** in town is Estrelão Shopping, in Pça. dos Garimpeiros. (☎401 1600. Open M-F 8am-8pm, Sa 8am-noon.) Other services include: a **laundromat,** Lavanderia Q'Linda, Rua Moreira Cabral 714 (☎401 1203; R$8 per kg; open M-F 8am-6pm, Sa 8am-noon); the **police station,** Rua Goiás 794, near the old *rodoviária* (☎401 2525, 401 1200); a **pharmacy,** Drogaria Santa Cruz, Av. Min. João Alberto 678 (☎401 2279; open M-F 7am-7pm, Sa 7am-noon); **Hospital Santa Julia,** Rua Padre Cobialchina 190 (☎401 2385); **Internet Access** at Navega.net, in Estrelão Shopping, in Pça. dos Garimpeiros (R$4 per hr.; open M-F 8am-6pm, Sa 8am-noon); a **post office,** Av. Min. João Alberto 843 (☎401 4027; open M-F 8am-5pm). **Postal code:** 78600-000.

ACCOMMODATIONS. There is a handful of hotels surrounding the old *rodoviária*. Although quarters in this area tend to be somewhat cramped, hotels here are in an ideal location near the waterfront and Parque Salome José Rodrigues. Better places to stay are generally located 20-30min. from town. Prices double during June and July. The most comfortable option close to the waterfront is **Discanauta Palace Hotel ❶,** Rua Antônio Côrtes 5, just off Av. Antônio Bilego, near Parque Salome José Rodrigues. All rooms have fan and private bath, and overlook a small pebble garden courtyard. (☎401 4121. Singles R$20, with A/C, TV, and *frigo-bar* R$30; doubles R$36, with A/C, TV, and *frigo-bar* R$52; triples R$54, with A/C, TV, and *frigo-bar* R$69; quads R$64, with A/C, TV, and *frigo-bar* R$80.) **Pousada Tropical ❷,** Rua Waldir Rabeio 1520, is 20min. from the *centro* and waterfront. Follow Rua Francisco Dourado from the old *rodoviária*, take the fourth left, then the first left, and it will be on the left. The *pousada* has a pool, dart board, and some exercise equipment. Rooms are spacious and all very similar. (☎401 4213; www.pousadatropical.tur.br. Laundry R$2 per piece. Singles R$30, with A/C and *frigo-bar* R$38; doubles R$45, with A/C and *frigo-bar* R$63.) Another good option a bit farther from town is **Pousada Sol do Araguaia ❷,** Av. Marechal Rondon 48. Turn right after you cross the bridge and follow Av. Antônio Bilego past Parque Salome José Rodrigues. At the roundabout, bear right onto Av. Marechal Rondon; it's 20min. farther along the waterfront. The *pousada* has a pool, basic exercise room, and can arrange fishing trips. Rooms are comfortable, with large double beds and clean bathrooms. (☎401 4819. Laundry R$3 per piece. Singles R$35. Suites with small veranda R$60.) **Hotel Santa Rica ❶,** Rua Goiás 345, is the best of the *rodoviária* hotels. Rooms are basic, but the price is right, and the hotel is popular with young Brazilians and international travelers. (☎401 5177. Dorms R$8. Singles R$8, with bath R$12; doubles R$16, with bath R$20.)

FOOD. The *centro* tends to shut down at night; luckily there are plenty of restaurants around Parque Salome José Rodrigues. Most are *lanchonetes*, and the better restaurants usually double as nightspots. **Botos ❷,** on Escadaria do Porto do Baé, in front of Parque Salome José Rodrigues, is a floating restaurant with an all-wood interior and thatched roof. It specializes in seafood, and has good soup (R$3.50). Most non-fish dishes cost R$10-15. (☎401 4545. Open M-F 11am-3pm and 7pm-1am, Sa-Su 11am-1am.) **Hasriel Pizzeria e Pamonharia ❸,** Rua Cristino Cortes 66, serves thick-crust pizza in a pleasant open-air seating area. The house pizza *(a moda do casa)* with mozzarella, bacon, chicken, and tomato, is just R$15. The friendly staff can also prepare a limited number of pasta dishes upon request. (☎401 8813. Open Tu-F 5pm-midnight, Sa-Su 5pm-2am.) **Choupana's Grill ❸,** Parque Salome José Rodrigues s/n, offers inexpensive seafood dishes and an excellent selection of soups (R$3). On the weekends, the sea of plastic tables outside is filled with people who come for the best live bands in town. (☎401 9664. Open M-F 4pm-midnight, Sa-Su 2pm-2am.) Another place that has live music (Th-Sa) is **Caribe ❶,** Rua Antônio Côrtes 82, near Parque Salome José Rodrigues. This restaurant/bar offers an array of mixed drinks, as well as seafood, hamburgers, and some Italian dishes. Their sandwiches are a good value (R$7). On weekend nights it can be hard to find a spot in the outdoor seating area. (☎401 1533. Open daily 4pm-1am. MC/V.) One of the few ice cream shops in the *centro* is **Sorvette Expresso ❶,** Av. Min. João Alberto 421. There are tons of toppings and flavors to choose from. (☎401 1050. R$13 per kg. Open daily 10am-11:30pm.)

OUTDOOR ACTIVITIES. The closest beach to Barra do Garças is the pretty **Praia de Rio Araguaia,** located away from town on the opposite bank of the river. To reach the beach you must follow the bridge over the river and into the town of Aragarças; turn left when you get to the mainland and the beach is only 20min.

away along the waterfront. Located on the island between the two towns is another popular beach, **Praia de Arara.** Cross the bridge from Barra do Garças to the island and the road to your right leads directly to the beach. You'll probably want a moto-taxi to take you; the beach is 10km from the bridge. The beaches around town only reveal themselves when the river waters recede during the dry season in June and July. The rest of the year, visitors spend time at **Estadual da Serra Azul,** a small wooded park with 14 waterfalls and several walking trails. The park is six kilometers east of the city along Rua Waldir Rabeio and, although guides are not required, they are highly recommended. (☎402 2021. Open daily 7am-8pm.) One kilometer farther along the road is **Aguas Quentes,** a park with hot springs and a couple of heated outdoor pools where one can float about in yellow inner tubes. (Open daily 8am-6pm. R$5.)

CACÉRES ☎65

Cacéres was once a busy port that saw a considerable number of vessels traveling to and from Corumbá, though today few boats make the journey. In September the city hosts the largest freshwater fishing contest in the world, and every March there is a piranha fishing contest, but the rest of the year there isn't much reason to visit unless you're on your way to or from Bolivia. **Buses** leave **Terminal Rodoviario de Cacéres,** 10 blocks north of the waterfront. **Real Norte** (☎223 2136) sends a bus to Cuiabá (4hr.; 8 per day 6am-7pm; R$23) and **Trans Jaó** (☎223 1122) runs to Bolivian border town Santa Matias (2½hr.; 6 per day 5am-4pm; R$10). Cacéres can also be used as a base for Pantanal trips to nearby *barcos* (p. 315).

To get to the *centro* from the *rodoviária*, follow Av. 7 de Setembro toward the waterfront and Pça. Barão do Rio Branco. **SEMATUR,** Rua Riachuelo 1, is the local tourist office and can help arrange stays at nearby *fazendas* and *barcos*. (☎223 5918; sematur@caceres.mt.gov.br. Open 8am-5pm.) **Banco do Brasil,** Rua José Dulce 234, exchanges currency and traveler's checks. (☎223 1900. Open M-F 10am-3pm.) **Bradesco,** Rua José Dulce 183, has a Visa-friendly ATM. (☎223 1700. Open M-F 10am-3pm.) **Cantó do Rio,** Rua Marechal Deodoro 9, facing the waterfront, has all the fishing and camping supplies you could ever want. (☎223 8030. Open M-F 7:30am-7pm, Sa 7:30am-3pm.) The **police** have an office at the *rodoviária* (☎223 1371). Try **Drogaria Povão,** Comandante Balduino 207, on the corner of Rua Cel. José Dulce, for medications and bugspray. (☎223 3045. Open M-F 7am-8pm, Sa 7am-noon.) **São Luís Municipal Hospital,** Pça. Major João Carlos s/n, has basic facilities. (☎223 1000.) For Internet access go to **Top Cybercafé,** Pça. Barão do Rio Branco 27, in the main *praça*. (☎223 5479. R$3.50 per hr. Open 10am-10pm.) The **post office** is on Av. 7 de Setembro. (☎223 1016. Open M-F 9am-5pm, Sa 9am-noon.) **Postal code:** 78200-000.

The closest thing to a hostel in town is the **Rio Hotel ❶,** Pça. Major João Carlos 61, on the corner of Rua Padre Cassemiro. *Apartamentos* are comfortable and welcoming, with A/C, bath, and *frigo-bar*. (☎223 3387. Breakfast included. Kitchen. Laundry R$1.50 per piece. *Quarto* singles R$20; doubles R$30; triples R$50. *Apartamento* singles R$35; doubles R$60; triples R$80.) Cheaper is **Charm Hotel ❶,** Rua José Dulce 408. Rooms have private bath, A/C, and *frigo-bar*. (☎223 5349, 223 5149. Singles R$15; doubles R$30; triples R$40.) **Kaskata Flutuante ❷,** a floating restaurant that sits in the port at the end of Rua Coronel José Dulce, has fresh fish and *jacaré* (alligator). At night Flutante becomes a bar popular with locals and tourists alike. (☎223 2916. 10% service charge. Open daily 10am-midnight. Visa.) Kilos can be found around the main *praça*, the best of which is **Hispano Restaurante ❷,** Pça. Barão do Rio Branco 64. Aside from the usual dishes, they also offer potato pudding, rolled pancakes, and fried banana. (☎223 1486. R$14 per kg. Open M-Sa 7am-3:30pm.)

BORDER CROSSING: TO BOLIVIA Corixo is a small Brazilian frontier town on the border with Bolivia, about 2hr. east of Cacéres by bus. Travelers looking to cross the border must get their exit stamp in Cacéres; **exit stamps** are available at the **Delegacia de Polícia Federal,** Rua Getúlio Vargas 2125 (☎223 1110), next the town hall. Open daily 7am-8pm. With your passport stamped proceed to the **Terminal Rodoviário de Cacéres** (☎223 5279, 223 4594). Yellow fever vaccinations are available at the *rodoviária;* Bolivian law requires you have a vaccination to enter the country. Free vaccinations are offered by the small clinic near the ticket offices. Open daily 7:30am-8pm. Trans Jaó (☎223 1122) sends **buses** to Corixio (2hr.; 6 per day 5am-4pm; R$7). Buses from Corixio across the border to Santa Matias, Bolivia, are available at the *rodoviária* in Corixio (10min.; R$3). Don't forget to get your **entrance stamp** as you cross the border. Few nationalities require **visas** to enter Bolivia, but check before you cross the border.

BARÃO DO MELGAÇO ☎65

Barão do Melgaço is a small fishing village on the banks of the Rio Cuiabá. Though there is little to do in the town itself, the nearby rivers and lakes offer excellent fishing opportunities. Most travelers use Barão do Melgaço as a staging ground for excursions to the northern Pantanal; the *fazendas* and *pousadas* surrounding the town are among the most beautiful and scenic in the wetlands area (p. 317).

Most services are found around **Praça Manuel Silva Tagues.** From here **Rua Fernando Correa** and **Rua Francisco de Assis** run four blocks south toward the river, where they eventually meet **Avenida Augusto Leverger,** which continues along the length of the waterfront. **Buses** to town stop on Rua Francisco de Assis, just past Pça. Tagues. From here **Tut** (☎331 1151) sends buses to Cuiabá (3½hr.; 2 per day 11am-2pm; R$15). **Seniema Tours,** Av. Augusto Leverger 1350, runs a mini-van service that will make hotel drop-offs in Cuiabá at no additional charge. (☎331 1441. 3hr.; 2 per day 5am-1am; R$18.) There are **no banks** in town. **Mercadinho do Povo,** Av. Augusto Leverger 1344, has groceries. (☎331 1149. Open M-Sa 6:30am-7pm.) **Mercado Gomes,** Av. Toto Paes 412, just off Av. Francisco de Assis, sells bamboo fishing poles (R$3-8) and hooks. (☎331 1245. Open M-Sa 6am-7pm, Su 7-11am.) The **Municipal Hospital,** Av. Augusto Leverger 1440, has only simple facilities. (☎331 1332.) The local **post office,** Rua Fernando Correa 116, is just off Av. Toto Paes. (Open M-F 9-11am and 1-4pm.) **Postal code:** 78190-000.

The cheapest lodging is at the convenient **Hotel Nossa Senhora do Carmo ❶,** Av. Augusto Leverger 1468, facing the waterfront. All rooms are clean and have private bath. (☎331 1141. Singles R$15; doubles R$25.) **Barão Tour Hotel ❸,** Av. Toto Paes 529, one block from the waterfront, is the town's only upscale option, with a swimming pool to help ease the heat. *Apartamentos* have A/C and *frigo-bar*. (☎331 1166. Singles R$50; doubles R$70.) Decent eats can be found at **Restaurant Peixe Vivo ❷,** Av. Augusto Leverger 1572, facing the waterfront. The restaurant offers a daily selection of *pratos feitos*. (☎9952 7673. R$10. Open 10am-3pm and 6-10pm.)

POCONÉ ☎65

Perched at the beginning of the Transpantaneira, the 165km road that cuts right into the heart of the northern Pantanal, Poconé is the primary entry point for travelers looking to explore the vast wetland area and its numerous *fazendas* (p. 315). The town sees most traffic from tour buses that pause briefly to stock up on supplies, but with no attractions of its own Poconé is more a pit stop than a finish line. Independent travelers sometimes come with the hope of thumbing a free ride to the Transpantaneira, but as the town lacks a healthy tourist infrastructure, those who fail are usually left stranded; it's far better to make arrangements with the *fazenda* to pick you up—or grab a cheap moto-taxi.

Rodoviária do Poconé is 2km from town on **Avenida Anibal de Toledo.** To reach the *centro* from the *rodoviária*, you must turn left on Av. Anibal de Toledo and walk for two blocks; when you reach **Rua Antônio João** turn right. Eight blocks farther the street connects with **Rua Campos Sales,** where most services and restaurants can be found. From the *rodoviária* **Tut** (☎345 1677) goes to Cuiabá (2hr.; 7 per day 5:30am-7:30pm; R$9.50). **Taxis** from the *rodoviária* to *centro* cost R$10. Those with limited luggage are better off going to the small **moto-taxi** stand on Av. Anibal de Toledo, two blocks from the *rodoviária*. (☎9621 9382. Ride to the *centro* R$3.) **Banco do Brasil,** Rua Campos Sales 449, near Rua Antônio João, has a Visa **ATM.** (☎345 1447. Open M-F 9am-2pm.) **Mercado Eskinao,** on the corner of Av. Anibal de Toledo and Av. Justino Francisco, near the *rodoviária*, sells all the basics. (☎345 1125. Open M-F 7:30am-9pm.) The **police** (☎345 1456) have an office at the very beginning of the Transpantaneira. Sunblock can be found at any of the town's several pharmacies; **Drogaria Correa** has the latest closing hours (☎345 2175; open daily 6am-2pm and 6-10pm). For medical emergencies contact the **Municipal Hospital,** Rua Dom Aquino s/n (☎345 1963). **Internet access** is available at **Bi-Link Informatica,** Rua Cel. Salvador Marques 316, across from the post office. (☎345 2105. R$5 per hr. Open M-F 8am-9pm, Sa 8am-4pm.) The **post office,** Rua Cel. Salvador Marques 335, is one block south of Rua Campos Sales. (☎345 1587. Open M-F 9am-5pm.) **Postal code:** 78175-000.

Four blocks from the *rodoviária* is **Hotel Tuiuu ❶,** Av. Anibal de Toledo 1709, which has clean dorms and large bathrooms. (☎345 1438. Breakfast included. Laundry R$1.50 per piece. Dorms R$12-15. Doubles R$25.) In the *centro* is **Hotel Skala ❶,** Pça. Bem Rondon 64. Rooms have soft beds and A/C but little natural light; doubles come with TV and *frigo-bar*. (☎345 1407. Breakfast included. Laundry R$1.50 per piece. Singles R$25, with TV R$30; doubles R$40, with TV R$50.) **Petiscaria Shanandoah ❷,** Pça. Matriz s/n, is a diner that serves pizzas (R$10-14), french fries, and a variety of burgers (R$3.50). The restaurant is also a popular nightspot, with a second-floor dance hall. (☎345 2634. 10% service charge. Open daily 8am-11pm.) **Restaurante e Peixaria Skala ❷,** Pça. Bem Rondon 64, in the same building as Hotel Skala, specializes in fish. The accommodating staff prepares vegetarian plates upon request. (☎345 1902. Chicken R$12; steak R$15; salads R$5-10. Open 11am-2pm and 7:30-10pm.) For cheaper eats, try the local favorite, **Churrascaria e Pousada Pantaneira ❷,** which serves grilled meat and a good selection of desserts. The restaurant is the first on the Transpantaneira highway, which makes it popular among hitchhikers and tour groups. (☎345 1630. Lunch buffet R$10. Dinner plates R$8. Open daily 11am-2:30pm and 6-8pm.)

THE PANTANAL

The Pantanal is one of the world's most important ecological sanctuaries, a vast flooded plain that stretches across parts of Brazil, Paraguay, and Bolivia. It's the largest area of inland wetlands on the planet, covering over 230,000 square kilometers, 130,000 of which are found in the Brazilian states Mato Grosso and Mato Grosso do Sul. The Pantanal is crossed by a number of rivers, all of which flow into the Rio Paraguai and eventually drain southward into the Atlantic. Often dubbed the "poor man's Amazon," it offers a large variety of open landscapes, dominated by low-lying grasslands and lush forested islands. It is inhabited by an

SEASONS IN THE PANTANAL In the **wet season** (Nov.-Mar.), the Pantanal is inundated with heavy rains, and the entire region becomes flooded as the rivers overflow. In April, the rivers drain south and the wetlands in the north recede as the south becomes even more flooded. The flooding forces animals to congregate on the scattered forested islands; tour activities revolve around horseback rides to these islands in this season. In the **dry season** (May-Nov.) the waters recede and grasslands become visible. Animals roam the plains and are best spotted when they converge at lakes and rivers; tour activities usually involve walks and boat trips. The **early dry season** (May-June) is undoubtedly the best time to visit the Pantanal, when there is a rich explosion of color as the flowers blossom throughout the wetlands. Migratory birds return at this time, and *caiman* are found in colossal numbers in the disappearing lakes.

incredibly diverse number of mammals, reptiles, birds, and fish, many of which are easily spotted roaming the open landscape; this is the place for those looking to observe jaguars, anteaters, and *tapirs* in the wild.

The untamed wetlands are virtually uninhabited by humans, and what few towns it has are sprinkled along the outskirts. The inaccessibility of the wetlands has helped preserve the environment and made it one of the least explored regions in Brazil. The Pantanal is officially divided into eleven subdivisions, but for the most part the area is thought of as having two distinct regions, the northern Pantanal and the southern Pantanal. Life in both regions is governed by seasonal flooding, during which the water level fluctuates by between four and six meters. Though seasonal flooding has prevented large settlements from arising, cattle farmers have managed to prosper; *fazendas* (farm ranches) are scattered throughout the wetlands.

WHO TO CHOOSE & WHAT TO BRING

Choosing the right tour will often make or break your experience in the Pantanal. The competition between operators is fierce, which makes bargains easy to come by. Unfortunately the market is riddled with sharks, so pick your operator well. The operators listed in this book are among the most reputable, but **always check with the local tourist office for recent reports and complaints.** Complaints usually revolve around skipped activities and late departures, but there have been more serious reports of sexual harassment and drug use by guides, especially in the southern Pantanal. In general the guides in the north are more professional and knowledgeable than their southern counterparts.

Regardless of your tour operator and final trip plans, there are certain ways to protect yourself from being ripped off by tour agencies. The most important thing while booking tours is to get everything in writing; for maximum protection include a clause that provides for a small refund for each activity missed. Also ask to meet the guide before your trip. In choosing how long your tour should last take into consideration that it often takes half a day to reach your accommodations. A 3-day trip is enough for a small taste but tours of 4-5 days are most recommended. If possible request to spend half your time at a "*wet fazenda*" and half your time at a "*dry fazenda*" (p. 315); operators in the north tend to be much more flexible with this than those in the south.

No matter which operator you choose for your trip(s) into the Pantanal, it is advised that you bring along the following: binoculars, a 300m lens for photos, long pants for horseback riding, sturdy boots for trekking in the swamps, suntan lotion, mosquito repellent, and a hat.

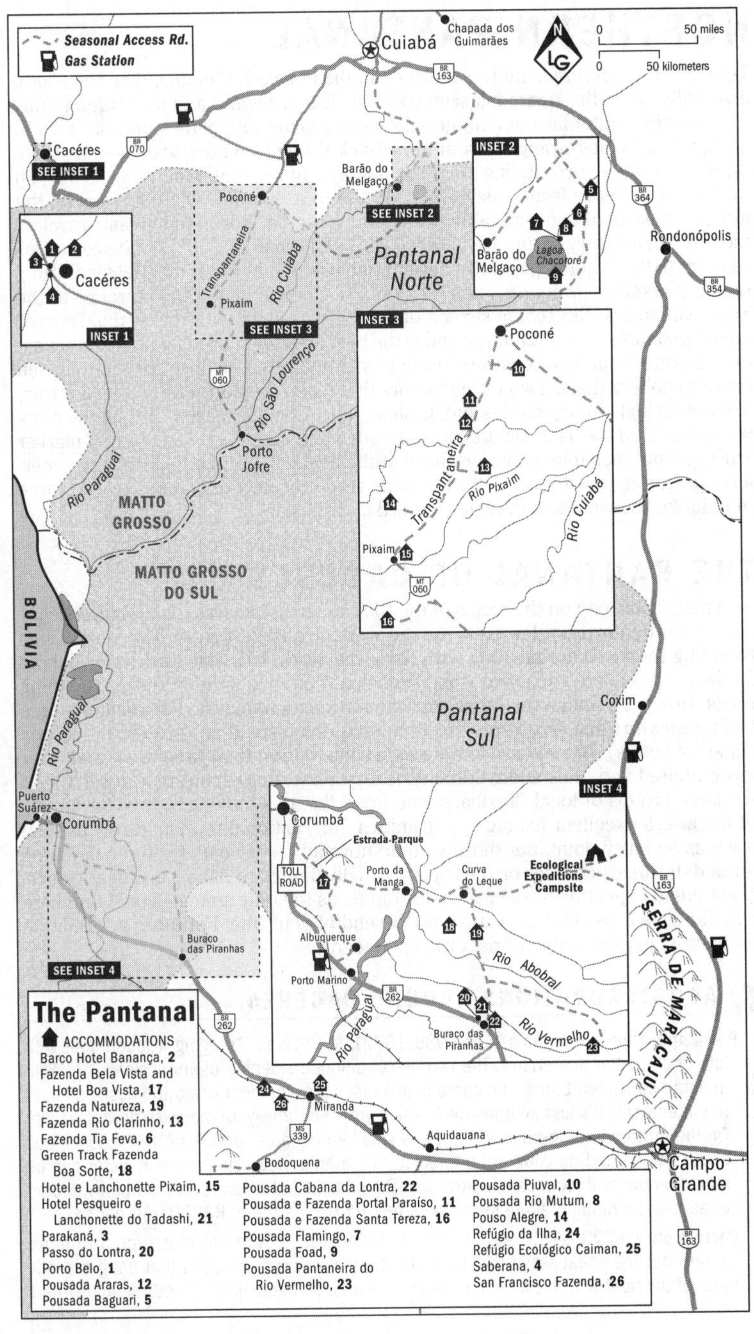

The Pantanal

ACCOMMODATIONS

Barco Hotel Banança, **2**
Fazenda Bela Vista and Hotel Boa Vista, **17**
Fazenda Natureza, **19**
Fazenda Rio Clarinho, **13**
Fazenda Tia Feva, **6**
Green Track Fazenda Boa Sorte, **18**
Hotel e Lanchonette Pixaim, **15**
Hotel Pesqueiro e Lanchonette do Tadashi, **21**
Parakaná, **3**
Passo do Lontra, **20**
Porto Belo, **1**
Pousada Araras, **12**
Pousada Baguari, **5**
Pousada Cabana da Lontra, **22**
Pousada e Fazenda Portal Paraíso, **11**
Pousada e Fazenda Santa Tereza, **16**
Pousada Flamingo, **7**
Pousada Foad, **9**
Pousada Pantaneira do Rio Vermelho, **23**
Pousada Piuval, **10**
Pousada Rio Mutum, **8**
Pouso Alegre, **14**
Refúgio da Ilha, **24**
Refúgio Ecológico Caiman, **25**
Saberana, **4**
San Francisco Fazenda, **26**

NORTHERN PANTANAL

Tourist infrastructure is more developed in the northern Pantanal than the south, especially along the **Transpantaneira** (p. 321). The *fazendas* and *pousadas* in this region offer high-class accommodations at reasonable prices and have well-designed activities—ranging from horseback riding to nature walks—that make the most of their surrounding area. The majority of international travelers sign up for tours that leave from Cuiabá (p. 298); the tour operators here are among the most professional and reputable in the entire region. For independent travelers the three main entry towns are **Cacéres** (p. 309), **Poconé** (p. 310), and **Barão de Melgaço** (p. 310). Cacéres primarily deals in *barcos*, while Barão de Melgaço offers scenic *pousadas*, *fazendas*, and *pesqueiros*. Poconé marks the entrance to the Transpantaneira, the 145km stretch of road that is lined with the wetland's most famed *pousadas* and *fazendas*, and is the best area for spotting wildlife. Independent travelers can take buses to these towns and often arrange for their chosen lodge to collect them. Two of the factors that make the northern Pantanal attractive are its high-quality guides and its short rainy/flooded season. During the rainy season most of the Transpantaneira is flooded and the *pousadas* south of marker km60 are unreachable; however, those at the beginning of the highway are generally accessible year-round. After the rains stop it usually only takes two to three months for the waters to drain southward and subside.

THE PANTANAL OF CACÉRES

As a major port city on the banks of the Rio Paraguai, Cacéres (p. 309) offers easy access to the northern Pantanal via the wetland's largest river. The waters surrounding the town are teeming with fish—the world's largest freshwater fishing festival is held here each year—and snakes are often sighted in the surrounding reeds. However, unlike the other entry points surrounding the Pantanal, the area lacks *fazendas* and *pousadas;* accommodations instead are offered by *barcos* (floating hotels). *Barcos* are a more expensive option than *fazendas*, and offer more limited activities and wildlife-spotting opportunities, but that doesn't stop the large groups of local Brazilians who flood the area looking to take advantage of the area's excellent fishing opportunities. International tourists rarely use the town as an entry point, but those who do normally rent boats for three-day trips around the area; activities on the trip are usually limited to fishing and beer games. Don't come expecting to see jaguars or tapirs, as the only animals you'll find here will likely be those that get caught on the end of your line. For more information on *barcos*, inquire at the tourist office in Cacéres.

ACCOMMODATIONS AROUND CACÉRES

Parakaná, Rua Las Vegas s/n (☎9989 1072), in Cacéres. An aging wooden craft with lots of character and charm. The two air-conditioned sleeping quarters sleep 12. Well-maintained shared baths. The captain advertises that the boat has a top-deck solarium but in actuality it's just an open deck where you can throw your mattress down and tan. On the bottom floor there is a kitchen, a small eating area, and TV/VCR. Those serious about fishing and drinking will appreciate the ample fridge space. Fresh water can be stored on board if requested in advance. The price includes food and board only. Motorboats can be brought along for an extra fee (R$100 per day). R$800-960 per day.

Porto Belo (☎223 8185, 223 4370). A narrow vessel with not much room to move about, but the cheapest at the dock. The captain has set up cages that hang over the side of the boat and thrown some mattresses on top–the makeshift beds sleep 8. There

ACCOMMODATIONS IN THE PANTANAL. The Pantanal offers something for everyone, from beautiful scenery to abundant wildlife to some of the best fishing in the world. Here you will find the opportunity to explore swamplands on horseback, walk through forests in search of animals, and fish for piranha or the coveted *pintado* and *dourado*. Your experience in the Pantanal, however, will largely depend upon where you stay. The wetlands offer four types of accommodations; *pesqueiros* and *barcos* are most frequented by local Brazilian fishermen while *fazendas* and *pousadas* draw large international crowds. **Pesqueiros** are wooden cabins, usually on stilts, that offer the cheapest accommodations, the fewest amenities, and only the most basic of facilities. The activities offered here are mostly fishing and boat excursions; expect few sightings of mammals. **Barcos** are pricier floating hotels on boats that have been equipped with comfortable bedrooms and lounge areas. They range in quality from luxurious to ludicrous, are primarily rented by large groups, and also offer only fishing and boat excursions. *Fazendas* and *pousadas* offer the most comfortable lodging and a wide array of activities, including horseback rides, trekking, and boat trips. **Fazendas** are typical Pantanal homesteads that rent out rooms to make extra money. The rooms are usually more basic than those in *pousadas,* but the Pantanal experience here is much more authentic. **Pousadas** lack the character and charm of *fazendas* but have the same activities and better amenities. Most excursions in the Pantanal offer a combination of *pousada* and *fazenda* lodging; these are the most popular among international travelers. The type of activities offered at *pousadas* and *fazendas* will be determined by whether or not it is a dry facility or a wet facility. **Wet facilities** are surrounded by shallow swamplands; activities are based around boat trips and, sometimes, horseback rides to nearby islands. They can be hard to get to, especially during the rainy season, but are favored among birdlife and fishing enthusiasts. **Dry facilities** are on higher ground and have more firm land on which to roam; activities are based around walks and horseback riding. Swamplands and rivers are always close by so they also offer boat trips. The dry facilities are usually the easiest to access, and offer the most complete of Pantanal experiences, with good fishing and wildlife sightings.

is no A/C, and make sure to request mosquito nets before leaving. There is just 1 bathroom on board and a very small kitchen. Travelers usually climb up on the boat's roof to get fresh air. String up a hammock and get a tan. It's the most basic option available but will get you where you want to go. The price of rental includes accommodations only; bring food. Motorboats can be brought along for an extra fee (R$100 per day). R$350 per 4hr.; R$440 per 10hr.; R$500 per 24hr.

Barco Hotel Banança (☎9989 1634, 223 6666; www.caceres.com.br/guialocal/portobelo). The best of the luxury options, most popular with suburban Brazilians on holiday. The boat has 4 suites, each of which has 4 beds, A/C, and private bath. On the bottom floor there is a cozy air-conditioned lounge area with couches, cable TV, and a *frigo-bar* stocked with complimentary beers. On the top deck there is an open-air shower for exhibitionists and some sun chairs for tanning; bring your own hammock for extra comfort. Attached to the side of the large vessel are 6 small motorboats included in the cost of rental. Meals, bait, and whiskey are also included in rental price (bring your own fishing rod). R$3000-3840 per 24hr. Less expensive outside of June and July.

Saberana (☎223 4956). A sturdy 8-man *barco* with tight quarters and little character. It has 4 double rooms, each of which have clean sheets, central A/C, and firm beds, as well as a small kitchen and 2 clean shared baths. There is no lounge area so most hop

NORTHERN PANTANAL TOUR OPERATORS

The following operators are all based out of Cuiabá (see p. 298), which is considered the northern gateway into the Pantanal.

Eco-Verde Wildlife Tours, Rua Pedro Celestino 391 (☎624 1386, 9282 3201; joelsouza@terra.com.br), run out of the Eco-Verde Pousada. Wildlife ecologist and all-round-nice guy Joel Souza oversees the operation. His personable approach—best demonstrated in the send-off song he performs the morning of you departure—keeps things lighthearted and fun, while his experience and knowledge brings great insight to the tours. His guides are among the best in the region, and all speak excellent English. Accommodations are provided in a range of *pousadas* and *fazendas* along the Transpantaneira, allowing visitors to see a host of environments in a limited time period. Offers the most reliable, rewarding, and professional tours in the entire Pantanal. Period. 4-day/3-night R$400 per person; 5-day/4-night R$450 per person. Open daily 8am-6pm.

Natureco, Rua Cel. Benedicto Leite 570 (☎321 1001, 322 8080; www.natureco.com.br). Near the corner of Rua Barão de Melgaço behind a large white gate; call ahead and the owner will come to your *pousada.* Run by the always colorful Munir, a local guide in the area for over 10 years, Natureco offers some of the more innovative tours in the north, including 3-6 day "dynamic tours" for those with limited time, as well as 15-day "explorer tours." Photo safari tours and 8-day adventure trips are also available. They have tours leaving weekly and are an excellent option for small groups who want to craft their own itinerary. 5-day/4-night trip R$450 per person (min. 2); R$331 per person (min. 4). 6-day dynamic tour R$770 per person (min. 2); R$700 per person (min. 4). 15-day explorer tour R$2400 per person (min. 2); R$1980 per person (min. 4). Open 24hr.

Anaconda Tours, Rua Mal. Deodoro 2142 (☎624 4142, 9981 0171). On the right as you walk toward the river and airport. All tours include meals, transport, accommodations, and activities. Like other tour operators in town they offer extended tours to the Pantanal but are most useful for their 1-3 day options. The guides are professional and the trucks are new, ensuring a pleasant trip for visitors. However, trips lack the personality found in those run by Eco-Verde and Natureco. Their 2-day option includes a night's accommodation, a boat trip, night safari, alligator spotting, and trekking; longer visits may include a stay at a local farm. 1-day R$165 per person (min. 2). 2-day/1-night R$380 per person (min. 2). 3-day/2-night R$440 per person (min. 2). Open M-F 9am-6pm, Sa 9am-noon.

Confiança, Av. São Sebastião 2852 (☎314 2700; www.confiancaturismo.com.br). A professionally run ticket agency that also arranges tours in the Pantanal, usually at luxurious *fazendas* and *pousadas* along the Transpantaneira. Tours are more expensive than elsewhere in town, but also dependable and more upscale. They also make advance bookings, for a small fee, at accommodations throughout the Pantanal for independent travelers who want to explore the area sans tour bus. 1-day tour R$375 per person (min. 2); R$120 per person (min. 4). 3-day/2-night R$605 per person (min. 2); R$530 (min. 4). 5-day/4-night R$920 per person (min. 2); R$810 per person (min. 4). Open M-F 8am-6pm, Sa 8am-noon.

up onto the roof, string up a hammock, and socialize up there. It's hard to fish from the boat itself but they have 2 attached motorboats for more private fishing excursions (R$120 per day). There are nicer boats on offer at the dock but its cheap price makes this more attractive. Price of rental includes accommodations only; bring your own food and beer. R$750 per 24hr.

THE PANTANAL OF BARÃO DO MELGAÇO

The mellow town of Barão de Melgaço (p. 310) beckons travelers seeking to explore the scenic side of the Pantanal. Resting on the banks of the Rio Cuiabá and surrounded by several mountain ranges, the area encircling the town has a beauty not found anywhere else in the wetlands. The *fazendas* here are known more for their isolation and tranquil views than they are for their abundance of wildlife, and almost all are located near Lago Siá Mariano and Lago Chacororé. The area has two *pesqueiros* (fishing hotels), two *pousadas*, and one *fazenda*. The *pousadas* and *fazenda* are limited in their terrestrial activities due to the heavy waters the area receives; most activities revolve around boat trips and some horseback rides. The area is best reached by taking a bus from Cuiabá to the town of Barão de Melgaço (3hr.) and then having the owners of your *pousada* or *fazenda* come pick you up in their boat (one-way transport by boat R$100-150; 1-4 people).

ACCOMMODATIONS AROUND BARÃO DO MELGAÇO

Pousada Foad, Av. Augusto Leverger 1272 (☎9958 5929, office 331 1202), in Barão do Melgaço. Another *pesqueiro* on stilts, much smaller than its counterpart Pousada Flamingo, with simpler facilities. Guests are confined to a small platform during the wet season, though the beach out front provides walking space July-Dec. Dorms are basic, but all have private bath and some have A/C. It's a good option for non-claustrophobic budget travelers satisfied with boat excursions. Horseback riding R$25 per hr. (June-Nov. only). Transfer from Barão de Melgaço R$100 (1-4 people). Motorboat rental R$80 per day. Dorms R$20, with A/C R$25. Room and board R$55, with A/C R$69.

Pousada Baguari, Rua Rui Barbosa 719 (☎391 1175, 9983 4203, office 322 3585; baguari@vsp.com.br), in Cuiabá. This modern complex is one of the easiest to access by road, though it is the farthest from Barão de Melgaço by boat. It has several comfortable lounges with TV/VCR, a lovely outdoor swimming pool, and a game room with table tennis and snooker tables. The *pousada* is set on a small sunken island, protected from the encompassing swampland by a series of bunkers. Lacking the scenery and rustic feel of other *pousadas* in the area, it's best suited for those seeking comfort and conveniece. All rooms have A/C, *frigo-bar,* mosquito netting, and private bath. Among the activities offered are horseback riding (R$20 per hr.) and boat excursions including fishing, bird watching, and alligator spotting (boat rental R$100 with guide and motor; R$50 per activity). Walking trails are accessible in the dry season. Laundry R$5 per piece. Transfer from Cuiabá R$400 (1-4 people); from Barão de Melgaço R$150 (1-4 people). Dorms R$105. Singles R$125.

Pousada Flamingo (☎623 7888, 391 1198). The best equipped *pesqueiro* in the area, catering almost exclusively to fishing crowds of local Brazilians. A wooden lodge on stilts on the very edge of Lago Siá Mariano, Flamingo's greatest draw may be its gorgeous sunsets and scenic views. During the dry season (July-Dec.) a small beach reveals itself out front; however, in the wet season guests are confined to the deck's platforms. The shallow water on which it stands makes alligator spotting relatively easy. There are no walking trails or horseback riding opportunities offered. All 10 *apartamentos* have private bath and A/C. There are limited snacks on sale so come stocked with your favorite treats; the meals here are simple to say the least (fish, fish, fish, and fish). The *pousada* also offers 5 luxury fishing boats for rent (with motor R$70 per day; without motor R$25). Singles R$60.

Pousada Rio Mutum, Av. Issac Póvoas 1539 (☎623 7022; www.pousadamutum.com.br), in Cuiabá. A self-consciously rustic homestead, lacking the authenticity of an actual ranch but boasting similar character and extra comfort. Expect the service to be more hands-off than at the family-run competitors, but first class all the same. It has sprawling grounds and charming chalets, hammocks strung up around the gardens, and a swampside swimming pool. It's most famous for the varied bird life surrounding the ranch, in addition to its numerous alligators. Has a well-equipped game room, TV lounge, and bar. All accommodations have A/C and *frigo-bar.* Activities include horseback riding (R$25 per hr.), boat rental (R$135 per hr.), fishing excursions (R$150 per day), and alligator spotting (R$20 per hr.). Transfer from Cuiabá R$500 (1-4 people); from Barão de Melgaço R$200 (1-4 people). 8-person cottages R$220 per person. 4-night tours including food, accommodations, and all activities R$1000 per person.

Fazenda Tia Feva (☎391 1259, 9956 3322, office 661 1376). A family-run *fazenda* with only the most basic facilities, good for quiet getaways and those interested in learning about how a Pantanal *fazenda* operates. Milking of the cows happens at 6am (guests are welcome to lend a hand). The *fazenda* is run by the very entertaining Clenoice, who will go out of her way to make guests feel happy. The 11 *apartamentos* have mosquito netting, plush mattresses, A/C, and private bath. Communal kitchen. Activities include horseback riding (R$15 per hr.), boat rental (R$70 per day), wandering several walking trails, and fishing excursions (R$100 per day; rods included). Transport from Barão de Melgaço R$100 (1-4 people). Singles R$65; doubles R$130; triples R$180; quads R$235.

THE PANTANAL OF TRANSPANTANEIRA

Starting from the town of Poconé (p. 310) and heading south, the Transpantaneira cuts deep into the marshy wetlands; tourists visiting the northern Pantanal will likely spend their time exploring this region. To each side of the highway are some of the Pantanal's most well-developed *fazendas* and *pousadas*, which generally offer excellent accommodations and activities. Though pricier than those in the south, they have better facilities, English-speaking guides, and well-planned excursions ranging from alligator spotting to fishing for piranha. The highway itself is often lined with thousands of *jacaré*, and at night *capivaras* are easy to spot. The rest of the day there are good opportunities to spot everything from anteaters to jaguars. Tours from Cuiabá operate throughout this area, though you'll also find several independent tourists traveling by car. Travelers without a car can take a bus from Cuiabá to Poconé (3hr.) and arrange for *fazendas* and *pousadas* to pick them up there (R$30-150; one-way). Taxis and moto-taxis are also available; taxis from Poconé to Pixaim (km65) cost R$130 for up to four people. An entrance fee to the Transpantaneira is paid at the gateway at Poconé (R$3).

ACCOMMODATIONS AROUND TRANSPANTANEIRA

Pousada e Fazenda Portal Paraíso, Transpantaneira km17, down a dirt road. This small family *fazenda* offers excellent value for both overnight and day visitors. Flat grasslands crawling with alligators surround the *fazenda* while pigs, chickens, and cows run around the farmstead. The facilities are more basic than others, with tree stumps substituting for dinner tables, but the large *apartamentos* have A/C. The area is more wet than dry, though there are several nearby walking trails and horseback riding tends to dominate the day's activities. Their nocturnal alligator catch-and-release trip is very popular. All activities and meals are included in the price for overnight visitors. Daytrippers can buy meals (R$15 per meal) and join in the activities for a small fee; horseback riding R$12 per hr., bike rental R$5 per 2hr., canoes R$20 per hr. Singles R$90; doubles R$160; triples R$200; quads R$280. MC/V.

Fazenda Rio Clarinho, Transpantaneira km42 (☎9977 8966, 9998 8888). The journey to the *fazenda* involves a 3km drive from the main road and a 10min. canoe trip across lily-covered waters filled with piranha and alligators. The most authentic *fazenda* open to tourists, with the friendliest of staff and the most rural of settings. It offers only the most basic of amenities, but has plenty of activities and character. It's a wet/dry *fazenda* surrounded by ankle-high water and large islands nearby that are good for spotting wildlife. The rustic accommodations lack A/C and mosquito nets, so bring your own net and plenty of repellent. Guests are encouraged to help with the milking of the cows in the morning (5am). Room prices include all meals and activities, including horseback riding, boat trips, alligator catch-and-release, piranha fishing, trekking, and bird watching boat trips. Be aware that during wet season the water can come all the way up to the front door, so it's best visited at other times of the year. Singles R$80; doubles R$150; triples R$200.

Pouso Alegre, Transpantaneira km52 (☎626 1545; www.pousalegre.com.br), 8km off the highway. One of the more picturesque options, known for its gorgeous scenery and abundant animal life. A good combination of *fazenda* and *pousada,* with the comforts of a hotel and the appearance of a ranch. This dry *fazenda* is near several forested islands and fishing holes. Horseback riding trips (R$50 per 3hr.) to explore the islands are very popular, as are the walking trails (R$10 per hr.); bring sturdy boots and a change of pants and expect to be tramping through waist-high waters. The dirt track leading into the *fazenda* is lined with alligators, and at night scores of *capivara* flood the road. The 8 lovely *apartamentos* have fan, private bath, and mosquito netting. Draws an international crowd and is a favorite with small tour groups. Offers all the usual activities, including boat rental (R$100 per day), fishing excursions (R$30 per hr.), and alligator spotting (R$40 per 2hr.) Best visited during the wet season but good year-round. Room prices include all meals and a 3hr. horseback ride. Dorms R$80. Singles R$120; doubles R$160; triples R$210. 15% price increase during high season.

Pousada Piuval, Transpantaneira km7 (☎9968 6300, 9968 6366, office 345 1338; www.pousadapiuval.com.br), 3km off the highway on a dirt road. Resting peacefully by a small lake, surrounded by tall swamp grasses that hide alligators and tapirs, this *pousada* has lovely views which can be enjoyed from the swampside swimming pool. It has the character of a rural homestead with the amenities and luxury of a hotel. The eggs served at breakfast come from the *pousada's* chickens, and the milk and cheese are all homemade. Their well-furnished *apartamentos* have A/C and private hot-water bath. There is a playground and volleyball court out front. Among the activities offered are horseback riding trips (R$20 per hr.), treks along extensive walking trails (R$10 per hr.), and boat and fishing excursions (motorboat R$50 per hr.; rowboat R$10 per hr.). All meals included in price. Singles R$150; doubles R$200; triples R$245; quads R$300. 10% price increase July-Oct.

Pousada Araras, Transpantaneira km32 (☎682 2800; www.araraslodge.com.br). The owners of this farmstead have gone to great lengths to make it look as rustic as possible, and for accommodations that offer this much luxury and style, they have largely succeeded. It has a swimming pool, hammocks, and 2 treetop lookout towers. The brick-walled dining area has a country cottage feel, and each of the charming *apartamentos* has hardwood floors, handmade blankets, A/C, and private hot-water bath. The small kiosk selling t-shirts seems out of place, but sells snacks throughout the day. Best-suited for those seeking all the comforts of a hotel without the gaudiness. In spite of the fact that it is surrounded by shallow swampland, this wet *pousada* offers a very complete set of ecological expeditions, including boat trips (R$30 per 3hr.), horseback riding (R$30 per 3hr.), walking treks (R$10 per 2hr.), and a popular night safari (R$15 per 2hr.). Fee for daytrippers R$2. Room prices include meals. Singles R$140; doubles R$200; triples R$280; quads R$320. Children ages 8-11 50% off; ages 4-7 70% off; under 3 free.

Hotel e Lanchonete Pixaim, Transpantaneira km64 (☎345 1383, 9983 8893). Functions predominately as a stopover for tourists on their way south, though it does have some *apartamentos* in the back. It's a wet *fazenda* and all activities revolve around boat trips (R$100 per day) and fishing excursions (R$30 per hr.). The entire complex is housed on stilts next to the main road; from the platforms it's easy to see the alligators squirming in the waters below. The 10 *apartamentos* have A/C, but some are better than others. It's best suited for fishermen or those looking to wake up early in the morning. The restaurant has a limited menu featuring 3-4 types of fish and no vegetarian options. Restaurant open daily 6:30-8:30am, noon-2pm, and 7-8:30pm. Room prices include all meals. Singles R$80; doubles R$110; triples R$150.

Pousada e Fazenda Santa Tereza, Transpantaneira km70 (☎9971 9417; www.santaterezahotel.hpg.com.br), down a 2km dirt trail that is often difficult to navigate. Though Santa Tereza has been a *fazenda* for more than 80 years, the family owners are moving more to becoming a *pousada,* which means that the grounds lack the rustic feel you find at other *fazendas* but are well-maintained and comfortable all the same. Today it's more of a farm resort, resting on the banks of the Rio Pixaim and surrounded by shallow swamplands that hold *capivara,* alligators, and giant otters. The encompassing farmland is picturesque, with several streams and forested islands. The 10 spacious *apartamentos* have A/C and private hot-water bath. In addition to the encircling wetlands, guests can also take dips in the swimming pool. Access to the *pousada* is restricted in the wet season; call ahead to check the roads. There are a couple of walking trails accessible June-Nov., but most activities revolve around boat trips and horseback riding. Room prices include meals. Horses R$30 per 3hr. Guided walks R$10 per 3hr. 1hr. photo safari R$300 for 6-8 people. Transportation from Cuiabá R$450 (1-4 people); from Poconé R$250 (1-4 people). Singles R$100; doubles R$150; triples R$200; quads R$240. 20% price increase during high season.

SOUTHERN PANTANAL

Fazendas and *pousadas* in the south are not as comfortable as their northern counterparts, but the wildlife and scenery is relatively similar. Although they offer nearly identical activities, the *fazendas* in the south tend to be cheaper, making the area popular with budget travelers. The majority of international travelers who tour this area sign up in one of two cities, Campo Grande (p. 325) or Corumbá (p. 331). Unless continuing to Bolivia, travelers tend to avoid the six-hour journey to Corumbá and opt instead for tours from Campo Grande. However, Corumbá has better tour operators and the bus ride there offers a mini-tour of the Pantanal, as the highway cuts directly through it. Ignore the claims of any operator who says they go "deeper" into the Pantanal than the others; all tours operate along the Estrada Parque (p. 321) and any *fazenda* or *pousada* along this stretch of road is already quite deep in the Pantanal. Independent travelers can also reach the *pousadas* along the Estrada Parque by taking the Corumbá-Campo Grande bus and getting off at Buraco das Piranhas; accommodations will pick you up from here for a small fee. Those with limited time can visit the day-use *fazendas* surrounding the town of Miranda (p. 337), close to Campo Grande (p. 325).

Travelers should note that the seasons in the south are slightly different from those in the north; while the north has just two seasons, a rainy/flooded season and a dry season, the south has three. The rainy season occurs at the same time as

THE TRANSPANTANEIRA & THE ESTRADA PARQUE The most exploited gateways to the Pantanal are the Transpantaneira in the north and the Rodovia Estrada Parque Pantanal in the south. International tour groups most often frequent *fazendas* and *pousadas* along these roads. The **Transpantaneira** is a bare-earth highway that was originally meant to cut through the heart of Pantanal and connect Poconé to towns in the southern Pantanal. The swamp-lands proved too wild to tame and the project was never completed; today the failed highway ends 145km south of Poconé at a small outpost called Porto Jofre. The road is lined with the best-equipped accommodations in the Pantanal, in addition to scores of alligators, *capivara,* and birds. Aside from a small out-post at km65, the Pixiam Hotel e Lanchonete, there are no restaurants or service stations along the highway. Independent travelers can take a bus from Cuiabá to Poconé (3hr.) and either hire a taxi or arrange pick-up with a *fazenda* or *pousada.* The latter option is highly recommended, as the afternoon heat along the highway can make hiking extremely unpleasant. The dirt road crosses over many wooden bridges, and though well maintained, it is often flooded. In the rainy season (Nov.-Feb.), the *fazendas* south of km60 are often inaccessible. Always call in advance to book accommodations and inquire about road conditions. The **Estrada Parque** in the south is just off the BR-242, which connects Corumbá and Campo Grande. There is a turnoff for the Estrada Parque 10km from Corumbá and a second turnoff, locally referred to as Buraco das Piranhas, near Miranda. The *fazendas* and *pousadas* along the highway are located near the Buraco das Piranhas turnoff and most offer pickups from this point; to reach Buraco das Piranhas take the Campo Grande-Corumbá bus and ask to be dropped off. The 117km Estrada Parque is a well-maintained dirt track, like the Transpantaneira, but it rarely floods so most of its *fazendas* and *pousadas* are accessible year-round. Both the Estrada Parque and the Transpantaneira offer excellent opportunities to spot wildlife, as many animals flock to the area during the wet season.

in the north (Nov.-Mar.). However, although the area gets flooded during this time, the most intense flooding doesn't occur until two or three months later, when the waters from the north drain southward, causing the water level to rise by up to three meters. A few months after this, the waters subside and the dry season begins. Although the south is waterlogged for a greater part of the year than the north, roads in this area—and the *fazendas* and *pousadas* off of them—are accessible year-round.

THE PANTANAL OF ESTRADA PARQUE

Most *fazendas* and *pousadas* in the southern Pantanal are located along the Estrada Parque, a 117km stretch of well-maintained dirt road just north of the BR-242 expressway. The highway turns off from the BR-242 about 10km east of Corumbá (p. 331). It eventually curves back toward the BR-242 near Buraco das Piranhas, a small outpost with a police station, telephone booth, bus stop, and nothing else. All the tour companies in the south operate along this stretch of road. If you enter the highway at the turnoff nearest Corumbá you're likely to spot anacondas bathing in the sun during the mid-afternoon; entering at Buraco das Piranhas will mean spotting small mammals. Unlike the Transpantaneira, the Estrada Parque is always dry and offers year-round accessibility. Also, the *fazendas* and *pousadas* are generally located right beside the road. Independent travelers look-

SOUTHERN PANTANAL TOUR OPERATORS

Green Track Tours, Rua Antônio João 216 (☎9611 3862, 231 2258; greentk@terra.com.br), in the travel office of Green Track Hostel in **Corumbá.** Green Track is a cooperative union of local guides that offers tours to an authentic *fazenda* surrounded by rugged scenery and abundant wildlife. Visitors are given the chance to work on the farm, rounding up cattle or fixing broken stirrups and cabana huts. They can also go on horseback riding trips, treks, boat rides, and excursions in search of wildlife. Tours feature basic accommodations but offer the best chance in the south for spotting wildlife and getting to know how *fazendas* work. 3-day/2-night R$225 per person. 4-day/3-night R$285 per person. 5-day/4-night R$335 per person.

Ecological Expeditions, Rua Antônio Maria Coelha 78 (☎9609 6309), in **Corumbá.** Owned and operated by the parent company in Campo Grande, they offer the same trips as those offered in the capital. The advantage of taking trips with the company from Corumbá lies in a shorter commute to the campsite. On the trip along the Estrada Parque toward the camp there is a good chance of seeing anacondas sunning themselves in the afternoon. Like its Campo Grande counterpart, they offer 1 free night of accommodations for trips of 3 days or more. 3-day/2-night R$250 per person. 4-day/3-night R$280. 5-day/4-night R$310. Office open daily 8am-6pm.

Gil's Pantanal Discovery Tours, with an office inside the mall at the **Rodoviária de Campo Grande** (☎9994 7774, 384 7636; gilstour@starbox.com.br). Far and away the most reliable option in town, with over 15 years of experience in the southern Pantanal. They offer the most comfortable accommodations of all the tour groups in the south, based out of Pousada Cabana do Lontra on the Estrada Parque. Among the usual activities offered they also have a unique river cruise down the Rio Vermelho. All guides speak English. Offers a free night's stay for tours of 3-5 days. Transport to the *pousada* takes 4hr. 3-day/2-night R$300 per person. 4-day/3-night R$350 per person. 5-day/4-night R$400 per person. Office open daily 8am-6pm.

Ecological Expeditions, Rua Joaquim Nabuco 185 (☎321 0505), based out of the Nosso Novo Campo Grande Youth Hostel in **Campo Grande.** Boasting the largest staff of bilingual guides and fancy new trucks to transport guests, they send more truckloads of tourists into the south than anyone else. Expect large crowds and more of a party atmosphere than a nature lover's paradise. Offering only simple camping accommodations, they can afford to offer the cheapest prices in the south. 3-day/2-night R$250 per person. 4-day/3-night R$280. 5-day/4-night R$310. Office open daily 7am-8pm.

ing to explore the *fazendas* here can catch the Campo Grande-Corumbá bus and get off at Buraco das Piranhas; accommodations offer pick-up from this point for a small fee (R$20-100). Make sure to call the *pousada* or *fazenda* on the day you expect to arrive as several travelers have been left stranded at this point; the town of Miranda (p. 337) is 35km east for those stuck in this situation. There are no fees to enter the highway, though cars entering from the Corumbá turnoff will have to pay a ferry fee (R$12) to cross the Rio Paraguai. The only official restaurant on the highway is **Posto e Lanchonete Passo do Lontra,** 7km from the Buraco das Piranhas turnoff, on the right. It sells very simple meals like piranha soup (R$3.50), hamburgers (R$3), and palmito salads (R$5). They also have a large stock of canned goods, fruits, and vegetables, in addition to eating/cooking supplies. The gas tanks out front sell expensive fuel. (☎231 6569. Open daily 7am-8:30pm.)

ACCOMMODATIONS AROUND ESTRADA PARQUE

Green Track Fazenda Boa Sorte, 36km from the Buraco das Piranhas turnoff (☎9611 3862, office 231 2258; greentk@terra.com.br). The main office is in the Green Track Hostel, Rua Antônio João 216, in Corumbá. The *fazenda* sits next to the Estrada Parque but is poorly marked. The favorite among international travelers, Boa Sorte is a rural *fazenda* with a rustic atmosphere and well-organized activities. It features some of the most knowledgeable and colorful guides operating in the southern Pantanal. The *fazenda* is well-located and features a host of activities, from horseback riding to fishing. Visitors can also help out with the operation of the farm, from milking the cows to rounding up the cattle in the afternoon. Accommodations are very simple–cabana huts with mosquito nets for walls–but anything more luxurious would be completely out of place. The steady flow of tourists from the Green Track Hostel ensures company for independent travelers, but don't expect more than 5-10 people at a time. Meals are included in the room price. The *fazenda* has no hot water, but it does have a bar. Transfer from Buraco das Piranhas R$100 (round trip; 1-4 people). 3hr. activities R$30 per person. Dorms R$40.

Passo do Lontra, 7km from the Buraco das Piranhas turnoff and a farther 3km along a dirt road (☎231 6569, 245 2407; www.passodolontra.com.br); turn right at the Posto Passo do Lontra. A self-consciously rustic *fazenda* reconstruction set on stilts overlooking the Rio Vermelho; it's one of the most attractive options in the entire Pantanal. Elevated wooden walkways connect the large stilted complex to the mainland, but otherwise it's relatively isolated and separated from the other *pousadas* nearby. It offers top-class accommodations with varying degrees of comfort. The most plush are the private chalets with A/C, separate lounge area, double bed, and *frigo-bar.* The *apartamentos* have kitchen but lack furniture and closet space. The real deal is found in the pleasant *quartos* with shared bath, fan, and firm beds. Those really on a budget can also pitch a tent on one of the designated wooden platforms. The *pousada* offers all the usual activities, though the horseback riding and walking treks are located 30km north in their own private farm. Has a cozy lounge area with TV, pool table, couches, an elegant restaurant serving international cuisine (meals are not included in price), and a small shop that sells sunscreen and repellent to the forgetful. Boat rental with guide R$120 per day. Treks with guide R$70 per day. 3hr. boat safari R$35 (min. 5 people). *Quartos* R$60. *Apartamentos* R$90. Chalets R$211. Camping R$12 per person. Discounts available for groups of 2 or more.

Fazenda Natureza, 33km from the Buraco das Piranhas turnoff (☎9601 1804, 321 3143), at the turnoff for Fazenda São João; call in advance to be picked up. An authentic *fazenda* in operation for more than 50 years, with the friendliest farm hands on the Estrada Parque. It lacks a good tourist infrastructure but the pastoral character and rustic atmosphere leads many to stay. The surrounding area is good for spotting tapirs and anteaters, and the nearby rivers are foaming with piranhas. Accommodations are basic to say the least, but they do have mosquito nets and fans. The *fazenda* offers horseback riding, boat trips, and fishing excursions, and you can spot wildlife from the excellent walking trails. Little English spoken. Transfer from Buraco das Piranhas R$100 (round-trip; 1-4 people). Prices include all meals and activities. 1-day visit R$90; 3-day visit R$250; 4-day visit R$280.

Fazenda Bela Vista and Hotel Boa Vista, 26km from the Corumbá turnoff (☎9987 1009, 067 9987 3660). A magnificently tranquil ranch set in the hills that overlook the Pantanal wetlands around Corumbá. The *fazenda* has been in operation for years but has only recently opened a hotel on its premises. Aside from the horse and cows that freely roam the grounds, the only chance to see wildlife is during the day activities when you are transported to the wetlands. The lack of a surrounding swampland allows guests the opportunity to explore the region alone, on foot or horseback. The *fazenda* has an exceptionally friendly staff and lovely rooms with A/C, *frigo-bar,* firm beds, and

TV; some rooms even have small libraries. Among the activities are fishing in the Rio Paraguai (R$100), horseback riding (R$30 per 2hr.), kayaking (R$30 per 2hr.), and exploring nearby caves. Amenities include a swimming pool, *futebol* field, and restaurant. Transport from Corumbá turnoff R$30. Room prices include all meals. Singles R$70, with activities R$160; doubles R$120, with activities R$300.

Hotel Pesqueiro e Lanchonete do Tadashi, 7km from the Buraco das Piranhas turnoff (☎231 9400; www.tadashihotel.net), before the sign for Posto Passo do Lontra. The most accessible of the *pesqueiro* fishing lodges, with the best facilities of any in the Pantanal. It's located on the banks of the Rio Vermelho, which means enthusiastic fishermen can be on the water by sunrise. The small *apartamentos* are comfortable and there is a lovely open-air dining area. Visitors are mainly international, though you may meet a few suburban Brazilians on holiday. All meals included. They have 25 6m boats for rent, in addition to bait, fishing tackle, and ice. Boat rental R$120 per day (includes fishing rods). Dorms R$90.

Pousada Pantaneira do Rio Vermelho (☎9987 4373, 321 4737). Located on the banks of the Rio Vermelho; best accessed by taking a boat from Cabana do Lontra. Set in idyllic surroundings, the countryside around the *pousada* is home to a matchless variety of plants and animals. Some of the best walking trails in the south are found on these lands. The accommodations offered are refreshingly pleasant. Each *apartamento* has A/C, *frigo-bar,* private bath, and closet. The *pousada* owns a fine group of horses, around which most of the activities revolve. Accessible only by river or four-wheel-drive vehicle, it's best to arrange pickup from Bracos das Piranhas (R$150; one-way). Prices include all meals and activities. Singles R$145.

Pousada Cabana da Lontra, 7km from the Buraco das Piranhas turnoff and a farther 2km along a dirt road (☎9602 2358). Boasts one of the best tourist infrastructures in the Pantanal, offering a host of activities that leave regularly each day. It's most frequented by tour groups from Gil's Pantanal Discovery Tours, though the odd independent traveler sometimes pays a visit. The wooden *pousada* is built on stilts and overlooks the Rio Vermelho. It provides hearty meals and its comfortable *apartamentos* with A/C and private bath are fully protected from mosquitoes. Activities are centered on the water though they do have some interesting alternatives, including sunrise walks (R$20) and photo safaris along the Estrada Parque (R$60 per 4-5hr.). Among the more standard activities, such as horseback riding and trekking (R$20 per day), they have a wonderful full-day river cruise down the Rio Vermelho to Pousada Rio Vermelho, where visitors spend a few hours horseback riding before hopping on the boat for the booze cruise home (R$75 per day). Round-trip transportation from Buraco das Piranhas R$20. Prices include breakfast and dinner. Dorms R$30, with lunch R$50.

THE PANTANAL OF MIRANDA

Travelers with limited time are encouraged to pay a visit to one of the several day-use *fazendas* that surround the little town of Miranda (p. 337), 230km east of Campo Grande. Access to the town and many of its *fazendas* is via the highway that connects the capital with Corumbá, which makes them easy for independent travelers to access. Among the more generic *fazendas* and *pousadas* hides the Pantanal's foremost ecological wildlife refuge, Refúgio Ecológico Caiman. Day-trips to all *fazendas* usually include transfer from the town of Miranda, especially for groups of four or more people. At each facility you can expect to learn about the flora and fauna of the area and the operation of *fazendas*. While the area is known for its bird life, you are not likely to see many larger animals. The scenery in this area is striking and often clouded by large groups of white herons taking to the sky, and the sunsets here are magical. If you only have a day to spend exploring the wetlands, this is where you'll want to be.

ACCOMMODATIONS AROUND MIRANDA

Refúgio da Ilha, about 78km east of Miranda, 10km of which is along a dirt road (☎784 3270; www.refugiodailha.com.br). Located on an island on the Rio Salobra, this family-run ranch covers 20 square kilometers and offers opportunities to see the larger mammals not found at the other nearby *fazendas.* The ranch has a good infrastructure with amenities that include a swimming pool and restaurant. Day visitors arrive at 9am, have breakfast, and then head out for a day of activities that includes boat trips and walking treks. Snorkeling in the Rio Salobra is available upon request, as are bike tours around the farmland in search of animals. It's a quaint facility with a lot of character and more secluded than most, making it attractive to travelers looking to get away from the tourist hordes. Prices include all meals and activities. Day-visit R$100 (min. 2 people); 2-day visit R$140 (min. 2 people); 3-day visit R$240 (min. 2 people).

Refúgio Ecológico Caiman (☎242 1450, office 11 3079 6622; www.caiman.com.br); main office at Rua Campos Bicudo 98, São Paulo. 140 mi. east of Campo Grande and 40km north of Miranda, this ecological refuge, which covers 530 square kilometers, is the Pantanal's premier luxury option. It's a self-consciously rustic lodge with 5 separate cabins, each of which has its own infrastructure and style. All cabins have swimming pool, international restaurant, and lavish lounge area. The lodge is surrounded by a diverse landscape of savanna grasslands, seasonal wetlands, and thickly forested islands. The guides here are far and away the most professional in the area; each is bilingual and holds a degree in their area of expertise. Rooms are luxuriously decorated and the food is delicious, though spending the night will not be an option for many. The cheapest way to take advantage of the lodge's offerings is on a daytrip from Miranda; you'll get the opportunity to see *capivara* and alligators, and go on boat trip and jungle tour. Daytrip from Miranda R$100 (including transportation). Prices include transportation, meals, and activities. 2-night stay US$300 (4 person min.); US$530 (1 person).

San Francisco Fazenda, 36km west of Miranda on the highway that connects Corumbá and Campo Grande (☎242 1088, 242 1242; www.fazendasanfrancisco.tur.br). Easily visited by independent travelers. Take the bus between Corumbá and Campo Grande and ask to be dropped off at the entrance. An excellent day-use *fazenda* that offers guests the chance to see how a working farm operates in the Pantanal. The daytrip includes riverside walking trails, horseback riding, photo safaris, and barge trips along the Rio Miranda. The *fazenda* has 1500 cows, but visitors are generally more interested in trying to spot the deer, *capivara,* and monkeys that call the farm home. Piranha fishing is one of the more popular activities, but the *fazenda* enforces a strict catch-and-release program. R$70 per day, includes lunch and transportation from Miranda.

MATO GROSSO DO SUL

CAMPO GRANDE ☎67

As a major transportation hub and gateway to the southern Pantanal, Campo Grande sees more tourist traffic than any other city in the Center-West. The city started to grow with the 1914 arrival of a railway, and really took off when it was named capital of the newly formed state of Mato Grosso do Sul. Today it is a busy metropolis with pretty parks and popular market places, and little else of interest to tourists. The city's saving grace is the buzzing nightlife fueled by its many university students. The tour companies that eagerly greet you at the *rodoviária* will try to convince you that this is the best place from which to take tours into the Pantanal (p. 311), but it might be better for those going on to Bolivia to base their tours in the more welcoming city of Corumbá (p. 331).

TRANSPORTATION

Flights: Aeroporto Internacional de Campo Grande, Av. Duque de Caxias s/n (☎368 6000), 7km from town on the road to Corumbá.

Buses: Rodoviária de Campo Grande, on the corner of Rua Joaquim and Rua Barão do Rio Branco (☎383 1678), is located in the *centro* next to a large mall. **Andorinha** (☎382 3699) sends buses to: **Corumbá** (6hr.; 7 per day 6:30am-midnight; R$49) via **Miranda** (3hr.; R$24); **Cuiabá** (10hr.; 5 per day 5:10am-9:10am; R$57); **Rio de Janeiro** (22hr.; 4 per day 9:45am-9:25pm; R$116) **via São Paulo** (14hr.; R$86).

Taxi: Campo Grande Moto-Taxi has a station beside the bus stop at Rua Aquino 693 (☎325 2001). Open 24hr. Regular taxis from **Rádio Taxi** (☎387 1414). Open 24hr.

Car Rental: Localiza has an office at the airport (☎363 1401; open daily 7am-1am), and at Av. Afonso Pena 318 (☎382 8786; open M-F 8am-8pm, Sa-Su 8am-2pm), beside Hotel Indiaiá. **Unidas** also has an office at the airport (☎368 6120; open daily 7am-1am) and at Av. Afonso Pena 607 (☎384 5626; open M-F 8am-6pm, Sa-Su 8am-noon). **Avis** (☎363 1010; open daily 8am-1am) and **Interlocadora** (☎363 4005; open daily 7am-1am) also have airport offices. Class A cars with unlimited km begin at R$76. You must be at least 21 years of age and have a credit card to rent.

ORIENTATION & PRACTICAL INFORMATION

The streets follow a grid system, which makes the city easy to navigate. Most services are found along **Avenida Afonso Pena,** which connects the *rodoviária* at one end of the city to **Parque das Nações Indígenas** and **Shopping Campo Grande** at the other. Parallel to Av. Afonso Pena are **Rua Barão do Rio Branco** and **Rua Dom Aquino;** most of the city's shops and restaurants are found on these streets between **Rua João Antônio** and **Rua 14 de Julho.** The **rodoviária,** on Av. Joaquim Nabuco, is just 5 blocks from the *centro.* The area around the *rodoviária* is best avoided at night.

TOURIST & FINANCIAL SERVICES

Tourist Office: Morado dos Baís Information Center, Av. Noreste 5140 (☎382 9244), at Av. Afonso Pena, in the Morado dos Baís Museum. One of the state's best run tourism offices, with a knowledgeable English-speaking staff and dozens of pamphlets about the Pantanal. Don't leave without picking up a free map of the city and the Estrada Parque map (R$3). **Internet** R$3 per hr. Open Tu-Sa 8am-7pm, Su 9am-noon.

Banks: Banco do Brasil, Av. Afonso Pena 2202 (☎389 1300). Charges a flat rate of US$15 for cash exchange. ATM Visa withdrawals also available. Open M-F 11am-4pm. **HSBC,** Rua Dom Aquino 1663 (☎312 4600). Cheaper than normal exchange fees (US$10) for cash and traveler's checks. ATM MasterCard withdrawals also available. Open M-F 11am-4pm. **Bradesco,** Rua Barão do Rio Branco 1582 (☎321 2616). Open M-F 11am-4pm.

ATM: Banco 24hr. ATM, on the corner of Rua Dom Aquino and Rua Nabuco, beside the *rodoviária,* accepts AmEx/Cirrus/MC/Maestro cards.

LOCAL SERVICES

Luggage Storage: Hotels are usually unwilling to store luggage during your trip to the Pantanal; both Gil's Pantanal Discovery and Natureza are happy to hold your bags. Luggage storage is available at **Postal,** a small airport convenience store (☎368 6110; R$3 per day; open when flights arrive), and at the *rodoviária* (R$2 per 24hr.).

English-Language Bookstore: Maciel, Rua 14 de Julho 1696 (☎321 0362), on Pça. Coelho, has a diverse collection of second-hand books in English hidden in a secret room; ask the staff for access, but don't tell anyone. Open M-F 8am-7pm, Sa 8am-2pm.

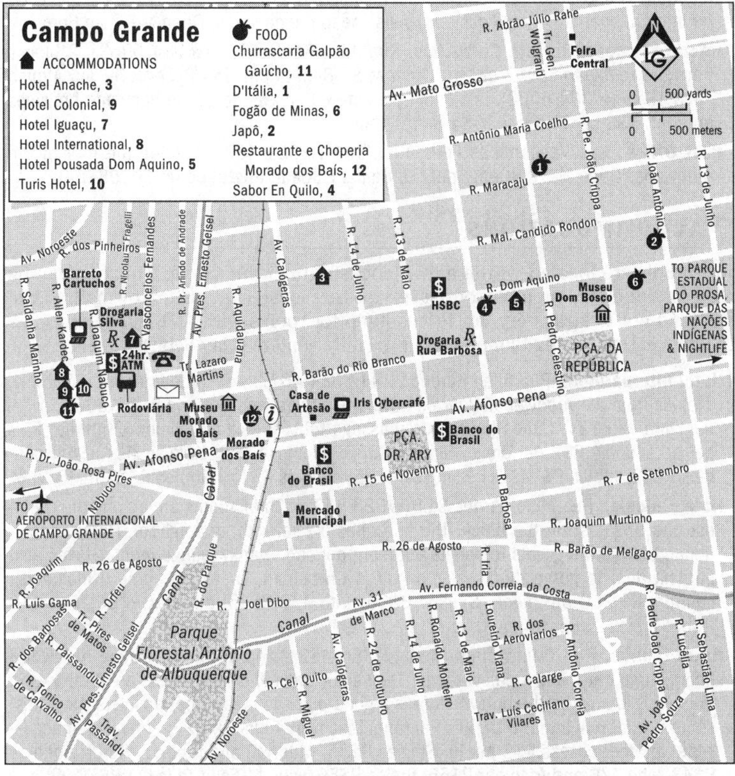

Airlines: Gol (☎368 6128) has the cheapest flights and serves all the nearby cities. **Varig** (☎368 6174). **VASP** (☎363 2389). **Gensa** (☎0800 647 7200).

Ticket Agencies: Vox Tour, Rua Barbosa 1777 (☎324 3335; voxtour@msinter-net.com.br), at Rua Candido Mariano Rondon, has discount tickets for flights and buses and also arranges rental cars. Their 4-day package to San Francisco Fazenda (p. 325) is a good deal at just US$130. Also has trips to Bonito. Open M-F 8am-6pm, Sa 8am-noon. **N&T Japan Tour,** Av. Afonso Pena 2081, rm. 20 (☎382 9425, 384 2820; www.japantour.com.br), in Galeria Dona Neta, offers good deals on flights but its package deals to *fazendas* in the Pantanal are very expensive (2 nights R$600-1200). Open M-F 9am-6pm, Sa 9am-2pm. **Palm Tur,** Rua Joaquim Nabuco 169-B (☎324 6012), in front of the *rodoviária,* arranges flights and buses. Open M-F 6am-8pm.

Laundry: Lavanderia Oriente, Av. Afonso Pena 276 (☎324 9512), 15min. north of the *rodoviária*. R$1 per piece. Open M-F 8am-6pm, Sa-Su 8am-noon.

EMERGENCY & COMMUNICATIONS

24hr. Pharmacy: Drogaria Silva, Rua Dom Aquino 861 (☎784 1102), next to the *rodoviária,* and **Drogaria Rua Barbosa** (☎314 3737), at Rua Barão do Rio Branco.

Hospital: Santa Casa, Rua Eduardo Santos Pereira 88 (☎321 5151), is the municipal hospital, but the more central **Clínica Campo Grande,** Rua Candido Mariano Rondon 1703 (☎327 9000), is a better bet.

Telephone: Posto Telefônico, inside the mall near the *rodoviária* (☎321 1360), is good for international and local calls, and sells cheap phone cards. Open M-F 7am-6pm.

Internet Access: Barreto Cartuchos, Rua Allen Kardec 374 (☎384 5963), 2 blocks from the *rodoviária.* R$2 per hr. Open M-Sa 8am-10pm. **Iris Cybercafé,** Av. Afonso Pena 1975 (☎384 6002), is a cool little café with chess boards in back and brownies up front. R$3 per hr. Open M-Sa 8am-11pm.

Post Office: Rua Vasconcilos Fernandes 164 (☎321 4837), facing the rear of the *rodoviária.* Open M-F 8:30am-6pm, Sa 8am-11:30am. **Postal code:** 79008-000.

ACCOMMODATIONS

Most hotels are located within a few blocks of the *rodoviária.* The area can be dangerous at night, but most tourist services are located in the nearby mall, so visitors tend not to stray very far. Prices jump for rooms with A/C, but such rooms are unnecessary during Campo Grande's chilly winters (May-Sept.).

Hotel International, Rua Allen Kardec 223 (☎384 4677; www.hotelintermetro.com.br), 1 block from the *rodoviária. Quartos* have plush beds, and *luxo* rooms have A/C, *frigo-bar,* and cable TV. Suites have hydromassage tubs. Breakfast included. Internet R$8 per hr. Laundry R$2 per piece. Singles R$38; doubles R$62. *Luxo* singles R$54; doubles R$72; triples R$94. Suite singles R$85; doubles R$110; triples R$125. MC/V. ❷

Hotel Colonial, Rua Allen Kardec 211 (☎383 5422). Small rooms are among the cleanest and brightest on the block. The hotel has a deal with its neighbor, Hotel International, that allows guests to use its outdoor pool and swanky lounge room. Guests also go next door to gorge themselves on the overwhelming breakfast spread (included). Laundry R$1.50 per piece. Singles R$30, with A/C R$35; doubles R$50, with A/C R$55; triples R$65, with A/C R$70. MC/V. ❷

Hotel Iguaçu, Rua Dom Aquino 761 (☎384 4621). *Apartamentos* have hardwood floors, large bath, and small veranda. The yellow walls and pink sheets are cheery, and the comfy lounge on the bottom floor is a good place to meet other travelers. Hefty discount if you book a tour with Gil's Pantanal Discovery Tours (p. 322). Wheelchair accessible. Internet access R$8 per hr. Singles R$35, with A/C and *frigo-bar* R$48; doubles R$43, with A/C and *frigo-bar* R$55; triples R$56, with A/C and *frigo-bar* R$70. ❷

Hotel Pousada Dom Aquino, Rua Dom Aquino 1806 (☎382 9373), near Rua Barbosa. For those who require lodging close to the *centro,* Pousada Dom Aquino offers the best value around. The owners work hard to make the hotel as inviting as possible, and happily offer advice about surrounding sights. All rooms have A/C, *frigo-bar,* and shower. Popular with Brazilian business travelers. Singles R$30; doubles R$50; triples R$80. ❸

Turis Hotel, Rua Allen Kardec 200 (☎382 7688), opposite Hotel Colonial. A run-of-the-mill hotel with basic services and simple rooms; some have couches, and all have sparklingly clean baths. Breakfast included. Kitchen. Singles R$20, with TV R$23, with A/C R$30; doubles R$38, with TV R$40, with A/C R$45. 20% low-season discount. Visa. ❶

Hotel Anache, Rua Candido Mariano Rondon 1396 (☎383 2841), is a few blocks from the *rodoviária,* closer to the *centro.* Spacious, furnished rooms have lots of light but nothing that merits leaving the area around the *rodoviária.* There's no lounge, but people get to know each other over breakfast. Parking. Singles R$25, with A/C R$30; doubles R$35, with A/C R$45; triples R$50, with A/C R$65. MC/V. ❷

FOOD

Campo Grande's few decent dining options can be found in the vicinity of the the *centro.* There are also a number of identical 24hr. cafés and *lanchonetes* around the city's *rodoviária.*

Sabor En Quilo, Rua Dom Aquino 1786 (☎325 5102), is one of the best self-service joints around, combining fast-food seating with quality dining. It has a huge selection of fresh salads, fruits, and even some sushi. Careful presentation makes even the beans and rice appear appetizing. In addition to the standard fare they also serve pasta salads and chicken curries. M-F R$14 per kg, Sa-Su R$16.50 per kg. Open M-F 11am-2:30pm, Sa-Su 11am-3pm. MC/V. ❷

Restaurante e Choperia Morado dos Baís, Av. Afonso Pena s/n (☎383 1227), behind Museu Morado dos Baís at Av. Noreste, is a pricey restaurant with a wide selection of regional dishes. The menu has a section of Pantanal cuisine, including *jacaré* (alligator meat) served with onion and tomato (R$34 serves 2). Fish dishes include the popular *pintado* and *pacu.* Chicken and steak options are available for the less adventurous. Live music nightly. Open daily 11am-2:30pm and 7pm-midnight. MC/V. ❸

D'Itália, Rua Maracaju 863 (☎324 0770), on the corner of Rua Pedro Celestino, serves a slew of healthful options ranging from soups and sandwiches to diet *sorvetes* (ice cream) and natural *sucos* (juices). An excellent choice for vegetarians and sweet-tooths alike. Open daily noon-midnight. MC/V. ❶

Fogão de Minas, Rua Dom Aquino 2200 (☎325 5287), has limited salad and fruit options, but the majority of people come here for the meat, including plates of pork, chicken, lamb, and alligator, all kept warm over a wood stove. Local diners consistently praise the restaurant, and it has more charm and character than Campo Grande's other self-service choices. Wheelchair accessible. Live music Tu-Th. M-F R$15 per kg, Sa-Su R$17 per kg. Open M-F 11am-2:30pm, Sa-Su 11am-4pm. MC/V. ❷

Japô, Rua João Antônio 1277 (☎383 2388), is a bit of a walk from the hotels near the *rodoviária* but worth the trek. Sampler plates of sushi generally start at R$25; the *cambinado matsu* plate serves over 50 pieces of sushi and offers the best value for small groups. In the back of the restaurant is a private room furnished with traditional seating and tables, great for large groups returning from the Pantanal. Reservations for the private room (R$10 extra per person) must be made in advance. Open daily 7pm-1am. ❸

Churrascaria Galpão Gaúcho, Rua Allen Kardec 187 (☎329 3474), is next to Hotel Colonial and is the only decent eatery near the *rodoviária.* The decor lacks appeal but the food is clean and fresh, unlike most nearby competitors. Vegetarians will be pleased with the cold pasta dishes but saddened by the lack of fruit. Buffet R$6.50. Open daily 10am-3pm and 5:30-10pm. ❶

SIGHTS

PARQUE ESTADUAL DO PROSA. This wonderfully run ecological reserve near the *centro* is filled with flora and fauna of the southern Pantanal. Guides lead you along one of three trails through magnificent woodlands and across elevated platforms and suspended bridges (1-1½hr.). The reserve has an animal rehabilitation center (CRAS) that cares for injured wildlife found in the Pantanal. The center opens for visits every Friday, but these must be booked in advance; this is best done at the Morado da Baís tourist office. *(At the end of Av. Afonso Pena, past Shopping Campo Grande and Parque das Naçóes Indigenas. Open Tu-Su 8am-5pm. R$4; students R$2.)*

PARQUE DAS NAÇÕES INDÍGENAS. This park was built to pay homage to the area's indigenous communities and is today a popular weekend escape for residents of Campo Grande who hope to see animals roaming freely throughout the park's 1.2 square kilometers of woodlands, including *capivara* and wetland deer, but sightings are limited as the park has just four kilometers of hiking tracks. More commonly seen are the colorful toucans and parrots that soar through the forest. The park also contains a lagoon and a cultural center that hosts occasional shows. *(On Av. Afonso Pena, next to Shopping Campo Grande. ☎326 2987. Open Tu-Su 6am-9pm.)*

CASA DA ARTESÃO. Housed in one of Campo Grande's oldest commercial buildings, this shop has two floors filled with souvenirs and some genuinely interesting works of local artists. Among the more intricate pieces are wooden replicas—complete with working wells—of the ranch houses typical of the Pantanal (R$60-500). On the top floor are some larger works, including sculptures of animals and some religious figures. Cowboy drinking flasks (R$20), cow horns (R$15), and glazed piranha (R$3) round out the tackier souvenir collection. *(Av. Calógeras 2050, on the corner of Av. Afonso Pena. ☎383 2633. Open M-F 8am-6pm, Sa-Su 9am-2pm.)*

MUSEU MORADO DOS BAÍS. This museum is housed in a colonial building famous as the birthplace of Campo Grande's most prominent artist, Lidia Baís. Leaning toward the unconventional and controversial, Baís was renowned for the spirited temperament that animated her often fiery paintings. The museum displays some of her more private works, including some murals she painted while living in the house. Among the personal effects on exhibit are her childhood bed, some musical instruments, and her rocking chair. *(Av. Nordeste 5140, at Av. Afonso Pena, next to the tourist office. ☎382 9244, 324 5830. Open Tu-Sa 8am-7pm, Su 9am-noon.)*

MUSEU DOM BOSCO. The museum's sterile exhibit cases detract from what is otherwise the finest collection of natural and indigenous artifacts in the state. The museum is home to an enormous number of pieces gathered from indigenous communities across the country. Highlights include crystal-tipped spear heads and intricate headdresses. The museum also has rooms dedicated to the birds and butterflies of the Pantanal. *(Rua Barão do Rio Branco 1843. ☎312 6491. Open Tu-Sa 8am-6pm, Su 8am-noon and 2-6pm. R$3; students R$1.)*

NIGHTLIFE

The city is home to four universities and a correspondingly active nightlife. Most clubs are near Shopping Campo Grande, a 30min. walk from the *rodoviária.*

Bar Acustic, Rua 13 de Junho 945 (☎383 5500), is just north of Rua Candido Mariano Rondon. This small venue is always jam-packed with Campos Grande's coolest crowd, primarily consisting of university students. It lacks the pretension of the town's other clubs and has a chill atmosphere conducive to meeting others. Live bands nightly. Cover R$10. Open F-Sa 11pm-4:30am.

Limit, Rua Zerbine 39 (☎331 3484), 2 blocks from Shopping Campo Grande. Though clubs open and close in the city with remarkable frequency, Limit has established itself as a favorite among locals, and with good reason. The best DJs in town somehow manage to switch smoothly between MPB, *samba,* and rock. It has more of a pulse than the other clubs and tends to be busiest on Saturdays. Regulars are a diverse crowd, from professional to professionless and young to young long ago. Cover R$12, or R$24 for a book of drink coupons. Open F-Sa 11pm-6am.

Cabral, Rua Zerbine 38 (☎326 2463), across from Limit, is a self-consciously hip establishment. It is frequented most often by the city's up-and-coming professionals who show up to mingle and listen to the live bands that play nightly (mostly MPB). Two floors offer indoor seating and outdoor patio escapes. Despite the classy decor it boasts the cheapest cover in town (R$2.50). Open W-Su 6pm-4am.

Mr. Dam, Rua Jose Eduardo Rolin 197 (☎341 0123), 10min. from Shopping Campo Grande. Similar to Limit but draws a more affluent crowd. It has a fancy interior with stylish curves and funky lights, a central dance floor where most action takes place, and some luxurious couches to collapse on after hours of bopping to techno and trance. The bouncers tend to be choosy about who to let in, but you'll appreciate that once you're inside. Cover R$10. Open F-Su midnight-5am.

COXIM ☎67

Coxim is a quiet village 250km north of Campo Grande, on the way to Cuiabá. Located near the intersection of Rio Taquari and Rio Capivari, it offers excellent fishing opportunities and excursions into the Pantanal. The limited tourist infrastructure leads many to bypass the town altogether, but travelers passing through between November and February should definitely stop to witness the impressive *piracema*, when the river's fish migrate upstream to spawn—fighting strong currents and jumping rapids and rocks.

The town is divided into the old and new districts, both of which are on the riverfront and which are connected by Rua Flinte Muller. The new part of town has most services and hotels while the old part is where most of the fishing boats and stores are located. The **rodoviária** is three kilometers from both. To reach the newer area of town from the *rodoviária*, walk one block south to Av. Gasper Ries Coelho, turn right and continue for two kilometers, then turn left when you reach Rua Delmira de Meto Bandeira, just after the gas station. Alternatively, you can hire a **moto-taxi** to make the trip (☎291 3318; R$3-4). **Andorinha** (☎291 1552) has buses to Campo Grande (4hr.; 6 per day 6am-11pm; R$26), Cuiabá (7hr.; 5 per day 5am-11pm; R$36), and São Paulo (18hr.; 4 per day 6am-11:10pm; R$94).

Comtur, the municipal tourist office, is near the old part of town next to the bridge. They can help arrange all-inclusive fishing tours, trips to the Pantanal, and *fazenda* stays. They can also arrange guides for daytrips to the nearby waterfalls. (☎291 1643. Open M-F 7am-6pm.) **Peixe Viva,** Rua Vargas 350, has good a selection of fishing rods and live bait. They also rent motorboats for R$90 per day. (☎291 1798. Open M-F 6am-7pm.) **Bradesco,** Rua Flinte Muller 85, has a Visa ATM. (☎291 1120. Open M-F 10am-3pm.) Other services include: the pharmacy **Drogaria Sáo Joáo,** Rua Flinte Muller 580 (☎291 1077; open M-F 7:30am-6pm, Sa 7:30am-noon); **Internet access** at Mundial Informática, Rua Antonio João 110 (☎291 4489; R$5 per hr.; open M-F 8am-8pm, Sa 8-11am); and the **post office**, Rua Antônio João 111, which is opposite Mundial Informática (☎291 2244; open M-F 8:30am-5pm, Sa 8am-11:30pm). **Postal code:** 79400-000.

The town offers a limited choice of accommodations. A good option in the old town is **Hotel Pousada Granado ❶**, Rua Vargas 2078, on the riverfront. The hotel has 12 simple rooms, each with fan and private bath. (☎291 1809. Breakfast included. Singles R$8; doubles R$15; triples R$22; quads R$30.) In front of the *rodoviária* is **Hotel Neves ❶**, Av. Gasper Coelho 1931, which offers the best value in town. The rooms look out on a central courtyard, and rooms are cheery if sparsely furnished. (Singles R$13, with TV and A/C R$20; doubles R$24, with TV and A/C R$35; triples R$33, with TV and A/C R$40.) The floating restaurant **Paradinha Chopp & Cia ❸**, Av. Virínia Ferreira 390, is one block south of Rua Flinte Muller. It has friendly service, and specializes in fish, although they also have several vegetarian and meat dishes. (Open M-Sa 11am-3pm and 6pm-midnight, Su 11am-3pm).

CORUMBÁ ☎67

Corumbá is a principal gateway to the southern Pantanal and the easiest entrypoint into Bolivia. Located on a hill smack-dab in the middle of the Pantanal wetlands, the city makes a great launching point for excursions farther into the swamps, especially given its proximity to the many *fazendas* along the Estrada Parque (p. 321). Many travelers—especially those not continuing on to Bolivia—opt to leave on tours from Campo Grande instead of from Corumbá, but miss out on the city's distinct frontier feel. Though tourists are largely shielded from this side of the city, Corumbá's reputation for smuggling dates back to the 1800s, when the city was an important port for the Spanish and Portuguese.

BORDER CROSSING: TO BOLIVIA Crossing the border is a relatively simple affair. Those needing a **visa** to enter Bolivia must first go to the Consulado de Bolivia, Rua Antônio Maria Coelho 881 (☎231 5605. Open M-F 8am-noon and 2-4pm); few European and American travelers will need a visa. If you don't need a visa proceed directly to the federal police station (☎231 1224), at the *rodoviária,* to receive your **exit stamp** from Brazil (open daily 8-11:30am and 2-5:30pm); the federal police station in the main *praça* can not help with exit stamps. With your exit stamp and visa in hand, head to the border. Here you will receive your **entrance stamp** and passage into the country, so long as you remember to bring your yellow fever certificate. **Buses to the border,** which is 2km from Corumbá, leave from the *rodoviária* in Pça. da República; ask for the bus to the *"fronteira"* (20min.; several per day; R$1.50). Across the border is the small town of Quijarro. To get from here to the train station at Puerto Suarez you must hire a taxi for the 15km journey. There are several currency exchange offices in Quijarro and Puerto Suárez. If you are passing into Bolivia for the day just to get bus or train tickets you do not need to get an exit or entry stamp.

TRANSPORTATION

The city is located 400km west of Campo Grande and 20km east of Puerto Suárez, Bolivia. A well-maintained road connects the three cities. Most tourists arrive in Corumbá by bus, though the city also has a small airport.

Flights: Aeroporto Internacional de Corumbá, Rua Porto Cabrero s/n (☎231 3322). Upon leaving the *rodoviária,* turn left onto Rua Porto Cabrero; the tiny airport is 20min. away at the end of the street. The airport has just one airline, **Gensa** (☎232 3851), which makes daily flights to **Campo Grande** (1hr.; 2:40pm; R$227). There are no luggage storage facilities or car rental agencies inside the airport.

Buses: Rodoviária de Corumbá is 20min. south of town. To reach the *centro* turn left on Rua Porto Cabrero and then take a quick right onto Rua Anotônio João, which will lead you to the main *praça.* **Andorinha** (☎231 2033) sends buses to **Campo Grande** (6hr.; 11 per day 7am-noon; R$48) via **Miranda** (3hr.; R$25); **Cuiabá** (14hr.; noon; R$104); **Rio de Janeiro** (26hr.; 11:30am; R$151); **São Paulo** (22hr.; 2 per day 11:30am-6pm; R$123). **Cruzeiro do Sol** (☎231 2383) goes to **Bonito** (8½hr.; M-Sa 1:30pm; R$65). For information on **transport to Bolivia** see p. 332. Luggage storage at **Guarda Volumes.** R$2 per day. Open 5:30am-8pm. Tour operators will usually meet you at the *rodoviária* and offer a free ride into town.

Car Rental: Localiza, Rua Cabral 2064 (☎231 6000; www.localiza.com.br), in front of the airport on the corner of Rua Rocha. Class A cars R$29 per day plus R$0.46 per km; R$89 with unlimited km. You must be at least 21 years of age and be able to provide a credit card to rent. Open M-F 9am-5pm, Sa 9am-noon.

Taxi: Taxis can always be found in front of the *rodoviária* and around Pça. da República. **Moto-taxis** (☎232 2956) congregate outside the *rodoviária* on Rua Antônio Coelho, near Pça. da República.

ORIENTATION & PRACTICAL INFORMATION

The town is divided into the **lower city,** where you'll find the port, and the **upper city,** where most of the tourist activity takes place. The lower city consists of just one street, **Rua Manoel Cavassa,** which runs along the Rio Paraguai. Tourists come here to rent boats for fishing excursions into the Pantanal. The upper city is centered on **Praça da República,** where the intercity *rodoviária* and most sights are located.

From here **Rua Antônio João** runs north-south, connecting the town with the local *rodoviária*. **Rua Delamare** extends west from Pça. da República and is a popular restaurant strip. One block west of the *praça*, running perpendicular to Rua Antônio João, is **Rua Frei Mariano,** where most banks and services are found. If you follow Rua Frei Mariano north the street curves down to the lower city, changing its name to **Rua José Banifacio de Piso** as it does so.

TOURIST & FINANCIAL SERVICES

Tourist Office: Tourists often have trouble finding the local **SEMATUR Tourist Office,** Rua José Banifacio de Piso 275 (☎231 7336). Follow Rua Frei Mariano north toward the port and as the street curves left and descends to the port, look for the office on your right. The office stocks a pile of brochures about the Pantanal and can help with choosing a reputable tour operator. Be sure to pick up the Estrada Parque map (R$3) before leaving. Open M-F 8:20-11am and 1:30-6pm.

Consulates: Bolivia, Rua Antônio Maria Coelho 881 (☎231 5605). Issues entry stamps to Bolivia and can help with obtaining visas, though few nationalities require visas to enter the country. Open M-F 8am-noon and 2-4pm.

Currency Exchange: There are no official currency exchange offices in the city, though most of the merchants on Rua 13 de Junho will change Brazilian, Bolivian, and US currency. **Tentaça,** Rua 13 de Junho 883 (☎232 4267), is a toy shop that offers good rates. Open M-Sa 8am-6pm. To change traveler's checks try **Banco do Brasil,** Rua 13 de Junho 914 (☎231 2686), near Pça. Independência. Open M-F 10am-3pm.

Banks: Bradesco, Rua Delamare 1067 (☎231 6917), has Visa ATMs. Open M-F 10am-3pm. **HSBC,** Rua Delamare 1068 (☎231 5455), has 24hr. Cirrus and MC ATMs. Open M-F 10am-3pm.

LOCAL SERVICES

Luggage Storage: At the *rodoviária*. Open 5:30am-8pm. R$2 per day.

Ticket Agencies: Mutum Turismo, Rua Frei Mariano 17 (☎231 1818; mutum@pantanalnet.com.br), sells bus and flight tickets. They also have a good line of tours including a 3hr. city tour (min. 6 people, R$20 per person), a 3hr. Puerto Suárez tour (min. 6 people, R$20 per person), and a full-day Pantanal "photo safari" (min. 6 people, R$105 per person). Open M-F 7:30am-6pm, Sa 7:30am-noon. MC/V. **Pantur,** Rua Frei Mariano 1013 (☎231 2000), has similar services and tours, and can arrange stays at local *fazendas* for a commission. Open M-F 8am-6pm, Sa 8am-noon, Su 9am-noon.

Camping Equipment: Casa São Miguel, Rua Frei Mariano 295 (☎231 3208), on Pça. Independência. In addition to outdoor equipment, the store also stocks cowboy hats, saddles, stirrups, and boots. Open M-F 7:30am-7:30pm.

Markets: Ohara Supermercado, Rua Dom Aquino 621 (☎231 5920), on the corner of Rua Antônio João. Overflowing with fresh fruits, breads, and canned goods. Open daily 7am-7pm. **Supermercado Frutal,** Rua 13 de Junho 538 (☎231 1423), 1 block from Pça. da República. Sells food and bamboo fishing rods. Open M-Sa 7:30am-8pm.

Laundry: Lav-Bem Lavanderia, Rua Antônio João 730 (☎232 8001), between the *rodoviária* and the *centro*. R$1 per piece. Open daily 7:30-11:30am and 1:30-6pm.

EMERGENCY & COMMUNICATIONS

Police: Polícia Federal, Pça. da República 51 (☎231 5848). Open M-F 7:30am-5:30pm. Another office at the *rodoviária*. Open M-F 7:30am-5:30pm.

Hospital: Hospital Candade, Rua 15 de Novembro 854 (☎231 2993).

Telephone: Posto de Serviço Telefônico, Rua Cuiabá 941 (☎232 8154), housed inside a tiny mall. Open M-F 8-11:30am and 1:30-5pm.

Internet Access: Terra Net, Rua América 677 (☎231 1221). R$4 per hr. Open M-F 8-11:30am and 1:30-6pm, Sa 8am-noon.

Post Office: The **post office,** Rua Delamare 708 (☎231 5877), in front of Pça. da República, has fax and telegram services. Open M-F 8:30am-5pm, Sa 8-11:30am. **Postal code:** 79300-000.

ACCOMMODATIONS

Don't expect much from the hotels in Corumbá: most accommodations here lack both comfort and character. Avoid the *simples* and splurge on the *apartamentos.* All hotels are located around Pça. da República and Rua Delamare, which allows travelers to check out a few options before committing.

Green Track Hostel, Rua Antônio João 216 (☎231 2258; greentk@terra.com.br), near Pça. da República. A superb hostel with superior amenities and atmosphere, run by a good-natured family that makes every effort to make guests feel at home. The dorms are decent, with firm beds but no A/C. The hostel's reputation for friendliness earns it a great deal of traffic from international travelers, which makes organizing groups for Pantanal excursions relatively easy. The hostel also organizes some of the best tours available to the southern Pantanal. Free pick-up from the *rodoviária.* Laundry R$4 per load. Dorms R$15. Doubles R$30. ❶

Hotel Angola, Rua Antônio Maria Coelho 524 (☎231 7727). The modest reception area belies spacious, comfortable *apartamentos.* Each room has TV, closet, and small couch. Popular with vacationing Brazilians and international tourists. Internet access R$4 per hr. Singles R$13, with A/C R$18; doubles R$25, with A/C R$25; triples R$25, with A/C R$35. ❶

Nacional Palace Hotel, Rua América 936 (☎231 6202; hnacion@brasinet.com.br), near the corner of Rua Frei Mariano. The city's only upscale lodging option, equipped with swimming pool and slide, football field, pool tables, and sports room. All 98 rooms have A/C, TV, phone, and *frigo-bar.* Spacious suites have a separate lounge and veranda, and are great for couples and families. Internet R$8 per hr. Singles R$67; doubles R$84; triples R$105; quads R$120. 1-2 person suites R$100. MC/V. ❹

Laura Vicuña Hotel, Rua Cuiabá 775 (☎231 5874; hulan@terra.com.br). A decent option close to the *centro.* All rooms have TV and A/C. The wooden animals in the lounge and reception area were carved by the owner himself. Free parking. Breakfast included. Laundry R$1 per piece. Singles R$30, with bath R$35; doubles R$40, with bath R$45; triples R$55, with bath R$60. MC/V. ❷

Saliette Hotel, Rua Delamare 889 (☎231 6246). The best of the budget hotels that line Rua Delamare, with bigger rooms and broader beds. Aside from their size, these basic rooms are similar to the others on the strip. Singles R$12, with A/C and TV R$20, with private bath R$25; doubles R$22, with A/C and TV R$35, with private bath R$40. ❶

Hotel Rimoneiro, Rua Cabral 879 (☎231 5530), near the *rodoviária.* An otherwise excellent hotel too far from the *centro* to be popular, as the nearest restaurants are more than 20min. away. Those looking to catch an early bus in the morning would do well to take advantage of the hotel's 18 *apartamentos,* each of which comes equipped with private bath, A/C, and TV. The hotel's best feature is the gregarious staff. Singles R$25; doubles R$35; triples R$45. ❶

FOOD

Corumbá has some decent dining options, most of which are located in the upper part of the city near the *centro.* With the notable exception of Baís do Chopp there are no restaurants by the port.

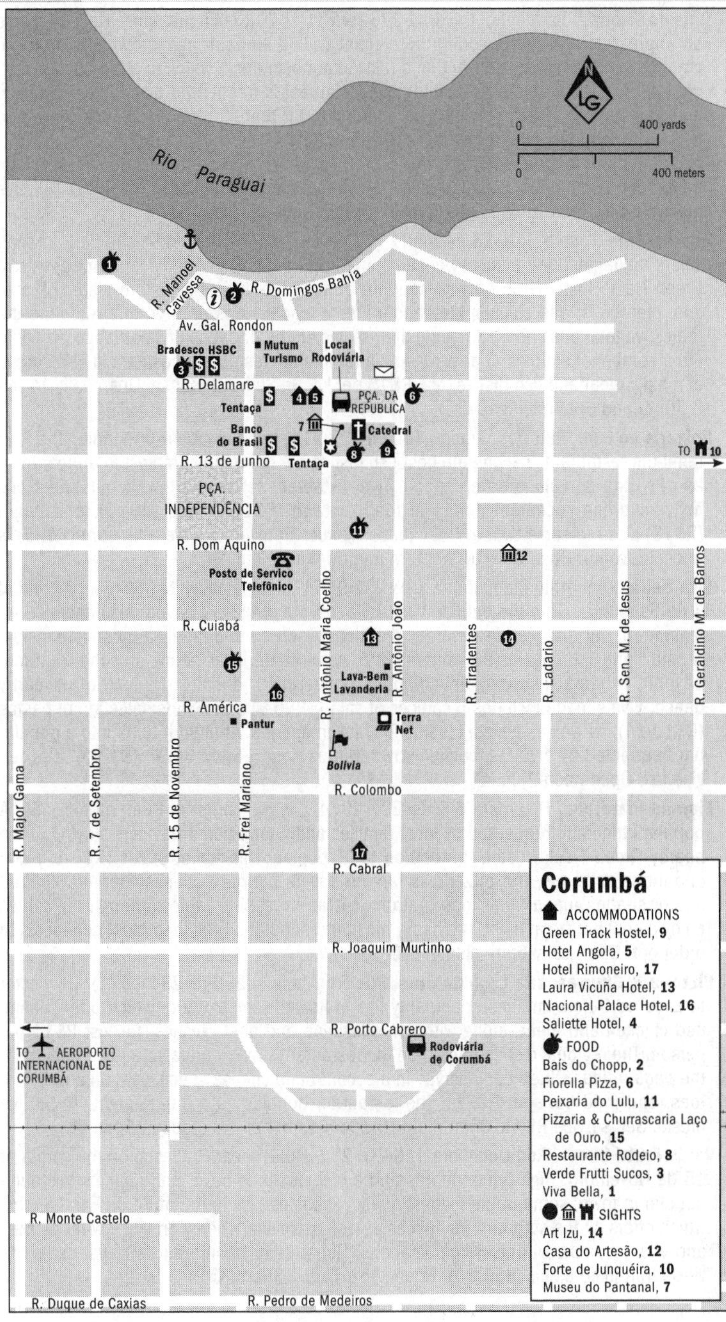
Rio Paraguai
400 yards
400 meters
R. Manoel Cavessa
R. Domingos Bahia
Av. Gal. Rondon
Bradesco HSBC
Mutum Turismo
Local Rodoviária
R. Delamare
Tentaça
PÇA. DA REPUBLICA
Banco do Brasil
Catedral
R. 13 de Junho
Tentaça
TO 10
PÇA. INDEPENDÊNCIA
R. Dom Aquino
Posto de Servico Telefônico
R. Cuiabá
Lava-Bem Lavanderia
R. América
Pantur
Terra Net
Bolivia
R. Colombo
R. Cabral
R. Joaquim Murtinho
R. Porto Cabrero
Rodoviária de Corumbá
TO AEROPORTO INTERNACIONAL DE CORUMBÁ
R. Monte Castelo
R. Duque de Caxias
R. Pedro de Medeiros
R. Major Gama
R. 7 de Setembro
R. 15 de Novembro
R. Frei Mariano
R. Antônio Maria Coelho
R. Antônio João
R. Tiradentes
R. Ladario
R. Sen. M. de Jesus
R. Geraldino M. de Barros
Corumbá
ACCOMMODATIONS
Green Track Hostel, 9
Hotel Angola, 5
Hotel Rimoneiro, 17
Laura Vicuña Hotel, 13
Nacional Palace Hotel, 16
Saliette Hotel, 4
FOOD
Bais do Chopp, 2
Fiorella Pizza, 6
Peixaria do Lulu, 11
Pizzaria & Churrascaria Laço de Ouro, 15
Restaurante Rodeio, 8
Verde Frutti Sucos, 3
Viva Bella, 1
SIGHTS
Art Izu, 14
Casa do Artesão, 12
Forte de Junquéira, 10
Museu do Pantanal, 7

CENTER-WEST

Baís do Chopp, Rua Manoel Cavessa 275 (☎231 1079), facing the port. Housed inside an impressive colonial building, the elegant ceiling and soft lighting work together to create a simultaneously polished and relaxed atmosphere in which to enjoy savory international dishes. In the early evening the restaurant is frequented by couples, families, and tourists, but at night it becomes a popular bar that features live bands playing to twenty-somethings. Among the favorite dishes are *filé de pintado com legumes* (R$12) and chocolate fondue with fresh fruit (R$40 serves 2). The menu also features several Italian and Asian options, including sampler plates of sushi (R$20). Cover R$1.50. Live music Th-Sa. Open Tu-W 5:30-10pm, Th-Sa 5:30pm-1am. ❸

Restaurante Rodeio, Rua 13 de Junho 760 (☎231 6477), behind Museu do Pantanal. Offers the largest and tastiest per-kilo spread in Corumbá, and a discount for guests of Green Track Hostel (R$5 off with coupon). Among the usual dishes are plates of lasagna, meatballs, and chicken stroganoff. Fresh, tender slabs of meat rotate around the tables; vegetarians choose to gorge themselves on the 45 types of salad. Also available are a number of soups and deserts. At dinnertime the restaurant has an a la carte menu of mainly meat and fish dishes. M-F R$15 per kg, Sa-Su R$20 per kg. Open daily 11am-3:30pm and 6pm-midnight. ❷

Peixaria do Lulu, Rua Dom Aquino 700 (☎232 2142). In the cities surrounding the Pantanal the restaurants serving the best fish dishes are often the humblest in appearance, and Peixaria do Lulu is no exception. This restaurant serves the town's most delicious fish, including succulent plates of fried *pintado* (R$16), *pacú* (R$15), and *bagre* (R$18) sized to serve two, at the cheapest prices in town. The *filé a urucum* (R$25) is a local favorite. Open daily 10am-4pm and 6pm-midnight. ❷

Viva Bella, Rua Arthur Mangabeira 1 (☎232 9464), in a small white house at the end of 7 de Setembro. From the outside Viva Bella looks more like a private residence than a restaurant, but that just underscores the friendly service and family atmosphere inside. A small and intimate establishment with views of the port below and the Pantanal beyond, it has a distinctly beach-house atmosphere, despite the lack of a nearby beach. Viva's menu includes 6 choices of salad (R$6-8) and a wide selection of pastas (R$10-14), as well as typical steak and chicken options. At night it turns into a popular bar frequented by a young, casual crowd. Happy Hour 5-6pm. Cover R$1.50. 10% service tax. Open noon-2am. ❷

Fiorella Pizza, Rua Delamare 647 (☎231 2974), on the corner of Rua Antônio João. A popular little joint frequented by local families and international travelers staying at the nearby Green Track Hostel. In addition to its popular thick-crust pizzas (R$8-12) and enormous calzones, the pizzeria is famous for its *catipury* cheese topping. Limited indoor seating means that most patrons eat at street-side tables. Though the tables enjoy a cool breeze at night, the heavy mosquito population will lead most non-locals to order out. Open daily 6pm-midnight. ❷

Pizzaria & Churrascaria Laço de Ouro, Rua Frei Mariano 556 (☎231 7371). The secret to Laço de Ouro's immense popularity lies in its self-serve *rodízio,* which offers unlimited chicken and meat—along with some lasagna and pasta dishes—for just R$11 per person. The regional dishes offered on the restaurant's menu are also a good option; try the *paçu urucum* (fried *paçu* served in a coconut and cheese sauce, with onions, tomatoes, and fried banana; R$21). The restaurant doubles as a bar at night. Th-Sa live music. Self service R$11. Open daily 10:30am-1am, per-kilo stops at 1pm. ❷

Verde Frutti Sucos, Rua Delamare 1164 (☎231 3032), near Bradesco on the corner of 15 de Novembro. High temperatures and a lack of shade have made juice stalls quite popular in town; some of the highest quality *sucos* can be found at Verde Frutti Sucos, which offers all the standard fruit juices as well as several energy drinks, low-fat blends, and vitamin-packed tropical combinations. Guaranteed to cure all that ails you is the verde fruit juice blend (R$3.30). Open M-Sa 7am-7:30pm. ❶

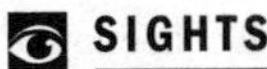 SIGHTS

Corumbá enjoyed prominence as a busy port city in the early 1800s, but once speedier land routes were developed the city's importance dwindled. Today only an imposing row of colonial buildings along the waterfront survives to remind visitors of the city's former glory. Worth checking out is Báis do Chopp (p. 336), one such colonial building that has been fully restored to its original condition.

ART IZU. No visit to Corumbá would be complete without paying a visit to the home of the city's most eccentric local artist. As you approach you'll see colorful engravings in the sidewalk, most of which were carved by visitors as a sign of appreciation for the artist's work. Looking up you'll notice giant sculptures of cranes and herons from the Pantanal looming down from the gates. In the front garden stands a 10-foot bronze statue of Jesus surrounded by bronze goats, alligators, and birds. Roman soldiers guard the doorway, to either side of the house stand colorful life-size Christian figures carved from wood and stone, and on the front balcony sit three ample "busts" carved from stone and decorated with five-*centavo* coins. Knock on the front door to speak with the artist herself, but don't interrupt her during lunchtime. *(Rua Cuiabá 558. ☎231 2040, 231 3115. Open M-F 8-11am and 1:30-5pm.)*

MUSEU DO PANTANAL. This museum contains some fascinating local artifacts that have been divided into four separate rooms. Among some of the exhibits in the "Colonist Room" are a cappuccino machine from the early 1900s, a dentist's chair with spit bowl from the mid-1800s, and a tombstone with accompanying coffin from the early 1800s. The "Pantanal Room" features a collection of stuffed animals and birds. *(Pça. da República s/n. ☎231 5757. Open M-F 8am-noon and 2-5:30pm.)*

CASA DO ARTESÃO. At first glance the grounds may seem abandoned, but inside the small buildings you'll find local artisans hard at work. Tourists usually come to commission crafts or to buy pre-made goods, but travelers interested in learning how to make the crafts themselves are welcome to join the artists at work for a small fee. Among the craft shops are stalls selling woolen clothes, hand-woven baskets, pottery, and fine lace. *(Rua Dom Aquino 405. ☎231 2715. Open M-F 8-11:30am and 2-5:30pm, Sa 8am-noon.)*

FORTE DE JUNQUÉIRA. Back when Corumbá was an important frontier town this fort helped guard the state from enemies across the Rio Paraguai. Though many forts were built near the city, only Forte De Junquéira remains intact. The hexagonal fort has 12 75mm cannons on display which date back to 1887, and tours are given upon request. *(Follow Rua Dom Aquino east out of town, bear left at the athletic track and walk along the waterfront for 10min. Open M-Sa 8am-5pm.)*

MIRANDA ☎67

Miranda saw most of its action in the early 1800s as a defensive outpost on the frontier. Today the town is significantly quieter, with most people making their money through tourism and cattle farming. The town is strategically located between all of the state's major attractions: the Pantanal to the north, Cuiabá to the east, Corumbá to the west, and ecotourism boomtown Bonito to the south. As the town has no attractions of its own, most tourists usually just pass through on their way to someplace else. However, Miranda is most useful to travelers with limited time who wish to sample the Pantanal; surrounding the town are some of the finest day-use *fazendas* in the southern Pantanal (p. 320). Miranda is also a good place to stock up on supplies before heading down the Estrada Parque, which begins a few dozen miles down the road.

Most tourists arrive at Miranda's *rodoviária* and mistake the small collection of stores that surround it as the *centro*, but in fact the *centro* is a 20min. walk down **Rua Barão do Rio Branco.** Those heading into town usually opt for a taxi, but travelers who want to walk should follow Rua Barão do Rio Branco and ask along the way for directions to **Praça Ageno Carrilho.** The **rodoviária** has **Andorinha** (☎242 1249) buses to Campo Grande (3hr.; 11 per day 10:15am-1:55am; R$23) and Corumbá (3hr.; 11 per day 9:20am-2:50am; R$23), via the entrance to the **Estrada Parque** (1hr.; R$10). Travelers looking to catch a bus to Bonito will have to head into the *centro*. **Cruzeira do Sul,** Rua General Camaro 311 (☎242 1060) has a small office about three blocks from Pça. Ageno Carrilho and sends a daily minibus to Bonito (3hr.; 5pm; R$18). For taxis between the *rodoviária* and *centro* (R$7) call **Moto-taxi Barão** (☎242 1564) or **Fimoto Taxis** (☎242 2768). To arrange daytrips to nearby *fazendas* or to organize local fishing trips contact **Aguas do Pantanal,** Av. Afonso Pena 367, the best travel agency in town. They charge a small commission for all travel arrangements. (☎242 1242; www.aguasdopantanal.com.br. Open M-F 7am-11pm.) Stock up on fishing and camping gear at **Tudo para Pesca e Camping,** across from the *rodoviária*. The store also rents motorboats (R$100 per day) for fishing excursions. (☎242 1312. Open M-F 7am-6pm.) There are Visa ATMs at **Bradesco,** Rua 13 de Junho 89 (☎242 1453; open M-F 10am-3pm) and **Banco do Brasil,** Rua Tiradentes 364 (☎242 1042; open M-F 11am-4pm). **Farmácia Nossa do Carmo,** Rua 13 de Junho 217, supplies the townspeople with drugs. (☎242 4007. Open M-Sa 7am-6pm, Su 7am-noon.) The **post office** is at Av. Afonso Pena 185. (☎242 1203. Open M-F 8:30am-4pm, Sa 8-11:30am.) **Postal code:** 79380-000.

Pousada Aquas do Pantanal ❹, Av. Afonso Pena 367, just two blocks from the main *praça*, is a tranquil place that has many hanging plants and palm trees. Spacious rooms have A/C, TV, and *frigo-bar;* the suites even offer private saunas and tiny hydromassage tubs. (☎242 1840. Internet access R$3 per hr. *Luxo* singles R$70; doubles R$90; triples R$120. Suite singles R$80; doubles R$110; triples R$170.) **Hotel Roma ❶,** Pça. Ageno Carrilho 356, on the main *praça*, has rooms with soft beds and big-screen TVs. (☎242 1321. Laundry R$1.50 per piece. Singles R$12, with A/C R$25; doubles R$20, with A/C R$45. Suite singles with A/C and private bath R$35; doubles with A/C and private bath R$55.) **Pastelaria Harmonia ❶,** Rua Francisco Rebuá 90, one block from the *rodoviária*, serves meat and chicken pies, pastries, and juices. (☎242 3521. Open M-Sa 6am-8pm.) For more filling meals you'll have to journey into the *centro* to **Restaurante Caneão ❷,** Rua General Camaro 308. The restaurant serves surprisingly filling *pratos feitos* (R$7) of rice, beans, and a serving of meat or chicken. (☎242 1309. Open daily 11am-8pm.)

BONITO ☎67

The secret of Bonito's impressive natural environment remained hidden until the early 1990s, but since then a huge influx of local and international travelers have descended on the town to take advantage of its spectacular surroundings. A series of subterranean caves, towering waterfalls, and underground lakes are strewn throughout the landscape surrounding Bonito, but the region's unbelievably crystal-clear rivers are what have made it the ecotourism capital of Brazil. Teeming with several hundred species of fish, the incredibly lucid waters give travelers to the area the opportunity to swim hand in fin with scores of fish, some of which grow to over a meter in length.

Though the area around Bonito is full of attractions, the town itself has little to offer visitors. The more than 30 major sights in the region are each located anywhere between eight and sixty kilometers from Bonito and are spread out in all directions; a car can be very useful and even then a full day may be necessary just to visit a single sight.

TRANSPORTATION

Bus Station: Rodoviária de Bonito is 10min. from the *centro.* Follow Rua Pedro Álvares Cabral from the *rodoviária* for 3 blocks and turn right when you reach Rua Cel. Pilad Rebuá; this street will take you to the main *praça.* **Cruzeiro do Sul** (☎255 1606) sends buses to: **Campo Grande** (5hr.; 2 per day 6am-4pm; R$32); **Corumbá** (6hr.; M-Sa 6am; R$40); **Miranda** (3hr.; M-Sa 6am; R$19); **Ponta Porã** (5hr.; M-Sa noon; R$32). There are no lockers or luggage storage facilities.

Car Rental: The attractions surrounding the town are best reached by car. **Yes Rent-a-Car,** Rua Sen. Felintro Müller 656 (☎255 1702), is the only rental agency in town. Class A cars with 150km per day begin at R$73; R$80 with unlimited km. You must be 21 years of age and be able to provide a credit card to rent. The insurance liability is R$1800. Open M-F 8am-5pm, Sa-Su 8am-noon.

Taxi: If you can't rent a car to explore the nearby attractions you'll have to rely on cabs and moto-taxis to take you around town. **Arara Moto-taxi,** Rua Cel. Pilad Rebuá 1541 (☎255 1238), has good rates; R$60 round-trip to Rio do Prata and R$18 round-trip to Rio de Sucre. Open daily 6am-midnight.

ORIENTATION & PRACTICAL INFORMATION

Bonito is a small town with roads laid out in an easily navigable grid. **Rua Cel. Pilad Rebuá** is the town's main boulevard. Here you'll find almost all hotels, restaurants, and services for the traveler, all in an area bounded to the north by **Rua Nelson dos Santos** and to the south by **Rua Pedro Alvares Cabral.** At the intersection of Rua Cel. Pilad Rebuá and **Rua 15 de Novembro** is the town's primary meeting place, known as the **Praça da República.**

TOURIST & FINANCIAL SERVICES

Tourist Office: While there is no official tourist office most tour agencies moonlight as info booths. The most reliable of these is the **Muito Bonito Travel Office,** Rua Cel. Pilad Rebuá 1448 (☎255 2555, 255 1645; reservas@muitobonito.com.br), in Pousada Muito Bonito. They offer tons of information about the surrounding sights, and trips to the Pantanal. English spoken.

Banks: Bradesco, Rua Cel. Pilad Rebuá 1942 (☎255 1341), has Visa ATMs. Open M-F 9am-2pm. **Banco do Brasil,** Rua Luís da Costa Leite 2279 (☎255 1659), in Pça. da República, exchanges currency and traveler's checks. Open M-F 9am-2pm.

LOCAL SERVICES

Ticket Agencies: Panttour, Rua Sen. Felintro Müller 578 (☎255 1000, 255 3535; panttur@bonitonline.com.br), next to VoVo Restaurante. Sells tickets for buses and airlines. Open M-F 7am-6pm.

Tour Operators: To visit the sights surrounding Bonito travelers must be accompanied by an accredited guide; tour operators in the city usually arrange for the guide to meet you at the sights. When you pay for a tour you are usually only paying for the cost of the tour and the guide. Transportation to the sight is *not* included and can sometimes be as much as the tour itself, if not more. Unless you rent a car to visit the sights (which is recommended) you'll have to split the cost of a cab with other travelers or wing it solo on a moto-taxi. Most agents are happy to help you arrange tour groups.

Muito Bonito Travel Office, Rua Cel. Pilad Rebuá 1448 (☎255 2555, 255 1645; reservas@muitobonito.com.br), located inside Pousada Muito Bonito Pousada. Has the most informed and helpful staff in town and can arrange groups to split the cost of transportation. English spoken. Open M-F 7am-9pm.

Tamandúr, Rua Cel. Pilad Rebuá 1890 (☎255 5000). Caters mostly to families and groups. One of the more reputable operations in town. Open M-F 7am-9pm.

Igarape Tour, Rua Cel. Pilad Rebuá 1853 (☎255 1733). Has a large-screen TV and videos of the tours. Limited English spoken. Open M-F 7am-10pm.

Carandá Ecotours, Rua Cel. Pilad Rebuá 1521 (☎255 1695; www.carandatour.com), just off Novo Jerusalém. Based out of Pousada Remusa. Expect more personalized service than elsewhere. Open M-F 7am-8:30pm.

Canaã Tour, Rua Cel. Pilad Rebuá 1376 (☎255 1282, 255 2090; canaatour@hotmail.com). Operating for over 7 years, making it one of the safer bets. Open M-F 7am-8pm.

Camping Supplies: Central de Adventuras, Rua Cel. Pilad Rebuá 1861 (☎255 2026), next to Ritz Burger. Sells wetsuits, snorkeling gear, and sandals. Open daily 8am-midnight. **Agrofar,** Rua Cel. Pilad Rebuá 165 (☎255 1680). Stocks hiking equipment, cowboy hats, knives, and inner tubes. Open M-F 7am-6pm, Sa-Su 8am-noon.

Markets: Mercado do Praça, Rua 15 de Novembro 798 (☎255 1698), sells all the canned regulars. Open daily 6:30am-midnight. **Sacolão Bonito,** Rua Cel. Pilad Rebuá 1707 (☎9606 4107), has fresh fruit. Open M-Sa 7am-7:30pm, Su 7am-noon.

Laundry: Omega Lavanderia, Rua Cel. Pilad Rebuá 873 (☎9986 4115, 255 1341), at the corner of Rua Nestor Fernandes about 9 blocks from Pça. da República. R$1 per piece. Open M-Sa 7am-7pm.

EMERGENCY & COMMUNICATIONS

Police: Delegacia Districtal de Polícia, Rua Nova Mato Grosso s/n (☎661 2132).

24hr. Pharmacy: Farmácia Drogacruz, Rua Cel. Pilad Rebuá 1699 (☎255 1554, 255 1559). Open M-Sa 7am-9pm, Su 7am-noon.

Hospital: Darcy João Bigattan, Rua Pedro Apóstolo 201 (☎255 3448, 255 3455).

Internet Access: Cybernet Café, Rua 29 de Maio 912 (☎255 3341). Drinks and small snacks are available while you type. R$6 per hr. Open daily 8am-11pm. Faster connections can be found at **Central de Adventuras,** Rua Cel. Pilad Rebuá 1861 (☎255 2026). R$7 per hr. Open daily 8am-midnight.

Post Office: Rua Cel. Pilad Rebuá 1759 (☎255 1723). Open M-F 8:30am-4pm, Sa 9-11:30am. **Postal code:** 79290-000.

ACCOMMODATIONS

Almost all the hostels are within two blocks of Rua Cel. Pilad Rebuá. Most operate travel agencies that can be helpful for planning trips into the area. Expect prices to increase by 25% on the weekends at most places, and 30% during the holidays.

Pousada Muito Bonito, Rua Cel. Pilad Rebuá 1448 (☎255 2555, 255 1645; reservas@muitobonito.com.br). A charming hostel that lives up to its auspicious name, run by local guide Mario and his son Vincius. Hanging plants and hammocks contribute to the hostel's relaxing feel, as do the small pond and garden. Each room comes with exceedingly comfortable mattresses, A/C, TV, and private bath. The owner works hard to make guests feel at home, and the hostel's travel agency is the best in town at organizing transportation to the nearby attractions. English spoken. Breakfast included. *Quartos* R$25, with *frigo-bar* R$30. ❶

Hotel Pirá Miúna, Rua Luís da Costa Leite 1792 (☎255 1058; www.piramiunahotel.com.br), 1 block off Rua Cel. Pilad Rebuá. An upper-end wooden lodge overflowing with charm; it offers the amenities of a hotel and the comfort of a home. The *apartamentos* converge around a large swimming pool with nearby hydromassage tub and barbecue. All rooms have A/C, TV, *frigo-bar,* and phone. The lounge downstairs has a big-screen TV and is an excellent place to socialize. *Luxo* rooms are slightly bigger than standard *apartamentos.* Wheelchair accessible. Laundry R$2 per piece. Singles R$70; doubles R$90; triples R$120; quads R$150. *Luxo* singles R$80; doubles R$100; triples R$130; quads R$170. MC/V. ❹

Pousada Rio Bonito, Rua Cel. Pilad Rebuá 1800 (☎225 1877). The modest entrance belies the quality rooms and personable service found within. Each *apartamento* is differently decorated and furnished. All are incredibly comfortable and have A/C, TV, and private bath. Guests can return as late as they wish in spite of the fact that reception closes at 11pm. Breakfast included. Reception 7am-11pm. High season singles R$30; doubles R$60; triples R$90. Low-season singles R$15; doubles R$30; triples R$45. ❶

Bonito Youth Hostel (HI), Rua Lúcio Burralho 716 (☎255 1462, 255 1022; www.ajbonito.com.br), 30min. from the *centro;* the hostel offers free pick-up from the *rodoviária.* With a swimming pool, BBQ grill, lounge area, and pool table, the hostel is well fitted to entertain visitors during their stay in Bonito. The only drawback is the distance from town. Rooms are basic but include private lockers. The hostel also offers bicycles for guests to cycle into town and back. Towels R$2. Lunch and dinner R$10. Laundry R$1 per piece. Camping R$10 per person (includes breakfast). Dorms R$22, non-members R$29. Singles R$23, non-members R$30. ❶

Hotel Canaá, Rua Cel. Pilad Rebuá 1376 (☎255 1255, 255 1958; www.hotelcanaa.com.br). The hotel's exterior hides inviting rooms. The lounge has comfortable couches, and *apartamentos* have large baths. Wheelchair accessible. Breakfast included. Laundry R$3 per piece. Internet R$7 per hr. Singles R$25; doubles R$40. ❶

Pousada Gaivota Pantaneira, Rua Das Flores 1066 (☎255 2597), on the corner of Pedro Álvares Cabral, 2 blocks from the *rodoviária* on the way to Rua Cel. Pilad Rebuá. A good choice for travelers looking for cheap digs. Roomy dorms are well-maintained. Breakfast R$5. Reception 6:30am-9pm. Dorms with A/C R$15. ❶

FOOD

Cantinho do Peixe, Rua 31 de Março 1918 (☎255 3381, 9959 2726). Walking along Rua Cel. Pilad Rebuá toward Pça. da República, turn left at Droga Cruz onto Rua 29 de Maio. Walk 3 blocks farther and turn right onto Rua 31 de Março. Don't be surprised to see limos parked alongside pickup trucks—you'll find all sorts eating at this little gem. From visiting politicians to cowboys from nearby *fazendas,* the delectable regional fish dinners served here demand attention from everyone. The restaurant operates out of a private residence, underscoring the amiable, familial atmosphere. The hands-down favorite is *moqueca pantaneira* (fried catfish with palmito, tomato, and banana, served with salad, rice, and potato chips; R$28 serves 2). If you haven't eaten all day you might want to start with the piranha soups (R$3) or share a sampler plate with a friend (R$7). Most of the dishes range in price from R$11-15 (for 1) and R$22-25 (for 2). English menu available. Open M-Sa 11am-2pm and 6-10pm. ❷

Sale & Pepe, Rua 29 de Maio 971 (☎255 1822). An intimate dining establishment specializing in Asian cuisine, decorated with wooden sculptures and contemporary artwork. Standard options include the *carne com brocolli* (meat with broccoli and noodles; R$15) and vegetable tempura (R$14). During the week the menu includes dishes like grilled salmon with rice and vegetables (R$18). Among the regional dishes offered is fried catfish with banana (R$22). Open Tu-Su 6:30-11:30pm. ❷

Churrascaria Pantanal, Rua Cel. Pilad Rebuá 1808 (☎255 2763). Hordes of locals converge here every night. Some come for the plates of catfish but the vast majority are here for the huge portions of meat and chicken. Among the more popular dishes is the *jacaré na telha* (alligator meat with coconut milk, potato, onions, and peppers; R$38 serves 2). Equally good and significantly cheaper is the *bonito picanha* (roasted beef with garlic bread and wine; R$22 serves 2). Backpackers often opt for the economical *jarra de vinho* (R$10). Open daily 11am-3pm and 6-11pm. ❷

Padaria Santa Rita, Rua Cel. Pilad Rebuá 1745 (☎255 2825). This bakery serves enough sweets to keep the local dentist in business for the forseeable future; the strawberry rolls (R$2) are topped with chocolate and the lemon pies come with extra whipped cream upon request. The bakery also offers some filling sandwiches (R$2). If you have the time, sit down and enjoy one of the tasty pizzas. For a change of pace order a *Paulistinha* (french bread topped with shredded chicken, palmito, and onion; R$4.20). English menu available. Open daily 5:30am-10:30pm. ❶

O Casarão, Rua Cel. Pilad Rebuá 1835 (☎255 1970), housed in a quaint thatched hut. Tourists looking to sample the local dishes are well advised to try the self-serve lunch option (R$9.50) at this relatively upscale establishment. The spread includes over 10 plates of native fish, 12 plates of regional meat, and 5 types of local desserts. Included in the options are *caldo de piranha* (piranha soup; R$6) and *carne do sol* (sun-dried meat; R$15). Open daily 11am-3pm and 6:30-11pm. MC/V. ❷

Castellababe, Rua Cel. Pilad Rebuá 2168 (☎255 1713), housed in a large building that resembles a medieval castle, about a block from Pça. da República. More of a take-out joint than a sit-in restaurant, serving heaping portions of BBQ meat and tasty pizza (R$13-18). The *bonito pizza* (palmito, mushrooms, onions, and mozzarella) is highly recommended. Has a few pasta options, but most come for the cheap plates of *jacaré* (R$38) and fried catfish (R$30), which are meant to be shared. Tourists have asked for pizzas topped with *jacaré*; an alligator pie usually costs R$30-35. Open daily 11am-2:30pm and 6-11pm. MC/V. ❷

SIGHTS & OUTDOOR ACTIVITIES

Bonito has no sights within the city itself, but there is an abundance of natural attractions in the surrounding countryside. The *fazendas* and private farms upon which the attractions are located collaborate with the tourist offices in arranging tours for visitors. Although these offices promote anywhere between 25 and 30 of these attractions, only a handful are truly exceptional. Tour prices can fluctuate by as much as 20% between the high and low seasons.

RIO DA PRATA. A trip to Rio da Prata begins with a 50min. trek through virgin rainforest; tourists must wear wetsuits for the duration of the hike but thankfully the trail is well-shaded and has several rest stops to cool down. Once at the entrance to Rio da Prata tourists are asked to slowly ease into the water—so as not to disturb the wildlife—and then spend about 20min. acclimating to the water and its resident fish. This done, tourists begin a three-kilometer swim downstream through crystalline waters filled with *dourados*, *pintados*, *pacús*, and *pirapu-tangas*. Rio da Prata boasts a larger variety of fish than the other rivers around Bonito—and also larger fish than other rivers—and tourists should expect to come face to face with some huge specimens. After the swim tourists regain their strength and energy with a delicious self-service buffet. *(Located 52km south of Bonito. Tour and guide R$54-74. Buffet R$12. Tour and buffet 5hr., with transportation 8hr.)*

RIO SUCURI. Those with limited time or funds can skip the expensive journey out to Rio da Prata and swim with the fishes of Rio Sucuri instead. Though not as large as Rio da Prata it contains many of the same fish and some delicate sub-aquatic gardens. In addition to the standard tour, one can float downstream for two hours surrounded by giant *pintados* and *dourados*. Horseback riding and hiking are also options. Another favorite among international tourists is the one-hour **Quad Bike Trip,** which leads visitors through a series of winding trails that cut through the surrounding forests. *(18km southwest of Bonito. Tour and guide R$58-84. Quad Bike Trip R$70. Buffet R$11. Tour and buffet 3hr., with transportation 4½hr.)*

AQUÁRIO NATURAL BAÍA BONITA. Back in the days before Bonito's beauty had been discovered by the rest of the country, locals came to Aquário Natural Baía to frolic with fish. It's a beautiful natural spring with over 30 varieties of fish and a 900m tributary along which visitors can float gently downstream. However, the

TOURING AROUND BONITO. The private farmsteads upon which most of the natural sights are located have established a strict set of regulations to ensure protection of the sights and their surrounding environment. These regulations include limits on the number of daily visitors, with some sights closing down for weeks at a time in order to ensure sustainability. Visitors are forbidden to wear suntan lotion when visiting the rivers, and all guests must be accompanied by a locally accredited guide. Tours should be booked at least a day in advance; expect large groups of people when you arrive. There are 25 travel agencies in the town offering over 30 different tours. Each agency offers the same tours at similar prices, though some are better at arranging groups than others, especially Muito Bonito Turismo. The price of a tour includes admission to the sight and a private guide, but transportation costs extra. Those without a car will have to find others to share a cab with (a group of 4 is perfect, though 2 makes the price of transport reasonable). To hire a taxi for the day costs R$110; half-day costs R$60. Taxis will generally drive you to the farmstead and wait for the duration of your trip.

close proximity of the natural springs to the *centro* has made it the most abused of the surrounding rivers; the heavy traffic of careless tourists has made the water murkier and left the reserve with the feel of an amusement park. Aquário Natural Baía Bonita is the only place in the area that offers a glass-bottomed boat tour, perfect for those uninterested in the tiring swim downstream. It also has several trails around the river, a floating trampoline, and a dash-and-splash zipline. *(Located 7km southeast of Bonito. 3hr. tour and guide R$45-90. 6hr. tour and guide R$77-128. Tour 3-6hr., with transportation 4-7hr.)*

ABISMO DE ANHUMAS. Under what appears to be a small crack in the dirt lies an enormous cavern that stretches 72m down to a clear lake below. The tour involves rappeling down through the cavern to the lake's surface. The descent is breathtaking and once at the surface visitors simply unhook themselves and fall into the water. Your wetsuit provides buoyancy while you snorkel along the water's surface, using your flashlight to illuminate the cavern. Looking down you can see gargantuan cone-shaped rock formations, some over 100m in height; pay a little extra and your guide will equip you with diving gear so you can get a closer look. Some of the formations are spectacular, especially those known as "the fingers" and "the cascades." The clear pool allows for excellent visibility for both divers and snorkelers alike. *(Located 22km west of Bonito. 6hr. tour and guide R$315. 7hr. tour and guide with dive R$450. PADI certification required to dive. Tour 6-7hr., with transportation 8-9hr.)*

GRUTA DO LAGO AZUL. The countryside surrounding Bonito is full of small caves and underground lakes, the most dramatic of which is Gruta do Lago Azul. Tourists approach the cave's monstrous mouth via a short trail through the surrounding forest. The descent through the cave reveals rock formations of varying shapes and sizes, some of which contain crystals and marble. After 100m a lake of solid blue water reveals itself. The colors of the lake change as the sun sets and rises, smoothly transitioning from green to turquoise to blue. During one month of the year, for about 45min. each day, the sun penetrates through the cave and shines directly on the lake's surface, causing the water to turn an electric blue. *(Located 22km west of Bonito. 1½hr. tour with guide R$10 year-round. Tour 1½hr., with transportation 3hr.)*

NORTHEAST

Encompassing the states of Alagoas, Bahia, Ceará, Maranhão, Paraíba, Pernambuco, Piauí, Rio Grande do Norte, and Sergipe, the Northeast is one of Brazil's top draws, and with good reason. Most travelers spend their time along the narrow coastal strip where a majority of Nordestinos live, in part due to the long stretches of stunning sand and sea here. Beautiful beaches are complemented by year-round tropical temperatures which sun-worshippers and surfers alike will appreciate. Those who venture into the more arid interior will be rewarded with beautiful vistsas from the fantastic Chapada Diamantina, mountains which rise like an island of green from the surrounding sere *sertão*. Because of the region's former involvement in the slave trade, the Northeast has the largest and most vibrant Afro-Brazilian population in Brazil, its influence felt in everything from cuisine to dance to religion—and perhaps most apparent in the country's cultural capital (and one of Brazil's must-see cities), Salvador.

HIGHLIGHTS OF THE NORTHEAST

SURF the sand dunes of **Jacumã** (p. 424).

APPLAUD the performers of the Passion Plays in **Nova Jerusalém** (p. 419).

SIT BACK and watch the sunset from the shores of **Jericoacoara** (p. 437).

MOTOR down the beach between Natal and Fortaleza in a **dune buggy** (p. 428).

WANDER the cobblestone streets of **Olinda** (p. 414), a well-preserved colonial town.

BOULDER HOP along the trails of the lush **Chapada Diamantina** (p. 387).

BAHIA

SALVADOR ☎71

When Amerigo Vespucci laid eyes upon the Baía de Todos os Santos in 1501, he could never have imagined that the small peninsula to the west of the bay would eventually become one of the world's most impressive cultural melting pots. Just 48 years after he landed, Portuguese colonists brought with them old-world architectural styles and religious traditions. After 300 more years, the surrounding areas were full of sugar plantations, which had become the engines of economic growth in Brazil and the reason for importing slave labor from West Africa. Unlike other parts of the Americas, slaves in Bahia managed to keep elements of their African heritage alive in their syncretic religious practices (p. 37) and in recipes handed down over generations. Long suppressed under colonial rule, this Afro-Brazilian community flourished after the end of slavery, which is reflected in the Salvador of today. Despite its poverty, the city has given birth to everything from fusion music styles (Paul Simon was one of the first Westerners to incorporate Baiano drumming in his albums) to Candomblé religious practices and forms of *capoeira* (p. 41). Today, Portuguese colonial mansions house African art, and Candomblé ceremonies take place at the feet of staircases leading to spectacular baroque cathedrals. Salvador is and always will be the cultural highlight of Brazil, and is not to be missed.

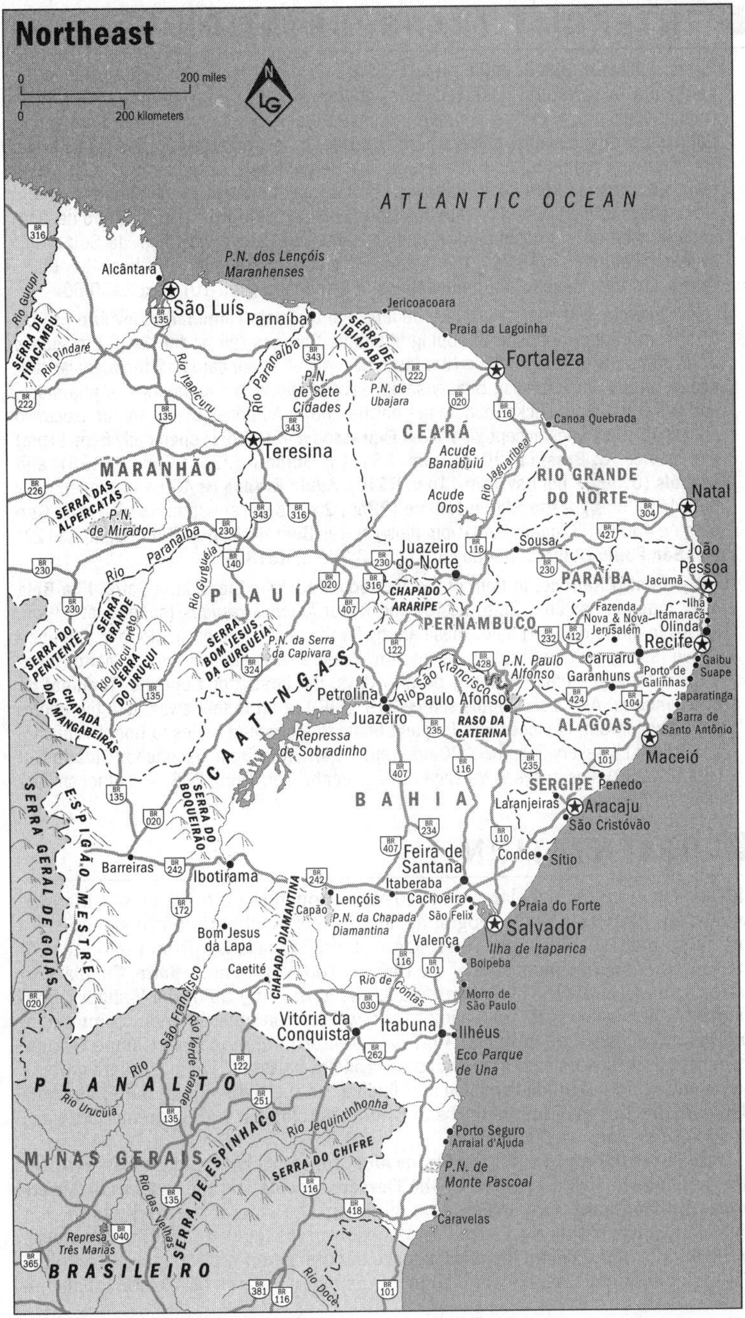

Northeast

0 200 miles
0 200 kilometers

ATLANTIC OCEAN

P.N. dos Lençóis Maranhenses
Alcântara
São Luís
Parnaíba
Jericoacoara
Praia da Lagoinha
Fortaleza
Canoa Quebrada
Serra de Ibiapaba
P.N. de Sete Cidades
P.N. de Ubajara
Serra de Tiracambu
Rio Gurupi
Rio Pindaré
Rio Itapicuru
Rio Parnaíba
Teresina
Ceará
Acude Banabuiú
Acude Oros
Rio Jaguaribe
Rio Grande do Norte
Natal
Maranhão
Serra das Alpercatas
P.N. de Mirador
Paranaíba
Rio Gurguéia
Sousa
Juazeiro do Norte
João Pessoa
Paraíba
Jacumã
Ilha Itamaracá
Olinda
Recife
Fazenda Nova & Nova Jerusalém
Chapado Araripe
Pernambuco
Piauí
Serra do Penitente
Serra Grande
Rio Uruçuí Preto
Serra do Uruçuí
Serra Bom Jesus da Gurguéia
P.N. da Serra da Capivara
Caatingas
Caruaru
P.N. Paulo Alfonso
Garanhuns
Porto de Galinhas
Gaibu
Suape
Japaratinga
Barra de Santo Antônio
Petrolina
Rio São Francisco
Paulo Afonso
Juazeiro
Raso da Caterina
Alagoas
Maceió
Chapada das Mangabeiras
Repressa de Sobradinho
Penedo
Sergipe
Laranjeiras
Aracaju
São Cristóvão
Bahia
Serra do Boqueirão
Espigão Mestre
Serra Geral de Goiás
Feira de Santana
Conde
Sítio
Barreiras
Ibotirama
Itaberaba
Chapada Diamantina
Lençóis
Capão
Cachoeira
São Felix
Praia do Forte
Salvador
Ilha de Itaparica
P.N. da Chapada Diamantina
Bom Jesus da Lapa
Valença
Boipeba
Caetité
Rio de Contas
Morro de São Paulo
Vitória da Conquista
Itabuna
Ilhéus
Eco Parque de Una
Rio São Francisco
Rio Verde Grande
Planalto
Rio Urucuia
Rio Jequitinhonha
Serra do Espinhaço
Porto Seguro
Arraial d'Ajuda
Minas Gerais
Serra do Chifre
P.N. de Monte Pascoal
Rio das Velhas
Serra de Espinhaço
Caravelas
Represa Três Marias
Brasileiro
Rio Doce

BR 316, BR 135, BR 222, BR 343, BR 020, BR 116, BR 226, BR 230, BR 304, BR 427, BR 140, BR 316, BR 407, BR 232, BR 412, BR 122, BR 428, BR 324, BR 135, BR 424, BR 104, BR 235, BR 101, BR 020, BR 242, BR 234, BR 110, BR 172, BR 030, BR 262, BR 251, BR 418, BR 040, BR 365, BR 381

INTERCITY TRANSPORTATION

Flights: Salvador Dois de Julho Airport (SSA; ☎204 1010), on the eastern side of the peninsula near Itapuã, is served by all major domestic and international airlines (though flights to/from SSA are more expensive than those to/from Rio or São Paulo). Contains shops, a tourist office, travel agencies, a post office kiosk, and 24hr. ATMs. The cheapest option to/from the airport is a **seletivo bus,** complete with A/C, plush reclining seats, and the latest Hollywood flicks. They run between the airport's *acarajé* stand (beyond the taxi and private bus stops outside the arrivals terminal) and destinations marked on the dashboard, including Barra and Pelourinho's Pça. da Sé (1½hr.; every hr. 7am-9pm; R$3.70). The Pça. da Sé stop is in the middle of busy Rua Chile. Take a taxi from there to accommodations in Pelourinho (R$5-10). **Taxi** R$50-60.

Buses: Intercity and interstate buses depart from the main **Terminal Rodoviário** (☎900 1555), in Pituba, opposite Shopping Iguatemi. Services (all on the 1st fl.) include a 24hr. ATM outside the entrance (Bradesco accepts all major cards), 24hr. luggage storage, a tourist office, police, beauty salon, several shops, a supermarket, a pharmacy, and a travel agency. Ticket booths are on the 2nd fl. All prices below are for *executivo* buses; all companies accept Visa. **Real Expresso** (☎450 2991; open daily 6am-11pm) has service to: **Brasília** (20hr.; 9pm; R$120); **Goiânia** (22hr.; 9pm; R$128); and **Lençóis** (6½hr.; 2 per day 7am-11pm; R$40). **Águia Branca** (☎450 4400; open daily 5am-10:30pm) goes to **Rio de Janeiro** (28hr.; 2 per day 7am-3pm; R$170). **São Geraldo** (☎450 9793; open 6am-10pm daily) serves **Belo Horizonte** (24hr.; 6pm; R$127) and **São Paulo** (33hr.; 3 per day 8:30am-10:20pm; R$183).

Boats: Centro Naútico, in front of the Mercado Modelo in the Cidade Baixa. **Ilha Bela** runs catamarans (2hr., 2pm, R$40) and faster *lanches rápidas* (speedboats; 9am, R$50) to Morro de São Paulo. These are by far the best transport to Morro as the alternative (a ferry to Itaparica, bus transport to Valença, and another ferry to Morro) takes at least triple the time; on windy or rainy days, the boats don't operate. **Terminal do São Joaquim,** Av. Oscar Pontes s/n (☎319 2890), a bit farther away from the *centro* on the waterfront, launches less frequent boats to Morro and ferries to Bom Despacho, Ilha Itaparica (every 30min. 7:20am-9pm; R$4). From Bom Despacho, **Cidade Sol** (☎450 7290) runs buses to Valença (2hr.; 2 per hr. 7am-9pm; R$8) and other smaller cities on Itaparica.

ORIENTATION

Salvador is intimidatingly large and provides enough to do for at least a lifetime. Luckily for tourists, several geographically distinct neighborhoods divide the city into more manageable areas. The Baiano capital spreads out from the bottom of the eastern V-shaped peninsula of the Baía de Todos os Santos. **Barra,** the place to go for beaches and a Rio-style boardwalk, sits at the very tip of the V-shaped peninsula; the left side (with your back to the water) contains the main commercial and historical districts. In Barra, Av. 7 de Setembro, running from Campo Grande to Vitória and Barra, is also known as the **Ladeira da Barra.** The best nightspots in Bahia can be found in **Rio Vermelho** and **Ondina,** on the right side of the V; this area also contains the wealthier suburbs of Ondina and **Pituba,** and Iguatemi Shopping, along with the airport, 20km away.

At the heart of Salvador are the **Cidade Alta** (upper city) and Cidade Baixa (lower city) neighborhoods, connected by the **Elevador Lacerda** and the **Ladeiras da Misericorda** and **Montanha,** two streets that snake up the side of the rocky bluff that divides the city. Within the Cidade Alta, most tourists head straight for **Pelourinho,** in the middle of the **Centro Histórico,** a maze of cobblestone streets packed with the city's architectural splendors and some of the major centers of Afro-Brazilian cul-

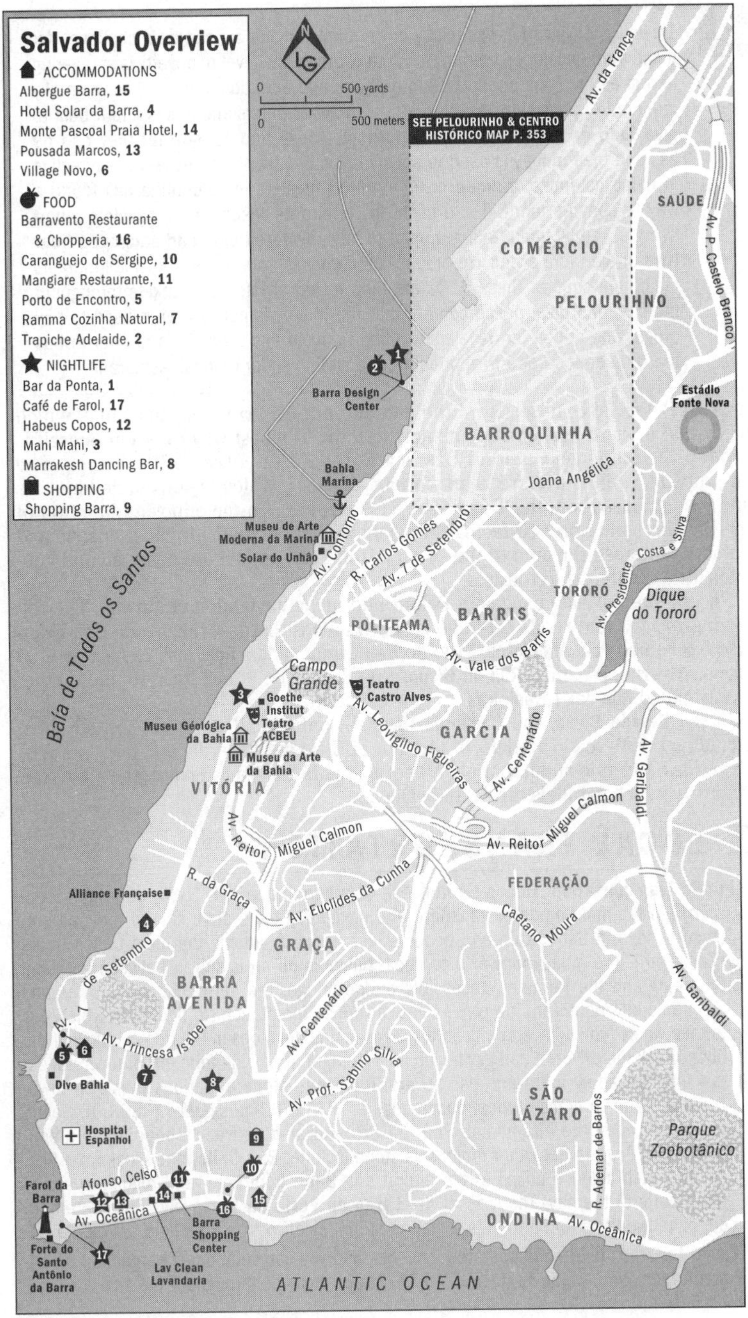

Salvador Overview

ACCOMMODATIONS
Albergue Barra, **15**
Hotel Solar da Barra, **4**
Monte Pascoal Praia Hotel, **14**
Pousada Marcos, **13**
Village Novo, **6**

FOOD
Barravento Restaurante & Chopperia, **16**
Caranguejo de Sergipe, **10**
Mangiare Restaurante, **11**
Porto de Encontro, **5**
Ramma Cozinha Natural, **7**
Trapiche Adelaide, **2**

NIGHTLIFE
Bar da Ponta, **1**
Café de Farol, **17**
Habeus Copos, **12**
Mahi Mahi, **3**
Marrakesh Dancing Bar, **8**

SHOPPING
Shopping Barra, **9**

0 500 yards
0 500 meters

SEE PELOURINHO & CENTRO HISTÓRICO MAP P. 353

Av. da França
SAÚDE
Av. P. Castelo Branco
COMÉRCIO
PELOURIHNO
Barra Design Center
Estádio Fonte Nova
BARROQUINHA
Joana Angélica
Bahia Marina
Museu de Arte Moderna da Marina
Solar do Unhão
Av. Contorno
R. Carlos Gomes
Av. 7 de Setembro
Av. Presidente Costa e Silva
Dique do Tororó
TORORÓ
BARRIS
POLITEAMA
Baía de Todos os Santos
Av. Vale dos Barris
Campo Grande
Teatro Castro Alves
Goethe Institut
Teatro ACBEU
Museu Geológica da Bahia
Museu da Arte da Bahia
Av. Leovigildo Figueiras
GARCIA
Av. Centenário
Av. Garibaldi
VITÓRIA
Av. Reitor Miguel Calmon
Av. Reitor Miguel Calmon
R. da Graça
Alliance Française
Av. Euclides da Cunha
FEDERAÇÃO
Caetano Moura
GRAÇA
Av. 7 de Setembro
BARRA AVENIDA
Av. Garibaldi
Av. Princesa Isabel
Av. Centenário
Dive Bahia
Av. Prof. Sabino Silva
SÃO LÁZARO
Hospital Espanhol
R. Ademar de Barros
Parque Zoobotânico
Farol da Barra
Afonso Celso
Av. Oceânica
Barra Shopping Center
ONDINA
Av. Oceânica
Forte do Santo Antônio da Barra
Lav Clean Lavandaria
ATLANTIC OCEAN

NORTHEAST

Traveling in Salvador, especially in the Centro Histórico, can be a challenge for those from developed countries; in many areas, the level of poverty is staggering and street beggars abound, from orphans and abandoned children to mentally impaired or physically disabled adults. Many travelers and locals find it best to give **food or non-monetary handouts** to these people, so that they can be assured their money is used to satisfy basic needs. While this tactic is effective in most instances, a group of enterprising hustlers in Pelourinho has found a way to convert goodwill into cash. In Terreiro de Jesus, many travelers report being asked by infant-toting women to buy **powdered milk and packaged flour** (two of the more expensive prepackaged goods) from one of the small markets facing the square. These items are then resold at informal markets throughout the city, and local police confirm that the money is nearly always used to buy drugs. One option for travelers wanting to avoid this scenario is to offer to buy ready-made food or a fresh meal from a street vendor or local restaurant.

ture. In Pelourinho, buses from the city and airport arrive on Rua Chile, which meets the modern **Pça. da Sé** at its northern tip. The best way to orient oneself is around the immense Catedral Basílica at the north corner of the *praça*. The entrance faces Pelourinho's heart, **Terreiro de Jesus,** which is surrounded by bars and restaurants. From the Terreiro, streets run east (in the opposite direction of the Basílica) and north (if facing the Basílica, on your right) to most hostels and points of interest; the area to the south of the Terreiro is more deserted and contains little of interest to tourists.

Recent **street name** changes in Pelourinho make navigation confusing. The following *praças* and roads often go by both names: Largo Cruzeiro de São Francisco, renamed **Pça. Anchieta;** Largo do Pelourinho, a.k.a. **Pça. José de Alencar;** Rua Monte Alverne, renamed **Rua do Bispo;** Rua Francisco Muniz Barreto, more commonly called **Rua das Laranjeiras.**

In the **Cidade Baixa,** the **Comércio** district contains all the most visited sites, including the Mercado Modelo, at the foot of Elevador Lacerda, and ferry ports to Morro de São Paulo and Itaparica. All ports are off **Avenida da França,** the main traffic artery which parallels the Atlantic Ocean.

LOCAL TRANSPORTATION

Public Transportation: Buses (Portuguese only info line ☎371 1580; open M-F 9am-8pm) are the main mode of transport, and navigating the system can be a nightmare. Local buses run 6am-11pm and become less frequent outside the main transit hours (7am-7pm). The main **rodoviária** for local buses is on an island in between Iguatemi Shopping and the Terminal, accessible by footbridge. The perplexing station has one electronic info booth and no other signs or tourist information; to figure out which bus to take where, you'll have to rely on the signs listing the stops in the front window of the bus, or ask the driver. It can get hectic here at night; if arriving from out of town, take a taxi into Salvador. There are also several **local bus stops** at various points in town. There are 2 main types of local buses, regular (R$1.30) and *seletivo* (R$2.60). *Seletivos* go between the airport and Pça. da Sé, and also between Shopping Iguatemi, Barra, and Pça. da Sé. Other major bus stops include: **Rua Chile,** one block from Pça. da Sé; catch *seletivo* buses to the airport and Barra from here, and regular buses to other parts of the city. The stop at the **Largo do Porto da Barra,** Av. 7 de Setembro opposite the Praia do Porto, has a map of stops; *seletivos* run from here to Pça. da Sé.

Taxis: *Taxistas* are often desperate for clients, and you can sometimes bargain for an off-meter rate. 24hr. **Ligue Taxi** (☎357 7777) does pick-ups throughout the city.

Car Rental: Localiza, Av. Oceânica 3057 (☎332 1999), Ondina. Open M-Sa 8am-8pm. Also has a 24hr. airport branch (☎377 2272) and a stand in Pça. Anchieta in Pelourinho. Daily rates for a mid-size vehicle start at R$30.

PRACTICAL INFORMATION

TOURIST & FINANCIAL SERVICES

Tourist Office: Bahiatursa, the extremely useful state tourist agency with offices in all major neighborhoods, arranges tours, provides info on Candomblé and *capoeira,* and helps with just about anything else. Agents at the following offices speak several languages (mainly English, French, Spanish, and German). **Pelourinho,** Rua das Laranjeiras 12 (☎321 2133), at Rua Gregório de Matos. Open daily 8:30am-10pm. **Airport** (☎204 1244). Open daily 7:30am-11pm. **Mercado Modelo** (☎241 0242). Open M-Sa 9am-6pm, Su 9am-2pm. **Terminal Rodoviário** (☎450 3871). Open daily 7:30am-9pm.

Travel Agents and Tours: Several travel agencies in Pelourinho have English-speaking staff and can arrange group packages. **C&C Turismo,** Ladeira do Carmo 30 (☎243 7347; www.cecturismobahia.com), organizes city tours of Salvador (3hr.; R$48), tours of neighboring islands (8hr.; R$45), guided Candomblé ceremonies (3hr.; R$35), and trips to Morro de São Paulo and Chapada Diamantina (2-3 days, R$150-500). Open daily 9am-7pm. **Pelourinho Turismo,** Rua Alfredo de Brito 20 (☎326 3777; tourpelourinho@hotmail.com), opposite Hotel Pelourinho, can arrange car rental, city tours, and flights; there's also an in-house Internet café. Open M-Sa 10am-6pm.

Airlines: In addition to the central offices listed below, all airlines have ticketing agents at the airport; travel agencies can also book tickets. **Gol,** Pça. Gago Coutinho s/n (☎375 2093 or 0800 701 2131; www.voegol.com.br). Open M-F 9am-6pm. **Nordeste,** Pça. Gago Countinho 282 (☎377 0130 or 0800 71 0737). **TAM,** Av. Tancredo Neves 2421 (☎340 0123 or 0800 12 3100; www.tam.com.br), Pituba. Open M-F 9am-6pm. **Varig,** Av. Centenário 2992 (☎245 5198 or 0800 99 7000). **VASP,** Av. A.C. Magalhães 2487 (☎353 7044 or 0800 99 8277).

Consulates: Canada, Av. Pres. Vargas (☎331 0064; 2402), Ondina. **Denmark,** Av. 7 de Setembro 2244 (☎336 9861), Vitória. **France,** Rua Francisco Gonçalves 01 (☎241 0168), Comércio. **Germany,** 281 Lucaia (☎334 7106), Rio Vermelho. **Japan,** Rua Vieira 39 (☎266 0527), Centro Histórico. **Portugal,** Largo do Carmo 04 (☎241 1633), Centro Histórico. **Spain,** 21 Mal Floriano (☎336 9055), Canela. **Switzerland,** Av. Tancredo Neves 3343 (☎341 5827). **UK,** Av. Estados Unidos 18 (☎243 7399), Comércio. **Uruguay,** Pça. Anchieta 18 (☎322 7093), Pelourinho. **US,** Rua Pernambuco 51 (☎345 1550, 345 1545), Pituba.

Currency Exchange, Banks & ATMs: *Câmbios* line Pça. Anchieta in front of Igreja de São Francisco in Pelourinho; these give worse rates for traveler's checks and cash than banks but are open daily, most from 9am-7pm. **Banco do Brasil,** in the same *praça* across from the police station, has ATMs for Visa cards and offers the same services. Open M-F 9am-5pm. ATM open daily 7am-10pm. **Bradesco** has an ATM for all major cards at Terreiro de Jesus, in front of Cantina da Lua restaurant. In Barra, there are **Banco do Brasil** ATMs in the Largo do Porto da Barra and in many other locations; the main bank branch is on Rua Miguel Brunier near Barra Shopping.

Work Opportunities: One of the best options for work is teaching English at one of the many language academies in Salvador. Pay at the following academies is generally R$10 per hr. Private tutoring usually pays better; check the classified section of the newspaper to find openings. **CNA Inglês,** Av. 7 de Setembro 2792 (☎336 4422). Open M-Sa 9am-7pm. **Wise Up,** Av. Tancredo Neves 1186 (☎272 1211; wiseup.com.br). Open M-Sa 9am-7pm. **Cultura Inglesa,** 481 M. Grosso (☎248 0255; www.culturainglesa-ba.com.br). Open M-F 9am-8pm.

THE HIDDEN DEAL

JINGA, GRINGO!

The *jinga,* the most basic step in both major forms of *capoeira,* is the first thing you'll learn at the fast-paced **Mestre Bimba School** in Pelourinho, which teaches the the so-called *capoeira regional,* which is thought to have originated in movements created by slaves to fight their masters. The more energetic *capoeira Angola* style, which is fought closer to the ground, is thought to have Old World origins. *Capoeristas* of all levels and ages can sign up for classes with a senior member of Mestre Bimba's school.

Classes, which are held daily from 9am onwards, are not for the weak of heart—beginners train alongside experienced locals, and some people are thrown into an informal *roda* (fighting circle) to battle other group members having completed just one class. Top-notch instructors and the school's international reputation make it popular among travelers and undoubtedly worth the cash—the instant respect you'll get from Brazilian kids with a few well-timed moves is priceless. Make sure to wear loose clothes; *capoeira* pants with the school's logo are available for sale in the main office (R$40).

Rua das Laranjeiras 1. ☎322 0639. R$80 for 12 1½hr. classes. Classes M-F 9am-noon and 2-8pm, Sa 9am-12:30pm.

Other Alternatives to Tourism: Many foreigners rent apartments in Salvador to stay a while and study Portuguese, *capoeira,* Afro-Brazilian dance, or music. Classes are inexpensive and easy to find. A few of the major schools are listed below.

Dance: Escola de Dança, Rua da Oração, located just 1 block from Pelourinho's Terreiro de Jesus. Afro-Brazilian, flamenco, ballet, and modern dance classes offered. R$30 per month for 1 twice-per-week course.

Capoeira: Several schools in Pelourinho teach different styles with different philosophies. For regional-style *capoeira,* try the **Associação de Capoeira Mestre Bimba,** Rua das Laranjeiras 1 (☎322 0639), 1 block from Terreiro de Jesus. 1hr. classes with plenty of individual attention costs R$10; packages of 5-12 classes are also available at a discount. *Rodas de capoeira* are well worth R$5 (Tu, F 7-9pm). Open M-F 9am-noon and 2-8pm, Sa 9am-12:30pm. **Associação Brasileira de Capoeira Angola,** opposite Teatro Miguel Santana off Rua João de Deus, has a number of *mestres* offering different styles; you can take classes for R$120 per month, or watch a class or *roda* for R$2. Open M-Sa 9am-8pm; *rodas* F 7:30pm.

Portuguese: Hundreds of institutes can be found all over Salvador; Bahiatursa can provide a list of options in each neighborhood. In Barra, **Gurgel Idiomas,** Rua Barão de Itapuã 60 (☎264 1379, 9924 5744; www.gurgelidiomas.com.br), has classes of up to 8 students, as well as individual instruction. Prices vary based on number of classes and students.

Music: Pelourinho is the best place to learn from the pros, from drumming to jazz to *capoeira's* string instrument, the *berimbau.* **Grupo Cultural Olodum,** Rua Gregório de Matos 22 (☎321 5010), in Pelourinho, is the production house and official store of the drum band, and has the best information on drumming classes and performances at their nearby school. Open M-Sa 11am-6pm. **Swing do Pelo,** Theatro XVIII, Rua Frei Vicente 15 (☎9998 4382), a percussion band that performs Tu and Sa nights in Pelourinho, can also arrange classes.

LOCAL SERVICES

Luggage Storage: Many of the *albergues* in Pelourinho and Barra have luggage storage rooms and charge R$2-3 per day. The long-distance bus terminal also has 24hr. storage (☎460 8344), on the 1st fl. near the departure area. R$2-3 per day.

English-Language Bookstore: Livraria Brandão (☎243 5383) has a giant collection of second-hand books, including many paperback titles available in English, French, and German. Brandão also exchanges used titles. Open M-F 9am-6pm.

Libraries: Biblioteca Público do Estado da Bahia, Rua General Labatut 27 (☎328 4555), in Barra, is the city's main library. Open M-F 9am-noon and 2-6pm. **Casa de Jorge Amado** (☎321 0070), in Pelourinho, has a quiet reading room with all of Amado's works. Open M-Sa 9am-6pm.

Cultural Centers: Alliance Française, Av. 7 de Setembro 401 (☎336 7599), Vitória, has a theater, library, café, and restaurant. Also offers French classes. Open M-F 9am-6pm. **Goethe Institut,** a.k.a. Instituto Cultural Brasil-Alemanhã, Av. 7 de Setembro 1809, offers similar services. **Nigerian Cultural and Information Center,** Rua Alfredo de Brito 26 (☎241 3667; nigerianculture@naijanet.com), in Pelourinho, has information on Nigerian religions and culture. Staff have a good knowledge of Yoruba religious practices for those curious about the African origins of Candomblé. They also organize the annual Dia da África, on May 25th. English spoken. Open M-F 10am-6pm.

GLS: Grupo Gay de Bahia, Rua Frei Vicente 24 (☎322 2176 or 322 2552), next to the Theatro XVIII in Pelourinho. Info on queer nightlife and events. Open M-F 9am-6pm.

Markets: Perini, Rua Miguel Burnier 24 (☎245 0122), opposite Shopping Barra, is an excellent, gourmet-style market with a fine selection of pastries, imported cheeses, and organic fruits and vegetables. Open M-Sa 6am-10pm, Su 6:30am-2pm. **Bompreço** supermarkets are everywhere. Next to Shopping Iguatemi are a few **24hr. hipermercados,** some large enough to warrant their own zip codes.

Laundromat: Wash Well, Rua Riberão dos Santos s/n, Pelourinho, 1 block past Albergue do Carmo. R$6 per load. Open M-F 9am-6pm, Sa 9am-5pm. **Lav Clean Lavandaria** (☎339 0077), off Rua Marques de Leão in the Farol Barra Flat building on Av. Oceânica, in Barra. R$14 to wash and dry up to 15 pieces, R$23 with ironing.

Weather and Surf Conditions: Meterologia (☎337 0491) is the weather information service. Operators have info on tide tables and weather forecasts (Portuguese only).

PUBLICATIONS

A Tarde is the largest newspaper in circulation in Bahia; the classifieds are the best source for apartment and part-time job hunting in the city. There are also movie listings and showtimes, plus nightlife and cultural events listed in the Arts section. *Bahia Cultural*, a monthly publication distributed by Bahiatursa and available at any of their offices, is a very helpful guide to seasonal activities, theatrical shows, traveling museum exhibitions, and nightlife in the city.

EMERGENCY & COMMUNICATIONS

EMERGENCIES	The emergency numbers for all of Brazil are: **Police** ☎190. **Ambulance** ☎192. **Fire** ☎193.

Tourist Police: DELTUR, in Pça. Anchieta (☎322 7155 or 1188 7804), in Pelourinho, opposite Banco Brasil, offer information on personal safety and can file police reports. English, Spanish, German, French, and Italian spoken. Open 24hr.

Tourist Information Hotline: Disque Turismo (☎131) can be dialed free from any payphone. 24hr. service in English and Portuguese.

24hr. Pharmacy: Estrela Galdino (☎264 8343) has branches in Shopping Barra (☎264 8340) and Shopping Iguatemi (☎462 7231). In Pelourinho, the only option is **Farmácia Drogaleve** (☎322 6921).

Hospital/Medical Services: Hospital Espanhol, Av. 7 de Setembro 4161 (☎264 1999; emergency line ☎264 1573), in Barra. A reputable facility with good doctors. Centrally located. Pelourinho does not have any major hospitals.

Fax Office: The Pituba post office (☎346 8888) has fax service. R$5-20 per page depending on destination. Many Internet cafés also have fax machines.

Internet Access: In Pelourinho, cafés abound. **Internetcafé.com,** Terreiro de Jesus at Rua Francisco Barreto and Rua João de Deus (☎321 2147), has decent cappucino. R$4 per hr. Open daily 9am-9pm. Another option is **Bahia.com,** facing Pça. da Sé at Rua José Gonçalves and Rua 3 de Maio (☎322 1266). Cigars and oil canvases (both for sale) add to the ambience. Open daily 9am-midnight. In Barra, **Internet Café.com,** Av. Oceânica 3701, has many computers and international phone service. Staff also arrange apartment and car rental. Open daily 8:30am-10pm.

Post Office: Av. Paulo IV 191 (☎346 8888), in Pituba. In Pelourinho, there is a branch in Pça. Anchieta (☎346 9520), opposite Igreja de São Francisco. Open M-F 9am-5pm, Sa 9am-1pm. **Postal code:** 41810-000. Street signs list the 8-digit postal code for each city block.

SAFETY & SECURITY. Unfortunately, the extreme disparity of wealth in northeastern Brazil has produced its fair share of hustlers and petty thieves. While the city has made a valiant effort in recent years to keep Pelourinho's touristed streets safe, unsavory types still prowl the Centro Histórico, even during the day. At night, every street corner in Pelourinho has a stand of officers outfitted in intimidating combat gear; stick near them to avoid trouble. Thieves pray on obvious-looking tourists, so it helps to reduce attention by leaving backpacks, fancy watches, and expensive-looking items safely locked in your hostel. Even after taking these precautions, some people can't help looking foreign and are likely to attract thieves anyway. To minimize your losses, don't carry your money in one place, even if it's in a hidden moneybelt. Some travelers recommend stashing cash in shoes and hidden pockets, and keeping a fake wallet with a few bills and expired ID cards in it. In the event that you do get robbed, cooperate with the thieves, then go immediately to the nearest police office or stand and try to provide all the relevant details. The DELTUR Tourist Police office at Pça. Anchieta in Pelourinho has multi-lingual staff, available 24hr., and pamphlets on personal safety (☎322 7155).

ACCOMMODATIONS

Accommodations run the gamut from centrally located five-star luxury hotels to dives in outlying neighborhoods. The city is also home to a number of excellent HI-affiliated youth hostels, clustered in the main tourist areas of Pelourinho and Barra. If you're looking to meet other backpackers, stay in a hostel; otherwise, the best deals are in renting beachfront suites or apartments in Barra, which is generally calmer and more relaxed than the historical center. Rates go up considerably in the high season (before/after Carnaval—Dec.-Mar.—and July); outside these times, many lodgings are desperate and willing to bargain, especially for long-term stays or groups. Discounts are facilitated with youth/student ID cards.

PELOURINHO & THE CENTRO HISTÓRICO

This is the cultural heart of Salvador and a haven for tourists and backpackers; unfortunately, street hustlers have become increasingly common, and tourist police are now stationed at every corner. If you like peace and quiet, stay away from Pelourinho, where live music often floats through the air until the wee hours, especially along Rua Alfredo de Brito and the Largo do Pelourinho. Inexpensive hostels and *pousadas* abound.

Albergue das Laranjeiras (HI), Rua Inácio Accioli 13 (☎321 1366; www.alaranj.com.br), at Rua Inácio. From Terreiro de Jesus, it's 3 blocks down Rua das Laranjeiras. Always packed, this cheery hostel has spotless high-ceilinged dorms, a snack bar, Internet café, and lounge. Breakfast, lockers, and linens included. Shared baths. Towels R$1.50. Laundry R$10 per 4kg. Reception 7am-9pm. High-season dorms R$24; singles R$40; doubles R$60; triples R$82. Low-season dorms R$20; singles R$36; doubles R$56; triples R$78. Discount with ISIC or HI membership. Visa. ❷

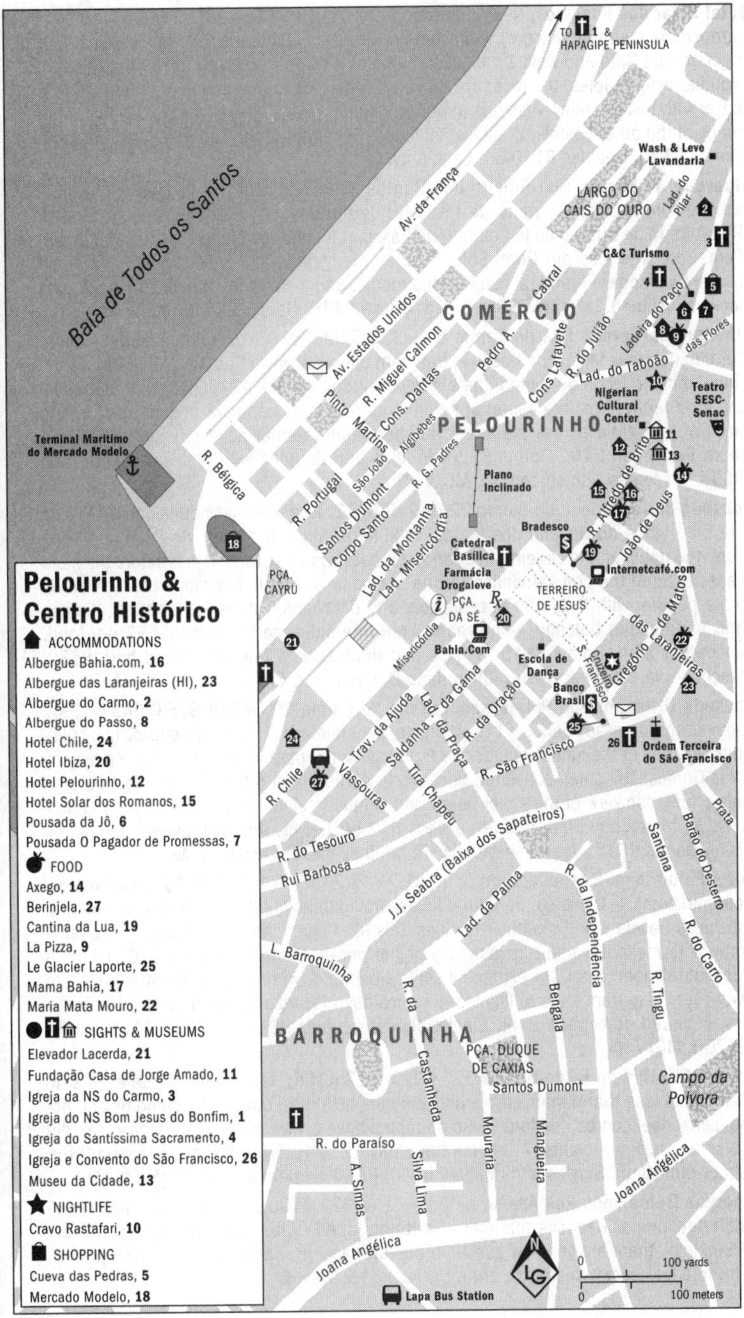

Pelourinho & Centro Histórico

ACCOMMODATIONS

Albergue Bahia.com, **16**
Albergue das Laranjeiras (HI), **23**
Albergue do Carmo, **2**
Albergue do Passo, **8**
Hotel Chile, **24**
Hotel Ibiza, **20**
Hotel Pelourinho, **12**
Hotel Solar dos Romanos, **15**
Pousada da Jô, **6**
Pousada O Pagador de Promessas, **7**

FOOD

Axego, **14**
Berinjela, **27**
Cantina da Lua, **19**
La Pizza, **9**
Le Glacier Laporte, **25**
Mama Bahia, **17**
Maria Mata Mouro, **22**

SIGHTS & MUSEUMS

Elevador Lacerda, **21**
Fundação Casa de Jorge Amado, **11**
Igreja da NS do Carmo, **3**
Igreja do NS Bom Jesus do Bonfim, **1**
Igreja do Santíssima Sacramento, **4**
Igreja e Convento do São Francisco, **26**
Museu da Cidade, **13**

NIGHTLIFE

Cravo Rastafari, **10**

SHOPPING

Cueva das Pedras, **5**
Mercado Modelo, **18**

Hotel Solar dos Romanos, Rua Alfredo de Brito 14A (☎322 6158, 321 6264; hotelsolardosromanos@hotmail.com). From Terreiro de Jesus facing the Catedral Basílica, turn right on Rua Brito and walk 1½ blocks; the hotel is on your left after Sorvetaria Cubano. Popular with couples, the recently-renovated hotel has roomy dorms and doubles (the latter with private bath). Also has a rooftop balcony with a view of the city. Quieter than many of the other hostels. Breakfast included. Reception 24hr. Laundry R$10 per load. Dorms R$20. Doubles R$40-60. Cash only. ❶

Albergue do Passo, Rua Ribeiro dos Santos 3 (☎326 1951; www.passoyouthhostel.hpg.com.br). From Terreiro de Jesus facing the Basílica, turn right and walk down Rua Alfredo de Brito, then left on Rua do Passo at Kilinho restaurant. Owners Diane and Fernando, who also run Hotel Solar, are knowledgeable and well-traveled. The small hostel has modern furniture, comfortable rooms, and a cozy feel. Breakfast, linens, and lockers included. Laundry R$8 per load. Dorms R$18. Doubles R$45. MC/V. ❶

Albergue do Carmo, Rua do Carmo 6 (☎326 3750; www.albergue.bol.com.br). From Terreiro de Jesus facing the Basílica, turn right and walk down Rua Alfredo de Brito. Continue uphill to Igreja do Carmo; the *albergue* is opposite the church. A very modern hostel, a bit farther from the center of Pelourinho. *Rodas de capoeira* frequent the area in front of the *igreja* across the street. Kitchen. Free Internet access. Laundry R$8 per load. Reception 24hr. Dorms R$20. Singles and doubles with fan and shared bath R$35. Discounts with student ID. MC/V. ❶

Pousada da Jô, Ladeira do Carmo 22 (☎243 8172; josetepalma@hotmail.com). Facing the blue Igreja do Rosário dos Pretos, walk left through the Largo do Pelourinho and continue uphill on the Ladeira do Carmo; the *pousada* is on the left just before the staircase. Lacking the commercialism of the big hostels, this family-run establishment is more popular with long-term backpackers and Brazilians. Dorms are smallish. Kitchen and picturesque balcony/game room. Free Internet access. Laundry R$7 per load. Reception 24hr. Dorms R$15. Singles and doubles with fan and shared bath R$30. Discounts for longer stays or with student ID. Cash only. ❶

Pousada O Pagador de Promessas, Ladeira do Carmo 19 (☎242 8753, 3491 1332; pousadappromessa@bol.com.br), opposite the staircase. Housed in one of the buildings featured in the film *O Pagador de Promessas,* adapted in the 1960s from a play by Dias Gomes. The small converted house is less glitzy than others, but the lounge area has a fantastic view of the street below and is much quieter than other Pelourinho hostels. All rooms have fan. Internet access R$2.50 per hr. Airport transfers. Reception 24hr. Dorms R$15. *Quarto* singles R$30; doubles R$35. Cash only. ❶

Hotel Pelourinho, Rua Alfredo de Brito 20/22 (☎243 2324, 321 7149; www.hotelpelourinho.com). In the Largo do Carmo across from Igreja dos Pretos. Long a favorite with business travelers and wealthier families, this old Pelourinho hotel is undergoing renovations to make it warrant its generally higher prices. Some rooms lack A/C; ask for a renovated room. Staff are extremely service-oriented, with a concierge who can help with everything from tours to flights. All rooms have TV, *frigo-bar,* bath, and A/C. Breakfast included. Reception 24hr. Singles R$75; doubles R$100; triples R$150; quads R$200. MC/V. ❹

Hotel Ibiza, Rua do Bispo 6/8 (☎322 6929, 322 4305), facing Pça. da Sé at Rua do Bispo, has less charm than surrounding colonial buildings, but the clean rooms and no-nonsense feel can be comforting. Some rooms have a view of the *praça*; these can get noisy on weekend nights. All rooms have private bath, TV, and fan. Reception 24hr. Check-out 10am. Singles and doubles R$40, R$10 extra for A/C. AmEx/MC/V. ❷

Albergue Bahia.com, Rua Alfredo de Brito 41 (☎321 0700), is more basic than its HI-affiliated peers. Decor is minimal and its cramped dorms have a sardine-can feel (thankfully, there are very few guests in the low season). Kitchen. Internet R$5 per hr., 1hr. free for guests. Reception 24hr. Dorms R$15. Visa. ❶

Hotel Chile, Rua Chile 4 (☎321 0245, 321 8421), near Pça. da Sé. Stands out from its Pelourinho peers in that it doesn't attract many tourists. While the facility doesn't offer the modern luxuries of Pelourinho hostels, excellent prices and lack of backpackers lure guests to Hotel Chile. Breakfast included. Check-out 10am. Singles R$17, with fan and private bath R$30, with A/C R$40; doubles R$30, with fan and private bath R$50, with A/C R$70. DC/MC. ❷

BARRA & VITÓRIA

Set away from the most touristed areas, Barra is Salvador's laid-back, breezy coastal strip, filled with joggers and health food-lovers. Easy bus access to the rest of the city and several excellent beaches make the area a good base for exploring Salvador, especially for those seeking to avoid the constant buzz of drumbeats in Pelourinho or the hustlers in other parts of the city. Accommodations here can be a bit expensive, and many longer-term travelers find it cheaper to rent an apartment. Some excellent ocean-view places go for as little as R$700 per month (check the listings at **Internet Café.com,** Av. Oceânica; p. 351). Vitória, Barra's upscale neighbor, on the hill overlooking the ocean on Av. 7 de Setembro, is mainly filled with apartment buildings and luxury hotels.

Village Novo, Av. 7 de Setembro 3659 (☎267 4362; www.villagenovo.com). Facing the ocean half a block from the Largo do Barra. This 125-year-old house has been converted into 11 stylish *apartamentos,* some with stunning ocean views. Central water heating, custom-made art, and original wooden floors distinguish this establishment from its peers, as does a rooftop balcony, Internet café, and communal kitchen. The American owner has other properties available for longer-term rent. All rooms have private bath, A/C, cable TV, and phone. Breakfast included. Reception 24hr. Dec.-Mar. and July rooms R$70, with ocean view R$80. Rooftop *apartamento* with kitchen R$100. Apr.-June and Aug.-Nov. all rates R$20 lower. Visa. ❷-❹

Monte Pascoal Praia Hotel, Av. Oceânica 591 (☎203 4000, 336 6611; www.montepascoal.com.br), opposite Barra Shopping Center. This gleaming, colorful 4-star complex is an excellent value for the price. Modern rooms have ocean and city views, and the pool patio overlooks the Atlantic. Sauna, fitness room, and game room are free for guests. Other services include a beauty salon, business center, private parking, laundry service, bar, and restaurant. English spoken. Breakfast included. Singles and doubles R$145; triples R$190; quads R$247. 5% hotel tax. AmEx/MC/V. ❺

Pousada Marcos, Av. Oceânica 281 (☎264 5117, 264 4599; www.cpunet.com.br/pmarcos), just after the lighthouse, has mediocre rooms and unenthusiastic service at decent prices. Some *apartamentos* have dorm-style beds, good for families. Rooms facing the ocean have an indoor patio area, though bars on the windows spoil the view. Breakfast included. 24hr. reception (ring buzzer). Singles R$40, with view R$50; doubles R$80, with view R$100. *Apartamentos* for up to 8 people can be rented for negotiable prices. Cash only. ❷

Albergue Barra, Rua Dr. Artur Neiva 4 (☎245 2600, 9963 8110; www.alberguebarravento.com.br), behind Hotel San Marino. Any "Barra Shopping" bus to the mall stop, or any "Campo Grande" bus from the airport to the Barravento stop, near Rua Neiva. This quiet hostel tucked away from the action is between the beach and Barra Shopping. Dorms are nothing special, and some doubles, though spotless, are windowless and sterile. Friendly staff don't speak much English. Kitchen. Reception 24hr. Dorms R$20. Doubles with fan R$45, with A/C R$55. 15% discount with ISIC. Visa. ❶

Hotel Solar da Barra, Rua 7 de Setembro 2998 (☎336 4917), at Rua Tenente Pires Fereira between Barra and Vitória. Walk down Rua 7 de Setembro (Ladeira da Barra) from Campo Grande, or take any "Campo Grande" bus from Largo do Porto da Barra. Smallish rooms with little style but good value for the pricey address. Ocean-front *apar-*

tamentos have tiny windows; get a cheaper back room and savor the view from outside. All rooms have A/C, TV, *frigo-bar,* and private bath. Breakfast included. Reception 24hr. Singles R$36; doubles R$54, with ocean view R$72. Cash only. ❷

FOOD

Salvador's culinary traditions embrace their African and Brazilian roots in such dishes as *acarajé,* made with manioc flour, okra stew, and palm oil (called *dendê* in Portuguese and not for the weak of heart); these are found at streetside booths all over the city, especially in Pelourinho. In Barra, *suco* stands and healthful sandwich shops dot the waterfront. Supermarkets are also abundant; the best pastries and deli sandwiches are at **Perini,** while **Bompreço** is the cheapest.

PELOURINHO & THE CENTRO HISTÓRICO

There are countless restaurants with excellent spicy African cuisine in this region; don't miss the flavorful *moquecas* (hearty coconut milk stews). Most travelers stroll the restaurant-crammed streets and let the savory smells direct them.

Berinjela, Travessa da Ajuda 01 (☎322 0247), opposite the Rua Chile *rodoviária.* This used bookstore, music store, and all-natural café (with Internet access) has a sophistication that defies its commercial location. Guilt-free menu options include soy-bread sandwiches (R$3-5), whole-wheat fruit tarts and cakes (R$1.70), and giant, delicious vegan-friendly salads (R$4.50). Occasional live music. Book exchange. Internet access R$2.50 per hr. Open M-F 9am-7pm, Sa 9am-2pm. Visa. ❶

Cantina da Lua, Terreiro de Jesus (☎241 7383), at Rua Alfredo de Brito, has been popular since it opened in the 1950s. The streetside patio features constant live music and an a la carte menu (entrees R$10-20). Upstairs kilo (R$17 per kg) has the freshest fruits, veggies, and meat dishes in town; antique address plates with the names of celebrity diners (including Danny Glover) fill the walls. 24hr. Bradesco ATM takes AmEx/MC/V. Beer R$2. Open Su-Th 11am-midnight, Th-Sa 11am-2am. ❷/❸

Marrom Marfim, Rua Gregório de Mattos 17 (☎321 8272), opposite Largo de Tereza Batista, offers a small dinner menu, friendly, attentive service, and a mouth-watering selection of homemade chocolates (R$1 per piece, boxes from R$6). Excellent *moquecas* for 2 (R$45). Free musical theater (in Portuguese) M 7pm. Open daily 8am-1am. ❺

Mama Bahia, Rua Alfredo de Brito 21 (☎322 4397). Well-known for spicy takes on western favorites like filet mignon (R$25) and shrimp in garlic sauce (R$28), Mama opens her doors to a trendy crowd of tourists and wealthy locals. Old wooden furniture and an upstairs dining room make patrons feel at home. Open M-Th 11am-midnight, F-Su 11am-1:30am. AmEx/MC/V. ❹

Maria Mata Mouro, Rua Inácio Accioli s/n (☎321 3929), opposite Albergue das Laranjeiras (HI). This swanky Pelourinho favorite has a tiny wooden interior with romantic candlelight dining and fantastic, pricey entrees. Popular with couples and tourists in the evenings. Consistently ranked as one of Salvador's best restaurants. Salmon in champagne sauce R$34.50, filet au poivre R$31. Good selection of local and imported wines and whiskeys. Open daily 11am-midnight. AmEx/MC/V. ❺

Le Glacier Laporte, Pça. da Anchieta (☎266 3649), opposite the post office. This French-owned ice cream shop has over 20 creamy flavors, from cappuccino to *cajú,* all made on the premises with natural ingredients. Open daily 9am-9pm. ❶

Axego, Largo do Pelourinho 7 (☎242 7481), opposite Museu da Cidade. Tiny 2nd fl. eatery with a daily menu of excellent local dishes in a modest setting. Remote location keeps it from getting packed like other Pelourinho spots. *Caranguejo* (crab) and *moquecas* are the specialties here (R$25-30 for 2). Open daily noon-1am. ❹

La Pizza, Rua Ribeiro dos Santos 7 (☎241 1717). Head down Largo do Pelourinho and turn left at the bottom onto Rua Ribeiro dos Santos. Tucked away from the hubbub and high prices of the rest of Pelourinho, this Italian-owned eatery has the area's best thin-crust pizza and tons of topping choices. R$1.50 per slice. Open daily 9am-9pm. ❶

BARRA, VITÓRIA, & ONDINA

Popular during the evenings, Barra and Vitória and the nearby suburb of Ondina have a different atmosphere from Pelourinho. International cuisine and seafood are more popular here, and several of the restaurants in these areas double as nightspots. Until 11pm, inexpensive city buses traverse the main waterfront road, which starts as Av. 7 de Setembro and becomes Av. Oceânica in Barra and Ondina.

Caranguejo de Sergipe, Av. Oceânica s/n (☎245 9826), opposite Barravento. Whacking crabs with little mallets was never a social phenomenon before Caranguejo opened; now the outdoor eatery is packed at all hours with locals sipping beer and hammering away. In addition to crustaceans (R$11.20 for a giant crab), the popular bar-restaurant serves excellent mixed drinks and tasty mains (R$10-20). Mojitos R$5, *Drink de Absinto* (absinthe) R$6.50. Beer R$2. Open M 6pm-2am, Tu-Su 4pm-2am. MC/V. ❸

Barravento Restaurante & Chopperia, Av. Oceânica 814 (☎247 2577), under a giant white tent along the ocean. A bit glitzier than the other beachfront bars, Barravento may be the perfect spot to sip champagne or imported wine (R$6-8) while watching the sun sink into the Atlantic. *Moquecas* R$25, steaks R$20-30, and in-house *acarajé* stand (R$7.50). Open M-Th 11am-11pm, F-Su 11am-midnight. MC/V. ❸

Churrascaria Taverna do Porto, Largo do Porto da Barra (☎267 2188), at the Grande Hotel de Barra. An outdoor *churrascaria* with a *rodízio* of beef, chicken, pork, and sausage—a great value for R$10. *Comercial* is a full meal of chicken, rice, beans, salad and *farofa* for R$5. Beer R$1.50. Open daily 11am-2am. ❷

Late Clube da Bahia, Av. 7 de Setembro, 1km toward *centro* from Porto da Barra. The city's most chic dining (with prices to match) is quite a contrast to the slums next door: plush leather chairs and jazz, with a dining room often with more waiters than guests. Caters to Salvador's wealthy set, who come to enjoy dishes like *lagosta ao buerre noir* (lobster in black butter; R$55) and *crêpe suzette* (R$10). A cheaper alternative is to come for sunset drinks (Kir royale R$6.30, Bloody Mary R$5.30, beer R$2-3). Open M-Th noon-midnight, F-Sa noon-1am, Su noon-6pm. AmEx/MC/V. ❺

THE HIDDEN DEAL

BUFFET ON A BUDGET

With a restaurant like this within walking distance, it's remarkable that any per-kilo restaurant in Barra manages to stay open. **Brasil Legal** is a veritable mecca for hungry locals, tempting empty stomachs with 16 hot dishes and 25 salad and fresh fruit options, not to mention a selection of mouth-watering cuts of meat, grilled to taste and brushed with butter. R$4.99 buys you unlimited buffet access, which amounts to a total of 5½ hours of eating time if you arrive at 11am and stay until closing. Understandably, the place is immensely popular, and private tables are hard to come by. It's completely acceptable to pull up a chair and join another group, although conversation between bites is rare. Unlike at kilos, this buffet is constantly replenished—since dishes disappear so quickly—so you're sure to get fresh food even 15 minutes before closing. If you're in Barra be sure to drop by—it's one meal that'll be great on your wallet, if not your waistline.

On the corner of Rua Alfonso Celson and Rua Dias Dávila, 1 block from the lighthouse (Farol da Barra). ☎267 6162. Open daily 11am-4:30pm. Visa. ❶

Mangiare Restaurante, Rua Marques de Leão 483 (☎3491 4069), opposite Barra Shopping and Banco Itaú, is a lunch-only kilo with a good selection of tasty entrees, including some vegetarian dishes and fish *moquecas* (R$12 per kg). Cheaper than the waterfront eateries, with better quality as well. Ambience is more functional than fashionable. Next door are a few *açaí* and ice cream shops perfect for a cooling dessert. Open daily 11:30am-3:30pm. MC/V. ❷

Porto de Encontro, Rua César Zama 41 (☎267 2355), 1 block inland from Av. 7 de Setembro in Barra, is an American-owned, Cuban-themed bar and restaurant, specializing in zesty salads and pastas and possibly the best piña coladas in the city. Entrees have a distinct edge; try *peixe à cubana* (fish wrapped in banana leaves, curried rice, and fried bananas; R$21) or *spaghetti à Maria Bonita* (with smoked ham, tomatoes, and olives; R$8.50). Live MPB F, informal salsa lessons Sa (both at 8:30pm). ❸

Dolce Vita Pizzaria e Restaurante, Rua César Zama 60 (☎267 2070), opposite Porto de Encontro, has less ambience than its neighbor, but tasty food nonetheless. Over 19 types of gourmet pizza, with toppings like gorgonzola and *palmito* (palm heart). R$10-20 per pizza. Decadent desserts R$6-8. Open daily 5:30-11:30pm. ❷

Ramma Cozinha Natural, Rua Lord Cochrane 76 (☎264 0044). Head away from Largo do Porto in Barra on Av. 7 de Setembro, and turn left after 3 blocks onto Rua César Zama. Walk 5 blocks, then turn left on Rua Cochrane. This organic food restaurant has a number of healthy options, from tofu to mouthwateringly convincing vegetarian meat substitutes, all served buffet-style (R$19 per kg). Open M-F 11:30am-8:30pm, Su and holidays 11:30am-3:30pm. MC/V. ❷

Sukiyaki, Av. Pres. Vargas 3562 (☎247 5063), in Ondina, is Salvador's staple for Japanese food. *Sashimi* cuts of salmon and tuna are extremely fresh, and the highly recommended all-you-can-eat buffet has tantalizing selections including tuna carpaccio, stewed eggplant, sweet tofu, sushi rolls made to order, and several desserts (Tu, W, Su; R$30 per person). A la carte menu items include *shabu-shabu* for 2 (R$47), 8-piece California roll (with strawberry and mango; R$20), and grilled salmon teriyaki (R$30). Open Tu-Su 11:30am-2:30pm and 6:30pm-last client. AmEx/MC/V. ❹

Trapiche Adelaide, Av. Contorno 2 (☎326 2211), on the waterfront in the trendy Barra Design Center, is without a doubt Salvador's swishiest eatery. The converted warehouse was renovated 6 years ago into an ultramodern loft, where the city's beautiful people lounge on plush white sofas and sip champagne at marble tables. Chef Luciano Boseggia prepares an array of sophisticated European dishes, from risotto with green asparagus (R$39) to *salada Rica* with salmon, foie gras, and parmesan (R$19). Live piano music Sa-Su. Open M-Th noon-4pm and 7pm-1am, F-Sa noon-1am, Su noon-4pm. ❹

SIGHTS

Most of Salvador's sights are concentrated in the Centro Histórico, home to a handful of the country's finest churches and restored colonial buildings. Outside this area, sights are limited to churches and forts. The best way to appreciate these is simply to walk around; guides are available at some locations and can be useful, but many are unaccredited. Bahiatursa has a series of brochures outlining bus and walking tours of the city, complete with maps and information on each sight.

For a breakdown of Salvador's worthwhile museums, see p. 360.

PELOURINHO & THE CENTRO HISTÓRICO

The historical district is the old home of Brazil's first capital, founded in 1549 and funded by the extremely profitable sugar plantations in the northeast of Brazil. Much of this profit was earned on the backs of forced labor; Brazil was one of the last countries in the world to outlaw slavery, and the capital developed several slave neighborhoods, one of which (Pelourinho) derives its name from the Portuguese term for "whipping post." This neighborhood of cobblestone streets and baroque cathedrals and churches is now home to a fascinating Afro-Brazilian resurgence, evident in drumming and dance styles and syncretic movements like Candomblé and *capoeira*. Thanks to UNESCO funding, which declared the Centro Histórico a World Heritage Site in 1985, the area is undergoing major reconstruction and has become something of a pastel tourist mecca.

IGREJA E CONVENTO DO SÃO FRANCISCO. It's easy to see why it took over 40 years to construct this immense church; every square inch of the interior is covered in gold leaf and ornate detail, making it one of the finest examples of early baroque architecture in the country, if not the world. The first foundation was laid in 1587, and the building was officially inaugurated in 1713. The neighboring convent contains the outdoor Teatro das Azulejos, the largest collection of *azulejos* (distinctive blue tiles) outside of Portugal, laid out in preachy murals. Freelance guides are available for tours (around R$15 per group); many are very knowledgeable and speak several languages. *(Facing Pça. Anchieta, on Rua Inácio Accioli. Walk through the praça from Terreiro de Jesus. ☎322 6430. English spoken. Open M-Sa 8:30am-5:30pm. R$3; students R$1.50; children under 10 free.)*

ELEVADOR LACERDA. Connecting the Upper and Lower cities, the 72m elevator was originally constructed in 1873 using hydraulic technology, as part of an ambitious city development plan. Today, the elevator remains one of the busiest spots in Salvador. Its base is in front of the Mercado Modelo in the Cidade Baixa; it travels to Pça. Tomé de Souza, near Pça. da Sé in the Centro Histórico. Afternoon crowds create long lines, especially if you haven't purchased a ticket; try to take the elevator earlier in the day to avoid waiting in the heat. Several ice cream and *acarajé* stands at the top make it a great place to relax and enjoy the city view. *(Mercado Modelo, Cidade Baixa. Open daily 5am-midnight. R$0.05 per ride.)*

CATEDRAL BASÍLICA. This central architectural splendor was built in the 1700s and is considered one of the finest examples of religious architecture in the New World. Despite being burned down in the early 1900s, the cathedral retains much of its original design thanks to faithful rebuilders. The sacristy contains wooden carvings and a delicate hand-painted ceiling by master artists. It all comes to life at nightly masses, when locals gather to worship in one of Brazil's oldest religious centers. *(Facing Terreiro de Jesus. ☎321 4573. Open daily 9-11am and 2-5pm.)*

FUNDAÇÃO CASA DE JORGE AMADO. This interactive museum, dedicated to the life and contributions of Brazil's most prolific writer, offers a glimpse into Ilhéus-born Amado's colorful Baiano world. The front lobby contains a display illustrating the popularity of the author's works, published in 45 different languages as well as in Braille. The library has a collection of his writing for in-house reading; there's also a café and quality gift shop, and knowledgeable English-speaking staff everywhere. *(Largo do Pelourinho. Walk down Rua Alfredo de Brito from Terreiro de Jesus and turn left. ☎321 0070. www.jorgeamado.org.br. Open M-Sa 9am-6pm. Free.)*

IGREJA DO SANTÍSSIMA SACRAMENTO. Perched at the top of a sweeping staircase connecting the Ladeira do Carmo and the Ladeira do Passo, this small church, with its molded façade and dilapidated exterior, was the site of Anselmo Duarte's award-winning film adaptation of Dias Gomes's play, *O Pagador de Promessas*, as well as a music video by Paul Simon. Today, the steps outside are often used as an impromptu spot for jazz performances and poetry readings, and provide a perfect vantage point for savoring city views.

IGREJA DA NOSSA SENHORA DO ROSÁRIO DOS PRETOS. The bright blue rococo church facing the Largo do Pelourinho was built by slaves and freedmen in the 1600s as a site for their religious ceremonies; elite whites banned all unorthodox religious activity in the church for a time before it returned to the hands of Salvador's Afro-Brazilian community. The neoclassical style is evident in the three interior altars, one of which is dedicated to Nossa Senhora do Rosário. *(Largo do Pelourinho. Open daily 8am-6pm.)*

PALÁCIO RIO BRANCO. The first seat of the colonial government of Brazil, this majestic building now serves as a memorial to former Baiano governors and houses a cultural foundation. The memorial is worth a look if only to admire the grandeur of Brazil's heyday, when sugar plantation revenues allowed colonial administrators free license in building construction. The interior of the *palácio* is done in marble, bronze, and crystal, providing quite a contrast to the poverty of the surrounding city. *(Facing Pça. Municipal and the Elevador Lacerda on Rua Chile. ☎322 7255. Open Tu-F 10am-noon and 2-6pm.)*

BEYOND PELOURINHO

IGREJA DO NOSSA SENHORA BOM JESUS DO BONFIM. The site of the annual **Lavagem do Bonfim,** a ritualistic washing of the church (amidst much revelry) that takes place during the second week in January, this church has a special spiritual significance for most Baianos. *Candomblistas* come to the church to pray outside, while Catholics believe one of the back rooms inside the church has a miraculous healing power. Baianos from all over the state bring images and casts of diseased or wounded loved ones to the room so that they may be cured. These special *ex-votos*, as the objects are called, are left behind in the room and make up quite a bizarre collection of plastic limbs and grim photographs. The church itself was built between 1745 and 1772, and remains one of the holiest sites in all of northeastern Brazil. *(Largo do Bonfim. Take any "Bonfim" or "Ribeira" bus from Pça. Cairu or Av. da França. ☎316 2196. Open daily 8am-7pm. Masses M 8am; Tu, Th, Sa 2pm and 6pm; F and Su 5:30am, noon, 2:30, 7pm.)*

FORTE DO SANTO ANTÔNIO DA BARRA. The black-and-white striped *farol* (lighthouse) seated atop the fort makes this 16th-century structure a Barra landmark. The building has historical significance for its role in aiding the defeat of the Dutch in Brazil's early days as a Portuguese colony. Today the fort houses a museum and restaurant; the grassy area around it is popular with couples and students in the evenings. *(Av. Oceânica, Barra. ☎264 3296. Open daily 9am-7pm. Restaurant open until 9pm. R$3; students with ID, children under 10, and seniors R$1.50.)*

FORTE MONTE SERRAT & PONTA DA HUMAITÁ. At the very tip of the Itapagipe peninsula, the white-washed fort near the newly-built Humaitá lighthouse is a treasure for military architecture buffs. Construction on the edifice began in the early 16th century. The fort's large upper level provides amazing views of the entire city on one side and the Baía de Todos os Santos on the other. *(At the Ponta da Humaitá in the Cidade Baixa. Take any "Ribeira" bus from the Cidade Baixa; the fort is along the waterfront. Open Tu-Su 2-6pm.)*

MUSEUMS

Salvador has a phenomenal collection of museums, from Afro-Brazilian themed cultural centers to contemporary art showrooms. They are spread out across several neighborhoods, with a good number of them in Vitória and Barra and an even greater amount in Pelourinho, where many privately-owned galleries feature contemporary pieces for sale; artists here will often accept commissions as well. The *Bahia Cultural* guide from Bahiatursa lists current exhibitions and changes in hours or scheduling for all the major museums of Salvador.

MUSEU DE ARTE MODERNA DA BAHIA. The Museum of Modern Art's collection is housed in several colonial buildings in the historical Solar do Unhão complex, constructed nearly four centuries ago. The Solar facility includes a theater, several temporary and permanent exhibition halls, a restaurant, a public garden, and even a small research library. The collections represent the best of Brazilian modern art, much of it on loan from contemporary art capital São Paulo. The waterfront views from the restaurant and garden are not to be missed. Solar do Unhão is a bit out of the way, but well worth the trek. *(Av. Contorno, Solar do Unhão. From the Mercado Modelo, head toward Barra on Av. do Cotorno; the complex is 2km down the road on the right, past the Barra Marina. ☎329 0660. Galleries open Tu-F 1-7pm, Sa-Su 2-8pm. Gardens open Tu-F 9am-7pm, Sa 9am-8pm, Su 9am-6pm. Free.)*

MUSEU DA CIDADE. Facing the Largo do Pelourinho, this museum was inaugurated in 1975 and is dedicated to the Afro-Brazilian traditions of Bahia. The exhibit on Terreiros de Candomblé is a must-see: colorful life-sized *papier-mâché* women in full dress represent the various *orixás*, with English placards describing their meaning and connections to Yoruba traditions. There are also excellent paintings depicting Baiano life and culture. *(Largo do Pelourinho 3, next to the Jorge Amado Center. Head down Rua Alfredo do Brito from Terreiro de Jesus. ☎321 1967. Open M, W-F 9am-6:30pm; Sa-Su 1-5pm. R$1.)*

MUSEU AFRO-BRASILEIRO. Housed in the old medical school along with the Medical Memorial and Museu de Arqueologia e Etnologia da UFB (Ethnology and Archeology Museum of the Federal University of Brazil; ☎321 3971; open M-F 9am-5pm), this superb collection of religious art contains over a thousand pieces, from wooden sculptures depicting slave life to more modern paintings. Worth noting are the old photographs of Baiano architecture, which illustrate the level of reconstruction the historical center has undergone since it was declared a World Heritage Site. *(Terreiro de Jesus, in the old Faculdade de Medicina, facing the Terreiro adjacent to the Basílica. ☎321 0386. Open M-F 9am-5pm. R$2; students and children under 10 R$1.)*

MUSEU DA ARTE DA BAHIA. Set in an old colonial mansion opposite the waterfront on the Ladeira da Barra, this collection contains a permanent exhibit of Bahia's most famous painters, among them the well-known Manoel Lopes Rodrigues. Be sure to see *O Adeus*, one of his larger works, which depicts a woman with an enigmatic smile and is often cited as characteristic of Rodrigues's style. In the opposite facing gallery, an exhibit on Igreja do Bonfim contains oil paintings and sketches of the church and the famous Lavagem do Bonfim ceremony. *(Av. 7 de Setembro 2340. Head down the Ladeira da Barra from Pça. Campo Grande; the museum is on the right, after Museu Geológica. ☎336 9450. Open Tu-F 2-7pm, Sa-Su 2:30-6:30pm. R$4; students, seniors, and children under 10 R$2; Th free.)*

MUSEU GEOLÓGICA DA BAHIA. Amethyst geodes and giant chunks of rose quartz welcome the visitor to Bahia's official gem collection, which may be interesting to first-time viewers but doesn't contain many finely-cut or rare stones. The museum is divided into two buildings: the one facing the street houses rocks, while the more modern gallery behind it has dinosaur skeletons and displays perfect for children. *(Av. 7 de Setembro 2195. Head down the Ladeira da Barra from Pça. Campo Grande. ☎336 6922. Open Tu-F 2-7pm, Sa-Su 2pm-6:30pm. Free.)*

MUSEU CARLOS COSTA PINTO. On the waterfront side of the winding Ladeira da Barra is this fully converted mansion from the 1950s, which houses an opulent display of period furniture, jewelry, and paintings from the 17th to 20th centuries. Worth checking out are the fine silver and crystal pieces on display, as well as the incredible view. *(Av. 7 de Setembro 2490. ☎336 6081. Open W-M 2:30-7pm. R$5; students with ID R$3; Th free.)*

BEACHES

Beaches in Salvador have distinct personalities: the more deserted, rocky areas attract crowds of surfers, while others attract families and hordes of vendors. Heading westward from the beginning of Barra, one can find a range of beach scenes. The most crowded, **Praia do Porto da Barra,** is centered on a small cove that faces west, making it perfect for gazing at the sunset. Vendors peddle everything from the famed grilled cheese on a stick (*queijo coalho;* R$0.75 and worth every *centavo*) to *shiatsu* massages (R$30 per hr.) The water here is calm and clear, and many more serious swimmers make the deeper areas their training ground. There's also a volleyball net and designated football area. Farther west past the *farol* (lighthouse), the **Praia do Farol** gets big waves and crowds of surf-seeking teenage boys. Stick to the sand and watch, as many tourists have been injured on the craggy rocks jutting out of the water, even at high tide. **Praia de Ondina,** three kilometers farther west, has outdoor basketball courts and a wheelchair accessible point opposite a rehabilitation center. The best *barracas* are at **Praia de Aleluia** and **Praia do Flamengo,** both of which have showers and public bathrooms, and are more popular in the afternoons and evenings.

All beaches are accessible by bus: all airport routes run along the waterfront, and buses to Rio Vermelho pass the Farol and Ondina beaches along the way. Salvador's last major beach, **Praia do Forte,** is far from the *centro*—55km from the airport—but well worth the trip for its crystal waters, Technicolor array of fish, and TAMAR sea turtle project headquarters (see **Daytrips,** p. 368).

OUTDOOR ACTIVITIES

Salvador's main attractions are its beaches, and most activity is centered on the waterfront. **Surfing** is a popular sport; even the rockiest beaches attract hoards of talented *surfistas* careening down waves. **Escola Espírito do Surf** in Barra is a popular school that also offers *capoeira* classes. (☎351 5162; www.espiritodosurf.hpg.com.br. Classes from R$10. Course schedules vary according to season.)

Diving is another popular option in Salvador because of the number of *naufrágios* (shipwrecks) off the coast; visibility is usually better outside the Apr.-July rainy season, when the water isn't cloudy from run-off. **Bahia Scuba,** in the Bahia Marina on Av. do Contorno, is a PDIC-associated facility offering a number of courses, from beginning open-water to advanced and instructor-levels. Guided night- and wreck-dives are well worth the R$150. (☎321 0156; www.bahiascuba.com.br.) SSI- and PADI-affiliated **Dive Bahia,** Av. 7 de Setembro 3809, near the Praia do Porto, is another reputable agency, with an English-speaking instructor who can accommodate first-timers. (☎264 3820; www.divebahia.com.br. Complete equipment rental and guided dive with 2 tanks R$150.)

During the summer, it is possible to go skydiving on Itaparica Island. Prices vary according to season and availability; contact **Skydive Itaparica** for details. (☎9953 1000; www.skydiveitaparica.com.br.)

NIGHTLIFE

As is the case in most parts of Brazil, Salvador's nightlife is incredibly varied, and caters to every budget, age, and musical taste. At the cheap end, live music in several Pelourinho *praças* is often free and open to the public; *barracas* from Barra to Itapuã are another inexpensive option where you can get beer and *caipirinhas.* For a more formal scene, head to one of the countless bar/restaurants in Rio Vermelho and Pituba, Salvador's wealthier suburbs. Generally, the dress code in bars and clubs is casual; you can party in anything from sneakers to stilettos and feel at home. At the most expensive places, it's better to dress the part, if only to avoid disapproving looks from other patrons.

PELOURINHO & THE CENTRO HISTÓRICO

Home to Salvador's highest concentration of bars and live music spots, the Centro Histórico is one of the best places to enjoy samba, *bossa nova*, and *axé*. All establishments listed below are within one mile of Terreiro de Jesus, making it easy to simply follow the music to nightspots. Most action occurs on Tuesday and Saturday nights, when live percussion bands perform in the Largo do Pelourinho and often on stages in Terreiro de Jesus and the Largo Tereza Batista. Check **Entertainment** (p. 365) for more details on this legendary scene.

Cinema Paradiso, Pça. Quincas Berro d'Água 30 (☎322 9891), is a film-themed bar with delightfully appropriate menu choices, including the Fred Astaire sandwich (ham, tomato, and mozzarella; R$8). *Caipirinha* R$3. *Kiwirinha* R$4. Beer R$2-3. Open Tu-Sa 7pm-late, Su 7pm-1am. Visa.

Kibe & Cla, Pça. Quincas Berro d'Água 50 (☎322 1673), next to Cinema Paradiso. A chain bar that specializes in *chopp* (R$1.50). The outdoor patio area is a popular nightspot, with free live music from the *praça*. Like many Pelo bars, this place is highly touristed and non-*chopp* drinks are a bit expensive. Open Tu-Su 6:30pm-2am. MC.

Cravo Rastafari (☎241 3625), facing the Largo do Pelourinho opposite Igreja dos Pretos, is popular with reggae-lovers. Live bands pump their sounds into the open-air patio, and the bar is filled with photographic tributes to Bob Marley. It's the perfect atmosphere for dancing, made even better by the availability of cheap beer, whiskey, and mixed drinks (R$1-3). Live music Tu and Sa nights, starting at 9pm; cover R$5. Open Tu-F 6pm-1am, Sa 10pm-1am, Su 6-10pm.

Quereres, Rua Frei Vicente 7 (☎321 1616), off Rua Gregório Mattos, is a stylish bar/restaurant with live MPB and rock and a phenomenal menu, voted "Best of Bahia" by *Veja* magazine. Formal upstairs dining area and downstairs bar with a funky vibe (complete with antique saxes and exposed brick). Red Bull R$6, beer R$2-3. Live music Tu-Su 8pm. Cover R$5. Open M-Tu noon-midnight, W-Sa noon-2am, Su 6pm-2am. MC/V.

BARRA & VITÓRIA

Discounting the historic district's live music and percussion, the best spots to spend an evening are outside Pelourinho, in the Vitória and Barra neighborhoods, as well as in the sprawling suburbs of Rio Vermelho and Pituba. From glittery bars to sweaty dance clubs, this is where to find Salvador's most vibrant nightlife, away from the touristy vibe of the Centro Histórico. Barra has a few busy clubs and waterfront bars, plus a seedy but harmless area of the Largo do Porto da Barra which is home to a strange blend of beer-sipping backpackers, stray dogs, prostitutes, and inexpensive Chinese food.

Bar da Ponta, Barra Design Center, Av. Contorno 2 (☎326 2211), along the waterfront, makes guests feel like they're walking on water—glass walls line the posh bar, which juts into the bay for extraordinary sunset views. Funky orange suede chairs, inviting appetizers (buffalo cheese and pineapple R$5), imported liquors, and exotic cocktails make it a top Salvador nightspot. Frangelico R$5.50. Strawberry daiquiri R$6.50. AmEx/MC/V.

Gloss, Rua Alfonso Celso 60 (☎264 2621), is the city's bumping electronica club, with smooth lounge decor and a VIP room. Weekend theme parties feature disco and 80s music, while F caters to a younger crowd. Drinks are not as overpriced as in some clubs (shots start at R$4). Snack menu for late-night munchies includes tiny pizzas (R$3). 18+. Cover R$18-20. Open Th-Sa 11pm-late, Su 6pm-2am. Visa.

Marrakesh Dancing Bar, Rua Augusto Frederico Schmidt 312 (☎247 2260), in the Jardim Brasil. It's not the bar but the patrons who swing their hips to lounge music and relax on plush sofas. Th live pop-rock ("poppy hock") and F dance music attracts a twenty-something crowd. Tasty Middle Eastern appetizers round out the scene (falafel R$8). Beer R$2. 21+. Cover F-Sa R$15 men, R$10 women; Th and Su R$10. Open Th-Sa 10pm-late, Su 8pm-late. DC/MC/V.

Mahi Mahi, Av. 7 de Setembro 2068 (☎336 7736), in a charmless luxury hotel in Vitória. This bar's main (only?) virtue is its position high above the rocky cliffs overlooking the Baía de Todos os Santos. Thai-influenced entrees will burn a hole in most budgets, but drinks are cheaper and include exotic selections like the *lychee caipirinha* (R$5.50). Downstairs poolside café is a good daytime spot with similarly stunning views. Open M-Th 10am-midnight, F-Sa 9am-1am, Su 9am-midnight. AmEx/MC/V.

Habeus Copos, Rua Marques de Leão 172 (☎247 4996), near the lighthouse. Named for a famous Carnaval *banda,* this has been a Barra favorite since it opened in the late 70s, and is popular with politicians and celebrities. The crowd is older (30s-40s) and the atmosphere relaxed; don't miss the fruit *caipiroskas,* made with kiwi and strawberry (R$3.50). Also at Pça. Berro d'Água, Pelourinho. Open daily 10pm-2am. AmEx/MC/V.

Café do Farol, Pça. Alminrante Tamandaré s/n (☎267 8881), inside the ancient Forte Santo Antônio, is a relaxing place for sunset drinks. The live piano (Tu-Sa 6pm), combined with the sound of the waves, is perfect for easing limbs sore from climbing around the lighthouse. Cheesy nautical decor popular with tourists and a younger crowd. Beer R$2-3. Cover F-Su R$4. Entrance to fort (before 7pm) R$3; students and seniors R$1.50. Open 9am-11pm Tu-Su.

RIO VERMELHO & PITUBA

Farther from the *centro* but accessible by bus or taxi, these suburbs house Salvador's hottest *discotecas* and bars, as well as an up-and-coming restaurant scene. If you're looking for a cluster of generic clubs in a safe environment, head to the **Aeroclube Plaza Show** in Boca do Rio (near Pituba), an outdoor shopping complex with a collection of decent *chopperias* and bars (all of which are packed on weekend nights); clubs in this area are all within stumbling distance.

French Quartier, Av. Otávio Mangabeira 2323 (☎240 1491), in the Jardim dos Namorados, recreates the sounds of New Orleans with excellent live bluegrass, soul, and jazz and the only cajun-creole menu in Bahia—including spicy shrimp plates (R$20+) and jambalaya (R$26). Cover Su-W R$6, Th-Sa R$7. Open daily 5pm-3am. AmEx/MC/V.

Fashion Clube, Av. Otávio Mangabeira 2472 (☎346 0012), in the Jardim dos Namorados, is the newest watering hole for *fashionistas* and Baianos with money to burn. The 2-level dance club has several VIP rooms and a DJ stage with a giant video screen above it, complete with theme dancers. The club pumps a dancey mix of Brazilian sounds from the likes of DJ Patifé. Drinks are overpriced and unspectacular, but you certainly won't notice while getting down with the hottest crowd north of Ipanema. Smirnoff Ice R$7; Red Bull R$8. Beer R$3-4. Women 18+, men 21+. Cover R$20-25 women, R$25-35 men. Open W-Sa 10pm-5am. AmEx/MC/V.

Café Cancun, Aeroclube Plaza, Av. Otávio Mangabeira 6000 (☎461 0600), is Mexican-themed, with a south-of-the-border snack menu including nachos and burritos (R$6-10). After midnight, the café gets funky with a young crowd and Latin music, from Paulina Rubio to Ricky Martin. 18+. Cover R$15-25. AmEx/MC/V.

Rock in Rio, Aeroclube Plaza (☎461 0300), has live bands on weeknights, mainly playing rock and *samba.* In between, DJs spin the latest dance music. The balcony and mezzanine is popular with an older crowd, while the lower dance floor packs in twenty-something Brazilians belting out rock lyrics or swinging to *samba* beats. *Caipirinhas* R$3, beer R$1-2. 17+. Cover R$8-20. Open W-Su 10pm onward. AmEx/MC/V.

Salvador Pub, Rua do Meio 154 (☎334 3704, 3495 0794; www.salvadorpub.com.br), in Rio Vermelho, is a genuine English pub, complete with a selection of draft beers on tap and themed decor. The crowded Happy Hour attracts local businessmen and professionals. Music is a sophisticated mix of blues and jazz. Highly recommended are the *chopp cremoso* (creamy *chopp;* R$3.20) and *calabresa* appetizers (R$9-11). Cover R$3.50. Open daily 6pm-onward. AmEx/MC/V.

Cien Fuegos, Rua Alexandre Gusmão 60 (☎334 7915), in Rio Vermelho. A mirror-lined Mexican bar and taqueria known for its quality imported tequilas (R$3-6) and popular with couples. Nachos are delicious, with fresh *queijo Minas* (cheese from Minas Gerais; R$9). Drink minimum R$10 for women; R$15 for men. AmEx/DC.

Satélite Bar, Av. Otávio Mangabeira 940 (☎363 5151), outside Pituba in Patamares, is known for its Sa night "flashback" parties, with music from the 70s-90s. The bar/*danceteria* has a late-night snack menu with fries and sandwiches (R$4-6). Despite having opened quite recently, this place gets packed on weekend nights. Cover R$25-30. Open Th-Sa 10pm-late. AmEx/MC/V.

GAY & LESBIAN NIGHTLIFE (GLS)

Possibly the only city in northern Brazil with an active gay and lesbian scene, Salvador has a few clubs that are popular with the GLS (*Gay, Lesbian, Sympatizantes*) crowd and many places with GLS nights. Like most of Brazil, Salvador's club culture is surprisingly accepting, and gay and lesbian couples usually aren't hassled even in non-GLS-only places. For listings of seasonal events, parties, and GLS nights, contact the helpful **Grupo Gay da Bahia** (☎322 2176), in Pelourinho.

OFF Club, Rua Dias d'Ávila 33 (☎267 6215; www.offclub.com.br), in **Barra.** Bumping with international dance music, OFF has 3 floors and outrageous live dancers with moves not suited for the timid. Weekly ladies-only (Clube da Luluzinha) and gentlemen-only (Clube do Bolinha) nights. Monthly "flashback" parties have music from the last few decades, popular with a mixed crowd. 18+. Cover R$15. Open Th 11:30pm-4am, F-Sa 11:30pm-6am, Su 7pm-1am. AmEx/MC/V.

Boate YES, Rua Gamboa de Cima 24, far from the *centro* in **Gamboa,** is another popular GLS spot, less flashy than OFF and Gloss. The bi-level club has DJs spinning dance music on the lower level and an upstairs area with video games and occasional live music. 18+. Cover R$7-10. Open F-Su until later. Visa.

Gloss, Rua Alfonso Celso 60 (☎264 2621), has a GLS night on Su, which features its standard electronica fare. See p. 363.

ENTERTAINMENT

CINEMA

Brazilians love the latest Hollywood blockbusters, which play not long after their US release with Portuguese subtitles. Popular European films occasionally make it to big theaters, but are more common at the cinemas in Salvador's libraries and galleries. For indie and art film listings, check Bahiatursa's *Bahia Cultural* guide.

Multiplex Iguatemi, Shopping Iguatemi (☎450 9500), off Av. Magalhães in the 3rd-floor food court. A 12-screen multiplex with the latest American flicks, as well as a handful of European and Brazilian films. Wheelchair accessible. R$14; students with ID, seniors, and children under 10 R$7. Open daily 1pm-midnight. MC/V.

UCI Cinemas Aeroclube, Aeroclube Plaza, Av. Otávio Mangabeira 6000 (☎461 0604), in Boca do Rio, is a 10-theater cinema with plush seats; crowds are common on weekends and holidays. M, T, and Th R$12; W R$8; F-Su R$14. Students with ID, seniors, and children under 10 half-price. Wheelchair accessible. AmEx/MC/V.

Cine Barra, Av. Centenário 2992 (☎264 5795), on the 1st fl. of Shopping Barra, has 2 screens and cheaper prices. F-Tu R$8; W and Th R$6. Students with ID, seniors, and children under 10 half-price.

Cine Teatro do ICBA, Av. 7 de Setembro 1809 (☎337 0120), has occasional art films. Admission prices vary depending on the film.

LIVE MUSIC

Pelourinho is the place to go for live outdoor music; many of the percussion groups that have achieved international fame outside of Salvador play for free here (among them *axé* progenitors **Olodum** and Carlinhos Brown's alma mater, **Timbalada**). The *Bahia Cultural* guide, available at Bahiatursa, has a listing in the back called *Pelourinho Dia & Noite*, which contains a monthly calendar of all live music in the Centro Histórico. Most of the bands and musicians listed perform in one of three areas: the **Largo Tereza Batista,** an open-air stage and dance floor on Rua Gregório de Matos at Rua Barreto, and at **Terreiro de Jesus** and **Largo do Pelourinho.** The following listings are for regular live music performances in Pelourinho; many bars and restaurants also have live music (see **Nightlife,** p. 362).

Olodum (☎321 5010), a Carnaval group that achieved international fame in the early 1990s for its unique African drumming style, also performs in the Largo Tereza Batista, every Tu Dec.-Carnaval, with infrequent off-season shows. The group also has a cultural center (p. 350) that offers music courses. Shows 8pm-midnight. Cover R$20; students with ID R$10.

Swing do Pelo, a percussion-only group specializing in *axé,* plays for free every Tu and Sa night in the Largo do Pelourinho (8:30-10:15pm). The group of 20-odd young men is unbelievably talented; some band members entertain audiences with furious *samba* moves or by tossing their giant drums into the air and flipping their drumsticks. The band's CD, on sale at the performances for R$20, is an excellent buy.

Didá Banda Feminina (☎321 9145). Didá is an all-female band that plays a mix of Brazilian sounds at least twice every month in Pelourinho, usually at the Largo Tereza Batista. The tourist office has a schedule of their performances, which are lively and popular with locals.

Filhos de Gandhy (☎321 7073), the legendary Carnaval group, has a permanent location in the Cidade Baixa at Rua Marcel de Baixo 53; they have frequent performances leading up to Carnaval and in June-July at various locations throughout the Centro Histórico, most free to the public. Call ahead for times and locations; watching the band perform live is a rare treat that should not be missed.

THEATERS

As the artistic center of Salvador, Pelourinho has several theaters showing plays, dance shows, and the like; Bahiatursa's *Bahia Cultural* guide lists shows and times. A must-see is the colorful *balé foclórico* show at the Theatro XVIII, which combines African rhythms with Brazilian dance styles. Other major theaters offer musical theater, comedy shows, dance and vocal performances. The inexpensive ticket prices and extraordinary variety of shows make Salvador's theaters an interesting alternative to standard city nightlife, and one that is quickly growing in popularity among tourists. Many of the theaters offer discounts for students with ID, children, and seniors—ask when you buy tickets.

Theatro XVIII, Rua Frei Vicente 18 (☎322 0018; www.theatroxviii.com.br). From Terreiro de Jesus facing Igreja de São Domingos, walk down Rua Francisco Barreto; make a left onto Rua Accioli (at Albergue das Laranjeiras); the theater is 2 blocks down, across the street. Tickets R$3-5. Ticket office open M-F 9am-6pm.

Teatro SESC-Senac, Largo do Pelourinho 19 (☎322 8273), the local campus of a national trade school, SESC-Senac also has a popular *balé foclórico* in an outdoor amphitheater that includes audience participation at the end. In the thick of sweltering Brazilian summers, it's a favorite of A/C-hating theater-lovers.

Teatro Castro Alves, Pça. Dois de Julho s/n (☎532 2323, 339 8000), in Campo Grande, is by far the city's largest theater and cultural venue, and the top place to go for various big-name Brazilian shows and dance troupes. Ticket office open M-F 9am-6pm, Sa 9am-2pm.

Teatro ACBEU (☎337 4395) is a smaller theater affiliated with a local academic program that features plays and music concerts, as well as occasional student recitals. There is also an art cinema with artsy films.

SHOPPING

Shopaholics can get their fix in the myriad markets and malls of Salvador. The latter get packed at night and many have gourmet restaurants and cinemas as well. Street vendors all over Pelourinho sell overpriced necklaces and the like, mainly designed for tourists; a better place to buy jewelry is outside the Mercado Modelo or on the Porto da Barra beach. For bootleg CDs, try the vendors at the late-night juice bars on Rua Miguel Brunier near Barra Shopping; if you bargain, you can pick up three CDs for as little as R$10.

Shopping Iguatemi, on Av. Antônio Carlos Magalhães (☎0800 71 2020), opposite the Terminal Rodoviário, is a challenge to navigate, even for die-hard shoppers. At night, the food court is quite a scene. Houses all major department stores and Bahia's largest movie theater, the 12-screen Multiplex. Open M-Sa 10am-10pm, Su 1-10pm.

Shopping Barra, Av. Centenário s/n (☎339 8222), 1 block in from Av. Oceânica, is a bit smaller than Iguatemi but nonetheless has a good selection of shops and a surprisingly varied food court, including the buffet-style Middle-Eastern **Rabbune** and **Califa** restaurants. **Bourbon Café** at the main entrance is one of the only places in Salvador with iced coffee (R$3-4). Open M-Sa 10am-9pm, Su 1-9pm.

Barra Design Center, Pça. dos Tupinambás 2, at Av. Contorno (tucked away behind the Petrogas station), is an ultramodern converted warehouse where prominent interior designers and artists have set up shop. While you may not be interested in buying sofas or carpets, there are a few jewelry stores, a cigar and wine shop, and several art-filled galleries for browsing, plus the excellent Trapiche Adelaide restaurant, perfect for a cup of tea or an afternoon martini.

Aeroclube Plaza Show, Av. Otávio Mandabeira 6000 (☎462 8000), Boca do Rio. Take any "Aeroclube" bus (30min., R$1.30-1.50) from Pça. da Sé or along the waterfront in Barra. This outdoor strip mall has 143 stores—from surf shops to high fashion outlets, plus an outdoor food court with sushi, gourmet sandwiches, and ice cream parlors. There's also a playground for children, a giant movie theater, and a number of bars and clubs. Shops open M-Sa and holidays noon-11pm, Su noon-10pm; bars and restaurants open daily noon-1am. Nightclub hours vary.

Mercado Modelo, Pça. Cayru 250, opposite the Elevador Lacerda. Built in 1861 as a maritime customs post, the market now houses nearly 300 *barracas* or stalls, specializing in touristy goods and fabulous handicrafts from the region, including woven hammocks, baskets, and jewelry made from Amazonian seeds and nuts. In the late afternoon, the Mercado hosts frequent live music shows and *capoeira rodas,* though these are not as good as in Pelourinho and cater to tourists. There are also food stalls and a waterfront restaurant with decent views of the port from the upper level. Better prices on hammocks and clothing can be found at the stalls outside the building, facing the elevator. Open M-Sa 9am-6pm, Su 9am-2pm.

La Cueva da las Pedras, Ladeira do Carmo 72 (☎243 2259), opposite C&C Turismo in Pelourinho, is the place to go if you're looking for gemstones. An unassuming closet-sized shop packed with all sorts of stones, from finely cut emeralds to chunks of amethyst. The Argentine owners cut stones on site, and often sell their pieces to H. Stern and other expensive jewelers. Open M-Sa 9am-6pm.

FESTIVALS & EVENTS

Salvador is—without a doubt—one of the party powerhouses of South America. The city packs in over two million visitors for Carnaval, the largest street celebration in Brazil, and the momentum barely slows during the rest of the year, when celebrations and holidays occur with mind-numbing frequency. The **Lavagem do Bonfim,** on the second Sunday in January each year, may be Bahia's most interesting religious event, in which thousands of white-robed worshippers scrub the steps of Igreja do Bonfim with scented water. Traditionally, people following syncretic cults (such as Candomblé) were forbidden from entering Catholic churches; the ritual washing is a symbol of solidarity for many in the Afro-Brazilian community. The **Festa da Iemanjá,** held each year on Feb. 2, commemorates the Yoruba goddess of the sea, celebrated in Candomblé as the mother of all deities. In Rio Vermelho, worshippers head to the beaches with offerings to the goddess, including flowers and mirrors, which are left in the sea to be carried to her. On this night, the beaches are crowded, and live music drifts in from every corner of the neighborhood. Salvador's version of the **Festas Juninas** are centered on the Festa São João. During July 19-24, many shops and government buildings close, and employees get a chance to enjoy live *forró* and traditional Baiano cuisine, plus bonfires and fireworks, in the evenings. The **Festas de São Cosme & Damião** are celebrated on September 27 each year, in the main church of the suburb of Liberdade. *Candomblistas* prepare the African-based *caruru* for revelers, and parties stretch into the night. (See p. 58 for more on Carnaval in Salvador.)

DAYTRIPS FROM SALVADOR

CACHOEIRA ☎75

This quiet colonial village is a perfect break from the bustle of Salvador. The crumbling facades and decaying cathedrals hint at Cachoeira's former grandeur as Brazil's richest and most populated city. Declared a national historical monument in 1971, the small *centro* is packed with museums, churches, and restored buildings, all a short walk from the tranquil waterfront where most accommodations and services are located. **Conjunto do Carmo,** an imposing cathedral with attached convent, boasts a gold-leaf interior with Asian architectural influences. (Open M-F 9am-noon and 2-5pm, Sa-Su 6am-2pm and 6-8pm.) Another must-see is the **Fundação Museu Hansen Bahia,** Rua 13 de Maio 13, which houses a collection of bold prints and sculptures by Karl Hansen, a German veteran who moved to Bahia in the 1950s. (☎425 2478; hansenbahia@uol.com.br. Open Tu-F 9am-5pm, Sa-Su 9am-2pm.) The interior of **Igreja Matriz,** on Rua Av. Nery Destacamse, is lined with *azulejos* (imported blue ceramic tiles from Portugal) and gold leaf, reminding visitors of the sugar barons' former extraordinary wealth. (Open daily 7am-6pm.)

Santana (☎450 4951) has **buses** that depart for Cachoeira via Santo Amaro from the central *rodoviária* in Salvador (2hr.; 1 every hr. 5:30am-9:30pm; R$11), and arrive in the market area at Pça. Macie off Rua Lauro de Freitas, where a Santana ticket office is located. Uphill on the left, Rua Lauro de Freitas runs parallel to the waterfront and passes Pça. Doutor Milton, where you'll find **Farmácia da Nossa Senhora do Rosário** (☎425 1256; open M-F 7am-11pm, Sa 8am-8pm) and the **post office**

(☎425 1621; open M-F 9am-6pm). The road then becomes Rua Ana Nery, which ends one block after Igreja Matriz at Pça. da Aclamação, home to the helpful Conjunto do Carmo **tourist office.** (☎425 4887. Open daily 8am-noon and 2-5pm.) Hungry daytrippers can head to the open-air market in Pça. Macie, where cheerful **vendors ❶** serve *milho grelhado* (grilled corn on the cob) and *acarajé.* You can also stock up here on fresh cheese, fruits, and vegetables. (Open daily 6am-8pm.)

SÃO FELIX ☎75

Set on a series of picturesque hills overlooking the Rio Paraguaçu, São Felix is less popular and has fewer sights than its sister city, Cachoeira. The 18th-century **Igreja Matriz de Senhor Deus Menino,** Pça. José Ramos s/n, fills with locals December 16-25, during the Deus Menino festival. (Open 7am-7pm.) **Centro Cultural Dannemann,** Av. Salvador Pinto 29, is housed in an old German *charuto* (cigar) factory on the waterfront. The space now hosts art exhibitions and occasional music performances and festivals; from Tuesday to Saturday, you can also watch cigars being made by traditional methods. (☎425 1220. Open M-F 9am-5pm, cigar viewing Tu-Sa 8am-noon and 1-4:30pm.)

All **Santana buses** to Cachoeira continue across the Dom Pedro II Bridge in São Felix and end up at Pça. Rui Barbosa, where onward transport is available to Maragojipe (30min., every hr. 7am-8:30pm, R$3.50). Vans also go to Maragojipe and Valença (2hr.; every other hr. 7am-6pm; R$7). The *praça* itself is situated at the end of Rua Dr. Seabra, which runs parallel to the waterfront and the second major road, Av. Salvador Pinto. Both begin roughly at the entrance to the Ponte Dom Pedro II, at Pça. José Ramos. Most services are located in neighboring Cachoeira, but São Felix contains the **Hospital Nossa Senhora da Pompéia,** Rua Bocaiúva s/n (☎425 2616), and a **Banco do Brasil,** Rua Seabra 1, complete with Visa ATMs (☎425 2611; open M-F 9am-noon and 2-5pm). There's a small **post office** on Rua Seabra 7. (☎425 2906. Open M-F 9am-5pm.) **Postal code:** 44360-000. For inexpensive on-the-go snacks, try the **lanchonetes** in Pça. Ramos.

ELSEWHERE IN BAHIA

PRAIA DO FORTE ☎71

Praia do Forte has it all, from walks on the beach to treks through the forest to dips in the lake. Regulations restrict urban sprawl and preserve young coconut trees, preventing Forte's tourist infrastructure from overwhelming the town.

TRANSPORTATION & PRACTICAL INFORMATION. Buses run from the bus stop on Av. do Farol to Salvador (1½hr.; every 30min.; R$4). Praia do Forte itself is easy to navigate. From the bus stop, walk straight down the main street, **Avenida ACM,** which veers toward Igreja São Francisco and is home to most of the shops. Rua da Aurora and Alameda da Lua run parallel to Av. ACM. Within the town itself, buggies called *quadriciclos charretes* cost about R$10. The tourist office, **Agência de Viagens–Centro Turistico,** Av. ACM, exchanges money. (☎676 1367; www.prdoforte.com.br. Open daily 9am-7pm.) There is a **24hr. ATM** on Av. ACM. Other services include: **Farmácia do Forte,** Av. ACM (☎676 1476); **police,** Av. do Farol and the beach (☎676 1132); and the **post office,** Av. ACM, next to the bank. (☎676 0311; open M-F 9am-noon and 2-4pm.) **Postal code:** 48280-000.

ACCOMMODATIONS & FOOD. Albergue Praia do Forte ❶, Rua Aurora 3, has friendly staff and is a relatively cheap way to experience clean, communal living. (☎676 1094. Kitchen. Laundry room. Dorms R$24. Singles with TV and fan R$24; doubles with TV and fan R$48. AmEx/MC/V.) Between the forest and beach, **Casa das Praças ❸,** Pça. dos Artistas 8/9, is a more secluded option. The 20 *apartamentos* have TV, *frigo-bar*, and decks with hammocks, and most have A/C. (☎676 1362; pousada@casadepraia.tur.br. High-season singles R$100; doubles R$120. Low-season singles R$65; doubles R$80.) **Sabor da Vila ❷,** Av. ACM, has authentic Baiano food in a cheerful setting. (☎676 1156, 676 1777. Entrees R$14-22. D/DC/MC/V.) **Taverna ❸,** Av. ACM, offers elaborate desserts (R$5.50), a wide varieta of pizzas (R$10-20), and Italian liquors. (Open Tu-Su 11am-1am. AmEx/MC/V.)

SIGHTS & ACTIVITIES. The most popular activities in Praia do Forte are visits to **Projeto TAMAR** (on the beach 5min. from the *centro*) and the **Garcia D'Ávila Castle.** The former is a marine preserve for three species of endangered sea turtles. (☎675 1045. Tours R$4, children R$2.) The castle was once home to a wealthy family who owned land throughout the Northeast. The castle is in the forest far from town roads, and is only accessible by rented buggy or a guide hired from the **Centro Turistico** on Av. ACM (☎676 1367). Other activities—all of which can be arranged through the Centro Turistico—include **parasailing** (9-11:30am; R$7), **snorkeling** (low tide; R$25), **horseback riding** through the dunes (8am-5pm; R$50), and guided tours through the lush **saparinga forest** (4 per day 8:15am-3:45pm; R$25 per person), which end at the D'Ávila Castle.

MORRO DE SÃO PAULO ☎71

On the northern tip of the Tinharé archipelago, Morro de São Paulo is a vacationer's dream: palm trees and airy *pousadas* line four pristine coves, ideal for swimming, diving, and kayaking. Locals depend heavily on the tourist industry, and the town has developed an excellent network of tour operators and travel guides who can arrange nature walks, horseback rides, and rappeling. Outside the high season (Dec.-Apr.), rates drop dramatically and quality accommodations can be found for as little as R$15 per night, with breakfast included. It's an excellent place during June and July, when beaches are less crowded and the Festa de São João (part of the Festas Juninas) attracts nightly live *forró* bands and dancing crowds on a temporary stage across from the Hotel Casarão. The neighboring island of **Boipeba** (see **Daytrips**, p. 373) is easily accessible by boat, and has glassy *piscinas naturais* (pools formed in the ocean by coral reefs), ideal for snorkeling. Despite its increasing popularity, Morro remains an inexpensive and tranquil paradise, and most travelers find themselves spending at least three days here.

TRANSPORTATION. From Salvador, there are two ways to get to Morro: a direct **catamaran** from Salvador, which is fast and easy, or a **ferry-bus-boat** combination that costs slightly less but takes at least five hours and plenty of patience. Catamarans depart (2hr.; 2pm; R$40) from the terminal opposite the Mercado Modelo, and tickets are available at most travel agencies in Salvador and in the terminal itself. (Open daily 9am-5pm.) The alternative begins with a 30min. ferry ride to Bom Despacho on Ilha da Itaparica, leaving from the São Joaquim Ferry Terminal off Av. da França in the Cidade Baixa (2 per hr. 6am-10pm, R$3). From Bom Despacho, **Cidade Sol** runs frequent buses to Valença's *rodoviária* (2hr., 2 per hr. 8am-7pm, R$9). It's a short walk to Valença's port, where there are speedboats to Morro's port, a single dock with an old stone arch leading the way into town (30min., 2 per hr. 8am-5pm, R$7).

An expensive alternative is **Aerostar,** which runs an *aero-taxi* from Salvador's international airport to an airstrip at Praia Terceira in just 20min. Rates per flight depend on the number of passengers; the seven-seater plane costs roughly R$900 per flight. (☎377 4406, 483 1312; www.aerostar.com.br. Salvador airport office open M-F 9am-6pm.)

ORIENTATION & PRACTICAL INFORMATION. The town's dirt road, **Caminha da Praia,** leads from the port to the central **Praça Aureliano Lima,** passes by the Pousada O Casarão, and then heads toward the four main beaches, which are numbered from the *centro* outwards. The main attraction at local favorite **Praia Primeira** is the rappeling cable that leads from the overhanging cliff into the water. **Praia Segunda** is a busy beach perfect for swimming and home to most of the action in Morro, including the city's two *discotecas*, a few bars, and restaurants. Next is **Praia Terceira,** longer and quieter than Segunda and lined with *pousadas*. Beyond this is **Praia Quarta,** which stretches along the town's wild side; there's a small bar and deserted, windswept sands.

The one-room **Centro de Informações ao Turista** is on the left side as you walk toward town from the port. The English-speaking staff can arrange accommodations and tours. (☎483 1083; www.morrosp.com.br. Open Nov.-Mar. daily 9am-6pm, Apr.-Oct. M-F 9am-5pm.) **Supermercado Estevão,** on the same side of the road a few storefronts toward the beach, stocks canned and fresh vegetables, toiletries, and other basic supplies. (☎483 1064. Open daily 7am-9pm.) The **police office** is behind the payphone before Caminho da Praia descends a small hill. (24hr. line ☎9987 0870.) **Farmácia São Lucas** is at the start of Caminho da Praia near the *praça*. (☎483 1164. Open daily 8:30am-11pm. MC/V.) **Morro Digital** is an excellent high-speed Internet café where you can also make international calls and sip cappuccino. (☎483 1159. Open 8am-midnight. R$6 per hr.) Outside the *centro*, there are a few minimarkets with cheap *cachaça*, fruits, and canned food—try **Mercadinho Morro de São Paulo,** adjacent to Pousada Aradinha on the Praia Terceira. (☎483 1253. Open daily 7am-8pm.) **Postal code:** 45400-000.

ACCOMMODATIONS. Morro has a range of options, though the most popular are the abundant mid-range *pousadas*. During the high season (Nov.-Mar. and July) prices nearly double, and advance reservations are highly recommended, even for the least expensive options. The best place to stay on the island is the stylish **Pousada O Casarão ❹,** Pça. Aureliano Lima near the start of Caminho da Praia, a renovated 18th-century mansion with an elegant poolside patio, sauna, and Japanese- and Indian-themed bungalows with A/C, TV, bath, *frigo-bar*, and veranda. (☎483 1049, 483 1022; www.ocasarao.net. Breakfast included. Singles and doubles R$85. MC/V.) **Mareia Pousada ❸** has an in-house sushi bar (high-season only) and impeccable rooms with hammocks, tasteful paintings, A/C, TV, *frigo-bar*, and private bath. (☎483 1224; www.zanzi.com.br/mareia. Breakfast included. Singles R$60; doubles R$80. AmEx/MC/V.)

On Praia Terceira, there are several nearly identical *pousadas;* those not facing the beach should be at least R$10 per night less than places with ocean views. A good option is **Pousada Aradinha ❷,** toward the middle of the strip with a wooden exterior and patio—its breezy doubles are right on the beach. The *pousada* has a pool and all rooms come with A/C, TV, *frigo-bar*, and private bath. (☎483 1116. Breakfast included. Singles and doubles R$35-45.) **Camping Girassol ❶,** inland between the second and third beaches, has some shady spots to pitch a tent. The staff can arrange horseback riding for R$10 per hr. (☎483 1144; atendimento@morrotour.com.br. R$6 per person. Cash only.)

FOOD. For its size, the town has some amazing restaurants catering to all tastes. **Pizzaria Forno a Lenha ❸,** opposite O Casarão, prepares 38 delectable combinations, including savory *rúcula* (with arugula, mozzarella, and sundried tomatoes; R$16-20). For dessert, try *gabriela* (with mozzarella, banana, and cinnamon; R$12-16). (☎482 1101. Open daily 5pm-midnight. MC/V.) **Sabor da Terra ❷,** farther down Caminho da Praia, has the best *moquecas* in town, available without palm oil (*sem dendê*) for weak stomachs; their *moqueca com peixe branco e camarão* (white fish and shrimp with white rice) is R$25 for three people. (☎483 1156. Open Tu-Su noon-2:30pm and 5-11pm.) **Alecrim Restaurante ❹,** on the opposite side of the road, cooks up spicy lobster (*agosta catupiry*; R$27) and a number of seafood dishes; there's also a lunch buffet for R$15 per kg. (☎483 1255. Open daily noon-3pm and 6-11pm. MC/V.) Farther along, **Bar e Restaurante Piscina ❶,** on Praia Quarta, is a good spot for drinks and hot, crisp french fries (R$5). (☎483 1072. Open M-Th 9am-10pm, F-Su 9am-11pm. Visa.) For cheap eats, there are **lanchonetes** all over town, and a cluster of **barracas** at the end of Praia Segunda selling *açaí*, *pastel* (hot savory pastries with various fillings), and fresh *sucos* (R$3-6). Praia Segunda's 24hr. snack bar is perfect for late-night munching.

OUTDOOR ACTIVITIES. The main points of interest on the island are nature-related. **Horseback riding** along the beach is popular, and if you can spare at least two hours, the local guides can take you to forested inland areas, some with streams and tiny waterfalls. (R$10-15 per hr.) Guides walk the beaches with horses in tow, and can also be caught on Praia Terceira before Pousada Aradinha. More adventurous types can try their luck dangling from the cable linking the base of Morro's lighthouse, set on a cliff above town, down into the waves of Praia Primeira, a trip otherwise known as rappeling. This is best arranged with a tour

COBRA CONFUSION. Morro's clean, clear waters make it easy to see the ocean floor, especially on the stiller second beach. Unfortunately, this means many travelers also get to see what they're bathing with: the occasional sand-colored snake slithering around. Panic attacks are usually fueled when locals inform you that the seemingly benign creatures are *cobras;* luckily, this Portuguese term refers to *all* varieties of snakes, even this harmless species. To avoid unpleasantness, drag your feet in the sand if you can't see the bottom.

company; **Morro Tour,** on the main road in town near the post office, has knowledgeable and reputable guides who also lead hikes and boat trips to neighboring islands, including Boipeba. (☎483 1144; www.morrotour.com.br. Rappeling R$30.) **Scuba diving** is popular during the summer (Nov.-Mar.); outside of this season, dive shops are closed. The professional staff at **Morro Dive,** between Segunda and Praia Terceira, provide courses for first-timers and rent equipment to licensed divers. (☎483 1333; omdas@morroaovivo.com.br.) Coordinating dive packages in Morro from Salvador is a headache; to plan ahead, call dive operators directly.

SIGHTS. The island's few old landmarks are all within walking distance. Start at the faded **Portaló,** a stone archway at the top of a ramp leading to the pier, built in the 1600s at the same time as the nearby **Fortaleza** (if heading up the ramp, it's on your left down a grass pathway), constructed to protect the strategically located island and its flour mills from Dutch invaders. It's hard to imagine the run-down walls sheltering hundreds of soldiers and over 50 cannons, as they did during its peak in the 1740s. Head back to the Portaló and up the stairs into town to view **Igreja da Nossa Senhora da Luz,** built in 1845 with subtly detailed gold leaf and silver decorations. Across the road behind the Centro de Informações ao Turista, you'll find a small dirt path leading up to the best sight on the island, the small **Farol do Morro** (lighthouse). Here, you can savor lovely views of the island, particularly when the sun sets and bathes the rocky cliffs in amber light.

NIGHTLIFE & ENTERTAINMENT. During the evenings, most restaurants are open until midnight and serve double duty as bars. There are two open-air nightclubs *(discotecas)* on the island, **Ilha Bela** and **Caitu,** both at the end of Praia Segunda near the *barracas* which open on alternating nights from Wednesday to Sunday. (Open Nov.-Mar. Cover R$5.) Fill up on drinks before you go in at the stands outside, where a *kiwiroska*, *caipirinha*, or *chopp* will set you back only R$1-3. During the **Festa do São João,** held annually the week of June 24, the party moves to the *centro*, where a temporary stage in Pça. Aureliano Lima hosts live *forró* bands and scores of dancing revelers, plus snack and drink booths.

DAYTRIP FROM MORRO DE SÃO PAULO. When Portuguese colonialists arrived in **Boipeba,** they found a pristine island wilderness, and even today the tiny island bears few marks of habitation or development. For this reason, most travelers enjoy the island as a daytrip from Morro de São Paulo. Packages that combine transport, lunch, and snorkeling or diving in the area's crystal-clear *piscinas naturais* (natural pools) are inexpensive and easy to arrange through the **Centro de Informações ao Turista** in Morro. (☎483 1083. Packages R$30+ per person.) An alternative is to go directly from Valença—*lanchas* depart from Valença's port down the mangrove-filled Rio do Inferno (3hr.; 2 per day; R$8). Boipeba and Tinharé are separated by the narrow Rio do Inferno; from here, Boipeba is framed by a series of good, nearly identical beaches including Boca da Mata, Moreré and, at the end of the strip, the Ponta de Castelhanos, ideal for snorkeling and diving. Excursions to the latter can be arranged through **Morro Dive** (see p. 372).

PORTO SEGURO ☎73

One of the first spots to be settled by Portuguese in the early 1500s, Porto Seguro is now a thriving beach town and a top draw for sun-worshipping tourists. During your stay in Porto Seguro, you'll never be far from beautifully calm waters, hot sun, or the seductive beats of *axé* and *forró* that fill the beach air nightly. It is almost impossible not to be drawn into the city's rhythm of daytime relaxation and nighttime partying. If you can stand to drag yourself away, know that Porto Seguro is also the gateway to the even more laid-back and seductive beach town of **Arraial d'Ajuda** (see p. 377), just minutes away by ferry from the mainland.

TRANSPORTATION. The **rodoviária** (☎288 1914) is within walking distance of the *centro.* **São Geraldo** (☎288 1198) has buses to: Belo Horizonte (17hr.; 2pm; R$95); Goiânia (27hr.; every other day 9am; R$121) via Brasília (24hr.; R$107); Rio de Janeiro (19hr.; 5pm; R$97); São Paulo (26hr.; 2:40pm; R$136). **Águia Branca** (☎288 1039) has buses to Salvador (11hr.; 7:30pm; R$83) and Vitória (10hr.; 3 per day 6:30am-9:30pm; *convencional* R$44, *semi-leito* R$64). A **ferry** down Rio Buranhém connects Porto Seguro and Arraial d'Ajuda. Many city buses (R$0.90) run along the coastal Av. Beira Mar, between the *centro*, the *rodoviária*, and the beaches. Buses marked "Cabrália" (R$2) run the entire length of Porto Seguro's beachfront, and continue to Coroa Vermelha and beyond.

ORIENTATION & PRACTICAL INFORMATION. The *centro* occupies a small area between Rio Buranhém and the ocean, and Porto Seguro's beaches are to the north. **Taperapuan,** Porto Seguro's liveliest beach, is 8km from the *centro*, and the popular Coroa Vermelha is just past the city limits. In the *centro*, shopping, bars, and restaurants concentrate on **Passarela do Álcool,** parts of which are known officially as Rua Assis Chateaubriand and Av. Portugal. The **tourist office** is in front of Pça. da Bandeira. (☎268 1390. Open daily 9am-10pm.) Other services include: **24hr. ATMs** in Pça. do Relógio and in a gas station just south of the beach; **Supermercado Marabá,** Av. Getúlio Vargas 296 (☎288 2053; open M-Sa 8am-7:30pm); **Lavanderia Automática,** on Av. dos Navegantes (open M-Sa 8am-noon and 1-5pm); a **24hr. pharmacy** in the *centro* (☎288 1698); and the **post office** (☎288 3117; open M-F 9am-5pm, Sa 9am-1pm).

ACCOMMODATIONS. Porto Seguro seems in places to consist only of hotels, and as soon as you enter the city you will be approached by many city-accredited promotional agents—look for their distinctive t-shirts—with files full of accommodation listings in the city. Their assistance should by no means be dismissed; they will almost always point out a fine hotel in your price range, and can secure you a better rate than you would otherwise be offered. **Tarifa's ❶,** Av. Antônio Osório 65, is somewhat minimal, but is close to lively Passaréla do Álcool. (☎288 1027. High-season singles R$18; doubles R$30. Low-season singles R$15; doubles R$25. Carnaval singles R$45; doubles R$70.) **Hotel Terra Brasil ❷,** Rua do Cajueiro 5, is an impeccably modern hotel, and all rooms come fully equipped with verandas looking outside or into one of the two interior courtyards. (☎288 2502; www.hotelterrabrasil.com.br. High-season singles R$80; doubles R$100. Low-season singles R$30; doubles R$35. Seven-night Carnaval package for two R$1000.) **Pousada Praia dos Lençóis ❶,** Rua Antônio Osório 35, is a good deal with a charming interior garden. (☎288 2877. High-season singles R$18; doubles R$30. Low-season singles R$15; doubles R$20. Carnaval doubles R$45.) **Hotel Navegantes ❷,** Av. 22 de Abril 212, has very appealing rooms and a charming breakfast area. (☎288 2390; www.hotelnavegantes.com.br. High-season singles R$35; doubles R$70. Low-season singles R$30; doubles R$40. Seven-night Carnaval package for two R$800.)

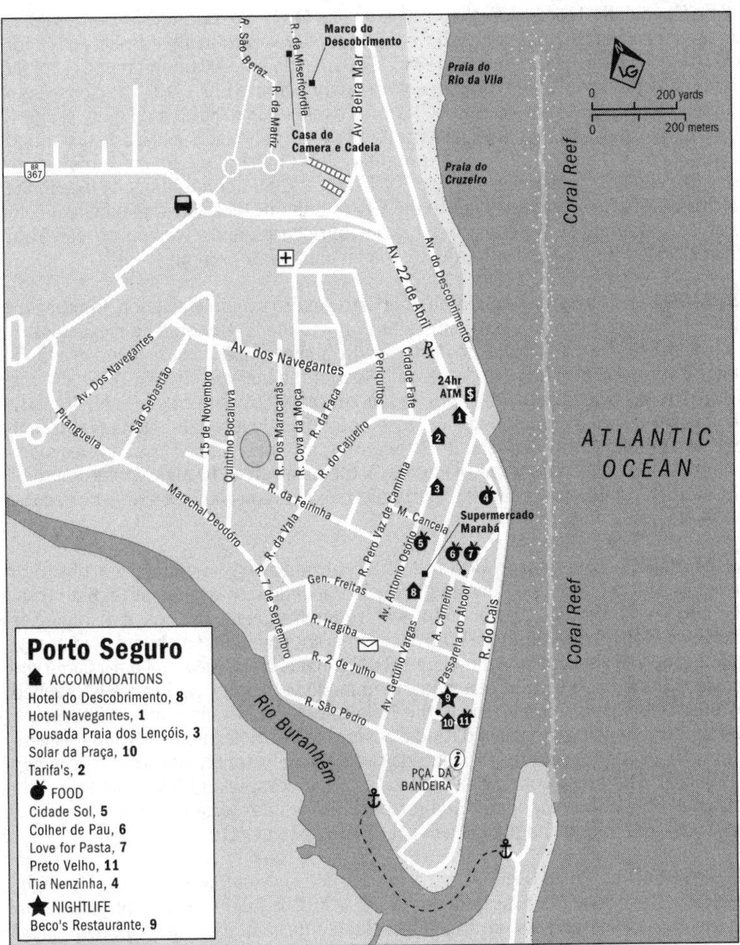

Beira Mar Praia Hotel ❷, Av. Beira Mar 5580, is a relatively simple hotel with an unbeatable location in the *centro* of Taperapuan. (☎679 0881; www.porto-net.com.br/beiramar. High-season *quartos* R$50. Low-season *quartos* R$35.) **Solar da Praça ❷**, Rua Assis Chateaubriand 75, is a simple but attractive hotel right in the tourist center. (☎288 2585. High-season doubles R$50. Low-season singles R$30; doubles R$40. Seven-day Carnaval package R$500.) **Hotel do Descobrimento ❸**, Av. Getúlio Vargas 330, has appealing green rooms with small verandas. (☎288 1795; www.hoteldescobrimento.com.br. High-season doubles R$60. Low-season singles R$30; doubles R$40. Carnaval doubles R$100.)

FOOD. Most restaurants line the Passarela do Álcool. **Tia Nenzinha ❸**, Av. Portugal 170, is a simply decorated restaurant with exquisite seafood and regional cuisine. *Moquecas* for two (R$25-70) are excellent; try the *bobó de camarão* (R$20 for two) for a lighter meal. The house specialty is lobster (R$83 for two). (☎288

1846. Open daily 11am-midnight.) **Colher de Pau ❹,** Travessa Augusto Borges 28, is a popular restaurant claiming to have the best *caldeirada* in all of Brazil (R$69 for two). Most seating is outdoors. (☎288 1574. Open daily 11:30am-midnight.) **Love for Pasta ❸,** Av. Portugal 268, prepares your pasta before your eyes. The house specialty is *tagliatelle con gamberi* (R$26 for two). (☎288 2861. Open daily 4:30pm-1am.) **Preto Velho ❹,** Pça. da Bandeira 30, is the city's longest-established seafood restaurant, with live music and a nightly show by the legendary transvestite Margô. (☎288 3221. Lobster for two R$75. Open M-Sa noon-midnight.) **Cidade Sol ❶,** Rua Antônio Osório s/n, next to the CCAA building, is a tiny but excellent self-service restaurant (R$7 per kg) outside the tourist area, and a welcome break from the prices on the Passarela do Álcool. (Open daily 11am-7:30pm.)

SIGHTS. Beaches and nightlife are Porto Seguro's main attraction, but the city and region are also of great historical importance in Brazil. The **monument** to Cabral's discovery of Brazil is in Porto Seguro's **historic city,** best reached by climbing the staircase at the Trevo de Cabral. Most of the historic city dates back to the 18th century, when the captainship was incorporated by the crown. The 1772 **Casa de Camera e Cadeia,** today housing Museu de Porto Seguro, and **Igreja Matriz** face each other near the monument. Porto Seguro is also part of the Costa do Descobrimento (literally, "Coast of the Discovery"), the name given to the extreme south of the state of Bahia, where the first Portuguese expeditions landed and explored the area in colonial times.

BEACHES. The entire Costa do Descobrimento is famous for beautiful beaches, but the most popular and lively is Porto Seguro's **Taperapuan,** 8km from the *centro*. If the soft sand and still water is not enough, the beach also parties hard: **Axé Moi,** the legendary beachfront restaurant and club, has bikini-clad booty-shaking action going all afternoon. (☎689 3237. Open daily 8:30am-6pm.) **Coroa Vermelha** is the most beautiful beach in the immediate vicinity, and is easily reached by bus. You will not regret a trip to the **Praia do Espelho,** which is about 60km south of the ferry crossing to Arraial d'Ajuda. Several of Porto Seguro's ecotourism agencies have excursions there (R$55 per day). Alternately, rent a motorcycle or buggy (R$30-50). The most popular excursion is to the coral island **Recife de Fora.** The island is only above the water line for part of each day, and has many *piscinas naturais* full of fish and the occasional turtle (R$16 per 4hr. tour).

NIGHTLIFE. Porto Seguro's party infrastructure is unlike any other. The night begins in the *centro* on Pássarela do Álcool, which is full of restaurants, bars, and shops. **Beco's Restaurante,** on Rua Assis Chateaubriand, has outdoor seating and live music nightly. The kitchen specializes in crepes (R$4-6) and Baiano food (R$22-45 for two). (Open 6pm-2am.) The Pássarela do Álcool is an excellent place to sample the Baiano drink *capeta*, for which Porto Seguro is famous. The drink is made from vodka, *guaraná* powder, condensed milk, cinnamon, sugar, and pineapple, and is sold for about R$3 from stands along the beach.

Porto Seguro's main dance clubs open on separate days, and each day has a different party; each club has three or four dance floors, each with its own type of music, so the open-air clubs are sure to satisfy all tastes. Wednesday's **Barramares** and Friday's **Ilha dos Aquarios,** on an island just off the *centro*, are recommended options. (Cover R$20; special acts R$25, including transportation.) **Porto Night** (☎268 2828) coordinates the parties. The club of the day tends to leave Passarela do Álcool and the nearby beaches entirely devoid of activity. For those craving a night on the beach and a few drinks, **Barraca do Gaúcho** at the northern end of Taperatuan is one of very few options; it also has a *rodízio* (R$15). (☎679 2142. Open daily 8am-late.)

ARRAIAL D'AJUDA ☎73

Arraial d'Ajuda has for years been a home for hippies from as far away as São Paulo, Argentina, and Europe, and the mood here is more Bob Marley than *axé*. Arraial d'Ajuda's three main beaches are **Mucugê, Parracho,** and **Pitinga.** The beachfront waterpark, **Eco Parque,** boasts dozens of slides, pools, and sports facilities (R$36). To get to Arraial d'Ajuda, take the **balsa** (ferry) from Porto Seguro (R$1.80). Once you arrive you will need to take a **bus** to the *centro* (R$0.90). The bus will leave you at Pça. Brigadeiro Gomes. **Broduei,** a street full of bars and shops, connects this square to **Praça São Braz,** a block down. **Estrada do Mucugê** leads from Praça São Braz to the beach, Mucugê. From there, you can walk along the water to the beaches Parracho and Pitinga. **Rua Nova,** which has several accommodations and restaurants, also begins at Pça. São Braz. There is a **supermarket** in Pça. São Bento (open M-Sa 8am-6pm). You can find a **pharmacy** (☎575 1239; open daily 8am-midnight) and **Internet access** (☎575 2925; open M-Sa 10am-10pm) on Broduei. The **post office** is in Pça. São Bento. (Open M-F 9am-5pm.)

Arraial d'Ajuda is full of excellent places to stay and eat. An excellent accommodations option is the **Pousada do Paulista ❶,** Rua Nova 180, located in a charming house. (☎575 2004. High-season doubles R$50. Low-season *quartos* R$10.) The family-run **Estalagem Manga Rosa ❶,** Rua Fábio Nobre 172, is half a block from Pça. São Braz, with simple, well-kept *apartamentos* opening onto a front lawn. (High-season doubles R$50. Low-season singles R$15; doubles R$25.) **Pousada Lua Azul ❸,** Rua Ipê 112, is a charming and relaxing *pousada* with a pool and many hammocks. (☎575 1555. High-season singles R$40; doubles R$80. Low-season singles R$25; doubles R$50.)

Bar Bohêmio ❷, on Rua Nova, a block from Pça. São Braz, is a tiny restaurant that makes up in character what it lacks in size, specializing in Israeli food like kebabs (R$7), falafel (R$6), and hummus (R$6). (☎9141 5838. Open daily 7pm-3am.) **Don Fabrizio ❸,** Estrada do Mucugê 402, is a beautiful Italian restaurant, serving several dishes featuring homemade pasta. (☎575 1123; donfabrizio@arraial.net. High-season open daily 1-11:30pm; low-season Th-Su 2pm-11pm.) **Portinho ❷,** Rua do Campo 1, is an excellent self-service restaurant with daily themes to its offerings (R$13 per kg). (☎575 1289. Open daily noon-10pm.) **Boi nos Aires ❸,** Estrada do Mucugê 200, is a very attractive Argentinian steakhouse, with *picanha* (steak; R$16 for 200g or R$31 for 400g). (☎575 2554.) There are several bars on Broduei, Estrada do Mucugê, and in Beco das Cores.

The groovy **Girassol,** Estrada do Mucugê 298, is a favorite gathering place for locals and tourists of all ages coming to drink (R$5-10), or play pool (R$2). (☎575 1717; www.arraialdajuda.com.br. Open daily 6pm-4am.) On Broduei, **Lala's Bar** is small and pleasant; try the *broduei,* a cocktail made from whisky, coconut milk, and chocolate liqueur (R$5). (☎9993 1927. Open daily 10am-5am.)

LENÇÓIS ☎75

Founded by diamond miners in the mid-1800s, Lençóis got its name from the ad hoc communities formed by the pioneers along the river's edge; viewed from above, the white tents of the miners looked to visitors like sheets—in Portuguese, *lençóis*—stretched out to dry. Now an attractive historic town overflowing with colonial charm, Lençóis sits amid a lush mountain forest surrounded by cascading waterfalls and natural swimming pools. Popular with Brazilians and foreigners alike, the town serves primarily as a base for wilderness lovers seeking to explore neighboring Chapada Diamantina (p. 387). While most come for the park, the town itself, with its cobblestone streets and terra-cotta roofs, leads many to extend their stay, and a number of short-term visitors have become long-term residents.

TRANSPORTATION

The town is 12km off the BR-242 highway that connects Salvador and Brasília. While several companies run buses between the two cities, most ignore the turn-off to Lençóis, stopping instead at the small town of **Seabre,** 60km west along the highway. From here there are a limited number of connecting buses to Lençóis, though catching them may necessitate a nighttime layover, especially for travelers arriving from Brasília.

Buses: The *rodoviária* is by the river across from the *centro* at the end of Av. Senhor dos Passos. **Real Expresso** (☎334 1112) sends buses to: **Brasília** (14hr.; 1-2 per day; R$79-87) via **Seabre** (1½hr.; $R6); **Feira de Santana** (4hr.; 2:30pm; R$20); **Palmeiras** (1hr.; M-Sa 2 per day 4:30am-12:30pm; R$5); **Salvador** (6hr.; 1-3 per day; R$31). **Entram** (☎334 1185) connects Lençóis to **São Paulo** (30hr.; F 9:30am; R$110) via **Andarai** (1½hr.; R$6). **São Geraldo** (☎334 1185) goes to **Recife** (18hr.; R$85).

Taxis: Most taxi drivers moonlight as guides and can be hired to get to nearby but otherwise inaccessible towns, hiking spots, caves, and waterfalls. **Eco-Taxi,** Rua Silva Jardim 14 (☎334 1226, 9966 1055), has 4x4 cars that can accommodate up to nine. R$20 per hour. English-speaking guide. Also **Renato Táxi** (☎358 2187, 9966 0154) and **Dilson Taxi Tours** (☎334 1664), both 24hr.

Car Rental: Lukdon Car Rental, Pça. Horâcio de Matos 16 (☎334 1995). Drivers must be 18 and have a credit card. R$80 per 24hr., unlimited km. R$50 per 12hr., 300km.

Bike Rental: Cicloturismo Mountain Bikes, Rua da Lagedo 68 (☎334 1700; ronybikes@bol.com.br). R$40 per day, all gear included. Guided tours also available (see **Tours,** p. 378).

Horse Rental: Sr. Dazim, Rua São Benedito 27, just down the road from Camping Luminar. R$40 per person per day, including guide; R$70 per 2 days, including guide. Bookings best arranged through your local *pousada*. **Rancho Talismá** also rents magnificent horses, though at a higher premium. Booking can be made at the Pousada Verde Puerto (see p. 381). 3hr. R$35 per person; 5hr. R$55 per person; two days R$160 per person, including guide. Min. 2 people.

ORIENTATION & PRACTICAL INFORMATION

Most of the action takes place in the triangular area formed by **Rua da Baderna** and its intersecting streets, **Rua das Pedras** and **Avenida 7 de Setembro.** Pça. Horâcio de Matos houses most local services, along with many tour agencies, bars, and restaurants. *Pousadas* are scattered throughout the town and easy to find.

TOURIST & FINANCIAL SERVICES

Tourist Office: Secretaria de Turismo, Pça. Otaviano Alvas (☎334 1380). Housed in the old Prefeitura Municipal building. Don't leave without picking up the excellent *Guia Lençóis* and maps of the surrounding park. Staff speaks Portuguese, French, and English. Open daily 8am-noon and 5-9pm.

Guides: Associaçao dos Conductores de Visitantes de Lençóis (ACVL), Av. Senhor dos Passos 61 (☎334 1425). Representing over 105 local guides, the ACVL can direct you to English-speaking guides, experts on flora, and guides who specialize in multi-day hiking. Expect to pay R$50-70 for day hikes. Open daily 8am-noon and 3-7pm.

Tours: Several companies offer packaged tours to sights around Lençóis and Chapada Diamantina. Most can be found on Pça. Horâcio de Matos and Rua dos Pedras, and all offer similar tours at similar prices. Some of the more reliable are listed below. For a one day car tour into the park (see **Packaged Trekking,** p. 386) expect to pay R$35-65; 3-day adventures cost R$70-180, depending on your bargaining skills.

Lentur Turismo Ecológico, Av. 7 de Setembro 10 (☎334 1274). The most established and reliable of the bunch. Open daily 8:30am-6:30pm.

Ecotrekking Turismo e Adventura, Pça. Horâcio de Matos 656 (☎334 1491). One of the more experienced and environmentally sensitive. Open daily 7:30am-10pm.

Cirtur, Rua da Baderna 41 (☎334 1113). Offers all the standard tours, sometimes at cheaper prices than competitors. Open daily 7:30am-10pm.

H2O Expedições, Rua do Pires s/n (☎334 1229). Run by the amiable crowd at the Pousada dos Duendes (p. 380). They also arrange bike tours. Open daily 7am-8pm.

Cicloturismo, Rua da Lagedo 68 (☎334 1700). Arranges bike tours into the Chapada Diamantina. Most popular is the 18km Pai Inácio-Lençóis route, which passes swimming holes and waterfalls along the way. 3-4hr. tour R$50 per person; 1-day tour R$70 per person.

Nativos da Chapada, Rua Miguel Calmon 29 (☎334 1314; www.nativosdachapada.com.br). Specializes in rappeling adventures. The Poço do Diabo rappeling/zipline combo, which ends in a zipline swan-dive into a lake, is a bargain at just R$40. The 2-day Fumaça adventure offers the chance to rappel the full 340m down. (R$350 per person. Min. 5 people.) Open daily 8am-noon and 1-10pm.

Pede Trilha, Pça. Horâcio de Matos s/n (☎334 1124). More expensive than the other agencies if you request an English-speaking guide, but many claim the price is worth it. Open daily 8am-noon and 5-10pm.

Currency Exchange: Avoid the exorbitant rates at Banco do Brazil and change money instead at the **Posto Telefônico Lençóis,** Av. 7 de Setembro 219. Even more attractive rates can be found down the street toward Pça. Horâcio de Matos, at **Internet Lençóis** (see **Internet Access,** p. 380).

Banks: Banco do Brasil, Pça. Horâcio de Matos 56 (☎334 1101). To change traveler's checks (fee R$20) or currency (fee R$20) you'll probably have to visit the ATM first. No-fee Visa withdrawals are available at the ATM on your right. Open M-F 10am-3pm.

LOCAL SERVICES

Luggage Storage: The *rodoviária,* on Av. Senhor dos Passos, has luggage storage facilities, but the lockers are small and are only accessible 7am-11pm.

Outdoor Equipment: Doislemâos, Pça. Horâcio de Matos 13 (☎334 1405). A wide array of hiking equipment, including boots, sandals, and rain jackets. Excellent backpacks for cheap. Open daily 8am-11pm. Right next door is **Venturas & Adventuras,** Pça. Horâcio de Matos 20 (☎334 1428), which offers an overpriced and more limited selection than its neighbor. Open daily 7:30am-11pm. Both sell maps of the local area. Many *pousadas,* including Pousada dos Duendes (p. 380), rent equipment: sleeping bags R$5 per day; tents R$10; hiking packs R$5.

Library: Biblioteca Pública, Av. 7 de Setembro 35 (☎335 1121). Includes a small collection of English books. Open M-F 8am-noon and 2-6pm.

Markets: Rua das Pedros is lined with local craft stores. Stalls selling gems and knitwear can be found next to the post office in **Praça Horâcio de Matos.** There is a large market at the **Novo Mercada Municipal,** where you can buy plenty of fruits, cheap clothing, and even cheaper CDs (R$5). To get there from Pça. do Rosârio, follow Rua São Benedito as it crosses the stone bridge and ascends the steep hill; at the top of the hill, a sign will direct you to the road on your left. Open M and F 9am-6pm.

Laundromat: Lavanderia Brilhante, Av. 7 de Setembro 109 (☎334 1844). R$2.50 per kg; R$3 per kg with ironing. Open M-Sa 7am-7:30pm. **Lavanderia Lençóis,** Rua 10 de Novembro 8 (☎334 1694). R$3 per kg with ironing. Open M-Sa 8am-9:30pm.

EMERGENCY & COMMUNICATIONS

Police: Delegacia de Polícia de Lençóis, on Rua Fundo do Papagaio (☎334 1269).

Pharmacy: Pharmâcia Maciel, Av. 7 de Setembro 40 (☎334 1224). Sells all the usual suspects, including sunscreen. Open M-Sa 7:30am-10pm, Su 8am-2pm and 5-9pm.

Hospital: Municipal Hospital de Lençóis, Rua Vai Quem Quer s/n (☎334 1587), just off Av. Senhor dos Passos. Offers free dengue vaccinations.

Telephones: Posto Telefônico Lençóis, Av. 7 de Setembro 219. Offers Internet access, fax services, and local and long-distance phone service. Open daily 9am-11pm.

Internet Access: Internet Lençóis, Pça. Horâcio de Matos s/n (☎334 1635). The cheapest access in town. Offers Internet (R$4 per 10min.) and printing services (R$0.50 per page). Open daily 8am-noon and 5-10pm. **Café.Com,** Rua Afrânio Peixoto 17 (☎334 1047). Hot chocolate, espresso, and a wide range of teas are served along with fast web access. Open daily 7am-7pm. Limited Internet access is also available at **Posto Teléfonio Lençóis** (see above) and **Pousada dos Duendes** (p. 380).

Post Office: Av. 7 de Setembro 213 (☎334 1122). Open M-F 8am-5pm. **Postal code:** 46960-000.

ACCOMMODATIONS

Lençóis is full of attractive, affordable accommodations, each of which makes a special effort to provide the best breakfast spread in all of Brazil. *Pousadas* provide sheets, towels, 24hr. reception, noon check-out, and free breakfast, unless otherwise noted. None but the most expensive accept credit cards. Bookings are recommended during the high season (Dec.-Feb. and June-July).

Casa da Hélia, Rua da Murtiba s/n (☎334 1143). From the *rodoviária*, facing the river, take the road to your right; it's 200m up the small hill. The *pousada* is surrounded by a labyrinth of interconnecting paths, pleasant mountain views, and hammocks strung up for lazy days. A favorite among travelers, the *pousada* arranges tours and reputedly serves the best breakfast in town. Spacious dorms, cable TV and VCR, and tire-swing. English spoken. Dorms R$20. Singles with bath R$30; doubles with bath R$50. ❶

Pousada Daime-Sono, Rua dos Pedras 102 (☎334 1445), on the main drag. More like a hostel than a *pousada,* with guitars hanging on the walls, funky decor, and a communal dorm upstairs full of hammocks. The eclectic decoration and small quarters lend a bohemian edge, while having only 14 beds means that the service is personable, and reservations are useful. Also offers one of the best 3-day Fumaça trips in town (R$180). Some English spoken. Dorms R$20. Singles R$25; doubles R$35. ❶

Pousada dos Duendas, Rua do Pires s/n (☎334 1229; www.pousadadosduendestripod.com). Follow Rua dos Pedras to Rua da Durante, take a left, then the first right, and after that the second left; continue down the street for about 3min. A bit of a hike from town, but travelers are well rewarded. Pool table, bar, Internet access (R$4 per 10min.), and a travel shop. The staff speak excellent English and can provide a wealth of information on the nearby area and the town itself. Laundry R$1 per piece. Reception 6am-11pm. Dorms R$15. Singles R$25, with veranda R$35; doubles R$40, with veranda R$50; triples R$60, with veranda R$70. Camping R$5 per person. ❶

Estalagem Alaciao, Rua Tomba Surrão 139 (☎334 1171). From the *rodoviária,* walk away from town along Av. Senhor dos Passos. Turn left at the fork, up the cobblestone street, and this large yellow colonial building will be on your left. Artist and hostel owner Alaciao makes a special effort to make visitors feel welcome in his home. Guests are encouraged to join him in his ceramics workshop, but are asked not to feed the three pet turtles that roam the grounds. Ideal for families and quiet types. Singles R$40, with bath R$60; doubles R$60, with bath R$90; triples R$80, with bath R$110. ❷

Albergue Algadoy, Rua da São Francisco 55 (☎334 1334), near Pça. do Rosário. Not as much traffic as the other *pousadas* but just as many services, including a warm living room and free use of the kitchen. The well-ventilated dorms have lovely views. Funky singles have faux fireplaces and mirror mosaics on the wall. Top-floor voyeurism provided by the shower's lack of walls. Dorms R$15. Singles R$20. ❶

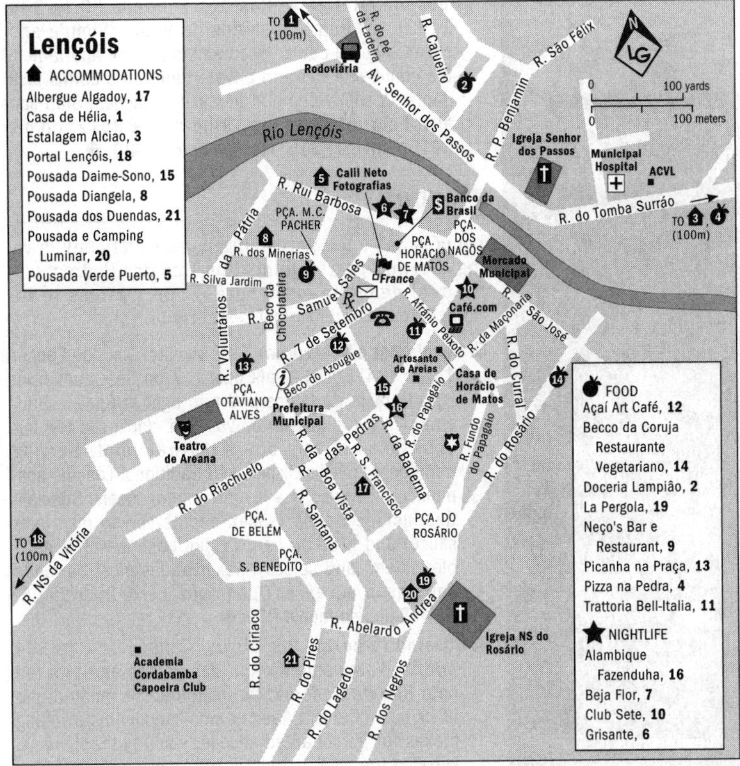

Portal Lençóis, Rua Chacâra Groto s/n (☎334 1233; www.portalhoteis.tur.br). Follow Rua Nossa Senhora da Vitória from the tourist office away from town. Curve around Hotel Lençóis and follow the road on your right to its end. A 5-star retreat with sauna, weight room, swimming pool, and a children's playground with mini-zip line. Despite all this, most guests spend their time relaxing in the comfortable hammock chairs listening to the sound of nearby waterfalls. The sprawling layout is curved into the hills and offers excellent views of the town below. 10% discount Mar.-May and Aug.-Nov. The 4-person bungalows are a great value at R$85 per person. Singles R$207. *Luxo* doubles R$230; mezzanine *luxo* triples R$310. Bungalows R$345. ❺

Pousada e Camping Luminar, Pça. do Rosário 70 (☎334 1241; lumiar@send-net.com.br), next to Igreja Nossa Senhora do Rosário. Shady campsites make this a favorite with trekkers. Only minimal facilities are provided, though campers are allowed to use the *pousada's* TV room and common area. With large peaceful rooms and soft beds the *pousada* offers comfort for a small premium. Quiet time 10pm-6am. Singles R$30; doubles R$50; triples R$70. Camping R$8 per person, R$15 with breakfast. ❷

Pousada Verde Puerto, Av. Rui Barbosa 56 (☎334 1317), off Pça. Horâcio de Matos. Despite its central location, travelers can expect privacy and quiet. The *pousada's* friendly owner can arrange tours and horse rental. *Frigo-bar* and pleasant garden. Yoga classes offered (Tu and Th.; R$5 per hr.). Dorms R$25, with bath R$35. Singles R$40, with bath R$50; doubles R$50, with bath R$70; triples R$75, with bath R$95. ❷

HE HIDDEN DEAL

SIGHTS & SOUNDS

Ristorante Italiano os Artistas la Massa is run by an Italian mmigrant who has a passion for azz. Like most restaurants, this place has a a menu for food, but unlike most places, there is also a nenu for music: after choosing rom the array of handmade pas-as (R$15-17) and wines, patrons hen select musical accompani-nent for their meal from a wide ibrary heavy on the bebop and cool jazz. Patrons can even equest a CD be made for them as hey eat (R$15). ❷/❸

Rua da Baderna 4. ☎334 1886. Open daily 12:30-10:30pm; ometimes closes in low season.

Sorveteria Verde Lima is a well-stocked ice cream store with 20 ropical flavors, which can be aug-nented with 5 sauces and 6 top-pings, including chocolate peanuts and jelly beans. The ice cream itself is a deal at R$12 per kg, but what makes this place spe-cial is that it doubles as the local video rental store and cinema. For R$2 patrons can pick a video and watch it on the 19in. television. The steel seats can get a little uncomfortable after an hour or two, but you can distract yourself with more ice cream or some of he shop's liquors (R$18). ❶/❷

Rua da Baderna 36, across from Ristorante Italiano. ☎334 1631. Open daily 8am-11pm.

Pousada Diangela, Rua dos Minerias 60 (☎334 1192), off Rua Voluntârios da Patria. Simple and cheap. A good bet for when others are full. *Apartamentos* come with fan and private bath; attic dorms lack doors. TV with video and free use of kitchen. Staff can also help arrange tours. Attic dorms R$12; dorms R$15. Singles R$15. *Apartamentos* R$20. ❶

FOOD

Lençóis has enough restaurants to satisfy any craving. *Gringo*-geared joints line Rua das Pedras, but the real gems lie elsewhere. Expect prices to be higher than usual at most restaurants.

Neço's Bar e Restaurant, Pça. Maestro Clarindo Pacher 15 (☎334 1179). Walk up Av. 7 de Setembro from Pça. Horâcio de Matos and turn right at Rua da Baderna; it's two blocks in on your left. You'll see few foreign faces at this out-of-the-way joint. Serving traditional Lençóis dishes with traditional Lençóis hospitality, this place is a favorite among locals. Specialities include *palma* (sliced cactus served in a light sauce) and *godo de banana* (hot banana with vegetables, meat, and spices). Reservations must be made one day in advance. Open daily 11am-2pm and 5-7pm. 2-course meals R$9. ❷

Cossinha Aberta, Rua Miguel Calmon 111 (☎334 1066). Walk uphill on Rua das Pedras and turn left onto Rua da Baderna; the restaurant is located one block up on the left. Aberta's small and intimate setting makes for personalized service; you'll probably leave knowing the chef as well as you know her food. Menu changes daily but there is always at least one Thai, Italian, and Indian dish to choose from. Entrees R$18-22. Open daily 1-11pm. ❸

Pizza na Pedra, Av. Senhor dos Passos 20 (☎334 1476), on the way out of town toward the main highway, past Canto dos Aguas. The open-air courtyard and riverside location attract locals and tourists alike. Serves the best pizza in town along with several pasta and lasagna dishes. The creative selection of pizzas includes the none-too-popular Smelly 1 (with anchovies, capers, and chili sauce; R$20). Large pizzas (R$21-23) are big enough for two. 10% service charge. Open W-M 7-11pm. ❸

Picanha na Praça, Pça. Otaviano Alves 62 (☎334 1248), near the tourist office at the top of Av. 7 de Setembro. White-washed walls and a lack of decoration remind you that you're here to eat, not fraternize: this is functional dining at its best. One of the tastiest options is the *picanha na praça,* 4 sizzling slabs of beef served with onions and a collection of small side dishes

(R$20). Meals can be ordered half-size, which feeds one person (R$15) or full-size, which feeds two (R$20). Vegetarians beware–this carnivore's paradise is not for you. Open Tu-Su noon-10:30pm. ❷/❸

La Pergola, Pça. do Rosário 70 (☎334 1241), to the right of the church. Run by the owner of Camping Luminar, the restaurant serves French and traditional dishes in the most inviting of atmospheres. One of the town's classier establishments: the soft lights, stained glass, and an entirely stone interior lend old-world charm. Try the *tucuharé moqueca* (fish served in a cream sauce; R$25). Open Tu-Su noon-4pm and 6-11pm. ❹

Doceria Lampiâo, Rua Cajueiro 33 (☎334 1402), just off Av. Senhor dos Passos, a block from the *rodoviária*. An exclusive *sorvete* café run by local guide Jair and his wife Regina. Bob Marley beats and a funky interior complement the establishment's original desserts. Travelers often grab a quick meal here while waiting for the bus. The *brigraideiro* (a chocolate and mint combo; R$3) is decadence at its most tempting. Open daily 10am-11:30pm. ❶

Becco da Coruja Restaurante Vegetariano, Rua do Rosârio 172 (☎334 1652). Take Rua José Florêncio from Pça. das Nagôs; it's near the corner three blocks up on your right. Serves omelettes (R$7), tortillas (R$7), veggie burgers (R$6), and sandwiches (R$4) in a small restaurant that seats just 12. A haven for the otherwise overlooked vegetarian diner in Lençóis. Open daily noon-10:30pm. ❶

Açaí Art Café, Rua Baderna 10 (☎334 1838). Açaí Art Café's various sandwiches and 6 types of lasagna (R$9-11) are just a ruse to draw you in; the desserts will keep you coming back for more. Serves great fruit cakes, mousses, and hot chocolate. *Açaí na tigela* with banana and granola is a bargain at R$3.50. Also a popular night spot. Open daily 6pm-midnight. ❶

Trattoria Bell-Italia, Rua das Pedras 68 (☎334 1454). For better or worse, most tourists end up eating here. Expect typical Italian fare served on stereotypical red-and-white checkered tablecloths. One of the cheaper options in town for pizza (R$11-13). Pasta R$10. Crepes R$5. 10% service charge. Open daily noon-3pm and 6:30-11:30pm. ❷

SIGHTS

COLONIAL ARCHITECTURE. Among the more attractive buildings in town is the **Subconsulado France,** in Pça. Horâcio de Matos. Though never an actual consulate, this narrow yellow building once served as a place for French nobles to buy diamonds. The building is most noted for the tall arches of its windows and doors. The nearby **Mercado Municipal** (under renovation at time of publication) was used as a stable until a roof was added in the 1940s, and it has since served as the local marketplace. North of the *centro*, at the end of Av. 7 de Setembro, the **Prefeitura Municipal,** originally a private residence, became the town hall when local warlord Horâcio de Matos kicked the family out of town in the 1920s. Protruding from either side of the building are the black lamp posts which have become the unofficial symbol of the town. In the same *praça* lies the **Teatro de Areana,** just behind the gazebo. This theater was originally intended to be a church, but when funding disappeared the building fell into disrepair. It has since been graced by a limited number of productions.

CHURCHES. Igreja Senhor dos Passos, on Av. Senhor dos Passos, across the river from town, served as a church for miners in the mid-1800s and toward the end of the century came to be used by slaves. The large wooden cross and statue of Jesus that sit on the altar were carved in Portugal and brought to the church in 1900. The two side columns on the church's exterior are capped by mosaics of blue and green glass. Opposite the church sits a large white cross that is lit up at night. **Igreja**

Nossa Senhorado do Rosário, in the *praça* of the same name, is Lençóis's largest church and has a reputation as traditionally being the church of the upper class, though its spartan interior and shabby exterior suggest otherwise.

ENTERTAINMENT

The **Academia Cordabamba Capoeira Club,** Pça. Altino Alves 42, has been operating in Lençóis for over 80 years, and is now run by local master Mercais Cacudo. Visitors are invited to watch practices or—for the more adventurous—to take lessons. The location of the club changes often but it can presently be found in the Alto Elstruea area of town. Turn left coming out of Pousada dos Duendes and take the first narrow alley on your left; the club is two blocks uphill. (☎334 1716. Lessons and shows M, W, and F 6-8pm. Lessons R$15, best booked through your *pousada.*)

FESTIVALS

The most fun among Lençóis's regional celebrations is the **Festa de São João** (June 23-25), when locals dress up to look like farmers, donning straw hats, patched pants, and painted mustaches. The festivities usually last into the night with light provided by the bonfires lit in the farms outside town. The **Festival da Lençóis** (3-day weekend in late Aug. or early Sept.) brings dozens of Brazilian pop artists to the small town. Running for several years now, the festival has become a favorite with tourists. Inquiries can be made at Portal Lençóis. Held during Lent, the **Lamentaça das Almas** is a mystical festival that brings the town to an eerie halt. Many people stay indoors during the day only to emerge at night, dressed all in white, to pray at the local cemetery. The **Semana de Afrânio Peixoto** (Dec. 11-18), held to honor the famous local author, brings heavy drumbeats to the town. **Festa de Senhor dos Passos** (Jan. 24-Feb. 2) celebrates the patron saint of the miners, Senhor dos Passos. The most important night comes at the end of the festival with the Noite dos Garimperos (Night of the Miners), when the town is lit up with rockets.

NIGHTLIFE

Lençóis has a limited number of bars and clubs; most locals spend their nights chatting at restaurants, cafés, and dessert houses. Rua das Pedras and Pça. Horâcio de Matos are always buzzing.

Alambique Fazenduha, Rua das Pedras 125. Lining the walls of this popular watering hole are relics from the town's mining days, including saddles and stirrups. Patrons come for the 48 varieties of homemade *cachaças* (R$1), though, not a lesson in history. Open daily 3pm-2am.

Beja Flor, Pça. Horâcio de Matos 30 (☎334 1986). One of the more popular restaurants, where tourists and locals mingle at night. Conversations are usually accompanied by fruit crepes (R$5) and damaging amounts of alcohol. Feel free to add to the growing wall of napkin art. Open daily 2pm-2am.

Grisante, Pça. Horâcio de Matos 36 (☎334 1527), next to Beja Flor. Similar to its neighbor, but without as much atmosphere. Everyone mingles at the tables outside where the radio usually pumps out MPB into the night. People tend to hop between here and Beja Flor during the evening. Open daily 11am-11:30pm.

Club Sete, Rua das Pedras 23. Known as *inferno inho* (little hell), Club Sete is crowded, sweaty, and very, very dark; a strobe light and two disco balls provide the only lighting. The night usually begins with traditional *forró* and finishes with US pop songs. The kind of place where *gringos* go to "meet the locals," who are often younger than they look. R$2 for a giant jug of beer. Open F-Sa 10pm-4am.

 OUTDOOR ACTIVITIES

TRAIL SAFETY. Although many of the trails around Lençóis are well-marked, few may be safely attempted alone, because of the flash floods that often occur in the area.

The town's prime location makes for easy excursions into the Chapada Diamantina; for information on the extremely popular hikes (which range in length from one to four days) into the park, see p. 390. Below is a list of the hikes and tours that operate outside the park's boundaries.

INDEPENDENT TREKKING

RIBEIRÂO DO MEIO ROCK-SLIDE. An easy and well-beaten track that leads to one of the area's biggest attractions. From Pça. do Rosário, follow Rua São Benedito away from town, across the small stone bridge and up the steep hill. Bear right at the fork, staying on the main road, and take your first sharp left at Pousada das Henrique. At the bottom of the road is a small stone gate to the left of which a small narrow path leads downhill toward the **natural rock-slide.** The hike rises and falls gently, eventually leading to the Rio Ribeirão. Here you find a large 100m sloping rock face over which the river flows. Climb up the left-hand side of the rock face, walking only on the dry areas, and jump on when you feel comfortable; many people have hurt themselves trying to climb up the slippery right-hand side. Though a little bumpy the slide is smooth and perfectly safe. Just watch the local kids and you should have no problem. It's particularly rewarding to hike to the slide as dawn breaks—you'll have the place to yourself and the sunrise from the top of the slide is breathtaking. *(6km, 1½hr. round-trip. Difficulty: easy.)*

RIO LENÇÓIS. A wonderful introduction to the park's flora and waterfalls, this is one of the more popular trails. The hike begins along a paved path that starts at Portal Lençóis and leads first to the Rio Lençóis' **serrano rapids.** Here the smooth river bed is punctuated by several cauldrons that make for excellent swimming holes. The trail then leads through thick vegetation toward **Cachoeirinha,** a large and impressive waterfall with a wide and swimmable pool. Twenty minutes away lies a second waterfall, **Cachoeira da Primavera,** some 4m in height. From there you boulder-hop downstream on the left bank until you reach the Rio Lençóis. The trail on the opposite side of the river brings you back to *serranos*, though on the opposite side of the river. Before crossing, ask someone to direct you to the **Salão de Areia,** a small canyon filled with the soft and colorful sands used by local artists to create bottle pictures. *(7km, 2hr. round-trip. Difficulty: easy.)*

GUIDED TREKKING

Of the several hiking opportunities available outside the park proper, these are among the best. Guides can be arranged at the tourist office, ACVL guide association (see **Guides** p. 378), or your *pousada*. Day trips cost R$50-70 per person.

CACHOEIRA DO SOSSEGO. The **Sossego Falls** are located on the same river as the Ribeirâo do Meio rock-slide (p. 385), but because the trail is a bit more complicated and potentially dangerous during the rainy season (Dec.-Mar.), it requires a guide. It's a rigorous hike to the falls but there are plenty of places to stop for swimming breaks along the way. The trail starts at the same stone gate where the trail to the rock-slide begins, only you turn left at the gate. The hike follows the Rio Ribeirão upstream and involves much boulder-hopping. Along the way there are canyons and smaller waterfalls. On the way to the falls, rest at the **Ribeirão de Cima,** a good place to picnic and swim. *(14km, 6hr. round-trip. Difficulty: medium.)*

GRUTA DO LAPÃO. This hike brings you face to face with the largest quartz cave in South America, **Gruta do Lapão,** which is very different from the common soft-rock limestone caves of the area. Formed in quartzite rock—which is highly resistant to water erosion—the cave lacks the stalactites, stalagmites, and other impressive rock formations that decorate most caves. However, it certainly provides an adventure: its huge caverns with uneven floors stretch for an entire kilometer. It is connected to Lençóis by an uneventful 3km trail. It takes one hour to go through the cave, and if you enter through the cave's back entrance the hike will be all downhill. Going in the back will also mean you end the hike at the mouth of the cave, providing a more spectacular conclusion to the trip. Don't forget to bring a flashlight or lantern. *(7km, 4-5hr. round-trip. Difficulty: medium.)*

PACKAGED TREKKING

Most of the best sights around Lençóis require a car. Tour companies (see **Tours** p. 378) in town offer the following daytrips. Expect to pay R$35-55.

MUCUGEZINHO/PAI INÁCIO DAYTOUR. This popular excursion begins with a visit to **Poço do Diabo** (Devil's Pool), a deep basin at the bottom of an imposing 50m waterfall formed by the Rio Mucugezinho. An optional zipline ride from the top of the waterfall into the pool is offered (R$5-10). Next is a short hike to the top of **Morro do Pai Inácio,** which provides magnificent panoramic views of the surrounding park. Visitors are then taken to a series of caves and pools including **Gruta da Lapa Doce,** which features soft-stone rock formations, and **Gruta da Pratinha,** a large, bright blue lake suitable for swimming and snorkeling (R$5). Heavy rains can flood the *grutas* (caves) with dirty water, so inquire about conditions. *(140km by car and 5km on foot.)*

POÇO ENCANTADO DAYTOUR. One of the more distant sights popular among tourists is **Poço Encantado** (the Enchanted Pool), a crystal-clear lake, 61m deep, that lies inside a shallow cave. From April to September, the reflection of the sun on the lake's water results in an amazing electric blue. The trip to the lake can be combined with a visit to **Poça Azul,** a similar though smaller pool where visitors are free to swim and snorkel, or with a trip to the stone cities of **Xique-Xique de Igatu** and **Mucuge.** *(300km by car and 2km on foot.)*

CACHOEIRA DA FUMAÇA DAYTOUR. For those lacking the time to take the immensely popular three-day trip to the bottom and top of the **Cachoeira da Fumaça** waterfall (see p. 390), this day-long tour at least offers the chance to see the spectacular 340m falls from the top at the edge of the waterfall. On the way down from the waterfall, a quick visit is paid to **Cachoeira do Riachinho** and **Vista do Morrão.** *(250km by car and 9km on foot.)*

MIRIMBUS DAYTOUR. Dubbed "the poor man's Pantanal," the **Mirimbus** is a vast expanse of wetlands accessible only by boat or kayak. Though the wildlife in the area is not as exotic as that found in the Pantanal, you can expect to see common Pantanal denizens like *caimans*, *capybaras,* colorful fish, and tons of wild birds. The trip includes a stop at the **Rio Roncador** for lunch and a swim. The long trip back to Lençóis is avoided with a 4x4 ride along the old miners' road. (60km by car, 2hr. by boat, and 2km on foot.)

NEAR LENÇÓIS: CAPÃO ☎75

Most travelers see the tiny village of Capão (Caeté-Acú) for only an hour or two at the end of their three-day Fumaça trek. Located at the base of the mountain from which the 340m Cachoeira da Fumaça tumbles, it is the jumping-off point for many of the park's longer hikes. The town would be the logical base for those seeking to explore Chapada Diamantina, if not for its lack of services and general inaccessibility. However, for many independent travelers these are the town's most attractive qualities. Located in the Vale de Capão—on the opposite side of the park as Lençóis—the village is surrounded by tall green mountains and roaring waterfalls, is more secluded than Lençóis, and offers cheaper guides and more scenic views.

Capão is 76km west of Lençóis, about 35km off the main BR-242 highway. The village is best accessed from the town of Palmeiras, 20km north. **Real Expresso** (☎334 1112) sends buses from Lençóis to Palmeiras (1hr.; M-Sa 2 per day 4:30am-12:30pm; R$5) and from Palmeiras to Lençóis (1-2 per day 6:30am-2:30pm). Private **taxis** connect Palmeiras to Capão via a bumpy, unpaved road (R$50). Taxis can also connect Capão directly to Lençóis (R$150). Reliable services are provided by **Cris e Jubileu** (☎334 1097), **Fátima** (☎244 1078), and **Zé Augusto** (☎332 2172). There is no hospital, bank, or post office in town—what few services can be found are located in the *centro*, Vila da Capão. Guides can be contacted through your *pousada* or the local guiding association, **ACVVS** (☎344 1087). The **Mercedinho Flamboyam,** Vila do Capão, provides all the usual foodstuffs. (☎344 1177. Open M-Sa 8am-noon and 1-7:30pm, Su 8am-2pm.) **Pé no Mato,** Vila da Capão, across from the pharmacy, has a wide array of hiking equipment for sale and rent. (☎344 1180. Open daily 9am-9pm.) **Farmácia José Bettos,** Vila do Capão, has bugspray and sunscreen. (☎344 1206. Open M-Th 9am-noon and 3-8pm, F-Su 9am-noon and 3-9pm.)

Just 150m from the beginning of the Fumaça trail and 50m from the day-long trail to Lençóis, **Pousada Canto Gala ❷,** Vale do Capão, is the most convenient and pleasant place to rest between hikes. Located 1km north of the *centro* and run by local guide extraordinaire Cris Pascoli, the *pousada* is popular among the independent hikers that come to town. (☎344 1097; crisejubileu@holistica.com.br. Singles R$30; doubles R$45; triples R$65.) **O Tatu Feliz Pousada ❶,** in Vila do Capão, is more central but much less attractive, with basic rooms and no breakfast. (☎344 1088. Singles R$10.) **Palmital Pizzeria & Comida Caseira ❷,** Vila da Capão, is across the street from the hiking shop. It offers cheap pizzas (R$8-14) and hearty soups (R$3). (Open M-F 11:30am-4pm, Sa-Su noon-2pm.) Just down the street, **Comida Caseira da Dona Beli ❷,** Vila do Capão, offers home-cooked meals in the living room of the owner's house. It primarily serves regional dishes, like chicken with *palma* (R$10). (☎344 1085. Open daily 2-10pm). The hiking shop, **Pé no Mato ❶,** has tempting brownies (R$1) that make an excellent snack for short hikes; their health bars provide sustenance for multiple-day trekking.

P.N. DA CHAPADA DIAMANTINA ☎75

Six hours from the eastern coast's beaches and ocean-front condos lies Chapada Diamantina, an island of lush forest that towers above the semi-arid *sertão* (grasslands) below. Covering an area larger than Israel, the botanic diversity found on this 1000m high plateau is overwhelming, similar to that of the Amazon rainforest. But plants are not what draw the crowds; most come for the natural swimming holes, idyllic waterfalls, and dense forest. The park also has a number of spectacular hiking trails, the most popular of which is the three-day hike to the 340m waterfall, **Cachoeira Fumaça.**

Opened in 1985, the park was created after a five-year uphill battle between local environmentalists and government authorities. Led by Roy Funch, a former American Peace Corps volunteer who had come to live in the area, the environmentalists sought to protect the area from encroaching loggers. Since it was granted national park status almost 20 years ago, little has been done to develop any sort of infrastructure. In fact, most of the park remains in the hands of private owners who graciously allow hikers to pass through their lands.

AT A GLANCE: P.N. DA CHAPADA DIAMANTINA

AREA: 1000 square kilometers.

FEATURES: Marrão Mountain, Cachoeira do Capivarí, Cachoeira Fumaça, Vale do Capão, Gerais da Vieira, Vale do Pati, Morro Branco, Cachoeirão.

CLIMATE: Wet season (Nov.-Mar.) makes for bigger waterfalls and more dangerous conditions. Dry season (Apr.-Nov.) is the best time to visit the sparkling lakes that lie just outside the park.

HIGHLIGHTS: Sleeping in caves on the 3-day Fumaça trek; the stunning scenery of the Vale do Pati; spectacular views from the top of Cachoeira Fumaça; diverse vegetation; majestic waterfalls; deep pools perfect for rock-diving.

GATEWAY TOWNS: Lençóis (p. 377) and Capão (p. 386).

FEES: None.

ALTITUDE: 400-1700 meters.

TRANSPORTATION

There are no official entrances to the park; most visitors enter from the towns of **Lençóis** and **Capão,** from which the major hikes begin. Transportation within the park is achieved by foot, hoof, or tire. While guides and taxis can be found in Capão and Lençóis, only the latter has cars, bikes, and horses for rent. For more information on transport to and within the park refer to the transportation sections for Lençóis (see p. 378) and Capão (see p. 386).

ORIENTATION & PRACTICAL INFORMATION

The park is on a 1000m high plateau, six hours from Salvador and 18 hours from Brasília. It is bordered by Lençóis, Palmeiras, and Capão in the north, and Andaraí in the south, making access relatively easy. Lençóis (p. 377) has the most services, though Capão (p. 386) is better located. Park trails are well-worn but frequent river crossings make them hard to follow; guides are strongly recommended.

Park Information: The official **Park Department** (☎332 2229) is inconveniently located in the town of Palmeiras. The office has no tourist facilities or maps; tour offices and *pousadas* in Lençóis are much better sources of information.

Luggage Storage: The *pousadas* in the surrounding towns are happy to store luggage during your trek, as are some tour companies. The *rodoviária* in Lençóis has luggage storage facilities, but the lockers are small and are only accessible 7am-11pm.

Supplies: Because of the abundance of waterfalls and freshwater streams in the park, a small bottle of water will suffice. Sunscreen, hat, and swimming trunks are all prerequisites for hiking. There are two hiking equipment stores in Lençóis (p. 379) and one in Capão (p. 386), both of which are well stocked.

Groceries: Supermercado Senina, Av. 7 de Setembro 34 (☎334 1231), beside the post office in Lençóis. Open daily 8am-9pm. **Lefru,** Rua das Pedras 73 and 81 (☎334 1983), has fresh breads, cheeses, fruits, and vegetables. Open daily 7am-10pm.

Maps: The maps on tour company brochures give a good idea of the park's hiking routes. For serious independent hiking, *Trilhas e Caminhos,* available from **Pede Trilha,** Pça. Horâcio de Matos s/n, in Lençóis, is an excellent survey map. Roy Funch's *A Visitor's Guide to the Chapada Diamantina Mountains* has good descriptions of the hikes, but no maps. It's available at **Doislemâos,** Pça. Horâcio de Matos 13, in Lençóis.

Tours: Several tour companies in Lençóis (see **Tours,** p. 378) organize treks through the park, and most *pousadas* are happy to arrange guides for their guests. Package tours to the sights that surround the park are especially popular (see p. 386), as are the 3-day Fumaça trek and 3-day Vale do Pati trek.

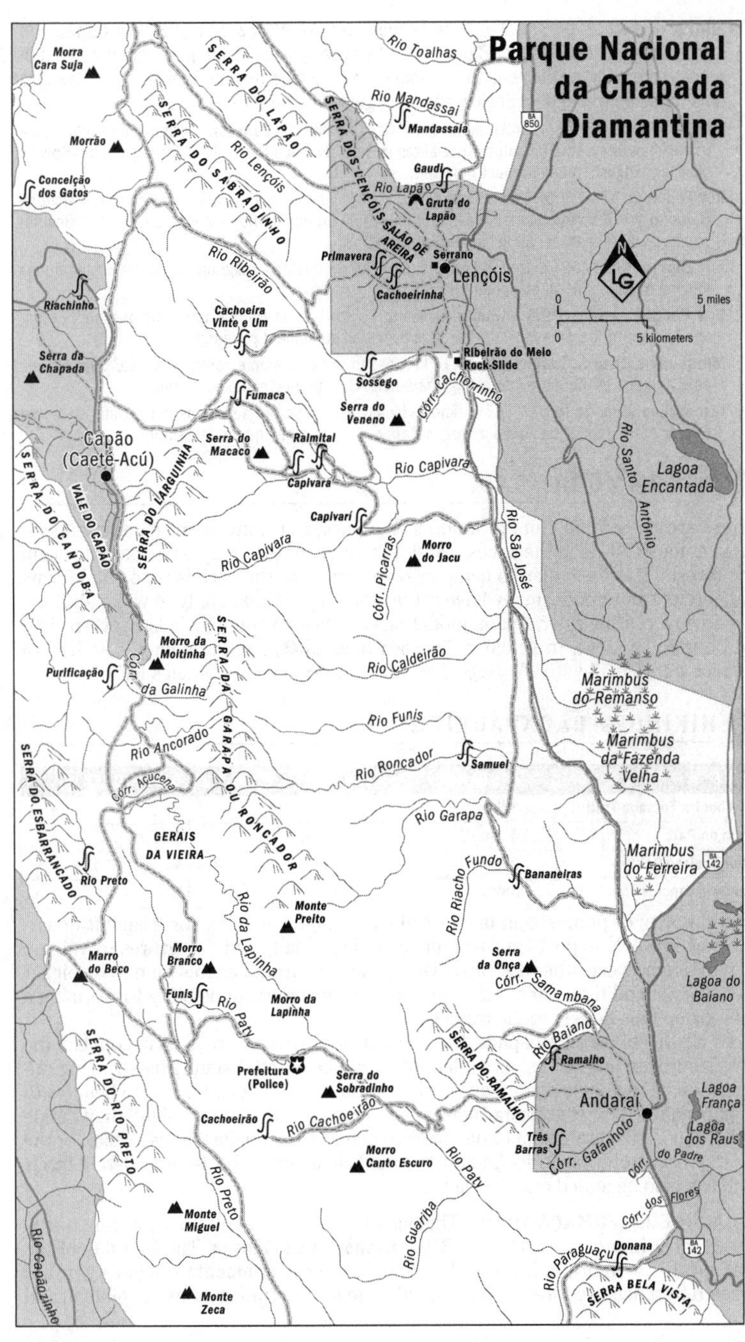
Parque Nacional
da Chapada
Diamantina
Lençóis
Capão
(Caeté-Açú)
Andaraí
Lagoa
Encantada
Marimbus
do Remanso
Marimbus
da Fazenda
Velha
Marimbus
do Ferreira
Lagoa do
Baiano
Lagoa
França
Lagoa
dos Raus
0
5 miles
0
5 kilometers
Rio Toalhas
Rio Mandassai
Mandassaia
Gaudi
Rio Lapão
Gruta do
Lapão
Serrano
Primavera
Cachoeirinha
Ribeirão do Meio
Rock-Slide
Sossego
Serra do
Veneno
Córr. Cachorrinho
Rio Lençóis
Rio Ribeirão
Cachoeira
Vinte e Um
Fumaça
Serra do
Macaco
Ralmital
Capivara
Rio Capivara
Capivarí
Morro
do Jacu
Córr. Picarras
Rio São José
Rio Santo Antônio
Rio Caldeirão
Rio Funis
Rio Roncador
Samuel
Rio Garapa
Rio Riacho Fundo
Bananeiras
Serra
da Onça
Córr. Samambana
Rio Baiano
Ramalho
Três
Barras
Córr. Gafanhoto
Córr. do Padre
Córr. dos Flores
Donana
Rio Paraguaçu
SERRA BELA VISTA
Morra
Cara Suja
Morrão
Conceição
dos Gatos
Riachinho
Serra da
Chapada
SERRA DO LAPÃO
SERRA DO SABRADINHO
SERRA DOS LENÇÓIS
SALÃO DE AREIRA
SERRA DO CANDOBA
VALE DO CAPÃO
SERRA DO LARGUINHA
Morro da
Moitinha
Purificação
Córr. da Galinha
SERRA DA GARAPA OU RONCADOR
Rio Ancorado
Córr. Açucena
SERRA DO ESBARRANCADO
GERAIS
DA VIEIRA
Rio Preto
Rio da Lapinha
Monte
Preito
Morro
Branco
Marro
do Beco
Funis
Rio Paty
Morro da
Lapinha
Prefeitura
(Police)
Serra do
Sobradinho
SERRA DO RAMALHO
SERRA DO RIO PRETO
Cachoeirão
Rio Cachoeirão
Morro
Canto Escuro
Rio Guariba
Monte
Miguel
Monte
Zeca
Rio Capãozinho
BA
850
BA
142

NORTHEAST

Guides: The **ACVL** (☎334 1425) in Lençóis and **ACVVS** (☎344 1087) in Capão can help arrange guides for 1- to 8-day treks. Because Lençóis is the most common point of entry to the park, guides tend to be more expensive here than in Capão. The following is a list of some of the best English-speaking guides in the area.

Trajano Alañtara (☎334 1143), works out of Casa da Héila, in **Lençóis.** A genuine love of the area makes him one of the favorites. Specializes in 3-day Fumaça tours. Good for big groups. Speaks excellent English. All equipment provided.

Roy Funch (☎334 1305), based in **Lençóis.** Former director of the park and author of *A Visitor's Guide to the Chapada Diamantina Mountains.* More expensive than the rest, but worth it. Best for smaller, quieter parties. All equipment provided.

Jair Zion (☎334 1402), based in **Lençóis.** Runs an overnight Fumaça trip. Good for bigger groups looking to have fun. All equipment provided.

Cris Pascoli (☎344 1097), owner of Pousada Canto Gala, in **Capão.** Energetic and tons of fun, she has a mad passion for waterfalls and rivers. All equipment provided.

Marquinhos Brito S. Borges (☎344 1117), based out of a hippie community near **Capão.** Reliable and one of the more interesting characters. Can arrange equipment rental.

Wanderlino Macedo (☎344 1176), known locally as Wando, he also owns the popular **Camping Pomar** at the foot of the Fumaça trek in **Capão.** Can arrange equipment rental.

ACCOMMODATIONS

There are no official campgrounds in the park, nor convenient camping spots. Most guides tent up in the caves that dot the area, or throw up some hammocks in the forests. It is forbidden to camp next to a river, as the park is renowned for its dangerous flash floods; many have set up camp by a stream only to wake up floating down a roaring river. Accommodations are easy to come by in Lençóis (p. 380) and Capão (p. 386). In Andaraí, **Pousada Andaraí ❹,** Av. Paraguaça 550, has 15 *apartamentos*, all with TV, *frigo-bar*, and fan. (☎335 2008. Singles R$70.)

HIKING & BACKPACKING

HIKE	DISTANCE	TIME	DIFFICULTY
Cachoeira Fumaça Trail	37km	3 days	Hard
Vale do Pati	47km	3-4 days	Medium
Rio Ribeirão Valley	25km	5-7hr.	Medium
Andaraí-Lençóis Trek	38km	8hr.	Easy

The majority of people sign up for treks in Lençóis, making for frequent departures each week; expect trips to Fumaça to leave daily and departures to Vale do Pati to occur every other day or so. Groups leaving from Lençóis tend to be bigger and more social than ones arranged in Capão, where responsibility for forming a tour group falls largely to the traveler.

As all the hikes in Chapada Diamantina are one-way treks that connect the park's surrounding towns, extended hikes can be created simply by stringing different hikes together. If you have a week in the area you can hike from Lençóis to Capão via the 3-day **Cachoeira Fumaça** trail, rest in Capão for one night, then tackle either the 1-2 day trail from Capão back to Lençóis via the **Rio Ribeirão Valley,** or the 3-4 day trail from Capão to Andaraí via the **Vale do Pati.** The 1-day **Andaraí-Lençóis** trek can also be added onto the latter.

CACHOEIRA FUMAÇA TRAIL. This superb trail takes you on a journey to the park's most impressive sight, the 340m **Cachoeira da Fumaça.** The first day of the trek entails a rigorous hike to the top of the **Veneno Mountain** where you are greeted by a densely forested and humid plateau. The trail crosses the plateau and soon descends to meet the Rio Capivara. After some light boulder-hopping the trail passes by **Cachoeira do Capivarí** and finally comes to *toca* (cave); the first night is spent sleeping here. Another option for the first day is to walk the 9km road to the **Rio Capivara** and then simply follow the river all the way to the *toca*. Being the longer of the two options, it is rarely used. The second day involves an easy walk through a 400m high canyon lush with palms, ferns, and tropical trees. Eventually the canyon reaches the base of Fumaça, where hikers can swim, have lunch, and take copious pictures. You return the way you came and spend your second night again in the *toca*. On day three you ascend the steep mountain from which Fumaça tumbles to view the falls from above. Later in the day you descend to the town and valley of Capão where you either spend the night or arrange a taxi back to Lençóis. *(37km one-way, 3 days. Difficulty: hard.)*

VALE DO PATI. Easily the most striking of all the hikes in the park, this trek from Capão to Andaraí, via the **Vale do Pati,** sees less tourist traffic than many of the park's other trails. The trek begins with a strenuous climb out of Capão valley and onto the open grassland area of **Gerais da Vieira.** In addition to the inspiring panoramic views of the valley below and Sincorá mountain range to the right, straight ahead you will see the **Morro Branco** (White Mountain), which is visible throughout most of the 3-4 day hike. After climbing out of the Capão valley the trail crosses the Gerais da Vieira toward the Morro Branco Mountain and leads into the **Vale do Pati,** passing high mountain escarpments along the way. The first night is usually spent in one of the caves along the trail. Day two of the trail leads though a boggy forest to the base of Morro Branco and on toward the **Cachoeirão,** though there is an optional one-day hike to the top of the mountain that is very popular. Day three begins with a refreshing dip in the Cachoeirão followed by a vigorous hike through a deep canyon. After climbing out of the canyon along a terrifyingly narrow path, it's a flat march to the town of Andaraí. *(47km one-way, 3-4 days. Difficulty: medium.)*

RIO RIBEIRÃO VALLEY. Beginning from the picturesque town of Capão, this trek takes you right into the heart of the Chapada Diamantina, eventually depositing you in the nearby town of Lençóis. Upon leaving Capão the trail veers left and gently winds around the tall plateau that borders the town. Two hours later the trail presents a splendid view of the **Morrão** mountain, and an optional sidetrail appears to the left and will lead hikers to the top of the mountain where they can camp for the night (7km round-trip). From this trail, the main trail continues to wind around the mountains until it reaches the **Rio Ribeirão Valley,** which runs behind the Capão plateau. Lunch is usually eaten at the first large swimming hole the trail encounters, which also conveniently marks the halfway point of the trek. The trail then crosses the river, climbs high above it, and continues parallel to the river valley for just under an hour, providing wonderful views of the valley and river below. A steep ascent leads you through a narrow passage and over the peak of the plateau that looks down on Lençóis; from here it's all downhill. During the descent you'll see pleasant views of the terra-cotta roofs of Lençóis resting in a carpet of green. *(25km one-way, 5-7hr. Difficulty: medium.)*

ANDARAÍ-LENÇÓIS TREK. For over 100 years this well-used trek was the only link between Lençóis and the rest of the world. Though the trailhead is difficult to find (ask locals for directions), once you're on the right path its a straight shot to Lençóis. Some very beautiful rivers cross the trail every once in a while, and at the Rio Roncador there is a sandy beach perfect for lounging for an hour or two. Rather dull when compared to the other hikes in the area, the trail is still much more interesting than the hour-long car ride from Andaraí to Lençóis. *(38km one-way, 8hr. Difficulty: easy.)*

SERGIPE

ARACAJU ☎79

Spread out for 30km between the Rio Poxim and the Atlantic, Aracaju replaced São Cristóvão as Sergipe's capital in 1855. The city's cooling ocean breezes and colonial charm are the main attraction, with pale stone churches and brightly lit palaces scattered all over town. Aracaju is named after the *cajú* (cashew), which skippers of merchant ships once used to pay the river tax.

TRANSPORTATION. **Aeroporto de Aracaju,** Av. Senador Júlio C. Leite, is accessible by local bus from Rodoviária Velha and has both domestic and international flights (☎212 8500). Long-distance buses leave from the **Terminal Rodoviária Nova,** in Bairro America; buses for nearby towns depart the **Terminal Rodoviaría Velha** in the *centro.* City buses (R$1.40) leave from *terminais de integração* in Bairro Santo Antônio (Terminal do Mercado), Atalaia, and Ponto Novo. If you're uncertain about which bus to catch, ask one of the *fiscais* (traffic cops) at the terminals. **Ferries** depart the Terminal Hidroviário, on the water between Av. Coelho e Campos

NORTHEAST

and Av Barão de Maruim, for the city island of Santa Luzia (daily 4am-11pm; R$0.60-1.20). **Taxis** from any of the *rodoviárias* to the *centro* cost R$10-17. Catamarans head to the nearby beaches: **Catamaran Parnamirim** runs along the Rio Sergipe and to Ilha de Santa Luzia (☎214 3876; 3 per day 10am-8pm); **Catamaran Velho Chico** goes along the Rio Vaza-Barris (☎246 2520; 2 per day 10am-2pm); **Nozestur,** Av. Santos Dumont 478, in Atalaia, next to the Hotel Jatoba, runs to various tourist hotspots (☎243 177, 9972 7314). **Paseos en Catamaran,** a.k.a. Catamarã Pomonga, sails down the Rio São Francisco past the Angico Cave (☎346 1245; Sa-Su 9am); **Catamará Zé Peixe** travels to Mangue Seco (☎243 3744).

ORIENTATION & PRACTICAL INFORMATION. The city's northern end is spacious and residential, while the southern end is more touristy, with the airport, campgrounds, and high-end beachside hotels. Aracaju is laid out in a grid, with roads running parallel to each other between **Terminal Rodoviária Nova** (long-distance bus terminal) and the beach. **Rua Laranjeiras** is the main drag, running straight through the **commercial center,** a white *praça* with rows of stores. **Av. Beira Mar,** the road parallel to the beach, changes names several times and runs through the **Bairro Industrial,** home to the city bus terminal **Terminal Integração,** and the **centro,** home to various city markets and **Terminal Rodoviária Velha** (regional bus terminal). After crossing the Rio Poxim, Av. Beira Mar becomes **Av. Santos Dumont,** which passes the lighthouse and the Delegacía de Turismo and has a long line of tourist hotels.

The **tourist office,** Bureau de Informações Turisticas, Centro de Turismo, on Rua Própria, is in the *centro*, only a few blocks from the *rodoviária*. Ask to be pointed toward the commercial center on Rua Laranjeiras and look for Rua 24 Horas, which connects Rua Laranjeiras and Rua Própria. It has tour info, but no maps. (☎3179 1947. Open M-F 8am-8pm.) Currency exchange is possible at **Banco do Brasil,** Pça. General Valadão (☎212 1144; open M-F 10am-3pm), in the *centro*, and **ITAPOAN Câmbio e Turismo,** Av. Delmiro Gouveia, Shopping RioMar, loja 102 (☎3041 1615; open M-Sa 10am-10pm). Other services include: **federal police** (☎213 0030); **Hospital São José,** on Av. João Ribeiro (☎215 3864; open 24hr.); **Internet access,** Av. Hermes Fondez 2120 (☎211 9359; R$1.50 per hr.); and the **post office,** Rua Acre 1084 (☎241 1934). **Postal code:** 49000-000.

ACCOMMODATIONS. Most accommodations in Aracaju are by the beach, and are generally quite pleasant, if pricey. The *centro* has cheaper options which are often just as comfortable. **Hotel Amado ❶,** Rua Laranjeiras 532, provides the best inexpensive lodging in the *centro*. The rooms are airy, spacious, and relatively quiet, despite all the nearby traffic. Most *apartamentos* have A/C and *frigobar;* all have TV, phone, and private bath. (☎211 9937; www.infonet.com.br/hotelamado. Breakfast included. Mar.-Sept. singles R$20; doubles R$47. Oct.-Feb. singles R$36; doubles R$52.) **Hotel Brasília ❷,** Rua Laranjeiras 580, is not as welcoming as Hotel Amado, but it is safe, comfortable, and one of the quieter places to stay in the *centro*. All *apartamentos* have TV, A/C, phone, and private bath. (☎214 2964. Breakfast included. Singles R$36; doubles R$55. DC/MC.) The main selling point of **Hotel Algos Marinhas ❸,** Rua Santos Dumont 690, is its view of the sea. All rooms have A/C, *frigo-bar*, phone, and TV. The hotel also has a pool, parking lot, and restaurant. (☎218 1983. Breakfast included. Group discounts available. Reservations required during Carnaval. Singles R$65-75; doubles R$80-90. AmEx/MC/V.)

FOOD. There are many **food stands ❶** along Rua Laranjeiras, Rua São Cristóvão, and Rua Própria in the *centro*, which sell a variety of kebabs, sandwiches, and pastries. (R$0.50-2.50. Open daily 9am-7pm.) **Panificação Sergipana e Delicatessan ❶,** Av. Própria 681, is a supermarket with a speedy deli and the best fruit

THE LOCAL LEGEND

ROBBIN' HOOD

Somewhere among the glitzy birds of paradise and drag queens of Carnaval, you may spot a leather-clad figure with glasses and a gun. Perhaps he will be dancing with a tough-looking lady, or roughhousing with boys eagerly looking for adventure. If so, you are watching yet another Brazilian entranced by the true-to-life story of the infamous *bandeirante* Lampião, his lady Maria Bonita, and their gang of *canguaceiros.*

Born in the Northeast, Lampião spent his adult life leading a gang of bandits in the harsh *caatinga.* According to lore, the gang stole from—and often slaughtered—the rich who had forcibly taken land from the poor. As they fled the authorities, the gang returned this land to its rightful owners. On July 28, 1938, the gang was finally caught at the Angico Cave in Sergipe: most members were killed, and Lampião was decapitated. This Brazilian Robin Hood has become a hero, remembered as one who fought social inequality and lived outside the law until the bitter end.

But history proves Lampião to be more complicated than this ideal. Apparently, he manipulated both the police and their opponents, and terrorized the poor as well as the rich. At the same time he reputedly loved French perfume, and could sometimes be found dancing *forró* in the lush summertime *caatinga.*

shakes in town. (R$1-3. ☎211 3071. Open M-Sa 8am-midnight, Su 6pm-midnight.) Fifteen minutes from the *centro* you'll find **O Miguel ❷**, Av. Antônio Alves 340, named one of the ten best restaurants in northeastern Brazil. It dishes up generous helpings of seafood and meat (entrees R$20-22 for 2 people), including the fish filet *surubim na brasa.* (☎243 1444. Open daily 11am-4:30pm and 6:30-11:30pm. AmEx/MC/V.) **Churrascaria Grilha Azul ❸**, Av. Santos Dumont, owned by an Italian Paulista Húgo Mileo, is a *churrascaria* serving beef, lamb, rabbit, pork, and buffalo. (☎243 4204. M-F R$17, Sa-Su R$28 per couple. Open daily 11:30am-3:30pm and 6:30-11pm. AmEx/MC/V.) Nearby is the waterfront **Cantina d'Italia ❷**, Av. Santos Dumont, the best Italian restaurant in Aracaju. This family establishment offers beautiful views and pasta dishes for two (R$12-25), including the house special, *lasagna de camarão.* (☎243 3184. Open daily 11am-1am. AmEx/MC/V.)

SIGHTS & OUTDOOR ACTIVITIES. Museu do Homem Sergipano, Pça. Camerino 227 in the *centro*, documents the history of the city. (☎214 1700. Open M-F 8-11am and 2:30-5pm. Free.) **Museu do Artesanato,** Pça. Olímpio Campos in the *centro* opposite the tourist office, crams an array of local artwork into a tiny space. Displays include the renowned lacework of the Northeast, wood carvings, religious icons, and modern art made from recycled paper. (☎3179 1943. Open M-F 8am-7pm. Free.) **Museu de Sergipe,** Av. Beira Mar, focuses on Sergipe's historical and cultural traditions. (☎211 3579. Any "Bairro 13 de Julho" bus. Open M-F 10am-5pm, Sa 9am-noon.) Aracaju's 30km stretch of **beach** is probably the city's top attraction, while charming **Atalaia Nova** beach is just a ferry ride away on the Ilha da Santa Luzia. **Catamarans** from the Agência de Viagens e Turismo, Av. Santos Dumont 478, can take you on daytrips to gorgeous natural points in Sergipe, including **Canyon Xingó, Angico Cave** (where Brazil's most famous bandit couple was killed; see **Robbin' Hood,** at left), and the **Rio São Francisco delta** (☎243 7177; R$50-55).

LARANJEIRAS ☎79

Things move at a relaxed pace along the cobblestone streets of Laranjeiras, which weave steeply along the surrounding circle of hills. The several churches of Laranjeiras, most of which were built in the 19th century, stand out in the valley for their color and the stories behind them. Two of the churches, **Igreja da Comandoroba** and **Igreja do Retiro,** are rumored to have tunnels leading to the Pedra Furada cave. **Capela Santa Aninha** was constructed by a local man for his daughter Ania. After he had a falling out with the local priest, he forbid Ania to attend church and built a chapel so that she could still have a place to worship. **Museu Afro-Brasileiro,** on Rua José do Prado Franco, documents the history of slavery in Laranjeiras and houses a tourist information booth. (☎281 1710, 281 2389. Open Tu-F 10am-5pm, Sa-Su 1-5pm. R$1.) The 19th-century **Trapiche,** a long white building across from the *rodoviária* near the river, serves the town's cultural center. It also has an tourist information booth that provides free guides. (Open daily 8am-6:30pm.) Larenjeiras once had more than 70 sugar mills. **Engenho,** the largest remaining mill, is near Igreja da Comandaroba. (☎281 1414. Open M-F 7am-5pm.)

Laranjeiras's roads can be confusing. The **rodoviária** is located on one of the main roads, **Avenida Municipal,** at the edge of a small *praça.* Av. Municipal runs parallel to Rio Cotinguiba; bridges cross over the river at both ends of the street. One bridge is near Igreja Bom Jesus dos Navegantes. The other bridge, **Ponte Nova,** is near Igreja Nossa Senhora da Conceição dos Pardos. Running perpendicular to Av. Municipal, **Rua Calcadão** begins at Cine-Teatro Iris, changes its name to **Rua Júlio Vargas,** and ends at the intersection with Rua José de Prado Franco. **Buses** run from the *rodoviária* to Aracaju (every hr. 5am-10:45pm; R$1.40). The **tourist office,** Secretária de Turismo e Cultura, on the Rua José de Prado Franco, is opposite Igreja São Benedicto. (☎287 1297. Open M-F 7am-5pm.) There are two **banks** in town, both with ATMs: **Banese,** on Pça. da Matriz (☎281 1050), and **Banco do Nordeste,** on Rua Calçadão (☎287 1145). Other services include: **police,** at Pça. de Conceição (☎281 1256); two **pharmacies,** one in Pça. Coronel José de Faro (☎281 1346; open M-F 7am-10pm), and one in Pça. Agosto Maynard (☎281 1857; open M-F 7am-10pm); **Hospital São João de Deus,** near Igreja Nossa Senhora Conceição dos Pardos (☎281 1149), and the **post office,** Pça. Marcolino Ezequiel (☎281 1259; open M-F 8-11am and 2-4pm). **Postal code:** 49170-000.

There are only two places to stay in Laranjeiras. **Pousada Vale dos Outeiros ❶,** Rua José Prado Franco 124, is a simple and quiet option, with a casual restaurant/bar next door, a comfortable common area, and laundry facilities. All rooms have private bath. (☎281 2434. Singles R$15; doubles R$40. Cash only.) **Pensão & Restaurante ❶,** Rua José do Prado Franco 17, is a dormitory in a family home. The four rooms all have fans, and there is a common room with a TV. (☎281 1162, 9136 0623. Breakfast included, other meals R$4. Dorms R$15.) **Nices Restaurante ❸,** Pça. da Matriz, serves large portions of traditional dishes, such as *churrasco* (R$6-10) of beef, pork, chicken, and mixed meat. (☎281 2883. Open daily 11am-3pm.) Pça. da Matriz often has a cluster of **food stands,** especially on weekends. Many sell simple sandwiches (R$1-4) and regional favorites like *beijú* and *acarajé.*

ALAGOAS

MACEIÓ ☎82

The clear waters and sunbaked streets of Maceió are reminiscent of the Caribbean. After spending a day relaxing on the beach or wandering through easily navigable streets, visitors can pick up the pace by taking part in the city's active nightlife, much of which takes place on the waterfront. Maceió's romantic landscape and the friendliness of its residents make it a difficult place to leave.

TRANSPORTATION. Aeroporto Zumbi dos Palmares, on C Palmares (☎214 4000; fax 214 4055) is 20km from the *centro.* The airport can be reached by Rio Largo buses that leave from the train station on Pça. dos Palmares in the *centro* (R$1.50) or by taxi (R$3). Flight carriers with offices in the airport include: **TAM** (☎214

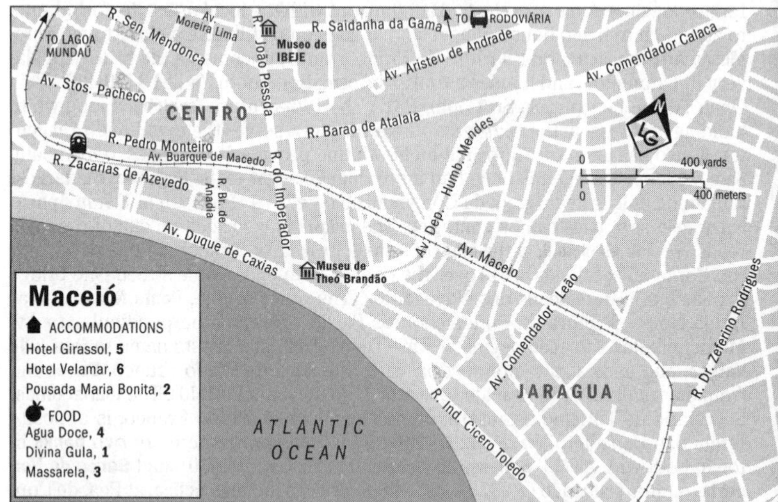

4112); **Varig** (☎214 4100, 322 1175); **VASP** (☎322 1414, 322 1099). Several carriers have offices in the city proper as well: **BRA,** Eng. M Gusmão 738 (☎322 1433, 377 1111); **Varig,** Av. Dr. Antônio Gouveia 759 (☎337 5030); **VASP,** on Av. Antônio Gouveia (☎327 8484). **Intercity buses** leave from the *rodoviária* is located in the central northern section of the city. (☎221 4615. Open 24hr.) **Local buses** in Maceió (R$1.25) are clearly marked with both their *volta* (origin) and *ida* (destination). However, bus stops are unmarked, so ask the ticket collector where to get off. **Taxis** cluster at the *rodoviária.* A ride from *centro* to the beaches costs R$6-9.

ORIENTATION & PRACTICAL INFORMATION. About half of Maceió's coast touches the Atlantic Ocean, and half borders **Lagoa Mundaú.** The affluent Atlantic shore neighborhoods—**Pajuçara, Ponta Verde,** and **Jatiúca**—are more popular with visitors, with the best beaches and most hotels and restaurants. The less popular **Jacintinho** is inland near the *rodoviária* and not far from the airport. At night, Jacintinho, the **centro,** and **Ponta Grossa** can be dangerous, and you should avoid walking them alone. The beautiful **Avenida Assis Chateaubriand,** the road along the Atlantic coast, begins at the southernmost point on Maceió's coast and runs north, passing through the neighborhoods of Trapiche and Prado. Upon reaching the *centro* (look for Museu Theó Brandão), it becomes **Avenida Duque de Caxias,** before it forks left into **Rua Sá E. Albuquerque. Avenida Antônio Gouveia** passes along Pajuçara, which is recognizable for its many hotels and *barracas.* When Av. Antônio Gouveia reaches Ponta Verde, it becomes **Avenida Silvio Viana,** which then veers sharply to the left, into the neighborhood of Jatiúca.

The several **tourist offices** in Maceió include **Aeroturismo,** Br. Penedo 61 (☎218 2000; open M-F 8am-noon and 2-6pm, Sa 8am-noon) and **Transalagoas,** Av. Paz 1318 (☎336 1004; open M-F 8am-noon and 2-6pm). There is also a **information booth** at the beach on Av. Dr. Antônio Gouveia. (☎315 1603, 315 1600. Open M-F 7am-6pm.) **Tour agencies** that run excursions to the area's nine islands include: **LUAU Turismo,** Rua José Laranjeiras 171 in Jacintinho (☎321 1856; www.luaturismo.com.br; open M-F 8am-noon and 2-6pm); **Marção Turismo,** Rua B 24 (☎9981 7896; open daily 8:30am-5:30pm); **Edvantur,** Rua Dr. José Correia Filho 356 (☎337 3919; open daily 8am-7pm); **Maceió Turismo,** Av. Júlio Marques Luz 1030 (☎327 7711; open 24hr.).

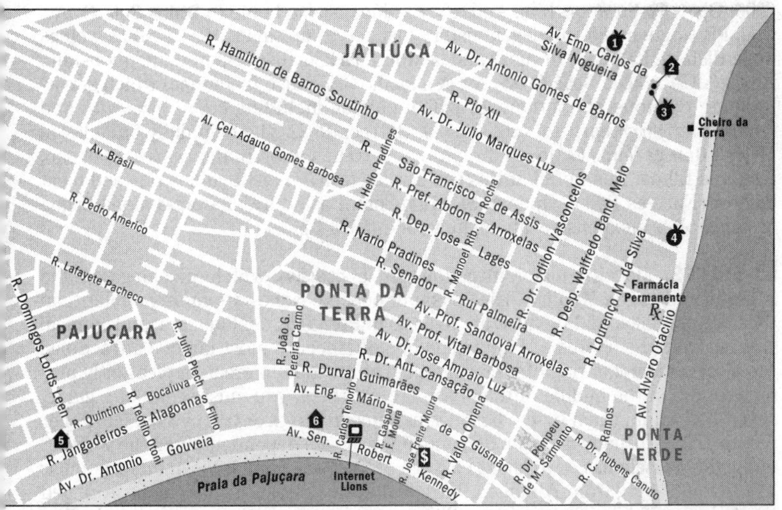

There are **banks** throughout the city, including **Banco do Brasil,** Principal Livramento 20 (☎216 1212; open M-F 10am-4pm), and **HSBC,** Av. F Lima 2229 (☎338 2001; open M-F 10am-4pm). Other services include: **laundry,** Lav Sempre, Av. J Sampião 1787A (☎320 3787); **24hr. pharmacy,** Farmácia Permanente, Av. Alvaro Otacílio 2901 (☎327 9251, 327 9290); **Hospital Unimed,** on Av. D. A. Brandião (☎215 2000, 326 1100; open 24hr.). There is **Internet access** at Internet Lions, in Shopping Lions in Ponta Verde's Pça. Leão. (☎327 4198, 327 0105. R$3 per 30min., R$5 per hr. Open M-Sa 9am-9pm). There is a **post office** at Rua do Sol 57. (☎216 7082. Open M-F 9am-5pm.) **Postal code:** 57020-000.

ACCOMMODATIONS. The best places to stay in Maceió are near the beaches of Pajuçara, Ponta Verde, and Jatiúca. **Hotel Velamar ❷,** Rua Antônio Gouveia 1359, is right across from the beach and the *barracas* and next to the city's prime handicrafts market. To get there, take any "Ponta Verde" or "via Ponta Verde" bus. The comfortable and clean rooms all have A/C, TV, *frigo-bar*, private bath, and safe. (☎327 5488; fax 231 6849; www.hotelvelamar.com.br. Singles R$60-70; doubles R$70-80. AmEx/MC/V.) Right by the sea sits **Pousada Maria Bonita ❷,** Rua JP Magalhães 321. To get there, take any "Circular Cidade 1" or "Jatiúca" bus. The staff is friendly, and all rooms have TV, A/C, *frigo-bar*, and private bath. (☎325 3713. Breakfast included. Singles R$30; doubles R$50. Visa.) **Hotel Girassol ❷,** Rua Jangadeiro Alagoanas 535, in Pajuçara, near Shopping Pajuçara, has rooms with TV, A/C, *frigo-bar*, and private bath. (☎231 4000; fax 231 0651. Breakfast included. Singles R$25; doubles R$40. Cash only.) To get to **Pousada Cavalo Marinho ❷,** Rua da Praia 55 in Riacho Doce, catch any "Jardim/Vaticano—Iguatemi" bus; at Iguatemi, switch to a bus marked "Militante" or "Ipioca." This *pousada* has well-kept quarters in a gorgeous location. Bikes, canoes, and body boards are available for use. (☎355 1247; fax 355 1265; cavalomarinho@dialnet.com.br. English spoken. Singles R$24, with breakfast R$30-54; doubles R$36-63. Cash only.)

FOOD. Great restaurants pepper Maceió, though the most popular are found in Jatiúca. **Massarela ❷,** Rua JP Magalhães 271, in Jatiúca, serves mostly Italian food, including pizza (R$17-20) with toppings that give it a Brazilian spin. (☎325

6000. Open Tu-Su noon-1am. AmEx/V.) Jatiúca is also home to **Divina Gula ❹**, Av. Eng. PB Nogueira 85, an elegant eatery that serves up salads (R$10-26) as well as huge dishes (R$30-35) of meat and seafood. (☎235 1016. Open daily noon-1am. AmEx/MC/V.) **Agua Doce ❸/❹**, Av. Á Otacílio 3977, also in Jatiúca, which serves up huge portions of southern Brazilian cuisine including *carne picanha* and *carne filet parmegiana*. (☎235 5580. Entrees R$22-24. Open daily 5pm-dawn. MC/V.) **Barriga Verde ❶**, located right by the train station in the *centro*, is cheap, fast, and filling. The buffet at this self-service *lanchonete* includes rice and meat dishes. (Entrees R$3-5. Open M-Sa 11am-2pm. Cash only.) **Barracas** along Lagoa Mundaú offer inexpensive late-night goodies (R$1-3).

SIGHTS. Maceió's major attractions are its **beaches**, which run along both the Atlantic and Lagoa Mundaú. The 230km of ocean beaches are more popular than those on the lake, and the best are located in Ponta Verde, Pajuçara, and Jatiuca. Not far from the shores of Pajuçara is one of Maceió's most famous attractions, the **piscina natural**, a ring of reefs emerging at low tide to create a pleasantly protected pool in the middle of the ocean. To get there, you must seek out a guide, several of whom roam by the beaches in Pajuçara, to take you by boat (R$13 per person). They usually leave on demand, but trips are dependant upon the weather and light. **Passeio das Nove Ilhas** (Passage of the Nine Islands) is another popular excursion leaving from Pontal da Barra by Lagoa Mundaú. Tours can be arranged through one of several agencies (p. 396), or you can purchase a passage at the **Restaurante Peixarão**, a small place in Pontal da Barra at the end of Ponte Devaldo Suruagi. (Tours R$15; R$22 with lunch.) There are also several worthwhile museums in Maceió. **Museu de Miza,** at Pça. dos Leões in Jaragua, contains an interesting collection of images and sounds. (☎315 1924. Open M-F 8am-5pm. Free.) **Museu de Theó Brandão,** Av. da Paz 1490 in the *centro*, documents the culture and history of Alagoas. (☎221 2651. Open Tu-F 8am-noon and 2-6pm. R$1.) **Museu de IBEJE (Instituto Histórico e Geográfico de Alagoas),** located at the Ladeira do Brito on Rua do Sol in the *centro*, focuses on the geography of Brazil. (☎223 2655, 221 1531. Open M-F 8am-noon and 2-6pm. R$1.50.)

ENTERTAINMENT & NIGHTLIFE. If you're looking for nightlife in Maceió, head down to the beaches, where there's usually something going on, or check out one of several dance clubs in town. **Lampião,** Av. Álvaro Otacílio s/n, is an enormous club which plays *forró* and *axé*. Their wide selection of drinks start at R$3. (☎325 4376. Cover R$5. Open daily 6pm-late.) **Aeroporto,** Rua Sáe Albuquerque 588, is popular with a young crowd in search of techno. (☎326 4762. Open Th-Sa evening-late. 18+. Cover R$12.) A calmer evening can be had at any of Maceió's three **cinemas.** There's one in each shopping center: **Shopping Iguatemi,** Av. Com G Paiva 2990 (☎357 1010; open M-Sa 10am-10pm, Su 3-9pm); **Shopping Cidade,** Av. F Lima 679 (☎336 6565; open M-Sa 10am-10pm); and **Shopping Farol,** Av. F Lima 2551 (☎338 1090; open M-Sa 10am-10pm). Admission is R$8 for adults, R$4 for students.

SHOPPING. There are several lively markets in Maceió, a few of which also serve as venues for live entertainment. All markets are open daily 10am-10pm and only accept cash. The biggest and best market, **Cheiro da Terra,** is in Jatiúca, right near the Hotel Meliá, on the corner of the beachside road and Rua Emp. Carlos da Silva Nogueira. There are free daily performances by folkloric groups and *capoeira* schools on its centrally located stage. Vendors come to **Feira do Artesanato,** on Rua Antônio Gouveia, in Pajuçara opposite Hotel Velamar, to sell lace, wood carvings, jewelry, and clothes. Just opposite stands the **Pavilhão do Artesanato,** an indoor market which sells similar handiwork, as well as hammocks and t-shirts. **Centro do Artesanato,** in Pontal da Barra, also sells handicrafts.

PRAIA DO FRANCÊS ☎82

Praia do Francês has become riddled with tourists, but even so its six kilometers of unfailingly clean beaches welcome all those who wish to swim and surf. Accommodations and restaurants, all of which cater to beach-bound visitors, can be a bit pricey. Reserve in advance during the peak season (Dec.-Feb.). Tiny Praia do Francês is easily reached from Maceió by bus. From the *rodoviária*, on Rua Arecifes, in front of the Mercadinho João Paulo II, **buses** go to Maceió (every 15min. 5am-10:40pm; R$2). As you walk toward the coast, Rua Arecifes splits in two: **Rua Massonil,** on the left, and **Rua dos Pescadoes,** to the right, both head to the beach. Parallel to Rua Arecifes is **Rua Carapeba,** where most upscale *pousadas* are located. Most restaurants and bars are located along the beach. Free **guides** are available at the beachside *barracas* and along Rua Arecifes. There is **no currency exchanges or ATMs** in town, so bring some cash with you.

Pousada Miroku ❶, Rua Cavalo Marinho 16, is close to the sand but also relatively quiet. All rooms have private hot-water bath, TV, A/C, *frigo-bar*, and safe. The *pousada* also has a pool. (☎260 1187. Breakfast included. Singles R$15; doubles R$30; triples R$45; quads R$60; quints R$75.) **Pousada Graciosa ❷,** Rua Cavalo Marinho 21, is a very friendly place with an English-speaking owner. All rooms have A/C, TV, and *frigo-bar*. (☎260 1197. Breakfast included. Mar.-Nov. singles R$30; doubles R$40. Dec.-Feb. singles R$50; doubles R$100. DC/V.) **Pousada Aconchego ❸,** Rua Carapeba 159, is a lovely wood building built around a pool, with a veranda and hammocks for every *apartamento*. The staff is friendly and all rooms have TV, A/C, *frigo-bar*, and private hot-water bath. (☎260 1193. Breakfast included. Singles and doubles R$60. Cash only.) **Pousada Maho-Mar ❹,** on Av. Caravelas, is a grand place with pool and poolside bar, sports field, a playground, and verandas with hammocks in each *apartamento*. All *apartamentos* have A/C, TV, *frigo-bar*, and private hot-water bath. (☎260 1223. Breakfast included. Check-out 10am. Singles and doubles R$70. Student group discounts negotiable. MC/V.) Most restaurants are located along the beachfront, and many *barracas* have color-coded seating directly on the beach. For a quick bite, try **Ovídio Lanche ❶,** on Rua Massonil, which serves sandwiches (R$1.80-5.00), fruit shakes (R$1.50-1.80), and a variety of meat dishes (R$5-10) served with rice. (☎260 1138. Open daily 9am-midnight.) **Beleza Tropical ❸** has green tables on the beach and serves regional dishes like *moqueca de peixe* (R$42) and *peixada* (R$28), all big enough for two. (☎260 1215. Open daily 8am-5pm. AmEx/DC/MC/V.)

BARRA DE SANTO ANTÔNIO ☎82

Beaches are Barra de Santo Antônio's pride and joy: the town boasts what *Veja* magazine named the fourth best beach in Brazil, on **Ilha da Crua.** Actually, the title of fourth best beach is shared by two of the island's beaches: **Praia de Carro Quebrado** and **Praia de Capitão Nikolas.** The river which winds around the island leads to a *piscina natural* (a natural pool formed by surrounding reefs) in the middle of the sea. The beaches are located off of Rodovia Al Norte, which can be reached by crossing Rio Santo Antônio via **canoe** from Rua Antônio Balthazar (R$0.70) or a **ferry** from Av. Pedro Cavalcante (R$7 per car).

Barra is located off a highway leading out of Maceió. The first section of the town's main thoroughfare is called **Av. Benedito Casado** until the medical post, after which it is named **Av. Pedro Cavalcantes,** which eventually forks, the left fork descending to **Rio Santo Antônio.** From here, you can catch a canoe or ferry to cross the river to Ilha da Crua. The easiest way to reach Barra do Santo Antônio is by **bus** from Maceió (R$2.50-5); ask the driver to stop at Barra. Larger buses will drop you off at the bus stop at the entrance of Av. Benedito Casado. Smaller buses stop at the **rodoviária,** at the end of Av. Pedro Cavalcantes (open daily 5am-5pm). Buses back to Maceió leave from the *rodoviária* (1hr.; every hr. 9am-6:30pm; R$2.5-5). **Tours** of the town can be arranged with **guides** from Maceió (p. 396). Other services include: **Banco do Brasil,** Av. Pedro Cavalcantes s/n (open M-F 8am-noon and 2-5pm); **police,** Av. Pedro Cavalcante 612 (open M-F 8am-2pm); a **health center,** on Av. Benedito Casado (☎291 1198); and a **post office,** on Av. Pedro Cavalcantes (open M-F 8am-noon and 2-5pm). **Postal code:** 57925-000.

Most of Barra's accommodations and restaurants are on the Ilha da Crua. **Brisas e Sonhos ❶**, Av. Pedro Cavalcantes 51, in the town proper, is a family-run *pousada* near the river, with simple rooms that have TV, private bath, and fan. (☎291 1359. Breakfast R$5. Rooms R$20. Visa.) On the island is the snazzy **Pousada Arco Iris ❷/❸**, which has *apartamentos* with *frigo-bar*, TV, fan or A/C, private hot-water bath, and veranda. The friendly staff can also arrange aquatic adventures for visitors. (☎291 1250; fax 291 1326; arcoiris@gmx.net. Mar.-June and Aug.-Nov. singles R$40; doubles R$50-70; suites R$90-120. Dec.-Feb. and July singles R$50; doubles R$60-90; suites R$120-150.) **Pousada Vila da Crua ❷**, also on Ilha da Crua, has large, comfortable rooms with kitchen, *frigo-bar*, TV, fan, and private hot-water bath. (☎355 2221. Mar.-Sept. rooms R$40. Oct.-Feb. rooms R$60. Cash only.) **Restaurante do Capitão Nikolas ❷**, Rodovia Al 101 Norte 40, attached to the hotel of the same name, serves a range of seafood dishes. House specialties include *filet de peixe* (R$25) and *molho de camarão* (R$25), and most dishes serve two. (☎291 2124. Open daily 8am-10pm. AmEx/MC/V.)

PERNAMBUCO

RECIFE ☎81

The sprawling but charming capital of one of Brazil's more picturesque states (and the largest city in the Northeast, with a population of 3.5 million), Recife has something for everyone, from architecture buffs to rabid clubbers. Named for the coral reefs *(recifes)* that still line its coast, this fast-growing hub is often called the "Venice of Brazil" for its many winding waterways and bridges. A city of rainbow hues—pink and blue colonial relics, blackened churches, blue rivers flowing to an emerald green sea—Recife ("heh-SEE-fee") shows its true colors at night, when the bars and clubs of the happening Boa Viagem district come to life. Recife is best visited along with its perfectly preserved sister city, historic **Olinda** (p. 414).

TRANSPORTATION

INTERCITY TRANSPORTATION

Flights: Aeroporto Internacional dos Guararapes, Av. Magalhães Mascarenhas de Morais 6211 (☎3464 4188), in Imbiribeira. M: Aeroporto (Linha Sul-Blue) or any "Aeroporto" bus. Services include: first aid, international vaccinations, luggage check, currency exchange, a post office (open M-F 9am-10pm, Sa 9am-5pm, Su and holidays 9am-1pm), tourist office, shops and eateries, a 24hr. pharmacy, and a Banco do Brasil with 24hr. ATM (open M-F 10am-4pm, Sa 4pm-7pm). **BRA** (☎3464 4655), **Gol** (☎0300 789 2121), **TAM** (☎0300 123 1000), **TRIP** (☎0800 701 8747), **Varig** (☎0300 788 7000), and **VASP** (☎0300 789 1010) all serve the airport.

Buses: Terminal Integrado dos Passageiros (TIP), Av. Central (☎3452 2824, 3452 1103; www.tiketes.com.br), off Rodovia BR-232/Av. Getúlio Vargas, in the Distrito Industrial do Curado. M: Rodoviária (Linha Centro-Red). Services include: phone and

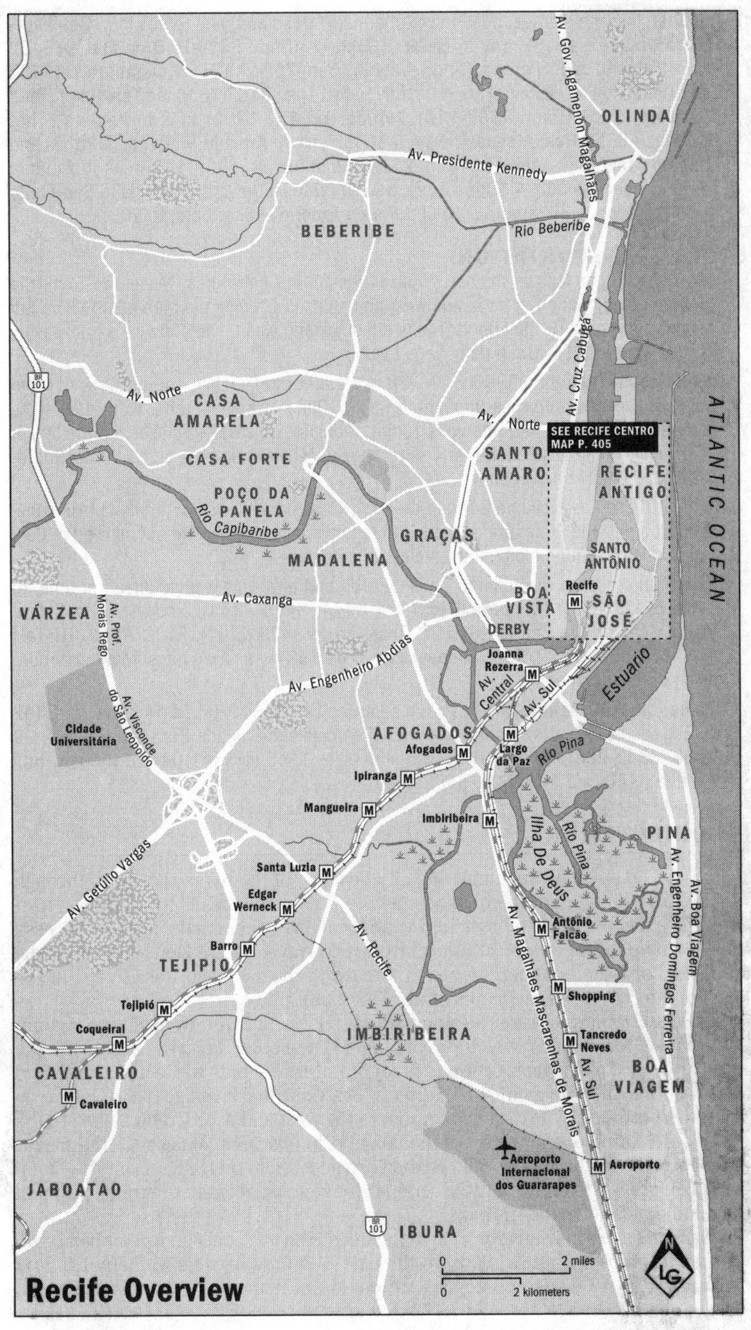
Recife Overview
OLINDA
Av. Gov. Agamenon Magalhães
Av. Presidente Kennedy
Rio Beberibe
BEBERIBE
Av. Cruz Cabugá
Av. Norte
CASA AMARELA
CASA FORTE
POÇO DA PANELA
Rio Capibaribe
SANTO AMARO
SEE RECIFE CENTRO MAP P. 405
RECIFE ANTIGO
ATLANTIC OCEAN
GRAÇAS
MADALENA
SANTO ANTÔNIO
Recife
SÃO JOSÉ
BOA VISTA
DERBY
Av. Caxanga
VÁRZEA
Av. Prof. Morais Rego
Av. Engenheiro Abdias
Joanna Rezerra
Av. Central
Av. Sul
Estuario
Av. Visconde do São Leopoldo
Cidade Universitária
AFOGADOS
Afogados
Largo da Paz
Rio Pina
Ipiranga
Mangueira
Imbiribeira
Ilha De Deus
Rio Pina
PINA
Av. Getúlio Vargas
Santa Luzia
Edgar Werneck
Av. Recife
Antônio Falcão
Barro
TEJIPIO
Av. Magalhães Mascarenhas de Morais
Shopping
Tejipió
Coqueiral
IMBIRIBEIRA
Tancredo Neves
Av. Sul
BOA VIAGEM
Av. Engenheiro Domingos Ferreira
Av. Boa Viagem
CAVALEIRO
Cavaleiro
Aeroporto Internacional dos Guararapes
Aeroporto
JABOATAO
BR 101
IBURA
0
2 miles
0
2 kilometers
N
LG

Internet, luggage storage. post office, pharmacy, taxi stand, and tourist info. **Boa Esperança** (☎3452 1618) runs to **Belém** (35hr.; 1:40pm; R$140). **Bom Fim** (☎3452 1155) runs to **João Pessoa** (2hr.; every hr. 5am-7pm; R$13). **Guanabara** (☎3452 1159) runs to **Fortaleza** (12hr.; 4 per day 9am-11pm; R$63-165) and **Teresina** (26hr.; 2 per day 7:30-10am; R$87-125). **Jotude** (☎3452 1300) runs to **Penedo** (7hr.; 9:30pm; R$35). **Real Alegoas** (☎3452 1511) runs to **Aracaju** (8hr.; noon: R$53) and **Maceió** (4hr.; 3 per day 8am-4pm; R$23). **Rodotur** (☎3626 0130) runs to **Goiânia** (1½hr.; 3 per day 8am-4:50pm; R$7). **São Geraldo** (☎3452 2733) runs to **São Paulo** (46hr.; 2 per day 3-7pm; R$246) and **Rio de Janeiro** (36hr.; 6pm; R$203).

LOCAL TRANSPORTATION

Metrô: Recife has 2 lines radiating from M: Recife in Centro, near Museu de Trem: the red *(vermelho)* Linha Centro heads west and splits in 2, while the blue *(azul)* Linha Sul heads south, passing the airport. Trains are quick and clean, and come by approx. every 15min. Fare R$0.80. Open daily 5am-11pm.

Buses: Local Buses (☎0800 810 158; www.emtu.pe.gov.br). The network of local buses is excellent and runs throughout Recife, Olinda, and Jaboatão. Front door signs list both *ida* (destination) and *volta* (point of origin). Boa Viagem buses run the length of Av. Eng. Domingos Ferreira. In Centro, they pass the main post office. Fare R$0.30-2.20. Open daily 5am-10pm.

Kombis: These are available 24hr. in the city (R$1-2), but it is safer to take a taxi, especially at night. The Prefeitura is starting to regulate *kombis.* They are not allowed in Centro, but can be found along many streets in other areas.

Taxis: Tourist offices recommend phoning taxis and arranging a price ahead of time, to avoid overcharging. **Coopetaxi** (☎3424 8944, 3424 4254). *Rodoviária* to Centro R$35, aeroporto to Centro R$15-20. **Tele-Taxi** (☎3429 4242). R$23/R$18. **TIP-Taxi** (☎3452 2552). R$22/R$25. **Copseta** (☎3462 1584) has fixed rates from the airport, listed at its post there.

Car Rental: ABC Rent-a-Car, Rua Carlos Pereira Falcão 311/04 (☎3463 1828, 3462 1827; abcrecife@hotmail.com). **Localiza,** Pça. Ministro Salgado Filho s/n (☎0800 99 2000, 3341 2082) and Av. Visc. Jequitinhonha 1145 (☎3341 0477). **Budget,** Rua Batalha 2140 (☎3341 2505, 3468 1671).

ORIENTATION

Recife can be a somewhat confusing city because of the rivers that wind through it—the town didn't earn its nickname as the "Venice of Brazil" for nothing. However, the excellent tourist information and local bus system make it easily accessible. The neighborhoods of primary interest to travelers are Boa Viagem, at the south end of the city along the beach; Centro in the east; and Casa Forte, at the heart of the city, along the banks of the Rio Capibaribe.

Rua Eng. Domingo Ferreira (along which buses run), Av. Conselheiro Aguiar, and Rua dos Navegantes, which run parallel to each other along the beach, are the main drags of **Boa Viagem. Centro** is made up of the islands of Recife Antigo and Santo Antônio and the mainland district of **Boa Vista. Recife Antigo** (a.k.a. Bairro de Recife) is bordered by Rua Cais do Apolo to the west and Av. Alfredo Lisboa to the east. Santo Antônio is made up of the neighborhoods **Santo Antônio** (to the north) and São José (to the south). The islands are accessible by bridge from the mainland; **São José** is served by the M: Recife *metrô* stop, adjacent to the train station in the middle of this neighborhood.

Casa Forte is a suburban area, which includes **Poço da Panela** on its southern end, right by the Rio Capibaribe, **Derby** to the east, and **Casa Amarela** to the north. It is cut through by Av. 17 de Agosto, or Estrada do Encanameto.

PRACTICAL INFORMATION

TOURIST & FINANCIAL SERVICES

Tourist Offices: Empetur, Centro de Conveções, 1st fl. (☎3427 8183), Olinda. Take any "Rio Doce/Piedade" bus to Shopping Tacaruna and cross the viaduct, or any "Jardim Brasil/Estrada de Belém" bus direct. Open M-F 8am-6pm. Also in **Boa Viagem,** Pça. da Boa Viagem (☎3463 3621). Take any bus along Av. Eng. Domingos Ferreira to Rua Tomé Gibson. Open daily 8am-8pm. **Casa da Cultura,** Rua do Sol at Av. Floriano Peixoto. M: Estaçao Central. Open daily 9am-7pm. Also has **booths** at the airport and *rodoviária*. All branches have English-speaking staff. **Disque Recife Turistico** (☎3425 8409). **Diretoria Geral do Turismo** (☎3425 8070).

Tours: Most of the following also arrange flights and buses. **BBtur Viagens e Turismo,** Pça. Ministro Salgado Filho (☎3462 4881), and Rua Padre Carapuceiro 733, loja 201 (☎3467 0377). **Casa Forte Viagens e Turismo,** Estrada dos Ubaias 758, loja 8 (☎3441 3670; casaforteturismo@hotlink.com.br), Casa Forte. **Dolphin Travel Câmbio e Turismo,** Av. Eng. Domingos Ferreira 4267 (☎3465 7855).

Consulates: UK, Av. Conselheiro Aguiar 2941, 3rd fl. (☎3465 0230; fax 3465 0247), Boa Viagem. Open M-Th 9am-12:30pm, F 9am-noon. **US,** Rua Gonçalves Maia 163 (☎3421 2441; fax 3231 1906), Boa Vista.

Banks: Banco do Brasil, Av. Conselheiro Aguiar 3600 (☎3465 4055), Boa Viagem; Av. Dantas Barreto 541 (☎3419 3197), Santo Antônio; Av. Rio Branco 240, Cais do Apolo (☎3425 7111), Recife Antigo. All open M-F 10am-4pm.

Currency Exchange: All the following charge R$3-4 exchange fees for traveler's checks (US dollars or euros) and dollars. **Bank Boston,** Av. Conselheiro Aguiar 4310 (☎3467 4343). Open daily 11am-3pm. **Brasicor Turismo,** Rua Padre Carapuceiro 777 (☎3464 9300). Open daily 10am-10pm. **Norte Câmbio Turismo,** Av. Boa Viagem 5000, loja B (☎3462 4600). Open 24hr. **Banco do Brasil,** Av. Rio Branco 240 (☎3425 7111). Open daily 10am-4pm. **Citibank,** Av. Marquês de Olinda 126 (☎3216 1262), Recife Antigo. Open M-F 10am-4pm.

ATMs: ATMs are everywhere. **Banco 24 Horas** has 24hr. ATMs at the airport and: Av. A. Magalhães 2977 and Av. Conde da Boa Vista 785, Centro; Shopping Center Recife; Av. Conselheiro Aguiar 3670; Av. Dantas Barreto 507. **HSBC,** Av. Conselheiro Aguiar 4432.

American Express: Av. Eng. Domingos Ferreira s/n, at Rua Ribeiro de Brito, Boa Viagem (look for the "Blue Tower 4060" sign).

LOCAL SERVICES

Cultural Centers: Centro Cultural Americano, Av. Montevideo 276 (☎3221 2828), Boa Vista, offers Portuguese language classes. Open M-F 7am-9pm, Sa 8am-1pm. Also in **Casa Forte,** Av. 17 de Agosto 1248 (☎3266 9000).

Markets: Feira de Artesanato de Boa Viagem, Pça. de Boa Viagem s/n (☎3445 5990), Boa Viagem. Open M-F 3-11pm, Sa-Su 8am-11pm. **ArtÍndia/FUNAI,** Av. João de Barros 668 (☎3421 1073), Boa Vista. Open M-F 8am-noon and 2-6pm. **Casa da Cultura,** Rua Floriano Peixoto s/n (☎3224 2850; webmaster@cultura.pe.gov.br), São José. Open M-Sa 9am-7pm, Su 9am-2pm. **Mercado de São José,** Pça. Dom Vital s/n (☎3224 5460), São José. Open M-Sa 6am-6pm, Su and holidays 6am-noon.

Laundromat: Acqua Clean Laundry, Av. Eng. Domingos Ferreira 4023, loja 8 (☎3466 6858), Boa Viagem. R$3.50 per kg. Open M-F 7am-7pm, Sa 7am-4pm. **VIP Lavanderia,** Av. Conselheiro Aguiar 2775 (☎3466 3755), Boa Viagem. R$29 wash and dry per 20 pieces. Open M-F 7am-7pm, Sa 7am-3pm. **Laundromat Lavanderia,** Rua G. Pires 143 (☎3221 2599), Centro. **Lavanderia Casa Forte,** Av. 17 de Agosto 2008 (☎3441 3434), Casa Forte. Open M-F 8am-6pm, Sa 8am-1pm.

PUBLICATIONS

Recife's three principal publications are the **Diario de Pernambuco** (R$2; Su R$3), **Jornal do Comércio** (R$1.80; Su R$3), and the more popular entertainment journal **Folha de Pernmabuco** (R$1). All have entertainment sections, though the **Jornal do Comércio** publishes a weekend magazine on Fridays, which contains a program of activities in the city.

EMERGENCY & COMMUNICATIONS

Tourist police: Av. Eng. Domingos Ferreira 4420 (☎3326 3030), Boa Viagem. Open 24hr. Rua Frei Casimiro s/n (☎3222 2622), Largo da Feira. Open M-F 8am-6pm. There is also an office at the airport (☎3464 4088). Open 24hr.

24hr. Pharmacies: Farmácia Pague Menos, Av. Conselheiro Aguiar 4635, lojas 1 and 4 (☎3465 9833), Boa Viagem. **Farmácia dos Pobres,** Av. Conselheiro Aguiar 3595 (☎3428 6055), Boa Viagem; Rua Fernandes Vieira 741 (☎3421 8879), Boa Vista.

Hospitals: Hospital Oswaldo Cruz, Rua Arnóbio Marques 310 (☎3421 1077, 3413 1300; fax 3421 2129), Centro. **Hospital Agamenon Magalhães,** Estrada do Arraial 2723 (☎3441 5888), Casa Amarela, near Casa Forte. **Hospital Barão de Lucena,** Av. Caxangá 3860 (☎3453 3566), Iputinga. **Hospital das Clínicas da UFPE,** Av. Professor Moraes Rêgo s/n (☎3454 3633), Cidade Universitária. **Hospital Getúlio Vargas,** Av. General San Martin s/n (☎3445 4800), Cordeiro.

Telephones: Telemar posts are all over the city. All of those listed offer fax services, calling cards (Telemar and Embratel, 30-60 call units), make calls to the US and Europe, and sell cards for cell phones (TIM, Oi, and BCP). **Boa Viagem:** Rua Bruno Veloso 268, loja 1-2 (☎3465 9484); Rua Barão de Souza Leão 545, loja 2 (☎3461 3307); Hotel Boa Viagem, Av. Boa Viagem 5000, loja 7B (☎3462 4523); Av. Conselheiro Aguiar 942 (☎3465 3597). **Centro:** Rua Imperador Pedro II 239 (☎3224 4403); Rua do Riachuelo 189, loja 4 (☎3423 0331); Rua Dona Ana Xavier 60, loja 5 (☎3241 9622).

Internet Access: Multlink, Av. Conselheiro Aguiar 2966 (☎3463 8932). R$5 per hr. Open M-W 6am-5pm, Th-Sa 24hr. **Pl@ylink,** Av. Domingos Ferreira 2284-A (☎3327 6849). R$6 per hr. Open daily 9:30am-10:30pm. There are also Internet cafés in several of the city's shopping malls.

Post Office: Correio Central, Av. Guararapes 250 (☎3424 3252), Santo Antônio. Open M-Sa 8:30am-7pm. Branch post offices at: Av. Conselheiro Aguiar 4955 (☎3465 3969), Boa Viagem; Rua 24 de Maio 59 (☎3424 2099), São José. Open M-F 9am-5pm. **Postal code:** 50010-970.

ACCOMMODATIONS

Recife offers accommodations for all price ranges, and affordable places to stay can be found even in the city's popular historic Centro.

BOA VIAGEM

The Boa Viagem area has the highest number of hotels and *pousadas* in the entire city. Most places are conveniently located—close to bus stops, the beach, and various restaurants and markets. There are usually young people and couples—as well as police—on the beachside road, and Boa Viagem Beach is a relatively safe place to be at night.

Vitória, Rua Capitão Zuzinha 234 (☎3462 6446), is a gorgeous place on a side street offering some peace and quiet. Take any "Aeroporto" bus. *Quartos* have TV, *frigo-bar*, and fan, while *apartamentos* have A/C and hot-water bath. Breakfast included. Laundry available. Reserve 2-3 days ahead. *Quarto* singles R$28; doubles R$38. *Apartamento* singles R$40; doubles R$60. DC/MC/V. ❷

NORTHEAST

Recife Centro

ACCOMMODATIONS

Hotel 4 de Outubro, **5**
Hotel Recife Plaza, **2**

NIGHTLIFE

Arsenal do Chopp, **1**
Downtown Club, **4**
Fashion Club, **3**

Av. Norte
Ponte de Limoeiro
Forte do Brum
Av. Alfredo Lisboa
R. 2 de Julho
R. Pedro Afonso
R. Araripina
Prefeitura da Cidade
R. Cais do Apolo
R. do Brum
R. Bernardo V. de Melo
R. São Jorge
Estuário
R. do Sossego
R. Coelho Leite
Av. Cruz Cabugá
R. do Veiga
Rio Beberibe
R. Capitão Lima
R. da Fundição
R. do Ocidente
RECIFE ANTIGO
R. Bione
R. Bom Jesus
Av. Mario Melo
Trav. Tiradentes
PÇA. ARTUR OSCAR
Torre Malakoff
Policia Federal
R. João Lira
R. do Observatório
R. do Hospício
Parque 13 de Maio
R. da Saudade
R. da União
R. da Aurora
Palácio do Governo
R. Barão de Mendes
Sinagoga Kahal Zur Israel
Pólo Bom Jesus
Teatro Santa Isabel
Palácio do Campo das Princesas
Av. Barbosa Lima
Marco Zero
R. Princessa Isabel
Ponte Buarque de Macedo
Av. Rio Branco
PÇA. DA REPÚBLICA
R. Álvares Cabral
R. de Olinda
Palácio da Justiça
Capela Dourada
R. do Sol
Av. Marquez
R. do Riachuelo
Unibanco
Ponte Maurício de Nassau
R. Mariz e Barros
BOA VISTA
Mercantil do Brasil
Av. Martins de Barros
R. 7 de Setembro
Ponte Duarte Coelho
R. Siqueiro Campos
R. do Imperador
Igreja de Madre de Deus
R. Madre de Deus
R. Cais da Alfândega
SANTO ANTÔNIO
Av. Condeda Boa Vista
Museu de Arte Moderna Aloísio Magalhães
Av. Guararapes
Teatro de Parque
PÇA. DA INDEPEDENCIA
Matriz de Santo Antônio
Rio Capibaribe
Ponte da Boa Vista
R. Nova
R. Estraita
R. das Flores
R. de Imperatriz Tereza Cristina
Av. N. Sra. do Carmo
R. da Praia
R. do Sol
R. da Palma
Igreja NS do Carmo e da Ordem Terceira
R. Velha
PÁTIO DE SÃO PEDRO
R. da Concórdia
R. Cais de Santa Rita
Mercado de São José
Casa da Cultura
Basílica de NS da Penha
Ponte 6 de Março
R. Tobais Barreto
Recife (Estação Central)
R. Barão da Vitória
Museo do Trem
R. Dr. José Mariano
Av. Dantas Barreto
R. das Calçadas
R. São José de Riba
R. Santa Rita
R. Rio Capibaribe
Negreiros
R. Floriano Peixoto
R. de São João
Forte das Cinco Pontas (Museu da Cidade do Recife)
COELHOS
SÃO JOSÉ
R. Vidal de
R. do Peixoto
R. do Muniz
0 400 yards
0 400 meters

Albergue de Juventude Maracatus do Recife, Rua Maria Carolina 185 (☎3326 1221, 9292 5670; www.geocities.com/alberguemaracatus), is extremely basic, but full of youthful travelers. All dorms have fan, locking closet, bath (inside for female dorms, outside for male dorms). Breakfast included. Laundry available. Reception 5am-midnight. Dorms R$20. Cash only. ❶

Albergue Boa Viagem, Rua Aviador Severiano Lins 455 (☎/fax 3326 9572; www.albergueboaviagem@hpg.com.br), near Colégio de Boa Viagem and Forte America. A comfortable, new place that is still being expanded. There are dorms, and a few smaller rooms meant for families and couples, plus a pool, garage area with chairs and hammocks, and a *quadra* for games and exercise. Breakfast included. Fans, locking closet, and sheets available. Dorms R$35. Doubles R$50. Cash only. ❷

Navegantes Praia Hotel, Rua dos Navegantes 1997 (☎3326 9609), is a smart little place near the sea with spacious, comfy rooms. All rooms have A/C, *frigo-bar,* TV, phone, and hot-water bath. Breakfast included. Feb.-Aug. singles R$39; doubles R$50. Sept.-Jan. singles R$51; doubles R$60. Group discounts available. AmEx. ❷

Gaivota, Av. Fernando Simóes Barbosa 632 (☎3326 3685; fax 3326 8793), is a bare, clean place alongside a major (noisy) road leading to the airport. Though rooms are not elegant or spacious, they are comfortable, and all have A/C, TV, *frigo-bar,* closet, and hot-water bath. There is a common space with TV and lines to connect PCs to Internet. English spoken. Breakfast included. Laundry. Reception 24hr. Singles R$40; doubles R$45; triples R$55; quads R$65. Cash only. ❷

Hotel Aconchego, Rua Felix de Brito Melo 382 (☎3464 2989; fax 3326 8059; aconchego@novaera.com.br), is a spotless, bustling place served by an efficient, well-informed staff and frequented by families and couples. All rooms have A/C, TV, *frigo-bar,* closet, phone, and hot-water bath. Hotel has a pool, a 24hr. restaurant, and a pet monkey. English spoken. Breakfast included. Reception 24hr. Singles R$70-80; doubles R$80-90. Service charge 10%. AmEx/MC/V. ❹

CENTRO

Centro consists of several neighborhoods that together make up old Recife. Recife Antigo is full of bars, clubs, and restaurants, and it is not unusual to stumble across some festival in the winding streets anywhere of Centro. Although it is a fun place to stay, accommodations here are more expensive than in Boa Viagem.

Hotel 4 de Outubro, Rua Floriano Peixoto 141 (☎3224 4900), is a 30s-style hotel conveniently located in a lovely, shaded part of Centro between the river and the Casa da Cultura. All rooms have A/C, TV, *frigo-bar,* phone, and hot-water bath. Breakfast included. Reception 24hr. *Quarto* singles R$55; doubles R$65. Suite singles R$85; doubles R$95. *Luxo* singles R$67; doubles R$75. *Luxo* suite singles R$85; doubles R$95. 25% extra per additional person. AmEx/DC/MC/V. ❸

Hotel Recife Plaza, Rua da Aurora 225 (☎32331 1200), is a large, elegant place right by the river, near the commercial heart of Centro. All rooms have A/C, TV, *frigo-bar,* closet, and hot-water bath. Hotel has a pool and restaurant (6am-10pm) with a café. Breakfast included. Reception 24hr. Mar.-Oct. standard singles R$50, doubles R$66; *luxo* singles R$83, doubles R$95; suite doubles and triples R$118. Nov.-Feb. standard singles R$83, doubles R$95; *luxo* singles R$96, doubles R$118; suite doubles and triples R$118. 10% service tax. AmEx/MC/V. ❸

CASA FORTE

Casa Forte is primarily a residential area; getting between this neighborhood and other sections of Recife can be time-consuming. However, if you're looking for a place to spend a quiet night or two, this is a decent place to do it, although you will probably pay more than you would in Boa Viagem.

Pousada Casa Forte, Av. 17 de Agosto 735 (☎3268 7699, 3268 0524). This quiet *pousada* reserves only 6 of its rooms for visitors (the rest are for local students), so reservations 15 days ahead of time are necessary. All *apartamentos* have A/C, TV, *frigobar,* phone, and hot-water bath. Spanish, French, German, and English spoken. Breakfast included. Restaurant open daily 6:30-1:30pm and 6-9:30pm. Laundry. Check-out 1pm. Standard *apartamento* singles R$72; doubles R$91. Superior *apartamento* singles R$85, doubles R$109. R$27 for an extra bed. Cash only. ❹

FOOD

The major food neighborhoods in Recife are the northern **Três Jardins** area of Boa Viagem and the **Pólo Bom Jesus** section of Recife Antigo, where there are blocks and blocks of restaurants, chic cafés, and little stands selling *tapioca* and popcorn. Recife's many **shoppings** (malls) are also a good bet, full of good quality, reasonably priced fast food stands. Unlike most of their American and European counterparts, Recife's malls usually have healthy options (like Shopping Recife's Siriguela natural food chain) in addition to heartier, greasier fare. The best *shoppings* for food are Shopping Recife (at M: Shopping), Shopping Guararapes, and Plaza Shopping Casa Forte.

BOA VIAGEM

Boa Viagem offers the best selection of restaurants in Recife, most of which are clustered around the "Três Jardins," near the north end of Boa Viagem beach. If you need a break from seafood, this neighborhood has an impressive array of alternatives, from Chinese to Middle Eastern cuisine.

Parraxaxá, Rua Baltazar Pereira 32 (☎3463 7874; www.parraxaxá.com.br), is a must-eat for anyone seeking Northeastern cuisine—all in an atmosphere dedicated to famous bandit Lampião (p. 16), with waiters dressed as *canguaceiros* and police. The buffet (R$18 per kg) includes traditional Northeastern fare, or you can try the popular meat dish *sarapatel* or *buxada* (*sarapel* meat in a sack; R$19). Casa Forte branch, Av. 17 de Agosto s/n. Both open M-F 11:30am-11pm, Sa-Su 6am-11pm. DC/MC/V. ❷

Venetia, Rua Júlio Pires 75 (☎3326 3550). Escape to Venice in the "Venice of Brazil" at this elegant Italian eatery voted one of the best in Recife. Beautiful setting with a warm staff and exquisite traditional Venetian cuisine (entrees for 2 R$29), plus 62 types of pizza and decadent European desserts (R$9). Open M-Th from 6am, F-Su from noon. ❸

Papaya Verde, Av. Pe. Bernardo Pessoa 287 (☎3325 6198), is a lively place with an eclectic buffet of international dishes (R$15 per kg), from Chinese to Indian fare, with lots of vegetarian options. Sa Middle Eastern buffet with music and bellydancing. Open M-F 11:30am-3pm, Sa-Su 11:30am-4pm. AmEx/MC/V. ❷

La Capannina, Av. Conselheiro Aguiar 538 (☎3465 9420), is a cozy, congenial place that caters to night-owls and intellectuals with plenty of great food and speedy, unobtrusive service. Be sure to try the house specialty pizza, or choose from 30+ types of sweet and savory *crêpes.* Plates for 2 average R$15. Open Su-Th 5:30pm-2am, F-Sa 5:30pm-4am. AmEx/DC/MC/V. ❶

Sabor de Beijo, Av. Conselheiro Aguiar 2994 (☎3325 2141), is an excellent self-service place near the Internet café Multlink (R$16-18 per kg). Also has excellent, rich cakes and Brazilian sweets (R$0.50-2). AmEx/DC/MC/V. ❷

Famiglia Giuliano, Av. Domingos Ferreira 3980 (☎3465 9922). An elegant place in a medieval-style castle. Cross the drawbridge to sample an Italian *antipasto* buffet or the 2nd fl. Shiro Sushi bar (open Tu-Sa 6pm-2am). Famed for Italian dishes like *fettucine alla pescatora* (pasta with cognac and shrimp; R$39) and their extensive international wine menu (R$15-350). Open daily 11am-2am. AmEx/DC/MC/V. ❺

Restaurante Canton, Rua Desembargador João Paes 123 (☎326 6709). This spacious, dim Chinese place serves lunch buffet-style and dinner a la carte (R$7-11). Popular *rolinhos fritos* (spring rolls) R$9. Open M-F 11:30am-3pm and 6pm-midnight, Sa 11:30-4pm and 6pm-1am, Su 8:30am-midnight. DC/MC. ❷

CASA FORTE

Although this neighborhood is known more for its museums than its restaurants, there are a number of inexpensive and satisfying places where you can take a break from sightseeing.

Famintos, Rua Sant'Anna 12 (☎3268 6364), serves a popular, giant buffet with an enormous array of options (R$16-20 per kg). Open M-Sa 11:30am-5:30pm. ❷

Planeta John's, Av. 17 de Agosto s/n, at Rua Samuel Farias, is a white-and-pink ice cream joint (pay per kg) with peaceful space for teens, couples, families, and anyone else, as well as 21 ice cream flavors (don't miss the unusual but surprisingly good corn flavor). Open daily 10am-11pm. Cash only. ❶

Budega Bar e Restaurante, Av. Conselheiro Rosa e Silva 1834 (☎3267 7777), is a cheerful pink restaurant catering to restless hipsters and families, with a menu of grilled Japanese cuisine, pasta, pizza, *crêpes,* and *feijoada*. Entrees (for 2) average R$30. Open M-F from 5pm, Sa-Su from 11:30am. MC/V. ❸

SIGHTS

Centro is the city's main sightseeing district, with a host of magnificent churches, palaces, and museums in a quaint canal setting amidst bridges and rivers. Casa Forte showcases both the old and new, from the cafés and boutiques of Shopping Casa Forte to the historic architecture of Poço da Panela, not to mention some of the best museums in the Northeast.

BOA VIAGEM

Although this neighborhood is home to far more *pousadas* than museums, it does have a beautiful (7km) **beach,** which is one of the cleanest in Brazil (because of the reefs—*recifes* in Portuguese—that protect the coast and keep the water unusually warm). There are also a few *piscinas naturais* here, and sharks are extremely rare on this stretch of the coast (unlike some surrounding beaches). Watch for signs that mark the boundaries of the safe area. *Barracas* line the road along the beach, and are open late into the night.

PÁTIO DAS ESCULTURAS. In the garden of Shopping Recife you'll find this Sculpture Patio, a collection of odd and interesting works of art, including several pieces by prominent Brazilian artists. *(Rua Padre Carapuceiro 777. M: Shopping. ☎3464 6000. Open daily 10am-10pm. Free.)*

CENTRO

The collection of neighborhoods that make up Recife Antigo is home to a plethora of old buildings and churches, with breathtaking interiors. Wandering this part of the city is an adventure in itself; the several bridges cross rivers which are splendid at any time of day. The island neighborhood of Recife Antigo is where the city of Recife began, and has numerous impressive monuments and churches which give testimony to the city's rich past.

PARQUE 13 DE MAIO. This is the largest state-planned park in Pernambuco, covering nearly 69 square kilometers. It is perfect for people of all ages, and has a playground, small lake, and small zoo. *(Rua Treze de Maio s/n, in Boa Vista. ☎3221 9723. Open M-Su 5am-11pm.)*

TORRE MALAKOFF. This tower once functioned as an observatory, but has been converted into a popular cultural center, with various photo exhibits and even a virtual library. The old observatory deck is still open to visitors, and telescopes are accessible 6-8pm. *(Rua do Observatório s/n, in front of Pça. do Arsenal da Marinha. ☎3424 8704. Open Tu-Su 3-8pm.)*

IGREJA DE MADRE DE DEUS. This church dates back to the colonial 18th century, and its altar is done in the baroque style. The church contains several religious paintings and an image of Senhor do Bom Jesus dos Passos. *(Rua Madre de Deus s/n, Recife Antigo. ☎3224 5587. Open M-F 8-11:30am and 2-4pm.)*

MATRIZ DO SANTÍSSIMO DE SANTO ANTÔNIO. The beautiful works within this church were begun in 1753, but not completed until 1862. It is an impressive baroque construction, with a gilded altar and pulpit. *(Pça. da Independencia, Santo Antônio. ☎3224 9494. Open M-F 7:30am-noon and 2-6pm, Sa 7am-7:30pm, Su 7:30am-noon and 5-7:30pm.)*

PÓLO DE BOM JESUS. Besides being a great place to eat, this area showcases wide stone streets and beautiful old buildings. Sundays, from 2pm to 10pm, there is an open-air market called "Domingo na Rua," which sells everything from clothes and jewelry to puppets and cookies. *(Bordered by Rua Bom Jesus, Rua do Apolo, Av. Barbosa Lima, and Pça. Arturo Oscar.)*

SINAGOGA KAHAL ZUR ISRAEL. Built in 1637, this was the first synagogue in the New World. In the same location is the Centro Cultural Judaico de Pernambuco, which contains an archive of Jewish history; many of the documents contained within it were excavated from the synagogue during its restoration. *(Rua do Bom Jesus 1214, Recife Antigo. ☎3224 2128. Open Tu-Su 9am-5pm. R$1-2.)*

FORTE DO BRUM. Built to protect the entrance into Recife's principal port, this fort was begun by the Portuguese in 1629. It changed hands, and was actually completed by the Dutch two years later. Although it was partially destroyed in 1669, it was restored 21 years later, and today it contains Museu Militar. *(Rua Cais do Apolo. ☎3224 4640. Open Tu-F 10am-4pm, Sa and Su 2-4pm.)*

PRAÇA DA REPÚBLICA. Located in the old Campo de Honra da Provincia, this *praça* contains three gardens and several stately buildings: the 19th-century Teatro Santa Isabel, the Palácio do Campo das Princesas (built in 1841), and the Palácio da Justiça, which houses sculptures of classical deities, a floodlit fountain, and an old *baobab* tree. *(North end of Santo Antônio. Walk along Rua do Sol past the post office, or along Av. Martins de Barros, keeping the Rio Capibaribe to your right. Accessible 24hr., though not recommended late at night.)*

TEATRO SANTA ISABEL. Designed by the French architect Louis Lerger Vauthier in 1841, this theater was completed in 1850. It has hosted grand operas and other theatrical spectacles, and is certainly worth a look, even if you can't attend a show. *(Pça. da República s/n, Santo Antônio. ☎3224 1020.)*

CAPELA DOURADA. This beautiful baroque chapel was constructed during the 17th and 18th centuries, and houses a gilded altar. Within are intricate works of art as well as dazzling architecture. Museu Franciscano de Arte Sacra is housed in the chapel annex. *(Rua do Imperador s/n, Santo Antônio. ☎3324 0530. Open M-F 8-11:30am and 2-5pm, Sa 8-11:30am. R$2.)*

CASA DA CULTURA. Built in 1885, this was once the Casa da Detenção do Recife (city prison). Today, cells have been replaced with various artesanal shops containing beautiful work done in the Nordestino style. *(Rua Floriano Peixoto s/n, Santo Antônio. ☎3224 2850. Open M-F 9am-7pm, Sa 9am-6pm, Su 9am-2pm.)*

MUSEU DE ARTE MODERNA ALOÍSIO MAGALHÃES. This museum has two floors, showcasing more than 700 works by artists from the Northeast and elsewhere. Past exhibits have featured Pernambucanos like Abelardo da Hora and Lula Cardoso Ayres, as well as the French sculptor Auguste Rodin. *(Rua da Aurora 265, Boa Vista. ☎3423 2761. Open M-F noon-6pm. R$1.)*

PÁTIO DE SÃO PEDRO. Recently renovated, this is now one of the major spaces for cultural events. From Thursday to Saturday, dance and music shows attract a diverse audience. On the patio sits the Catedral de São Pedro dos Clérigos (1782), as well as bars and restaurants which make it a major nightlife spot. *(Rua de São Pedro, São José. ☎3224 6368. Open M 10am-midnight, F-Sa 10am-2am.)*

MERCADO DE SÃO JOSÉ. This marketplace is modeled on one in Paris. It was designed by French engineer J.L. Lieutier, and perfected by Louis Léger Vauthier in France. Today, the Mercado has more than 500 stalls and is one of the major open-air markets in Recife. *(Along Rua da Praia, just before Rua da Santa Rita. Open M-Sa 6am-5:30pm, Su 6am-11:30pm.)*

BASÍLICA DE NOSSA SENHORA DA PENHA. This is one of the few churches in the Northeast done in an Italian style, built in 1870. Inside, there are frescoes by the Pernambucan artist Murillo La Greca. Fridays, the Basilica holds the traditional "Blessing of São Felix." Next to the church is a small museum containing exhibits on Dom Vidal, a bishop known for his involvement in the Religious Question of the 19th century, which was concerned with the power balance between Church and State. *(Pça. Dom Vital s/n, São José. ☎3424 8500. Basílica open Tu-Th 8am-noon and 3-5pm, F 6am-6pm, Sa 3-5pm, Su 7-9am. Museum open F 6am-6pm.)*

MUSEU DA CIDADE DO RECIFE. This museum traces the history of Recife, and contains more than 150,000 photographs as well as objects like a key that once belonged to Dom Pedro II (1859) and original maps of the city. It also houses a library with 1500 volumes focusing on Recife Antigo. *(Forte das Cinco Pontas s/n, São José. ☎3224 8492. Open M-F 9am-6pm, Sa-Su 1-5pm.)*

MUSEU DA IMAGEM E DO SOM. This is an extensive archive of Brazilian musical and artistic works. It consists of over 4000 objects including photos, theatrical pieces, tapes, videos, postcards, slides, and literature. *(Rua da Aurora 379. ☎3221 4990. Open M-F 8am-5pm.)*

MUSEU DO INSTITUTO ARQUEOLÓGICO HISTÓRICO DE PERNAMBUCO. This museum is full of pieces from Brazil's colonial period, including the stoneworks which marked the divisions between the districts of Pernambuco and Itamaracá. It also houses rare books and relics from the Dutch invasions. *(Rua do Hospício 130, Boa Vista. ☎3222 4952. Open M-F 1-5pm, Sa 8am-noon. R$1.)*

MUSEU DO TREM. Since its opening in 1972, this museum has gathered together more than 2000 objects, including historical documents, photographs, telegraphs, and various types of locomotives. *(Pça. Visconde de Mauá, by the Estação Ferroviária in São José. ☎3424 3141. Open M-F 9am-noon and 2–5pm.)*

CASA FORTE

This neighborhood contains the city's best museums, which display some of the finest artwork in the Northeast. Many of the museums also keep textual and photographic records of the city's past. Of additional interest is **Poço da Panela,** at the south end of Casa Forte and one of the oldest, loveliest neighborhoods in Recife.

MUSEU DO HOMEM DO NORDESTE. If you go to only one museum in Recife, make it this one. Part of the Joaquim Nabuco Foundation, it has a collection of more than 3500 items which give insight into the particular history and culture of

Northeastern Brazil. The sections on anthropology, the sugarcane industry, and popular art are particularly good. There is also a guide who speaks English. *(Av. 17 de Agosto 187. From Av. Conde da Boa Vista in Centro, take the "Alto Santa Isabel" bus to the front of the museum. Open Tu, W, F 11am-5pm; Th 8am-5pm; Sa-Su and holidays 1-5pm. R$2.)*

MUSEU-OFICINA CERÂMICA FRANCISCO BRENNAND. This is both a museum and a ceramics factory, and has more than 15 square kilometers of greenery where visitors can wander among the works of one of the greatest figures of Brazilian contemporary art, Francisco Brennard. *(Propriedade dos Santos Cosme e Damião s/n, in Várzea. ☎3271 2466. Open M-F 8am-5pm. R$2.)*

POÇO DA PANELA. This is a beautiful suburban district that served as a summer residence for Recife's wealthy denizens during the 19th century. It overlooks the Rio Capibaribe, and is characterized by mansions and terraced houses preserved from that period. Other highlights of this area are the **Church of Nossa Senhora da Saúde,** at the intersection of Estrada Real do Poço and Rua Visconde de Araguara, and the **Poço Atelier,** Rua Antônio Vimivio 113, which is both an art museum and a studio for local artists. (Open M-F 9am-6pm.)

FUNDAÇÃO GILBERTO FREYRE. This was once home to the sociologist, anthropologist, and internationally known writer Gilberto Freyre. The house, built in the 19th century, now contains an artistic and literary collection, as well as a memorial to the previous owners. *(Rua Dois Irmãos 320, in Apipucos. ☎3441 1733. Open M-F 9am-5pm. R$2.)*

MUSEU DO ESTADO. Housed in an old mansion that once belonged to the family of the Baron of Beberibe, this museum showcases diverse artifacts from the 16th to 19th centuries, including furniture, jewels, coins, paintings, and ceremonial items. *(Av. Rui Barbosa 960, Graças. ☎3427 0766. Open Tu-F 9am-5pm, Sa-Su 2-5pm. R$2.)*

PARQUE DOIS IRMÃOS. This reserve of Atlantic rainforest (Mata Atlântica) covers almost four square kilometers and functions as a zoo, botanical garden, and Environmental Education Center. The park has ecological trails with specialized guides; it also has lakes and a British building that once functioned as the pump station of the Companhia do Beribe, which was responsible for Recife's water supply in the 1980s. *(Pça. de Dois Irmãos s/n, Dois Irmãos. ☎3268 5707. Open daily 8am-4pm. R$2.)*

NIGHTLIFE & ENTERTAINMENT

The places to be on Recife's warm, breezy nights are right by Boa Viagem's shore or in swinging Centro, as both neighborhoods have great bars and clubs. Centro also has several beautiful theaters if you're looking for lower-key entertainment. Alternately, you can head to Shopping Center Recife in Boa Viagem, where there are any number of movies playing in the complex's 10 theaters.

BOA VIAGEM

Biruta Bar, Rua Bem-te-vi 15 (☎3326 5151), Pina, is a calm beach bar chosen the best in Recife for 3 years running. Excellent musical selection and fun crowd, fueled by the potent *Caipifruta Pernambucana Gostosa* (R$4). Open M-Th from 5pm, F-Su from noon.

Butterfly, Rua Azevedo 165 (☎3076 7298), is a happening GLS-friendly place right in the beach district. It is often inundated with an energetic young crowd itching to have a good time. Heavy on the crazy-fun side, with regular drag shows. 18+. Cover R$15-20.

Multiplex Recife, Shopping Recife (☎3464 6669). M: Shopping. First-run cinema with 10 screens, comfortable seating, and digital sound. Tickets R$9-12; over 65 and under 11 R$4.50-6. Check newspapers or *Veja* magazine for times.

CENTRO

Arsenal do Chopp, Pça. do Arsenal da Marinha 59 (☎3224 6259), in Pólo Bom Jesus, is a sophisticated bar-restaurant with its own brand of beer (R$2.20). Popular nighttime dish is the *escotilha* (chicken with fries; R$12 for 2 people). Open daily from 5pm. MC.

Fashion Club, Av. Marques de Olinda s/n, is a popular, super-hip club true to its name. Renowned for its lively dance scene and bar, the club is a trendy place to spend an evening. 18+. Cover R$15-20. Open Th-Su 10pm-dawn.

Downtown Club, Rua Vigário Tenório s/n, is another hotspot for Recife's locals. It tends to be less touristy than Fashion Club, with the same great quality music and bar (and fashion-conscious dress code). 18+. Cover R$15-20. Open Th-Su 10pm-dawn.

Teatro Santa Isabel, Pça. da República (☎3224 1020), Santo Antônio, was designed by the French architect Louis Lerger Vauthier in 1841 and completed in 1850. Call for an up-to-date list of performances.

Teatro de Parque, Rua do Hospício 81 (☎3423 6044), Boa Vista, has various programs, from dance festivals to theater and film projects.

Teatro do Valdemar de Oliveira, Rua Oswaldo Cruz 412 (☎3222 1200), Boa Vista, hosts comedy shows, usually by local groups. The small theater, which bears the name of its founder, suffered from a fire but was re-inaugurated in 1982.

CASA FORTE

Expand Wine Bar, Rua Sebastião Malta Arcoverde 80 (☎3266 4202), is elegance itself. The wine cellars have 400+ selections of the best wines from around the world, served only in the famous Riedel glass. Menu included treats like bruschetta, carpaccio, and fondue (R$25). Open M-W 5:30-11:30pm, Th-Sa 5:30pm-12:30am. AmEx/V.

Cinema da Fundação José Cavalcanti Borges, Rua Henrique Dias 609 (☎3421 3266), Derby, screens art flicks. R$6; Mondays R$3. Open Sa-Th until 6:30pm.

DIVING

SHARKS. Boa Viagem beach is bordered by a reef, and so sharks rarely infiltrate this part of the shore. However, they do appear occasionally on neighboring beaches, so you should check with the tourist offices for shark warnings.

Diving into the waters off Boa Viagem, where there are about 20 wrecks—including Portuguese galleons—is a popular activity. To organize an outing, contact **Expedição Atlântica,** Rua Comendador Bento Aguiar 520/101, in Madalena. (☎3227 0458, 3445 5233. Open M-F 8am-noon and 2-6pm.) Another option is **Projeto Mar,** Rua Padre Bernadino Pessoa 410, in Boa Viagem. (☎3326 0162; www.projetomar.com.br. Open M-Sa 10am-10pm.) Recife's three major sports clubs, all in the middle of the city, allow visitors and non-members to use some of the facilities (call clubs for specific information). To reach **Sport,** Ilha do Retiro (☎3227 1213), take the "Torrões" bus from Av. Guararapes in Centro. **Santa Cruz** (☎3441 6811) is accessible by the "Casa Amarela" bus. **Náutico** (☎3423 8900) can be reached by any "Água Fria" or "Afflitos" bus.

DAYTRIPS FROM RECIFE

GAIBU & SUAPE ☎81

The two standouts among the many seaside towns near Recife are Gaibu and Suape, twin towns with clear, calm waters ideal for relaxing or kayaking and boating around nearby islands along the 24km coastline. While Suape is the more picturesque destination and the main hub for local-guided boat tours of the area, Gaibu has services and amenities like the police and ATMs. Both towns have beachfronts and main areas lined with numerous identical *pousadas* and bars.

Suape's central **Praça da Suape** draws visitors wanting to experience the regional dances called **forrós de chiquinho** (Su 7pm-midnight). From Praia do Suape, you can take boat tours to the nearby islands of Cocáia, Ilha do Francês, and Ilha Tatuoca, with a local guide: Chico (☎9969 2852), Admário (☎9165 7805), Totonho (☎9147 3873), Ronaldo (☎9951 7982), Antônio (☎3522 5253), or Zé Dantas (☎9145 8201). Hours vary but boats leave from Praia do Suape. (Several daily 9am-5pm. R$30 per trip.) You can also take the same tour on the **Olinda II,** with Alexandre (☎3062 0341, 9168 6866), or the **Scuna Summer,** with Ane (☎3559 0684, 9947 0444), both of which leave from the neighboring beach of **Praia de Calhetas** (R$30 per trip). You can rent **kayaks** (R$15) and arrange guides (R$30) at the Pólo Naútico, a.k.a. **Marina Porto Verde.** (☎9933 1818, 3327 7551. Open daily 8am-5pm.)

To get to either town, take any "Cabo Centro" or "Cohab Aeroporto" bus from Recife's airport, or the "Cohab Centro" bus from Recife's Centro. Any of these will drop you off in the *centro* of Cabo de Santo Agostinho (30min.), from which you can take a "Gaibu/Suape" bus right to either town (20-30min., daily 8am-5pm, R$2.20). There are also **taxis** at the *rodoviária* in Cabo de Santo Agostinho that will transport you to either town (15min., R$15-20). Suape has one **posto de médico,** Rua Professora Maria Mendes Barros s/n. (☎3522 6686. Open daily 7am-5pm.) Most other services are in Gaibu. The **tourist office** is in Gaibu, at Av. Laura Cavalcante 110, near the bus stop, and has free maps of the area. (☎3512 7006. Open Tu-Su 8am-7pm.) Other services (all in Gaibu) include: **Banco do Brasil,** Av. Laura Cavalcante, near Farmácia Santa Rosa, which exchanges money and has a **24hr. ATM** (open M-F 8am-10pm); **Pharmacy Paixão,** Rua Joaquim Rodrigues (☎3522 6035; open daily 8am-10pm); and **police**, Av. Laura Cavalcante 57 (☎3521 2228).

PORTO DE GALINHAS ☎81

Man-sized chickens *(galinhas)*, carved from the stumps of coconut trees, speckle Porto de Galinhas. The name (and the giant chickens) are derived from the era after slavery was abolished in 1850, when traders in this area continued to smuggle slaves into Brazil beneath cages of Angolan chickens. While these bizarre sculptures are the most striking feature of this tiny beach town, Porto de Galinhas is worth a visit more for its natural wonders: three sparkling natural pools, a vivid reef, a muddy mangrove swamp, and of course its 18km of beach.

TRANSPORTATION. Princesa (☎3527 9461) runs buses from the end of Rua da Esperança to Recife (18 per day 4am-6pm; R$5) and Cabo de Santo Agostinho (18 per day 4:20am-6:30pm; R$2.70). **Taxis** in front of Shopping Porto Rico, Rua da Esperança, will take you straight to Maracuípe (R$15) and Muro Alto (R$20). **Mototaxis** take you around town. (☎3552 2247. R$3.)

ORIENTATION & PRACTICAL INFORMATION. Muro Alto is along the coastal highway, PE-09. The main road into Porto de Galinhas (and its beach) is **Rua da Esperança,** which branches off PE-09 and intersects with **Rua Beijupirá** (both streets run to the beach), which becomes Estrada Para Maracaípe (the main road to Pontal da Maracaipe). The *estrada* is home to several excellent, similar pousadas. The **Centro de Turismo,** Rua da Esperança 188, provides excellent information and an English-speaking staff. (☎3552 1480, 3552 1900. Open daily 9am-5pm.) Other services include: **24hr. ATMs** at Banco do Brasil, Rua Beijupirá, the gas station on Rua da Esperança, and Pça. de Artesanato by the beach; **bike rental** and **surfboard rental,** from a store at the end of Rua da Esperança, near Galeria Aquarius (open daily 10am-5pm; bikes R$10 per day, surfboards R$15); **police,** PE-09 km 8, Merepe 1 (☎3552 1658); and a **posto médico,** at the end of Rua Manoel Luiz Uchoa (☎3552 2997; open 24hr.).

ACCOMMODATIONS & FOOD. Estrada Para Maracaipe (the end of Rua Beijupirá) has many excellent, identical *pousadas*. A different option is **Pousada Marahú ❹,** Rua Carauna 12, which has a pool, sauna, cheerful staff, and rooms with hot-water bath, veranda with hammocks, safe box, TV, A/C, *frigo-bar*, and phone. (☎3552 1700. Breakfast included. Some English spoken. Oct.-Feb. singles R$90; doubles R$100. Mar.-Sept. singles R$68; doubles R$75. Visa.) **Pousada Beira Mar ❷,** Av. Beira Mar 12, is right on the beach. All rooms have A/C, TV, *frigo-bar*, hot shower, and hammock, plus access to a pool and outside bar. (☎3552 1052. Breakfast included. Dec.-Feb. singles R$85, doubles R$125; *luxo* singles R$110, doubles R$160. Mar.-Nov. singles R$45, doubles R$55; *luxo* singles R$90, doubles R$95. 10% discount for student groups. AmEx/MC/V.)

Dirt-cheap *lanchonetes* line Rua da Esperança, just after the gas station, while *barracas* line the beach. **La Creperia ❶,** Rua Beijupirá, near Galeria Picoola, serves over 40 types of crêpe, both savory and sweet (R$8-9), plus salads, soups, and pasta (R$9-11). (☎3552 1831. Open M-F 5-10pm, Sa-Su and holidays 2-10pm. Cash only.) **Carne de Sol do Cunha ❷,** Rua Manoel Luís Cavalcante Uchoa, which intersects Rua Esperança, offers overflowing plates of Northeastern fare (from *picanha* to *maminha*) for a great price: R$20-30 (feeds 2) gets you a huge, hearty entree and several side dishes, including rice and beans, *pirão*, *farofa*, and fried manioc. (☎3552 1340. Open daily 11:30am-10pm. Visa.) **Restaurante Beijupirá ❹,** Rua Beijupirá s/n, is a garden-like eatery with outdoor seating, specializing in seafood (R$26-30). (☎3552 2354. Open daily noon-midnight. AmEx/DC/MC/V.)

WATERFRONT ACTIVITIES. The 18km Porto de Galinhas **beach** stretches for 18km from the reef of **Muro Alto** to **Pontal da Maracaípe,** where Rio Maracaípe meets the sea, forming a "fragrant" mangrove swamp. Self-guided buggy and kayak trips or guided boat tours are the most popular way to experience the area's outdoor attractions, but some people choose to venture no farther than their beach towel. **Cabina de Bugeiros,** Rua Beira Mar, by Pça. Artesanato, runs buggy tours from Muro Alto to Pontal da Macaraípe. (Daily 9am-5pm. R$40-50.) **Pé no Mangue,** Rua da Esperança 101, 1st fl., arranges kayak tours. (☎3552 1612; www.penomangue.com. Open daily 2-10pm.) To visit a *piscina natural*, you must travel by **jangada,** which can be rented from **Cabina dos Janguadeiros,** Rua da Esperança, on Pça. das Piscinas Naturais. (Daily at low tide. R$6 per person.)

OLINDA ☎81

The attractive, well-preserved older sibling to sister city Recife's sprawling modern chaos, Olinda is a gorgeous UNESCO World Heritage Site and home to some of Brazil's most majestic, breathtaking churches. While tourism is heavy in this colonial setting, the city's charm is worth the higher prices.

TRANSPORTATION

Olinda is most easily accessible from neighboring Recife, and the two are so close that buses running between them are not considered to be on an intercity route.

Buses: Local buses run between Recife and Olinda (every 20min. 5am-11pm; R$1.30-2). Catch the bus for Olinda on Recife's Av. Olinda, and the bus for Recife on Olinda's Av. Getúlio Vargas.

Taxis: Taxis cluster around Pça. do Carmo (near the Prefeitura in Viradouro) and the Mercado Eufrasio Barbosa. **Teletaxi** (☎3429 4242).

Kombis: Legal *kombis* run between Olinda and Recife (R$3-5).

ORIENTATION & PRACTICAL INFORMATION

Olinda has two districts: the southern **Centro Histórico** bordering Recife and the northern residential/commerical area (centered on **Bairro Novo**), home to many of Olinda's services. The Centro Histórico consists of the neighborhoods Milagres, Varadouro, Amparo, Alto da Sé, and Carmo, the last bordering the commercial district's Bairro Novo and home to most of historic Olinda's local services). The Centro Histórico's main streets (running parallel to the coast) are **Rua Manoel Borba,** which becomes **Avenida Beira Mar,** and **Avenida Sigismundo Gonçalves** farther inland, which becomes **Rua do Sol.**

Tourist Offices: Empetur, Centro de Conveções, 1st fl. (☎3427 8183), connected by viaduct to Shopping Tacaruna. See the listing in **Recife,** p. 403. Open M-F 8am-6pm. **Tourist Hotline** (☎3429 9153). Open M-F 8am-1pm.

Tours: Both Empetur and the Secretaria de Turismo can help you arrange tours with reputable guides, who will be cheaper than those who wait in Pça. Do Carmo. Another option is to take a tour with one of the **guias mirins**—teenagers who give free tours as part of a program with the Prefeitura–found at the intersection of Rua do Bomfim and Av. da Liberdade. In the Bairro Novo, try: **Felitur,** Av. Getúlio Vargas 1411 (☎3439 5885; www.felitur.com), or **Ostra,** Av. Getúlio Vargas 70 (☎3429 0700).

Banks: Bandepe Bank, Mercado Eufrasio Barbosa, Centro Histórico. Open M-F 9am-2pm. **Banco do Brasil,** Av. Getúlio Vargas 1470, Barrio Novo. Open M-F 10am-4pm; ATM open daily 7am-8pm. **24hr. ATMs: HSBC,** Av. Getúlio Vargas 1050. **Bradesco,** Av. Getúlio Vargas at Rua Pedro de Assis Rocha. **Currency exchange:** Banco do Brasil, in Shopping Tacaruna. Open M-F 10am-4pm.

24hr. Pharmacies: Dropersa, Largo do Varadouro, Mercado Eufrasio Barbosa, Centro Histórico. Open M-Sa 7am-8pm. **Farmácia,** Pça. João Lapa. Open M-Sa 8:30am-7pm.

International Phones: Pça. Do Carmo 57 (☎3439 8998). Open daily 8am-7:30pm.

Internet Access: Olindanetcafé.com, Pça. Do Carmo 5B (☎3429 5528), Centro Histórico. R$3.50 per 30min., R$6 per hr. Open M-Sa 9am-8pm.

Post Office: Pça. João Pessoa s/n, Carmo. Open M-F 9am-5pm. **Bairro Novo,** Av. Getúlio Vargas 1180. Open M-F 9am-5pm, Sa 9am-noon. **Postal code:** 53120-970.

ACCOMMODATIONS

Olinda is a popular destination for both locals and tourists for Carnaval, with a reputation as an even wilder party town than Salvador. If you will be in town for the holiday, be sure to book in advance and be prepared for steep price hikes.

Pousada São Francisco, Rua do Sol 127 (☎3429 1418; pousadasaofrancisco.com.br), Carmo. A spacious, quiet place with cheerful staff, just off Pça. Do Carmo. All rooms have A/C, TV, *frigo-bar,* closet, phone, and hot-water bath. Laundry service available. Breakfast included. Reception 24hr. Standard singles R$60; doubles R$66. *Luxo* singles R$80; doubles R$93. 10% service tax. AmEx/DC/MC/V. ❸

Pousada Peters, Rua do Amparo 215 (☎3439 2171), is a large, beautiful place popular with youth and families alike. Common area with TV. All rooms have A/C, TV, fan, *frigo-bar,* safe, and hot-water bath. Pool and lovely terrace area. English spoken. Breakfast included. Reception 24hr. Make reservations 3 days in advance. Small *quartos* R$50; large *quartos* R$85. Cash only; US dollars accepted. ❸

Pousada dos Quatro Cantos, Rua Prudente de Morais 441 (☎3429 0220; www.pousada4cantos.com.br), is a shaded place near good restaurants, offering luxury for a decent price. All rooms have A/C, TV, *frigo-bar,* hot-water bath, closet, and phone. English spoken. Breakfast included. Reception 24hr. Reserve 1 month in advance. Singles R$90-153; doubles R$103-176. AmEx/DC/MC/V. ❹

Pousada da Olinda, Pça. João Alfredo 178 (☎3494 2559; www.pousada-olinda.com.br), is an elegant place. All rooms have fan or A/C; most have *frigo-bar,* TV, and hot-water bath. The *pousada* has a pool, and offers city tours of Olinda and Recife (R$50-100). Also can provide transportation to Recife's airport (R$20). English spoken. Lavish breakfast included. Laundry service available. Apr.-Sept. dorms R$12; singles R$30; doubles R$50; triples R$20-40; quads R$20-40. R$3-5 extra Oct.-Mar. ❶/❷

Pousada d'Olinda no Aradouro, Rua 15 de Novembro 98 (☎3439 1163, 9965 5229) Varadouro. All rooms have A/C, TV, *frigo-bar,* and private bath, and an attached self-service restaurant (open M-F 11:40am-3pm). English spoken. Breakfast included. Reception 24hr. Make reservations 1 week in advance. Mar.-May singles R$20; doubles R$35. July-Feb. singles R$30; doubles R$60. DC/MC/V. ❶

Albergue São Francisco (HI), Rua do Sol 233 (☎3429-1592; fax 3439 1913; www.alberguedeolinda.com.br), Carmo. Laid-back, with hammocks and fans for every room and some hot-water baths. Laundry facilities. Breakfast included. Reception 24hr. Dorms R$20. Doubles R$48. HI discount. DC/MC/V. ❶

FOOD

Trattoria Don Francesco, Rua Prudente de Morais 358 (☎3429 3852), is a family restaurant with quiet veranda, offering superb Venetian food—including vegetarian dishes—made using ingredients from their garden. Lasagna R$14-18, ravioli R$16, tagliatelle R$14-18. Italian wines R$15-36. Dessert means *tiramisu* and Italian ice (R$6). Open M-F noon-3pm and 7-11pm, Sa 7pm-midnight. Cash only, including US dollars. ❸

Restaurante Mourisco, Pça. João Alfredo 7, 2nd fl. (☎3429 1390), is a 33-year-old eatery in Olinda's oldest house, dating from 1516 and decorated in a Spanish-Brazilian style. The menu is mostly seafood (R$10-30), like *camarão mourisco* (shrimp grilled with cheese and corn over rice; R$20). Open daily noon-3pm and 7pm-late. DC/MC. ❸

Tian an Men, Pça. do Carmo 742 (☎3439 6069). Unimpressive exterior hides an elegant, lantern-hung interior. Regional food and Chinese dishes, from fried bananas (R$1-3) to spring rolls (R$2-4.50). Entrees (for 2-3) R$12-16. Hours vary. ❷

Creperia, Pça. João Alfredo s/n (☎3429-2935), is a small place that serves satisfying *crêpes* (R$10) and salads (R$8-13). Open Tu-Su 4-11pm. Visa. ❷

Olinda Café & Arte, Rua Prudente de Morais 256 (☎3439 8561), Carmo. A small, classy space to rest after all those hills. The owner, Simone, sells her own artwork and that of local artists, both porcelain and sculpture. Sandwiches and soups (R$1-3). Cappuccino, juices, and teas R$1-2. Open Th-Su 4-9:30pm. Cash only. ❶

SIGHTS

Olinda has an incredible array of churches, and those interested in religious artwork will find much of interest. The churches listed below are only a few of the many throughout the city. For a different perspective on the area, head to the hilltop neighborhood of Alto da Sé, where you can marvel at a panorama of Recife that rivals that of Rio de Janeiro in grandeur.

CHURCHES

IGREJA DE SÃO JOSÉ DOS PESCADORES. This simple but lovely blue and white structure was built by the area's fishermen. It was constructed because of the reputed appearance of an image of St. Joseph in the spot where the church now stands. *(Rua do Sol, past Pça. do Carmo. Open daily 9-11am. ☎3429 9349.)*

IGREJA DA NOSSA SENHORA DAS NEVES & CONVENTO DE SÃO FRANCISCO. This church is home to the oldest Franciscan convent in all of Brazil. Although the building was partially destroyed by the Dutch shortly after its 1585 construction, it was fully repaired in the second half of the 17th century. Especially lovely are the Portuguese tiles and the ceiling in the chapter house which portrays images of Jesus and Mary. *(Rua de São Francisco, just off of Av. da Liberdade. ☎3429 0517. Open M-F 8am-noon and 2-5pm.)*

IGREJA DA NOSSA SENHORA DA GRAÇA. This church was originally constructed in 1550, and was restored in the 17th century after having been damaged during the Dutch fires that destroyed so many of Olinda's architectural treasures. After it was donated to Jesuit priests, the chapel was used to teach catechism to the area's indigenous peoples. The church's side altars are some of the oldest stone monuments in Brazil. *(Rua de São Francisco, just before the Feirinha da Sé. ☎3429 0627. Open Feb.-June and Aug.-Nov. M-F 2-4:30pm.)*

IGREJA NOSSA SENHORA DA MISERICÓRDIA. When it was first built, the Misericórdia church shared this site with a local hospital. However, after the Dutch burnt both church and hospital down to the ground, only the church was restored, in 1654. The sacristy contains an interesting marble washbasin made by Portuguese stonemasons. *(On Rua Saldanha Marinho, off Rua Bispo Coutinho. ☎3429 2922. Mass Su 7:30am, M-Sa 6:20am.)*

IGREJA DE NOSSA SENHORA DO AMPARO. This church is interesting not only because of its architecture, but because of its origins. It was founded about 400 years ago by a group of young bachelors and musicians. Although it—like many other churches in the city—was burned down in 1631, it has been restored several times, most recently in 1992. *(Rua Saldanha Marinho. ☎3429 7339. Open daily 7:30am-1pm; go to the side entrance.)*

IGREJA DA NOSSA SENHORA DE GUADALUPE. This church is one of the few in Olinda that survived the Dutch burnings unscathed, and so is a rare example of some of the earlier architecture from this region. Its high altar is reputedly from the destroyed Church of Saint Peter the Martyr. *(Off Rua São Jose, on an unnamed road to the left. ☎3429 1914. Open Tu-F 3-5pm.)*

IGREJA DA NOSSA SENHORA DO ROSÁRIO DOS HOMENS PRETOS DE OLINDA. This church was built by liberated slaves in the early 1600s, and a hospice was founded next door in 1702. Restoration work in 1988 uncovered an interesting series of paintings, which imitate the precious stones and marbling of wooden altars in Olinda's wealthiest churches. *(Travessa do Rosário, off Estrada do Bonsucesso. ☎3439 2495. Open daily 9-11am.)*

IGREJA DA NOSSA SENHORA DO MONTE. This church possesses the state's oldest historical records, some of which date back to before 1537. It currently serves as a residence to a group of Benedictine nuns, who sell homemade wafers and liqeurs. *(Rua Dom Bonifácio Jansem, just off of Estrada do Bonsucesso. ☎3429 0317; call from the gate to be admitted. Open daily 8:30-11:30am and 2:30-6pm.)*

IGREJA DE SÃO BENTO. This is considered one of the most beautiful churches in Olinda, and was restored in baroque style after the Dutch fires destroyed much of it. The sacristy and high altar are carved and done in gold leaf, and were exhibited in New York City in 2002. *(On Rua de São Bento, near Pça. Mons. Fabrício. ☎3429 3288. Open M-Sa 8-11:30am and 2-4pm. Gregorian chants performed Su 10am.)*

IGREJA DE SÃO SEBASTIÃO. This church was built and dedicated to Saint Sebastian in 1686, in an appeal for protection against a plague that had struck Olinda. One of its altars moves, and allows a view of an earlier altar done in fresco. *(On Rua 15 de Novembro. ☎3439 9699. Open Sa 4-6pm.)*

IGREJA NOSSA SENHORA DO DESTERRO & CONVENTO DA SANTA TEREZA. This church was built to fulfill a promise João Fernandes Vieira made upon defeating the Dutch on Mt. Tabocas. The altar is covered with beautiful carvings. *(On Av. Olinda. ☎3429 3686. Open M-F 8am-noon and 2-5pm, Sa 8am-noon.)*

MUSEUMS & OTHER COLLECTIONS

MUSEU DE ARTE SACRA. This museum contains a collection of religious artwork and relics from the region, many of which date back to colonial times. *(On Rua Bispo Coutinho. ☎3429 0032. Open M-F 9am-2:45pm.)*

MUSEU REGIONAL. For those interested in the origins of the city, this is an excellent place to learn a little bit of history. The museum contains information and exhibits on the development of Pernambuco State, as well as Olinda. *(Rua do Amparo. ☎3429 0018. Open M-F 9am-5pm, Sa-Su 2-5pm.)*

MUSEU DE MAMULENGO. This museum showcases puppets used as popular entertainment, as well as those which have performed for governors, royalty, and other major figures throughout history. The curator may explain the puppets' history for you by asking the puppets themselves. *(On Rua do Amparo. ☎3429 6214. Open Tu-F 9am-5pm, Sa 10am-5pm. R$1.)*

CASA DO BONECOS GIGANTES. This establishment is dedicated to a collection of literally larger-than-life Carnaval puppets. They are housed in what is actually the home of their creator, a local artist. This place is definitely worth a visit: the experience is both eerie and exhilarating. *(Rua do Amparo, a few doors down from Museu de Mamulengo. Open weekends; hours vary. R$2.)*

MUSEU DE ARTE CONTEMPORÂNEA. This chapel worked in conjunction with the old Diocesan Prison, and was originally used as a place of prayer for religious prisoners. *(On Rua 13 de Maio. ☎3429 2587. Open Tu-F 9am-1pm, Sa-Su 2-5pm.)*

NIGHTLIFE & ENTERTAINMENT

Those interested in nightlife should really head back to the superclubs and varied bars of Recife. Small bars and *barracas* are plentiful around Pça. do Carmo, along the beach (Av. Beira Mar), and in Feirinha da Sé. **Clube Atlântico,** in Pça. do Carmo, is a spacious place that's lots of fun, with a varying schedule featuring everything from classical dance performances to club nights. **Bar e Restaurante Cantinho da Sé,** Ladeira da Sé 305, near the Feirinha do Sé, is Olinda's swankiest bar by far. (☎3439 8815. Cocktails R$2-7. Open Tu-Sa 11am-1am, Su 11am-10pm).

FAZENDA NOVA & NOVA JERUSALÉM ☎81

Ten minutes from the town of Fazenda Nova is a **Nova Jerusalém,** a full model of Jerusalem, one-third the size it was during Jesus's lifetime. Nova Jerusalém is also home to the largest open-air theater in the world, and every year during Semana Santa (the week before Easter), 70,000 people come here to witness the nightly passion plays, Paixão de Cristo. (☎3732 1129, 3732 1154. Open daily 7am-5pm. R$3; R$2 for children and students; R$35-45 during Semana Santa). Also worth a visit while in town is Fazenda Nova's **Parque das Esculturas,** to the left four blocks after the town's entrance on the main road, which harbors old stone sculptures. (Open daily 7am-5pm. Free.)

The road entering the town, **Avenida Soares da Costa,** passes a *praça* to the left, then Igreja da Nossa Senhora da Conceição and a tiny *praça* to the right. Immediately following is a huge arc with the town name "Fazenda Nova" inscribed on it. Close to the inside right of the arc is the Diretoría de Cultura. The road leading off right immediately after this Diretoría is **Rua Agamenon Magalhães,** which leads to a residential neighborhood. To reach Nova Jerusalém, keep walking straight down Av. Soares da Costa. During most of the year, Fazenda Nova is accessible only via **jeep** from Caruaru (40min.; R$4). These jeeps can be found in Caruaru in front of Sicamel and A Confiança Loteria; ask the driver to stop just before Brejo, at Fazenda Nova. The **last jeep** returns to Caruaru at 4:30pm. **Buses** leave from Recife for Fazenda Nova and Nova Jerusalém only during Easter week as part of package tours. **Tourist information** can be obtained from the Directoría de Cultura, to the inside right of the arch at the beginning of town. Other services include: a **medical post,** near Igreja da Nossa Senhora da Conceição at the start of town (open M-F 7am-5pm); an **ambulance** to nearby hospitals in Caruaru or Brejo (☎9608 7861); a **post office,** by the *praça* at the start of town. **Postal code:** 55175-000.

Accommodations in Fazenda Nova tend to be pricey, especially during the Semana Santa. **Pousada Mora Antiga ❷,** three streets after the arc into Nova Jerusaém and off to the left, is one of the better options for those on a budget. (☎3732 1206. Breakfast included. Check-out 10am. Dorms R$40. Cash only.) For a fast and filling meal, try **Restaurante Nego Bom ❷,** Av. Soares da Costa 75. This self-service restaurant has a buffet (R$13 per kg) with typical Brazilian fare and some regional specialties. (☎3732 1456. Open daily noon-3pm and 7pm-midnight. Cash only.)

ILHA ITAMARACÁ ☎81

Itamaracá is set apart from other beach towns on this stretch of coast by its neighboring island of **Ilha Coroa do Avião,** which has five *piscinas naturais.* The main road onto Av. João Pessoa Guerra passes **Praia Jaguaribe** and ends at **Praia do Pilar. Forte Orange,** at the end of PE-15, is an expansive fort built by the Dutch, which is today crowded with *barracas.* (Open daily 9am-4:30pm. R$3.) To get to the Ilha Coroa do Avião, several types of transportation wait by the side of the fort: you can catch a *canoa* (daily 7am-7pm; R$5) or a *lancha* (daily 7am-7pm; R$5-10). **Vilha Velha,** in the *centro* of Ilha Itamaracá, was the first port in the Northeast.

The main bridge to the island, **Ponte Getúlio Vargas** becomes **PE-15** when it reaches the island. It forks by a sugar mill: the fork which continues straight is still PE-15 and ends at the Forte Orange, while the fork to the left is called **Avenida João Pessoa Guerra** and heads for the *centro*, passing Jaguaribe, and ending at Pilar. **Taxis** are the easiest way to get around the island and are found at the entrance of Itamaracá. There is also a **bus** around the island, which stops at the entrance of town and the various beaches (every 30min. M-Sa 4am-midnight, Su 4:30am-11pm; R$2). **Tourist information** can be had from the **Prefeitura,** in the *centro.* (☎3544 1156. Open M-Sa 7am-1:30pm.) Other services include: a **24hr. ATM** at Caixa Econômica Federal, near the Prefeitura (☎3544 1186; open M-F 10am-3pm); **Hospital Alzira Figuerido,** on Av. João Pessoa Guerra (☎3544 1226); and the **post office,** on Av. João Pessoa Guerra (☎3544 1135; open M-F 7:30am-1pm). **Postal code:** 53900-000.

Hotel Pousada ❷, Rua Fernando Lopes 205, in the *centro*, is a clean and affordable option. All *apartamentos* have A/C, TV, *frigo-bar,* and hot-water bath. The hotel has a pool and bar. (☎3544 1152. Breakfast included. Reception 24hr. Check-out 2pm. Singles R$40; doubles R$50. AmEx/MC/V.) The neighborhoods of Jaguaribe, Pilar, and Forte all have many good restaurants and *lanchonetes* which are open until late.

JAPARATINGA ☎82

Japaratinga is a sleepy beach town. Stop by for an undisturbed swim, but don't expect much more. The **beaches** are just 10min. from the start of town. They can be reached via Rua Maria das Mercés, which changes its name to Rua Francisco dos Barros Pedes. **Banho de Bica,** a small waterfall, is in the **Povoado de Barreiras,** six kilometers from the *centro.* The highway passing by Japaratinga is **PR-101 Norte.** Off of it is the main road entering town, **Rua Antônio Alvim.** After a two-minute walk, the road intersects **Praça Nossa Senhora das Candeias,** where the *centro* is located. A road to the left of the Pça. NS das Candeias runs to the beach. The main road continues as **Rua Maria das Mercés,** which eventually hits **Praça Padre Cicero,** where most accommodations are located. As you continue down Rua Maria das Mercés, its name changes to **Rua Francisco dos Barros Pedes,** and to its left lies the Praia de Japaratinga.

Real Alegoas and **São Domingo** buses stop by the town entrance. From town, you can catch **buses** to Maceió (every hr. 6am-midnight; R$8), Maragoji (every 30min. 6am-midnight; R$2), and Recife (3 per day 8am-4pm; R$10-15). **Secretária de Turismo,** in Pça. NS das Candeias, can arrange excursions to nearby *piscinas naturais.* (Open daily 7:30am-1:30pm; Jan. daily 7:30am-6:30pm. 1hr. tours R$15 per person.) At the central *praça,* there are two banks with **ATMs:** Caixa Postal Bradesco (open M-F 9am-noon and 2-4pm) and Caixa Econômica Federal (open

M-F 9am-noon and 2-4pm). Other services include: **police,** on the left side of Rua Antônio Alvim (☎297 1195; open 24hr.); a **pharmacy,** Farmácia Santa Rita, on Rua Maria das Mercés, a short walk from Pça. NS das Candeias (☎297 1135; open daily 9am-noon and 2-7pm); a 24hr. **posto de saúde,** on the right side of Rua Antônio Alvim just after entering town (☎297 1178); a **telephone post,** on the corner of Rua Maria das Mercés and Travessa Bernadino Calaça da Silva (☎297 1314; open M-Sa 7am-8pm, Su 7am-noon); and **post office,** in Pça. NS das Candeias (☎297 1143; open M-F 9am-noon and 2-4pm). **Postal code:** 57950-000.

Pousada Raio do Sol ❷, Rua Francisco dos Barros Pede 36, is just a minute from the beach. All *apartamentos* have A/C, TV, *frigo-bar*, and hot-water bath. (☎297 1140. Breakfast included. Reception 24hr. Singles R$35; doubles R$50. Cash only.) To get to **Pousada dos Mares ❶,** follow the winding dirt off Rua Maria das Mercés, just after Pça. Padre Cicero. Most rooms have fan, and all have private bath. (☎297 1384; pdosmares@hotmail.com. Breakfast included. Kitchen. Internet R$6 per hr. Reception 24hr. Mar.-Aug. dorms R$10; doubles R$35; triples R$40. Sept.-Feb. dorms R$15; doubles R$45; triples R$50. MC/V.) For a bite to eat, try **Restaurante e Pizzaria Mama Perreira ❶/❷,** at the end of Rua Sebastião Lins de Melo in front of the beach, an excellent place with a spectacular view of the sea. The diverse menu includes seafood (R$10-20), pizza (R$13.50-17), pastas (R$11-R$13), and lighter fare like sandwiches (R$1.30-3). All plates serve two people. (☎297 1222. Open daily 9am-10:30pm. Visa.)

PARAÍBA

JOÃO PESSOA ☎83

Mild-tempered João Pessoa lacks the history and excitement of the neighboring state capitals, but will satisfy those looking for a city's conveniences combined with a town's security. Most sights are located in orderly Centro, and most hotels and restaurants lie along the shore, not far from a *piscina natural* and an island of red sand. The city has only recently begun to develop a tourist infrastructure.

TRANSPORTATION

Flights: Aeroporto Internacional Presidente Castro Pinto (☎232 1562; fax 232 3255), in Bayeux. To get there, take any "Aeroporto" bus from the *rodoviária* (20-30min.). Flight carriers with offices in the airport include: **BRA** (☎232 4638); **TAM** (☎232 2002); **Varig** (☎232 1515); **VASP** (☎232 1757). Numbers operate daily 11:30am-4pm.

Buses: Intercity buses leave from **Terminal Rodoviária Severino Camelo** (☎221 9611). Luggage storage available. **Nordeste** has buses to **Fortaleza** (Su-F 3 per day 7-10pm) and **Natal** (8 per day 5:30am-7:30pm). **Boa Vista** (☎241 1454) goes to **Goiânia** (2hr.; 11 per day 5am-4pm; R$5). **Progresso** (☎241 1122) runs to: **Aracaju** (8hr.; 7:30pm; R$76); **Recife** (2hr.; 13 per day 5:30am-7:30pm; R$15); **Salvador** (14hr.; 7:30pm; R$103); **São Luís** (19hr.; 7pm; R$129). **Itapemirim** (☎241 1080) goes to **Rio de Janeiro** (39hr.; 2 per day 2-3pm; R$217) and **São Paulo** (46hr.; 1pm; R$247). **São Geraldo** (☎241 1464) has buses to: **Belém** (36hr.; 10am; R$159); **Maceió** (6hr.; M, W, F 7:30pm; R$33); **Teresina** (22hr.; 2 per day 10am-5pm; R$100).

Public Transportation: From the *ferroviária* (☎241 4240), right next to the *rodoviária,* a **commuter rail** runs along the west end of João Pessoa, between Santa Rita and Porto de Cabedero (28 per day 8am-4pm; R$0.45). Local **buses** stop at the *rodoviária* and at the *lagoa,* both in Centro Histórico. Buses also run along Av. Pres. Epitácio Pessoa (R$1.15). **Ferries** leave from the dock (☎228 3459) in Cabedero, in the northwestern end of the city, to **Lucenha** (25min.; 15 per day 6am-9:30pm; R$1 per person, R$5 per car) via **Costinha** (15min.).

Taxis: Taxis can be found at the airport, *rodoviária*, the *lagoa* in the Centro Histórico, and Shopping Manaíra. **Disk Taxi** ☎222 3135. **Transtaxi** ☎232 4167.

Car Rental: Localiza, Av. Epitácio Pessoa 4910 (☎247 4030), in Cabo Branco. **USA Rent A Car,** Av. NS dos Navegantes 950 (☎247 3203, 9985 2299; www.usarentac-arpb.com.br), in Tambaú.

ORIENTATION & PRACTICAL INFORMATION

João Pessoa is a thin strip of a city stretching north-south along the coast. **Centro Histórico** is located on the midwestern edge of the strip, at the edge of the huge **lagoa,** by which all buses pass, 20min. from the **rodoviária.**

Connecting Centro Histórico to the **beaches** is João Pessoa's principal road, **Avenida Presidente Epitácio Pessoa,** which runs along before dead-ending at the popular **Praia de Tambaú.** South of Tambaú is **Praia de Seixas,** the easternmost point in the Americas. **Praia de Cabedoro,** at one end of the commuter rail, is located at the northern tip of the city.

Tourist Offices: Centro Turistico, on Av. Almirante Tamandaré (☎214 8279), next to the Feirinha de Tambaú. Open daily 8am-7pm. Branch at the **airport,** 1st fl. (☎253-4010). Open daily 10am-4pm. Branch at the **rodoviária,** 1st fl. (☎218 6655). English spoken. Open daily 8am-6pm.

Tours: Navega Turismo, Av. João Maurício 1341 (☎246 6548), in Manaíra. **Passear Turismo,** Rua José Clemtinho de Oliveira 130, rm. 102 (☎247 8087; fax 983 0093), runs tours by buggy as well as by boat. **Green Tour Receptivo,** Av. Nego 99, rm. 1 (☎247 5900, 245 9223) offers van tours of the city (R$15 per person) as well as tours to the beaches of Litoral Sul and Litoral Norte (R$25 per person). Also offers buggy tours of the beaches, and nautical tours of Ilha da Areia Vermelha (R$25 per person).

Banks: There are many banks located along Rua Duque de Caxias and Pça. 1817, near the *lagoa* in Centro. Most banks are open M-F 10am-4pm. Those in Centro include: **Banco do Brasil,** Pça. 1817 129 (☎221 8907); **Banco Itaú,** Rua Duque de Caxias 524 (☎241 1006); **HSBC,** Av. Pres. E. Pessoa 1797 (☎244 8611). In Praia Tambaú there is a **Banco do Brasil,** Av. Sen. Rui Carneiro 186 (☎247 5577).

Currency Exchange: PB Câmbio e Turismo, Av. Visc. Pelotas 54 (☎241 4555). **Mondeo Tour,** Av. Nego 46 (☎226 3100), in Praia Tambaú.

Supermarket: Bompreço, Av. Pres. Epitácio Pessoa 1450 (☎244 5030). Open 24hr.

24hr. Pharmacies: Dia e Noite, Av. Pres. Epitácio Pessoa 1370 (☎214 7160). **Pague Menos,** Pça. 1817 58 (☎214 2880).

Hospitals: Hospital de Emergência e Trauma Sen. Humberto Lucena, BR-230 km 17 (☎216 5700). **Hospital Municipal Santa Isabel,** Pça. C. Brandão s/n (☎214 1808).

Internet Access: Available at **Centro Turistico,** on Av. Almirante Tamandaré, near Feirinha de Tambaú. R$1 per 10 min., R$0.10 per additional min. R$5 per hr.; R$20 per 5 hr. Also sends **faxes:** to US R$5 per page, to Europe R$8 per page. Open M-Sa 8am-9pm, Su and holidays 2-9pm.

Post Office: Correio Central (Main post office), Pça. Pedro Americo 70 (☎214 1901; fax 221 8014), in Centro. Open M-F 8am-5pm. Branch office on Av. Senador Rui Carneiro, right by Pça. da Independência in Praia de Tambaú. Open M-F 8am-6pm. **Postal code:** 58000-000.

ACCOMMODATIONS

The best accommodations and restaurants in João Pessoa are located by Tambaú, but if you plan to use the city as a base for excursions to the nearby beach towns, it is much more convenient to stay in Centro Histórico, because of its close proximity to the *rodoviária.*

Pousada de Caju, Rua Infante Dom Henrique 750 (☎247 3960; www.pousadadocaju.com.br), is a colorful and comfortable place with cashews everywhere. All rooms have A/C, TV, *frigo-bar,* phone, and private bath. Hotel also has a pool and *lanchonete.* Breakfast included. Reception 24hr. Apr.-Oct. singles R$25; doubles R$45; triples R$115; quads R$120-130. Nov.-Feb. singles R$35; doubles R$55; triples R$95; quads R$140. Group discounts. MC. ❶/❷

Pouso das Aguas, Av. CC 2348 (☎226 5103, 226 5003), is a popular tourist hangout. All rooms have A/C, TV, *frigo-bar,* phone, closet, and hot-water bath. Breakfast included. Laundry service available. Reception 24hr. Singles R$40; doubles R$55; triples R$70; quads R$90. Nov.-Feb. 20% price increase. AmEx/MC/V. ❷

Veleiros Praia Hotel, Av. NS dos Navegantes 602 (☎247 5406), is plain but clean, and conveniently located 5min. from Centro Histórico. All rooms have A/C, TV, *frigo-bar,* phone, closet, and hot-water bath. Hotel has a pool, living room, garage, and playground. English spoken. Breakfast included. Laundry service available. Reception 24hr. Singles R$35; doubles R$45; triples R$55. AmEx/DC/MC/V. ❷

Rhema, Av. Antônio Lira 127 (☎247 1900, 226 1406), is a small place near the beach. All its clean, quiet rooms have A/C, TV, *frigo-bar,* and hot-water bath. Breakfast included. Reception 24hr. Reserve 2-3 days in advance. July, Nov.-Feb. singles R$51; doubles R$66; triples R$86; quads R$96. Mar.-June and Aug.-Oct. singles R$40; doubles R$56; triples R$76; quads R$86. MC/V. ❷

Pousada dos Estrangeiros, Rua Alberto Falcão 67 (☎226 4667); ring doorbell to enter. All rooms have A/C, TV, *frigo-bar,* closet, and hot-water bath. Breakfast included. Reception 24hr. Singles R$40; doubles R$50; triples R$65; quads R$80. Group discounts available. MC. ❷

Nossa Senhora das Neves, Rua Dom Carlos de Goveia Poelho (☎222 2917), has some of the city's least expensive rooms. All rooms have fan, TV, sofa, and bath. Breakfast included. Reception 24hr. R$20 per person. Cash only. ❶

FOOD

For a quick bite to eat, head to the open-air market **Feirinha de Tambaú,** on Av. Almirante Tamandaré, located between the Tropical Hotel Tambaú and the Centro Turistico. Here, vendors sell various inexpensive light meals and an impressive array of *sucos.* (Open daily 8am-10pm.)

Tabua de Carne, Av. Rui Carneiro 648 (☎247 5970), serves largely regional dishes, like *carne do sol* (R$17-29) and *picanha* (R$24-32), all big enough for 3-4 people. Open M-Sa 11:30am-10:30pm, Su 11:30am-5pm. AmEx/DC/MC/V. ❷/❸

Salutte, Rua Geraldo Costa 150 (☎247 4080; www.salutte.com.br), at the intersection of Av. Edson Ramalho. An upscale, airy self-service place that serves international cuisine, including Italian, French, and Japanese dishes. R$16.90 per kg. Open daily 11am-5pm. AmEx/DC/MC/V. ❷

Cheiro Verde, Rua Carlos Alvergas 43 (☎226 4802, 226 2700), is a popular kilo (R$11.80 per kg) known for its wide selection of regional and seafood dishes. Open daily 11am-3pm. MC/V. ❷

China In Box, Av. Duarte da Silveira 610 (☎222 6699; www.chinainbox.com.br), offers a variety of delicious Chinese dishes–including fried rice with egg, meat, or seafood–to go (in a box, no less). Plates average R$16, and usually serve two. Try the *yakisoba* (noodles with shrimp, chicken, and lentils; R$11.60). Open M-F 11am-3pm and 5-11pm, Sa-Su 11am-11pm. DC/MC/V. ❷/❸

A Fazenda Nova, Av. Epitácio Pessoa 5060 (☎227 0343, 9984 4371), has hearty northeastern specialties. Some dishes are a la carte, like the popular tapioca (R$1-3) and *cartola* (banana with cheese; R$3). Filling and delicious soups (R$2 per bowl). Open daily 7am-10pm. Cash only. ❷/❸

SIGHTS

BEACHES & THE OUTDOORS. Beaches are João Pessoa's main attraction. Those within the city proper run from Praia Seixas to Praia Cabedoro, and span about 30km. At Praia Seixas you will find **Ponte Seixas,** the easternmost point in the Americas. *(From the rodoviária, take Bus #508.)* A lovely outdoor excursion is to visit the **piscina natural** of Picãozinho at low tide. *(Purchase tickets on Praia Tambaú, or through any travel agency. R$7-15 per person.)* Boats also leave for the lovely red-sand island of **Areia Vermelha.** *(Boats can be found along Praia de Camboinha. Departures at low-tide. R$7 per person.)* Another option is to explore the **Parque Arruda Câmara,** a zoo that also contains an aviary, walking trails, an 18th-century fountain, all on 17 hectares of land. *(Off Av. Mons. W. Alfredo Leal. Open daily 8am-7pm. R$1-1.20 per person.)* The **Manacial do Bouraquinho** (a.k.a. Mata) is a reserve of 471 hectares that show-cases much of the region's native wildlife. *(Take Bus #301 or #302 from the* lagoa *in Centro Histórico, and ask to be dropped off near the reserve. Open daily 8am-4pm. Free. Guides can be arranged through IBAMA; call ☎244 4100).*

MUSEUMS & CHURCHES. The most interesting buildings in João Pessoa are located in Centro Histórico, along the *lagoa.* The church most worth seeing is **Igreja de São Francisco,** which dates back to the 16th century. *(Pça. São Francisco. Open daily 8am-6pm. R$1.)* Another beautiful church to visit is **Igreja do Carmo,** also in Centro Histórico. *(Open M-F 2:30-5:30pm, Sa 3:30-5:30pm. Free.)* **Casa da Póvora** is an old gunpowder store that has been converted into a museum. *(Near Igreja São Francisco. Open M-F 8am-4pm. Free).*

NIGHTLIFE

Most bars are in Tambaú, by Av. Coração de Jesus and Av. Cabo Branco. Things get started late, and usually last until dawn on the weekend. Most clubs are 18+, and there is usually a cover charge.

JACUMÃ ☎83

Jacumã is a peaceful town encircled by red roads, rolling hills, and the sea. Its clean beaches, multi-colored sandbars, and mineral water springs attract quite a few visitors. Particularly popular is the central **Praia de Jacumã.** Near the entrance to town is **Praia de Amor,** site of the Pedra do Amor, a huge hollow stone overlooking the beach. Legend has it that any couple who passes through the stone will remain together forever. Farther north is **Praia Barra de Gramame,** famous for its beautiful sandbars. **Buses** labeled "Jacumã" make their last stop in **Praia Carapibus,** just south of town. Praia Jacumã and Praia Carapibus have several *piscinas naturais,* which can be reached at low tide by walking through the water. A short walk from Praia Carapibus is **Praia de Coqueirinhas,** home to the town's refreshing **mineral water spring.**

Jacumã is connected to the surrounding beaches by PB-008. Roads within Jacumã proper do not have posted street signs, but the small town is easy to navigate. **Buses** run between Jacumã and João Pessoa daily via Conde (every 30min. 5am-10pm; R$2.30-3.20). You can catch them in Jacumã at the intersection of PB-008 and PB-18, or from the *centro*. Another option is a **taxi** from João Pessoa (R$30). The **Secretaria de Turismo,** on PB-008 in the *centro*, can provide tourist information. (☎298 1081. Open M-F 9am-noon and 2-5pm.) **Tours** can be arranged with Hotel Viking, including **buggy rides** along the beach (R$50). The **police** are located on PB-008, near the bus stop by Colégio José Maris. (☎298 1122. Open 24hr.) Other services include: **bank,** Multibank, on Rua Riuza Ribeiro, in the *centro* (☎290 1272; open M-F 8am-6pm); **ATM,** Banco do Brasil, at the start of BR-8, near Mercadinho Jacumã; **telephones,** Telemar, across the street from the bank, next to the Prefeitura; **post office,** next to the pharmacy and Paderia Brasiluso (open M-F 8am-noon and 2-5pm). **Postal code:** 58322-000.

Pousada do Inglês ❶/❷, Av. Beira-Mar s/n, before Praia de Tambaba, is around the corner from the Prefeitura. All rooms have *frigo-bar*, TV, hot-water bath, and fan or A/C. (☎290 1168; www.pousadadoingles.com.br. Breakfast included. Reception 24hr. Check-out 2pm. Reservations recommended. Singles R$25, with A/C R$30; doubles R$40, with A/C R$55. Visa.) **Hotel Viking ❷,** Rua Projetada 330, on a hill between Jacumã and Praia Carapibus, with a Viking ship atop the building. The hotel has a pool and also organizes tours. (☎290 1015; www.hotelviking.com.br. English spoken. Breakfast included. Reservations recommended. Singles with fan R$30-45, with A/C and *frigo-bar* R$40-70; doubles with fan R$35-50, with A/C and *frigo-bar* R$50-80; triples with fan R$40-60, with A/C and *frigo-bar* R$60-95. 10% service tax. AmEx/DC/MC/V.) For great seafood, try **Peixada ❸,** Av. Beira-Mar s/n, at the end of the first road turning left after Prefeitura, right by the sea. (☎290 1518, 290. Open daily 9am-5pm. Entrees R$13-36. Cash only.)

RIO GRANDE DO NORTE

NATAL ☎84

Aside from sun, surf, and sand, Natal offers little to visitors, but the small city nevertheless sees its fair share of travelers using the city as a base for exploring the area beaches. Most coastal buggy rides from Fortaleza (p. 428) end here, and quiet Natal is a good place to catch your breath. Aside from its beaches and a few churches and museums, there's not much here; even the liveliest areas are dormant on weekends. The city's biggest attraction is the world's largest cashew tree, in neighboring Parnamirim.

TRANSPORTATION. Flights leave from **Aeroporto Internacional Augusto Severo,** 12km southwest in neighboring Parnamirim. Flight carriers with offices in Natal include: **TAM,** Rua Seridó 746 (☎202 3385; fax 202 3802); **TAP Air Portugal,** Rua Mossoró 576 (☎221 0037); **TransBrasil,** Av. Deodoro 429 (☎211 1805, 221 6025); **TRIP,** Av. Prudente de Morais 4283 (☎234 1717); **Varig,** Rua Mossoró 598 (☎221 4453, 0800 997 000); **VASP,** Rua João Pessoa 429 (☎221 4453, 0800 998 277). Intermunicipal and interstate buses depart from **Rodoviária Nova,** Av. Capitão Mor Gouveia 1237 (☎205 4377), in southwest end of the city. **Rodoviária Velha,** in Pça. Augusto Severo, between the Centro and Centro Histórico, serves as a stopping point for various local buses (daily 6am-midnight; R$1.30). **Taxi** companies include: Coopertaxi (☎743 1183); Disque Taxi Natal (☎213 0800); Rádio Taxi (☎221 5666).

ORIENTATION & PRACTICAL INFORMATION. Natal is spread out over a peninsula. The most touristed areas are near the north end of the city, and include the *praias urbanas* (urban beaches), on the northeast side of the peninsula on the Atlantic shore. **Centro** and **Centro Histórico** are adjacent to each other, on the northwest side by Rio Potengi. The airport is in the city of Parnamirim, southwest of Natal. The main road near the *praias urbanas* is **Avenida Presidente Filho,** which becomes **Avenida Gov. Sívio Pedrosa** as it moves south past Praia dos Artistas. Heading westward, Av. Pres. Filho becomes **Ladeira do Sol,** a road that rises up the main hill of this city into the *centro,* which is also referred to as **Cidade Alta.**

The main **tourist office,** Av. Pres. Filho s/n, is at Praia dos Artistas. (☎232 7312. English spoken. Open daily 8am-noon and 2-10pm.) There are information booths at Rodoviária Nova, Rua Capitão Morgoveia 1237 (☎205 1000; open M-F 8am-10pm), and at the airport (☎644 1000, 743 1811; open M-F 8am-10pm). Information is also available from the **tourist hotline** (☎0800 841 516). There are **ATMs** at **Banco do Brasil,** Pça. Albuquerque 534 (☎201 0682) and Av. Duque Caxias 20 (☎211 5942, 211 5986), and **HSBC,** Av. P. Morais 3346 (☎2113 6699) and Pça. Mal. Deodoro 745 (☎201 9672). **Currency exchange** is available at **Dunas Câmbio,** Av. Eng. Roberto Freire 1776, loja B11 (☎219 3840), and **Super Câmbio,** Via Direta Shopping, box 11 (☎234 2689). In case of emergencies you can contact either the **tourist police** (☎232 7404) or the **polícia federal** (☎0800 841 536). There are many **24hr. pharmacies** in the city, including **Drogaria Globo,** Av. Eng. Freire 2960 (☎215 1642), and **Drogaria Guararapes,** Av. Eng. R. Morais 8790 (☎215 1700). **Internet access** is available at Infotec, Rua Princesa Isabel 461, loja 1, in Shopping Centro (☎221 2507; open daily 8am-9pm; R$2 per hr.), and **Hotel Miami Beach,** Av. Gov. Sílvio Pedrosa 24, in Praia do Meio (☎202 3377; open daily 7am-10pm; R$5 per hr.). The main **post office,** Av. Rio Branco 510 538, is in Centro. (☎211 6757, 220 2492. Open M-F 8-11am and 2-5pm.) **Postal code:** 59000-000.

ACCOMMODATIONS. Natal's best accommodations are by the beaches, but there are also some decent options in Centro and Centro Histórico. **Hotel Miami Beach ❷,** Av. Gov. Sílvio Pedrosa 24, at Praia de Meio, is a bright and bustling place with an Internet café and a restaurant. All rooms have A/C, TV/DVD, phone, *frigo-bar,* and private bath. (☎202 3377. Reception 24hr. Internet access R$5 per hr. Restaurant open Tu-Su 11am-9:30pm. Singles R$40; doubles R$60; triples R$70; quads R$85. DC/MC/V.) **Bruma Praia Hotel ❷,** Av. Pres. Filho 1176, is a clean and airy place right by the sea. It has 25 *apartamentos,* all with A/C, TV, phone, *frigo-bar,* closet, and hot-water bath. The hotel also has a small pool and a bar. (☎/fax 211 4308. Breakfast included. Reception 24hr. Reserve one month ahead in high season. Dec.-Feb., July singles R$79; doubles R$98; triples R$110; quads R$135. Mar.-June and Aug.-Nov. singles R$40; doubles R$60; triples R$80; quads R$100. AmEx/DC/MC/V.) **Pousada Albergue Cidade do Sol ❶,** Av. Duque de Caxias 190, is conveniently located in Centro Histórico near Rodoviária Velha. All rooms have bath, fan, towels, and closet space. (☎211 3233. Dorms R$16. Visa.) **Casa Grande ❷,** Rua Princesa Isabel 159, in Centro, is a swankier spot with slightly higher prices. All rooms have A/C, TV, *frigo-bar,* closet, and hot-water bath. (☎211 4895; fax 211 0555. Breakfast included. Reserve two days in advance. Singles R$29; doubles R$41; triples R$56; quads R$71. Discounts for cash. Visa.) **Albergue Pousada Meu Canto ❶,** Rua Manoel Dantas 424, in Centro, has rooms with fan. (☎212 2811. English spoken. Breakfast included. Dorms R$16. Cash only.) **Pousada Lua Cheia (HI) ❶/❷,** Rua Dr. Manoel Augusto Bezerra de Araújo 500, in Ponta Negra, has rooms with fan and hot-water bath. (☎236 3696; www.luacheia.com.br. Breakfast included. Reserve at least one week in advance. Dorms R$22, non-members R$30. Doubles R$66; triples R$88. DC/MC/V.)

FOOD. The best restaurants are located primarily near the *praias urbanas*. Cheap eateries popular with locals abound in **Shopping Natal,** Av. Senador Salgado Filho 2234, in Candelária. Vegetarians will love **Marietta ❶,** in Shopping Natal, which serves up a fantastic array of sandwiches (R$2-8), as well as juices. (Shopping Natal open M-Sa 11am-10:30pm, Su 11:30am-10:30pm.) **Restaurante Pequim ❷,** Rua Floriano Peixoto 498, in Centro, has cheap and excellent food and a chef who specializes in Chinese cuisine. (☎211 9007. Lunch buffet R$2.90 per kg. Dinner entrees for two R$10-23. Open daily 11:30am-3pm and 6-10:30pm. DC/MC/V.) **Mama Italia ❸,** Rua Sílvio Pedroso 43, has a warm family atmosphere and Italian fare. (☎202 1622. Pasta dishes R$11-19. Pizzas R$10-23. Open M-W 6pm-midnight, Th-Sa 6pm-1am, Su 11:30am-3:30pm. DC/MC.) **Sorveteria Tropical ❶,** at the intersection of Rua Sílvio Pedrosa and Av. Pres. Filho, is a popular ice cream place overlooking the sea with more than 25 flavors (R$1.25-4.50) and excellent milkshakes. (Open daily 10am-midnight.) **Marenosso ❷,** Rua Aderbal de Figueiredo 980, inside Centro de Turismo, is a classy café that serves as both a quick stop and a nice eat-in place. (☎211 6149. Entrees R$10-14. Open F-W 10am-6pm, Th 10am-midnight. Cash only.)

SIGHTS. Although Natal is not known for its sights, it does have a few nice beaches and museums. Natal's **beaches** stretch for a total of 15km. The principal ones are referred to as the *praias urbanas* (urban beaches), and span three kilometers in the southern end of the city, where the blue-gray waters are clean, safe, and popular with surfers. To reach the *praias urbanas*, catch Bus #33. The star-shaped **Forte dos Reis Magos,** on Av. Pres. Filho, is near Praia do Forte at the tip of Natal's peninsula. (Open M-F 8am-4:30pm. R$2.) **Museu do Mar,** on Av. Dinarte Mariz, at Praia de Mãe Luiza, contains tanks with local sea life and exhibits of preserved specimens. (☎221 3611. Open M-F 8-11:30am and 2-5pm. Free.) Also at Praia de Mãe Luiza is **Farol de Mãe Luiza,** a lighthouse that affords a great view of the city. To get here, take any "Mãe Luiza" bus. Get off when you see the lighthouse, and obtain the key from the house next door. (Open M-F 8am-5pm. R$2.) Natal's Centro (a.k.a. Cidade Alta) and Centro Histórico have some good museums and beautiful buildings. **Catedral Nossa Senhora da Apresentação** is in Pça. André de Albuquerque. (Open M-F 8am-5pm. Free.) Also in Pça. André de Albuquerque is the **Memorial Câmara Cascudo.** (☎211 8404. Open Tu-F 9am-5pm, Su 7am-7pm. Free.) Another interesting church to visit is **Igreja de Santo Antônio,** Rua Santo Antônio 683, which has a lovely wood altar and contains a museum of sacred art. (Open M-F 8am-5pm, Sa 8am-2pm; museum open Tu-Sa 8am-5pm. Free.) **Museu Câmara Cascudo,** Av. Hermes de Fonseca 1398, is largely a historical museum, containing exhibits on archaeological digs and displays on former regional industries. (☎212 2795. Open Tu-F 8-11am and 1-5pm. R$2.) In the neighboring city of Parnamirim is the **Cajueiro de Pirangi do Norte,** the world's biggest cashew tree. The tree's branches cover 8500 square meters, and the tree itself produces over 60,000 cashews annually.

NIGHTLIFE & ENTERTAINMENT. The best weekly party, especially for visitors looking to get a feel for the city, is held at the **Centro de Turismo (Forró com Turista),** Rua Aderbal Figueiredo 980. (☎211 6218; www.forrocomturista.com.br. Open Th 10pm-dawn.) **Zás-Trás Shopping Show,** Rua Apodi 500, has some of the most glamorously eye-catching shows around. Stop by to watch traditional dances, comedy shows, *capoeira* performances, and the band Zás-Trás. (☎211 1444, 211 1457. Open M-Sa 8:30pm-1am. Cash only.) **Downtown Pub,** Rua Chile 11, tries its hand at resembling an English pub. There is also a dance floor and a game room. (☎611 1950. Cover varies. Open Th-Sa 9pm-dawn. AmEx/DC/MC/V.)

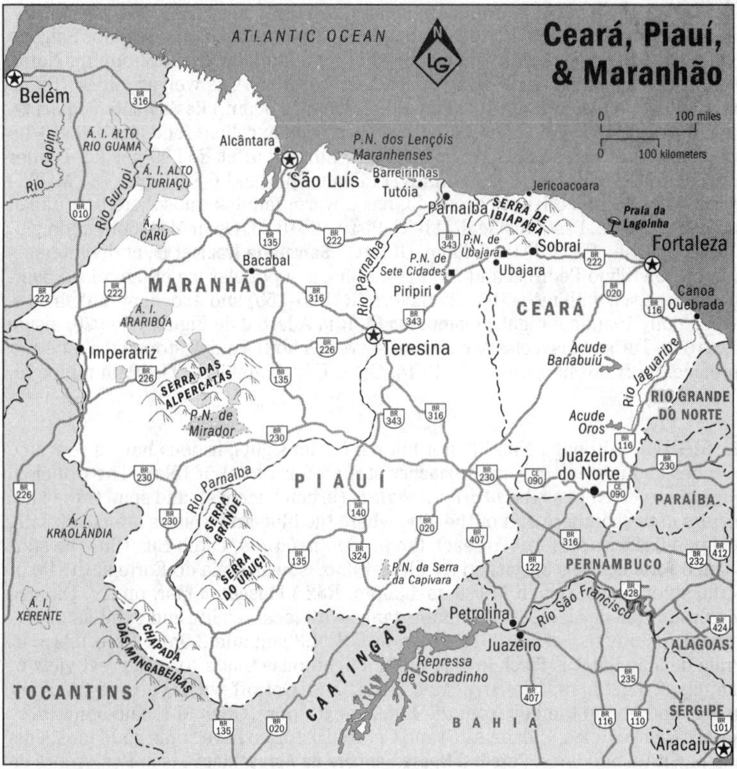

Ceará, Piauí, & Maranhão

CEARÁ

FORTALEZA ☎85

Fortaleza, Brazil's fifth biggest city, may be the capital of one of Brazil's poorest states, but that doesn't stop its inhabitants from enjoying life. Even outside of Carnaval and the Festa Junina, there are plenty of opportunities to *forró* the night away. Because it is an urban center, the shores of Fortaleza itself are far from pristine, but it is still a good jumping-off point for the unspoiled and magnificent beaches of Lagoinha (p. 436), Canoa Quebrada (p. 435), and the increasingly famous Jericoacoara (p. 437).

TRANSPORTATION

Flights: Aeroporto Internacional Pinto Martins, Av. Senador C. Jereissati 2000 (☎0800 991 516, 477 1200). Services available: ATMs, luggage storage, restaurants, travel agents, car rental agencies.

Buses: The **rodoviária** (☎256 4080) is 6km from Centro. Services available: ATMs, restaurants, luggage storage (12hr.; R$2 per small bag, R$4 per large bag). **Boa Esperança** (☎256 5006) has buses to **Belém** (25hr.; 4:30pm; R$115) and **Natal** (7hr.; 5:30pm; R$37). **Guanabara** has buses to: **Aracaju** (21hr.; 7:15pm; R$98); **Brasília** (42hr.; 3 per day 9am-8:30pm; R$178); **Recife** (12hr.; 4 per day 8am-8pm; R$60); São Luís (17hr.; 4 per day 12:30-9pm; R$78); **Teresina** (10hr.; 5 per day 7am-8:30pm; *convencional* R$45, *leito* R$78) via **Piripiri** (7½hr.; R$34). **Itapemerim/Penha** has buses to: **Belém** (24hr.; 2 per day 9am-8pm; R$134); **Porto Alegre** (70hr.; 8am; R$325); **Rio de Janeiro** (48hr.; 9am; R$230); **Salvador** (22hr.; 7pm; R$130); **São Paulo** (55hr.; 9:30am; R$237). **Nordeste** runs to **Natal** (8hr.; 8 per day 9am-11pm; R$39). **Redençao** (☎256 1973) serves **Jericoacoara** (6hr.; 2 per day 10:30am-6:30pm; R$29). **São Benedito** (☎272 2544) runs to **Canoa Quebrada** (3hr.; 4 per day 8:30am-3:45pm; R$13). **Transbrasilia** (☎256 1306) has buses to **Brasília** (48hr.; 8am; R$206) and **Teresina** (11hr.; 2 per day 8am-7pm; R$53).

Public Transportation: The local bus station is **Terminal Papicu.** From there buses can be caught to anywhere in Fortaleza and are clearly marked with destinations. Running a couple of blocks up from the coast, Grand Circular 1 (East-West) and Grand Circular 2 (West-East) connect Praia Iracema, Praia Meireles, and Praia Mucuripe as well as pass through the *centro* and Terminal Papicu. Minibuses called **Top Buses** run throughout the city; one runs down Av. Beira Mar right along the beachfront. Fare R$1.40.

Taxis: Rádio Taxi Ceará (☎2438 1111) and Rádio Taxi Fortaleza (☎800 5744). Average prices: airport to Praia Iracema R$20-25; *rodoviária* to Praia Iracema R$10-12; *rodoviária* to Centro R$10-12; airport to Centro R$20-25.

Car Rental: Hertz (☎477 5055) and Localiza (☎477 8933) both have offices at the **airport.** The following agencies have offices in the city proper: **Avis,** Av. Br. Studart 1425 (☎261 6785) and Av. Abolição 2480 (☎242 3115); **Hertz,** Rua Osvaldo Cruz 175 (☎242 5425); **Localiza,** Pça. do Vanqueiro, s/n. (☎272 5744).

ORIENTATION & PRACTICAL INFORMATION

The main beaches are on the northern edge of the city. From west to east they are: **Praia Iracema,** which has the cheapest accommodations and vibrant nightlife; **Praia Meireles,** full of glitzy hotels and a few bars; **Praia Mucuripe,** the city's major fishing port; and **Praia Futuro,** the only unpolluted beach and the best for swimming. **Centro** lies to the west of Praia Iracema, and is where you will find most of the museums and cultural centers. **Avenida Beira Mar** runs between Praia Iracema, Praia Meireles, and Praia Mucuripe. Parallel to it and farther back from the shore is **Avenida Abolição,** which has more services and a few hotels.

Tourist Office: Central Tourist Information, Centro Administrativó Virgilio Távora (☎488 3900; www.turismo.ce.gov.br). There are **tourist offices** at the airport (☎477 1667; 24hr.); Centro de Convenções, Av. Washington Soares 1147 (☎488 3904; 8am-8pm); Rua Senador Pompeu 350, in Centro, toward the beach (☎231 3566).

Tours: Resetur, Av. Barão de Studart 1105 (☎268 2627; fax 268 2462; www.resetur.com.br). **Oceanview,** Av. Mensenhor Tabosa 1165 (☎219 1300; fax 219 1666; www.brazilamerica.com). **Lisa tur Viagens e Turismo,** Av. Dom Luiz 88, rm. 507 (☎244 7812; fax 244 7813; www.lisatur.com.br). **24hr. central reservations:** ☎264 5404.

Embassies & Consulates: Britain, Sede Grupo Edson Queiroz, Pça. da Impresa (☎466 888; fax 261 8763); **US,** Rua Noguieira Acioly 891 (☎/fax 252 1539).

Bank & ATMs: Banco do Brasil, Central Agency, Duque de Caxias 560 (☎255 3000), at Barão do Rio Branco. Open 10am-3pm. **Bradesco ATMs** are the most likely to accept AmEx/MC/V. There are **24hr. ATMs** at the *rodoviária,* airport, on Av. Abolição opposite Habibs, and at Shopping Iguatemi.

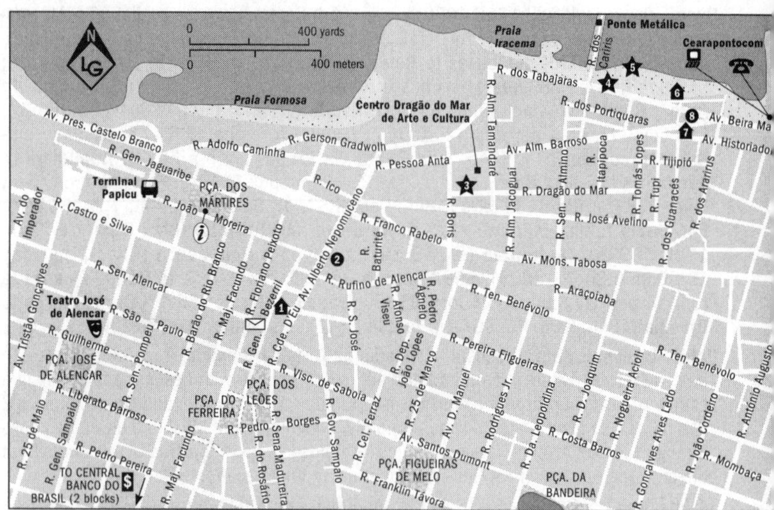

American Express: Av. Beira Mar 3960, loja 6, Pisso Térreo da Via Scala.

Luggage Storage: Available at the airport and the *rodoviária* (12hr.; R$2 per small bag, R$4 per large bag).

Cultural Center: Centro Dragão do Mar de Arte e Cultura, Rua Dragào do Mar 81 (☎488 8600, 219 1816; wwww.dragaodomar.org.br). Houses cinemas, theaters, an amphitheater, Museu de Arte Contemporâna do Ceará, Memorial da Cultura Cearense, and the public library. Library open Tu-Th 9am-8:30pm, F-Su 10am-9:30pm.

Markets: Mercado Central, Rua Alberto Nepomuenco 199 (☎454 8586), sells arts and crafts. Open M-F 7:30am-6:30pm, Sa 8am-4pm, Su 8am-noon. There is also an evening arts and crafts **market** on Praia Meireles. Open daily 5-11pm.

Laundromats: Lavanderia Doméstica Ltda., in Praia Iracema. R$11 per kg. Open M-F 8am-7pm, Sa 8am-1pm. **Lav & Lev,** Av. Abolição 2685 (☎242 3343), in Praia Meireles. Wash R$6.50 per kg, dry R$6.50 per kg. Open M-F 8am-7pm, Sa 8am-6pm.

Public Toilets & Showers: Along Praia Iracema, Praia Meireles, and Praia Futuro there are showers and toilets for public use, usually affiliated with the nearby *barracas.*

Police: ☎185 (civil); ☎295 3022 (federal).

Crisis Line: ☎221 6355 (Centro de Valorização da Vida).

24hr. Pharmacies: Drogajafre, Av. 13 de Maio 1081 (☎227 2505). **Drogajafre,** Av. Abolição 2655 (☎242 6181). **Pague Menos,** Av. Santos Dumont 1256 (☎488 8060).

Hospital: Hospital SOS Socorros Médicos, Av. Tristão Gonçalves 1367 (☎231 6099).

Fax Office: Centro Copy, Rua Pedro Borges 66 (☎226 8917, 254 6079).

Internet Access: Cearapontocom, Av. Beira Mar 728 (☎3081 6380; www.cearapontocom.com.br), in Praia Iracema. R$3 per hr. Open Su 8am-12:30pm, M 8am-midnight, Tu-F 24hr. **Clube dos Diáros,** Av. Beira Mar 2120A (☎248 8324, 9114 0405; www.beiranet.com.br), in Praia Meireles. R$4 per 30min. Open daily 8am-2am.

Post Office: The central post office is at Rua Senador Alencar 38 (☎255 7100). There there are other branches at Av. Beira Mar 4452 (☎248 7519), in Mucuripe, and Av. Senador Virgílio Távora 867 (☎224 6906), in Aldeota. All open M-F 9am-5pm, Sa 9am-noon. **Postal code:** 60001-000.

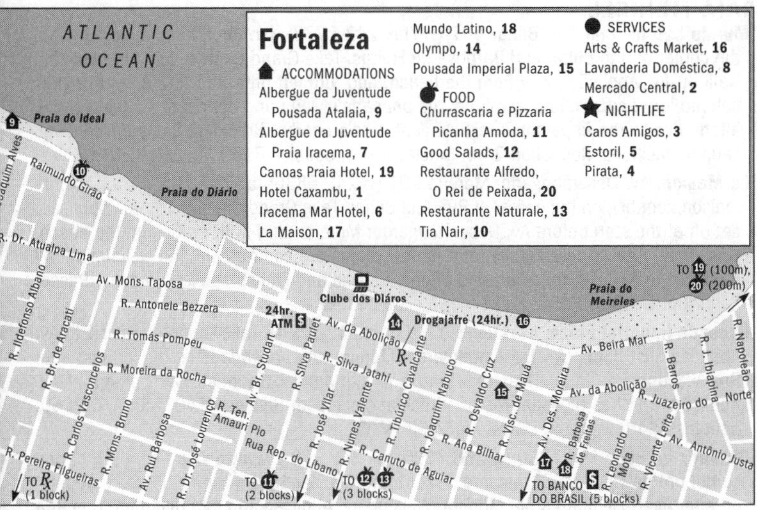

ACCOMMODATIONS

There are a wide variety of accommodations to be had in Fortaleza. Generally, hotels and *pousadas* are on or very close to the beachfront. Praia Meireles is renowned for its luxury hotels, but on the nearby streets there are some less expensive places to stay. The cheapest accommodations are found in Praia Iracema. Prices generally rise from December to March, and during July. Prices quoted below are low season prices.

PRAIA IRACEMA

Albergue da Juventude Pousada Atalaia (HI), Av. Beira Mar 814 (☎219 0755; fax 219 0658; www.alberguedajuventudeatalaia.com.br). To get there, take the Grand Circular 1 to Praia Iracema, continue along Av. Beira Mar for about 300m, and look to the left; the *pousada* will be right there. Atalaia may be fairly small, and the quality of rooms may vary, but the staff here are quite friendly and the *pousada* itself is kept clean. Kitchen. Breakfast included. Reception 24hr. Dorms R$20, non-members R$25. Singles R$55; doubles R$70. Visa. ❶

Albergue da Juventude Praia Iracema, Av. Almirante Barroso 998 (☎219 3267; fax 219 3720; www.aldeota.com/albergue). To get there, take the Grand Circular 1 to Praia Iracema, walk up Av. Beira Mar, and then take the left fork when the road splits right by a church. The hostel is 50m up Av. Almirante Barroso. It is the cheaper of the two hostels, but has fewer amenities and less atmosphere. Linens R$5. Reception 24hr. Dorms R$17. ❶

Iracema Mar Hotel, Rua dos Tabajaras 532 (☎219 3600; fax 219 1424). To get there, take the Grand Circular 1 to Praia Iracema, walk up Av. Beira Mar, and then take the right fork by the church. Follow this road until it becomes Rua dos Trabajaras; the hotel will be directly up on the left. A slightly more expensive option, but with more luxuries to make up for it. All *apartamentos* at the Iracema Mar come complete with A/C, TV, *frigobar,* and phone. The hotel is also located just minutes from the bars and clubs on Rua dos Tabajaras. Breakfast included. Reception 24hr. Singles R$35; doubles R$45; triples R$55. AmEx/MC/V. ❷

PRAIA MEIRELES

Mundo Latino, Rua Ana Bilhar 507 (☎/fax 242 8778; www.mundolatino.com.br), on the corner of Ana Bilhar and Barbosa de Freitas. Take Grand Circular 1 to Av. Abolição, walk up Av. Abolição away from the beach, and turn left onto Rua Ana Bilhar. Brightly colored in orange, yellow, and blue, the *pousada's* warm and open feel makes it a nice alternative to the impersonal, extravagant hotels nearby. Breakfast included. Parking. Laundry facilities. Reception 24hr. Singles R$40; doubles R$50. AmEx/MC/V. ❶

La Maison, Av. Desembagador Moreira 201 (☎242 6836; fax 242 7017; www.hotellamaison.com.br), on the corner of Rua Ana Bilhar. Take Grand Circular 1 to Av. Abolição, get off at the stop before Av. Desembargardor Moreira, and walk away from the beach. This small hotel is very homey, and its few rooms are comfortable and welcoming. All rooms have A/C, TV, *frigo-bar,* and phone. English and French spoken. Parking. Reception 24hr. Doubles R$55; R$12 for an extra bed. ❸

Pousada Imperial Plaza, Av. Abolição 2456 (☎242 1224). Take Grand Circular 1 to Av. Abolição, just before Av. Desembargardor Moreira; the *pousada* is on the left just after Rua Visconde de Mau. This small *pousada* sits amidst the hustle and bustle of Av. Abolição, and has pleasant rooms. Breakfast included. Singles R$40, with A/C R$50; doubles R$45, with A/C R$60. AmEx/MC/V. ❷

Olympo, Av. Beira Mar 2380 (☎266 7200; fax 248 2793; www.olympo.com.br), on the corner of Rua Tibúricio Cavalcante. Take Grand Circular 1 from Terminal Papicu and get off after Av. Desembargardor Moreira. Walk up Av. Abolição and turn right onto Rua Rua Tibúricio Cavalcante. Plush and elegant, this hotel makes a nice place to splurge on a luxurious room. It has a pool, in-house restaurant, information on trips, wake-up calls, Internet access, and room service, all only a step away from the beach. Breakfast included. Reception 24hr. *Quarto* singles R$180; doubles R$220. *Apartamento* singles R$200; doubles R$240. R$65 for an extra bed. AmEx/MC/V. ❺

PRAIA MUCURIPE & CENTRO

Canoas Praia Hotel, Rua Senador Machado 12 (☎248 7751; fax 248 7786; www.canoaspraiahotel.com.br). From the eastern end of Av. Beira Mar, turn onto Rua Manuel Jacare, then left onto Rua Senador Machado; the hotel is on the right. Offers clean rooms close to the glitz of Murcuripe beach. No hot water. Singles R$40. ❷

Hotel Caxambu, Rua General Bezerril 22 (☎231 0339; caxambu@accvia.com.br), near Mercado Central, opposite the Cathedral Metropolitana de Fortaleza. The hotels and *pousadas* on the beach are generally nicer, but if you need somewhere to stay in Centro, this is a decent option. All rooms have A/C, TV, and *frigo-bar.* Breakfast included. Reception 24hr. Singles R$50; doubles R$70; triples R$90. ❸

FOOD

Fortaleza is a veritable heaven for fans of seafood. Most restaurants have an impressive array of seafood dishes, although some places can be rather pricey. Late afternoon on Praia Mucuripe's boat-filled shoreline provides an opportunity to buy fish, shrimp, and lobster at relatively cheap prices from local fishermen. Along the beachfront, every 20 meters or so, there are *barracas* serving a variety of light meals. Light meals usually cost R$3-6, while full meals run R$7-15.

Tia Nair, Rua Idelfonso Albano 68 (☎219 1461), at Praia Iracema. Specializes in seafood and has occasional promotional discounts (R$16) that make it an affordable way to sample Fortaleza's seafood. Entrees R$18-30. Open daily 11am-midnight. ❸/❹

Restaurante Alfredo, O Rei de Peixada, Av. Beira Mar 466 (☎263 1803). Alfredo is indeed a kingly option for sampling Fortaleza's seafood, but you'll have to spend like royalty if you plan to eat here. Nonetheless, the elegant setting–just steps from the waterfront—as well as the excellent, incredibly fresh dishes of this self-proclaimed "King of Seafod" might make the meal worth the extra cash you'll be shelling out. Entrees R$20-50. Open daily 4pm-late. MC/V. ❹

Churrascaria e Pizzaria Picanha Amoda, Av. Santos Dumont 2287 (☎261 3737; fax 264 7100). If you're feeling the need for a big juicy steak, this is the place to go. Serves excellent (albeit meat-heavy) cuisine. Entrees R$10-30. Open daily 8am-2pm. ❷

Assis, O Rei da Picanha, Rua Frederico Borges 505 (☎267 4759). If Alfredo is king of seafood, then Assis is king of the steak. Or so the signs indicate. Also serves a good array of seafood and pasta dishes. Entrees R$10-23. Open daily 11am-1am. ❷

Náutico Athletico Cearense, Av. da Abolição 2727, with entrance on Av. Beira Mar. Yes, it is an athletic center, but it looks more like a mansion. Although an athletic club might not be the first place you'd think to go for a meal, it does offer a beautiful view of the Atlantic from the grand terraced balcony. Entrees R$11-21; fish R$25-35. Open daily 11am until late. ❷/❸

Good Salads, Av. Santos Dumont 2390 (☎261 4166). Here pastel greens and soft yellows light up the room, enticing you to try the remarkable and interesting salad combinations and warm pies. Simple buffet R$21 per kg, with meat R$23.5 per kg. Open daily 11:30am-3pm. AmEx/DC/MC/V. ❷

Restaurante Naturale, Av. Santos Dumont 2511 (☎261 8976). Set in the Centro Aquariano, with a few arts and crafts also on sale. Serves delicious food made strictly from organically grown ingredients. Buffet R$17 per kg. Open M-F 11am-3pm. ❷

SIGHTS

There are a number of small, interesting museums in Fortaleza, but most all of them are quite specialized in their collections. If you don't have much time in Fortaleza, however, you would do well to check out the massive cultural center known as the Centro Dragão; it has a plethora of attractions, and will be able to provide something to please virtually anyone.

CENTRO DRAGÃO DO MAR DE ARTE E CULTURA. This cultural center is a mega-complex comprising **Museu de Arte Contemporânea do Ceará,** the city's contemporary art museum, as well as the **Memorial da Cultura Cearense (MCC),** which displays a folk art collection. The center also includes a planetarium with occasional evening shows, a cinema, and theater. For a list of current performances, get a Centro Dragão brochure either from the center itself or from one of the many tourist sites around town. *(Rua Dragão do Mar 81. Near Praia Iracema, on the main road heading to Centro. ☎488 8600; www.dragaodomar.org.br. Open Tu-Th 9am-9pm, F-Su 10am-10pm. Adults R$8, children R$4, under 6 and over 65 free. Free Su.)*

MUSEU HISTÓRICO DO CEARÁ. The Ceará History Museum is a worthwhile visit only if you have an ardent interest in the anthropological history of the state. If this is your cup of tea, though, there are plenty of exhibits on the region's development to enjoy at the museum. *(Rua São Paulo 51. ☎251 1502. Open W-F 8:30am-5:30pm, Sa 10am-4pm, Su 2-5pm. Free.)*

TEATRO JOSÉ DE ALENCAR. The theater was constructed between 1908 and 1910, but soon began to fall into disrepair. Several revamps over the last fifty years have left the theater one of the most intricately designed, artistically interesting, and well-kept buildings in Fortaleza. With a capacity of up to 800 people, it has now become a popular location for big theatrical performances and cultural extravaganzas. Check with the tourist office or theater to see what is playing and when. *(Pça. José de Alencar s/n. ☎252 2324.)*

MUSEU DE IMAGEM E DO SOM. The Museum of Image and Sound has interesting displays of old slides, negatives, and photographs, as well as a collection of old discs, cassettes, and records. *(Av. Barão de Studart 598. ☎264 2462. Open M-F 9am-5pm.)*

MUSEU DO AUTOMÓVEL. Opened in 1981, the Automobile Museum may well please car-lovers with its collection of Cadillacs, Fiats, Chevrolets, Dodges. One of the more interesting vehicles on display is a 1917 Ford. *(Av. Desembargador Manoel Sales de Andrade 70. ☎273 3129. Open Tu-Sa 9am-5pm, Su 9am-4pm. R$0.50)*

PARQUE ECOLÓGICO DE CÔCO. This park covers 446 hectares of protected forest and mangrove swamps, right in the middle of a rapidly expanding city. The park is open all day, and is a great place to check out some of the local flora. *(Take any "Grand Circular" bus to Shopping Iguatemi. The stop closest to the park entrance is next to a big car dealership; watch for the Chevrolet signs. Free.)*

BEACHES & OUTDOOR ACTIVITIES

Fortaleza has four main beaches: Praia Iracema, Praia Meireles, Praia Mucuripe, and Praia Futuro. Only **Praia Futuro** is clean enough for swimming, and with up to 8km of unspoiled coastline it is not surprising that most visitors to the city—and the inhabitants themselves—head here when they want to take a dip. The northernmost 5km are the cleanest; the polluted Rio Côco meets the sea at the southern end of the beach. Praia Futuro has *barracas* along most of it, where meals can be obtained throughout the day and shower, toilet, and some locker facilities can be found. The best way to get there is to take any "Caca e Pesca" bus. The bus does not run directly to the beachfront, but from the main road there are many side roads that lead down to it. Get off the bus once you see the beach from the bus, and walk along it until you find that perfect spot. Although Fortaleza's other beaches are not suitable for swimming, they do have enough restaurants, bars, and clubs to satisfy any urbanite. Connecting Praia Iracema, Praia Meireles, and Praia Mucuripe is a wide beach promenade that gets filled with runners and walkers throughout the day, especially in the early morning and late afternoon.

Lying around on the beach all day is not for everyone; the more active may want to head to Praia Mucuripe, where you can take a two-hour **boat tour** around the coast, visiting several beaches and being presented with an impressive view of the city skyline. To arrange an excursion, contact either Martur, Av Beira Mar 430 (☎263 8000, 263 3081), or Ceará Saveiros, Av. Beira Mar 4293 (☎263 1085, 8817 8895). Tours leave daily at 10am, 4pm, and 8pm, and generally cost R$20 per person. If you'd like to try your hand at **windsurfing,** Brother's Wind School, Av. Beira Mar s/n (☎9984 1967), near the Estatua de Iracema, has classes to show beginners the ropes (R$80). They also rent equipment to those with experience (windsurfs R$30 per hr.). If windsurfing's not exactly your style, but you'd like to spend some time on the water, they also rent canoes (R$10 per hr.) and small catamarans (R$200 per hr.).

NIGHTLIFE

Fortaleza is known for its active nightlife, and perhaps the best way to experience the city is to relax on the beach all day in preparation for dancing the night away. Fortaleza's many outdoor bars spill into one another, and all *barracas* have a lively atmosphere. Most people start their evenings at the bars on Rua dos Tabajaras, near Praia Iracema. **Estoril,** Rua dos Tabajaras 379 (☎219 8389), has occasional comedy acts. The square around the **Centro Cultural Dragão do Mar** (see p. 433) in Praia Iracema is fast overtaking Rua dos Tabajaras as the popular hotspot. The bars here are open from about 6pm onward. On Tuesdays and Sundays, **Caros**

Amigos, Rua Dragão do Mar 108 (☎226 6567), has live music ranging from *samba* to jazz, blues, and MPB. If you feel the need to party a little harder, there are several nightclubs in town, although they are usually open only on the weekends.

Pirata, Rua dos Tabajaras 325 (☎219 8030). The owners bill it as "the craziest Monday night in the world," and it just may be, if you're willing to let go to the live *forró, axé, pagode,* and *samba.* 18+. Cover R$20. Open M 10pm-late.

Mucuripe, Av. Beira Mar 4430 (☎263 1006). Watch for the big fish. This megaclub has 3 different dance floors, playing techno, MPB, and *forró*. The night begins on F-Sa with some live music on an outdoor stage, and the dancing begins as the small hours approach. Dress to impress. 18+. Cover R$18. Open F-Su 10pm-3am.

Barraca Chico da Caranguejo, Av. Zezé Diogo 4930 (☎234 6808). Its location right on the beach makes it a popular place for Thursday night dancing. No cover. Open daily 10pm-late.

SHOPPING

Ceará is famous for its lacework, a skill passed down to current inhabitants by immigrants from the Azores (a group of islands off the coast of Portugal), and Fortaleza is a great place to invest in a hammock. The **Mercado Central,** Rua Alberto Nepomuceno 199 (☎454 8586), in Praia Meireles, has a nightly open-air market on the beachfront, which runs from 5-11pm.

DAYTRIPS FROM FORTALEZA

CANOA QUEBRADA ☎88

This small fishing village has fast become one of Ceará's top attractions. Despite the influx of tourists, Canoa retains a certain village charm: there is only one paved road, and fishermen still draw their nets as the sun rises. Besides its beaches, Canoa Quebrada is also famous for handicrafts made from its rainbow-colored sands and rocks. There are several **buggy trips** that travel along the coast in either direction. Heading south takes you to **Ponto Grosso,** where erosion has carved interesting shapes in the rock. Along the way to Ponto Grosso is **Majorlândia,** where artists have sculpted intricate scenes into the rock face (R$1 donation). Buggies also go to **Cumbe, Rio Jaquaribe,** and **Lagoa no Mato,** where there is a water-slide into the lagoon. There is no central agency with which to reserve buggy trips but drivers usually congregate on **Broadway,** the village's main road. Most *pousadas* can also arrange trips. (Half-day buggy trips around Lagoa to Mato R$72; Cumbe R$110; Rio Jaquaribe R$110; Ponto Grosso R$140.) **Buses** stop on the corner of the main road into the village and Broadway, and go to Fortaleza (3hr.; 3-5 per day 6am-5pm; R$11.50). Along Broadway you'll find a small **pharmacy** (☎421 7112; open M-Sa 8am-6pm), and a few bars and restaurants. There are **no ATMs or currency exchanges** in the village. **Postal code:** 62800-000

Canoa Quebrada can get crowded, so it is best to reserve ahead if you plan to arrive on the weekend or during the holiday seasons (July-Aug. and Dec.-Jan.). To get to **Pousada Caleidoscópio ❶,** walk down the main road leading into town toward the beach. After about 200m, turn left at the sign; Caleidoscópio will be the second building. Rooms are in little chalet-type houses with very useful mosquito nets. (☎421 7102; www.pousadacaleidoscopio.com.br. Singles R$20-25; doubles R$30.) To reach **Pousada Europa ❶,** walk down the main road and take a right at the *pousada* sign. Rooms are basic but have balconies, and the *pousada* has a pool. (☎421 7433. Breakfast included. Singles R$20; doubles R$30). **Pousada Luna Rosa ❶**

ROM THE ROAD

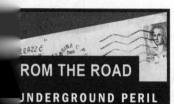

JNDERGROUND PERIL

'he beachside buggy ride south of ;anoa Quebrada had made for an ›xcellent morning: all day I had elt the sun on my back as we ;ruised past the area's famous)rightly colored rocks. Our guide ;topped the buggy, and motioned or us to follow, presumably to ;ome and see yet another of the ırea's many hidden marvels. We ollowed him to a small patch of ;and that seemed almost to be)ubbling. The guide pointed at it ınd said *"Agua doce."* As I stared, rying to figure out what he meant)y that phrase, I suddenly realized hat I was sinking, rapidly. Well, ıot exactly rapidly; certainly slowly ›nough that I had a chance to ›scape, but also fast enough that could be in real trouble if I did ıot act soon.

The guide pulled me to safety, ınd once safe I realized this was ıuicksand. I walked forward to get closer look, but after only a sin-gle step the ground gave way)eneath me. I'd never experienced ınything like it: what had been ;olid ground a moment before col-apsed into a strange mix of water ınd sand that came all the way to ny chest. I called for help, and by he time my guide came to my aid, he quicksand had almost com-)letely enveloped me. Thankfully ıe extracted me, but as we left the ırea I shuddered, realizing that he whole time I was sinking there ıad not been even the slightest ;uggestion of a bottom.

—Adeline Boatin

is off the main road, closer to Broadway than the beach. There is an immaculate garden, great decor, and the beds have mosquito nets. (☎421 7189. Singles R$20; doubles R$35.) **Pousada Oasis do Rei ❸**, Rua Nascer do Sol 112, is close to Broadway but a more expensive option. The hosts speak English, and the comfortable rooms and great pool on a terrace overlooking the ocean might be worth the extra cash. (☎421 7081; www.oasisdorei.com. Singles R$45; doubles R$60. MC/V.) Most restaurants are on the main street, and beachside *barracas* are a great option for seafood. **Restaurante Casa Verde ❶**, on Broadway, has the cheapest meals, with basic *pratos feitos* for R$6. (Open daily 11am-10pm.) At night, locals head to the bars on the upper end of Broadway.

PRAIA DA LAGOINHA ☎85

Lagoinha is one of those blissful beaches for which Ceará is famous, although it can fill up on the weekends with daytrippers from nearby Fortaleza, especially during the holiday seasons. Close to the beach are the **lagoons,** Lagoa das Almécegas, Lagoa do Jeque and Coqueirais. Along the beach you can pick up a **buggy** to any of these lagoons and dunes along the nearby coast. (Daily 9am-4pm. R$40 per hr.). The wide strip of sand is a great place for parasailing, even if it is from the back of a pick-up truck. You'll see the truck driving up and down the beach, perhaps with an adventurous person or two in tow. (Runs daily 9am-4pm, dependent on weather. R$15 per person.)

Aside from the beach, there is not much in Lagoinha. **Buses** stop at the town's only *praça* and run to Fortaleza (4hr.; 5 per day 6:30am-3:30pm; R$7). From the *praça*, **Rua Francisco Henrique de Azevedo** runs to the beach in both directions. All accommodations and restaurants are either here or on the beachfront. The **tourist office,** on Rua Franciso Henrique de Azevedo, doubles as a **post office.** (☎9609 1939. Open daily 8am-6pm.) There is a small **pharmacy** on the *praça*, which has limited supplies. (Open M-F 2:30-6:30pm.) There are no ATMs or currency exchanges.

Accommodations in Lagoinha are somewhat impractical for the budget traveler, as nothing costs under R$60. **Pousada Mar á Vista ❹,** Rua Henrique de Azevedo s/n, is about 100m from the *praça*. Rooms are clean and comfortable and most have a small balcony with a sea view. (☎363 5034, 9997 3016; fax 363 5049; www.pousadamaravista.cjb.net. Doubles R$70. R$15 per additional person.) Farther down the road is **Hotel e Restaurante Plato ❹,** Rua Henrique de Azevedo s/n. It's set in a large gray building with interesting architecture that attempts to allow all rooms to have views of the sea, although some are much better than others. (Doubles with fan R$60, with A/C R$80. R$10 per additional person.) The best place to eat is the beachfront, where *barracas* serve the usual light meals (R$6-14), and an array of seafood (R$10-30). *Barracas* are usually open daily 11am-late. Try **Restaurante Briscio D'oste ❷,** Rua Henrique de Azevedo s/n, for something other than seafood. (☎363 5115. Salads R$15-28. Entrees R$13-50. Open daily 11:30am-late.)

JERICOACOARA ☎88

Known simply as "Jeri" to everyone who has fallen under its spell, this small town is a paradise of palm trees, sand dunes, and unspoiled beaches. Almost every traveler to the Northeast coast stops here, intending to spend a day and ending up staying for a week (or more). The only thing you *have* to do in Jeri is make the trek up the dunes to watch the sunset. Relaxing on the beach, tanning on the beach, and sleeping on the beach are favorite pasttimes for the rest of the sunlight hours, while the more adventurous can try their hand at sandboarding and windsurfing, both activities popular with locals and visitors alike.

The 200 sq. km area surrounding (and including) Jeri has been a special Environmental Protection Area since 1984, meaning this paradise will never be spoiled: as an EPA, Jeri cannot have any paved roads and must cap the number of hotels and *pousadas* that can be built on its premises.

TRANSPORTATION. As with any paradise, Jericoacoara is difficult to get to and even harder to leave. The easiest route is from Fortaleza, where **Redençao** has **buses** to Gijoca (6hr.; 2 per day 10:30am-6:30pm). From Gijoca, a truck called the **Jardineira** drives the rest of the way along the coast (truck is the only option here, as the area's protected status forbids roads). The entire trip costs R$28.50. The same truck returns to Gijoca at 2pm and 10:30pm, and the Redençao bus meets you at Gijoca and continues to Fortaleza. Traveling west from Jericoacoara is more difficult. Catch the Jardineira to Gijoca and then pick up the 2am bus to Sobral, where connections can be made to Belém (23hr.; 2 per day 4:30pm-12:30am; R$98); Brasília (46hr.; 9am; R$170); Parnaíba (5hr.; 2 per day 3-10:30pm; R$23); São Luís (13hr.; 3 per day 4:30-11:30pm; R$62); Teresina (6hr.; 5 per day 11am-midnight; R$30) via Piripiri (5hr.; R$17).

ORIENTATION & PRACTICAL INFORMATION. There are three main roads in Jericoacoara: **Rua do Forró, Rua Principal,** and **Rua São Francisco** run approximately parallel to each other and all lead to the beach. The **tourist office,** on Rua Principal, has information on activities and excursions. (☎/fax 669 2000; www.jericoacoara.com). Also on Rua Principal is a **supermarket** (open daily 7am-10:30pm), a **currency exchange** (open M-F 9am-2pm and 4-10pm), and a **police station.** There is **Internet access** on Av. Beira Mar. (Open daily 11am-12:30am. R$10 per hr.) **Postal code:** 62598-000.

ACCOMMODATIONS. Pousada Tirol (HI) ❶, Rua São Francisco 202, has clean dorms which are rather comfortable despite being a bit small. The hammocks outside are a great place to relax and share stories with other travelers. (☎669 2006, 9955 3927; www.jericoacoara-tirol.com. Breakfast included unless camping. Internet access R$8 per hr. Dorms R$17, non-members R$20. Singles R$50; doubles R$60. Camping R$8.) **Pousada Avalon ❶,** Rua Principal 84, has funky and fairly comfortable rooms. (☎669 2066, 669 2161; www.jericoacoara.tur.br/avalon. Dorms R$25.) **Jeri Praia Hotel ❷,** Rua São Francisco s/n, is a good upmarket option with plenty of personality and character. All rooms have A/C. (☎603 1602. Singles R$35; doubles R$45.)

FOOD. The best eatery in town is **Naturalmente ❶**, Av. Beira-Mar s/n, next to the Internet cafe. This small restaurant and cafe serves an array of wonderful crepes, both savory and sweet—just try and resist the latter. (Crepes R$6-12. No phone. Open daily from 6pm onward.) Pizza lovers can get their fix at **Pizza Banana ❶/❷**, on a side road between Rua do Forró and Rua Principal. (Pizzas R$9-30. Open daily 5pm-late.) **Espaço Aberto,** on Rua Principal, is known for its seafood. (☎669 2154. Open daily 11am-late).

ACTIVITIES. All visitors to Jeri should make the trek up the **dunes** to watch the sunset. The more adventurous can try **windsurfing** or **sandboarding. Clube dos Ventos,** at the end of Rua São Francisco, rents windsurfing equipment and sandboards. (Open daily 8:30am-5pm. Windsurfing US$18 per hr., US$44 per day; R$700 deposit required. Sandboards R$3 per hr., R$50 deposit required.)

Jericoacoara is also famous for the unusual **Pedra Furada,** a large arched rock formation 3km from the town. If following the shore there, be sure to allow plenty of time to return before the tide comes in, as it can get quite dangerous. The rock and dunes can also be visited on **horseback** (R$10 per hr.; full-day excursions R$50 per person). **Lagoa Paraiso** and **Lagoa Azul** lie to the east of Jericoacoara, and are famed for their clear sparkling waters, as is nearby Tajatuba. **Buggy rides** are a great way to go; prices quoted are for two people and are often negotiable (Lagoa Azul R$50; Tatajuba's lakes and dunes R$120).

NIGHTLIFE. The nightlife in Jericoacoara starts late. There is something pretty much every night, although Saturday and Wednesday are particularly lively. Most nights begin with a hike up the dunes to catch the sunset, while the less adventurous head to the balcony of the aptly named **Bar Panorâmico.** After that, it's time for a nap—you'll need to save up energy for the non-stop **forró** that starts near the beach nightly, around midnight.

P.N. DE UBAJARA ☎88

This is Brazil's smallest national park and remains relatively unknown. Still, its small area encompasses six rivers, three waterfalls, and a system of caves where underground rivers and streams have carved out odd shapes in the rock. Above ground, tropical flora covers steep slopes, creating a lush green valley surrounded by sharp, irregular peaks.

The small town of Ubajara lies 2km from the park. It is quite far from the usual travelers' routes, and with your backpack in tow you might cause a bit of a stir here. The town does have basic travel services: a bank, post office, pharmacy, supermarket, and a telephone office.

AT A GLANCE: P.N. DE UBAJARA	
AREA: 5.63 square kilometers. **CLIMATE:** Tropical, with a average temperature 24-26°C; Min 12-16°C, Max 38-40°C. Rainy season Dec.-Mar. **HIGHLIGHTS:** Gruta de Ubajara; Cachoeira do Cafundó; Cachoeira Gavião; Cachoeira Murimbeca. **GATEWAY:** Ubajara. **CAMPING:** Prohibited.	**FEES:** Entrance R$2; cable car rides including tours of the caves R$4. **WHEN TO GO:** The park is open Tu-Su from 9am-5pm. Cable cars run 9am-3pm. The caves are accessible all year round. The waterfalls are most impressive just after the rainy season, but during the drier months (May-Nov.) may be reduced to small trickles not worth the trek.

TRANSPORTATION

The main mode of transport to the town is public bus. However, there are no buses from the town to the park, and you will either have to walk or take a taxi (R$10). The **rodoviária** is about 300m out of town on Rua dos Constituintes. **Buses** travel to: Belo Horizonte (35hr.; 7am; R$180); Foz do Iguaçu (7am; R$285); Rio de Janeiro (48hr.; 7am; R$199); São Paulo (54hr.; 7am; R$222); Teresina (6hr.; 2 per day 7:30am-11:30am; R$21) via Piripiri (3hr.; R$11).

ORIENTATION & PRACTICAL INFORMATION

The park itself is fairly mountainous, with a few sharp peaks rising out of the valleys. There are six rivers running through the park: Rio Gavião, Rio Murimbeca, Rio Ubajara, Rio Bela Vista, Rio Miranda, and Rio Gameleira. Trails through the park are often steep and can get slippery, so make sure to wear shoes with good grip. In the park itself there is a Vistor's Center with some info on the local flora and fauna, and close to the main entrance sits a small *lanchonete*. Basic services can be found in the nearby town of Ubajara.

Park Information: IBAMA office (☎634 1388; www.ibama.gov.br).

Fees: Entrance R$2; cable car rides including tours of the caves R$4.

Maps: Free maps of the park are available at the park entrance, or from the tourist office at Ubajara's *rodoviária*.

Gear: The only specialized gear necessary for the park is a pair of good shoes.

Tours: Organized tours begin at the park entrance. Guides accompany hikers through the trails in the park, and the price is included in the entrance fee.

ACCOMMODATIONS

Conveniently, the best accommodations are situated less than 50m from the park entrance, which makes an early start in the park very feasible.

Pousada Neblina, Estrada do Telerifico s/n (☎634 1270, 223 9327). This is the nicest place to stay and is located right next to the park. The *pousada* is surrounded by 30,000 square meters of terrain with trails for short walks; it also has a pool, a restaurant and bar and even a heliport. Doubles with fan R$40; with *frigo-bar* and TV R$50. *Luxo* doubles with fan R$60; with *frigo-bar* and TV R$70. ❷

Hotel Paraíso, Av. dos Constituintes s/n (☎634 1320, 9961 1482). Paraíso is a good place to stay the night, although it is located some 2km from the park. Rooms are large and simple, but pleasant and very clean. Parking. Laundry facilities. Singles R$20; doubles R$35; triples R$45. ❶

Pousada Gruta de Ubajara, Estrada do Telerifico s/n (☎634 1375). Also close to the park, and a much cheaper place to stay. Rooms are very basic, providing a place to rest your head and very little else. Breakfast R$3. Singles R$12. ❶

FOOD

There are no restaurants in the park and for full meals it is best to head to the town of Ubajara or to Pousada Neblina just outside the park.

Pousada Neblina, Estrada do Telerifico s/n (☎634 1270, 223 9327), has a fairly nice restaurant attached and is conveniently near the park entrance. The restaurant is on an open terrace. Pizza R$8-15; seafood R$15-35. Open daily 11am-10pm. ❶/❷

Restaurante Rodizío and Churrascaria, Av. Cel. Francisco Calvacante s/n (☎634 2289), a little way out of town, but it's worth the walk, as you can be assured a tasty and juicy grill. Buffet R$7. Open daily 8am-11pm. ❶/❷

Restaurante Nevoar, Av. Mons. Gonçalo Eurasio 167 (☎634 1312). En route to the park but closer to town. Simple restaurant with open-air seating. Entrees R$11-20; Pizza R$3.50-15. Open daily 9am-11pm. ❷/❸

Restaurante Cozhina Caseirão de Assis, Av. dos Constituintes s/n (☎9961 0352), is fairly basic but has extremely cheap *prato feitos* (R$3) and other meals under R$7. Open M-F 8am-9pm, Sa 8am-4pm. ❶

HIKING & BACKPACKING

There is a circular trail through the park that leads past **Cachoeira da Cafundó** and **Cachoeira Gavião.** The trail ends at the caves, where you can take a one-hour guided tour through them and then pick up the cable car to the Visitor's Center. (5-6hr., 12km. Difficulty: medium.) Some parts of the trail are fairly steep. There is also a shorter trail which leads directly to the caves. The trail is pretty steep but you can always hike down and take the cable cars up. (1½hr., 3km. Difficulty: medium.)

PIAUÍ

TERESINA ☎86

Teresina's city anthem proclaims it "Joyful, between the two rivers that embrace it...Teresina, eternal sunbeam". Although this state capital—the only one in the Northeast without a beach—is seldom visited by travelers, it presents a rare chance to see Brazilian city life unadulterated by tourism. The best time to visit is either in the first week of July—when the **Bumba-Meu-Boi** festival is celebrated—or during October when the city hosts the **Salão Internacional Festivale Humor do Piauí.**

TRANSPORTATION. The **airport** (☎225 2947), on Av. Centenário, has direct flights to **São Luís** and **Brasília;** from there connections can be made to other major cities. The **rodoviária** (☎218 1514) is 6km from the *centro*. Local buses travel from the bus station on Pça. Cons. Saraiva to the *rodoviária* (R$1.40). **Boa Esperança** (☎229 1785) has buses to Belém (15hr.; 5 per day 7am-3am; R$70) and Natal (27hr.; 2 per day 8am-11pm; R$83). **Barroso** (☎218 1707) runs to Piripiri (3hr.; 14 per day 5:40am-7:15pm; R$14). **Itapemirim** (☎218 3686) goes to Rio de Janeiro (44hr.; 6pm; *convencional* R$200, *executivo* R$212, *leito* R$234) and São Paulo (48hr.; 2 per day 8am-1:30pm; *convencional* R$207, *executivo* R$219), while **São Geraldo** (☎218 2655) travels to Salvador (20hr.; 1pm; R$109). **Guanabara** (☎0800 610 300) has buses to: Brasília (30hr.; 8pm; R$137); Fortaleza (10hr.; 3 per day 7:30pm-9pm; *convencional* R$51, *leito* R$81); Recife (22hr.; 12:30am; R$78), São Luís (7hr.; 6 per day 7am-11pm; R$50); Piripiri (3hr.; 7 per day 6am-11:30pm; R$14).

PRACTICAL INFORMATION. The most convenient **tourist office,** on Pça. Pedro II, is in the Centro de Artesano. However, hours are not set and there is no telephone. Another option is the office in the Centro de Convençoes, Rua Acre s/n (☎222 6202; fax 222 4377; piemtur@piemtur.pi.gov.br). **Miracéu Turismo,** Rua 7 de Setembro 159, changes cash and serves as a travel agent. (☎221 3388, 221 3735; miraceu@miraceu.com.br. Open M-F 8am-5pm.) Other services include: a **supermarket,** Pão du Açúcar, Av. Frei Serafim 1754; **police** (☎221 5924); **Hospital Getulio**

Vargas, Geral Av. Frei Serafim 2352 (☎221 3040); **Internet access,** in Riverside Shopping (☎230 2200; open daily 8am-10pm; R$3 per hr.); **post office,** on Pça. Rio Branco (☎221 8465; open M-F 9am-5pm, Sa 9am-noon). **Postal code:** 64000-000.

ACCOMMODATIONS. There are a good number of hotels in Teresina, prices are stable, and you rarely need to book ahead outside of October (when Piaui State's version of Carnaval occurs). To reach **Metro Hotel ❷,** Rua 13 de Maio 85, turn left onto Rua Barroso from the local bus station, then turn right onto Rua Paissandu, and left onto Rua 13 de Maio. The well-equipped and immaculate rooms are surprisingly cheap and the staff are extremely friendly. (☎226 1010; fax 2261 0111; metrohotel@triade.com.br. Singles R$30; doubles R$50. AmEx/MC/V.) To reach the inexpensive but basic **Hotel São Raimundo ❶,** Rua Senador Teodoro Pacheco 1199, turn right onto Rua Rui Barbosa from the bus station and then left onto Rua Senador Teodoro Pacheco. Its small entrance is to the left just after Rua Simplicio Mendes. The rooms are fairly small, and most don't have windows. (☎/fax 222 0181. Singles R$20; doubles R$30.) **Royal Palace Hotel ❷,** Rua 13 de Maio 233, is near the Metro Hotel, but farther up the street. It's not as royal or elegant as the name suggests, but the rooms are okay, the owner is friendly, and the reception area is lively. (☎221 7708, 221 7709. Singles R$30; doubles R$45. MC/V.) **Real Palace Hotel ❹,** Rua Areolino de Abreu 1217, can be reached from the local bus station by turning left onto Rua Barroso: walk until you reach Rua Areolino de Abreu and take a left onto it. This is a nice upmarket alternative with a good restaurant, exquisite rooms, and a pool. (☎221 2768; fax 221 7740; wwwrealpalacehotel.com.br. Parking. Standard singles R$89; doubles R$99; triples R$129. *Luxo* singles R$99; doubles R$109; triples R$139. AmEx/MC/V.)

FOOD. In the *centro* there are a number of excellent and inexpensive self-service options. **Bom Bocado ❷,** Rua 13 de Maio 120, near the Centro do Artesana, is very popular with locals and has a diverse selection of salads, stews, and meats for R$10 per kg. (☎221 7517. Open M-Sa 11am-3pm.) Another good self-service restaurant is attached to the **Metro Hotel ❷,** Rua 13 de Maio 85. Also popular with locals, the excellent food reflects the quality of the hotel. (☎226 1010; metrohotel@triade.com.br. Open daily 11:30am-3pm.) There are a number of dishes unique to Piauí and most common in Teresina. Maria Isabel is a mixture of rice and dry crushed beef, Baião-de-Dois a mixture of rice and beans, and Cajuína is a popular drink made from cashew fruit. A good place to sample these regional specialties is **Restaurante Flutante ❸,** Av. Boa Esperança s/n, in the Parque Ambiental Encentro. This floating restaurant serves great food near the confluence of Rio Poty and Rio Parnaíba. (☎217 5213, 9401 8342. Open daily 8am-6pm.) Both **Riverside Shopping** and **Teresina Shopping** have food courts where a quick burger or stir-fry can be obtained for under R$12. To get there take any "Shopping" bus. Both malls are open daily 8am-10pm.

SIGHTS. There is not much to see in Teresina, but if you do visit make sure to catch a sunset over the Rio Parnaíba from **Ponte Metalica,** at the upper end of Av. Maranhão: to get here face the river, turn right, and walk up the *avenida* from the *centro*. During the day, **Parque Ambiental Encontro dos Rios,** Av. Boa Esperança s/n, at the confluence of Rio Poty and Rio Parnaíba, is the nicest place to visit. It was created in 1996 and has a number of paths along the rivers and beautiful gardens. (☎217 9514; singtur-pi@bol.com.br. Open daily 8am-6pm. Free.) On the edge of the *centro* **Museu do Piauí,** Pça. Marechal Deodoro, is housed in a huge building and has displays on prehistoric times, indigenous cultures, and the colonial era. The most interesting chamber has a series of framed legends from the region; if you can read Portuguese they are worth a look. (☎221 6027. Open Tu-F 8am-5pm, Sa-

Su 8am-noon. R$1.) Piauí is famous for its arts and crafts, and the **Centro do Artesano,** Pça. Pedro II, is a good place to browse. It was originally a prison, but fear not, the originally gloomy cells have been transformed into small shops displaying the skill of local artists. (Open M-Sa 8am-6pm.)

ENTERTAINMENT. Between festivals, Teresina's nightlife could use some spicing up. The best place to head is **Bar Clube dos Diarios,** on the corner of Rua 13 de Maio and Rua Antônio Freire. On Wednesday night you can sit on the balcony sipping a cool drink and enjoying some live music. (☎221 4657. Open daily 5:30pm-late.) Nearby **Ed's Bar,** on Rua Antônio Freire, has open seating on a terrace near the brightly lit Igreja São Benedito. (Drinks R$0.40-6.50. Open daily 7pm-midnight.) Another pleasant way to spend an evening is watching a performance at the **Teatro Quatro de Setembro,** Pça. Dom Pedro II (☎222 7100). **Cine Teresina,** Av. Raul Lopes 100 (☎230 1070), in Shopping Teresina, and **Cine Riverside,** Av. Ininga s/n (☎230 1131), in Riverside Shopping. Both show Brazilian and foreign movies, sometimes in English (both charge R$8 F-Su, and R$7 M-Th).

PARNAÍBA ☎86

In the sections of Parnaíba closest to the river, colonial architecture—some restored, some decaying—is a constant reminder of this town's former status as a bustling port. Right on the river banks, **Porto das Barcas** is the best-maintained remnant of this past; its old warehouses have been restored and converted into bars, restaurants, and artisanal shops. Parnaíba has become a major tourist attraction, partially because of the more than 70 lush islets just offshore. The *centro* lies close to the river along **Avenida Presidente Vargas,** and around the **Praça da Graça** area. **Moto-taxis** rule the town (R$3), but if you're uncomfortable on a bike, minivans dash around the town and go anywhere (until about 10pm; R$1).

The **rodoviária,** on Av. Pinheiro Machado, is a 5min. bus ride from the *centro.* **Guanabara** (☎323 7619) has buses to: Fortaleza (9-10hr.; 2 per day 7:15am-7pm; R$44); Piripiri (3hr.; R$14); São Luís (9-10hr.; 2 per day 7:30am-9pm; R$36). **Boa Esperança** goes to Belém (19hr.; 2 per day 8:30am-11am; R$85) and Salvador (27hr.; 8am; *convencional* R$114, *executivo* R$134). **Itapemerim** (☎323 2944) has buses to Rio de Janeiro (48hr.; Th, F; *executivo* 9am, R$253.50, *convencional* noon, R$224) and São Paulo (55hr.; M-Sa 8am; R$227). **Transbrasilia** (☎323 7621) goes to Brasília (38hr.; 5pm; R$148). From Porto Salgado a **boat** leaves for Parnaíba (8hr.; M, Th, Sa; R$25); sling a hammock on deck and relax.

The main **tourist office** in town is PIEMTUR, Rua Dr Oscar Clark 575, which mainly acts as a referral center to the many tour companies. (☎321 1532. Open M-F 9am-12:30pm.) **Tour companies** include: **Morais Brito Viagens,** Porto das Barcas 13 (☎321 1969; www.deltadorioparnaiba.com.br); **Clip Turismo,** Av. Pres. Vargas 5 (☎322 3129, 322 2072; www.clipecoturismo.com.br); **EcoAdventure Tour,** Porto das Barcas 26 (☎323 9595, 9983 6333; www.adventure.tur.br); **Iguatur,** Porto das Barcas (☎322 2141; www.deltaamerica.com.br). These companies are open M-F 8:30am-6pm, and all run tours of the delta (8hr.; daily in high season; R$35). The **Banco do Brasil,** Pça. Graça 340, changes cash and traveler's checks. (☎321 2939. Open M-F 10am-3pm.) Other services include: a Visa **ATM** at Bradesco, Av. Pres Vargas 403 (☎321 3032); **police** (☎322 4299, 322 4399); **24hr. pharmacy,** Av. Gov. Chagas Rodrigues 980 (☎322 4564); a **hospital,** Av. São Sebastião s/n (☎323 2918); **Internet access,** Porto das Barcas 26, at EcoAdventure Tour (☎323 9595; open M-F 2-9pm, Sa 7-11am and 2-9pm; R$10 per hr.). The main **post office** is at Pça. Graça 356. (☎322 4841. Open M-F 8am-5pm, Sa 8am-noon.) **Postal code:** 64200-000.

Pousada Porto das Barcas ❶, Porto das Barcas, at the very end of the narrow street, has simple rooms in a renovated warehouse, and a charming craft store in the reception area. (☎322 2307. Reception 7:30am-10pm. High-season singles R$20; doubles R$40. Low-season singles R$15; doubles R$30.) To get to **Pousada dos Ventos ❹**, Av. São Sebastião 2586, from the *rodoviária*, take a bus heading toward the *centro*. After the bus goes down Av. Pinheiro Machado it will make a right onto Av. São Sebastião, and the *pousada* will be on the left side of the road. It has a sauna, pool, tennis court, restaurant, and helpful staff. (☎323 2555; www.pousadadosventos.com.br. Standard singles R$87; doubles R$120; triples R$143. *Luxo* singles R$94; doubles R$129; triples R$160.) Porto das Barcas and the Beira Rio strip are the most popular places to get a meal. **Rio's Restaurant & American Bar ❷/❸**, Rua da Praia 45, is the biggest in the Porto das Barcas area, and has a good variety of international and regional foods. (☎323 9627. Entrees R$14-50. Open daily 10am-11:50pm.) **Taverna Restaurante e Bar ❸**, Av. Gov. Chagas Rodrigues 624, is set in a charming house that lends a classy feel to the place. There is live music on Friday and Saturday nights. (☎322 1893. Open Th-Su 7pm-late.)

P.N. DE SETE CIDADES ☎86

Sete Cidades is one of those places that illustrate the power of nature to create weird and wonderful spectacles. They are so weird, in fact, that the park's strange, ribbed rock formations have been attributed to Phoenicians, Vikings, and even aliens. Rock paintings confirm the presence of life, but nothing more specific than that. Even among these, one print of a six-fingered hand calls into question the nature of the beings responsible for them.

AT A GLANCE: P.N. DE SETE CIDADES

AREA: 77 square kilometers.

CLIMATE: Average temp 26°C. June-Dec. dry and very hot, Jan.-May cooler and wetter.

HIGHLIGHTS: A series of rock formations; Cachoeira do Riachão.

GATEWAYS: The park is 3½hr. from Teresina (p. 440). The closest town is Piripiri, 26km away.

CAMPING: Prohibited.

FEES: Entrance R$3; mandatory guide R$20.

WHEN TO GO: The best time to visit is Jan.-June, when the waterfall is biggest and it is slightly cooler. In the dry season the waterfall is no more than a trickle, and it gets very hot during midday. The park is open daily 8am-5pm.

TRANSPORTATION

Buses: Buses leave Piripiri for: **Belém** (15hr.; 2 per day 7:30pm-4am; R$83); **Fortaleza** (7hr.; 4 per day 6:30am-11pm; R$36); **Parnaíba** (3hr.; 5 per day 8:40am-9:15pm; R$15); **São Luís** (10hr.; 2 per day 7:30pm-2:30am; R$47-50); **Teresina** (3hr.; 8 per day 7:45am-7:30pm; R$14); **Ubajara** (3hr.; 3pm; R$11). At the *rodoviária* there are a couple of *lanchonetes*.

Public Transportation: From Piripiri's main *praça,* IBAMA runs a free bus to the park. It leaves daily at 7am and returns at 5pm.

Taxis: From the *rodoviária* to Piripiri's *centro* R$6; from the *rodoviária* to the park R$40.

ORIENTATION & PRACTICAL INFORMATION

The terrain is very flat, and mostly shadeless. In the early 1990s a forest fire wiped out 70% of the vegetation in the park and remnants of burnt trees are still scattered about. Trails are clearly marked, and the mandatory guides will prevent anyone getting lost. There is a Visitor's Center six kilometers from the park entrance, where there are free maps, a small *lanchonete*, and public toilets. Piripiri is the closest town and has basic services.

Stations and Park Information: Centro do Visitante, Rodovia Min. Vicente Fialho s/n (☎343 1342), 6km from the entrance. Hotel Sete Cidades (☎223 3366, 223 2423) lies 2km from the Centro do Visitante and is also a good place for information.

Fees & Reservations: Entrance R$3. At the Centro do Visitante, mandatory guides are available but most do not speak English (R$20). Cars are allowed, but beyond certain points walking is the only way to see the park.

Maps: Free maps come in the basic pamphlets available at the Centro do Visitantes; these provide a good overview of the park and have trail distances clearly marked.

Gear: Some food can be obtained in the park, but bring lots of water. It is advisable to wear good shoes, a hat to provide some shade, and strong sunscreen.

Supermarket: Varejao Piripiriense, Av. 4 de Julho 173 (☎276 1685), in Piripiri. Open M-Sa 8am-6pm.

Bank: There are no ATMs, but there is a Banco do Brasil in Piripiri, Av. 4 de Julho 211 (☎276 1600). Open M-F 10am-3pm.

Post Office: Rua Severiand Medeiros 323 (☎276 1600), in Piripiri. Open M-F 9am-12pm and 2-5pm.

ACCOMMODATIONS & FOOD

There are a couple of excellent options for accommodations in the area. In Piripiri, **Hotel California ❷**, Rua Dr. Antenor Freitas 546, is a modern, comfortable place to stay. It is a 15min. walk from the *rodoviária:* turn left out of the *rodoviária*, take the first left and then the first left again. Follow the signs to the hotel. All rooms have A/C, TV, *frigo-bar*, and very clean bath. (☎276 1645. Laundry. Singles R$28; doubles R$30; triples R$45). Two kilometers from the park's Centro do Visitantes is the **Parque Hotel Sete Cidades ❷.** The hotel is well equipped and has a natural swimming pool. (☎223 3366, 223 2423; www.hotelsetecidades.com.br. Singles R$40; doubles R$50; triples R$55; quads R$65).

The best place to get a meal while here is at the restaurant attached to the **Parque Hotel ❶.** Meals are well-prepared, and their portions are not only large but also tasty. They have good *pratos feitos* and some regional dishes. (Entrees R$12-30. Open daily 11am-7pm.)

HIKING & BACKPACKING

As its name suggests, the park is divided into seven *cidades* (cities). Each *cidade* is a group of rocks which either have a set of petroglyphs, or look surprisingly like some object or animal. On the outskirts of the park are the Cachoeira do Riachão and a small natural pool. There are several trails through the park; to see everything involves walking 14 kilometers and takes about six hours.

ROUTE 1. This is the shortest worthwhile trail—a vaguely circular route that winds from the Visitor's Center to the sixth, second, third, fourth and fifth *cidades* and then back to the Centro. The sixth *cidade* has the **Pedra da Tartaruga, Pedra do Elefante,** and **Pedra do Cachorro.** These are huge mounds of rock with scaly surfaces that could belong to an extremely oversized turtle. The second *cidade* has a lookout from which you can view the entire park. It also includes the **Arc de Triomphe,** which was named for its similarity to the original, and the famous rock painting of the **Mão dos Seis Dedos** (six-fingered hand). The third *cidade* is famous for the **Três**

Reis Magos, the fourth *cidade* for a hole in a rock face that mirrors a map of Brazil. This trail is flat all the way, except for a 400m climb in the second *cidade. (5.5km, 3½hr. Difficulty: easy.)*

ROUTE 2. This trail is an extended version of Route 1, which also involves a 1.5km trail out to the first *cidade* and a longer route back to the Visitor's Center via the seventh *cidade. (10.5km, 4-5hr. Difficulty: easy.)*

ROUTE 3. This trail leads directly to **Cachoeira do Riachão** and back (via the seventh *cidade*). The waterfall has two drops, one seven meters high and the other 16 meters. The water pours into a deep natural pool that makes a great place to swim after the hot and dusty walk there. *(4.4km, 2½hr. Difficulty: easy.)*

MARANHÃO

SÃO LUÍS ☎98

A colonial city, an Afro-Brazilian city, a beach city, and the reggae capital of Brazil—São Luís is all of these and more. It was founded in 1612 by the French, but two years later was taken over by the Portuguese, and soon became an important port. The African slaves who were used to support the trade system have left an indelible mark on the city; many generations later the descendents of the slaves remain in the city, adding greatly to the culture of the region.

São Luís is known for its weather; the tropical climate means it rains virtually every day and the humid air has posed a threat to the city's buildings for centuries. The best-kept colonial buildings have survived because of the imported Portuguese tiles which were used to protect their surfaces. Today the difference between the decaying buildings and the colorful tiled survivors is dramatic. Perhaps even more striking is the fact that many families live in the decaying and decrepit historical buildings that attract tourists by the dozens to the city. One can only hope that the city's initial restoration project, Projeto Reviver (begun in the 1980s) and the UNESCO status of the *centro* will mean that funds continue to support renovation of not only museums, but also the homes of the city's inhabitants.

TRANSPORTATION

Flights: Aeroporto Marechal Cunha Machado (☎217 6101) is a 20min. car ride from the *centro*. All major airlines have offices both at the airport and in town: **TAM,** Rua dos Afogados 16; **Varig,** Av. Dom Pedro II 221 (☎231 5066); **VASP,** Rua do Sol 43 (☎231 4422). All of these offices are open M-F 8am-6pm, Sa 8am-noon. Buses to the airport leave from Pça. Deodoro, and are usually marked "Aeroporto."

Buses: The *rodoviária* (☎243 2320) is 8km from the historical *centro*. From the Terminal da Integraçao near Praia Grande and the bus stop at Pça. Deodoro you can take any "Rodoviária" bus (R$1.40). **Ribeiro Turismo** (☎231 1621), on Pça. João Lisboa, at the corner of Rua do Sol and Rua God Viana, sells tickets for **Itapemerim** and **Guanabara.** Open M-F 8am-6pm, Sa 8am-noon. From the *rodoviária* **Açalândia** (☎249 2795) goes to **Belém** (12hr.; 2 per day 7:30am-7pm; R$79). **Continental** (☎243 1426) has a bus to **Salvador** (27hr.; W 1pm; R$116). **Guanabara** has buses to **Fortaleza** (18hr.; 3 per day 11:30am-9:30pm; R$84) via **Piripiri** (12hr.; R$47) and **Teresina** (8hr.; 6 per day 6:30am-11pm; *convencional* R$35, *leito* R$51). **Itapemerim** (☎249 2347) goes to **Rio de Janeiro** (51hr.; 11am; R$259) and **São Paulo** (48hr.; 9am; R$215). **Transbrasília** (☎243 2077) goes to **Brasília** (36hr.; 3pm; R$183).

Ferries: Near Terminal da Intergraçao is **Terminal de Passageiros,** where there are boats to Alcântara, Guimarães, and Lusitana. Boats to Guimarães and Lusitana leave on Tu and F and return M and Th. **Diamantina** (☎232 0692, 232 6929) has a service to Alcântara (departs 7am, 9am; returns 4pm; R$10). Buy tickets the night before, and check with the boat staff to confirm departure times.

Catamarans: This is a cheaper but bumpier way to get to Alcântara. Fare is R$6, but the schedule varies: check at the Terminal da Passageiros for departure and return times.

Public Transportation: Buses to São Francisco and the beaches across the bay leave from the **Terminal da Intergraçao** fairly frequently. A more direct route to the beaches is to pick up the buses from the **Refesa** on Av. Beira Mar, just before Ponte José Sarney. Buses are clearly marked with their destinations: "São Francisco"; "Calhau"; "Calhau Litorâneo." The last two reach the beaches via Ponta d'Areia.

ORIENTATION & PRACTICAL INFORMATION

Historic **centro** lies close to **Baía São Marcos.** The *praça* between Rua da Alfândega and Rua Portugal is essentially the center of all historic buildings and makes a good point of reference. Navigating this area is fairly easy, as there are tourist maps placed at convenient points throughout the district. It is compact enough that all locations can be reached by walking, although hilly terrain and steep staircases connecting streets can be tiring. The **commercial centro** lies between Rua do Sol and Rua de Santana, and is where most services are located. Across the bay is **São Francisco,** a more modern sector of São Luís where you will find hotels, restaurants, bars, and access to the **beaches.** Praia Ponte d'Areia has become quite polluted, so crowds now head to **Praia do Calhau** and **Praia do Olho d' Água.** Of the two, Praia do Calhau is more developed, with public toilets and showers.

Tourist offices: FUMTUR, Pça. Benedito Leite, at the end of Av. Dom Pedro II, is the best place to go for information. They also have a **head office,** Rua da Palma 53 (☎212 6212; www.saoluis.ma.gov/fumtur). Open M-F 8am-7pm, Sa-Su 9am-5pm. There is also a **24hr. office** at the airport, and offices at the *rodoviária* (open daily 8am-10pm) and at Pça. Deodoro (open M-F 8am-6pm, Sa-Su 9am-noon). Brochures and maps of the city are available from these offices in English.

Tours: Giltur–Viagens e Turismo, Rua Montanha Russa 22 (☎231 7065; fax 232 6041; www.giltur.com.br). Open M-F 8am-6pm, Sa 8am-2pm. MC/V. **Carvelas Turismo,** Av. Dom Pedro II 231 (☎232 6606, 976 6606; fax 221 2519; caravelas@elo.com.br). Open M-F 8:30am-6pm, Sa 8:30am-noon. MC/V. **Babicu Turismo,** Av. Dom Pedro II 258 (☎231 4747, 231 0737; fax 231 5485; babaçu@elo.com.br). Open M-F 8am-6pm, Sa 8am-noon. AmEx/MC/V.

24hr. ATM: HSBC, Rua do Sol 105, near Pça. João Lisboa. Accepts AmEx/Cirrus/MC.

Currency Exchange: Banco do Brasil, Pça. Deodoro, changes cash and traveler's checks. Open M-F 10am-3pm. **Banco Amazonia,** Av. Dom Pedro II 140 (☎231 5553), changes cash and traveler's checks with no commission. Open M-F 10am-4pm. **Barcelona Câmbio e Turismo,** Pça. Benedito Leite 264 (☎222 8064, 221 3975), also changes cash and traveler's checks. Open M-F 8am-6pm, Sa 8-11am.

Police: ☎232 7395.

Internet Access: São Luís has several **free Internet posts** around the city. However, there is usually a long wait, and you only get 15min. of surf time. There are posts at Pça. Deodoro, near Av. Silva Maia, and in front of Refesa in Beira Mar, near the Ponte José Sarney. All open M-F 8am-9pm, Sa-Su 9am-6pm. There is also access at **Poem-Se,** on Rua Humberto de Campos. R$4 per hr. Open M-F 9am-7pm, Sa 9am-1pm.

Post Office: Pça. João Lisboa 292 (☎221 2113). Open M-F 9am-5pm, Sa 9am-1pm. **Postal code:** 65000-000.

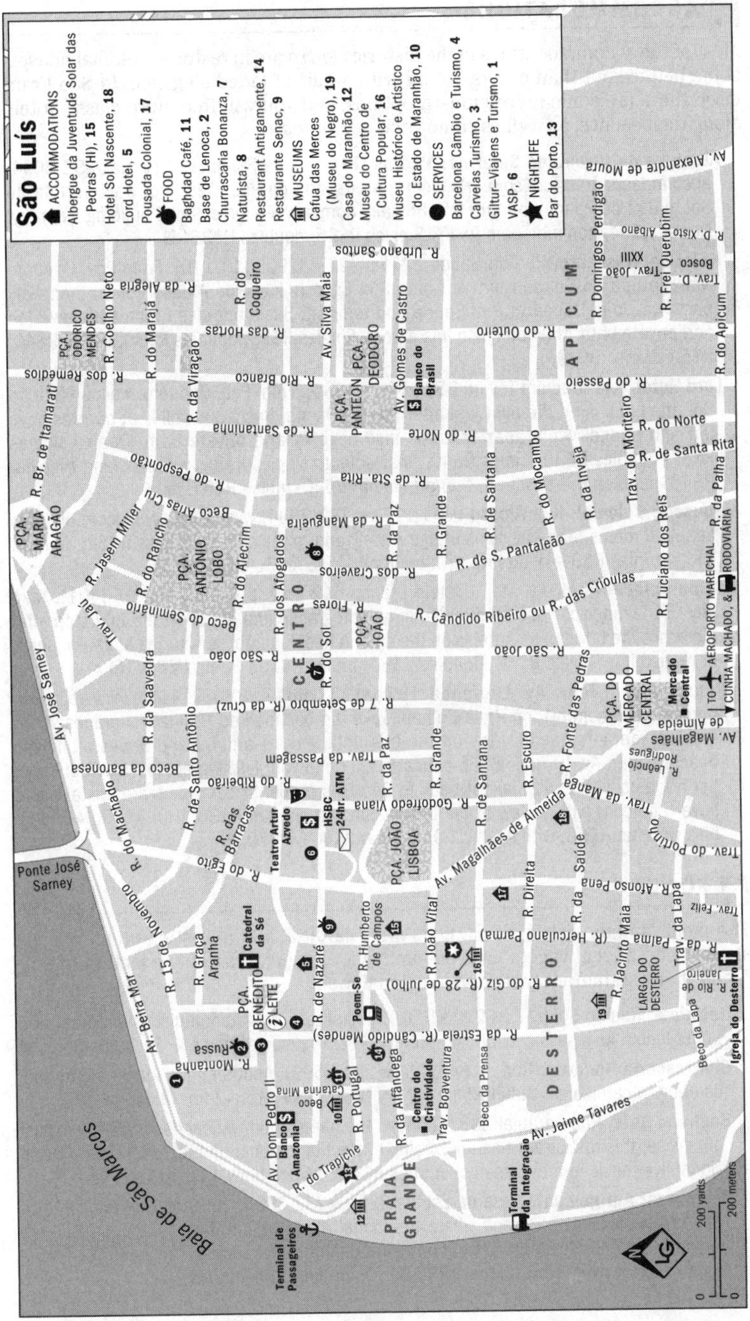

São Luís

ACCOMMODATIONS
Albergue da Juventude Solar das Pedras (HI), **15**
Hotel Sol Nascente, **18**
Lord Hotel, **5**
Pousada Colonial, **17**

FOOD
Baghdad Café, **11**
Base de Lenoca, **2**
Churrascaria Bonanza, **7**
Naturista, **8**
Restaurant Antigamente, **14**
Restaurante Senac, **9**

MUSEUMS
Cafua das Merces (Museu do Negro), **19**
Casa do Maranhão, **12**
Museu do Centro de Cultura Popular, **16**
Museu Histórico e Artístico do Estado de Maranhão, **10**

SERVICES
Barcelona Câmbio e Turismo, **4**
Carvelas Turismo, **3**
Giltur–Viajens e Turismo, **1**
VASP, **6**

NIGHTLIFE
Bar do Porto, **13**

ACCOMMODATIONS

Most of the accommodations in the historic *centro* are in restored colonial houses, some better kept than others but all with an air of faded elegance. In São Francisco there are some more modern options, and you will find more classy hotels along the beaches, as well as some good *pousadas*.

Albergue da Juventude Solar das Pedras (HI), Rua da Palma 127 (☎/fax 232 6694; aj.solardaspedras@bol.com.br). From the bus stop on Pça. Deodoro, walk up Rua do Sol to Rua da Palma and turn left. Has airy dorms in a huge colonial building. Laundry. Dorms R$14, non-members R$17. Singles R$25; doubles R$35. ❶

Hotel Sol Nascente, Rua da Saúde 221 (☎222 4329, 211 0119). From Pça. Deodoro walk up Rua do Sol and turn left onto Rua Egito (a.k.a. Rua Afonso Pena), then walk past Pça. João Lisboa to Rua Saudé and turn left. Basic but clean rooms all have fan and private bath. The hotel also has a pool. Singles R$23; doubles R$30; triples R$40. R$5 extra for TV. ❶

Lord Hotel, Rua Joaquim Távora 258 (☎221 4655). From Pça. Deodoro, walk up Rua do Sol: the hotel is on the right just after Rua da Palma. Basic but well-kept *quartos* have fan and phone, while *apartamentos* also have TV and private bath. *Quarto* singles R$22; doubles R$30; triples R$40. *Apartamento* singles R$30, with A/C and *frigo-bar* R$40; doubles R$38, with A/C and *frigo-bar* R$40; triples R$57. ❶

Pousada Colonial, Rua Afonso Pena 112 (☎232 2834; www.guiasaoluis.com.br). Has beautiful rooms, and any signs of age merely add to the charm. Singles R$52; doubles R$75; triples R$91; quads R$120; quints R$150. AmEx/MC/V. ❸

Skina Palace Hotel, Av. Mal. Castelo Branco 512 (☎235 6020; fax 235 6301). Take any "São Francisco" bus from the Terminal Integração and get off at the 2nd stop after it crosses the bridge; the hotel is on the right. A fresh alternative with the squeaky gleam of modernity. Singles R$70; doubles R$84; triples R$105. AmEx/MC/V. ❸

Pousada Vela Mar, Av. Litorânea 186 (☎233 6517, 8803 1468; www.velamar-pousada.hpg.com.br), on Praia Calhau. Take the bus marked "Calhau/Litorânea" from the Terminal Integração. Stay on the bus until it turns around and drives along the beachfront on Av. Litorânea; the *pousada* will be to your left. Perfect for beach bums or bar hoppers who don't make it back to São Luís proper. Nicer rooms are upstairs and have a balcony with a view of the beach. Singles with fan R$30, with A/C R$40; doubles with fan R$50, with A/C R$60; triples with A/C R$70. ❷

FOOD

The most famous dish in São Luís is **Arroz de Cuxá,** an interesting blend of rice, shrimp, and a local vegetable. You can try it along with a good selection of seafoods at any restaurant that serves regional food.

Naturista, Rua do Sol 517 (☎222 4526), specializes in vegetarian dishes and has good buffet lunch. Also sells cookbooks. Buffet R$12.50 per kg. Open M-F 11:30am-3pm. ❷

Churrascaria Bonanza, Rua do Sol 325 (☎221 5599). Another good lunchtime option, catering to carnivores. Buffet R$10 per kg. Open M-Sa 11am-2pm. ❷

Baghdad Café, Rua Portugal 243. Although the name and mystical decor might suggest otherwise, this restaurant has an excellent selection of local and regional foods. Occasional live music in the evenings. Entrees R$4-25. Open daily 11am-11pm. ❷

Restaurant Antigamente, Rua da Estrela 220 (☎232 3904; antigamente@elo.com.br). Just off the corner of a *praça* where traditional Afro-Brazilian dance performances are regularly held. Seating spreads out into surrounding streets and live music M-Sa spices up an already lively crowd. Meals R$7-30. Open daily 4pm-late. ❷

Base da Lenoca, Rua Montana Russa 181 (☎227 5545). Beautiful hilltop view and great local food (try the *caranguejo*). Entrees R$14-30. Open daily noon-11pm. ❶/❷

Restaurante Senac, Rua de Nazaré 452 (☎232 6377). Leave those flip-flops behind: this elegant restaurant may usually only open for lunch, but class, style, and grace are the name of the game here. Buffet R$16. Open M-Th 11am-3pm, F 11am-midnight. ❹

Pizzaria Internacional Sapori D'Italia, Av. Castelo Branco 451 (☎235 4452, 227 5935). Serves pizzas, and several excellent pastas R$9-17. Pleasant open-air seating. Delivery available. Open Su-Th 11:30am-11pm, F-Sa 11:30am-midnight. ❷

Restaurante Maracangalha, Av. Litorânea 45 (☎233 6769), on Praia Calhau. It's more expensive than most, but it certainly has the most attractive and creative decor. Palm stems, pottery, and brightly colored ornaments create a permanently festive feel. Entrees R$15-25. Open daily 11am-midnight. AmEx/MC/V. ❸

SIGHTS

The historical *centro* is a sight in itself, and it's worth spending a few hours milling around the Projeto Reviver area. The tourist office offers a free walking tour departing Benedito Leite Plaza (2hr., W-F 4pm) if you want a more structured visit.

IGREJA DO DESTERRO. This is the first and oldest church in São Luís, begun in the early 17th century but damaged during a Dutch siege in 1641. It took until 1863 to complete the structure, notable now as Brazil's only Byzantine-influenced church. *(At the end of Rua da Palma, on Largo do Desterro. Open M-F 9am-noon. Free.)*

CAFUA DAS MERCES (MUSEU DO NEGRO). This former slave market has been transformed into a museum dedicated to the history of the area's African slaves. It has a only a few artifacts from the era of slavery, but houses an impressive exhibition of African art, including wood carvings and sculptures of Yoruba, Bante, Malinke, Benin, and Dogon origin. *(Rua Jacinto Maia 43. Open M-F 9am-6pm. Free.)*

TEATRO ARTUR AZVEDO. This theater is famous for its neoclassical architecture. Interestingly, it is also the birthplace of Apolonia Pinto, a famous Brazilian actress born in 1854. *(Rua do Sol 180, at Rua Godofredo Viana. Open M-F 3-5pm.)*

MUSEU HISTÓRICO E ARTÍSTICO DO ESTADO DE MARANHÃO. This large and elegant building was originally the mansion of the famous Brazilian philosopher and mathematician Gomes de Souza, and is a good example of a typical colonial manor. The mansion was converted into a museum in 1973, but much of the original furnishings remain. It also houses a number of religious statues, and its hallways are hung with photographs and short bios of famous figures in Maranhão history. *(Rua do Sol 302. Open Tu-Su 9am-6pm. R$2; students free.)*

CATEDRAL DA SÉ. This is now the official church of Maranhão State. It was originally built in 1692, to honour "Our Lady of Victory," who is supposed to have supported the Portuguese against the French in the battle of Guaxenduba, when the French were defeated and forced from the island. The main altar is an ornate example of the Portuguese baroque style. *(At the end of Av. Dom Pedro II, facing the impressive Palácio dos Leões. No set visiting hours.)*

CASA DO MARANHÃO. This huge building is dedicated to the history of the Bumba-Meu-Boi festival. It has four chambers detailing the four different steps of the festival, as well as displays of festival dancers' attire and instruments. Guides take you through the exhibits, explaining clearly and thoroughly their significance and origin; these tours are available in English and Portuguese. There is also a small gift shop with CDs of Bumba-Meu-Boi music, and postcards. *(Av. Jaime Tavares, opposite the Terminal de Passageiros. Open Tu-Su 9am-7pm. Free.)*

MUSEU DO CENTRO DE CULTURA POPULAR. This building originally housed Bumba-Meu-Boi displays, but now contains photography exhibits by locals and a section on the history of the different Candomblé houses, Casa Fanti-Ashanti, Casa das Minas, and Casa de Nagô. *(Rua 28 de Julho 221. Open Tu-Sa 9am-6pm.)*

NIGHTLIFE & ENTERTAINMENT

The best way to start an evening is to the head to the *praça* in the *centro's* heart, between Rua Estrela and Rua do Giz. After 8pm you will usually find some performance here, often Afro-Brazilian dance. Many of the bars in the city are open-air affairs, where the bar itself is really a collection of chairs and tables on the street, and the building behind it is only used to serve drinks and house the band.

Reggae: If you came to find the reggae bars São Luís is famed for, worry not: the chill beats will soon draw you to their doors. Most of these bars are little more than one-room buildings with a patio where patrons sit or dance under the gleam of the stars. In the historic *centro,* **Canto do Tônico,** Rua Portugal, and **Bar do Porto,** Rua do Trapiche, are highly recommended. The most famous reggae bar is probably **Bar do Nelson,** on Praia Calhau. Cover R$2-3. Open daily 10pm-late.

Other Live Music: If reggae ain't your thing, there are lots of other options. Head across the bay to the beaches, where there are bars packed back to back. **Flamingo,** in the Rio Poty Hotel on Praia d'Areia, is very popular and has MPB. Cover R$15-20. Open F-Sa evenings. On Praia Calhau, **Restaurante Calhau and Club,** Av. Litorânea 60 (☎233 6508; restaurantedocalhau@terra.com.br), has bands which play a variety of music from MPB to *samba.* Cover R$3. Live music Tu-Sa after 10:30pm. Open daily 6pm-3am.

Theater: Centro do Criatividade, Rua da Alfândega 200 (☎231 4058), is a space for plays, dance performances, films, and live music. Shows generally happen Tu-F 8pm: ask at the tourist office for a schedule.

ALCÂNTARA ☎98

Twenty-two kilometers from São Luís, across the Baía de São Marco, lies Alcântara. This former state capital is now a small town with a few colonial buildings interspersed with ruins of the former city. In strange contrast to its colonial origins, it is here that the Aviation Ministry built the Centro do Lançamento de Alcântara, the most modern satellite launching center in South America. There are a few *pousadas* in the town, but everything of interest can be seen in a couple of hours, and the beaches near São Luís are bigger and much more pleasant. From São Luís, Diamantina (☎232 0692, 232 6929), runs **boats** to and from Alacântara (depart from São Luís 7am and 9am, return from Alcântara 4pm; R$10). Buy your tickets the night before at the Terminal de Passageiros in São Luís.

To reach the central **Praça da Matriz** from the port, walk straight up the main road, **Rua das Merces.** At one end of the *praça* stands the ruins of **Igreja Matriz de São Matia,** built in 1648. In front of the church is the **pelourinho** (whipping post), once a symbol of Portuguese power, which was used as a post against which African slaves were tied and beaten or sold. Just off Pça. Matriz is **Museu Histórico,** on Rua de Baixo. This former mansion remains an example of the luxurious lives lived by the original colonial masters of the town. Most of the house's original furniture and china remains on exhibit. (Open Tu-Sa 8am-2pm, Su and holidays 8am-1pm. R$1.) The **Festival do Divino Espírito Santo,** held in May, is Alcântara's biggest festival. It has a distinctly African influence, as well as elements of the Catholic tradition, and so illustrates the heterogeneous culture of this town.

If you do plan on staying in Alcântara, the best place is **Pousada Guarás ❶,** on Praia da Baronesa, which is named for bright red birds that live nearby. From the *centro*, walk up Rua Grande and turn onto Rua da Silva, then follow the dirt road down to the beach. The beach is very isolated, and is a calm place perfect for relaxing. The *pousada* has small chalets with hammocks on each doorstep, as well as an attached restaurant with tasty local cuisine. If you call ahead you can arrange to be picked up at the port or in the *centro*. (☎337 1339; pousadadosguaros@aol.com. Meals R$15-21. Singles R$20; doubles R$40; triples R$54.) In the historic *centro* the **Sítio Tijupá Bar, Restaurante e Pousada ❶**, on Rua de Baixo, is another good option. To find it just look for the bright yellow doors. Rooms are simple and clean, but have no hot water. (☎337 1291. Restaurant open daily 11am-3pm; meals R$8-10. *Quartos* R$15 per person.) Another good place to eat is **Restaurante Palácio dos Nobres ❶**, Rua Direta 14. It has a friendly host and cheap *pratos feitos* (R$4). (☎337 1405. Open Su-Th 7am-11pm, F-Sa 7am-midnight.)

P.N. DOS LENÇÓIS MARANHENSES ☎86

This park gets its name from the similarity between the peaks and falls of the sand dunes and the wrinkles in *lençóis* (sheets). This immense area of shifting sand dunes interspersed with sparkling lakes is surprisingly desert-like; if you turn your back to the ocean and look out over the dunes, you might easily imagine yourself in the middle of the Sahara. As hard as it might be to imagine life on these sands, the resilience and adaptability of certain birds and reptiles (like the endangered giant turtle) has resulted in this area having a unique ecosystem.

AT A GLANCE: P.N. DOS LENÇÓIS MARANHENSES	
AREA: 71,550 square kilometers. **CLIMATE:** Tropical. Dry season Aug.-Dec. **HIGHLIGHTS:** Sand dunes as far as the eye can see; sparking lakes and hidden lagoons. **GATEWAYS:** From the northwest, Barreirinhas. From the northeast, Tutóia.	**CAMPING:** Not necessary but for 2- to 3-day hikes it is a possibility. Camps use tarps not tents. No facilities: all food and water must be carried. **FEES:** None. **WHEN TO GO:** Just after the rainy season when water has seeped through the dunes to fill the area's lakes and lagoons.

TRANSPORTATION

Transportation to the park itself is slightly out of the ordinary: the popular modes of transport here are four-wheel-drive vehicles, motorboats, speedboats or—failing that—horse and bicycle. **Four-wheel-drive vehicles** make the journey from Barreirinhas to Tutóia via Paulino Neves (R$20). In Barreirinhas, they depart in front of the Banco do Brasil, Av. Joaquim Soeiro de Carvalho (daily 10am). In Tutóia, ask your *pousada* owner for more information as times are not set, although they generally leave around 9am from the main *praça*. To get from Barreirinhas to Caburé you can take a motorboat (4hr.; R$5) or speedboat (1hr.; R$30-35). There is no set schedule, so ask at the riverfront. **Buses** are run by **Cisne Branco** (☎243 2847, 245 1233) to São Luís (4hr.; 4-5 per day 6am-7pm; R$25); the ticket office is on Av. Brasil, opposite the tourist office, which is where buses depart.

ORIENTATION & PRACTICAL INFORMATION

The park lies along 50km of coastline to the west of Barreirinhas. Close to the eastern edge of the park, Rio Preguisça winds its way to the coast and the tiny villages of Atins and Caburé rest at its mouth. East of Caburé is another 50km stretch of coastline, and inland near the villages of Rio Novo and Paulino Neves is another system of sand dunes and lakes called Pequenos Lençóis. Tutóia is farther east.

The park itself has no infrastructure, but arranging trips from Barreirinhas is very feasible. Barreirinhas is the most developed of the settlements in the park environs, and a night here or in Tutóia will probably be necessary to reach the park. Tranquil Caburé is merely a few beach shacks and a couple of *pousadas* alongside a freshwater and saltwater beach: it's so small all power comes from a generator and is only available 8am-10pm.

Park Information: At the tourist office, Av. Brasília 126 (☎349 0099) in Barreirinhas. Open M-Sa 8am-8pm, Su 8am-noon.

Fees & Reservations: No entrance fee. Tours to the park require reservations.

Maps: There are no good maps of the park proper, but the tourist office or any of the tour companies can provide free maps of the general area.

Gear: If hiking and camping, you must bring along all food, water, and supplies. Camping equipment is provided by the tour companies who organize excursions into the park.

Tours: Organized tours are usually daytrips that visit the lakes on the eastern edge of the park. Trips to the interior are 2-4 days long and involve hiking and camping. Daytrips also go to the villages of Caburé, Mandacaru, and Atins. Excursions to the park usually leave from Tutóia or Barreirinhas. Daytrips cost R$25 per person; camping trips are arranged on an individual basis but cost R$100+ per person. Trips to Caburé and the other fishing villages R$35 per person.

Bank: Banco do Brasil, Av. Joaquim Soeiro de Cavalho 550 (☎349 11720), in Barreirinhas. Open M-F 10am-3pm.

Pharmacy: Farmácia Nayane, Av. Brasília s/n (☎349 1191), in Barreirinhas. Open daily 8am-9pm.

Post Office: Av. Brasília s/n (☎349 1175), in Barreirinhas. Open M-F 8am-noon and 2-4pm. **Postal code:** 65590-000.

ACCOMMODATIONS

There are *pousadas* and hotels in all the towns mentioned. During the holiday season (July-Aug. and Dec.-Feb.), it is advisable to book ahead. Camping is permitted in most areas, but there are no specific campsites or facilities available.

BARREIRINHAS

Pousada Iguape, Rua Coronel Godinho s/n (☎349 0641). From the riverfront take any road perpendicular to the river and cross over Av. Joaquin de Cavalho; the 2nd perpendicular road is Rua Coronel Godinho. Rooms are large, clean, and comfortable, although some have large metal windows that open right onto the *pousada's* main hallway. Singles R$30, with A/C R$42; doubles R$50, with A/C R$70. ❷

Albergue Paraiso das Dunas, Av. Joaquim Soeiro de Carvalho 650 (☎9962 4940, 349 0008). The town's only youth hostel has basic dorms with shared bath. Dorms R$15. ❶

Pousada Lins, Av. Joaquim Soeiro de Cavalho 550 (☎349 1494), is a very popular option with an attached restaurant and a nice open communal area. Singles R$45; doubles with A/C and TV R$65. ❸

Hotel Pousada do Buriti, Rua Inâcio Lins s/n. This road runs perpendicularly into the town from the riverfront; the *pousada* is on the left just after Rua Coronel Godinho. More costly, but offers a little more luxury. Singles R$70; doubles R$108; triples R$137. ❹

CABURÉ & TUTÓIA

Pousada do Paulo, on Praia do Caburé (☎349 9010), is the cheapest of 3 *pousadas* on the freshwater beach. Like the others it has an attached restaurant and rooms are in little chalets built in the style of local traditional huts. Singles R$45; doubles R$70. ❸

Pousada Tremembés, in Pça. Tremembés (☎479 1819, 479 1354). This is the most conveniently located *pousada,* as it is close to the *centro* and the riverfront. It does get pretty busy, so make sure you book ahead. Single R$25; doubles R$40. ❶

FOOD

In the smaller villages and towns, restaurants are rare and *pousadas* either have restaurants attached or will make meals upon request. In Caburé all *pousadas* have restaurants. The seafood here is excellent and fairly cheap (under R$15). In Tutóia, the restaurant attached to **Pousada Tremembes** ❷ is open to the public and serves a small buffet. (Buffet R$10. Open daily until 8pm). There is a little more choice in Barreirinhas. Along the riverfront **Restaurante Preguiças** ❶, has an excellent selection of dishes. Try their Salada Tropical (R$12). (Entrees R$5-28. Open daily 11am-11pm.) **Pizzaria** ❶, on Av. Brasília at Pça. Matriz, has a good variety of pizzas for R$6-19. (☎349 1004, 249 4455. Open daily 6pm-midnight.)

HIKING & BACKPACKING

There are a few options for hiking. All trails and hikes require a guide, because the dunes are constantly shifting, which makes it extremely easy to get lost. Hiking through the dunes is very challenging, because it gets very hot and the terrain is often steep. Popular dayhikes include the trek from Lagoa da Esperança to Lagoa Azul via Lagoa Bonita. It is possible to hike to the park from Barreirinhas, but it is long, difficult, and unrewarding. A better use of time and energy is to take a tour to the park and from there hike to the different lakes. Two-day trips include the above-mentioned lakes and then a hike to Baixa Grande in the interior of the park. Three-day hikes include a trek from Baixa Grande to Queimada dos Britos, and four-day hikes continue to Queimada dos Britos and along the coast to Atins.

GUIDES & TOURS

Barreirinhas is packed full of reputable tour companies all charging similar prices. Daytrips to the park start at R$25 per person, while camping trips start at more than R$100 per person. Tours to Caburé and the other fishing villages on the way cost about R$35.

Freeway Adventures (☎349 1410; www.freeway.tur.br; mandacuruecoturismo@elo.com.br), in Barreirinhas. Offers a week-long package to the Lençóis area including trips to the park, Caburé, and smaller fishing villages. Guides, accommodations, breakfast, and round-trip flight from São Luís included (R$885).

Off Road Adventure, Av. Joaquim Soeiro de Carvalho. (☎349 0546, 9991 3762, 9962 0788), in Barreirinhas. Best for longer hikes that involve camping in the park.

Ecotrilhas Empreedimentos Turisticos, Av. Joaquim Soeiro de Carvalho 682 (☎349 0372, 9114 3829; www.ecotrilhas.com.br), in Barreirinhas.

Giltur—Viagens e Turismo, Rua Montanha Russa 22 (☎231 7065; fax 232 6041; www.giltur.com.br), in São Luís. Two-day trips depart at 5am and return 5pm the next day, and include walks to Lagoa Azul and Lagoa Peixe. Includes accommodations with A/C, *frigo-bar,* and breakfast. R$340 per person; R$270 per person for 2 people; R$261 per person for 3 people.

Lopez Turismo e Adventura, Travessa Marcelino Almeida 85 (☎221 0942, 9992 6330; www.lopezturismo.com.br), in São Luís. Daytrip to the Lençóis R$140; 2-day trips R$280. Transportation, accommodations, and breakfast included.

NORTH

Home to the highest peak in Brazil (Amazonas's Pico de Neblinha, 3104m) and covered by nearly four million square kilometers of lush Amazon rainforest, the sprawling, uncharted North of Brazil looms large on the map and the imagination. (The North includes the states of Acre, Amapá, Amazonas, Pará, Roraima, Rondônia, and Tocantins.) The dwindling tropical forest that surrounds the Amazon River (Rio Amazonas)—not to mention the region's exotic wildlife—are far and away the main attraction here, for better or for worse. For although the river influences the alluringly laid-back and rustic pace of life here (travel is almost exclusively boat), it also ensures that a pre-packaged "back-to-nature" experience is always around the corner. Regardless, the region is worth a visit, if only for its distance from the hectic pace of the more touristed cities and beaches.

HIGHLIGHTS OF THE NORTH

SWING in your hammock on an **Amazon riverboat** as the jungle rolls by (p. 455).

NAVIGATE flooded forests in a canoe at the **Mamirauá Reserve** (p. 507).

SIP some of the sweetest *sucos* (fruit juices) imaginable in **Belém** (p. 454).

DISCOVER the rainforest on **jungle trips** around Manaus (p. 500).

PARÁ

BELÉM ☎91

The surprisingly cosmopolitan Cidade das Mangueiras, named for the thousands of mango trees downtown, is the busy hub of the North, situated at the Amazon Basin's mouth. Wealth came to Belém in the 1800s rubber boom, and most of the city's spectacular belle epoque architecture (notably the ornate Theatro da Paz) was created during this period. In the 1920s, Art Deco had a major influence on the buildings in the *comércio* (commercial district), creating a faint resemblance to Rio de Janeiro's Copacabana district. At the crossroads of two worlds, the city weaves the culinary and artistic influences of indigenous Amazonian groups into the fast-paced, glitzy lifestyle of a growing urban culture. Recent timber industry revenues have funded renovations, resulting in the Estação das Docas and Casa das Onze Janelas, which combine artsy eateries and functional cultural centers. All this allows for great flexibility—one could feasibly spend the morning sipping *guaraná* and watching jaguars, later take in Louis XV period furniture at Museu de Arte de Belém, and dine on Amazonian cuisine in Pça. da República. at night.

TRANSPORTATION

Flights: Aeroporto Val de Cães, on Av. Júlio César (☎210 6000), 10km away from the *centro,* is the city's international airport. Available services include Banco do Brasil and Bradesco ATMS, a 24hr. Internet café, Paratur tourist office, and several restaurants, gift shops, and newsstands. **Buses** to various locations in the *centro* leave from a blue stand near Terminal A (35min.; several per hr.; R$1). To get to the airport, take the "Marex" bus from Av. Vargas or the *rodoviária.* The **Coopertaxí** service has a booth in the arrivals area; a cab to the *centro* will cost at least R$25.

Buses: The central **rodoviária** is in a giant blue building in São Bras, 3km west of the *centro* along Av. Governador Malcher. Most buses heading away from the *centro* on this street pass by the *rodoviária.* Available services include 24hr. luggage storage (*guarda volumes;* ☎266 2635), an ATM, newsstand, and Sinetel/Telemar phone office with Internet access (R$6 per hr.) and phone cards. (Open M-Sa 8am-8pm.) **Transbrasiliana** has air-conditioned buses to: **Brasília** (34hr.; 3 per day noon-1am; R$173); **Rio de Janeiro** (50hr.; 3pm; R$251) via **Belo Horizonte** (45hr.; R$219); **São Luís** (13hr.; 8pm; R$75); **São Paulo** (48hr.; 10am; R$246).

Ferries: Terminal Hidroviário, Av. Marechal Hermes, south of Av. Visconde de Souza Franca. Open daily 5:30am-midnight. The area gets deserted at night, so be cautious. Services include luggage storage and a small *lanchonete*. The bus stop outside services all major city routes. **Rodrigues Alves Navegação** (☎212 2424, 241 7508) runs clean, new boats to **Manaus** (5 days; M, Tu, W 6pm; hammock R$220, suite R$320) via **Santarém** (2½ days; hammock R$140, suite R$240). (Open M-F 8am-6pm. Visa.) **Bom Jesus** (☎225 5559) is the best option for trips to **Macapá** (24hr.; 10am; R$90). (Open M-F 8am-6pm.) **Rodofluvial Banav** (☎9961 2203, 249 8617) goes to **Camará** on **Ilha de Marajó** (2½hr.; 3 per day M-Sa, 1 per day Su; R$9.50), from which onward transport to Soure and Salvaterra is readily available. (Open daily 6am-6pm.)

Public Transportation: Belém's bus network is easy to navigate and operates until roughly 11pm. Routes are written clearly on the dashboard and note all major stops. Buses to the airport pass along Av. Hermes in front of the Estação das Docas; to get to the *rodoviária,* catch a bus to São Braz anywhere along Av. Pres. Vargas. Several buses shuttle around the *comércio* area and Ver-o-Peso market.

Taxis: The most reliable (though more expensive) option is the 24hr. **Coopertaxí** (☎257 1720, 257 1041), with centers throughout the city and a main airport office. Visa.

Car Rental: Avis, Av. Pres. Vargas 882 (☎225 1699, 24hr. airport line 257 2222), in the Hilton Hotel. From R$35 per day. **InterBrasil,** Rua Oliveira Belo 122 (☎230 1989, 8111 2755). Slightly more expensive (from R$45 per day), but includes free mileage.

ORIENTATION

Easy to navigate on foot, Belém's *comércio*, waterfront, and Cidade Velha are the most interesting for visitors, with plenty of aging colonial architecture and most hotels and services. Nightlife and restaurants are in the trendier Umarizal and Docas neighborhoods, along Travessa Almirante Waldenkolk. **Avenida Presidente Vargas** cuts through the *comércio*, starting at the **Estação das Docas,** some warehouses with restaurants and cafés along the waterfront, and leads inland to *centro's* **Praça da República.** The waterfront starts at the Estação and continues south along **Rua Castilho França,** ending at the Ver-o-Peso market and the Cidade Velha, oriented around **Praça Dom Pedro II** and the giant white Catedral da Sé, opposite the rebuilt Forte do Castelo and Casa das Onze Janelas. Branching out from the *centro* to the east is **Avenida Nazaré** (called **Avenida Governador Barata** after a few blocks) which leads to the Basílica, Parque Zoobotânico, *rodoviária*, and, 12km farther, the airport. The parallel **Av. Governador Malcher** runs to Pça. da República.

PRACTICAL INFORMATION

TOURIST & FINANCIAL SERVICES

Tourist Office: The **Paratur** office, in Pça. Waldemar Henrique (☎242 1118, late-night tourist line 242 0900; www.paratur.pa.gov.br; turismo@prodepa.gov.br), on Av. Marechal Hermes, has free city maps and the extremely handy *Informativ Cultural,* a monthly guide to cultural activities in the city published by the Secretary of Tourism. The helpful,

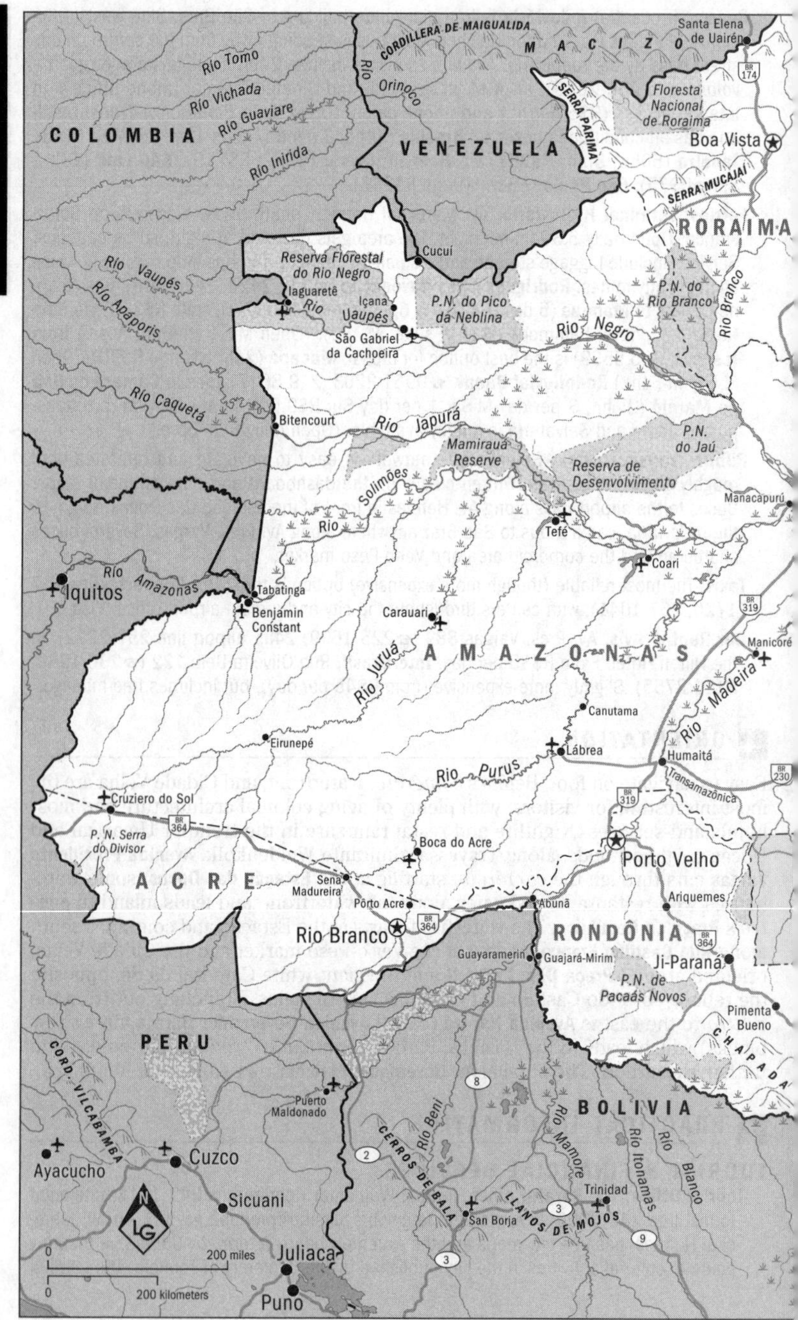

COLOMBIA
VENEZUELA
RORAIMA
AMAZONAS
ACRE
RONDÔNIA
PERU
BOLIVIA
CORDILLERA DE MAIGUALIDA
MACIZO
SERRA PARIMA
SERRA MUCAJAI
Floresta Nacional de Roraima
Boa Vista
Santa Elena de Uairén
Río Tomo
Río Vichada
Río Guaviare
Río Inirida
Río Orinoco
Río Vaupés
Río Apaporis
Río Caquetá
Reserva Florestal do Rio Negro
Cucuí
Iaguaretê
Içana
Rio Uaupés
São Gabriel da Cachoeira
P.N. do Pico da Neblina
Rio Negro
P.N. do Rio Branco
Rio Branco
Bitencourt
Rio Japurá
P.N. do Jaú
Mamirauá Reserve
Reserva de Desenvolvimento
Manacapurú
Rio Solimões
Tefé
Coari
Río Amazonas
Iquitos
Tabatinga
Benjamin Constant
Carauari
Rio Juruá
Manicoré
Rio Madeira
Canutama
Eirunepé
Lábrea
Humaitá
Rio Purus
Transamazônica
Cruziero do Sol
P. N. Serra do Divisor
Boca do Acre
Porto Velho
Sena Madureira
Pôrto Acre
Abunã
Ariquemes
Rio Branco
Guayaramerín
Guajará-Mirim
Ji-Paraná
P.N. de Pacaás Novos
Pimenta Bueno
CHAPADA
CORD. VILCABAMBA
Puerto Maldonado
Río Beni
CERROS DE BALA
Río Mamore
Río Itonamas
Río Blanco
Trinidad
LLANOS DE MOJOS
San Borja
Ayacucho
Cuzco
Sicuani
Juliaca
Puno
200 miles
200 kilometers

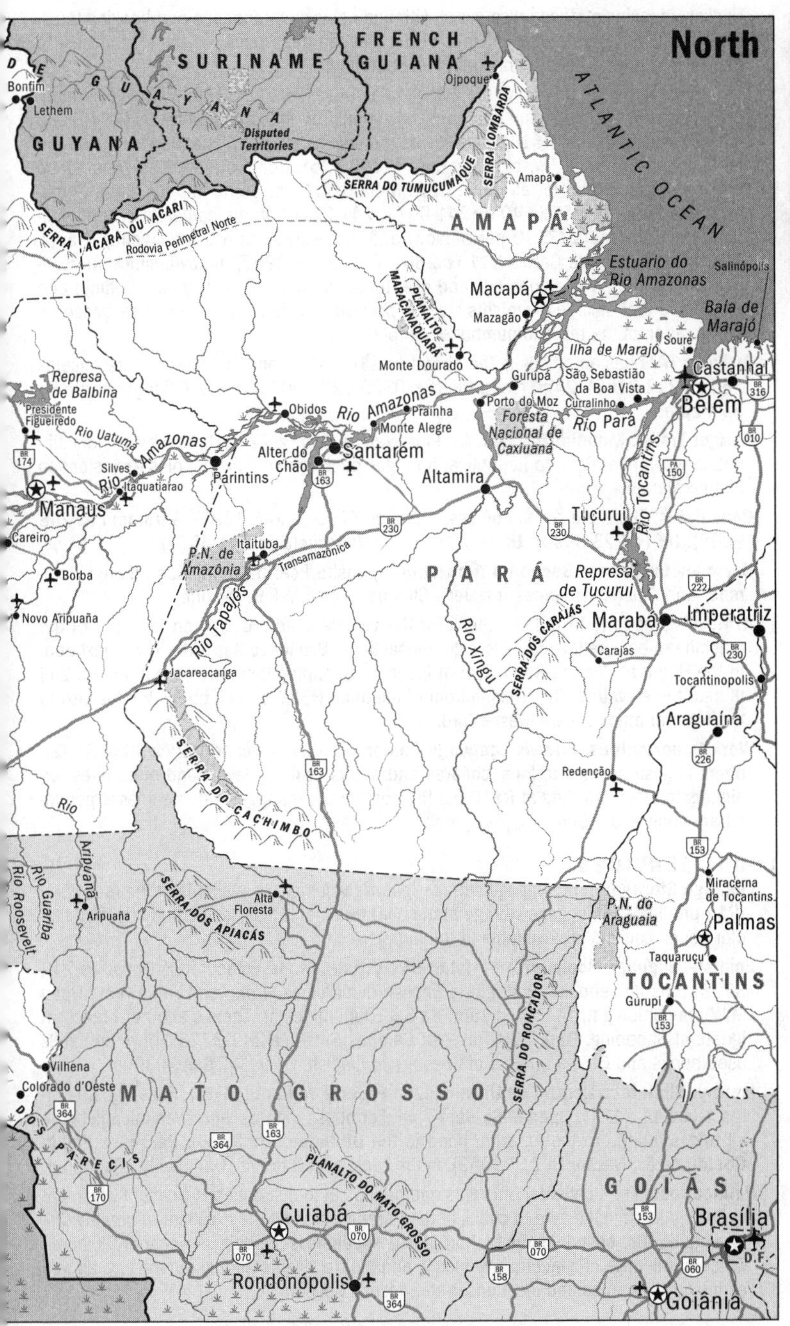
North
FRENCH GUIANA
SURINAME
GUYANA
ATLANTIC OCEAN
AMAPÁ
PARÁ
TOCANTINS
MATO GROSSO
GOIÁS
Bonfim
Lethem
Disputed Territories
Ojpoque
SERRA LOMBARDA
SERRA DO TUMUCUMAQUE
Amapá
SERRA ACARA OU ACARI
Rodovia Perimetral Norte
Estuario do Rio Amazonas
Salinópolis
Macapá
Mazagão
PLANALTO MARACANAQUARA
Baía de Marajó
Soure
Ilha de Marajó
Monte Dourado
Gurupá
São Sebastião da Boa Vista
Castanhal
Represa de Balbina
Presidente Figueiredo
Obidos
Rio Amazonas
Prainha
Porto do Moz
Curralinho
Belém
Monte Alegre
Foresta Nacional de Caxiuanã
Rio Pará
Rio Uatumã
Santarém
Alter do Chão
Silves
Parintins
Altamira
Rio Tocantins
Manaus
Itaquatiarao
Tucuruí
Careiro
Itaituba
P.N. de Amazônia
Transamazônica
Borba
Represa de Tucuruí
Novo Aripuaña
Rio Tapajós
Rio Xingu
SERRA DOS CARAJÁS
Marabá
Imperatriz
Carajás
Jacareacanga
Tocantinopolis
Araguaína
SERRA DO CACHIMBO
Redenção
Rio
Aripuanã
Rio Guariba
Rio Roosevelt
Aripuaña
SERRA DOS APIACÁS
Alta Floresta
P.N. do Araguaia
Miracerna de Tocantins
Palmas
Taquaruçu
Gurupi
SERRA DO RONCADOR
Vilhena
Colorado d'Oeste
DOS PARECIS
PLANALTO DO MATO GROSSO
Cuiabá
Brasília
D.F.
Rondonópolis
Goiânia

English-speaking staff can also assist with finding accommodations and booking tours. Branch offices operate on weekends at the Estação das Docas (on the side closest to Ver-o-Peso) and at the airport. Open M-F 8am-5pm.

Tours: Veleverde, at the end of the Estação das Docas (☎212 3388; www.valeverdeturismo.com.br), offers bus and boat tours, including 3hr. trips around the city (R$40) and a 1½hr. sunset cruise (R$18), plus several excursions to nearby islands Mosqueiro and Marajó, ranging from 7hr. to a few days (R$80-225). Boats often have live *foclórico* music. 2 person min. for all tours. Open M-Sa 9am-8pm, Su noon-6pm. **Casa Francesa,** Rua Padre Prudêncio 40 (☎241 0071, 241 2716), in the *comércio* district, specializes in city tours (R$30 per person) and also serves as a travel agency. **Happy Travel,** Av. Duque de Caixas 311 (☎266 0761, 9992 3967; happyturismo@interconnect.com.br), runs afternoon city and river tours, as well as longer trips to Marajó and Mosqueiro that include overnights stays in *pousadas* or *fazendas.* Prices vary based on the duration of the trip and number of people.

Airlines: TAM has an offices in the airport (☎210 6400), and Av. Assis de Vasconcelos 265 (☎212 2166). 24hr. reservations ☎0300 123 1000. Open M-F 8am-6pm, Sa-Su 8am-2pm.

Budget Travel: Mundial Turismo, Av. Pres. Vargas 780 (☎223 1981; www.mundial.libnet.com.br), near Pça. da República, arranges packages and flights, plus excursions to Ilha de Marajó.

Consulates: There are several offices in Belém: **Chile** (☎248 1333); **Suriname** (☎248 9008); **UK** (☎223 0990); **US** (☎223 0800); **Venezuela** (☎241 7574).

Currency Exchange: Banco da Amazônia, opposite Pça. da República, changes currency and American Express Traveler's Cheques. Open M-F 9am-5pm.

ATM: ATMs abound in Belém; check for the Visa/MasterCard logo on the front of the machine to be sure it accepts foreign transactions. **Bradesco** has 24hr. ATMs next door to the Hilton at Pça. da República; at Iguatemi Shopping there are several on the 2nd fl. near the elevators. The ATMs in front of the main **HSBC** branch on Av. Vargas next to the Telemar office accept MasterCard.

Work Opportunities: Friends Language Center, Av. Gov. Malcher 352 (☎3086 3632), offers English courses to local children and adults at many levels and often hires foreigners to teach, starting at R$10 per hr.; contact the manager with inquiries. Open M-F 8am-noon and 2-9pm.

LOCAL SERVICES

Luggage Storage: 24hr. luggage storage *(guarda volumes)* is available at the *rodoviária* (R$2 per day); the luggage storage at the boat terminal is less secure and not open regular hours. Lockers are available at the airport.

English-Language Bookstore: Revistaria Newstime, in the Estação das Docas (☎212 3298), has guidebooks, Portuguese-English dictionaries, *Time,* and *Newsweek*. Open M-W noon-midnight, Th-F noon-1am, Sa-Su 10am-midnight. There's another branch at Iguatemi Shopping. **Baú,** 529 Travessa Campos Sales (☎242 3426), buys and sells used books and CDs; a number of titles are in English. Open M-F 9am-4:30pm.

Library: Biblioteca Central da Universidade Federal do Pará (UFPA), Rua Augusto Correa 1 (☎211 2121). Open M-Sa 9am-7pm. For books, photos, and even microfiche on all things related to the Amazon, head to the **Biblioteca do Museu Paraense Emílio Goeldi,** on Av. Nazaré (☎217 6052), in the Zoological Gardens. Open daily 10am-5pm.

Publications: For a calendar of events and periodical tourist bulletins (most of which are in Portuguese), make sure to check at the Paratur office for the excellent *Informativ Cultural* guide. The best resource for Portuguese speakers is the daily newspaper *O Liberal,* which has listings of concerts, live music, and theater events throughout the city, as well as movie showtimes and locations in the *Agenda* section.

Cultural Centers: A good place for cultural information and events is the **Centro Cultural Brasil Estados Unidos (CCBEU),** Av. Padre Eutíquio 1309 (☎242 9455). Open M-F 9am-5pm. The **Escola de Teatro e Dança da UFPA,** Av. Magalhães Barata 611 (☎249 6400), in the Anfiteatro Claudio Banadas, is the university's main theater and dance group and schedules occasional performances and workshops.

Market: The immense department stores **Visão** and **Y.Yamada** have locations in the Castanheira and Iguatemi Shopping Centers (see **Shopping** p. 468); they stock virtually everything. For a giant supermarket, try the **Lojas Americanas** in Iguatemi Shopping or **Almirante** across from the *rodoviária* on Av. José Malcher. Both open daily 9am-9pm.

Laundromat: Lav & Lev, Travessa Dr. Moraes 576 (☎223 7247), has 1hr. service. Dry cleaning *(lavagem a seco)* is available at Iguatemi Shopping.

EMERGENCY & COMMUNICATIONS

EMERGENCIES The emergency numbers for all of Brazil are: **Police** ☎190. **Ambulance** ☎192. **Fire** ☎193.

Emergency: 24hr. emergency line (*pronto soccoro*) ☎241 2246.

24hr. Pharmacy: Farmácia Zero Hora, on Av. Almirante Barroso past the *rodoviária* (☎243 3100), is the city's only 24hr. facility. There are several locations scattered throughout Belém, but none in the *centro.* Another option during the day is **Extrafarma,** Av. Pres. Vargas 404 (☎225 4563), which stocks most medications and has a good selection of toiletries. Open 8am-8pm daily. MC/V.

Hospital/Medical Services: Hospital Madre Teresa, Av. Governador José Malcher 651 (☎241 2444), is close to the *centro.*

Telephones: You can make and receive international phone calls at **Telemar,** Av. Pres. Vargas 620 (☎241 4965). English spoken. **Internet access** (R$6 per hr.) Also has a branch at the *rodoviária,* also with Internet access. Both open daily 8am-9pm.

Internet Access: The cheapest option is **Serviços de Informática,** at the intersection of Av. Vasconcelos and Rua Gaspar Viana (☎9996 3223), in the Shopping Popular arcade. Open M-F 9am-7pm, Sa 9am-3pm. R$4 per hr. **CyberCafé,** in the 3rd fl. food court of Iguatemi Shopping, has 10 computers and is always packed. Open daily noon-10pm. R$4.80 per hr. Internet access is also available at the centrally located **Telemar** office (see above) and there is 24hr. access at the **airport.**

Post Office: The **main post office,** Av. Pres. Vargas 491 (☎211 3174), offers basic services as well as international faxing and FedEx express delivery. Open M-F 9am-5pm. There are several other **branches** throughout the city with the same hours, including one at the corner of Travessa Campos Sales and Rua 13 de Maio. **Postal code:** 66000-000.

ACCOMMODATIONS

Accommodations options range from insect-ridden shacks along the waterfront to architectural wonders in the *centro* and periphery, some of which are an excellent value. Most medium- and top-end hotels offer discounts for longer stays, and in low season (outside Carnaval and October's Círio de Nazaré) it is worth asking. All hotels listed have 24hr. reception and a standard noon check-out, unless otherwise noted; most include breakfast *(café de manha)*, often a sumptuous buffet of fruit and cakes. Because the Ver-o-Peso and Cidade Velha neighborhoods are reportedly unsafe at night, *Let's Go* lists accommodations outside of these areas.

Hotel Central, Av. Pres. Vargas 290, between Rua 28 de Setembro and Rua Manuel Barata. High-ceilinged, airy rooms with antique Art Deco furniture make the aging Hotel Central, built in the 1920s, a diamond in the rough. Popular with travelers. Rooms close

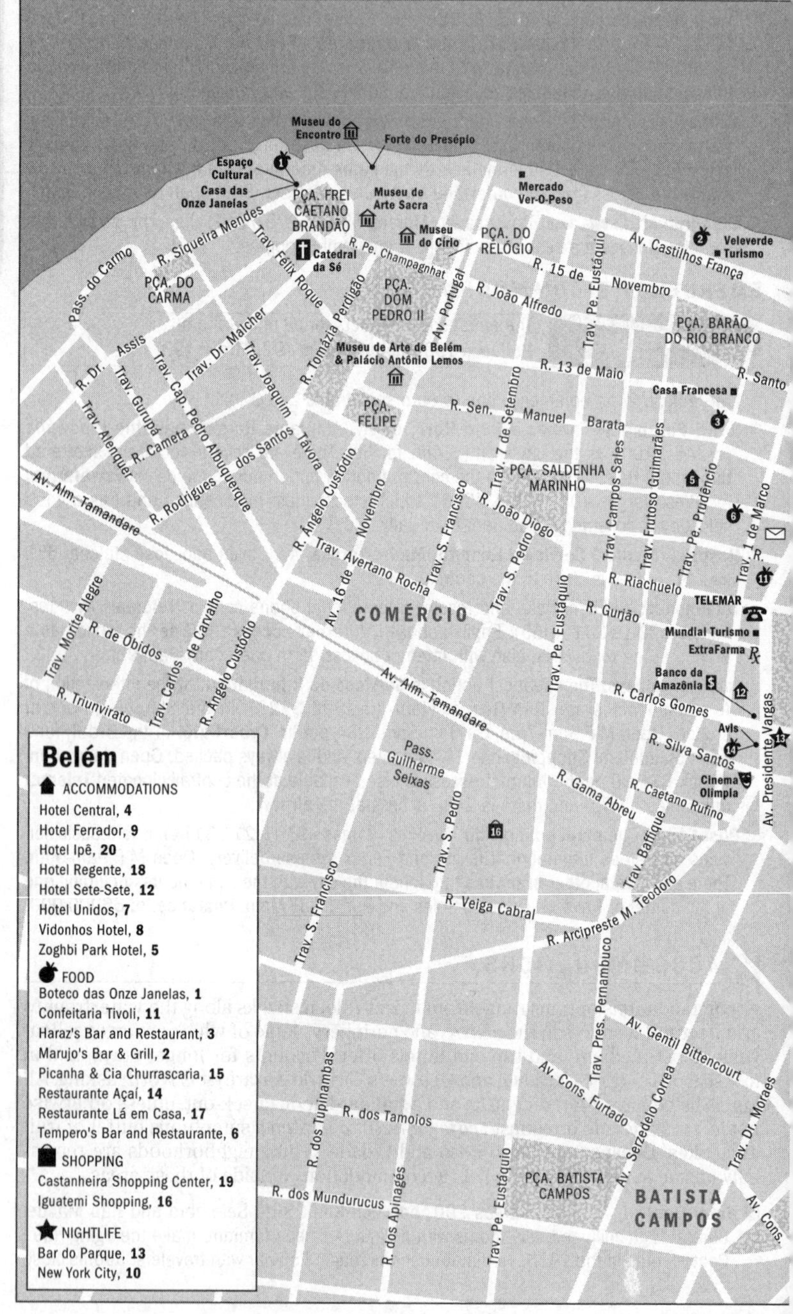

Belém
ACCOMMODATIONS
Hotel Central, 4
Hotel Ferrador, 9
Hotel Ipê, 20
Hotel Regente, 18
Hotel Sete-Sete, 12
Hotel Unidos, 7
Vidonhos Hotel, 8
Zoghbi Park Hotel, 5
FOOD
Boteco das Onze Janelas, 1
Confeitaria Tivoli, 11
Haraz's Bar and Restaurant, 3
Marujo's Bar & Grill, 2
Picanha & Cia Churrascaria, 15
Restaurante Açaí, 14
Restaurante Lá em Casa, 17
Tempero's Bar and Restaurante, 6
SHOPPING
Castanheira Shopping Center, 19
Iguatemi Shopping, 16
NIGHTLIFE
Bar do Parque, 13
New York City, 10
Museu do Encontro
Forte do Presépio
Espaço Cultural
Casa das Onze Janelas
PÇA. FREI CAETANO BRANDÃO
Museu de Arte Sacra
Museu do Círio
PÇA. DO RELÓGIO
Mercado Ver-O-Peso
Veleverde Turismo
Catedral da Sé
PÇA. DO CARMA
PÇA. DOM PEDRO II
Museu de Arte de Belém & Palácio Antônio Lemos
PÇA. FELIPE
PÇA. BARÃO DO RIO BRANCO
Casa Francesa
PÇA. SALDENHA MARINHO
TELEMAR
Mundial Turismo
ExtraFarma
Banco da Amazônia
Avis
Cinema Olimpia
COMÉRCIO
Pass. Guilherme Seixas
PÇA. BATISTA CAMPOS
BATISTA CAMPOS
R. Siqueira Mendes
Pass. do Carmo
Trav. Félix Roque
R. Pe. Champagnhat
R. 15 de Novembro
Av. Castilhos França
R. João Alfredo
R. Tomázia Perdigão
Av. Portugal
Trav. Pe. Eustáquio
R. 13 de Maio
R. Santo
R. Dr. Assis
Trav. Dr. Malcher
Trav. Joaquim Távora
Trav. Gurupá
Trav. Cap. Pedro Albuquerque
Trav. Alenquer
R. Cametá
R. Rodrigues dos Santos
R. Sen. Manuel Barata
Trav. 7 de Setembro
Trav. Campos Sales
Trav. Frutoso Guimarães
Trav. Pe. Prudêncio
Trav. 1 de Marco
Av. Alm. Tamandare
R. Ângelo Custódio
Av. 16 de Novembro
Trav. S. Francisco
R. João Diogo
Trav. Avertano Rocha
Trav. S. Pedro
R. Riachuelo
R. Gurjão
Trav. Morite Alegre
R. de Óbidos
Trav. Carlos de Carvalho
R. Triunvirato
R. Carlos Gomes
R. Silva Santos
Av. Presidente Vargas
R. Gama Abreu
R. Caetano Rufino
Trav. Baffique
R. Veiga Cabral
R. Arcipreste M. Teodoro
Trav. Pres. Pernambuco
Av. Gentil Bittencourt
Av. Cons. Furtado
Av. Serzedelo Correa
Trav. Dr. Moraes
R. dos Tupinambas
R. dos Tamoios
R. dos Mundurucus
R. dos Apinagés
Av. Cons.

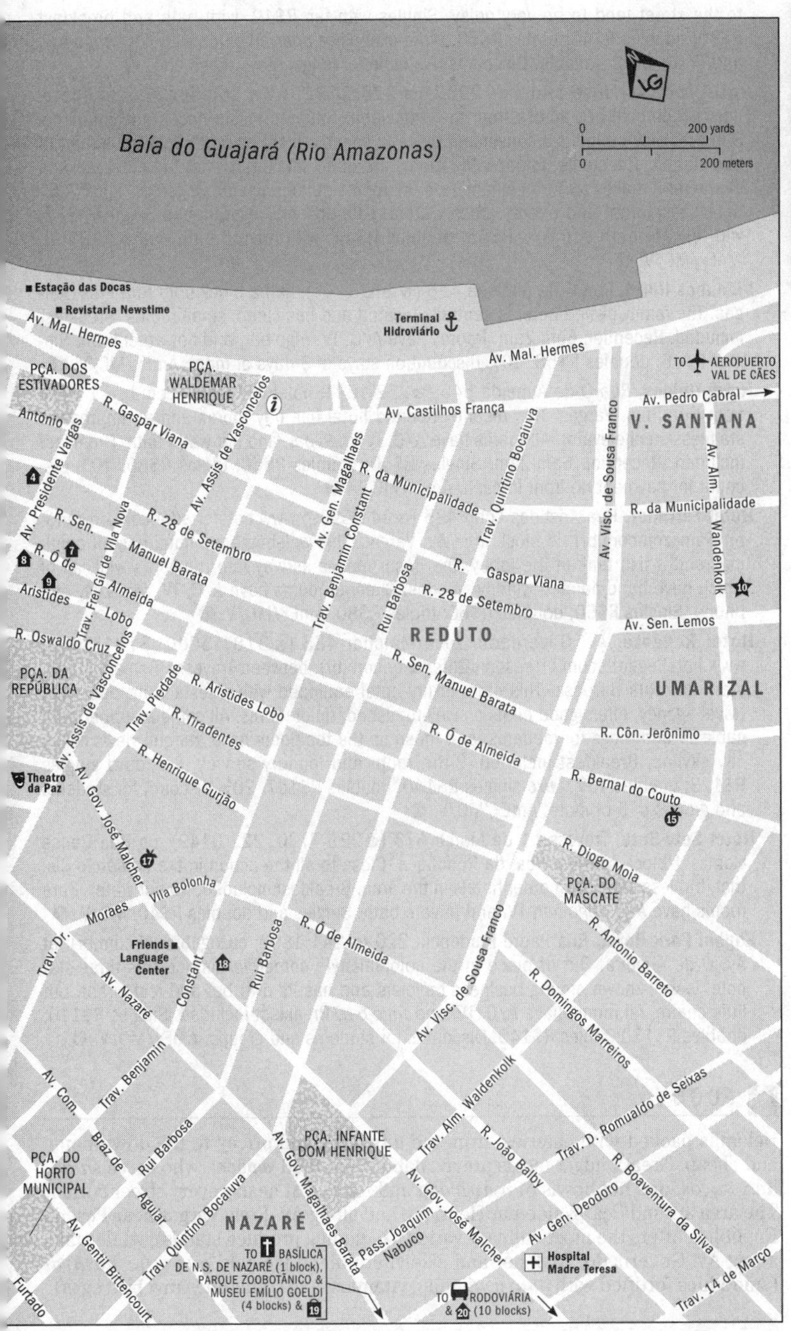
Baía do Guajará (Rio Amazonas)
0 200 yards
0 200 meters
Estação das Docas
Revistaria Newstime
Terminal Hidroviário
Av. Mal. Hermes
PÇA. DOS ESTIVADORES
PÇA. WALDEMAR HENRIQUE
TO AEROPUERTO VAL DE CÃES
Av. Pedro Cabral
Av. Castilhos França
V. SANTANA
R. Gaspar Viana
Antônio
Av. Presidente Vargas
Av. Assis de Vasconcelos
Av. Gen. Magalhaes
R. da Municipalidade
Trav. Quintino Bocaiuva
Av. Visc. de Sousa Franco
Av. Alm. Wandenkolk
R. Sen. Manuel Barata
R. 28 de Setembro
Trav. Frei Gil de Vila Nova
R. Ó de Almeida
Aristides Lobo
Trav. Benjamin Constant
Rui Barbosa
Av. Sen. Lemos
REDUTO
R. Oswaldo Cruz
PÇA. DA REPÚBLICA
UMARIZAL
Trav. Piedade
R. Aristides Lobo
R. Tiradentes
R. Côn. Jerônimo
R. Henrique Gurjão
R. Bernal do Couto
Theatro da Paz
Av. Gov. José Malcher
R. Diogo Moia
PÇA. DO MASCATE
Vila Bolonha
Moraes
R. Antonio Barreto
Friends Language Center
Trav. Dr.
Av. Nazaré
Constant
R. Domingos Marreiros
Trav. Benjamin
Av. Com. Braz de Aguiar
Trav. Alm. Waldenkolk
Trav. D. Romualdo de Seixas
PÇA. INFANTE DOM HENRIQUE
Av. Gov. Magalhaes Barata
R. João Balby
PÇA. DO HORTO MUNICIPAL
R. Boaventura da Silva
Trav. Quintino Bocaiuva
NAZARÉ
Pass. Joaquim Nabuco
Av. Gen. Deodoro
Av. Gentil Bittencourt
Furtado
TO BASÍLICA DE N.S. DE NAZARÉ (1 block), PARQUE ZOOBOTÂNICO & MUSEU EMÍLIO GOELDI (4 blocks) & 19
Hospital Madre Teresa
TO RODOVIÁRIA & 20 (10 blocks)
Trav. 14 de Março

to the street tend to be very noisy. Singles with fan R$19, with bath and breakfast R$30; doubles R$40; triples R$50. More expensive *apartamentos* with A/C, *frigo-bar,* and TV are also available. Discounts available for longer stays. Cash only. ❶

Hotel Ipê, Av. José Malcher 2953 (☎228 2121; www.hotelipe.com.br, hotelipe@yahoo.com.br), across from the *rodoviária.* Situated in the hectic and industrial São Braz district, Ipê is a convenient place to spend a night en route from the airport or bus station. The sterile, impeccable rooms are quite small, but what the hotel lacks in character it makes up for in cleanliness. All rooms at Ipê have fan, *frigo-bar,* and TV. In-house restaurant and nearby grocery store. Laundry service available. Singles R$33, with private bath and A/C R$55; doubles R$44, with private bath and A/C R$66. AmEx/MC/V. ❷

Vidonhos Hotel, Rua Ó de Almeida 476 (☎242 1444), half a block from Rua Pres. Vargas. The family-owned hotel is centrally located and has clean, small rooms. Breakfast included. Reception 6am-2am. Rooms have A/C, TV, *frigo-bar,* and hot-water bath. Singles R$46; doubles R$58. 10% discount on stays of 3 days or more. AmEx/MC/V. ❸

Hotel Unidos, Rua Ó de Almeida 545 (☎252 1891; hotelunidos@bol.com.br), 1 block from Rua Pres. Vargas. This recently opened hotel has tidy rooms and an impressive stainless-steel elevator. All rooms have A/C, TV, *frigo-bar,* and hot-water bath. Breakfast included. Reception 6am-2am. Singles R$50; doubles R$60; triples R$80. 10% discount for payment up front in cash. AmEx/MC/V. ❸

Hotel Ferrador, Rua Aristides Lobo 485 (☎241 5999; www.hoteferrador.com.br; ferrador@amazon.com.br), ½ block from Av. Vargas. This well-managed hotel has oil paintings and a fish tank in the lobby; the decor makes its way into rooms as well, all of which have hand-painted window shades. Cheerful rooms have A/C, TV, *frigo-bar,* and phone. Singles R$50; doubles R$60; triples R$80. AmEx/MC/V. ❸

Hotel Regente, Av. Governador José Malcher 485 (☎3181 5000, 3181 5003; www.hotelregente.com.br; reserva@hregente.com.br), between Travessa Benjamin Constant and Rua Barbosa. This older luxury hotel equipped with a restaurant, pool, and travel agency, offers good deals on well-furnished, quiet rooms. All come equipped with cable TV and plugs for modems, and those on the top floors have tranquil views of the city skyline. Breakfast included. 24hr. room and laundry service. Standard singles R$123; doubles 137. *Luxo* singles R$140; doubles R$157. 20% discount for students and groups of 5 or more. AmEx/MC/V. ❺

Hotel Sete-Sete, Travessa 1 de Março 673 (☎222 7730, 222 0149), on Rua Carlos Gomes 1 block south of Pça. da República. Close to all the action in the *comércio* district, but less noisy than other hotels in the area. Breakfast included. No hot water. Bare rooms have A/C, *frigo-bar,* TV, and private bath. Singles and doubles R$40. MC/V. ❷

Zoghbi Park Hotel, Rua Padre Prudencio 220 (☎241 1800; cazoghbi@uol.com.br), at Av. Ó de Almeira. Out of place in the colonial-style *comércio* district, this three-star hotel is well-known among business travelers and has its own bar and restaurant, but little charm. All rooms have A/C, TV, and *frigo-bar.* Breakfast included. Singles R$110; doubles R$130; triples R$140. Discounts for students and groups. AmEx/MC/V. ❺

FOOD

Belém is packed with eateries, from the ultra-chic and pricey to the down-home and cheap. Great budget meals are available from food **vendors,** who serve *salgados*, *sucos*, and hot bowls of *maniçoba* and *vatapá* at nearly every street corner. The area around Pça. Waldemar Henrique and along Av. Pres. Vargas near Pça. da República offers the most culinary variety (including produce stands), while stalls along Av. Governador Malcher and elsewhere blend ice-cold *guaraná natural* (smoothies fortified with *guaraná*, nuts, vitamins, and sometimes raw bird eggs).

Estação das Docas, a series of renovated warehouses along the waterfront across from Av. Pres. Vargas (☎212 5525). Nothing short of culinary paradise: guests here can choose from dozens of excellent restaurants serving everything from sushi to Italian food. The ice cream chain **Cairu** and several popular cafés have stalls on the lower levels of the building; up above **Spazzio Verde** offers a per-kilo buffet. On Sundays the restaurants serve buffet brunch and the warehouses fill to the brim with families. During the evenings, candlelit place settings and romantic waterfront lighting make the Docas equally appealing. ATMs are available at the entrance, though all restaurants accept AmEx/MC/V. Open M 10am-11pm, Tu-Su 10am-midnight. ❶-❺

Restaurante Lá em Casa, Rua José Malchera 247 (☎223 1212), is 3 blocks east of Pça. da República. The collection of awards displayed proudly on Lá em Casa's walls don't lie; the restaurant serves up some of the city's best cuisine in a vine-filled patio which exudes Amazonian elegance. The varied menu includes regional dishes like *pato no tucupi* (duck in manioc root sauce; R$25) and *haddock paraense* (grilled haddock; R$22) as well as unique desserts like *sabor Pará*, a combination of *açaí*, tapioca, and ground cashews (R$5). Beer R$3-4. Wheelchair accessible. Open daily noon-3:30pm and 7pm-1:30am. Reservations recommended on weekends. MC/V. ❸

Restaurante Açaí, Rua Vargas 882 (☎217 7000), inside the Hilton Hotel facing Pça. da República. While the restaurant seems to lack character with bland decor and subdued guests, its menu is excellent. Perhaps the most vegetarian-friendly establishment in Belém. Vegetarian "steak" R$13. Hamburger R$10. Seafood risotto R$19. Shrimp thermidor R$24. Wheelchair accessible. Open daily 24hr. AmEx/MC/V. ❷/❸

Boteco das Onze Janelas, in Pça. da Sé (☎241 8255, 241 8599), in the Casa das Onze Janelas. This incredibly chic new restaurant is where the beautiful people in Belém flock to enjoy live jazz and *bossa nova* on the waterfront. The grotto-like interior displays art borrowed from the gallery next door, and the exposed wood beams along the ceiling date back to the late 1700s. Filet mignon with poivre vert sauce R$30. Creme brulée (*creme de leite*) R$9. Cocktails and liquors R$6-10. R$3 cover after 9pm. Wheelchair accessible. Open Tu-Th noon-4pm and 7pm-1am, F-Su noon-3am. MC/V. ❹

Picanha & Cia Churrascaria, Travessa Almirante Waldenkolk 260 (☎224 3343, 224 3317), at Rua Bernal do Couto. Locals come here for the immense platters of sizzling meat, some of which are large enough to comfortably serve 5 people. Prices are a bit higher than elsewhere, but the extra buck pays for quality cuts, making Picanha one of the best values in town. All

ON THE MENU

(ALMOST) FREE ENERG

According to legend, the firs **guaraná** bush sprung up at th spot where a lightning bolt struc a pair of star-crossed lovers fron rival indigenous tribes. With al these sparks flying as *guaran* supposedly came into existence it's no wonder that the berry-lik fruit contains even more caffein than a cup of coffee. Despite th fact that the ripe *guaraná frui* looks remarkably like a giant eye ball ripped from someone's head this little fruit has become incredi bly popular in Brazil, particularly i its native North region (namel around the Amazon). Its od appearance has also not stoppe *guaraná* from becoming more an more common as a fashionabl ingredient in souped-up energ drinks and diet pills throughou the western world.

In the Amazon, *guaraná* ha been used as a pick-me-up fo ages, and can be purchased fro any of the region's ubiquitou *suco* stands, blended into del cious shakes made from nativ fruits like *graviola*, *açaí*, an guava *(goiaba)*, usually for les than R$2. Brazilians (and energy seeking travelers) also get their fi in a bubblegum-flavored sod (labeled as a "Champagne"); o the many brands, **Antarctica** i the most popular.

After a long day on the road, refreshing *suco* with *guaraná* i the perfect reward, and all for les than half the price of your favorit energy drink.

dishes come with complementary sides, including salad and *feijão* (beans); the menu also includes a selection of vegetarian-friendly baked potatoes (R$10-17). *Picanha na manteiga* (beef steak in butter sauce; R$38). The patio area is wheelchair accessible. Open Tu-Su 11:30am-3pm and 6:30pm-1am. Visa. ❹

Confeitaria Tivoli, on Av. Pres. Vargas at Rua Riachuelo (☎224 7345). The modest setting in an unmarked open-air storefront doesn't do justice to Tivoli's excellent fresh pastries and breads, made on the premises throughout the day. The bistro fills up in the afternoons with everyone from mothers and sons munching on *queijo quente* (grilled cheese sandwiches; R$1.70) to older men chatting over cappuccinos (R$1.50). *Sucos* R$1.20. Hamburgers R$2-3. Open M-Sa 6:30am-8pm. ❶

Tempero's Bar and Restaurante, on Rua Ó de Almeida at Travessa 1 de Março (☎223 8874), is 1 block south of Av. Vargas. A family-style restaurant with checkered tablecloths and a cheap buffet (R$11 per kg) with several vegetarian dishes. A la carte meals like *feijoada carioca* (Rio-style bean stew) are filling and cost as little as R$4. Simple beef and fish dishes R$7. Open M-Sa 11am-11pm. ❷

Haraz's Bar and Restaurant, Travessa Padre Prudêncio 104, in the heart of the *comércio* district. Far from stylish but cheap enough to draw budget travelers. Haraz's is popular with locals and has a pleasant patio overlooking Pça. Maranhão. Huge servings of fish filet (with rice, beans, and salad R$5) and steaming bowls of soup (R$1) are a steal. *Caipirinhas* R$2. Open M-Sa 8am-8pm. ❶

Ver-o-Peso Market, on Rua Castilho França, along the waterfront. Ver-o-Peso has a section devoted to over 100 food vendors, serving local dishes like *maniçoba* and *pato no tucupi,* as well as basic *refeições* (fried fish or beef with rice and beans) for around R$3. The side facing the street is perfect for enjoying a *suco* or *salgado* (R$1) while people-watching, provided you don't mind being downwind of the nearby fish market. ❶

Marujo's Bar & Grill, at the Ver-o-Peso end of Estação das Docas (☎212 0835), has a delightful evening atmosphere, as couples cluster around wooden tables with white umbrellas. The chic bar/restaurant provides excellent waterfront views at sunset. The menu includes seafood dishes like *paelha marinheira* (seafood paella; R$35 serves 2-3) and frozen cocktails like *frapê de menta* (mint frappe; R$5) and *marujita* (ice-blended *caipirinha;* R$3.50). Open M-W 10am-midnight, Th-Su 10am-3am. MC/V. ❺

SIGHTS

Belém has several excellent museums and historical buildings, mainly concentrated in the *centro* in the Cidade Velha, as well as to the east in Nazaré. Most can be conveniently explored on foot; unfortunately, guides at most sites are hard to find unless you are part of a larger group. One option if you speak Portuguese—and if you don't mind tagging along with kids at least half your age—is to join a school tour (most are on Tuesdays in the Cidade Velha): these are often excellent, detailed, and free.

CIDADE VELHA

Thanks to the December 2002 inauguration of the highly anticipated Feliz Lusitânia project, the Cidade Velha has been revamped and daytime security guards patrol the entire area. The project, sponsored by the state government as part of its emphasis on social programs, included the renovation of an old military hospital into the Casa das Onze Janelas, one of Belém's cultural jewels and home to several contemporary art galleries. Other additions include a waterfront pier, several restaurants, and a new location for Museu do Círio, formerly at the old Basílica in Nazaré. One of the benefits of the Feliz Lusitânia project is that all museums are now integrated into a Núcleo Cultural. A museum pass, available at any of the sights listed below except the cathedral, costs R$10; the facilities are free on Tuesdays and all offer a 50% student discount with ID. Plan to spend at least a day or two wandering around the Cidade Velha absorbing the unique atmosphere and baroque architecture.

CATEDRAL DA SÉ. The immense and ornate white facade of the giant cathedral towers over the Cidade Velha; the dark interior, restored in 1965, is lined with oil paintings and stained glass depicting major saints. From June 15-24, the Festa de São João is held here; check with Paratur for information on nightly events. *(On Rua Champagnhat at Pça. Dom Frei Caetano Brandão, near the end of Ver-o-Peso market. Open daily 10am-9pm. Mass M-F 6pm; Sa 7pm; Su 7, 9am, 7pm.)*

FORTE DO PRESÉPIO & MUSEU DO ENCONTRO. This orange fort, built in the 1600s by the Portuguese colonial administration, contains manicured lawns and old cannons; far more interesting is the one-room museum at the entrance, which houses the highlights of recent archaeological excavations on both Ilha de Marajó and the grounds of the fort itself. The fascinating collection includes an array of finely crafted ceramic and bone pipes *(cachimbos)*, some dating from the 1500s, as well as thousand-year-old Marajó funeral urns, created by an indigenous group that arrived on the island around 1900 BC. *(At Pça. Caetano Brandão, across from the Casa das Onze Janelas. ☎219 1134. Open Tu-F 10am-6pm, Sa-Su 10am-8pm, holidays 9am-1pm. R$2, students and seniors R$1.)*

MUSEU DE ARTE SACRA. The spectacular Igreja de Santo Alexandre, constructed in 1698, contains masses of exquisite baroque wood carvings, done by Jesuit and indigenous communities in a unique style which incorporates tropical elements. The immaculate gilt altar is a testament to the former colony's wealth. There are roughly 320 sacred objects in the other galleries of the museum as well as a pleasant courtyard. The café with courtyard patio and overpriced museum shop are located to the right of the entrance. *(Pça. Caetano Brandão, across from Forte do Presépio. ☎219 1151; sim@nautilus.com.br. Open Tu-F 1-6pm, Sa-Su 9am-1pm. Free English and Portuguese tours available for groups of 5 or more. R$4, students and seniors R$2.)*

MUSEU DO CÍRIO. This two-room structure contains memorabilia and old photographs of the famous Círio de Nazaré Catholic festival, celebrated in Belém since 1793. The displays include *objetos de cera*, wax castings of body parts representing promises, which are deposited in large containers during the festival. Be sure to check out the scaled miniature replica of the procession done in 1998 by Silvana Passos, containing over 500 tiny individuals marching through the streets. *(On Rua Champagnhat facing Pça. Dom Pedro II, in the same building as Museu de Arte Sacra. Open Tu-F 1-6pm, Sa-Su and holidays 9am-1pm. R$2, students and seniors R$1.)*

ESPAÇO CULTURAL CASA DAS ONZE JANELAS. The orange Casa, facing the waterfront and bordered on one side by the fort, was built in the 18th century to serve as the residence of Domingos da Costa Bacelar, a wealthy sugar plantation owner. The government took ownership of the complex in 1768, after which it served as a military hospital; in December 2002 it was reopened as a cultural space and collection of contemporary art galleries. Since its inception, the Casa has hosted a number of important exhibitions, including the extraordinary documentary images of up-and-coming Paraense photographers Guy Veloso and Eduardo Kalif. The downstairs area is reserved for mixed media pieces, many of which are on loan from art museums in São Paulo and Rio. Across from the entrance to the galleries is the elegant restaurant Boteca das Onze Janelas, a great spot for an afternoon drink. The Jardim da Casa, the garden through the main archway, has benches, fountains, and a breathtaking view of the waterfront. *(At Pça. Caetano Brandão on the waterfront. Open Tu-F 10am-6pm, Sa-Su 10am-8pm, holidays 9am-1pm. R$2, students and seniors R$1. Wheelchair accessible.)*

PALÁCIO ANTÔNIO LEMOS & MUSEU DE ARTE DE BELÉM. The former administrative headquarters of Belém, this immense structure now houses private state offices and the city's primary art museum in its refurbished themed rooms. The Sala Waldemar da Costa, across from the entrance, is dedicated to popular images; the Sala de Legislativo, down the hallway on the right, has a wall-sized canvas depicting the first state assembly in 1892, an all-white group of aristocrats operating in stark contrast to the heterogeneous mix of today's Belenense government. The painting has a hole in it near the bottom, which some speculate is a bullet hole from when the Palácio was taken over by rebels. Don't miss the collection of Louis XV and XVI gilt furniture, possibly the most complete sets in Brazil. The collections in the front hall feature sketches and prints by local artists. *(At Pça. Dom Pedro II. ☎242 3344. Open Tu-F 10am-6pm, Sa-Su and holidays 9am-1pm. Free tours in Portuguese for groups of 4 or more. R$2, students and seniors R$1. Wheelchair accessible.)*

NAZARÉ

The two main attractions of this part of Belém, situated east of the *centro* along Av. Nazaré, include the expansive Basílica and Zoological Gardens, which are well worth the detour from the *centro*. To get here, take any Nazaré bus. Alternatively, the pleasant 1.5km walk takes about 20min. and the street is lined with vendors selling tasty snacks.

BASÍLICA DE NOSSA SENHORA DE NAZARÉ. Completed in 1909, the Basílica was designed by Italian architect Gino Coppede to resemble the Basilica of St. Paul in Rome. One of its most famous functions is housing the small statue of Nossa Senhora de Nazaré (the Virgin Mary), the centerpiece of the annual Círio de Nazaré procession for which Belém is famous. The structure's ornate detailing is the result of major rubber boom investment; patrons certainly spared no expense here. Museu do Círio, formerly housed in the basement, has been relocated to the Cidade Velha as part of the Feliz Lusitânia project (p. 464). *(On Rua da Basílica at Pça. Justo Chermont. Open Tu-Su 6:30-11:30am and 2:30-6:30pm.)*

PARQUE ZOOBOTÂNICO & MUSEU EMÍLIO GOELDI. It's hard to imagine jaguars, capybaras, and alligators strutting through central Belém, but a couple of metal bars between you and them make it all possible at this splendid public garden. Also among the bamboo and giant ferns are colorful macaws and intimidatingly large anacondas. Nestled at the center of the park is the Emílio Goeldi Museum, which is scheduled to reopen in 2004. The holdings include an incredible collection of archaeological findings and information on the Amazon region. *(Rua Magalhães Barata 376. ☎219 7033. Open Tu-Su 9am-5pm.)*

NIGHTLIFE & ENTERTAINMENT

Like most large Brazilian cities, Belém's streets come alive after sundown, and live music can be found at several local bars on the weekends. Nightlife here ranges from casual grassy *praças* with vendors selling *choppes* and grilled meat to swanky, smoke-filled lounges in Docas. Many restaurants that are open for dinner, like the Boteco das Onze Janelas and the Estação das Docas (see **Food**, p. 463), transform into evening bars with live jazz and *bossa nova*. The city often plans fairs and other nighttime events, so it's worth checking the listings in *Informativ Cultural* (available at the Paratur office) or the Agenda section of the local paper *O Liberal* to make sure you aren't missing out on anything.

Theater: Theatro da Paz, in Pça. da República (☎224 7355, 212 7915), is a magnificent 4-story building with intricate gilt detailing and chandeliers. Several music and drama festivals grace the theater, including the Pará Classical Music festival, held annually in June; check the *Informativ Cultural* for listings of events and showtimes. The café inside serves espresso and beer (R$2-3). Box office open Tu-F 9:30am-5pm, Sa 9:30am-12:30pm. Tours (in Portuguese) R$2.

Movies: Cinema Olímpia, on Rua Pres. Vargas (☎223 1882), across from Pça. da República next to the giant Lojas Americanas, shows the latest American movies, plus the occasional Brazilian film. (M-Th R$8, F-Su R$10. 50% student discount with ID. Open M-Th 10am-11pm, F-Su 10am-midnight.) **Cine Arte,** on the 3rd fl. of Castanheira Shopping on Rua Almirante Barroso (☎250 4105), has 2 screens and a better selection for the same prices, as long as you are willing to trek the 6km or take a bus. **Cine Estação,** at the Estação das Docas (☎212 5525), often features foreign films for free.

Bar do Parque, in Pça. da República next to Theatro da Paz, has a shady outdoor patio that gets packed on weekend afternoons with Belenenses and hippies sipping beers. A jukebox adds to the eclectic ambience. Beer R$2. Open daily 24hr.

Interpretação in London, on Travessa Quintino Bocaiúva between Rua Tiradentes and Rua Boaventura da Silva in the Docas area (☎212 4610). Decor is eclectic, with old photographs of London adorning the walls and rustic antique furniture; the wealthy clientele are the local equivalent of yuppies. Menu items and drinks celebrate all things British—try the tangy *sangria in London* (white wine, vodka, and green apple mix; R$13) or *frango Beatles* (fried chicken in butter; R$16). Live pop/rock F and Sa, DJs on Th. Cover R$3. Half-price Happy Hour M-Th 6-8pm. Open M-Th 6pm-1am, F-Sa 6pm-3am.

Groove ME, on the corner of Rua Boaventura da Silva and Travessa Bocaiúva (☎225 5661), attracts the 18-25 crowd for its reputation as the best—and the only—electronica club in Belém, with a mix of Goa, house, and trance music. Upstairs, black lights and neon polka dots cover the walls, while the 1st fl. "Chill Out" room is strewn with plush white lounge chairs and teenagers draped across them. Groove is famous for themed parties and internationally renowned DJs; call in advance for the schedule. Red Bull™ R$7; Hi-Fi (vodka and orange juice) R$5. Cover R$10-20. Open F-Sa midnight-5:30am.

Lithium, Travessa Bocaiúva 1214 (☎241 1371), attracts rockers with live local bands that cover American and British pop/rock. Less plush than most other bars in Docas, Lithium has a definite edge and a unique cocktail menu (try the *Madrugada* with gin, coconut milk, and strawberry juice; R$6). Crowd ranges from punky teenagers to middle-aged couples. 18+. Cover R$5. Open F-Sa 10pm-6am.

New York City, near the intersection of Travessa Almirante Waldenkolk and Av. Senador Lemos (☎225 1313), in a black building covered in the silhouette of the Big Apple's skyline. Belém's most popular nightclub is frequented by the fashionable. Dress to impress: the flashier, the better. Well-known DJs spin the top international dance music, and drinks here are pricier than elsewhere. Dry martini R$7. *Amarula* R$6. Flashback 70s F nights. 18+. Cover R$10-15. Open F-Sa midnight-6am. Visa.

FESTIVALS & EVENTS

Each year since 1793 on the second Sunday in October, Belém's streets swell with participants in the region's largest religious festival, the Círio de Nazaré, honoring Nossa Senhora de Nazaré (the Virgin Mary). As legend has it, the celebrated statue of the Virgin, found by a poor cattle farmer named Plácido in the 18th century, is endowed with spiritual significance. On the evening before the Círio, the image is taken from the Basílica to the Catedral da Sé; the following Sunday morning, a giant procession of the faithful follows the statue back to the Basílica. Crowds anxiously reach for the 350m *corda* (string) attached to the carriage, which is believed to have a powerful effect on those who touch it, and others simply walk behind the image offering prayers and promises to the Virgin. After the procession, families return to their homes to enjoy a traditional lunch of *pato no tucupi*. The two weeks following the Círio are filled with feasting and *festas*, much like the December holiday season in the US. During this time, strangers greet each other on the streets with a "*bom Círio*" (the local equivalent of "Merry Christmas") and children receive colorful wooden *brinquedos de Mirití*, toys named for the palm tree from which they're made. The city virtually shuts down during this period, and it may be difficult to find accommodations. Make sure to book in advance, or consult the Paratur office for possible homestays.

The second major festival period in Belém is the Festas Juninas, a series of celebrations all over the country honoring St. John the Baptist (São João). According to local lore, the young saint sleeps in the heavens during his own holiday and is unable to wake up; in the evening, giant bonfires are lit to shake São João from slumber and draw him to earth for the festivities. While the actual birth of the saint was in late June, the entire month is filled with *forró* bands, Carnaval-style *samba* troupes, and thousands of local food vendors taking to the streets. The useful *Arraial da Alegria* guide, available at the Paratur office, provides specifics on daily planned events, most of which are free.

SHOPPING

Shopaholics will adore Belém: from Amazonian handicrafts and herbal elixirs to bikinis and tropical fruits, the city is alive with street vendors and storefronts calling for customers. The old **Mercado Ver-o-Peso** (literally "see the weight") has undergone a recent face-lift: an expanse of white tents now shades the sprawling marketplace along Rua Castilho França and municipal police guards patrol the area. Here, you can observe grassroots capitalism by navigating the aisles and engaging in some friendly bargaining; most vendors are amused (if not delighted) to meet foreigners. Walking toward the Cidade Velha from the Estação das Docas, you'll first find stalls selling clothes and colorfully woven *redes* (hammocks); after these you can stop and sample local dishes (R$2-4), *sucos*, snacks (R$0.50-1), and fresh fruits from over 100 vendors.

By far the best place to buy baskets and other woven goods, plus beautifully made replicas of indigenous-style pottery, is the blue-and-white **Sala do Beira,** near the end of the Mercado Ver-o-Peso along Rua Castilho França. The building itself is a joy to behold; head upstairs for views of the waterfront area. (Open M-F 6am-6pm, Sa 6am-4pm, Su 6pm-noon.) Outside is the equally fascinating tip of Ver-o-Peso, where friendly old women sell a number of elixirs and scents to cure any malady under the sun. When added to a bath, *Chama Dinheiro* and *Sexo da Bota* are reported to make one richer and more attractive (respectively); *Garaffa Pulmonar*, if taken orally, is said to cure a cough or respiratory problem. Rua Mercado Occidental, a small perpendicular street, has several stores that sell dried Amazonian seeds, roots, and leaves by the kilogram. **Produtos Naturais da Amazônia** has an excellent selection at bargain prices, labelled by name and indication. (☎212 3552. Open M-Sa 8am-5pm, Su 8am-noon.)

On weekends, the **Feira do Artesanato,** lining the entire side of Pça. da República along Av. Pres. Vargas, is an excellent place to pick up jewelry (some made from forest seeds), bags, baskets, CDs, and most other locally produced goods. There are also vendors selling cheap eats (R$1 for *salgados* and *sucos*) near the entrance. (Open F-Su 8am-5pm.) **Rua Santo Antônio,** a cobblestone pedestrian street parallel to the waterfront, is the best place to pick up swimwear and inexpensive clothing. Street vendors at most corners also have benches where you can stop to enjoy a plateful of *maniçoba* and other local dishes.

A good alternative to the high-priced malls is **Shopping Popular,** a modest block of stores selling handicrafts, at Av. Assis de Vasconcelos and Rua Gaspar Viandra. There's also an Internet café here (see **Internet Access,** p. 459). For mall-lovers,

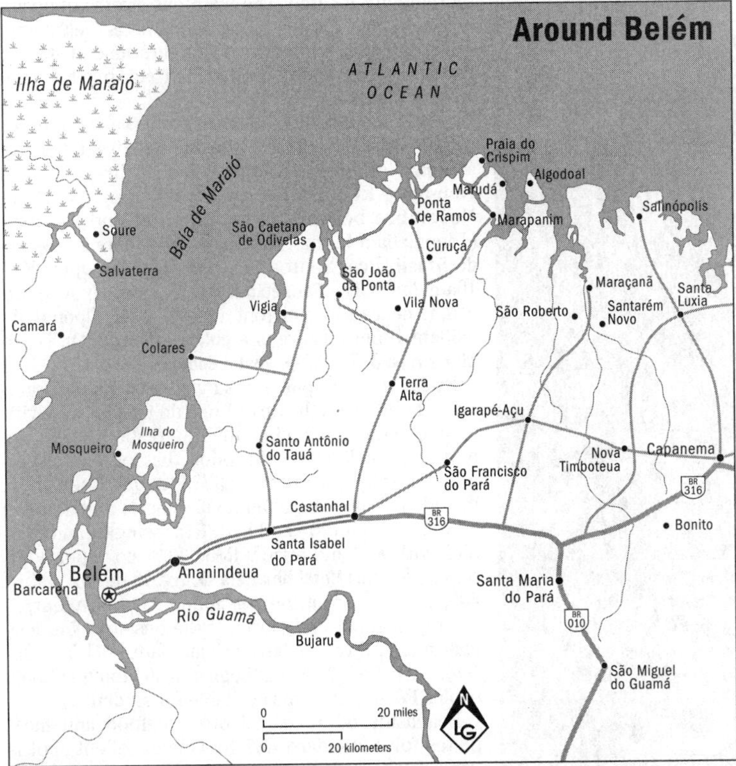

Iguatemi Shopping, on Travessa Padre Eutiquio and Rua Viega Cabral, does not disappoint. The giant building houses several large department stores and a *praça de alimentação* (food court) with kilos and fast food chains. There's a convenient shoe repair near the entrance, and several shops that process film. (Open M-Sa 10am-10pm, Su 1-10pm). Iguatemi's bigger sibling (with more stores, a bigger cinema, and even a post office) is the **Castanheira Shopping Center,** 6km from the *centro* along Av. Almirante Barrosa. To get there, take any Castanheira bus from the *rodoviária* or *comércio;* the ride takes about 40min.

AROUND BELÉM

ILHA DO MOSQUEIRO ☎91

Mosqueiro is the preferred summer destination for wealthy Belenenses, many of whom have impressive homes along the Av. Beira Mar overlooking the waterfront. There isn't much to do in Mosqueiro other than bake on the beach and sip drinks in shady *barracas*, but it's an excellent place to get away from the city for a day or two. The main road running parallel to the beach is Av. Beira Mar; at Pça. Condurú (look for the giant Tony Lanches restaurant), the street branches off into Av. 16 de Novembro, leading to the *vila* (center) 3km away, where some services and res-

ꟷIE LOCAL LEGEND

MUST'VE BEEN THE BOTO

'he legend of the mysterious boto *s one of the most popular in the mazon, and can be heard in a ariety of versions throughout the Amazon Basin.*

'he *boto* (a type of river dolphin) oves a good party, and can often e seen hanging out in nearby vaters whenever people are celeorating near the shore). When the noon is full, however, things change—literally. During the full noon, the *boto* can supposedly ransforms himself (temporarily) nto a handsome and charismatic oung man, usually dressed ntirely in white.

At this point the *boto* is free at ast to join the party. Apparently, his charming character also has a vay with young, unmarried vomen. Under the full moon's ight, the *boto* is said to sweep one lady off her feet. He is completely indistinguishable from any other young man, except for one hing: if someone were to remove nis hat, they would find the blownole of a dolphin. Of course, it never occurs to any of his dancing partners to check.

Just before dawn, the *boto* supposedly slips away, back to the mazon, where he resumes his life is a dolphin. His lady friend nakes her way back to the village. Should she happen to give birth nine months later, she will explain o her parents (as unwed mothers n the Amazon have been known o do), "it was the *boto.*"

taurants are located. The main bus stop is opposite Pça. Condurú. Farther along Beira Mar is the tranquil **Praia do Farol,** named for the lighthouse at its tip. Buses are infrequent along this road, but the 1km walk is pleasant.

Several companies run buses from the *rodoviária* in Belém to Mosqueiro. **Beira-Dão** (☎226 1162) stops at Pça. Condurú and in the *vila* (1½hr.; every hr. 7am-5pm; R$2.50). **City buses** run along Av. 16 de Novembro between the waterfront and the *vila* (15min.; 6am-11pm; R$1). In the *vila* there is a **Banco do Brasil,** Pça. Santos 17. (☎3771 2803. Open M-F 10am-3pm.) The **Farmácia Nova,** Av. 16 de Novembro 540, is near the waterfront. (☎3771 1021. Open daily 6:30am-10pm.) There is a **police office** at Av. Beira Mar s/n (☎3771 3509). **Postal code:** 66000-000.

By far the best place to stay is **Hotel Farol ❷**, in a 1920s building on the tip of Praia do Farol beach with an exquisite view and an inviting restaurant. In the morning check out the tide pools that form in the volcanic rocks outside. (☎3771 2095. Breakfast included. Singles with fan R$35. Singles and doubles with fan, *frigo-bar*, and bath R$55; singles and doubles with A/C and a view R$60. 20% extra per additional person.) **Hotel Ilha Bela ❷,** Av. 16 de Novembro 409, 2 blocks from the beach and Av. Beira Mar, is slightly cheaper and closer to the bus stop, but less charming. All rooms have private bath, A/C, TV, and *frigo-bar*. (☎3771 1612. Singles R$40; doubles R$50; triples R$60. Discounts available for students.)

Beachside *barracas* all offer seafood and meat plates for a standard R$7-15. One excellent spot is **Ponto de Encontro ❶,** on Av. Beira Mar after the Av. 16 de Novembro junction, surrounded by trees. The friendly chefs can prepare vegetarian plates (R$5) with salad, beans, and rice. (☎3771 3230. Open Tu-Th 8am-11pm, F-Su 8am-1am. Live music Sa and Su. Cover R$1.50.) A bit farther down the beach, **Barraca Nativa ❶** offers healthier options, including various types of sandwiches (R$2) and fresh *sucos* (R$1). (Open Tu-Su 11am-9pm.) **Tony Lanches ❶,** at the corner of Av. Beira Mar and Av. 16 de Novembro, is a 24hr. place with creative burgers like the "Big Boss" (egg, ham, cheese, and a giant chicken patty; R$4) as well as blended juices and yogurt drinks (R$1-3). Across the street, the **Mercadinho Talismã** has basics. (☎3771 2268. Open M-Sa 7am-1pm and 3-8:30pm, Su 7am-1pm. Visa.)

SALINÓPOLIS ☎91

Salinas, as the town is commonly known, is a seasonal beach resort that gets packed in July. It boasts several **beaches** and a well-developed tourist infrastructure resulting from several years of major investment by Pará state. Salinas is the optimal summer holiday spot, with long boardwalks, ice cream parlors, and a lively evening bar scene. However, outside of July, it becomes something of a ghost town. During the peak season, there are often live bands and other events organized nightly; it's best to check with the Paratur office in Belém (☎242 1118; www.paratur.pa.gov.br) for information before you go.

The *vila* (center) is located along **Avenida Miguel Santa Brigada,** where the *rodoviária* and several small restaurants are found. At one end of the avenue is the entrance to **Praia Maçarico.** Two kilometers farther along the road is the newly renovated **Orla de Maçarico,** a bike path and boardwalk along which there are a few bars and hotels. The boardwalk, which runs along rolling dunes and mangroves, attracts joggers and bikers by day and barhopping revelers by night. **Praia da Corvina,** at the end of the Orla, is a calm, windswept beach with fewer people and more privacy than Praia Maçarico. During the day, most people head to the packed white sand of **Praia da Atalaia,** a strip of dunes and beach 14km from the *vila* filled with bars blasting *samba.* To get to this beach, catch one of the yellow municipal buses that pass by the Orla and *vila* (30min.; every hr. 9am-8pm; R$1.40).

Buses leave from Salinópolis's Terminal Rodoviário, on Avenida Miguel Santa Brigada (☎423 1783, 423 4400). **Viação Princesa** (☎423 1148) runs comfortable *frescão* buses to Belém (3½hr.; 5 per day; R$11). Services in town include: an ATM at **Banco do Brasil,** Av. Miguel Brigada s/n (☎423 3890; open M-F 10am-3pm); the **Mercadinho Junior,** at the entrance to Atalaia, which stocks ice, canned food, and other basic supplies (☎464 1227; open daily 9am-6pm); a **police hotline,** for reporting crime or theft (☎423 1443); a pharmacy, **Farmácia Leão,** Av. Miguel Santa Brigada s/n (☎423 1039; open M-Sa 9am-7pm); and a **hospital** (☎423 1787; open daily 6am-midnight). **Postal code:** 68721-000.

Along Praia do Atalaia, there are several *pousadas* right on the beach overlooking the waves. However, it's best to stay on the Orla; it's close to the beach, within walking distance of the *vila*, and quieter than Praia Atalaia. **Hotel Mar e Onda ❷,** on the left side of the Orla after the main arch, has friendly owners and spotless rooms with A/C. (☎423 3045. Breakfast included. Singles and doubles with private bath, TV, and *frigo-bar* R$40.) **Hotel Flórida ❸,** one block further down the Orla, rents out furnished, spacious suites with private bath, A/C, *frigo-bar*, satellite TV, and small front patio for the entire weekend (F-M)—a good value for families. (☎423 2155. Daily rates: doubles R$50; triples R$60; quads R$70. Weekend rates: doubles R$200; triples R$230; quads R$270. AmEx/MC/V.) Salinópolis has some excellent restaurants and food stalls that cater to almost every budget. At Pça. de Alimentaçao, next door to Hotel Mar e Onda, small **stalls ❶** cook up hot soups, fish dishes, and a variety of pizzas for about R$3. **Cia. Paulista ❷,** along the Orla, has an enormous selection of pizzas. (☎423 1201. Pizzas R$9-11. Open M-Sa noon-11pm.)

ILHA DE MARAJÓ

Ilha de Marajó is nicknamed Ilha de Paraíso by its inhabitants, and with good reason: with a terrain larger than several European countries (Marajó is 50,000 square kilometers) and relatively few people, nature here is at its essence. Belém—with its fast-paced atmosphere, hordes of traffic, and immense buildings—couldn't seem farther away: countless beaches, many only accessible by boat, adorn the island's perimeter and herds of buffalo roam the center. Locals, many of whom are descended from the indigenous Marajó and continue the culture's traditions of pottery and leather work, and warmly welcome visitors. The tourist infrastructure on the island is minimal, and most visitors make arrangements to stay in all-inclusive *fazenda*, many of which arrange island tours and have camping facilities. Bring insect repellent and a mosquito net if your accommodation does not provide one. There are very limited supplies in Soure (food, basic medicines, and toiletries), so you might find it easier to stock up in Belém prior to arrival. Because many of the island's natural attractions are far apart, it's best to come here for at least a few days to leave ample time for transport and absorbing the scenery.

AT A GLANCE: ILHA DE MARAJÓ

AREA: Mostly flat and surrounded by mangrove swamps and beaches; the interior has several rivers and waterfalls, many of which appear seasonally.

CLIMATE: Seasonal temperature variation is minimal—the island benefits from perpetually sunny skies and warm weather. However, the rainy season peaks Jan.-June with 400cm of rain, when many roads become impassable and boat transport is recommended.

WHEN TO GO: To avoid the rainy season and resulting transportation difficulties, July-Dec. is the best time to go.

HIGHLIGHTS: Herds of buffalo; isolated beaches; and a vast saltwater marshland perfect for bird-watching (and alligator-avoiding).

GATEWAY TOWNS: Most people arrive at the tiny port area of Camará and travel by bus to Salvaterra or Soure (p. 472), Marajó's two largest towns. From either town, you can book accommodations at a *fazenda* and explore nearby beaches.

CAMPING: Camping alone is not permitted on the beaches; inland the hoards of insects might make it nearly impossible. Some *fazendas* also run campgrounds.

SOURE ☎91

The tiny capital of Ilha de Marajó, filled with bicycles and buffalo, provides the perfect base from which to explore the island's attractions and stock up on supplies or souvenirs, including the excellent locally produced cheese, *queijo marajoana*. Leather goods can be found at the artisan's collective **SOMA,** on Rua Quarta (Rua 4) near the Mercado Municipal. (Open M-Sa 8am-noon and 2:30-6pm, Su 8am-noon. MC.) Navigating the town is a breeze, because it is built on a grid system of *ruas* running parallel to the waterfront and perpendicular *travessas*. Rua Primeira (Rua 1) traces the waterfront and the main pier *(trapiche)*, where ferries arrive from across the river. The *centro* is at the intersection of Rua 4 and Travessa 16.

You can fly directly into Soure (the airstrip is off Rua 4 near the waterfront); see the Ilha de Marajó Transportation section for more information. **Puma Air** (☎3741 2225, 9963 8670) has direct **flights** from Belém to Soure (20min.; R$200-250). From Camará and Salvaterra, municipal **buses** take passengers to the dock at the Rio Paracauary (R$2), where tiny vessels chug across to Soure's shore (10min.; R$0.75). Or, for R$2 more, you can sit in an air-conditioned **minivan** while the driver navigates the roads and the river barge across the Paracauary. **Enasa** (☎257 2774, 257 1400) is the only operator with direct **boats** to Soure from Belém (3hr.; departs Belém F 8pm, returns Su 3pm; R$9.50). There are several companies that run from Belém to Camará and Salvaterra, from which public transport is readily available for the 30-45min. ride to Soure. Most road transport is based on the boat schedules; outside of these times, transport to Soure can be more difficult. **Bike Tur,** on Rua 3 at Travessa 14, rents bikes (R$20 per day). Services available in Soure include: **tourist office,** on Rua 3 in front of the Mercado Municipal (open daily 7:30am-5pm); **Banco do Brasil,** on Rua 3 (☎3741 1385; open M-F 10am-3pm); **police station** Travessa 15 259 (☎3741 1350); the very basic **Farmácia Celeste,** on Rua 2 (☎3741 1487). The **post office** is at the intersection of Rua 2 and Travessa 14 (open M-F 10am-3pm). **Postal code:** 66000-000.

Hotel Marajó ❷, off Rua 4 near the Mercado Municipal at Pça. Inhangaíba, is the best place to stay in town, though it's far from the beaches. Pleasant, airy rooms with TV, A/C, *frigo-bar*, and private bath overlook a pool and patio, and the bar becomes a popular dance spot on Saturday nights. (☎3741 1396. Singles R$40; doubles R$60; triples R$65. MC/V.) Most prefer to arrange accommodations at a *pousada* or *fazenda* elsewhere on the island (p. 473). The best place for food is the collection of stalls at the **Mercado Municipal ❶**, where you can enjoy a filling meal of buffalo, chicken, or fish with rice, beans, pasta, and salad for R$3. (Open daily 11am-9pm.) Next door at the market, fresh fruits and vegetables are for sale. The **Restaurant/Bar Patú Anú ❶**, at the corner of Rua 2 and Travessa 14, is owned by an exceedingly friendly woman named Eunice who serves large portions and excellent stuffed crab. (Meals R$7. Drinks R$2. Open daily 7am-1am.) There are also a couple of waterfront bars with snacks (R$1-2). (Open daily from 9pm.)

ELSEWHERE ON ILHA DE MARAJÓ ☎91

From Belém, most boats head to the closest port town of **Camará. Salvaterra** is about 20km north along the shore, and Soure is 8km farther, situated inland on the Rio Paracauary. Buses meet the boats arriving from Belém to take travelers to these towns; several ferries cross the Paracauary, one of which takes vehicles as well. Aside from buses, there is very little visitor infrastructure on Marajó, most of which is based in Soure or the smaller town of Salvaterra. Navigating the wilderness on your own is not recommended; *fazendas* and most hotels organize trips to the island's interior or more remote beaches. Package tours can also be purchased through a number of agents in Belém. **Valeverde,** at Belém's Estação das Docas, offers 2-day excursions that include animal watching and one night in a *fazenda.* (☎212 3388; valeverdeturismo.com.br. 2-day excursions R$160 per person.)

Puma Air (☎3741 2225, 9963 8670) has flights from Belém to Soure and Salvaterra (20min.; R$200-250); schedules vary, so check in Belém. Outside of Soure, island transport is limited to municipal buses, private minivans, and boats. From Camará, city **buses** head to Salvaterra (30min.; every hr.; R$2) and then on to Rio Paracauary (45min.; R$2) for the crossing to Soure. A more comfortable option is to ride in an air-conditioned **minivan,** which can drop you off right at your hotel or *fazenda;* these operate only around the scheduled ferry arrivals and departures from Belém (45min.; R$4). From Belém, several **boat** companies serve Marajó daily from the Terminal Hidroviário, on Av. Marechal Hermes just south of Av. Visconde de Souza Franca (departs for Camará 6, 10am; returns 2:30, 3pm). **Rodofluvial Banav** (☎9961 2203, 249 8617) has comfortable, large boats with airy decks to Camará (3½hr.; 1 per day; R$9.50). Boats arrive at the port in Camará, a tiny dock with a couple of snack shops and buses waiting to take passengers to Soure. Another option on the island is the cheap and efficient **moto-taxis,** identifiable by the driver's uniform or extra helmet. These operate within the towns and can take you to nearby beaches; to get from town to town, take either a city bus or minivan.

Most accommodations elsewhere on Marajó are in *fazendas* and campsites either on the outskirts of towns or in the island's interior. Camping on beaches is not permitted, and it is not advisable to pitch a tent outside designated campgrounds. Check with the Paratur office in Belém for accommodations listings. Reservations should be made at *pousadas* and *fazendas* from Belém or Soure. **Pousada & Camping Boto ❶/❷**, on Rodovia Alcindo Cacela at Travessa 5, on the outskirts of Salvaterra, has cheap cabins and hammocks with breakfast included, plus a decent in-house restaurant. (☎3765 1539; www.botoonline.hpg.com.br; pousadaboto@bol.com.br. 2-person suites with fan R$35; with TV, *frigo-bar*, A/C, and bath R$45. Hammocks R$15. 2-person tents with locker and bath R$15). **Fazenda Araruna ❸**, outside of Soure in a large clearing, is accessible by moto-taxi. Pleasant cottages include all meals, some with local foods like buffalo milk and tapioca cake. Araruna also offers *folclórico* shows and canoe rides along the Rio Paracauary. (☎3741 1474, 9605 8674; www.cruzeirinho.hpg.com.br. Singles R$50;

doubles R$70.) **Fazenda Camburupy ❶**, also near the outskirts of Soure, has well-decorated rooms with hammocks and beds, and a front lobby filled with traditional-style pottery. The management can arrange tours and visits to see *vaqueiros* (buffalo cowboys) in action. Breakfast included; other meals R$5-15. (☎9969 8160; fazendacamburupy@yahoo.com.br. Hammocks R15. Dorms R$20. Seasonal discounts available.)

SANTARÉM ☎93

Santarém, the third largest city on the Brazilian stretch of the Amazon River, sits at the meeting of the Rio Tapajós and Rio Amazonas, halfway between Belém and Manaus. Jesuits started the Tapajós mission here in 1661, and the village that sprang up around it was christened Santarém in 1758. Today Santarém is a pleasant city of refreshing breezes and slowly decaying buildings with ornately tiled facades. Riverboats dock along a renovated waterfront where fishermen sell their morning's catch. There are several nearby beaches, including an excellent one at Alter do Chão (see p. 480), a relaxed village 35km away.

TRANSPORTATION

Flights: Aeroporto Santarém, Estrada Eduardo Gomes s/n (☎522 4328; fax 523 2127), is about 13km from the *centro*. Taxis into town R$35. Buses labelled "Aeroporto" leave from the stop in front of Santarém Palace Hotel at 6:30am, then hourly 9:30am-5:30pm. Avoid the "Aeroporto V. Cuiabá" bus. Buses from the airport leave daily on the hour 5am-9pm. New City, Rio Dourado, and Amazon Park hotels offer an airport shuttle for guests. The small terminal has counters for carriers **Meta, Penta, Rico, TAM, Tavaj, Varig,** and smaller *aero-taxi* companies. Lockers available.

Buses: Terminal Rodoviário Dr. Jonathas de Almeida e Silva, Av. Cuiabá s/n. From the *centro,* take the "Rotagem" bus (R$1), which stops around the corner from the station, just beyond the overpass. Taxi R$8. Most long-distance routes past Rurópolis become virtually impassable or take a week during the wet season, and most bus service ceases Mar.-June. **Expresso Maringa** (☎522 5227) runs to Cuiabá (min. 48hr.; M, Th, Sa 6pm; R$202). There is no bus service Mar.-June.

Boats: Docas do Pará, about 2.5km from the *centro,* behind the Cargill building. Take any "Orla Fluvial" or "Orla via Museu" bus from the waterfront (R$1). Taxi R$6. A line of agencies sell passage on the same boats headed up or down river. Two are **Agência Tarcisio Lopes** (☎522 2034) and **Agência P.C. Almeida** (☎523 0547). Boats sail to **Belém** (48hr.; W-Su noon; R$100-120) and **Manaus** (48-56hr.; M-Sa 3-4pm; R$100). They also sell tickets on the Lancha Ajato 2001 speedboat to **Manaus** (14hr.; W, Sa 7am; R$140) via **Parintins** (6hr.; R$70).

Car Rental: Bill Car, Av. Mendonça Furtado 1603 (☎522 1705; billcar@stm.inter-conect.com.br). Minimum rental age 21. R$70 per day with 100km. Basic insurance R$13 per day. Open M-F 7am-6pm, Sa 7am-2pm. AmEx/V.

ORIENTATION & PRACTICAL INFORMATION

The *centro* is on a bulge of land between the waterfront and **Avenida Rui Barbosa,** and has a cluster of shops, hotels, and restaurants. A 3.5km renovated waterfront promenade runs from the **Praça São Sebastião** along Rua Adriano Pimentel, which becomes **Avenida Tapajós.** Boats from Belém and Manaus arrive at the **Docas do Pará** behind the giant Cargill building at the end of the waterfront.

Tourist Office: There is no tourist office but there are several travel agencies that can provide information. Try one of the following:

Santarém Tur, Rua Adriano Pimentel 44 (☎522 4877; fax 522 3141; www.santaremtur.com.br), 1 block to the right of Restaurante Mascote on the waterfront. A helpful travel agency that can book flights and offers tours around Santarém. These include: half-day (R$70 per person for 2 people, R$60 for 4) city tours and visits to Santa Lúcia Forest; full-day visits (R$170) to the Mirante dos Tapajós and Maicá Lake for bird watching, piranha fishing, and canoe trips. Group discounts, but with a lack of visitors to Santarém, it can be hard to scrape a group together. English brochure and mediocre maps of Santarém. Little English spoken in office, but guides speak English, French, and Spanish. Open M-F 8am-6pm, Sa 8am-noon. AmEx/MC/V.

Amazon Tours, Travessa Turiano Meira 1084 (☎522 2620, 9122 0299; www.amazonriver.com), 7 blocks up from Av. Rui Barbosa. Run by American Steve Alexander, a long-time resident of Santarém. Steve is full of information about things to see and do around Santarém. Offers daytrips to Bosque Santa Lúcia and Tapajós National Forest as well as multi-day river tours. These include a 3-night trip to Monte Alegre to see the prehistoric rock paintings at Serras Paituna and Ererê that are estimated to be 900-12,000 years old. Trips average US$125 per day for 2 people, and US$100 for 4. Steve can also refer you to reputable local guides. Tours are best organized by email or telephone. Open M-F 7-11am.

Airlines: All flight carriers accept AmEx/MC/V. **Meta,** Av. Rui Barbosa 528 (☎/fax 522 6221). Open M-F 7am-6pm, Sa 7am-noon. **Penta,** Travessa 15 de Novembro 183 (☎523 2220; fax 512 5000). Open M-F 8am-noon and 2-5:30pm, Sa 7:30am-noon. **Rico,** Travessa Floriano Peixoto 556 (☎/fax 523 3997). Open M-F 7am-noon and 2-6pm, Sa 7am-noon. **TAM,** Av. Mendonça Furtado 913 (☎523 9450, fax 523 9452). Open M-F 8am-6pm, Sa 8am-noon. **Tavaj,** Travessa Otaviano de Matos 95 (☎522 7666). Open M-F 8am-noon and 2-6pm, Sa 8am-noon. **Varig,** Av. Rui Barbosa 790 (☎523 2488, fax 523 5145). Open M-F 8am-noon and 2-5:30pm, Sa 8:30am-noon.

Ticket Agencies: Curuá-Una Turismo, Travessa 15 de Novembro 123 (☎522 6611; fax 522 6318), between Rua Floriano Peixoto and Rua Galdino Veloso. Sells domestic and international flights. Open M-F 8am-6pm, Sa 8am-noon.

Currency Exchange: Ourominas, Travessa dos Mártires 198 (☎522 7655), at Rua Galdino Veloso. Changes US dollars. Open M-F 7am-5:30pm, Sa 7am-noon. An unmarked **exchange office,** Av. Rui Barbosa 646 (☎522 2281), at Travessa 15 de Novembro, exchanges US dollars and traveler's checks. Open M-Sa 8am-noon and 2-5:30pm.

ATMs: HSBC, Rua Floriano Peixoto 743 (☎523 255), across from Travessa Francisco Corrêa. 24hr. ATMs accept Cirrus/PLUS/AmEx/MC/V cards. **Bradesco,** Av. Rui Barbosa 756 (☎523 2502), at Travessa 15 de Agosto. 24hr. ATMs accept Visa cards. **Banco do Brasil,** Av. Rio Barbosa 794 (☎523 2600), at Travessa dos Mártires, has 2 ATMs that accept Visa/PLUS cards. Open daily 6am-10pm.

Public Market: There are two public markets along the waterfront. **Mercado Municipal e Modelo,** 200m left of Pça. da Matriz, has a wide selection of hammocks, fishing gear, and fish, as well as smaller meat and produce sections. **Mercado 2000,** about 1km farther along Av. Tapajós toward the Docas do Pará, is a large indoor market with a larger choice of produce as well as meat, fish, and a few artisanal stalls. There is also a **morning market** to the left of the Mercado Modelo that sells fish and fresh produce.

Supermarket: Cristo Rei Supermercado, Av. Tapajós 384 (☎522 4496), at Travessa Padre João, just left of the Mercado Municipal. Open M-Sa 7am-8pm, Su 7am-noon.

Laundromat: Lavanderia Storil, Travessa Turiano Meira 167 (☎523 1329), on the 2nd fl. above Planet Arcade. R$5 per kg. Same-day service. Open M-F 8am-noon and 2-6pm, Sa 8am-noon and 2-4pm.

Police: Polícia Militar (☎533 2477), Pça. Rodrigues dos Santos opposite the post office.

Hospital: Hospital Imaculada Conceição, Travessa 7 de Setembro 611 (☎522 5051), 100m up from Av. Mendonça Furtado.

Telephones: TeleTrin, Rua Siqueira Campos 511 (☎523 2701), opposite Pça. Rodrigues dos Santos. Calls to US R$2.30 per min., Europe and Australia R$4 per min., rest of the Americas R$3.68 per min. Open M-F 7:30am-6pm, Sa 7:30am-2pm. Visa.

Internet Access: Cyber Café Orla, Av. Tapajós 418 (☎523 0023), at Travessa dos Mártires. R$1.50 per 30min. Open M-Sa 8am-11pm, Su 4-11pm. **Amazon.net,** Av. Mendonça Furtado 1120 (☎523 3223). R$3 per hr. Open M-Sa 8am-10:30pm.

Crafts: Loja Regional Muiraquitá, Rua Sen. Lameira Bittencourt 131 (☎522 7164), opposite Pça. do Pescador. Every inch is jam-packed with quality curiosities including masks, pottery, baskets, walking sticks, *licor de tamarindo,* slingshots, and *cuia* gourd castanets. Open M-Sa 8am-noon and 2-6pm. MC/V. **Casa do Artesanato,** Rua Sen. Lameira Bittencourt 69A (☎9975 3943). Sells a smaller selection of pots, postcards, and woven purses. Open M-F 8am-noon and 2-6pm, Sa 8am-noon and 2-4pm.

Post Office: Pça. da Bandeira 801 (☎523 1178), at Travessa Octaviano de Matos and Rua Siqueira Campos. Open M-F 8am-4pm. **Postal code:** 68000-000.

ACCOMMODATIONS

Santarém's accommodations run the gamut from simple cells to poolside luxury suites. Mid-range hotels are often a good value with discounts given for paying cash. All hotels listed below include breakfast.

Hotel Brasil, Travessa dos Mártires 30 (☎523 5177), 1 block from Pça. da Matriz down Rua Senador Lameira Bittencourt. A good, affordable choice set in an old building with high ceilings and wood floors. There are 2 rooms with A/C, but rooms with fan have large windows overlooking the bustle below. In some rooms, the walls only go part-way up so you might hear your neighbor over your fan. The lobby wall sports an impressive collection of baseball caps. Common bath. Singles with fan R$25, with A/C R$35; doubles with fan R$30, with A/C R$35. ❶

Rio Dourado Hotel, Rua Floriano Peixoto 799 (☎523 2174), behind the Mercado Municipal. This modern hotel has sizable rooms with good mattresses, A/C, TV, phone, and *frigo-bar.* Watch out for the 60s egg chairs and the aquarium with a disconcerting skull in the lobby. Upstairs air-conditioned common room has a good view of the market and river. Upstairs rooms are brighter. Free van from airport. Singles R$45; doubles R$60; triples R$75. 30% more if you pay by credit card. AmEx/MC/V. ❷

New City Hotel, Travessa Francisco Corrêa 200 (☎522 0355), between Travessa Floriano Peixoto and Rua Galdino Veloso. New City focuses on the little details, from toilet lid cozies with little plastic flowers to black-light pictures of the forest in your room. Comfortable rooms all have A/C, TV, phone, and *frigo-bar.* Hot shower R$3 per 10min. Free airport van. Singles R$45; doubles R$60; triples R$75. ❷

Alvorada Hotel, Rua Senador Lameira Bittencourt 179 (☎522 5340), overlooking Pça. do Pescador, behind Restaurante Mascote. This pleasant family-run hotel has front rooms with fans and a good view of the Mirante does Tapajós. Shared bath. Singles with fan R$15, with A/C R$28; doubles with fan R$25, with A/C R$36. ❶

Brisa Hotel, Rua Senador Lameira Bittencourt 5 (☎/fax 522 1018), on the opposite corner of Pça. do Pescador from Restaurante Mascote. The minimalist yet colorful design (a bit heavy on the lime green) is reminiscent of a Miami retirement home. A/C rooms have TV, *frigo-bar,* and bath. The upstairs room with fan has large windows and common bath. Singles with fan R$20, with A/C R$30; doubles R$30; triples R$50. ❶

Mirante Hotel, Travessa Francisco Corrêa 115 (☎523 1361; www.mirantehotel.com), between Rua Siqueira Campos and Travessa Floriano Peixoto. A popular and central hotel. All rooms have A/C, TV, *frigo-bar,* phone, and hot-water bath. Several rooms have small safes. Free Internet access. Singles R$59; doubles R$69; triples R$78. MC/V. ❸

Amazon Park Hotel, Av. Mendonça Furtado 4120 (☎523 2800; fax 522 2631; amazon@netsan.com.br), an R$8 taxi ride from the *centro.* Set on a hill overlooking the river on the outskirts of town, the luxurious Amazon Park has it all: swimming pool, nightclub,

restaurant, gift shop, good views, and even native plants in the bathroom. Each room comes with its own balcony—the best place to check out the pool or the Mirante dos Tapajós. Sept.-Apr. singles R$130; doubles R$141. May-Aug. singles R$89; doubles R$98. 10% hotel tax. AmEx/MC/V. ❺

Brasil Grande Hotel, Travessa 15 de Agosto 213 (☎522 5660), between Rua Floriano Peixoto and Rua Galdino Veloso. The sombre lobby of the Brasil Grande has dark wood walls and a brooding Mona Lisa, but rooms are bright and large. All have A/C, TV, phone, and *frigo-bar.* Also has a decent restaurant upstairs. Singles R$50; doubles R$60; triples R$78. ❸

Central Hotel, Av. Tapajós 208 (☎522 4920), on the waterfront between Travessa 15 de Agosto and Travessa 15 de Novembro. A straightforward place on the water, Central features several decent white rooms done up with orange trim. The balcony has a good view of the river nearby. Singles with fan R$25, with A/C R$30; doubles with fan R$30, with A/C R$45. ❶

Equatorial Hotel, Travessa Silvino Pinto 14 (☎522 1135), at Rua Rui Barbosa. This hotel is near the bus to Alter do Chão, and has prominent world flags painted on its shutters. A simple and cheap option that's still relatively central. The outside rooms are brighter and all share a common bath. Singles with fan R$15; with TV and window R$20, with A/C and *frigo-bar* R$35; doubles with fan R$20; with TV and window R$25; with A/C and *frigo-bar* R$45. ❶

FOOD

Options for dining out in Santarém are primarily kilos and outdoor restaurants serving a la carte dinners along the waterfront. There are numerous food stalls past the market toward the **Docas do Pará** which sell cheap, filling meals, and several stalls spring up after dark in **Pça. do Pescador.**

Peixaria Piracatu, Av. Mendonça Furtado 174 (☎523 5098). From the *centro,* walk down Rui Barbosa and past Pça. São Sebastião 2 blocks. This culinary highlight of Santarém takes fish seriously, and it shows. House specialty is *Juarez Simões* (shredded *pirarucú* with melted cheese and banana; R$30 for 2). Also excellent is *casebre* (*pirarucú* stuffed with shrimp and cheese; R$15). Open daily 8am-2am. MC/V. ❸

Restaurante Mascote, Pça. do Pescador 10 (☎523 2844). A Santarém institution for over 50 years, Mascote has outside seating next to Pça. do Pescador and air-conditioned indoor seating. They have steak (R$12-16), chicken (R$10-18), and pizza (R$7-10), and their *tucunaré* and *pirarucú* are excellent. Try the *peixe grelhado à Belle Munier* (tender *tinharé* filet with a shrimp and caper sauce; R$17). Open daily 10am-2:30pm and 5pm-1am. AmEx/MC/V. ❷

Restaurante Mistura Brasileira, Av. Tapajós 23 (☎523 2991), at Travessa 15 de Novembro. The bright and shiny Mistura Brasileira is smack in the center of the waterfront walk and a popular place to take a break for a good lunch or dinner buffet (R$11), steak (R$4.50), burger (R$2-3), or a beer. Open daily 11am-2am. ❷

Pecado da Gula, Travessa 15 de Novembro 4 (☎523 2254), on the waterfront opposite Mistura Brasileira. Pecado da Gula serves up good pizza (R$12-15) and burgers (R$2-4), as well as delicious juices (R$1-2). Open daily 7am-1am. ❶

Restaurante Santo Antônio, Av. Tapajós 2051 (☎523 1556). About 1.5km from the *centro* toward the Cargill building, behind the Shell station. Despite looking like a highway rest stop on the outside, Santo Antônio is a refined open-air restaurant with Spanish tile and cactus. *Rodízio* lunch (R$10) and dinner a la carte. Steaks (R$15-20) and huge servings of fish including *filé de pirarucú ao creme de camarão* (*pirarucú* in a shrimp sauce; R$20). English menu. Open daily 10am-2pm and 6-11pm. ❸

Delicias Caseiras Restaurante, Travessa 15 de Agosto 121 (☎523 5525), between Rua Siqueira Campos and Travessa Floriano Peixoto. Load up your plate with the self-service buffet (R$15 per kg), sit back in an air-conditioned corner, listen to the soothing music, and stare out at the sweating people who walk by. Open daily 11am-3pm. ❷

Restaurante Regional Toka do Pagode, Rua Siqueira Campos 164 (☎523 5284), at Travessa Francisco Corrêa, 1 block up from Mascote. Locals flood in for the buffet (R$12 per kg), complete with fresh and tender charcoaled meats. Dining area in a cool courtyard with ferns and paintings of tropical birds. Open M-Sa 10:30am-2:30pm. ❷

Restaurante Sacy Caseiro, Rua Floriano Peixoto 521 (☎523 2672), between Travessa dos Mártires and Travessa 15 de Agosto. A straightforward place for a good buffet (R$16 per kg) with a good meat and fish selection. Tablecloths and river paintings add a bit of style to the air-conditioned interior. Open M-Sa 11am-3pm. ❷

Bonzão Lanche, Av. Tapajós 115 (☎523 2027), at Travessa 15 de Agosto. Juice with a view. They specialize in whipping up your favorite tropical fruit concoction (R$1.20-2). Sandwiches and pizza (R$8-10) also served. Open M-Sa 7am-midnight. ❶

Brasil Grande Hotel Restaurante, Travessa 15 de Agosto 213 (☎522 5660), on the 3rd fl. of the hotel. The nicest part about this restaurant is the view from the windows on three sides. The all-you-can-eat lunch buffet (R$5.50) and all-the-meat-you-can-handle *rodízio* (R$7) are also hard to beat. Dinner is a la carte (entrees R$8-15), including their specialty *tucunaré à Maestro Isoca* (fried *tucunaré* with rice, vegetables, and *farofa;* R$9.50). Open daily 11am-2:30pm and 6:30-8:30pm. ❷

Churrascaria e Restaurante Mutum, Travessa Otaviano de Matos 190 (☎522 6084), at Rua Galdino Veloso, 2 blocks up from the post office. A decent buffet (R$12 per kg) served under cool *barracãos* (thatched huts). Open M-Sa 10am-3pm. ❷

SIGHTS

CENTRO CULTURAL JOÃO FONA (MUSEUM DE SANTARÉM). Housed in the former city hall in pretty Pça. São Sebastião, this small museum has an interesting collection of paintings and archaeological artifacts, including Tapajós pottery, burial urns, and small human figurines. *(Pça. São Sebastião s/n. ☎522 1383. Open M-F 8am-5pm. Admission by donation.)*

MUSEU DICA FRAZÃO. For well over 50 years, Dica Frazão has been meticulously creating fabrics and women's clothing solely from her imagination and all-natural wood and grass fibers. Her home is also her workshop, and houses a small museum displaying some of her creations. Dica herself eagerly shows visitors around, and the tour includes a basket of her raw materials and the spectacular finished products that can take up to three months to make. These include festival costumes, a replica of a dress made in 1972 for a Belgian queen, a woven tablecloth for Pope John Paul II, hats, and baskets of flowers made from feathers. *(Rua Floriano Peixoto 281. ☎522 1026. Open daily whenever Dona Dica is around, usually 7am-7pm. Admission by donation.)*

PRAIA DO MARACANÃ. This popular beach is 20min. from town by bus, and its white sand is lined with bars and restaurants. There is a quieter beach to the left of the main stretch. During the wet season, the beach virtually disappears. *(Take any "Maracanã" bus from the stop opposite the cinema.)*

MIRANTE DOS TAPAJÓS. The meeting of the dark blue waters of Rio Tapajós with the muddy brown of Rio Amazonas can clearly be seen from the waterfront. The viewpoint on a small hill between Museu Dica Frazão and Centro Cultural João Fona has a better vantage point. You would never guess it, but this hill used to be the site of the Santarém fort.

NIGHTLIFE & ENTERTAINMENT

Nightlife in Santarém usually entails sitting at outdoor bars and restaurants along the waterfront with a cold *chopp*. Locals stroll the promenade to catch the breeze, and music is supplied by car stereos with the trunk open to better let their huge subwoofers pump out the base. On the weekends, several dance clubs provide a change of scene. If you're in the mood to just sit back and relax, consider catching one of the Hollywood action films screened nightly at **Cinerama,** Av. Rui Barbosa. (☎522 5277. Shows at 7:30pm. R$4.)

Fun House, Av. Mendonça Furtado s/n, next to the Boaslojas store at Av. Barão do Rio Branco. The best dance club for many a mile spins techno all night on Th and Su. Young and beautiful locals jam the air-conditioned, split-level dance floor and exclusive VIP area, or let go under the flashing lights and amidst the machine-generated smoke and multimedia screens. Beer in plastic bottles R$2. Dress is dressy-casual. Cover R$15. Open Th, Sa 11:30pm-dawn.

Restaurante Mascotinho, Travessa Adriano Pimentel s/n (☎523 2399). The terrace seating over the water is an ideal place to enjoy a breeze, beer, and sunset. The full menu features pasta (R$6-12), steak (R$10), hamburgers (R$3), and pizza (medium R$8-12), for those who like something to go with their *cerveja gelada.* Open daily 5pm-1am. AmEx/MC/V.

MPBar, Av. São Sebastião 970 (☎523 2050), at Travessa Silvino Pinto, 1 block up from Rua Rui Barbosa. A relaxed and unpretentious place to have a beer and listen to good live MPB (Th-Sa after 9pm). Open Tu-Su 5pm-late.

Picanha Grill, Av. Mendonça Furtado 1031, at Travessa Dom Amando, 100m to the right of TAM. Specializes in steaks (R$14-16) and live music (F-Sa after 9pm). Another good place to sit under the stars with a cold one. Open Tu-Su 6:30pm-1am.

ALTER DO CHÃO ☎93

Located 33km from Santarém and over 700km from the Atlantic, the laid-back village of Alter do Chão, on the shores of the Rio Tapajós, has the best **beach** on the Amazon. On the weekend, the picture-perfect white sands fill with locals from Santarém. Here, the toughest parts the day will be choosing where to eat and making sure your tan is even. Alter do Chão is a beautiful and relaxed place and a perfect place to throw away your watch and lose track of the days (or weeks), though travelers should note that the beaches are underwater in June and July.

TRANSPORTATION. **Buses** run to Santarém (1hr.; M-Sa 10 per day 6am-7:20pm, Su 10 per day 7am-5pm; R$1.80). Four-person **rowboats** run to and from the beach (R$1). **Locaiaque Borari,** by the string of shacks on the beach 400m to the left of the *praça*, rents **kayaks** (R$2 per hr.). **Mingote Mercantil,** next to the Pousada do Mingote in the *praça*, sells essentials. (Open daily 6am-8pm.)

ORIENTATION & PRACTICAL INFORMATION. Buses stop in front of the corner store at the only real **intersection** in town. Walking down **Travessa Agostinho A. Labato,** you pass a couple *pousadas* and good artesanal shops before reaching the small *praça* and yellow church overlooking the water. Straight ahead a long sandbar juts toward you, lined with a string of thatched roof shacks. To the left of the *praça* is another beach with several more shacks.

There is a **police** booth in the *praça* by the river. For medical services, follow the red cross signs from the intersection to the **Centro de Saúde de Alter do Chão,** Rua Lauro Sodré s/n. (Open M-F 7am-7pm.) The **post office** is 200m up Travessa Agostinho A. Lobato from the intersection. (Open M-F 8am-noon.) There is **no currency exchange** in town, as cash is king in Alter do Chão. **Arte Nativa,** Av. Turiano Meira 127, opposite the church, has a good selection of pottery, wood carvings, and masks. (☎527 1295. Open daily 8am-8pm.) **Araweté Indigenous Arts,** Av. Turiano Meira 567, sells swimwear in addition to various with carvings and baskets. (☎9125 5605. Open daily 8am-6pm.)

ACCOMMODATIONS. There are a small number of *pousadas* geared toward the needs of backpackers clustered near the beach. Prices vary, and during the low season (May-Aug.), bargaining can pay off, especially for longer stays. **Pousada e Restaurante Alter do Chão ❶,** Rua Lauro Sodré 74, to the right of the *praça* 200m toward Pizzaria D'Italia, has rooms with fan or A/C for up to five, all around a hanging garden. (☎527 1215. Breakfast for 2 included. Singles with fan R$15, with A/C R$30; doubles with fan R$30, with A/C R$45. R$5 per additional person.) **Pousada Tia Marilda ❶,** Travessa Agostinho A. Lobato 559, on the right walking from the bus stop to the water, is a popular *pousada* with five rooms all in a row, opening onto a small garden. (☎527 1144. Breakfast included. Singles with A/C and TV R$15; doubles with fan R$15, with A/C and TV R$25.) **Pousada do Mingote ❷,** Travessa Agostinho A. Lobato s/n, halfway between the bus stop and the *praça* on the right, is the nicest place in town, with suites that have A/C, TV, and *frigo-bar*. The best rooms are upstairs, with a balcony and a view. (☎527 1158. Breakfast included. Singles R$30; doubles R$40; triples R$50; quads R$60.)

FOOD. The string of restaurants by the river all serve similar menus of beef, chicken, and fish. **Restaurante Alter do Chão ❷,** in front of the Pousada Alter do Chão, has fish specialties including *pirarucú no leite de côco recheado* (stuffed *pirarucú* in coconut milk; R$20). (Open daily 10am-2pm and 6pm-late.) **Churrascaria e Pizzaria D'Italia ❷,** on Rua Lauro Sodré, serves large portions of pizza (R$12-R$15), fish (R$8), and a nightly *rodízio* (R$12), plus a weekend kilo lunch (R$12 per kg, F-Su 10:30am-3pm). (☎523 0277. Open M-Sa 10am-10:30pm, Su 10am-3pm.)

AMAPÁ

MACAPÁ ☎96

Located at the juncture of the Amazon River and the Atlantic Ocean, Macapá is known for its remarkably low crime rate and its easily accessible downtown area. This location makes the humble capital an excellent starting point for journeys into the interior of the Amazon, or up north to the border of French Guyana. Amapá state is renowned for its efforts to support the arts and traditions of several indigenous communities residing within its borders, including the Waiãpi, Karipuna, Palikur, Galibi, Aparai-Waiana, Tirió, and Kaxuyana, to name but a few; visitors can buy products made by these groups at the **Casa do Índio** near the waterfront. The city (population 277,000) is a mix of efforts at cultural and environmental preservation (like the **Sacaca Museum of Sustainable Development** and **Forest Products Market**), faded colonial architecture, weedy *praças*, and busy storefronts, as well as a tranquil waterfront area complete with a wharf and passenger tram. There are several annual festivals and events, including the fantastic **Pororoca** in March, when Atlantic ocean tides break the water balance and send giant waves up the Amazon River (see **Pounding the Pororoca,** p. 11).

TRANSPORTATION. The international **airport** (☎223 2323) is 4km west of the waterfront on Rua Hildemar Maia. **Gol** (☎222 4857, 223 7481; www.voegol.com.br), the regional airline, has the best rates on flights. There are daily departures to: Belém (1hr.; 2:50am; R$118); Brasília (2hr.; 2 per day; R$600); Manaus (2hr.; 2 per day; R$517); São Paulo (3½hr.; 2 per day; R$700). The main ticket office is at the airport. **Rio Norte Aero Taxi** runs between smaller towns in the Amazon. Contact the airport ticket office for details. (☎222 0033. Open M-F 9am-5pm.) Most long distance travel cannot be done by road. **Buses** linking Macapá to other cities within Amapá state leave from the *rodoviária*, 5km south of the *centro* along Rodovia Kubitschek. Several bus operators have offices there, nestled between restaurants, a small pharmacy, and a Banco do Brasil with **ATMs. Serrano** has buses to Serra do Navio (5hr.; 5:45pm; returns 7:30am; R$15) via Pedra Branca (4½hr.; R$14) and Porto Grande (2hr.; R$8). (☎251 5642. Open daily 8am-6pm.) **Local buses** from the *rodoviária* to the *centro* leave from the opposite side of the street, near the BP gas station (15min.; 4 per hr.; R$1.40). **Trains** leave the central station at Santana, 23km south of the city; to get there, take any bus labeled "Santana" heading south (on the church side) on Rua São José. Trains run to Serra do Navio (M and W 7am, F 10am; returns M and W 2pm, F 5pm; R$6). (☎281 1845. Open M-F 6am-6pm.) **Boats** also leave from the dock at Santana to Belém (14hr.; 4 per day; R$70). There are also boats to Almerim, Santarém, and Manaus. Various companies operate boats and understanding the schedule in Portuguese abbreviations can be frustrating; it's best to contact the DETUR office or a travel agent to book tickets in advance. **Agência Sonave,** on Rua São José between Av. Lombaerd and Av. Mendonça Jr., specializes in boat travel. (☎223 9090, 222 3135. Open M-F 9am-5pm.)

City buses are fairly simple; all display destinations on placards to the right of the driver, and most pass in front of the main bus stand opposite Igreja São José at some point on their routes. A thrilling alternative to buses are zippy **moto-taxis** (identifiable by bright yellow handlebar signs or the extra helmet strapped on the back seat), provided you don't mind jamming your head into a sometimes smelly spare helmet and hanging on for dear life whenever the driver makes a turn. Rates are negotiable, but within the *centro* should be no more than R$3-4.

ORIENTATION & PRACTICAL INFORMATION. All major points of interest are located within the *centro*, which is bordered on one side by the waterfront area and Complexo Beiro Rio, a collection of small restaurants and bars. **Revoada das Andorinhas** and **Rua São José** run parallel to the water; the latter passes in front of the large white Igreja of the same name. Across the street is the central bus stop and **Praça Viega Cabral.** The town's major downtown area is between perpendicular streets **Avenida Padre Lombaerd** at the south end and **Avenida FAB** at the north end, bordered by Rev. das Andorinhas to the east and Rua São José to the west. DETUR, the state **tourist office,** Rua Independência 29, has an excellent city map as well as English-speaking staff, and can help with finding accommodations. There is also a branch at the airport. To get there from Igreja São José, walk across Pça. Cabral on Av. Mário Cruz (lining the right side of the square if your back is to the church) and turn right on Rua Independência. (☎212 5335; fax 212 5337; www.detur.ap.gov.br. Open M-F 7:30am-noon and 2:30-6pm.) **Banco do Brasil,** on Av. Mendes at Av. Jucá, exchanges traveler's checks, and cash. (☎223 7123. Open M-F 10am-4pm.) **BBV Banco,** on Av. Independência at Av. Carvalho (☎223 0044), has an international 24hr. ATM. There is a pharmacy, **FarmaBem,** at Av. Pres. Vargas 166. (☎217 5555. Open daily 8am-8pm.) The **Telemar phone office,** at the corner of Rua São José and Av. Gurjão, is the distinctive bright blue building (☎215 6444. Open M-Sa 9am-5pm.) For Internet access, try **Cyberpl@y Internet Café,** on Rua Gen. Rondon at Av. Iracema Nunes. (☎223 9439. Open daily 8am-midnight. R$2 per hr.) At the **post office,** on Rua General Rondon, across from Pça. da Bandeira, you can send faxes (☎223 3803. Open M-F 9am-3pm.) There's also another small **branch** at Macapá Shopping. (Open M-Sa 10am-10pm.) **Postal code:** 68900-000.

ACCOMMODATIONS. Many of the budget hotels in Macapá have a stale odor to them and, like the surrounding jungle, are teeming with local fauna. Generally, this has more to do with the city's hot and humid climate than hygiene standards, so come prepared with insect repellent no matter where you decide to stay. Most hotels are located close to the *centro*, within walking distance of Pça. Cabral. The cheapest and most obvious choice for backpackers is **Hotel Santo Antônio ❶,** on Av. Coriolano Jucá between Rua Tiradentes and Rua Rondon near some excellent restaurants and an Internet café. The windowless, musty rooms come with breakfast (*cafezinho* with bread and margarine), and the occasional six-legged visitor. (☎222 0226, 222 0244. Dorms R$10. Singles R$12, with fan R$18, with A/C R$25; doubles with fan R$28, with A/C R$34; triples with A/C R$48. Cash only.) The **Mercúrio Hotel ❷,** on Rua Candido Mendes between Av. Cora Carvalho and Av. Maria Lombaerd, has clean *apartamentos* with A/C and a communal balcony overlooking the busy shopping district below. The entrance is between two shops; reception is located up the old marble staircase. (☎222 5622. Breakfast included. Singles R$40, with TV and *frigo-bar* R$50; doubles R$56, with TV and *frigo-bar* R$66; triples with TV and *frigo-bar* R$87. 15% student discount with ID.) The **Hotel Frota Palace ❹,** on Rua Tiradentes at Av. Coaracy Nunes, is a gleaming exception to most accommodations in Macapá. The decorated rooms are impeccable and include private bathrooms with hot water, TV, A/C, *frigo-bar*, and telephones. There's also a balcony on every floor and an in-house restaurant for the free breakfast buffet and other meals. Popular with local businessmen. (☎223 3999; frotapalacehotel.com.br. Singles R$76; doubles R$94; triples R$120. 20% discount for cash payments. R$4 airport transfers. MC/V.) If you're stuck for another budget option, try the run-down but cheap **Hotel Merco Sul ❶**, on Av. Coaracy Nunes one block before Rua Tiradentes. Thirteen tired-looking rooms are available, all with A/C, TV, and *frigo-bar*. (☎224 2214. Singles R$25; doubles R$35; triples R$50. Cash only.) **Macapá Hotel ❺**, at the opposite end of the price and quality spectrum, is a pink luxury hotel on the waterfront, opposite the pier, with a pool table, swimming pool, and sauna. All rooms have A/C, TV, *frigo-bar*, and phone. (☎217 1350; macapa.hotel@uol.com.br. Breakfast included. Singles R$135; doubles R$167; triples R$189. Suites R$250. MC/V).

FOOD. Most of Macapá's restaurants are downtown and on the waterfront. An inexpensive and fascinating place for home cooked cuisine is outside the Casa do Artesão, opposite the waterfront Beira Rio complex. There, **vendors ❶** dish out heaping plates of *maniçoba* (a stew made from manioc leaves) and *feijoada* with rice for R$4. The cool river breezes and nearly panoramic views of the Rio Amazonas make the nearby **Trapiche Restaurant ❸**, at the end of the Eliezer Levy pier, the most enjoyable place to sip a *suco* (R$2) or dive into regional cuisine (crayfish in coconut milk R$20). Trapiche has a great, well-priced menu and incredibly cordial service. (☎225 2665. Live MPB F and Sa nights. Open M 5pm-midnight, Tu-Su 10am-1am.) The **Sorveteria Crema ❶**, at the foot of the pier, is pricier than ice cream stalls but maintains the best selection of ice creams freshly made from Amazonian fruits. (☎217 1383. Cone R$2. Open M-F 4-10pm, Sa-Su 5pm-midnight.) **Sarney Lanches ❷**, on Rua Rondon at Rua Coriolano Jucá, is an excellent kilo with a wide selection of fresh vegetables, salads, stews, and desserts. The *churrascaria* is the best in Macapá; be prepared to wait for a table, as it's a local favorite. (☎223 7557. Open daily 11am-3pm and 6-9pm. Visa.) Just one block east on Gen. Rondon across from the *praça*, **Pastelaria do Goiano ❶** churns out delicious fried empañadas with beef, chicken, shrimp, and cheese fillings for R$2, as well as *pão de queijo*, *salgados*, and various *sucos*. (☎9965 0867. Open M-Sa 8am-midnight, Su 3pm-midnight). The **food court** at Macapá Shopping has sandwich and pizza shops, dessert cafés, and a formal restaurant. It's especially popular after 7pm on weekend nights, when live *bossa nova* masks the buzz of escalators and fluorescent lighting. (Open M-Th 10am-10pm, F-Sa 10am-11pm.)

THE BIG SPLURGE

POUNDING THE POROROCA

Every May, some of the world's best surfers and a few adventurous wannabes gather to conquer the **Pororoca,** which derives its name from *"poroc poroc,"* the Tupi phrase for "great thundering." This name refers to a bizarre phenomenon in which every 12 hours the Atlantic tides shift and create massive waves—some as tall as 5m—that sweep into the mouth of the Amazon and can continue upriver for as long as 40 minutes. During these surges, an astounding 24,000 cubic meters of water per second flush down the many tributaries of the Amazon delta.

The best waves are said to be along the Rio Araguari, 150km north of Macapá, where waves can tear through the normally silent wilderness at up to 20km per hour. Thus far, the longest recorded surf upriver is a whopping 26 minutes and 39 seconds, set by pro surfer Adilton Mariano.

Brave souls who'd like to follow Mariano's lead should plan to start their journey at Cutias, not far from the mouth of the Rio Araguari and accessible from Macapá by road. A boat traverses the remaining 70km downstream to the tiny town of Bom Amigo, where the waves (and the fun) begin.

For information on accommodations, equipment rental, and logistics during the Pororoca, *contact DETUR (☎212 5335; www.detur.ap.gov.br).*

SIGHTS. The best place to start exploring Macapá is from the waterfront. Start at the base of the **Trapiche Eliezer Levy,** a pier built in the 1930s and rebuilt in 1998. A free tram traverses the length of the long wooden pier and brings you to Trapiche Restaurante (see **Food,** above), with a view of the river. Heading back down the pier, the **Casa do Artesão** and **Casa do Índio,** opposite the Beira Rio complex on the left, are interesting places to check out indigenous artwork. At the Casa do Artesão, over 50 artisans create characteristic black pottery with shiny manganese detailing (medium-sized vases up to R$10), as well as intricately designed boxes made from Amazonian woods. (☎212 9156. Open M-Sa 7:30am-6pm.) Next door, the Casa do Índio sells dramatic *tamoko* masks, made of dyed plant fibers and wood, which are used in festivals of the Tumucumaque group. You can also buy such curios as paddle-like *borduna* weapons and inexpensive seed jewelry (R$3-6), including some with monkey and *onça* (leopard) teeth for good luck. (Open M-Sa 7:30am-6pm.)

From here, exit the Casa and turn right on Av. Mendonça Jr. after crossing the canal, then turn left on Rev. Andorinhas to get to the **Fortaleza São José.** Inaugurated in March 1782, this large stone structure was designed by Portuguese architect Antônio Henrique Galúcio and has since undergone four major renovations (the most recent completed about five or six years ago). A free guide can show you around the small museum, on the left side of the main courtyard as you enter it, filled with old photographs of Macapá and information on the Wajãpi Indians, whose labor was exploited alongside that of thousands of African slaves for the construction of the fort. The adjacent room has information on the recent archeological expeditions around Amapá state, which have uncovered earthenware anthropomorphic statuettes and other pottery dating from the 16th century and earlier. (Open Tu-Su 9am-6pm. Free.)

With your back to the fort entrance, head left on Rev. Andorinhas and, after two blocks, turn right on Rio Matapi. A 15min. walk through town from this point will land you at the engaging **Sacaca Museum of Sustainable Development,** a tribute to the state's focus on environmental awareness and social justice and the result of the newly initiated PDSA, the sustainable development program for the state of Amapá. One exhibit highlights a series of technological advances that may be implemented for improving the quality of life of residents. (☎212 5342. Open M-Sa 8:30am-noon and 3-6pm. Free.)

The phenomenal **Mercado dos Produtos da Floresta,** at the corner of Av. FAB and Rua São José, stocks liquors distilled from Amazonian fruits as well as a wide range of chocolates, jams, bath products, and homeopathic medicines made using local forest plants. (☎223 0110. Open M-F 8am-6pm, Sa-Su 8am-2pm.) Other points of limited interest include the **Marco Zero,** on Rodovia Kubitschek, a giant concrete obelisk (from which you can observe the equinox in March and November) marking the location of the equator. Across the road, the **Estádio Zerão** sports arena is divided in half by the same line.

NIGHTLIFE. Nightlife in Macapá is surprisingly vibrant; many places that appear deserted by day undergo a transformation at sunset, when everyone gets out of work and flocks to bars and restaurants. The best place for a relaxed beer or cocktail is on the waterfront. On Rua Francisco Azarias Neto across the street from Pça. Zagury, about 30 **vendors** have small kiosks with beer (R$2) and fresh *leite de côco* (coconut milk, R$1), along with plastic chairs from which to people-watch. Across the street, the *praça* fills with cartoon-like inflatable slides and rides (R$1) and gets packed with kids in the early evening.

The **Complexo Beira Rio,** a collection of small restaurants and bars on the opposite side of the pier, has a slightly more upscale bar scene than elsewhere in town, with whiskeys and caipirinhas (R$3) as well as a variety of light food dishes and beer. In town, the area around Pça. Bandeira gets packed with students and is a nice place for a stroll around sunset. On most Friday nights, Macapá's glitterati head to **Broadway,** which is actually located on Av. Feliciano Coelho close to the Museu Sacaca. Macapá's only real *boate* (dance club), Broadway draws crowds of chic locals looking to shake their *bundas* to Brazilian and European dance music throughout the night; things get started after midnight. (18+. Cover R$10. Open F 11pm-5:30am.)

ENTERTAINMENT. Those looking for a little local culture should check out the **Theatro das Bacabeiras,** where various plays, concerts, and dance shows are performed throughout the year; check the newspaper for listings. (☎212 5272. Box office open daily 8am-noon and 2pm-10pm.) **Ciné Macapá,** in the Macapá Shopping, plays American flicks in English with Portuguese subtitles. (☎217 2000. R$8, R$4 on Wednesday or before 7pm.)

NEAR MACAPÁ

CURIAÚ ☎96

Ten kilometers from the center of Macapá, the village of Curiaú sits in the middle of a large ecological marsh reserve, where the *afrodescendentes* raise herds of buffalo. Curiaú's pastoral landscape, distinctive wood-plank architecture, and religious traditions make it an interesting daytrip possibility for visitors to Macapá. The central panoramic deck of the reserve surrounds a crystal clear lagoon, providing the perfect spot for swimming or having a nearby picnic. There are plans to construct a small information center here as well. It's best to visit during the evenings to enjoy a meal or nurse a chilled *chopp* in one of the restaurants overlooking the Rio Curiaú.

To get to Curiaú's **tourist center** (Centro de Cultura), exit the bus from Macapá when you see the large arch. On your left you'll find the small office, which contains plenty of information on the town (in Portuguese only) and offers an array of guided tours; however, it's best to organize a tour from Macapá, before you arrive.

Just beyond the tourist office, on the right, is the tiny **Capela Santo Antônio.** Outside of the major **São Joaquim festival** (when residents head to the cultural center for dance and songs honoring the saint each August), there's not much to do here on a weekday afternoon, unless you've arranged a tour beforehand. The DETUR office in Macapá can contact local guides to take you on a tour of the surrounding nature reserve—which teems with all manner of birds, fish, and colorful dragonflies—on foot or by canoe (R$1-3 per guide); that office can also provide specifics on the annual festival.

Across the street from the *capela* (church) are a few bars where locals go to pass the time. Chief among these is the **Bar e Dancetaria Marabaixo,** a relaxed place for sipping a beer with music and dancing on weekend nights. (Open M-Sa 6pm-2am.) There are a couple of open-air restaurants located about 1km farther down the same road, directly in front of the bus station. **Bar do Dico,** across from the panoramic deck, prepares tasty *carne do sol* (R$13) and *maniçoba* (a stew made from ground manioc paste; R$4), and has several beers available for around R$1-2. (Open daily 10am-8pm.)

Buses marked with the destination "Curiaú" leave from opposite Igreja São João in Macapá and pass by the *rodoviária* on the main highway (30min.; every hr.; R$1.40). The tourist office and a cluster of restaurants are located near the main arch welcoming visitors to the town; the deck, bus station, and waterfront bars are nearly a kilometer farther down the highway.

TOCANTINS

PALMAS ☎14

Palmas (pop. 210,000), the sleepy capital of the state of Tocantins, is a testament to Brazilian urban planning. In 1989, the city was little more than a cluster of dirt roads and fields; now, thanks to the work of former Governor Siqueira Campos, Palmas boasts a large artificial lake and pleasant Ilha da Canela (Cinnamon Island), several hotels and restaurants, as well as the highest per-capita amount of "green space" (parks, trees, and forests) of any city in Brazil. The state capital is located in the geographical center of Tocantins, a region known for its progressive environmental policies and diverse landscape (ranging from the lush, forested north to the desert-like Jalapão of the east). While the city itself doesn't contain much of interest to the visitor, it's an excellent rest stop and the surrounding area is filled with *cachoeiras* (waterfalls, many of which are suitable for rappeling and swimming), forest trails, and sandy beaches along the massive Rio Tocantins, a tributary of the Amazon.

TRANSPORTATION. The international **airport** is a sparkling white complex in the middle of red-earthed countryside, a 45min. bus ride from the *centro* along Av. Teotônico. **TAM** (☎215 7722, 219 3782) operates flights to São Paulo and Rio de Janeiro via Brasília (1½hr.; 2 per day 5am-4:50pm; R$880). **Gol,** a smaller regional airline, also flies to Brasília (1½hr.; 10am; R$770). (☎0300 789 2121; www.voe-gol.com.br.) Bus #71 leaves from the bus stand opposite the main exit to Pça. dos Girassóis (45min.; every hr.; R$1.40). **Taxis** line the airport exit; expect to pay upwards of R$30 to save 20min. in transport time.

Intercity buses run from the modern **rodoviária,** 10km south of the *centro* (☎225 3030. Open daily 9am-8pm. Visa.) The following companies operate only *executivo* buses, with A/C and reclining seats: **União** (☎217 5611; www.expressouniao.com.br) runs to Rio de Janeiro (36hr.; 8:30pm; R$138); **Reunidas** (☎217 5631) runs to São Paulo (24hr.; 7am; R$131) and Goiânia (12hr.; 3 per day; R$51); **Novo Horizonte** (☎217 5606) serves northern destinations, including Salvador (22hr.; 10pm; R$76) and Recife (32hr.; 10pm; R$139). Several local buses shuttle downtown from the *rodoviária* (15min.; 2 per hr.; R$1.40).

Despite its environment-friendly mantra, the state designed Palmas for cars and so pedestrians will have a difficult time getting around. The **local bus** system has no central station within town and no published schedules, but most hotel and shop owners will be able to direct you to the right bus. Most follow simple paths to/from Pça. dos Girossóis on Av. J-K or Av. Teotônico. Stops are hard-to-miss colorful concrete arches along the sidewalk. Board at the front and have the R$1.40 fare ready when you enter. **Taxis** are readily available outside Palmas Shopping and the airport; otherwise you'll have to call for one. **Taxi Rápido** (☎215 1444) offers a 24hr. pickup service; fares are about R$2.50 per km. **Hertz** has an office on Av. Teotônico in front of the Palácio; cars start at R$126 per day. (☎215 1900, 24hr. 9978 1900. Open M-F 9am-5pm.)

ORIENTATION & PRACTICAL INFORMATION. Palmas is difficult to navigate on foot and resembles a sprawling suburb much more than an urban capital. All roads are based on a grid-like pattern of streets intercepted by grass-covered roundabouts. In the *centro* is the impressive **Praça dos Girossóis,** which derives its name from the state symbol, the sunflower *(girassol)*, and houses the **Palácio,** the governor's imposing office. Facing the southern entrance of the *praça*, **Av. Jus-**

celino Kubitschek (affectionately known as **J-K,** pronounced "Jota-Ka" in Portuguese), runs left (west) to the Henrique Cardoso Bridge and artificial lake, and right (east) to the old Palacinho. **Avenida Teotônico Segurado** is the town's major north-south artery which at its southernmost tip meets the airport; most hotels and services, however, are within one block of the main *praça.*

The municipal tourist office, **AMATUR,** offers limited information in Portuguese on ecotourism projects in Palmas and its environs. To get there from the *praça,* take any bus heading away from the Palácio on Av. Teotônico; the office is on the left side of the street 1.5km from the square. (☎218 5339, 218 5238; www.amatur.palmas.to.gov.br.) **Batista Pereira Turismo,** on Av. J-K across from the Hotel Vitória on the lake side of the Palácio, can book flights, tours, transport, and accommodations. (☎215 1228; www.tna-brazil.com/batistapereiraturismo. Open M-Sa 9am-5pm.) **Banco Amazônia,** on the lake side of Av. J-K facing the Palácio, has an **ATM,** exchanges traveler's checks, and does Visa cash advances. (☎215 1121. Open M-F 9am-5pm.) The central **police office,** on the south side of Av. Teotônico across from Hotel Casa Grande, will file reports and deal with missing passports. (☎218 5726, 218 5700. Open M only, 8am-noon and 2-6pm.) The **post office** is in a giant yellow compound on Av. Teotônico, three blocks south of the Palácio on the same side of the street as Palmas Shopping. (Open M-F 8:30am-noon and 2-5pm.) **Palmas Shopping,** a giant red-and-orange mall with a food court, cinema, and several shops facing the southwest corner of Pça. dos Girassóis, is always packed with locals. (☎223 1141. Open M-Sa 10am-10pm.)

ACCOMMODATIONS. The tourist industry in Palmas is still in its infancy and there are few budget accommodations. Most hotels, however, are a very good value and all offer private rooms, hot water, and breakfast ranging from bread and coffee to a full buffet with *salgados* (salty pastries) and fruit. Those that are more expensive usually have some type of weekend special; ask before you book. **Alfredu's Hotel ❶,** on an unnamed street across from Batista Turismo on Av. J-K, is a budget traveler's only real option in Palmas. To get there, walk two blocks toward the lake from Pça. dos Girassóis and turn left onto the unmarked street one block before Hotel Vitória. The small guesthouse has simple but airy *quartos,* most facing a pleasant courtyard with hammocks. (☎215 3036. Singles with fan R$22, with A/C R$30; doubles with fan R$34, with A/C R$45. Cash only.) **Hotel Casa Grande ❸,** on Av. Teotônico Segurada four blocks in front of the southern side of Pça. dos Girassóis, is highly recommended by locals. Starting with your back toward the front entrance of the Palácio, walk four blocks past Palmas Shopping and the post office; the hotel is on the right side of the street next to the bus stop. All rooms have A/C, TV, and *frigo-bar.* It's worth the extra R$20 for the immense buffet breakfast, sparkling-clean rooms, pool, and professional staff. (☎215 1713. Singles R$60; doubles R$70. MC/V.) Next door is the orange **El Colorado Palmas Hotel ❷,** which has simpler rooms and a smaller breakfast, but compensates with equally modest prices. All rooms have A/C, TV, and *frigo-bar.* (☎215 1586, 215 2006. Singles R$35; doubles R$45; triples R$60. Visa.) The **Rio do Sono ❹,** at the intersection of Av. Teotônico and the *praça,* offers luxury for less; the four-star hotel rivals the grandeur of the neighboring Palácio with its 61-item *café da manhã* (breakfast) and popular poolside patio. All rooms come equipped with A/C, TV, and *frigo-bar.* (☎215 1065, 215 2857. Singles R$94; doubles R$115. Wheelchair accessible. MC/V.)

FOOD. Surprisingly, the young capital of Tocantins offers an excellent array of dining options—from self-serve kilos to elegant Italian restaurants. **Fogão a Lenha ❷,** located on a small street behind the Hotel Vitória, specializes in traditional *comida mineira*. The kilo lunch-only buffet is packed with simmering pots of freshly-cooked stews and the finest cuts of meat in town, best enjoyed on the premises in the vine-covered patio. (☎215 5868. R$12.50 per kg. Open daily 11am-2pm. Visa.) On Sundays, the vendors at the **Feira do Bosque ❶** (p. 488) serve hamburgers, sandwiches, skewers of beef, and *salgados* for R$1; fresh juices and desserts go for R$1-3. **Restaurante Muralha Chinesa ❷**, on Av. Teotônico three blocks south of the *praça* near Hotel Casa Grande, is the only Chinese restaurant in Tocantins. Tofu and soft-noodle dishes (R$10-12) make it a vegetarian's paradise; other offerings include *chop suey de camarão* (shrimp chop-suey; R$25 serves 2) and *maçã caremelada* (caramelized apple; R$5). (☎215 2552. Open Tu-Su 11am-3pm and 6-11:30pm. Free dessert on orders of R$25 or more with ISIC. Visa.) **Frango Assado ❷**, on the same street three blocks closer to the *praça*, serves a buffet (R$10 per kg) that revolves around chicken. Dishes like *frango em molho roso* (chicken in red sauce) are a mere R$3. (☎225 8097. Open M-Sa 11am-3pm and 6-8:30pm, Su 11am-3pm.)

SIGHTS. Sights are few and far between in this practical capital. The handful of attractions that do exist are spread out, and only the small *centro* around the *praça* can be explored on foot. The marble **Palácio,** built in 1990, houses the state offices and contains a small floor inset which all Tocantinenses consider to be the actual geographical center of Brazil. The **Praça dos Girossóis** was given its name for the sunflower-packed field that Siqueira Campos discovered upon arriving here, and you'll see its image displayed everywhere inside the Palácio. If you're facing the Palácio's south entrance, about 50m to the left in the direction of the lake is the white dome-shaped **Memorial Coluna Prestes,** which honors a group of 19th century explorers who trekked 2500km across 14 states, including Tocantins, to promote democracy and an end to dictatorial rule. The small museum houses a few photos and some old rifles. (☎218 2419, 218 3316. Open Tu-Su 8am-6pm. Free.)

Farther down Av. J-K is the **artificial lake,** created as part of a major dam project designed to provide all the energy and water for Palmas. The unspectacular **Praia de Graciosa,** a 500m strip of beach along the lake, has a swimming area, playground, and a couple of restaurants. On weekends, **Travessia** runs boats to nearby **Ilha da Canela,** a tiny island with a few bars and restaurants. (☎9991 0447. Every hr. Sa-Su 8am-8pm; round-trip R$10).

The **Feira do Bosque,** on Av. Teotônico 2km south of the *praça*, is an excellent place to spend a Sunday night. There, you can buy anything from Peruvian earrings to pudding to tupperware, and popular bands perform live for free. (Open Su 5-11pm.) To get to the fair/market, take any bus heading south on Av. Teotônico; getting back after 7pm is nearly impossible by bus, so plan to walk or spend a few *reais* extra for a taxi.

NIGHTLIFE & ENTERTAINMENT. The city's nightlife may leave urbanites unsatisfied; most places are low-key, very far apart, and away from the major bus routes. Taking a taxi is the best option for getting to these places; rates average R$2.50 per km. Dress codes in Palmas are relatively casual, but keep in mind that most people like to get dressed up and you'll stand out if you decide to wear sneakers and a t-shirt.

The best place in Palmas for live music is **Oca,** at Quadra NE11, Conj. 4, Lote 22, in the northeast section of the city, where *samba* and *forró* bands get wild on the club's small palm-roofed stage. Don't be fooled by the modest wooden chairs, R$3 *caipirinhas*, and open-air seating; this place gets packed on weekend nights and carries the excellent reputation of inviting only the best bands. (☎215 2154. Cover R$2-3, up to R$15 for special events. Open W-Sa 9pm-4am.) **Amazônia Green,** at Quadra NE103, Lote 4, is known for offering quality dining and peaceful *bossa* *nova* beats in a vine-covered patio with several fountains. Beef carpaccio with arugula and fresh tomatoes R$14. (☎215 2411. Live MPB, *bossa nova*, and *samba* F and Sa nights. Open Tu-Sa noon-3:30pm and 6pm-2am, Su noon-3:30pm. Visa.) **Choppileque Bar,** between the Banco do Brasil and fairgrounds on Av. Teotônico 2km south of the *praça*, is another popular place with excellent cocktails (frozen daiquiri R$7; piña colada R$6) and a cold buffet (imported cheeses, olives, and salami; R$38 per kg). (☎214 3838. Open daily 6pm-4am. Visa.) Next door, **Carrangueijo's Bar** has an interesting wine selection (from R$18 per bottle) and exotic seafood dishes like *tartaruja ao leite de côco* (turtle in coconut milk; R$40). (☎214 5296. *Caipirinhas* R$5. Open M-Sa 5pm-4am. Visa.) The only thing in Palmas that approximates a night club is **Atlanta Bolliche's Bar,** a bowling alley/outdoor club where you can dance with Tocantins teenagers. (☎212 1090. *Caipirinhas* R$2.50-4.50; *salgados* and snacks R$5-10. 18+. Cover R$10, R$5 with student ID. Bowling R$15 per hr. Open W-Su 7pm-5am. MC/V.)

NEAR PALMAS: TAQUARUÇU ☎63

Several tributaries of the Rio Tocantins cut through the forested hills around Taquaruçu, making the small village a perfect base for camping or hiking near one of 80 pristine waterfalls. Some of the most spectacular include the 70m **Cachoeira do Roncador,** 2km from the *centro* on the main road, and the wide **Cachoeira das Três Quedas,** 18km farther along with pleasant campsites. Here and at many of the other falls, you can arrange **rappeling** (R$15) with a local guide. **Diego Sommer** (☎9977 8968, 213 1451) speaks English and is recommended; he also arranges mountain bike tours (R$60 per day). The Hotel Fazenda Encantada offers 10 guided **hikes,** ranging from moderate to high difficulty and lasting from 45min. to 3hr. (R$3 per hike), as well as **horseback riding** (R$5 for 40min.) and rappeling (R$15). Other points of interest include the **Casa do Artesão,** 500m behind the main tourist office on an unmarked road. The artist's collective sells locally produced jewelry, stationery, and finely-woven bags and baskets made of *capim dourado*, a shiny gold-colored fiber found only in Tocantins state. (☎554 1556. Open M-Sa 9am-5pm.)

To get to Taquaruçu from Palmas, take **Bus #90** from the stop in front of the Casa Grande Hotel, on Av. Teotônico three blocks south of Pça. dos Girassóis; there are only a few buses per day, so be sure to leave enough time for the return trip (45min., 2 per day 7:30am-1pm, R$1.40). The main bus stop in Taquaruçu is at Pça. Joaquim Maracaípe, a grass-covered square with a large fountain at its center. From here, walk left to the yellow **CATUR** office (Centro de Atendimento ao Turista; a division of AMATUR), behind the bright pink *dormitório* on the left side of Rua 24 where it intersects the *praça*. They can arrange guides for day trips (R$4 per waterfall) and camping (guide mandatory; R$30 per group per day), provide maps, and help find accommodations at one of the local *pousadas*. (☎554 1515; amatur@uol.com.br. Open daily 8am-6pm.) There are a few shops and small markets facing the *praça* where you can buy food and bottled water; for anything else—including medical assistance—you'll need to head back into Palmas.

Accommodations in Taquaruçu are very basic and often don't include hot water or a large breakfast, but *pousadas* here have pleasant, familial atmospheres. Camping requires a guide; solo travelers should pair up, as locals warn theft is a concern. **Pousada Lugar Comum ❶,** on Rua 8, Lote 12, is recommended by travelers for its clean, airy rooms with high ceilings and tasty breakfast, which includes eggs, bread, coffee, and fruit for R$3. (☎554 1532. Singles R$20; doubles R$25). **Pousada Serra do Carmo ❶,** 300m south of the main *praça* on quiet Rua 33, has small private rooms with mosquito nets and bathrooms. On weekends groups can rent an entire three-bedroom house, complete with TV and kitchen. Serra do

Carmo also offers camping facilities. (☎554 1183. Singles R$15. Camping R$6 per person. 12-person house R$100.) There are several restaurants open 9am-11pm around the *praça,* serving a variety of meat-heavy dished with rice and salad. A **quiosque ❶** in the *praça* serves chilled beer (R$1-3), *salgados* (R$2), and hamburgers (R$3). (Open daily 11am-midnight.) **Sorveteria Pinguim ❶,** also in the *praça,* has over 20 flavors of ice cream made on the premises, most from local fruits (R$1.50 per cone), as well as soda floats *(vaca preta)* and milkshakes (R$2-3). (Open M-Sa 10am-7pm.) **Supermercado Lopes,** on the opposite side of the *praça* from the bus stop, sells biscuits and basics. (Open M-Sa 9am-7pm.)

AMAZONAS

MANAUS ☎92

Manaus is a modern city of 1.4 million on the shores of the Rio Negro. It is 10km upstream from the meeting of the Rio Negro and the Rio Solimões, which merge to form the Amazon River. Some 1600km from the Atlantic coast, Manaus sits only 67m above sea level. As the center for ecotourism and a transport hub for the region, most travelers get in and out of this state capital as quickly as possible, using the city as a base for nearby jungle trips (p. 500). However, Manaus is worth several days, as there are good museums and parks, the opera house has frequent performances, and the beach at Ponta Negra is only 13km away.

Founded in 1699 around the São José do Rio Negro fort, the settlement became a city in 1856, taking the name Manaus after the indigenous Manaos who lived upstream. Manaus became the center of the 1890-1910 Brazilian rubber boom, and the population increased tenfold to 50,000 by 1900. Many new buildings sprang up around town—including the opera house—and were constructed by renowned European artists using expensive materials shipped from overseas. Manaus's fortunes languished after the end of the rubber boom, until 1967, when the Brazilian government created the Zona France de Manaus (ZFM), a low-tax area that encouraged industry and development. Today, Manaus is a busy, steamy city with high-rise buildings popping up, a large industrial district filled with international companies, and transport by river and air to the rest of Brazil, as well as to Venezuela and Guyana via the BR-174 highway.

INTERCITY TRANSPORTATION

Flights: Aeroporto Internacional Eduardo Gomes (MAO), Av. Santos Dumont 1350 (☎652 1210), about 13km from the *centro,* in Tarumã. Official taxi rate to town R$42. Taxis waiting by the bus stop will head to the *centro* for less, but make sure they take you to the hotel that you want. Bus #306 ("Aeroporto Centro") to town (R$1.50) stops 200m to the right of the terminal exit after the road makes a left turn. Shorter domestic flights depart from Terminal 2, 800m before the international terminal behind the gas station. Domestic departure tax R$9.15. Yellow fever card and return ticket required for flights to Bolivia.

Buses: Empresa Municipal de Transportes Urbanos, Rua Recife 2784 (☎643 5500), in Flores. Take Bus #301, #306, or any "Cidade Nova" bus past the stadium. Ring the bell when you see the AmBev building, and get off at the Shell station; walk over the pedestrian bridge. Open daily 5:30am-midnight. **União Casavel** (☎648 1493). Open 6:30am-midnight. MC/V. To: **Boa Vista** (12hr.; 5 per day 10am-midnight; R$70); **Puerto de la Cruz,** Venezuela (26hr.; 8pm; R$120); **Santa Elena de Vairén,** Venezuela (16hr.; 8pm; R$80). **Aruanã Transportes** (☎642 5757). Open daily 5am-7:15pm.

Boats: Boats leave from the **Porto Flutante,** opposite Pça. da Matriz. There are no posted times, but the helpful information counter (open daily 7am-6pm) has a list of departures, and the *A Critica* newspaper prints a list of daily departures. Ticket windows are behind glass to the rear of the info counter. To: **Belém** (2½ days; M, W, F 5pm; hammock R$236); **Tabatinga** (6 days; W, F, Sa 6pm; R$268); **Porto Velho** (4 days; Tu, Th 6pm; R$202). Additional boats to various destinations leave from the waterfront next to the market.

ORIENTATION

Manaus's *centro* stretches from the Rio Negro up 1km to the **Teatro Amazonas** and is easily covered on foot. Long-distance passenger boats dock at the **Porto Flutante** (Floating Dock), opposite **Praça da Matriz,** where one finds the cathedral and local bus station. Old buildings and free-trade shops cluster around the **Mercado Municipal,** along the waterfront to the right. Manaus's cheaper accommodations are also in this area, around Rua dos Andrades. **Avenida Eduardo Ribeiro,** the main shopping street, runs up a gentle hill from the port to the opera house. Perpendicular to Av. Eduardo Ribeiro is the busy **Avenida 7 de Setembro.** Parallel to Av. Eduardo Ribeiro runs **Avenida Getúlio Vargas,** which is lined with restaurants and more expensive hotels. **Avenida Constantino Nery** runs north from the *centro* toward the bus station, airport, and the BR-174 highway to Boa Vista and Venezuela.

LOCAL TRANSPORTATION

Local Buses: The easiest place to catch a bus is at the local bus station in Pça. da Matriz. Buses stop at different points along the two islands. Signs clearly list origins and destinations. The bus stops at Av. Floriano Peixoto, between Rua dos Andrades and Rua Quintino Bocaiúva, and at Av. Getúlio Vargas are also convenient. Heavy traffic (11am-1pm and 5-7pm) can substantially increase transit time. Buses run daily 5:30am-11:30pm. Fare R$1.50.

Taxis: Associação Amazonas Rádio Taxi (☎232 3005, 233 1625). Booth at intersection of Rua Quintino Bocaiúva and Rua Dr. Moreira. **Tucuxi Rádio Taxi,** Av. Eduardo Ribeiro 520, rm. 601 (☎622 4040, 622 4041).

Car Rental: Bill Car, Av. Constantino Nery 111 (☎233 0093; fax 233 9946), opposite Hotel Mônaco. 21+. Compact car R$71 with 100km and basic insurance. R$0.35 per additional km. Open M-F 8am-6pm, Sa 8am-noon. AmEx/MC/V. **Localiza,** at the airport (☎652 1176). R$124 per day with 100km; insurance R$17. Open daily 7am-11pm.

PRACTICAL INFORMATION

TOURIST & FINANCIAL SERVICES

Tourist Office: Centro de Atendimento ao Turista (CAT), Av. Eduardo Ribeiro 666 (☎231 1998; www.visitamazonas.com.br). Booths at the airport (☎652 1120; open daily 7am-11pm), Amazon Shopping Center (☎648 1396; open M-Sa 9am-10pm, Su noon-9pm), and the Porto Flutante (☎233 8689; open M-F 8am-5pm). Very helpful, with numerous brochures, maps, and lists of registered travel and tour agencies. Staff at all locations speak some English. **Manaus Tur—Fundação Municipal de Turismo,** Av. 7 de Setembro 157 (☎622 4948; www.manaustur.com.br). The city tourist authority has several brochures and the useful book *Walking Around Manaus* (R$5) in English.

Airlines: Gol (☎652 1634). Open daily 8am-4am. **Lab,** Av. Eduardo Ribeiro 520, rm. 1105 (☎633 4511). Open M-F 8:30am-4:30pm. AmEx/MC/V. **Meta,** Rua Barroso 316 (☎633 5801). Open M-F 8am-6pm, Sa 8am-noon. AmEx/MC/V. **Rico,** Rua 24 de Maio 60 (☎633 4651). Open M-F 8am-6pm, Sa 8am-noon. AmEx/MC/V. **TAM** (☎652

Manaus

ACCOMMODATIONS
Central Hotel, **32**
Hotel 10 de Julho, **4**
Hotel Continental, **43**
Hotel Doral, **33**
Hotel Ideal, **45**
Hotel Rio Branco, **46**
Lider Hotel, **20**
Pensão Sulista, **40**

FOOD
Casa do Pamonha, **9**
Churrascaria Búfalo, **34**
Filosóphicus, **26**
Ki-Tempero, **7**
Restaurante Himawari, **6**
Restaurante Mandarim, **13**
Restaurante Pizzaria Scarola, **5**
Ristorante Fiorentia, **27**
Texas Churrascaria, **10**

SIGHTS & SERVICES
Alfândega, **35**
Amazon Book, **17**
Amazon Explorers, **37**
Amazonas Indian Turismo, **41**
Arqueôlogo Usados CDs e Livros, **1**
Artesanato da Amazônia, **8**
Carrefour, **14**
Catedral Nossa Senhora da Conseição, **25**
Centro de Artes Usina Chaminé, **42**
Centro Cultural Palácio Rio Negro, **29**
Cortez Câmbio, **21**
Eco Planet Turismo, **30**
Foto Nascimento, **28**
Igreja NS dos Remédios, **44**
Lavalux Lavanderia, **39**
Loja Artíndia, **36**
Manaus Tur, **19**
Meta, **12**
Museu de Ciências Naturais da Amazonas, **2**
Museu do Homem do Norte, **22**
Museu do Índio, **23**
Rico, **11**
Selvatur, **38**
Tavaj, **15**
Tukano Turismo, **18**
Varig, **31**

NIGHTLIFE
Bar do Armando, **3**
Club A2, **16**
Club Ts GLST, **24**

1300). Open daily 9am-3am. AmEx/MC/V. **Tavaj,** Rua Rui Barbosa 200 (☎622 6699). Open M-F 8am-6pm, Sa 8am-noon. AmEx/MC/V. **Varig,** Rua Marcílio Dias 284 (☎621 4522). Open M-F 8:30am-6pm, Sa 8:30am-noon. AmEx/MC/V.

Ticket Agencies: Tucunaré Turismo (☎234 5071; www.tucunareturismo.com.br), main office located at the airport. Open daily 7am-7pm. **Tukano Turismo,** Av. Getúlio Vargas 275 (☎233 1112). Open M-F 8am-6pm, Sa 8am-noon. Both agencies accept AmEx/MC/V.

Consulates: UK, Rua Poraquê 240 (☎613 1819), in the Distrito Industrial. Open M-F 7-11:30am and 3-5pm. **US,** Rua Recife 1010 (☎633 4907), in Adrianópolis. Open M-F 9:30am-noon and 3:30-5:30pm.

Visa Extensions: Polícia Federal, Av. Domingos Jorge Velho 150 (☎655 1586, 655 1500), in Dom Pedro. Open M-F 9am-2pm. The process is quite time-consuming: first, you have to go to their office to purchase an R$5 extension form *(prorrogação de visto);* next you must go to a nearby Banco do Brasil (the official national bank), deposit the appropriate extension fee (R$22 for US passport holders; amount differs by nationality), and get a receipt; finally, you must return to the office and have your passport and visa stamped.

Currency Exchange: Cortez Câmbio, Av. 7 de Setembro 1199 (☎621 4444). Changes US dollars and traveler's checks (AmEx and Thomas Cook). Open M-F 9am-5pm, Sa 9am-noon. **Amazônia Câmbio,** Rua Dr. Moreira 88 (☎622 7206; fax 234 8564). Changes US dollars and traveler's checks (AmEx, Thomas Cook, and Visa). Open M-F 9am-5pm, Sa 9am-noon. **União Alternativa Câmbio,** at the airport (☎652 1293). Offers poor rates for US dollars, traveler's checks, euros, Swiss francs, and Canadian dollars. Open 24hr.

Bank: Banco do Brasil, Rua Guilherme Moreira 315, 1st fl. (☎621 5500). Changes US dollars (US$15 fee), traveler's checks (US$20 fee), and gives Visa cash advances (US$10 fee). Also accepts international wire transfers. Open M-F 9am-3pm.

ATMs: HSBC, Rua Dr. Moreira 226 (☎622 2737). ATMs give cash on AmEx/Cirrus/MC/PLUS/Visa networks. ATMs open 24hr. **Banco do Brasil** (see **Banks**) has PLUS/Visa ATMs. ATMs at the airport accept Cirrus/MC/PLUS/V cards.

American Express: Selvatur, Pça. Adalberto Vale 17 (☎622 2577; fax 622 2177; www.selvatur.com.br), is a representative of American Express Travel Service. Sells and refunds Traveler's Cheques. Open M-F 8am-6pm, Sa 8am-noon.

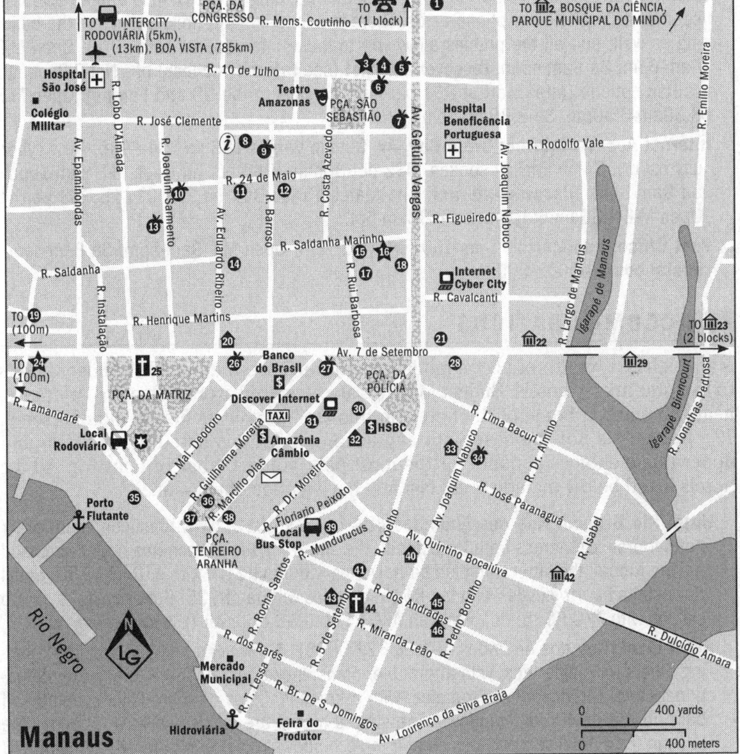

LOCAL SERVICES

Bookstores: Arqueôlogo Usados CDs e Livros, Av. Getúlio Vargas 766 (☎234 0965). Sells used books, comic books, records, CDs, and DVDs. There is a carousel of paperback books in English (R$2.50) in the room behind the counter. Open M-F 8:30am-6:15pm, Sa 9am-2pm. AmEx/MC/V. **Amazon Book,** Rua Rui Barbosa 184 (☎637 7637; fax 637 7164). The best bookstore downtown has a Manaus tourist map and Portuguese/English dictionaries. Open M-F 8am-6pm, Sa 8am-1pm.

Supermarket: Carrefour, Av. Eduardo Ribeiro 516 (☎633 2008), at the corner of Rua Saldanha Marinho. Open M-Sa 7am-9pm, Su 7am-2pm. AmEx/MC/V.

Laundry: Lavalux Lavanderia, Rua Mundurucus 77 (☎233 7672; fax 234 0466), behind Av. Floriano Peixoto, off Rua dos Andrades, 200m on the left. 3hr. wash and dry R$6 per kg. Open M-F 8am-6pm.

EMERGENCY & COMMUNICATIONS

Police: Politur (the official tourist police) has several posts: one at the tourist information complex located by the Opera House (☎231 1998; open M-F 9am-5pm) and one at the airport (☎652 1120; open 24hr.). The **24hr. Polícia Federal** post is opposite the bus stop in Pça. da Matriz.

Hospital: Universitário Getúlio Vargas, Pça. 14, Av. Apurinã 752 (☎622 1838).

Telephones: Located inside the former Telemar building at Av. Getúlio Vargas 950 is a counter selling Telemar phone cards. There is a long line of public phones in the building as well, and all the phones allow you to make international calls (DDI). Open M-F 8am-6pm, Sa 8am-noon. **Discover Internet** (see **Internet Access**) has Net-2-Phone to call any phone (rates start at R$1 per min. for calls to the US and Europe). Open M-F 8:30am-6:30pm, Sa 8:30am-5pm.

Internet Access: Internet Cyber City, Av. Getúlio Vargas 188 (☎234 8930; www.cybercity.psi.br). Some English spoken. R$2 per 30min., R$3 per hr. Open M-F 8am-10pm, Sa 9am-8pm. **Discover Internet,** Rua Marcílio Dias 304 (☎233 0121). R$3 per hr. Open M-F 8:30am-6:30pm, Sa 8:30am-5pm.

Post Office: Rua Marcílio Dias 160 (☎215 2522). Open M-F 9am-5pm, Sa 8am-noon. **Postal code:** 69005-000.

ACCOMMODATIONS

Manaus has a wealth of accommodations options, from minimalist budget hotels to five-star luxury hotels. Budget lodgings are clustered around Rua dos Andrades, near the market. Some of the hotels in this area double as hourly motels (see p. 79), but this is not the case with any accommodations listed below. Mid- and upper-range choices abound; for the most part, you get what you pay for. All the hotels listed below include breakfast and have a noon check-out.

Hotel Rio Branco, Rua dos Andrades 484 (☎233 4019; www.brasilcomercial.com/hotelriobranco). Across from Hotel Ideal, the sprawling Rio Branco has both dorms and private rooms, the latter with tiled bath. Dorms with fan R$10, with A/C R$17.50. Small downstairs *quarto* singles with fan R$15; doubles with fan R$25. Better upstairs *quarto* singles with A/C R$25; doubles with A/C R$35. R$3 extra for TV and *frigo-bar.* ❶

Hotel Ideal, Rua dos Andrades 491 (☎622 0038). A traveler's hangout good for meeting others for jungle trips, with affordable rooms, locker rental, and a phone for international calls. The decor is prison chic, with a functional gray-on-white color scheme and bars on the back room windows. The simple rooms are clean and have phones. The ones in front have small balconies and large windows. Singles with fan R$17, with A/C R$26, with *frigo-bar* R$35; doubles with fan R$26, with A/C R$35, with *frigo-bar* R$44; triples with fan R$32, with A/C R$42, with *frigo-bar* R$50. ❶

Hotel 10 de Julho, Rua 10 de Julho 679 (☎232 6280; fax 232 9416; htjd@internext.com.br). The good location by the opera house, recently completed expansion, terraces, and rooftop bar create a traveler-friendly atmosphere. The older rooms downstairs are darker, while the newer are larger and brighter. All come with A/C, TV, and *frigo-bar.* Singles R$35; doubles R$40; triples R$50; quads R$60. ❷

Hotel Doral, Av. Joaquim Nabuco 687 (☎232 4102). A functional choice with large, rather empty rooms with ancient TV and tired bath. Singles with fan R$15, with A/C and phone R$20; doubles with fan R$20, with A/C and phone R$25; triples R$30.

Pensão Sulista, Av. Joaquim Nabuco 347 (☎234 5814). Those looking for a cheap place to crash could do worse than the downstairs rooms with fan and common bath. Upstairs rooms have A/C, TV, bath, *frigo-bar,* windows, and high ceilings. Downstairs singles R$15; doubles R$25; triples R$37.50. Upstairs doubles R$35; triples R$45. ❶

Hotel Continental, Rua Coronel Sergio Pessoa 189 (☎234 3626; fax 233 3342). This reasonable choice has outside rooms with balconies overlooking Igreja Nossa Senhora dos Remédios. All rooms have A/C, TV, *frigo-bar,* and temperamental hot water. Singles R$30; doubles R$40; triples R$50. ❷

Central Hotel, Rua Dr. Moreira 202 (☎622 2600; fax 622 2609; www.hotelcentralmanaus.com.br). The 70s survive at Central Hotel, from the light fixtures to the old typewriter sitting at reception. The hotel's standard rooms have A/C, TV, phone, *frigo-bar,* and hot-water bath. Upstairs, superior rooms are brighter and have newer TV and *frigo-bar.* Standard singles R$66; doubles R$77. Superior singles R$72; doubles R$88; triples R$112. AmEx/MC/V. ❹

Lider Hotel, Av. 7 de Setembro 827 (☎621 9700, 633 1673; www.internext.com.br/liderhotel). The most central mid-range choice has 60 good rooms with A/C, cable TV, desk, *frigo-bar,* and safe. Internet access. Laundry services. *Quarto* singles R$99; doubles R$120. *Luxo* singles R$123; doubles R$149; triples R$180. AmEx/MC/V. ❹

FOOD

In Manaus, you are never far away from tropical *sucos, churrasco,* and fresh fish. Small stalls line the streets selling *salgados* and *côcos gelados* (coconuts). Kilos open for lunch and are everywhere, but dinner choices are more limited: a good number of them line Av. Getúlio Vargas.

Ki-Tempero, Av. Getúlio Vargas 615 (☎633 3957). The best value buffet lunch in town (R$9 per kg) can be found in this air-conditioned indoor and breezy outdoor restaurant. Piles of salads, *churrasco,* tender fish, and excellent shrimp *vatapá.* At night, they serve a la carte meat and fish entrees including *picanha* and *dourado filé* (fish fillet; R$13-17). Open daily 11am-3pm and 4-11pm. MC/V. ❷

Filosóphicus, Av. 7 de Setembro 752, 3rd fl. (☎234 2224). This vegetarian oasis opens for a good buffet lunch (R$14.50 per kg) with unique salads and lentil, tofu, and chick-pea dishes, as well as lasagne and pastries. Open M-F 11am-2:30pm. ❷

Churrascaria Búfalo, Av. Joaquim Nabuco 628 (☎633 3773). The best *churrascaria* in town takes meat seriously. Waiters bring savory spits of meat until you admit defeat and fly the red flag. All-you-can-eat R$24 plus 10% service tax. Complete wine and dessert carts. Open M-Sa 11am-2:45pm and 6:30-11pm, Su 11am-3:45pm. AmEx/MC/V. ❸

Restaurante Mandarim, Rua Joaquim Sarmento 221 (☎234 9834, 232 0562). Sick of *churrasco?* The impressive lunch buffet (R$16.80 per kg) features an extensive selection of fresh vegetables, salads, tofu dishes, sushi, egg rolls, fish, noodles, and fried rice, while classical music soothes the traveling spirit. Dinner entrees for two (R$15-22) include Szechuan shredded pork (R$16), vegetable chop suey (R$17), and tofu served a variety of ways (R$17). English menu. Open daily 11am-3pm and 6-10pm. ❷

Ristorante Fiorentia, Rua José Paranaguá 44 (☎215 2233; www.ristorantefiorentina.com.br). This Manaus institution serves good Italian pastas (R$9-16), pizzas (medium R$9-17), filet mignon (R$20-24), and a Saturday *feijoada* (R$20). Open daily 11am-3pm and 6-10:30pm. AmEx/MC/V. ❸

Restaurante Pizzaria Scarola, Rua 10 de Julho 739 (☎234 8542). You can find pizza all over town, but Scarola churns out some of the best (R$10-27), to go with ice-cold *chopp.* They can also drum up *churrasco* (R$22-24) and fish (R$15-21), if you so desire. Open daily 10am-1am. AmEx/MC/V. ❸

Restaurante Himawari, Rua 10 de Julho 618 (☎233 2208), opposite the opera house. Himawari has a huge menu of Japanese food including *sashimi* (R$38), sushi (R$45), and *teppan* (R$20-30). Sake R$15. Open Tu-Th 11:30am-2pm and 6:30-10pm, F-Sa 11:30am-3pm and 6:30-11pm, Su 11:30am-3pm and 4:30-10pm. AmEx/MC/V. ❹

Casa da Pamonha, Rua Barroso 375 (☎/fax 233 1028). Vegetarian restaurant serving breakfasts of *tapiocas,* homemade breads, and cakes (including Brazilnut; R$3). Simple lunch buffet (R$15 per kg) varies daily and often includes eggplant lasagna, lentils, rice and beans, and green salads. Open M-F 7am-7pm, Sa 8am-2pm. Visa. ❷

Texas Churrascaria, Rua 24 de Maio 188 (☎232 3752). The only thing Texan about this lunch buffet is the name and its supply of good beef. The huge buffet (R$16 per kg) includes tons of salads and meat dishes including beef, fish, and pork. Try to save room for dessert. Open M-Sa 10:30am-3pm. AmEx/MC/V. ❷

Restaurante Ginatório, Av. Getúlio Vargas 741 (☎627 3737), atop the Taj Mahal Hotel. Good food is complimented by excellent views of downtown and the opera house as the restaurant slowly rotates beneath you. Local specialties include fish (try *filé de peixe au Gratin;* R$18) and chicken *(frango ao catupiry;* R$16) as well as international staples like steak and shrimp. Open daily noon-3pm and 7-11pm. AmEx/MC/V. ❸

SIGHTS

TEATRO AMAZONAS

Pça. São Sebastião s/n. ☎*622 1880; teatroamazonas@visitamazonas.com.br. Open M-Sa 9am-4pm; orchestra rehearsals M-F 9am-noon. 20min. tour with English-speaking guide R$5.*

The Teatro Amazonas opera house is the most enduring symbol of the luxury and power that Manaus enjoyed during the rubber boom. Construction began in 1884, but was paralyzed from 1886 until 1893, when the governor Eduardo Ribeiro imported the workers, artists, and raw materials from Europe needed to complete the project. It was Ribeiro's idea to add the incongruous dome (the tiles were imported from Alsace, France): the Brazilian flag atop it could be seen from boats docking at the port. The theater opened on December 31, 1896. The neoclassical theater was constructed with the most expensive and ostentatious materials available. The bricks surrounding it were originally made with a rubber base so that the noise from late-arriving carriages would be muffled. Most have disintegrated, but a few remain in the rear of the theater. The wavy tiled sidewalk *(calçadão)* in front symbolizes the Meeting of the Waters and inspired Roberto Burle Marx's design for the sidewalks of Rio's Copacabana sidewalks (p. 148).

The theater seats 681, with 266 in the orchestra and the rest in 90 boxes. The curtain is original, and shows a scene of the Meeting of the Waters, painted by the Brazilian Crispim do Amaral in Paris. It is done in only one color (blue) because in Paris the color difference between Rio Solimões and Rio Negro was unknown. In order not to damage the 195 square meters of painting the curtain is not rolled up, but raised as a whole into the ceiling. The 220 square meters of ceiling was also painted in Paris and then reassembled in Manaus. Looking up, it appears that you are under the Eiffel Tower, which had been recently built. The upstairs **Noble Salon** was used during concert intermissions and for balls: its floor is made of 12,000 pieces of wood, alternating dark Baiano rosewood and light Latvian wood (riga pine, which was also used to make Stradivarius violins). On the terrace, you can see the descendants of imported European pigeons. European opera companies made the pilgrimage to perform in the theater until 1907, when the rubber boom began to decline. During WWII, the theater was used to store rubber, and it was closed for eight years during the military dictatorship. In 1974 it was renovated, and air-conditioning was added in 1990. Now the theater hosts regular concerts and an opera festival (Apr.-May).

OTHER SIGHTS IN CENTRO

CENTRO CULTURAL PALÁCIO RIO NEGRO. Waldemar Sholtz, a rich German rubber baron, built this stately neoclassical palace to be his home in 1903. In 1918, after the collapse of Brazilian rubber, the state bought it and it served as the governor's executive offices until 1995. The palace and surrounding buildings were then remodeled to be a cultural center. The beautiful complex now houses painting, coinage, and sound and image museums, as well as a theater, and often hosts classical and popular music concerts. Outside there are replicas of a river boat, a rubber tapper's home, and a traditional indigenous dwelling. *(Av. 7 de Setembro 1546.* ☎*633 2850. Open Tu-F 10am-5pm, Sa-Su 2-6pm. English-speaking guides. Free.)*

PORTO FLUTANTE & ALFÂNDEGA. There are few floating piers like this in the world. Built in 1912, it was operated by the British company Manaos Harbor Ltd. until 1963, when control of it was transferred to the Brazilian government. It is almost 300m long and 20m wide, and can rise and fall over 10m. With a deep approach channel, ocean-going container ships are able to dock, and cruise ships periodically appear. On the right of the pier there is a metal chart plotting the high water levels of every year since 1904. Buses run from the passenger terminal to the dock, and you need a boat ticket to enter. The neighboring white and yellow Alfândega (Customs House) was opened in 1906, and is considered to be the world's first prefabricated building. Made in England, blocks suitable to the tropical climate were transported in British ships. *(Alfândega open daily 8am-5pm.)*

MERCADO MUNICIPAL. Liveliest in the mornings, the Mercado Municipal and the larger Feira do Produtor nearby are bustling waterfront markets selling the best the Amazon has to offer. In 1855, a market called Ribeira dos Comestíveis ("Food Riverbank") already existed here. The main building of the **Mercado Municipal** was constructed in 1883. At the outset of the 20th century, two cast-iron pavilions were built on either side of the main building, in the same style as Les Halles in Paris, with ornate ironwork and stained glass. Today they house aromatic meat and fish sections. The central building houses a number of artesanal shops selling woven bags, jewelry, *guaraná*, and stuffed piranha, as well as stalls selling traditional herbs and medicines.

FEIRA DO PRODUTOR. The Feira do Produtor (part of the Mercado Municipal) is a large, more recent warehouse full of stalls overflowing with vegetables and tropical fruits like *maracujá*, *açaí*, *cupuaçu*, avocados, at least four types of banana, and piles of oranges and pineapples. The yellow stuff in plastic bottles is *tucupi*—made from manioc—and is used in local soups. The right side of the warehouse is given over to cuts of meat and the morning's catch of striped catfish, *tucunaré* (recognizable by the spot on the tail which looks like an eye), *jaraqui*, *matrinxã*, large *tambaquí*, and even larger *pirarucú*.

MUSEU DO ÍNDIO. Salesian nuns created and continue to run this museum dedicated to the cultures of the indigenous peoples of the upper Rio Negro and Rio Amazon, including the Yanomami and Tukano. There are exhibits on clothing, hunting and fishing, pottery, dance, religion, and funeral rites. *(Rua Duque de Caxias 356. ☎ 635 1922. Open M-F 8-11:30am and 2-4:30pm, Sa 8:30-11:30am. R$5.)*

MUSEU DO HOMEM DO NORTE. The Man of the North Museum (opened in 1985 and recently renovated) houses ethnographic and anthropological collections of the local indigenous populations, with a focus on the river-dwelling *caboclos*. Displays include models of various means of river transport, religious and medical objects, traditional foods, musical instruments, and tools for rubber extraction and mining. The ethnographic collection includes an interesting selection of Karajá ceramics collected by the Russian Noel Nutels. *(Av. 7 de Setembro 1385. ☎ 232 5373; fax 233 5220; iesam@internext.com.br. Open M-F 9am-noon and 1-4pm. R$3.)*

CENTRO DE ARTES USINA CHAMINÉ. The Chaminé Arts Center is housed in a building from the rubber-boom era, originally used by the English firm Manaos Improvements, which held the lease for the city's water and sanitation services. Abandoned for decades, the building was renovated in the 1990s to house the state's art gallery. The center hosts temporary art and photography exhibitions, concerts, plays, movies, and other events. *(Av. Lourenço da Silva Braga s/n. ☎ 633 3026; usinachamine@hotmail.com. For details of current exhibits and events see www.madrugadadentro.com.br. Open Tu-F 10am-5pm, Sa-Su 4-8pm. Free.)*

FARTHER AFIELD: PARKS & BEACHES

BOSQUE DA CIÊNCIA (SCIENCE FOREST). Bosque da Ciência is a small but interesting island of forest in the suburbs, with tanks of manatee, river otters, and *caiman*, as well as turtles, eels, parrots, and beehives. If you are lucky you may see some of the free-range monkeys and sloths in the forest canopy. The forest is a project of the adjoining Instituto Nacional de Pesquisas da Amazônia (INPA; the National Institute of Amazonian Research). In the center of the forest, the **Casa da Ciência** describes (in Portuguese) the numerous INPA projects in ecology, agronomy, entomology, hydrometeorology, and health sciences. The highlight of the Casa is a gigantic two-meter leaf from a *cocoloba* tree. *(Av. André Araújo 2936, in Petrópolis. ☎/fax 643 3192; www.inpa.gov.br. Take Bus #519, which drops you just past the entrance. Open Tu-F 9-11am and 2-4pm, Sa-Su 9am-4pm. R$2.)*

MUSEU DE CIÊNCIAS NATURAIS DE AMAZONAS. On the outskirts of Manaus, the Amazonas Museum of Natural Sciences has a large collection of stuffed fish, manatees, *caiman*, insects, and some angry-looking turtles. Fish include the armored sucker catfish, the *piraiba* (which can weigh up to 200kg and grows to be 2m long), the tasty *tambaquí*, *tucunaré*, and the huge *pirarucú*. Around the corner, a case of about 20 piranhas look as if they are about to eat the wall. The insect section is not for the squeamish. They start you off gradually with beautiful butterflies with iridescent blue wings before the locusts, scorpions, tarantulas, spiders, and the huge Hercules beetle appear. An aquarium out back houses five bored *pirarucú*. There are signs in English, and you can buy your own stuffed piranha at the gift shop. *(Estrada dos Japoneses 34. ☎644 2799. Easily combined with the Bosque da Ciência (see above). Take Bus #519 and get off at the blue and white Aços da Amazônia factory, then follow the small "Museu" signs: it's a 15min. walk. Open M-Sa 9am-5pm. R$10; students with ID R$4.50.)*

PARQUE MUNICIPAL DO MINDU. This ecological reserve in the middle of the Parque 10 suburb has several interesting walking trails and elevated walkways, as well as an amphitheater and library. It hosts occasional programs on conservation. *(Av. Perimental s/n. ☎236 7702. Take Bus #351, #422, or #423, which pass the entrance to the narrow end of the park; watch for the sign on the right. Open Tu-Su 8am-5pm. Free.)*

PRAIA DE PONTA NEGRA. On the weekends, locals head to the beach at Ponta Negra. Once home to the indigenous Manaos, after which the city is named, this renovated waterfront with a strip of high-rise apartment buildings is popular with runners, cyclists, water-skiers, and dog walkers. The beach is lined with an amphitheater, a totally rad skateboard park, and a string of bars and restaurants. The beach disappears under rising waters from about March to July, but even then the waterfront is hopping. *(Take Bus #120, labeled "Ponta Negra"; about 30min.)*

NIGHTLIFE & ENTERTAINMENT

Manaus offers a wide variety of things to do after dark. Cinemas, concert halls, art galleries, bars, and clubs mean that there's something going on every night. Most city squares sprout stalls selling cheap food and cold *chopp* (beer), and dance clubs in the suburbs of Cachoeirinha, Adrianópolis, and on the road to Ponta Negra keep going until dawn. See the *Guia Rápido* in the newspaper *A Critica* or www.madrugadadentro.com for more information. **Teatro Amazonas,** in Pça. São Sebastião, hosts regular concerts by the Orquestra Amazonas Filarmônica, as well as visiting orchestras and theater groups. The opera season is Apr.-May, and throughout the year there are at least two free concerts a month. (☎622 2420; www.visitamazonas.com.br, operaamazonas.com.br. Performances R$10-35. 50%

student discount.) The six-screen **Cinema Amazonas Shopping,** Av. Djalma Batista 482, 2nd fl., screens subtitled English-language movies. Buy tickets early, as lines can get long. (☎236 0730. R$6-10. Shows daily after 11:30am.)

Choppicanha Beer & Grill, opposite Pça. da Matriz (☎631 1111), in the "International Departure" section of the Porto Flutante. A relaxed place for an afternoon beer. It overlooks the port, so you can watch riverboats load and unload. Both indoor and outdoor seating is removed from the bustle of the city. *Chopp* R$2. Drinks R$3-7. Open M-Sa 10am-10pm, Sa 10am-3pm. MC/V.

Clave de Sol Piano Bar, Rua Belo Horizonte 320 (☎663 4433, www.clavedsol.com), in Adrianópolis. Taxi R$12. This place just can't help being sexy, with its dim blue lighting, sensuously comfortable chairs, and couples moving slowly on the dance floor to good jazz. The pianist works his magic nightly after 9pm. Subtle waiters serve grilled *petiscos* (R$5-15) and *chopp* (R$2-3). Cover F R$5, Sa R$6. Open Th-Sa 6pm-late. MC/V.

Amazon Bowling, Rua Belo Horizonte 97 (☎631 0087), in Adrianópolis. Taxi R$12. For leisurely sports, this place is hard to beat. Downstairs there is a bar, foosball table, and a 10-lane bowling alley. (R$20-35 per lane per hr.) Upstairs houses 10 pool tables (R$10 per hr.) and another bar. Open M-Sa 5pm-late, Su 3pm-late. AmEx/MC/V.

Bar do Armando, Rua 10 de Julho 593 (☎232 1195). This Manaus institution provides outdoor seating opposite the opera house, perfect for *chopp* (R$2) and conversation. Drinks R$3-5. Open M-Sa 1pm-2am.

Jack and Blues Music Bar, Calçadão da Ponta Negra s/n (☎658 5259). A trendy outdoor bar with good music, good *chopp,* and uncomfortable bar stools. W MPB; Th rock; F-Sa jazz, blues, and soul; Su reggae. Cover R$3. Open W-Su 6pm-late.

Bar O Laranjinha, Estrada da Ponta Negra 10675 (☎658 6666), in Ponte Negra. The largest outdoor bar on the Ponta Negra waterfront has live *boi* and MPB Th-Su after 7:30pm. Open daily 4:30pm-4am. AmEx/MC/V.

Allegro Bar, Pizza, and Grill, Av. Djalma Batista 482, Amazonas Shopping, ground fl. (☎216 5099). Allegro produces good pizza (R$13-15) and steaks (R$17-22), to accompany nightly live music upstairs. Cover R$3. Opens daily 11am. AmEx/MC/V.

Club Ts GLST, Blvd. Dr. Vivaldo Lima 33 (☎232 6793). A tropically themed gay club with a mixed crowd dancing to techno and house. Drag shows after 2am. R$5 cover. Open Sa-Su 11pm-6am.

Club A2, Rua Saldanha Marinho 780 (☎9116 6969). DJs spin dance, techno, tribal, and drum'n'bass at this GLS club. There's a bar, lounge, crowded dance floor, and both drag and strip shows after 3am. Cover R$8 after midnight. Opens Th-Sa after 11pm.

SHOPPING

In addition to a number of shops, Manaus has a **crafts fair** (Su 7am-2pm) which springs up on Av. Eduardo Ribeiro, between Av. 7 de Setembro and Rua 24 de Maio. Stalls sell wood carvings, masks, jewelry, plants, sandals, and used books. There are also numerous food stalls for a cheap refueling. In **Praça Tenreiro Aranha** there are usually a number of stalls selling crafts and hammocks. Hammock sellers also line the nearby area around the port (single hammocks R$20, doubles R$30, depending on your haggling skills). **Loja Artíndia,** Rua Guilherme Moreira s/n, is housed in the rubber boom-era Pavilhão Universal, in the center of Pça. Tenreiro Aranha. It has a wide selection of wood carvings, masks, baskets, purses, jewelry, and blowguns, with more up the wrought-iron circular staircase. (☎232 4890. Open M-Sa 8am-6pm.) **Artesanato da Amazônia,** Rua José Clemente 500, opposite the opera house, is a larger shop selling postcards, T-shirts, baskets, pottery, and paintings. (☎232 3979. Open M-F 8am-6pm. AmEx/MC/V.) **Foto Nascimento,** Av.

7 de Setembro 1194, with other locations scattered around town, is the best place for photographic supplies. (☎633 4995; fax 633 4772; www.fotonascimento.com.br. Open M-F 8am-6pm. MC/V.) **Amazonas Shopping Center,** Av. Djalma Batista 482, is the largest shopping mall in Amazonas and caters to every shopping impulse. There is a six-screen theater, a huge Carrefour supermarket, travel agencies, ATMs, currency exchange, three food courts, several good restaurants, and scores of shops selling everything from gourmet soap to fridges. Take Bus #203, #207, #209, or #214, or the yellow Transgold minibus and get off at TVlândia mall; Amazonas Shopping is 300m up on the right. (☎642 3555. Open daily 10am-10pm.)

DAYTRIPS FROM MANAUS

ENCONTRO DAS ÁGUAS & ECOLÓGICO JANUARY

Tours can be arranged with one of two agencies, both of which offer similar excursions at identical prices. ***Amazon Explorers,*** *Pça. Tenreiro Aranha. ☎633 3319, 232 3052. Open M-F 7:30am-noon and 2-5:30pm, Sa 7:30am-noon, Su 7:30-9am. Tours R$50; R$70 with pick-up from your hotel.* ***Selvatur,*** *Pça. Adalberto Vale 17. ☎622 2577; fax 622 2177; www.selvatur.com.br. Open M-F 8am-6pm, Sa 8am-noon. Tours R$50; R$70 with pick-up from your hotel. AmEx/MC/V.*

The dark waters of the Rio Negro meet the light muddy waters of the Rio Solimões about 10km downstream from Manaus. Due to the different temperatures, densities, and speeds of the two rivers, they flow side-by-side for several kilometers without mixing. Organized daytrips to Encontro das Águas (the Meeting of the Waters) also head to the Parque Ecológico January. These trips are very touristy with large groups herded from sight to sight to gift shop. Boats leave from the Porto Flutante at 9am and cruise the shores of Manaus before visiting the Meeting of the Waters. They then sail up to Lake January. The herds troop on elevated walkways to see the giant Vitória-Régia waterlilies, and take covered ten-person boats with outboard motors through small waterways or, during high water (May-July), through the flooded forest itself. There are several pointed stops during the day at tacky tourist shops before a late lunch (included) at a floating restaurant and heading back to Manaus by 4pm. Many multi-day jungle trips also include a stop at the Meeting of the Waters, but for those with limited time, this packaged tour gives a brief taste of the forest. Guides usually speak English.

AMAZON JUNGLE TRIPS

The highlight of any visit to the Amazon Basin is a trip on its rivers and through its famed tropical rainforest. Most trips into the Brazilian Amazon begin in Manaus. As ecotourism and the population around Manaus have expanded, getting to true wilderness takes an increasingly long bus ride and/or boat journey. Manaus is filled with dozens of tour agencies and guides that cater to every budget, and can organize a trip in a day or two.

ORIENTATION

Manaus is situated at the point where Rio Negro and Rio Solimões become the **Rio Amazonas.** Just 60km up the **Rio Negro** is the start of the **Anavilhanas Archipelago,** the largest inland archipelago in the world, made up of 400 islands. The Rio Negro's water is acidic, so mosquitoes are not normally a problem. The rainforest around Rio Negro has a higher elevation and treks through it are possible year-round. The **Rio Solimões** is home to more wildlife, including birds and *caiman* (as well as mosquitoes), and floods the surrounding rainforest for six months a year. The more remote jungle treks are northeast of Manaus, up tributaries of the Rio Amazonas.

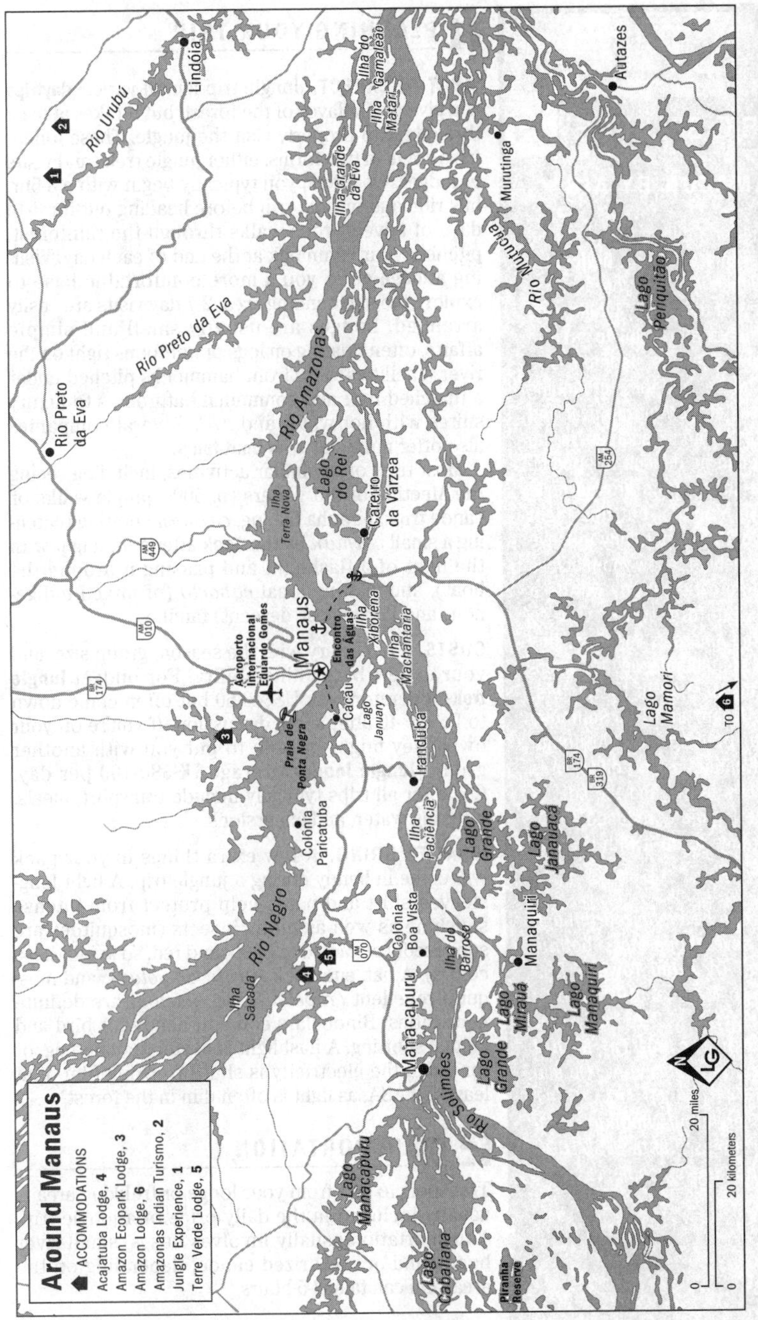
Around Manaus
ACCOMMODATIONS
Acajatuba Lodge, 4
Amazon Ecopark Lodge, 3
Amazon Lodge, 6
Amazonas Indian Turismo, 2
Jungle Experience, 1
Terre Verde Lodge, 5
Lindóia
Rio Urubu
Rio Preto da Eva
Rio Preto da Eva
Rio Amazonas
Ilha do Gamaleão
Ilha Matari
Ilha Grande da Eva
Autazes
Murutinga
Rio Mutuca
Lago Periquitão
AM 254
Lago do Rei
Careiro da Várzea
Ilha Terra Nova
AM 449
AM 010
BR 174
Aeroporto Internacional Eduardo Gomes
Manaus
Encontro das Águas
Ilha Xiborena
Ilha Machantaria
Cacau
Lago January
Praia de Ponta Negra
Iranduba
Colônia Paricatuba
Ilha Paciência
Lago Mamori
TO 6
BR 174
BR 319
Lago Grande
Lago Janauacá
Rio Negro
Colônia Boa Vista
AM 070
Ilha do Barroso
Manaquiri
Lago Manaquiri
Lago Miraúá
Ilha Sacada
Manacapuru
Lago Grande
Rio Solimões
Lago Manacapuru
Lago Cabaliana
Piranha Reserve
20 miles
20 kilometers
LG

HE BIG SPLURGE

AMAZON BY AIR

ooking for a different way of seeng the Amazon? Try a **helicopter ide,** which will give you a bird's-ye view of the mighty jungle. One our flights allow you to take in owntown Manaus, its impressive pera house, and the surrounding xpanses of the Amazon river and ainforest. With skyscrapers in the vay, it can be difficult to appreciate the jungle from ground level vhile in Manaus, but this flight ives you the opportunity to leave he city behind. A low zoom across he rainforest's canopy will be a nique, unforgettable way to rasp the Amazon's vastness. This s also the ultimate way to experince the Meeting of the Waters, s Rio Negro and Rio Solimões low far beneath you. Although his adventure is a bit pricey, it is ertainly worth it, and the cost of he ride is greatly reduced if you an arrange to do it with a group f travelers.

lights can be organized through ne of several operators, both in lanaus. Try ***Ariaú Towers,*** *Rua eonardo Malcher 699 (☎622 000; fax 233 5615; www.ariau.tur.br).* ***Taj Mahal lotel's*** *travel agency, Av. Getúlio /argas 741 (☎627 3737, 9141 919; sergiotour@hotmail.com), lso arranges flights. US$1000 er flight. Max. 5 people.*

PLANNING YOUR TRIP

WHAT TO EXPECT. Jungle trip length varies: **daytrips** can give you a flavor of the forest, but it takes at least three days to properly visit the jungle. These longer trips come in two forms: either jungle treks and visits to lodges. On a **trek,** you typically begin with a 3-5hr. bus ride and/or boat trip before heading out for 3-10 days of adventurous walks through the rainforest, pitching your hammock at the end of each day. Visiting a **lodge** gives you a more comfortable base to explore the surrounding area; 2-7 day visits are easily arranged. Lodges are usually small and simple affairs, often floating on logs or pontoons right on the river. Facilities vary, from hammocks pitched under a thatched roof and communal bathrooms to luxury suites with hot water and A/C. Several companies also offer multi-day **river boat tours.**

Most trips offer similar activities, including seeing the Meeting of the Waters (p. 500), jungle walks or canoe trips, piranha fishing, *caiman* spotting (catching a small *caiman* by the neck after stunning it with the light of a flashlight and passing it around the boat), and visiting local *caboclo* (of mixed indigenous and Portuguese descent) families.

COSTS. Prices vary with the season, group size, and your expert bargaining ability. For budget **jungle treks,** operators ask US$40-60 but often come down to US$25-40 after some discussion. If you're on your own, they might be able to put you with another group. **Jungle lodges** average US$80-100 per day. Costs for all trips typically include transport, meals, drinking water, and excursions.

WHAT TO BRING. A few extra things in your pack will come in handy during a jungle trip. A light long-sleeved shirt and pants help protect from intense sunshine as well as biting insects (mosquitoes are supposedly attracted to black and red, so avoid those colors). A hat, sunblock *(proteção solar)*, and mosquito repellent *(repelente de insetos)* are definite necessities. Binoculars come in handy for bird and animal spotting. A flashlight is useful for camping, or for when the electricity is shut off. Bring film of at least 400 ASA, as light is often dim in the forest.

TRANSPORTATION

Transport to and from your lodge or trekking area is usually included in the daily price of a jungle trip. Transportation usually involves buses, small river boats, and/or motorized canoe, depending on the area, and can take 2-5 hours.

TOUR AGENCIES & OPERATORS

Be sure to book your trip only with a reputable agency or guide, either by email before you arrive or at their office in Manaus. Although you will be accosted at the airport and downtown by people offering tours (some of whom may even mention the names of reputable operators), do not make arrangements with such characters, as it may not always be safe. Check into your hotel, and then start getting information on trips. The tourist office has a list of EMBRATUR-certified agencies and guides. Always clarify exactly what is included in the trip (whether hammocks, beds, tours, food, or drinks). Most companies now have you sign a contract for both your protection and theirs. The tourist office and police by the Teatro Amazonas also have EMBRATUR complaint forms if anything goes wrong. The following organizations are all in Manaus unless otherwise indicated.

DAYTRIPS

Amazon Explorers, Rua Nhamundá 21, Pça. NS Auxiliadora (☎633 3319, 633 1978; fax 234 5753; www.amazonexplorers.com.br). They also have booths at Pça. Tenreiro Aranha (☎232 3052; fax 234 6767), near Selvatur; and TVlândia Mall, Av. Djalma Batista 2100 (☎642 0055; fax 642 4777). An agent for many area jungle lodges. Also run city tours and trips to Encontro das Águas and Ecológico January (R$50 from downtown booth, R$70 including pick-up from hotel). Open M-F 7:30am-noon and 2-5:30pm, Sa 7:30am-noon, Su 7:30-9am. AmEx/MC/V.

Selvatur, Pça. Adalberto Vale 17 (☎622 2577; fax 622 2177; www.selvatur.com.br). Selvatur runs 3hr. city trips and 6hr. boat trips to Encontro das Águas and Ecológico January (R$50 from office, R$70 including pick-up from hotel). They can also organize stays at jungle lodges listed below. Open M-F 8am-6pm, Sa 8am-noon. AmEx/MC/V.

JUNGLE TREKS

Amazonas Indian Turismo, Rua dos Andradas 311 (☎/fax 633 5578). Offers adventurous 2- to 10-day trips to the remote Rio Urubú region, 200km (4hr.) northeast of Manaus by bus and boat. English-speaking guides share their knowledge of the region during flexible excursions that include canoe trips through the *igarapé* channels and flooded forest *(igapó),* alligator spotting, fishing, and trekking and sleeping in the rainforest. They are geared toward trips for younger backpackers. US$30-43 per day. 1- to 5-person groups. Open M-F 8am-6pm, Sa 8am-5pm, Su 8am-noon. Cash only.

Jungle Experience, Rua dos Andradas 491 (☎233 2000; www.geocities.com/hotelidealmanaus). Christopher Gomes works out of the Hotel Ideal and offers camping trips to the Rio Urubú region, 200km northeast of Manaus. He can organize flexible trips of 3-10 days that include treks, canoe trips through *igapós* (flooded forest), and bird watching with English-speaking guides. Trips are for the active and adventurous, accommodations are in hammocks, and camping in the jungle is possible. The region is accessible by a 3hr. bus and 1½hr. boat trip. US$60 per day. 2- to 10-person groups.

JUNGLE LODGES

Terra Verde Lodge, Hotel Monaco, Rua Silva Ramos 20, rm. 305 (☎622 7305, 622 4114; www.internext.com.br/terraverde). 2½hr. from Manaus, Terra Verde Lodge sits on the 27,000 acre private Floresta Vida (Forest of Life) Ecological Reserve. Founded by Polish filmmaker Zygmunt Sulistrowski, the lodge is on the site of the Fazenda São Francisco, a historic cattle ranch. Zygmunt formed the NGO Cepecam in 1988 to preserve one of the largest primary rainforests still intact in the Manaus region. The lodge is simple but peaceful. Each bungalow has a private bathroom and balcony overlooking the water, where there is also a protected swimming area. 2-day/1-night package US$170; 3-day/2-night package US$200. Open M-F 8am-6pm.

Amazon Ecopark Lodge, Rua Lauro Müller 36, ste. 510, in Rio de Janeiro (in Manaus ☎622 2612; in Rio ☎21 2275 5285; fax in Rio 21 2275 6544; www.amazonecopark.com). Forty minutes by boat from the Tropical Hotel dock, the Amazon Ecopark Lodge and Monkey Forest are on the 4500-acre private nonprofit Floresta Vida Reserve. The lodge has 60 comfortable rooms with A/C and hot water, contained in 20 bungalows spread through the forest, along with a good buffet restaurant, 10km of walking trails, cascading natural swimming pools, and a private beach. A 2min. boat ride across the river is the Monkey Forest, where confiscated or captured monkeys receive medical treatment and time to reacclimatize to the forest before being returned to the wild. Six species of monkeys were in residence as of August 2003, including *vakari,* howler, spider, and capuchin. 2-day/1-night package US$240-260; 3-day/2-night package US$280-350; 4-day/3-night package US$360-400. US$35 extra for solo travelers. Cash or traveler's checks only.

Swallows and Amazons, Rua Quintino Bocaiúva 189, rm. 13 (☎/fax 622 1246; www.swallowsandamazonstours.com). Owned by American Mark Aitchison and his Brazilian wife Tania, Swallows and Amazons specializes in 3- to 4-day boat trips on the Rio Negro. These trips include visiting the Meeting of the Waters, Lake January, and the Anavilhanas Archipelago. They also offer longer personalized 7- to 15-day trips and organize expeditions to Pico da Neblina (the highest peak in Brazil). Additionally, they run the **Overlook Lodge** on the Rio Negro near the Anavilhanas Archipelago. The rustic lodge has 8 double rooms with common bath. Boat trips (where you sleep on board in hammocks) R$70-120. Min. 3 people.

Nature Safaris, Rua Flávio Espírito Santo 1 (☎656 6033; www.naturesafaris.com), in Kissia II. Nature Safaris manages a guesthouse in Manaus as well as 2 floating lodges located in private reserves. **Amazon Lodge,** 80km (4hr.) from Manaus, opened in 1982 and was the first floating lodge in the Amazon. It can hold up to 36 people, in rooms with fans and common bath. **Piranha Lodge** opened in 2003 in the 1030 square kilometers that comprise Piranha Reserve, 120km from Manaus. It has 20 double rooms with A/C and private bath. Built on a flat-bottom barge, the lodge moves around the reserve depending on the season and water level. Visitors receive discounts at the Mango Guest House (US$50 per night) in the suburbs of Manaus. Amazon Lodge 3-day/2-night package US$495; 4-day/3-night package US$555; each excursion from the lodge US$10-15. Piranha Lodge has a 5-day/4-night package (depart W; US$640) and a 4-day/3-night package (depart Su; US$490), with excursions included. US$65 extra for solo travelers.

Eco Planet Turismo, Rua Dr. Moreira 270, rm. 204 (☎/fax 234 8551; www.ecoplanetturismo.com). Eco Planet Turismo offers 1- to 5-day boat trips on Rio Negro and Rio Solimões, sport fishing excursions (Oct.-Jan.), stays at **Acajatuba Lodge,** and more adventurous 5-day trips to Lagoa Mamori and Lagoa Juma. Their multilingual website is definitely worth checking out. Guides speak English. US$45-110 per day (including drinks and airport transfers). 2-8 people per boat trip. Open M-F 8am-6pm, Sa 8am-2pm. AmEx/MC/V.

Green Planet Tours, Rua 10 de Julho 481 (☎232 1398; fax 232 5671; www.planettours.com.br). Green Planet is a budget-oriented agency that makes boat trips up the Rio Negro to their lodge at Jacaré Ubau and 3-day trips to their cabanas at Mamori and Juma Lakes. US$40-50 per day, in either simple rooms or hammocks. Max. 10 people. Open daily 8am-6pm. Cash only.

Eco-Discovery Tours, Rua Leovegildo Coelho 301 (☎664 3536; www.ecodiscovery.hpg.com.br). This outfit runs excursions to the waterfalls at Presidente Figueiredo and the Jaú Reserve, but specializes in 4-day/3-night packages to Lagoa Mamori via the Meeting of the Waters. At Lagoa Mamori, they share Green Planet's simple lodge (see above). US$60-80 per day. 3-person min. Cash only.

PARINTINS ☎92

Parintins has become increasingly famous in Brazil and abroad for its annual **Boi-Bumba Festival** (p. 39), the biggest party in the Amazon, held June 28-30. In the weeks leading up to the festival, everything gets a new coat of paint, costumes receive finishing touches, and performances are perfected. The usually quiet town transforms with the arrival of tens of thousands of visitors; the waterfront is lined with boats, restaurants and shops stay open all night, and dance clubs greet the sun.

TRANSPORTATION. Aeroporto Júlio Belém is located about 8km from the heart of the *centro;* a fixed-price taxi from the *centro* costs R$20. **Rico,** Av. Amazonas 2046 (☎533 3400), has the most flights. **Total, Tavaj,** and **Varig** have offices at the airport, which are only open before flights. **Boats** leave from the dock at the end of Rua Gomes de Castro. **Agência Prestes,** Pça. Cristo Redentor 2118, 100m to the right of the market, has information and sells passage on all boats. (☎533 1783. Open daily 7am-noon and 2-5:30pm). Most stop briefly in Parintins to drop off and pick up passengers as they sail to Manaus (20hr.; M noon and Tu-Su 6pm; R$40) or Santarém (14-20hr.; daily around noon; R$40). The Ajato **speed boat** goes to Manaus (8hr.; W, Sa noon; R$90) and Santarém (5hr.; Tu, F 2pm; R$60).

ORIENTATION. Activity is centered between the **port, cathedral,** and the **Bumbódromo** stadium. The **Mercado Municipal** is to the right of the port. **Rua Clarindo Chaves** runs from the market square past the cathedral to the stadium. The cathedral is on the main street, **Avenida Amazonas,** lined with eateries, bars, and hotels. The airport is down **Rua Lindolfo Monte Verde.** The Caprichoso and Garantido schools are on opposite sides of town: Caprichoso at the end of **Avenida Nações Unidas** and Garantido by the water on the way to the airport. Their huge flags can be seen from all over. All directions below are given with your back to the water.

PRACTICAL INFORMATION. The **Secretaria Municipal de Cultura e Turismo (Sectur),** Av. Nações Unidas 708, next to Supermercado Triunfante and three blocks to the left of the Bumbódromo, has information on the festival. (☎533 3109. Open M-F 8am-7pm.) **Tucunaré Turismo,** Rua Jonathas Pedrosa 89, opposite Banco do Brasil, sells tickets for all local flights and is the agent for Tavaj and Total. (☎533 3330. Open M-F 8am-6pm, Sa 8am-noon and 1-5pm. AmEx/MC/V.) **Turis Par,** Av. Amazonas 2046, one

NO WORK, ALL PLAY

BOI-BUMBÁ

The Amazon's biggest party is the **Boi-Bumbá** folk festival in Parintins, when tens of thousands of people fly, boat, and paddle their way to the small town to watch two *boi* schools, the Caprichoso and the Garantido, as they compete in song, dance, and percussion. The festival's origins lie in a dispute between two wealthy families, the Monteverds and the Cids, whose would challenge each other to sing the better song.

The schools were formed in 1913 and are symbolized by bulls, Garantido's in red and Caprichoso's in blue and white. Every resident has loyalty to either red or blue. These factions divide the festival's home—the 35,000 seat Bumbódromo—into two seas, one of red Garantido loyalists and one of blue Caprichoso supporters. The performances are spectacular, as hundreds of locals dress in elaborate costumes and act out local legends involving a bull's death and resurrection.

As the show has become more and more technically sophisticated, Parintins's Boi-Bumbá has become increasingly famous both in Brazil and abroad. Accommodations become extremely scarce and expensive during the festival.

The Boi-Bumbá occurs June 28-30 every year. The following websites have information on the festival: www.boideparintins.com.br or www.parintins.com.

block left of the cathedral, is the agent for Rico. (☎533 2700. Open M-Sa 8am-1pm. AmEx/MC/V.) There is **no currency exchange** in town. The leftmost ATM at **Banco do Brasil,** Pça. Eduardo Ribeiro 2024, at the corner of Rua Jonathas Pedrosa, accepts Visa and Cirrus cards. (☎533 2021. Open daily 6am-10pm.) **Bradesco,** Rua Benjamin da Silva 3711 (☎533 1765), up one block from the dock on the right, has **24hr. ATMs** that accept Visa. Other services include: **Supermercado Baranda,** Rua Paes de Andrade 229, on the corner of Av. Amazonas. (☎533 1372; open M-Sa 7am-noon and 2-8pm, Su 7am-noon; MC/V); **police,** Av. Nações Unidas s/n, to the left of the Bumbódromo (☎533 3735); the **Hospital Padre Colombo,** Rua Oneldes Martins 3515, off Av. Nações Unidas toward the airport (☎533 1614); **Internet access** at Dabela.com, Av. Amazonas 2500, three blocks to the right of the cathedral (☎533 5645; R$3 per 30min., R$4 per hr.; open daily 8-10am and 4-10pm); **international phones** outside Telemar, Av. Amazonas 1916, at Rua Paes de Andrade (☎533 1717); and the **post office,** Rua Rui Barbosa 1958, on the waterfront 100m right of the dock (☎533 2105; open M-F 8am-4pm). **Postal code:** 69151-000.

ACCOMMODATIONS. Pousada Tia Marlene ❶, Rua Hebert Azevedo 1354, is one block to the left of Hotel Uyrapuru. This family-run *pousada* with a garden is in a quiet neighborhood. All rooms include A/C, TV, and *frigo-bar.* (☎533 1590. Singles R$20; doubles R$30; triples R$45.) **Hotel Amazonas ❶,** Av. Amazonas 2351, just one block to the right of the cathedral, is in the center of things. Amazonas has large rooms with A/C and TV, and some have *frigo-bar.* Big windows make outside rooms along the balcony the best. (☎533 4395. Singles R$25; doubles R$50.)

FOOD. Restaurante Barraco do Boi ❷, Rua Boulevard 14 de Maio s/n, is one block up from the dock and to the left. It serves a great *pato no tucupí* (spicy duck soup made with manioc powder; R$8). (☎9145 8984. Entrees R$4-10. Open daily 8am-midnight.) **Churrascaria Carne na Tábua ❷,** Rua Rui Barbosa s/n, is right above the dock at the corner of Rua Gomes de Castro. Meat is the order of the day, with heaping servings on wooden boards from the BBQ. (☎9129 1472. Entrees R$13-15. Open daily 9am-midnight.) **Kais Bar,** Rua Rui Barbosa s/n, on a breezy terrace overlooking the dock and river, is an excellent place to catch a *futebol* match on the big-screen TV or slowly sip an evening beer as the river boats putter by. (Open daily 10am-3am.) **Plataforma 1,** Rua Paes de Andrade 210, between the dock and Av. Amazonas on the right, draws revelers with *forró*, techno, and its large air-conditioned dance floor. (Cover R$15. Open F-Su 11pm-late.)

TEFÉ ☎97

At the halfway point of the Amazon's journey from the Andes to the Atlantic, Tefé is the largest stopover town for riverboats chugging up the Rio Solimões. Located between Manaus and the Columbian border, this town is most often visited by travelers on their way to the **Mamirauá Sustainable Development Reserve** (p. 507). The jungle is never far away in Tefé, and the cars and moto-taxis which travel the few stretches of local road were all brought by barge. There is little reason to tarry in Tefé, but during the dry season you can charter a *lancha* (R$5) to your own private beach on Lago Tefé. Tefé's main road, the Estrada do Aeroporto, stretches 4km from the airport to the port. The *centro* is located between the fork where Estrada Aeroporto splits into Rua Olavo Bilac and Pça. Santa Teresa, which runs toward Igreja Santa Teresa. Ferries to Manaus leave from the Capitalia do Portos, behind the central market.

Varig and Rico fly to Manaus and Tabatinga from the small **airport** which lies 4km from the *centro*. **Varig,** Estrada do Aeroporto 269, is located 100m on the right toward the airport after the Estrada do Aeroporto fork. (☎343 2466. Open M-F 8-

11am and 2-5pm, Sa 8-11am. AmEx/MC/V.) **Rico,** Estrada do Aeroporto 793, is across the street. (☎/fax 343 3636. Open M-F 8am-noon and 2-5pm. AmEx/MC/V.) A **taxi** from the airport to the *centro* costs R$15, and a **moto-taxi** costs R$5. **Riverboats** leave daily from the dock to Manaus (2½ days; R$30 lower deck, R$40 upper deck, R$150 cabin). Those in a rush can take the weekly Ajato **speedboat** to Manaus (11hr.; Su 7am; R$130). Boats to Tabatinga pass by Tefé at least once a week (6-7 days; R$150), but you need to rent a *lancha* (R$5) at the port to meet these boats as they head up the Rio Solimões. There is **currency exchange** at Bradesco Bank, Rua Benjamin Constant 122 (☎343 2514; fax 343 2514). Banco do Brasil, Rua Olavo Bilac 268, across from the market, has **ATMs** that accept Cirrus/Plus/MC/V cards. (☎343 2556. Open M-F 9am-2pm; ATMs open daily 6am-10pm). Other services include: **police,** Estrada do Aeroporto 1036; **Hospital São Miguel,** Marechal Deodoro 660 (☎343 2446); phones at **Telemar,** Pça. Santa Teresa 395 (☎343 3939; open M-F 7:30-11am and 1:30-5:30pm, Sa 7:30am-noon); and the **post office,** Estrado do Aeroporto 697 (☎343 2871; open M-F 8am-2pm). **Postal code:** 69470-000.

Tefé's hotels cluster in the few blocks between the market on Rua Olavo Bilac, Igreja Santa Teresa, and the fork in Estrada do Aeroporto. The centrally located **Hotel Panorama ❶,** Rua Floriano Peixoto 90, on the corner of Rua Olavo Bilac, has an attached restaurant and overlooks the river: the best views are on the third floor. (☎743 2483; fax 743 2526. Breakfast included. Singles with fan R$20, with A/C and *frigo-bar* R$30; doubles with fan R$25, with A/C and *frigo-bar* R$45.) Between the Panorama and Banco do Brasil sits the **Raydienne Hotel ❶,** Rua Olavo Bilac 342. This electric-blue hotel is only a few steps from the market, and the most affordable place in town. (☎343 4871. Breakfast included. Singles R$8, with bath R$12; doubles R$15; triples R$20.) The slightly more upscale **Anilçe's Hotel ❷,** Pça. Santa Teresa 264, is just across from the church. This is probably Tefé's most well-known hotel, and the only one with monogrammed sheets: it also has a TV lounge where guests can mingle. (☎343 2416. Breakfast included. Singles with A/C R$30; doubles with A/C and TV R$40.) The only *churrascaria* in town is **Churrascaria Boî na Brassa ❷,** Pça. Santa Teresa 476, next to the church. It offers *churrasco* for one (R$9-13) or two (R$11-18) and has a full bar. (☎343 4553. M-Sa lunch R$5. Drinks R$3-4. Open daily 8am-11pm.) The waterfront side of the Mercado Municipal has a number of **food stalls** and after dark (generally 6-10pm), more stalls appear in the square in front of Igreja Santa Teresa: this is a great place to get beef and sausage kebabs (R$0.50), as well as to people-watch.

MAMIRAUÁ RESERVE ☎97

Mamirauá is one of the best places in Brazil to view Amazonian wildlife. The **Mamirauá Sustainable Development Reserve** is also a pioneering attempt to protect and study the largest *várzea* (flooded forest) in the world, while assisting the development of the surrounding communities. The reserve was founded in 1996 by a non-profit organization, the Instituto de Sustentável Mamirauá. It consists of over 11,000 square kilometers of *várzea* forest, inhabited by about 5000 *ribeirinhos* (literally, "river people"). For as many as nine months of the year, the *várzea* is flooded to depths of up to 12m. The plants and wildlife of the forest are well-adapted to this yearly deluge, and the forest is a unique ecosystem with a number of endemic species. Researchers first came to Mamirauá in search of the rare white uakari monkey, which is found only in the area now covered by the reserve. Pink dolphins, manatees, and caimans inhabit Mamirauá's rivers, and its forests are home to howler and capuchin monkeys, jaguars, and the three-toed sloth. The world's largest rodent, the *capivara*, can also be found in Mamirauá, as can the *pirarucú*, one of the world's largest freshwater fish. There are over 400 species of bird in the area covered by the reserve, including 19 species of parrot.

AT A GLANCE: MAMIRAUÁ RESERVE

AREA: Over 11,000 square kilometers. **CLIMATE:** Partially flooded for most of the year. The temperature varies little throughout the year (averaging 27°C), and it tends to be humid. **WHEN TO GO:** During the peak of the wet season (May-June), canoe trips are possible through the flooded forest near the canopy. In the middle of the dry season (Sept.-Oct.), you can walk through the jungle and the wildlife is easier to spot.	**HIGHLIGHTS:** Canoe trips; guided walks; visiting the Mamirauá Lake; meeting researchers studying the ecosystem. **GATEWAY TOWNS:** Tefé (p. 506). **FEES:** A 3-night/4-day package costs US$360 per person. **CAMPING:** Camping is not possible in Mamirauá: you can only enter the reserve on a package tour with the Instituto de Desenvolvimento Sustentável Mamirauá.

The Mamirauá Reserve lies adjacent to the Amanã Reserve and Parque Nacional do Jaú: together they form the world's largest contiguous area of protected tropical forest. Mamirauá is divided into nine sectors, and ecotourism is permitted only in one section—with an area of 2600 square kilometers—in the southeast. This sector is the closest to the small town of Tefé (p. 506), where all trips to the reserve begin and end. **Mamirauá vehicles** meet Varig's Wednesday flight from Manaus (1hr.; R$203) in Tefé and transport their guests to the port. From the port, 10-seater **lanches** take about 1½hr. to reach the Uakari Lodge. The only way to visit the Mamirauá Reserve is on an all-inclusive organized excursion with the **Instituto de Desenvolvimento Sustentável Mamirauá,** Av. Brasil 197 in Tefé. (☎/fax 343 4160; www.mamiraua.org.br. Open M-F 8am-noon and 2-6pm, Sa 8am-noon.) The Instituto offers a 3-night/4-day package, which includes transportation from the Tefé airport, double accommodations, food, and excursions. (US$360 per person; US$25 extra for solo travelers. Max. 20 people per tour. Cash or traveler's checks.) **Supplies** to bring include sunglasses, sunblock, mosquito repellent, binoculars, a rain jacket, and film of at least 400ASA (the light can get quite dim under the forest canopy). The **Ukari Lodge** has five floating bungalows, attached to the central lodge by flower-lined walkways. Each bungalow has two large double rooms with queen-sized beds and mosquito nets, as well as a porch and hammock. In the interests of minimizing the lodge's environmental impact, all the lights and hot-water showers are solar-powered. **Food** is also included in the package tour of Mamirauá. Dietary restrictions should be reported when the excursion is booked.

The Mamirauá package includes a series of **guided excursions** in groups of four or less. English-speaking guides accompany trips to local communities, research stations, and the Mamirauá Lake. Local *ribeirinho* guides take you on canoe trips (**nighttime canoe trips** allow you to spot nocturnal wildlife). Activities vary with the weather and season, but typically include hiking, fishing trips, and canoeing.

RORAIMA

BOA VISTA ☎95

Boa Vista, the sprawling capital of the state of Roriama, is on the paved road that runs between Manaus and the Venezuelan border. It is a planned city of parks, wide streets, and government buildings. For many travelers it is a stopover, and they get in and out as quickly as possible. Boa Vista is 758km from Manaus and 230km from Santa Elena de Vairén (Venezuela) on the BR-174, and 125km from Lethem (Guyana) on the BR-401.

TRANSPORTATION

Flights: Aeroporto Internacional de Boa Vista, Pça. Santos Dumont 3110 (☎623 9394; fax 623 9363), 4km from the *centro*. Take Bus #206 ("Aeroporto") to the *centro*. Services include: luggage storage, 24hr. tourist booth, yellow fever station. Taxis R$20. There are two carriers with offices in town. **Varig,** Rua Araújo Filho 91 (☎224 2269), near Av. Getúlio Vargas. Open M-F 8am-6pm, Sa 8am-noon. AmEx/MC/V. **Meta,** Av. Benjamin Constant 79W (☎224 7677; fax 623 9500). Open M-F 8am-6pm, Sa 8am-noon. AmEx/MC/V.

Intercity Buses: Long-distance buses leave from **Rodoviária Internacional José Oliveira Amador Baton,** Av. das Guianas 1523 (☎623 2233), 3km from the *centro*. Take Bus #215 ("Novo Cidade" or "Jockei Clube"). **Amatur Amazônia Turismo** (☎224 0004; www.amatur.com.br) runs to **Manaus** (12hr.; Tu, Th, Su 7pm; R$70). **Eucatur** (☎624 1322; open 6am-midnight) runs to: **Caracas,** Venezuela (24hr.; 6am; R$100); **Manaus** (12hr.; 5 per day 10am-8:30pm; R$69-76); **Santa Elene de Vairén,** Venezuela (4hr.; 3 per day 6am-5pm; R$20). AmEx/MC/V.

Local Buses: Leave from **Rodoviária Urbano,** Av. Dr. Sílvio L. Botelho, between Av. Getúlio Vargas and Av. Sebastião Diniz (R$1.50). The fenced-off upper area is only for reduced-fare passengers; use the lower section.

Taxis: Ponto de Taxi, Av. Glaycon de Paiva 1536 (☎224 2441). There are numerous metered taxis prowling the streets. White taxis with yellow and blue stripes (marked "Lotação") follow fixed routes around town—mostly along the streets radiating from the *centro*—and can easily be flagged down (R$1.80).

Car Rental: Localiza Rent-A-Car, Av. Benjamin Constant 1044E (☎224 5222), at Rua Alfredo Cruz. Compact car R$85 with unlimited mileage. Open M-F 8am-noon and 2-6pm, Sa 8am-noon. AmEx/MC/V.

ORIENTATION & PRACTICAL INFORMATION

Eighteenth-century Portuguese established cattle ranches and the Forte São Joaquim in the area which is today Boa Vista. In the 1960s, the gargantuan modern city plan was created. The spread-out city is completely unsuited for walking (although it does have Brazil's most courteous drivers). It is laid out in an arc, with **Rio Branco** at its base and six main streets. **Avenida Major Williams** is the outermost in the arc. At the center of the arc is **Praça do Centro Cívico,** which contains the Palácio do Governo Estadual as well as the Monumento ao Garimpeiro, a crude monument to the gold prospectors who flooded the Yanomami reserve in the 1980s. Main streets radiate from this large unkempt *praça*. The **airport** is about 4km from the *praça* on the road directly behind the palace. Intercity buses arrive at the **rodoviária,** 3km from the *centro*. The main shopping district and local bus station are between the Palácio and Rio Branco.

Tourist Office: Detur, Av. Cap. Júlio Bezerra 196 (☎/fax 623 1230; turismo.seplan@cei.rr.gov.br), near Av. Getúlio Vargas in the Seplan Building. Helpful brochure on Roriama with a map of Boa Vista. Open M-F 8am-6pm. Branches in the intercity *rodoviária* (open daily 7:30am-11pm) and airport (open 24hr.).

Consulates: Guyana, Av. Benjamin Constant 1020 (☎224 1333; consulgny@technet.com.br), 1 block from the *praça* at Rua Col. Pinto. To obtain a visa, bring a passport valid for 6 months, a copy of your yellow fever certificate, and 2 photos. Fee is paid at the nearby post office. Open M-F 9am-1pm. **Venezuela,** Av. Benjamin Constant 525 (☎623 9285), at Rua Barão do Rio Branco. Same-day tourist cards for those that need them. Bring a passport valid for at least 6 months, 1 photo, and copies of your passport, yellow fever card, and Brazilian entry card. Open M-F 8am-noon.

Currency Exchange: Best rates are at jewelry store **Safira Jóias,** Av. Benjamin Constant 64 (☎224 5983, 624 4104). Changes US dollars and traveler's checks. Open M-F 8am-5:30pm. **Pedro José,** Rua Araújo Filho 287 (☎224 9797), in the back of BV Tours, between Av. Benjamin Constant and Av. Getúlio Vargas. Changes US dollars and traveler's checks. **Banco do Brasil,** Av. Glaycon de Paiva 56 (☎623 2727), on Pça. do Centro Cívico. Gives Visa advances, exchanges US dollars and euros for a 3% commission, and traveler's checks for a flat US$20 fee. Open for exchange 9am-noon.

24hr. ATMs: HSBC, Av. Ville Roy 292E (☎623 2174), 2 blocks from the *praça* behind the Legislative Assembly, to the right. Gives cash on AmEx/Cirrus/MC/PLUS/V cards. **Bradesco,** Av. Jaime Brasil 441 (☎623 2620), at Av. Getúlio Vargas. Accepts MC/V cards. **Banco do Brasil** has PLUS/V ATMs at the airport and the intercity *rodoviária.*

Ticket Agencies: Anaconda Tours, Av. Dr. Sílvio L. Botelho 12 (☎224 4132; anaconda@uze.com.br). Open M-F 8am-noon and 2-6pm, Sa 8am-noon. AmEx/MC/V. **Tours Águia,** Av. Benjamin Constant 115W (☎624 1516; afonsoaguia@aol.com), next to Meta Airlines. Open M-F 8am-noon and 2-6pm, Sa 8am-noon. AmEx/MC/V.

Supermarket: Supermercado Butekão, Av. Getúlio Vargas 75W (☎224 9100; fax 224 7542), behind local bus station at corner of Av. Dr. Sílvio L. Botelho. Open 24hr. MC/V.

Police: Polícia Federal, Av. Ville Roy 2801 (☎621 1500, 627 2460), in Caçari. Take any "Caçari" bus. Also at the airport.

24hr. Pharmacy: Drogaria Megafarma, Av. Cap. Júlio Bezerra 1225 (☎623 7285), in São Francisco.

Hospital: Hospital Coronel Mota, Av. Col. Pinto 626 (☎623 0161), at the intersection of Av. Ville Roy.

Telephones: International calls can be made from the public telephones outside **Telemar,** Av. Cap. Ene Garcez 126, behind the Palácio.

Internet Access: Nobel Mega Store Café Internet, Av. Glaycon de Paiva 172A (☎621 3422). R$3 per 30min.; R$5 per hr. Open M-Sa 9am-7pm.

Post Office: Pça. do Centro Cívico 176 (☎621 3525), on the right side of the *praça.* Open M-F 8am-5pm, Sa 8am-noon. **Postal code:** 69301-970.

ACCOMMODATIONS

Boa Vista is a horizontal city, and even the budget hotels are not cramped. Mid-range hotels are mad about swimming pools (and poolside bars). The hotels listed below all include breakfast and have a noon check-out.

Hotel Monte Libano, Av. Benjamin Constant 319W (☎224 7232), 2 blocks left of the *praça.* A centrally located no-frills budget hotel. Singles with fan R$14, with bath R$15, with A/C R$25; doubles R$18, with bath R$24, with A/C R$28; triples with bath R$30, with A/C R$35. ❶

Hotel Ideal, Rua Araújo Filho 393 (☎224 6342), at Av. NS da Consolata. Ideal might not quite live up to its name, but it does provide sizable rooms. Rooms with fan are in a separate annex and a bit older than the brighter A/C rooms. Singles with fan R$25, with A/C R$30; doubles with fan R$30, with A/C R$40. R$6 extra for TV or *frigo-bar.* ❶

Hotel Euzebio's, Rua Cecília Brasil 1107 (☎623 0300; fax 623 9131; hoteleuzebios@uol.com.br), 20m left of Av. Cap. Ene Garcez, 2 blocks behind the Palácio. Euzebio's is a good value: the hotel has a pool, poolside bar, and standard rooms with A/C and TV. Larger, brighter *luxo* rooms upstairs have a *frigo-bar,* larger bathrooms with hot water, and the occasional balcony. Excellent breakfast included. Laundry available. Complimentary airport van. Standard singles R$42; doubles R$52. *Luxo* singles R$68; doubles R$85; triples R$100. MC/V. ❷

Hotel Imperial, Av. Benjamin Constant 433 (☎224 5592), 100m past Rua Cecília Brasil. Simple but popular, Imperial has 26 rooms and a small pool out back. Singles with fan R$20, with A/C and TV R$25; doubles with fan R$25, with A/C and TV R$30. ❶

Hotel Barrudada, Rua Araújo Filho 228 (☎623 9335). The tall building between Av. Benjamin Constant and Av. Getúlio Vargas. A sparkling, newish hotel with bright rooms and good views. All rooms have A/C, TV, *frigo-bar,* and telephone. Singles R$60; doubles R$80; triples R$90. MC/V. ❸

Hotel Farroupilha, Av. das Guianas 1400 (☎224 9499, 624 4226), opposite the intercity *rodoviária* on the left. A good choice for those who arrive in town late at night. Modern rooms are clean and have A/C, TV, *frigo-bar,* phone, and hot-water showers. Singles R$30; doubles R$38; triples R$45. ❷

Uiramutam Palace Hotel, Av. Cap. Ene Garcez 427 (☎624 4700; uiramutam@technet.com.br), located 3 blocks behind the Palácio. A cool hotel in whites and blues, Uiramutam Palace has all the luxuries you could want, including a full restaurant, pool, room service, and spotless standard rooms with *frigo-bar,* A/C, TV, and phone. Upstairs *luxo* rooms are similar, but also have hot-water showers. Standard singles R$85; doubles R$110; triples R$130. MC/V. ❹

 FOOD

Boa Vista's culinary scene relies heavily on fish dishes, which are generous and fresh. For a quick, cheap bite to eat, there are many lunch buffets and *lanchonetes* scattered around the *centro.*

Crepe & Cia, Rua Araújo Filho 1765 (☎623 9869), at Av. Benjamin Constant. Create your own *pièce de resistance* at the best (and only) place for a crepe for many a mile. Choose between savory (R$13-15) and sweet (R$10) fillings. Live MPB Sa after 9pm. Open daily 6pm-midnight. ❷

Restaurante La Gôndola, Av. Benjamin Constant 35W (☎224 9547), opposite the central *praça.* A popular choice for a lunch or dinner buffet, which includes *churrasco* and a variety of meat and fish dishes (R$12.50 per kg). Outside seating is good with a cold drink, but the cool inside features A/C, checked tablecloths, and artwork to distract you from the *novelas* on TV. Open daily 10:30am-3pm and 5:30-10:30pm. MC/V. ❷

Café Expresso, Av. Ville Roy 5023E (☎224 0490), in São Pedro, 2 blocks past Av. Major Williams. Well worth the 10min. walk, Café Expresso is a relaxed place for breakfast or afternoon tea. Light food served includes fruit plates (R$3.50-5), sandwiches (R$3-4.50), and *cuscuz* (couscous; R$2) to go with a good cappucino (R$2.50). Open daily 7:15am-noon and 2-7:30pm. Visa. ❶

Mister Quilo, Rua Inácio Magalhães 246 (☎224 0032), 1 block to the right of the local bus station. A huge bustling lunch place with a large buffet (R$15 per kg), *churrasco,* and excellent *vatapá.* Open M-Sa 11am-1:30pm. MC/V. ❷

Pigalle Pizzaria, Av. Cap. Ene Garcez 153 (☎224 6838), next to Hotel Euzebio's. Pizza, burgers, and beer are calling you. You know they are. Pigalle has what you need with a large selection of pizzas (R$10-13) and burgers (R$3-4.50). Delivery available. English menu. Open daily 6pm-midnight. Cash only. ❷

Restaurante Panorama Macuchik, Rua Floriano Peixoto 114 (☎624 1882), overlooking the river by Pça. Barreto Leite. Macuchik is perfect for enjoying excellent fish. They will serve ½ portions as these are meant for a hungry 2. Entrees R$18-24. Live music F-Sa after 9pm. Cover R$2. Open daily 11am-midnight. Visa. ❹

Marina Meu Caso, Av. Santos Dumont 40 (☎624 3911), in São Pedro. To get there, head east on Av. Getúlio Vargas, then turn right on Av. Santos Dumont. Tucked in by the river under leafy trees, this simple local restaurant specializes in large plates of fresh fish for 2, including piping-hot *caldeiradas* of the local favorites, *dourado* and *matrinxã* (R$25-35), as well as an excellent grilled *tambaqui* (R$20). English menu. Open daily 11am-midnight. ❸

Restaurante e Pizzaria Brasil, Av. Getúlio Vargas, at Rua Araújo Filho. This affordable corner pizzeria serves up cheap pies (R$8-13), including the vegetarian house special—Pizza Boa Vista—with cream cheese, hearts of palm, corn, and green beans. Meat lovers can dig into sausage pizzas as well as steak, fish, and chicken dishes (R$12-26). Open daily 11am-3pm and 5pm-midnight. ❷

SIGHTS

Besides lounging by the pool or going for a sweaty walk, there are not many ways to keep yourself busy in Boa Vista. **Praia Grande** is a popular river beach on the opposite shore of the Rio Branco, which appears during the dry season (Dec.-Mar.). There are full moon "luau" parties on the beach at this time. Small boats (round-trip R$3) shuttle people to the beach from the dock at the end of Av. Major Williams. **Parque Anauá,** on Av. Brigadeiro Eduardo Gomes (☎623 1733), is next to the airport about two and a half kilometers from the *centro*. This is the city's largest park; it has a lake, amphitheater, areas for skateboarding, *lanchonetes*, and a museum on its sprawling grounds.

Half-day trips can be made to visit the site of the former Portuguese fort, **Forte São Joaquim,** and the historic former cattle ranch **Fazenda São Marcos,** which is now located in an indigenous reserve administered by FUNAI. **Iguana Tours,** Rua Floriano Peixoto 505, is run by the English-speaking Eliezer Rufino, who offers these trips for R$50 per person (min. 3 people). He also organizes two-hour city tours (R$30 per person) and can arrange week-long stays with indigenous families to learn traditional ways of making pottery and baskets. (☎623 0787, 9971 7076; iguana@technet.com.br.) Detur (see **Tourist Office**) has a list of other EMBRATUR-registered guides.

NIGHTLIFE & ENTERTAINMENT

The *centro* has a number of small bars to knock back a few beers, but there's not much else to be had in terms of nightlife.

Restaurante Ver O Rio, Rua Floriano Peixoto 116 (☎624 1683), at Pça. Barreto Leite. One of the best places to have a sunset *chopp,* with a view over the Rio Branco to the distant rolling hills. They also serve seafood dishes for 2 (R$27-40), including grilled *pirarucú,* shrimp, and *tambaqui caldeirada* (R$27). Open 10am-1am. AmEx/MC/V.

Video-Q, Rua Floriano Peixoto s/n, at Av. Jaime Brasil. This open-air club overlooking the Rio Branco spins a mix of *forró, brega, pagode,* and MPB. Open F-Sa 7pm-dawn.

Cine Super K, Av. Cap. Ene Garcez 1555 (☎224 2138), 2km from the *centro* toward the airport, on the left, at Av. Brigadeiro Eduardo Gomes. This 2-screen cinema has subtitled Hollywood movies and local offerings. Shows at 5, 7, and 9pm. R$10. MC/V.

ACRE

RIO BRANCO ☎68

Rio Branco (pop. 252,800) is an active city that retains a frontier feel, where most parks and public spaces are lined by well-maintained buildings from the turn of the century. The parks are uniformly immaculate, which testifies to the efforts to improve the city for the 2002 celebration of Acre's independence.

TRANSPORTATION

Flights: Aeroporto Rio Branco, BR-364 km19-21 (☎211 1000), about 20km from the *centro.* Bus #303 ("Custódio Freire") runs between the city bus terminal and the airport (30min.; R$1.50). From the airport, catch it 100m to the left of the main entrance. Taxis to town R$40. **Inácio's Tur,** Rua Rui Barbosa 450 (☎223 7191), runs a comfortable bus to the airport (2 per day 5:30am-11pm; R$20). There are **aero-taxi** agencies at the airport that fly to smaller airports. They usually need 3-6 passengers and cost about R$1200 per hr.

Intercity Buses: Terminal Rodoviário, Av. Uirapuru km2 (☎221 4195). Bus #101 ("Norte-Sul") runs between this *rodoviária* and the city's local bus terminal. Buses to the *centro* stop outside the station on the right, in front of the blue shelter opposite Droga Numes II. **Eucatur** (☎221 4180; open daily 6:30am-10pm) has buses to: **Brasília** (52hr.; Tu, Th, and Su 11pm; R$188); **Fortaleza** (90hr.; Tu, Th, and Su 11pm; R$404); **Porto Alegre** (72hr.; 10pm; R$336) via **Curitiba** (56hr.; R$296) and **Rio de Janeiro** (65hr.; R$296); **Porto Velho** (8-10hr.; 5 per day 7am-11pm; R$30-43); **São Paulo** (56hr.; Tu, Th, and Su 11pm; R$245). **Rotas** (☎221 1880; open daily 7am-11pm) runs to **São Paulo** (52hr.; 10:30pm; R$254) via **Cuiabá** (34hr.; R$113) and **Goiânia** (48hr.; R$160). **Viação Rondônia** (☎221 1177; open daily 6am-11pm) has buses to **Guajará-Mirim** (10hr.; 11am; R$36) and **Porto Velho** (8-10hr.; 5 per day 7am-11pm; R$30-43).

Local Buses: Terminal Urbano, on Av. Ceará at Rua Sergipe opposite the Mercado Municipal. From the palace, head down Rua Benjamin Constant, which turns into a pedestrian mall halfway to the station. City buses routes begin and end here (5am-11:30pm; R$1.50).

Car Rental: Localiza, Rua Rio Grande do Sol 310 (☎224 7746; fax 224 8478; localizarbr@uol.com.br), 100m off Rua Floriano Peixoto near Av. Ceará. Standard A/C compact with unlimited mileage and limited insurance costs R$130 per day. Open M-F 7am-6pm, Sa 8am-noon. AmEx/MC/V.

ORIENTATION & PRACTICAL INFORMATION

The Rio Acre snakes through Rio Branco and divides it into two districts—the **Primeiro (1°)** and the **Segundo (2°).** The *centro* is in the 1° district and forms a rough "T" with **Avenida Ceará** on the top, which leads to the airport and **Avenida Getúlio Vargas.** Av. Getúlio Vargas runs from Av. Ceará down past the main square, **Praça Plácido de Castro** and its nearby **cathedral,** then past the **Palácio Rio Branco** to the river. The 2° district has the *rodoviária*, several cheap hotels, and Rio Branco's oldest street, **Calçadão da Gameleira,** which is now a pedestrian promenade. There are two one-way bridges that connect the two districts, one at the end of Av. Getúlio Vargas and another at the end of **Rua Marechal Deodoro.**

Tourist Office: There is no tourist office, but you can get some information from the **Secretâria de Turismo (Setur),** Av. Silvestre Coelho 280 (☎223 1390; fax 223 2699; promocao.turismo@ac.gov.br). From the *praça* on Av. Vargas at Rua Rui Barbosa, head toward the Consultório Médico on Av. Vargas; walk 800m down the hill. Just past the bike path at the Parque da Maternidade sign, turn left and go up the hill 200m. No English spoken. Open M-F 7:30am-6pm.

Currency Exchange: Banco do Brasil, Pça. Eurico Dutra 85 (☎223 9510), between Rua Benjamin Constant and Rua Epaminondas Jácome. Changes US dollars, traveler's checks, and gives Visa cash advances, all for a flat US$15 fee. Open M-F 8-11am. **Viaje Agência de Viagens e Turismo** (see **Ticket Agencies,** p. 514) changes US dollars for a US$2.70 fee.

24hr. ATMs: HSBC, Rua Rui Barbosa 399 (☎223 2240), at Rua Marechal Deodoro, 200m to the right of Mira Shopping. ATMs accept AmEx/Cirrus/MC/PLUS/V cards. ATMs at **Bradesco Bank,** Pça. Eurico Dutra 65 (☎223 3484), accept MC/V cards.

Airlines: Rico, Av. Ceará 2090 (☎223 5902; fax 223 5125.) Open M-F 8am-noon and 2-6pm, Sa 8am-noon. **Tavaj,** Av. Ceará 2395 (☎226 1666; fax 226 2228.) Open M-F 7:30am-5:30pm, Sa 8am-noon. **Varig,** Rua Marechal Deodoro 115 (☎224 2226; fax 224 2814.) Open M-F 8am-6pm, Sa 8am-noon. **VASP,** Rua Quintino Bocaiúva 1276 (☎224 6535; fax 224 6155). Open M-F 8am-6pm, Sa 8am-noon.

Ticket Agencies: Viaje Agência de Viagens e Turismo, Rua Rui Barbosa 51 (☎224 9977; fax 224 0403; viaje.ac@uol.com.br), 300m to the right of Mira Shopping at Av. Ceará, sells domestic and international phone tickets and can change US dollars. Open M-F 7am-6pm, Sa 8am-noon. **Inácio's Tur,** Rua Rui Barbosa 450 (☎223 7191), inside Pinheiro Palace Hotel, sells plane tickets, rents cars, and runs an airport bus (see **Flights,** p. 513). Open M-F 8am-noon and 2-6pm; Sa 8am-noon. AmEx/MC/V.

Public Market: Mercado Municipal, on Rua Elias Mansour, opposite the Terminal Urbano at the end of the Rua Benjamin Constant pedestrian mall. The main building has sections for meat, fish, and produce. The building on the other side of Rua Sergipe has a number of small food stalls. The **pedestrian mall** on Rua Benjamin Constant and Rua Quintino Bocaiúva has stores selling everything from towels to antennae.

Police: Polícia Federal, Rua Floriano Peixoto 874 (☎223 3500), near Rua Rui Barbosa.

Hospital: Hospital Santa Juliana, Rua Alvorada 806 (☎212 4700), in the suburb of Bosque.

Internet Access: Both of the following charge R$2 per 20min.; R$3 per hr. **Viarena Lan House & Cyber Café,** Rua Rui Barbosa 507 (☎223 8738), 100m from Inácio Palace, down Rui Barbosa away from the *praça,* has a fast connection and even faster crowds of young boys playing video games. Open Su-Th 8am-10pm, F-Sa 24hr. **Sala de Internet,** Rua Rui Barbosa 226 (☎223 0971), in Mira Shopping. Open M-Sa 9am-8pm.

Telephones: There are public phones and a kiosk selling Brasil Telecom cards in front of **Teleacre,** Av. Brasil 378. Kiosk open daily 6am-8pm.

Post Office: Rua Epaminondas Jácome 2858 (☎244 2226), near the river between Av. Vargas and Rua Marechal Deodoro. Open M-F 7am-4pm, Sa 8am-noon. **Postal code:** 69900-000.

ACCOMMODATIONS

Accommodations in Rio Branco range from rock-bottom to three-star. You get what you pay for, but there are usually cash and long-term discounts available, making the mid-range hotels a good deal.

Hotel Triangulo, Rua Floriano Peixoto 893 (☎224 9206). To get there from the *praça,* head down Rua Rui Barbosa past Pinheiro Palace and turn right at the Polícia Federal. Not the classiest joint ever, Hotel Triangulo is still a great deal. All rooms have A/C, TV, phone, and hot water. The *luxo* rooms have *frigo-bar.* Breakfast included. Laundry available. With cash discount singles R$25; doubles R$35. *Luxo* singles R$35; doubles R$45; triples R$65. MC/V. ❷

Hotel Guapindáia, Rua Floriano Peixoto 550 (☎/fax 223-5747; www.hotelguapindaia.hpg.com.br). With the palace on your right, walk down Rua Benjamin Constant and turn right when the street ends. This new yellow hotel relies heavily on checkerboard tile floors and solid wood furniture; try not to look at yourself in the mirrors in the stairwell. The rooms in front have a balcony with an amazing view. All rooms are new with A/C, satellite TV, hot-water bath, and *frigo-bar.* Excellent breakfast included. Laundry available. With cash discount singles R$40; doubles R$54; triples R$74. MC/V. ❷

Albemar Hotel, Rua Franco Ribeiro 109 (☎224 1396), is 100m off Rua Rui Barbosa toward Pinheiro Palace. The walls in the Albemar have had many a coat of paint, but this small hotel is friendly and convenient. Rooms have A/C, TV, hot-water bath, *frigo-bar,* and phone. The only difference between standard and *luxo* rooms is size. Breakfast included. Laundry available. Standard singles R$25; doubles R$32; triples R$50. *Luxo* singles R$30; doubles R$42; triples R$60. ❷

Hotel Loureiro, Rua Marechal Deodoro 304 (☎224 3110). Just to the left when entering the Rua Benjamin Constant pedestrian mall. The good location helps make up for the narrow singles with small bath and dim corridors; the upstairs doubles are better. All rooms have A/C, TV, phone, hot-water bath, and *frigo-bar.* Breakfast included. Laundry available. Singles R$40; doubles R$60; triples R$80; quads R$90. ❷

Pinheiro Palace Hotel, Rua Rui Barbosa 450 (☎/fax 223 7191; www.irmaospinheiro.com.br). From the *praça,* head toward the Colégio down Rua Rui Barbosa 1 block. Rio Branco's finest has all the necessities including a pool, *lanchonete,* travel agency/airport bus operated by Inácio's Tur (see **Ticket Agencies,** p. 514). Sizable *luxo* rooms have A/C, satellite TV, phone, *frigo-bar,* and hot-water bath. Breakfast included. Laundry available. With discounts singles R$75; doubles R$110; triples R$140. The presidential suite will set you back R$220. AmEx/MC/V. ❹

Inácio Palace Hotel, Rua Rui Barbosa 469 (☎223 6397; inacio@irmaospinheiro.com.br). Opposite the Pinheiro Palace sits its younger and cheaper cousin. Run by the same management, the Inácio Palace has a good restaurant, car rental, Internet access (R$10 per hr.), and meeting rooms. The standard *apartamentos* are slightly older than the *luxos,* which have better mattresses. Breakfast included. Laundry available. With cash discount singles R$35; doubles R$60; triples R$90. *Luxo* singles R$75; doubles R$105; triples R$140. AmEx/MC/V. ❷

Hospedaria Camelo, Rua Floriano Peixoto 553. Opposite Hotel Guapindaia at Rua Benjamin Constant. The cheapest *centro* option has rooms with wooden shutters and floors, a bed, and not much else. Singles with fan and tiny bath R$15, with larger bath and A/C R$20; doubles with small bath and fan R$15; with larger bath and A/C R$25. ❶

Hotel Rodoviária, Rua Palmeiral 468 (☎221 4434). Across the street from the *rodoviária* exit and on the left. An affordable option for early departures and late arrivals. The yellow walls help liven up this otherwise standard (and popular) place. Breakfast included. Musty singles in the back R$6, better singles with A/C and TV R$20; doubles R$10, with fan and bath R$15, with A/C and TV R$30. ❶

 FOOD

There are several very good restaurants and food stalls in the market serving cheap, filling meals, including the famous *tacacá* and *pato no tucupí.*

Anexo Espaço Gastronómico, Rua Franco Ribeiro 99 (☎224 1396, 224 1938). The best restaurant in town offers an unbeatable combination of excellent food and artistic decor. Locals flock to Anexo for the amazing buffet (R$15 per kg), or the salad bar that may include roasted vegetables, sushi, or *tabouli.* Meat and fish dishes include the local specialty *pato no tucupí* (duck in manioc sauce). Desserts like the *maracujá* mousse are lick-your-plate good. Dinner is an a la carte affair (entrees R$16-22). Come hungry. Open daily 11am-2pm and 4-8pm. Visa. ❸

Elcio Restaurante, Av. Ceará 2395 (☎226 1629). From the *centro,* it is a 10min. walk down Av. Ceará toward the airport, across from Pça. da Maternidade. This brightly colored 2-fl. restaurant specializes in *moqueca baiana* (tender pieces of fish cooked in a coconut milk and olive oil and served in a large clay pot; R$22), which easily serves two. They also have steak, chicken, and shrimp dishes (R$16-26). Open M-F 11am-2pm and 6-10pm, Sa 11am-3:30pm and 6-10pm, Su 11am-3pm. Visa. ❸

Churrascaria Triângulo, Rua Floriano Peixoto 893 (☎224 9206), attached to Hotel Triângulo. The mounted steer's head and blazing charcoal beckon carnivores to this excellent bargain *rodízio.* All-you-can-eat lunch is R$10 and dinner is R$12. Open M-F 11am-2pm and 6-10pm, Sa-Su 11am-2pm. MC/V. ❷

Pizzaria e Sorveteria Água na Boca, Av. Nações Unidas 672 (☎224 7475), at the corner of Rua Silvestre Coelho, 500m from Setur. This open-air restaurant is popular with families and those after a good pizza. The portions are huge, and it's a good place to sip a *chopp* in one of the surprisingly comfortable plastic chairs. There are 25 types of pizzas (R$10-18), steaks (R$18-20), chicken (including *risotto de frango;* R$16), and an ice cream bar to finish you off (R$3-5). Open Tu-Su 5pm-midnight. Visa. ❸

Restaurante Matsuo, Rua Rio Grande do Sul 320 (☎224 1541). Next to Localiza car rental, 100m from the intersection of Av. Ceará and Rua Floriano Peixoto. Matsuo serves up good Chinese and Japanese food and is filled with locals eating *teppanyaki:* stir-fried beef, chicken, or fish and vegetables with a brown sauce (R$20). They also have chop suey (R$16), curried chicken (R$18), and fried rice (R$16). All dishes serve 2, but half-portions are available. Open daily noon-2pm and 6:30-10pm. Visa. ❷

Lanchonete e Restaurante Rio Branco, Av Getúlio Vargas 70 (☎223 9567). Opposite the Legislative Assembly and in the same building as the Rio Branco Football Club. The buffet lunch (R$8 per kg) has salad and pasta selections. Open M-Sa 7am-3pm. ❷

SIGHTS

Most of the sights in Rio Branco are clustered within several blocks of the green Pça. Plácido de Castro in the 1° district, or are a five-minute walk down Av. Getúlio Vargas and over the bridge in the 2° district. Rio Branco's recently renovated public spaces make it a great walking city. All of the sights listed are free.

1° DISTRICT

MUSEU DA BORRACHA (RUBBER MUSEUM). This interesting little museum housed in a picturesque rubber boom-era house has exhibits on local archaeology, indigenous peoples, rubber tappers, and the Santo Daime cult. There is a replica of a rubber tapper's home and workshop, complete down to the red accordion. *(Av. Ceará 1441. Leaving Mira Shopping, turn left then left again at Thenny Video, then right onto Av. Ceará. ☎223 1202. Open M-F 8am-6pm, Sa-Su 4-9pm. Free.)*

MEMORIAL DOS AUTOMISTAS. The most stunning building in Rio Branco houses a theater, café, and a small museum dedicated to Acre's struggle for autonomy and statehood. Opened in 2002, the building is more interesting than the exhibits, which are few—from old newspapers and pictures to a jubilantly huge picture of the signing of Law 4070, which made Acre a state on June 15, 1962. The museum is exquisitely designed, with circular glass walls and wood ceiling and columns. A circular path in the center winds down to the tombs of José Guiomard dos Santos, the territory's governor before it became a state, and his wife. The museum also houses periodic art exhibits. *(On Av. Brasil at Av. Getúlio Vargas, at the corner of Pça. Plácido de Castro and behind the Palace. Open Tu-F 9am-5pm, Sa-Su 4-9pm. Free.)*

PALÁCIO RIO BRANCO. This neoclassical palace built in 1930 houses both the governor's ceremonial office and a small museum that is well worth a look; women in red lead tours through the museum's rooms. The first room has walls and floors made of gigantic, enlarged pictures of the palace, and the next holds many relics of indigenous cultures like flutes, baskets, and feather headdresses; its walls are painted with giant photos of local indigenous peoples. The next room is empty but for gigantic wall pictures of the diverse Brazilians who populate Acre. Headphones allow you to hear them talk (in Portuguese). There is a collection of old bottles from around the world, imported during the rubber boom, including "Humphrey's Marvel of Healing," as well as a small, incongruous collection of modern art. Upstairs is a series of immaculately stark meeting rooms and offices decorated 1960s style, with lots of smooth wood. The inescapable 6x8m painting is of Plácido de Castro. *(Av. Getúlio Vargas, at Av. Benjamin Constant, 1 block below the* praça. *Open Tu-F 9am-6pm, Sa-Su 4-9pm. Free.)*

CRAFTS. Mira Shopping's **Florestar,** Rua Rui Barbosa 226, loja 204, has a good selection of jewelry, chimes, and latex products from purses to little rubber *caimans*. (☎224 1254. Open M-Sa 9am-8pm. Visa.) **Casa d'Art Rivasplata,** Rua Rui Barbosa 344, at Av. Getúlio Vargas on the edge of the *praça*, sells postcards, small carvings, necklaces, bracelets, and feather headdresses. *(☎223 5820. Open M-F 8am-noon and 2-6pm, Sa 8am-noon. AmEx/MC/V.)*

2° DISTRICT

CALÇADÃO DA GAMELEIRA. Across the Rio Acre from the *centro*, this promenade is a pleasant place for a sunset stroll. The promenade along Rio Branco's first street, Rua Eduardo Asmar, was renovated for the 2002 centenary celebration. It leads from the Ponte Juscelino Kubitschek bridge along a row of brightly colored turn-of-the-century storefronts and iron lampposts, past a gigantic flagpole flying the Acre flag, to the **Gameleira Tree.** The city's first settlement began under this 20m tree back in 1882. *(From Pça. Plácido de Castro, head downhill along Av. Getúlio Vargas and over the bridge.)*

PARQUE URBANO CAPITÃO CÍRIACO. This small 4.6 hectare park is a good place to escape the city's bustle and traffic. Locals come for a stroll or a picnic under the shade of one of its 600 rubber trees. An elevated walkway leads to old buildings and an open space popular for birthday parties and city celebrations. *(At the AC-01 roundabout. Walk over the iron bridge, then turn left onto Rua 6 de Agosto and walk around the block to the right. Open M-F 7:30am-noon and 2-5pm. Free.)*

BEYOND THE 1° & 2° DISTRICTS

PARQUE AMBIENTAL CHICO MENDES. This is Rio Branco's best park, with a small zoo, several kilometers of walking paths, and a memorial to Chico Mendes. The small building near the entrance commemorates the life of Francisco (Chico) Alves Mendes, who helped found the first union of *seringueiros* (rubber tappers) and became famous outside of Brazil for his passionate calls to protect the Amazon rainforest. Boards hanging from the

IN RECENT NEWS

A MIXED LEGACY

On December 22, 1988 th *seringueiro* (rubber tapper) an rainforest activist **Francisc (Chico) Mendes** was gunne down outside of his home i Xapuri, Acre, allegedly at th behest of local ranchers. Fiftee years later his legacy has becom a mixture of hope and disappointment. Chico's enduring influenc is due to his understanding tha the fates of the *seringueiros* an the rainforest were intimatel linked. With the help of international NGOs his rural labor movement received global attention and his influence only grew afte he received the UN Global 50 award in 1987. Chico has becom a martyr for Brazilian environmentalists, and in the years since hi death, Chico's political associate have gone on to positions o power—including the governorshi of Acre—where they have contin ued Chico's defense of the rainfo est and the *seringueiros*.

Today, roughly 31% o Amazônia is protected, and man cooperative factories have bee created to help provide sustai able income. However, Brazil ha pressed forward with its progra to pave more highways throug the Amazon Basin, an *seringueiros* still struggle with pov erty, a 34% illiteracy rate, an 20% unemployment. Despit increased acknowledgment an protection, the rainforest and it *seringueiros* remain at risk.

memorial's rafters chronicle (in Portuguese) Chico Mendes's growing influence before his assassination in December 1988, the life of the *seringueiros*, and the religious and scientific roles of the rainforest. A rubber tree grows through the center of the building. The **zoo** houses various species of parrots, monkeys, panthers, pigs, turtles, and the small rat-like *cutia preta*. Besides a model *seringueiro* home, there is an interesting (if slightly scary) collection of mythical forest creatures. The two-meter tall, hairy one-eyed Sasquatch-looking thing is the *mapinguarí*. The less frightening *caboquinho de mata* looks like a small hairy child, although it is supposed to be invisible. Paved **nature trails** lead through the forest (watch out for the *mapinguarí!*), and there are several good picnic spots. *(AC-040 km9. Take Bus #103 ("Santa Maria/Vila Acre") for about 10km and get off at the stop right past the Mercantil Quero Mais. ☎221 1933. Open Tu-Su 7am-noon and 2-5pm. Free.)*

PARQUE ZOOBOTÂNICO. On the sprawling campus of the state university, Universidade Federal do Acre (UFAC), five kilometers from the *centro*, lies this quiet stretch of rainforest with several kilometers of walking trails, a scenic lagoon populated with a number of birds, and the classrooms and laboratories of ongoing studies. The Viveiro de Mudas is a moderately interesting garden of young plants. *(UFAC, BR-364. Take any "UFAC" bus to campus and get off at the small yellow sign before the large brick column on the right. The park is behind the classrooms. Take a right at the small café. Open M-Sa 7-11am and 2-5pm. Free.)*

IGREJINHA DE FERRO (LITTLE IRON CHURCH). This small pink and lime-green chapel is a result of a promise made by Joaquim Victor, an overeager farmer from Acre. He pledged to build a monument to the Virgin Mary that would last forever if Plácido de Castro was victorious over the Bolivians in the Acrean Revolution. To make a timeless building, he enlisted two German engineers to make the chapel from prefabricated galvanized iron plates, which were shipped from Germany to Rio Branco. The interior is tiny and while it may be eternal, it isn't pretty, despite the Miami Vice color scheme. Now the small church sits surrounded by the Fourth Battalion Infantry Base. *(Rua Columbia s/n, in the suburb of Bosque. Take Bus #901 ("Cohab do Bosque/Cadeivelha") and get off at the Hotel Guapindaia at Rua Alvorada and Av. C.J. Galdino. Walk past the Banco do Brasil and take Rua Don Bosco, the right fork, down 300m. When the road turns right, ask a soldier for entrance through the small gate straight ahead. ☎224 0510. Open M-F 7:30am-5pm. Free.)*

NIGHTLIFE & ENTERTAINMENT

The **food court** at Mira Shopping, Rua Rui Barbosa 226, is a popular place to escape the heat and catch up with friends over a cold *chopp*. The local students are not shy about practicing their English (especially after a beer or two). **Cine João Paulo I & II,** Av. Ceará 1848 (☎223 3828), next to João Paulo Hotel, screens American movies nightly, 7pm and 9pm (R$6-9).

Chopperia Sahara, Rua 17 de Novembro s/n (☎223 5847). Along the Calçadão da Gameleira, to the left of Hotel Vitória. Relaxed and romantic rooftop restaurant, perfect for a beer by the river. Live music after 9pm, which tends toward sexy acoustic guitars. Open Tu-Su 5pm-2am. AmEx/MC/V.

Varandas do Porto Restaurante e Choperia, Rua Eduardo Asmar 618 (☎9987 7726). At the end of the Calçadão, on a terrace jutting out over the Rio Acre, Varanda do Porto has *choppes* in *very* frosty glasses and nightly live MPB (after 7pm). Open Tu-Su 11am-1am.

Restaurante Rio Branco II, Rua 17 de Novembro 257 (☎9974 4970). Along the Calçadão da Gameleira behind the gigantic flagpole. Sidewalk tables perfect for a beer while watching people watching other people on the promenade. Open daily 7am-1am.

Restaurante e Chopperia A Princezinha, Travessa da Catedral 14 (☎222 7207). In the park opposite the cathedral. Tables fill up under the trees at this popular place with excellent beer, pizza, and music. Open M 7am-4pm, Tu-Su 7am-1am. AmEx/MC/V.

RONDÔNIA

PORTO VELHO ☎69

Over the last century, Porto Velho has seen more than its share of ups and downs. It began as the starting point for the Madeira-Mamoré Railway, which was constructed during the rubber boom in the late 19th century. However, the rubber boom did not last, nor did the timber industry and gold rush which followed it. As an epicenter for three economic booms, it is not surprising that people from all over Brazil flocked to this area to seek their fortunes. The city still has a certain roughness to it—the sort of thing one would expect from a frontier town—and the newspapers tell of drug traffickers being nabbed while transporting Bolivian and Peruvian cocaine downriver.

TRANSPORTATION. The **Aeroporto Internacional Governador Jorge Teixeira,** on Av. Lauro Sodré (☎225 1675), is about 7km from the *centro*. To get into town you can either hire a taxi (R$25) from the stand outside the terminal, or catch Bus #201B, labeled "H. Base/Aeroporto," which stops to the left of the cabstand (30min.; R$1.50). Several operators run flights out of Porto Velho. **Varig** has an office at Av. Campos Sales 2666 (☎224 2262; fax 224 2278. Open M-F 8am-noon and 2-6pm, Sa 8am-noon. AmEx/MC/V.) **Rico's** office is at the airport itself. (☎225 1299. Open daily 8am-5:30pm. AmEx/MC/V.) **TAM** also has an office at the airport (☎222 6666. Open M-F 8am-noon and 2-6pm, Sa 8am-noon and 2-4pm. AmEx/MC/V.) **Tavaj** is at the airport as well and, although it only flies to Manaus, Rio Branco, and Belém, it is often the cheapest option. (☎225 2999, 229 5908. Open daily 8am-5:30pm. AmEx/MC/V.) **VASP,** Rua Gonçalves Dias 438, is one block behind the cathedral. (☎223 3755; fax 224 4690. Open M-F 8am-noon and 2-6pm, Sa 8am-noon. AmEx/MC/V.)

The **rodoviária,** on Av. Jorge Teixeira, is about 3km from the river between Av. Carlos Gomes and Rua Dom Pedro II. A taxi from the *centro* costs about R$5, or you can catch Bus #201B, labeled "H. Base/Aeroporto," Bus #201, which is marked "Hosp. de Base," or Bus #301, labeled "Presidente Roosevelt," all of which run down Av. 7 de Setembro from the *centro* and pass the *rodoviária* (R$1.50). From the *rodoviária*, **Andorinha** (☎225 3025; MC/V) runs to: Cuiabá (22hr.; 4 per day; R$106); Goiânia (36hr.; 2 per day; R$171); Belo Horizonte (40hr.; noon; R$250); São Paulo (48hr.; 3 per day; R$244); Rio de Janeiro (60hr.; 2 per day; R$274); Fortaleza (96hr.; 2 per day; R$382). **Viação Rondônia** (☎223 3033; Visa) runs to Guajará-Mirim (5½hr.; 6 per day; R$20-R$27) and Rio Branco (8hr.; 4 per day; R$30-R$43).

Boats leave Porto Velho from the **Porto Cai n'Água** dock. Facing the entrance to the Madeira-Mamoré train station, turn left and walk down Av. Farquar 500m to the stop sign, then turn right. Three agencies sell tickets for the same boats: **Agência Amazonas,** Rua João Alfredo 185 (☎223 9743); **Agência Parintins,** Rua 13 de Maio 58 (☎223 0046); **Manaus Turismo,** Rua João Alfredo 175 (☎9281 0927). Boats leave for Manaus (3 days; Tu, Th 6pm; R$100, 2-person cabin R$300). Bring a **hammock** to sling on deck, and set up early because the best places fill up fast. Also, be sure to check out the boat and your sailing companions before buying a ticket, to make sure everything's above-board.

You can rent a car from **Avis,** Rua Júlio de Castilho 208, on the corner of Rua Afonso Pena. (☎224 6686; fax 224 4688. R$70 per day up to 100km, R$90 per day with unlimited mileage. Open M-F 7:30am-7pm, Sa 7:30am-noon. AmEx.) **Localiza Rental Car,** Rua Dom Pedro II 1208, is 100m from Rua Marechal Deodoro. (☎224 6530; localiza-pvh@enter-net.com.br. Unlimited miles R$107 per day, with A/C R$149. Basic insurance R$23. Open M-F 8am-7pm, Sa 8am-1pm. AmEx/MC/V.)

ORIENTATION & PRACTICAL INFORMATION. Modern Porto Velho is a sprawling city of 310,000, overlooking a stretch of the Rio Madeira. The main street is Av. 7 de Setembro, which runs up a gentle hill away from the now-defunct railway station at the riverside until it intersects with Av. Jorge Teixeira. The market, port, and busier shops are all off Av. 7 de Setembro, while the nicer hotels and restaurants cluster around Av. Carlos Gomes.

The **tourist office,** Setur, is located at Rua Dom Pedro II 3004. (☎/fax 223 2461; seturo@ibest.com.br. Open M-Th 7:30am-noon and 2-6pm, F 7:30am-1:30pm.) **Nossa Viagense Turismo,** Rua Tenreiro Aranha 2125, has helpful staff who speak English and German and can help you organize flights as well as trips to the Guaporé Valley and several ecotourism reserves. (☎224 4777; fax 223 5270; nossatur@ronet.com.br. Open M-F 8am-6pm, Sa 8am-noon. AmEx/MC/V.) **Vip'stur,** Rua Carlos Gomes 1700, is a tourist agency which sells airplane tickets and exchanges US dollars. (☎224 2144; fax 221 3311; vipstur@mailcity.com. Open M-F 8am-6pm, Sa 8am-noon. MC/V.) You can change cash and traveler's checks at **Marco Aurélio Câmbio,** Rua José de Alencar 3353. (☎221 4922. Open M-F 8:30am-3pm.) **Banco do Brasil,** Rua Dom Pedro II 607, will also exchange cash and traveler's checks, but at much higher rates. (☎221 3337. Open M-F 9am-2pm.) There are **ATMs** at HSBC, Av. Lauro Sodré 2600, which give cash on the AmEx/Cirrus/MC/Plus/Visa networks. (☎221 0153. Open 8am-8pm.) **Luggage storage** is available at the *rodoviária* (☎225 0132. Open 6am-6pm. R$3 per bag, per day.) There is **Internet access** at the airport. (☎9984 1959. Open M-Sa 24hr. M-F R$3 per hr., Sa R$4 per hr.) **Games and Videos,** Av. 7 de Setembro 1925, provides Internet access in a more convenient location. (☎224 2724. Open M-Sa 9am-10pm, Su 2-10pm. R$3 per 30min., R$5 per hr. MC/V.) Other services include: **police,** in the Prefectura, opposite the cathedral and next to the library; **Hospital Central,** Rua Júliode Castilho 149 (☎224 6428, 224 5225); **telephone office,** Telemania, Rua Carlos Gomes 714 (☎224 5507; open M-Sa 8am-6pm; MC/V); and the **post office,** Av. Pres. Dutra 2701, three blocks from the train station (☎217 3667; open M-F 8am-5pm, Sa 9am-noon). **Postal code:** 78900-000.

ACCOMMODATIONS. Porto Velho's accommodations range from spartan dorm rooms to the '*especial suite.*' Hotels along Av. 7 de Setembro are more budget-oriented, but keep in mind that upper-end hotels often offer discounts. **Hotel Samaúma ❷,** Rua Dom Pedro II 1038, on the corner of Av. Campus Sales, is an oasis of stained wood, shade trees, and Spanish tile. All rooms have A/C, telephones, hot showers, satellite TV, and a fully-stocked *frigo-bar.* The attentive owner and her daughter speak English. They also run trips to their ranch-turned-park, Sausalito, which feature jungle walks, horseback riding, and waterskiing. (☎/fax 224 5300; samauma.samauma@bol.com.br. Breakfast included. Singles R$40; doubles R$60.) Two blocks from the *centro* you'll find **Hotel Tia Carmen ❶,** Av. Campos Sales 2895, a popular spot with the few travelers who visit Porto Velho. They offer friendly service and quiet, simple rooms, all with private bath. (☎221 7910. Breakfast included. Laundry service available. Singles with fan R$13, with TV R$15, with A/C and *frigo-bar* R$28; doubles R$35; triples R$55.) One kilometer from the railway station, near bus stop #5 and across from Tubo d'Água Surf Shop, is **Hotel Messianico ❶,** Av. 7 de Setembro 1180, which has 17 simple rooms arranged around a red tiled courtyard. The beds are hard but the price is right.

(☎221 4084. Breakfast included. Singles with fan and bath R$15, with A/C R$20; doubles with fan and bath R$20, with A/C R$25; triples R$30.) The five-story **Hotel Central ❸**, Rua Tenreiro Aranha 2472, is between Av. Carlos Gomes and Rua Dom Pedro II. Businessmen flock to this reasonable mid-range hotel. All rooms have TV, A/C, hot water, phone, soft beds, and unimpressive artwork. (☎224 2099; fax 224 5114; hcentral@enter-net.com.br. Laundry and Internet access available. Singles R$62; doubles R$85; triples R$102. MC/V.) A substantially cheaper option is the basic but central **Sonora Hotel ❶**, Av. 7 de Setembro 1205, across from the Hotel Messianico. (☎224 1861. Singles with fan R$10; doubles R$15, with A/C, private bath, and TV R$20.) The small, monastic singles of **Hotel Amazonas ❶**, Av. Carlos Gomes 2838, are an acceptable option for those arriving late or leaving early. From the *rodoviária*, turn left at HSBC and walk 100m. (☎221 7735. Singles with fan R$9, with private bath R$13; doubles with fan R$18, with A/C R$30.)

FOOD. Kilos, *lanchonetes*, and market stalls dominate the Porto Velho food scene. If you want to do-it-yourself, try the **Super Bem Plus Supermercado,** Av. 7 de Setembro 1414. (☎224 2112. Open 24hr. MC/V.) Alternatively, head down Rua Gonçalves Dias past the military marching grounds to **Gonçalves Supermercado,** on Rua Abunã. (☎224 1444. Open daily 7am-9:30pm. AmEx/MC/V.) The **Emporium Restaurante e Choperia ❹**, Av. Pres. Dutra 3366, is a relaxed Spanish restaurant with inlaid tile tables, iron railings, and seriously good food. They specialize in huge portions of *paella* (R$40) and *bacalhau* (R$65), and also do a beautiful beef fillet gorgonzola (R$27). (☎221 2665. Appetizers R$7-14. Entrees R$20-65. Open Tu-Sa 6pm-1am. Visa.) At the corner of Av. Campos Sales sits **Café Restaurant ❷**, Av. Carlos Gomes 1097. They serve a sizable buffet lunch (R$13 per kg) with more than 10 salads, pastas, fish, and meat dishes. The large dining room fills with businessmen by noon. (☎224 3176. Open M-Sa 11am-2pm. MC/V.) To get to **Remanso do Tucunaré ❹**, Av. Brasília 1506, walk up Av. 7 de Setembro, turn right at the diagonal Av. Nações Unidas, then turn right at the BR station. This restaurant dishes up large bowls of *caldeira de tucunaré* (large tender pieces of fish and vegetables in a savory broth). The walls are lined with aquariums and the names of celebrities, veterans, and friends that have eaten here. (☎221 2353. Live music Th-Sa after 8pm. Open 11am-3pm and 6pm-midnight.) For a great lunch, head to **Chá Self-Service ❷**, Av. Pres. Dutra 3024, next to Setur and behind the Paláçio do Governador. Help yourself to mounds of salads, fish, meat, and enchilada-like *pancaqueca de carne*. (☎221 5839. R$16 per kg. Open 11am-3pm. AmEx/MC/V.) The most popular pizza joint in town is **Pizza & Cia ❷**, Av. Abunã 1625. From the *centro*, walk seven blocks down Rua Marechal Deodoro past Av. Carlos Gomes, and turn right at Drogaria Village. They serve over 60 kinds of pizza under an open red tiled roof. The small (R$11-14) is medium and the *gigante* (R$22-24) lives up to its name. (☎221 9953. Delivery available. Open 6pm-midnight. MC/V.) The vegetarian **Shopping Vida Natural ❶**, Rua Dom Pedro II 1251, is both a shop—selling organic tea, granola, and vitamins—and an air-conditioned *lanchonete*. They serve *sopa de legumes* (R$2.50), banana torte (R$1.50), and the best *sucos* in town (R$1.50-3). (Open M-Th 11am-2:30pm, F 8am-5pm. MC/V.) Create your own ice cream masterpiece at **Dullim Sorvetes ❶**, Av. Pinheiro Machado 3314. With 36 flavors (from *doce de leite* to *açaí*), 10 sauces, and 30 toppings, choosing may be the hardest part. (☎221 1040. R$21 per kg. Open M-Sa 2-11pm, Su 3-11pm. MC/V.)

SIGHTS. Down by the river, **Praça Madeira-Mamoré** is lined with huge rusted railroad sheds. One of them houses **Museu Ferroviário,** which contains relics of the ill-fated Madeira-Mamoré railroad. Faces of politicians and railroad workers stare out of faded pictures and Coronel Church—the first steam locomotive to ply the initial 6km of track in 1878—sits at the far end of the shed. Several other Pennsylvania Baldwin and Berlin Schwartzkopff engines rust outside. (Open M-F 8am-6pm. Free.) Across the street from the *praça* sits the lime-green EFMM building (complete with clock tower) that used to house the railroad management offices. It now holds the small **Museu Geológico,** which displays a number of rocks. Try to find the house of small pebbles. (Open M-F 8am-6pm. Free.) More interesting is **Museu Estadual de Rondõnia,** next door, which contains a number of baskets and pots, as well as several jaguar and anaconda skins. (Open M-F 8am-6pm. Free.) Walk three blocks up Av. 7 de Setembro, then take a left up the hill above Pça. Getúlio Vargas, and you will come across the stately **Paláçio do Governador,** the current seat of power in Rondônia. Around the corner, at the top of the hill, sits the **Catedral do Sagrado Coração de Jesus.** The cathedral, built between 1927 and 1930, sits smack in the center of Pça. João Nicoletti. Piped music inspires the faithful, and the bright and ornate stained-glass windows are definitely worth a look. Keep an eye out for the vanquished Roman soldiers and the suitably terrifying fire-breathing demon. After the rigors of walking Porto Velho's hills, a **boat trip** on the Rio Madeira can provide a welcome break from the heat. Departing from the dock in front of Museu Ferroviário, boats meander along the coast and up to the **Cachoeira de Santo Antônio Rapids,** 7km from the town (1hr.; several 8am-8pm; R$4.) The shore at Santo Antônio is popular place for splashing around during the dry season, but in the wet season swimming can be dangerous due to high water. From 1981-2002, the **Maria Fumaça** ("Smoking Mary") locomotive ran to and from Santo Antônio on Sundays. Service stopped in late 2002 due to the track washing out and is not expected to start again any time soon.

ENTERTAINMENT. In the evening, the yellow plastic tables of open-air bars spread across **Praça Marechal Rondon,** just across from the post office on Av. 7 de Setembro. Locals fill the square nightly from dusk until just after midnight, knocking back cold *chopp* (R$2.50) and munching on bags of fried banana chips, *churros,* and skewers of meat (all R$0.50). Alternatively, you can listen to live music (Th-Sa after 9pm) at **Tacacá Dona Izaura,** Rua Herbert de Azevedo 160. This open-air café and bar serves *tacacá* soup (R$6) and *peixe frito* (fried fish; R$10). (☎224 4299. Open 4pm-1am.) A slightly classier option is **The Wood River,** Av. Carlos Gomes 1901, two blocks past the high-rise Hotel Vila Rica. This romantic bar is a great place to recline in a cane chair while sipping a martini (R$3) or Johnny Walker Black (R$9). They sell not only imported alcohol, but also foreign cigarettes and wines. The walls are covered with images of Elvis Presley and Marilyn Monroe, complimented by leopard-skin curtains and subdued music. (☎223 7300. Drinks R$3-10. Open M-F 6pm-midnight, Sa 4pm-1am. Visa.) For a more relaxed atmosphere, check out the several thatched huts by the riverside, which sell coconuts (R$1) and frosty Kaiser beer (R$2.50), and are a good place to kick back in a plastic chair and watch the sun set. On the hill above the railway station you will find **Mirante II,** at the intersection of Rua Dom Pedro II and Rua Major Amarante. This open-air bar has a great view and live MPB after 9pm (W, F-Sa), and serves cold beer for R$3. (Open M-Sa 3pm-1am.) If you've had enough of the bar scene, head to **Cine Brasil,** Av. 7 de Setembro 534, across the street from Pça. Marechal Rondon. You can catch Hollywood blockbusters complete with fresh popcorn. (☎221 8296. Three shows daily. R$3). If you're looking for a souvenir, check out **Artes Brasil,** Rua Euclides de Cunha 1952, behind the EFMM building. They have the best quality and selection of crafts in town, including pottery and baskets. (☎/fax 224 4774. Open M-F 8:30am-6pm, Sa 8:30am-3pm, Su 9am-noon.)

GLOSSARY

LANGUAGE

Portuguese is the official language of Brazil, and it's spoken everywhere. Few people speak English outside the tourist infrastructure, so arm yourself with as many of the phrases below as possible. Travelers who speak **Spanish** will do well: many in the tourist industry know the language, and most Brazilians will be able to understand Spanish if you speak very slowly.

For most English speakers, **pronunciation** is the hardest part of this melodious language. One sentence out of a Brazilian's mouth and the rhythms of *samba* will make perfect sense, though not much else will. As with Spanish, every letter is pronounced (except for diphthongs).

In words without written accents, the **stress** falls on the next-to-last syllable, unless the word ends in "r" or a nasalized vowel (when it falls on the last syllable). Vowels with tildes (ã and õ) or those followed by "m" or "n" are heavily **nasalized**—with air escaping through the nose, similar to "so**ng**." Other letters except the following are pronounced as they are in English:

c	**c**ity before e or i; **c**ountry everywhere else	**l**	"w" at end of a word; **l**unch everywhere else
ç	"s" as in fa**ç**ade	**lh**	bi**ll**ionaire
ch	ca**ch**e or sta**sh**	**m, n**	makes the previous letter nasalized (am = ã)
d	ba**dg**er before e or i; **d**og everywhere else	**nh**	onion, like the Spanish ñ
g	lo**dg**ing before e or i; **g**as everywhere else	**r**	"h" at the start or end of a word; **r**at elsewhere
j	"zh" as in rou**g**e	**rr**	"h" as in **h**ouse

PHRASEBOOK

The phrases that follow should help you navigate most basic situations that you might encounter while you're in Brazil, from buying a bus ticket to reporting a robbery to just looking for a good beach. Brazilians are usually impressed by *gringos* who speak even a few words of Portuguese, so even mastering just the **Basics** (outlined below) should get you far.

BASICS

ENGLISH	PORTUGUÊS
Hello.	*Oi.*
Goodbye.	*Tchau.*
Good morning.	*Bom dia.*
Good afternoon.	*Boa tarde.*
Good evening/night.	*Boa noite.*
Yes.	*Sim.*
No.	*Não.*
Thank you (very much).	*(Muito) obrigado. [masc]*
Thank you (very much).	*(Muito) obrigada. [fem]*
You're welcome.	*De nada.*
Please.	*Por favor.*

ENGLISH	PORTUGUÊS
Excuse me.	*Da licença.*
I'm sorry.	*Desculpe.*
Help!	*Socorro!*
Leave me alone!	*Deixa-me em paz!*
Do you speak English?	*Você fala inglês?*
Anyone speak English?	*Alguem fala inglês?*
I don't speak Portuguese.	*Não falo português.*
I (don't) understand.	*(Não) entendo.*
Speak slower.	*Fale mais devagar.*
Where is ...?	*Onde é ...?*
How much is ...?	*Quanto é ...?*

DIRECTIONS & SIGNS

ENGLISH	PORTUGUÊS
How do I get to ... ?	*Como chega a/à ... ?*
Is it near/far from here?	*É perto/longe de aqui?*
corner; block	*esquina; quadra*
north; south; east; west	*norte; sul; este; oeste*
straight ahead	*na frente*
left/right	*esquerda/direita*

ENGLISH	PORTUGUÊS
near/far	*perto/longe*
behind/in front	*atrás/na frente*
here/there	*aqui/lá*
more/less	*mais/menos*
open/closed	*aberto/fechado*
entrance/exit	*entrada/saida*

SMALL TALK

ENGLISH	PORTUGUÊS
How are you?	*Tudo bem?*
I'm fine; I'm well.	*Tudo bom; Tudo legal.*
What's your name?	*Qual é seu nome?*
My name is ...	*Meu nome é ...*
Where are you from?	*De onde é?*
I'm from ...	*Sou de ...*
How old are you?	*Quantos anos tem?*
I am ... years old.	*Tenho ... anos.*
I; you; he; she; we	*eu; você; ele; ela; a gente o nós*

ENGLISH	PORTUGUÊS
I have/we have	*Eu tenho/nós temos*
I need/we need	*Preciso/Precisamos*
I will/we will	*Vou/vamos*
I can/we can	*Posso/Podemos*
I want, I would like	*Queria*
Do you have ...?	*Você tem ...?*
and; but; or; with	*e; más; ou; com*
good; bad; awful	*bom; mal; ruim*
Can I buy you a drink?	*Quer beber alguma coisa?*

TRANSPORTATION

ENGLISH	PORTUGUÊS
I want to go to ...	*Quero ir pra ...*
I want to buy a ticket for ...	*Quero comprar um bilhete pra ...*
Do you pass by/go to ...?	*Passa pra ...?*
What time does ... leave?	*A que horas sai ...?*
What time does ... arrive?	*A que horas chega ...?*
airport; bus station	*aeroporto; rodoviária*
ticket	*bilhete (transport)* *ingresso (non-transport)*
ticket office	*bilheteria*
timetable, schedule	*quadro de horários*
one-way/round-trip	*ida/ida e volta*
Stop!	*Pare!*
Slower, please!	*Mais devagar, por favor!*
That [fare] is too much.	*É demais.*

ENGLISH	PORTUGUÊS
bus	*ônibus*
bus company	*companhia, empresa*
stop	*parada*
train	*trem*
boat	*barco*
airplane	*avião*
airline flight	*linhas aereas* *vôo*
ferry	*ferry* [FEH-hee]
metro	*metrô*
car	*carro*
taxi	*táxi*
bicycle	*bicicleta*
horse	*cavalo*

PRACTICAL INFORMATION

ENGLISH	PORTUGUÊS
street, road	*rua*
neighborhood	*bairro*
town, city	*cidade*
plaza; square	*praça (pça.); largo*

ENGLISH	PORTUGUÊS
Internet café	*Internet* [in-ter-NET-chee]
tourist office	*informações turísticas*
bookstore	*livraria*
laundromat	*lavanderia*

ENGLISH	PORTUGUÊS
currency exchange	*câmbio*
bank	*banco*
ATM	*caixa automática*
credit card	*cartão de crédito*
police	*polícia*
hospital	*hospital*
pharmacy, chemist	*farmácia, drogaria*
post office	*correio*
letter; postcard	*carta; cartão-postal*
stamps	*selos*

ENGLISH	PORTUGUÊS
restaurant	*restaurante*
newsstand	*banca*
consulate; embassy	*consulado; embaixada*
passport	*passaporte*
visa extension	*prorrogação de visto*
backpack; backpacker	*mochila; mochileiro*
fort	*forte*
hill; mountain; range	*morro; montanha; serra*
lake; lagoon	*lago; lagoa*
hiking trail	*trilha, caminhada*

MEDICAL EMERGENCIES

ENGLISH	PORTUGUÊS
doctor	*médico*
syringe	*seringa*
prescription	*receita médico*
diarrhea	*diarréia*
fever; ache; sickness	*febre; dor; doença*

ENGLISH	PORTUGUÊS
headache	*dor de cabeça*
earache	*dor de orelha*
stomachache	*dor de barriga*
sunburn	*queimadura (de sol)*
tablet	*comprimido*

ACCOMMODATIONS

ENGLISH	PORTUGUÊS
campground	*camping*
guesthouse, B&B	*pousada*
hotel	*hotel*
hostel	*albergue*
owner	*dono/dona, gerente*
Do you have vacancies?	*Tem vagas?*
Is breakfast included?	*O café da manhã tá incluído?*
Can I see the room?	*Posso ver o quarto?*
Do you have a discount?	*Tem desconto?*
Is there a better price?	*Pode fazer um melhor preço?*
daily rate	*diária*
room	*quarto*
room with private bath	*apartamento*
bed	*cama*

ENGLISH	PORTUGUÊS
single	*solteiro*
double; twin beds	*casal; duas camas*
bathroom	*banheiro*
shower	*chuveiro*
hot water	*água quente*
toilet paper, loo roll	*papel higiênico*
A/C	*ar condicionado, condicionado de ar*
fan	*ventilador*
key	*chave*
sheets; towel	*lençóis; toalha*
safe; safe location	*cofre; seguro*
mini-bar	*frigo-bar*
dirty; noisy; dark; broken	*sujo; barulhento; escuro; quebrado*

FOOD

ENGLISH	PORTUGUÊS
cup; plate	*copo; prato*
fork; knife; spoon	*garfo; faca; colher*
daily set meal	*prato do dia, refeição*
One more ...	*Mais um ...*

ENGLISH	PORTUGUÊS
money; change	*dinheiro; troco*
the bill	*a conta*
waiter	*moço; garçom*
I don't have smaller bills.	*Não tenho menor.*

SHOPPING

ENGLISH	PORTUGUÊS
market	*mercado, feira*
store; mall	*loja; shopping*
Just looking	*Só estou olhando.*
I'll come back.	*Vou voltar.*
That's too much!	*É demais!*
cheap/expensive	*barato/caro*
shoes; sneakers	*sapatos; tênis*
socks	*meias*
watch	*relógio*
shirt	*camisa*
shorts	*calção*

ENGLISH	PORTUGUÊS
skirt	*saia*
Speedo© swimsuit	*sunga*
bikini; thong; sarong	*bikini; fio dental; canga*
hat	*chapéu*
sun cream, sunblock	*proteção solar*
bug spray	*repelente (de insetos)*
shopping bag; bag	*sacola; bolso*
book(s)	*livro(s)*
soap	*sabonete*
condom	*camisinha*
souvenir	*lembrança*

AT THE BEACH

ENGLISH	PORTUGUÊS
beach	*praia*
sand	*areia*
wave; surf	*onda; ondas*
surfboard	*prancha*
high/low tide	*maré alta/baixa*
lifeguard	*salva-vida*

ENGLISH	PORTUGUÊS
beach towel	*toalha da praia*
beach umbrella	*guarda-sol*
beach chair	*cadeira*
flip-flops	*chinelos, Havaianas*
marijuana	*maconha*
Can I swim here?	*Posso nadar aqui?*

AT THE BARS

ENGLISH	PORTUGUÊS
beautiful; ugly	*lindo; feio*
beautiful girl/boy	*gata/gato*
dude	*cara*
flirt; kiss; have sex	*paquerar; beijar; transar*

ENGLISH	PORTUGUÊS
nice ass	*bum-bum, bunda*
Do you like me?	*Gosta de mim?*
I love you.	*Te quero.*
Can I buy you a drink?	*Quer beber alguma coisa?*

AT THE POLICE STATION

ENGLISH	PORTUGUÊS
police; fireman	*polícia; bombeiro*
robber, thief	*ladrão*
crime	*crime* [CREE-mee]
police report	*boletin de ocorrência*

ENGLISH	PORTUGUÊS
prostitute	*garota de programa*
strip club	*boîte*
mugging, assault	*assalto*
I was/we were attacked.	*Fui/Fomos atacado.*

NUMBERS

1	2	3	4	5	6	7	8	9	10
um	dois	três	quatro	cinco	meia	sete	oito	nove	dez
11	**12**	**13**	**14**	**15**	**16**	**17**	**18**	**19**	**20**
onze	doze	treze	catorze	quinze	dezesseis	dezessete	dezoito	dezenove	vinte
21	**30**	**40**	**50**	**60**	**70**	**80**	**90**	**100**	**1000**
vinte e um	trinta	quarenta	cinqüenta	sessenta	setenta	oitenta	noventa	cem	mil

DAYS & TIME

ENGLISH	PORTUGUÊS
Monday	*Segunda-feira (Seg.)*
Tuesday	*Terça-feira (Ter.)*
Wednesday	*Quarta-feira (Qua.)*
Thursday	*Quinta-feira (Qui.)*
Friday	*Sexta-feira (Sex.)*
Saturday	*Sábado (Sab.)*
Sunday	*Domingo (Dom.)*
hour; day; month; year	*hora; dia; mês; ano*
yesterday; today; tomorrow	*ontem; hoje; amanhã*
what?; when?; where?	*quê?; quando?; onde?*
always/never	*sempre/nunca*
What time is it?	*Que horas são?*
What day is it today?	*Que dia é hoje?*

ENGLISH	PORTUGUÊS
now	*agora*
January	*Janeiro*
February	*Fevereiro*
March	*Março*
April	*Abril*
May	*Maio*
June	*Junho*
July	*Julho*
August	*Agosto*
September	*Setembro*
October	*Outubro*
November	*Novembro*
December	*Dezembro*

MENU READER

LUNCH & DINNER

CARNES (MEATS)					
bacalhau	cod	*frutos do mar*	seafood	*picanha*	beef rump roast
camarão	shrimp	*linguíça*	pork sausage	*porco*	pork
carangueijo	crab	*pato*	duck	*presunto*	cured ham
carne/bife/ filet	beef	*peixe*	fish	*salsicha*	beef sausage
frango	chicken	*peru*	turkey	*siri*	stuffed crab
GUARNIÇÕES (SIDE DISHES/ACCOMPANIMENTS)					
alho & oléo	garlic & oil	*farofa*	manioc flour	*puré de batata*	mashed potatoes
açúcar	sugar	*manteiga*	butter	*queijo*	cheese
arroz	rice	*massas*	pasta	*sal & pimenta*	salt & pepper
batatas fritas	(French) fries	*pão*	bread	*salpicão*	creamy slaw
VEGETAIS (VEGETABLES)					
aipim	cassava/manioc	*cebola*	onion	*feijão*	beans
abóbora	pumpkin, squash	*cenoura*	carrot	*milho*	corn
alface	lettuce	*couve*	kale, cabbage	*palmito*	heart-of-palm
batatas	potatoes	*espinafre*	spinach	*tomate*	tomato
SOBREMESAS (DESSERTS)					
arroz doce	rice pudding	*prato do verão*	fruit salad	*sorvete*	ice cream
bolo	cake	*pudim*	pudding	*tapioca*	manioc crêpe
doces	sweets	*quindim*	coconut custard	*torta*	torte, cake, or pie
BEBIDAS (DRINKS)					
água mineral	bottled water	*cerveja, chopp*	beer	*refrigerante*	soft drink
café, cafezinho	coffee	*chá*	tea	*suco*	juice (see below)
cachaça	white rum gutrot	*gelo*	ice	*vinho*	wine

GLOSSARY

SUCOS & FRUTAS

FRUIT JUICES & FRUITS					
abacaxí	pineapple	*fruto-do-conde*	custard apple	*maçã*	apple
açaí	grapey Amazon power berry	*guaraná*	sweet Amazon power berry	*mamão*	papaya
				manga	mango
acerola	Amazon cherry	*gengibre*	ginger	*maracujá*	passionfruit
cacau	cocoa pod	*goiaba*	guava	*melancia*	watermelon
caju	cashew fruit	*graviola*	sugar apple	*melão*	honeydew
caldo de cana	sugarcane juice	*hortelã*	mint	*morango*	strawberry
clorofila	chlorophyll	*jaca*	jackfruit	*pêssego*	peach
côco; cocô	coconut; poop	*laranja*	orange	*tangerina*	tangerine
cupuaçú	Amazon pear	*limão*	lemon	*uva*	grape
damasco	apricot	*lima*	lime	*3 em 1*	orange, beet, & carrot

COMMON WORDS & PHRASES

a cobrar: local collect call
aberto: open
acarajé: Baiano fried bean patties filled with shrimp, *vatapá,* and tomato sauce
aeroporto: airport
afoxé: the music of Bahian religious cult Candomblé
água quente: hot water
alamadea: lane
albergue: hostel
albergue da juventude: youth hostel
álcool: fuel made from a blend of alcohol and petroleum
aldeia: village, usually populated by an indigenous community
andar: floor, story
apartamento: room with private bath
ar condicionado (A/C): air conditioning
areia: sand
artesanato: workmanship
autobol: autoball, a variation on soccer played in cars with man-sized balls
avenida (Av.): avenue
avião: airplane
axé: Bahian-born fusion style of samba, funk, reggae, pop, *afoxé,* and more
azulejo: blue-and-white Portuguese tile
bacalhau: cod
Baiano: local of Bahia; from Bahia
bairro: neighborhood
balsa: ferry
banca: newsstand
banco: bank
bandito: druglord
banheiro: bathroom
barco: boat; floating fishing hotel popular in the Pantanal
barraca: beach bar
batidas: fruit juice with milk and *cachaça*
beco: alley
Belenense: local of Belém
beleza: (slang) perfect; literally, beautiful
bicho de pé: foot worm; a parasite found in the Northeast; literally, foot monster
bicicleta: bicycle
bife: steak
bilhete: ticket (for transportation)
bilheteria: ticket office
blocos afros: pulse-pounding Bahian tribal beats of special "drum corps" bands
bobó: Amazonian dish of dried shrimp, coconut, *dendê,* and various nuts
boîte: strip club
boletin de ocorrência: police report
bolso: bag
bombeiro: fireman
bossa nova: smooth, sexy musical cousin to *samba,* created in Rio
boto: river dolphin
caboclo: of mixed indigenous and Portuguese descent.
cachaça: a gutrot rum-style liquor
cachoeira: waterfall
cadastro: identification card required by many parks in Brazil
cadeira: chair
café da manha: breakfast
cafezinho: shot of strong, sweet coffee
caipirinha: Brazil's brutal national cocktail of *cachaça* rum, limes, and sugar
caipivodka: the vodka version of a *caipirinha;* a.k.a *caipiroska*
caixa automática: ATM
calçadão: sidewalk

calção: shorts
caldeirada: stewed
cama: bed
cama casal: double bed
câmbio: currency exchange
caminhada: hiking trail
camisa: shirt
camisinha: condom
camping: campground
canga: sarong
canja: hearty chicken vegetable soup
canoa: canoe
capela: chapel
capeta: drink made with *guaraná* powder, condensed milk, and vodka
capivara: capybara, world's largest rodent
capoeira: acrobatic Brazilian martial art
Carioca: local of Rio de Janeiro city
carne: meat, beef
carne do sol: sun-dried salty beef cubes
carro: car, automobile
carta: letter
cartão-postal: postcard
cartão de credito: credit card
cartão telefônico: prepaid Brazilian telephone card
catedral: cathedral
carteira de estrangeiro: entry card
caruru: Amazonian shrimp and okra curry, made with peppers, *dendê,* and garlic
casal: married couple
catamarã: catamaran
cavalo: horse
celular: mobile phone, cellular phone
centavo: cent
centro: center; downtown
centro histórico: historical center
cerrado: grassland, savanna
cerveja: beer
chafariz: fountain
chantilly: whipped cream
chapéu: hat
chave: key
cheio: full
chinelos: flip-flops
chopp: draft beer
choro: a more lyrical style of *samba*
churrascaria: barbecue house
churrasco: barbecued
chuveiro: shower
cidade: city
cobra: snake
cofre: safe, lockbox
comércio: commerce; downtown
companhia: bus company
comum: metered taxis; literally, common
consulado: consulate
conta: bill
convencional: standard single-level buses, usually without A/C, that serve shorter routes
corredor: aisle; hallway
correiro: mail; postal service; post office
correiro aéreo: airmail
cozido: stew where everything is boiled to grayness; typically eaten on Sundays
cuscuz: couscous
delegacia: police station
dendê: heavy, yellow palm oil used in Northeastern cuisine
desconto: discount
diária: daily rate
dica: tip, advice
dinheiro: money
direita: right
Discagem Direta a Distância (DDD): phone restricted to domestic calls
Discagem Direta Internacional (DDI): phone capable of making international calls
doces: sweets
drogaria: pharmacy, chemist
embaixada: embassy
empresa: bus company
engenho: any plantation or distillery
entrada: entrance
esquerda: left
esquina: corner
estação: station
estação ecológica: ecological station
este: east
executivo: buses equipped for overnight travel (with amenities like A/C, bathroom, and reclining seats) that stop more frequently than *leito* buses
farmácia: pharmacy, chemist
farofa: sawdust-like powdered manioc baked or fried in oil
favela: shantytown, often built on the outskirts of major cities
fechado: closed
feijão: beans
feijoada: Brazil's national dish, typically eaten on Saturdays; a hearty, salty stew of beans simmered with pork and sausage
feira: marker, fair
ferroviária: train station
fio dental: thong; literally, dental floss
Fluminense: local of Rio de Janeiro state
forró: Brazil's twangy "country" music, featuring accordions and a shuffling backbeat
forte: fort
frango: chicken
freguês: client
frevo: a frenetic Carnaval music style
frigo-bar: mini-bar, small refrigerator
frutos do mar: seafood
fuso horário: time zone
futebol: soccer, football
futevolei: a variation on and combination of soccer (football) and volleyball

GLOSSARY

Gaúcho: local of the South; cowboy
gíria: slang
GLS: *gay, lésbica, e simpatizante;* gays, lesbians, and supporters
guarda-chuva: umbrella
guarda-sol: beach umbrella
guarda volumes: luggage storage
gringo: any non-Brazilian; not considered derogatory in Brazil
gruta: cave
guaraná: energizing Amazon berry
Havaianas: flip-flops
hora: hour
horário: schedule
hospedaria: hostel
ida: one-way
ida e volta: round-trip
idoso: elderly
igreja: church
ilha: island
inconfidente: participant in the Inconfidência Mineira
Inconfidência Mineira: failed 1789 pro-independence uprising led by a group of *inconfidentes* based in Minas Gerais
informações turística: tourist office
ingresso: ticket
jacaré: alligator
jaganda: raft
jambu: tongue-numbing leaves used to flavor *tacacá no tucupi*
janela: window
jangada: sailboat
jardim: garden
kilo: restuarant selling food by weight
kombi: mini-van
lago: lake
lagoa: lagoon
lancha: motorboat
lanchonete: lunch counter, snack bar
largo: square, plaza
lavanderia: laundromat
legal: (slang) cool, great
leito: express buses equipped for overnight travel (with amenities like A/C, bathroom, and reclining seats); more expensive than *executivo* buses
lembrança: souvenir
lençóis: sheets
ligação a cobrar: international collect call
linha aérea: airline
litoral: coastal region
livraria: bookstore
livro: book
locadora: car rental agency
loja: store, shop
lotado: full
maconha: marijuana
mata, mato: forest
mate: tea popular in the South
meia: six; half
meias: socks
mercado: market, fair
metrô: metro, subway
Mineiro: local of Minas Gerais; from Minas Gerais
mochila: backpack
mochileiro: backpacker
moeda: coin
montanha: mountain
moqueca: delicious Bahian clay-pot seafood stew made with coconut milk, *dendê*, peppers, and tomatoes
morro: hill
motel: hotel that rents rooms by the hour
MPB: *música popular brasileira;* literally, Brazilian pop music; used to refer to any and every Brazilian musical style
museu: museum
norte: north
Nossa Senhora (NS): Our Lady, a term usually found in church names
novela: overwrought Brazilian soap opera
oeste: west
onda: wave
ondas: surf
ônibus: bus
orelhão: public pay phone; literally, big ear
orixá: deity
pacote: package, parcel
padaria: bakery
pagode: lyrical, softer form of *samba*
papel higiênico: toilet paper, loo roll
papelaria: stationary store
parada: stop
Paraense: local of Pará
parque: park
parque estadual: state park
parque nacional (P.N.): national park
passaporte: passport
pato no tucupi: roast duck in *tucupi* sauce, made with garlic, manioc juice, and the exotic vegetable *jambu*
Paulista: local of São Paulo state
Paulistano: local of São Paulo city
pinga: white rum
peixe: fish
pesada: ranking of a hiking trail meaning difficult.
pesqueiro: wooden cabin on stilts in the Pantanal, usually inhabited by fishermen
polícia: police
poltrona: seat (on a bus)
ponte: bridge
posto: post, marker along a beach
posto telefônico: international phone office
pousada: privately run guest house; similar to a bed and breakfast
praça (Pça.): plaza, square
praia: beach

prancha: surfboard
prato feito: lit. "made plate;" one-plate dish served at cheap eateries
prorrogação de visto: visa extension
proteção solar: sunblock
quadra: block
quadro de horários: timetable, schedule
quarto: room with communal bath
quiosque: kiosk, newsstand
rappel: rappeling, abseiling
real, reais: Brazilian currency
rede: hammock
refeição: meal
relógio: watch
repelente de insetos: insect repellent
restaurante: restaurant
rio: river
rodízio: same as *churrascaria*
rodovia: highway
rodoviária: bus station
rua: street, road
sabonete: soap
sacola: shopping bag
saia: skirt
saida: exit
salgado: savory pastry
salva-vida: lifeguard
samba: rhythmic two-step musical style
sapatos: shoes
seguro: safe location
selo: postage stamp
sem gelo: without ice
sem número (s/n): literally, without number; used in street addresses
semi-cama: the term for *executivo* elsewhere in South America
seringvero: rubber tapper
serra: mountain range
sertão: Brazil's arid interior
shopping: shopping mall
show: (slang) cool
solteiro: single
solução dos lentes de contato: contact lens solution
sorvete: ice cream
sorveteria: ice cream shop
suco: fruit juice; juice bar
sul: south
sunga: Speedo© swimsuit
tacacá no tucupi: manioc-based soup flavored with *jambu* leaf, served in a decorative gourd and eaten with a fork; popular in the North
tapioca: manioc flour crêpe
taxa: fee, duty
taxa de câmbio: exchange rate
táxi: taxi, cab
taxista: taxi driver
teleférico: cable car
telelista: telephone book
tênis: sneakers
tinto: red wine
toalha: towel
torta: torte, cake, or pie
travessa: side street
travesti: transvestite
trem: train
trilha: hiking trail
trios eléctricos: funk- and reggae-influenced music of the bands that parade atop trucks during Salvador's Carnaval
troco: small bills, change
Tropicália: fusion protest musical style
tutu à mineira: a thick paste-like refried bean sauce
unidade: unit on a *cartão telefônico*
vaqueiro: buffalo cowboy
vatapá: a famous Indian dish of coconut milk, *dendê*, and *farofa* paste
várzea: rainforest lowlands that often flood
ventilador: fan
vila: district; small town
visto: visa
vôo: flight

INDEX

D

E

F

INDEX

R

S

INDEX

MAP INDEX

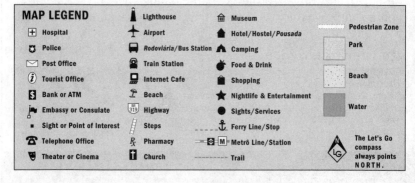

MAP LEGEND

Hospital
Police
Post Office
Tourist Office
Bank or ATM
Embassy or Consulate
Sight or Point of Interest
Telephone Office
Theater or Cinema
Lighthouse
Airport
Rodoviária/Bus Station
Train Station
Internet Cafe
Beach
Highway
Steps
Pharmacy
Church
Museum
Hotel/Hostel/*Pousada*
Camping
Food & Drink
Shopping
Nightlife & Entertainment
Sights/Services
Ferry Line/Stop
Metrô Line/Station
Trail
Pedestrian Zone
Park
Beach
Water
The Let's Go compass always points NORTH.